Mariëlle Hoefnagels
The University of Oklahoma

BIOLOGY
THE ESSENTIALS

Mc Graw Hill
Connect Learn Succeed™

The McGraw-Hill Companies

BIOLOGY: THE ESSENTIALS
Published by McGraw-Hill, a business unit of The McGraw-Hill Companies, Inc., 1221 Avenue of the Americas, New York, NY 10020.

This book is printed on acid-free paper.

1 2 3 4 5 6 7 8 9 0 RJE/RJE 1 0 9 8 7 6 5 4 3 2

ISBN 978–0–07–809692–1
MHID 0–07–809692–8

Vice President, Editor-in-Chief: *Marty Lange*
Vice President, EDP: *Kimberly Meriwether David*
Senior Director of Development: *Kristine Tibbetts*
Publisher: *Michael S. Hackett*
Sponsoring Editor: *Eric Weber*
Director of Digital Content Development: *Tod Duncan, Ph.D.*
Senior Developmental Editor: *Anne L. Winch*
Senior Marketing Manager: *Tamara Maury*
Lead Project Manager: *Sheila M. Frank*
Senior Buyer: *Kara Kudronowicz*
Lead Media Project Manager: *Judi David*
Manager, Creative Services: *Michelle D. Whitaker*
Cover/Interior Designer: *Elise Lansdon*
Cover Image: © *George Grall/Getty Images*
Senior Photo Research Coordinator: *John C. Leland*
Photo Research: *Emily Tietz/Editorial Image, LLC*
Art Studio and Compositor: *Electronic Publishing Services Inc., NYC*
Typeface: *10/12 Times Roman*
Printer: *R. R. Donnelley*

All credits appearing on page or at the end of the book are considered to be an extension of the copyright page.

Library of Congress Cataloging-in-Publication Data

Hoefnagels, Mariëlle.
Biology : the essentials / Marielle Hoefnagels. -- 1st ed.
p. cm.
Includes index.
ISBN 978–0–07–809692–1 (hard copy : alk. paper) 1. Biology--Study and teaching (Higher) I. Title.
QH315.H634 2013
570.71--dc23
2011035414

www.mhhe.com

Brief Contents

Student's Guide *To Using This Text*

I have been teaching nonmajors biology at the University of Oklahoma since 1997, and over that time I have encountered many students who fear science in general and biology in particular. The complexity, abstractions, and unfamiliar terms can be overwhelming, and some students believe they can't do well because they're just not "into science." In writing this book, I have focused on students and what they need to be successful in a nonmajors biology class.

In my experience, a big part of the problem is that many students just don't have the right study skills—they focus too much on superficial learning such as memorizing definitions, but they don't immediately grasp the power of UNDERSTANDING the material.

If you are a student who needs help learning biology, I have created the following features for you. Each of these tools should help you make the transition from memorizing to understanding.

- **Learn How to Learn:** Each chapter in this book contains a tip focusing on study skills that build understanding.
- **What's the Point?** This brief introduction helps set the stage for the rest of the chapter's content.
- **Summary Illustrations:** Created specifically for the summary, these figures tie together the material in a visual way to help you learn relationships among the topics in the chapter.
- **Progress Bar:** The bar found at the bottom of most pages should help you keep in mind where you are in the chapter's big picture.
- **Why We Care:** These boxes reinforce the applications of biology to the real world.
- **Burning Question:** In this feature I answer questions from students who are either in my classes or who have written to me with a "burning question" of their own.
- **Essential Content:** My goal in writing this book has been to simplify the material to the elements that you need to actually understand it.
- **Connect:** The content in this textbook is integrated with a wide variety of digital tools available in Connect that will help you learn the connections and relationships that are critical to understanding how biology really works.

I hope that you enjoy this text and find that the study tips and tools help you develop your understanding of biology.

Mariëlle Hoefnagels

About the Author

Mariëlle Hoefnagels is an associate professor in the departments of Zoology and Botany/Microbiology at the University of Oklahoma, where she teaches both traditional and online courses in introductory biology for nonmajors. She has received the University of Oklahoma General Education Teaching Award and the Longmire Prize (the Teaching Scholars Award from the College of Arts and Sciences). She has also been awarded honorary memberships in several student honor societies.

Dr. Hoefnagels received her B.S. in environmental science from the University of California at Riverside, her M.S. in soil science from North Carolina State University, and her Ph.D. in plant pathology from Oregon State University. Her dissertation work focused on the use of bacterial biological control agents to reduce the spread of fungal pathogens on seeds. In addition to authoring *Biology: Concepts and Investigations* and *Biology: The Essentials*, her recent publications have focused on the creation of investigative teaching laboratories and methods for teaching experimental design in beginning and advanced biology classes. She frequently gives presentations on study skills and related topics to student groups across campus.

The Essentials: *Relevant to Your Life*

What's the Point?

The animal kingdom is full of intriguing reproductive strategies. Consider, for example, the male sea horse pictured on the opposite page. These fish look unusual, with their elongated snouts and upright swimming posture. Their reproductive habits are unique as well: the males become pregnant!

As in other sexually reproducing animals, the female sea horse produces eggs. But she deposits the eggs into a brood pouch on the male's abdomen. He then fertilizes the eggs with his sperm. The young develop in the wall of his brood pouch for 2 to 4 weeks. At the end of the pregnancy, he gives birth to dozens or hundreds of miniature sea horses.

Humans are no less amazing. Sperm and egg cells come together in a woman's body. The resulting cell begins to divide, first into two cells, then four, then eight, and so on. The resulting ball of cells soon hollows out and develops an outside and an inside. Slowly, organs develop and begin to work together. After nine months, a brand new baby emerges into the world.

This chapter explores these two interrelated topics—reproduction and development—with a focus on our own species.

What's the Point?

This brief introduction provides a quick overview of the chapter's topic and its importance.

Burning Questions

Students come into class with their own questions. Burning Questions come from the author's students or from students who have written her with their own Burning Questions.

Burning Questions

Is male baldness really from the female side of the family?

Male pattern baldness is the distinctive hair loss that many men (and some women) experience as they enter their 20s, 30s, and 40s. The baldness spreads outward from the temples and crown of the head in a characteristic pattern.

Two conditions are required for male pattern baldness to develop. First, hormones called androgens must be present in high concentrations. Testosterone and dihydrotestosterone (DHT) are androgens; they bind to and enter hair follicle cells, interacting with the DNA to stop growth of the hair follicle. Second, the individual must have a genetic predisposition for the condition. The gene(s) controlling this trait reside on autosomes, not on the sex chromosomes. Therefore, either parent can pass the baldness allele(s) to a child.

Why don't women suffer from baldness as often as males? The answer is that pattern baldness is a so-called "sex-influenced" condition in which males and females can carry the same pair of alleles yet express them differently. In this case, the amount of testosterone is the deciding factor. The higher the concentration of testosterone, the stronger the influence of the "baldness allele." Men typically have more of this sex hormone than women—hence the name, *male* pattern baldness.

Submit your burning question to:
marielle_hoefnagels@mcgraw-hill.com

Why We Care | Invasion of the Zebra Mussels

Introduced species sometimes displace native species by competitive exclusion. Zebra mussels, for example, are native to the Caspian Sea in Asia. These mollusks were accidentally introduced to the Great Lakes in the 1980s and have since spread to many waterways in the United States and Canada. The tiny filter feeders reproduce rapidly and have crowded out native mussel species, with which they compete for food and oxygen. ▸ invasive species, p. 417

The effects of the zebra mussel invasion have rippled through the rest of the lake community as well. Zebra mussels have greatly increased water clarity, which has changed aquatic plant communities. In turn, the altered plant species composition has triggered changes in the community of fishes.

Why We Care

These boxes apply chapter concepts to biological phenomena that you may have experienced or noticed in your own life.

Art in Context

Difficult concepts are put into a familiar context to help you bridge the gap between textbook concepts and real world situations.

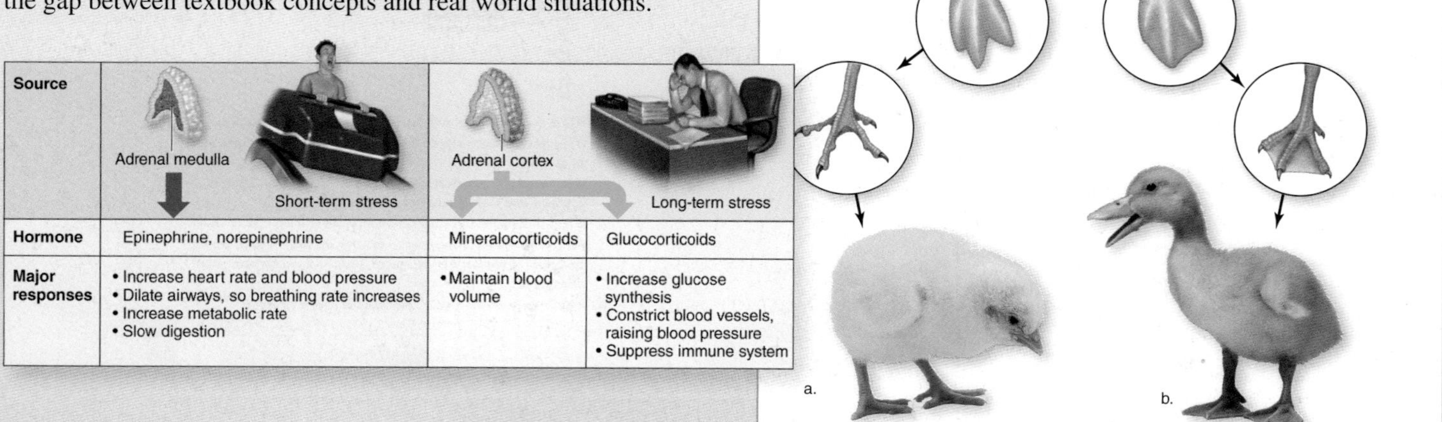

Source	Adrenal medulla / Short-term stress		Adrenal cortex / Long-term stress
Hormone	Epinephrine, norepinephrine	Mineralocorticoids	Glucocorticoids
Major responses	• Increase heart rate and blood pressure • Dilate airways, so breathing rate increases • Increase metabolic rate • Slow digestion	• Maintain blood volume	• Increase glucose synthesis • Constrict blood vessels, raising blood pressure • Suppress immune system

The Essentials: *Learning How to Learn*

Learning Outline

This outline previews the major ideas discussed in the chapter.

Learning Outline

5.1 Life Depends on Photosynthesis
5.2 Photosynthetic Pigments Capture Sunlight
5.3 Chloroplasts Are the Sites of Photosynthesis
5.4 Photosynthesis Occurs in Two Stages
5.5 The Light Reactions Begin Photosynthesis
A. Photosystem II Produces ATP
B. Photosystem I Produces NADPH
5.6 The Carbon Reactions Produce Carbohydrates
5.7 C_3, C_4, and CAM Plants Use Different Carbon Fixation Pathways
5.8 Investigating Life: Solar-Powered Sea Slugs

Chapter Summary

The outline headings are integrated into a helpful Chapter Summary at the end of the chapter. A unique summary illustration helps you organize key ideas from the chapter.

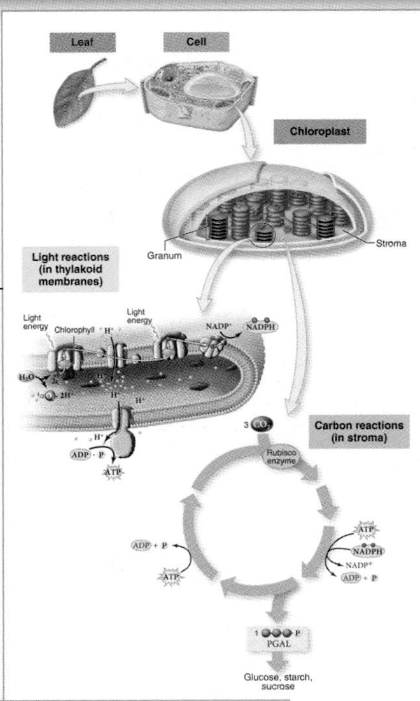

Learn How to Learn
A Quick Once-Over

Unless your instructor requires you to read your textbook in detail before class, try a quick preview. At the very least, read the Learning Outline to identify the main ideas. It is also a good idea to look at the figures and the key terms in the narrative. Previewing a chapter should help you understand the lecture, because you will already know the main ideas. In addition, note-taking will be easier if you recognize new vocabulary words from your quick once-over. Return to your book for an in-depth reading after class to help nail down the details.

Learn How to Learn

Learning anything takes daily practice. These tips, found at the beginning of each chapter, are designed to help you use your study time productively.

Pull It Together

This visual concept map integrates chapter content and art. Follow-up questions ask students about the relationships illustrated in the map.

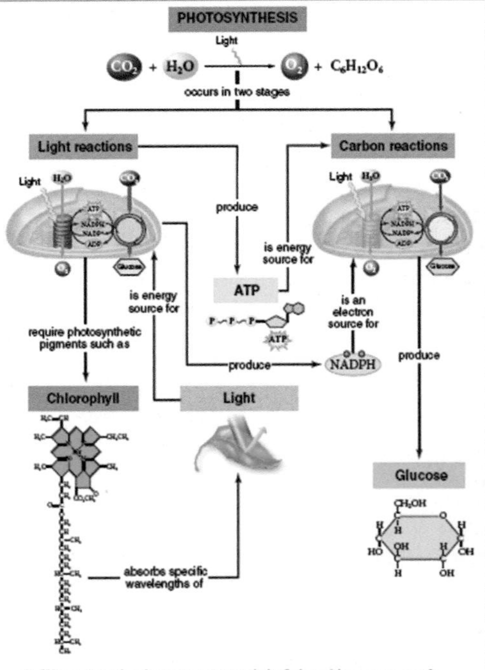

Progress Bar

A progress bar, found at the bottom of each page, helps show where you are in the chapter's big picture.

The Light Reactions Begin Photosynthesis | The Carbon Reactions Produce Carbohydrates | C_3, C_4, and CAM Plants | Investigating Life: Solar-Powered Sea Slugs

The Essentials: *Building Understanding Through Practice*

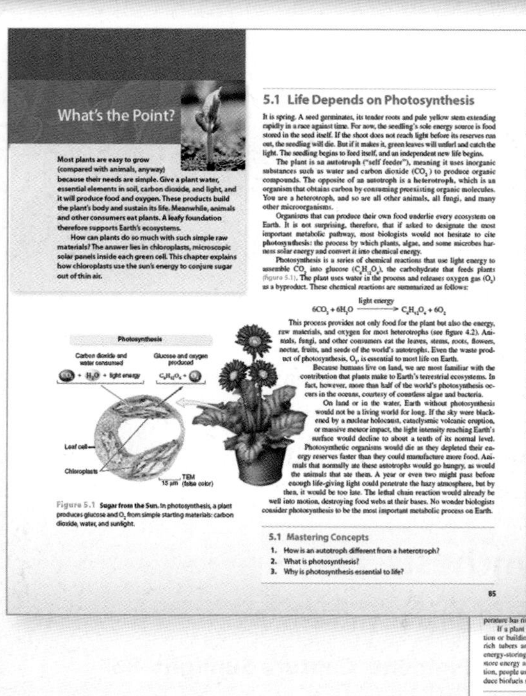

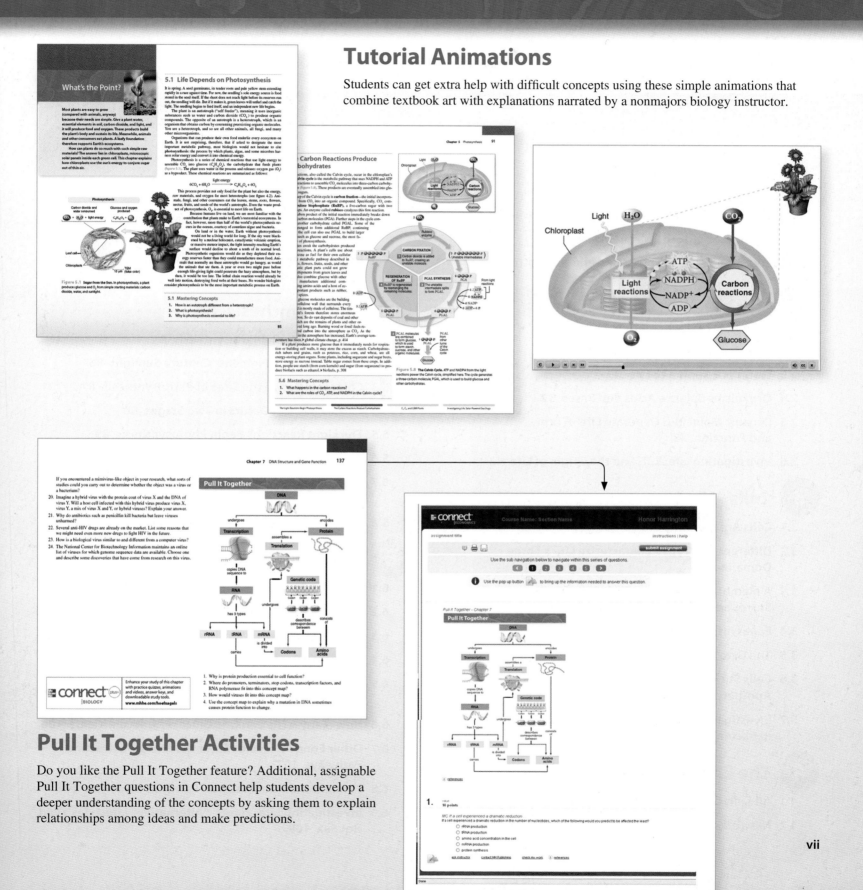

Tutorial Animations

Students can get extra help with difficult concepts using these simple animations that combine textbook art with explanations narrated by a nonmajors biology instructor.

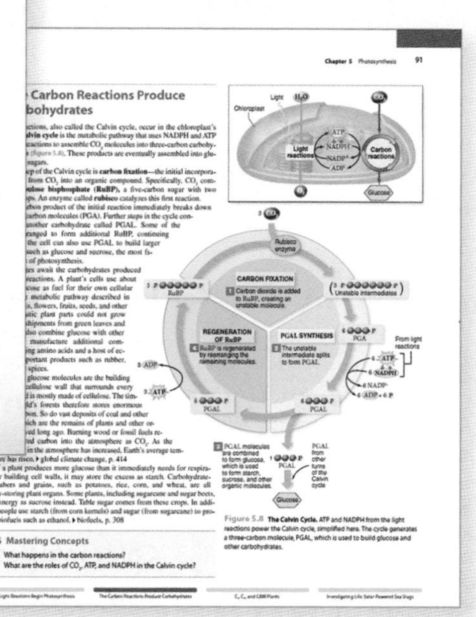

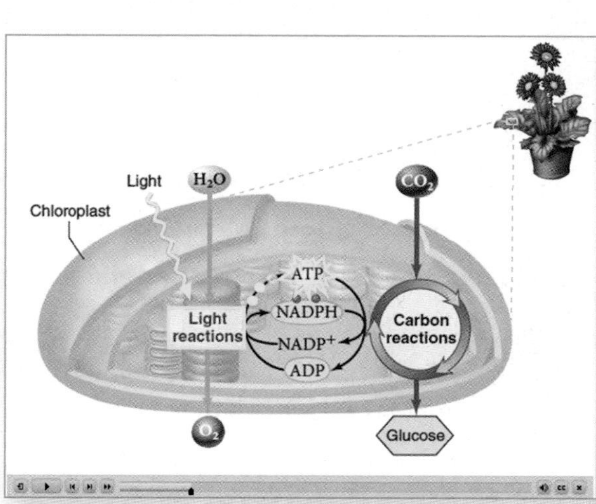

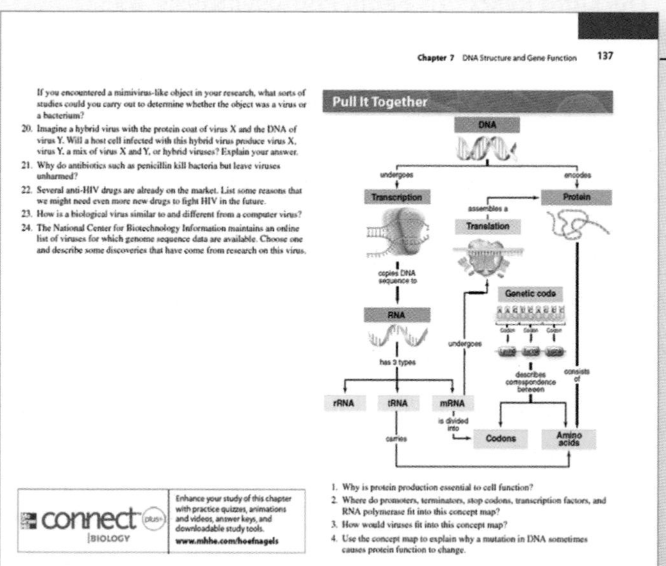

Pull It Together Activities

Do you like the Pull It Together feature? Additional, assignable Pull It Together questions in Connect help students develop a deeper understanding of the concepts by asking them to explain relationships among ideas and make predictions.

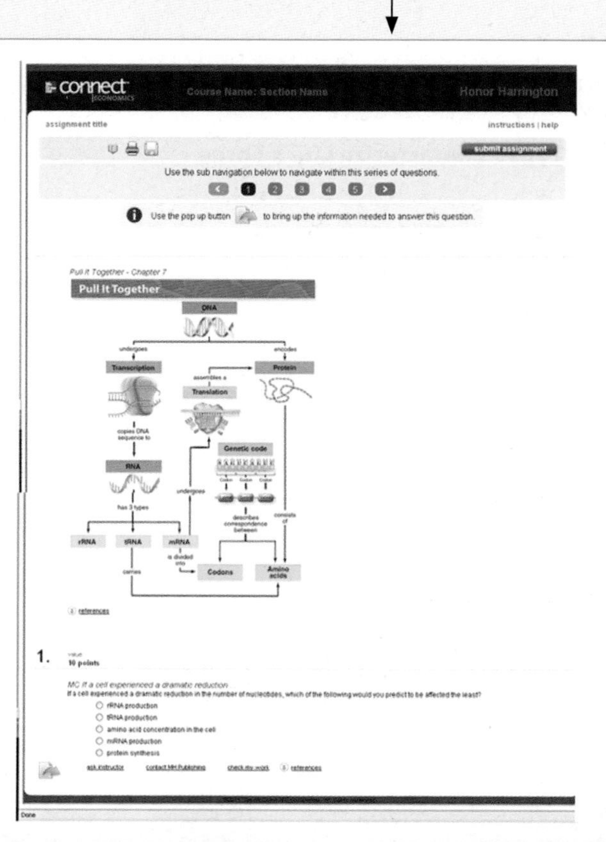

Detailed Contents

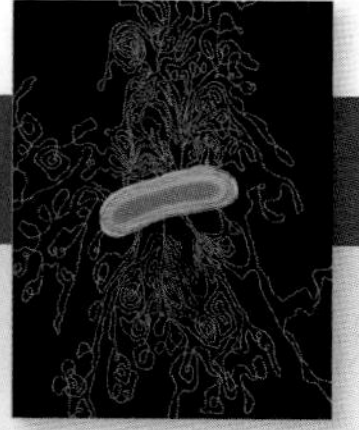

UNIT 2 Biotechnology, Genetics, and Inheritance

7 DNA Structure and Gene Function 112

8 DNA Replication and Cell Division 138

9 Sexual Reproduction and Meiosis 154

10 Patterns of Inheritance 170

11 DNA Technology 198

UNIT 3 Evolution and Diversity

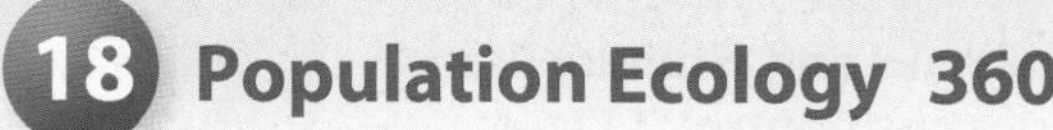

UNIT 4 Ecology

18 Population Ecology 360

19 Communities and Ecosystems 378

20 Preserving Biodiversity 408

UNIT 5 Plant Physiology

21 Plant Form and Function 426

22 Reproduction and Development of Flowering Plants 448

UNIT 6 Animal Physiology

Acknowledgments

This book would not exist without the help and support of many people. Matt Taylor assisted with every stage of development, from first draft to finished product; I value his hard work, careful eye, insights, and friendship. Caleb Cosper has read every word and scrutinized every illustration, contributing a student perspective that has improved this book in many ways.

I could not be happier with my team at McGraw-Hill. I thank publisher Michael Hackett for his support and friendship and for teaching me so much about the publisher's side of the textbook world. Eric Weber, sponsoring editor, is devoted to creating quality products that really help students learn. Anne Winch, developmental editor extraordinaire, is friendly, supportive, funny, and responsive. I can't imagine doing this project without her. Sheila Frank keeps the entire production team moving forward, and I appreciate designer Michelle Whitaker's keen eye for detail. Emily Tietz of Editorial Image and photo research coordinator John Leland provide patient and outstanding service in photo selections. Kari Voss and Christine Foushi are my software lifelines. Jane Peden has been helpful in arranging travel, processing payments, ordering books, and doing many other small things that make life easier. On the marketing side, Tamara Maury and Patrick Reidy build extraordinary connections with sales reps and customers. Finally, I appreciate my friend Michael Lange, without whose support I would not be writing textbooks at all.

The team at EPS produced the art and composed the beautiful page layouts. I appreciate their artistic talent and creative ideas for integrating the narrative with the illustrations. I remain in awe of their ability to turn my rough sketches into new art.

I also benefit greatly from the help of my colleagues at the University of Oklahoma, including Ari Berkowitz, Ken Hobson, David Durica, and J. P. Masly, each of whom has provided timely advice or helped me solve a writing dilemma. OU students have also offered suggestions and feedback along the way, notably my good friend Elise Knowlton. Conversations with students enrolled in my classes, along with Andrea Knowlton and Danielle Martin, have also been helpful.

My family and friends continue to encourage me in what is, at times, an all-consuming occupation. Thank you to my parents and sister for their pride and continued support. I also thank my friends Nicole Campbell, Kelly Damphousse, Phil Gibson, Ben Holt, Karen Renfroe, Clarke Stroud, Robin Stroud, and Mark Walvoord. Scoops and Sidecar do their part by livening up the office. Finally, my husband Doug Gaffin is always there for me, doing everything from offering advice to preparing tea and meals. I could not do this work without him.

Reviewers

Sylvester Allred, *Northern Arizona University*
Paul Assanah, *Prince George's Community College*
Andrew S. Baldwin, *Mesa Community College*
Joseph Beuchel, *Triton College*
Cheryl Boice, *Lake City Community College*
Matthew Burnham, *Jones County Junior College*
Wilbert Butler, *Tallahassee Community College*
Marilyn Caldwell, *Saint Louis Community College–Florissant Valley Campus*
Kelly S. Cartwright, *College of Lake County*
Aaron Cassill, *University of Texas at San Antonio*
Maitreyee Chandra, *Diablo Valley College*
Yvonne E. Cole, *Saint Louis Community College–Florissant Valley Campus*
Scott Cooper, *University of Wisconsin–LaCrosse*
Chris Davison, *Long Beach City College*
Danielle M. DuCharme, *Waubonsee Community College*
Angela Foster, *Wake Technical Community College*
Brandon Foster, *Wake Technical Community College*
Tamar Goulet, *University of Mississippi*
Monica L. Hall-Woods, *St. Charles Community College*
Angela Harper-English, *Hinds Community College*
Jessica Hopkins, *Flathead Valley Community College*
Timothy Hoving, *Grand Rapids Community College*
Meshagae Hunte-Brown, *Drexel University*
Diana E. Hurlbut, *Irvine Valley College*
Evelyn Jackson, *University of Mississippi*
Scott Johnson, *Wake Technical Community College*
Anthony Jones, *Tallahassee Community College*
Hinrich Kaiser, *Victor Valley College*
Ragupathy Kannan, *University of Arkansas–Fort Smith*
Arnold Karpoff, *University of Louisville*
Judy Kaufman, *Monroe Community College*
Brenda Knotts, *Eastern Illinois University*
Delia Lister, *Pittsburg State University*
Suzanne Long, *Monroe Community College*
Joshua Loomis, *Nova Southeastern University*
Eric Lovely, *Arkansas Tech University*
Jose Maldonado, *El Paso Community College*
Cindy Malone, *California State University–Northridge*
Lisa Maranto, *Prince George's Community College*
Lance McBrayer, *Georgia Southern University*
Santina Mongold, *Diablo Valley College*
Jamie C. Moon, *University of North Florida*
Scott Murdoch, *Moraine Valley Community College*
Elizabeth Tisei Nash, *Long Beach City College*

Rodney K. Nelson, *University of Arkansas–Fort Smith*
Judith D. Ochrietor, *University of North Florida*
Charlotte K. Omoto, *Washington State University*
Joanna Padolina, *Virginia Commonwealth University*
Usha Rani Palaniswamy, *Excelsior College*
Roger Ramsammy, *Palm Beach State College*
Matthew P. Rowe, *Sam Houston State University*
Albert S. Rubenstein, *Ivy Tech Community College of Indiana*
Michael Rutledge, *Middle Tennessee State University*
Sydha Salihu, *West Virginia University*
Georgiana Saunders, *Missouri State University*
Brian W. P. Seymour, *Edward Waters College*
Kathryn Shows, *Longwood University*
Del William Smith, *Dixie State College*
Jennifer R. Smith, *Triton College*
Kelly J. Smith, *University of North Florida*
Ayodotun O. Sodipe, *Texas Southern University*
Jim Stegge, *Rochester Community and Technical College*
Bethany Stone, *University of Missouri*
Todd Tarrant, *Michigan State University*
Fernando Tenjo, *Virginia Commonwealth University*
Jeffrey Thomas, *Queens University of Charlotte*
Kip Thompson, *Ozarks Technical Community College*
Muatasem Ubeidat, *Southwestern Oklahoma State University*
Susan Wadkowski, *Lakeland Community College*
Daniel W. Ward, *Waubonsee Community College*
Chris Wendtland, *Monroe Community College*
Leslie Whiteman-Richardson, *Virginia State University*
Calvin Young, *Fullerton College*

Focus Group Participants

Lena Ballard, *Rock Valley College*
Peggy Brickman, *University of Georgia*
Lori Buckley, *Oxnard College*
Jane Caldwell, *Washington and Jefferson College*
James Claiborne, *Georgia Southern University*
Scott Cooper, *University of Wisconsin–La Crosse*
David Cox, *Lincoln Land Community College*
Bruce Fink, *Kaskaskia College*
Brandon Foster, *Wake Tech Community College*
Douglas Gaffin, *University of Oklahoma*
Carlos Garcia , *Texas A&M University–Kingsville*
Phil Gibson, *University of Oklahoma*
Kelly Hogan, *University of North Carolina at Chapel Hill*
Jessica Hopkins, *University of Akron*
Tim Hoving, *Grand Rapids Community College*
Dianne Jennings, *Virginia Commonwealth University*
Leslie Jones, *Valdosta State University*
Hinrich Kaiser, *Victor Valley Community College*
David Lemke, *Southwest Texas State University*
Mark Lyford, *University of Wyoming*
Richard Musser, *Western Illinois University*
Ikemefuna Nwosu, *Lake Land College*
Murad Odeh, *South Texas College*
Karen Plucinski, *Missouri Southern State University*
Maretha Roberts, *Olive-Harvey College*
Frank Romano, *Jacksonville State University*
Felicia Scott, *Macomb Community College–Clinton Twp*
Cara Shillington, *Eastern Michigan University*
Brian Shmaefsky, Lone Star College–Kingwood
Wendy Stankovich, University of Wisconsin–Platteville
Bridget Stuckey, *Olive-Harvey College*
Sharon Thoma, *University of Wisconsin–Madison*
Kip Thompson, *Ozarks Technical Community College*
Sue Trammell, *John A. Logan School*
Valerie Vander Vliet, Lewis University
Mark Walvoord, *University of Oklahoma*
Daniel Ward, *Waubonsee Community College*
Scott Wells, *Missouri Southern State University*
Stephen White, *Ozarks Technical Community College*
Sonia Williams, *Oklahoma City Community College*
Jo Wu, *Fullerton College*

UNIT 1 Science, Chemistry, and Cells

1 Scientific Study of Life

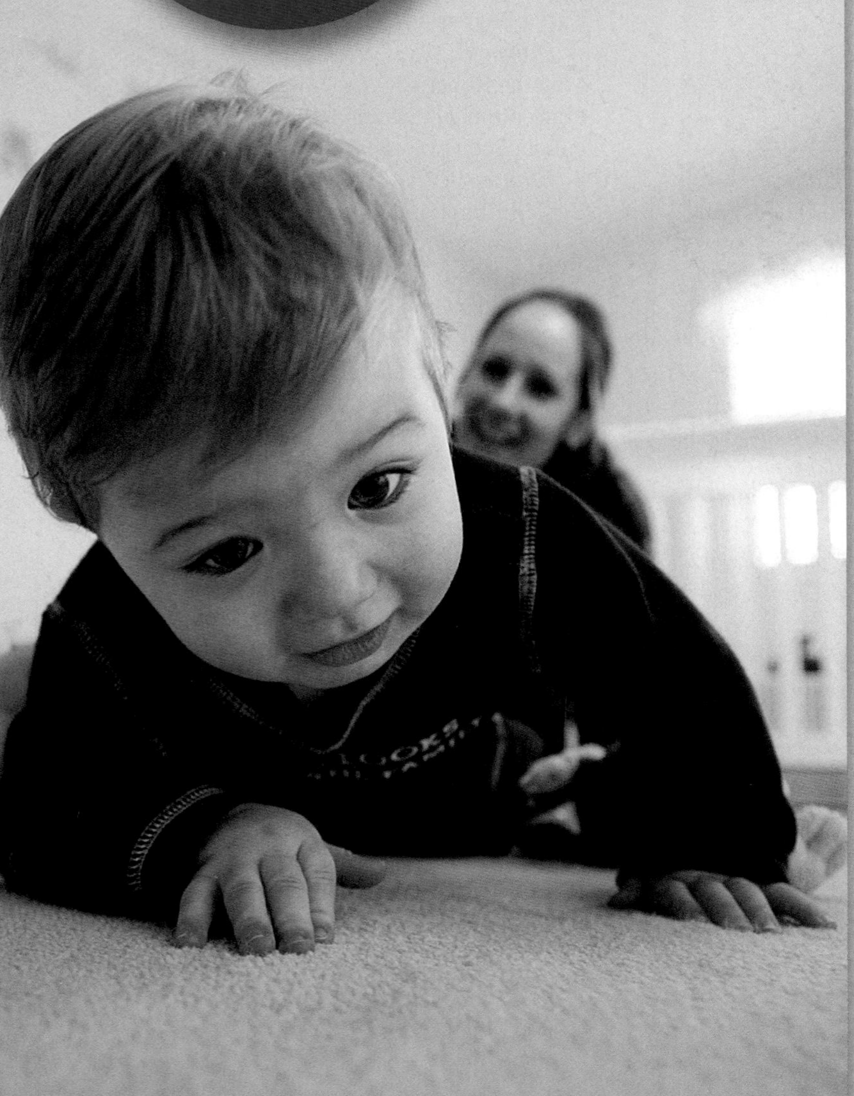

Lifesaving DNA Technology. This boy was born with a rare genetic immune disorder. He underwent experimental gene therapy, an attempt to replace his faulty gene with healthy DNA intended to restore his immune system.

Learning Outline

1.1 What Is Life?
- A. Life Is Organized
- B. Life Requires Energy
- C. Life Maintains Internal Constancy
- D. Life Reproduces, Grows, and Develops
- E. Life Evolves

1.2 The Tree of Life Includes Three Main Branches

1.3 Scientists Study the Natural World
- A. The Scientific Method Has Multiple Interrelated Parts
- B. An Experimental Design Is a Careful Plan
- C. Theories Are Comprehensive Explanations
- D. Scientific Inquiry Has Limitations

1.4 Investigating Life: The Orchid and the Moth

Learn How to Learn

Real Learning Takes Time

You got good at basketball, running, dancing, art, music, or video games by putting in lots of practice. Likewise, you will need to commit time to your biology course if you hope to do well. To get started, look for the "Learn How to Learn" tip in each chapter of this textbook. Each hint is designed to help you use your study time productively.

What's the Point?

Welcome to biology, the scientific study of life. Biology is everywhere: you are alive, and so are your friends, your pets, and the plants in your home and yard. Countless other organisms thrive on and in your body. The food you have eaten today was (until recently, anyway) alive. And the news is full of biology-related stories about fossils, weight loss, cancer, genetics, climate change, and the environment.

Stories such as these enjoy frequent media coverage because this is an exciting time to study biology. Not only is the field changing rapidly, but its new discoveries and applications might change your life. DNA technology has brought us genetically engineered bacteria that can manufacture pharmaceutical drugs—and genetically engineered corn plants that produce their own pesticides. The same technology may one day enable physicians to routinely cure inherited diseases by replacing faulty DNA with a functional "patch."

DNA technology is only a small part of modern biology. This book will bring you a taste of what we know and help you make sense of the science-related news you see every day. Chapter 1 begins your journey by introducing the scope of biology and explaining how science teaches us what we know about life.

1.1 What Is Life?

Biology is the scientific study of life. The second half of this chapter explores the meaning of the term *scientific,* but first we will consider the question, "What is life?" We all have an intuitive sense of what life is. If we see a rabbit on a rock, we know that the rabbit is alive and the rock is not. But it is difficult to state just what makes the rabbit alive. Likewise, in the instant after an individual dies, we may wonder what invisible essence has transformed the living into the dead.

One way to define life is to list its basic components. The **cell** is the basic unit of life; every **organism,** or living individual, consists of one or more cells. Every cell has an outer membrane that separates it from its surroundings. This membrane encloses the water and other chemicals that carry out the cell's functions. One of those biochemicals, deoxyribonucleic acid (DNA), is the informational molecule of life (figure 1.1). Cells use genetic instructions—as encoded in DNA—to produce proteins, which enable cells to specialize and to function in tissues, organs, and organ systems.

A list of life's biochemicals, however, provides an unsatisfying definition of life. After all, placing DNA, water, proteins, and a membrane in a test tube does not create artificial life. And a crushed insect still contains all of the biochemicals it had immediately before it died.

Figure 1.1 Informational Molecule of Life. All cells contain DNA, a series of "recipes" for proteins that each cell can make.

Figure 1.2 Levels of Biological Organization. This diagram uses an acacia tree as an example that illustrates how life is organized.

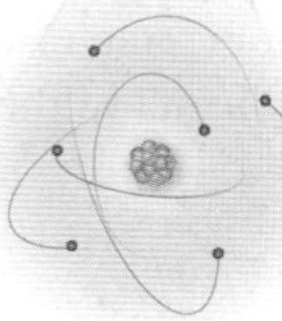

ATOM
The smallest chemical unit of a type of pure substance (element).
Example: Carbon atom

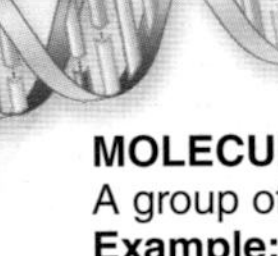

MOLECULE
A group of joined atoms.
Example: DNA

ORGANELLE
A membrane-bounded structure that has a specific function within a cell.
Example: Chloroplast

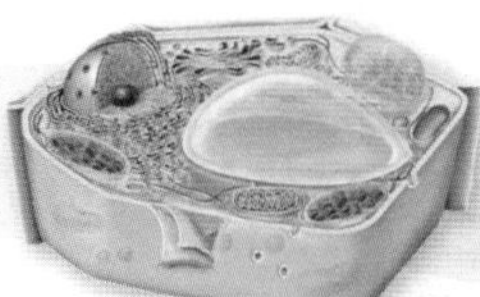

CELL
The fundamental unit of life.
Example: Leaf cell

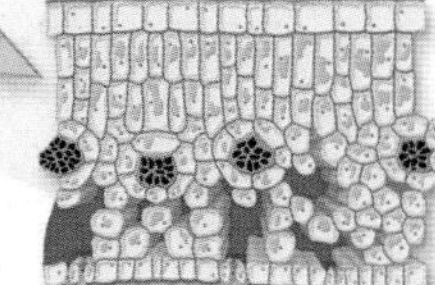

TISSUE
A collection of specialized cells that function in a coordinated fashion.
Example: Epidermis of leaf

ORGAN
A structure consisting of tissues organized to interact and carry out specific functions.
Example: Leaf

ORGAN SYSTEM
Organs connected physically or chemically that function together.
Example: Aboveground part of a plant

ORGANISM
A single living individual.
Example: One acacia tree

POPULATION
A group of the same species of organism living in the same place and time.
Example: Multiple acacia trees

COMMUNITY
All populations that occupy the same region.
Example: All populations in a savanna

ECOSYSTEM
The living and nonliving components of an area.
Example: The savanna

BIOSPHERE
The global ecosystem; the parts of the planet and its atmosphere where life is possible.

In the absence of a concise definition, scientists have settled on five qualities that, in combination, constitute life (table 1.1). An organism is a collection of structures that function together and exhibit all of these qualities. Note, however, that each of the traits listed in table 1.1 may also occur in nonliving objects. A rock crystal is highly organized, but it is not alive. A fork placed in a pot of boiling water absorbs heat energy and passes it to the hand that grabs it, but this does not make the fork alive. A fire can "reproduce" and grow very rapidly, but it lacks most of the other characteristics of life.

TABLE 1.1 Characteristics of Life: A Summary

Characteristic	Example
Organization	Atoms make up molecules, which make up cells, which make up tissues, and so on.
Energy use	A kitten uses the energy from its mother's milk to fuel its own growth.
Maintenance of internal constancy	Your kidneys regulate your body's water balance by adjusting the concentration of your urine.
Reproduction, growth, and development	An acorn germinates, develops into an oak seedling, and, at maturity, reproduces sexually to produce its own acorns.
Evolution	Increasing numbers of bacteria survive treatment with antibiotic drugs.

A. Life Is Organized

Just as the city where you live belongs to a county, state, and nation, living matter also consists of parts organized in a hierarchical pattern (figure 1.2). At the smallest scale, all living structures are composed of particles called **atoms,** which bond together to form **molecules.** These molecules can form **organelles,** which are compartments that carry out specialized functions in cells (note that not all cells contain organelles). Many organisms consist of single cells. In multicellular organisms such as the tree illustrated in figure 1.2, however, the cells are organized into specialized **tissues** that make up **organs** such as leaves. Multiple organs are linked into an individual's **organ systems.**

Organization in the living world extends beyond the level of the individual. A **population** includes members of the same species of organism living in the same place at the same time. A **community** includes the populations of different species in a region, and an **ecosystem** includes both the living and nonliving components of an area. Finally, the **biosphere** refers to all parts of the planet that can support life.

Biological organization is apparent in all life. Humans, eels, and evergreens, although outwardly very different, are all organized into specialized cells, tissues, organs, and organ systems. Single-celled bacteria, although less complex than animals or plants, still contain DNA, proteins, and other molecules that interact in highly organized ways.

An organism, however, is more than a collection of successively smaller parts. When those components interact, they create new, complex functions called **emergent properties** (figure 1.3). These characteristics arise from physical and chemical interactions among a system's components, much like flour, sugar, butter, and chocolate can become brownies—something not evident from the parts themselves.

Emergent properties explain why structural organization is closely tied to function. Disrupt a structure, and its function ceases. Shaking a fertilized chicken egg, for instance, disturbs critical interactions and stops the embryo from developing. Likewise, if a function is interrupted, the corresponding structure eventually breaks down, much as unused muscles begin to waste away. Biological function and form are interdependent.

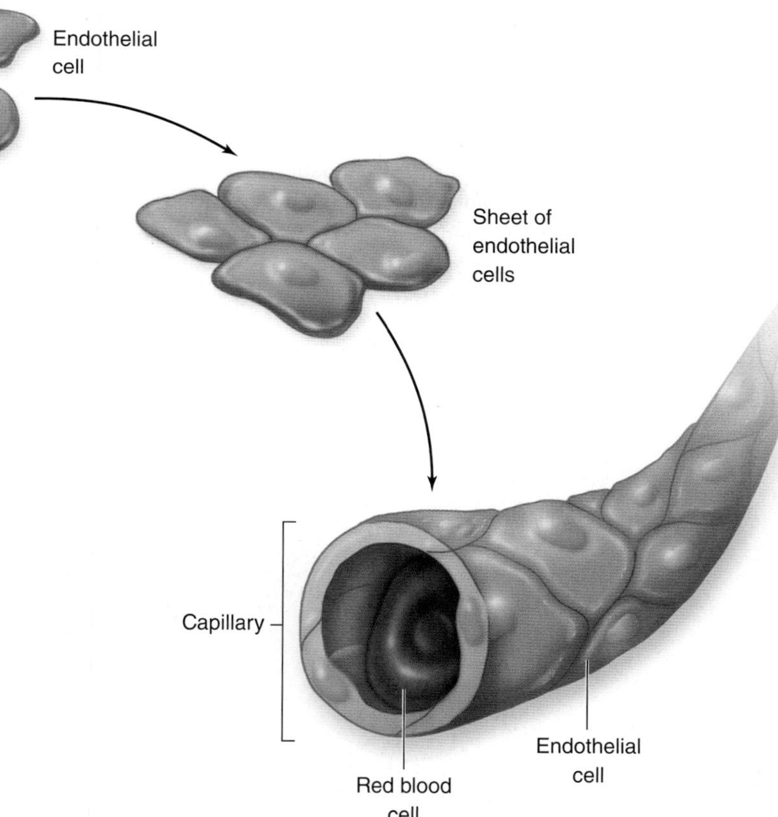

Figure 1.3 An Emergent Property—From Tiles to Tubes. Endothelial cells look like tiles that stick together to form a sheet. This sheet folds to form a capillary (a tiny blood vessel). The blood-carrying function does not "emerge" until the cells interact in a specific way.

B. Life Requires Energy

Inside each living cell, countless chemical reactions sustain life. These reactions, collectively called metabolism, allow organisms to acquire and use energy and nutrients to build new structures, repair old ones, and reproduce.

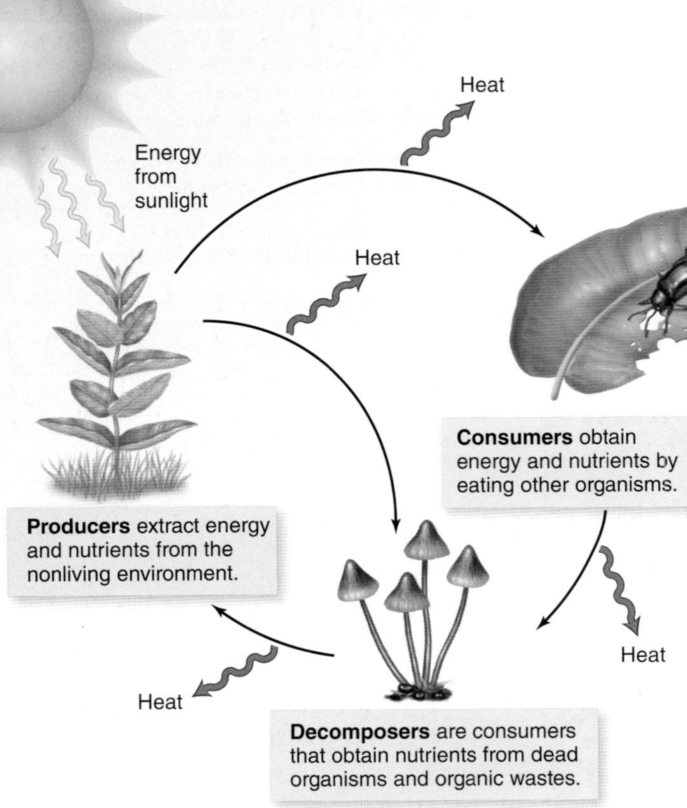

Figure 1.4 Life Is Connected. All organisms extract energy and nutrients from the nonliving environment or from other organisms. Decomposers recycle nutrients back to the nonliving environment. At every stage along the way, heat is lost to the surroundings.

Biologists divide organisms into broad categories, based on their source of energy and raw materials (figure 1.4). **Producers,** also called autotrophs, make their own food by extracting energy and nutrients from nonliving sources. The most familiar producers are the plants and microbes that capture light energy from the sun, but some bacteria can derive chemical energy from rocks. **Consumers,** in contrast, obtain energy and nutrients by eating other organisms, living or dead; consumers are also called heterotrophs (*hetero-* means "other"). You are a consumer, using energy and atoms from food to build your body, move your muscles, send nerve signals, and maintain your temperature. **Decomposers** are heterotrophs that obtain energy and nutrients from wastes or dead organisms. Fungi and many bacteria are decomposers.

Within an ecosystem, organisms are linked into elaborate food webs, beginning with producers and continuing through several levels of consumers (including decomposers). But energy transfers are never 100% efficient; some energy is always lost in the form of heat (see figure 1.4). Because no organism can use heat as an energy source, it represents a permanent loss from the cycle of life. All ecosystems therefore depend on a continuous stream of energy from an outside source, usually the sun.

C. Life Maintains Internal Constancy

The conditions inside cells must remain within a constant range, even if the surrounding environment changes. For example, a living cell must maintain a certain temperature—not too high and not too low. The cell must also take in nutrients, excrete wastes, and regulate its many chemical reactions to prevent a shortage or surplus of essential substances. **Homeostasis** is the process by which a cell or organism maintains this state of internal constancy, or equilibrium.

The ability to sense and react to changes in the environment is critical to maintaining homeostasis. Consider, for example, the mechanisms by which your body keeps its internal temperature steady at about 37°C. The brain detects any shift in temperature and coordinates the body's responses. When the brain senses that you are too cold, you may begin to shiver; heat from these involuntary muscle movements warms the body. In severe cold, your lips and fingertips may turn blue as your circulatory system sends blood away from your body's surface. Conversely, on a hot day, sweat evaporating from your skin helps cool your body.

D. Life Reproduces, Grows, and Develops

Organisms reproduce, making other individuals similar to themselves. Reproduction transmits DNA from generation to generation; this genetic information defines the inherited characteristics of the offspring.

Reproduction occurs in two basic ways: asexually and sexually (figure 1.5). In **asexual reproduction,** genetic information comes from only one parent, and all offspring are virtually identical. One-celled organisms such as bacteria reproduce asexually by doubling the contents of the cell and then dividing in half, yielding two new individuals. Many multicellular organisms also reproduce asexually. For example, a strawberry plant's "runners" can sprout leaves and roots, forming a new plant identical to the parent. The green, white, or black powder on moldy bread or cheese is made of the countless asexual spores of fungi (figure 1.5a). Some animals, including sponges, reproduce asexually when a fragment of the parent animal detaches and develops into a new individual.

In **sexual reproduction,** genetic material from two parent individuals unites to form an offspring, which has a new combination of inherited

Figure 1.5 Asexual and Sexual Reproduction. (a) This fungus, *Pencillium,* asexually produces identical cells on brushlike structures. (b) A tree seedling and (c) a newborn deer are products of sexual reproduction.

traits. By mixing genes at each generation, sexual reproduction results in tremendous diversity in a population. Genetic diversity, in turn, enhances the chance that some individuals will survive even if conditions change. Sexual reproduction is therefore a very successful strategy, especially in an environment where conditions change frequently; it is extremely common among plants and animals (figure 1.5b,c).

If each offspring is to reproduce itself, it must grow and develop to adulthood. The fawn in figure 1.5c, for example, started as a single fertilized egg inside its mother. That cell divided over and over, developing into an embryo. Continued cell division and specialization yielded the newborn fawn, which will eventually mature into an adult that can also reproduce—just like its parents.

E. Life Evolves

One of the most intriguing questions in biology is how organisms become so well-suited to their environments. A beaver's enormous front teeth are ideal for gnawing wood. Tubular flowers have exactly the right shapes for the beaks of their hummingbird pollinators. Some organisms have color patterns that enable them to fade into the background (figure 1.6).

These examples, and countless others, illustrate adaptations. An **adaptation** is an inherited characteristic or behavior that enables an organism to survive and reproduce successfully in its environment.

Where do these adaptive traits come from? The answer lies in natural selection. The simplest way to think of natural selection is to consider two facts. First, resources such as food and habitat are limited, so populations produce many more offspring than will survive to reproduce. A single mature oak tree may produce thousands of acorns in one season, but only a few are likely to germinate, develop, and reproduce. The rest die. Second, no organism is exactly the same as any other. Genetic mutations—changes in an organism's DNA sequence—generate variability in all organisms, even those that reproduce asexually.

Of all the offspring in a population, which will survive long enough to reproduce? The answer is those with the best adaptations to the current environment; poorly adapted organisms are most likely to die before reproducing.

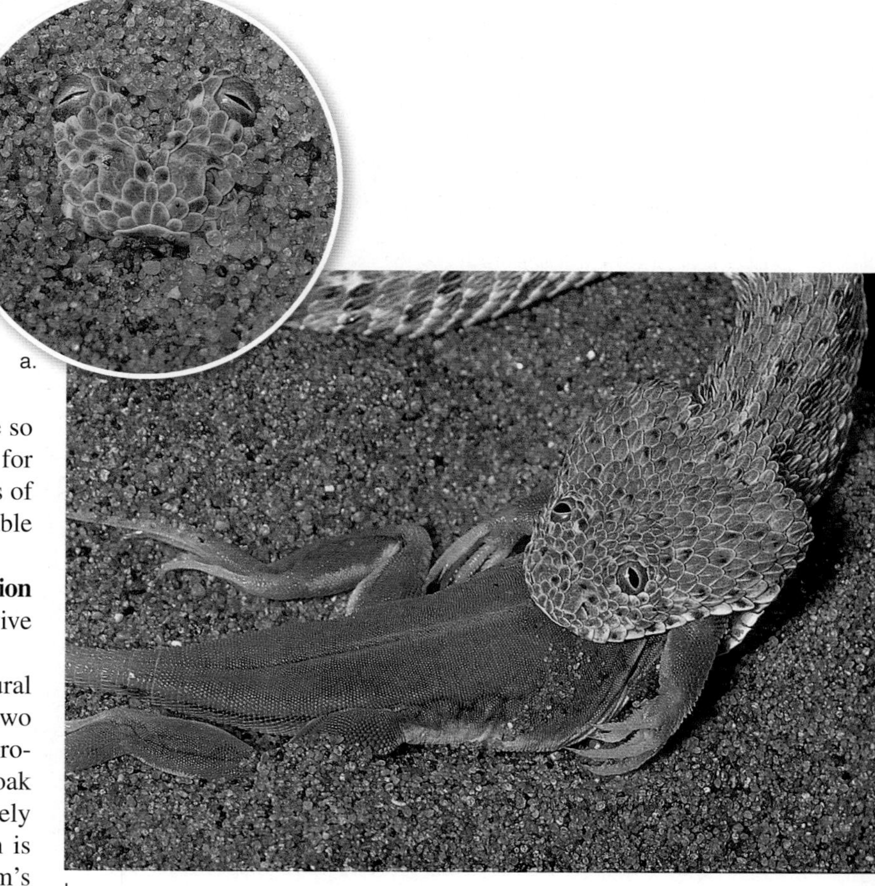

Figure 1.6 Blending In. (a) The superb camouflage of the adder snake makes it virtually undetectable buried in the sand in the Namib Desert, Namibia. (b) It is little wonder that this sand lizard soon became the meal of the snake.

A good definition of **natural selection,** then, is the enhanced reproductive success of certain individuals from a population based on inherited characteristics (figure 1.7). Over time, individuals with the best combinations of genes survive and reproduce, while those with less suitable characteristics fail to do so. Over many generations, individuals with adaptive traits make up most or all of the population.

But the environment is constantly changing. Continents shift, sea levels rise and fall, climates warm and cool. What happens to a population when the selective forces that drive natural selection change? Only some organisms survive: those with the "best" traits in the *new* environment. Features that may once have been rare become more common as the reproductive success of individuals with those traits improves. Notice, however, that this outcome depends on variability within the population. If no individual can reproduce in the new environment, the species may go extinct.

Natural selection is one mechanism of **evolution,** which is a change in the genetic makeup of a population over multiple generations. Although evolution can also occur in other ways, natural selection is the mechanism that selects for adaptations. Charles Darwin became famous in the 1860s after the publication of his book *On the Origin of Species by Means of Natural Selection,* which introduced the theory of evolution by natural selection; another naturalist, Alfred Russel Wallace, independently developed the same idea at around the same time.

Evolution is the single most powerful idea in biology. As unit 3 describes in detail, evolution has been operating since life began, and it explains the current diversity of life. In fact, the similarities among existing organisms strongly suggest that all species descend from a common ancestor. Evolution has molded the life that has populated the planet since the first cells formed almost 4 billion years ago, and it continues to act today.

1.1 Mastering Concepts

1. What characteristics distinguish the living from the nonliving?
2. List the levels of life's organizational hierarchy from smallest to largest, starting with atoms and ending with the biosphere.
3. What are the roles of natural selection and mutations in evolution?

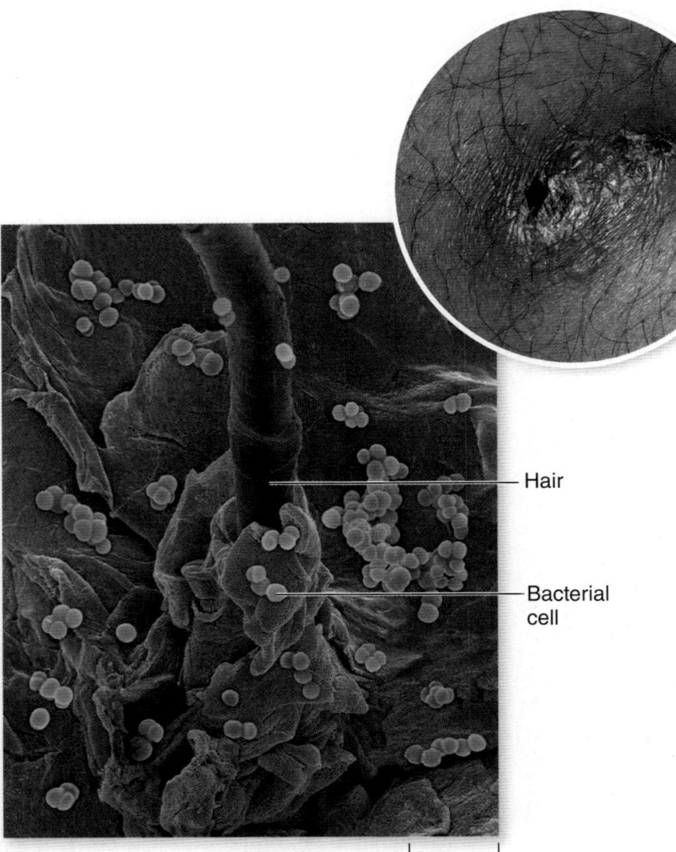

Generation 1

Generation 2

Multiple generations later

Antibiotic present

Time

Time

Reproduction and Selection

Staphylococcus aureus before mutation

Mutation occurs (red)

Antibiotic-resistant bacteria are most successful

b.

Figure 1.7 Natural Selection. (a) *Staphylococcus aureus* is a bacterium that causes skin infections. (b) A bacterium undergoes a random genetic mutation that happens to make the cell resistant to an antibiotic. The presence of the antibiotic increases the reproductive success of the resistant cell and its offspring. After many generations, nearly all of the bacteria in the population are antibiotic-resistant.

1.2 The Tree of Life Includes Three Main Branches

Biologists have been studying life for centuries, documenting the existence of everything from bacteria to blue whales. An enduring problem has been how to organize the ever-growing list of known organisms into meaningful categories. **Taxonomy** is the biological science of naming and classifying organisms.

The basic unit of classification is the **species,** which designates a distinctive "type" of organism. Closely related species, in turn, are grouped into the same **genus.** Together, the genus and species denote the unique scientific name of each type of organism. A human, for example, is *Homo sapiens* (note that scientific names are always italicized). By assigning each type of organism a unique scientific name, taxonomists help other biologists communicate with one another.

But taxonomy involves more than simply naming species. Taxonomists also strive to classify organisms according to what we know about evolutionary relationships; that is, how recently one type of organism shared an ancestor with another type of organism. The more recently they diverged from a shared ancestor, the more closely related we presume the two types of organisms to be. Researchers infer these relationships by comparing anatomical, behavioral, cellular, genetic, and biochemical characteristics.

Section 14.6 describes the taxonomic hierarchy in more detail. For now, it is enough to know that the evidence suggests that all species fall into one of three **domains,** the broadest (most inclusive) taxonomic category. Figure 1.8 depicts the

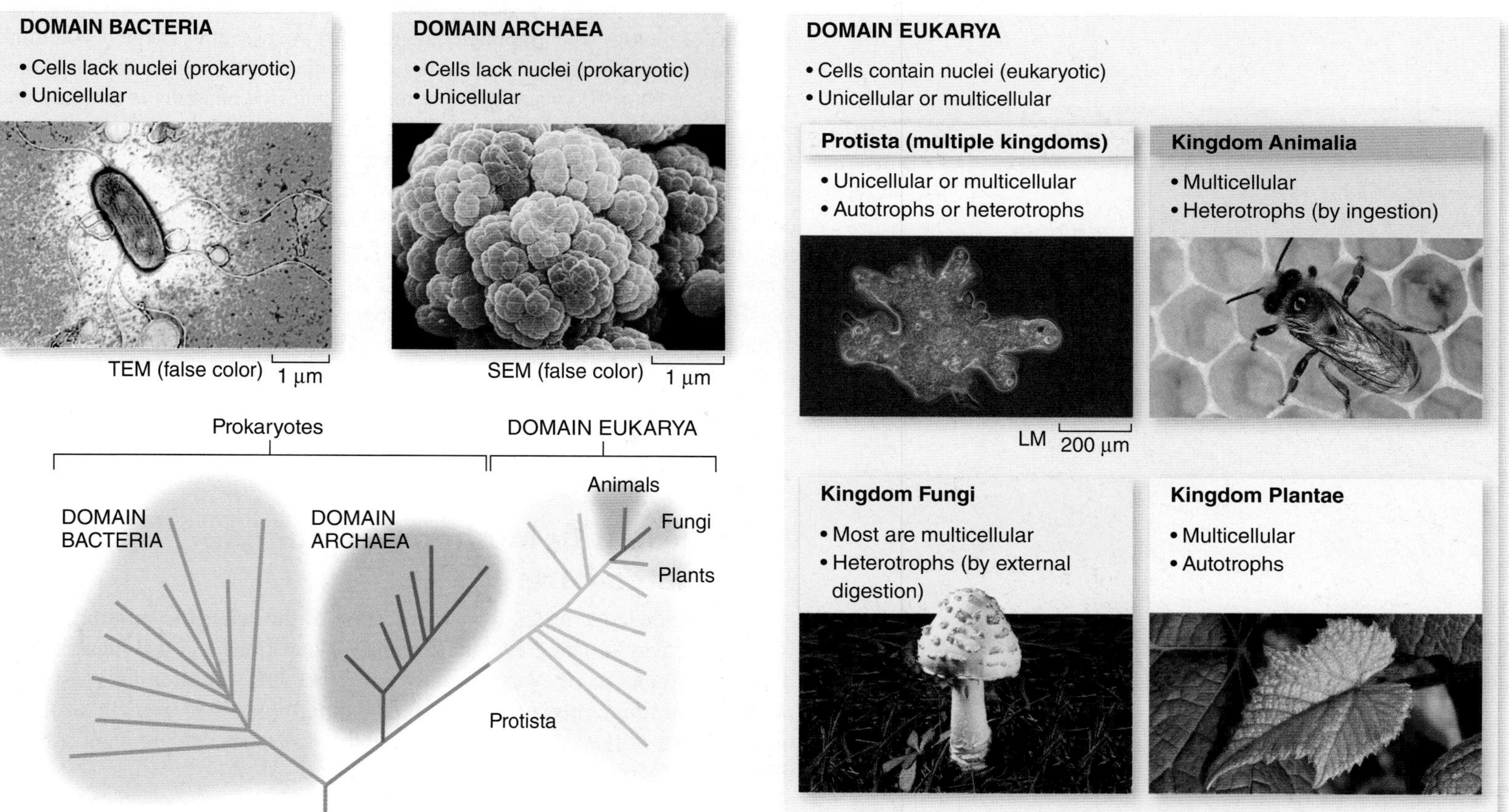

Figure 1.8 Life's Diversity. The three domains of life (Bacteria, Archaea, and Eukarya) arose from a hypothetical common ancestor, which forms the base of the evolutionary tree.

evolutionary relationships among the three domains: Bacteria, Archaea, and Eukarya. Species in domains Bacteria and Archaea are superficially similar to one another; all are single-celled prokaryotes, meaning that their DNA is free in the cell and not confined to an organelle called a nucleus. Major differences in DNA sequences separate these two domains from each other. Domain Eukarya contains all species of eukaryotes, which are unicellular or multicellular organisms whose cells contain a nucleus.

The species in each domain are further subdivided into **kingdoms;** the right half of figure 1.8 shows the kingdoms within domain Eukarya. Three of these kingdoms—Animalia, Fungi, and Plantae—are familiar to most people. Within each one, organisms share the same general strategy for acquiring energy. For example, plants are autotrophs. Fungi and animals are consumers, although they differ in the details of how they obtain food. But the fourth group of eukaryotes, the Protista, contains a huge collection of unrelated species. Protista is a convenient but artificial "none of the above" category for the many species of eukaryotes that are not plants, fungi, or animals.

1.2 Mastering Concepts

1. What are the goals of taxonomy?
2. How are domains related to kingdoms?
3. Which kingdoms contain eukaryotic organisms?

1.3 Scientists Study the Natural World

The idea of biology as a "rapidly changing field" may seem strange if you think of science as a collection of facts. After all, the parts of a frog are the same now as they were 50 or 100 years ago. But memorizing frog anatomy is not the same as thinking scientifically. Scientists use evidence to answer questions about the natural world. For example, if you compare a frog to, say, a snake, can you determine how those animals are related? How can the frog live in both water and on land, and how does the snake survive in the desert? Understanding anatomy simply gives you the vocabulary you need to ask these and other interesting questions about life.

Biology is changing rapidly because technology has expanded our ability to make observations. New microscopes allow us to spy on the inner workings of living cells, DNA sequencing machines are faster than ever, and powerful computers allow us to process huge amounts of data. Scientists can now answer questions about the natural world that previous generations could never have imagined.

A. The Scientific Method Has Multiple Interrelated Parts

Scientific knowledge arises from application of the **scientific method,** which is a general way of using evidence to answer questions and test ideas. Scientific inquiry consists of everyday activities: observing, questioning, reasoning, predicting, testing, interpreting, and concluding (figure 1.9). It includes thinking, detective work, communicating with other scientists, and noticing connections among seemingly unrelated events.

Observations and Questions The scientific method begins with observations and questions about the natural world. The observations may rely on

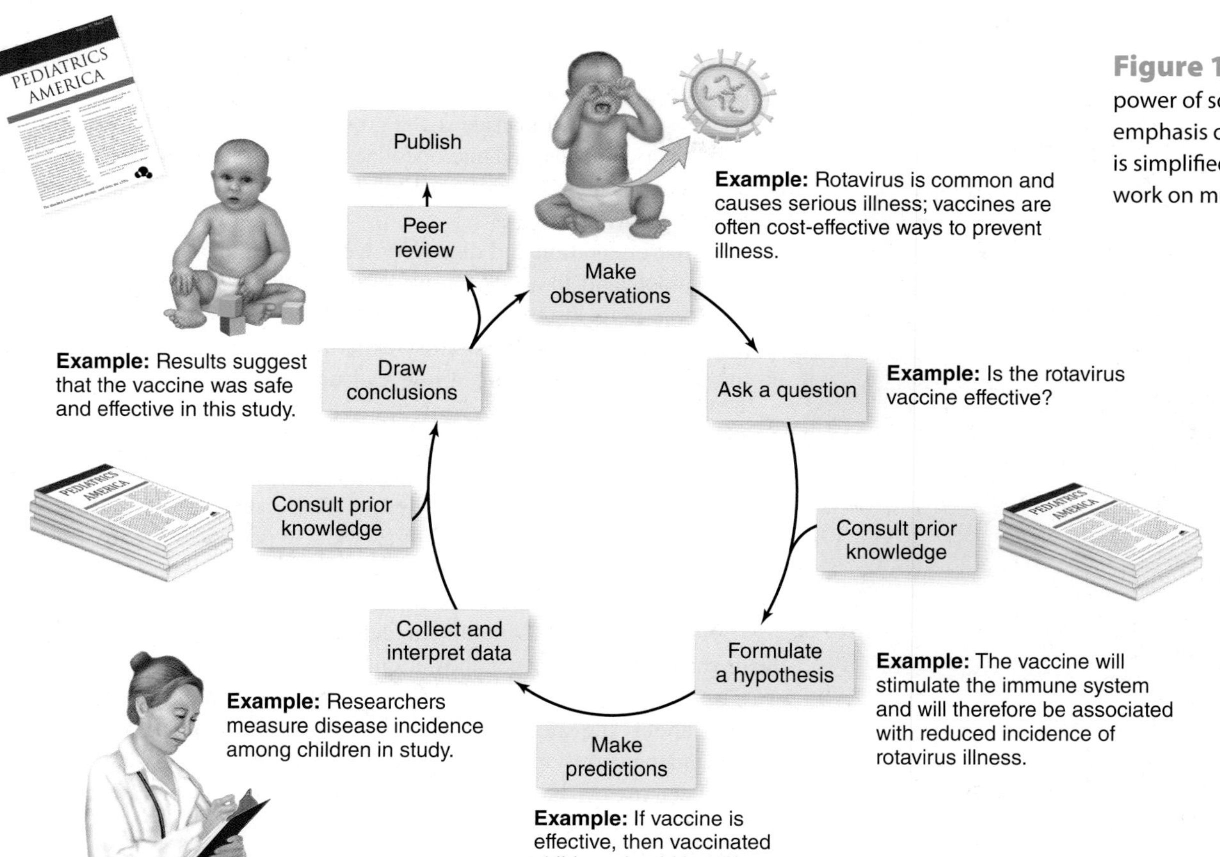
PEDIATRICS AMERICA
Publish
Peer review
Make observations
Example: Rotavirus is common and causes serious illness; vaccines are often cost-effective ways to prevent illness.
Ask a question
Example: Is the rotavirus vaccine effective?
Consult prior knowledge
Formulate a hypothesis
Example: The vaccine will stimulate the immune system and will therefore be associated with reduced incidence of rotavirus illness.
Make predictions
Example: If vaccine is effective, then vaccinated children should have lower incidence of rotavirus illness than children receiving placebo.
Collect and interpret data
Example: Researchers measure disease incidence among children in study.
Consult prior knowledge
Draw conclusions
Example: Results suggest that the vaccine was safe and effective in this study.

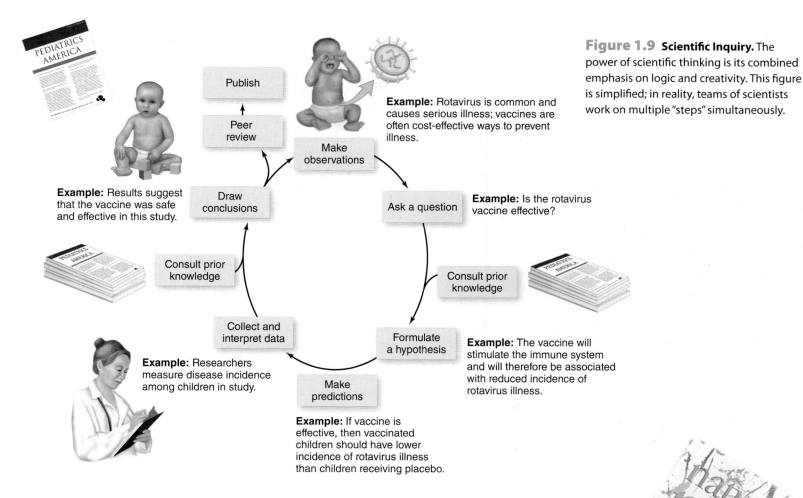

Figure 1.9 Scientific Inquiry. The power of scientific thinking is its combined emphasis on logic and creativity. This figure is simplified; in reality, teams of scientists work on multiple "steps" simultaneously.

the senses of sight, hearing, touch, taste, or smell, or they may be based on existing knowledge and experimental results. Often, a great leap in science happens when one person makes mental connections among previously unrelated observations. Charles Darwin, for example, developed the idea of natural selection by combining the study of geology with his detailed observations of organisms. Another great advance occurred decades later, when biologists realized that mutations in DNA generate the variation that Darwin saw but could not explain.

nature medicine
nature
Single-molecule electronics
Hydrogen bridges the gap
Nanostructured metals
Stretching the results
Colour vision
Blues in the night
Neurobiology of behaviour

Hypothesis and Prediction A **hypothesis** is a tentative explanation for one or more observations. The hypothesis is the essential "unit" of scientific inquiry. To be useful, the hypothesis must be testable—there must be a way to collect data that can support or reject the hypothesis. Interestingly, no hypothesis can be *proven* to be true, because scientific thinking is open to future discoveries that may contradict today's results.

A hypothesis is a general statement that can lead to specific **predictions.** Often, the prediction is written as an if-then statement. As a simple example, suppose you hypothesize that your lawn mower stopped working because it is out of gas. A reasonable prediction would be, "If I put fuel into the tank, then my lawn mower should start."

Data Collection Investigators draw conclusions based on data, which they can collect in many ways. Often, a scientist devises an experiment to test a hypothesis under controlled conditions; section 1.3B explores experimental design in more detail. But not all data are collected in the context of an experiment; instead, many

a.

b.

Figure 1.10 Different Types of Science. (a) Counting the number of migratory birds in a wildlife refuge is an example of discovery science. (b) Controlled experiments can help food scientists test hypotheses about new techniques for roasting or brewing coffee.

scientific investigations are based on discovery. For example, British anthropologist Jane Goodall used careful observations, not experimentation, to learn about the dynamics within chimpanzee social groups. Likewise, the discovery of new species of plants, animals, and microbes does not typically require an investigator to conduct experiments. Figure 1.10 shows two additional examples of discovery and experiments.

Experimentation and discovery work hand in hand. For example, we now understand the connection between cigarettes and cancer because scientists noticed that smokers are far more likely than nonsmokers to develop lung cancer. Laboratory experiments with cells growing in culture help fill in the details of how cancer develops.

Analysis and Peer Review After collecting and interpreting data, investigators decide whether the evidence supports or falsifies the hypothesis. Often, the most interesting results are those that are unexpected, because they force scientists to rethink their hypotheses. Figure 1.9 shows this feedback loop. Science advances as new information arises and explanations continue to improve.

Once a scientist has enough evidence to support or reject a hypothesis, he or she may write a paper and submit it for publication in a scientific journal. The journal's editors then send the paper to anonymous reviewers knowledgeable about the research. In a process called **peer review,** these scientists independently evaluate the validity of the methods, data, and conclusions. Peer review is not perfect. Some published papers are recalled or amended as unnoticed mistakes are later discovered. Overall, however, peer review ensures that published studies are of high quality.

B. An Experimental Design Is a Careful Plan

Scientists use experiments to test many hypotheses. An **experiment** is an investigation carried out in controlled conditions. This section considers a real study that tested the hypothesis that a new vaccine protects against rotavirus. This virus causes severe diarrhea that takes the lives of hundreds of thousands of young children each year. An effective, inexpensive vaccine would prevent many of these deaths.

Sample Size One of the most important decisions that an investigator makes in designing an experiment is **sample size,** which is the number of individuals that he or she will study. For example, several hundred infants participated in the rotavirus vaccine study. In general, the larger the sample size, the more credible the results.

Variables A systematic consideration of variables is also important in experimental design (table 1.2). A **variable** is a changeable element of an experiment, and there are several types. The investigator manipulates the levels of the **independent variable** to determine whether it influences some other phenomenon. For example, in the rotavirus study, the independent variable is the vaccine's dose. The **dependent variable** is the response that the investigator measures, such as the number of children who become ill during the study.

A **standardized variable** is anything that the investigator holds constant for all subjects in the experiment, ensuring the best chance of detecting the effect of the independent variable. For example, rotavirus infection is most common among very young children. The test of the new vaccine therefore included only infants younger than 12 weeks. Furthermore, vaccines work best in people with healthy immune systems, so the study excluded infants who were already ill or who were known to have weak immunity.

TABLE 1.2 Types of Variables in an Experiment: A Summary

Type of Variable	Definition	Example
Independent variable	What the investigator manipulates to determine whether it influences the phenomenon of interest	Dose of experimental vaccine
Dependent variable	What the investigator measures to determine whether the independent variable influenced the phenomenon of interest	Number of children with illness caused by rotavirus
Standardized variable	Any variable intentionally held constant for all subjects in an experiment, including the control group	Age of children in study

Controls Well-designed experiments compare a group of "normal" individuals to a group undergoing treatment. Ideally, the only difference between the normal group and the experimental group is the one factor being tested. The normal group is called an experimental **control** and provides a basis for comparison.

Experimental controls may take several forms. Sometimes, the control group simply receives a "zero" value for the independent variable. If a gardener wants to test a new fertilizer in her garden, she may give some plants a lot of fertilizer, others only a little, and still others—the control plants—none at all. In other types of experiments, a control group might receive a **placebo,** an inert substance that resembles the treatment given to the experimental group. In medical research, a placebo is often a stand-in for a drug being tested: a sugar pill or a treatment already known to be effective. The control infants in the rotavirus study received a placebo that contained all components of the vaccine except the active ingredient.

Statistical Analysis Once an experiment is complete, the investigator compiles the data and decides whether the independent variable affected the dependent variable. Look at the experimental results in figure 1.11. Did the rotavirus vaccine prevent illness? Apparently so, but the only way to know for sure is to apply a statistical analysis, using a set of mathematical tools that help the researchers interpret the data. The analysis considers both variation and sample size to yield a measure of **statistical significance,** which is the probability that the results arose purely by chance. Appendix B shows how scientists illustrate statistical significance in graphs.

C. Theories Are Comprehensive Explanations

Outside of science, the word *theory* is often used to describe an opinion or a hunch. For instance, immediately after a plane crash, experts offer "theories" about the cause of the disaster. These tentative explanations are really untested hypotheses.

In science, the word *theory* has a distinct meaning. Like a hypothesis, a **theory** is an explanation for a natural phenomenon, but a theory is typically broader in scope than a hypothesis. For example, the germ theory—the idea that some microorganisms cause human disease—is the foundation for medical microbiology. Individual hypotheses relating to the germ theory are much narrower, such as the suggestion that rotavirus causes illness. Not all theories are as "large" as the germ theory, but they generally encompass multiple hypotheses. Note also that the germ theory does not imply that *all* microbes cause disease or that all diseases have microbial causes. But it does explain many types of human diseases.

A second difference between a hypothesis and a theory is acceptance. A hypothesis is tentative, whereas theories reflect broader agreement. This is not to imply that theories are not testable; in fact, the opposite is true.

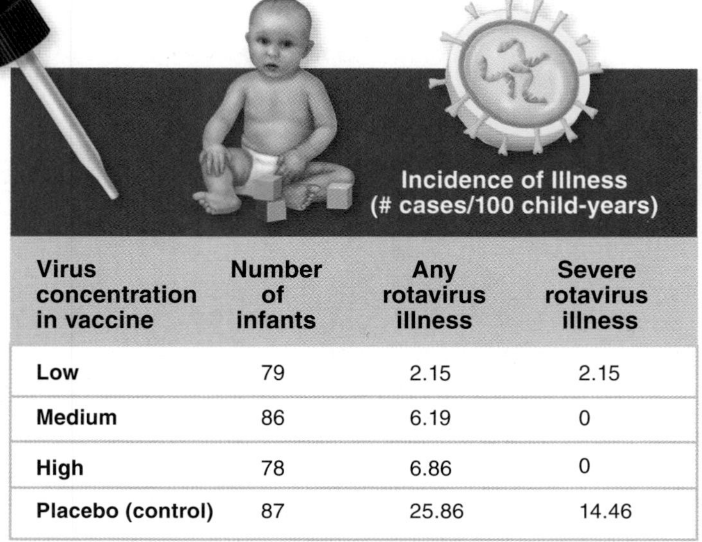

Virus concentration in vaccine	Number of infants	Incidence of Illness (# cases/100 child-years): Any rotavirus illness	Incidence of Illness (# cases/100 child-years): Severe rotavirus illness
Low	79	2.15	2.15
Medium	86	6.19	0
High	78	6.86	0
Placebo (control)	87	25.86	14.46

Figure 1.11 Vaccine Test. In this experimental test of a new vaccine against rotavirus, the independent variable was the dose of the vaccine. Control infants received a placebo. The data suggest that the vaccine was effective.

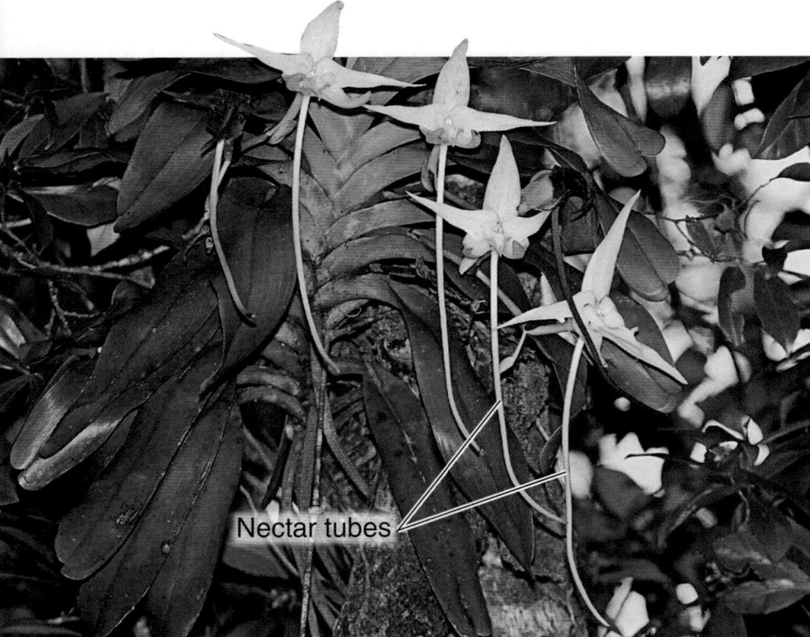

Figure 1.12 Prediction Confirmed. When Charles Darwin saw this orchid, he predicted that its pollinator would have long, thin mouthparts that could reach the bottom of the elongated nectar tube. He was right; the unknown pollinator turned out to be a moth with an extraordinarily long tongue.

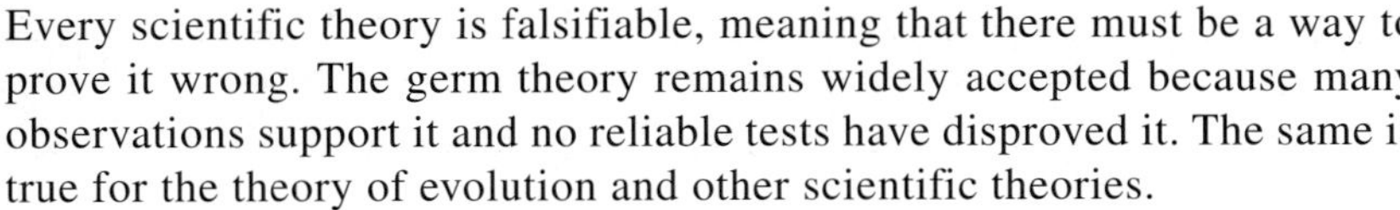

Every scientific theory is falsifiable, meaning that there must be a way to prove it wrong. The germ theory remains widely accepted because many observations support it and no reliable tests have disproved it. The same is true for the theory of evolution and other scientific theories.

Another quality of a scientific theory is its predictive power. A good theory not only ties together many existing observations, but it also suggests predictions about phenomena that have yet to be observed. Both Charles Darwin and naturalist Alfred Russel Wallace, for example, used the theory of evolution by natural selection to predict the existence of a then-unknown pollinator for a plant whose flowers had a distinctive shape (figure 1.12). Scientists discovered the pollinator, a moth, decades later (see section 1.4). A theory weakens if subsequent observations do not support its predictions.

At some point, a theory is so widely accepted that people regard it as a fact. The line between theory and fact is fuzzy, but the late paleontologist Stephen Jay Gould recognized a useful difference: "In science 'fact' can only mean 'confirmed to such a degree that it would be perverse to withhold provisional assent.'" Although a theory can never be proved 100% true, some theories are so well-supported that no educated person questions their validity. Gravity, for example, is a fact.

Biologists also consider biological evolution to be a fact. Yet the phrase "theory of evolution" persists, because evolution is both a fact *and* a theory. Both terms apply equally well. The evidence for genetic change over time is so persuasive and comes from so many different fields of study that to deny its existence is unrealistic. Nevertheless, biologists do not understand everything about how evolution works. Many questions about life's history remain, but the debates swirl around *how,* not *whether,* evolution occurred.

Science is just one of many ways to investigate the world, but its strength is its openness to new information. Theories change to accommodate new knowledge. The history of science is full of long-established ideas that changed as we learned more about nature, often thanks to new technology. For example, people thought that Earth was flat and at the center of the universe before inventions and data analysis revealed otherwise. Similarly, biologists thought all organisms were plants or animals until microscopes unveiled a world of life invisible to our eyes.

D. Scientific Inquiry Has Limitations

Scientific inquiry is neither foolproof nor always easy to implement (see the Why We Care box on page 15). One problem is that experimental evidence may lead to multiple interpretations, and even the most carefully designed experiment can fail to provide a definitive answer. Consider the observation that animals fed large doses of vitamin E live longer than similar animals that do not ingest the vitamin. So, does vitamin E slow aging? Possibly, but excess vitamin E causes weight loss, and other research has connected weight loss with longevity. Does vitamin E extend life, or does the weight loss? The experiment alone does not distinguish between these possibilities.

Another limitation is that researchers may misinterpret observations or experimental results. For example, centuries ago, scientists heated broth in a bottle, corked it shut, and observed bacteria in the broth a few days later. They concluded that life arose directly from the broth. The correct explanation, however, was that the cork did not keep airborne bacteria out. Science is self-correcting, in the sense that scientific thought is open to new data and new interpretations. But it is also fallible, especially in the short term.

A related problem is that the scientific community may be slow to accept new evidence that suggests unexpected conclusions. It is human nature to be cautious in accepting an observation that does not fit what we think we know.

Why We Care | The Saccharin Scare

You have probably heard reports that a food previously considered healthy is actually bad for you, or vice versa. Eggs are good and caffeine is bad! No, they're both bad! No, they're both good! If scientists can't make up their minds, does it mean that scientific studies are invalid? Or are scientists just out for publicity?

The reality is a bit more complex. Take, for example, the artificial sweetener saccharin (see the Why We Care box on sugar substitutes in chapter 2). Saccharin was discovered in 1879, and its popularity as a low-calorie sugar substitute peaked in the 1960s. But in 1977, the U.S. Food and Drug Administration (FDA) proposed a ban on saccharin, based on a handful of studies suggesting that the sweetener caused bladder cancer in rats. Because few alternative artificial sweeteners were available at the time, however, Congress instead required warning labels on products containing saccharin such as low-calorie soda pop. In 1991, the FDA withdrew its proposed ban, and in 1998, the International Agency for Research on Cancer rated saccharin as "not classifiable as to its carcinogenicity to humans." Two years later, legislation removed the warning label requirement.

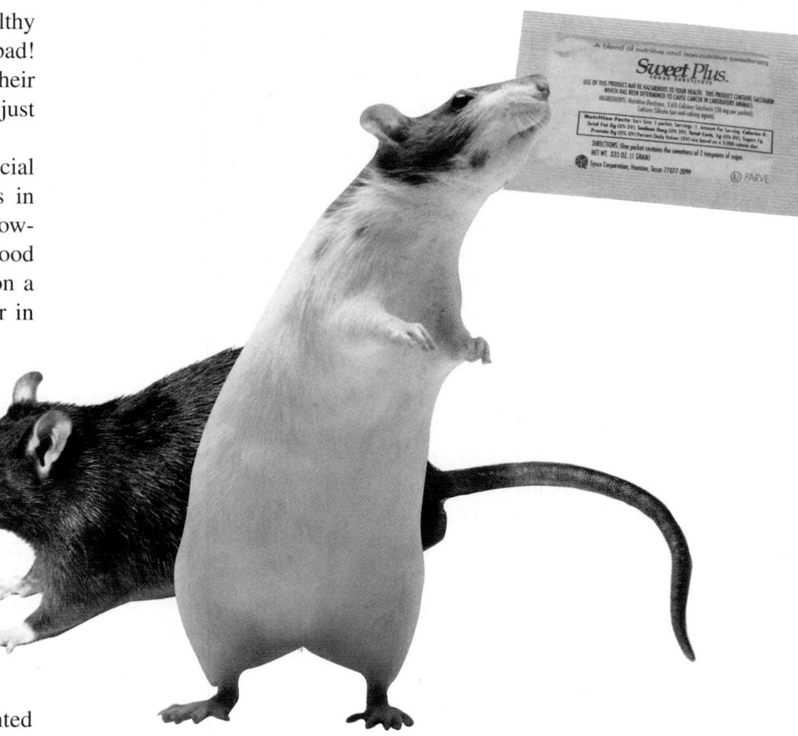

This tangled legislative history raises an important issue: Why can't science reply "yes" or "no" to the seemingly simple question of whether saccharin is bad for you? To understand the answer, consider one of the studies that prompted the FDA to propose the ban on saccharin in the first place. Researchers divided 200 rats into two groups. The control animals ate standard rodent chow, whereas the experimental group got the same food supplemented with saccharin. At reproductive maturity the animals were bred, and the researchers fed the offspring the same dose of saccharin throughout their lives as well. They measured the incidence of cancer in both generations of rats for 24 months or until the rats died, whichever came first. The results are in the table below.

At first glance, the conclusion seems inescapable: saccharin causes cancer in male lab rats. But closer study reveals several hidden complexities that make the data hard to interpret. First, the dose of saccharin was huge: 5% of the rats' diets, for life. The equivalent dose in humans would require drinking hundreds of cans of saccharin-sweetened soda every day. In addition, the experimental rats weighed up to 20% less than the control rats by the end of the study, suggesting that high doses of the sweetener are toxic. Rather than causing cancer directly, the saccharin may have simply weakened the animals and made them more susceptible to disease.

The researchers could have tested for that possibility by adding additional treatments with lower, less toxic saccharin concentrations. Then, if the sweetener really did cause cancer, they could have looked for a predicted "dose-response" relationship: low doses should yield just a few cases, and high doses should produce more. But the experiment was not designed to test for such a relationship. Furthermore, studies using mice, hamsters, and monkeys were inconclusive. The researchers who used these other animals created different designs for each experiment, so it is difficult to compare the results. The rat study, for example, followed two generations of animals; those with other animals used just one generation.

The animal studies did not yield uniform results, so maybe the scientists should have studied the saccharin-cancer connection in humans instead. Such research, however, is extremely difficult. It is obviously unethical to keep humans in captivity, control every facet of their environment and breeding, intentionally expose them to potentially harmful chemicals, and then kill and dissect them to check for tumors. The only way to approach the question in humans, therefore, would be to measure the incidence of cancer in saccharin users versus nonusers. But with so many other possible causes of cancer—smoking, poor diet, exposure to job-related chemicals, genetic predisposition—it is difficult to separate out just the effects of saccharin.

So what are we to make of the mixed news reports on eggs, caffeine, chocolate, wine, and soy? It is hard to say, but one thing is certain: No matter what the headlines say, one study, especially a small one, cannot reveal the whole story. Good, bad, or neutral? The complexities of real-world science mean that in most cases, the jury is still out.

Cancer Incidence in Rats

	Rats with Tumors/Rats Examined (% with tumors)	
	Parents	**Offspring**
Male rats		
Saccharin-fed	7/38 (19%)	12/45 (27%)
Controls	1/36 (3%)	0/42 (0%)
Female rats		
Saccharin-fed	0/40 (0%)	2/49 (4%)
Controls	0/38 (0%)	0/47 (0%)

Data adapted from Office of Technology Assessment Report, October 1977, *Cancer Testing Technology and Saccharin*, page 52.

Burning Questions

Why am I here?

The Burning Questions featured in each chapter of this book came from students. On the first day of class, I always ask students to turn in a "Burning Question"—anything they have always wondered about biology. I answer most of the questions as the relevant topics come up during the semester.

Why not answer *all* of the questions? It is because at least one student often asks something like "Why am I here?" or "What is the meaning of life?" Such puzzles have fascinated humans throughout the ages, but they are among the many questions that we cannot approach scientifically. Biology can explain how you developed after a sperm from your father fertilized an egg cell from your mother. But no one can develop a testable hypothesis about life's meaning or the purpose of human existence. Science must remain silent on such questions.

Instead, other ways of knowing must satisfy our curiosity about "why." Philosophers, for example, can help us see how others have considered these questions. Religion may also provide the meaning that many people seek. Part of the value of higher education is to help you acquire the tools you need to find your own life's purpose.

Submit your burning question to:
marielle_hoefnagels@mcgraw-hill.com

The careful demonstration that life does not arise from broth surprised many people who believed that mice sprang from moldy grain and that flies came from rotted beef. More recently, it took many years to set aside the common belief that stress causes ulcers. Today, we know that a bacterium (*Helicobacter pylori*) causes most ulcers.

Although science is a powerful tool for answering questions about the natural world, it cannot answer questions of beauty, morality, ethics, or religion (see the Burning Question box). Nor can we directly study some phenomena that occurred long ago and left little physical evidence. For example, many experiments have attempted to re-create the chemical reactions that might have produced life on early Earth. Although the experiments produce interesting results and reveal ways that these early events may have occurred, we cannot know if they accurately duplicate conditions at the beginning of life.

1.3 Mastering Concepts

1. What are the components of scientific inquiry?
2. Identify the elements of the experiment summarized in the Why We Care box on page 15.
3. What is the difference between a hypothesis and a theory?
4. What are some limitations of scientific inquiry?

Investigating Life

1.4 The Orchid and the Moth

Each chapter of this book ends with a section that examines how biologists use systematic, scientific observations to solve a different evolutionary puzzle from life's long history. This first installment of "Investigating Life" revisits the story of the orchid plant pictured in figure 1.12.

In a book published in 1862, Charles Darwin speculated about which type of insect might pollinate the unusual flowers of Madagascar's *Angraecum sesquipedale* orchid. The flowers have unusually long nectar tubes (also called nectaries). Darwin observed nectaries "eleven and a half inches long, with only the lower inch and a half filled with very sweet nectar." Darwin found it "surprising that any insect should be able to reach the nectar; our English sphinxes [moths] have probosces as long as their bodies; but in Madagascar there must be moths with probosces capable of extension to a length of between ten and eleven inches!"

Alfred Russel Wallace picked up the story in a book published in 1895, summarizing how natural selection could explain this unusual flower: "The pollen of this flower can only be removed by the base of the proboscis of some very large moths, when trying to get at the nectar at the bottom of the vessel. The moths with the longest probosces would do this most effectually; they would be rewarded for their long tongues by getting the most nectar; whilst on the other hand, the flowers with the deepest nectaries would be the best fertilized by the largest moths preferring them. Consequently, the deepest nectaried orchids and the longest tongued moths would each confer on the other an advantage in the battle of life."

Figure 1.13 Found at Last. More than 40 years after Charles Darwin and Alfred Russel Wallace predicted its existence, scientists finally discovered the sphinx moth, *Xanthopan morgani*.

At that time, the pollinator had not yet been discovered. However, as Wallace wrote, moths with very long tongues were known to exist: "I have carefully measured the proboscis of a specimen … from South America … and find it to be nine inches and a quarter long! One from tropical Africa … is seven inches and a half. A species having a proboscis two or three inches longer could reach the nectar in the largest flowers of *Angraecum sesquipedale* … That such a moth exists in Madagascar may be safely predicted."

A taxonomic publication from 1903 finally validated Darwin's and Wallace's predictions. The authors described a moth species, *Xanthopan morgani*, with a 225-millimeter (8-inch) tongue (figure 1.13). Given the correspondence between lengths of the orchid's nectary and the moth's tongue, the authors concluded that "*Xanthopan morgani* can do for *Angraecum* what is necessary [for pollination]…."

This story illustrates how theories lead to testable predictions and reflects the collaborative nature of science. Darwin and Wallace asked a simple question: Why are these nectar tubes so long? Decades later, biologists cataloging the world's insect species finally solved the puzzle.

Darwin, C. R. 1862. *On the Various Contrivances by Which British and Foreign Orchids Are Fertilised by Insects, and on the Good Effects of Intercrossing*. London: John Murray, pages 197–198.

Rothschild, W., and K. Jordan. 1903. A revision of the lepidopterous family Sphingidae. *Novitates Zoologicae* 9, supplement part 1, page 32.

Wallace, Alfred Russel. 1895. *Natural Selection and Tropical Nature: Essays on Descriptive and Theoretical Biology*. London: MacMillan and Co., pages 146–148.

1.4 Mastering Concepts

1. What observations led Darwin and Wallace to predict the existence of a long-tongued moth in Madagascar?
2. How does this story illustrate discovery science?

Chapter Summary

1.1 What Is Life?

- A combination of characteristics distinguishes life: organization, energy use, internal constancy, reproduction and development, and evolution.

A. Life Is Organized

- An **organism** consists of **atoms,** which form **molecules.** These molecules form the **organelles** inside **cells.** In most multicellular organisms, cells form **tissues,** which make up **organs** and, in turn, **organ systems.**
- Multiple individuals of the same species make up **populations;** multiple populations form **communities. Ecosystems** incorporate the nonliving environment, and the **biosphere** includes all of the world's ecosystems.
- **Emergent properties** arise from interactions between the parts that make up an organism.

B. Life Requires Energy

- Life requires energy to maintain its organization and functions. **Producers** make their own food, using energy and nutrients extracted from the nonliving environment. **Consumers** eat other organisms, living or dead. **Decomposers** are consumers that recycle nutrients to the nonliving environment.
- Because of heat losses, all ecosystems require constant energy input from an outside source, usually the sun.

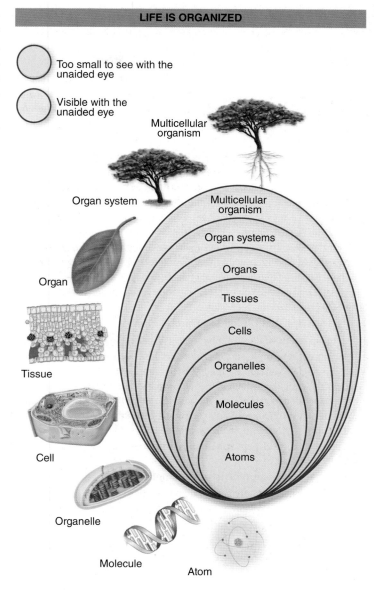

LIFE IS ORGANIZED

C. Life Maintains Internal Constancy

- Organisms must maintain **homeostasis,** an internal state of constancy in changing environmental conditions.

D. Life Reproduces, Grows, and Develops

- Organisms reproduce asexually, sexually, or both. **Asexual reproduction** yields virtually identical copies, whereas **sexual reproduction** generates tremendous genetic diversity.

E. Life Evolves

- In **natural selection,** environmental conditions select for organisms with inherited traits that increase the chance of survival and reproduction. The result of natural selection is **adaptations,** which are features that enhance reproductive success.
- **Evolution** through natural selection explains how common ancestry unites all species, producing diverse organisms with many similarities.

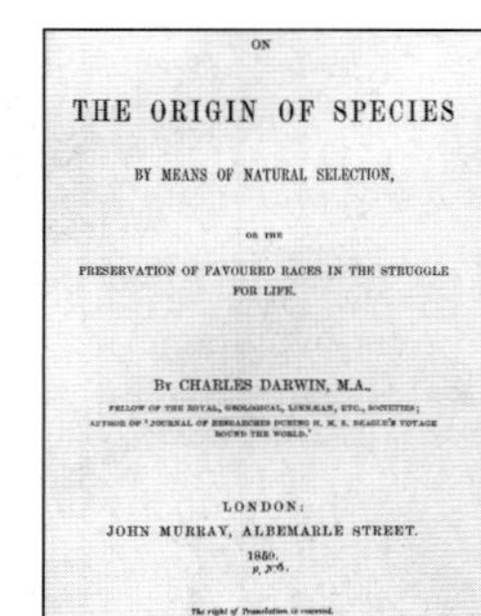
ON
THE ORIGIN OF SPECIES
BY MEANS OF NATURAL SELECTION,
OR THE
PRESERVATION OF FAVOURED RACES IN THE STRUGGLE FOR LIFE.
BY CHARLES DARWIN, M.A.,
LONDON:
JOHN MURRAY, ALBEMARLE STREET.

1.2 The Tree of Life Includes Three Main Branches

- **Taxonomy** is the science of classification. Biologists classify types of organisms, or **species,** according to probable evolutionary relationships. A **genus,** for example, consists of closely related species.
- The two broadest taxonomic levels are **domain** and **kingdom.**
- The three **domains** of life are Archaea, Bacteria, and Eukarya. Within each domain, mode of nutrition and other features distinguish the **kingdoms.**

1.3 Scientists Study the Natural World

A. The Scientific Method Has Multiple Interrelated Parts

- Scientific inquiry, which uses the **scientific method,** is a way of using evidence to evaluate ideas. Science involves observing, questioning, reasoning, predicting, testing, interpreting, concluding, and posing further questions.
- Scientific inquiry begins when a scientist makes an observation, raises questions about it, and uses reason to construct a testable explanation, or **hypothesis.** Specific **predictions** should follow from a scientific hypothesis.
- After collecting data and making conclusions based on the evidence, an investigator may seek to publish scientific results. **Peer review** ensures that published studies are high in quality.

B. An Experimental Design Is a Careful Plan

- An **experiment** is a test of a hypothesis carried out in controlled conditions.
- The larger the **sample size,** the more credible the results of an experiment.
- Experimental **controls** are the basis for comparison. The **independent variable** in an experiment is the factor that the investigator manipulates. The **dependent variable** is a measurement that the investigator makes to determine the outcome of an experiment. **Standardized variables** are held constant for all subjects in an experiment.
- Experimental results are **statistically significant** if they are unlikely to be due to chance.

C. Theories Are Comprehensive Explanations

- A **theory** is more widely accepted and broader in scope than a hypothesis.
- The acceptance of scientific ideas may change as new evidence accumulates.

D. Scientific Inquiry Has Limitations

- The scientific method does not always yield a complete explanation, or it may produce ambiguous results. Science cannot answer all possible questions, only those for which it is possible to develop testable hypotheses.

1.4 Investigating Life: The Orchid and the Moth

- Charles Darwin and Alfred Russel Wallace knew of an orchid in Madagascar with an extremely long nectar tube. They predicted that the orchid's pollinator would be a moth with an equally long tongue.
- Years later, other scientists discovered the moth, illustrating the predictive power of evolutionary theory.

Multiple Choice Questions

1. All of the following are characteristics of life EXCEPT
   a. evolution.
   b. reproduction.
   c. homeostasis.
   d. multicellularity.

2. Which property of life can a scientist directly observe in a single plant fossil?
   a. Homeostasis
   b. Organization
   c. Energy use
   d. Growth

3. Which of the following lists is ordered from smallest (least inclusive) to largest (most inclusive)?
   a. Cell < Tissue < Organelle < Individual < Community
   b. Community < Population < Ecosystem < Biosphere
   c. Organelle < Cell < Organ < Individual < Population
   d. Individual < Ecosystem < Community < Biosphere

4. Because plants extract nutrients from soil and use sunlight as an energy source, they are considered to be
   a. autotrophs.
   b. consumers.
   c. heterotrophs.
   d. decomposers.

5. Evolution through natural selection will occur most rapidly for populations of plants that
   a. are already well adapted to the environment.
   b. live in an unchanging environment.
   c. are in the same genus.
   d. reproduce sexually and live in an unstable environment.

6. Which of the following statements is true?
   a. Two of the three domains contain eukaryotes.
   b. The three main branches of life are animals, plants, and fungi.
   c. Humans and plants share the same domain.
   d. Two species in the same genus can be in different domains.

7. In an experiment to test the effect of temperature on the rate of bacterial reproduction, temperature would be the
   a. standardized variable.
   b. independent variable.
   c. dependent variable.
   d. control variable.

8. What is the role of a placebo in medical research?
   a. It ensures that all patients in a study have the same illness.
   b. It is the highest possible value of the dependent variable.
   c. It is a standardized treatment given to all patients.
   d. It is given to some patients as a control.

9. Can a theory be proved wrong?
   a. No, theories are the same as facts.
   b. No, because there is no good way to test a theory.
   c. Yes, a new observation or interpretation of data could disprove a theory.
   d. Yes, theories are the same as hypotheses.

10. Which of the following questions can NOT be answered using the scientific method?
    a. What was the first living organism on Earth?
    b. Does a particular gene influence aging in mice?
    c. How does migration affect the reproductive success of monarch butterflies?
    d. How does coastal development affect wetland biodiversity?

Write It Out

1. Describe each of the five characteristics of life, and list several nonliving things that possess at least two of these characteristics.
2. Draw and explain the relationships among producers, consumers, and decomposers.
3. What is homeostasis? Give an example other than those mentioned in the book.
4. Describe the main differences between asexual and sexual reproduction. Why are both types of reproduction common?

5. Describe a specific adaptation in an organism familiar to you, and explain how the environment could have selected for that adaptation.
6. How are the members of the three domains similar? How are they different?
7. Find an example of a news story that describes an experiment. Which components of the scientific method can you identify in the article?
8. Give two examples of questions that cannot be answered using the scientific method. Explain your reason for choosing each example.
9. If you dissect and label the parts of an earthworm, are you "doing science"? Why or why not? Give an example of a testable hypothesis that could result from dissecting organisms.
10. Studies show that research funded by drug companies is more favorable to new drugs than is publicly funded research. How can scientists avoid such systematic biases?
11. For each of the following examples, state whether each of the following faults occurred: (I) experimental evidence does not support conclusions; (II) inadequate controls; (III) biased sampling; (IV) inappropriate extrapolation from the experimental group to the general population; (V) sample size too small.
    a. "I ran 4 miles every morning when I was pregnant with my first child," the woman told her physician, "and Jamie weighed only half as much as a normal baby. This time, I didn't exercise at all, and Jamie's sister had normal birth weight. Therefore, running during pregnancy must cause low birth weight."
    b. Eating foods high in cholesterol was found to be dangerous for a large sample of individuals with hypercholesterolemia, a disorder of the heart and blood vessels. It was concluded from this study that all persons should limit dietary cholesterol intake.
    c. Osteogenesis imperfecta (OI) is an inherited condition that causes easily fractured bones. In a clinical study, 30 children with OI were given a new drug for 3 years. The children all showed less fatigue, improved bone density, and a lowered incidence of fractures compared with before treatment began. The conclusion: the drug is effective in treating OI.
    d. Researchers studied HIV in blood and semen from 11 HIV-infected men. In eight of the men, the virus was resistant to several medications. In two men, viruses from the blood were resistant to the class of drugs called protease inhibitors, but viruses from semen were not resistant. The researchers concluded that protease inhibitors do not reach the male reproductive organs.
12. Design an experiment to test the following hypothesis: "Eating chocolate causes zits." Include sample size, independent variable, dependent variable, the most important variables to standardize, and an experimental control.
13. Morgellons syndrome is a medical mystery. Patients experience sensations of stinging, biting, or crawling skin; they may also have rashes or sores that are slow to heal. Scientists have proposed several hypotheses to explain the symptoms: the patients may be imagining the disorder and creating the sores by picking at their skin; "Morgellons syndrome" may simply be a new name for a recognized skin disorder such as dermatitis or a bacterial infection; or exposure to toxins in the environment may cause the symptoms. If you had unlimited resources, what data might you collect to test each hypothesis?
14. Review "The Saccharin Scare" box on page 15. If you were investigating a possible saccharin-cancer link today, how would you improve on the design of the experiments conducted in the 1970s? Also, develop a hypothesis that could explain why more male than female rats developed tumors. Design an experiment that would help you test your hypothesis.

Pull It Together

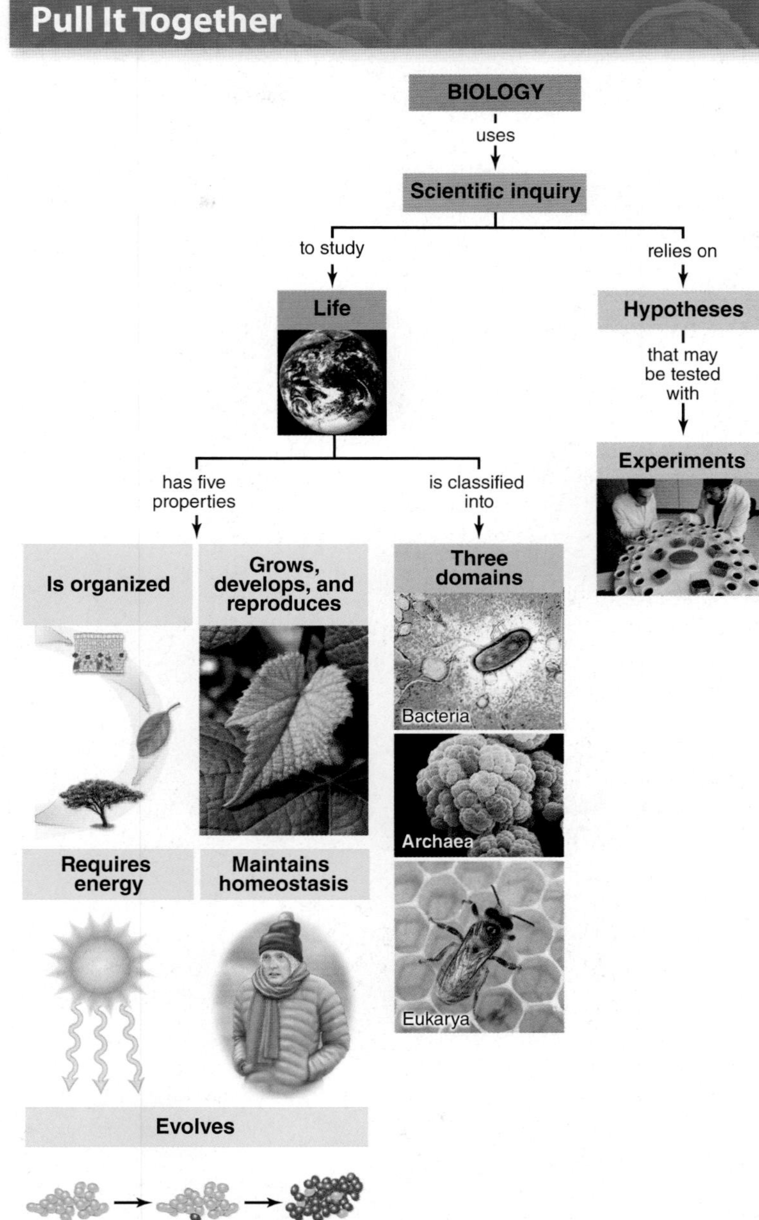

1. What are the elements of a controlled experiment?
2. What is the relationship between natural selection and evolution?
3. List the levels of biological organization, from atoms to the biosphere, and describe the relationships among them.
4. Where do the protists and kingdoms Plantae, Animalia, and Fungi fit into this concept map?

Enhance your study of this chapter with practice quizzes, animations and videos, answer keys, and downloadable study tools.
www.mhhe.com/hoefnagels

2 The Chemistry of Life

Life Is Chemistry. Soil, water, and air provide the elements that make up plants. When we eat the plants, these elements become part of our own bodies.

Learning Outline

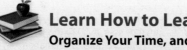

Learn How to Learn

Organize Your Time, and Don't Try to Cram

Get a calendar, and study the syllabus for every class you are taking. Write each due date in your calendar. Include homework assignments, quizzes, and exams, and add new dates as you learn them. Then, block out time before each due date to work on each task. Success comes much more easily if you take a steady pace instead of waiting until the last minute.

What's the Point?

If you are like many people, you may not feel as though chemistry has much to do with your life. But it does. The easiest connection to make is with your food. Look at any nutrition label from a food package. The chemicals listed on the label are a subset of the same ones that your own body is made of. You really are what you eat!

There are many other examples of everyday chemistry as well. Chemistry allows technicians to test urine for everything from drugs to sugar to the hormones that indicate pregnancy. Chemical reactions account for the damaging effects of acid rain and air pollution. The chemicals we add to swimming pools prevent the growth of algae and the spread of disease. The flea medicines we apply to our dogs and cats are chemicals that disrupt the insect life cycle. And we water and fertilize our plants because of chemistry. The list is literally endless.

Life is made of chemicals, and chemical reactions sustain the life of every individual. Understanding biology is impossible without an introduction to chemistry. This chapter describes how tiny particles called atoms come together to form the molecules of life.

2.1 Atoms Make Up All Matter

If you have ever touched a plant in a restaurant to see if it's real, you know that we all have an intuitive sense of what life is made of. A living leaf feels moist and pliable; a fake one is dry and stiff. But what does chemistry tell us about the composition of life?

Your desk, your book, your body, your sandwich, your dog, a swimming pool, a plastic plant—indeed, all objects in the universe, including life on Earth—are composed of matter and energy. **Matter** is any material that takes up space, such as organisms, rocks, the oceans, and gases in the atmosphere. This chapter and the next concentrate on the composition of living matter. **Energy,** on the other hand, is the ability to do work. In this context, *work* means moving matter. Heat, light, and chemical bonds are all forms of energy; chapters 4, 5, and 6 discuss the energy of life in detail.

A. Elements Are Fundamental Types of Matter

The matter that makes up every object in the universe consists of one or more elements. A chemical **element** is a pure substance that cannot be broken down by chemical means into other substances. Examples include pure oxygen (O), carbon (C), nitrogen (N), and hydrogen (H).

Scientists had already noticed patterns in the chemical behavior of the elements by the mid-1800s, and several had proposed schemes for organizing the elements into categories. Nineteenth-century Russian chemist Dmitry Mendeleyev invented the **periodic table,** the chart that we still use today. The chart is "periodic" because the chemical properties of the elements repeat in each column of the table. Figure 2.1 illustrates an abbreviated periodic table,

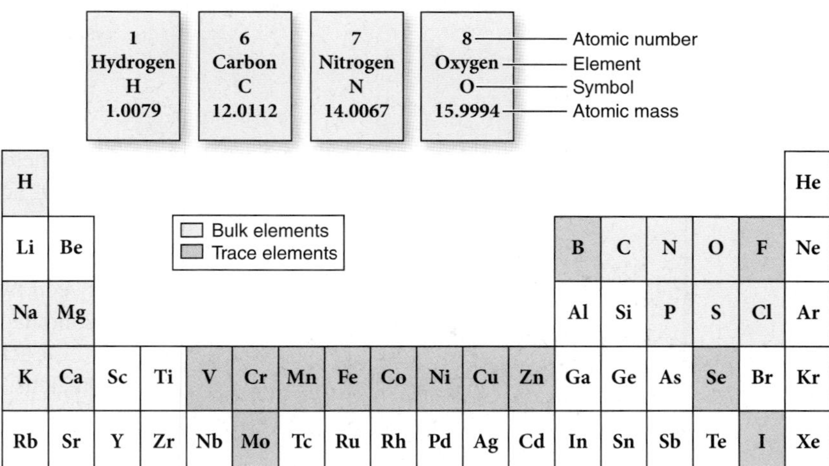

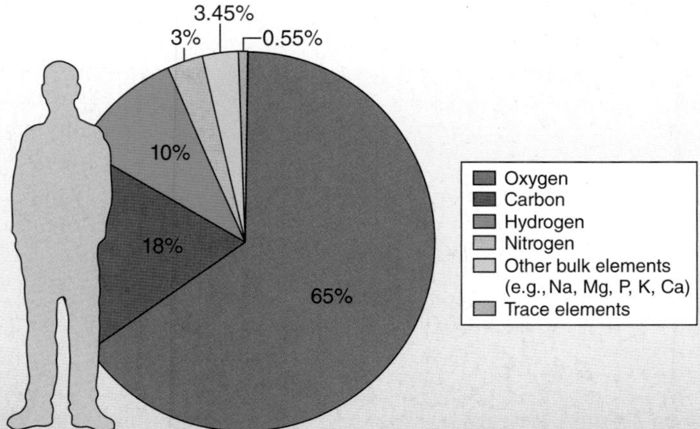

Figure 2.1 Chemical Elements. Each element has a unique atomic number and symbol; a complete periodic table appears in appendix D. The pie chart shows the distribution (by weight) of the elements that compose the human body.

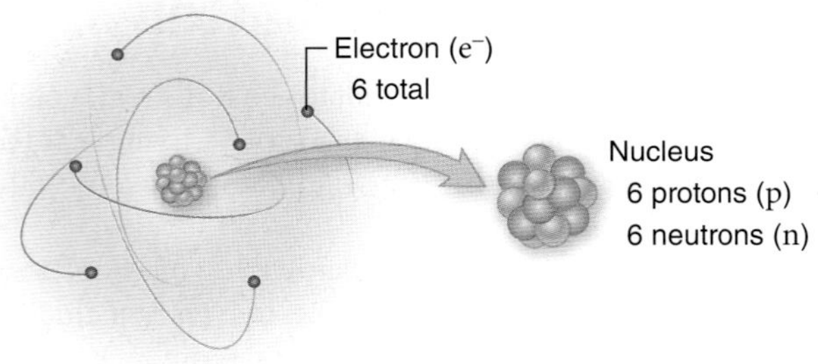

Figure 2.2 Atom Anatomy. The nucleus at the center of an atom is made of protons and neutrons. A cloud of electrons surrounds the nucleus. This example has six protons, so it is a carbon atom.

TABLE 2.1 Types of Particles in an Atom

Particle	Charge	Mass	Location
Electron	Negative (–)	0	Surrounding nucleus
Neutron	None	1	Nucleus
Proton	Positive (+)	1	Nucleus

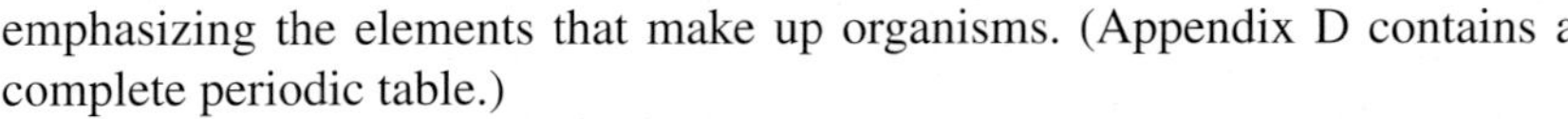

emphasizing the elements that make up organisms. (Appendix D contains a complete periodic table.)

Only about 25 elements are essential to life. Of these, the **bulk elements** are required in the largest amounts because they make up the vast majority of every living cell. For example, just four elements—carbon, hydrogen, oxygen, and nitrogen—account for 96% of the human body. **Minerals** are essential elements other than C, H, O, and N. Some minerals, including sodium (Na), magnesium (Mg), phosphorus (P), potassium (K), and calcium (Ca), are bulk elements, totalling about 3.5% of the human body by weight. The remaining minerals, such as iron (Fe) and iodine (I), are **trace elements,** meaning they are required in tiny amounts.

A person whose diet is deficient in any mineral can become ill or die. The thyroid gland, for example, requires iodine. If the diet does not supply enough iodine, the thyroid may become enlarged, forming a growth called a goiter. Similarly, blood requires iron to carry oxygen to the body's tissues. An iron-poor diet can therefore cause anemia.

B. Atoms Are Particles of Elements

An **atom** is the smallest possible "piece" of an element that retains the characteristics of the element. Atoms are composed of three types of particles (figure 2.2 and table 2.1). **Protons,** which carry a positive charge, and **neutrons,** which are uncharged, together form a central **nucleus.** Negatively charged **electrons** surround the nucleus. An electron is vanishingly small compared with a proton or a neutron.

For simplicity, most illustrations of atoms show the electrons closely hugging the nucleus. In reality, however, if the nucleus of a hydrogen atom were the size of a meatball, the electron belonging to that atom would be an invisible speck as much as 1 kilometer away from it! Thus, most of an atom's mass is concentrated in the nucleus, while the electron cloud occupies virtually all of its volume.

The electron whizzes around a hydrogen atom's nucleus at about 2200 kilometers per second. How can this electron cloud, which is mostly empty space, account for the solid "feel" of the objects in our world? The fact that the electrons are in constant motion helps explain this paradox. A good analogy is a ceiling fan. When the fan is not spinning, it is easy to move your hand between two blades. But when the fan is on, the rotating blades seem to form a solid disk.

Each element has a unique **atomic number,** the number of protons in the nucleus. Hydrogen, the simplest type of atom, has an atomic number of 1. In contrast, an atom of uranium has 92 protons. Elements are arranged sequentially in the periodic table by atomic number.

When the number of protons equals the number of electrons, the atom is electrically neutral; that is, it has no net charge. An **ion** is an atom (or group of atoms) that has gained or lost electrons and therefore has a net negative or positive charge. Common positively charged ions include hydrogen (H^+), sodium (Na^+), and potassium (K^+). Negatively charged ions include iodide (I^-) and chloride (Cl^-). Ions participate in many biological processes, including the transmission of messages in the nervous system. They also form ionic bonds, discussed in section 2.2. ▸ action potential, p. 486

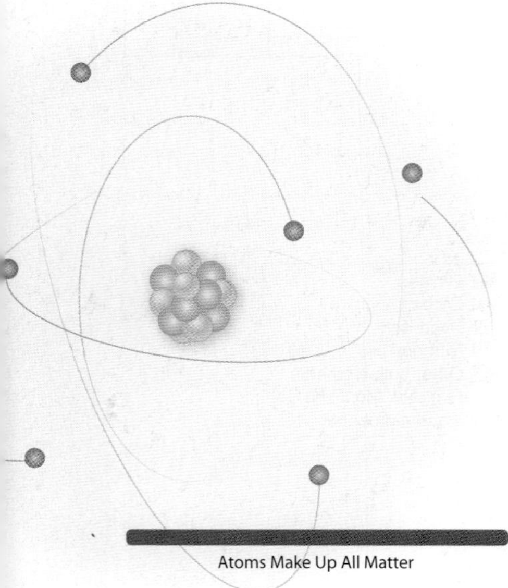

C. The Number of Neutrons May Vary

An atom's **mass number** is the total number of protons and neutrons in its nucleus. Because neutrons and protons have the same mass (see table 2.1), subtracting the atomic number from the mass number therefore yields the number of neutrons in an atom.

All atoms of an element have the same atomic number but not necessarily the same number of neutrons. An **isotope** is any of these different forms of a single element. Carbon, for example, has three isotopes, designated ^{12}C (six neutrons), ^{13}C (seven neutrons), and ^{14}C (eight neutrons). The superscript in each isotope's symbol denotes the mass number.

An element's **atomic mass** (also called atomic weight) is the average mass of all isotopes. Often one isotope of an element is very abundant, and others are rare. For example, about 99% of carbon isotopes are ^{12}C, and only 1% are ^{13}C or ^{14}C. Because nearly all carbon atoms contain six neutrons, carbon's atomic mass is very close to 12 in the periodic table (see figure 2.1).

Many of the known isotopes are unstable and **radioactive,** which means they emit energy as rays or particles when they break down into more stable forms. Every radioactive isotope has a characteristic half-life, which is the time it takes for half of the atoms in a sample to emit radiation, or "decay" to a different, more stable form. Scientists have determined the half-life of each radioactive isotope experimentally. Depending on the isotope, the half-life might range from a fraction of a second to millions or even billions of years (relatively large samples of isotopes are required to calculate the longest half-lives).

Radioactive isotopes have a variety of uses in medicine and science. For example, radiation can be used to kill microorganisms on medical equipment and on food surfaces. Likewise, directing radiation at a tumor kills cancer cells. In addition, a physician might give a patient a radioactive tracer, then track how the isotope moves in the body to search for tumors or examine a physiological process. (This is the basis of a PET scan.) Archaeologists and paleontologists use the known half-lives of radioactive isotopes to determine the ages of artifacts and fossils (see chapter 13).

But the same properties that make radioactive isotopes useful can also make them dangerous. Exposure to excessive radiation can lead to radiation sickness, and radiation-induced mutations of a cell's DNA can cause cancer (see chapter 8). The lead-containing "bib" that a dentist places on you during a mouth X-ray protects your chest from radiation.

Table 2.2 reviews the terminology of matter.

2.1 Mastering Concepts

1. Which chemical elements do organisms require in large amounts?
2. Where in an atom are protons, neutrons, and electrons located?
3. What does an element's atomic number indicate?
4. What is the relationship between an atom's mass number and an element's atomic mass?
5. How do all isotopes of the same element differ from one another?

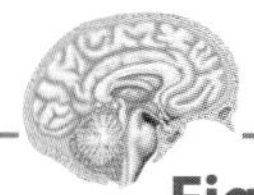

Figure It Out

The most abundant isotope of iron (Fe) has a mass number of 56. If Fe has an atomic number of 26, how many neutrons are in each atom of ^{56}Fe?

Answer: 30.

TABLE 2.2 A Miniglossary of Matter

Term	Definition
Element	A fundamental type of substance
Atom	The smallest unit of an element that retains the characteristics of that element
Atomic number	The number of protons in an atom's nucleus
Mass number	The number of protons plus the number of neutrons in an atom's nucleus
Isotope	Any of the different forms of the same element, distinguished from each other by the number of neutrons in the nucleus
Atomic mass	The average mass of all isotopes of an element

2.2 Chemical Bonds Link Atoms

Like all organisms, you are composed mostly of carbon, hydrogen, oxygen, and nitrogen atoms. But the arrangement of these atoms is not random. Instead, your atoms are organized into molecules (see figure 1.2). A **molecule** is two or more chemically joined atoms.

Some molecules, such as the gases hydrogen (H_2), oxygen (O_2), and nitrogen (N_2), consist of two atoms of the same element. More often, however, the elements in a molecule are different. A **compound** is a molecule composed of two or more different elements. Water (H_2O) is a compound made of two atoms of hydrogen and one of oxygen. Many large biological compounds, including DNA and proteins, consist of tens of thousands of atoms.

Scientists use molecular formulas to describe the chemical structure of a molecule. Each formula includes the symbol for each element in the molecule; subscripts indicate the number of atoms of each element. For example, methane is written CH_4, which denotes one carbon atom attached to four hydrogen atoms. Table salt's formula is NaCl, that of water is H_2O, and that of the gas carbon dioxide is CO_2.

What forces hold together the atoms that make up each of these molecules? To understand the answer, we must first learn more about how electrons are arranged around the nucleus.

A. Electrons Determine Bonding

Electrons occupy distinct energetic regions around the nucleus. They are constantly in motion, so it is impossible to determine the exact location of any electron at any instant in time. Instead, chemists use the term **orbitals** to describe the most likely location for an electron relative to its nucleus. Each orbital can hold up to two electrons. Consequently, the more electrons in an atom, the more orbitals they occupy.

Electron orbitals exist in several energy levels; an **energy shell** is a group of orbitals that share the same level. The number of orbitals in each shell determines the number of electrons the shell can hold. The lowest energy shell, for example, contains just one orbital and thus holds up to two electrons. The next shell contains up to eight electrons in four orbitals.

Electrons occupy the lowest energy level available to them, starting with the innermost one. As each energy shell fills, any additional electrons must reside in higher energy shells. For example, hydrogen has only one electron in the lowest energy orbital, and helium has two. Carbon has six electrons; two occupy the lowest energy orbital, and four are in the next energy shell. Oxygen, with eight electrons total, has two electrons in the lowest energy orbital and six in three orbitals at the next higher energy level.

We can thus envision any atom's electrons as occupying a series of concentric energy shells, each having a higher energy level than the one inside it (figure 2.3). An atom's **valence shell** is its outermost occupied energy shell. Atoms are most stable when their valence shells are full. The gases helium (He) and neon (Ne), for example, are inert. Because their outermost shells are full, they exist in nature without combining with other atoms.

For most atoms, however, the valence shell is only partially filled. Such an atom will become most stable if its valence-shell "vacancies" fill. To arrive at exactly the right number, atoms share, steal, or donate electrons. The result is a **chemical bond:** an attractive force that holds atoms together. The remainder of this section describes three types of chemical bonds that are important in biology (table 2.3).

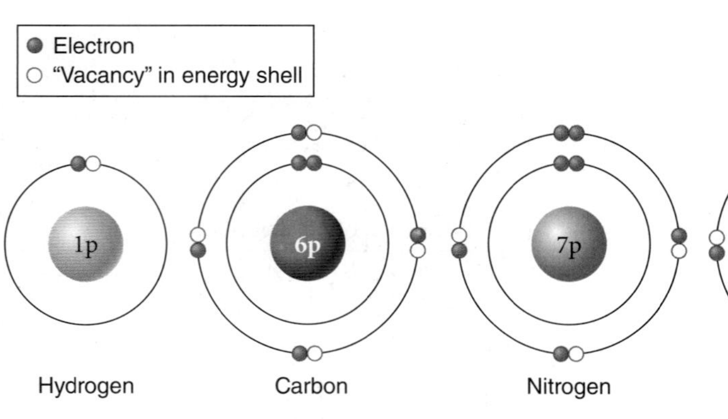

Figure 2.3 Energy Shells. Shown here are models of the four most common types of atoms in organisms.

TABLE 2.3 Chemical Bonds: A Summary

Type	Chemical Basis	Strength	Example
Covalent bond	Two atoms share pairs of electrons.	Strong	O—H bond within water molecule
Ionic bond	One atom donates one or more electrons to another atom, forming oppositely charged ions that attract each other.	Strong but breaks easily in water	Sodium chloride (NaCl)
Hydrogen bond	An atom with a partial negative charge attracts an atom with a partial positive charge. Hydrogen bonds form between adjacent molecules or between different parts of a large molecule.	Weak	Attraction between adjacent water molecules

B. In a Covalent Bond, Atoms Share Electrons

A **covalent bond** forms when two atoms share electrons. The shared electrons travel around both nuclei, strongly connecting the atoms together. Most of the bonds in biological molecules are covalent.

Methane provides an excellent example of how atoms share electrons to fill their valence shells. A carbon atom has six electrons, two of which occupy its innermost shell. That leaves four electrons in its valence shell, which has a capacity of eight. Carbon therefore requires four more electrons to fill its outermost shell. As shown in the top half of figure 2.4, a carbon atom can attain the stable eight-electron configuration by sharing electrons with four hydrogen atoms, each of which has one electron in its only shell. The resulting molecule is methane, CH_4. The bottom half of figure 2.4 shows how oxygen and hydrogen form covalent bonds as they combine to form water.

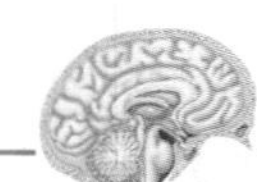

Figure It Out

Use the information in figure 2.1 to predict the number of covalent bonds that nitrogen (N) forms.

Answer: 3.

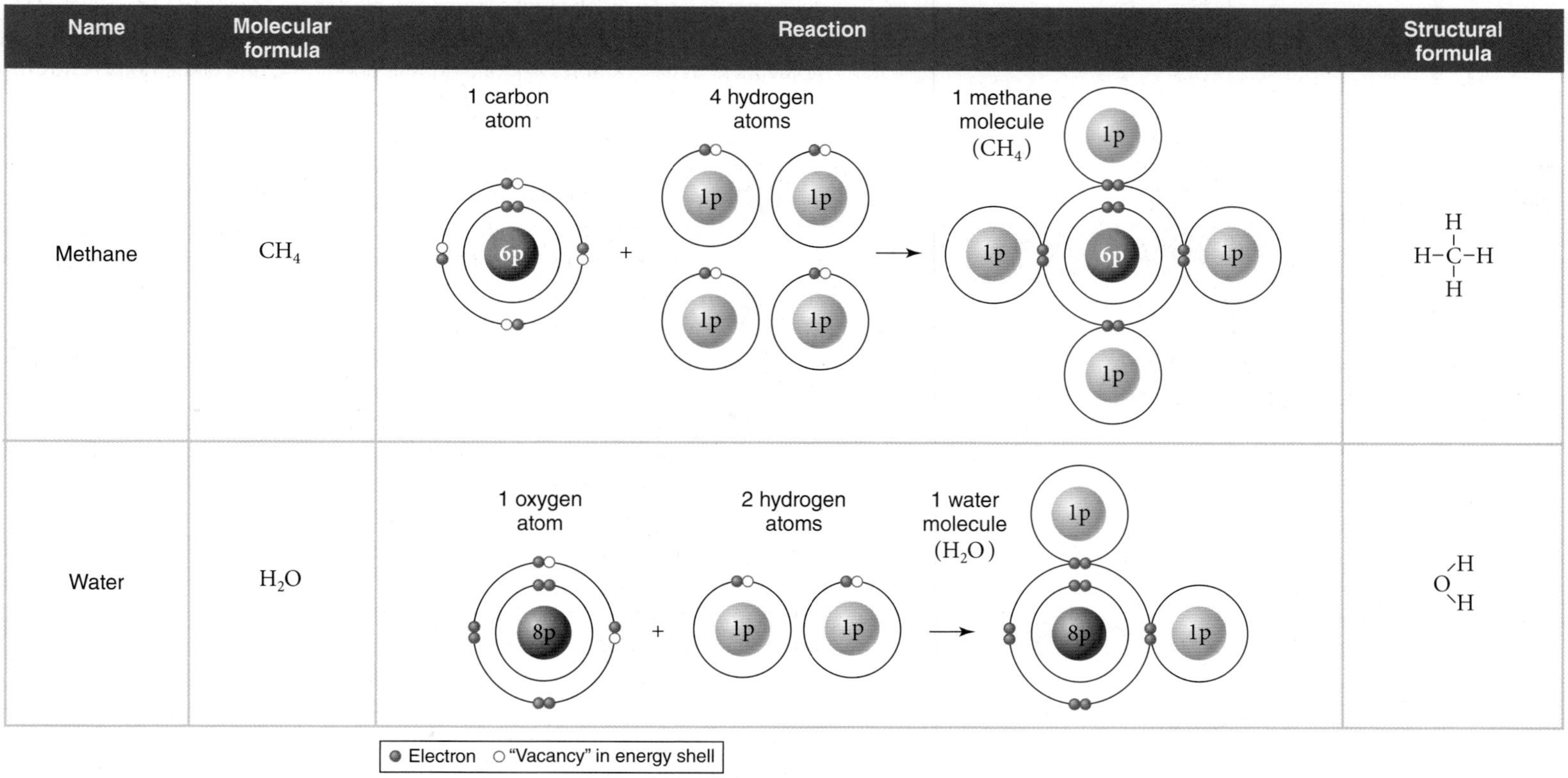

Name	Molecular formula	Reaction	Structural formula
Methane	CH_4	1 carbon atom (6p) + 4 hydrogen atoms (1p, 1p, 1p, 1p) → 1 methane molecule (CH_4)	H–C–H with H above and below C
Water	H_2O	1 oxygen atom (8p) + 2 hydrogen atoms (1p, 1p) → 1 water molecule (H_2O)	O bonded to two H

● Electron ○ "Vacancy" in energy shell

Figure 2.4 Atoms Share Electrons in Covalent Bonds. Methane (CH_4) contains four covalent bonds, formed when one carbon and four hydrogen atoms complete their outermost shells by sharing electrons. A water molecule (H_2O) has two covalent bonds.

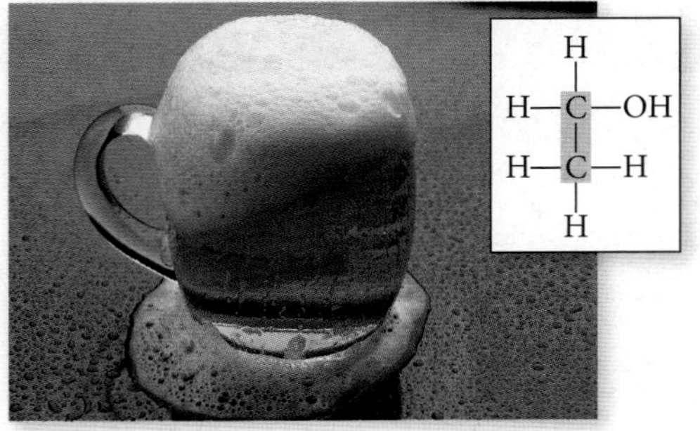

a. Ethanol

b. Ethylene

c. Acetylene

d. Caffeine

Figure 2.5 Carbon Atoms Form Four Covalent Bonds. (a) Ethanol is an alcohol built around two singly bonded carbon atoms. (b) Ethylene has two carbon atoms linked by a double bond. Ethylene is a plant hormone that triggers fruit to ripen. (c) Acetylene includes two carbons held together by a triple bond. Tremendous heat energy is released when the triple bond in this flammable gas is broken. (d) Caffeine illustrates a double-ring structure of carbon bonded with nitrogen, oxygen, and hydrogen atoms.

Covalent bonds are usually depicted as lines between the interacting atoms, with each line representing one bond. Each single bond contains two electrons, one from each atom. Atoms can also share two or three pairs of electrons, forming double and triple covalent bonds, respectively (figure 2.5). The molecule O_2, for example, has one double bond; a strong triple bond holds together the two atoms in N_2.

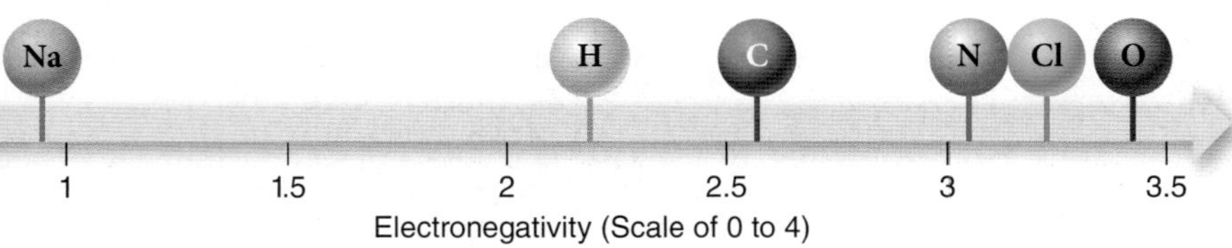

Figure 2.6 Unequal Attraction. Atoms vary widely in their electronegativity, which is the ability to attract electrons.

Covalent bonding means "sharing," but the partnership is not necessarily equal. **Electronegativity** is a measure of an atom's ability to attract electrons (figure 2.6). Oxygen, for example, strongly attracts electrons. Carbon and hydrogen have low electronegativity relative to oxygen. A **nonpolar covalent bond** is a "bipartisan" union in which both atoms exert approximately equal pull on their shared electrons. A bond between two atoms of the same element is nonpolar; after all, a bond between two identical atoms must be electrically balanced. H_2, N_2, and O_2 are all nonpolar molecules. Carbon and hydrogen atoms have similar electronegativity. A carbon–hydrogen bond is therefore also nonpolar.

A **polar covalent bond,** in contrast, is a lopsided union in which one nucleus exerts a stronger pull on the shared electrons than does the other nucleus. Polar bonds form whenever a highly electronegative atom such as oxygen shares electrons—albeit unequally—with a less electronegative partner such as carbon or hydrogen. Like a battery, a polar covalent bond has a positive end and a negative end.

Polar covalent bonds are critical to biology. As described in section 2.2D, they are responsible for hydrogen bonds, which in turn help define not only the unique properties of water (see section 2.3) but also the shapes of DNA and proteins (section 2.5).

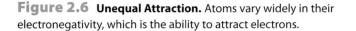

C. In an Ionic Bond, One Atom Transfers Electrons to Another Atom

So far, we have seen covalent bonds in which atoms share electrons either equally (nonpolar) or unequally (polar). Is it possible for two atoms to have such different electronegativities that one actually takes one or more of its partner's electrons?

The answer is yes. Recall that an atom is most stable if its valence shell is full. Not surprisingly, the most electronegative atoms, such as chlorine (Cl), are usually those whose valence shells have only one "vacancy." Likewise, sodium (Na) and other weakly electronegative atoms have only one electron in their outermost shells. Sodium would not benefit at all from sharing. Instead, sodium is most stable if it simply releases its extra electron to chlorine, which needs this "scrap" electron to complete its own valence shell.

An ion is an atom that has lost or gained electrons. The atom that has lost electrons carries a positive charge, whereas the one that has gained electrons acquires a negative charge. An **ionic bond** results from the electrical attraction between two ions with opposite charges. In general, such bonds form between an atom whose outermost shell is almost empty and one whose valence shell is nearly full. Thus, when sodium donates its electron to an atom of chlorine, the two atoms bond ionically to form NaCl (figure 2.7).

In NaCl, the most stable configuration of Na^+ and Cl^- is a three-dimensional crystal. Ionic bonds in crystals are strong, as demonstrated by the stability of the salt in your shaker. Those same crystals, however, dissolve when you stir them into water. As described in section 2.3, water molecules pull ionic bonds apart.

Nonpolar covalent bonds, polar covalent bonds, and ionic bonds represent points along a continuum. Two atoms of similar electronegativity share electrons equally in nonpolar covalent bonds. If one atom tugs at the shared electrons much more than the other, the covalent bond is polar. And if one atom is so electronegative that it rips electrons from another atom's valence shell, an ionic bond forms. Notice that the bond type depends on the *difference* in electronegativity, so the same element can participate in different types of bonds. Oxygen, for example, forms nonpolar bonds with itself (as in O_2) and polar bonds with hydrogen (as in H_2O).

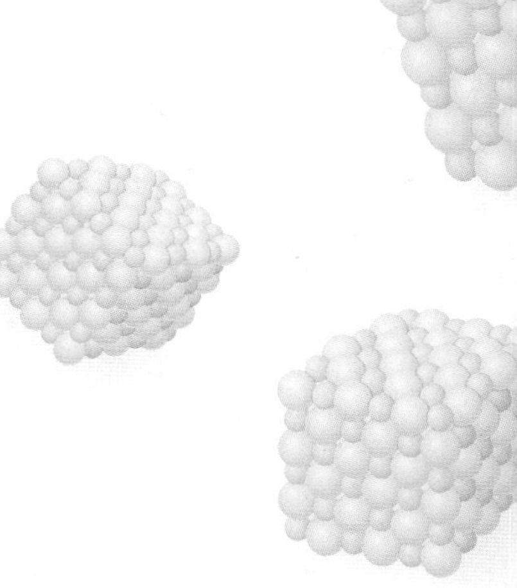

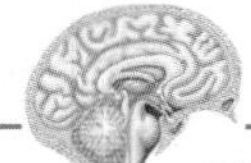

Figure It Out

The electronegativity of potassium (K) is 0.82. Using the scale in figure 2.6, what type of bond should form between K and Cl?

Answer: Ionic.

Figure 2.7 Table Salt, an Ionically Bonded Molecule. (a) A sodium atom (Na) can donate its "spare" electron to a chlorine atom (Cl), which has seven electrons in its outermost shell. The resulting ions (Na^+ and Cl^-) form the compound sodium chloride, NaCl. (b) Na^+ and Cl^- ions occur in a repeating pattern that produces salt crystals.

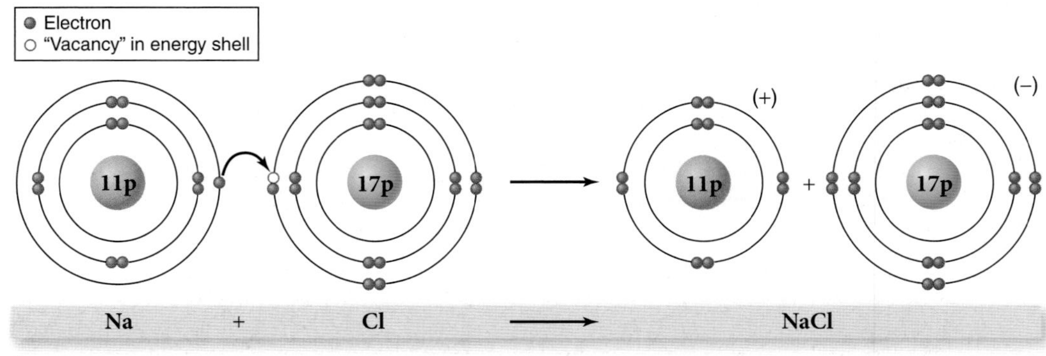

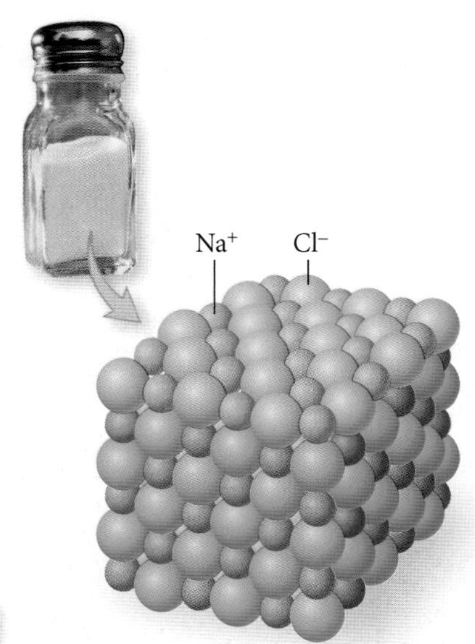

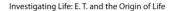

Whether it contains covalent or ionic bonds, a compound's characteristics can differ strikingly from those of its separate elements. Consider table salt, sodium chloride. Sodium is a silvery, highly reactive solid metal, whereas chlorine is a yellow, corrosive gas. But when equal numbers of these two atoms combine, the resulting compound forms the familiar white salt crystals that we sprinkle on food—an excellent example of an emergent property (chapter 1). Another example is methane, the main component of natural gas. Its components are carbon, a black sooty solid, and hydrogen, a light, combustible gas.

D. Partial Charges on Polar Molecules Create Hydrogen Bonds

When a covalent bond is polar, the negatively charged electrons spend more time around the nucleus of the more electronegative atom than around its partner. The "electron-hogging" atom therefore has a partial negative charge (written as "δ^-"), and the less-electronegative partner has an electron "deficit" and a partial positive charge (δ^+).

In a **hydrogen bond,** opposite partial charges on *adjacent molecules*—or within a single large molecule—attract each other. The name comes from the fact that the atom with the partial positive charge is always hydrogen. The atom with the partial negative charge, on the other hand, is a highly electronegative atom such as oxygen or nitrogen.

Water provides the simplest illustration of hydrogen bonds (figure 2.8). Each water molecule has a "boomerang" shape. Moreover, the two O—H bonds in water are polar, with the nucleus of each oxygen atom attracting the shared electrons more strongly than do the hydrogen nuclei. Each hydrogen atom in a water molecule therefore has a partial positive charge, which attracts the partial negative charge of the oxygen atom on an adjacent molecule. This attraction is the hydrogen bond. The partial charges on O and H, plus the bent shape, cause water molecules to stick to one another and to some other substances. (This slight stickiness is another example of an emergent property, because it arises from interactions between O and H.)

Hydrogen bonds are relatively weak compared with ionic and covalent bonds. In 1 second, the hydrogen bonds between a water molecule and its nearest neighbors break and re-form some 500 billion times. Although hydrogen bonds are weak, they account for many of water's unusual characteristics—the subject of section 2.3. In addition, multiple hydrogen bonds help stabilize some large molecules, including proteins and DNA (see section 2.5).

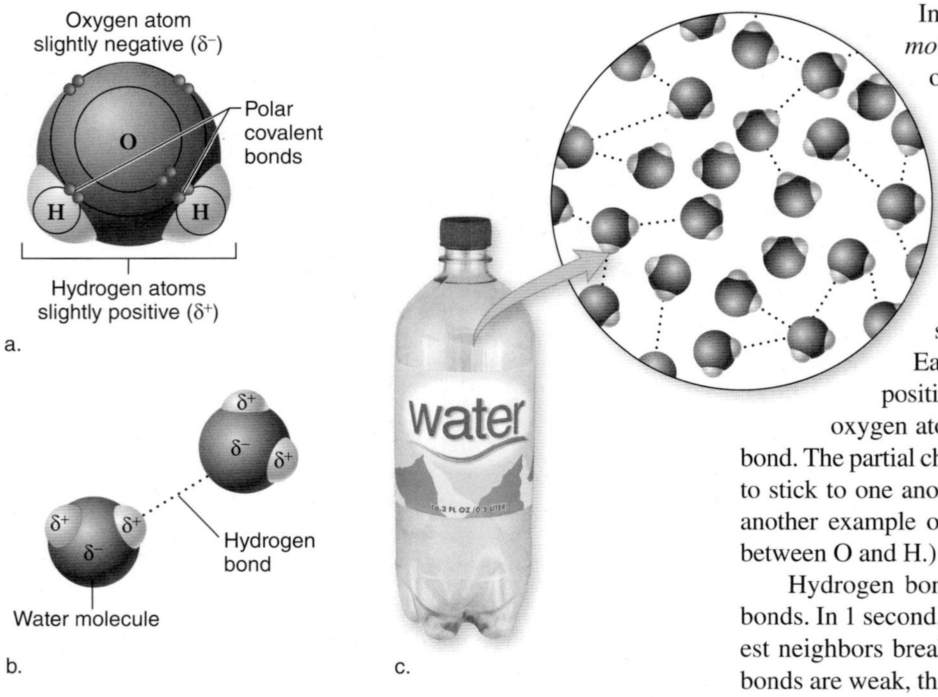

Figure 2.8 Hydrogen Bonds. (a) In water's polar covalent bonds, oxygen attracts the shared electrons more strongly than does hydrogen. The O atom therefore bears a partial negative charge (δ^-), and the H atoms carry partial positive charges (δ^+). (b) The hydrogen bond is the attraction between partial charges on adjacent molecules. (c) This bottle contains many water molecules that stick together with hydrogen bonds.

E. Bonds Break and Form in Chemical Reactions

In a **chemical reaction,** two or more molecules "swap" their atoms to yield different molecules; that is, some chemical bonds break and new ones form. Life exists because of thousands of simultaneous chemical reactions. Chemists depict these reactions as equations with the **reactants,** or starting materials, to the left of an arrow; the **products,** or results of the reaction, are listed to the right.

Consider what happens when the methane in natural gas burns inside a heater, gas oven, or stove (figure 2.9):

$$CH_4 + 2O_2 \longrightarrow CO_2 + 2H_2O$$
$$\text{methane + oxygen} \longrightarrow \text{carbon dioxide + water}$$

In words, this equation says that one methane molecule combines with two oxygen molecules to produce a carbon dioxide molecule and two molecules of water. The bonds of the methane and oxygen molecules have broken, and new bonds formed in the products.

Note that each side of the equation shows the same number of atoms of each element: that is, one carbon, four hydrogens, and four oxygens. The atoms were neither created nor destroyed in the reaction; rather, they were simply rearranged.

Figure 2.9 **Burning Gas.** When we burn natural gas (methane) in a stove, the products are carbon dioxide and water—and a lot of heat.

2.2 Mastering Concepts

1. How are atoms, molecules, and compounds related?
2. How does the number of valence electrons determine an atom's tendency to form bonds?
3. Explain how electronegativity differences between atoms result in nonpolar covalent bonds, polar covalent bonds, and ionic bonds.
4. What is the relationship between polar covalent bonds and hydrogen bonds?
5. What happens in a chemical reaction?

2.3 Water Is Essential to Life

Although water may seem to be a rather ordinary fluid, it is anything but. The tiny, three-atom water molecule has extraordinary properties that make it essential to all organisms, which explains why the search for life on other planets begins with the search for water. Indeed, life on Earth began in water, and for at least the first 3 billion years of life's history on Earth, all life was aquatic. It was not until some 475 million years ago, when plants and fungi colonized land, that life could survive without being surrounded by water. Even now, terrestrial organisms cannot live without it. This section explains some of the properties that make water central to biology.

A. Water Is Cohesive

Hydrogen bonds contribute to a property of water called **cohesion**—the tendency of water molecules to stick together. Without cohesion, water would evaporate instantly in most locations on Earth's surface. Cohesion also contributes to the observation that you can sometimes fill a glass so full that water is above the rim, yet it doesn't flow over the side unless disturbed.

This tendency of a liquid to hold together at its surface is called surface tension, and not all liquids exhibit it. Water has high surface tension because it is cohesive. At the boundary between water and air, the water molecules form hydrogen bonds with neighbors to their sides and below them in the liquid. These bonds tend to hold the surface molecules together, creating a thin "skin" that is strong enough to support the weight of a small insect (figure 2.10).

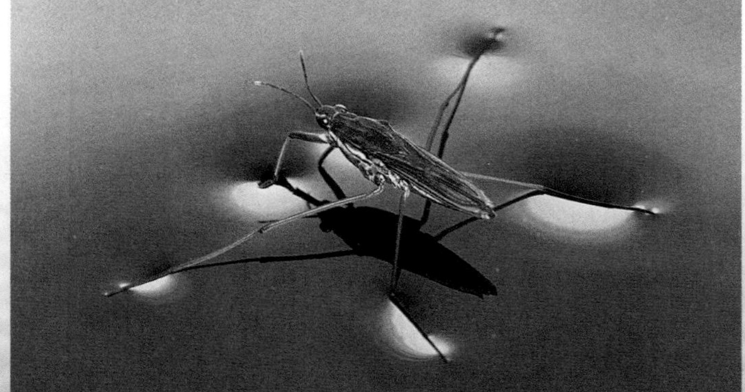

Figure 2.10 **Running on Water.** A lightweight body and water-repellent legs allow this water strider to "skate" across a pond without breaking the water's surface tension.

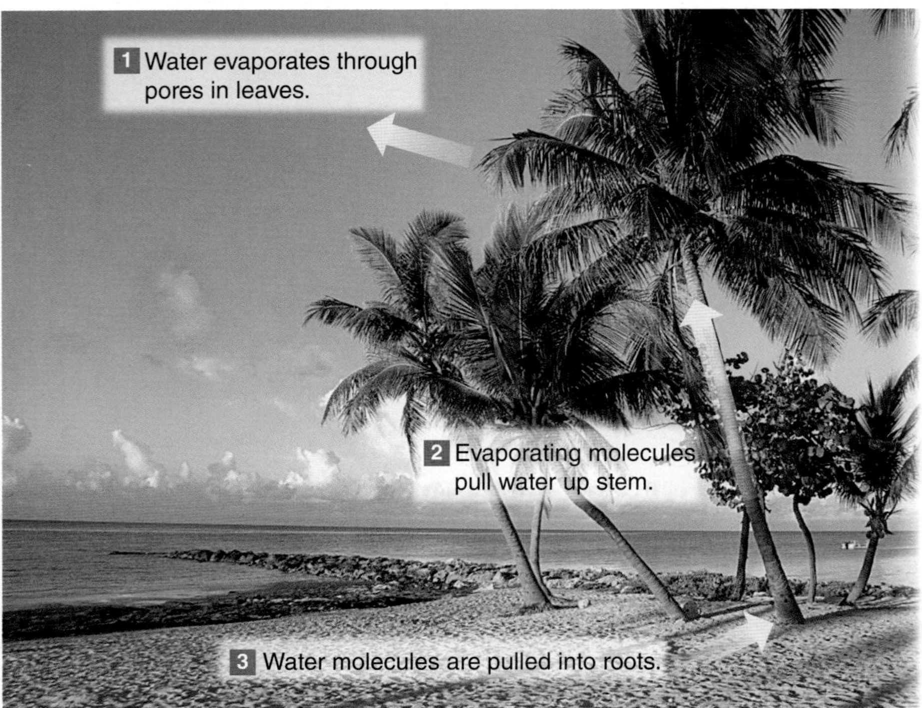
1 Water evaporates through pores in leaves.
2 Evaporating molecules pull water up stem.
3 Water molecules are pulled into roots.

Figure 2.11 Defying Gravity. Thanks to cohesion, water evaporating from the leaves of these palm trees is replaced by water pulled up from the soil and through the tree's trunk.

Cohesion is at work when water seemingly defies gravity as it rises from a plant's roots to its highest leaves (figure 2.11). Water entering roots is drawn up through internal conducting tubes as water molecules evaporate from leaf cells. ▸ transpiration, p. 440

B. Many Substances Dissolve in Water

Another reason that water is vital to life is that it can dissolve a wide variety of chemicals. To illustrate this process, picture the slow disappearance of table salt as it dissolves in water. Although the salt crystals seem to vanish, the sodium and chloride ions remain. Water molecules surround each ion individually, separating them from one another (figure 2.12).

In this example, water is a **solvent:** a chemical in which other substances dissolve. The **solutes** are the dissolved substances—in this case, the ions of sodium and chlorine. A **solution** consists of one or more solutes dissolved in a liquid solvent. In a so-called aqueous solution, water is the solvent. But not all solutions are aqueous. According to the rule "Like dissolves like," polar solvents such as water dissolve polar molecules; similarly, nonpolar solvents dissolve nonpolar substances.

Scientists divide chemicals into two categories based on solubility in water. **Hydrophilic** substances are either polar or charged, so they readily dissolve in water (the term literally means "water-loving"). Examples include sugar, salt, and ions. Electrolytes are ions in the body's fluids, and the salty taste of sweat illustrates water's ability to dissolve them. Sports drinks replace not only water but also sodium, potassium, magnesium, and calcium ions that are lost in perspiration during vigorous exercise. Electrolytes are essential to many processes, including heart and nerve function.

On the other hand, nonpolar molecules made mostly of carbon and hydrogen, such as fats, are **hydrophobic** ("water-fearing") because they do not dissolve in, or form hydrogen bonds with, water. This is why water alone will not remove grease from hands, dishes, or clothes. Dry cleaning companies use nonpolar solvents to remove oily spots from fabric. Detergents contain molecules that attract both water and fats, so they can dislodge greasy substances and carry the mess down the drain with the wastewater.

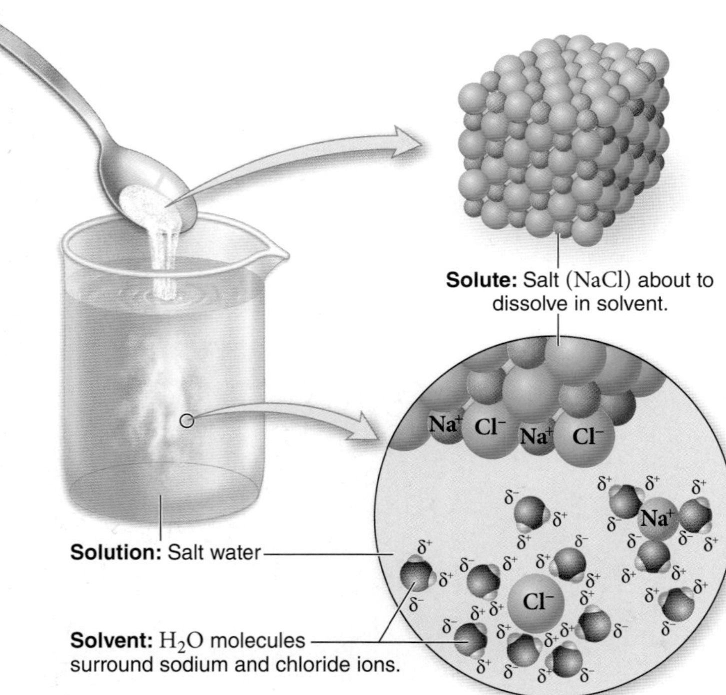
Solute: Salt (NaCl) about to dissolve in solvent.
Na+ Cl− Na+ Cl−
Na+
Cl−
Solution: Salt water
Solvent: H2O molecules surround sodium and chloride ions.

Figure 2.12 Solutions Are Mixtures of Substances. As salt crystals dissolve, polar water molecules surround each sodium and chloride ion.

C. Water Regulates Temperature

Another unusual property of water is its ability to resist temperature changes. When molecules absorb energy, they move faster. But the hydrogen bonds that hold water molecules together tend to counteract this movement. As a result, more heat is needed to raise water's temperature than is required for most other liquids, including alcohols. Because an organism's fluids are aqueous solutions, the same effect holds: an organism may encounter considerable heat before its body temperature becomes dangerously high. Likewise, the body cools slowly in cold temperatures.

At a global scale, water's resistance to temperature change explains why coastal climates tend to be mild. People living along the California coast have good weather year-round because the Pacific Ocean's steady temperature helps keep winters warm and summers cool. Far away from the ocean, in the central United States, winters are much colder and summers are much hotter. These differences in local climate contribute to the unique ecosystems that occur in each region (see chapter 19).

Hydrogen bonds also mean that a lot of heat is required to evaporate water. **Evaporation** is the conversion of a liquid into a vapor. When sweat evaporates from skin, individual water molecules break away from the liquid droplet and float into the atmosphere. Surface molecules must absorb energy to escape, and when they do, heat energy is removed from those that remain, drawing heat out of the body—an important part of the mechanism that regulates body temperature.

D. Water Expands as It Freezes

Water's unusual tendency to expand upon freezing also affects life. In liquid water, hydrogen bonds are constantly forming and breaking, and the water molecules are relatively close together. But in an ice crystal, the hydrogen bonds are stable, and the molecules are "locked" into roughly hexagonal shapes. Therefore, the less-dense ice floats on the surface of the denser liquid water below (figure 2.13).

This characteristic benefits aquatic organisms. When the air temperature drops, a small amount of water freezes at the pond's surface, forming a solid cap of ice that traps heat in the water below. If ice were to become denser upon freezing, it would sink to the bottom. The lake would then gradually turn to ice from the bottom up, entrapping the organisms that live there.

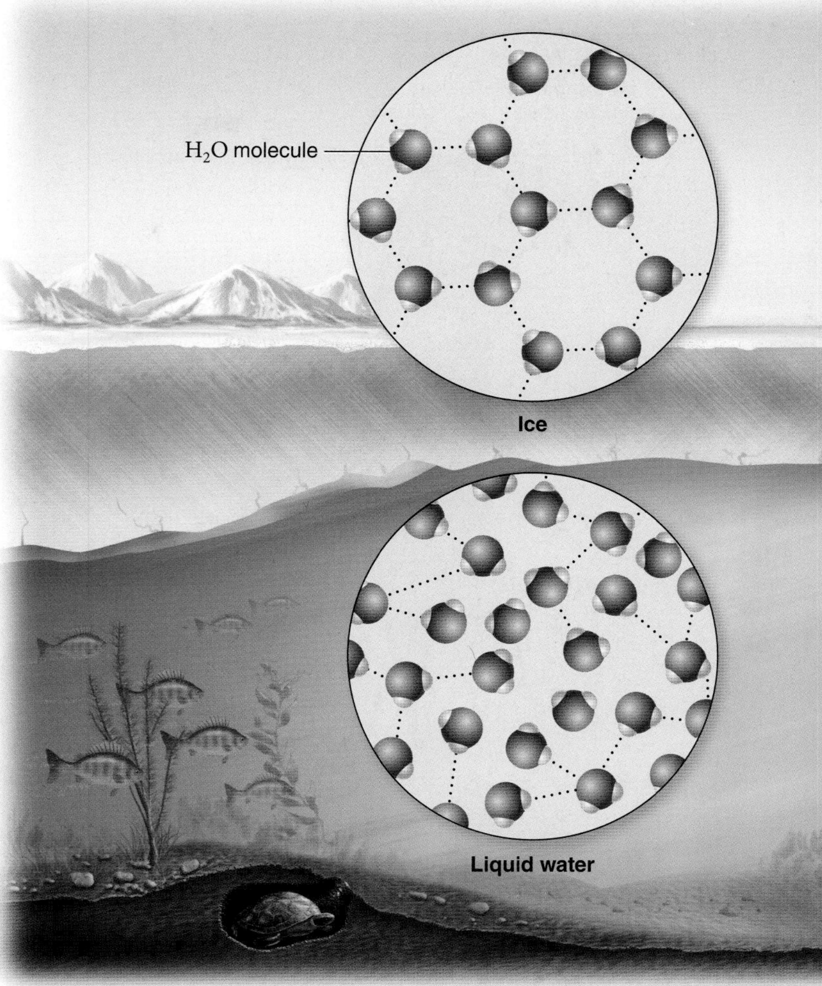

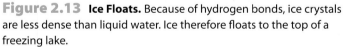

Figure 2.13 Ice Floats. Because of hydrogen bonds, ice crystals are less dense than liquid water. Ice therefore floats to the top of a freezing lake.

E. Water Participates in Life's Chemical Reactions

Nearly all of life's chemical reactions occur in the watery solution that fills and bathes cells. Moreover, water is either a reactant in or a product of many of these reactions. In photosynthesis, for example, plants use the sun's energy to assemble food out of just two reactants: carbon dioxide and water (see chapter 5). Section 2.5 describes two other water-related reactions, hydrolysis and dehydration synthesis, that are vital to life.

2.3 Mastering Concepts

1. How is cohesion important to life?
2. Differentiate between hydrophilic and hydrophobic molecules.
3. How does water help an organism regulate its body temperature?
4. How do the different densities of ice and water affect life?
5. How does water participate in the chemistry of life?

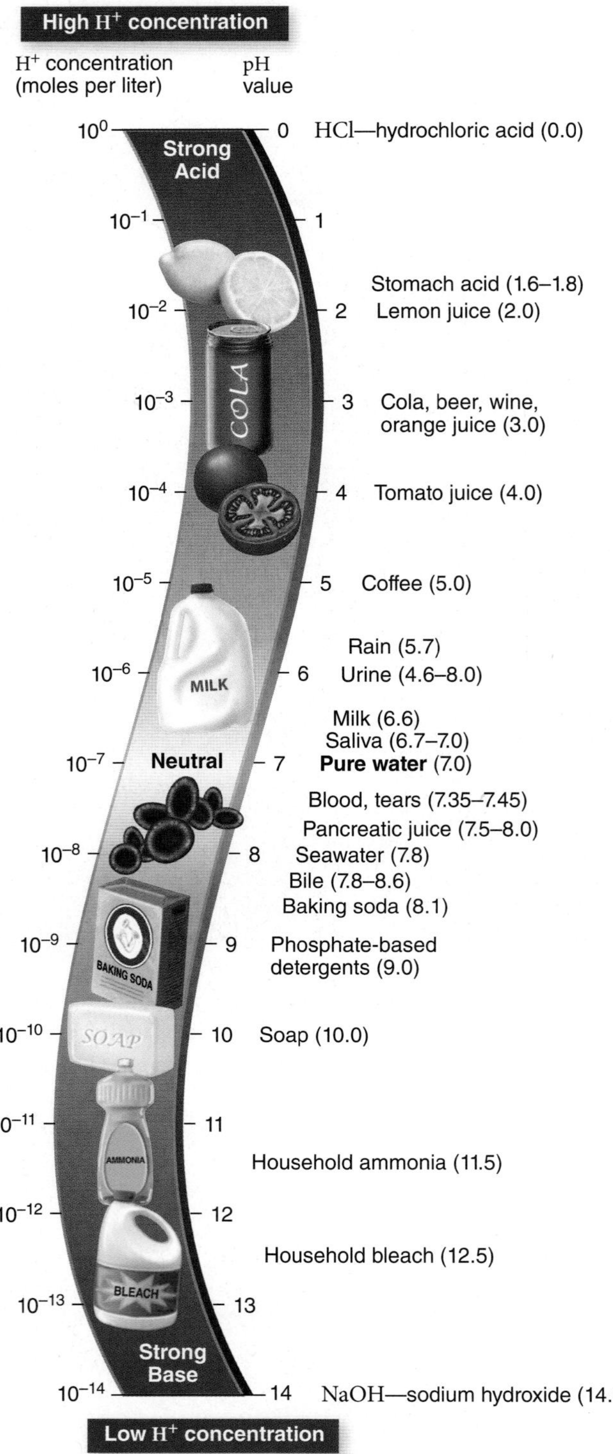

Figure 2.14 The pH Scale. The pH scale indicates the concentration of hydrogen ions (H^+). The lower the pH, the higher the concentration of free H^+ and the more acidic the solution. Conversely, the higher the pH, the more free hydroxide (OH^-) ions and the more basic (alkaline) the solution.

2.4 Organisms Balance Acids and Bases

One of the most important substances dissolved in water is one of the simplest: H^+ ions. Each H^+ is a hydrogen atom stripped of its electron; in other words, it is simply a proton. But its simplicity belies its enormous effects on living systems. Too much or too little H^+ can ruin the shapes of critical molecules inside cells, rendering them nonfunctional.

One source of H^+ is pure water. At any time, perhaps one in a million water molecules spontaneously breaks into two pieces, producing one hydrogen ion (H^+) and one hydroxide ion (OH^-). Pure water is a **neutral** solution because it has exactly the same amount of H^+ as OH^-.

Some substances, however, alter this balance. An **acid** is a chemical that adds H^+ to a solution, making the concentration of H^+ ions exceed the concentration of OH^- ions. Examples include hydrochloric acid (HCl) and sour foods such as vinegar and lemon juice (see the Why We Care box on page 33). Adding acid to pure water releases H^+ ions into the solution:

$$HCl \longrightarrow H^+ + Cl^-$$

A **base** is the opposite of an acid: it makes the concentration of OH^- ions exceed the concentration of H^+ ions. Bases work in one of two ways. They come apart to directly add OH^- ions to the solution, or they absorb H^+ ions. Either way, the result is the same: the balance between H^+ and OH^- shifts toward OH^-. Two common household bases are baking soda and sodium hydroxide (NaOH), an ingredient in oven and drain cleaners. When NaOH dissolves in water, it releases OH^- into solution:

$$NaOH \longrightarrow Na^+ + OH^-$$

What happens if a person mixes an acid with a base? The acid releases protons, while the base either absorbs the H^+ or releases OH^-. Acids and bases therefore neutralize each other.

Scientists use the **pH scale** to measure how acidic or basic a solution is. The pH scale ranges from 0 to 14, with 7 representing a neutral solution such as pure water (figure 2.14). An acidic solution has a pH lower than 7, whereas an **alkaline,** or basic, solution has a pH greater than 7. Thus, 0 represents a strongly acidic solution and 14 represents an extremely basic one.

Each unit on the pH scale represents a 10-fold change in H^+ concentration. A solution with a pH of 4 is therefore 10 times more acidic than one with a pH of 5, and it is 100 times more acidic than one with a pH of 6.

All species have optimal pH requirements. Straying too far from the normal pH can be deadly, yet organisms frequently encounter conditions that could alter their internal pH. They can maintain homeostasis because of **buffer systems,** pairs of weak acids and bases that resist pH changes. If the pH of a solution rises too high, the buffer releases H^+ into the solution, restoring acidity. Alternatively, if an acid contributes H^+ to the solution, the buffer consumes the excess H^+. This action keeps the pH of the solution relatively constant.

2.4 Mastering Concepts

1. How do acids and bases affect a solution's H^+ concentration?
2. How do the values of 0, 7, and 14 relate to the pH scale?
3. How do buffer systems regulate the pH of a fluid?

2.5 Organic Molecules Generate Life's Form and Function

Organisms are composed mostly of water and **organic molecules,** chemical compounds that contain both carbon and hydrogen. As you will learn later in this unit, plants and other autotrophs can produce all the organic molecules they require, whereas heterotrophs—including humans—must obtain them from food.

Life uses a tremendous variety of organic compounds. Organic molecules consisting almost entirely of carbon and hydrogen are called hydrocarbons; methane (CH_4) is the simplest example. Because a carbon atom forms four covalent bonds, however, this element can assemble into complex molecules with long chains, intricate branches, and rings (see figure 2.5). Many organic compounds also include other elements, such as oxygen, nitrogen, phosphorus, or sulfur.

The four most abundant types of organic molecules in life are carbohydrates, lipids, proteins, and nucleic acids. Vitamins are also biologically important organic compounds, but they are required in smaller amounts. Vitamin deficiencies can cause illnesses such as scurvy (vitamin C), beriberi (vitamin B_1), and pellagra (vitamin B_3).

Proteins, nucleic acids, and some carbohydrates all share a property in common with one another: they are chains of small molecular subunits called **monomers.** Linked together, these monomers form **polymers,** just as a train is made of individual railcars.

How does your body produce new muscle proteins and other polymers? Cells use a chemical reaction called dehydration synthesis, also called a condensation reaction, to link the monomers together (figure 2.15a). In a **dehydration synthesis** reaction, a protein called an enzyme removes an —OH (hydroxyl group) from one molecule and a hydrogen atom from another, forming H_2O and a new covalent bond between the two smaller components. (The term *dehydration* means that water is lost.) By repeating this reaction many times, cells can build extremely large polymers consisting of thousands of monomers.

The reverse reaction also occurs, breaking the covalent bonds that link monomers (figure 2.15b). In **hydrolysis,** enzymes use atoms from water to add

Why We Care: Acids and Bases in Everyday Life

Both acids and bases are important in everyday life. The tart flavors of yogurt, sour cream, and spoiled milk come from acid-producing bacteria. Also, some pigments in fruits and flowers are pH-sensitive, turning blue when basic and red when acidic. When baking cherry muffins, the fruit can turn blue when it reacts with the alkaline baking soda or baking powder. You can prevent this reaction by using sour cream instead of milk in the recipe; the acidic sour cream lowers the pH of the batter.

Acids also aid in digestion. Your stomach produces hydrochloric acid that kills microbes and activates enzymes that begin the digestion of proteins in food. Antacids contain bases that neutralize excess acid, relieving an upset stomach.

In the environment, some air pollutants return to Earth as acid precipitation. The acidic rainfall kills plants and aquatic life, and it damages buildings and outdoor sculptures.

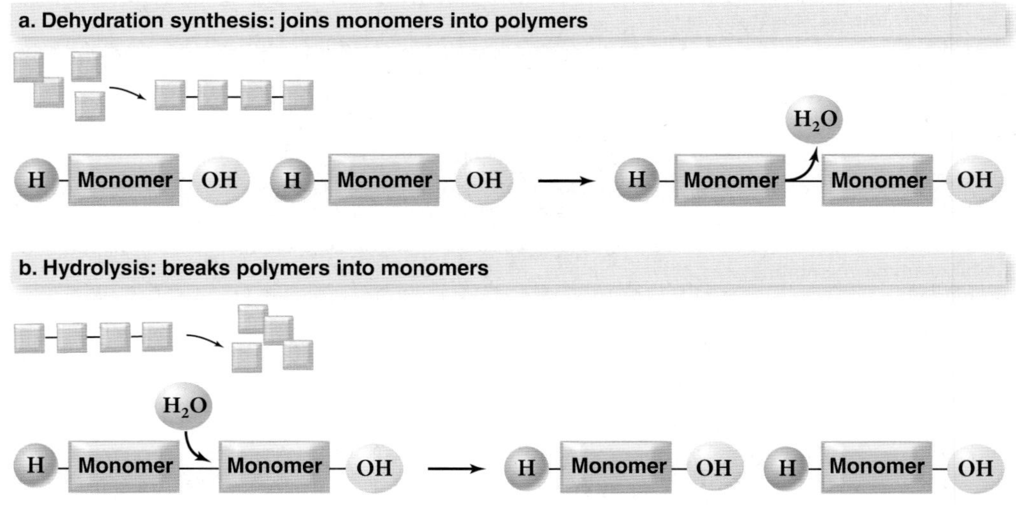

Figure 2.15 Opposite Reactions. (a) In dehydration synthesis, water is removed and a new covalent bond forms between two monomers. (b) In hydrolysis, water is added when the bond between monomers is broken.

Burning Questions

What does it mean when food is "organic" or "natural"?

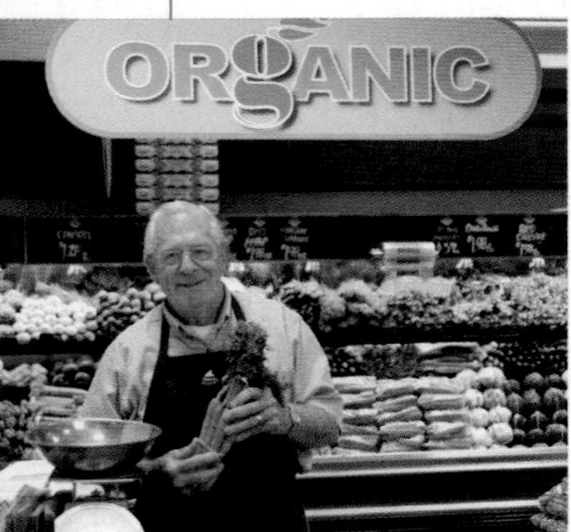

The word *organic* has multiple meanings. To a chemist, an organic compound contains carbon atoms. Chemically, all food is therefore organic. To a farmer or consumer, however, organic foods are produced according to a defined set of standards.

The U.S. Department of Agriculture (USDA) certifies crops as organically grown if the farmer did not apply pesticides (with few exceptions), petroleum-based fertilizers, or sewage sludge. Organically raised cows, pigs, and chickens cannot receive growth hormones or antibiotics, and they must have access to the outdoors and eat organic food. In addition, no food labeled "organic" may be genetically engineered or treated with ionizing radiation.

A natural food may or may not be organic. The term *natural* refers to the way in which foods are processed, not how they are grown. Standards for what constitutes a natural food are fuzzy. The USDA specifies that meat and poultry labeled as natural cannot contain artificial ingredients or added color, but no such standards exist for other foods.

Submit your burning question to:
marielle_hoefnagels@mcgraw-hill.com

a hydroxyl group to one molecule and a hydrogen atom to another (*hydrolysis* means "breaking with water"). Hydrolysis happens in your body when digestive enzymes in your stomach and intestines break down the proteins and other polymers in food.

Table 2.4 reviews the characteristics of the four major types of organic molecules in life. The rest of this section takes a closer look at each one.

A. Carbohydrates Include Simple Sugars and Polysaccharides

Anyone following a "low-carb" diet can recite a list of the foods to avoid: potatoes, pasta, bread, cereal, sugary fruits, and sweets. All of these foods are rich in **carbohydrates,** organic molecules that consist of carbon, hydrogen, and oxygen, often in the proportion 1:2:1.

Carbohydrates are the simplest of the four main types of organic compounds, mostly because just a few monomers account for the most common types in cells. The two main groups of carbohydrates are simple sugars and complex carbohydrates.

Simple Sugars **Monosaccharides,** the smallest carbohydrates, usually contain five or six carbon atoms (figure 2.16a). A **disaccharide** ("two sugars") is two monosaccharides joined by dehydration synthesis. Figure 2.16b shows how sucrose (table sugar) forms when a molecule of glucose bonds to a molecule of fructose. Lactose, or milk sugar, is also a disaccharide.

Together, the sweet-tasting monosaccharides and disaccharides are called sugars, or simple carbohydrates. Their function in cells is to provide a ready source of energy, which is released when their bonds are broken (see chapter 6). Sugarcane sap and sugar beet roots contain abundant sucrose, which the

TABLE 2.4 The Macromolecules of Life: A Summary

Type of Molecule	Chemical Structure	Function(s)
Carbohydrates		
Simple sugars	Monosaccharides and disaccharides	Provide quick energy
Complex carbohydrates (cellulose, starch, glycogen, chitin)	Polymers of monosaccharides	Support cells and organisms (cellulose, chitin); store energy (starch, glycogen)
Lipids		
Triglycerides (fats)	Glycerol + 3 fatty acids	Store energy
Phospholipids	Glycerol + 2 fatty acids + phosphate group (see chapter 3)	Form major part of biological membranes
Sterols	Four fused rings, mostly of C and H	Stabilize animal membranes; sex hormones
Proteins	Polymers of amino acids	Carry out nearly all the work of the cell
Nucleic acids (DNA, RNA)	Polymers of nucleotides	Store and use genetic information and transmit it to the next generation

Carbohydrates (starch); lipids
Proteins; lipids
Carbohydrates (cellulose)

plants use to fuel growth. The disaccharide maltose provides energy in sprouting seeds; beer brewers also use it to promote fermentation.

Short chains of monosaccharides on cell surfaces are important in immunity. For example, a person's blood type—A, B, AB, or O—refers to the combination of carbohydrates attached to the surface of his or her red blood cells. A transfusion of the "wrong" blood type can trigger a harmful immune reaction. ▸ blood type, p. 544

Complex Carbohydrates **Polysaccharides** ("many sugars"), also called complex carbohydrates, are huge molecules consisting of hundreds of monosaccharide monomers (figure 2.16c). The most common polysaccharides are cellulose, starch, glycogen, and chitin. They are all long chains of glucose, but they differ from one another by the orientation of the bonds that link the monomers.

Cellulose forms part of plant cell walls. Cotton fibers, wood, and paper consist largely of cellulose. Although it is the most common organic compound in nature, humans cannot digest it. Yet cellulose is an important component of the human diet; nutrition labels refer to it as "fiber." A high-fiber diet reduces the risk of colon cancer. No one knows exactly why fiber has this effect. One possible explanation is that fiber eases the movement of food through the digestive tract, so it may shorten the length of time that harmful chemicals linger within the intestines. ▸ plant cell wall, p. 63

Starch and glycogen are polysaccharides with similar structures and functions. Both are storage molecules that readily break down into their glucose monomers when cells need a burst of energy. Most plants store starch. Potatoes, rice, and wheat are all starchy, high-energy staples in the human diet. Glycogen occurs in animal and fungal cells. In humans, for example, skeletal muscle cells and the liver store energy as glycogen.

Chitin is another common polysaccharide. The cell walls of fungi contain chitin, as do the flexible exoskeletons of insects, spiders, and crustaceans. Chitin resembles a glucose polymer, except that it also contains nitrogen atoms. Because chitin is tough, flexible, and biodegradable, it is used in the manufacture of surgical thread.

a. Monosaccharides

Ribose $C_5H_{10}O_5$

Glucose $C_6H_{12}O_6$

Fructose $C_6H_{12}O_6$

b. Disaccharide formation and breakdown

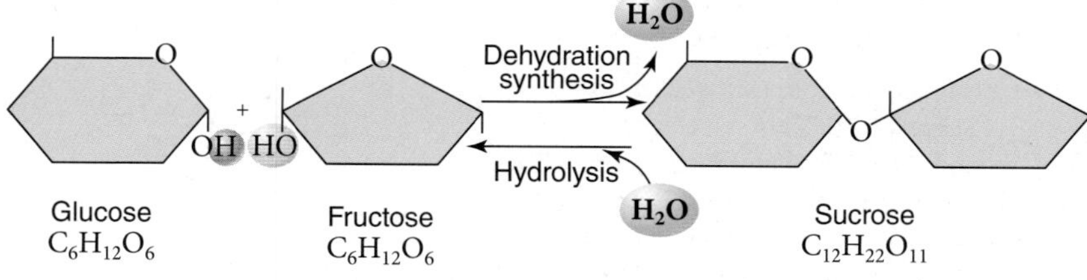

c. Polysaccharides

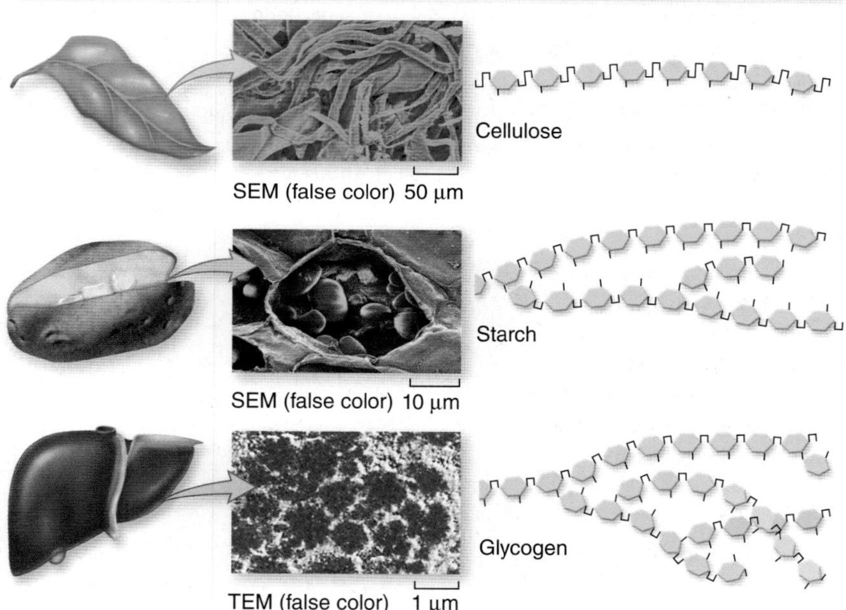

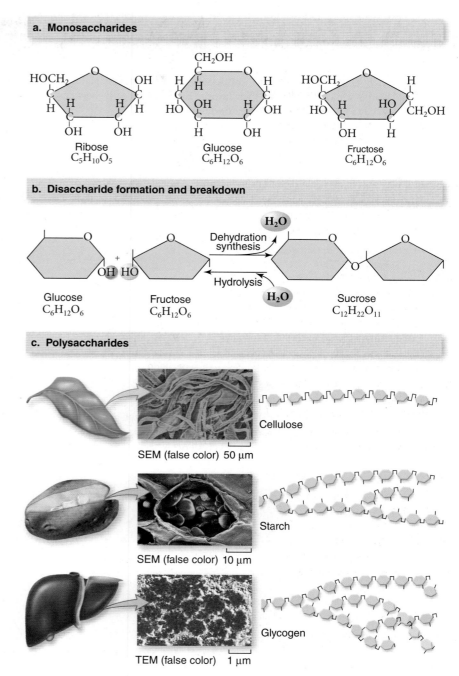

Figure 2.16 Carbohydrates—Simple and Complex. (a) Monosaccharides are composed of single sugar molecules. (b) Disaccharides form when two monosaccharides join by dehydration synthesis. (c) Polysaccharides are long chains of monosaccharides such as glucose. The orientations of the covalent bonds determine the properties of the polymers.

B. Lipids Are Hydrophobic and Energy-Rich

Lipids are organic compounds with one property in common: they do not dissolve in water. They are hydrophobic because they contain large areas dominated by nonpolar carbon–carbon and carbon–hydrogen bonds. Unlike carbohydrates, lipids are not polymers consisting of long chains of monomers. Instead, they have extremely diverse chemical structures.

This section discusses two groups of lipids: triglycerides and sterols. Another important group, phospholipids, forms the majority of cell membranes; section 3.3 describes them.

Why We Care | Sugar Substitutes and Fake Fats

Many weight-conscious people turn to artificial sweeteners and fat substitutes to cut calories while still enjoying their favorite foods. Chemically, how do these sugar and fat replacements compare with the real thing?

Artificial Sweeteners

Table sugar delivers about 4 Calories per gram. Using an artificial sweetener instead of sugar can reduce calorie intake in one of two ways. Some of these additives are calorie-free because our bodies cannot derive energy from them. Most, however, are hundreds of times sweeter-tasting than sugar, so a tiny amount of artificial sweetener achieves the same effect as a teaspoon of sugar. A few popular artificial sweeteners include:

- **Saccharin** (sold as Sweet'n Low and Sugar Twin): This sweetener, which has only 1/32 of a Calorie per gram, was originally derived from coal tar in 1879. It consists of a double-ring structure that includes nitrogen and sulfur. (Saccharin's eventful history as a food additive is the topic of the Why We Care box in chapter 1).

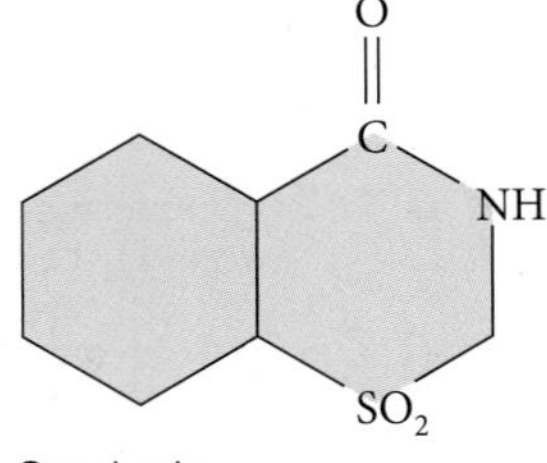

Saccharin

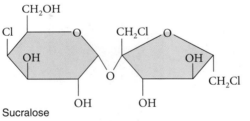

- **Aspartame** (sold as NutraSweet and Equal): Surprisingly, aspartame's chemical structure does not resemble sugar. Instead, it consists of two amino acids, phenylalanine and aspartic acid. Like sugar, it delivers about 4 Calories per gram, but it is about 200 times sweeter than sugar, so less is needed.
- **Sucralose** (sold as Splenda): This sweetener is a close relative of sucrose, except that three chlorine (Cl) atoms replace three of sucrose's hydroxyl groups. Sucralose is about 600 times sweeter than sugar, but the body digests little if any of it, so it is virtually calorie-free.

Sucralose

- **Acesulfame-K** (sold as Sweet One and Sunett): Structurally similar to saccharin, acesulfame-K is about 200 times sweeter than sugar. However, it is essentially calorie-free because the body cannot absorb or use it as an energy source. (The "K" in the name stands for potassium, since acesulfame is sold as a potassium salt.)

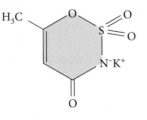

Acesulfame-K (potassium salt)

Fat Substitutes

Because fat is so calorie-dense (about 9 Calories per gram), cutting fat is a quick way to trim calories from the diet. Excess dietary fat can be harmful, leading to weight gain and increasing the risk of heart disease and cancer. It is important to remember, however, that some dietary fat is essential for good health. Fat aids in the absorption of some vitamins and provides fatty acids that human bodies cannot produce. Fats also lend foods taste and consistency.

Fat substitutes are chemically diverse. The most common ones are based on carbohydrates, proteins, or even fats, and a careful reading of nutrition labels will reveal their presence in many processed foods.

- **Carbohydrate-based fat substitutes:** Modified food starches, dextrins, guar gum, pectin, and cellulose gels are all derived from polysaccharides, and they all mimic fat's "mouth feel" by absorbing water to form a gel. Depending on whether they are indigestible (cellulose) or digestible (starches), these fat substitutes deliver 0 to 4 Calories per gram. They cannot be used to fry foods.
- **Protein-based fat substitutes:** These food additives are derived from egg whites or whey (the watery part of milk). When ground into "microparticles," these proteins mimic fat's texture as they slide by each other in the mouth. Protein-based fat substitutes deliver about 4 Calories per gram, and they cannot be used in frying.
- **Fat-based fat substitute:** Olestra (marketed as Olean) is a hybrid molecule that combines a central sucrose molecule with six to eight fatty acids. Its chief advantage is that it tastes and behaves like fat—even for frying. Olestra is currently approved only for savory snacks such as chips. It is indigestible and calorie-free, but some people have expressed concern that olestra removes fat-soluble vitamins as it passes through the digestive tract. Others have publicized its reputed laxative properties. Most people, however, do not experience problems after eating small quantities of olestra.

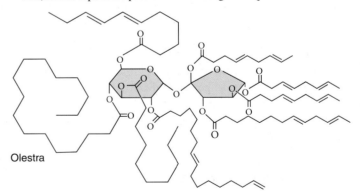

Olestra

Sugar and fat substitutes can be useful for people who cannot—or do not wish to—eat much of the real thing. But nutritionists warn that these food additives should not take the place of a healthy diet and moderate eating habits.

Triglycerides A **triglyceride** consists of three long hydrocarbon chains called **fatty acids** bonded to **glycerol,** a three-carbon molecule that forms the triglyceride's backbone. Although triglycerides do not consist of long strings of similar monomers, cells nevertheless use dehydration synthesis to produce them (figure 2.17). Each fatty acid has a **carboxyl group,** a carbon atom double-bonded to one oxygen and single-bonded to another oxygen carrying a hydrogen atom. Enzymes link the —OH groups from three fatty acids to glycerol, yielding three water molecules per triglyceride.

Many dieters try to avoid triglycerides, commonly known as fats. Red meat, butter, margarine, oil, cream, cheese, lard, fried foods, and chocolate are all examples of high-fat foods. Nutrition labels divide these fats into two groups: saturated and unsaturated. The degree of saturation is a measure of a fatty acid's hydrogen content. A **saturated** fatty acid contains all the hydrogens it possibly can. That is, single bonds connect all the carbons, and each carbon has two hydrogens (see the straight chains in figure 2.17). Animal fats are saturated and tend to be solid; bacon fat and butter are two examples. Most nutritionists recommend a diet low in saturated fats, which tend to clog arteries.

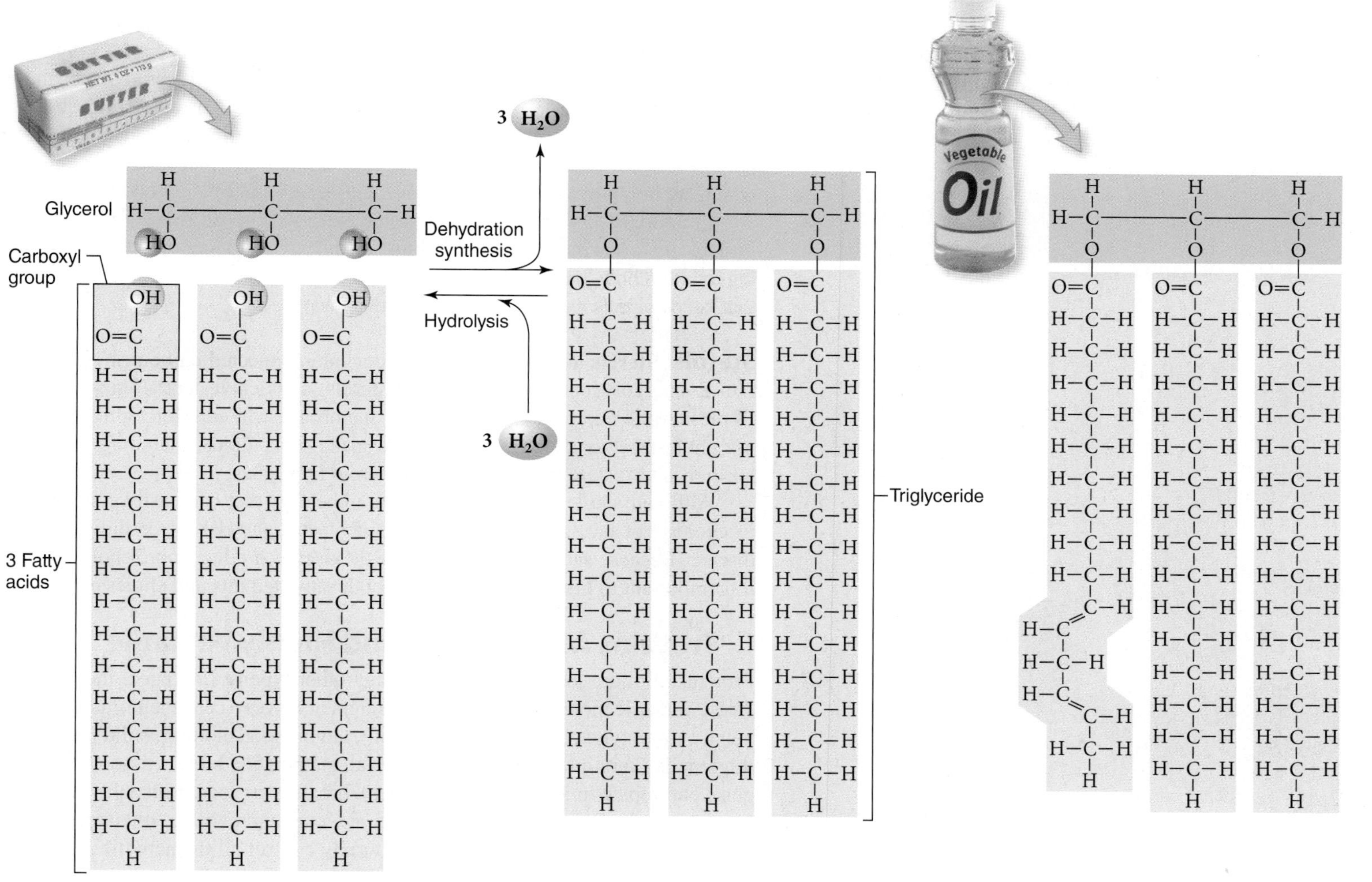

Glycerol
Carboxyl group
3 Fatty acids
Dehydration synthesis
Hydrolysis
3 H_2O
3 H_2O
Triglyceride
Vegetable Oil

Figure 2.17 Triglycerides. A triglyceride, or fat molecule, consists of three fatty acids bonded to glycerol. In saturated fats such as butter, the fatty acid chains contain only single carbon-carbon bonds. In unsaturated fats, one or more double bonds bend the fatty acid tails to make the lipid more fluid. Vegetable oil is an unsaturated fat.

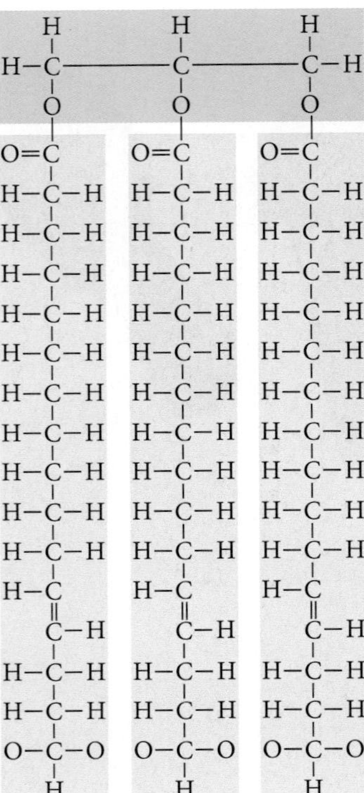

Figure 2.18 Trans Fats. Donuts are among the many foods that are high in trans fats. The fatty acids in a trans fat contain double bonds yet remain straight, so the fat remains a solid.

A fatty acid is **unsaturated** if it has at least one double bond between carbon atoms (see the right side of figure 2.17). A polyunsaturated fat has many such double bonds. These double bonds cause kinks to form in the fatty acid "tails," producing an oily (liquid) consistency at room temperature. Olive oil, for example, is an unsaturated fat. These fats are healthier than are their saturated counterparts.

Food chemists have discovered how to turn vegetable oils into solid fats. In the production of some brands of margarine, shortening, and peanut butter, for example, a technique called partial hydrogenation adds hydrogen to the oil to solidify it—in essence, partially saturating a formerly unsaturated fat. One byproduct of this process is **trans fats,** which are unsaturated fats whose fatty acid tails are straight, not kinked (figure 2.18). Trans fats are common in fast foods, fried foods, and many snack products, and they raise the risk of heart disease even more than saturated fats. Nutritionists therefore recommend avoiding trans fats entirely.

Despite their unhealthful reputation, fats and oils are vital to life. Fat is an excellent energy source, providing more than twice as much energy as equal weights of carbohydrate or protein. Animals must have dietary fat for growth; this requirement explains why human milk is rich in lipids, which fuel the brain's rapid growth during the first 2 years of life. Fats also slow digestion, and they are required for the use of some vitamins and minerals. Nutrition experts therefore recommend that people eat nuts and oily fish such as salmon, which contain polyunsaturated omega-3 fatty acids and other "good fats."

In animals, fat-storing cells combine to form adipose tissue. White adipose tissue forms most of the fat in human adults, cushioning organs and helping to retain body heat as insulation. Brown adipose tissue releases heat energy that keeps infants and hibernating mammals warm.

Sterols **Sterols** are lipids that have four interconnected carbon rings. Vitamin D and cortisone are examples of sterols, as is cholesterol (figure 2.19). Cholesterol is a key part of animal cell membranes. In addition, animal cells use cholesterol as a starting material to make other lipids, including the sex hormones testosterone and estrogen. ▸ steroid hormones, p. 510

Although cholesterol is essential, an unhealthy diet can easily contribute to cholesterol levels that are too high, increasing the risk of cardiovascular disease. Because saturated fats stimulate the liver to produce more cholesterol, it is important to limit dietary intake of both saturated fats and cholesterol.

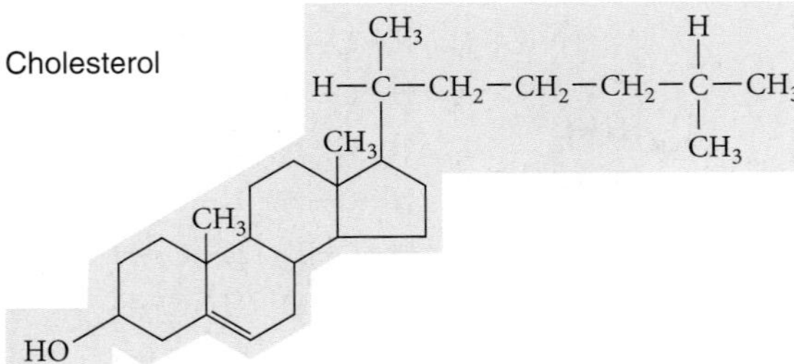

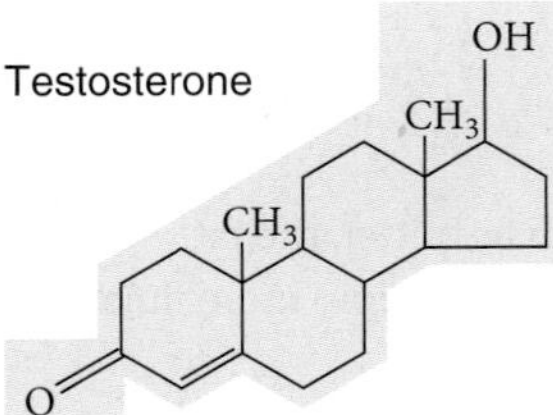

Figure 2.19 Steroids. All steroid molecules consist of four interconnected rings. Cholesterol and testosterone are two variations on this theme.

C. Proteins Are Complex and Highly Versatile

Proteins do more jobs in the cell than any other type of biological molecule. These versatile molecules control what enters or leaves a cell (membrane channels), carry oxygen in blood (hemoglobin), aid in blood clotting, build hair and fingernails (keratin), copy genetic material, support the body's tissues (collagen), participate in immunity (antibodies), break apart food molecules (digestive enzymes), allow for muscle contraction (actin and myosin), and participate in countless other processes. Proteins literally control all the activities of life, so much so that illness or death can result if even one is missing or faulty.

Amino Acid Structure and Bonding A **protein** is a chain of monomers called **amino acids.** Each amino acid has a central carbon atom bonded to four other atoms or groups of atoms (figure 2.20a). One is a hydrogen atom;

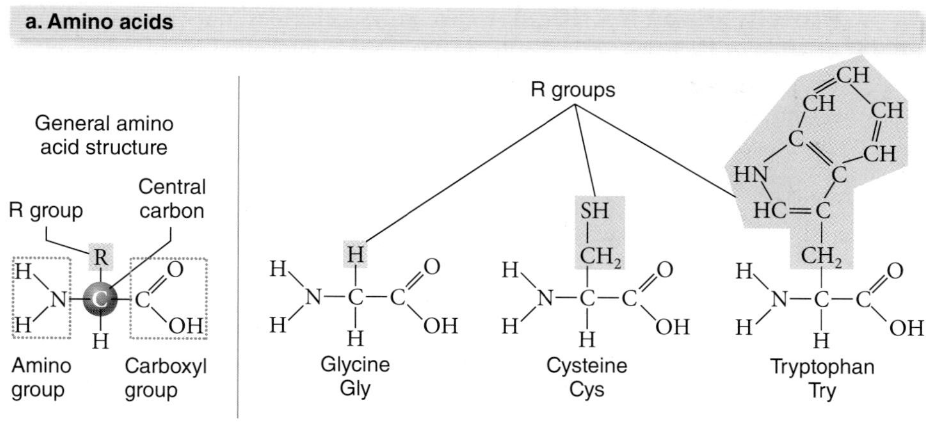

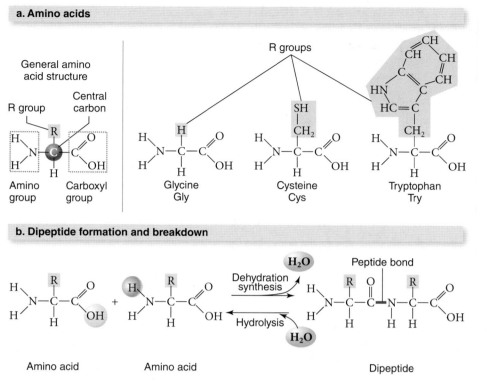

Figure 2.20 Amino Acids. (a) All amino acids consist of an amino group, a carboxyl group, and one of 20 R groups attached to a central carbon atom. This figure shows the general structure along with three specific examples. (b) A peptide bond forms by dehydration synthesis, the chemical reaction that links two amino acids.

another is a carboxyl group; a third is an **amino group,** a nitrogen atom single-bonded to two hydrogen atoms ($—NH_2$); and the fourth is a side chain, or **R group,** which can be any of 20 chemical groups.

Life's proteins are composed of 20 types of amino acids; figure 2.20a shows three of them. (Appendix E includes a complete set of amino acid structures.) The R groups distinguish the amino acids from one another, and they have diverse chemical structures. An R group may be as simple as the lone hydrogen atom in glycine or as complex as the two rings of tryptophan. Some R groups are acidic or basic; some are strongly hydrophilic or hydrophobic.

Just as the 26 letters in our alphabet combine to form a nearly infinite number of words in many languages, mixing and matching the 20 amino acids gives rise to an endless diversity of unique proteins. This variety means that proteins have a seemingly limitless array of structures and functions.

The **peptide bond,** which forms by dehydration synthesis, is the covalent bond that links each amino acid to its neighbor (figure 2.20b). Two linked amino acids form a dipeptide; three form a tripeptide. Long chains of amino acids are **polypeptides.** A polypeptide is called a protein once it folds into its functional shape; a protein may consist of one or more polypeptide chains.

Where do the amino acids in your own proteins come from? Humans can synthesize many of the 20 amino acids from scratch, but eight must come from protein-rich foods such as meat, fish, dairy products, beans, and tofu. Digestive enzymes catalyze the hydrolysis reactions that break peptide bonds and release amino acids from proteins in food. The body then uses these monomers to build its own polypeptides.

Protein Shape Is Critical Unlike polysaccharides, most proteins do not exist as long chains inside cells. Instead, the polypeptide chain folds into a unique three-dimensional structure determined by the order and kinds of amino acids. Biologists describe the conformation of a protein at four levels, described below and in figure 2.21.

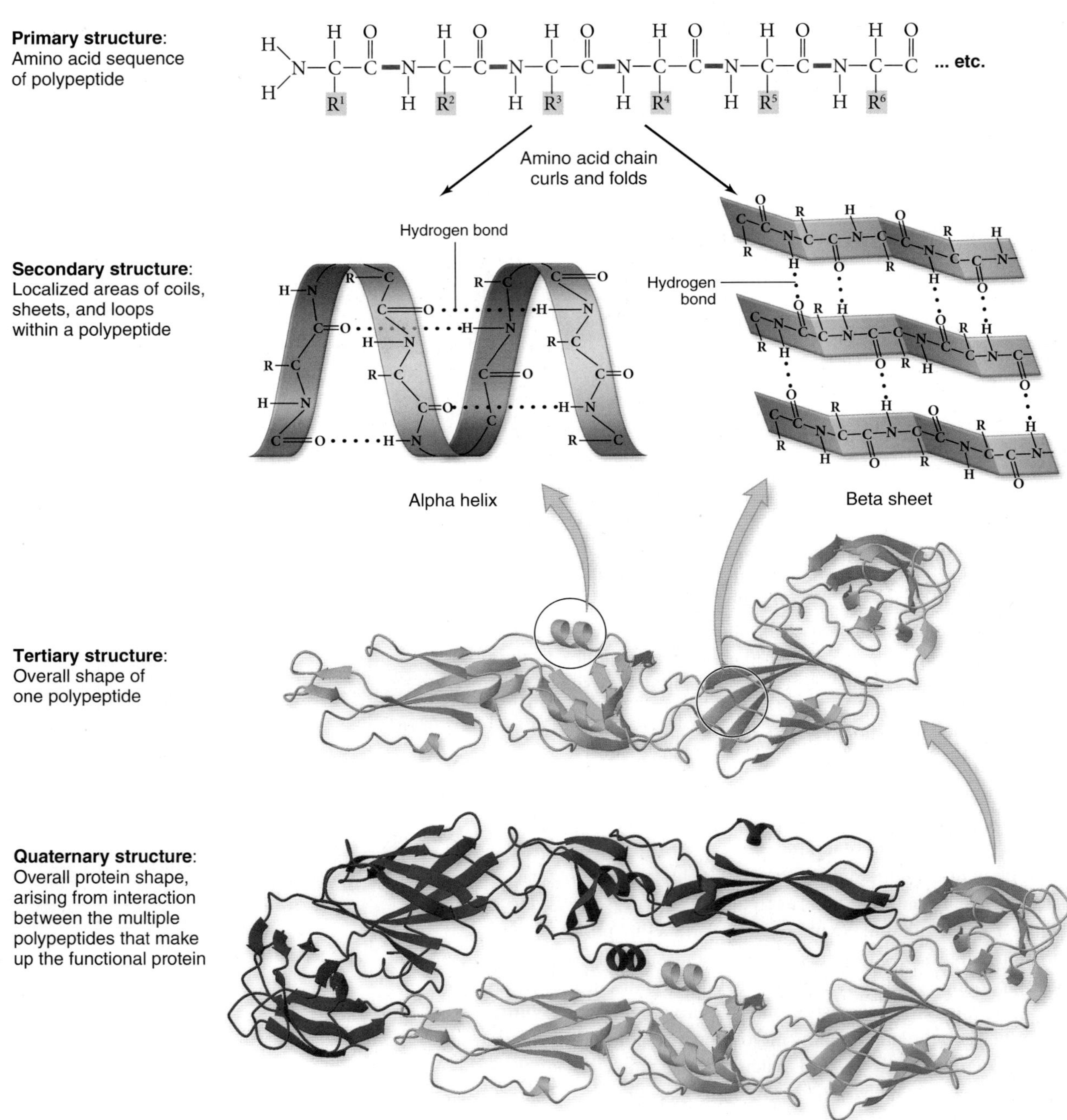
Primary structure: Amino acid sequence of polypeptide
... etc.
Amino acid chain curls and folds
Secondary structure: Localized areas of coils, sheets, and loops within a polypeptide
Hydrogen bond
Hydrogen bond
Alpha helix
Beta sheet
Tertiary structure: Overall shape of one polypeptide
Quaternary structure: Overall protein shape, arising from interaction between the multiple polypeptides that make up the functional protein

Figure 2.21 Four Levels of Protein Structure. The amino acid sequence of a polypeptide forms the primary structure, while hydrogen bonds create secondary structures such as a helix or sheet. The tertiary structure is the overall three-dimensional shape of a protein. The interaction of multiple polypeptides forms the protein's quaternary structure.

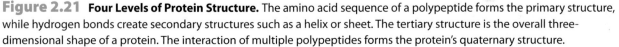

- **Primary (1°) structure:** The amino acid sequence of a polypeptide chain. This sequence determines all subsequent structural levels.
- **Secondary (2°) structure:** A "substructure" with a defined shape, resulting from hydrogen bonds between parts of the polypeptide. These interactions fold the chain of amino acids into coils, sheets, and loops. Each protein can have multiple areas of secondary structure.
- **Tertiary (3°) structure:** The overall shape of a polypeptide, arising primarily through interactions between R groups and water. Inside a cell, water molecules surround each polypeptide. The hydrophobic R groups move away from water toward the protein's interior. In addition, hydrogen bonds and (rarely) ionic bonds form between the peptide backbone and some R groups. Covalent bonds between sulfur atoms in some R groups further stabilize the structure.
- **Quaternary (4°) structure:** The shape arising from interactions between multiple polypeptide subunits of the same protein. The protein in figure 2.21 consists of two polypeptides; similarly, the oxygen-toting blood protein hemoglobin is composed of four polypeptide chains.

It is impossible to overstate the importance of a protein's shape in determining its function. Examine figure 2.22, which illustrates the major categories of protein function: structural, contraction, transport, storage, and enzymes. Notice the great variety of protein shapes, reflecting their different jobs in the cell. A digestive enzyme, for example, has a groove that holds a food molecule in just the right way to break the nutrient apart. Muscle proteins form long, aligned fibers that slide past one another, shortening their length to create muscle contractions. A membrane channel includes pores that admit some molecules but not others into a cell.

Proteins are therefore vulnerable to external conditions that alter their shapes. Heat, excessive salt, or the wrong pH can disrupt the hydrogen bonds that maintain the protein's secondary and tertiary structures. The protein is **denatured** if its structure is modified enough to destroy its function. Looking back at figure 2.22, consider what would happen if the holes in the membrane channel protein were closed or if the long, straight regions of the muscle proteins were bent. These proteins could no longer do their jobs.

Humans prevent microbes from spoiling food by denaturing proteins. These proteins are not necessarily those in the food itself. Rather, when we heat foods or preserve them in salt or vinegar, we are denaturing *microbial* proteins. Without functional proteins, the microbes die, and the food's shelf life is extended.

Genetic mutations can also cause a cell to produce misshapen proteins. As detailed in chapter 7, an organism's genetic code specifies the amino acid sequence of each protein. A genetic mutation, or change in the genetic code, may therefore alter a protein's primary structure. As you saw in figure 2.21, a protein's secondary, tertiary, and quaternary structures all depend upon the primary structure. Genetic mutations are often harmful because they result in misfolded, nonfunctional proteins.

As different as carbohydrates, lipids, and proteins are, food chemists have discovered ways to use all three substances to make artificial sweeteners and fat substitutes. The Why We Care box on page 36 describes how they do it.

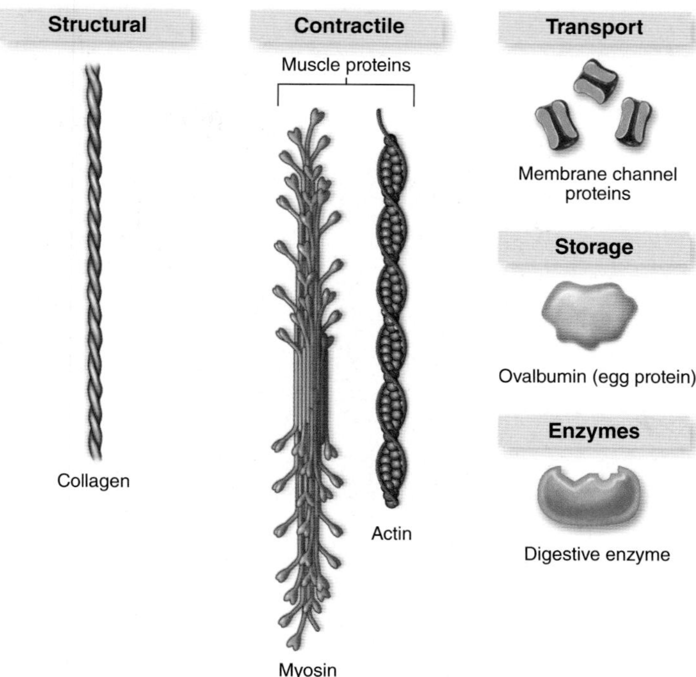

Figure 2.22 Protein Diversity. The function of a protein is a result of its shape. Shown are a few of the thousands of types of known proteins.

D. Nucleic Acids Store and Transmit Genetic Information

A **nucleic acid** is a polymer consisting of monomers called nucleotides. Cells contain two types of nucleic acids, **deoxyribonucleic acid (DNA)** and **ribonucleic acid (RNA).**

Each **nucleotide** monomer consists of three components (figure 2.23a). At the center is a five-carbon sugar—ribose in RNA and deoxyribose in DNA. Attached to one of the sugar's carbon atoms is at least one phosphate group (PO_4). The opposite side of the sugar is bonded to a **nitrogenous base:** adenine (A), guanine (G), thymine (T), cytosine (C), or uracil (U). DNA contains A, C, G, and T, whereas RNA contains A, C, G, and U.

Dehydration synthesis links nucleotides together (figure 2.23b). In this reaction, a covalent bond forms between the sugar of one nucleotide and the phosphate group of its neighbor.

A DNA polymer is a double helix that resembles a spiral staircase. Alternating sugars and phosphates form the rails of the staircase, and nitrogenous bases form the rungs (figure 2.24). Hydrogen bonds between the bases hold the two strands of nucleotides together: A with T, C with G. The two strands are therefore complementary, or "opposites," of each other. Because of complementary base pairing, one

a. Nucleotides and nitrogenous bases

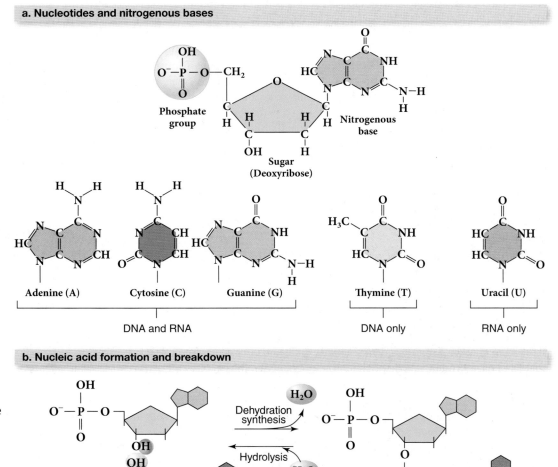

Phosphate group
Sugar (Deoxyribose)
Nitrogenous base

Adenine (A) | Cytosine (C) | Guanine (G) — DNA and RNA
Thymine (T) — DNA only
Uracil (U) — RNA only

b. Nucleic acid formation and breakdown

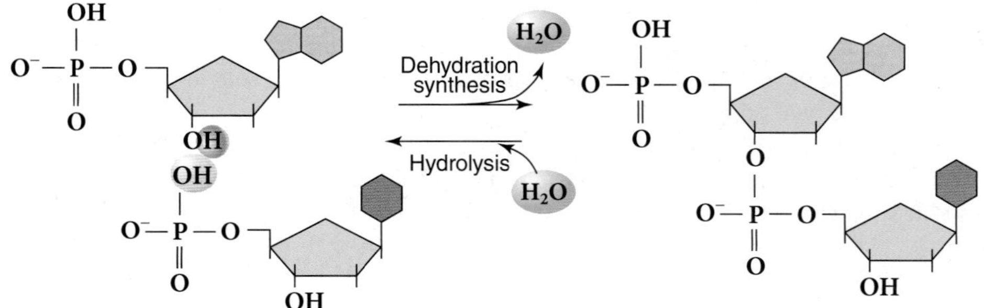

Figure 2.23 Nucleotides. (a) A nucleotide consists of a sugar, one or more phosphate groups, and one of several nitrogenous bases. In DNA, the sugar is deoxyribose, whereas RNA nucleotides contain ribose. In addition, the base thymine appears only in DNA; uracil is only in RNA. (b) Dehydration synthesis links two nucleotides together.

strand of DNA contains the information for the other, providing a mechanism for the molecule to replicate. ▶ DNA replication, p. 141

DNA's main function is to store genetic information; with the help of RNA, its sequence of nucleotides "tells" a cell which amino acids to string together to form each protein. (This process, which is summarized at the top of figure 2.24, is described in detail in chapter 7.) Every organism inherits DNA from its parents (or parent, in the case of asexual reproduction). Slight changes in DNA from generation to generation, coupled with natural selection, account for many of the evolutionary changes that have occurred throughout life's history.

Unlike DNA, RNA is typically single-stranded (see figure 2.24). One function of RNA is to enable cells to use the protein-encoding information in DNA. In addition, a modified RNA nucleotide, adenosine triphosphate (ATP), carries the energy that cells use in many biological functions. ▶ ATP, p. 72

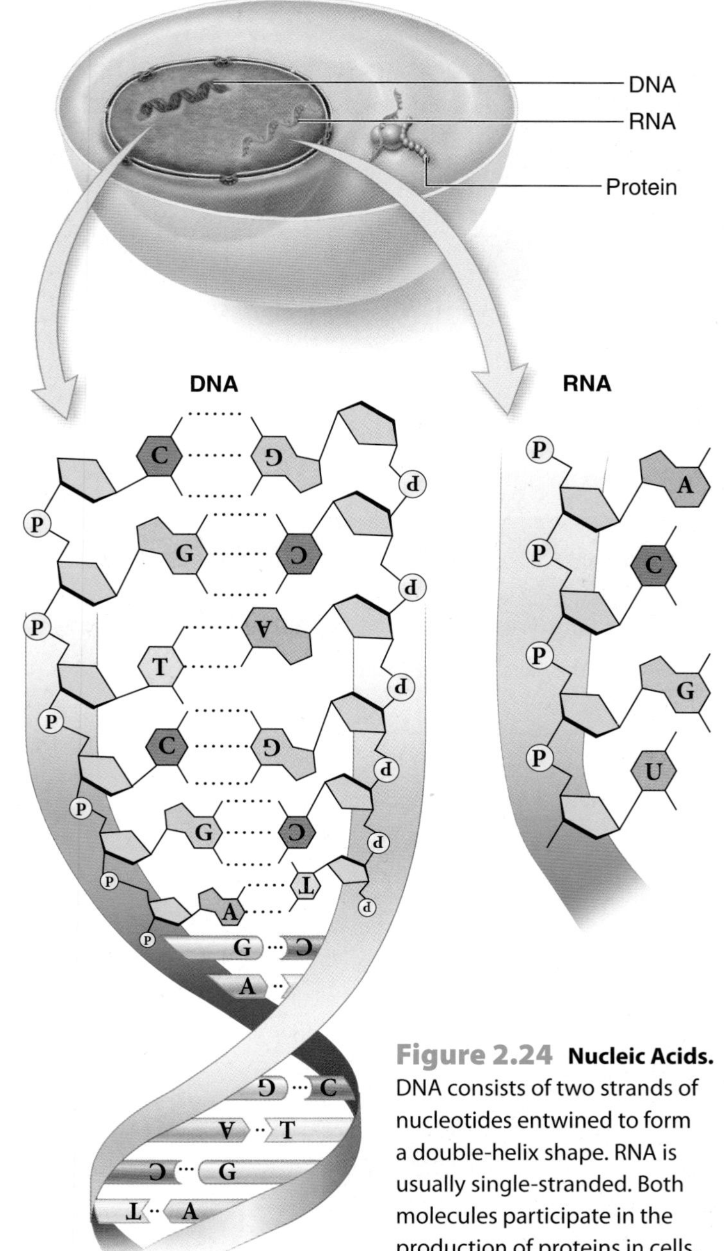

Figure 2.24 Nucleic Acids. DNA consists of two strands of nucleotides entwined to form a double-helix shape. RNA is usually single-stranded. Both molecules participate in the production of proteins in cells.

2.5 Mastering Concepts

1. What is the relationship between hydrolysis and dehydration synthesis?
2. Describe the monomers that form polysaccharides, proteins, and nucleic acids.
3. List examples of carbohydrates, lipids, proteins, and nucleic acids, and name the function of each.
4. What are the components of a triglyceride?
5. What is the significance of a protein's shape, and how can that shape be destroyed?
6. What are some differences between RNA and DNA?

Investigating Life

2.6 E. T. and the Origin of Life

Life's chemistry reflects life's unity: the same elements make up the same types of molecules in all organisms. This observation is consistent with evolution by common descent. After all, if one or a few ancient organisms gave rise to all of life's diversity, then contemporary life should reflect the chemistry of that ancestor.

The Question: Evolution accounts for the diversity of species on Earth, but it cannot explain how life started in the first place. We know that cells require carbohydrates, lipids, proteins, and nucleic acids. At the dawn of life on Earth, where did those first critical ingredients come from?

One hypothesis is that meteorites or comets carrying organic molecules seeded Earth with the precursors of life. Evidence for this explanation comes from a meteorite that fell to Earth near an Australian town called Murchison in 1969 (figure 2.25). Researchers discovered that the meteorite contained amino acids and other organic compounds. But an obvious question immediately arose: Did these molecules contaminate the meteorite after it fell, or did they really come from space?

Figure 2.25 Murchison Meteorite. When the Murchison meteorite struck Earth in 1969, it scattered rocks such as this one over a large area near Murchison, Australia.

The Approach: The atoms that make up organic molecules can help answer this question. Carbon and nitrogen are two of the most abundant elements in life, and each has multiple isotopes (see section 2.1C). On Earth, 98.89% of C atoms are

TABLE 2.5 ^{15}N in the Murchison Meteorite

Organic Compound	^{15}N (parts per thousand) Relative to Standard
Amino acids from the Murchison meteorite	
Glycine	+37
Alanine	+57
Aspartic acid	+61
Glutamic acid	+58
Typical terrestrial organic compounds	–5 to +10

TABLE 2.6 ^{13}C in the Murchison Meteorite

Organic Compound	^{13}C (parts per thousand) Relative to Standard
Bases from the Murchison meteorite	
Uracil	+44.5
Xanthine	+37.7
Typical terrestrial organic compounds	–110 to 0

^{12}C, with six protons and six neutrons. Just 1.11% of Earthly carbon atoms have seven neutrons (^{13}C). Likewise, 99.63% of nitrogen atoms on Earth are ^{14}N, and 0.37% are ^{15}N. But the heavier isotopes, ^{13}C and ^{15}N, are slightly more abundant in materials from outer space than they are on Earth. Scientists can use this small difference to distinguish between terrestrial and extraterrestrial materials.

Michael Engel, from the University of Oklahoma, and the University of Virginia's Stephen Macko tested the hypothesis that the Murchison meteorite's amino acids are extraterrestrial. They chemically extracted amino acids from a meteorite stone. Next, they measured the amounts of ^{14}N and ^{15}N in the amino acids. Engel and Macko predicted that the Murchison amino acids should be enriched in ^{15}N.

In another study, Zita Martins of Imperial College in London and an international group of colleagues analyzed the Murchison meteorite for the nucleotide bases that characterize RNA and DNA. They found uracil in the meteorite, along with xanthine, a base that today's cells need to produce thymine. Martins and her team then measured the amounts of ^{13}C and ^{12}C in the bases. Like Engel and Macko, the Martins group predicted that bases from the meteorite should contain more ^{13}C than do terrestrial organic molecules.

The Conclusion: Tables 2.5 and 2.6 show the results of both studies. In both tables, a positive number means that a sample contained more ^{15}N or ^{13}C than a known standard, and a negative number means that the sample contained less. As predicted, the amino acids and bases from the Murchison meteorite were enriched in both ^{15}N and ^{13}C relative to the same molecules on Earth. These results support the hypothesis that the Murchison meteorite carried amino acids, uracil, and xanthine to Earth.

Does this mean that life (or its key molecules) originally came from outer space? Not necessarily. As you will see in chapter 15, life's organic molecules may have arisen by chemical processes occurring entirely on Earth. We may never know how life started on our planet, but it is intriguing to think that some of its key ingredients may literally have fallen from the sky.

Engel, M. H., and S. A. Macko. 1997. Isotopic evidence for extraterrestrial nonracemic amino acids in the Murchison meteorite. *Nature,* vol. 389, pages 265–268.

Martins, Zita, Oliver Botta, Marilyn L. Fogel, and six coauthors. 2008. Extraterrestrial nucleobases in the Murchison meteorite. *Earth and Planetary Science Letters*, vol. 270, pages 130–136.

2.6 Mastering Concepts

1. What question were these researchers trying to answer?
2. Why are ^{15}N and ^{13}C called "heavy" isotopes? How are they different from ^{14}N and ^{12}C?
3. Both groups of researchers collected samples from the meteorite's interior. Why does the sample location matter?
4. How would the results have differed if the amino acids and bases were contaminants acquired after the meteorite fell to Earth?

Chapter Summary

2.1 Atoms Make Up All Matter

- All **matter** can be broken down into pure substances called **elements.**

A. Elements Are Fundamental Types of Matter

- **Bulk elements** are essential to life in large quantities, and **trace elements** are required in smaller amounts. **Minerals** are essential elements other than C, H, O, and N.

B. Atoms Are Particles of Elements

- An **atom** is the smallest unit of an element. Positively charged **protons** and neutral **neutrons** form the **nucleus,** and the negatively charged, much smaller **electrons** surround the nucleus.
- Elements are organized in the **periodic table** according to **atomic number** (the number of protons).
- An **ion** is an atom that has gained or lost electrons.

C. The Number of Neutrons May Vary

- **Isotopes** of an element differ by the number of neutrons. A **radioactive** isotope is unstable.
- An element's **atomic mass** reflects the average **mass number** of all isotopes, weighted by the proportions in which they naturally occur.

2.2 Chemical Bonds Link Atoms

- A **molecule** is two or more atoms joined together; if they are of different elements, the molecule is called a **compound.**

A. Electrons Determine Bonding

- Electrons move constantly; they are most likely to occur in volumes of space called **orbitals.** Orbitals are grouped into **energy shells.**
- An atom's tendency to fill its **valence shell** with electrons drives it to form **chemical bonds** with other atoms.

B. In a Covalent Bond, Atoms Share Electrons

- **Covalent bonds** form between atoms that can fill their valence shells by sharing one or more pairs of electrons.
- Atoms in a **nonpolar covalent bond** share electrons equally. Highly **electronegative** atoms in covalent bonds attract electrons away from less electronegative atoms, forming **polar covalent bonds.**

C. In an Ionic Bond, One Atom Transfers Electrons to Another Atom

- An **ionic bond** is an attraction between two oppositely charged ions. These ions form when one atom strips one or more electrons from another atom.

D. Partial Charges on Polar Molecules Create Hydrogen Bonds

- **Hydrogen bonds** result from the attraction between opposite partial charges on adjacent molecules or within a large molecule.

E. Bonds Break and Form in Chemical Reactions

- In a **chemical reaction,** the **products** are different from the **reactants.**

2.3 Water Is Essential to Life

A. Water Is Cohesive

- Water molecules stick together, a property called **cohesion.**

B. Many Substances Dissolve in Water

- A **solution** consists of a **solute** dissolved in a **solvent.**
- Water dissolves **hydrophilic** (polar and charged) substances but not **hydrophobic** (nonpolar) substances.

C. Water Regulates Temperature

- Water helps regulate temperature in organisms because it resists both temperature change and **evaporation.**
- Large bodies of water help keep coastal climates mild.

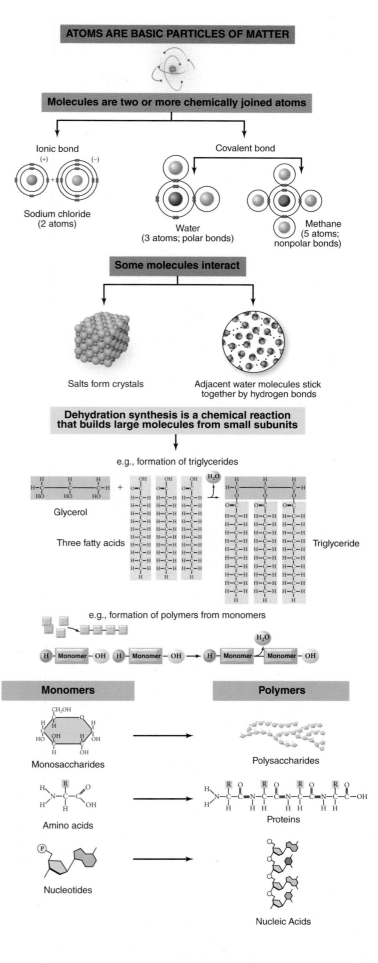

ATOMS ARE BASIC PARTICLES OF MATTER

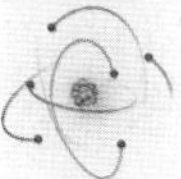

Molecules are two or more chemically joined atoms

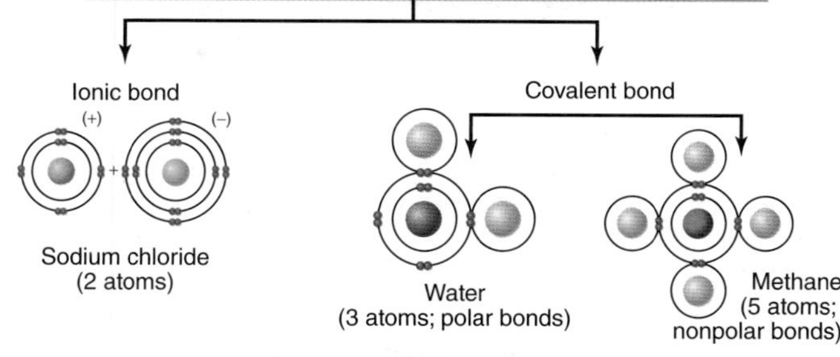

Some molecules interact

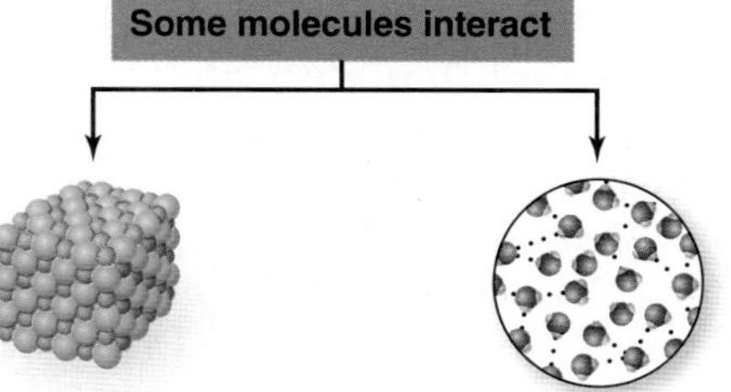

Dehydration synthesis is a chemical reaction that builds large molecules from small subunits

e.g., formation of triglycerides

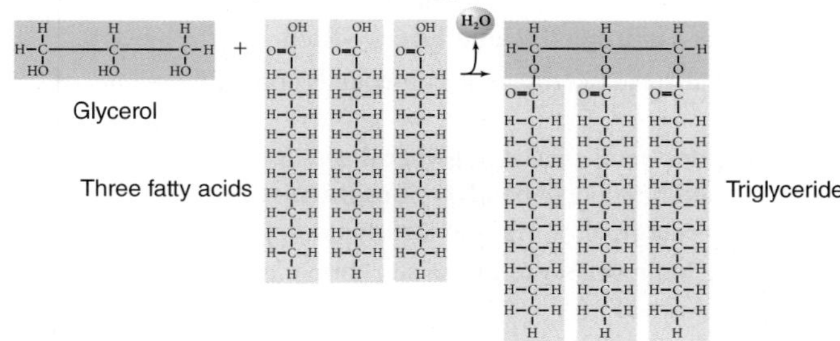

e.g., formation of polymers from monomers

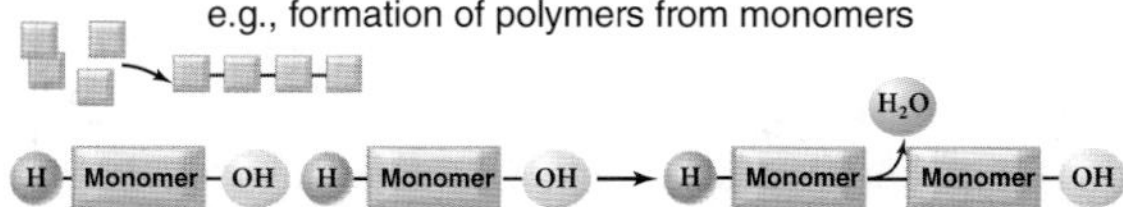

Monomers **Polymers**

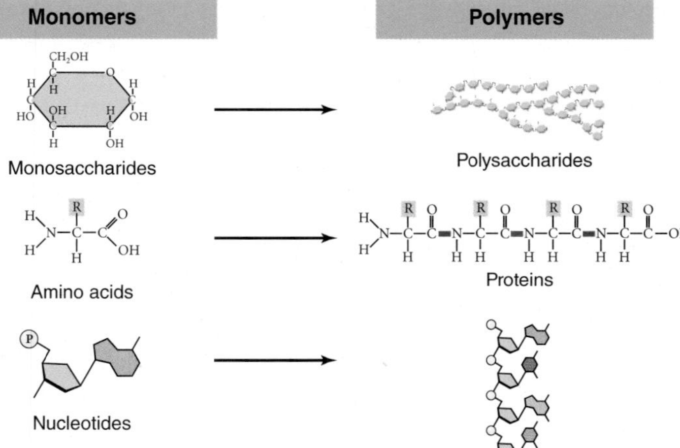

D. Water Expands as It Freezes

- Ice is less dense than liquid water. As a result, ice floats on the surface of lakes and oceans.

E. Water Participates in Life's Chemical Reactions

- Most biochemical reactions occur in a watery solution.

2.4 Organisms Balance Acids and Bases

- In pure water, the concentrations of H^+ and OH^- are equal, and the solution is **neutral.** An **acid** adds H^+ to a solution, and a **base** adds OH^- or removes H^+.
- The **pH scale** measures H^+ concentration. Pure water has a pH of 7, acidic solutions have a pH below 7, and an **alkaline** solution has a pH between 7 and 14.
- **Buffers** consist of weak acid–base pairs that maintain the optimal pH ranges of body fluids.

2.5 Organic Molecules Generate Life's Form and Function

- Many **organic molecules** consist of small subunits called **monomers,** which link together to form **polymers. Dehydration synthesis** is the chemical reaction that joins monomers together, releasing a water molecule.
- The **hydrolysis** reaction uses water to break polymers into monomers.

A. Carbohydrates Include Simple Sugars and Polysaccharides

- **Carbohydrates** consist of carbon, hydrogen, and oxygen in the proportions 1:2:1.
- **Monosaccharides** are single-molecule sugars such as glucose. Two bonded monosaccharides form a **disaccharide.** Monosaccharides and disaccharides are simple sugars that provide quick energy.
- **Polysaccharides** are complex carbohydrates consisting of hundreds of monosaccharides. They provide support and store energy.

B. Lipids Are Hydrophobic and Energy-Rich

- **Lipids** are diverse hydrophobic compounds consisting mainly of carbon and hydrogen.
- **Triglycerides** (fats) consist of **glycerol** and three **fatty acids,** which may be **saturated** (no double bonds) or **unsaturated** (at least one double bond). They store energy, slow digestion, cushion organs, and preserve body heat.
- **Sterols,** including cholesterol and sex hormones, are lipids consisting of four carbon rings.

C. Proteins Are Complex and Highly Versatile

- **Proteins** consist of **amino acids,** which join into **polypeptides** by forming **peptide bonds** through dehydration synthesis.
- A protein's three-dimensional shape is vital to its function. A **denatured** protein has a ruined shape.
- Proteins have a great variety of functions, participating in all the work of the cell.

D. Nucleic Acids Store and Transmit Genetic Information

- **Nucleic acids,** including **DNA** and **RNA,** are polymers consisting of **nucleotides.**
- DNA carries genetic information and transmits it from generation to generation. RNA copies the information, enabling the cell to make proteins.

2.6 Investigating Life: E. T. and the Origin of Life

- Amino acids and nucleotide bases extracted from the Murchison meteorite suggest that early life's organic molecules may have come from outer space.

Multiple Choice Questions

1. The *atomic mass* of an element reflects the total number of
   a. electrons.
   b. protons.
   c. neutrons.
   d. protons + neutrons.
2. The atomic number of the element neon (Ne) is 10. How many electrons does a neutral atom of neon contain?
   a. 5
   b. 10
   c. 20
   d. It can't be determined from this information.
3. A *covalent bond* forms when
   a. electrons are present in a valence shell.
   b. a valence electron is removed from one atom and added to another.
   c. a pair of valence electrons is shared between two atoms.
   d. one atom attracts electrons more strongly than another atom.
4. The atomic number of silicon (Si) is 14. Use the concept of energy shells to predict the number of covalent bonds that Si could form.
   a. 2
   b. 3
   c. 4
   d. 8
5. An *ionic bond* forms when
   a. an electrical attraction occurs between two atoms of different charge.
   b. a nonpolar attraction is formed between two atoms.
   c. a valence electron is shared between two atoms.
   d. two atoms have similar attraction for electrons.
6. A hydrophilic substance is one that can
   a. form covalent bonds with hydrogen.
   b. dissolve in water.
   c. buffer a solution.
   d. mix with nonpolar solvents.
7. What type of chemical bond is being broken when methane burns in oxygen?
   a. Ionic
   b. Hydrogen
   c. Polar covalent
   d. Nonpolar covalent
8. What type of chemical bond forms during a dehydration synthesis reaction?
   a. Covalent
   b. Ionic
   c. Hydrogen
   d. Polymer
9. A sugar is an example of a __________, whereas DNA is a __________ .
   a. protein; nucleic acid
   b. nucleic acid; lipid
   c. lipid; protein
   d. carbohydrate; nucleic acid
10. The shape of a protein is determined by
    a. the sequence of amino acids.
    b. chemical bonds between amino acids.
    c. temperature and pH.
    d. All of the above are correct.

Write It Out

1. Define the following terms: *atom, element, molecule, compound, isotope,* and *ion.*
2. The vitamin biotin contains 10 atoms of carbon, 16 of hydrogen, 3 of oxygen, 2 of nitrogen, and 1 of sulfur. What is its molecular formula?
3. Consider the following atomic numbers: oxygen (O) = 8; fluorine (F) = 9; neon (Ne) = 10; magnesium (Mg) = 12. Draw the electron shells of each atom, and then predict how many bonds each atom should form.
4. Distinguish between nonpolar covalent bonds, polar covalent bonds, and ionic bonds.
5. If oxygen strongly attracts electrons, why is a covalent bond between two oxygen atoms considered nonpolar?
6. Can nonpolar molecules such as CH_4 participate in hydrogen bonds? Why or why not?
7. Define *solute, solvent,* and *solution.*
8. Explain why each of the following properties of water is essential to life: cohesion, ability to dissolve solutes, resistance to temperature change.
9. Using your knowledge of the properties of water, explain the quote "Hydrogen bonds sank the *Titanic*."
10. Why would the formation of ice crystals inside a cell cause the cell to rupture?
11. Why are buffer systems important in organisms?
12. Compare and contrast the chemical structures and functions of carbohydrates, lipids, proteins, and nucleic acids.
13. How is an amino acid's R group analogous to a nucleotide's nitrogenous base?
14. Pickles and several other foods are preserved in acids such as vinegar. Why is an acid a good preservative? (*Hint:* Consider the effect of acids on protein shape.)
15. Complete and explain the following analogy: a protein is to a knitted sweater as a denatured protein is to a ____.
16. A topping for ice cream contains fructose, hydrogenated soybean oil, salt, and cellulose. What types of chemicals are in it?
17. Three very different proteins are silk, hair, and collagen. Chemically, how are they similar, and how are they different?
18. Why are proteins extremely varied in organisms, but carbohydrates and lipids are not?
19. Amyotrophic lateral sclerosis (also known as ALS or Lou Gehrig's disease) paralyzes muscles. An inherited form of the illness is caused by a gene (sequence of DNA) encoding an abnormal enzyme that contains zinc and copper. The abnormal enzyme fails to rid the body of a toxic form of oxygen. Which of the molecules mentioned in this description is a
   a. protein?
   b. nucleic acid?
   c. bulk element?
   d. trace element?
20. A man on a very low-fat diet proclaims to his friend, "I'm going to get my cholesterol down to zero!" Why is achieving this goal impossible (and undesirable)?
21. Using information in "Sugar Substitutes and Fake Fats" on page 36 and the amino acid structures in appendix E, draw the dipeptide called aspartame (NutraSweet).
22. Name three examples of emergent properties (see chapter 1) in chemistry.
23. Flask A contains 100 milliliters of a solution with pH 5. After you add 100 ml of solution from Flask B, the pH rises to 7. What was the pH of the solution in Flask B?

Pull It Together

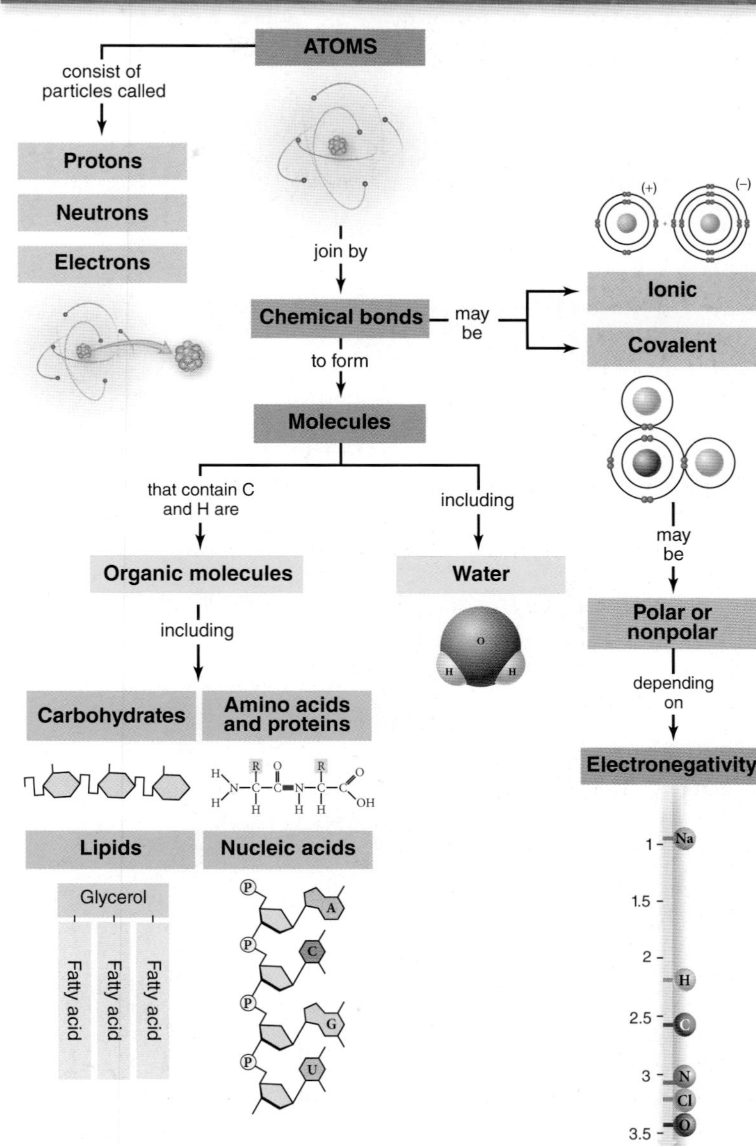

1. How do ions and isotopes fit into this concept map?
2. How does electronegativity explain whether a covalent bond is polar or nonpolar?
3. Add *hydrogen bonds* to this concept map and explain the relationship between hydrogen bonds and polar covalent bonds.
4. Besides water, what are other examples of molecules that are essential to life?
5. Add *monomers, polymers, dehydration synthesis,* and *hydrolysis* to this concept map.

3 Cells

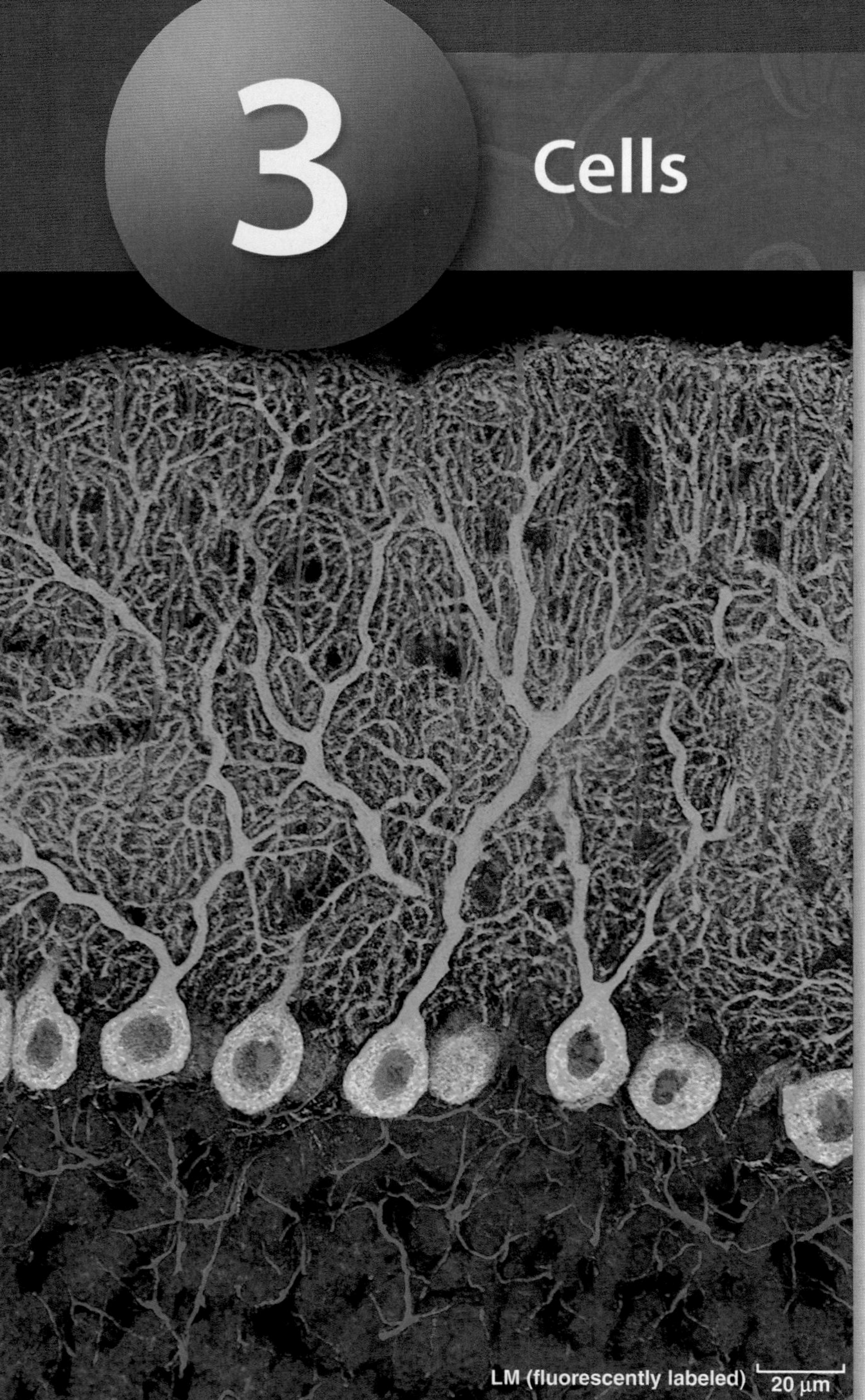

Brain Slice. Microscopes offer a detailed view of life's smallest components. The cells shown here, called neurons, occur in the brain. Each intricately branched neuron may form connections with more than 200,000 other cells.

Learning Outline

Learn How to Learn

Bite-Sized Pieces

Many students think they need to read a whole chapter in one sitting. Instead, try working through one topic at a time. Read just one section of the chapter, and compare it to your class notes. Think of each chapter as a meal: you eat a sandwich one bite at a time, so why not tackle biology the same way?

What's the Point?

"The cell is the fundamental unit of life." You have probably heard this line ever since you started learning about science in grade school. But who cares about tiny packets of life that you can only see with the help of a microscope?

Conquering cancer is one compelling reason to study cell biology. In cancer, a person's own cells multiply out of control. Research revealing how cancer cells differ from normal cells has yielded spectacular new treatments that target these differences, producing fewer side effects than older treatments that destroy healthy cells, too. Consider also the amazing power of antibiotics. These drugs kill bacteria inside our bodies but leave our own cells alone. How? By inhibiting processes that occur only in bacterial cells.

Cancer treatments, antibiotics, and many other wonder drugs owe their success to generations of cell biologists who painstakingly documented the structures in and on cells—the subject of this chapter.

3.1 Cells Are the Units of Life

A human, a rose bush, a mushroom, and a bacterium appear to have little in common other than being alive. However, on a microscopic level, these organisms share many similarities. For example, all organisms consist of microscopic structures called **cells,** the smallest unit of life that can function independently. Within cells, highly coordinated biochemical activities carry on the basic functions of life. This chapter introduces the cell, and the chapters that follow delve into the energy transformations that make the cell's life possible.

A. Microscopes Revealed the Cellular Basis of Life

The study of cells began in 1660, when English physicist Robert Hooke melted strands of spun glass to create lenses. When he used a lens to look at cork, which is bark from a type of oak tree, it appeared to be divided into little boxes, left by cells that were once alive. Hooke called these units "cells" because they looked like the cubicles (Latin, *cellae*) where monks studied and prayed. His discovery initiated a new field of science, now called cell biology.

Microscopes continued to improve into the nineteenth century, revealing details of the nucleus and other structures inside cells. In 1839, German biologists Mathias J. Schleiden and Theodor Schwann used their observations of many different plant and animal cells to formulate the **cell theory,** which originally had two main components: all organisms are made of one or more cells, and the cell is the fundamental unit of all life. German physiologist Rudolf Virchow added a third component in 1855, when he proposed that all cells come from preexisting cells (see the Burning Question on page 55).

Like any scientific theory, the cell theory is *potentially* falsifiable—yet many lines of evidence support each of its components, making it one of the most powerful ideas in biology.

B. Microscopes Magnify Cell Structures

Most cells are too small for the unaided human eye to see, so studying life at the cellular and molecular levels requires magnification. Cell biologists use a variety of microscopes to produce different types of images. This section describes several types of microscopes; figure 3.1 provides a sense of the size of objects that each can reveal.

Figure 3.1 Ranges of Light and Electron Microscopes. Biologists use light microscopes and electron microscopes to view a world too small to see with the unaided eye. This illustration uses the metric system to measure size (see appendix C), and each segment in the scale represents 1/10 of the length of the segment to its right.

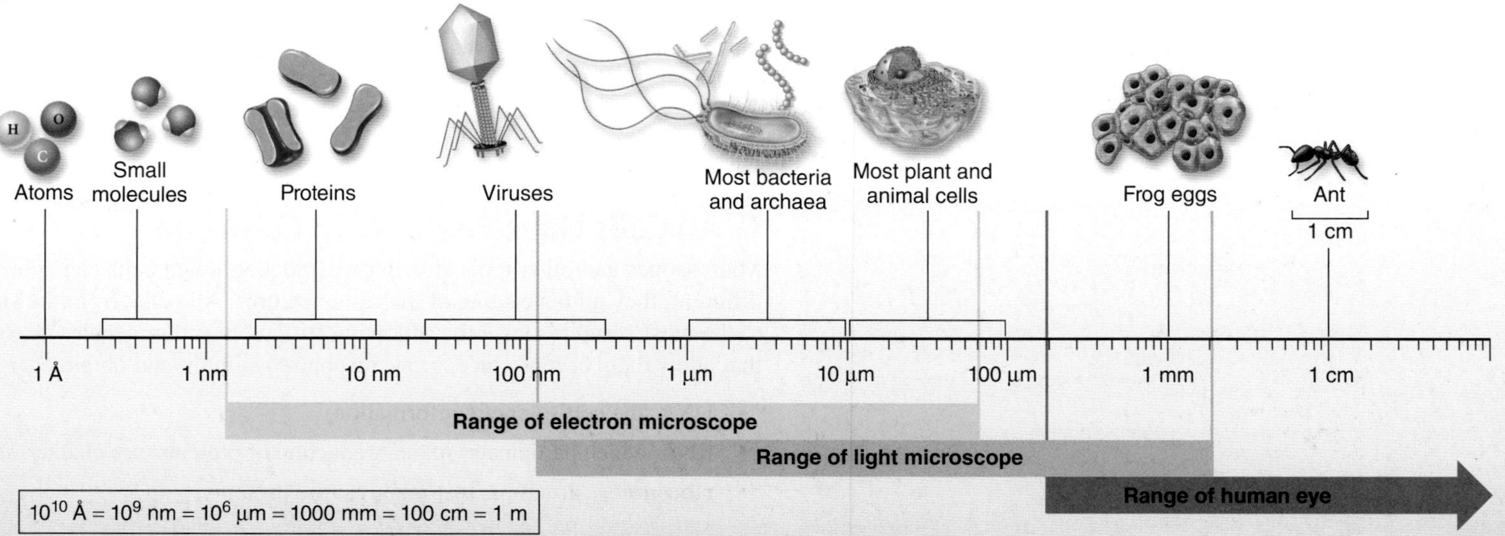

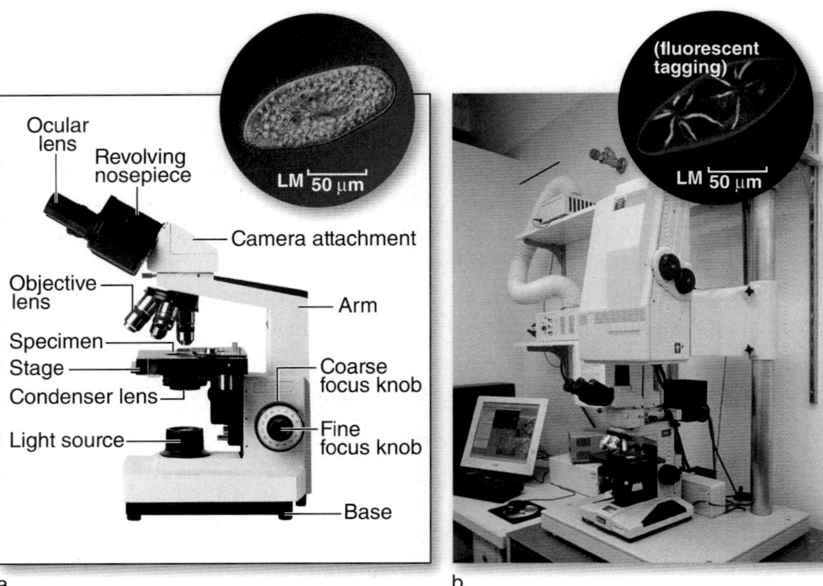

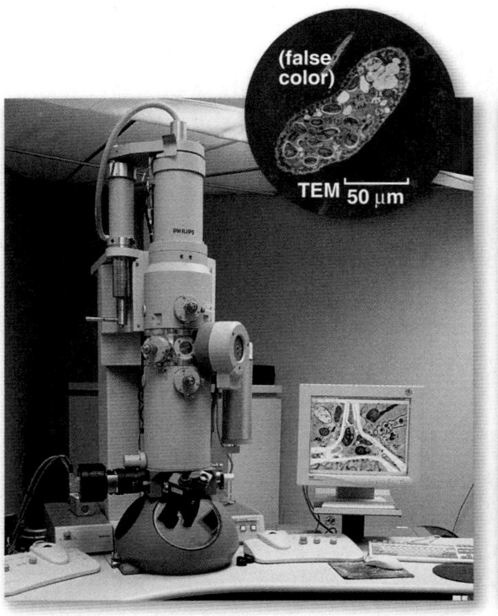

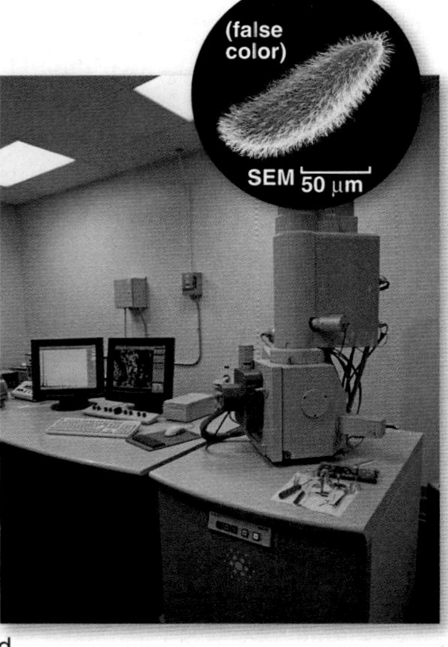

Figure 3.2 Light and Electron Microscopes: A Comparison. These photographs show four types of microscopes, along with sample images of a protist called *Paramecium*. (a) Compound light microscope. (b) Confocal microscope. (c) Transmission electron microscope. (d) Scanning electron microscope. The *Paramecium* images in (c) and (d) have been enhanced with false color.

Light Microscopes Light microscopes are ideal for generating true-color views of living or preserved cells. Because light must pass through an object to reveal its internal features, however, the specimens must be transparent or thinly sliced to generate a good image.

Two types of light microscopes are the compound microscope and the confocal microscope (figure 3.2a, b). A compound scope uses two or more lenses to focus visible light through a specimen; the most powerful ones can magnify up to 1600 times and distinguish between objects that are 200 nanometers apart. A confocal microscope enhances resolution by focusing white or laser light through a lens to the object. The image then passes through a pinhole. The result is a scan of highly focused light on one tiny part of a specimen. Computers can integrate multiple confocal images of specimens exposed to fluorescent dyes to produce spectacular three-dimensional peeks at living structures.

Transmission and Scanning Electron Microscopes Instead of using light, the transmission electron microscope (TEM) sends a beam of electrons through a very thin slice of a specimen. The microscope translates differences in electron transmission into a high-resolution, two-dimensional image that shows the internal features of the object (figure 3.2c). TEMs can magnify up to 50 million times and distinguish between objects less than 1 angstrom (10^{-10} meters) apart.

The scanning electron microscope (SEM) scans a beam of electrons over the surface of a metal-coated, three-dimensional specimen. Its images have lower resolution than the TEM; in SEM, the maximum magnification is about 250,000 times, and the resolution limit is 1 to 5 nanometers. The chief advantage of SEM is its ability to highlight crevices and textures on the surface of a specimen (figure 3.2d).

Both TEM and SEM provide much greater magnification and resolution than light microscopes. Nevertheless, they do have limitations. First, they are extremely expensive to build, operate, and maintain. Second, electron microscopy normally requires that a specimen be killed, chemically fixed, and placed in a vacuum. These treatments can distort natural structures. Light microscopy, in contrast, allows an investigator to view living organisms. Third, unlike light microscopes, all images from electron microscopes are black and white, although artists often add false color to highlight specific objects in electron micrographs. (In this book, each photo taken through a microscope is tagged with the magnification and the type of microscope; the presence of false color is also noted where appropriate.)

C. All Cells Have Features in Common

Microscopes and other tools clearly reveal that although cells can appear very different, they all have some of the same features. All cells, from the simplest to the most complex, have the following structures and molecules in common that allow them to reproduce, grow, respond to stimuli, and obtain energy:

- DNA, the cell's genetic information;
- RNA, which participates in the production of proteins (see chapter 7);
- **ribosomes,** structures that manufacture proteins;

- proteins that carry out all of the cell's work, from orchestrating reproduction to processing energy to regulating what enters and leaves the cell;
- **cytoplasm,** the fluid that occupies much of the volume of the cell; and
- a lipid-rich **cell membrane** (also called the plasma membrane) that forms a boundary between the cell and its environment (see section 3.3).

One other feature common to nearly all cells is small size, typically less than a tenth of a millimeter in diameter (see figure 3.1). Why so tiny? The answer is that nutrients, water, oxygen, carbon dioxide, and waste products enter or leave a cell through its surface. Each cell must have abundant surface area to accommodate these exchanges. As an object grows, however, its volume increases much faster than its surface area. Figure 3.3a illustrates this principle for a series of cubes, but the same applies to cells: small size maximizes the ratio of surface area to volume.

Cells avoid surface area limitations in several ways. Nerve cells are long (up to a meter or so), but they are also extremely thin, so the ratio of surface area to volume remains high. The flattened shape of a red blood cell maximizes its ability to carry oxygen, and the many microscopic extensions of an amoeba's membrane provide tremendous surface area for absorbing oxygen and capturing food (figure 3.3b). A transportation system that quickly circulates materials throughout the cell also helps.

Beyond the level of the cell, the concept of surface area is everywhere in biology. A pine tree's pollen grains have extensions that maximize flotation on air currents; root hairs provide a huge surface area for absorbing water; the broad, flat leaves of plants maximize exposure to light; a fish's feathery gills absorb oxygen from water; a jackrabbit's enormous ears help the animal lose excess body heat in the desert air—the list goes on and on. Conversely, low surface areas have the opposite effect, minimizing the exchange of materials or heat with the environment.

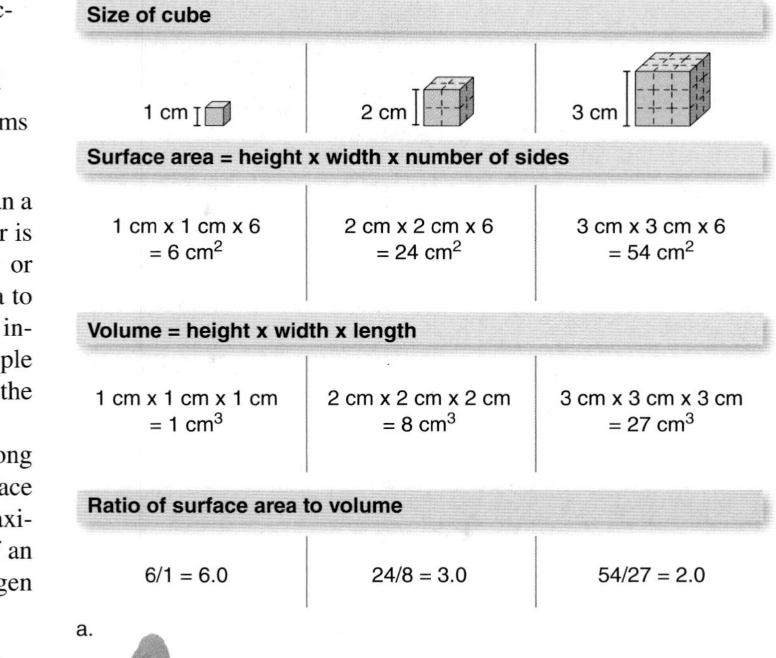

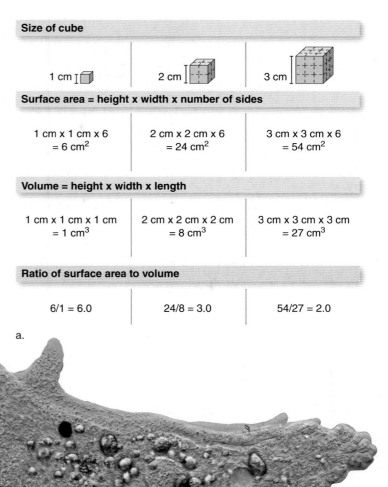

Size of cube		
1 cm	2 cm	3 cm
Surface area = height x width x number of sides		
1 cm x 1 cm x 6 = 6 cm^2	2 cm x 2 cm x 6 = 24 cm^2	3 cm x 3 cm x 6 = 54 cm^2
Volume = height x width x length		
1 cm x 1 cm x 1 cm = 1 cm^3	2 cm x 2 cm x 2 cm = 8 cm^3	3 cm x 3 cm x 3 cm = 27 cm^3
Ratio of surface area to volume		
6/1 = 6.0	24/8 = 3.0	54/27 = 2.0

a.

b.

Figure 3.3 The Relationship Between Surface Area and Volume. (a) This simple example shows that larger objects have less surface area *relative to their volume* than do smaller objects with the same overall shape. (b) The membrane of this amoeba is highly folded, producing a large surface area relative to the cell's volume.

3.1 Mastering Concepts

1. What is a cell?
2. How have microscopes contributed to the study of cells?
3. What are the three main components of cell theory?
4. Describe the differences between light and electron microscopes.
5. Which molecules and structures occur in all cells?
6. Describe adaptations that increase the ratio of surface area to volume in cells.

3.2 Different Cell Types Characterize Life's Three Domains

Until recently, biologists recognized just two types of cells, prokaryotic and eukaryotic. **Prokaryotes,** the simplest and most ancient forms of life, are organisms whose cells lack a nucleus (*pro* = before; *karyon* = kernel, referring to the nucleus). About 2.7 billion years ago, prokaryotes gave rise to **eukaryotes,** whose cells contain a nucleus and other membranous organelles (*eu* = true).

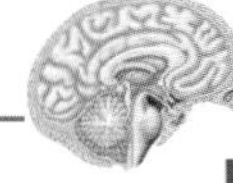

Figure It Out

For a cube 5 centimeters on each side, calculate the ratio of surface area to volume.

Answer: 1.2

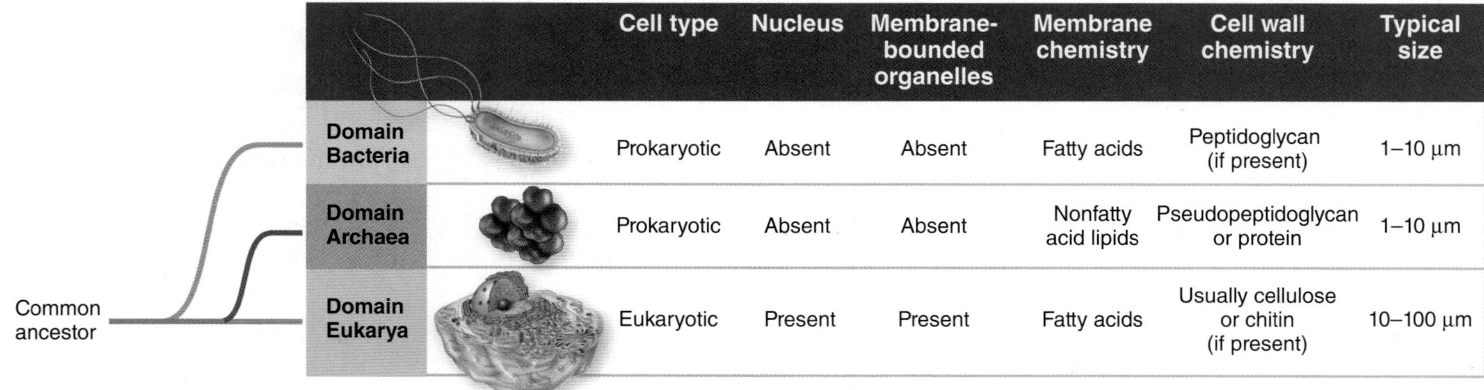

	Cell type	Nucleus	Membrane-bounded organelles	Membrane chemistry	Cell wall chemistry	Typical size
Domain Bacteria	Prokaryotic	Absent	Absent	Fatty acids	Peptidoglycan (if present)	1–10 μm
Domain Archaea	Prokaryotic	Absent	Absent	Nonfatty acid lipids	Pseudopeptidoglycan or protein	1–10 μm
Domain Eukarya	Eukaryotic	Present	Present	Fatty acids	Usually cellulose or chitin (if present)	10–100 μm

Figure 3.4 The Three Domains of Life. Biologists distinguish domains Bacteria, Archaea, and Eukarya based on unique features of cell structure and biochemistry. The small evolutionary tree shows that archaea are the closest relatives of the eukaryotes.

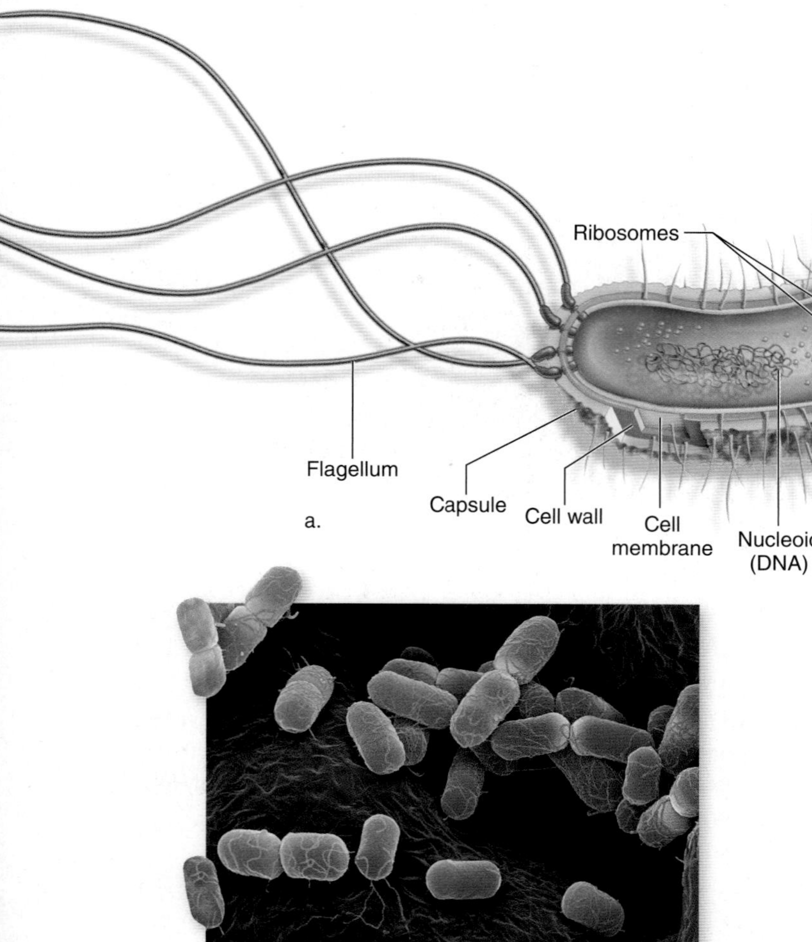

Figure 3.5 Anatomy of a Bacterium. (a) Bacterial cells are structurally simple. (b) Rod-shaped cells of *E. coli* inhabit human intestines.

In 1977, however, microbiologist Carl Woese studied key molecules in many cell types and detected differences that suggested that some prokaryotes represented a completely different form of life. Biologists subsequently divided life into three domains: Bacteria, Archaea, and Eukarya (figure 3.4).

A. Domains Bacteria and Archaea Contain Prokaryotic Organisms

Bacteria are the most abundant and diverse organisms on Earth. Some species, such as *Streptococcus* and *Escherichia coli*, can cause illnesses, but others living on your skin and inside your intestinal tract are essential for good health. Bacteria are also very valuable in research, food and beverage processing, and pharmaceutical production. In ecosystems, bacteria play critical roles as decomposers and producers.

Bacterial cells are structurally simple. The **nucleoid** is the area where the cell's circular DNA molecule congregates (figure 3.5a). Unlike a eukaryotic cell's nucleus, the bacterial nucleoid is not bounded by a membrane. Located near the DNA in the cytoplasm are the enzymes, RNA molecules, and ribosomes needed to produce the cell's proteins.

A rigid **cell wall** surrounds the cell membrane of most bacteria, protecting the cell and preventing it from bursting if it absorbs too much water. This wall also gives the cell its shape: usually rod-shaped (as in figure 3.5b), round, or spiral. Many antibiotic drugs, including penicillin, halt bacterial infection by interfering with the microorganism's ability to construct its protective cell wall. In some bacteria, polysaccharides on the cell wall form a capsule that adds protection or enables the cell to attach to surfaces.

Many bacteria can swim in fluids. **Flagella** (singular: flagellum) are tail-like appendages that enable these cells to move. A cell may have one or more flagella, which are anchored in the cell wall and underlying cell membrane. Bacterial flagella rotate like a propeller, moving the cell forward or backward.

Archaean cells resemble bacterial cells in many ways. Like bacteria, they are smaller than most eukaryotic cells, and they lack a nucleus and other organelles. Most have cell walls, and flagella are also common. However, the resemblance to bacteria is only superficial. Archaea have their own domain because their cells contain biochemicals that are different from those in either bacteria or eukaryotes. Their ribosomes, however, are more similar to those of eukaryotes than to those of bacteria. Archaea are therefore considered to be the closest relatives of eukaryotes.

B. Organisms in Domain Eukarya Have Complex Cells

An astonishing diversity of organisms, including humans, belong to domain Eukarya. Our fellow animals are eukaryotes, as are yeasts, mushrooms, and other fungi. Plants are also eukaryotes, and so are one-celled protists such as *Amoeba* and *Paramecium*.

Despite their great differences in external appearance, all eukaryotic organisms share many features on a cellular level. Figures 3.6 and 3.7 depict generalized animal and plant cells. Although both of the illustrated cells have many structures in common, there are some differences. Most notably, plant cells have chloroplasts and a cell wall, which animal cells lack.

One obvious feature that sets eukaryotic cells apart is their large size, typically 10 to 100 times greater than prokaryotic cells. The other main difference is that the cytoplasm of a eukaryotic cell includes multiple **organelles** ("little organs"), compartments that carry out specialized functions. Examples include the nucleus, mitochondria, and chloroplasts. An elaborate system of internal membranes creates these compartments.

In general, organelles keep related biochemicals and structures close enough to make them function efficiently, without altering or harming other cellular contents. Compartmentalization also means that the cell maintains high concentrations of each biochemical only in certain organelles, not throughout the entire cell. The rest of this chapter describes the structure of the eukaryotic cell in greater detail.

3.2 Mastering Concepts

1. How do prokaryotic cells differ from eukaryotic cells?
2. How are bacteria and archaea similar to and different from each other?
3. How do organelles contribute to efficiency in eukaryotic cells?

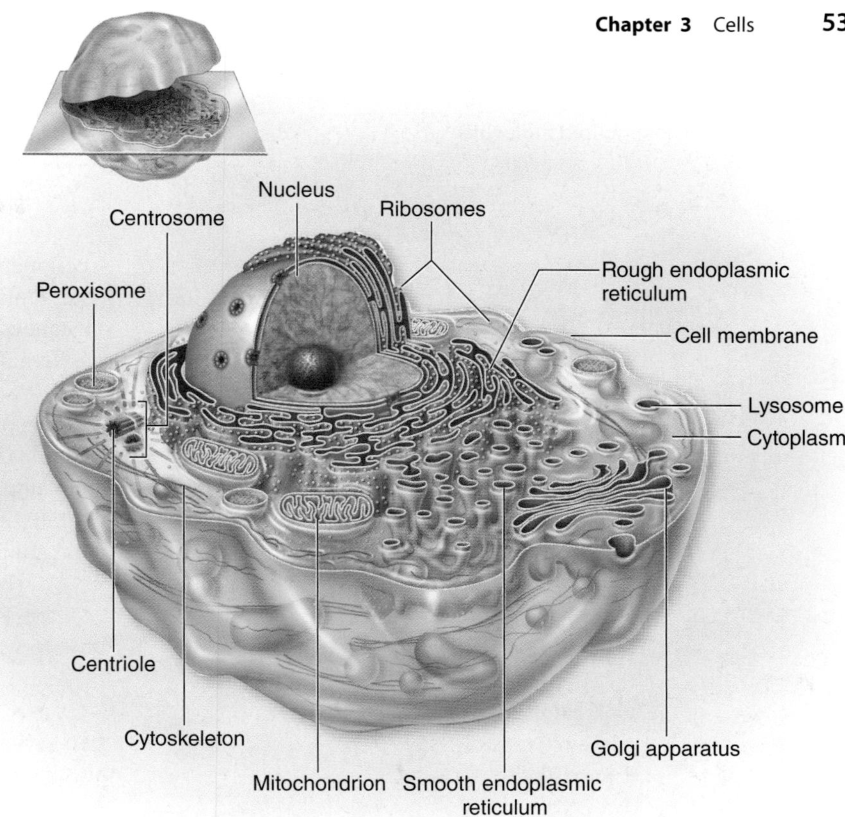

Figure 3.6 Anatomy of an Animal Cell. This illustration shows the relative sizes and locations of the components of an animal cell.

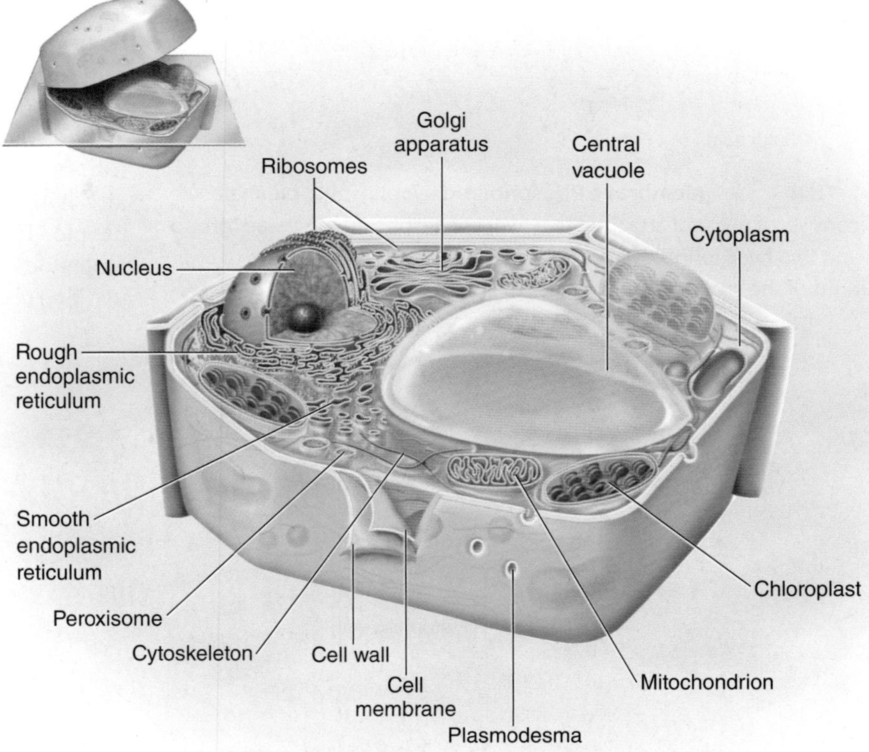

Figure 3.7 Anatomy of a Plant Cell. This generalized view illustrates key features of the plant cell. Note the cell wall, chloroplasts, and large vacuole.

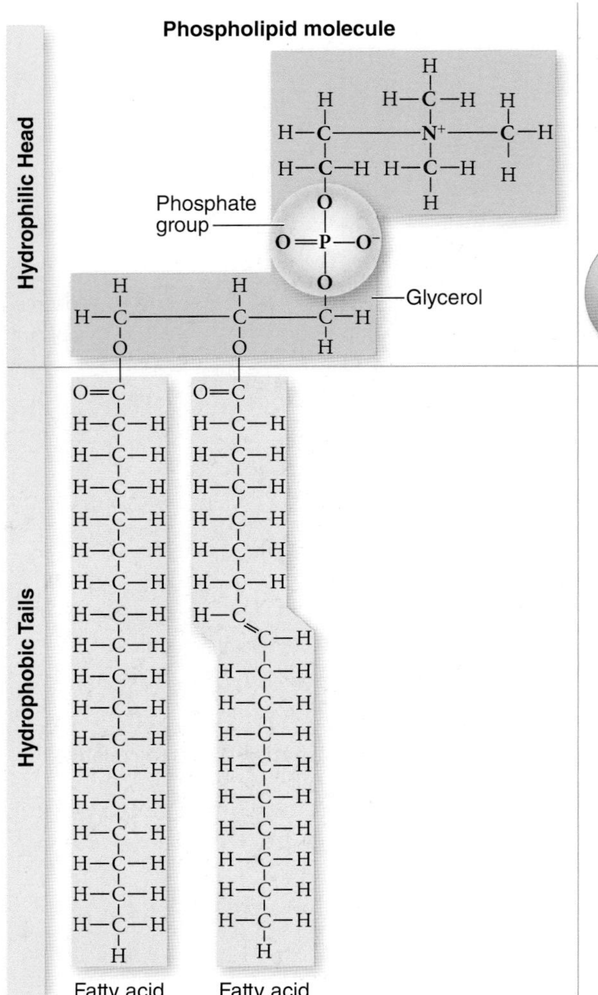

Figure 3.8 Membrane Phospholipids. A phospholipid molecule consists of glycerol attached to a hydrophilic phosphate "head" group and two hydrophobic fatty acid "tails." The simplified structure to the right of the molecule emphasizes the head and tails.

3.3 A Membrane Separates Each Cell from Its Surroundings

A cell membrane is one feature common to all cells. The membrane separates the cytoplasm from the outside of the cell. The cell's surface also transports substances into and out of the cell (see chapter 4), and it receives and responds to external stimuli. Inside a eukaryotic cell, internal membranes enclose the organelles.

The cell membrane is composed of phospholipids, organic molecules that resemble triglycerides (figure 3.8). In a triglyceride, three fatty acids attach to a three-carbon glycerol molecule. But in a **phospholipid,** glycerol bonds to only two fatty acids; the third carbon binds to a phosphate group attached to additional atoms. ▸ triglycerides, p. 37

This chemical structure gives phospholipids unusual properties in water. The phosphate "head" end, with its polar covalent bonds, is attracted to water; that is, it is hydrophilic. The other end, consisting of two fatty acid "tails," is hydrophobic. In water, phospholipid molecules spontaneously arrange themselves into a **phospholipid bilayer** (figure 3.9). In this two-layered, sandwichlike structure, the hydrophilic surfaces (the "bread" of the sandwich) are exposed to the watery medium outside and inside the cell. The hydrophobic tails face each other on the inside of the sandwich, like cheese between the bread slices. Unlike a sandwich, however, the bilayer forms a three-dimensional sphere, not a flat surface.

Thanks to the phospholipid bilayer, a biological membrane has selective permeability. The hydrophobic interior of the phospholipid bilayer prevents ions and polar molecules from moving freely into and out of a cell. The membrane does not, however, block the passage of lipids and small, nonpolar molecules such as O_2 and CO_2.

In both plants and animals, the cell membrane consists not only of a phospholipid bilayer but also of proteins and other molecules (figure 3.10). Many of the membrane's components are free to move laterally within the bilayer, a bit like pickpockets moving within a crowd of people. The cell membrane is often called a **fluid mosaic** because diverse molecules (the pieces of the "mosaic") drift freely among the phospholipids. Sterols, including cholesterol in animal cell membranes, maintain the membrane's fluidity.

Whereas phospholipids and sterols provide the membrane's structure, proteins are especially important to its function. Researchers estimate that about one third of every organism's genome encodes membrane proteins. Some of the proteins lie completely within the phospholipid bilayer, whereas others extend out of one or both sides. Membrane proteins have many functions:

- **Transport proteins:** Transport proteins embedded in the phospholipid bilayer create passageways through which water-soluble molecules and ions pass into or out of the cell. Section 4.5 describes membrane transport in more detail.

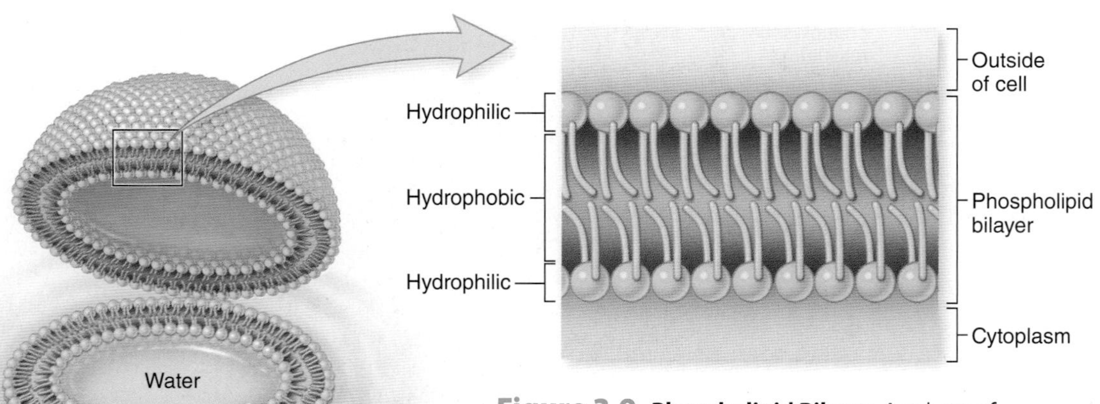

Figure 3.9 Phospholipid Bilayer. A sphere of phospholipids forms the basis of the cell membrane. These phospholipids form a bilayer in water. The hydrophilic head groups are exposed to the water; the hydrophobic tails face each other, minimizing contact with water.

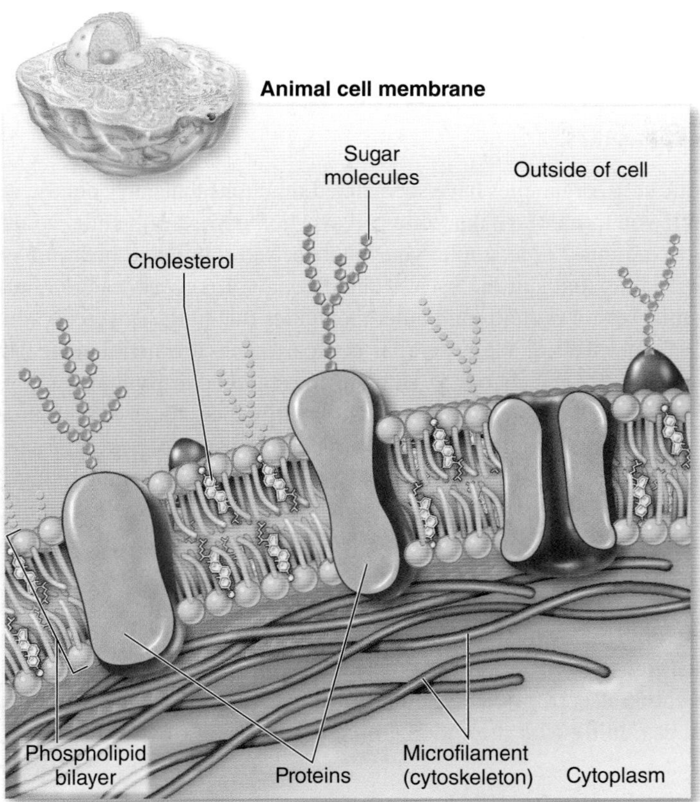

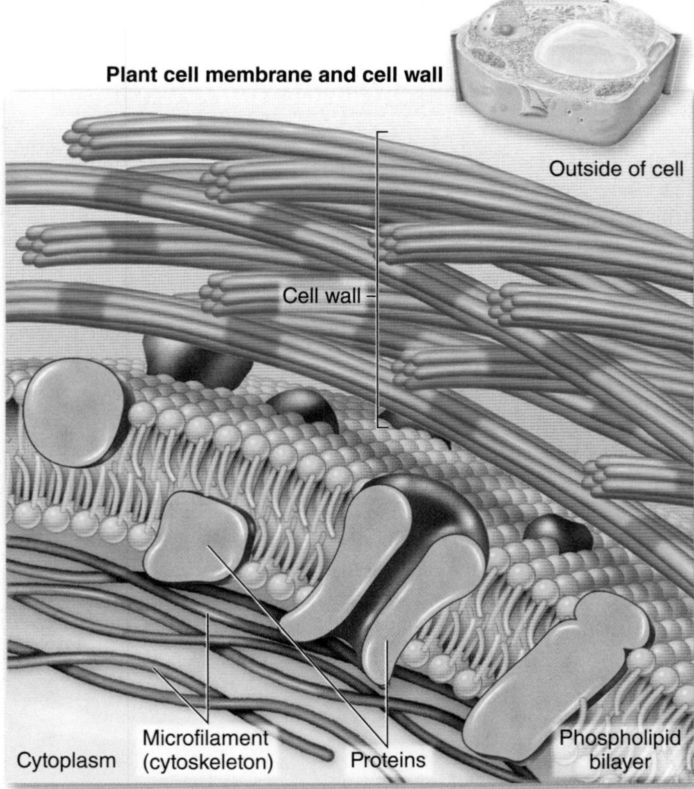

Figure 3.10 Anatomy of a Cell Membrane. The cell membrane is a "fluid mosaic" of proteins embedded in a phospholipid bilayer. Note that animal cell membranes, but not plant cell membranes, contain cholesterol. The outer face of the animal cell membrane also features carbohydrate molecules linked to proteins. A cell wall of cellulose fibers surrounds each plant cell.

- **Enzymes:** These proteins facilitate chemical reactions that otherwise would proceed too slowly to sustain life. ▸ enzymes, p. 74
- **Recognition proteins:** Carbohydrates attached to cell surface proteins serve as "name tags" that help the body's immune system recognize its own cells.
- **Adhesion proteins:** These membrane proteins enable cells to stick to one another.
- **Receptor proteins:** Receptor proteins bind to hormones and other molecules outside the cell and trigger a response inside the cell.

Understanding membrane proteins is a vital part of human medicine, in part because at least half of all drugs bind to them. One example is omeprazole (Prilosec). This drug relieves heartburn and gastric reflux by blocking some of the transport proteins that pump acid into the stomach. Another is the antidepressant drug fluoxetine (Prozac), which prevents receptors on brain cell surfaces from absorbing a mood-altering biochemical called serotonin.

3.3 Mastering Concepts

1. How does the chemical structure of phospholipids enable them to form a bilayer in water?
2. Where in the cell do phospholipid bilayers occur?
3. What are some functions of membrane proteins?

Burning Questions

Can biologists make synthetic cells?

One component of the cell theory is that cells come only from preexisting cells. Yet scientists have been inching closer to the possibility of creating cells in the laboratory.

A breakthrough in synthetic biology came in 2010, when headlines blared that scientists had created an artificial cell. In reality, a team led by J. Craig Venter had managed to replace the "natural" DNA in a bacterial cell with a synthetic genome. The scientists did not, however, build a cell from scratch. Instead, they inserted the instructions—the synthetic DNA—and let the cell build the membranes, enzymes, and other cellular components.

Synthetic cells do not have practical uses yet, but they may in the future. Biologists should be able to create strands of DNA that encode any protein, whether it currently exists or not. The artificial cells can therefore become miniature factories, churning out everything from biofuels to vaccines.

Submit your burning question to:
marielle_hoefnagels@mcgraw-hill.com

Why We Care — Most of Your Cells Are Not Your Own

Cells are so tiny that it is hard to imagine how many make up a human body. For adults, estimates range from about 10 trillion to 100 trillion. No one knows for sure, because counting living cells is much harder than estimating the number of candies in a jar. After all, the number of cells changes throughout life. A child's growth comes from cell division that adds new cells, not from the expansion of existing ones. Moreover, new cells arise as old cells die, so a "true" count is a moving target. Also, no one has found a good way to count them all. Cells come in so many different shapes and sizes that it is hard to extrapolate from a small sample to the whole body.

Surprisingly, nonhuman cells vastly outnumber the body's own cells. Microbiologists estimate that the number of bacteria living in and on a typical human is *10 times* the number of human cells! Although some of these bacteria can cause disease, most exist harmlessly on the skin and in the mouth and intestines. These inconspicuous guests, which so vastly outnumber your own cells, also can help extract nutrients from food and prevent disease.

3.4 Eukaryotic Organelles Divide Labor

In eukaryotic cells, organelles have specialized functions that carry out the work of the cell. If you think of a eukaryotic cell as a home, each organelle would be analogous to a room. For example, your kitchen, bathroom, and bedroom each hold unique items that suit the uses of those rooms. Likewise, each organelle has distinct sets of proteins and other molecules that fit the organelle's function. The "walls" of these cellular compartments are membranes, often intricately folded and studded with enzymes and other proteins.

Many of these internal membranes form a coordinated **endomembrane system,** which consists of several interacting organelles: the nuclear envelope, endoplasmic reticulum, Golgi apparatus, lysosomes, vacuoles, and cell membrane. As you will see, the organelles of the endomembrane system are connected by small "bubbles" of membrane that can pinch off of one organelle, travel within the cell, and fuse with another. These membranous spheres, which are also part of the endomembrane system, form **vesicles** that transport materials inside the cell.

This section describes the structures and functions of the most important organelles, beginning with the endomembrane system.

A. The Nucleus, Endoplasmic Reticulum, and Golgi Interact to Secrete Substances

The organelles of the endomembrane system enable cells to produce, package, and release complex mixtures of biochemicals. This section focuses on the production and secretion of one such mixture: milk (figure 3.11).

Special cells in the mammary glands of female mammals produce milk, which contains proteins, fats, carbohydrates, and water in a proportion ideal for development of a newborn. Human milk is rich in lipids, which the rapidly growing baby's nervous system requires. (Cows' milk contains a higher proportion of protein, better suited to a calf's rapid muscle growth.) Milk also contains calcium, potassium, and antibodies that help jump-start the infant's immunity to disease.

The milk-producing cells of the mammary glands are dormant most of the time, but they undergo a burst of productivity shortly after the female gives birth. How do the organelles of each cell work together to manufacture milk?

The Nucleus The process of milk production and secretion begins in the **nucleus** (see figure 3.11, step 1), the most prominent organelle in most eukaryotic cells. The nucleus contains DNA, an informational molecule that specifies the "recipe" for every protein a cell can make (such as milk protein and enzymes required to synthesize carbohydrates and lipids). As described in more detail in chapter 7, the cell copies the genes encoding these proteins into another nucleic acid, messenger RNA (mRNA).

The mRNA molecules exit the nucleus through **nuclear pores,** which are holes in the double-membrane **nuclear envelope** that separates the nucleus from the cytoplasm (figure 3.11, step 2, and figure 3.12). Nuclear pores are highly specialized channels composed of dozens of types of proteins. Traffic through the nuclear pores is busy, with millions of regulatory proteins entering and mRNA molecules leaving each minute.

Also inside the nucleus is the **nucleolus,** a dense spot that assembles the components of ribosomes. These ribosomal subunits leave the nucleus through

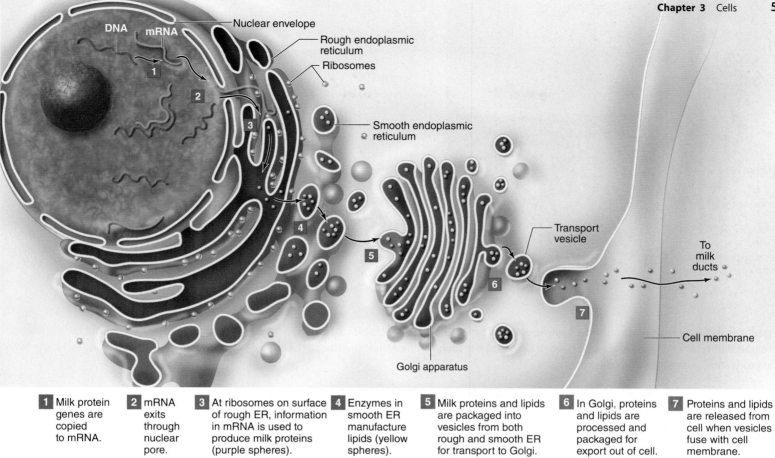

1 Milk protein genes are copied to mRNA.

2 mRNA exits through nuclear pore.

3 At ribosomes on surface of rough ER, information in mRNA is used to produce milk proteins (purple spheres).

4 Enzymes in smooth ER manufacture lipids (yellow spheres).

5 Milk proteins and lipids are packaged into vesicles from both rough and smooth ER for transport to Golgi.

6 In Golgi, proteins and lipids are processed and packaged for export out of cell.

7 Proteins and lipids are released from cell when vesicles fuse with cell membrane.

Figure 3.11 Making Milk. Several organelles participate in the production and secretion of milk from a cell in a mammary gland; the numbers (*1*) through (*7*) indicate the order in which organelles participate in this process.

the nuclear pores, and they come together in the cytoplasm to form complete ribosomes.

The Endoplasmic Reticulum and Golgi Apparatus The remainder of the cell, between the nucleus and the cell membrane, is the cytoplasm. In all cells, the cytoplasm contains a watery mixture of ions, enzymes, RNA, and other dissolved substances. In eukaryotes, the cytoplasm also includes organelles and arrays of protein rods and tubules called the cytoskeleton (see section 3.5).

Once in the cytoplasm, mRNA coming from the nucleus binds to a ribosome, which manufactures proteins (see figure 3.11, step 3). Ribosomes that produce proteins for use inside the cell are free-floating in the cytoplasm. But many proteins are destined for the cell membrane or for secretion (in milk, for example). In that case, the entire complex of ribosome, mRNA, and partially made protein is anchored to the surface of the **endoplasmic reticulum,** a network of sacs and tubules composed of membranes. (*Endoplasmic* means "within the cytoplasm," and *reticulum* means "network.")

The endoplasmic reticulum (ER) originates at the nuclear envelope and winds throughout the cell. Close to the nucleus, the membrane surface is studded with ribosomes making proteins that enter the inner compartment of the ER; these

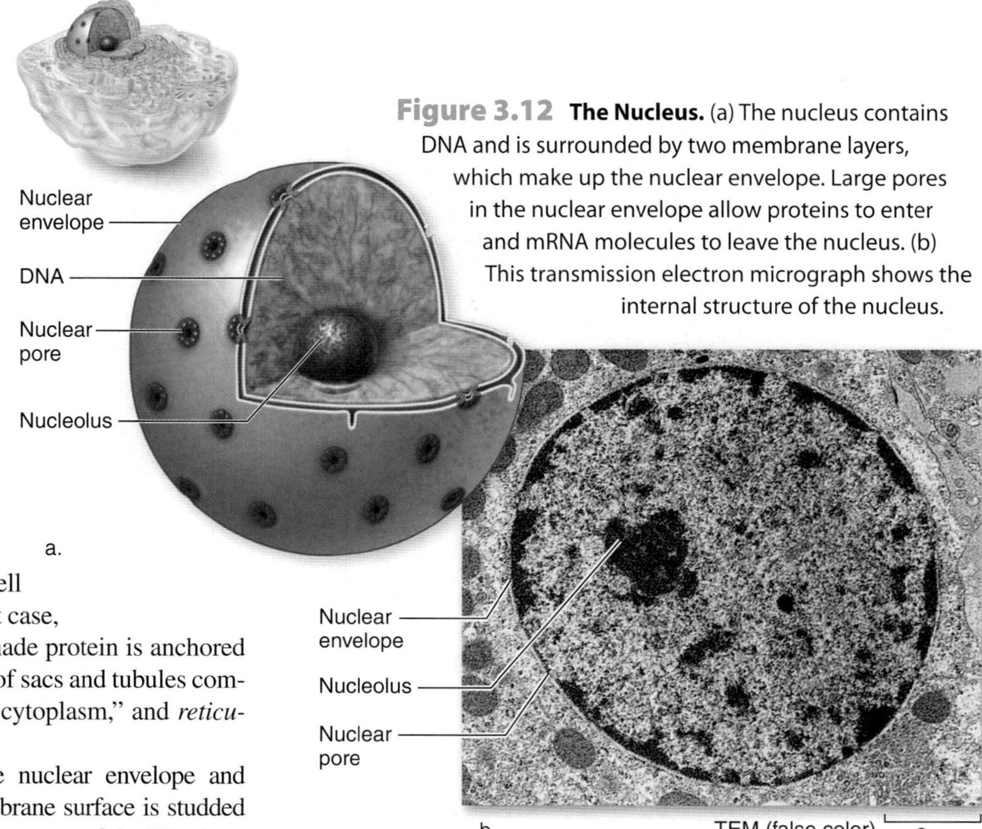

Figure 3.12 The Nucleus. (a) The nucleus contains DNA and is surrounded by two membrane layers, which make up the nuclear envelope. Large pores in the nuclear envelope allow proteins to enter and mRNA molecules to leave the nucleus. (b) This transmission electron micrograph shows the internal structure of the nucleus.

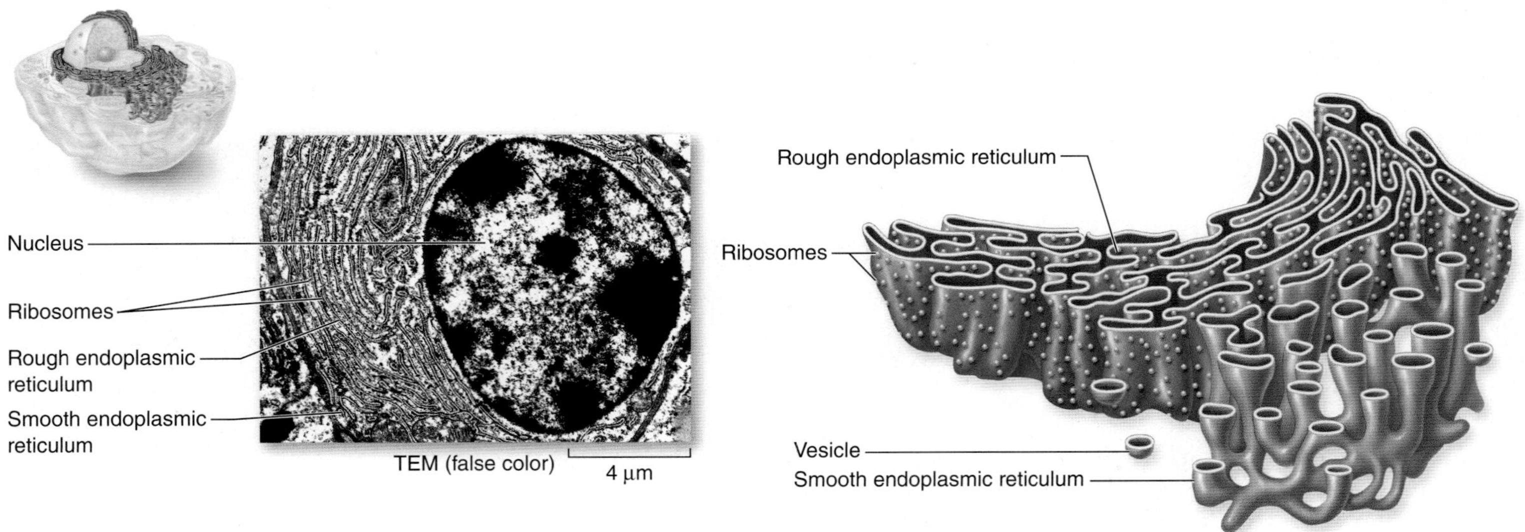

Figure 3.13 The Endoplasmic Reticulum, Rough and Smooth. The endoplasmic reticulum is a network of membranes extending from the nuclear envelope. Ribosomes dot the surface of the rough ER, giving it a "rough" appearance. The smooth ER is a series of interconnecting tubules and is the site for lipid production and other metabolic processes.

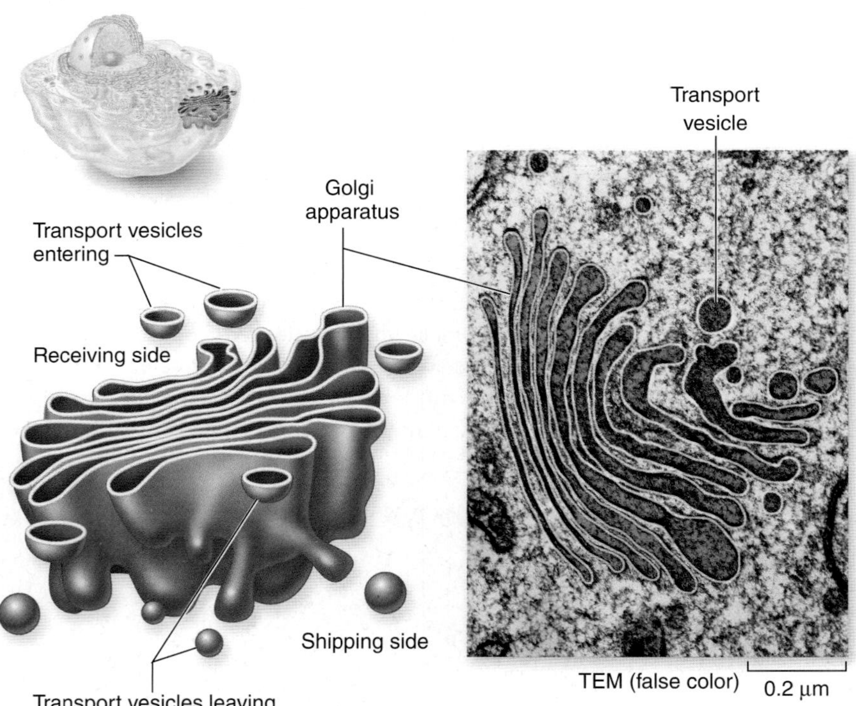

Figure 3.14 The Golgi Apparatus. The Golgi apparatus is composed of a series of flattened sacs, plus transport vesicles that deliver and remove materials. Proteins are sorted and processed as they move through the Golgi apparatus on their way to the cell surface or lysosomes.

proteins are destined to be secreted from the cell. This section of the network is called the **rough ER** because the ribosomes give these membranes a roughened appearance (figure 3.13).

Adjacent to the rough ER, a section of the network called **smooth ER** synthesizes lipids—such as those that will end up in the milk—and other membrane components (see figure 3.11, step 4, and figure 3.13). The smooth ER also houses enzymes that detoxify drugs and poisons. In muscle cells, a specialized type of smooth ER stores and delivers the calcium ions required for muscle contraction.

The lipids and proteins made by the ER exit the organelle in vesicles. A loaded transport vesicle pinches off from the tubular endings of the ER membrane (see figure 3.11, step 5) and takes its contents to the next stop in the production line, the **Golgi apparatus** (figure 3.14). This organelle is a stack of flat, membrane-enclosed sacs that functions as a processing center. Proteins from the ER pass through the series of Golgi sacs, where they complete their folding and become functional (see figure 3.11, step 6). Enzymes in the Golgi apparatus also manufacture and attach carbohydrates to proteins or lipids, forming the "name tags" recognized by the immune system (see section 3.3).

The Golgi apparatus sorts and packages materials into vesicles, which move toward the cell membrane. Some of the proteins it receives from the ER will become membrane surface proteins; other substances (such as milk protein and fat) are packaged for secretion from the cell. In the production of milk, these vesicles fuse with the cell membrane and release the proteins outside the cell (see figure 3.11, step 7). Fat droplets retain a layer of surrounding membrane when they leave the cell.

This entire process happens simultaneously in countless specialized cells lining the milk ducts of the breast, beginning shortly after a baby's birth. When the infant suckles, hormones released in the mother's body stimulate muscles surrounding balls of these cells to contract, squeezing milk into the ducts that lead to the nipple.

B. Lysosomes, Vacuoles, and Peroxisomes Are Cellular Digestion Centers

Besides producing molecules for export, eukaryotic cells also break down molecules in specialized compartments. All of these "digestion center" organelles are sacs surrounded by a single membrane.

Lysosomes **Lysosomes** are organelles containing enzymes that dismantle and recycle food particles, captured bacteria, worn-out organelles, and debris (figure 3.15). They are so named because their enzymes lyse, or cut apart, their substrates.

The rough ER manufactures the enzymes that end up inside lysosomes. The Golgi apparatus detects these enzymes by recognizing a sugar attached to them, then packages them into vesicles that eventually become lysosomes. The lysosomes, in turn, fuse with transport vesicles carrying debris from outside or from within the cell. The enzymes inside the lysosome break down the large organic molecules into smaller subunits by hydrolysis, releasing them into the cytoplasm for the cell to use.

What keeps a lysosome from digesting the entire cell? The lysosome's membrane maintains the pH of the organelle's interior at about 4.8, much more acidic than the neutral pH of the rest of the cytoplasm. If one lysosome were to burst, the liberated enzymes would no longer be at their optimum pH, so they could not digest the rest of the cell. Nevertheless, a cell injured by extreme cold, heat, or another physical stress may initiate its own death by bursting all of its lysosomes at once. ▸ pH, p. 32

Some cells have more lysosomes than others. White blood cells, for example, have many lysosomes because these cells engulf and dispose of debris and bacteria. Liver cells require many lysosomes to process cholesterol.

Malfunctioning lysosomes can cause illness. In Tay-Sachs disease, for example, a defective lysosomal enzyme allows a lipid to accumulate to toxic levels in nerve cells of the brain. The nervous system deteriorates, and an affected person eventually becomes unable to see, hear, or move. In the most severe forms of the illness, death usually occurs by age 5.

Vacuoles Most plant cells lack lysosomes, but they do have an organelle that serves a similar function. In mature plant cells, the large central **vacuole** contains a watery solution of enzymes that degrade and recycle molecules and organelles.

The vacuole also has other roles. Most of the growth of a plant cell comes from an increase in the volume of its vacuole. In some plant cells, the vacuole occupies up to 90% of the cell's volume (figure 3.16). As the vacuole acquires water, it exerts pressure (called turgor pressure) against the cell membrane. This pressure helps plants stay rigid.

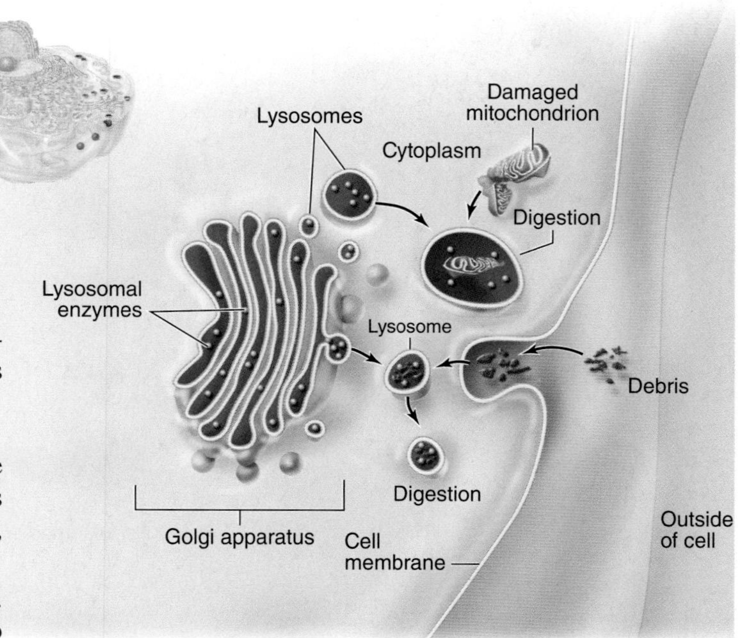

Figure 3.15 Lysosomes. Lysosomes contain enzymes that dismantle damaged organelles and other debris, then release the nutrients for the cell to use.

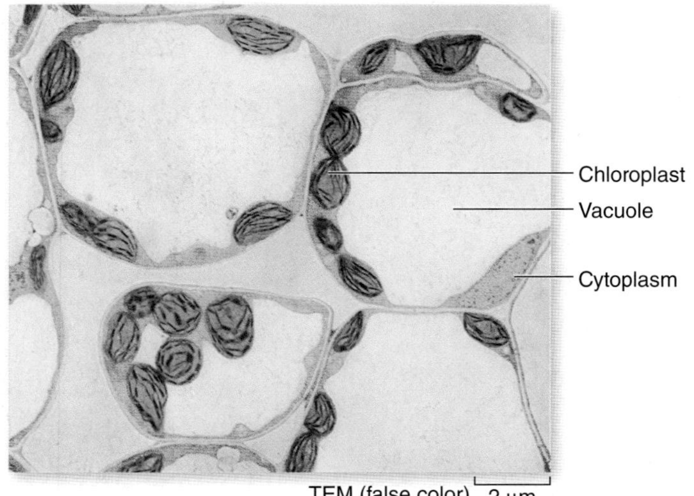

Figure 3.16 Vacuole. Much of the volume of a spinach leaf cell is occupied by the large central vacuole. The cytoplasm (containing numerous chloroplasts) is confined to the edges of the cell.

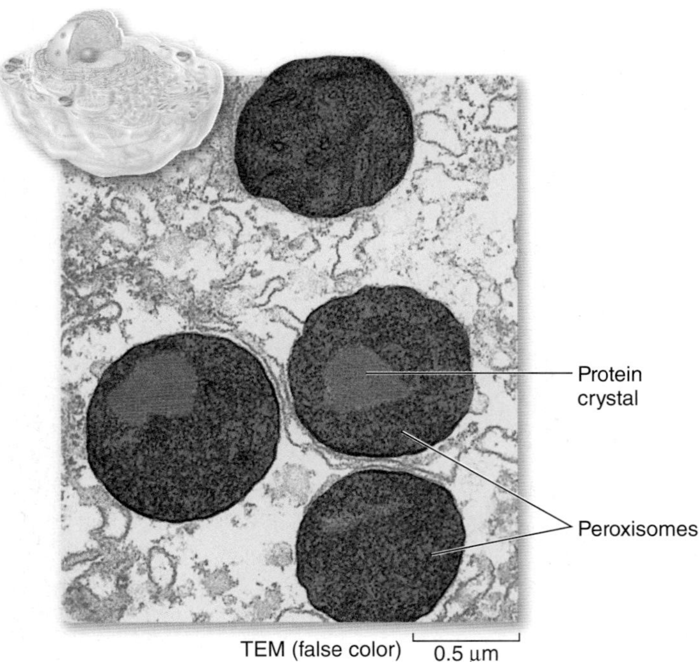

Figure 3.17 Peroxisomes. Crystals consisting of dense collections of enzymes give peroxisomes their characteristic appearance.

Besides water and enzymes, the vacuole also contains a variety of salts, sugars, and weak acids. Therefore, the pH of the vacuole's solution is usually somewhat acidic. In citrus fruits, the solution is very acidic, producing the tart taste of lemons and oranges. Water-soluble pigments also reside in the vacuole, producing blue, purple, and magenta colors in leaves, flowers, and fruits.

Some protists have vacuoles, although their function is different from that in plants. The contractile vacuole in *Paramecium*, for example, pumps excess water out of the cell. In *Amoeba*, a food vacuole digests nutrients that the cell has engulfed.

Peroxisomes All eukaryotic cells contain **peroxisomes,** organelles that contain several types of enzymes that dispose of toxic substances (figure 3.17). Although they resemble lysosomes in size and function, peroxisomes originate at the ER (not the Golgi) and contain different enzymes.

Liver and kidney cells contain many peroxisomes that help dismantle toxins from the blood. Peroxisomes also break down fatty acids and produce cholesterol and some other lipids. In a disease called adrenoleukodystrophy (ALD), a faulty peroxisomal enzyme causes fatty acids to accumulate to toxic levels in the brain. The film *Lorenzo's Oil* depicted a boy with this disease and his parents' struggle to find treatment options.

C. Photosynthesis Occurs in Chloroplasts

Plants and many protists carry out photosynthesis, a process that uses energy from sunlight to produce glucose and other food molecules (see chapter 5). These nutrients sustain not only the photosynthetic organisms but also the consumers (including humans) that eat them.

The **chloroplast** (figure 3.18) is the site of photosynthesis in eukaryotes. Each chloroplast contains multiple membrane layers. Two outer membrane

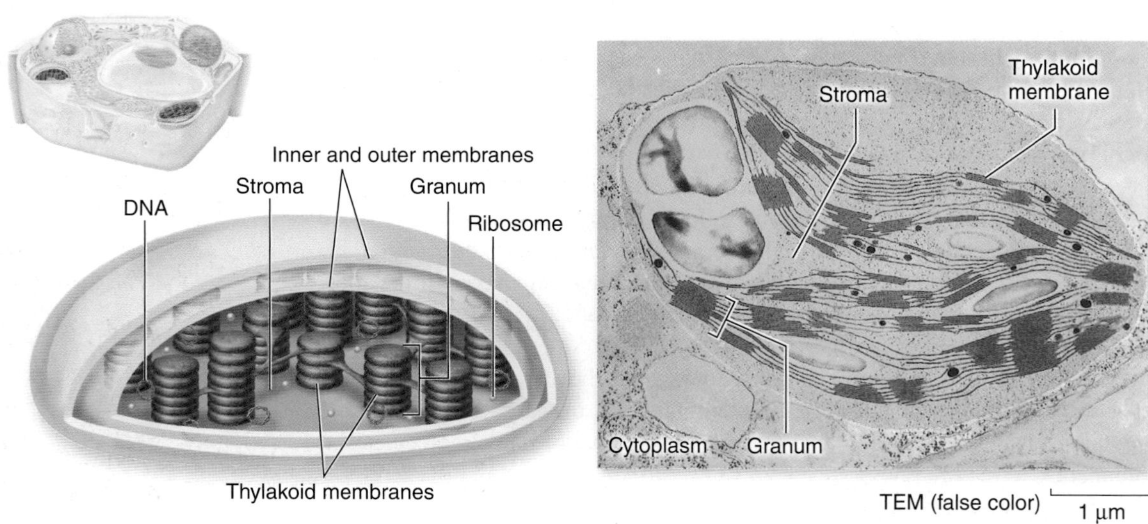

Figure 3.18 Chloroplasts. Photosynthesis occurs inside chloroplasts. Each chloroplast contains stacks of thylakoids that form grana within the inner compartment, the stroma. Enzymes and light-harvesting pigments embedded in the thylakoid membranes convert sunlight to chemical energy.

layers enclose an enzyme-rich fluid called the stroma. Within the stroma is a third membrane system folded into flattened sacs called thylakoids, which are stacked in interconnected structures called grana. Photosynthetic pigments such as chlorophyll are embedded in the thylakoid membranes.

A chloroplast is one representative of a larger category of plant organelles called plastids. Some plastids synthesize lipid-soluble red, orange, and yellow carotenoid pigments, such as those found in carrots and ripe tomatoes. Plastids that assemble starch molecules are important in cells specialized for food storage, such as those in potatoes and corn kernels. Interestingly, any plastid can convert into any other type. As a tomato ripens, for example, its green chloroplasts change into plastids that store red carotenoid pigments.

Unlike most other organelles, all plastids (including chloroplasts) contain their own DNA and ribosomes. The genetic material encodes proteins unique to plastid structure and function, including some of the enzymes required for photosynthesis.

D. Mitochondria Extract Energy from Nutrients

Growth, cell division, protein production, secretion, and many chemical reactions in the cytoplasm all require a steady supply of energy. **Mitochondria** (singular: mitochondrion) are organelles that use a process called cellular respiration to extract this needed energy from food (see chapter 6). With the exception of a few types of protists, all eukaryotic cells have mitochondria.

A mitochondrion has two membrane layers: an outer membrane and an intricately folded inner membrane that encloses the mitochondrial matrix (figure 3.19). Within the matrix is DNA that encodes proteins essential for mitochondrial function; ribosomes occupy the matrix as well. **Cristae** are the folds of the inner membrane. The cristae add tremendous surface area to the inner membrane, which houses the enzymes that catalyze many of the reactions of cellular respiration.

In most mammals, mitochondria are inherited from the female parent only. (This is because the mitochondria in a sperm cell stay in the sperm's tail, which never enters the egg.) Mitochondrial DNA is therefore useful for tracking inheritance through female lines in a family. For the same reason, genetic mutations that cause defective mitochondria also pass only from mother to offspring. Mitochondrial illnesses are most serious when they affect the muscles or brain, because these energy-hungry organs depend on the functioning of many thousands of mitochondria in every cell.

Chloroplasts and mitochondria have striking similarities: both have their own DNA and ribosomes, and both are surrounded by double membranes. These shared features provide clues to the origin of eukaryotic cells, an event that apparently occurred some 2.7 billion years ago. According to the endosymbiosis theory, some ancient organism (or organisms) engulfed bacterial cells. Rather than digesting them as food, the host cells kept them on as partners: mitochondria and chloroplasts. The structures and genetic sequences of today's bacteria, mitochondria, and chloroplasts supply powerful evidence for this theory. ▸ endosymbiosis, p. 288

Organelles divide a cell's work, just as the rooms in a house contain related items: pots and dishes are in the kitchen, whereas blankets and pillows are in the bedroom. But highly specialized buildings also exist. A restaurant, for example, has an enormous kitchen and no bedrooms at all. Likewise,

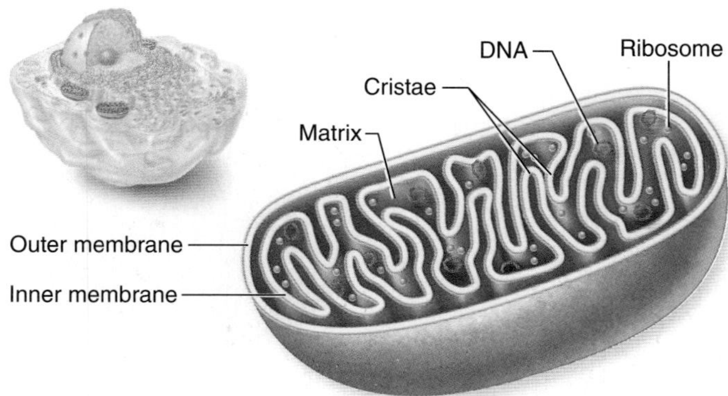

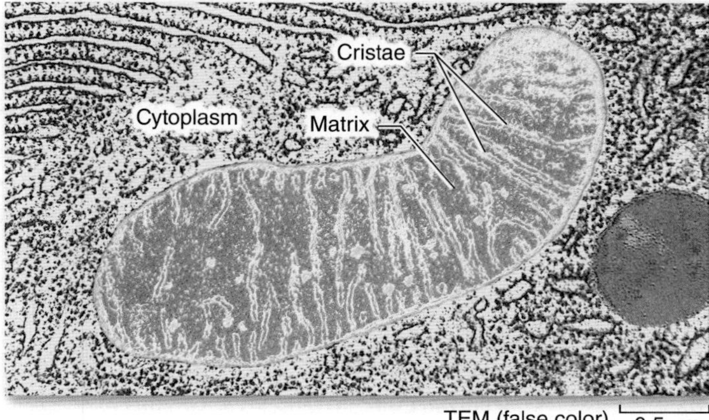

Figure 3.19 **Mitochondria.** Cellular respiration occurs inside mitochondria. Each mitochondrion contains a highly folded inner membrane, where many of the reactions of cellular respiration occur.

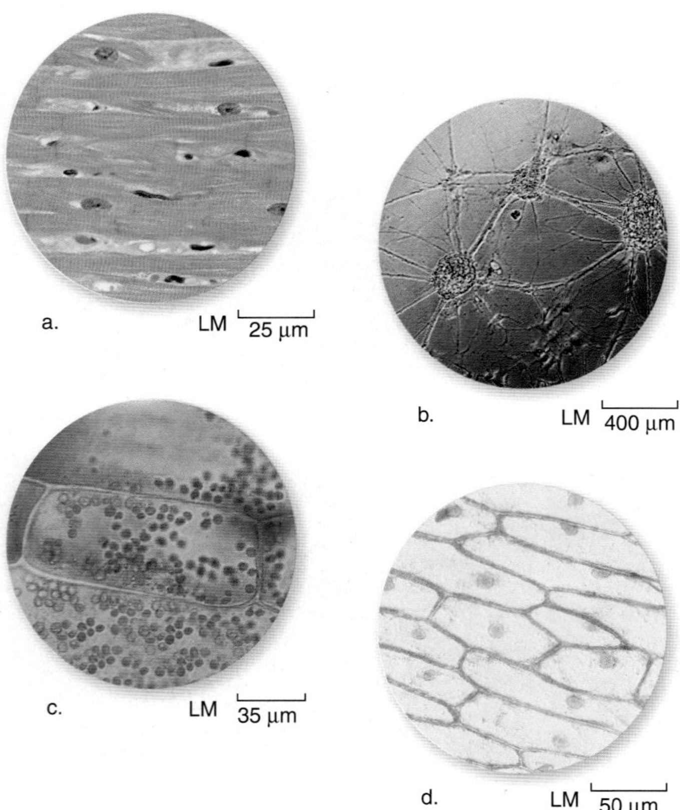

Figure 3.20 Specialized Cells. (a) Muscle cells in the heart look and behave differently from (b) the highly branched neurons that form the nervous system. (c) A plant's leaf cells contain chloroplasts, whereas (d) the cells making up the outer skin of an onion do not.

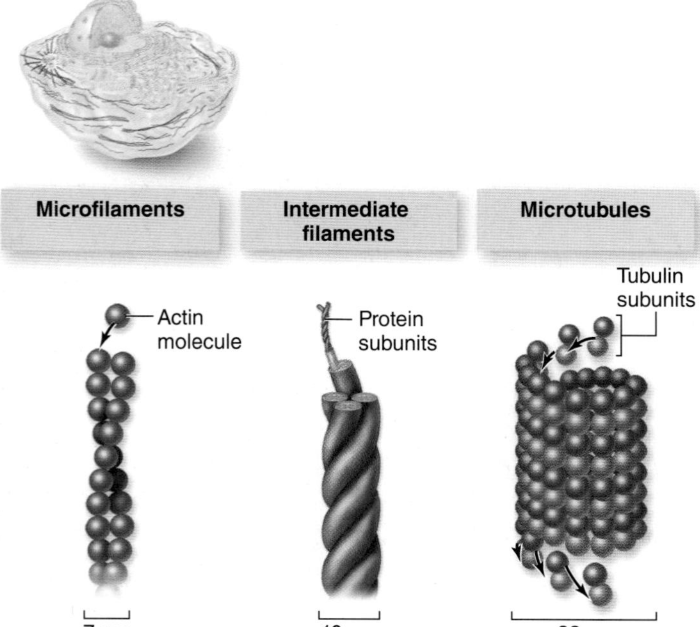

Figure 3.21 Elements of the Cytoskeleton. The cytoskeleton consists of three types of protein filaments, arranged in this figure from smallest to largest diameter.

many cells also have specialized functions (figure 3.20). Muscle cells, for example, are long and thin, whereas neurons produce multiple extensions that touch adjacent nerve cells. Leaf cells are packed with chloroplasts. The protective epidermis of an onion, on the other hand, forms underground; its cells therefore lack chloroplasts. Keep these specialized structures and functions in mind as you study cell processes throughout this book.

3.4 Mastering Concepts

1. Which organelles interact to produce and secrete a complex substance such as milk?
2. What is the function of the nucleus and its contents?
3. Which organelles are the cell's "recycling centers"?
4. What process occurs in a chloroplast?
5. Which organelle houses the reactions that extract chemical energy from nutrient molecules?
6. Which three organelles contain DNA?

3.5 The Cytoskeleton Supports Eukaryotic Cells

The cytoplasm of a eukaryotic cell contains a **cytoskeleton,** an intricate network of protein "tracks" and tubules. The cytoskeleton is an internal framework with many functions. It is a transportation system, and it provides the structural support necessary to maintain the cell's characteristic three-dimensional shape. It aids in cell division and helps connect cells to one another. The cytoskeleton also enables cells—or parts of a cell—to move.

The cytoskeleton includes three major components: microfilaments, intermediate filaments, and microtubules (figure 3.21). They are distinguished by protein type, diameter, and how they aggregate into larger structures. Other proteins connect these components to one another, creating an intricate meshwork.

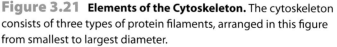

The thinnest component of the cytoskeleton is the **microfilament,** a long rod composed of the protein actin. Actin microfilament networks are part of nearly all eukaryotic cells. Microfilaments provide strength for cells to survive stretching and compression, and they help to anchor one cell to another (see section 3.6). Muscle contraction relies on actin filaments and another protein, myosin. ▸ muscle movement, p. 530

Intermediate filaments are so named because their diameters are between those of microfilaments and microtubules. Several different proteins form intermediate filaments. All form an internal scaffold in the cytoplasm and resist mechanical stress, both functions that maintain a cell's shape. Intermediate filaments also help bind some cells together (see section 3.6).

A **microtubule** is composed of a protein called tubulin. The cell can change the length of a microtubule rapidly by adding or removing tubulin molecules. Microtubules have many functions in eukaryotic cells. For example, chapter 8 describes how microtubules pull a cell's duplicated chromosomes apart during cell division. Microtubules also form a type of "trackway" along which organelles and proteins rapidly move within a cell. Some organisms, such as the squid, can change colors rapidly by using this process to rearrange pigment molecules in their skin cells.

In animal cells, structures called **centrosomes** organize the microtubules. The centrosome contains two centrioles, which are visible in figure 3.6. The centrioles also indirectly produce the extensions that enable some cells to move: cilia and flagella (figure 3.22).

Cilia are short and numerous, like a fringe. Some protists, such as the *Paramecium* in figure 3.2, have thousands of cilia that enable the cells to "swim" in water. In the human respiratory tract, coordinated movement of cilia sets up a wave that propels particles up and out; other cilia can move an egg cell through the female reproductive tract. ▸ ciliates, p. 295

Unlike cilia, flagella occur singly or in pairs, and a flagellum is much longer than a cilium. Flagella are more like tails, and their whiplike movement propels cells. Sperm cells in many species (including humans) have prominent flagella.

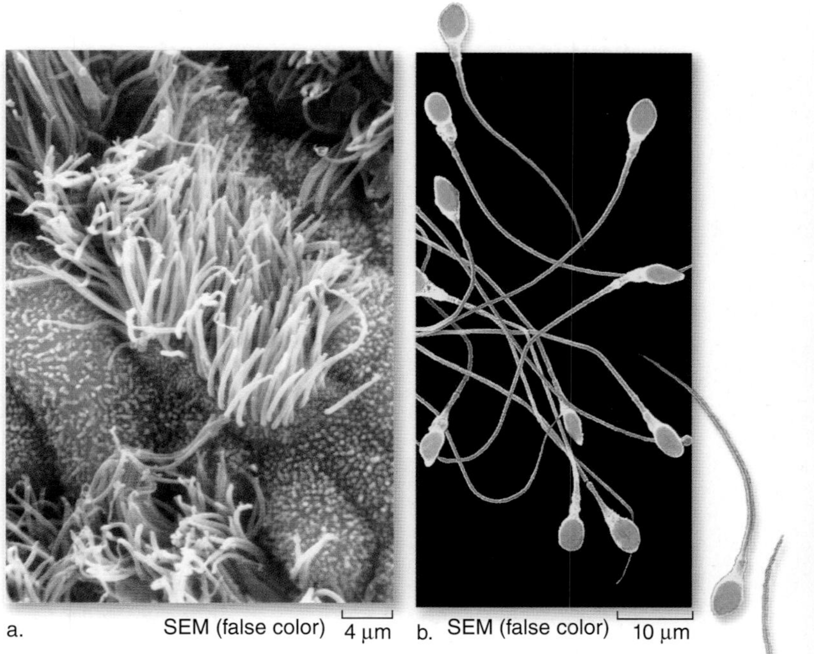

a. SEM (false color) 4 µm b. SEM (false color) 10 µm

Figure 3.22 Cilia and Flagella. (a) These cilia help eliminate dust and other foreign particles from the human respiratory tract. (b) The flagella on human sperm cells enable them to swim.

3.5 Mastering Concepts

1. What are some functions of the cytoskeleton?
2. What are the main components of the cytoskeleton?
3. How are cilia and flagella similar, and how are they different?

3.6 Cells Stick Together and Communicate with One Another

So far, this chapter has described individual cells. But multicellular organisms, including plants and animals, are made of many cells that work together. How do these cells adhere to one another so that your body—or that of a plant—doesn't disintegrate in a heavy rain? Also, how do cells in direct contact with one another communicate to coordinate development and respond to the environment? This section describes how the cells of plant and animal tissues stick together and how neighboring cells share signals.

Cell walls surround the cell membranes of nearly all bacteria, archaea, fungi, algae, and plants. But *cell wall* is a misleading term: it is not just a barrier that outlines the cell. Cell walls impart shape, regulate cell volume, and prevent bursting when a cell takes in too much water.

Much of the plant cell wall consists of cellulose molecules aligned into fibrils (figure 3.23a). This organization imparts great strength. Other polysaccharides glue adjacent cells together and add strength and flexibility. Each cell communicates with its neighbors through **plasmodesmata,** channels that connect adjacent cells (figure 3.23b). Plasmodesmata are essentially "tunnels" in the cell wall, through which the cytoplasm of one plant cell can interact with that of another. ▸ cellulose, p. 35

Animal cells lack cell walls. Instead, many animal cells secrete a complex extracellular matrix that holds them together and coordinates many aspects of cellular life. In these tissues, cells are not in direct contact with

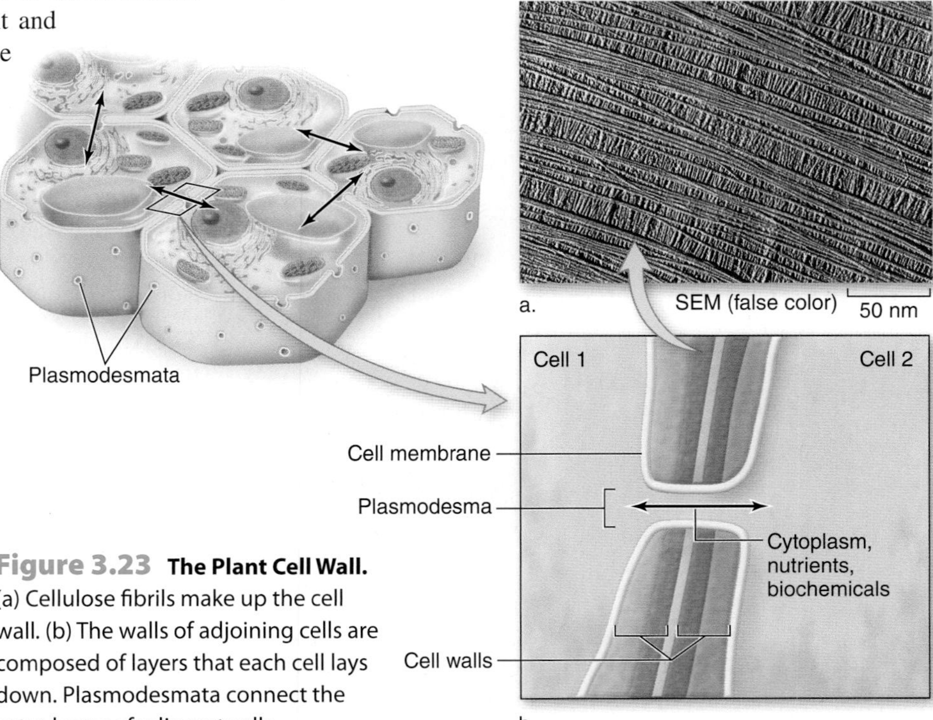

Figure 3.23 The Plant Cell Wall. (a) Cellulose fibrils make up the cell wall. (b) The walls of adjoining cells are composed of layers that each cell lays down. Plasmodesmata connect the cytoplasms of adjacent cells.

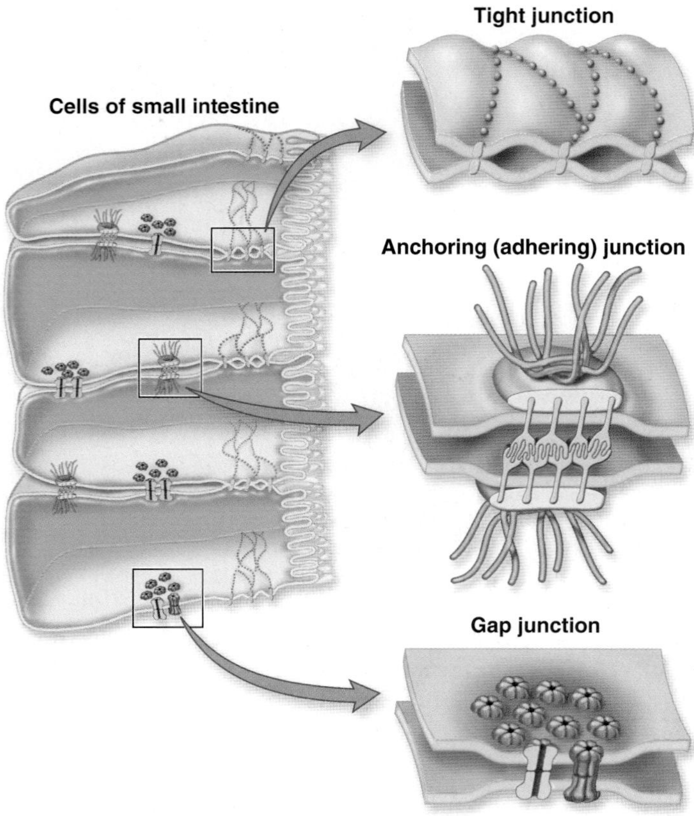

Figure 3.24 Animal Cell Connections. These cells illustrate all three types of animal cell junctions. Tight junctions fuse neighboring cell membranes, anchoring junctions form "spot welds," and gap junctions allow small molecules to move between adjacent cells.

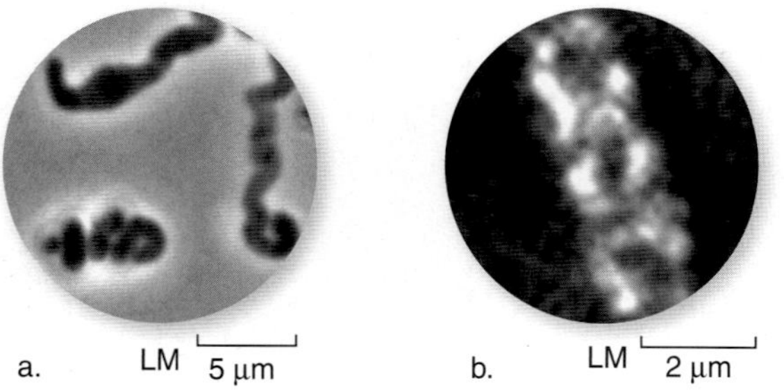

Figure 3.25 Cytoskeleton Precursor? (a) Mutated genes produced misshapen *Bacillus subtilis* cells. (b) An actinlike protein tagged with a fluorescent label accumulates in a helix just inside the cell wall.

one another. In other tissues, however, the plasma membranes of adjacent cells directly connect to one another via several types of junctions (figure 3.24):

- A **tight junction** fuses cells together, forming an impermeable barrier between them. Tight junctions create the "blood–brain barrier," densely packed cells that prevent many harmful substances from entering the brain. However, this barrier readily admits lipid-soluble drugs such as heroin and cocaine across its cell membranes, accounting for the speed with which these drugs act.
- An **anchoring** (or **adhering**) **junction** connects adjacent cells by linking their intermediate filaments in one spot, somewhat like rivets or "spot welds." These junctions hold skin cells in place by anchoring them to the extracellular matrix.
- A **gap junction** is a protein channel that links the cytoplasm of adjacent cells, allowing exchange of ions, nutrients, and other small molecules. It is therefore analogous to plasmodesmata in plants. Gap junctions link heart muscle cells to one another, allowing groups of cells to contract together.

3.6 Mastering Concepts

1. What functions do cell walls provide?
2. What is the chemical composition of a plant cell wall?
3. What are plasmodesmata?
4. What are the three types of junctions that link cells in animals?

Investigating Life

3.7 Did the Cytoskeleton Begin in Bacteria?

The Question: The cytoskeleton is one feature that distinguishes eukaryotic from prokaryotic cells. Because all eukaryotic cells have a cytoskeleton, these proteins must have been present in their last common (shared) ancestor. But the cytoskeleton does not occur in prokaryotic cells, which were the first organisms. Where did this essential part of the eukaryotic cell come from?

The Approach: Researchers tackled this mystery by revisiting the assumption that prokaryotic cells lack a cytoskeleton. For example, Laura Jones, Rut Carballido-López, and Jeffery Errington at the University of Oxford discovered a pair of intriguing proteins that lie just inside the cell surface of a bacterium called *Bacillus subtilis*. They used several tools to learn more about the two proteins.

Bacillus subtilis ordinarily forms rod-shaped cells, but the researchers noticed that when they experimentally "turned off" either of two genes, the cells had abnormal shapes. When the scientists turned off the gene encoding one protein, the cells were the correct length but appeared abnormally inflated or rounded. When they turned off the gene encoding the other protein instead, the cells were bent and twisted (figure 3.25a).

The team also used microscopes to learn where in the cell the two proteins are located. An individual protein, however, is far too small for even the most powerful microscope to resolve. So the researchers attached glowing fluorescent "tags" that made the proteins visible. The results were remarkable: each protein formed a helix just beneath the cell surface (figure 3.25b).

Could the same proteins that help determine cell shape in *B. subtilis* operate in other microbes as well? The team searched the DNA sequences of dozens of other bacteria and archaea. They found that most of the species with comparable genes had cells shaped like rods, filaments, or corkscrews, whereas most species lacking the genes had spherical cells. The scientists also searched databases of amino acid sequences for proteins from other species. The proteins turned out to share key similarities with actin from yeast and human cells, suggesting related functions.

The Conclusion: These studies strongly suggest that the actin in eukaryotic cells has a prokaryotic counterpart with a function that persists to this day. At least some elements of the cytoskeleton apparently evolved before the two cell types diverged some 2.7 billion years ago. This research has therefore brought biologists closer to answering the question of "Where did that come from?" for the cytoskeleton.

Jones, Laura J. F., Rut Carballido-López, and Jeffery Errington. 2001. Control of cell shape in bacteria: helical, actin-like filaments in *Bacillus subtilis*. *Cell*, vol. 104, pages 913–922.

3.7 Mastering Concepts

1. How did the researchers use multiple lines of evidence to answer their question?
2. How would the bacterial cells in figure 3.25b look different if the target proteins occurred throughout the cytoplasm?

Chapter Summary

3.1 Cells Are the Units of Life

A. Microscopes Revealed the Cellular Basis of Life

- **Cells** are the microscopic components of all organisms.
- The first person to see cells was Robert Hooke, who viewed cork with a crude lens in the late seventeenth century.
- The **cell theory** states that all life is composed of cells, that cells are the functional units of life, and that all cells come from preexisting cells.

B. Microscopes Magnify Cell Structures

- Light microscopes and electron microscopes are essential tools in cell biology.

C. All Cells Have Features in Common

- All cells have DNA, RNA, **ribosomes** that build proteins, **cytoplasm,** and a **cell membrane** that is the interface between the cell and the outside environment.
- Complex cells also have specialized compartments called **organelles.**
- The surface area of a cell must be large relative to its volume.

3.2 Different Cell Types Characterize Life's Three Domains

- Cells are **prokaryotic** (lacking a nucleus) or **eukaryotic** (having a nucleus and other **organelles**).

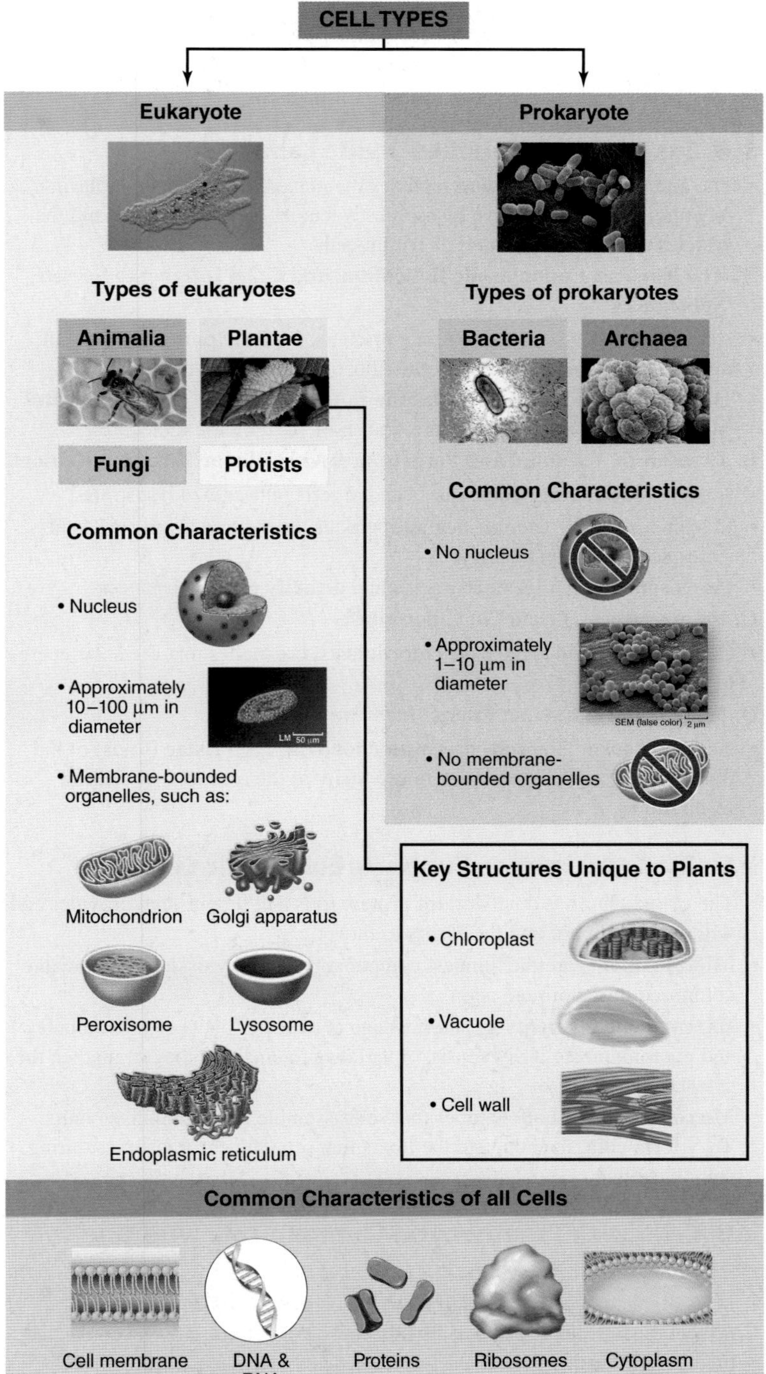

A. Domains Bacteria and Archaea Contain Prokaryotic Organisms

- Bacterial cells are structurally simple, but they are abundant and diverse. Most have a **cell wall** and one or more **flagella.** DNA occurs in an area called the **nucleoid.**
- Archaea share some characteristics with bacteria and eukaryotes but also have unique structures and chemistry.

B. Organisms in Domain Eukarya Have Complex Cells

- Eukaryotic cells include those of protists, plants, fungi, and animals. Most eukaryotic cells are larger than prokaryotic cells.

3.3 A Membrane Separates Each Cell from Its Surroundings

- A biological membrane consists of a **phospholipid bilayer** embedded with movable proteins and sterols, forming a **fluid mosaic.**
- Membrane proteins carry out a variety of functions.

3.4 Eukaryotic Organelles Divide Labor

- The **endomembrane system** includes the nuclear envelope, endoplasmic reticulum, Golgi apparatus, lysosomes, vacuoles, cell membrane, and the **vesicles** that transport materials within cells.

A. The Nucleus, Endoplasmic Reticulum, and Golgi Interact to Secrete Substances

- A eukaryotic cell houses DNA in a **nucleus. Nuclear pores** permeate the **nuclear envelope;** assembly of the ribosomes occurs in the **nucleolus.**
- The **smooth** and **rough endoplasmic reticulum** and the **Golgi apparatus** work together to synthesize, store, transport, and release molecules.

B. Lysosomes, Vacuoles, and Peroxisomes Are Cellular Digestion Centers

- A eukaryotic cell degrades wastes and digests nutrients in **lysosomes.**
- In plants, a watery **vacuole** degrades wastes, exerts turgor pressure, and stores acids and pigments.
- **Peroxisomes** help digest fatty acids and detoxify many substances.

C. Photosynthesis Occurs in Chloroplasts

- Cells of plants and algae have **chloroplasts,** organelles that use solar energy to make food.

D. Mitochondria Extract Energy from Nutrients

- Nearly all eukaryotic cells have **mitochondria.** The **cristae** (folds) of the inner mitochondrial membrane house many of the reactions of cellular respiration.

3.5 The Cytoskeleton Supports Eukaryotic Cells

- The **cytoskeleton** is a network of protein rods and tubules that provides cells with form, support, and the ability to move.
- **Microfilaments** are the thinnest components of the cytoskeleton. They are composed of the protein actin.
- **Intermediate filaments** are intermediate in diameter between microtubules and microfilaments. They consist of various proteins, and they strengthen the cytoskeleton.
- **Microtubules** are hollow tubes that self-assemble from tubulin subunits. They form **cilia,** flagella, and the fibers that separate chromosomes during cell division.

3.6 Cells Stick Together and Communicate with One Another

- Most organisms other than animals have cell walls, which provide protection and shape. Plant cell walls consist of cellulose fibrils connected by other molecules.
- **Plasmodesmata** are openings that extend between the cell walls of adjacent plant cells.
- Connections between animal cells include **tight junctions, anchoring junctions,** and **gap junctions.** Tight junctions create a seal between adjacent cells. Anchoring junctions are "spot welds" that secure cells in place. Gap junctions allow adjacent cells to exchange signals and cytoplasmic material.

3.7 Investigating Life: Did the Cytoskeleton Begin in Bacteria?

- Although the cytoskeleton occurs only in eukaryotic cells, bacteria do have actinlike proteins that help control cell shape.

Multiple Choice Questions

1. Why are cells considered to be the smallest unit of life?
   a. Because you need a microscope to see them
   b. Because a cell is the smallest thing that carries out all the functions of life
   c. Because they have an organized structure
   d. Because all cells have a nucleus with DNA
2. Which of the following is NOT a feature found in all cells?
   a. Proteins
   b. Ribosomes
   c. Cell wall
   d. Cell membrane
3. A cell membrane is said to be a *fluid mosaic* because
   a. there is water in the membrane.
   b. the membrane is made of lipids and proteins that can move.
   c. it forms a bilayer.
   d. transport proteins allow for the movement of water-soluble molecules.
4. One property that distinguishes cells in Domain Eukarya from those in Domain Bacteria is the presence of
   a. a cell wall.
   b. DNA.
   c. flagella.
   d. membrane-bounded organelles.
5. Which of the following organelles are associated with the job of cellular digestion?
   a. Lysosomes and peroxisomes
   b. Golgi apparatus and vesicles
   c. Nucleus and nucleolus
   d. Smooth and rough endoplasmic reticulum
6. Which of the following organelles does not belong to the endomembrane system?
   a. Golgi apparatus
   b. Endoplasmic reticulum
   c. Mitochondrion
   d. Lysosome
7. Within a single cell, which of the following is physically the smallest?
   a. Nuclear envelope
   b. Phospholipid molecule
   c. Cell membrane
   d. Mitochondrion
8. Which of the following organelles does NOT contain its own DNA?
   a. Nucleus
   b. Chloroplast
   c. Rough endoplasmic reticulum
   d. Mitochondrion
9. What cellular process is involved in the production of milk-specific mRNA molecules?
   a. Protein synthesis
   b. Digestion
   c. Lipid synthesis
   d. Cellular respiration

10. A human nerve cell that has an abnormal shape most likely has a defective
    a. cell wall.
    b. cytoskeleton.
    c. nucleus.
    d. ribosome.

Write It Out

1. How did microscopes contribute to the formulation of the cell theory?
2. List the features that all cells share, then name three structures or activities found in eukaryotic cells but not in bacteria or archaea.
3. In what ways is a prokaryotic cell like a baseball stadium, but a eukaryotic cell is more like an office building?
4. Biologist J. Craig Venter has designed and built an artificial bacterial chromosome. If he wants to build an entire cell from scratch, what other ingredients will he need? Can you foresee any benefits from, or ethical problems with, the ability to create artificial life? What do you need to know to be able to answer these questions?
5. Your friend claims that an ostrich egg is the largest single cell, but you are skeptical that one cell can be that large. If you had access to an ostrich egg and a high-quality light microscope, what features would you look for to resolve the argument?
6. Suppose you discover a new organism and that you have access to light and electron microscopes to examine its cells. List a specific question you could answer by using each type of microscope.
7. Why are large organisms made of numerous small cells instead of a few large ones?
8. Which has a greater ratio of surface area to volume, a hippopotamus or a mouse? Which animal would lose heat faster in a cold environment and why?
9. List the chemicals that make up cell membranes.
10. Compare and contrast the phospholipid bilayer with two pieces of Velcro sticking to each other.
11. One way to understand cell function is to compare the parts of a cell to the parts of a factory. For example, the Golgi apparatus would be analogous to the factory's shipping department. How would the other cell parts fit into this analogy?
12. This chapter used the endomembrane system to illustrate the organelles involved in milk production. Once a baby drinks the milk, which organelles in the infant's cells extract the raw materials and potential energy in the milk to fuel growth?
13. Why does a muscle cell contain many mitochondria? Why does a white blood cell contain many lysosomes?
14. List the components and functions of the cytoskeleton.
15. How do plant cells interact with their neighbors through the rigid cell wall?
16. Describe how animal cells use junctions in different ways.
17. List several examples of highly folded organelles with huge surface area.
18. Scientists can use nanoparticles (tiny objects smaller than 100 nanometers) to deliver DNA or drugs into animal cells. Are nanoparticles visible with the human eye? With a light microscope? With an electron microscope? What physical barrier makes it hard to use nanoparticles to place chemicals inside plant cells?

Pull It Together

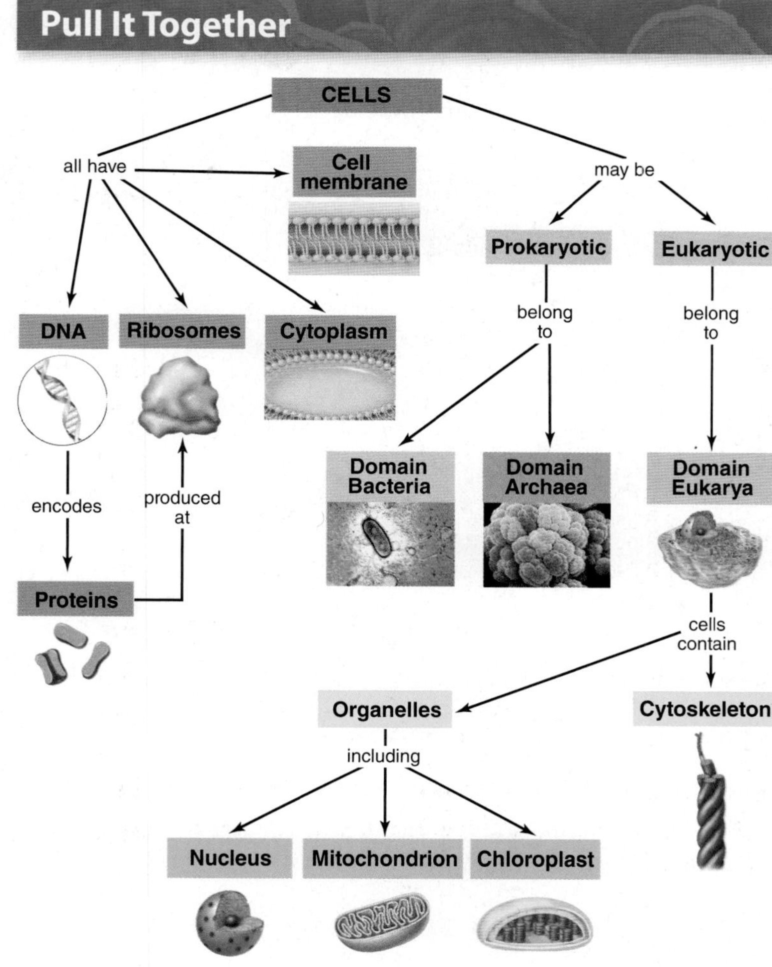

1. What are the functions of each part of a cell?
2. How do a cell's organelles interact with one another?
3. Add the eukaryotic kingdoms of life to this concept map.
4. Which structures occur in plant cells but not animal cells?
5. How do plant and animal cells stick together and communicate with their neighbors?
6. Which cell types have a cell wall?

4 The Energy of Life

Burning Calories. Riding a bicycle takes energy, which is provided by metabolic reactions inside cells.

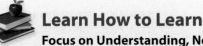

Learning Outline

4.1 All Cells Capture and Use Energy
- A. Energy Allows Cells to Do Life's Work
- B. Energy Is Converted from One Form to Another

4.2 Networks of Chemical Reactions Sustain Life
- A. Chemical Reactions Absorb or Release Energy
- B. Linked Oxidation and Reduction Reactions Form Electron Transport Chains

4.3 ATP Is Cellular Energy Currency
- A. Energy in ATP Is Critical to the Life of the Cell
- B. ATP Represents Short-Term Energy Storage

4.4 Enzymes Speed Biochemical Reactions
- A. Enzymes Bring Reactants Together
- B. Many Factors Affect Enzyme Activity

4.5 Membrane Transport May Release Energy or Cost Energy
- A. Passive Transport Does Not Require Energy Input
- B. Active Transport Requires Energy Input
- C. Endocytosis and Exocytosis Use Vesicles to Transport Substances

4.6 Investigating Life: Does Natural Selection Maintain Cystic Fibrosis?

Learn How to Learn

Focus on Understanding, Not Memorizing

When you are learning the language of biology, be sure to concentrate on how each new term fits with the others. Are you studying multiple components of a complex system? Different steps in a process? The levels of a hierarchy? As you study, always make sure you can see how each part relates to the whole.

What's the Point?

"I wish I had your metabolism!" Perhaps you have overheard a calorie-counting friend make a similar comment to someone who stays slim on a diet of fattening foods.

In that context, the word *metabolism* means how fast a person burns food. But biochemists define metabolism as all of the chemical reactions that build and break down molecules within any cell. How are these two meanings related?

Interlocking networks of metabolic reactions supply the energy that every cell needs to stay alive. In humans, teams of metabolizing cells perform specialized functions such as digestion, muscle movement, hormone production, and countless other activities. It all takes a reliable energy supply—food, which each of us "burns" at a different rate.

This chapter describes the fundamentals of metabolism, including how cells organize, regulate, and fuel the chemical reactions that sustain life.

4.1 All Cells Capture and Use Energy

You're running late. You overslept, you have no time for breakfast, and you have a full morning of classes. You rummage through your cupboard and find something called an "energy bar"—just what you need to get through the morning. But what is energy?

A. Energy Allows Cells to Do Life's Work

Physicists define **energy** as the ability to do work—that is, to move matter. This idea, as abstract as it sounds, is fundamental to biology. Life depends on rearranging atoms and trafficking substances across membranes in precise ways. These intricate movements represent work, and they require energy.

Although it may seem strange to think of a "working" cell, all organisms do tremendous amounts of work on a microscopic scale. For example, a plant cell assembles glucose molecules into long cellulose fibers, moves ions across its membranes, and performs thousands of other tasks simultaneously. Likewise, a gazelle grazes on a plant's tissues to acquire energy that will enable it to do its own cellular work. A crocodile eats that gazelle for the same reason.

The total amount of energy in any object is the sum of energy's two forms: potential and kinetic (table 4.1 and figure 4.1). **Potential energy** is stored energy available to do work. A bicyclist at the top of a hill illustrates potential energy. Likewise, unburned gasoline—and that energy bar you grabbed—contains potential energy stored in the chemical bonds of its molecules.

Kinetic energy is energy being used to do work; any moving object possesses kinetic energy. The bicyclist coasting down the hill in figure 4.1 demonstrates kinetic energy. Moving pistons, a rolling bus, and contracting muscles also have kinetic energy. Light and sound are other types of kinetic energy. Inside a cell, each molecule also has kinetic energy; in fact, all of the chemical reactions that sustain life rely on collisions between moving molecules, and many substances enter and leave cells by random motion alone.

TABLE 4.1 Examples of Energy in Biology

Type of Energy	Examples
Potential energy	Chemical energy (stored in bonds) Concentration gradient across a membrane
Kinetic energy	Light Sound Movement of atoms and molecules Muscle contraction

Figure 4.1 Potential and Kinetic Energy. Potential energy in the chemical bonds of food is converted to kinetic energy as muscles push the cyclist to the top of the hill. The potential energy of gravity provides a free ride by conversion to kinetic energy on the other side.

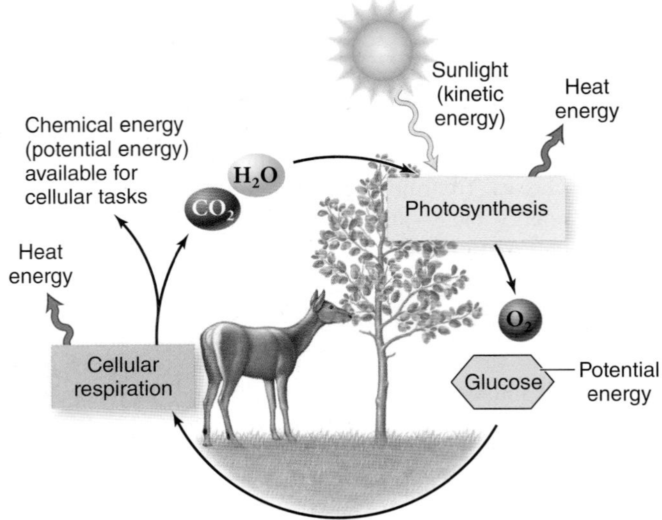

Figure 4.2 Energy Conversions. In photosynthesis, plants transform the kinetic energy in sunlight into the potential energy contained in the chemical bonds of glucose. Respiration, in turn, releases the potential energy in glucose. Heat energy is lost at every step along the way.

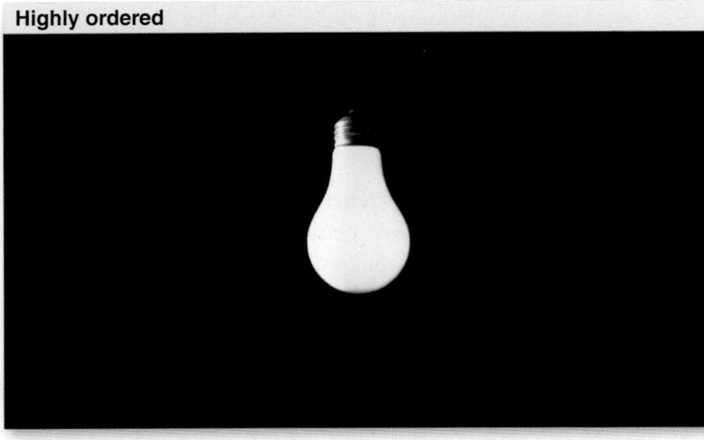

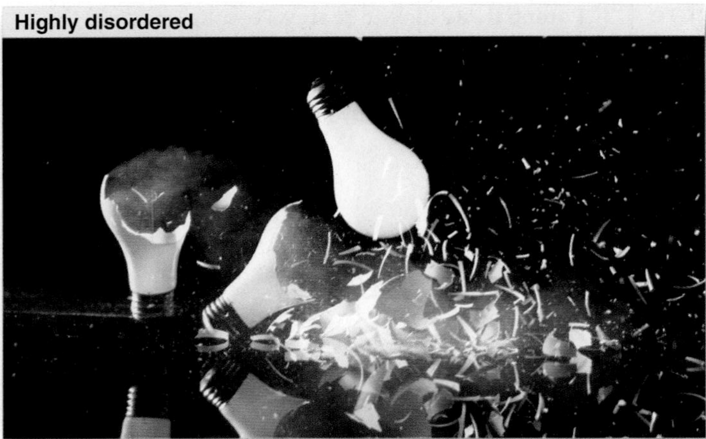

Figure 4.3 Entropy. In an instant, a highly organized light bulb is transformed into broken glass and metal fragments. Entropy has irreversibly increased; no matter how many times you drop the glass and metal, the pieces will not reorganize themselves into a light bulb.

Both forms of energy are measured in units called calories. One **calorie** (cal) is the amount of energy required to raise the temperature of 1 gram of water from 14.5°C to 15.5°C. The most common unit for measuring the energy content of food, however, is the **kilocalorie** (kcal), which equals 1000 calories. (In nutrition, 1 food Calorie—with a capital C—is actually a kilocalorie.) A typical energy bar, for example, contains 240 kilocalories of potential energy stored in the chemical bonds of its ingredients: mostly carbohydrates, proteins, and fats.

B. Energy Is Converted from One Form to Another

Physical laws describe the energy conversions vital for life, as well as those that occur in the nonliving world. They apply to all energy transformations—gasoline combustion in a car's engine, a burning chunk of wood, or a cell breaking down glucose. Two of these physical laws are especially relevant to the study of biology.

The first, called the law of energy conservation, states that energy cannot be created or destroyed, although energy can be converted to other forms. In fact, every aspect of life centers on converting energy from one form to another.

The most important energy transformations in life are photosynthesis and cellular respiration (figure 4.2). In photosynthesis, plants and some microbes use carbon dioxide, water, and the kinetic energy in sunlight to assemble glucose molecules. These carbohydrates contain potential energy in their chemical bonds. During cellular respiration, the energy-rich glucose molecules change back to carbon dioxide and water, liberating the energy necessary to power life. Cells translate the potential energy in glucose into the kinetic energy of molecular motion and use that burst of kinetic energy to do work.

A second physical law states that all energy transformations are inefficient because every reaction loses some energy to the surroundings as heat (see figure 4.2). If you eat your energy bar on the way to your first class, your cells can use the potential energy in its chemical bonds to divide, make proteins, or do other forms of work. But you will lose some energy as heat with every chemical reaction. This process is irreversible; the lost heat energy will not return to a useful form.

Heat energy results from random molecular movements. Because heat is disordered and all energy eventually becomes heat, it follows that all energy transformations must head toward increasing disorder. **Entropy** is a measure of this randomness. In general, the more disordered a system is, the higher its entropy (figure 4.3).

Because organisms are highly organized, they may seem to defy the principle that entropy always increases—but only when considered as closed systems. Organisms can increase in complexity *as long as something else decreases in complexity by a greater amount*. All organisms use incoming energy and matter from sources such as sunlight and food to maintain their organization and stay alive. Ultimately, life remains ordered and complex because the sun is constantly supplying energy to Earth. But the entropy of the universe as a whole, including the sun, is always increasing.

The ideas in this chapter and the two that follow describe how organisms acquire and use the energy they need to sustain life.

4.1 Mastering Concepts

1. What are some examples of the "work" of a cell?
2. Give examples of potential and kinetic energy in your body.
3. What are some energy conversions that occur in cells?
4. Why does the amount of entropy in the universe always increase?

4.2 Networks of Chemical Reactions Sustain Life

The number of chemical reactions occurring in even the simplest cell is staggering. Thousands of reactants and products form interlocking pathways that resemble complicated road maps.

The word **metabolism** encompasses all of these chemical reactions in cells, including those that build new molecules and those that break down existing ones. Each reaction rearranges atoms into new compounds, and each reaction either absorbs or releases energy. Digesting your morning energy bar and using its carbohydrates to fuel muscle movement are part of your metabolism. Photosynthesis and respiration are part of the metabolism of the grass under your feet as you hurry to class.

A. Chemical Reactions Absorb or Release Energy

Biologists group metabolic reactions into two categories based on energy requirements: those that require energy input to proceed, and those that release energy (figure 4.4).

If a reaction requires an input of energy, the products contain more energy than the reactants. Reactions that build complex molecules from simpler components therefore typically require energy input. One example is photosynthesis. Glucose ($C_6H_{12}O_6$), the product of photosynthesis, contains more potential energy than carbon dioxide (CO_2) and water (H_2O), the reactants. The energy source that powers this reaction is sunlight.

In contrast, if a reaction releases energy, the products contain less energy than the reactants. Such reactions break large, complex molecules into their smaller, simpler components. Cellular respiration, the breakdown of glucose to carbon dioxide and water, is an example. The products, carbon dioxide and water, contain less energy than glucose.

What happens to the released energy? As we saw in section 4.1, some is lost as heat; entropy always increases. But some of the energy can be used to do work. For example, the cell may use the energy to form bonds or to power reactions that require energy input. As we shall see, life's biochemistry is full of reactions that proceed only at the expense of energy released in other reactions.

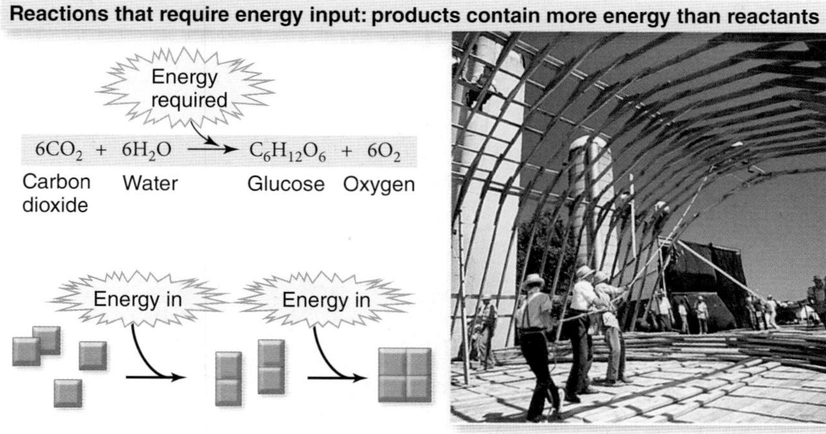

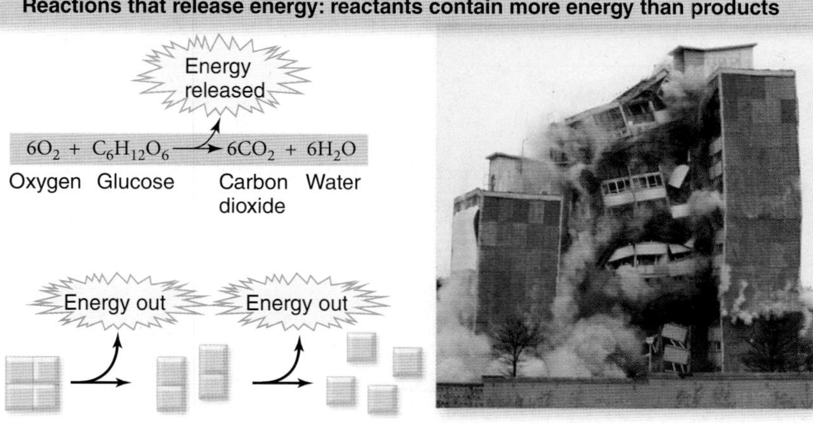

Figure 4.4 Energy Required or Released. Some reactions require an input of energy, such as those that build complex molecules from small components. This input is analogous to the energy used to build a barn out of boards and nails. Other reactions release energy, as when complex molecules (or old buildings) are dismantled.

B. Linked Oxidation and Reduction Reactions Form Electron Transport Chains

Electrons can carry energy. Most energy transformations in organisms occur in **oxidation–reduction ("redox") reactions,** which transfer energized electrons from one molecule to another. ▸ electrons, p. 22

Oxidation means the loss of electrons from a molecule, atom, or ion. Oxidation reactions, such as the breakdown of glucose to carbon dioxide and water, release energy as they degrade complex molecules into simpler products. Conversely, **reduction** means a gain of electrons (plus any energy contained in the electrons). Reduction reactions therefore require a net input of energy.

Oxidations and reductions occur simultaneously because electrons removed from one molecule during oxidation join

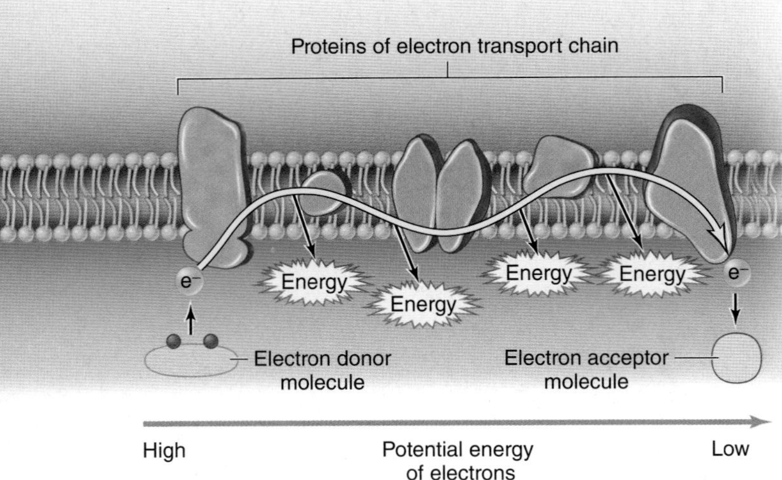

Figure 4.5 Electron Transport Chain. An electron donor transfers an electron to the first protein in the chain. This protein donates the electron to its neighbor, and so on, until the electron is transferred to a final electron acceptor. Energy is released at each step. As described in chapters 5 and 6, both photosynthesis and respiration use electron transport chains.

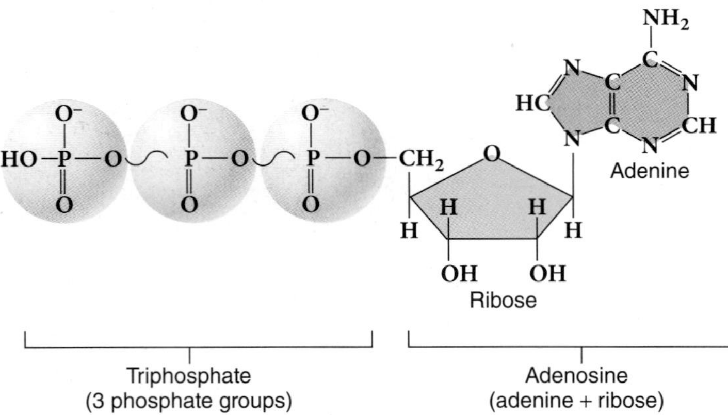

Figure 4.6 ATP's Chemical Structure. ATP is a nucleotide consisting of adenine, ribose, and three phosphate groups.

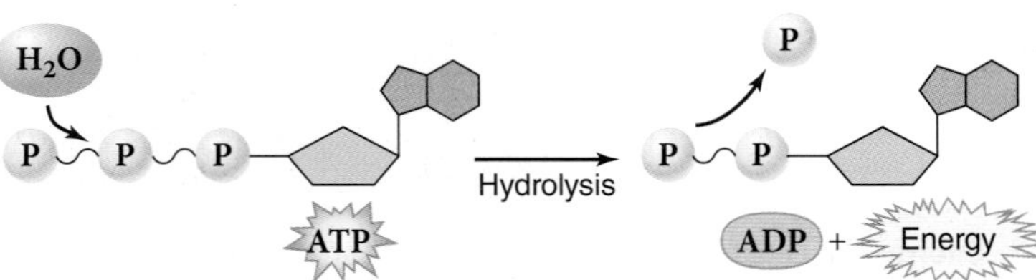

Figure 4.7 ATP Hydrolysis. Removing the endmost phosphate group of ATP yields ADP and a free phosphate group. The cell uses the released energy to do work.

another molecule and reduce it. That is, if one molecule is reduced (gains electrons), then another must be oxidized (loses electrons).

Some proteins are electron-shuttling "specialists." Groups of these electron carriers often align in membranes. In an **electron transport chain,** each protein accepts an electron from the molecule before it and donates the electron to the next in line (figure 4.5), like a basketball team passing a ball from one player to another. As a result, each protein in the chain is first reduced and then oxidized. Small amounts of energy are released at each step, and the cell uses this energy in other reactions. As you will see in chapters 5 and 6, electron transport chains play key roles in both photosynthesis and respiration.

4.2 Mastering Concepts

1. What is metabolism on a cellular level?
2. Which reactions require energy input and which release energy?
3. What are oxidation and reduction, and why are they always linked?
4. What is an electron transport chain?

4.3 ATP Is Cellular Energy Currency

All cells contain a maze of interlocking chemical reactions—some releasing energy and others absorbing it. The covalent bonds of **adenosine triphosphate,** a molecule more commonly known as **ATP,** temporarily store energy released in chemical reactions—such as the digestion of an energy bar—just long enough to power muscle contractions and all other reactions that require energy input.

Recall from chapter 2 that ATP is a type of nucleotide (figure 4.6). Its components are the nitrogen-containing base adenine, the five-carbon sugar ribose, and three phosphate groups (PO_4). These phosphate groups place three negative charges very close to one another. This arrangement makes the molecule unstable, so it releases energy when the covalent bonds between the phosphates break. ▸ nucleotides, p. 42

In eukaryotic cells, organelles called mitochondria produce most of a cell's ATP. As you will see in chapter 6, the mitochondrion uses the potential energy in the bonds of one glucose molecule to generate dozens of ATP molecules in cellular respiration. Not surprisingly, the most energy-hungry cells, such as those in the muscles and brain, also contain the most mitochondria.

A. Energy in ATP Is Critical to the Life of a Cell

All cells depend on the potential energy in ATP to power their activities. When a cell requires energy for a chemical reaction, it "spends" ATP by removing the endmost phosphate group (figure 4.7). The products of this hydrolysis reaction are adenosine *di*phosphate (ADP, since only two phosphate groups remain attached to ribose), the liberated phosphate group, and a burst of energy:

$$ATP + H_2O \longrightarrow ADP + \text{Ⓟ} + \text{energy}$$

In the reverse situation, energy can be temporarily stored by adding a phosphate to ADP, forming ATP and water:

$$ADP + \text{Ⓟ} + \text{energy} \longrightarrow ATP + H_2O$$

The energy for this reaction comes from molecules broken down in other reactions, such as those in cellular respiration.

These reactions are fundamental to biology because ATP is the "go-between" that links reactions that require energy input with those that release energy (figure 4.8). ATP hydrolysis drives the reactions that require energy input, such as those that do work or synthesize new molecules.

As an example, consider the dehydration synthesis reaction that builds proteins from individual amino acids (see figure 2.20b). This reaction requires energy, and it can only proceed when ATP is available as the energy source. ATP hydrolysis is therefore coupled to protein synthesis. ▸ dehydration synthesis and hydrolysis, p. 33

How does this coupling work? A cell uses ATP as an energy source by transferring its phosphate group to another molecule (figure 4.9). This transfer may have either of two effects. The presence of the phosphate may energize the target molecule, making it more likely to bond with other molecules. Alternatively, the added phosphate group may change the shape of the target molecule.

ATP is sometimes described as energy "currency" for the cell. Just as you can use money to purchase a great variety of different products, all cells use ATP in many chemical reactions to do different kinds of work. Besides muscle contraction, other examples of jobs that require ATP include transporting substances across cell membranes, moving chromosomes during cell division, and synthesizing the large molecules that make up cells.

ATP is also analogous to a fully charged rechargeable battery. A full battery represents a versatile source of potential energy that can provide power to many types of electronic devices. Although a dead battery is no longer useful as an energy source, you can recharge a spent battery to restore its utility. Likewise, the cell can use respiration to rebuild its pool of ATP.

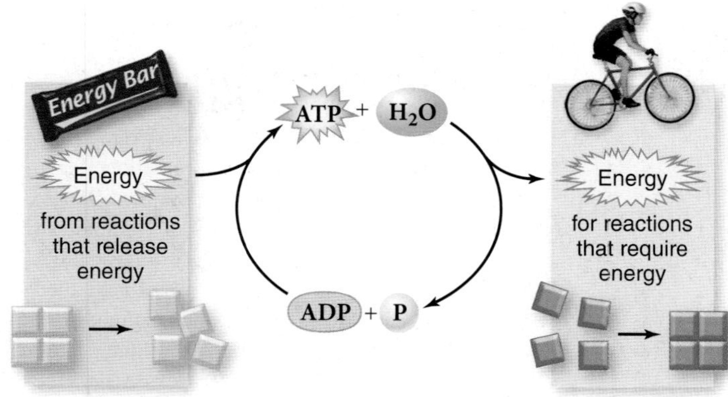

Figure 4.8 Coupled Reactions. Cells use ATP hydrolysis, a reaction that releases energy, to fuel reactions that require energy input. The cell regenerates ATP in other reactions, such as those that break down food.

B. ATP Represents Short-Term Energy Storage

Organisms require huge amounts of ATP. A typical adult human uses the equivalent of 2 billion ATP molecules a minute just to stay alive. Organisms recycle ATP at a furious pace, adding phosphate groups to ADP to reconstitute ATP,

a. ATP energizes target molecule, making it more likely to bond with other molecules.

E.g., ATP provides the energy to build large molecules out of small subunits

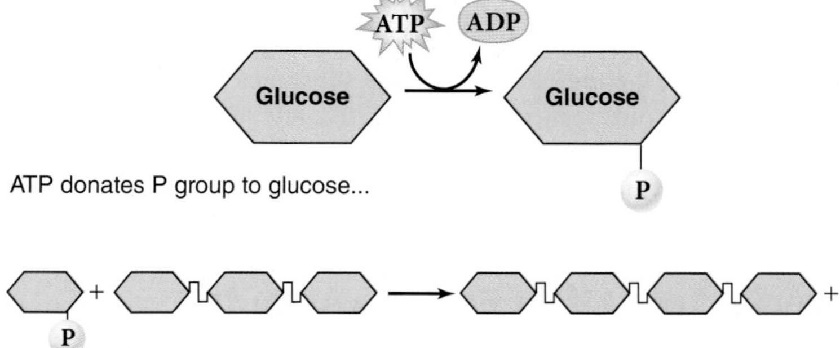

... glucose + P then reacts with short polysaccharide to build longer polysaccharide

b. ATP donates a phosphate group that changes the shape of the target molecule.

E.g., phosphate group changes shape of membrane transport protein

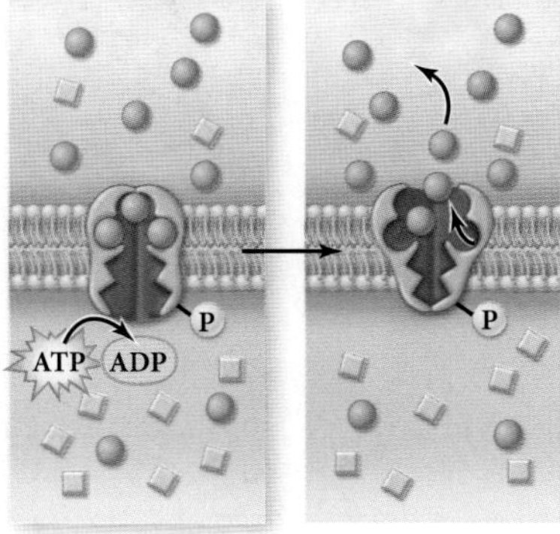

E.g., ATP binding changes shape of proteins involved in muscle contraction

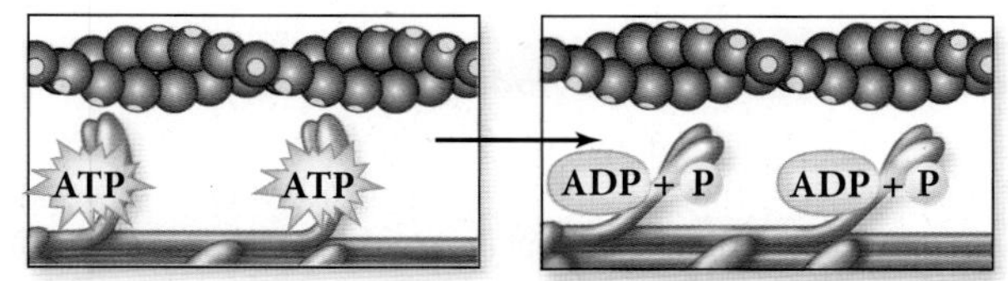

Figure 4.9 ATP Use. When ATP donates a phosphate group to a molecule, the recipient may (a) be more likely to bond or (b) change its shape in a useful way.

Why We Care | Enzymes Are Everywhere

Enzymes are so critical to life that just one faulty or missing enzyme can have dramatic effects. Lactose intolerance is one example. People whose intestinal cells do not secrete an enzyme called lactase cannot digest milk sugar (lactose). Fortunately, a product called Lactaid can supply the missing enzyme.

Phenylketonuria (PKU) is a much more serious disease. A PKU sufferer lacks an enzyme required to break down an amino acid called phenylalanine. When this amino acid accumulates in the bloodstream, it causes brain damage. People with PKU must avoid foods containing phenylalanine, including the artificial sweetener aspartame (NutraSweet). ▸ artificial sweeteners, p. 36

Enzymes also have household applications. Many detergents contain enzymes that break down food stains on clothing or dirty dishes, and contact lens cleaners have enzymes that remove protein buildup. Raw pineapple also contains an enzyme that breaks down protein, which explains why you cannot put this fruit in gelatin. The pineapple's enzymes will destroy the gelatin, which will not solidify. Some meat tenderizers contain the same enzyme, which breaks down muscle tissue and makes the meat easier to chew.

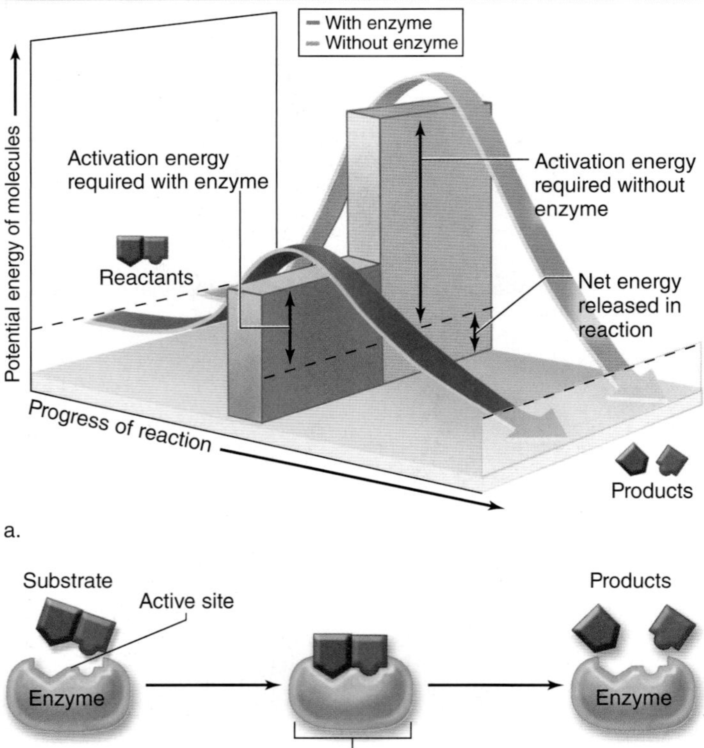

Figure 4.10 How Enzymes Work. (a) Enzymes lower the amount of energy required to start a reaction. These "walls" represent the activation energy for the same reaction, with and without an enzyme. (b) An enzyme's active site has a specific shape that binds to one or more substrates. After the reaction, the enzyme releases the products.

using the ATP to drive reactions, and turning over the entire supply every minute or so. If you ran out of ATP, you would die instantly.

Even though ATP is essential to life, cells do not stockpile it in large quantities. ATP's high-energy phosphate bonds make the molecule too unstable for long-term storage. Instead, cells store energy-rich molecules such as fats, starch, and glycogen. When ATP supplies run low, cells divert some of their lipid and carbohydrate reserves to the metabolic pathways of cellular respiration. This process soon produces additional ATP.

4.3 Mastering Concepts

1. How does ATP hydrolysis supply energy for cellular functions?
2. Describe the relationship between energy-requiring reactions, ATP hydrolysis, and cellular respiration.

4.4 Enzymes Speed Biochemical Reactions

Enzymes are among the most important of all biological molecules. An **enzyme** is an organic molecule that catalyzes (speeds) a chemical reaction without being consumed. Most enzymes are proteins, although some are made of RNA.

Many of the cell's organelles, including mitochondria, chloroplasts, lysosomes, and peroxisomes, are specialized sacs of enzymes. Enzymes copy DNA, build proteins, digest food, recycle a cell's worn-out parts, and catalyze oxidation–reduction reactions, just to name a few of their jobs. Without enzymes, all of these reactions would proceed far too slowly to support life.

A. Enzymes Bring Reactants Together

Enzymes speed reactions by lowering the **activation energy,** the amount of energy required to start a reaction (figure 4.10a). Even reactions that ultimately release energy require an initial "kick" to get started. The enzyme brings reactants (also called substrates) into contact with one another, so that less energy is required for the reaction to start. The lower the activation energy, the faster the reaction can proceed.

Most enzymes can catalyze only one or a few chemical reactions. An enzyme that dismantles a fatty acid, for example, cannot break down the starch in your energy bar. The key to this specificity lies in the shape of the enzyme's **active site,** the region to which the substrates bind (figure 4.10b). The substrates fit like puzzle pieces into the active site. Once the reaction occurs, the enzyme releases the products. Note that the reaction does not consume or alter the enzyme. Instead, after the protein releases the products, its active site is empty and ready to pick up more substrate.

B. Many Factors Affect Enzyme Activity

The intricate network of metabolic pathways may seem chaotic, but in reality it is just the opposite. Cells precisely control the rates of their chemical reactions. If they did not, some vital compounds would always be in short supply, and others might accumulate to wasteful (or even toxic) levels.

One way to regulate a metabolic pathway is by **negative feedback** (or feedback inhibition), in which the product of a reaction inhibits the enzyme that controls its formation. For example, the production of amino acids requires multiple steps. When an amino acid accumulates, it binds to an enzyme that acts early in the synthesis pathway. For a time, the synthesis of that amino acid stops. But when the level falls, the block on the enzyme lifts, and the cell can once again produce the amino acid.

Negative feedback works in two general ways to prevent too much of the reaction product from accumulating (figure 4.11). In **noncompetitive inhibition,** a product molecule binds to the enzyme at a location other than the active site. This action alters the enzyme's shape so that it can no longer bind the substrate. Alternatively, in **competitive inhibition,** the reaction product binds to the enzyme's active site, preventing it from binding substrate. It is "competitive" because the product competes with the substrate to occupy the active site.

Enzymes are also extremely sensitive to conditions in the cell. An enzyme can become denatured and stop working if the pH changes or if the salt concentration becomes too high or too low. Temperature also greatly influences enzymes (figure 4.12). Enzyme action generally speeds up as the temperature climbs because reactants have more kinetic energy at higher temperatures. If it gets too hot, however, the enzyme rapidly denatures and can no longer function. ▸ denatured proteins, p. 41

Pharmaceutical drugs can also inhibit enzyme function. Many antibiotics, including triclosan (an ingredient in antibacterial soap), kill microorganisms—but not people—by inhibiting enzymes not present in our own cells. Aspirin relieves pain by binding to an enzyme that cells use to produce pain-related molecules called prostaglandins. Likewise, some poisons are also enzyme inhibitors. For example, a chemical called glyphosate (the active ingredient in a herbicide called Roundup) competitively inhibits an enzyme found in plant cells but not in animals. ▸ weed killers, p. 92

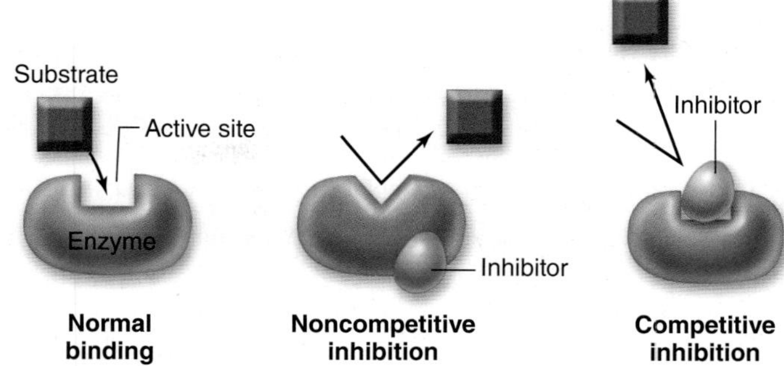

Figure 4.11 Enzyme Inhibitors. A noncompetitive inhibitor binds to an enzyme in a place other than the active site, changing the shape of the protein. A competitive inhibitor physically blocks the enzyme's active site, preventing the substrate from entering.

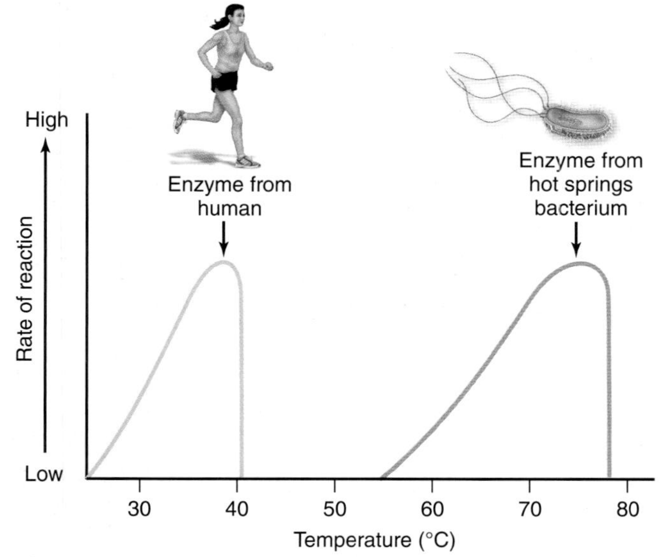

Figure 4.12 Temperature Matters. These graphs show how temperature affects the activity of enzymes from a human (left) and a bacterium that lives in hot springs (right). The microbes have heat-tolerant enzymes that function only at very high temperatures.

4.4 Mastering Concepts

1. What do enzymes do in cells?
2. How does an enzyme lower a reaction's activation energy?
3. What is the role of negative feedback in enzyme production?
4. List three conditions that influence enzyme activity.

4.5 Membrane Transport May Release Energy or Cost Energy

The cell membrane is a busy place. Like a well-used border crossing between two countries, substances enter and exit the cell in a continuous flow of traffic.

How do membranes regulate the traffic into and out of the cell? As described in chapter 3, a biological membrane is a phospholipid bilayer studded with proteins. This structure means that a membrane is "choosy," or **selectively permeable.** Some substances pass freely through the bilayer, but others—such as the sugar from a digested energy bar—require help from proteins.

Thanks to the regulation of membrane transport, the interior of a cell is chemically different from the outside. Concentrations of some dissolved substances (solutes) are higher inside the cell than outside, and others are lower. Likewise, the inside of each organelle in a eukaryotic cell may be chemically quite different from the solution in the rest of the cell.

The term *gradient* describes any such difference between two neighboring regions. In a **concentration gradient,** a solute is more concentrated in one region than in a neighboring region. For example, you can immediately see a concentration gradient when you first place a tea bag in a cup of hot water: near

TABLE 4.2 Movement Across Membranes: A Summary

Mechanism	Characteristics
Passive transport	Net movement is down concentration gradient; does not require energy input.
Simple diffusion	Substance moves across membrane without assistance of transport proteins. Area of low concentration Area of high concentration
Osmosis	Water diffuses across a selectively permeable membrane.
Facilitated diffusion	Substance moves across membrane with assistance of transport proteins.
Active transport	Net movement is against concentration gradient; requires transport protein and energy input, often from ATP. ATP ADP + P
Transport using vesicles	Vesicle carries materials into or out of a cell.
Endocytosis	Membrane engulfs substance and draws it into cell.
Exocytosis	Vesicle fuses with cell membrane, releasing substances outside of cell.

the tea bag, there are many more brown tea molecules than elsewhere in the cup (figure 4.13).

Over time, however, the brownish color spreads to create a uniform brew. This occurs because a concentration gradient dissipates *unless energy is expended to maintain it*. Random molecular motion always increases the amount of disorder (entropy). It costs energy to counter this tendency toward disorder. For the same reason, however, an existing concentration gradient represents a form of potential energy.

All forms of transport across membranes involve gradients. In the simplest types of transport, a gradient dissipates across the membrane. A substance moving from an area where it is more concentrated to an area where it is less concentrated is said to be "moving down" or "following" its concentration gradient. In other situations, a cell spends energy to maintain a concentration difference. This section describes three basic forms of traffic across the membrane; table 4.2 provides a summary.

A. Passive Transport Does Not Require Energy Input

In **passive transport,** a substance moves across a membrane without the direct expenditure of energy. All forms of passive transport involve **diffusion,** the spontaneous movement of a substance from a region where it is more concentrated to a region where it is less concentrated (see figure 4.13). Because diffusion represents the dissipation of a chemical gradient—and the loss of potential energy—it does not require energy input.

How does any substance "know" which way to diffuse? The answer, of course, is that atoms and molecules know nothing. Diffusion occurs because all substances have kinetic energy; that is, they are in constant, random motion. To simplify the tea example, suppose each molecule can move

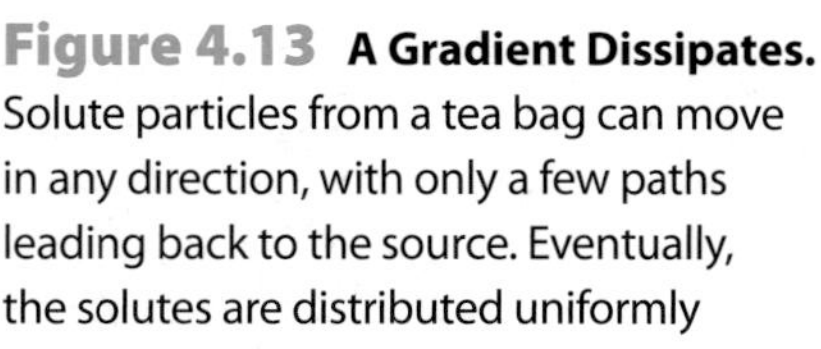

Figure 4.13 A Gradient Dissipates. Solute particles from a tea bag can move in any direction, with only a few paths leading back to the source. Eventually, the solutes are distributed uniformly throughout the cup.

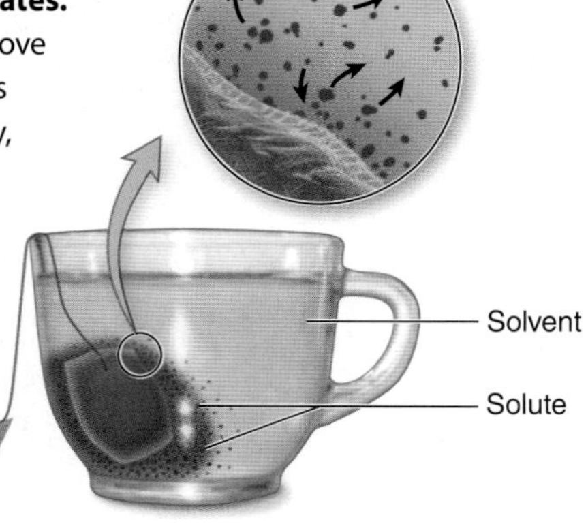

randomly along one of 10 possible paths (in reality, the number of possible directions is infinite). Assume further that only one path leads back to the tea bag. Since nine of the 10 possibilities point away from the tea bag, the tea molecules tend to spread out; that is, they move down their concentration gradient.

If diffusion continues long enough, the gradient disappears. Diffusion *appears* to stop at that point, but the molecules do not stop moving. Instead, they continue to travel randomly back and forth at the same rate, so at equilibrium the concentration remains equal throughout the solution.

Simple Diffusion: No Proteins Required **Simple diffusion** is a form of passive transport in which a substance moves down its concentration gradient without the aid of a transport protein (see table 4.2). Substances may enter or leave cells by simple diffusion only if they can pass freely through the membrane. Lipids and small, nonpolar molecules such as oxygen (O_2) and carbon dioxide (CO_2), for example, diffuse easily across the hydrophobic portion of a biological membrane.

If gradients dissipate without energy input, how can a cell use simple diffusion to acquire essential substances or get rid of toxic wastes? The answer is that the cell maintains the gradients, either by continually consuming the substances as they diffuse in or by producing more of the substances that diffuse out. For example, mitochondria consume O_2 as soon as it diffuses into the cell, maintaining the O_2 gradient that drives diffusion. Respiration also produces CO_2, which diffuses out because its concentration always remains higher in the cell than outside.

Osmosis: Diffusion of Water Across a Selectively Permeable Membrane Two solutions of different concentrations may be separated by a selectively permeable membrane through which water, but not solutes, can pass. In that case, water will diffuse down its own gradient toward the side with the high solute concentration. **Osmosis** is this simple diffusion of water across a selectively permeable membrane (figure 4.14).

A human red blood cell demonstrates the effects of osmosis (figure 4.15). The cell's interior is normally **isotonic** to the surrounding blood plasma (figure 4.15a), which means that the solute concentration inside the cell is the same as that of the plasma (*iso-* means "equal," and *tonicity* is the ability of a

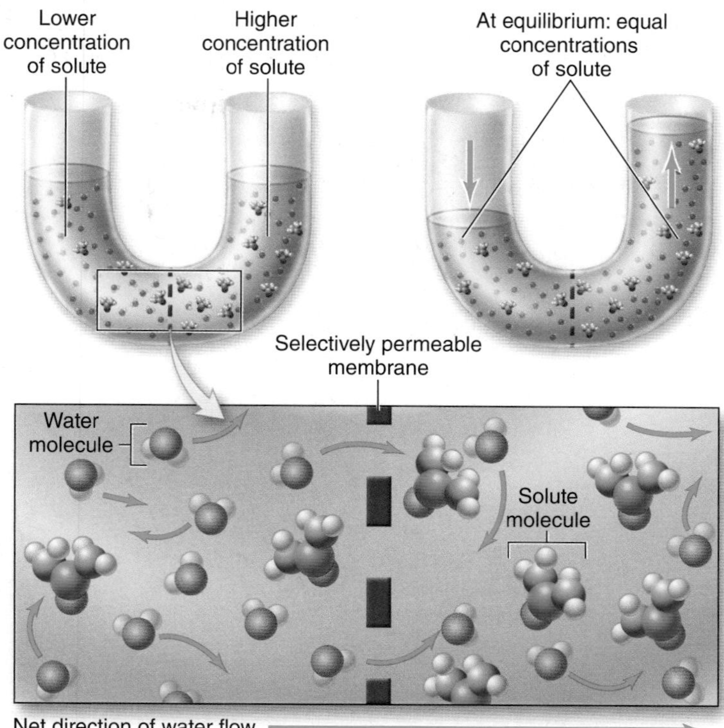

Figure 4.14 Osmosis. A selectively permeable membrane divides this U-shaped tube. The membrane permits water but not solutes to pass through. Water diffuses from the side with low solute concentration toward the side with high solute concentration. At equilibrium, water flow is equal in both directions, and the solute concentrations will be equal on both sides of the membrane.

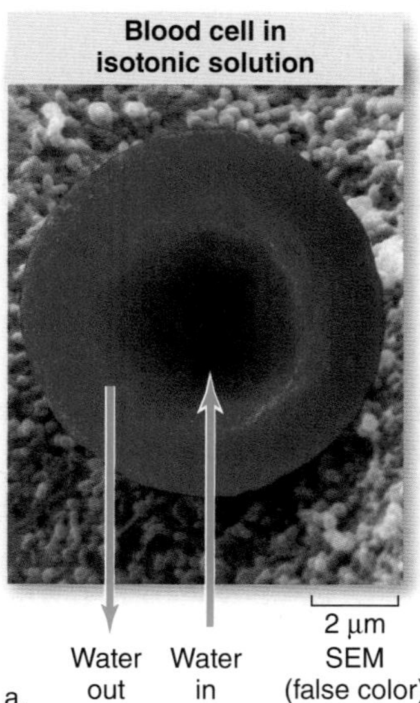

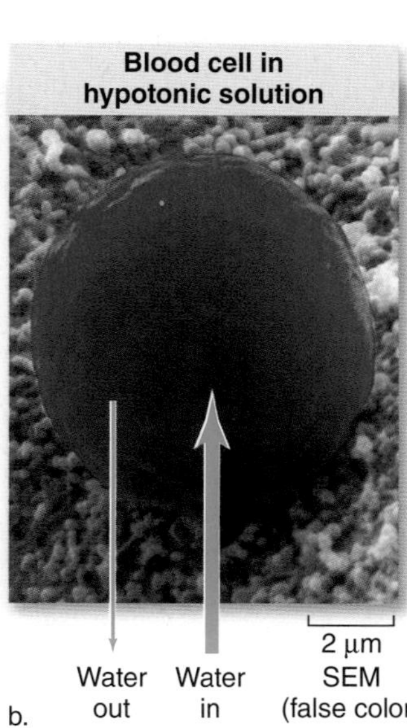

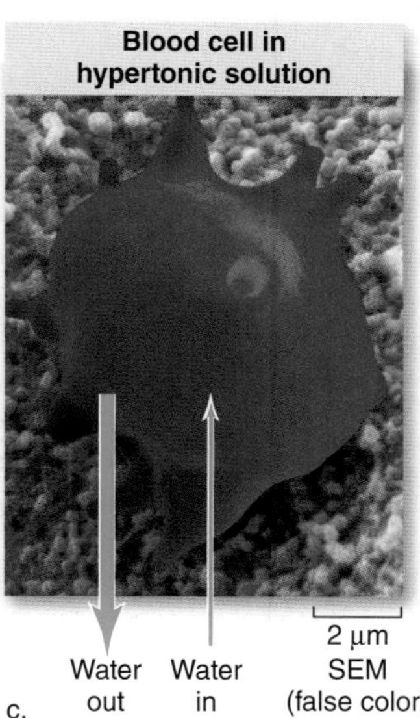

Figure 4.15 Osmosis and Red Blood Cells. (a) A human red blood cell is isotonic to the surrounding plasma. Water enters and leaves the cell at the same rate, and the cell maintains its shape. (b) When the salt concentration of the plasma decreases, water flows into the cell faster than it leaves. The cell swells and may even burst. (c) In salty surroundings, the cell loses water and shrinks.

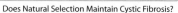

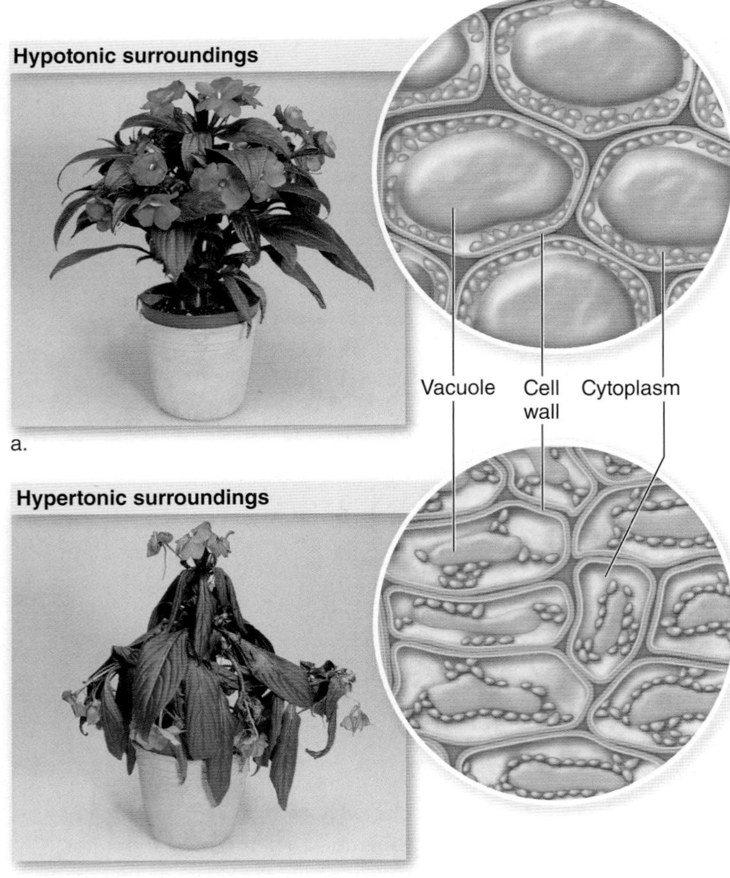

Figure 4.16 Osmosis and Plant Cells. (a) The interior of a plant cell usually contains more concentrated solutes than its surroundings. Water enters the cell by osmosis, generating turgor pressure. (b) In a hypertonic environment, turgor pressure is low. The plant wilts.

solution to cause water movement). Water therefore moves into and out of the cell at equal rates. If the environment is **hypotonic** to the cell, the external solute concentration is lower than it is inside the cell (*hypo-* means "under," as in hypodermic). Water moves by osmosis into a blood cell in hypotonic surroundings (figure 4.15b); the membrane may even burst. Conversely, **hypertonic** surroundings have a higher concentration of solutes than the cell's cytoplasm (*hyper-* means "over," as in hyperactive). In a hypertonic environment, a cell loses water, shrivels, and may even die (figure 4.15c).

Hypotonic and *hypertonic* are relative terms that can refer to the surrounding solution or to the solution inside the cell. The same solution might be hypertonic to one cell but hypotonic to another, depending on the solute concentrations inside the cells. No matter what the configuration, however, the net direction of water movement is from the hypotonic solution to the hypertonic one.

A plant's roots are often hypertonic to the soil, particularly after a heavy rain. Water rushes into the plant cells by osmosis, and the central vacuoles expand until the cell walls constrain their growth. **Turgor pressure** is the resulting force of water against the cell wall (figure 4.16). A limp, wilted piece of lettuce demonstrates the effect of lost turgor pressure. But the leaf becomes crisp again if placed in water, as individual cells expand like inflated balloons. Turgor pressure helps keep plants erect.

Facilitated Diffusion: Proteins Required Ions and polar molecules cannot freely cross the hydrophobic part of the phospholipid bilayer; instead, transport proteins form "pores" that help these solutes cross. **Facilitated diffusion** is a form of passive transport in which a membrane protein assists the movement of a polar solute along its concentration gradient (see table 4.2). Facilitated diffusion does not require energy because the solute moves from where it is more concentrated to where it is less concentrated.

Glucose moves into red blood cells via facilitated diffusion. This sugar is too hydrophilic to pass freely across the membrane, but glucose transporter proteins form channels that allow it in. Respiration inside the red blood cells consumes the glucose and maintains the concentration gradient.

Membrane proteins can enhance osmosis, too. Although membranes are somewhat permeable to water, osmosis can be slow. The cells of many organisms, including bacteria, plants, and animals, use membrane proteins called aquaporins to increase the rate of water flow. Kidney cells control the amount of water that enters urine by changing the number of aquaporins in their membranes.

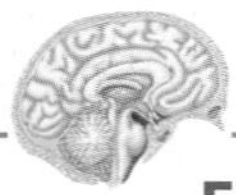

Figure It Out

A 0.9% salt solution is isotonic to human red blood cells. What will happen if you place a red blood cell in a 2.0% solution of salt water?

Answer: Water will leave the cell.

B. Active Transport Requires Energy Input

Both simple diffusion and facilitated diffusion dissipate an existing concentration gradient. Often, however, a cell needs to do the opposite: create and maintain a concentration gradient. A plant's root cell, for example, may need to absorb nutrients from soil water that is much more dilute than the cell's interior. In **active transport,** a cell uses a transport protein to move a substance *against* its concentration gradient—from where it is less concentrated to where it is more concentrated (see table 4.2). Because a gradient represents a form of potential energy, the cell must expend energy to create it; this energy often comes from ATP.

Cells must contain high concentrations of potassium (K^+) and low concentrations of sodium (Na^+) to perform many functions. In animals, for example, sodium and potassium ion gradients are essential for nerve and muscle function (see chapters 24 and 26). One active transport system in the membranes of most animal cells is a protein called the **sodium–potassium pump** (figure 4.17), which uses ATP as an energy source to expel three Na^+ for every two K^+ it admits. Sodium ions therefore become increasingly concentrated

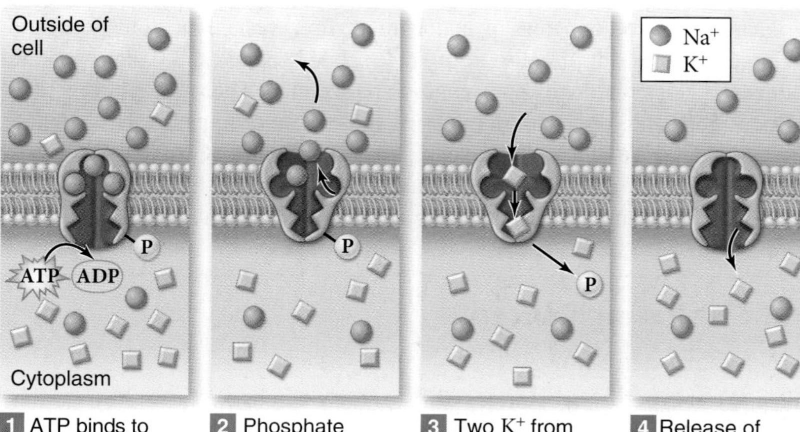
Outside of cell
Na+
K+
ATP
ADP
P
Cytoplasm
1 ATP binds to transport protein along with three Na+ from cytoplasm. ATP transfers phosphate to protein.
2 Phosphate changes the shape of the protein, moving Na+ across the membrane.
3 Two K+ from outside of cell bind to protein, causing phosphate release.
4 Release of phosphate changes the shape of the protein, moving K+ into the cytoplasm.

Figure 4.17 Active Transport. The sodium–potassium pump is a protein embedded in the cell membrane. It uses energy released in ATP hydrolysis to move potassium ions (K^+) to the inside of the cell and sodium ions (Na^+) to the outside. The process costs energy because both types of ions are moving from where they are less concentrated to where they are more concentrated.

outside the cell, while K^+ accumulates inside. Maintaining these ion gradients is costly: the million or more sodium–potassium pumps embedded in a cell's membrane use some 25% of the cell's ATP.

Concentration gradients are an important source of potential energy that cells can use to do work. For example, chapters 5 and 6 describe how cells establish concentration gradients of hydrogen ions (H^+) during photosynthesis and respiration. By controlling how and when H^+ diffuses back across the membrane, the chloroplast or mitochondrion can convert the potential energy stored in the gradient into another form of potential energy—chemical energy in the bonds of ATP.

C. Endocytosis and Exocytosis Use Vesicles to Transport Substances

Most molecules dissolved in water are small, and they can cross cell membranes by simple diffusion, facilitated diffusion, or active transport. Large particles, however, must enter and leave cells with the help of a vesicle—a small sac that can pinch off of, or fuse with, a cell membrane.

Endocytosis allows a cell to engulf fluids and large molecules and bring them into the cell (figure 4.18). First, a small indentation forms in the cell membrane. The indentation then becomes a "bubble" of membrane that closes in on itself, forming a vesicle that traps whatever was outside the membrane. The fully enclosed vesicle is free to transport the contents within the cell.

The two main forms of endocytosis are pinocytosis and phagocytosis. In pinocytosis, the cell engulfs small amounts of fluids and dissolved substances. In **phagocytosis,** the cell captures and engulfs large particles, such as debris or even another cell. The vesicle then fuses with a lysosome, where hydrolytic enzymes dismantle the cargo. ▸ lysosomes, p. 59

When biologists first viewed endocytosis in white blood cells in the 1930s, they thought a cell would gulp in anything at its surface. We now recognize a more specific form of the process called receptor-mediated endocytosis. A receptor protein on a cell's surface binds a biochemical; the cell membrane then indents, embracing the substance and drawing it into the cell. Liver cells use receptor-mediated endocytosis to absorb cholesterol-toting proteins from the bloodstream.

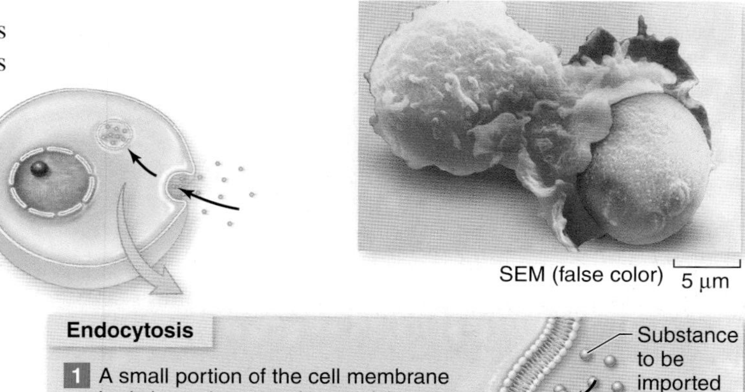
SEM (false color)
5 µm

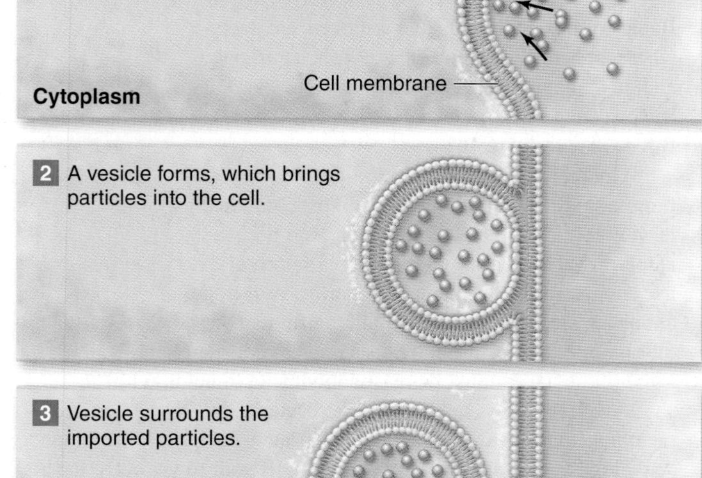
Endocytosis
1 A small portion of the cell membrane buds inward, entrapping particles.
Substance to be imported
Cell membrane
Cytoplasm
2 A vesicle forms, which brings particles into the cell.
3 Vesicle surrounds the imported particles.
Vesicle

Figure 4.18 Endocytosis. Large particles enter a cell by endocytosis. The inset shows a white blood cell engulfing a yeast cell by phagocytosis, a form of endocytosis.

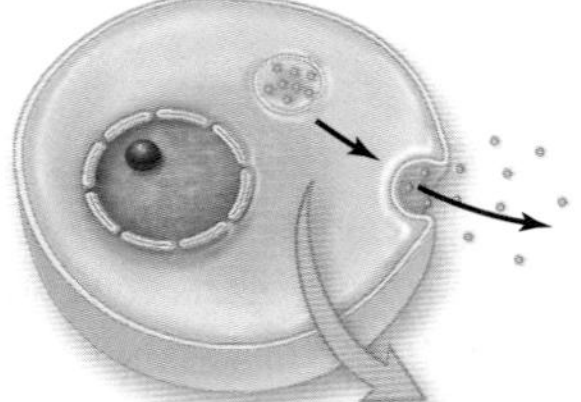

Figure 4.19 Exocytosis. Cells package substances to be secreted into vesicles, which fuse with the cell membrane to release the materials.

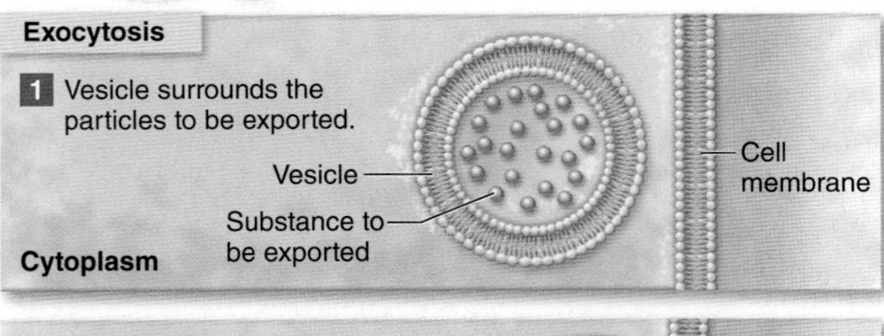

1 Vesicle surrounds the particles to be exported.

Substance to be exported

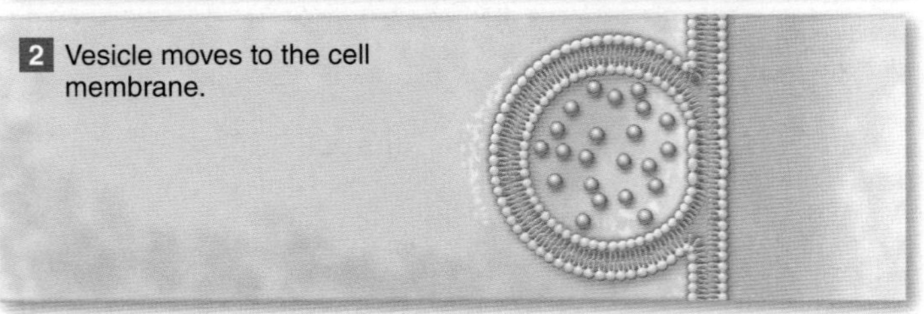

2 Vesicle moves to the cell membrane.

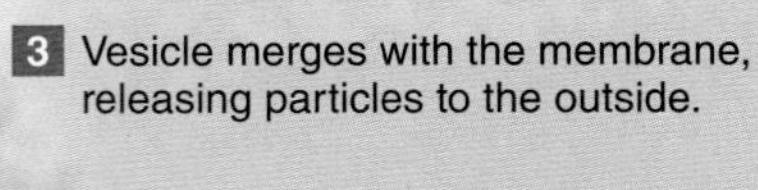

3 Vesicle merges with the membrane, releasing particles to the outside.

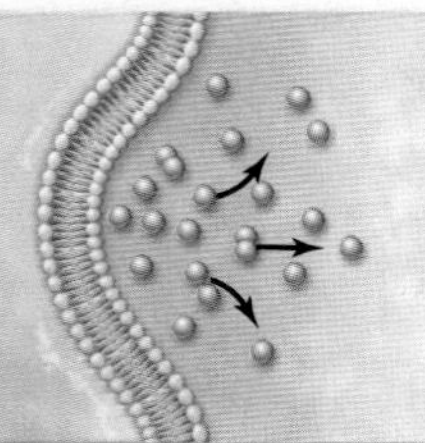

Exocytosis, the opposite of endocytosis, uses vesicles to transport fluids and large particles out of cells (figure 4.19). Inside a cell, the Golgi apparatus produces vesicles filled with substances to be secreted. The vesicle moves to the cell membrane and joins with it, releasing the substance outside the membrane. For example, the tip of a neuron releases neurotransmitters by exocytosis; these chemicals then stimulate or inhibit neural impulses in a neighboring cell. The secretion of milk into milk ducts, depicted in figure 3.11, is another example.

4.5 Mastering Concepts

1. What is diffusion?
2. What types of substances diffuse freely across a membrane?
3. How do differing concentrations of solutes in neighboring solutions drive osmosis?
4. Why does it cost energy to maintain a concentration gradient?
5. Distinguish between simple diffusion, facilitated diffusion, and active transport.
6. How do exocytosis and endocytosis use vesicles to transport materials across cell membranes?

Investigating Life

4.6 Does Natural Selection Maintain Cystic Fibrosis?

A single enzyme or membrane protein may seem too small to be very important—until you consider that a single faulty one can cause serious illness. Cystic fibrosis is one example. One in every 2500 babies born each year in the United States has cystic fibrosis. Each affected person lacks a membrane transport protein called CFTR.

CFTR normally occurs in tissues that secrete watery fluids such as mucus. Its function is to move chloride ions (Cl^-) out of cells by active transport. As it does so, the solute concentration outside the cell increases, drawing water out by osmosis. CFTR therefore helps thin the mucus in the lungs. Patients with cystic fibrosis, however, lack a working CFTR protein. The mucus in the lungs remains thick, making breathing difficult and creating a breeding ground for bacteria. The patient succumbs to chronic infections, often before age 30.

The Question: Cystic fibrosis may make patients too sick to have children; the disease may even take patients' lives before they are old enough to reproduce. Why hasn't natural selection eliminated cystic fibrosis from the human population?

A possible answer to this evolutionary mystery may lie in another organ system where cells produce CFTR proteins: the digestive tract. The bacteria that cause cholera (*Vibrio cholerae*) produce a toxin that overstimulates CFTR. As a result, Cl^- and water pour from the lining of the small intestine and leave the body (along with many *Vibrio* cells) in watery diarrhea. The resulting dehydration can be deadly if left untreated. Researcher Sherif Gabriel and his colleagues at the University of North Carolina hypothesized that the abnormal

Burning Questions

Do hand sanitizers work?

Bottles of alcohol-based hand sanitizers are everywhere: in handbags, in medical offices, at schools, and in shopping centers. They promise to kill bacteria and viruses, reducing the spread of disease. But do they really work?

Under ideal conditions, the answer is yes. For the sanitizer to be effective, it must contain at least 60% alcohol; check the label. And because alcohol evaporates so quickly, it is important to use enough of the product to kill germs. A dollop about the size of a dime is usually sufficient for the sanitizer to last through 30 seconds of constant hand-rubbing. Finally, the hands must be reasonably clean to begin with.

Alcohol-based sanitizers kill bacteria by disrupting cell membranes. Influenza and other viruses with outer membrane "envelopes" are also vulnerable. But if your own cells have membranes too, why don't hand sanitizers damage the skin? The explanation is that the cells that make up the outer layers of skin cannot be killed—they are already dead.

Submit your burning question to:
marielle_hoefnagels@mcgraw-hill.com

CFTR protein—the same one that causes cystic fibrosis—may actually help protect against cholera.

The Approach: The team knew that everyone has two versions (alleles) of nearly every gene; one version is inherited from each parent. The researchers therefore bred three groups of mice. The animals in one group had two normal (functioning) *CFTR* gene copies. A second set of mice had two defective copies, and a third group had one normal and one defective copy. The team then gave all the mice cholera toxin and measured the amount of fluid produced in the small intestine.

Mice with two normal copies of the CFTR-encoding gene produced the most fluid, indicating they were vulnerable to cholera (figure 4.20). Mice with two faulty genes resisted the toxin's effects, and those with two different versions lost intermediate amounts of fluid. The amount of faulty CFTR was therefore correlated with resistance to cholera.

The Conclusion: This study helps explain how natural selection might maintain cystic fibrosis in the human population. A person develops cystic fibrosis only if he or she receives a defective version of the CFTR-encoding gene from both parents. But inheriting just one normal *CFTR* gene is enough to keep cystic fibrosis from developing. Evolutionary biologists suggest that, in some areas of the world, cholera resistance gives people with one faulty *CFTR* gene a reproductive edge over people with two copies of the normal gene. From an evolutionary point of view, improved resistance to infectious disease apparently offsets losing some children to cystic fibrosis.

Gabriel, Sherif E., K. N. Brigman, B. H. Koller, et al. Oct. 7, 1994. Cystic fibrosis heterozygote resistance to cholera toxin in the cystic fibrosis mouse model. *Science,* vol. 266, pages 107–109.

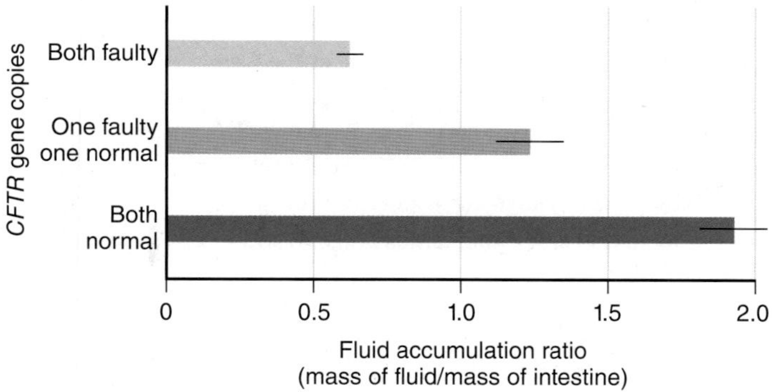

Figure 4.20 Cholera Toxin and *CFTR*. This graph shows the amount of fluid that accumulated in the small intestines of mice after exposure to the cholera toxin. Mice with normal CFTR proteins lost the most fluid and were therefore the most susceptible to cholera.

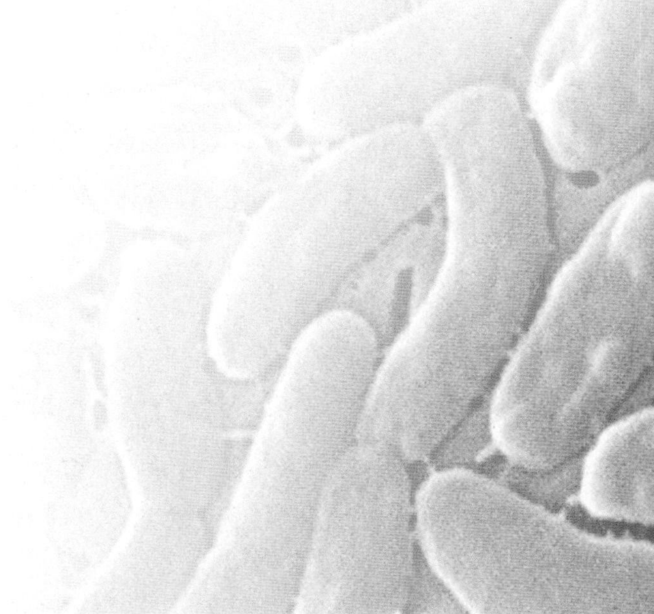

4.6 Mastering Concepts

1. What is the role of the CFTR protein in cystic fibrosis?
2. Summarize the question Gabriel and his colleagues asked, and explain how their experiment helped answer the question.
3. How would the results in figure 4.20 have been different if, before adding cholera toxin, the researchers had added a chemical that blocked the site at which the toxin binds to CFTR?

Chapter Summary

4.1 All Cells Capture and Use Energy

A. Energy Allows Cells to Do Life's Work

- **Energy** is the ability to do work. **Potential energy** is stored energy, and **kinetic energy** is action.
- Energy is measured in units called **calories.** One food Calorie is 1000 calories, or 1 **kilocalorie.**

B. Energy Is Converted From One Form to Another

- Energy cannot be created or destroyed but only converted to other forms.
- Every reaction increases **entropy** (disorder) and loses energy as heat.

4.2 Networks of Chemical Reactions Sustain Life

- **Metabolism** is the sum of the chemical reactions in a cell.

A. Chemical Reactions Absorb or Release Energy

- In reactions that require energy input, the products have more energy than the reactants. Conversely, in reactions that release energy, the products have less energy than the reactants.

B. Linked Oxidation and Reduction Reactions Form Electron Transport Chains

- Many energy transformations in organisms occur via **oxidation–reduction (redox) reactions. Oxidation** is the loss of electrons; **reduction** is the gain of electrons. Oxidation and reduction reactions occur simultaneously.
- In photosynthesis and respiration, proteins shuttle electrons along **electron transport chains.**

4.3 ATP Is Cellular Energy Currency

A. Energy in ATP Is Critical to the Life of the Cell

- **ATP** stores energy in its high-energy phosphate bonds. Cellular respiration generates ATP.
- Cells use the energy released in ATP hydrolysis to drive other reactions.

B. ATP Represents Short-Term Energy Storage

- ATP is too unstable for long-term storage. Instead, cells store energy as fats and carbohydrates.

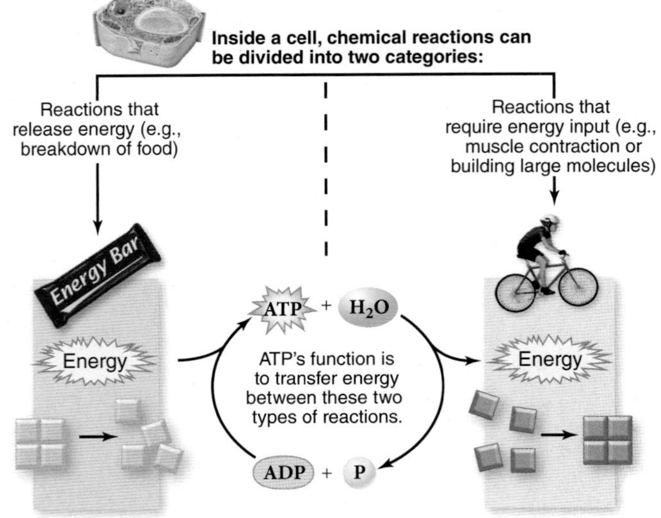
Inside a cell, chemical reactions can be divided into two categories:
Reactions that release energy (e.g., breakdown of food)
Reactions that require energy input (e.g., muscle contraction or building large molecules)
Energy Bar
Energy
ATP + H2O
ATP's function is to transfer energy between these two types of reactions.
ADP + P
Energy

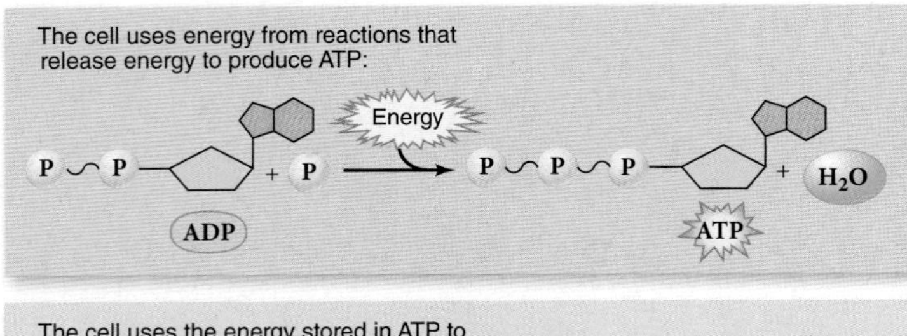
The cell uses energy from reactions that release energy to produce ATP:
P P + P
ADP
Energy
P P P
ATP
+ H2O

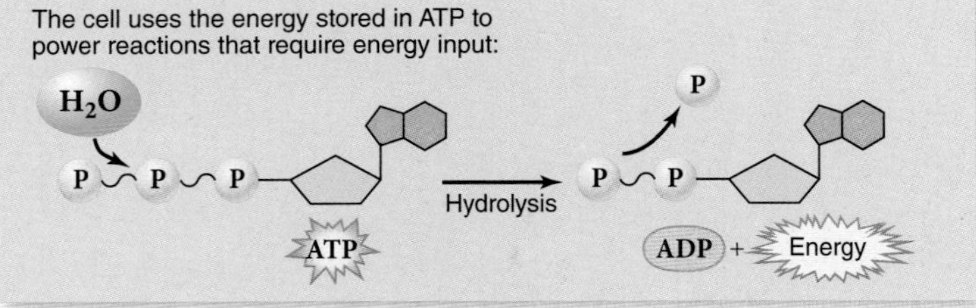
The cell uses the energy stored in ATP to power reactions that require energy input:
H2O
P P P
ATP
Hydrolysis
P
P P
ADP + Energy

4.4 Enzymes Speed Biochemical Reactions

A. Enzymes Bring Reactants Together

- **Enzymes** are organic molecules (usually proteins) that speed biochemical reactions by lowering the **activation energy.**
- Substrate molecules fit into the enzyme's **active site.**

B. Many Factors Affect Enzyme Activity

- In **negative feedback,** a reaction product temporarily shuts down its own synthesis whenever its levels rise. Negative feedback may occur by **competitive** or **noncompetitive inhibition.**
- Enzymes have narrow ranges of conditions in which they function.

4.5 Membrane Transport May Release Energy or Cost Energy

- Membranes have **selective permeability,** which means they admit only some substances.
- A **concentration gradient** is a difference in solute concentration between two neighboring regions. Gradients dissipate without energy input.

A. Passive Transport Does Not Require Energy Input

- All forms of **passive transport** involve **diffusion,** the dissipation of a chemical gradient by random molecular motion.
- In **simple diffusion,** a substance passes through a membrane along its concentration gradient without the aid of a transport protein.
- **Osmosis** is the simple diffusion of water across a selectively permeable membrane. Terms describing tonicity (**isotonic, hypotonic,** and **hypertonic**) predict whether cells will swell or shrink when the surroundings change. When plant cells lose too much water, the resulting loss of **turgor pressure** causes the plant to wilt.
- In **facilitated diffusion,** a membrane protein admits a substance along its concentration gradient without expending energy.

B. Active Transport Requires Energy Input

- In **active transport,** a carrier protein uses energy (ATP) to move a substance against its concentration gradient. In animals cells, the **sodium–potassium pump** uses active transport to exchange sodium ions for potassium ions.

C. Endocytosis and Exocytosis Use Vesicles to Transport Substances

- In **endocytosis,** a cell engulfs liquids or large particles. Pinocytosis brings in fluids; **phagocytosis** brings in solid particles.
- In **exocytosis,** vesicles inside the cell carry substances to the cell membrane, where they fuse with the membrane and release the cargo outside.

4.6 Investigating Life: Does Natural Selection Maintain Cystic Fibrosis?

- The faulty membrane protein that causes cystic fibrosis may help protect against cholera.

Multiple Choice Questions

1. Which of the following is the best example of potential energy in a cell?
   a. Cell division
   b. A molecule of glucose
   c. Movement of a flagellum
   d. Random molecular motion
2. Building proteins __ energy; ATP hydrolysis ___ energy.
   a. releases; releases
   b. requires; requires
   c. releases; requires
   d. requires; releases
3. How do proteins contribute to the function of an electron transport chain?
   a. They become oxidized and reduced.
   b. They undergo osmosis.
   c. They are involved in the hydrolysis of electrons.
   d. They consume electrons.
4. Where in a molecule of ATP is the stored energy that is used by the cell?
   a. Within the nitrogenous base, adenine
   b. Within the five-carbon ribose sugar
   c. In the covalent bonds between the phosphate groups
   d. In the bond between adenine and ribose
5. What is the role of an enzyme in a cell?
   a. To speed up chemical reactions
   b. To become consumed during a chemical reaction
   c. To increase the energy required to make a reaction occur
   d. To provide energy to the cell

6. Which of the following is true regarding noncompetitive inhibition?
   a. The amino acid sequence of an enzyme is altered.
   b. Excess product blocks the active site.
   c. The active site is unable to bind substrate.
   d. Excess product enhances enzyme activity.
7. The movement of water molecules during osmosis is due to
   a. diffusion. c. pinocytosis.
   b. active transport. d. endocytosis.
8. What would happen to a plant cell in a *hypertonic* environment?
   a. There would be no change.
   b. It would swell and burst.
   c. Its turgor pressure would increase.
   d. It would shrink.
9. A polar molecule moves across a membrane from a region of high concentration to a region of low concentration by a process called
   a. simple diffusion. c. active transport.
   b. facilitated diffusion. d. phagocytosis.
10. A concentration gradient is an example of
    a. oxidation–reduction. c. entropy.
    b. potential energy. d. hydrolysis.

Write It Out

1. Some people claim that life's high degree of organization defies the physical law that says that entropy always increases. What makes this statement false?
2. Why is ATP called the cell's "energy currency"?
3. How does an enzyme speed a chemical reaction?
4. Why would a cell's fat-digesting enzymes not be able to digest an artificial fat such as Olestra (chapter 2)?
5. Figure 4.12 shows the effect of temperature on enzyme activity. Draw similar curves that show the optimal pH for trypsin (an enzyme in the small intestine, pH 10), amylase (an enzyme in the saliva, pH 6.5), and pepsin (an enzyme in the stomach, pH 2).
6. When a person eats a fatty diet, excess cholesterol accumulates in the bloodstream. Cells then temporarily stop producing cholesterol. What phenomenon described in the chapter does this control illustrate?
7. Why does poking a hole in a cell's membrane kill the cell?
8. Diffusion is an efficient means of transport only over small distances. How does this relate to a cell's surface-area-to-volume ratio (chapter 3)?
9. A drop of a 5% salt (NaCl) solution is added to a leaf of the aquatic plant *Elodea.* When the leaf is viewed under a microscope, colorless regions appear at the edges of each cell as the cell membranes shrink from the cell walls. What is happening to these cells?
10. Seawater contains about 35 grams of salt per liter, whereas a liter of fresh water contains 0.5 g of salt or less. The blood of a fish has about 10 g of dissolved salt per liter. Cells in a fish's gills have transport proteins that pump salts across their membranes. In what direction would a saltwater fish pump ions? What about a freshwater fish?

Pull It Together

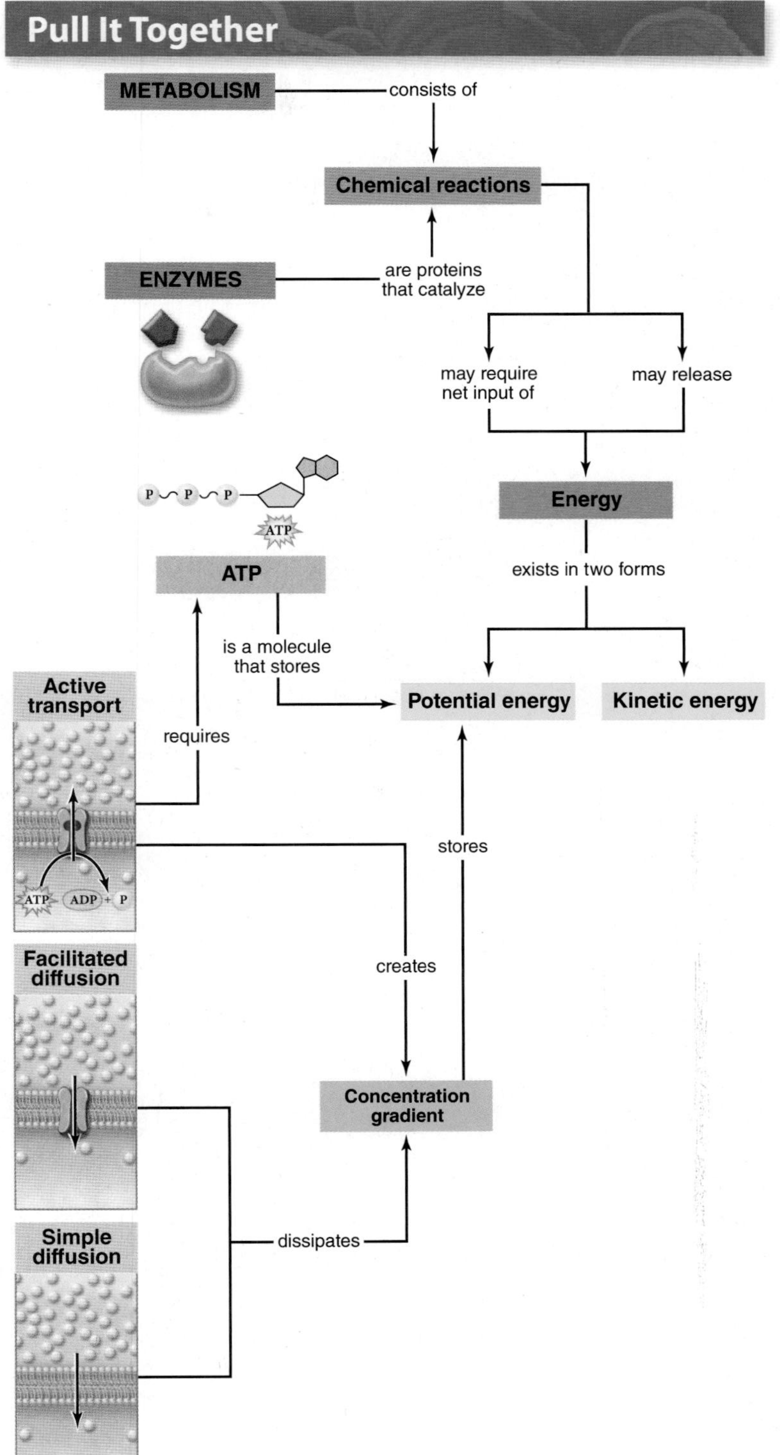

1. What types of organic molecules are ATP and enzymes?
2. What are some examples of potential energy and kinetic energy other than those included on the concept map?
3. Add the terms *substrate, active site,* and *activation energy* to this concept map.
4. Where does passive transport fit on this concept map?
5. Explain the differences among diffusion, facilitated diffusion, active transport, endocytosis, and exocytosis.

5 Photosynthesis

Learning Outline

5.1 Life Depends on Photosynthesis

5.2 Photosynthetic Pigments Capture Sunlight

5.3 Chloroplasts Are the Sites of Photosynthesis

5.4 Photosynthesis Occurs in Two Stages

5.5 The Light Reactions Begin Photosynthesis
- A. Photosystem II Produces ATP
- B. Photosystem I Produces NADPH

5.6 The Carbon Reactions Produce Carbohydrates

5.7 C_3, C_4, and CAM Plants Use Different Carbon Fixation Pathways

5.8 Investigating Life: Solar-Powered Sea Slugs

Food from Plants. A farmer works his way through a rice terrace in China. Rice grains are a food staple for much of the world's population.

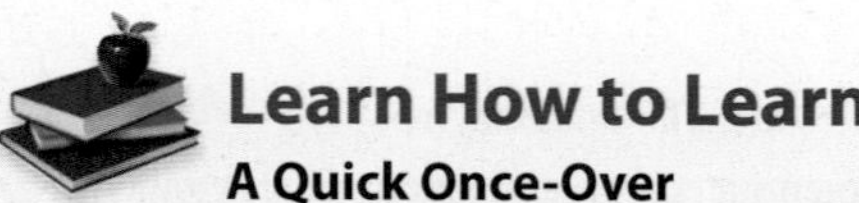

Learn How to Learn

A Quick Once-Over

Unless your instructor requires you to read your textbook in detail before class, try a quick preview. At the very least, read the Learning Outline to identify the main ideas. It is also a good idea to look at the figures and the key terms in the narrative. Previewing a chapter should help you understand the lecture, because you will already know the main ideas. In addition, note-taking will be easier if you recognize new vocabulary words from your quick once-over. Return to your book for an in-depth reading after class to help nail down the details.

What's the Point?

Most plants are easy to grow (compared with animals, anyway) because their needs are simple. Give a plant water, essential elements in soil, carbon dioxide, and light, and it will produce food and oxygen. These products build the plant's body and sustain its life. Meanwhile, animals and other consumers eat plants. A leafy foundation therefore supports Earth's ecosystems.

How can plants do so much with such simple raw materials? The answer lies in chloroplasts, microscopic solar panels inside each green cell. This chapter explains how chloroplasts use the sun's energy to conjure sugar out of thin air.

5.1 Life Depends on Photosynthesis

It is spring. A seed germinates, its tender roots and pale yellow stem extending rapidly in a race against time. For now, the seedling's sole energy source is food stored in the seed itself. If the shoot does not reach light before its reserves run out, the seedling will die. But if it makes it, green leaves will unfurl and catch the light. The seedling begins to feed itself, and an independent new life begins.

The plant is an **autotroph** ("self feeder"), meaning it uses inorganic substances such as water and carbon dioxide (CO_2) to produce organic compounds. The opposite of an autotroph is a **heterotroph,** which is an organism that obtains carbon by consuming preexisting organic molecules. You are a heterotroph, and so are all other animals, all fungi, and many other microorganisms.

Organisms that can produce their own food underlie every ecosystem on Earth. It is not surprising, therefore, that if asked to designate the most important metabolic pathway, most biologists would not hesitate to cite **photosynthesis:** the process by which plants, algae, and some microbes harness solar energy and convert it into chemical energy.

Photosynthesis is a series of chemical reactions that use light energy to assemble CO_2 into glucose ($C_6H_{12}O_6$), the carbohydrate that feeds plants (figure 5.1). The plant uses water in the process and releases oxygen gas (O_2) as a byproduct. These chemical reactions are summarized as follows:

$$6CO_2 + 6H_2O \xrightarrow{\text{light energy}} C_6H_{12}O_6 + 6O_2$$

This process provides not only food for the plant but also the energy, raw materials, and oxygen for most heterotrophs (see figure 4.2). Animals, fungi, and other consumers eat the leaves, stems, roots, flowers, nectar, fruits, and seeds of the world's autotrophs. Even the waste product of photosynthesis, O_2, is essential to most life on Earth.

Because humans live on land, we are most familiar with the contribution that plants make to Earth's terrestrial ecosystems. In fact, however, more than half of the world's photosynthesis occurs in the oceans, courtesy of countless algae and bacteria.

On land or in the water, Earth without photosynthesis would not be a living world for long. If the sky were blackened by a nuclear holocaust, cataclysmic volcanic eruption, or massive meteor impact, the light intensity reaching Earth's surface would decline to about a tenth of its normal level. Photosynthetic organisms would die as they depleted their energy reserves faster than they could manufacture more food. Animals that normally ate these autotrophs would go hungry, as would the animals that ate them. A year or even two might pass before enough life-giving light could penetrate the hazy atmosphere, but by then, it would be too late. The lethal chain reaction would already be well into motion, destroying food webs at their bases. No wonder biologists consider photosynthesis to be the most important metabolic process on Earth.

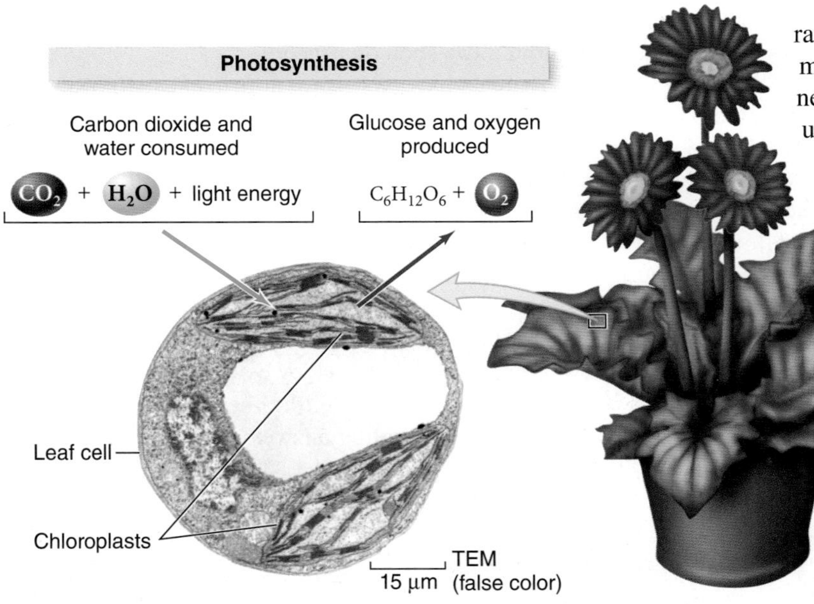

Photosynthesis

Carbon dioxide and water consumed

CO_2 + H_2O + light energy

Glucose and oxygen produced

$C_6H_{12}O_6$ + O_2

Leaf cell

Chloroplasts

15 µm

TEM (false color)

Figure 5.1 Sugar from the Sun. In photosynthesis, a plant produces glucose and O_2 from simple starting materials: carbon dioxide, water, and sunlight.

5.1 Mastering Concepts

1. How is an autotroph different from a heterotroph?
2. What is photosynthesis?
3. Why is photosynthesis essential to life?

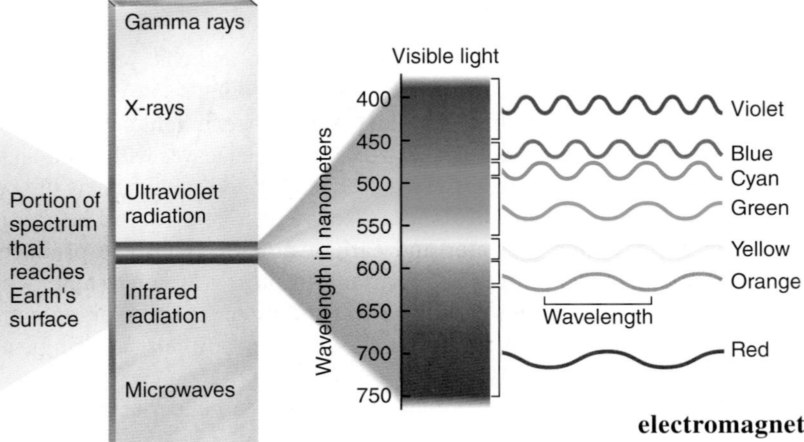

Figure 5.2 The Electromagnetic Spectrum. Sunlight reaching Earth consists of ultraviolet radiation, visible light, and infrared radiation, all of which are just a small part of a continuous spectrum of electromagnetic radiation. The shorter the wavelength, the more energy associated with the radiation.

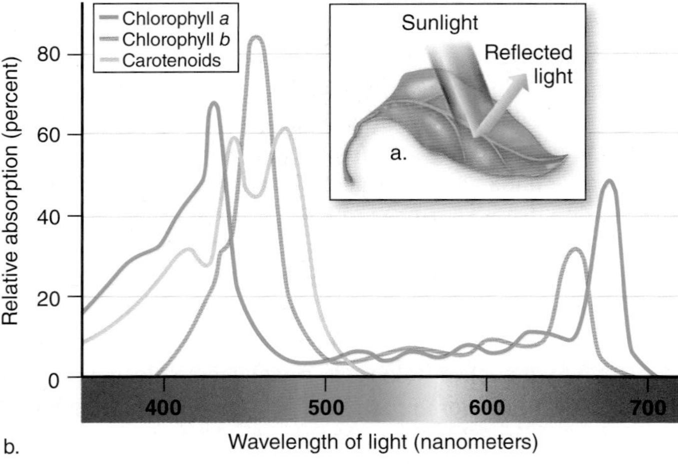

Figure 5.3 Everything but Green. (a) Chlorophyll molecules reflect green and yellow wavelengths of light and absorb the other wavelengths. (b) Each pigment absorbs some wavelengths of light and reflects others.

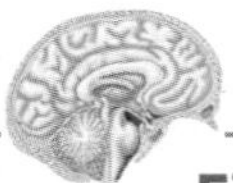

Figure It Out

If you could expose plants to just one wavelength of light at a time, would a wavelength of 300 nm, 450 nm, or 600 nm produce the highest photosynthetic rate?

Answer: 450 nm

5.2 Photosynthetic Pigments Capture Sunlight

Each minute, the sun converts more than 100 metric tons of matter to energy, releasing much of it outward as waves of electromagnetic radiation. After an 8-minute journey, about two billionths of this energy reaches Earth's upper atmosphere. Of this, only about 1% is used for photosynthesis, yet this tiny fraction of the sun's power ultimately produces nearly 2 quadrillion kilograms of carbohydrates a year! Light may seem insubstantial, but it is a powerful force on Earth.

Visible light is a small sliver of a much larger **electromagnetic spectrum,** the range of possible frequencies of radiation (figure 5.2). All electromagnetic radiation, including light, consists of discrete packets of kinetic energy called **photons.** A photon's **wavelength** is the distance it moves during a complete vibration. The shorter a photon's wavelength, the more energy it contains. The visible light that provides the energy that powers photosynthesis is in the middle range of the electromagnetic spectrum. We perceive visible light of different wavelengths as distinct colors.

Plant cells contain several pigment molecules that capture light energy. The most abundant is **chlorophyll *a*,** a green photosynthetic pigment in plants, algae, and cyanobacteria. Photosynthetic organisms usually also have several types of **accessory pigments,** which are energy-capturing pigment molecules other than chlorophyll *a*. Chlorophyll *b* and carotenoids are accessory pigments in plants (see the Burning Question on page 90).

The photosynthetic pigments have distinct colors because they absorb only some wavelengths of visible light, while transmitting or reflecting others (figure 5.3). Chlorophylls *a* and *b* absorb red and blue wavelengths; they appear green because they reflect green light. Carotenoids, on the other hand, reflect longer wavelengths of light, so they appear red, orange, or yellow. (Carrots, tomatoes, lobster shells, and the flesh of salmon all owe their distinctive colors to carotenoid pigments, which the animals must obtain from their diets.)

Only absorbed light is useful in photosynthesis. Accessory pigments absorb wavelengths that chlorophyll *a* cannot, so they extend the range of light wavelengths that a cell can harness. This is a little like the members of the same team on a quiz show, each contributing answers from a different area of expertise.

5.2 Mastering Concepts

1. What is the relationship between visible light and the electromagnetic spectrum?
2. How does it benefit a plant to have multiple types of pigments?

5.3 Chloroplasts Are the Sites of Photosynthesis

In plants, leaves are the main organs of photosynthesis. Most are broad and flat, exposing abundant surface area to sunlight. But light is just one requirement for photosynthesis. Water is essential, too; roots absorb this vital ingredient, which moves up stems and into the leaves. Plants also must exchange CO_2 and O_2 with the atmosphere through **stomata** (singular: stoma), tiny openings in the epidermis of a leaf or stem. (The word *stoma* comes from the Greek word for "mouth"). ▸ leaf epidermis, p. 432

Most photosynthesis occurs in cells filling the leaf's interior (figure 5.4). **Mesophyll** is the collective term for these internal cells (*meso-* means "middle," and *-phyll* means "leaf"). Leaf mesophyll cells contain abundant **chloroplasts,** the organelles of photosynthesis in plants and algae. Most photosynthetic cells contain 40 to 200 chloroplasts, which add up to about 500,000 per square millimeter of leaf—an impressive array of solar energy collectors.

Each chloroplast contains tremendous surface area for the reactions of photosynthesis. Two membranes enclose the **stroma,** a gelatinous fluid containing ribosomes, DNA, and enzymes. (Be careful not to confuse the *stroma* with a *stoma*, or leaf pore.) Suspended in the stroma of each chloroplast are between 10 and 100 **grana** (singular: granum), each composed of a stack of 10 to 20 disk-shaped thylakoids. Each **thylakoid,** in turn, consists of a membrane studded with photosynthetic pigments and enclosing a volume called the **thylakoid space.**

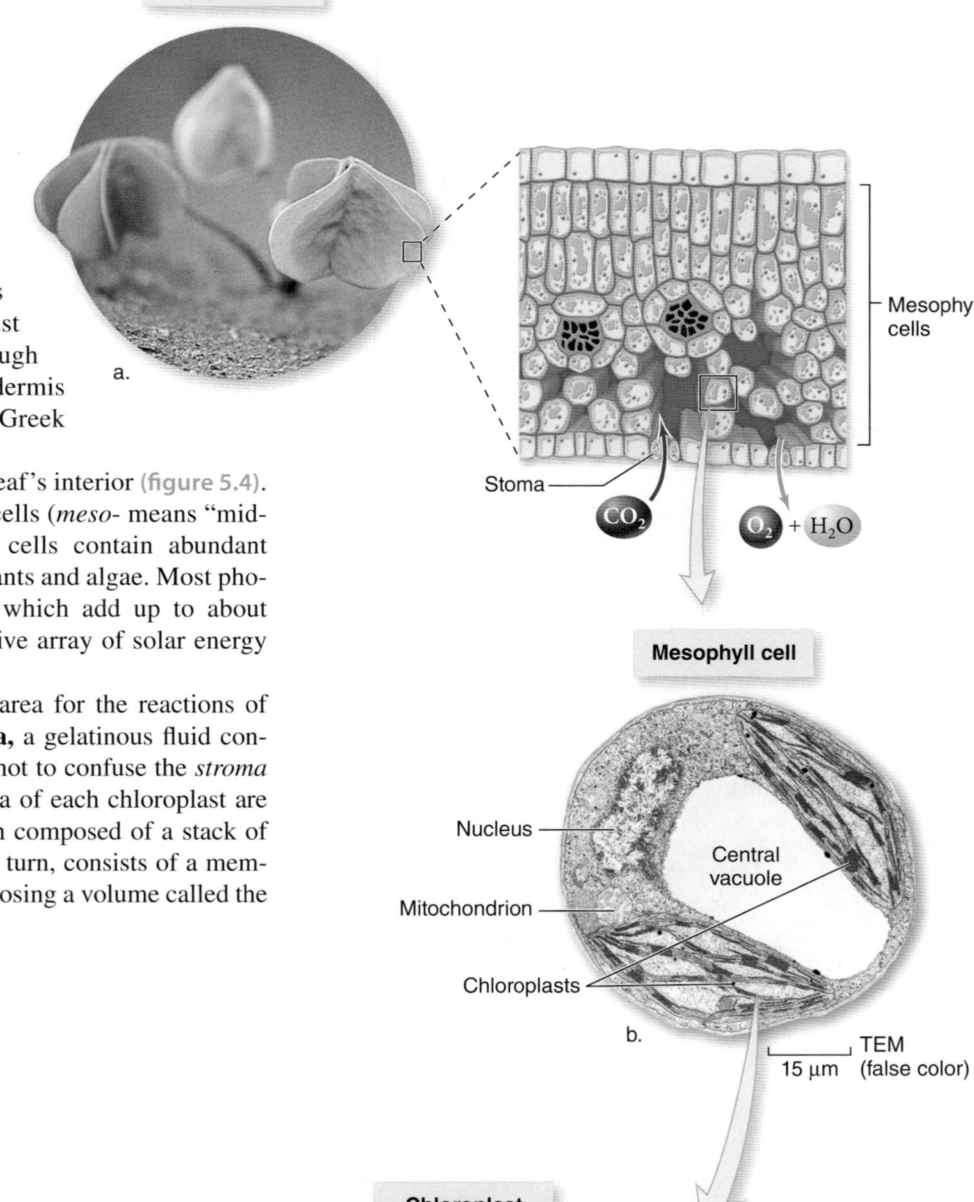

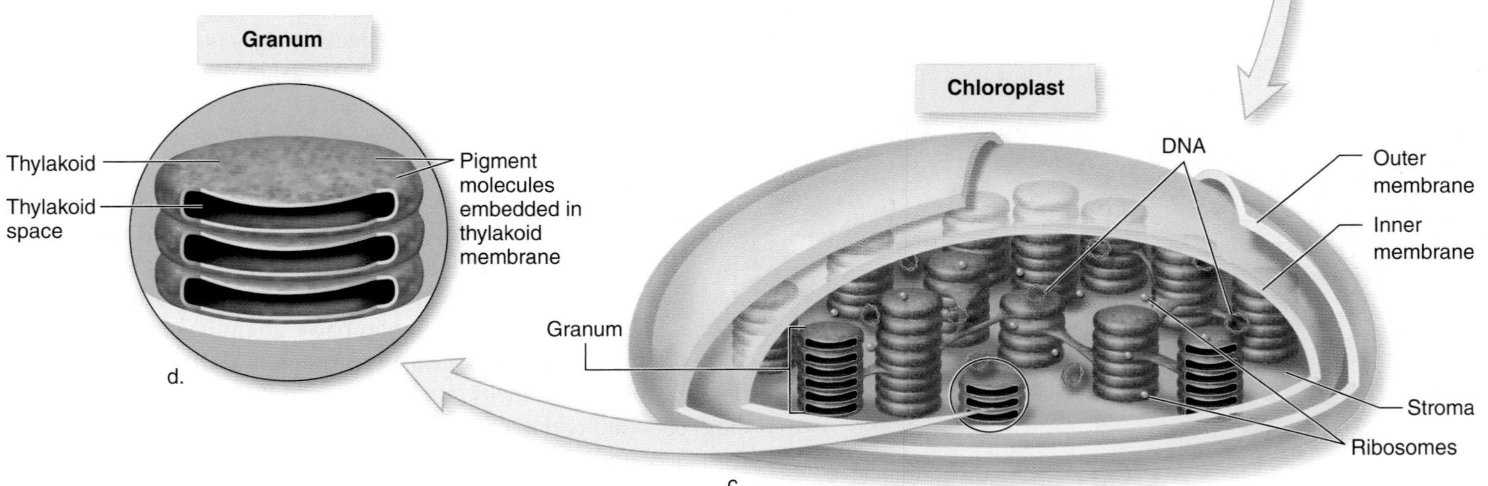

Figure 5.4 Leaf and Chloroplast Anatomy. (a) The tissue inside a leaf is called mesophyll. (b) Each mesophyll cell contains multiple chloroplasts. (c) A chloroplast contains light-harvesting pigments, embedded in (d) the stacks of thylakoid membranes that make up each granum.

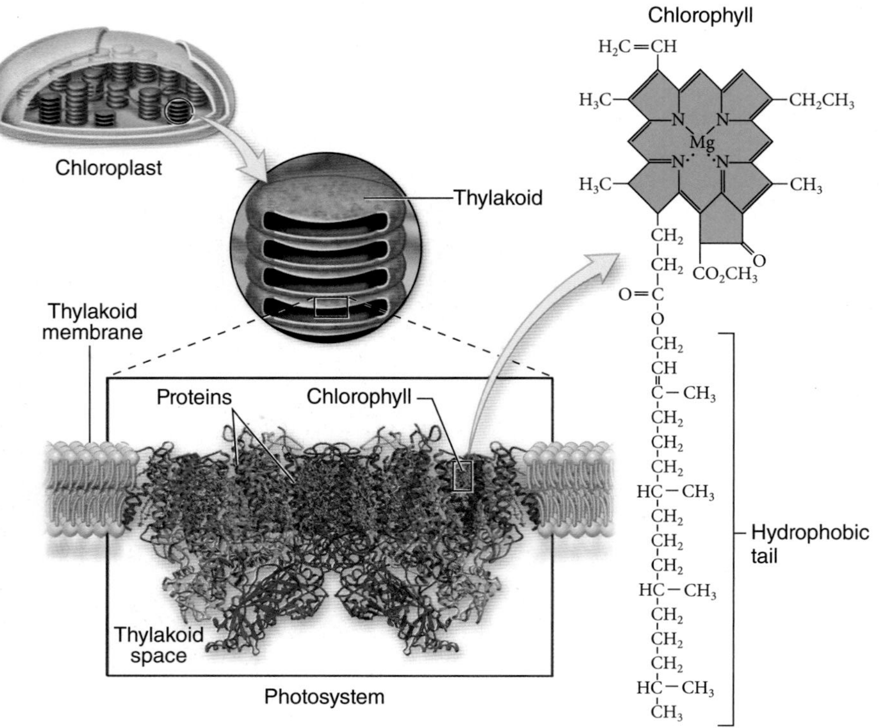

Figure 5.5 Thylakoid Membrane. This diagram of a photosystem shows a complex grouping of proteins and pigments (including chlorophyll) embedded in the chloroplast's thylakoid membrane.

The pigments and proteins that participate in photosynthesis are grouped into photosystems in the thylakoid membrane (figure 5.5). One **photosystem** consists of chlorophyll *a* aggregated with other pigment molecules and the proteins that anchor the entire complex in the membrane.

Within each photosystem are some 300 chlorophyll molecules and 50 accessory pigments. Although all of the pigment molecules absorb light energy, only one chlorophyll *a* molecule per photosystem actually uses the energy in photosynthetic reactions. The photosystem's **reaction center** is this chlorophyll *a* molecule and its associated proteins. All other pigment molecules in the photosystem are called **antenna pigments** because they capture photon energy and funnel it to the reaction center. If the different pigments are like a quiz show team, then the reaction center is analogous to the one member who announces the team's answer to the show's moderator.

Why does only one chlorophyll molecule out of a few hundred actually participate in photosynthetic reactions? A single chlorophyll *a* molecule can absorb only a small amount of light energy. Several pigment molecules near each other capture much more energy because they can pass the energy on to the reaction center, freeing them to absorb other photons as they strike. Thus, the photosystem's organization greatly enhances the efficiency of photosynthesis.

5.3 Mastering Concepts

1. Describe the relationship among the chloroplast, stroma, grana, and thylakoids.
2. How does the reaction center chlorophyll interact with the antenna pigments in a photosystem?

5.4 Photosynthesis Occurs in Two Stages

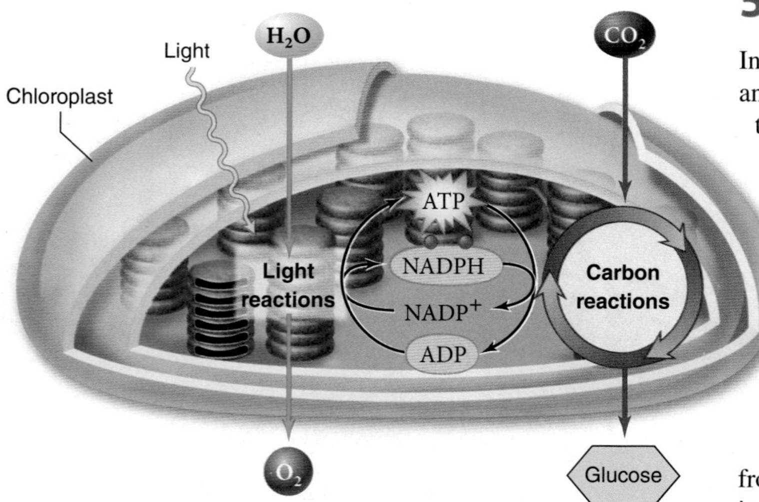

Figure 5.6 Overview of Photosynthesis. In the light reactions, pigment molecules capture sunlight energy and transfer it to molecules of ATP and NADPH. The carbon reactions use this energy to build glucose out of carbon dioxide.

Inside a chloroplast, photosynthesis occurs in two stages: the light reactions and the carbon reactions. Figure 5.6 summarizes the entire process, and sections 5.5 and 5.6 describe each part in greater detail.

The **light reactions** convert solar energy to chemical energy. (You can think of the light reactions as the "photo-" part of photosynthesis.) In the chloroplast's thylakoid membranes, pigment molecules in two linked photosystems capture kinetic energy from photons and store it as potential energy in the chemical bonds of two molecules: ATP and NADPH.

Recall from chapter 4 that **ATP** is a nucleotide that stores potential energy in the covalent bonds between its phosphate groups (see figure 4.6). ATP forms when a phosphate group is added to ADP. The other energy-rich product of the light reactions, **NADPH,** is a molecule that carries pairs of energized electrons. In photosynthesis, these electrons come from chlorophyll molecules. Once the light reactions are underway, chlorophyll, in turn, replaces its "lost" electrons by splitting water molecules, yielding O_2 as a waste product.

These two resources (energy and "loaded" electron carriers) set the stage for the second part of photosynthesis. The **carbon reactions** use ATP and the high-energy electrons in NADPH to reduce CO_2 to glucose molecules. (These reactions are the "-synthesis" part of photosynthesis.) The ATP and NADPH come from the light reactions, and the CO_2 comes from the atmosphere. Once inside the leaf, CO_2 diffuses into a mesophyll cell and across the chloroplast membrane into the stroma, where the carbon reactions occur.

Overall, photosynthesis is an oxidation–reduction (redox) process. "Oxidation" means that electrons are removed from an atom or molecule; "reduction" means electrons are added. As you will see, photosynthesis strips electrons from the oxygen atoms in H_2O (i.e., the oxygen atoms are oxidized). These electrons reduce the carbon in CO_2. Because oxygen atoms attract electrons more strongly than do carbon atoms (see chapter 2), moving electrons from oxygen to carbon requires energy. The energy source for this reaction is, of course, light. ▸ redox reactions, p. 71

5.4 Mastering Concepts

1. What happens in each of the two main stages of photosynthesis?
2. Where in the chloroplast does each stage occur?

5.5 The Light Reactions Begin Photosynthesis

A plant placed in a dark closet literally starves. Without light, the plant cannot generate ATP or NADPH. And without these critical energy and electron carriers, the plant cannot feed itself. Once its stored reserves are gone, the plant dies. The plant's life thus depends on the light reactions of photosynthesis, which occur in the membranes of chloroplasts.

We have already seen that the pigments and proteins of the chloroplast's thylakoid membranes are organized into photosystems (see figure 5.5). More specifically, the thylakoid membranes contain two types of photosystems, dubbed "I" and "II." An electron transport chain connects the two photosystems.

Recall from chapter 4 that an **electron transport chain** is a group of proteins that shuttle electrons from carrier to carrier, releasing energy with each step. As you will see, the electron transport chain that links photosystems I and II stores potential energy used in ATP synthesis. A second electron transport chain extending from photosystem I ends with the production of NADPH.

Figure 5.7 depicts the arrangement of the photosystems and electron transport chains in the thylakoid membrane. Refer to this illustration as you work through the rest of this section.

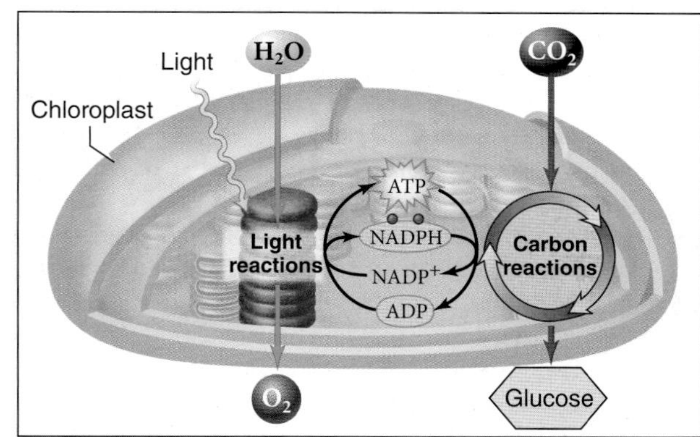

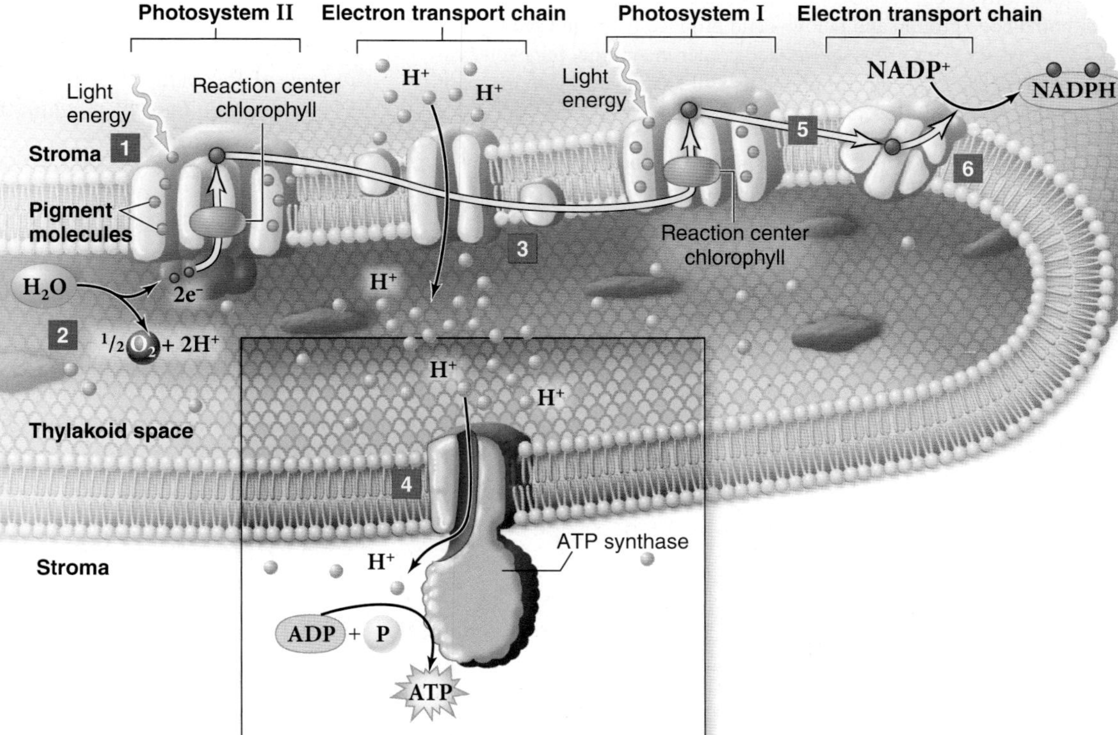

Figure 5.7 Two Photosystems Participate in the Light Reactions. [1] Chlorophyll molecules in photosystem II transfer light energy to electrons. [2] Electrons are stripped from water molecules, releasing oxygen. [3] The energized electrons pass to photosystem I via an electron transport chain. Each transfer releases energy that is used to pump hydrogen ions into the thylakoid space. [4] The resulting hydrogen gradient is used to generate ATP. [5] In photosystem I, the electrons absorb more light energy and [6] are passed to $NADP^+$, creating the energy-rich NADPH.

Burning Questions

Why do leaves change colors in the fall?

Most leaves are green throughout a plant's growing season, although there are exceptions; some ornamental plants, for example, have yellow or purple leaves. The near-ubiquitous green color comes from chlorophyll *a*, the most abundant pigment in photosynthetic plant parts.

But the leaf also has other photosynthetic pigments. Carotenoids contribute brilliant yellow, orange, and red hues. Purple pigments, such as anthocyanins, are not photosynthetically active, but they do protect leaves from damage by ultraviolet radiation.

These accessory pigments are less abundant than chlorophyll, so they usually remain invisible to the naked eye during the growing season. As winter approaches, however, deciduous plants prepare to shed their leaves. The chlorophyll degrades, and the now "unmasked" accessory pigments reveal their colors for a short time as a spectacular autumn display. These pigments soon disappear as well, and the dead leaves turn brown.

Spring brings a flush of fresh, green leaves. The energy to produce the foliage comes from glucose the plant produced during the last growing season and stored as starch. The new leaves make food throughout the spring and summer, so the tree can grow—both above ground and below—and produce fruits and seeds.

As the days grow shorter and cooler in autumn, the cycle will continue, and the colorful pigments will again participate in one of nature's great disappearing acts.

Submit your burning question to:
marielle_hoefnagels@mcgraw-hill.com

A. Photosystem II Produces ATP

Photosynthesis begins in the cluster of pigment molecules of photosystem II. These pigments absorb light and transfer the energy to a chlorophyll *a* reaction center, where it boosts two electrons to a higher energy level. The "excited" electrons, now packed with potential energy, are ejected from this chlorophyll *a* molecule and grabbed by the first protein in the electron transport chain that links the two photosystems (figure 5.7, step 1). ▸ electron orbitals, p. 24

How does the chlorophyll *a* molecule replace these two electrons? They come from water (H_2O), which donates two electrons when it splits into oxygen gas and two protons (H^+). Chlorophyll *a* picks up the electrons, and O_2 is the waste product that the plant releases to the environment (step 2).

Meanwhile, the chloroplast uses the potential energy in the electrons to create a proton gradient (step 3). As the electrons pass along the electron transport chain, the energy they lose drives the active transport of protons from the stroma into the thylakoid space. The resulting proton gradient between the stroma and the inside of the thylakoid represents a form of potential energy. ▸ active transport, p. 78

An enzyme complex called **ATP synthase** transforms the gradient's potential energy into chemical energy in the form of ATP (step 4). A channel in ATP synthase allows protons trapped inside the thylakoid space to return to the chloroplast's stroma. As the gradient dissipates, energy is released. The ATP synthase enzyme uses this energy to add phosphate to ADP, generating ATP. (As described in chapter 6, the same enzyme produces ATP in cellular respiration.)

This mechanism is similar to using a dam to produce electricity. As water accumulates, tremendous pressure (a form of potential energy) builds on the face of the dam. That pressure is released by diverting water through a large pipe at the base of the dam, turning massive blades that spin an electric generator.

B. Photosystem I Produces NADPH

Photosystem I functions much as photosystem II does. Photon energy strikes energy-absorbing molecules of chlorophyll *a,* which pass the energy to the reaction center. The reactive chlorophyll molecules eject electrons to an electron carrier molecule in a second electron transport chain (figure 5.7, step 5). The boosted electrons in photosystem I are then replaced with electrons passing down the first electron transport chain from photosystem II.

Unlike in photosystem II, however, the second electron transport chain does not generate ATP, nor does it pass its electrons to yet another photosystem. Instead, the electrons reduce a molecule of $NADP^+$ to NADPH (step 6). This NADPH is the electron carrier that will reduce carbon dioxide in the carbon reactions, while the ATP generated in photosystem II will provide the energy.

5.5 Mastering Concepts

1. Describe the events that occur after light strikes photosystem II, ending with the production of ATP.
2. How do electrons pass from photosystem II to photosystem I?
3. How are the electrons from photosystem II replaced?
4. What happens in photosystem I?

5.6 The Carbon Reactions Produce Carbohydrates

The carbon reactions, also called the Calvin cycle, occur in the chloroplast's stroma. The **Calvin cycle** is the metabolic pathway that uses NADPH and ATP from the light reactions to assemble CO_2 molecules into three-carbon carbohydrate molecules (figure 5.8). These products are eventually assembled into glucose and other sugars.

The first step of the Calvin cycle is **carbon fixation**—the initial incorporation of carbon from CO_2 into an organic compound. Specifically, CO_2 combines with **ribulose bisphosphate (RuBP),** a five-carbon sugar with two phosphate groups. An enzyme called **rubisco** catalyzes this first reaction.

The six-carbon product of the initial reaction immediately breaks down into two three-carbon molecules (PGA). Further steps in the cycle convert PGA to another carbohydrate called PGAL. Some of the PGAL is rearranged to form additional RuBP, continuing the cycle. But the cell can also use PGAL to build larger carbohydrates such as glucose and sucrose, the most familiar products of photosynthesis.

Several fates await the carbohydrates produced in the carbon reactions. A plant's cells use about half of the glucose as fuel for their own cellular respiration, the metabolic pathway described in chapter 6. Roots, flowers, fruits, seeds, and other nonphotosynthetic plant parts could not grow without sugar shipments from green leaves and stems. Plants also combine glucose with other substances to manufacture additional compounds, including amino acids and a host of economically important products such as rubber, medicines, and spices.

Moreover, glucose molecules are the building blocks of the cellulose wall that surrounds every plant cell. Wood is mostly made of cellulose. The timber in the world's forests therefore stores enormous amounts of carbon. So do vast deposits of coal and other fossil fuels, which are the remains of plants and other organisms that lived long ago. Burning wood or fossil fuels releases this stored carbon into the atmosphere as CO_2. As the amount of CO_2 in the atmosphere has increased, Earth's average temperature has risen. ▸ global climate change, p. 414

If a plant produces more glucose than it immediately needs for respiration or building cell walls, it may store the excess as starch. Carbohydrate-rich tubers and grains, such as potatoes, rice, corn, and wheat, are all energy-storing plant organs. Some plants, including sugarcane and sugar beets, store energy as sucrose instead. Table sugar comes from these crops. In addition, people use starch (from corn kernels) and sugar (from sugarcane) to produce biofuels such as ethanol. ▸ biofuels, p. 308

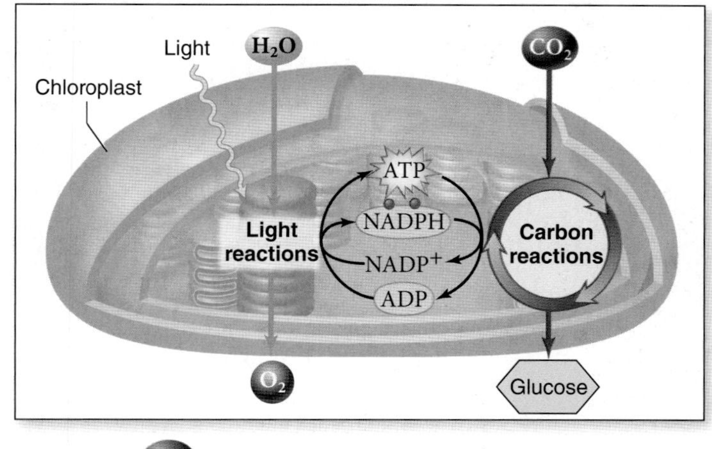

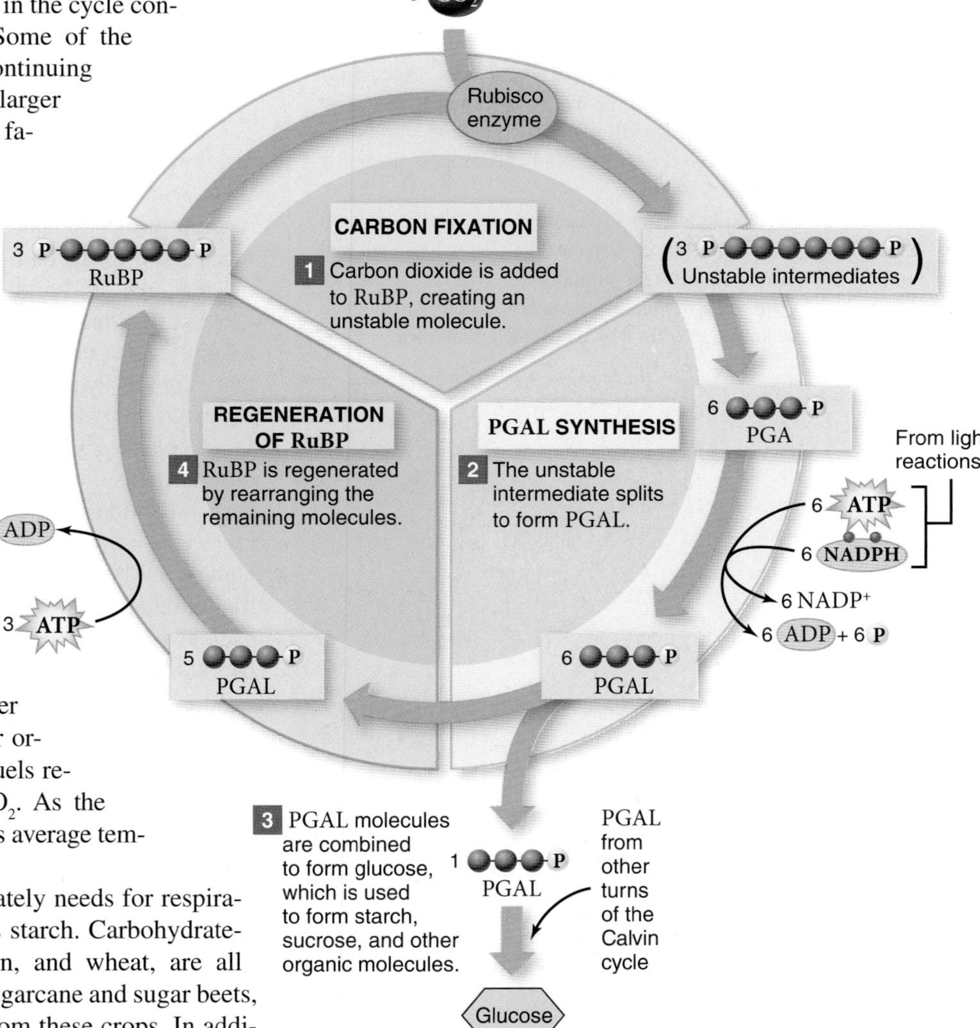

Figure 5.8 The Calvin Cycle. ATP and NADPH from the light reactions power the Calvin cycle, simplified here. The cycle generates a three-carbon molecule, PGAL, which is used to build glucose and other carbohydrates.

5.6 Mastering Concepts

1. What happens in the carbon reactions?
2. What are the roles of CO_2, ATP, and NADPH in the Calvin cycle?

Why We Care | Weed Killers

One low-tech way to kill an unwanted plant is to deprive it of light. Gardeners who want to convert a lawn into a garden, for example, might kill the grass by covering it with layers of newspaper or cardboard for several weeks. The light reactions of photosynthesis cannot occur in the dark; the plants die.

Many herbicides also stop the light reactions. For example, a weed killer called diuron blocks electron flow in photosystem II. Paraquat, noted for its use in destroying marijuana plants, diverts electrons from photosystem I.

Other herbicides take a different approach. Accessory pigments called carotenoids protect plants from damage caused by free radicals. Triazole herbicides kill plants by blocking carotenoid synthesis. No longer protected from free-radical damage, the cell's organelles are destroyed.

Still other weed killers exploit pathways not directly related to photosynthesis. For instance, glyphosate (Roundup) inhibits an enzyme that plants require for amino acid synthesis. Another herbicide, 2,4-D, mimics a plant hormone called auxin (see chapter 22); no one knows exactly why the treated plant dies.

5.7 C_3, C_4, and CAM Plants Use Different Carbon Fixation Pathways

The Calvin cycle is also known as the **C_3 pathway** because a three-carbon molecule, PGA, is the first stable compound in the pathway. Although all plants use the Calvin cycle, C_3 plants use *only* this pathway to fix carbon from CO_2. About 95% of plant species are C_3, including cereals, peanuts, tobacco, spinach, sugar beets, soybeans, most trees, and some lawn grasses.

C_3 photosynthesis is obviously a successful adaptation, but it does have a weakness: inefficiency. Photosynthesis has a theoretical efficiency rate of 30%, but on cloudy days, individual plants average only from 0.1% to 3% photosynthetic efficiency.

How do plants waste so much solar energy? One contributing factor is a metabolic pathway called **photorespiration,** a series of reactions that begin when the rubisco enzyme uses O_2 instead of CO_2 as a substrate. The net result of photorespiration is that the plant loses CO_2 that it has already fixed, wasting both ATP and NADPH.

Photorespiration is most likely in hot, dry climates. Plants in these habitats therefore face a trade-off. If the stomata remain open too long, a plant may lose water, wilt, and die. If the plant instead closes its stomata, CO_2 supplies in the leaves run low while O_2 builds up. Under those conditions, photorespiration becomes much more likely, and photosynthetic efficiency plummets. Plants may lose as much as 30% of their fixed carbon to this pathway, which has no known benefit.

In hot climates, plants that minimize photorespiration may therefore have a significant competitive advantage. One way to improve efficiency is to ensure that rubisco always encounters high CO_2 concentrations. The C_4 and CAM pathways are two adaptations that do just that.

C_4 plants physically separate the light reactions and the carbon reactions into different cells (figure 5.9). The light reactions occur in mesophyll cells, as does a carbon-fixation reaction called the C_4 pathway. In the **C_4 pathway,** CO_2 combines with a three-carbon molecule to form a four-carbon compound (hence the name C_4). This molecule then moves into adjacent **bundle-sheath cells** that surround the leaf veins. The CO_2 is liberated inside these cells, where the Calvin cycle fixes the carbon a second time by the C_3 pathway. Unlike mesophyll cells, bundle-sheath cells are not exposed directly to atmospheric O_2. The rubisco in bundle-sheath cells is therefore much more likely to bind CO_2 instead of O_2, reducing photorespiration. Meanwhile, at the cost of two ATP molecules, the three-carbon "ferry" returns to the mesophyll to pick up another CO_2.

About 1% of plants use the C_4 pathway. All are flowering plants growing in hot, open environments, including crabgrass and crop plants such as sugarcane and corn. C_4 plants are less abundant, however, in cooler, moister habitats. In those environments, the ATP cost of ferrying each CO_2 from a mesophyll cell to a bundle-sheath cell apparently exceeds the benefits of reduced photorespiration.

Another energy- and water-saving strategy, called crassulacean acid metabolism (CAM), occurs in about 3% to 4% of plant species, including pineapple and cacti. Plants that use the **CAM pathway** open their stomata to fix CO_2 only at night, when the temperature drops and the humidity rises. CO_2 diffuses in. Mesophyll cells incorporate the CO_2 into a four-carbon compound, which they store in large vacuoles. The stomata close during the heat of the day, but the stored molecule moves from the vacuole to a chloroplast and releases its CO_2. The chloroplast then fixes the CO_2 in the Calvin cycle. The CAM pathway reduces photorespiration by generating high CO_2 concentrations inside chloroplasts.

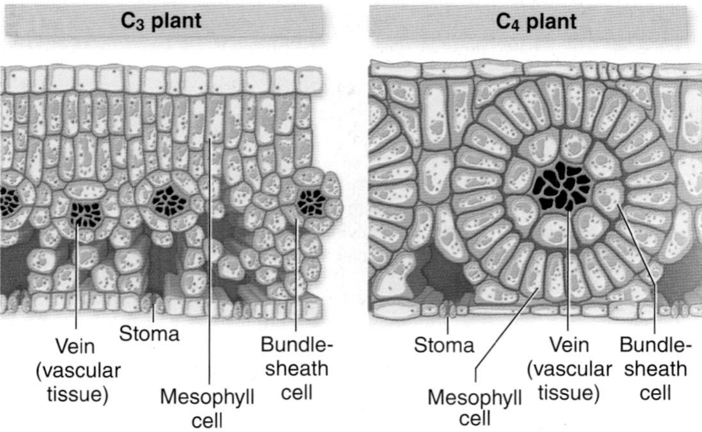

Figure 5.9 C_3 and C_4 Leaf Anatomy. In C_3 plants, the light reactions and the Calvin cycle occur in mesophyll cells. In C_4 plants, the light reactions occur in mesophyll, but the inner ring of bundle-sheath cells houses the Calvin cycle.

All CAM plants are adapted to dry habitats. In cool environments, however, CAM plants cannot compete with C_3 plants. Their stomata are only open at night, so CAM plants have much less carbon available to their cells for growth and reproduction.

Figure 5.10 compares and contrasts C_3, C_4, and CAM plants.

5.7 Mastering Concepts

1. Why is the Calvin cycle also called the C_3 pathway?
2. How does photorespiration counter photosynthesis?
3. Describe how a C_4 plant minimizes photorespiration.
4. How is the CAM pathway like C_4 metabolism, and how is it different?

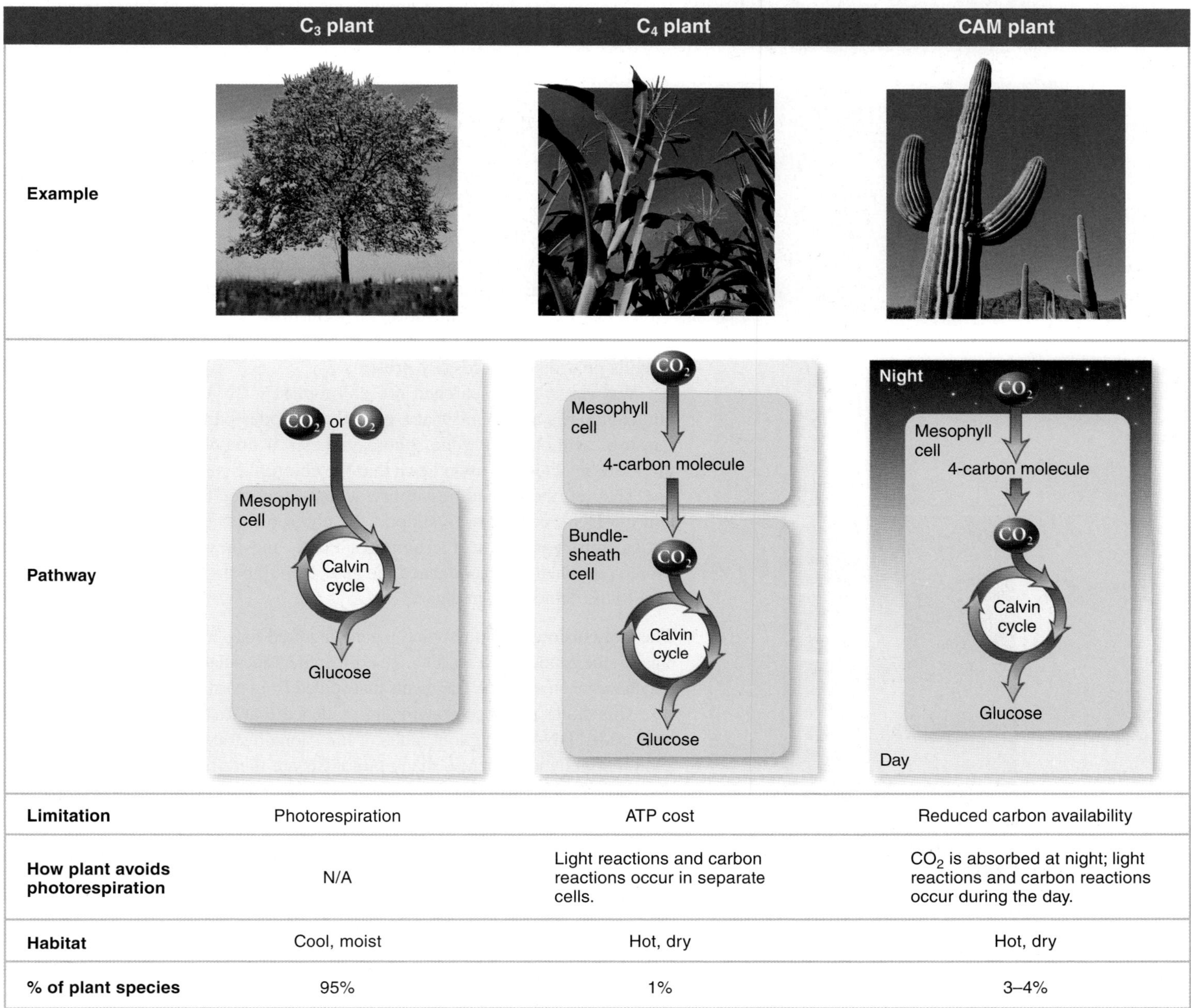

	C_3 plant	C_4 plant	CAM plant
Example			
Pathway			
Limitation	Photorespiration	ATP cost	Reduced carbon availability
How plant avoids photorespiration	N/A	Light reactions and carbon reactions occur in separate cells.	CO_2 is absorbed at night; light reactions and carbon reactions occur during the day.
Habitat	Cool, moist	Hot, dry	Hot, dry
% of plant species	95%	1%	3–4%

Figure 5.10 **C_3, C_4, and CAM Pathways Compared.** The C_4 and CAM pathways are adaptations that minimize photorespiration.

Investigating Life

5.8 Solar-Powered Sea Slugs

Most animals have an indirect relationship with photosynthesis: autotrophs make food, which animals eat. But *Elysia chlorotica* is an unusual animal (figure 5.11). This sea slug, which lives in salt marshes along the eastern coast of North America, is solar-powered: it has chloroplasts in the lining of its gut.

These invertebrate animals do not inherit their solar panels from their parents; instead, they acquire the chloroplasts by eating algae. As a young sea slug grazes, it punctures the filaments of the algae and sucks out the contents. The animal digests most of the nutrients, but cells lining the slug's gut absorb the chloroplasts. The organelles stay there for the rest of the animal's life. Like a plant, the solar-powered sea slug can live on sunlight and air.

The Question: A chloroplast requires a few thousand genes to carry out photosynthesis, yet chloroplast DNA encodes less than 10% of the required proteins. DNA in a plant cell's nucleus makes up the difference. But slugs are animals, so their nuclei presumably lack these genes. How can the chloroplasts operate inside their mollusk partners?

Head

Digestive tract

Figure 5.11 A Slug with Solar Panels. The sea slug *Elysia chlorotica* owes its green color to chloroplasts harvested from algae.

The Approach: Mary E. Rumpho, of the University of Maine, collaborated with James R. Manhart, of Texas A&M University, to find out the answer. They considered two possibilities. Either the chloroplasts can work inside the host slug's digestive tract without the help of supplemental genes, or the slug's own cells provide the necessary proteins.

The researchers searched the chloroplast's DNA for genes essential to photosynthesis and found that a gene that encodes part of photosystem II was missing. Without this gene, photosynthesis is impossible. The researchers therefore rejected the hypothesis that the chloroplasts are autonomous.

That left the second possibility, which suggested that the slug's cells contain the DNA necessary to support the chloroplasts. The team looked for the critical missing gene in the animal's DNA, and they found it (figure 5.12). Moreover, when they sequenced the gene from the slug's genome, it was identical to the same gene in algae.

The Conclusion: At some point, a gene required for photosynthesis moved from algae to the genome of a sea slug. The researchers speculate that cells in a slug's gut may have taken up DNA fragments that spilled from partially eaten algae.

This study provides convincing evidence that distantly related organisms have traded DNA throughout much of life's long history. In light of this research and other genetic evidence, many biologists are therefore discarding the notion of a tidy evolutionary "tree" in favor of a messier, but perhaps more fascinating, evolutionary thicket.

Rumpho, Mary E., and seven colleagues, including James R. Manhart. 2008. Horizontal gene transfer of the algal nuclear gene *psbO* to the photosynthetic sea slug *Elysia chlorotica*. *Proceedings of the National Academy of Sciences,* vol. 105, pages 17867–17871.

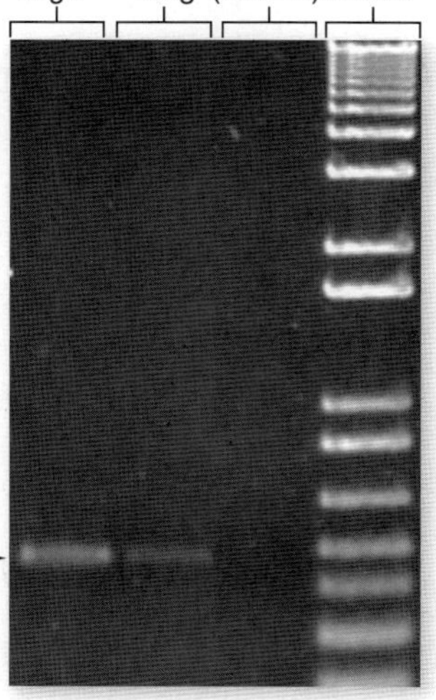

Alga
Slug
Water (control)
DNA ladder
Gene encoding part of photosystem II

Figure 5.12 Photosynthesis Gene. Both algae and the solar-powered sea slug contain a particular gene required for photosynthesis. This electrophoresis gel sorts DNA fragments by size as they migrate from the top to the bottom of the gel. The "ladder" contains DNA pieces of known size, allowing the researchers to estimate the size of the DNA being studied.

5.8 Mastering Concepts

1. Explain the most important finding of this study.
2. What evidence led the researchers to their conclusion?

Chapter Summary

5.1 Life Depends on Photosynthesis

- **Photosynthesis** converts kinetic energy in light to potential energy in the covalent bonds of glucose, according to the following chemical equation:

$$6CO_2 + 6H_2O \xrightarrow{\text{light energy}} C_6H_{12}O_6 + 6O_2$$

- **Autotrophs** produce their own organic molecules from atmospheric CO_2. Plants, algae, and some bacteria are autotrophs. **Heterotrophs** rely on organic molecules produced by other organisms.
- Food and oxygen produced in photosynthesis are critical to life in terrestrial and aquatic habitats.

5.2 Photosynthetic Pigments Capture Sunlight

- Visible light is a small part of the **electromagnetic spectrum.**
- **Photons** move in waves. The longer the **wavelength,** the less kinetic energy per photon. Visible light occurs in a spectrum of colors representing different wavelengths.
- **Chlorophyll *a*** is the primary photosynthetic pigment in plants. **Accessory pigments** absorb wavelengths of light that chlorophyll *a* cannot absorb, extending the range of wavelengths useful for photosynthesis.

5.3 Chloroplasts Are the Sites of Photosynthesis

- Plants exchange gases with the environment through pores called **stomata.**
- Leaf **mesophyll** cells contain abundant **chloroplasts.**
- A chloroplast includes a gelatinous matrix called the **stroma.** This fluid surrounds the **grana,** which are composed of stacked **thylakoid** membranes. Photosynthetic pigments are embedded in the thylakoid membranes, which enclose the **thylakoid space.**
- A **photosystem** consists of **antenna pigments** and a **reaction center.**

5.4 Photosynthesis Occurs in Two Stages

- The **light reactions** of photosynthesis produce **ATP** and **NADPH;** these molecules provide energy and electrons for the glucose-producing **carbon reactions.**
- Photosynthesis is a redox reaction in which water is oxidized and CO_2 is reduced to glucose.

5.5 The Light Reactions Begin Photosynthesis

A. Photosystem II Produces ATP

- Photosystem II captures light energy and sends electrons from reactive chlorophyll *a* to an **electron transport chain** that joins photosystem II to photosystem I.
- Electrons from chlorophyll are replaced with electrons from water. O_2 is the waste product.
- The energy released in the electron transport chain drives the active transport of protons into the thylakoid space. The protons diffuse out through channels in **ATP synthase.** This movement powers the production of ATP.

B. Photosystem I Produces NADPH

- Photosystem I receives electrons from the electron transport chain and uses them to reduce $NADP^+$, producing NADPH. Light provides the energy.

5.6 The Carbon Reactions Produce Carbohydrates

- The carbon reactions use energy from ATP and electrons from NADPH in **carbon fixation** reactions that incorporate CO_2 into organic compounds.

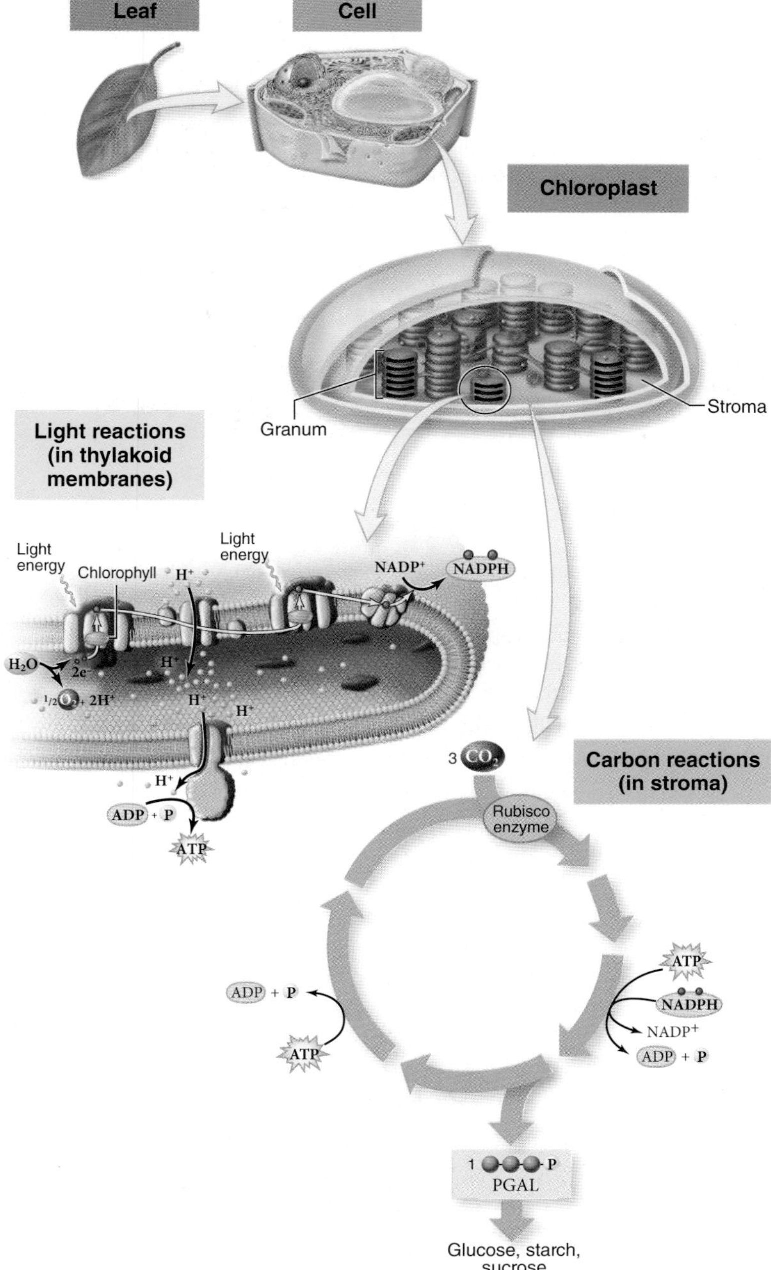

- In the **Calvin cycle, rubisco** catalyzes the reaction of CO_2 with **ribulose bisphosphate** (RuBP) to yield two molecules of PGA. These are converted to PGAL, the immediate carbohydrate product of photosynthesis. The cell later uses PGAL to produce glucose.
- Plants use glucose to generate ATP, grow, nourish nonphotosynthetic plant parts, and produce cellulose and many other biochemicals. Most store excess glucose as starch or sucrose.

5.7 C_3, C_4, and CAM Plants Use Different Carbon Fixation Pathways

- The Calvin cycle is also called the **C_3 pathway.** Most plant species are C_3 plants, which use only this pathway to fix carbon.
- **Photorespiration** wastes carbon and energy when rubisco reacts with O_2 instead of CO_2.

- The C_4 **pathway** reduces photorespiration by separating the light and carbon reactions into different cells. In mesophyll cells, CO_2 is fixed as a four-carbon molecule, which moves to a **bundle-sheath cell** and liberates CO_2 to be fixed again in the Calvin cycle.
- In the **CAM pathway,** desert plants such as cacti open their stomata and take in CO_2 at night, storing the fixed carbon in vacuoles. During the day, they split off CO_2 and fix it in chloroplasts in the same cells.

5.8 Investigating Life: Solar-Powered Sea Slugs

- The sea slug *Elysia chlorotica* contains chloroplasts acquired from its food, a filamentous alga. The slug's DNA includes a gene required for photosynthesis.

Multiple Choice Questions

1. Where does the energy come from to drive photosynthesis?
   a. A chloroplast
   b. ATP
   c. The sun
   d. Glucose
2. Algae in a swimming pool are ____; *Escherichia coli* bacteria in the human intestine are ___.
   a. autotrophs; autotrophs
   b. heterotrophs; heterotrophs
   c. autotrophs; heterotrophs
   d. heterotrophs; autotrophs
3. Photosynthesis is essential to animal life because it provides
   a. CO_2 for respiration.
   b. O_2.
   c. organic molecules.
   d. Both b and c are correct.
4. A plant appears green because
   a. its chloroplasts use green wavelengths of light.
   b. chlorophyll *a* absorbs red and blue light.
   c. chlorophyll *a* absorbs ultraviolet light.
   d. Both a and c are correct.
5. Only high-energy light can penetrate the ocean and reach photosynthetic organisms in coral reefs. What color light would you predict these organisms use?
   a. Red
   b. Yellow
   c. Blue
   d. Orange
6. Which part of the chloroplast is associated with the production of carbohydrates?
   a. The thylakoid
   b. The grana
   c. The thylakoid space
   d. The stroma
7. The ATP that is produced in the light reactions is used by the cell to
   a. reproduce and grow.
   b. build carbohydrate molecules.
   c. move electrons through the electron transport chain.
   d. split water into H^+ and O_2.
8. Besides ATP from the light reactions, the carbon reactions also require
   a. NADPH from the light reactions.
   b. glucose from the mitochondria.
   c. CO_2 from the atmosphere.
   d. Both a and c are correct.
9. What happens to the enzyme rubisco during photorespiration?
   a. The enzyme speeds up the formation of glucose.
   b. The enzyme's active site binds to O_2 instead of CO_2.
   c. The enzyme becomes denatured.
   d. The enzyme catalyzes the breakdown of glucose.
10. A plant that only opens its stomata at night is a
   a. C_2 plant.
   b. C_3 plant.
   c. C_4 plant.
   d. CAM plant.

Write It Out

1. Photosynthesis takes place in plants, algae, and some microbes. How does it affect a meat-eating animal?
2. What color would plants be if they absorbed all wavelengths of visible light? Why?
3. Define these terms and arrange them from smallest to largest: thylakoid membrane; photosystem; chloroplast; electron transport chain; reaction center.
4. Determine whether each of the following molecules is involved in the light reactions, the carbon reactions, or both and explain how: O_2, CO_2, carbohydrates, chlorophyll *a*, photons, NADPH, ATP, H_2O.
5. One of the first investigators to explore photosynthesis was Flemish physician and alchemist Jan van Helmont. In the early 1600s, he grew willow trees in weighed amounts of soil, applied known amounts of water, and noted that in 5 years the trees gained more than 45 kg, but the soil had lost only a little weight. Because he had applied large amounts of water, van Helmont concluded (incorrectly) that plants grew solely by absorbing water. What is the actual source of the added biomass? Explain your answer.
6. One of the classic experiments in photosynthesis occurred in 1771, when Joseph Priestley found that if he placed a mouse in an enclosed container with a lit candle, the mouse would die. But if he also added a plant to the container, the mouse could live. Priestley concluded that plants "purify" air, allowing animals to breathe. What is the biological basis for this observation?
7. In 1941, biologists exposed photosynthesizing cells to water containing a heavy oxygen isotope, designated ^{18}O. The "labeled" isotope appears in the O_2 gas released in photosynthesis, showing that the oxygen came from the water. Where would the ^{18}O have ended up if the researchers had used ^{18}O-labeled CO_2 instead of H_2O?
8. Over the past decades, the CO_2 concentration in the atmosphere has increased.
   a. Predict the effect of increasing carbon dioxide concentrations on photorespiration.

b. Scientists suggest that increasing CO_2 concentrations are leading to higher average global temperatures. If temperatures are increasing, does this change your answer to part (a)? If so, how?

9. How is the CAM pathway adaptive in a desert habitat?
10. Explain why each of the following misconceptions about photosynthesis is false:
    a. Only plants are autotrophs.
    b. Plants do not need cellular respiration because they carry out photosynthesis.
    c. Chlorophyll is the only photosynthetic pigment.

Pull It Together

PHOTOSYNTHESIS

$CO_2 + H_2O \xrightarrow{\text{Light}} O_2 + C_6H_{12}O_6$

occurs in two stages

Light reactions — produce → ATP; produce → NADPH

Carbon reactions

ATP is energy source for Carbon reactions

O_2 … H_2O is an electron source for NADPH

Carbon reactions produce → Glucose

Light reactions require photosynthetic pigments such as → Chlorophyll

Chlorophyll absorbs specific wavelengths of → Light

Light is energy source for Light reactions

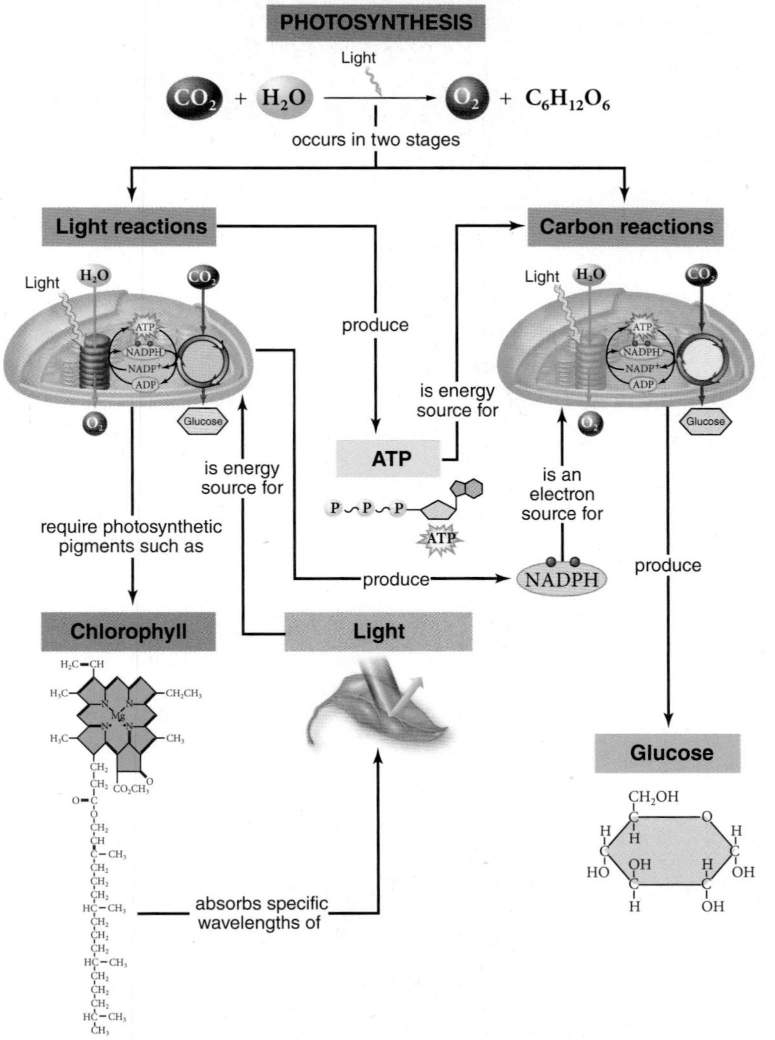

1. Where does the electron transport chain fit into this concept map?
2. What specific process in the light reactions gives rise to the waste product, O_2?
3. How would you incorporate the Calvin cycle, rubisco, C_3 plants, C_4 plants, and CAM plants into this concept map?
4. Where do humans and other heterotrophs fit into this concept map?
5. Build another small concept map showing the relationships among the terms *chloroplast, stroma, grana, thylakoid, photosystem,* and *chlorophyll.*
6. What happens to the glucose produced in photosynthesis?

6 How Cells Release Energy

Learning Outline

Precious Oxygen. This scuba diver could not survive underwater without a tank of oxygen, a gas our cells need to release energy from food.

Learn How to Learn
Don't Skip the Figures

As you read the narrative in the text, pay attention to the figures as well. Each one is trying to teach you something, but what is it? Sometimes, a figure summarizes the narrative and helps you see the chapter's "big picture." Other illustrations show the parts of a structure or the steps in a process; still others summarize a technique or help you classify information. Flip through this book and see if you can find examples of each type.

What's the Point?

Our need for oxygen is absolute; we lose consciousness after just a few minutes without it. We can extract it only from air, which explains why swimmers must emerge to breathe every few moments, and why scuba divers carry tanks filled with the gas.

Life also demands a steady supply of food. Plants make their own food, but animals—like the bluebird pictured above—have to eat.

There is an intimate relationship between our twin requirements to eat and breathe. Both are essential for the production of ATP, the power-packed molecule that supplies energy for life's activities. This chapter describes how cells make those little ATP molecules that nothing can live without.

6.1 Cells Use Energy in Food to Make ATP

No cell can survive without **ATP**—adenosine triphosphate. Without this energy carrier, you could not have developed from a fertilized egg into an adult. You could not breathe, chew, talk on the phone, circulate your blood, blink your eyes, walk, or listen to music. Without ATP, a plant could not take up soil nutrients, grow, or produce flowers, fruits, and seeds. A fungus could not absorb food or produce mushrooms. Like a car without gasoline, a cell without ATP would simply die. ▸ ATP, p. 72

ATP is essential because it powers nearly every activity that requires energy input in the cell: synthesis of DNA, RNA, proteins, carbohydrates, and lipids; active transport across the membranes surrounding cells and organelles; separation of duplicated chromosomes during cell division; movement of cilia and flagella; muscle contraction; and many others. This constant need for ATP explains the need for a steady food supply: all organisms use the potential energy stored in food to make ATP.

Where does the food come from in the first place? Chapter 5 explains the answer: In most ecosystems, plants and other autotrophs use photosynthesis to make organic molecules such as glucose ($C_6H_{12}O_6$) out of carbon dioxide (CO_2) and water (H_2O). Light supplies the energy. The glucose produced in photosynthesis feeds not only the autotrophs but also all of the animals, fungi, and microbes that share the ecosystem (see figure 4.2).

All cells need ATP, but they don't all produce it in the same way. In aerobic cellular respiration, the main subject of this chapter, a cell uses oxygen gas (O_2) and glucose to generate ATP. Plants, animals, and many microbes, especially those in O_2-rich environments, use aerobic respiration. Other pathways, including fermentation, generate ATP from glucose without using O_2. Section 6.8 describes fermentation, which is most common in microorganisms.

The overall equation for **aerobic respiration** is essentially the reverse of photosynthesis:

$$\text{glucose} + \text{oxygen} \longrightarrow \text{carbon dioxide} + \text{water} + \text{ATP}$$
$$C_6H_{12}O_6 + 6O_2 \longrightarrow 6CO_2 + 6H_2O + 36\text{ATP}$$

According to this equation, aerobic cellular respiration requires organisms to acquire O_2 and get rid of CO_2 (figure 6.1). In humans and many other animals, O_2 from inhaled air diffuses into the bloodstream across the walls of microscopic air sacs in the lungs. The circulatory system carries the inhaled O_2 to cells, where gas exchange occurs. O_2 diffuses into the cell's mitochondria, the sites of respiration. Meanwhile, CO_2 diffuses out of the cells and into the bloodstream. After moving from the blood into the lungs, the CO_2 is exhaled.

Many people mistakenly believe that plants do not use cellular respiration because they are photosynthetic. In fact, plants respire about half of the glucose they produce. But if plants consume O_2 in respiration, why do they have a reputation for releasing this gas into the atmosphere? The explanation is that plants retain the other half of the glucose they produce, using it to build cellulose, starch, and other organic molecules as they grow. Because they absorb much more CO_2 in photosynthesis than they release in respiration, they also release much more O_2 than they consume.

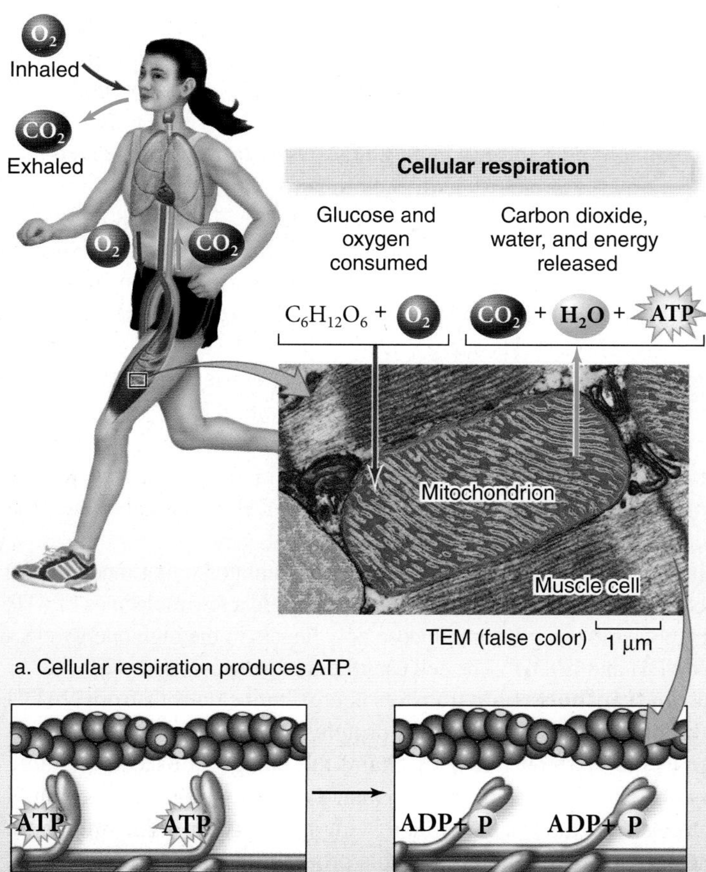

Figure 6.1 The Link Between Breathing and Cellular Respiration. (a) The athlete breathes in O_2, which enters the bloodstream in the lungs and is distributed to all cells. There, in mitochondria, the O_2 participates in the reactions of cellular respiration. CO_2, a metabolic waste, is exhaled. (b) ATP generated in cellular respiration is used in muscle contraction and many other cellular activities.

The rest of this chapter describes how cells use the potential energy in food to generate ATP. Like photosynthesis, the journey entails several overlapping metabolic pathways and many different chemicals. But if we consider energy release in major stages, the logic emerges.

6.1 Mastering Concepts

1. Why do all organisms need ATP?
2. What is the overall equation for cellular respiration?
3. How is cellular respiration related to breathing?
4. How can plants release more O_2 in photosynthesis than they consume in respiration?

6.2 Cellular Respiration Includes Three Main Processes

The chemical reaction that generates ATP is straightforward: an enzyme tacks a phosphate group onto ADP, yielding ATP. As described in chapter 4, however, ATP synthesis requires an input of energy. The metabolic pathways of respiration harvest potential energy from food molecules and use it to make ATP. This section briefly introduces these pathways; later sections explain them in more detail.

Like photosynthesis, respiration is an oxidation–reduction reaction. The pathways of aerobic respiration oxidize (remove electrons from) glucose and reduce (add electrons to) O_2. Because of oxygen's strong attraction for electrons, this reaction is "easy," like pushing a bike downhill. It therefore releases energy, which the cell traps in the bonds of ATP. ▸ redox reactions, p. 71

This reaction does not happen all at once. If a cell released all the potential energy in glucose's chemical bonds in one uncontrolled step, the sudden release of heat would destroy the cell; in effect, it would act like a tiny bomb. Rather, the chemical bonds and atoms in glucose are rearranged one step at a time, releasing a tiny bit of energy with each transformation. Some of this energy is lost as heat, but much of it is stored in the chemical bonds of ATP.

Biologists organize the intricate biochemical pathways of respiration into three main groups: glycolysis, the Krebs cycle, and electron transport (figure 6.2). In **glycolysis,** glucose splits into two three-carbon molecules of **pyruvate.** This process harvests energy in two forms. First, some of the electrons from glucose are transferred to an electron carrier molecule called **NADH**. Second, glycolysis generates two molecules of ATP.

Additional reactions, including the **Krebs cycle,** oxidize the pyruvate and release CO_2. Enzymes rearrange atoms and bonds in ways that transfer the pyruvate's potential energy and electrons to ATP, NADH, and another electron carrier molecule—**$FADH_2$**.

By the time the Krebs cycle is complete, the carbon atoms that made up the glucose are gone—liberated as CO_2. The cell has generated a few molecules of ATP, but most of the potential energy from glucose now lingers in the high-energy electron carriers, NADH and $FADH_2$. The cell uses them to generate more ATP.

The **electron transport chain** transfers energy-rich electrons from NADH and $FADH_2$ through a series of membrane proteins. As electrons pass from carrier to carrier in the electron transport chain, the energy is used to create a gradient of hydrogen ions. (Recall from chapter 2 that a hydrogen ion is simply a hydrogen atom stripped of its electron, leaving just a proton.) The mitochondrion uses the potential energy stored in this proton gradient to generate ATP.

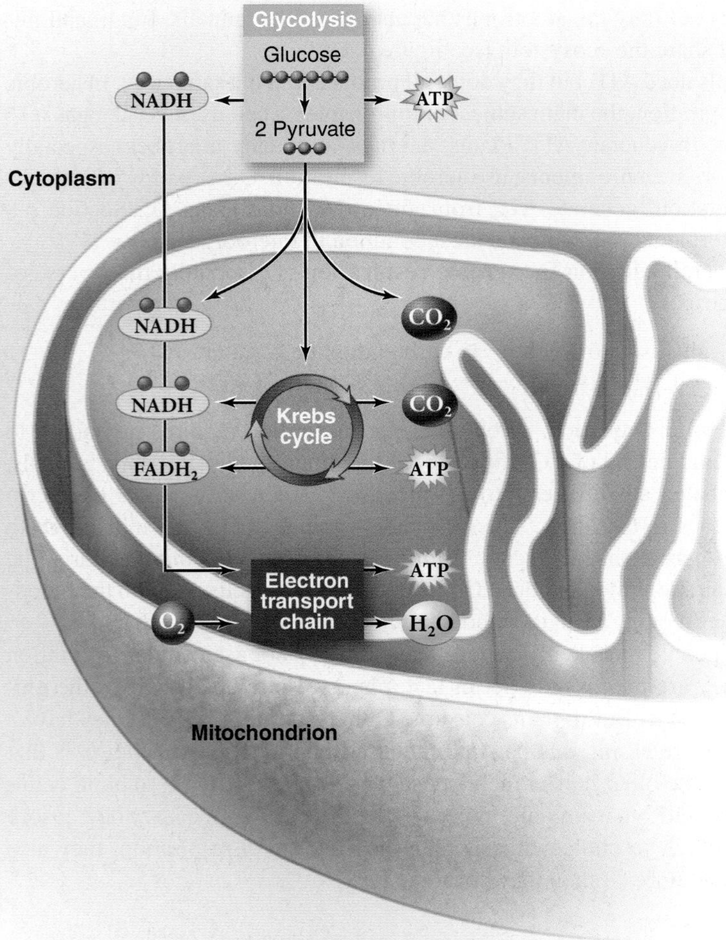

Figure 6.2 Overview of Aerobic Cellular Respiration. Glucose is broken down to carbon dioxide in three main stages: glycolysis, the Krebs cycle, and the electron transport chain. Along the way, energy is harvested as ATP. Except for glycolysis, these reactions occur inside the mitochondria of eukaryotic cells.

An enzyme called **ATP synthase** forms a channel in the membrane, releasing the protons and using their potential energy to add phosphate to ADP. (As described in section 5.5, the same enzyme generates ATP in the light reactions of photosynthesis.) In the meantime, the "spent" electrons are transferred to O_2, generating water as a waste product.

6.2 Mastering Concepts

1. Why do the reactions of respiration occur step-by-step instead of all at once?
2. What occurs in each of the three stages of cellular respiration?

6.3 In Eukaryotic Cells, Mitochondria Produce Most ATP

Glycolysis always occurs in the cytoplasm, but the location of the other two pathways depends on the cell type. In bacteria and archaea, the enzymes of the Krebs cycle are in the cytoplasm, and electron transport proteins are embedded in the cell membrane. The eukaryotic cells of protists, plants, fungi, and animals, however, contain organelles called **mitochondria** that house the other reactions of cellular respiration.

A mitochondrion consists of an outer membrane and a highly folded inner membrane (figure 6.3). **Cristae** are folds that greatly increase the surface area of the inner membrane. The **intermembrane compartment** is the area between the two membranes, and the mitochondrial **matrix** is the fluid enclosed within the inner membrane.

In a eukaryotic cell, the two pyruvate molecules produced in glycolysis cross both of the mitochondrial membranes and move into the matrix. Here, enzymes cleave pyruvate and carry out the Krebs cycle. Then, $FADH_2$ and NADH from glycolysis and the Krebs cycle move to the inner mitochondrial membrane, which is studded with electron transport proteins and ATP synthase. The inner membrane's cristae provide tremendous surface area on which the reactions of the electron transport chain occur.

Electron transport chains and ATP synthase also occur in the thylakoid membranes of chloroplasts, which generate ATP in the light reactions of photosynthesis (see chapter 5). Similar enzymes operate in the cell membranes of respiring bacteria and archaea, making ATP synthase one of the most highly conserved proteins over evolutionary time.

Mitochondria and chloroplasts also share another similarity: Both types of organelles contain DNA and ribosomes. Mitochondrial DNA encodes ATP synthase and most of the proteins of the electron transport chain. Not surprisingly, a person with abnormal versions of these genes may be very ill or even die. The worst of the mitochondrial diseases affect the muscular and nervous systems. Muscle and nerve cells are especially energy-hungry; each may contain as many as 10,000 mitochondria.

6.3 Mastering Concepts

1. What are the parts of a mitochondrion?
2. Which respiratory reactions occur in each part of the mitochondrion?

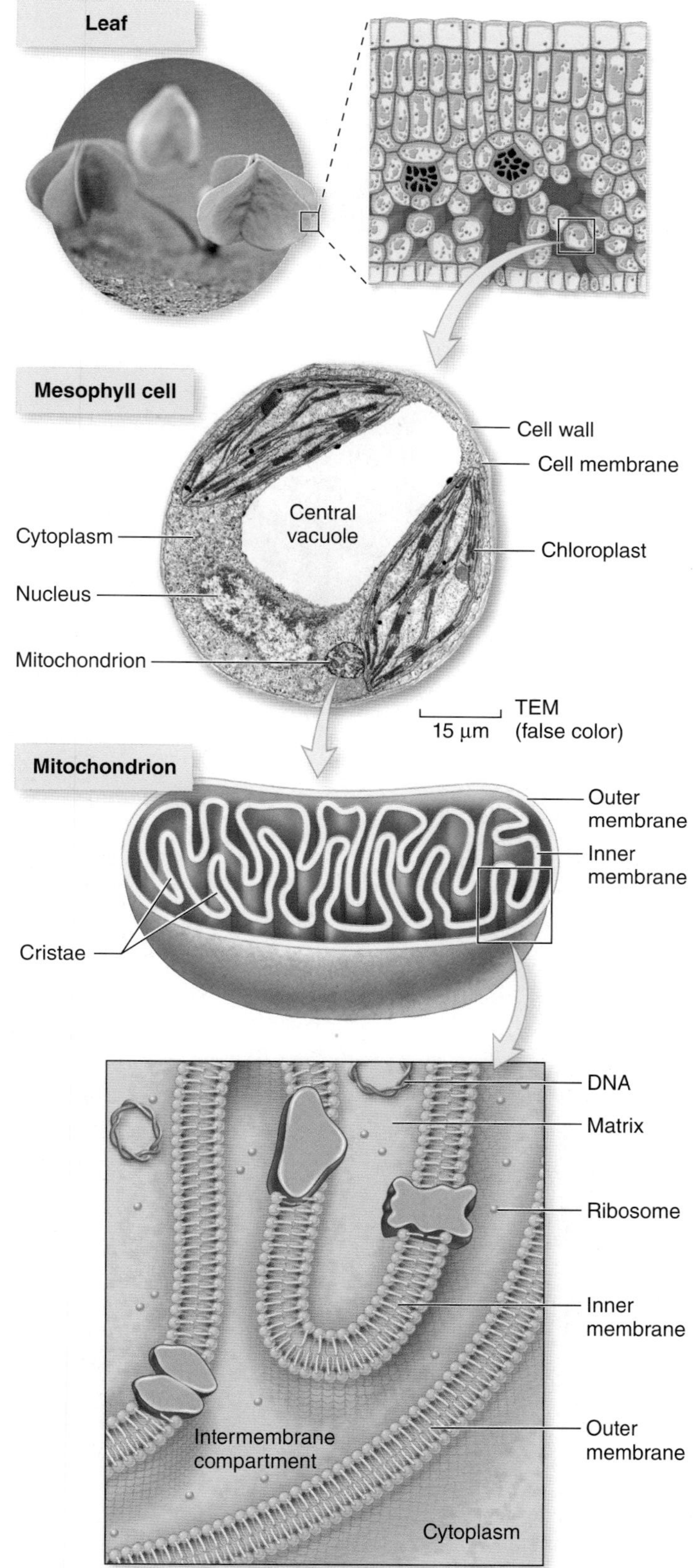

Figure 6.3 Anatomy of a Mitochondrion. Eukaryotic cells, such as the ones that make up a plant's leaves, contain mitochondria that provide most of the cell's ATP. Each mitochondrion includes two membranes. The inner membrane encloses fluid called the matrix, and the space between the inner and outer membranes is the intermembrane compartment.

6.4 Glycolysis Breaks Down Glucose to Pyruvate

Glycolysis is a more-or-less universal metabolic pathway that splits glucose into two three-carbon pyruvate molecules. The name of the pathway reflects its function: *glyco-* means sugar, and *-lysis* means to break.

The entire process of glycolysis requires many steps, all of which occur in the cell's cytoplasm. Figure 6.4 shows a simplified version, with an emphasis on the major steps. Note that none of the steps requires O_2, so cells can use glycolysis in both oxygen-rich and oxygen-free environments.

The first reactions of glycolysis use ATP to "activate" glucose. In steps 1 and 2, for example, ATP donates a phosphate group to the sugar. The two

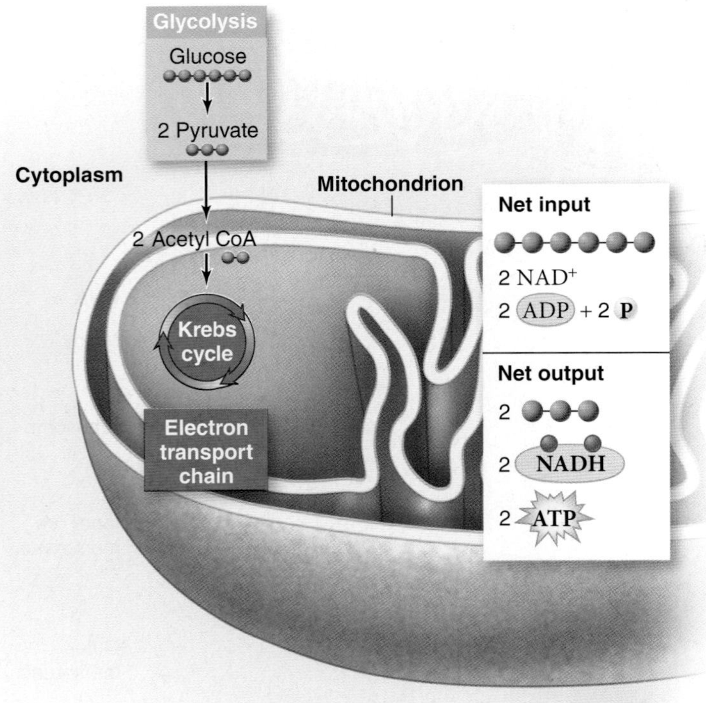

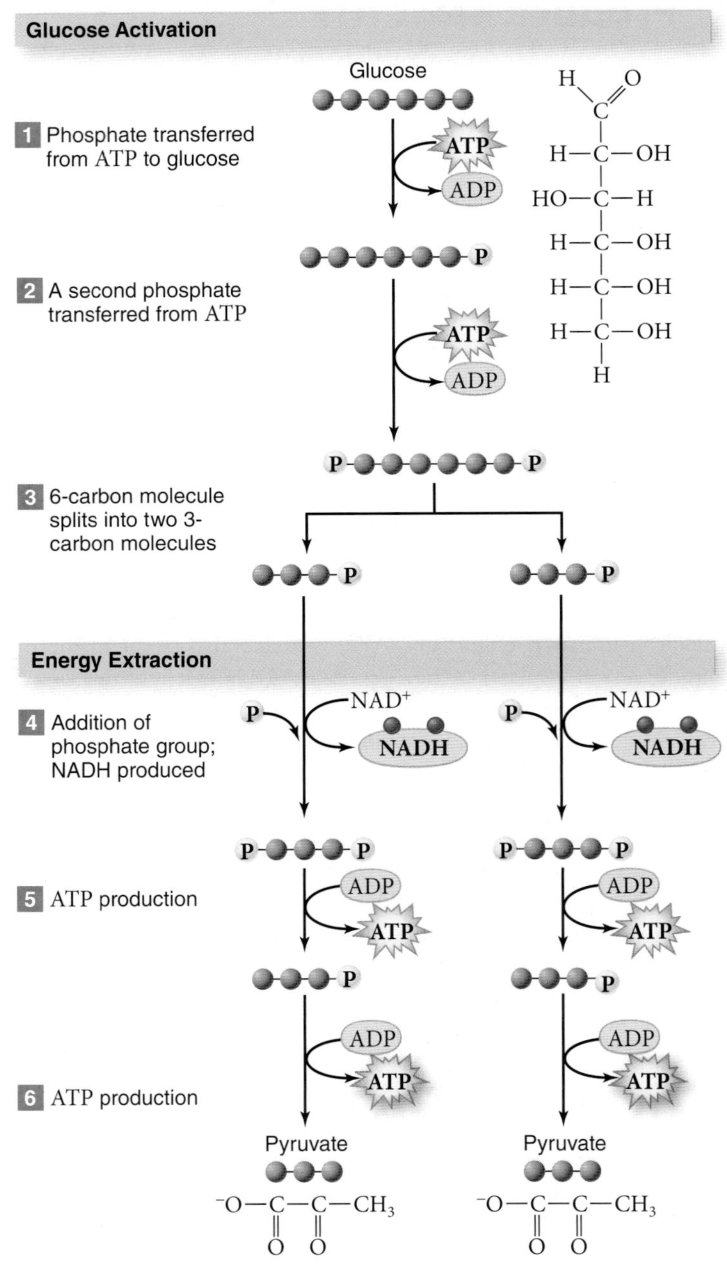

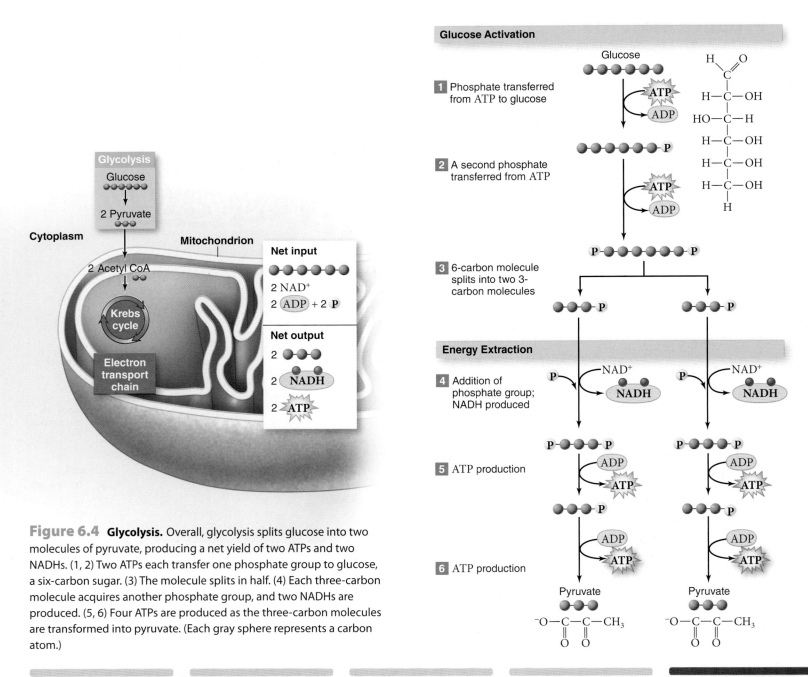

Figure 6.4 Glycolysis. Overall, glycolysis splits glucose into two molecules of pyruvate, producing a net yield of two ATPs and two NADHs. (1, 2) Two ATPs each transfer one phosphate group to glucose, a six-carbon sugar. (3) The molecule splits in half. (4) Each three-carbon molecule acquires another phosphate group, and two NADHs are produced. (5, 6) Four ATPs are produced as the three-carbon molecules are transformed into pyruvate. (Each gray sphere represents a carbon atom.)

high-energy phosphate groups redistribute energy in the molecule and cause it to split in half in step 3. The rest of the pathway then extracts some of the potential energy in the resulting pair of three-carbon molecules. In step 4, each of the molecules acquires another phosphate group and stores some energy in two molecules of the electron carrier, NADH. The four phosphate groups are transferred to ADP in steps 5 and 6. The overall pathway therefore regains the two ATP molecules invested earlier and produces two more. The net gain is two NADHs and two ATPs per molecule of glucose, plus the two pyruvate molecules that emerge from the last step of glycolysis.

Glucose contains considerable bond energy, but the reactions of glycolysis capture only a small portion of it as ATP and NADH. Cells that carry out fermentation, such as yeasts that produce wine and beer, survive on this paltry ATP yield (see section 6.8). Yet the two pyruvate molecules still retain most of the potential energy of the original glucose molecule. As you will see, the pathways of aerobic respiration extract much more of that energy.

6.4 Mastering Concepts

1. What are the starting materials and end products of glycolysis?
2. What is the net gain of ATP and NADH for each glucose molecule undergoing glycolysis?

6.5 Aerobic Respiration Yields Much More ATP than Glycolysis Alone

Overall, aerobic cellular respiration taps much of the potential energy remaining in the pyruvate molecules that emerge from the pathways of glycolysis. The Krebs cycle and electron transport chain are the key ATP-generating processes. This section explains how they work.

A. Pyruvate Is Oxidized to Acetyl CoA

After glycolysis, pyruvate moves into the mitochondrial matrix, but it is not directly used in the Krebs cycle. Instead, a preliminary chemical reaction further oxidizes each pyruvate molecule (figure 6.5). First, a molecule of CO_2 is

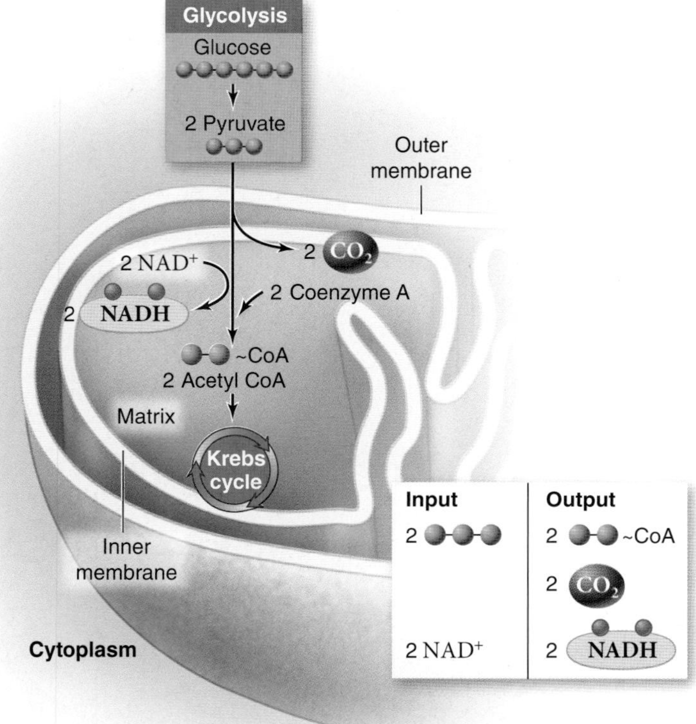

Figure 6.5 Transition to the Mitochondria. After pyruvate moves into a mitochondrion, it is oxidized to form CO_2, a two-carbon acetyl group, and NADH. The acetyl group joins with coenzyme A to form acetyl CoA. For every glucose molecule that entered glycolysis, two acetyl CoA molecules are now ready to enter the Krebs cycle.

Why We Care | Some Poisons Inhibit Respiration

Many toxic chemicals kill by blocking one or more reactions in respiration. Here are a few examples:

Krebs cycle inhibitor:

- Arsenic binds to part of a molecule needed for the formation of acetyl CoA. It therefore blocks the Krebs cycle.

Electron transport inhibitors:

- Some mercury compounds stop an oxidation–reduction reaction early in the electron transport chain.
- Cyanide blocks the final transfer of the electrons to O_2. When proteins in the electron transport chain have no place to "dump" their electrons, the process grinds to a halt.
- Carbon monoxide (CO) blocks electron transport at the same point as cyanide.

Proton gradient inhibitor:

- A poison called DNP makes the inner mitochondrial membrane permeable to protons, blocking formation of the proton gradient necessary to drive ATP synthesis.

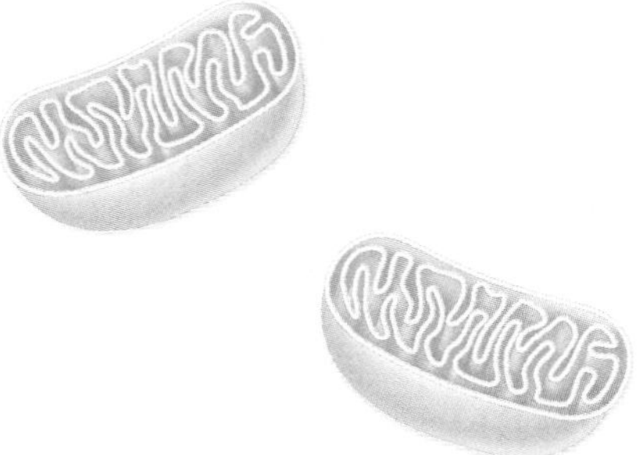

removed, and NAD^+ is reduced to NADH. The remaining two-carbon molecule, called an acetyl group, is transferred to a molecule called coenzyme A to form acetyl coenzyme A (abbreviated acetyl CoA). **Acetyl CoA** is the compound that enters the Krebs cycle.

B. The Krebs Cycle Produces ATP and Electron Carriers

The Krebs cycle completes the oxidation of each acetyl group, releasing CO_2 along the way (figure 6.6). The cycle begins when acetyl CoA sheds the coenzyme and combines with a four-carbon molecule (step 1). The resulting six-carbon molecule is called citrate, which is why the Krebs cycle is also known as the citric acid cycle.

The remaining steps in the Krebs cycle rearrange and oxidize citrate through several intermediates. As the molecules rearrange, two carbon atoms are released as CO_2 (steps 2 and 3). In addition, some of the transformations transfer electrons to NADH and $FADH_2$ (steps 2, 3, 5, and 6); others produce ATP (step 4). Eventually, the molecules in the Krebs cycle re-create the original four-carbon acceptor molecule. The cycle can now repeat.

The Krebs cycle turns twice per glucose molecule. Thus, the combined net output to this point (glycolysis, acetyl CoA formation, and the Krebs cycle) is four ATP molecules, 10 NADH molecules, two $FADH_2$ molecules, and six

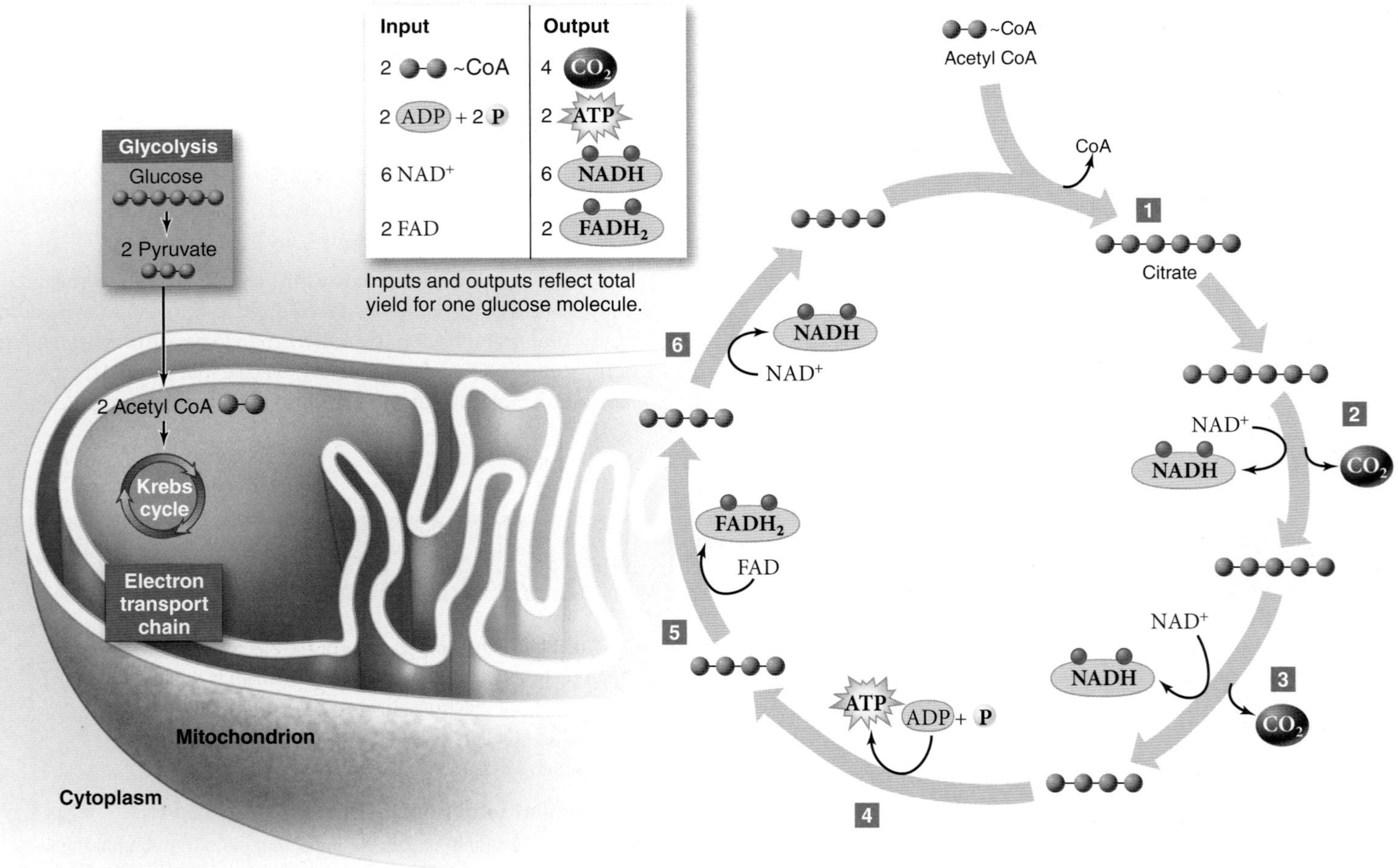

Input	Output
2 ~CoA	4 CO_2
2 ADP + 2 P	2 ATP
6 NAD^+	6 NADH
2 FAD	2 $FADH_2$

Inputs and outputs reflect total yield for one glucose molecule.

Figure 6.6 Krebs Cycle. In the mitochondrial matrix, (1) acetyl CoA enters the Krebs cycle and (2, 3) is oxidized to two molecules of CO_2. (4, 5, 6) In the rest of the Krebs cycle, potential energy is trapped as ATP, NADH, and $FADH_2$.

molecules of CO_2. Of course, this process does not capture all of the potential energy in glucose; some is lost as heat.

Besides continuing the breakdown of glucose, the Krebs cycle also has another function not directly related to respiration. The cell uses intermediate compounds formed in the Krebs cycle to manufacture other organic molecules, such as amino acids and fats. Section 6.7 explains that the reverse process also occurs; amino acids and fats can enter the Krebs cycle to generate energy from food sources other than carbohydrates.

C. The Electron Transport Chain Drives ATP Formation

What happens to the products generated in glycolysis, acetyl CoA formation, and the Krebs cycle? The cell disposes of the waste CO_2 and uses the ATP to fuel essential processes. The mitochondrion uses the potential energy in the electron carriers (NADH and $FADH_2$) to generate ATP, courtesy of an electron transport chain in the inner mitochondrial membrane.

The electron transport chain uses the energy from NADH and $FADH_2$ in incremental steps (figure 6.7). The first proteins in the chain accept electrons from NADH and $FADH_2$ (step 1). Subsequent proteins use some of the potential energy from the electrons to pump hydrogen ions (protons, or H^+) from the inner mitochondrial matrix into the intermembrane compartment (step 2). As the electrons continue along the chain, the process repeats. The final electron acceptor is O_2, which combines with hydrogen ions to form water (step 3). Breathing provides the O_2.

The electron transport chain therefore uses the energy in NADH and $FADH_2$ to establish a proton gradient across the inner mitochondrial membrane. As explained in chapter 4, a gradient represents a form of potential energy. The mitochondrion harvests this energy as ATP in the final stage of cellular respiration, with the help of the ATP synthase enzyme (figure 6.7, step 4). Protons

Burning Questions

How do diet pills work?

Ads for diet pills are everywhere. A few are for prescription drugs that the U.S. Food and Drug Administration (FDA) has approved as safe and effective. Others are for dietary supplements that are not subject to FDA approval at all. How do these products work?

All three prescription diet pills work by reducing calorie intake. Sibutramine (Meridia) and phentermine (Adipex-P) suppress a person's appetite. Orlistat (sold as Xenical or Alli), on the other hand, blocks the enzyme that digests fat in the small intestine. This drug therefore reduces the body's absorption of fat molecules.

Dietary supplements greatly outnumber prescription weight-loss drugs. Ads for "natural" products such as hoodia, green tea extract, and fucoxanthin make extraordinary promises of rapid, effortless weight loss, but the claims remain largely untested in scientific studies. The mechanism by which they work (if they work at all) usually remains unclear. Moreover, some dietary supplements have serious side effects. For example, many studies linked ephedra to fatal seizures, strokes, and heart attacks; the FDA subsequently banned the sale of ephedra in the United States. An herb called bitter orange has taken its place in many "ephedra-free" weight-loss aids. But bitter orange has side effects that are similar to ephedra's, and its safety remains unknown.

Submit your burning question to:
marielle_hoefnagels@mcgraw-hill.com

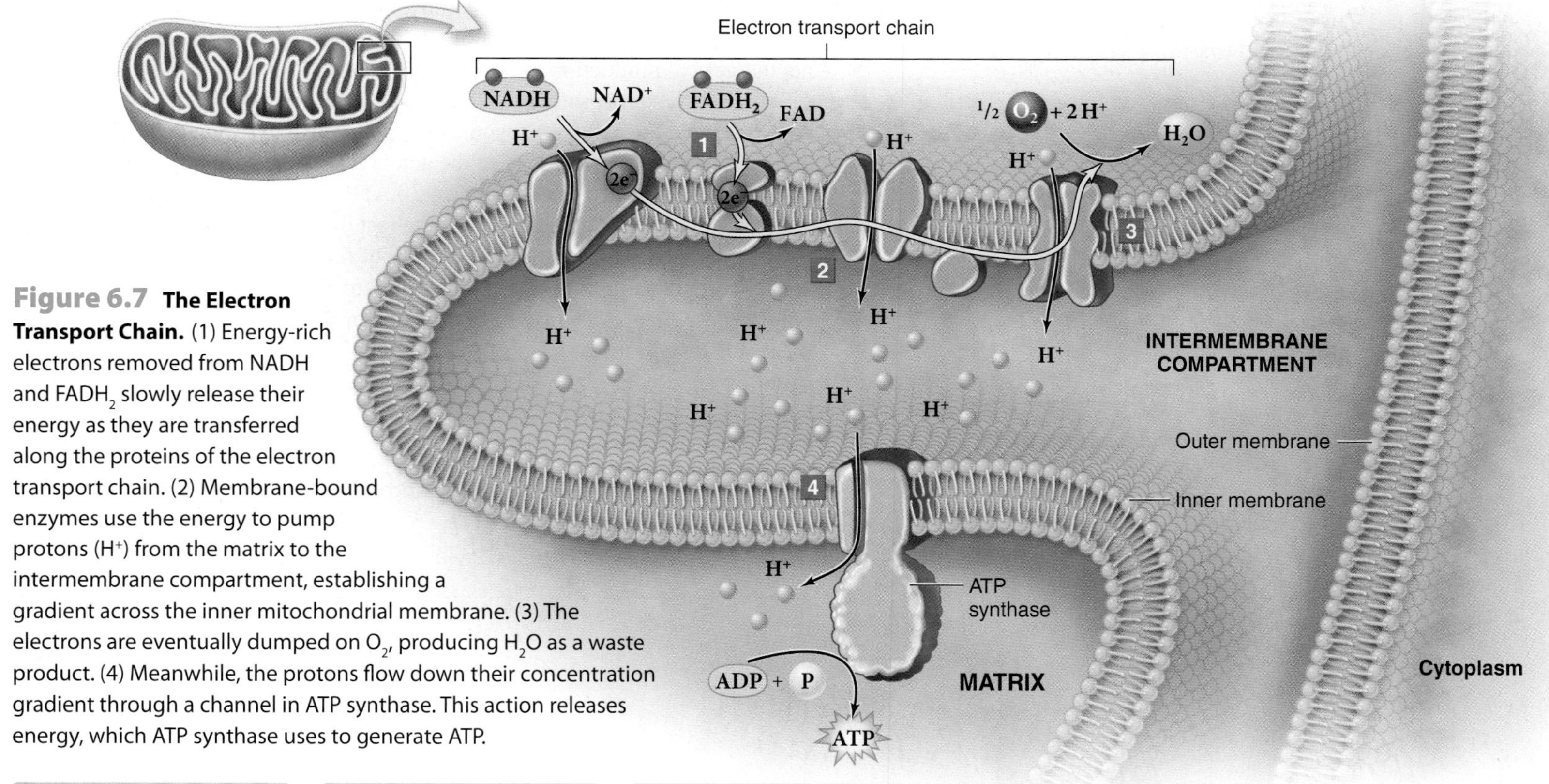

Figure 6.7 The Electron Transport Chain. (1) Energy-rich electrons removed from NADH and $FADH_2$ slowly release their energy as they are transferred along the proteins of the electron transport chain. (2) Membrane-bound enzymes use the energy to pump protons (H^+) from the matrix to the intermembrane compartment, establishing a gradient across the inner mitochondrial membrane. (3) The electrons are eventually dumped on O_2, producing H_2O as a waste product. (4) Meanwhile, the protons flow down their concentration gradient through a channel in ATP synthase. This action releases energy, which ATP synthase uses to generate ATP.

move down their gradient through ATP synthase channels back into the matrix, and a phosphate group is linked to ADP. The ATP synthase enzyme therefore captures the potential energy of the proton gradient and saves it in a form the cell can use: ATP.

6.5 Mastering Concepts

1. Pyruvate contains three carbon atoms; an acetyl group has only two. What happens to the other carbon atom?
2. How does the Krebs cycle generate CO_2, ATP, NADH, and $FADH_2$?
3. How do NADH and $FADH_2$ power ATP formation?
4. What is the role of O_2 in the electron transport chain?

6.6 How Many ATPs Can One Glucose Molecule Yield?

To estimate the yield of ATP produced from every glucose molecule that enters aerobic cellular respiration, we can add the maximum number of ATPs generated in glycolysis, the Krebs cycle, and the electron transport chain (figure 6.8).

Glycolysis and the Krebs cycle each directly produce two ATPs per molecule of glucose. In addition, each glucose yields two NADH molecules from glycolysis, two NADHs from acetyl CoA production, and six NADHs and two $FADH_2$s from two turns of the Krebs cycle.

In theory, the ATP yield from electron transport is three ATPs per NADH and two ATPs per $FADH_2$. The 10 NADHs from glycolysis and the Krebs cycle therefore yield up to 30 ATPs; the two $FADH_2$s yield four more. Add the four ATPs from glycolysis and the Krebs cycle, and the total is 38 ATPs per glucose. However, NADH from glycolysis must be moved into the mitochondrion by active transport, usually at a cost of one ATP for each NADH. This reduces the net theoretical production of ATPs to 36.

In reality, some protons leak across the inner mitochondrial membrane on their own, and the cell spends some energy to move pyruvate and ADP into the matrix. These "expenses" reduce the actual ATP yield to about 30 per glucose. The number of kilocalories stored in 30 ATPs is about 32% of the total kilocalories stored in the glucose bonds; the rest of the potential energy in glucose is lost as heat. This may seem wasteful, but for a biological process, it is reasonably efficient. To put this energy yield into perspective, an automobile uses only about 20% to 25% of the energy contained in gasoline's chemical bonds; the rest is lost as heat.

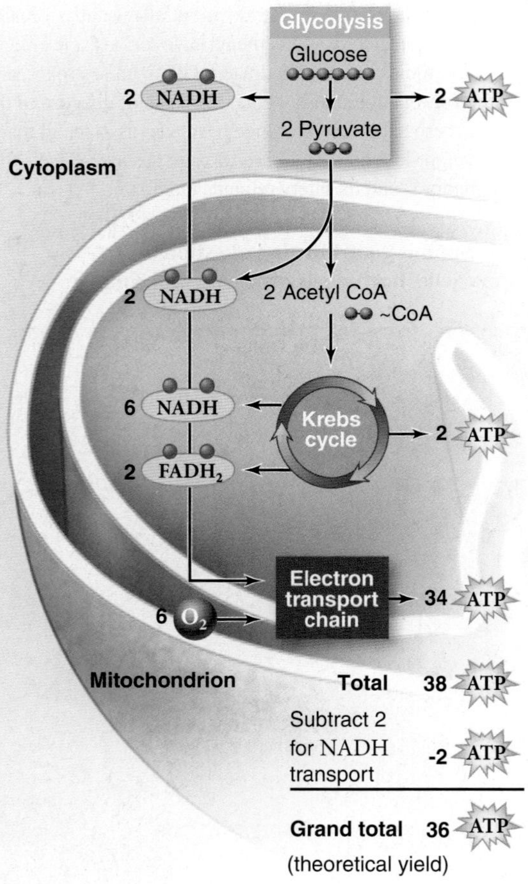

Figure 6.8 Energy Yield of Respiration. Breaking down glucose to carbon dioxide can theoretically yield as many as 36 ATPs, mostly from the electron transport chain.

6.6 Mastering Concepts

1. Explain how to arrive at the estimate that each glucose molecule theoretically yields 36 ATPs.
2. How does the actual ATP yield compare to the theoretical yield?

6.7 Other Food Molecules Enter the Energy-Extracting Pathways

So far we have focused on the complete oxidation of glucose. But food also includes starch, proteins, and lipids that contribute calories to the diet. These molecules also enter the energy pathways (figure 6.9).

The digestion of starch from potatoes, wheat, and other carbohydrate-rich food begins in the mouth and continues in the small intestine. Enzymes snip the long starch chains into individual glucose monomers, which generate ATP as described in this chapter. Another polysaccharide, glycogen, follows essentially the same path as starch. ▸ carbohydrates, p. 34

Proteins are digested into monomers called amino acids. The cell does not use most of these amino acids to produce ATP. Instead, most of them are incorporated into new proteins. When an organism depletes its immediate carbohydrate supplies, however, cells may use amino acids as an energy source. First, ammonia (NH_3) is stripped from the amino acid. The remainder of each molecule enters the energy pathways as pyruvate, acetyl CoA, or an intermediate of the Krebs cycle, depending on the amino acid. ▸ amino acids, p. 39

Meanwhile, enzymes in the small intestine digest fat molecules into glycerol and fatty acids, which enter the bloodstream and move into the body's cells. Enzymes convert the glycerol to pyruvate, which then proceeds through the rest of cellular respiration as though it came directly from glucose. The fatty acids enter the mitochondria, where they are cut into many two-carbon pieces that are released as acetyl CoA. From here, the pathways continue as they would for glucose. ▸ lipids, p. 35

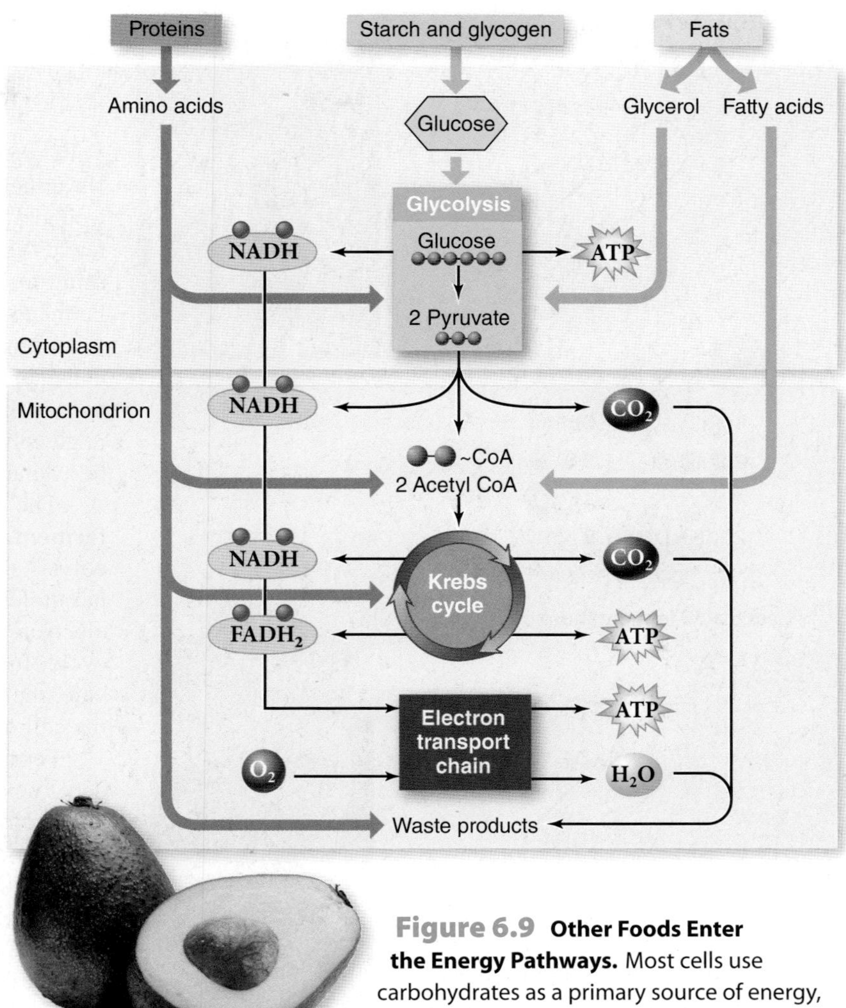

Figure 6.9 Other Foods Enter the Energy Pathways. Most cells use carbohydrates as a primary source of energy, but cells can also use amino acids and lipids to generate ATP.

Fats contain more calories per gram than any other food molecule. A fat molecule has three fatty acids, each of which may contain 20 or more carbon atoms. A single fat molecule therefore yields about 30 two-carbon acetyl CoA groups for the Krebs cycle. Conversely, the body can also store excess energy from either carbohydrates or fat by doing the reverse: diverting acetyl CoA away from the Krebs cycle and using the two-carbon fragments to build fat molecules. These lipids are stored in fat tissue that the body can use for energy if food becomes scarce.

6.7 Mastering Concepts

1. At which points do digested polysaccharides, proteins, and fats enter the energy pathways?
2. How does the body store extra calories as fat?

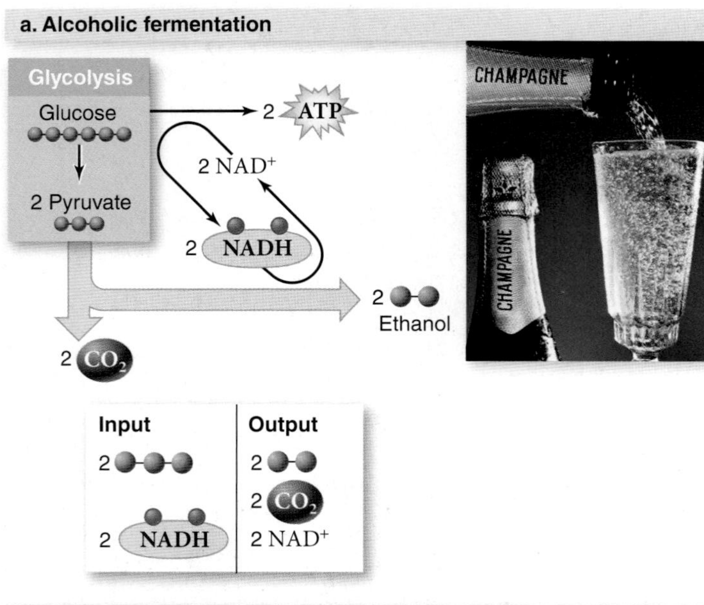

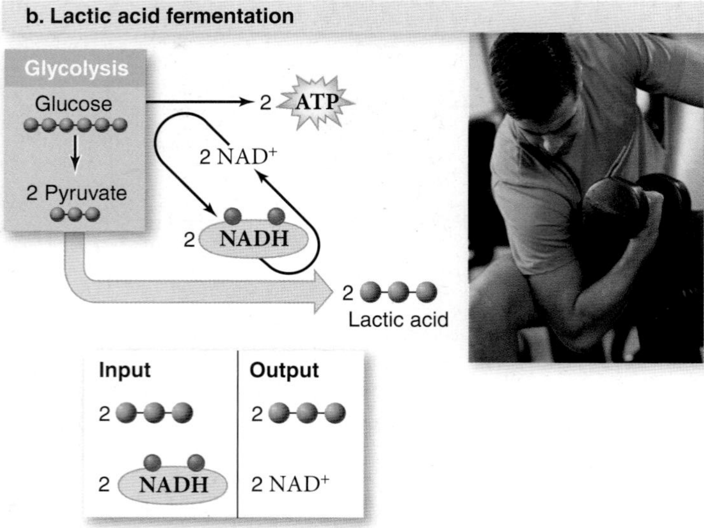

Figure 6.10 Fermentation. In fermentation, ATP comes only from glycolysis. (a) Yeasts produce ethanol and carbon dioxide by alcoholic fermentation; one possible product is champagne. (b) Lactic acid fermentation occurs in some bacteria and, occasionally, in mammalian muscle cells.

Figure It Out

Compare the number of molecules of ATP generated from 100 glucose molecules undergoing aerobic respiration versus fermentation.

Answer: 3600 (theoretical yield) for aerobic respiration; 200 for fermentation.

6.8 Fermentation Generates ATP Only in Glycolysis

Most organisms on Earth, including humans, use aerobic cellular respiration. Nevertheless, life thrives without O_2 in waterlogged soils, deep puncture wounds, sewage treatment plants, and your own digestive tract, to name just a few places. In the absence of O_2, the microbes in these habitats generate ATP using metabolic pathways that are anaerobic (meaning they do not use O_2). Fermentation is one such pathway.

Before studying the details of fermentation, consider for a moment an underappreciated role of the electron transport chain in respiration. The proteins in the electron transport chain accept electrons from the NADH produced in glycolysis and the Krebs cycle. This action regenerates the NAD^+ that must be available for both of these processes to continue.

The fermentation pathway regenerates NAD^+ in another way. In **fermentation,** electrons from NADH are used to reduce pyruvate. Glycolysis still yields two ATPs, two NADHs, and two molecules of pyruvate per molecule of glucose. But the NADH does not donate its electrons to an electron transport chain, nor is the pyruvate further oxidized in the Krebs cycle. Instead, when the electrons from NADH are "dumped" onto pyruvate, the product is an organic molecule such as an alcohol or an acid that the cell discards as waste.

Fermentation regenerates NAD^+ so that glycolysis can continue, but it produces no additional ATP. This pathway is therefore far less efficient than respiration. Not surprisingly, fermentation is most common among microorganisms that live in sugar-rich environments where food is essentially unlimited. Most multicellular organisms, however, require too much energy to rely on fermentation exclusively.

Of the many fermentation pathways that exist, one of the most familiar produces ethanol (a two-carbon alcohol). In **alcoholic fermentation,** pyruvate is converted to ethanol and CO_2 (figure 6.10a), regenerating NAD^+ along the way. Alcoholic fermentation produces the airy texture of breads, along with beverages such as wine, beer, cider, and champagne.

The products of **lactic acid fermentation,** in contrast, are NAD^+ and the three-carbon compound lactic acid (figure 6.10b). The bacterium *Lactobacillus,* for example, ferments the lactose in milk, producing lactic acid that gives yogurt its sour taste.

The same pathway also occurs in human muscle cells. During vigorous exercise, muscles consume their available oxygen supply. In this "oxygen debt" condition, the muscle cells can acquire ATP only from glycolysis. The cells use lactic acid fermentation to generate NAD^+ so that glycolysis can continue. If too much lactic acid accumulates, however, the muscle may become fatigued and begin to cramp. When the circulatory system catches up with the muscles' demand and O_2 is once again present, liver cells convert lactic acid back to pyruvate. Mitochondria then process the pyruvate as usual, by aerobic respiration.

6.8 Mastering Concepts

1. How many ATP molecules per glucose does fermentation produce?
2. What are two examples of fermentation pathways?

Investigating Life

6.9 Plants' "Alternative" Lifestyles Yield Hot Sex

Think of an organism that feels warm. Did you think of yourself? A puppy? Your cat? Chances are you did not picture a plant. Yet some plants, including one called *Philodendron solimoesense*, do warm their flowers to several degrees above ambient temperature (figure 6.11).

Philodendron flowers generate heat with a metabolic pathway involving the electron transport chain. As described in section 6.5, electrons from NADH and $FADH_2$ are normally passed along a series of proteins embedded in the inner mitochondrial membrane. The last protein in the electron transport chain dumps the electrons on O_2, yielding water as a waste product.

Plants have another pathway, dubbed "alternative oxidase," that diverts electrons from the electron transport chain. NADH and $FADH_2$ still donate electrons to a protein in the chain, but that electron acceptor transfers them immediately to O_2 instead of to the next carrier. The alternative oxidase pathway generates heat, but it does not help mitochondria produce ATP.

Figure 6.11 Hot Bloom. The central spike of this *Philodendron solimoesense* flower generates heat.

The Question: What does *Philodendron* gain by warming its flowers? One clue comes from the observation that the plant heats *just* its flowers, not its leaves or roots. Since flowers are reproductive organs, could the hot blooms somehow improve the plant's reproductive success?

The Approach: Australian researcher Roger Seymour and his colleagues wondered whether heat helped the flowers attract pollinators. They did a simple set of experiments to find out. First, they measured the temperature of *Philodendron* flowers and found that the central spike peaked at 40°C, about 15° above ambient temperature.

Next, the researchers turned their attention to beetles that pollinate the flowers. The team measured the amount of CO_2 produced by active and resting beetles at temperatures from 20°C to 35°C. (CO_2 production is an indirect measure of energy use.) Resting beetles emitted approximately the same amount of CO_2 at all temperatures, but active ones (such as those that would visit flowers) produced much less CO_2 at 30°C than they did at 20°C (figure 6.12).

The Conclusion: The pollinating insects save energy by loitering on or near the flowers, energy that they can use to find food or lure mates. The hot flowers—courtesy of the seemingly wasteful alternative oxidase pathway—therefore enhance the reproductive success of both *Philodendron* and the beetles.

Seymour, Roger S., Craig R. White, and Marc Gibernau. November 20, 2003. Heat reward for insect pollinators. *Nature,* vol. 426, pages 243–244.

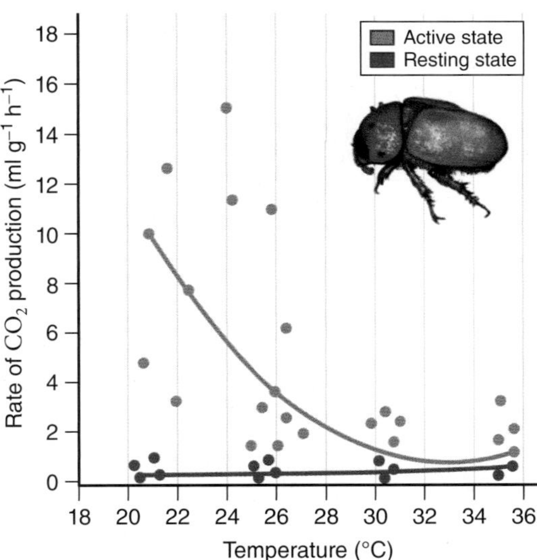

Figure 6.12 Energy Saver. Resting beetles respired at the same rate no matter what the temperature, but active beetles saved energy in warmer surroundings.

6.9 Mastering Concepts

1. What hypothesis were the researchers testing, and what experiment did they design to help them test the hypothesis?
2. Suppose you hold one group of active beetles at 20°C and another group at 30°C. After several hours, you measure how far each animal can fly at 20°C. Which group should fly farther?

Chapter Summary

6.1 Cells Use Energy in Food to Make ATP

- Every cell requires **ATP** to power reactions that require energy input.
- **Aerobic respiration** is a biochemical pathway that extracts energy from glucose in the presence of oxygen.
- The overall reaction for cellular respiration is

$$C_6H_{12}O_6 + 6O_2 \longrightarrow 6CO_2 + 6H_2O + 36ATP$$

- In humans and many other animals, the respiratory system provides the oxygen that aerobic cellular respiration requires.
- Photosynthetic organisms such as plants also use aerobic respiration.

6.2 Cellular Respiration Includes Three Main Processes

- In respiration, electrons stripped from glucose are used to reduce O_2.
- Nearly all cells use **glycolysis** as the first step in harvesting energy from glucose. The **Krebs cycle** and an **electron transport chain** follow.
- The electron transport chain establishes a proton gradient that powers the production of ATP by the enzyme **ATP synthase.**

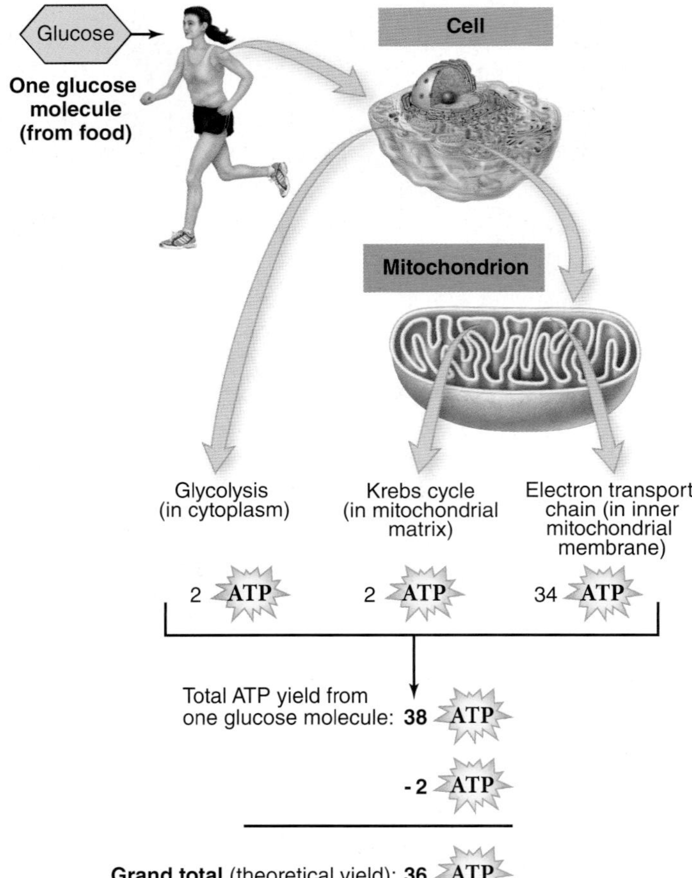

6.3 In Eukaryotic Cells, Mitochondria Produce Most ATP

- In eukaryotes, the Krebs cycle and electron transport chain occur in **mitochondria.**
- The two membranes of a mitochondrion enclose the **matrix. Cristae** are the folds of the inner membrane. The space between the two membranes is the **intermembrane compartment.**

6.4 Glycolysis Breaks Down Glucose to Pyruvate

- In glycolysis, glucose is split into two molecules of **pyruvate.**
- The reactions of glycolysis also produce **NADH** and two ATPs.

6.5 Aerobic Respiration Yields Much More ATP than Glycolysis Alone

A. Pyruvate Is Oxidized to Acetyl CoA

- In the mitochondria, pyruvate is broken down into **acetyl CoA** in a reaction that produces CO_2 and reduces NAD^+ to NADH.

B. The Krebs Cycle Produces ATP and Electron Carriers

- Acetyl CoA enters the Krebs cycle, a series of oxidation–reduction reactions that produces ATP, NADH, **$FADH_2$,** and CO_2.

C. The Electron Transport Chain Drives ATP Formation

- Energy-rich electrons from NADH and $FADH_2$ fuel an electron transport chain, which pumps protons from the matrix into the intermembrane compartment. As protons diffuse back into the matrix through channels in ATP synthase, their potential energy drives the production of ATP.
- Meanwhile, the electrons reduce O_2, producing H_2O as a waste product.

6.6 How Many ATPs Can One Glucose Molecule Yield?

- In the pathways of aerobic respiration, each glucose molecule theoretically yields 36 ATP molecules. The actual yield is about 30 ATP per glucose.

6.7 Other Food Molecules Enter the Energy-Extracting Pathways

- Polysaccharides are digested to glucose, which undergoes respiration.
- Amino acids enter the energy pathways as pyruvate, acetyl CoA, or an intermediate of the Krebs cycle.
- Fatty acids enter as acetyl CoA, and glycerol enters as pyruvate.

6.8 Fermentation Generates ATP Only in Glycolysis

- **Fermentation** pathways oxidize NADH to NAD^+, which is recycled to glycolysis, but these pathways do not produce additional ATP. **Alcoholic fermentation** produces ethanol and carbon dioxide, whereas **lactic acid fermentation** generates lactic acid as a waste.

6.9 Investigating Life: Plants' "Alternative" Lifestyles Yield Hot Sex

- *Philodendron* flowers use a modified respiratory pathway to create a "heat reward" for their insect pollinators.

Multiple Choice Questions

1. Which of the following best describes aerobic respiration?
   a. The production of ATP from glucose in the presence of oxygen
   b. The production of pyruvate in the absence of oxygen
   c. The production of pyruvate using energy from the sun
   d. The production of ATP from glucose in the absence of oxygen
2. Which stage in cellular respiration directly requires the presence of O_2?
   a. Glycolysis
   b. The Krebs cycle
   c. Electron transport
   d. Both a and b are correct.
3. What is the role of ATP synthase?
   a. It uses ATP to make glucose.
   b. It uses a proton gradient to make ATP.
   c. It uses ATP to make a proton gradient.
   d. It synthesizes ATP directly from glucose.

4. How many ATP are made in glycolysis?
   a. Two ATP are made.
   b. Four ATP are made.
   c. Two ATP are made, but two are consumed for a net gain of zero.
   d. Four ATP are made, but two are consumed for a net gain of two.
5. Which of the following molecules has the most potential energy?
   a. Pyruvate
   b. Acetyl CoA
   c. Glucose
   d. CO_2
6. If a substance causes holes to form in the inner mitochondrial membrane, which process would be affected first?
   a. The donation of electrons to O_2
   b. Glycolysis
   c. The production of ATP by ATP synthase
   d. The formation of acetyl CoA
7. The CO_2 produced in respiration comes mainly from
   a. glycolysis.
   b. the Krebs cycle.
   c. the electron transport chain.
   d. All of the above processes generate CO_2.
8. Which of the following molecules can be used to generate ATP energy?
   a. Carbohydrates
   b. Amino acids
   c. Fats
   d. All of the choices are correct.
9. The difference between aerobic respiration and fermentation is
   a. the amount of NADH that is produced in glycolysis.
   b. the electron carriers used in the electron transport chain.
   c. the electron acceptors used in the electron transport chain.
   d. the fate of the NADH and pyruvate produced in glycolysis.
10. Why is it important to regenerate NAD^+ during fermentation?
    a. To help maintain the reactions of glycolysis
    b. To transfer an electron to the electron transport chain
    c. To maintain the levels of pyruvate in a cell
    d. To produce alcohol or lactic acid for the cell

Write It Out

1. How are breathing and cellular respiration similar and different?
2. How are photosynthesis and cellular respiration related?
3. How does aerobic respiration yield so much ATP from each glucose molecule, compared with glycolysis alone?
4. Health-food stores sell a product called "pyruvate plus," which supposedly boosts energy. Why is this product unnecessary? What would be a much less expensive substitute that would accomplish the same thing?
5. At what point does O_2 enter the energy pathways of aerobic respiration? What is the role of O_2? Why does respiration stop if a person cannot breathe? Why would a cell die if it could not make ATP?
6. In a properly functioning mitochondrion, is the pH in the matrix lower than, higher than, or the same as the pH in the intermembrane compartment? If you add one or more poisons described in this chapter's Why We Care box, does your answer change?
7. Edgar is making bread. He begins by adding yeast to sugar and hot water; the mixture soon begins to bubble. What is happening? How would the outcome change if he forgot to add the sugar?
8. A student runs 5 kilometers each afternoon at a slow, leisurely pace. One day, she runs 2 km as fast as she can. Afterward she is winded and feels pain in her chest and leg muscles. She thought she was in great shape! What, in terms of energy metabolism, has she experienced?
9. Explain the fact that species as diverse as humans and yeasts use the same biochemical pathways to extract energy from nutrient molecules.
10. Birds and mammals are endotherms: they maintain a constant internal body temperature. An endotherm that gets too cold will increase its metabolic rate to generate heat. An ectotherm such as a lizard or snake, on the other hand, allows its body temperature to fluctuate with the environment. If you own a pet rat and a pet snake of equal weight, which will require more food and why?

Pull It Together

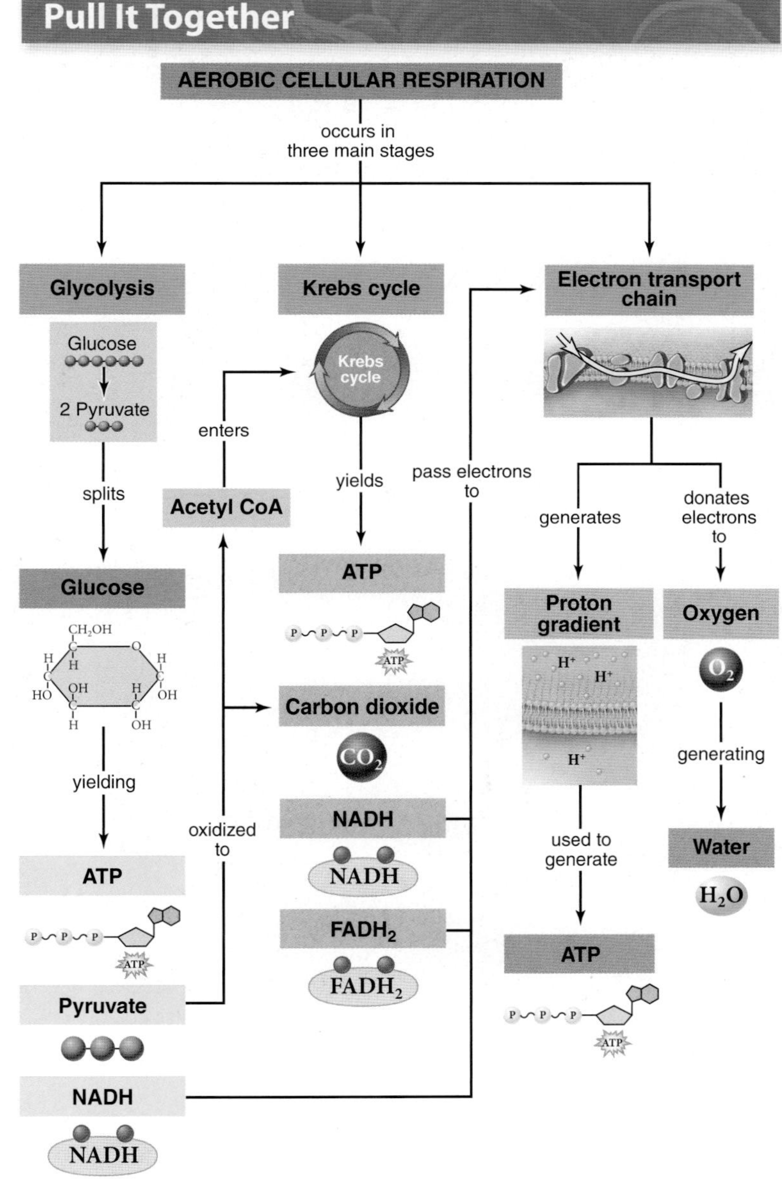

1. Where in the cell does each stage of respiration occur?
2. Where do the O_2 and glucose used in respiration come from?
3. How many ATP and CO_2 molecules are produced at each stage?
4. What happens to the CO_2 and H_2O waste products?
5. What do cells do with the ATP they generate in respiration?
6. Put photosynthesis, fermentation, and ATP synthase on this concept map.

UNIT 2 Biotechnology, Genetics, and Inheritance

7 DNA Structure and Gene Function

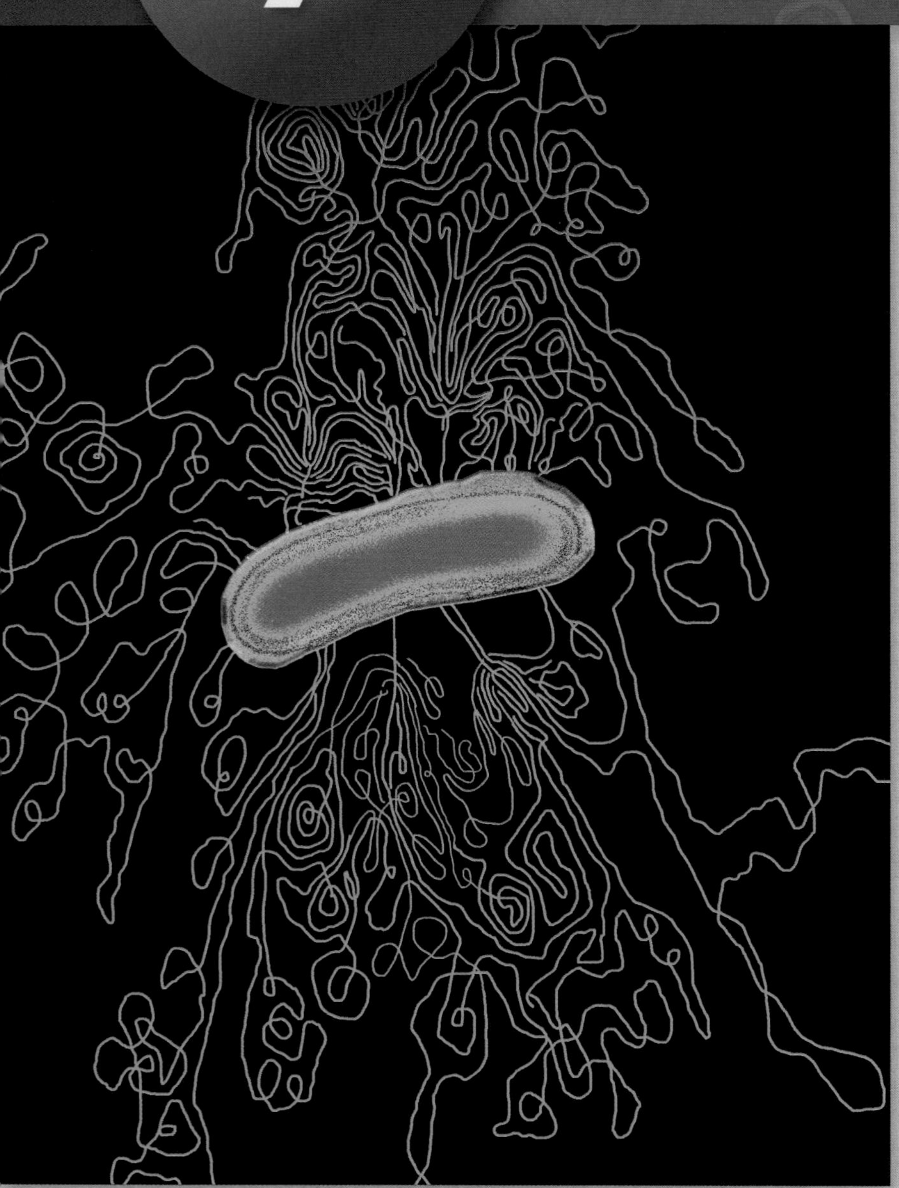

Lots of DNA. Genetic material bursts from this bacterium, illustrating just how much DNA is packed into a single cell.

Learning Outline

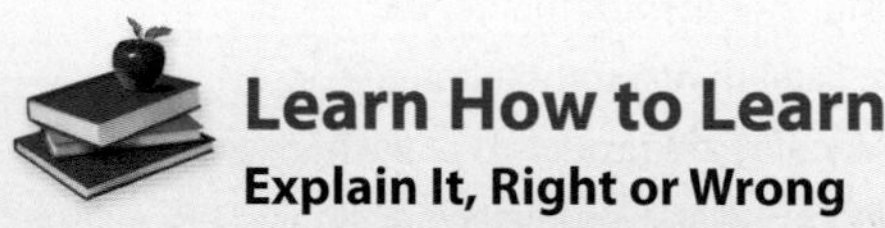

Learn How to Learn
Explain It, Right or Wrong

As you work through the multiple-choice questions at the end of each chapter, make sure you can explain why each correct choice is right. You can also test your understanding by taking the time to explain why each of the other choices is wrong.

What's the Point?

The nucleic acid DNA is one of the most familiar molecules, the subject matter of movies and headlines. Criminal trials hinge on DNA evidence; the idea of human cloning raises questions about the role of DNA in determining who we are; and DNA-based discoveries are yielding new diagnostic tests, medical treatments, and vaccines.

More important than DNA's role in society is its role in life itself. DNA acts as a sort of "library" that stores the information required for cells to function. Every species passes this vital molecule from generation to generation, with major or minor changes along the way. We begin this genetics unit with a look at DNA's structure and its role in the cell.

7.1 DNA Is a Double Helix

Life depends on **DNA,** a molecule with a remarkable function: it stores the information that each cell needs to produce proteins. These instructions make life possible. In fact, before a cell divides, it first makes an exact replica of its DNA. This process, described in chapter 8, copies the precious information that will enable the next generation of cells to live.

Given what we now know about DNA's structure and function, it may seem difficult to believe that scientists once hesitated to accept DNA as the biochemical of heredity. Early biochemists knew more about proteins than about nucleic acids. They also thought that protein, with 20 types of amino acids, could encode many more traits than DNA, which includes just four types of **nucleotides.** Their ideas changed by the 1950s. Biologists used a series of clever experiments to show that DNA—not protein—is the genetic material, even though nobody at that time completely understood the chemical structure of DNA.

The breakthrough came in 1953. U.S. biochemist James Watson and English physicist Francis Crick, working at the Cavendish laboratory in Cambridge in the United Kingdom, used two lines of evidence to deduce DNA's structure. First, Austrian-American biochemist Erwin Chargaff had shown that DNA contains equal amounts of the nucleotide bases adenine (A) and thymine (T) and equal amounts of the bases guanine (G) and cytosine (C). Second, English physicist Maurice Wilkins and chemist Rosalind Franklin used a technique called X-ray diffraction to determine the three-dimensional shape of the molecule. The X-ray diffraction pattern revealed a regularly repeating structure of building blocks.

Watson and Crick combined these clues to build a ball-and-stick model of the DNA molecule. The now familiar double helix included equal amounts of G and C and of A and T, and it had the sleek symmetry revealed in the X-ray diffraction pattern (figure 7.1).

a.

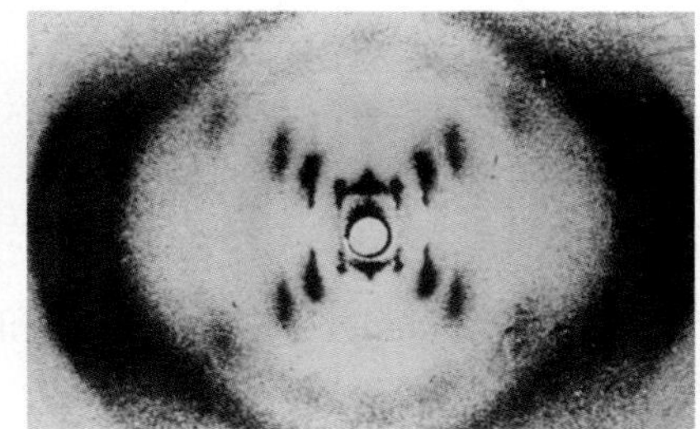

b.

c.

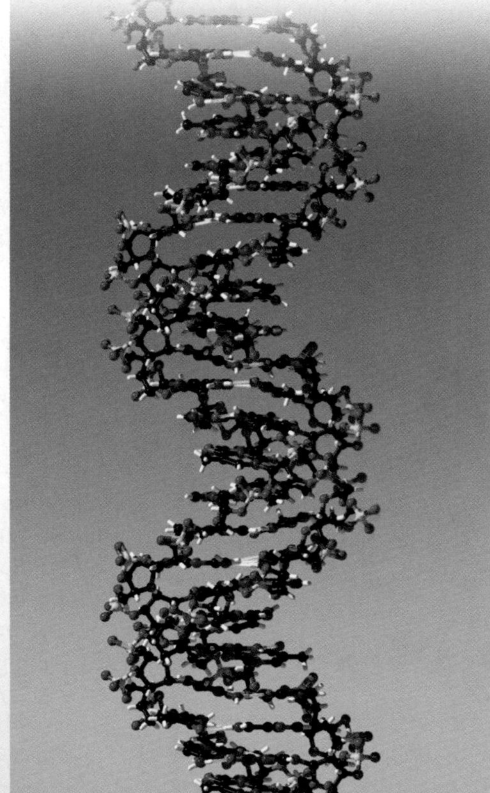

d.

Figure 7.1 Discovery of DNA's Structure. (a) Rosalind Franklin produced (b) high-quality X-ray images of DNA that were crucial in the discovery of DNA's structure. (c) Maurice Wilkins, Francis Crick, and James Watson (first, third, and fifth from the left) shared the Nobel Prize in physiology or medicine for their now-famous discovery. Franklin had already died, and by the rules of the award, she could not be included. (d) Franklin, Wilkins, Watson, and Crick all contributed to the discovery that DNA is a double helix.

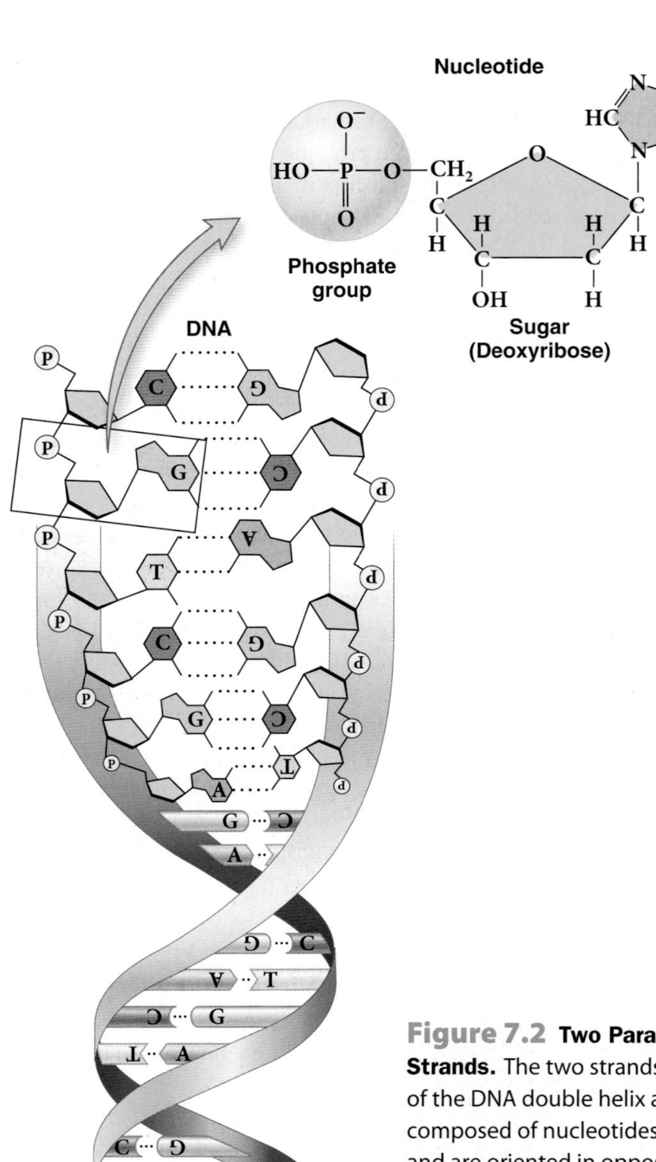

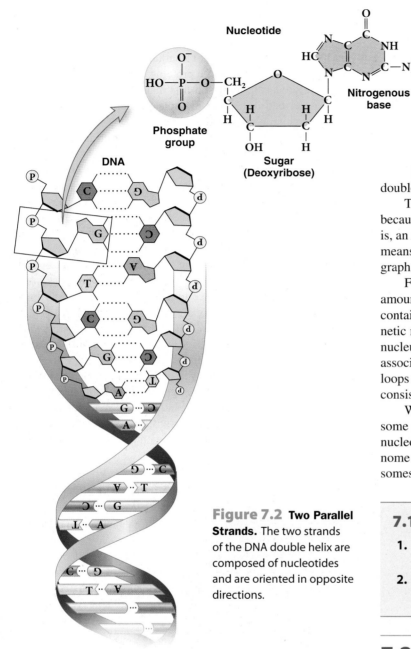

Figure 7.2 Two Parallel Strands. The two strands of the DNA double helix are composed of nucleotides and are oriented in opposite directions.

The DNA double helix resembles a twisted ladder (figure 7.2). The twin rails of the ladder, also called the sugar–phosphate "backbones," are alternating units of deoxyribose and phosphate joined with covalent bonds. The two chains are parallel to each other, but they are oriented in opposite directions, like the northbound and southbound lanes of a highway.

The ladder's rungs are base pairs joined by hydrogen bonds. These base pairs arise from the chemical structures of the nucleotides (see figure 2.23). Adenine and guanine are bases with a double ring structure. Cytosine and thymine each have a single ring. Each A–T pair is the same width as a C–G pair because each includes a double- and a single-ringed base.

The two strands of a DNA molecule are **complementary** to each other because the sequence of one strand determines the sequence of the other; that is, an A on one strand means a T on the opposite strand, and a G on one strand means a C on the other. The two strands are therefore somewhat like a photograph and its negative, since each is sufficient to define the other.

Figure 7.2 shows a small portion of one DNA molecule. In reality, the amount of DNA in any cell is immense; in humans, for example, each nucleus contains some 6.4 billion base pairs. An organism's **genome** is all of the genetic material in its cells. In a eukaryotic cell, most of the DNA resides in the nucleus and is divided into multiple **chromosomes**, long DNA molecules that associate closely with proteins. The mitochondria and chloroplasts also contain loops of DNA (see chapter 3). On the other hand, the genome of a bacterial cell consists of one circular chromosome.

What does all of that DNA do? Much of it has no known function, but some of it encodes the cell's RNA and proteins. A **gene** is a sequence of DNA nucleotides that codes for a specific protein or RNA molecule; the human genome includes 20,000 to 25,000 genes scattered on its 23 pairs of chromosomes. Likewise, a bacterial chromosome is also divided into multiple genes.

7.1 Mastering Concepts

1. What evidence enabled Watson and Crick to decipher the structure of DNA?
2. Describe the components of DNA and its three-dimensional structure.

7.2 DNA Stores Genetic Information: An Overview

In the 1940s, biologists deduced that a single gene somehow controls the production of each protein. In the next decade, Watson and Crick described this relationship between nucleic acids and proteins as a flow of information they called the "central dogma" (figure 7.3). First, in **transcription**, a cell copies a gene's DNA sequence to a complementary RNA molecule. Then, in the process of **translation**, the information in RNA is used to manufacture a protein by joining a specific sequence of amino acids into a polypeptide chain.

According to this model, a gene is therefore somewhat like a recipe in a cookbook. A recipe specifies the ingredients and instructions for assembling one dish, such as spaghetti sauce or brownies. Likewise, a protein-encoding gene contains the instructions for assembling a protein, amino acid by amino acid. A cookbook that contains many recipes is analogous to a chromosome,

Figure It Out

Write the complementary DNA sequence of the following:
ATCGGATCGCTACTG

Answer: TAGCCTAGCGATGAC

which is an array of genes. A person's entire collection of cookbooks, then, would be analogous to a genome.

To illustrate DNA's function with a concrete example, suppose a cell in a female mammal's breast is producing milk to feed an infant (see figure 3.11). One of the many proteins in milk is albumin. The steps below summarize the production of albumin, starting with its genetic "recipe":

1. Inside the nucleus, an enzyme first transcribes the albumin gene's DNA sequence to a complementary sequence of RNA.
2. After some modification, the RNA emerges from the nucleus and binds to a ribosome.
3. At the ribosome, amino acids are assembled in a specific order to produce the albumin protein.

The amino acid sequence in albumin is dictated by the sequence of nucleotides in the RNA molecule. The RNA, in turn, was transcribed from DNA. In this way, DNA provides the recipe for albumin and every other protein in the cell.

Clearly, RNA is central to the flow of genetic information. This multifunctional nucleic acid differs from DNA in several ways (figure 7.4). First, its nucleotides contain the sugar ribose instead of deoxyribose. Second, RNA has the nitrogenous base uracil, which behaves similarly to thymine—that is, in complementary base pairs, uracil binds with adenine. Third, unlike the DNA double helix, RNA can be single-stranded. Finally, RNA can catalyze chemical reactions, a role not known for DNA.

Cells produce three types of RNA, which interact to synthesize proteins:

- **Messenger RNA (mRNA)** carries the information that specifies a protein. Each group of three mRNA bases forms a **codon**, which is a genetic "code word" that corresponds to one amino acid.
- **Ribosomal RNA (rRNA)** forms part of a **ribosome**, the physical location of protein synthesis.
- **Transfer RNA (tRNA)** molecules are "connectors" that bind an mRNA codon at one end and the corresponding amino acid at the other. Their role is to carry each amino acid to the ribosome at the correct spot along the mRNA molecule.

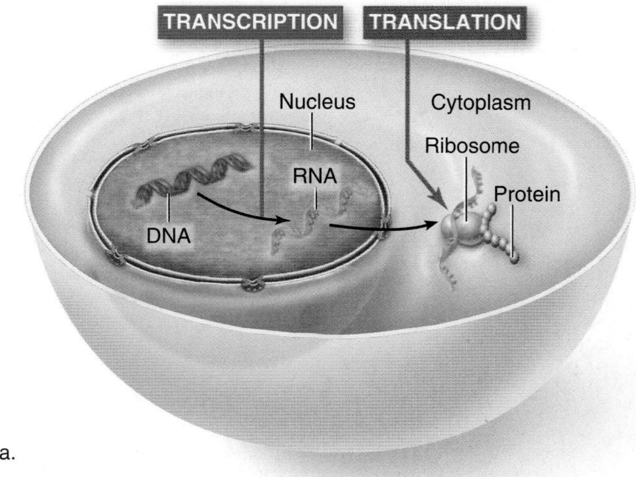

a.

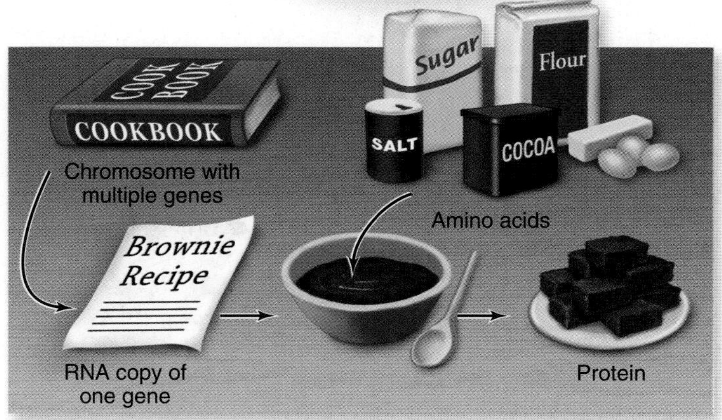

b.

Figure 7.3 DNA to RNA to Protein. (a) The central dogma of biology states that information stored in DNA is copied to RNA (transcription), which is used to assemble proteins (translation). (b) DNA stores the information used to make proteins, just as a recipe stores the information needed to make brownies.

a.	DNA	RNA
Sugar	Deoxyribose (HO—CH$_2$, OH, H, H, H, H, OH, **H**)	Ribose (HO—CH$_2$, OH, H, H, H, H, OH, **OH**)
Nucleotide bases	Adenine (A), Guanine (G), Cytosine (C), Thymine (T)	Adenine (A), Guanine (G), Cytosine (C), Uracil (U)
Form	Double-stranded	Generally single-stranded
Functions	Stores RNA- and protein-encoding information; transfers information to next generation of cells	Carries protein-encoding information; helps to make proteins; catalyzes some reactions

b. Complementary base pairs

DNA	pairs with	RNA
Adenine (A)	—	Uracil (U)
Cytosine (C)	—	Guanine (G)
Guanine (G)	—	Cytosine (C)
Thymine (T)	—	Adenine (A)

RNA	pairs with	RNA
Adenine (A)	—	Uracil (U)
Cytosine (C)	—	Guanine (G)
Guanine (G)	—	Cytosine (C)
Uracil (U)	—	Adenine (A)

Figure 7.4 DNA and RNA. (a) Summary of the structural and functional differences between DNA and RNA. (b) Complementary base pairs show that uracil in RNA behaves chemically like thymine in DNA.

The function of each type of RNA is further explained later in this chapter, beginning in the next section with the first stage in protein production: transcription.

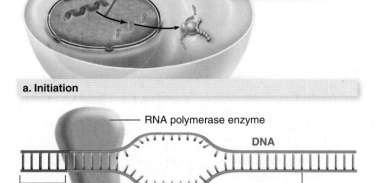

7.2 Mastering Concepts

1. What is the relationship between a gene and a protein?
2. How do transcription and translation use genetic information?
3. What are the three types of RNA?

7.3 Transcription Uses a DNA Template to Create RNA

Transcription produces an RNA copy of one gene. More specifically, RNA nucleotide bases bond with exposed complementary bases on the DNA template strand. The process occurs in three stages (figure 7.5):

1. **Initiation:** In the first stage, enzymes unwind the DNA double helix, exposing the **template strand** that encodes the RNA molecule. **RNA polymerase** (the enzyme that builds an RNA chain) binds to the **promoter,** a DNA sequence that signals the gene's start. Often, proteins called transcription factors must bind to the DNA for RNA polymerase to attach to the DNA (see section 7.5).
2. **Elongation:** RNA polymerase moves along the DNA strand, adding nucleotides to the growing RNA molecule.
3. **Termination:** RNA polymerase reaches a **terminator** sequence that signals the end of the gene. RNA, RNA polymerase, and the DNA template separate from each other, and the DNA molecule resumes its usual double helix shape.

As the RNA molecule is synthesized, it curls into a three-dimensional shape dictated by complementary base pairing within the molecule. The final shape determines whether the RNA functions as mRNA, tRNA, or rRNA. In fact, the definition of *gene* includes any DNA sequence that is transcribed to any type of RNA. Most genes, however, are transcribed to mRNA, and mRNA encodes protein. A common "shorthand" definition for a gene is therefore a DNA sequence that encodes a protein.

In bacteria and archaea, ribosomes begin translating mRNA to a protein as soon as transcription is complete. This can happen in eukaryotes too, but usually mRNA is altered before it leaves the nucleus (figure 7.6).

One modification that occurs in eukaryotic cells is that a short sequence of modified nucleotides, called a cap, is added to one end of the mRNA molecule. This cap helps the ribosome attach to the mRNA. Also, at the opposite end, 100 to 200 adenines are added, forming a "poly A tail." The length of the tail may determine how long an mRNA lasts before being degraded.

In archaea and in eukaryotic cells, only part of an mRNA molecule is translated into an amino acid sequence. **Introns** are first removed, and the

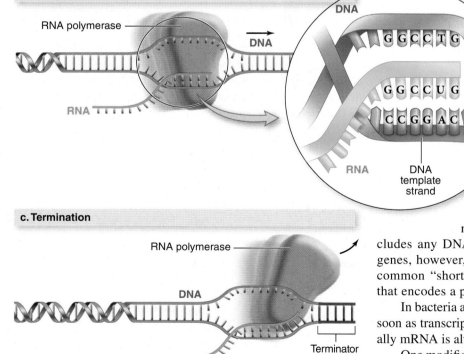

TRANSCRIPTION

a. Initiation

RNA polymerase enzyme

DNA

Promoter

DNA template strand

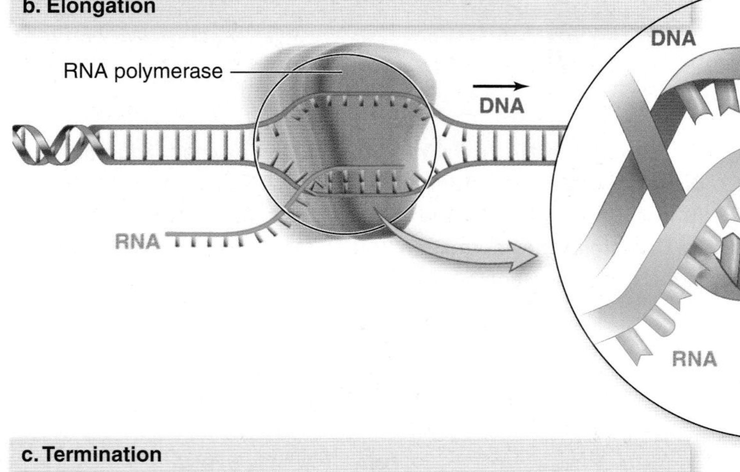

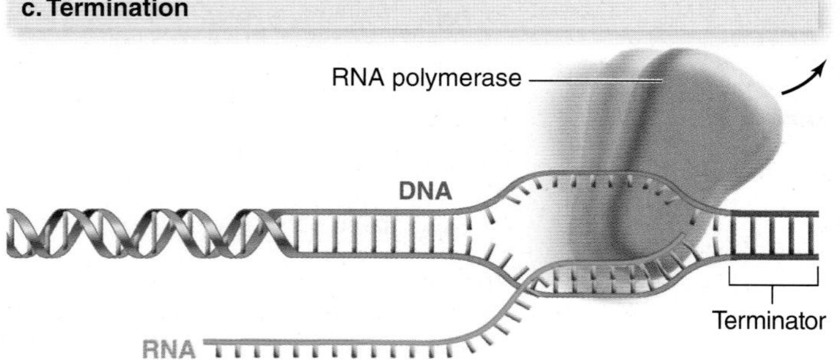

Figure 7.5 Transcription of RNA from DNA. Transcription occurs in three stages: initiation, elongation, and termination. (a) Initiation is the control point that determines which genes are transcribed and when. (b) RNA nucleotides are added during elongation. (c) A terminator sequence in the gene signals the end of transcription.

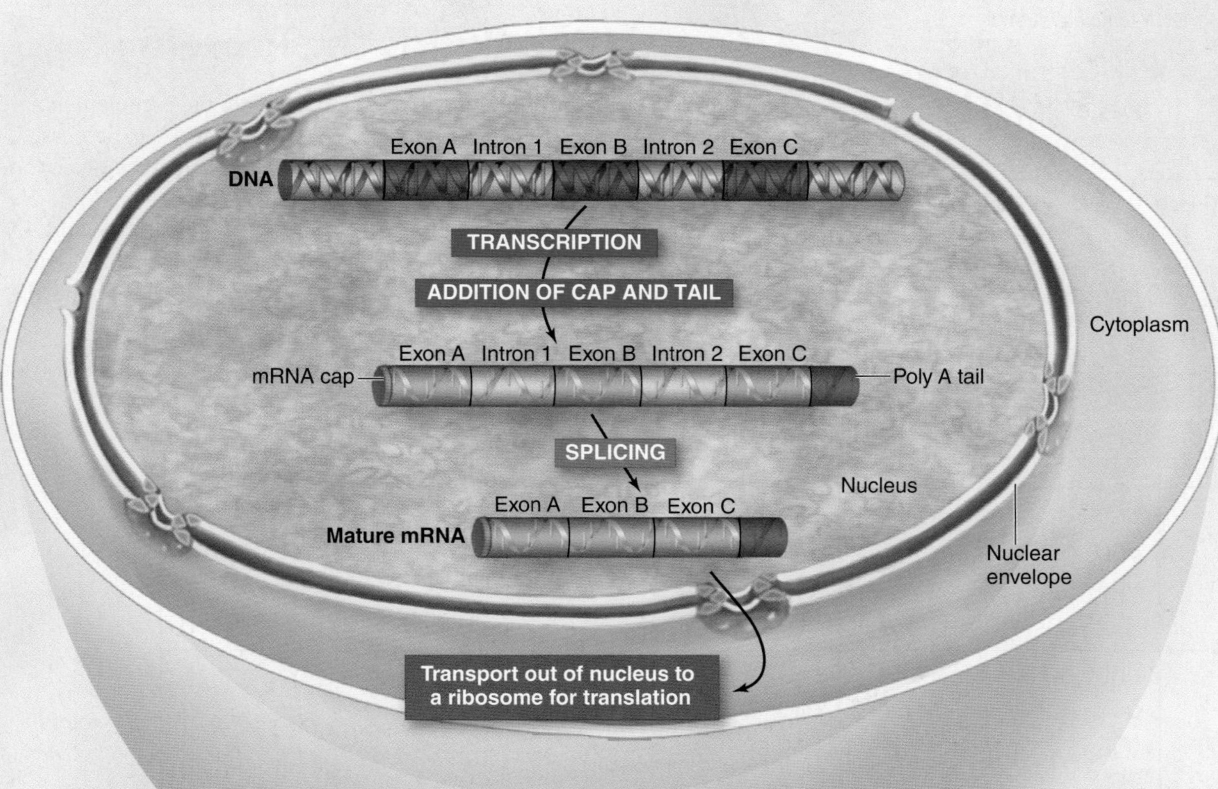

Figure 7.6 Processing mRNA. In eukaryotic cells, a nucleotide cap and poly A tail are added to mRNA, and introns are spliced out. Finally, the mature mRNA exits the nucleus.

remaining portions, called **exons,** are spliced together. These joined exons form the mature mRNA that leaves the nucleus to be translated. (One tip for remembering this is that *ex*ons are the parts of the mRNA that are *ex*pressed or that *ex*it the nucleus.)

The amount of genetic material devoted to introns can be immense. The average exon is 100 to 300 nucleotides long, whereas the average intron is about 1000 nucleotides long. Some unmodified mRNA molecules include 70 or more introns; the cell therefore simply discards much of the RNA created in transcription.

7.3 Mastering Concepts

1. What happens during transcription?
2. Where in the eukaryotic cell does transcription occur?
3. What is the role of RNA polymerase in transcription?
4. What are the roles of the promoter and terminator sequences in transcription?
5. How is mRNA modified before it leaves the nucleus of a eukaryotic cell?

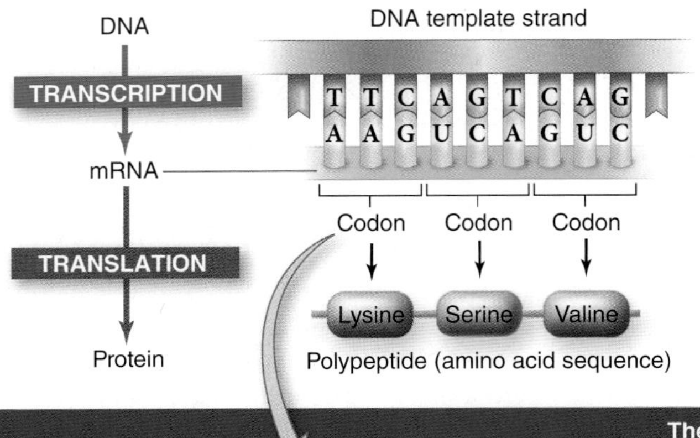

7.4 Translation Builds the Protein

Transcription copies the information encoded in DNA into the complementary language of mRNA. Once transcription is complete and mRNA is processed, the cell is ready to translate the mRNA "message" into a sequence of amino acids.

On paper, translating a molecule of mRNA is easy, thanks to the work of biologists who, in the 1960s, deciphered the **genetic code**—that is, they determined which codons correspond to which amino acids. Figure 7.7 shows the

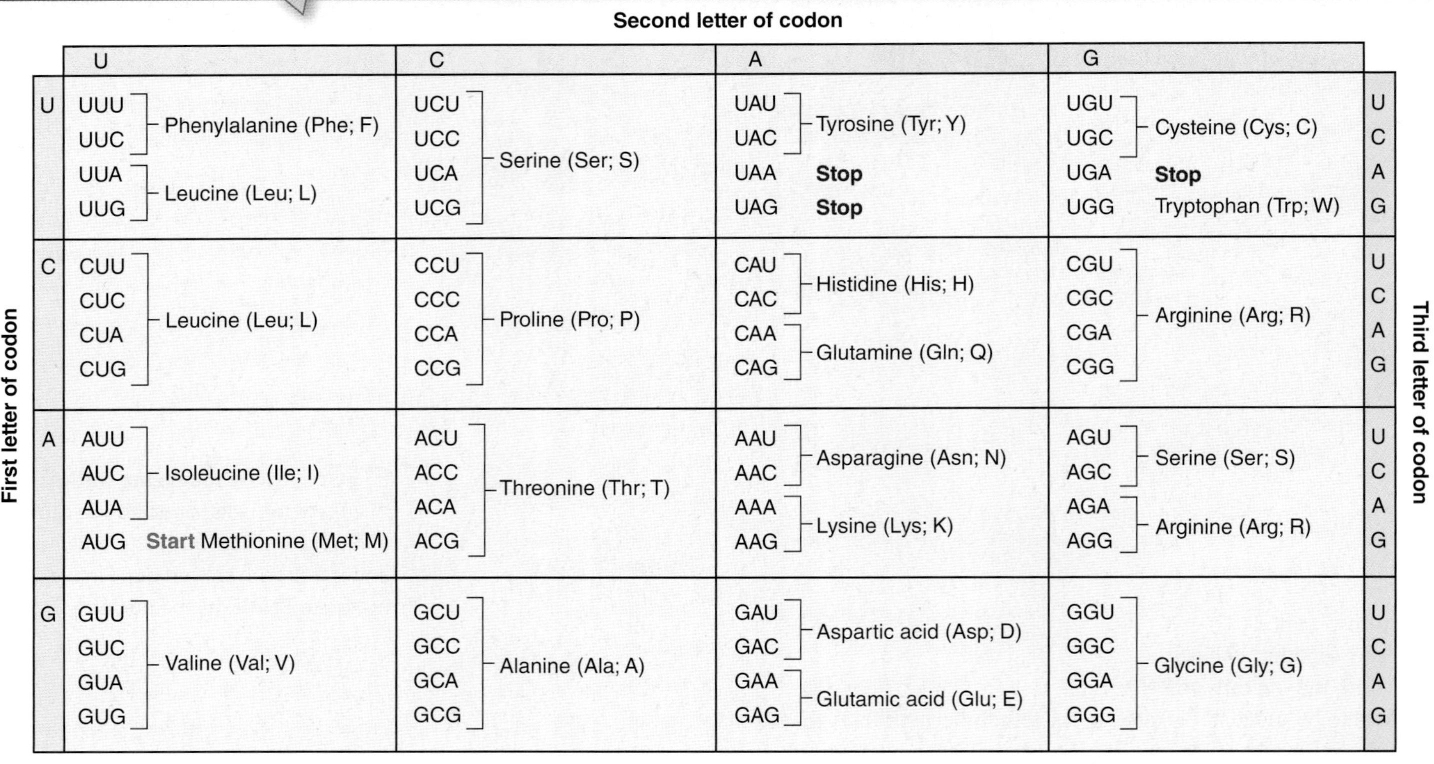

The Genetic Code

Second letter of codon

First letter of codon	U	C	A	G	Third letter of codon
U	UUU Phenylalanine (Phe; F)	UCU Serine (Ser; S)	UAU Tyrosine (Tyr; Y)	UGU Cysteine (Cys; C)	U
	UUC Phenylalanine (Phe; F)	UCC Serine (Ser; S)	UAC Tyrosine (Tyr; Y)	UGC Cysteine (Cys; C)	C
	UUA Leucine (Leu; L)	UCA Serine (Ser; S)	UAA **Stop**	UGA **Stop**	A
	UUG Leucine (Leu; L)	UCG Serine (Ser; S)	UAG **Stop**	UGG Tryptophan (Trp; W)	G
C	CUU Leucine (Leu; L)	CCU Proline (Pro; P)	CAU Histidine (His; H)	CGU Arginine (Arg; R)	U
	CUC Leucine (Leu; L)	CCC Proline (Pro; P)	CAC Histidine (His; H)	CGC Arginine (Arg; R)	C
	CUA Leucine (Leu; L)	CCA Proline (Pro; P)	CAA Glutamine (Gln; Q)	CGA Arginine (Arg; R)	A
	CUG Leucine (Leu; L)	CCG Proline (Pro; P)	CAG Glutamine (Gln; Q)	CGG Arginine (Arg; R)	G
A	AUU Isoleucine (Ile; I)	ACU Threonine (Thr; T)	AAU Asparagine (Asn; N)	AGU Serine (Ser; S)	U
	AUC Isoleucine (Ile; I)	ACC Threonine (Thr; T)	AAC Asparagine (Asn; N)	AGC Serine (Ser; S)	C
	AUA Isoleucine (Ile; I)	ACA Threonine (Thr; T)	AAA Lysine (Lys; K)	AGA Arginine (Arg; R)	A
	AUG Start Methionine (Met; M)	ACG Threonine (Thr; T)	AAG Lysine (Lys; K)	AGG Arginine (Arg; R)	G
G	GUU Valine (Val; V)	GCU Alanine (Ala; A)	GAU Aspartic acid (Asp; D)	GGU Glycine (Gly; G)	U
	GUC Valine (Val; V)	GCC Alanine (Ala; A)	GAC Aspartic acid (Asp; D)	GGC Glycine (Gly; G)	C
	GUA Valine (Val; V)	GCA Alanine (Ala; A)	GAA Glutamic acid (Glu; E)	GGA Glycine (Gly; G)	A
	GUG Valine (Val; V)	GCG Alanine (Ala; A)	GAG Glutamic acid (Glu; E)	GGG Glycine (Gly; G)	G

Figure 7.7 The Genetic Code. According to this "dictionary" of the genetic code, most mRNA codons correspond to an amino acid. Three codons, however, signal the ribosome to stop translating.

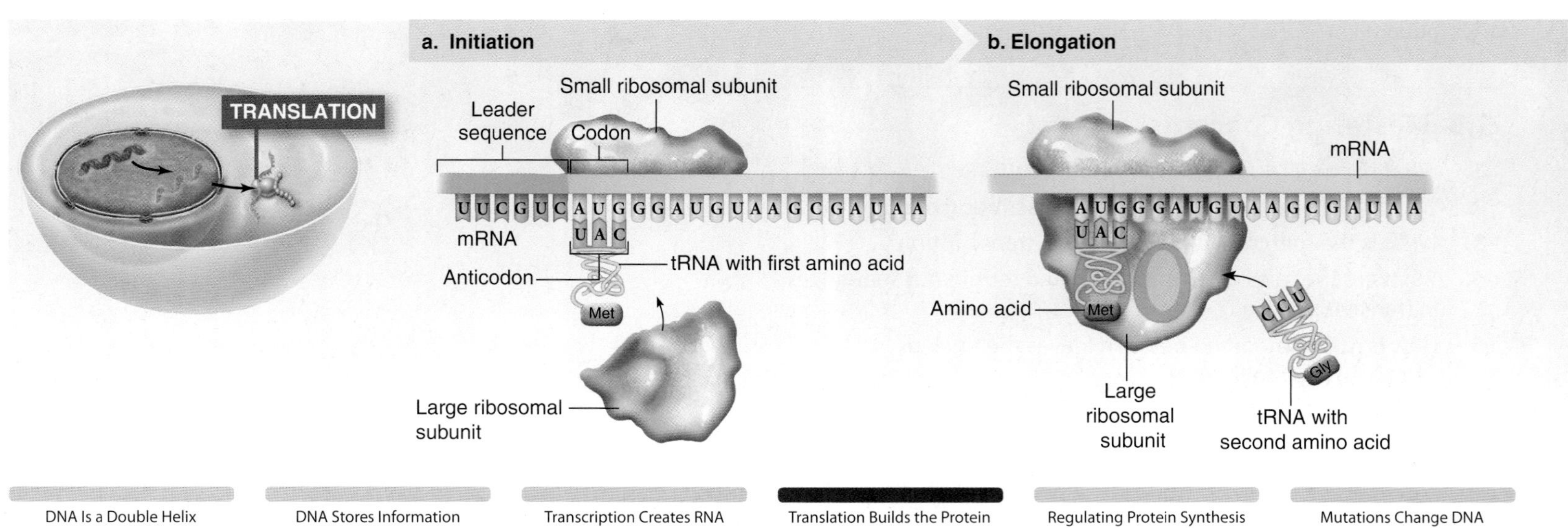

complete genetic code, the product of about a decade of research conducted in many laboratories. The rest of this section explains how cells implement the genetic code in protein synthesis.

A. Translation Requires mRNA, tRNA, and Ribosomes

Translation—the actual construction of the protein—requires the following participants:

- **mRNA:** This product of transcription carries the genetic information that encodes a protein, with each three-base codon specifying one amino acid.
- **tRNA molecules:** tRNA is a "bilingual" molecule that binds to both mRNA codons and amino acids (figure 7.8). A small part of each tRNA molecule, called the **anticodon,** is a three-base loop that is complementary to one mRNA codon. The other end of the tRNA molecule forms a covalent bond to the amino acid corresponding to that codon. For example, if the mRNA codon is UUC, the tRNA's anticodon sequence would be AAG. At the other end, this tRNA molecule would carry the amino acid phenylalanine (see figure 7.7).
- **Ribosome:** The ribosome, built of rRNA and proteins, anchors mRNA during translation. Each ribosome has one large and one small subunit that join at the start of protein synthesis.

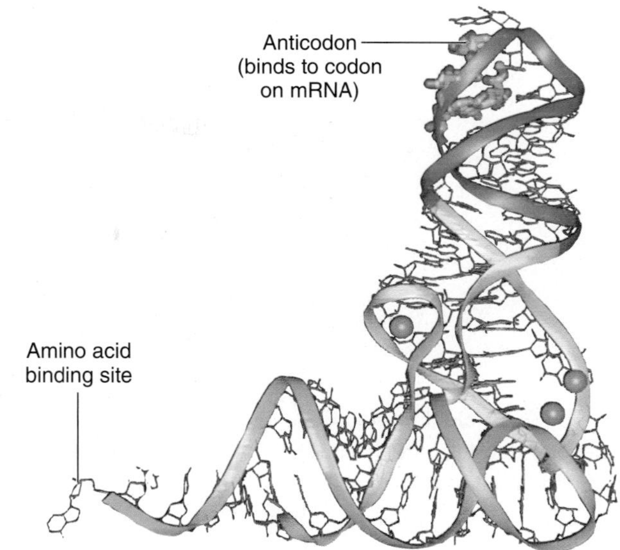

Figure 7.8 Transfer RNA. In this illustration of tRNA, the anticodon that binds to the mRNA is on top and the amino acid-binding region is at the opposite end.

B. Translation Occurs in Three Steps

The process of translation is divided into three stages (figure 7.9): initiation, elongation, and termination.

1. **Initiation:** In the first stage, the leader sequence of the mRNA molecule bonds with a small ribosomal subunit. A large ribosomal subunit attaches to the small subunit. The first mRNA codon to specify an amino acid is usually AUG, which attracts a tRNA that carries the amino acid methionine.
2. **Elongation:** To start the next stage, the second codon bonds to the anticodon of a tRNA molecule carrying the next amino acid. A covalent bond forms between two amino acids, and the ribosome releases the first tRNA. This tRNA will pick up another methionine and may be used again.

Figure 7.9 Translation Creates the Protein. (a) Initiation brings together the ribosomal subunits, mRNA, and a tRNA carrying the protein's first amino acid. (b) As elongation begins, the anticodon of a tRNA molecule bearing a second amino acid binds to the second codon. The first amino acid forms a covalent bond with the second amino acid. Additional tRNAs bring subsequent amino acids encoded in the mRNA. (c) Termination occurs when a release factor protein binds to the stop codon. All components of the translation machine are liberated, and the completed polypeptide is released.

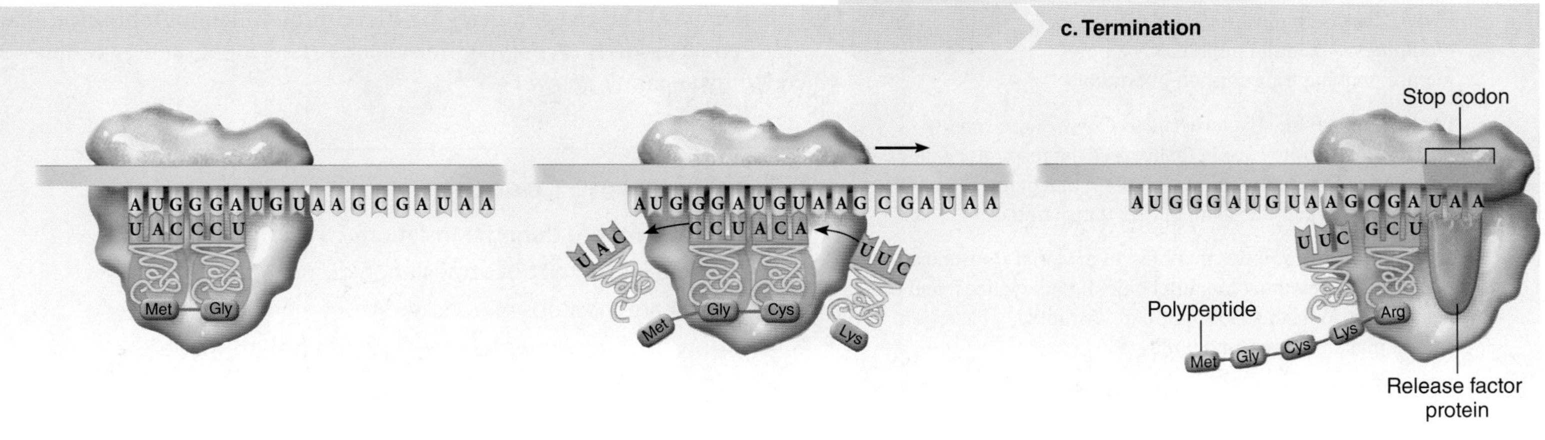

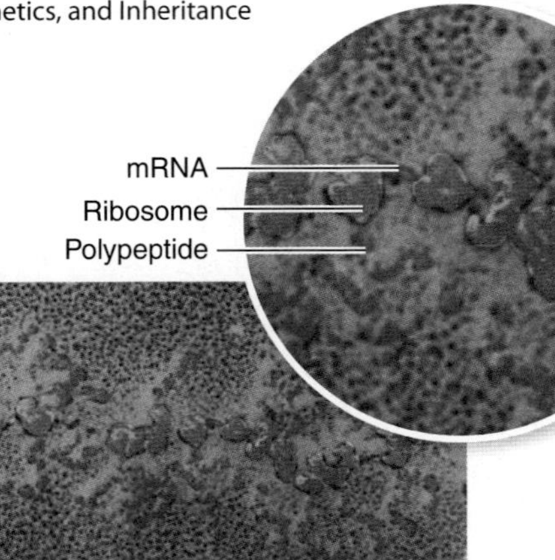

Figure 7.10 Efficient Translation. Multiple ribosomes can simultaneously translate one mRNA. This micrograph shows about two dozen ribosomes producing proteins from the same mRNA.

Next, the ribosome moves down the mRNA by one codon. A third tRNA enters, carrying its amino acid. This third amino acid aligns with the other two and forms a covalent bond to the second amino acid in the growing chain. In this way, the polypeptide grows one amino acid at a time, as tRNAs continue to deliver their cargo.

3. **Termination:** Elongation halts at a "stop" codon. No tRNA molecules correspond to these stop codons. Instead, proteins called release factors bind to the stop codon, prompting the release of the last tRNA from the ribosome. The ribosomal subunits separate from each other and are recycled, and the new polypeptide is released.

Overall, protein synthesis can be very speedy; a cell in the human immune system, for example, can manufacture 2000 identical antibody proteins per second. How can such a complex process occur so rapidly? A cell can maximize the efficiency of protein synthesis by producing multiple copies of each mRNA; moreover, dozens of ribosomes may simultaneously translate the same mRNA molecule (figure 7.10). These ribosomes zip along the mRNA, incorporating some 15 amino acids per second. A cell can therefore quickly make many copies of a protein from the same mRNA.

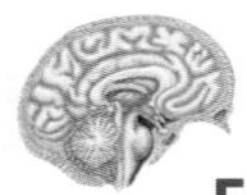

Figure It Out

If the sequence of a template strand of DNA is AAAGCAGTACTA, what would be the corresponding amino acid sequence?

Answer: Phe-Arg-His-Asp

C. Proteins Must Fold Correctly After Translation

The newly synthesized protein cannot do its job until it folds into its final shape. Some regions of the amino acid sequence attract or repel other parts, contorting the polypeptide's overall shape. Enzymes catalyze the formation of chemical bonds, and "chaperone" proteins stabilize partially folded regions. ▸ protein folding, p. 40

An improperly folded protein can cause illness. In some forms of cystic fibrosis, for example, a membrane protein that normally controls the flow of chloride ions does not fold correctly into its final form. Alzheimer disease is associated with a protein that forms an abnormal mass in brain cells because of improper folding. "Mad cow disease" and similar conditions in sheep and humans are caused by abnormal clumps of proteins called prions in nervous system cells (see section 7.10).

In addition to folding, some proteins must be altered in other ways before they become functional. For example, insulin, which is 51 amino acids long, is initially translated as proinsulin, an 80-amino-acid polypeptide. Enzymes cut proinsulin to form insulin. A different type of modification occurs when polypeptides join to form larger protein molecules. The oxygen-carrying blood protein hemoglobin, for example, consists of four polypeptide chains (two alpha and two beta) encoded by separate genes.

Why We Care | Poisons

We learned in chapter 6 that some poisons kill because they interfere with respiration. Here we list a few poisons that inhibit protein synthesis. A cell that cannot make proteins quickly dies.

- **Amanatin:** This toxin naturally occurs in the "death cap mushroom," *Amanita phalloides*. Amanatin inhibits RNA polymerase, making transcription impossible.
- **Diphtheria toxin:** Bacteria called *Corynebacterium diphtheriae* secrete a toxin that causes the respiratory illness diphtheria. The toxin inhibits a protein that helps add amino acids to a polypeptide chain during translation.
- **Antibiotics:** Antibiotics that bind to bacterial ribosomes include clindamycin, chloramphenicol, tetracyclines, and gentamicin. When its ribosomes are disrupted, a bacterium cannot make proteins, and it dies.

7.4 Mastering Concepts

1. What happens during translation?
2. Where in the cell does translation occur?
3. What are the steps of translation?
4. How does a polypeptide fold into its finished shape?

7.5 Protein Synthesis Is Highly Regulated

Producing proteins costs tremendous amounts of energy. For example, an *Escherichia coli* cell spends 90% of its ATP on protein synthesis. Transcription and translation require energy, as does the synthesis of the nucleotides, tRNA, rRNA, enzymes, and other molecules that make protein synthesis possible. In eukaryotes and archaea, splicing out introns and making other modifications to the mRNA require still more energy. ▸ ATP, p. 72

Given the enormous cost of making proteins, it makes sense that cells save energy by not producing unneeded proteins. Genes encoding proteins that are essential to life, such as those encoding the enzymes involved in respiration, must be expressed all the time. But cells transcribe other genes only under some conditions. This section describes some examples of the many mechanisms that regulate gene expression in cells.

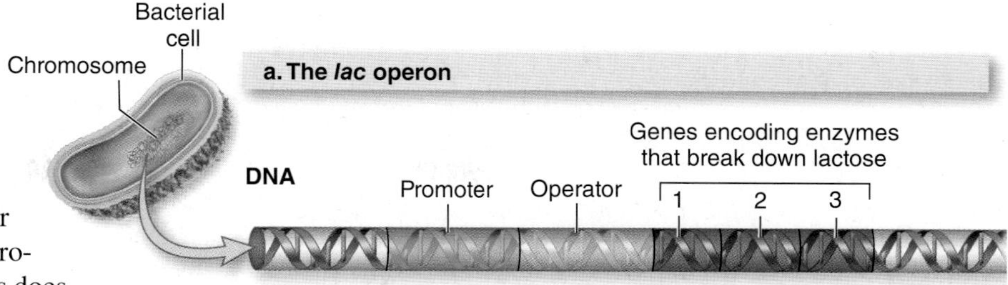

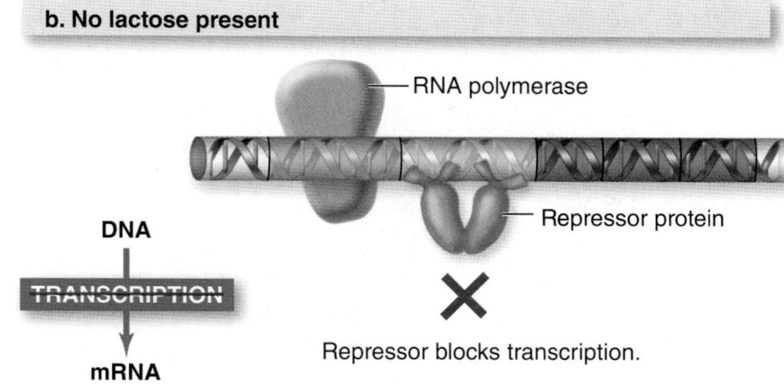

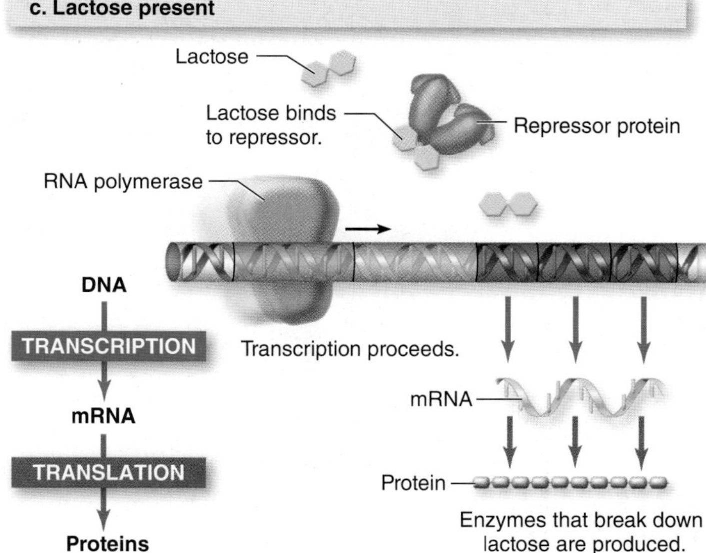

Figure 7.11 The *Lac* Operon. (a) One promoter controls the expression of three genes, which encode the enzymes that break down lactose. (b) In the absence of lactose, a repressor protein binds to the operator, preventing transcription of the genes. (c) If lactose is present, the sugar binds the repressor, changing the protein's shape and causing it to release the operator. Transcription proceeds.

A. Operons Are Groups of Bacterial Genes That Share One Promoter

Intestinal bacteria such as *E. coli* live in an environment where food sources can change from hour to hour. To maximize efficiency, the bacteria should produce enzymes that degrade only those food molecules that are actually available. For example, *E. coli* requires three enzymes to absorb and degrade the sugar lactose. How does the cell "know" to transcribe all three genes when lactose is present?

The answer relates to the way that genes are organized in *E. coli* and other bacteria. An **operon** is a group of genes plus regulatory sequences—a promoter and an operator—that control the transcription of the entire group at once. The promoter, as described earlier, is the site to which RNA polymerase can attach to begin transcription. The **operator** is a DNA sequence located between the promoter and the genes. When a protein called a **repressor** binds to the operator, the genes are not transcribed; when the repressor is released, the genes turn "on."

Many bacterial genes are organized as operons. Figure 7.11a shows one example: *E. coli's* ***lac*** **operon,** which consists of three genes plus a promoter and operator. To understand how the *lac* operon works, first consider *E. coli* in an environment lacking lactose. Producing lactose-degrading enzymes would be a waste of energy. The repressor protein therefore binds to the operator, preventing RNA polymerase from transcribing the genes (figure 7.11b). All three genes are effectively "off" in a lactose-free environment. But when lactose is present, the sugar attaches to the repressor, changing its shape so that it detaches from the DNA. RNA polymerase is now free to transcribe the genes (figure 7.11c).

B. Eukaryotic Organisms Use Many Methods to Regulate Gene Expression

In multicellular eukaryotes, the control of protein synthesis is more complex than in bacteria, because different cell types express different subsets of genes. A cell in an early animal embryo, for example, must express the proteins that dictate the formation of body parts in the correct places. A skin cell in an adult would not need those proteins but would need others, such as pigments that protect the body from the sun's ultraviolet radiation.

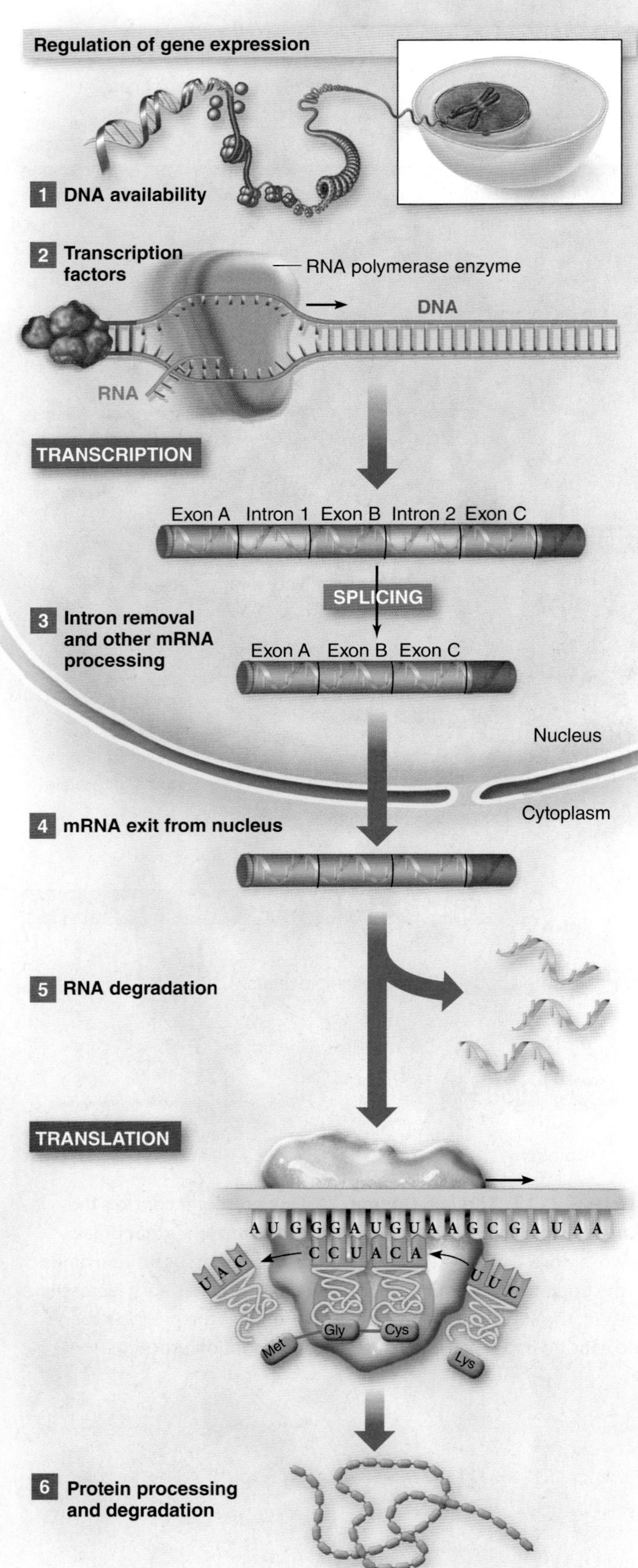

The rest of this section describes a few of the ways that eukaryotic cells control gene expression. Figure 7.12 illustrates where each mechanism fits into the overall process of gene expression.

DNA Availability Not all DNA in a eukaryotic cell is available to be transcribed (figure 7.12, step 1). For example, a cell can "tag" unneeded DNA with methyl groups (—CH_3). Proteins inside the cell bind to the tagged DNA, preventing gene expression and signaling the cell to fold that section of DNA more tightly. RNA polymerase cannot access highly compacted DNA, effectively turning off the genes.

Sometimes, entire chromosomes can be inactivated. For example, in mammals, only one X chromosome can be active in each cell. Female mammals inherit two X chromosomes per cell, but one is inactivated (see section 10.7).

Transcription Factors In eukaryotes (unlike in bacteria), RNA polymerase cannot bind to a promoter in the absence of specialized regulatory proteins. Groups of these proteins, called **transcription factors,** bind DNA at the promoter. The transcription factors form a pocket for RNA polymerase, activating transcription (figure 7.12, step 2).

Figure 7.13 shows in more detail how transcription factors combine with RNA polymerase before transcription can begin. The first transcription factor to bind is attracted to a DNA sequence called a TATA box. This transcription factor attracts others. Finally, RNA polymerase joins the complex, binding just in front of the start of the gene sequence.

Hundreds of transcription factors are known. Defects in transcription factors underlie some diseases, including cancer, by interfering with the production of proteins that regulate cell division. In addition, some drugs interfere with transcription factors. The "abortion pill" RU486, for example, indirectly blocks the action of transcription factors needed for the development of an embryo. ▸ cancer, p. 148

mRNA Processing One gene can encode multiple proteins if different introns are removed from the mRNA (figure 7.12, step 3). For example, one gene expressed in the nervous system of fruit flies can theoretically be spliced into more than 38,000 different configurations!

mRNA Exit from Nucleus For a protein to be produced, mRNA must leave the nucleus and attach to a ribosome (figure 7.12, step 4). If the mRNA is not allowed to leave, the gene is effectively silenced.

mRNA Degradation Not all mRNA molecules are equally stable (figure 7.12, step 5). Some are rapidly degraded, perhaps before they can be translated, whereas others persist long enough to be translated many times.

Protein Processing and Degradation Additional regulation may occur during and after translation (figure 7.12, step 6). Some proteins must be altered before they become functional. Proinsulin, for example, is cut in two places after translation to form the final insulin protein. If these modifications fail to occur, the protein cannot function.

Figure 7.12 Regulation of Gene Expression. Eukaryotic cells have many ways to control whether each gene is turned on or off.

In addition, to do its job, a protein must move from the ribosome to where the cell needs it. For example, a protein secreted in milk must be escorted to the Golgi apparatus and be packaged for export (see figure 3.11). A gene is effectively silenced if its product never moves to the correct destination. Finally, like RNA, not all proteins are equally stable. Some are degraded shortly after they form, whereas others persist longer.

A human cell may express hundreds to thousands of genes at once. Biologists are tackling the enormous challenge of unraveling the complex regulatory mechanisms that control the expression of each gene. The payoff will be a much better understanding of cell biology, along with many new medical applications. The same research may also help scientists understand how external influences on gene expression contribute to complex traits, such as the one described in the Burning Question on page 128.

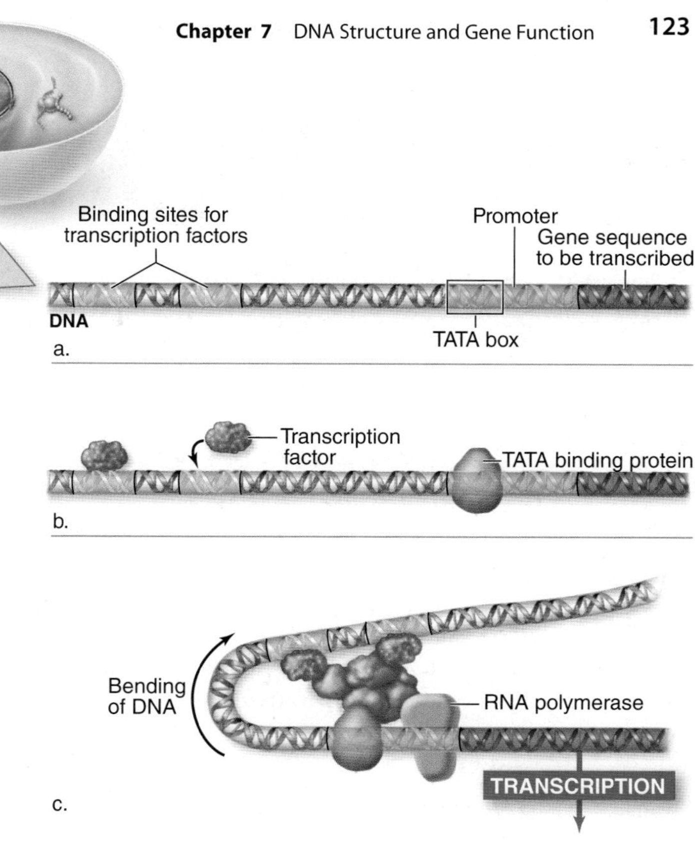

Figure 7.13 Transcription Factors. Transcription factors are proteins that bind to DNA and regulate gene expression in eukaryotic cells. RNA polymerase can initiate transcription only in the presence of transcription factors bound to a gene's promoter region.

7.5 Mastering Concepts

1. Which steps in protein synthesis require energy?
2. Why do cells regulate which genes are expressed at any given time?
3. How do proteins determine whether a bacterial operon is expressed?
4. What is the role of transcription factors in gene expression?
5. What are some mechanisms by which eukaryotic cells control gene expression?

7.6 Mutations Change DNA

A **mutation** is a change in a cell's DNA sequence. Many people think that mutations are always harmful, perhaps because some cause such dramatic changes (figure 7.14). Although some mutations do cause illness, they also provide the variation that makes life interesting (and makes evolution possible).

To continue the cookbook analogy introduced earlier, a mutation in a gene is similar to an error in a recipe. A small typographical error might be barely noticeable. A minor substitution of one ingredient for another might hurt (or improve) the flavor. But serious errors such as missing ingredients or truncated instructions are likely to ruin the dish.

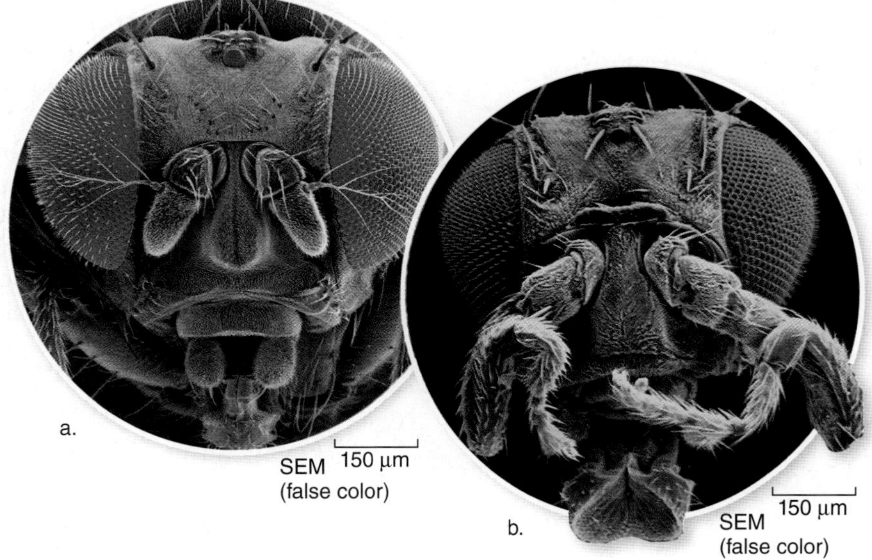

Figure 7.14 One Mutation Can Make a Big Difference. Mutations in some genes can cause parts to form in the wrong places. (a) Normally, a fruit fly has two small antennae between its eyes. (b) This fly has legs growing where antennae should be. It has a mutation in a gene that affects development.

A. Mutations Range from Silent to Devastating

A **point mutation** changes one or a few base pairs in a gene; larger-scale mutations may also occur. The mutation may be a single-base change, an insertion or deletion that shifts the codon "reading frame," or the expansion of repeated sequences. Some are not detectable except by DNA fingerprinting, while others

TABLE 7.1 Types of Mutations

Wild type	THE ONE BIG FLY HAD ONE RED EYE
Substitution	TH**Q** ONE BIG FLY HAD ONE RED EYE
Frameshift	THE ONE **Q**BI GFL YHA DON ERE DEY
Deletion of three nucleotides	THE ONE BIG HAD ONE RED EYE
Insertion of three nucleotides	THE ONE BIG **WET** FLY HAD ONE RED EYE

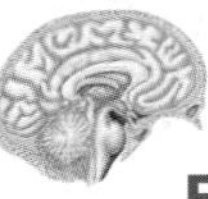

Figure It Out

Suppose that a substitution mutation replaces the first "A" in the following mRNA sequence with a "U":

A A A G C A G U A C U A

How many amino acids will be in the polypeptide chain?

Answer: Zero

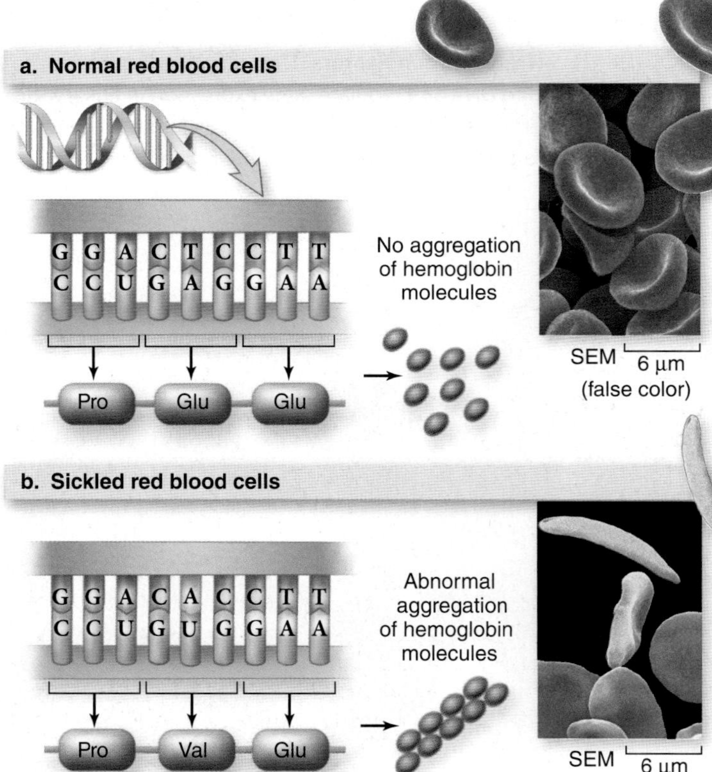

Figure 7.15 Sickle Cell Mutation. Sickle cell anemia usually results from a mutation in a hemoglobin gene. (a) Normal hemoglobin molecules enable the cell to assume a rounded shape. (b) In sickle cell disease, a substitution mutation causes hemoglobin molecules to clump (aggregate) into long, curved rods that deform the red blood cell.

may be lethal. Table 7.1 illustrates some of the major types of mutations, using sentences composed of three-letter words.

A **substitution mutation** is the replacement of one DNA base with another. Such a mutation is "silent" if the mutated gene encodes the same protein as the original gene version. Silent mutations are possible because more than one codon encodes most amino acids.

Often, however, a substitution mutation changes a base triplet so that it specifies a different amino acid. The substituted amino acid may drastically alter the protein's shape, changing its function. Sickle cell disease results from this type of mutation (figure 7.15).

In other cases, a base triplet specifying an amino acid changes into one that encodes a "stop" codon. This shortens the protein product, which can profoundly influence the organism. At least one of the mutations that gives rise to cystic fibrosis, for example, shortens a protein from the normal 1480 amino acids to only 493. The faulty protein cannot function.

One or more nucleotides can also be added to, or deleted from, a gene. In a **frameshift mutation,** nucleotides are added or deleted by a number other than a multiple of three. Because triplets of DNA bases specify amino acids, such an addition or deletion disrupts the reading frame. It therefore also disrupts the sequence of amino acids and usually devastates a protein's function. Some mutations that cause cystic fibrosis result from the addition or deletion of just one or two nucleotides.

Even if a small insertion or deletion does not shift the reading frame, the effect might still be severe if the change drastically alters the protein's shape. The most common mutation that causes severe cystic fibrosis, for example, deletes only a single group of three nucleotides. The resulting protein lacks just one amino acid, but it cannot function.

B. What Causes Mutations?

Some mutations occur spontaneously—that is, without outside causes. A spontaneous substitution mutation usually originates as a DNA replication error, but replication errors can also cause insertions and deletions. Mutations may also occur during meiosis, a type of cell division required for sexual reproduction (see chapter 9). ▸ DNA replication, p. 141

Exposure to chemicals or radiation may also damage DNA. A **mutagen** is any external agent that induces mutations, such as the ultraviolet radiation in sunlight, X-rays, radioactive fallout from atomic bomb tests and nuclear accidents, chemical weapons such as mustard gas, and chemicals in tobacco. The more contact a person has with mutagens, the higher the risk for cancer. Coating skin with sunscreen, wearing a lead "bib" during dental X-rays, and stopping smoking all lower cancer risk by reducing exposure to mutagenic chemicals and radiation.

C. Mutations Are Important for Many Reasons

One reason that mutations are important is that they create new **alleles,** which are alternative versions of the same gene. Some of these new alleles are "neutral" and have no effect on an organism's fitness. Your reproductive success, for example, does not generally depend on the color of your eyes or the size of your feet. As unit 3 explains, however, variation has important evolutionary consequences. In every species, individuals with some allele combinations reproduce more successfully than others. Natural selection "edits out" the less favorable allele combinations.

Mutations in disease-causing bacteria and viruses have enormous medical importance. Antibiotic drugs kill bacteria by targeting their unique membrane proteins, enzymes, and other structures. Random mutations in bacterial DNA encode new versions of these proteins, and the descendants of some of the mutated cells become new strains that are not susceptible to these antibiotics. Likewise, random mutations enable viruses to jump from other animals to humans. Evolving viruses have caused the global epidemics of HIV, influenza, and other diseases.

The importance of mutations in evolution became clear with the discovery of **homeotic genes.** These genes encode transcription factors that are expressed during the development of an embryo. If the transcription factors are faulty, the signals that control the formation of an organism's body parts become disrupted. The flies in figure 7.14 show what happens when homeotic genes are mutated. Having parts in the wrong places is, of course, usually harmful. But studies of many species reveal that mutations in homeotic genes have profoundly influenced animal evolution. Limb modifications such as arms, hooves, wings, and flippers trace their origins to mutations in homeotic genes.

Geneticists frequently induce mutations to learn how genes normally function. For example, biologists discovered how genes control flower formation by studying mutant *Arabidopsis* plants in which flower parts form in the wrong places.

Finally, plant breeders induce mutations to create new varieties of many crop species (figure 7.16). Some kinds of rice, grapefruit, oats, lettuce, begonias, and many other plants owe their existence to breeders treating cells with radiation and then selecting interesting new varieties from the mutated individuals.

Figure 7.16 **Useful Mutants.** (a) Rio Red grapefruits and several varieties of (b) rice and (c) cotton are among the many plant varieties that have been created by using radiation to induce mutations.

7.6 Mastering Concepts

1. What are the types of mutations, and how does each alter the encoded protein?
2. What causes mutations?
3. How are mutations important tools in biological research?

7.7 Viruses Are Genes Wrapped in a Protein Coat

So far, this chapter has explained the structure and function of DNA and RNA in cells. As we have seen, genes act as "recipes" for the cell's proteins. The rest of this chapter describes a logical extension of this idea: if a cell receives new genes, it can produce a new set of proteins. In this case, the genes come from viruses.

A **virus** is a small, infectious agent that is simply genetic information enclosed in a protein coat. The 2000 or so known species of viruses therefore straddle the boundary between the chemical and the biological (see the Burning Question on this page).

Viruses cause a long list of diseases that range from the merely inconvenient to the deadly. Smallpox, influenza, the common cold, rabies, polio, chickenpox, warts, mononucleosis, and AIDS are just a few examples. Because bacteria and viruses are microscopic and cause disease, many people mistakenly lump them together as "germs." Viruses, however, are not bacteria. In fact, they are not even cells.

Burning Questions

Are viruses alive?

Most biologists do not consider a virus to be alive because it does not metabolize, respond to stimuli, or reproduce on its own. Instead, a virus must enter a living host cell to manufacture more of itself.

Nevertheless, viruses do have some features in common with life, including genetic material. Both DNA and RNA can mutate, which means that viruses evolve just as life does. Each time a virus replicates inside a host cell, random mutations occur. The genetic variability among the new viruses is subject to natural selection. That is, some variants are better than others at infecting and replicating in host cells. Many mutant viruses die out, but others pass their successful gene versions to the next generation. Over time, natural selection shapes the genetic composition of each viral population.

Submit your burning question to:
marielle_hoefnagels@mcgraw-hill.com

TABLE 7.2 Some Viruses That Infect Humans

Genetic Material	Virus (Disease)
DNA	Variola major (smallpox) Herpesviruses (oral and genital herpes; chickenpox) Epstein–Barr virus (mononucleosis, Burkitt lymphoma) Papillomaviruses (warts, cervical cancer) Hepatitis B virus
RNA	Human immunodeficiency virus (AIDS) Poliovirus Influenza viruses Measles virus Mumps virus Rabies virus Ebola virus Rhinovirus (common cold) West Nile virus Hepatitis A and C viruses

A. Viruses Are Smaller and Simpler Than Cells

A virus is much smaller than a cell (see figure 3.1). At about 10 μm (microns) in diameter, an average human cell is perhaps one tenth the diameter of a human hair. A bacterium is about one tenth again as small, at about 1 μm (1000 nm) long. The average virus, with a diameter of about 80 nm, is more than 12 times smaller than a bacterium.

A virus does not have a nucleus, organelles, ribosomes, or even cytoplasm. Only a few types of viruses contain enzymes. All viruses share two features:

- **Genetic information.** All viruses contain genetic material that carries instructions to make their molecular components. The genetic material is either DNA or RNA (table 7.2). ▸ nucleic acids, p. 42
- **Protein coat.** A **protein coat** surrounds the genetic material and determines a virus's overall form (figure 7.17). Many viruses are spherical or icosahedral (a 20-faced shape built of triangular sections). Others are rod-shaped, oval, or filamentous.

Some viruses have other features as well. For example, some have a lipid-rich **envelope,** a layer of membrane outside the protein coat (see figure 7.17d). The envelope may include embedded proteins that help a virus invade a host cell. An example of an enveloped virus is the human immunodeficiency virus (HIV), which causes acquired immunodeficiency syndrome (AIDS). The influenza virus also has an envelope. ▸ cell membrane, p. 54

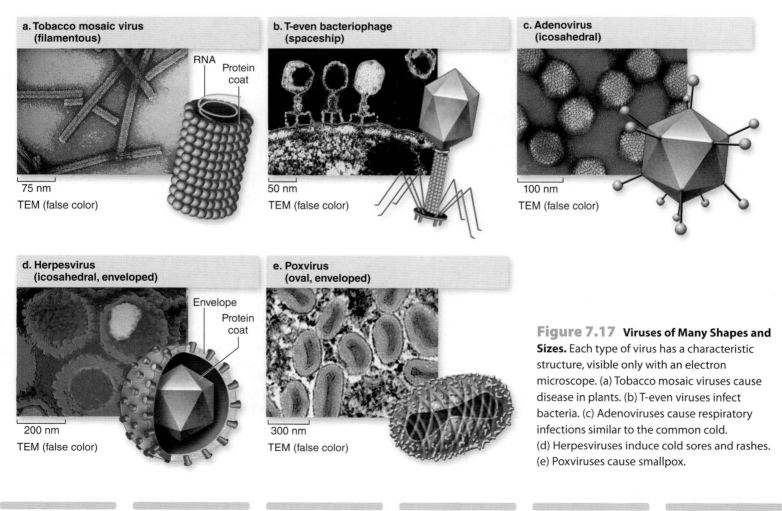

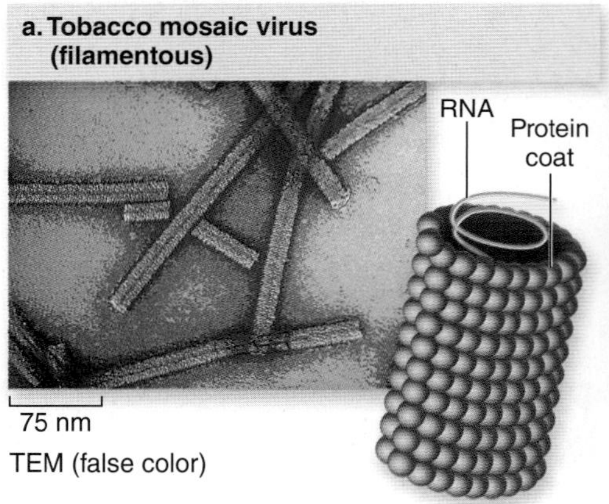

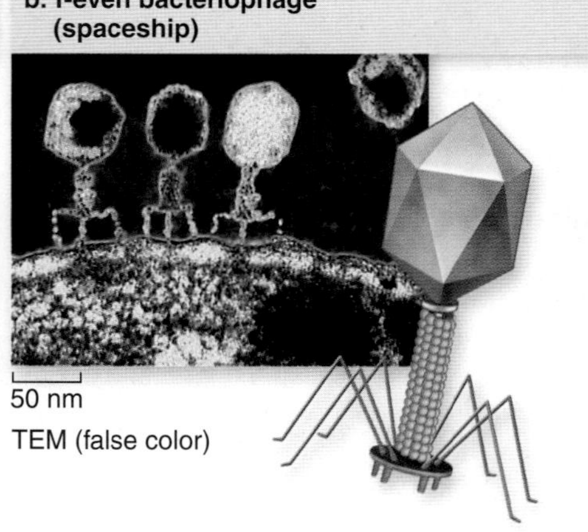

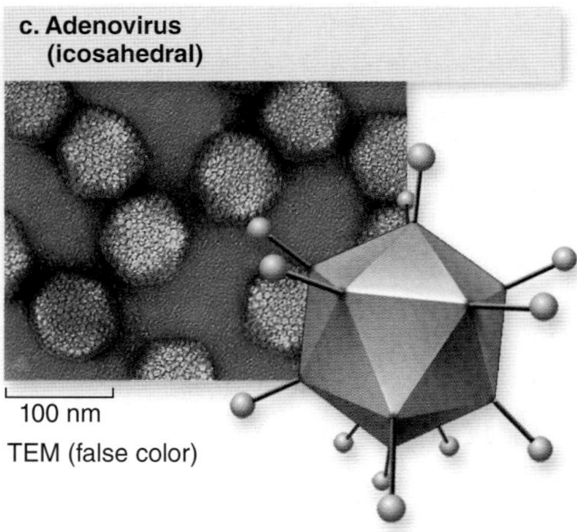

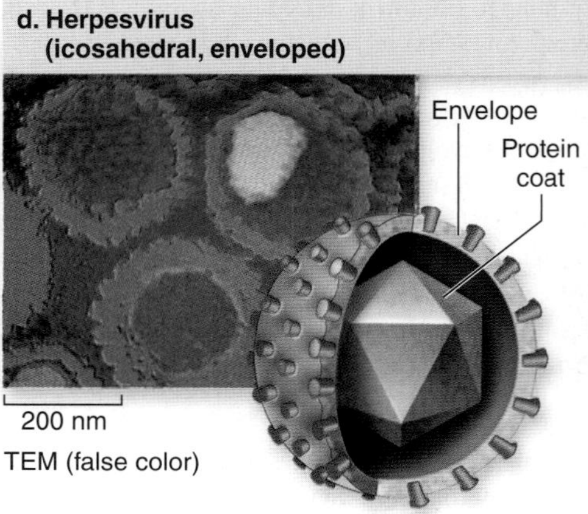

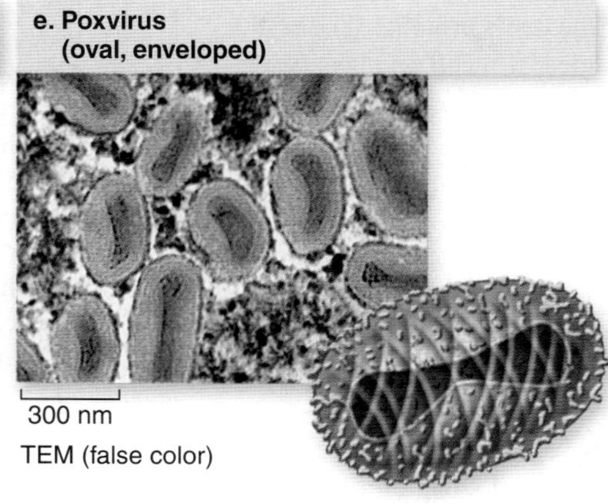

Figure 7.17 Viruses of Many Shapes and Sizes. Each type of virus has a characteristic structure, visible only with an electron microscope. (a) Tobacco mosaic viruses cause disease in plants. (b) T-even viruses infect bacteria. (c) Adenoviruses cause respiratory infections similar to the common cold. (d) Herpesviruses induce cold sores and rashes. (e) Poxviruses cause smallpox.

Despite having relatively few components, a virus's overall structure can be quite intricate and complex. For example, some **bacteriophages,** which are viruses that infect bacteria, have parts that resemble tails, legs, and spikes. These viruses look like the spacecrafts once used to land on the moon (see figure 7.17b).

B. Viral Replication Occurs in Five Stages

The production of new viruses is very different from cell division. When a cell divides, it doubles all of its components and splits in two. Virus production, on the other hand, resembles the way workers build new cars in a factory. The proteins in a virus-infected cell may assemble and release hundreds of new viral particles.

Whatever the host species or cell type, the same basic processes occur during a viral infection (figure 7.18):

1. **Attachment:** A virus attaches to a host cell by adhering to a receptor molecule on the cell's surface. Generally, the virus can attach only to a cell within which it can reproduce. HIV cannot infect skin cells, for example, because its receptors occur only on helper T cells.
2. **Penetration and uncoating:** The viral genetic material can enter the cell in several ways. Animal cells engulf virus particles and bring them into the cytoplasm via endocytosis. Viruses that infect plants often enter their host cells by hitching a ride on the mouthparts of insects that munch on leaves. Many bacteriophages inject their genetic material through a hole in the cell wall, somewhat like a syringe. ▸ endocytosis, p. 79
3. **Synthesis:** The host cell produces multiple copies of the viral genome; mutations during this stage are the raw material for viral evolution. In addition, the information encoded in the viral DNA or RNA is used to produce the virus's proteins. The host cell provides all of the resources required for the production of new viruses: enzymes, ATP, nucleotides, ribosomes, and amino acids.
4. **Assembly:** The subunits of the protein coat join, and then genetic information is packed inside. Enveloped viruses such as HIV are not complete until they bud from the host cell, acquiring their outer coverings from the host cell membrane.
5. **Release:** Once the virus particles are assembled, they are ready to leave the cell. Some bacteriophages induce production of an enzyme that breaks down the host's cell wall, killing the cell as it releases the viruses. HIV and herpesviruses, on the other hand, bud from the host cell by exocytosis. The cell may die as enveloped viruses carry off segments of the cell membrane. ▸ exocytosis, p. 80

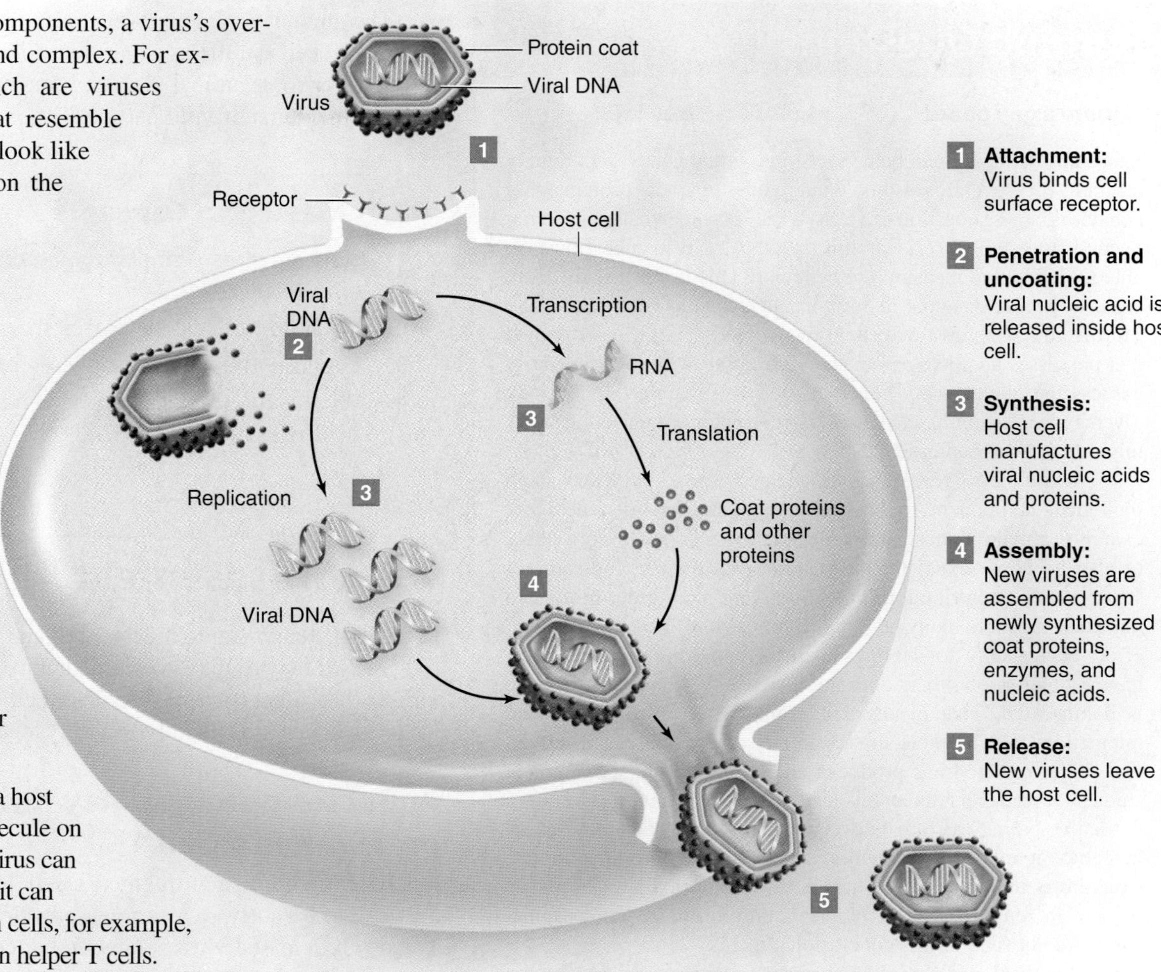
Protein coat
Viral DNA
Virus
1
Receptor
Host cell
Viral DNA
2
Transcription
RNA
3
Translation
Replication
3
Coat proteins and other proteins
4
Viral DNA
5
1 Attachment: Virus binds cell surface receptor.
2 Penetration and uncoating: Viral nucleic acid is released inside host cell.
3 Synthesis: Host cell manufactures viral nucleic acids and proteins.
4 Assembly: New viruses are assembled from newly synthesized coat proteins, enzymes, and nucleic acids.
5 Release: New viruses leave the host cell.

Figure 7.18 Viral Replication. The five basic steps of viral replication apply to any virus, whether the host cell is prokaryotic or eukaryotic.

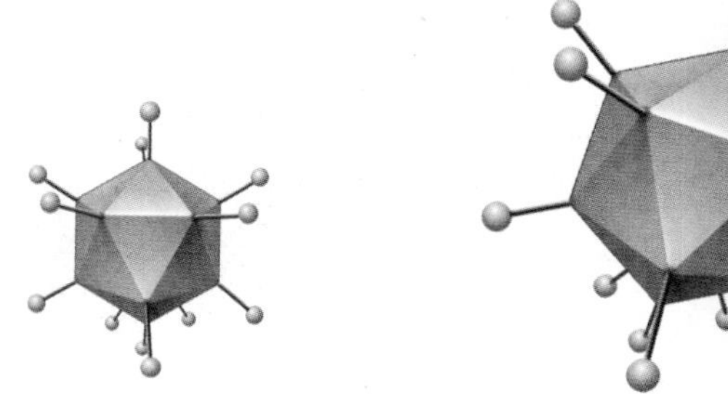

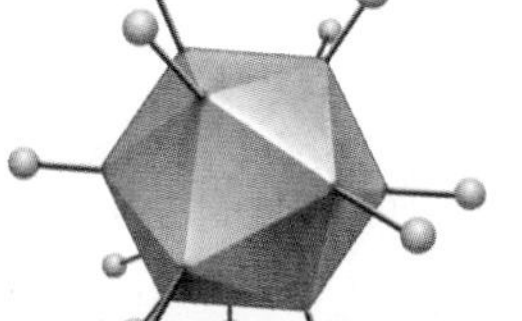

Burning Questions

Is there a gay gene?

Research linking human behavior to individual genes is extremely difficult for several reasons. First, genes encode proteins, not behaviors, so the question of a "gay gene" is somewhat misleading. Second, to establish a clear link to DNA, a researcher must be able to define and measure the behavior. This in itself is difficult, because people disagree about what it means to be homosexual. Third, multiple genes are likely to be involved. Fourth, an individual that possesses an allele associated with a trait will not necessarily express the allele; many genes in each cell remain "off" at any given time. To complicate matters, the environment contributes mightily to gene expression.

Nevertheless, research has yielded some evidence of a biological component to homosexuality, at least in males. For example, a male homosexual's identical twin is much more likely to also be homosexual than is a nonidentical twin, indicating a strong genetic contribution. In addition, the more older brothers a male has, the more likely he is to be homosexual. This "birth order" effect occurs only for siblings with the same biological mother; having older stepbrothers does not increase the chance that a male is homosexual. That means that events before birth, not social interactions with brothers, are apparently responsible for the effect.

Other research has produced ambiguous results. Anatomical studies of cadavers have revealed differences in the size of a particular brain structure between heterosexual and homosexual men, but the relative contribution of genes and environment to this structure is unknown. One study linked homosexuality in males, but not in females, to part of the X chromosome; a subsequent study did not support this conclusion.

So is there a gay gene? The answer remains elusive. But we can say without a doubt that both the environment and genetics play important roles.

Submit your burning question to:
marielle_hoefnagels@mcgraw-hill.com

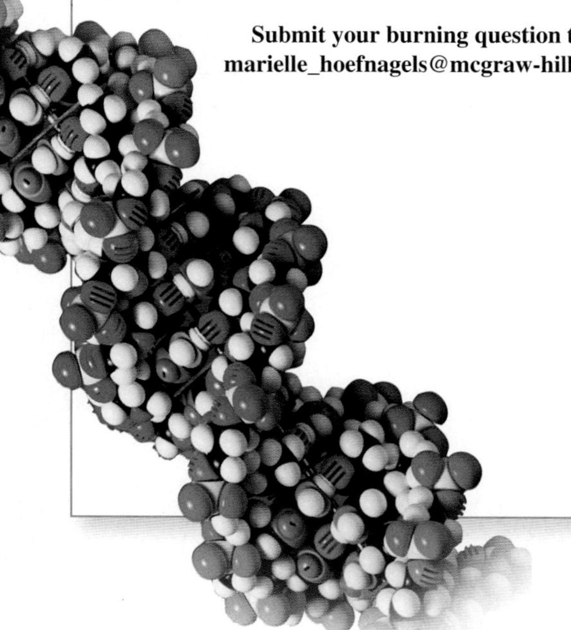

The amount of time between initial infection and cell death varies. Bacteriophages need as little as a half hour to infect a cell and replicate. At the other extreme, for some animal viruses, years may elapse between initial attachment and the final burst of viral particles.

7.7 Mastering Concepts

1. How are viruses similar to and different from bacteria and eukaryotic cells?
2. What features do all viruses share?
3. Describe the five steps in viral replication.
4. What is the source of energy and raw materials for the synthesis of viruses in a host cell?

7.8 Viruses Infect All Cell Types

Following attachment to the host cell and penetration of the viral genetic material, viruses may or may not immediately cause cell death. Bacteriophages, the viruses that infect bacteria, can do either. The two viral replication strategies in bacteriophages are called lytic and lysogenic infections (figure 7.19).

A. Bacteriophages May Kill Cells Immediately or "Hide" in a Cell

In a **lytic infection,** a virus enters a cell, immediately replicates, and causes the host cell to burst (lyse) as it releases a flood of new viruses (see figure 7.19a). The newly released viruses infect other cells, repeating the process until all of the bacteria in a culture are dead.

Some researchers have investigated the possibility of using lytic bacteriophages instead of antibiotics to treat bacterial infections in people. "Phage therapy" would have two main advantages over antibiotics. First, viruses evolve along with their bacterial hosts, and they keep killing until all host cells are dead. Bacterial populations are therefore unlikely to acquire resistance to the phages. Second, each phage targets only one or a few strains of bacteria. Because the treatment is tailored to the infection, side effects are unlikely.

Paradoxically, phage therapy's main weakness is related to this second advantage. Medical personnel must first identify the exact strain of bacteria causing infection before beginning phage therapy. This delay could be deadly.

In a **lysogenic infection,** the genetic material of a virus is replicated along with the host cell's chromosome, but the cell is not immediately destroyed (see figure 7.19b). At some point, however, the virus reverts to a lytic cycle, releasing new viruses and killing the cell.

Many lysogenic viruses use enzymes to cut the host cell DNA and join its own DNA with the host's. A **prophage** is the DNA of a lysogenic bacteriophage that is inserted into the host chromosome. Other lysogenic viruses

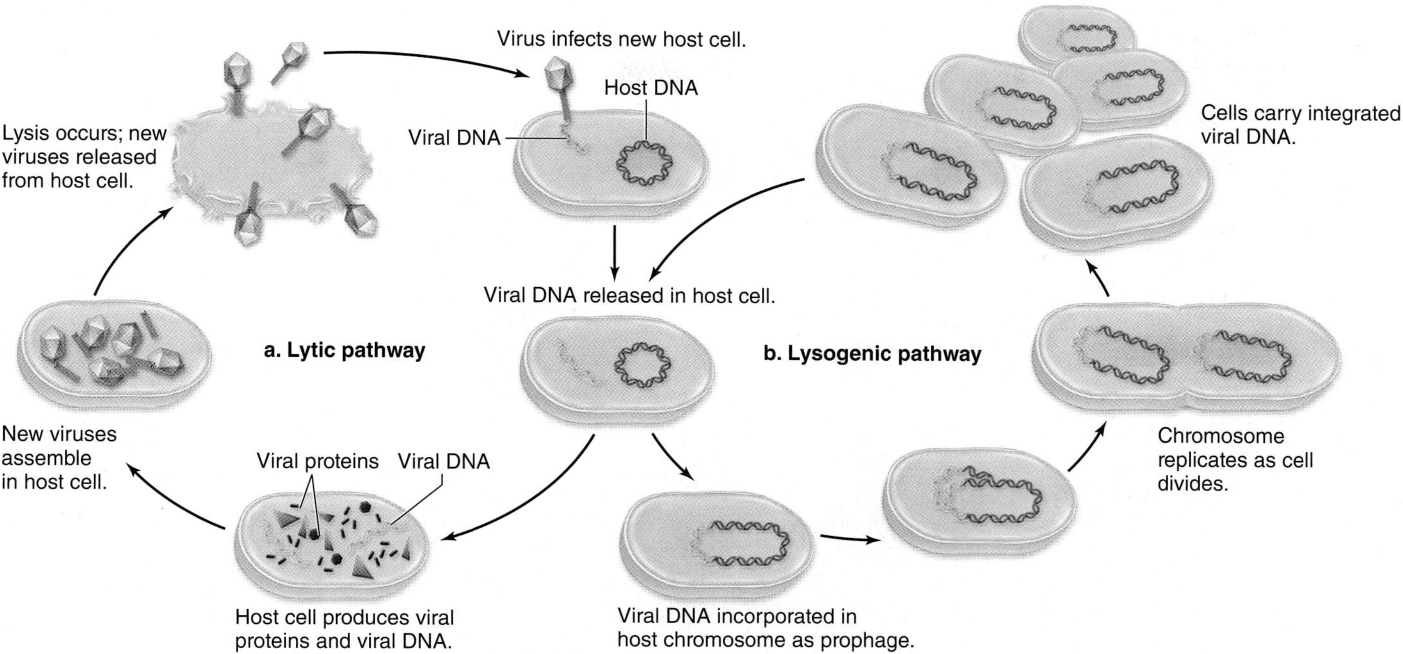
Virus infects new host cell.
Host DNA
Viral DNA
Lysis occurs; new viruses released from host cell.
Cells carry integrated viral DNA.
Viral DNA released in host cell.
a. Lytic pathway
b. Lysogenic pathway
New viruses assemble in host cell.
Viral proteins
Viral DNA
Chromosome replicates as cell divides.
Host cell produces viral proteins and viral DNA.
Viral DNA incorporated in host chromosome as prophage.

Figure 7.19 **Lysis and Lysogeny.** (a) In the lytic pathway, the host cell bursts (lyses) when new virus particles assemble and leave the cell. (b) In lysogeny, viral DNA replicates along with the cell, but new viruses are not produced. An environmental change may trigger a lysogenic virus to become lytic.

maintain their DNA apart from the chromosome. Either way, however, when the infected cell divides, the viral genes replicate, too.

During a lysogenic stage, the viral DNA does not damage the host cell. Only a few viral proteins are produced, most functioning as a "switch" that determines whether the virus should become lytic. At some signal, such as stress from DNA damage or cell starvation, these viral proteins trigger a lytic infection cycle that kills the cell and releases new viruses that infect other cells. The next generation of viruses may enter a lytic or lysogenic replication cycle, depending on the condition of the host cells.

B. Some Animal Viruses Linger for Years

Like a lysogenic bacteriophage, a virus infecting an animal cell may remain dormant as a cell divides. A **latent** infection does not produce disease symptoms, yet the viral genetic information is inside the cell.

Some animal viruses remain latent until conditions make it possible, or necessary, to replicate. An example is herpes simplex virus type I, which causes cold sores on the lips. After initial infection, the viral DNA remains in host cells indefinitely. When a cell becomes stressed or damaged, new viruses are assembled and leave the cell to infect other cells. Cold sores, which reflect the localized death of these cells, periodically recur at the site of the original infection.

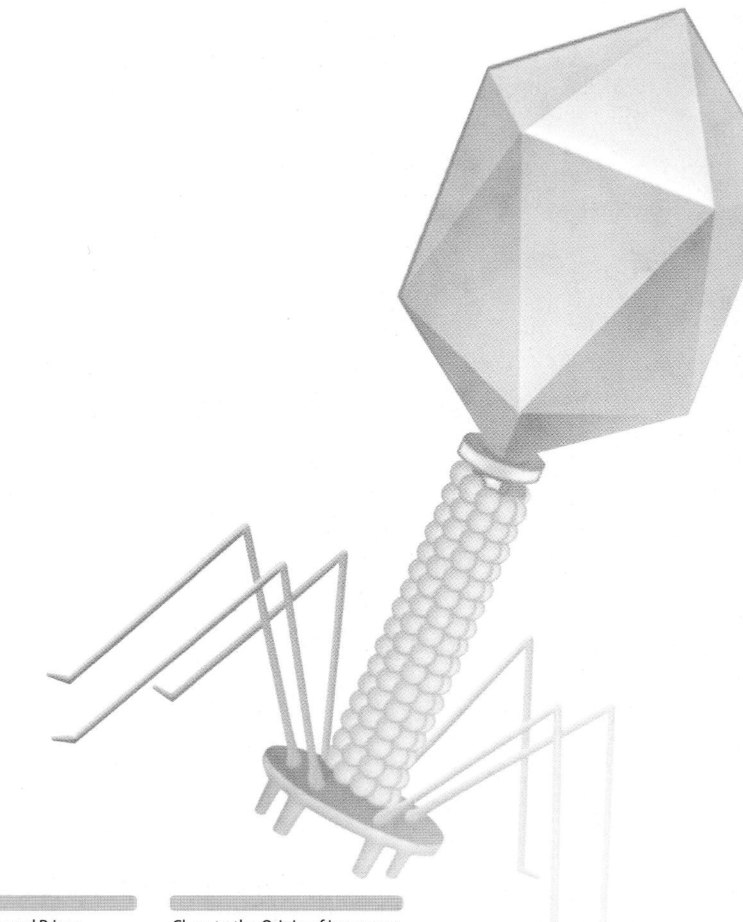

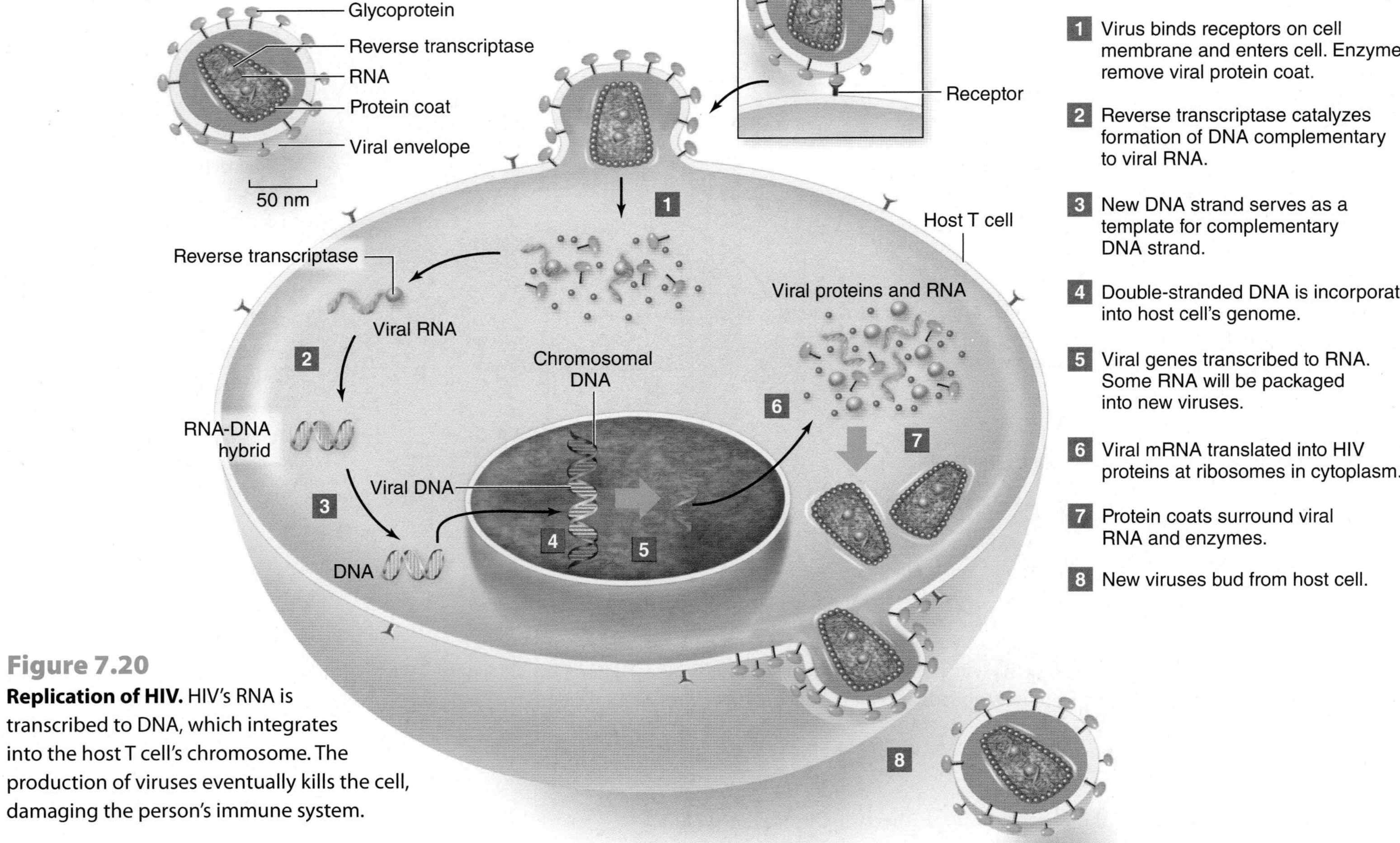

Glycoprotein
Reverse transcriptase
RNA
Protein coat
Viral envelope
50 nm
Receptor
Host T cell
Reverse transcriptase
Viral RNA
Viral proteins and RNA
Chromosomal DNA
RNA-DNA hybrid
Viral DNA
DNA
1
2
3
4
5
6
7
8
1 Virus binds receptors on cell membrane and enters cell. Enzymes remove viral protein coat.
2 Reverse transcriptase catalyzes formation of DNA complementary to viral RNA.
3 New DNA strand serves as a template for complementary DNA strand.
4 Double-stranded DNA is incorporated into host cell's genome.
5 Viral genes transcribed to RNA. Some RNA will be packaged into new viruses.
6 Viral mRNA translated into HIV proteins at ribosomes in cytoplasm.
7 Protein coats surround viral RNA and enzymes.
8 New viruses bud from host cell.

Figure 7.20

Replication of HIV. HIV's RNA is transcribed to DNA, which integrates into the host T cell's chromosome. The production of viruses eventually kills the cell, damaging the person's immune system.

HIV is another virus that can remain latent inside a human cell (figure 7.20). HIV belongs to a family of viruses called retroviruses, all of which have an RNA genome. The virus infects helper T cells, which are part of the immune system. Once inside the cell, HIV's reverse transcriptase enzyme transcribes the viral RNA to DNA. The DNA then inserts itself into the host cell's DNA. Shortly after infection, many HIV particles are produced and released by budding. A strong immune response soon greatly reduces virus production, but infected cells in the lymph nodes continue to release small numbers of viruses. Infected individuals have almost no symptoms, yet HIV is present in their bloodstreams and can be transmitted to others. This phase, called clinical latency, can persist for years.

Throughout this latent period, immune function appears normal, but the number of helper T cells gradually declines. Eventually, the loss of T cells leaves the body unable to defend itself from infections or cancer. AIDS is the result.

Because latent viruses persist by signaling their host cells to divide continuously, some cause cancer. A latent infection by some strains of human papillomavirus, which causes genital warts, can lead to cervical cancer. Epstein–Barr virus is another example. More than 80% of the human population carries this virus, which infects B cells of the immune system. A person who is initially exposed to the virus may develop mononucleosis. The virus later maintains a latent infection in B cells. In a few people, especially those with weakened immune systems, the virus eventually causes a form of cancer called Burkitt lymphoma. ▸ cancer, p. 148

C. Viruses Cause Diseases in Plants

Like all organisms, plants can have viral infections (figure 7.21). The first virus ever discovered was tobacco mosaic virus, which affects not only tobacco but also tomatoes, peppers, and more than 120 other plant species.

To infect a plant cell, a virus must penetrate waxy outer leaf layers and thick cell walls. Most viral infections spread when plant-eating insects such as leafhoppers and aphids move virus-infested fluid from plant to plant on their mouthparts. ▶ plant cell wall, p. 63

Once inside a plant, viruses multiply at the initial site of infection. The killed plant cells often appear as small dead spots on the leaves. Over time, the viruses spread from cell to cell through plasmodesmata (bridges of cytoplasm between plant cells). They can also move throughout a plant by entering the vascular tissues that distribute sap. Depending on the location and extent of the viral infection, symptoms may include blotchy, mottled leaves or abnormal growth. A few symptoms, such as the streaking of some flower petals, appear beautiful to us.

Although plants do not have the same forms of immunity as do animals, they can fight off viral infections. For example, in a process called "posttranscriptional gene silencing," a plant cell degrades viral mRNA, which prevents the production of new viruses. Researchers are learning more about the role of posttranscriptional gene silencing in the defense against viruses in both plants and animals.

Figure 7.21 Sick Plants. (a) Cucumber mosaic virus causes a characteristic mottling (spotting) of squash leaves. (b) A virus has also caused the streaking on the petals of these tulips.

7.8 Mastering Concepts

1. How is a lysogenic viral infection similar to and different from a lytic cycle?
2. What is a latent animal virus?
3. Describe how HIV replicates in host cells.
4. How are some latent viral infections linked to cancer?
5. How do viruses enter plant cells and spread within a plant?
6. What are some symptoms of a viral infection in plants?

7.9 Drugs and Vaccines Help Fight Viral Infections

Halting a viral infection is a challenge, in part because viruses invade living cells. Researchers have developed few medicines that inhibit viruses without killing infected host cells. Many viral diseases therefore remain incurable.

Antiviral drug development is complicated by the genetic variability of many viruses. Consider the common cold. Many different cold viruses exist, and their genomes mutate rapidly. As a result, a different virus strain is responsible every time you get the sniffles. Developing drugs that work against all of these variations has so far proved impossible. Even if a drug inactivated 99.99% of cold-causing viruses, the remaining 0.01% would be resistant. These viruses would replicate, and natural selection would rapidly render the drug ineffective.

Vaccination remains our most potent weapon against many viral diseases. A **vaccine** "teaches" the immune system to recognize one or more molecular components of a virus without actually exposing the person to the disease. Some vaccines confer immunity for years, whereas others must be repeated

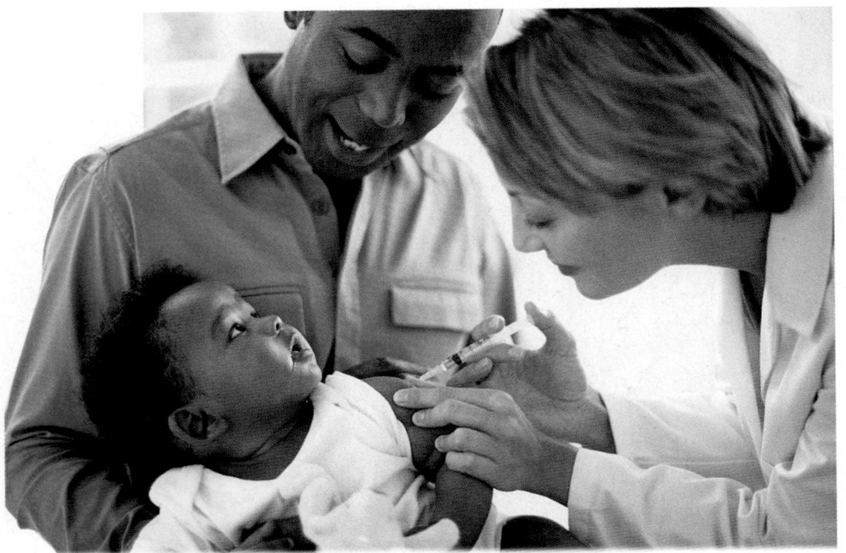

Figure 7.22 Childhood Vaccination. Countless lives have been saved by vaccines that medical researchers have developed against a suite of deadly diseases caused by viruses.

annually. The influenza vaccine is an example of the latter. Flu viruses mutate rapidly, so this year's vaccine is likely to be ineffective against next year's strains.

Childhood vaccinations have greatly reduced the incidence of measles, mumps, and many other potentially serious illnesses (figure 7.22). Unfortunately, researchers have been unable to develop vaccines against many deadly viruses, including HIV. High mutation rates in HIV's genetic material make this virus a moving target.

The antibiotic drugs that kill bacteria never work against viral infections. The reason is that viruses lack the cell walls, ribosomes, and enzymes targeted by antibiotics. Although antibiotics are useless against viruses, many patients demand that physicians prescribe them for viral infections. This behavior selects for antibiotic-resistant bacteria, an enormous and growing public health problem. ▸ antibiotic resistance, p. 233

Nevertheless, a viral infection can sometimes promote bacterial growth. For example, patients sometimes develop sinus infections as a complication of influenza or the common cold. Physicians may prescribe antibiotics to treat these secondary bacterial infections, but the drugs will not affect the underlying virus.

7.9 Mastering Concepts

1. How are viral infections treated and prevented?
2. Why are antibiotics ineffective against viruses?

Figure 7.23 Viroids Infect Plants. The plant on the left has a viroid-caused disease called "tomato bunchy top"; the one on the right is healthy.

7.10 Viroids and Prions Are Other Noncellular Infectious Agents

The idea that something as simple as a virus can cause devastating illness may seem amazing. Yet some infectious agents are even simpler than viruses.

A **viroid** is a highly wound circle of RNA that lacks a protein coat; it is simply naked RNA that can infect a cell. Although viroid RNA does not encode protein, it can nevertheless cause severe disease in many important crop plants, including tomatoes (figure 7.23). Apparently the viroid's RNA interferes with the plant's ability to produce one or more essential proteins.

Another type of infectious agent is a **prion,** which stands for "proteinaceous infectious particle." A prion protein (PrP for short) is a normal cellular protein that can exist in multiple three-dimensional shapes, at least one of which is abnormal and can cause disease. Upon contact with an abnormal form of PrP, a normal prion protein switches to the abnormal PrP configuration. The change triggers another round of protein refolding, and so on. As a result of this chain reaction, masses of abnormal prion proteins accumulate inside cells. ▸ protein folding, p. 40

The misshapen prion proteins cause cells of the nervous system to die. The brain eventually becomes riddled with holes, like a sponge. Mad cow disease is one example of an illness associated with prions (figure 7.24). Cattle and other animals acquire prions by ingesting an infected animal or receiving a transplant of infected tissue. Because of mad cow disease, governments now ban the practice of feeding cattle the processed remains of other cattle.

7.10 Mastering Concepts

1. How are viroids and prions different from viruses?
2. How do viroids and prions cause disease?

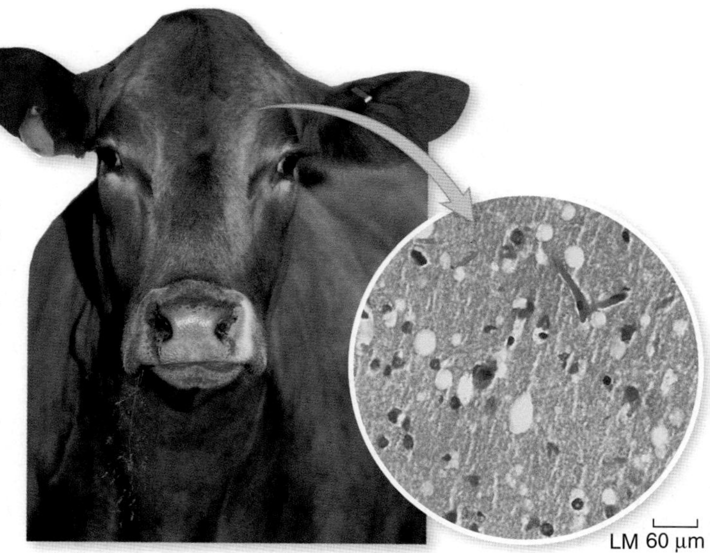

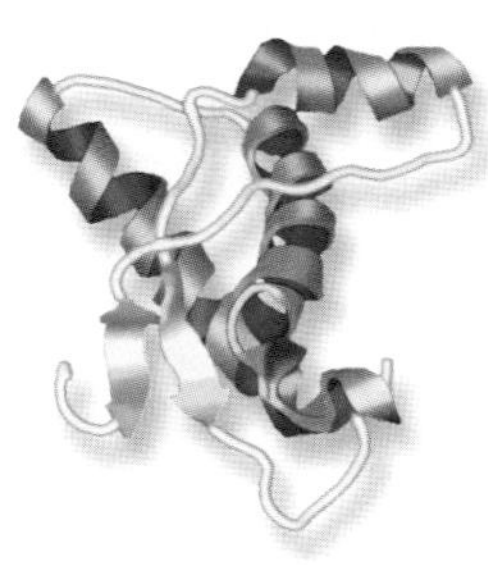

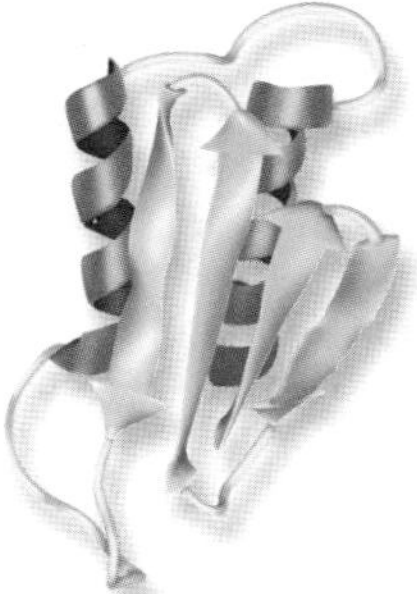

Figure 7.24 Prion Disease. The holes and clumps of abnormal proteins are evident in the brain of a cow with bovine spongiform encephalopathy, also known as "mad cow disease." The lower half of the figure shows models of normal and abnormal prion proteins.

Investigating Life

7.11 Clues to the Origin of Language

The Question: As you chat with your friends and study for your classes, you may take language for granted. Although communication is not unique to humans, a complex spoken language does set us apart from other organisms. Every human society has language; without it, people could not transmit information from one generation to the next, so culture could not develop. Its importance to human evolutionary history is therefore incomparable. But how and when did such a crucial adaptation arise?

The Approach: In the early 1990s, scientists described a family with a high incidence of an unusual language disorder. Affected family members had difficulty controlling the movements of their mouth and face, so they could not pronounce sounds properly. They also had lower intelligence compared with unaffected individuals, and they had trouble applying simple grammatical rules. Researchers traced the language disorder to one mutation in a single gene on chromosome 7. (Overblown media reports incorrectly dubbed this "the language gene" or "the grammar gene," even though many genes influence language capabilities.)

Further research revealed that the gene belongs to the large *f*orkhead b*o*x family of genes, abbreviated *FOX*. All members of the *FOX* family encode transcription factors, proteins that bind to DNA and control the expression of other genes. The "language gene" on chromosome 7, eventually named *FOXP2*, is not solely responsible for language acquisition. But the fact that it encodes a transcription factor explains how it can simultaneously affect both muscle control and brain structure.

To learn more about the evolution of language, scientists Wolfgang Enard, Svante Pääbo, and colleagues at Germany's Max Planck Institute and at the University of Oxford compared the amino acid sequence of the FOXP2 protein in humans, several other primates, and mice. Chimpanzees, gorillas, and the rhesus macaque monkey all have identical FOXP2 proteins; their version differs from the mouse's by only one amino acid out of the 715 amino acids that

Species	Number of differences relative to mouse protein
Mouse	N/A
Rhesus monkey	1
Gorilla	1
Chimpanzee	1
Human	3

Figure 7.25 FOXP2 Protein Compared. The mouse version of the FOXP2 protein differs from that of nonhuman primates by just one amino acid out of 715 in the protein. The human version has three differences when compared with that of the mouse.

make up the protein. Yet the human version differs from the mouse's by three amino acids (figure 7.25).

In a follow-up study published in 2007, several members of the same research team worked with colleagues in Spain and France to study yet another source of the *FOXP2* gene: the remains of two Neandertal individuals unearthed in Spain in 2006. DNA analysis showed that the Neandertal version of *FOXP2* had the same mutations as the version of the gene in modern humans.

The Conclusion: In the 70 million or so years since the mouse and primate lineages split, the FOXP2 protein changed by only one amino acid. Yet in the 5 million or 6 million years since humans split from the rest of the primates, the *FOXP2* gene changed twice. The results of the Neandertal study suggest that the human-specific mutations had already occurred by 300,000 to 400,000 years ago, the time when modern humans and Neandertals last shared a common ancestor.

The study of *FOXP2* is important because it helps us understand a critical period in human history. Apparently, individuals with the new, highly advantageous allele produced more offspring than those with any other version. By natural selection, the new allele quickly became fixed in the human population. Without those events, human communication and culture (including everything you chat about with your friends) might never have happened.

Enard, Wolfgang, Molly Przeworski, Simon E. Fisher, and five coauthors, including Svante Pääbo. August 22, 2002. Molecular evolution of *FOXP2*, a gene involved in speech and language. *Nature*, vol. 418, pages 869–872.

Krause, Johannes, and 12 coauthors, including Wolfgang Enard and Svante Pääbo. November 6, 2007. The derived *FOXP2* variant of modern humans was shared with Neandertals. *Current Biology*, vol. 17, pages 1908–1912.

7.11 Mastering Concepts

1. What question about the *FOXP2* gene were the researchers trying to answer?
2. What insights could scientists gain by intentionally mutating the *FOXP2* gene in a developing human? Would such an experiment be ethical?

Chapter Summary

7.1 DNA Is a Double Helix

- Watson and Crick combined many clues to propose the double-helix structure of DNA.
- **DNA** consists of building blocks called **nucleotides.** The rungs of the DNA double helix consist of **complementary** base pairs. Hydrogen bonds between adenine and thymine, and between cytosine and guanine, hold the two strands together.
- An organism's **genome** is all of the DNA in its cells. In eukaryotic cells, the genome is divided into **chromosomes.**
- **Genes** are sequences of DNA that encode a cell's proteins.

7.2 DNA Stores Genetic Information: An Overview

- To produce a protein, a cell **transcribes** a gene's information to mRNA, which is **translated** into a sequence of amino acids.
- Three types of RNA (**mRNA, rRNA,** and **tRNA**) participate in gene expression.

7.3 Transcription Uses a DNA Template to Create RNA

- Transcription consists of three stages: initiation, elongation, and termination.
- The process begins when **RNA polymerase** binds to a **promoter** on the DNA **template strand.** RNA polymerase then builds an RNA molecule. Transcription ends when RNA polymerase reaches a **terminator** sequence in the DNA.
- After transcription, the cell adds a cap and poly A tail to mRNA. **Introns** are cut out of RNA, and the remaining **exons** are spliced together. The finished mRNA molecule then leaves the nucleus.

7.4 Translation Builds the Protein

- Each group of three consecutive mRNA bases is a **codon** that either specifies one amino acid or signals translation to stop.
- The correspondence between codons and amino acids is the **genetic code.**

A. Translation Requires mRNA, tRNA, and Ribosomes

- mRNA carries a protein-encoding gene's information. rRNA associates with proteins to form **ribosomes,** which support and help catalyze protein synthesis.

- One end of a tRNA molecule has an **anticodon** sequence complementary to an mRNA codon; the amino acid corresponding to the codon binds to the other end of the tRNA molecule.

B. Translation Occurs in Three Steps

- The three stages of translation are initiation, elongation, and termination.
- Translation begins when mRNA joins with a ribosome and a tRNA, usually carrying methionine.
- A second tRNA binds to the next codon, and its amino acid bonds with the amino acid that the first tRNA brought in. The ribosome moves down the mRNA as the chain grows.
- Upon reaching a stop codon, the ribosome is released, and the new polypeptide breaks free.

C. Proteins Must Fold Correctly After Translation

- A protein does not function until it has folded into a specific shape. A polypeptide may also be shortened or combined with others before taking its final form.

7.5 Protein Synthesis Is Highly Regulated

- Protein synthesis requires substantial energy input because large, ordered molecules are created from many small components.

A. Operons Are Groups of Bacterial Genes That Share One Promoter

- In bacteria, **operons** coordinate expression of grouped genes whose encoded proteins participate in the same metabolic pathway. *E. coli*'s ***lac* operon** is a well-studied example. Transcription does not occur if a **repressor** protein binds to the **operator** sequence of the DNA.

B. Eukaryotic Organisms Use Many Methods to Regulate Gene Expression

- Proteins called **transcription factors** bind to DNA and regulate which genes a cell transcribes.
- Other regulatory mechanisms include inactivating regions of a chromosome; alternative splicing; and control over mRNA stability, translation, and protein folding and movement.

7.6 Mutations Change DNA

- A **mutation** adds, deletes, alters, or moves nucleotides in a DNA sequence.

A. Mutations Range from Silent to Devastating

- A **point mutation** alters one or a few DNA bases. A **substitution mutation** is a point mutation that replaces one base with another. The resulting mRNA may encode a different amino acid or substitute a stop codon for another codon. Substitution mutations can also be "silent."
- Altering the number of nucleotides in a gene (a **frameshift mutation**) may disrupt the reading frame, changing the amino acid sequence of the encoded protein.

B. What Causes Mutations?

- A gene can mutate spontaneously. **Mutagens,** such as chemicals or radiation, can also induce mutations.

C. Mutations Are Important for Many Reasons

- Mutations create new alleles, which are the raw material for evolution.
- Induced mutations help scientists deduce gene function and help plant breeders produce new varieties of fruits and flowers.

7.7 Viruses Are Genes Wrapped in a Protein Coat

A. Viruses Are Smaller and Simpler Than Cells

- A **virus** is a nucleic acid (DNA or RNA) in a **protein coat.** A membranous **envelope** surrounds some viruses.
- A virus must infect a living cell to reproduce.
- Many viruses, including some **bacteriophages,** have relatively complex structures.

B. Viral Replication Occurs in Five Stages

- The stages of viral replication within a host cell are attachment, penetration, synthesis, assembly, and release.

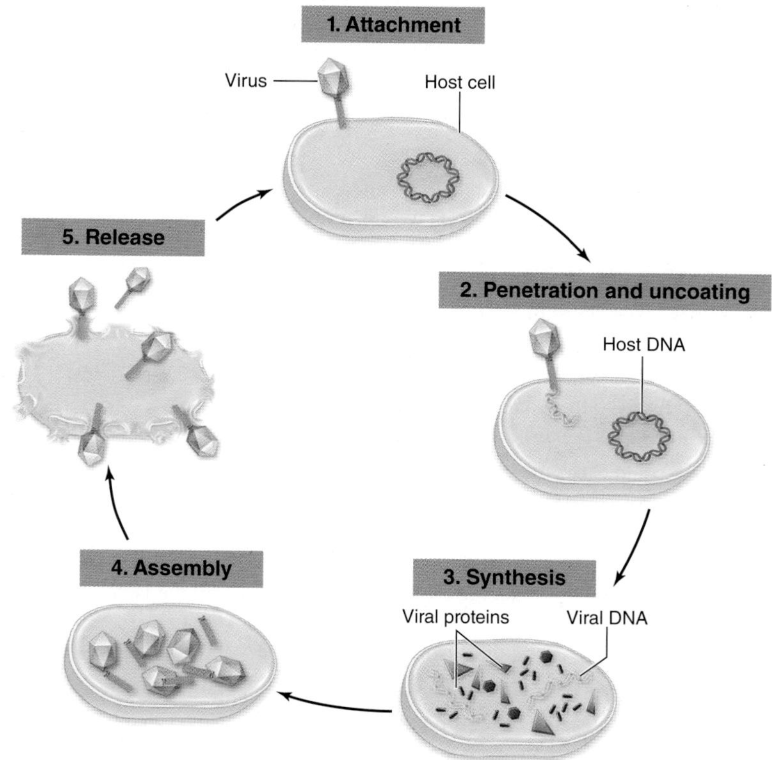

7.8 Viruses Infect All Cell Types

A. Bacteriophages May Kill Cells Immediately or "Hide" in a Cell

- In a **lytic infection,** new viruses are immediately assembled and released.
- In a **lysogenic infection,** the virus's nucleic acid replicates along with that of a dividing cell without causing symptoms. The viral DNA may integrate as a **prophage** into the host chromosome.

B. Some Animal Viruses Linger for Years

- HIV and some others remain **latent,** or hidden, inside animal cells.
- Some latent viruses are associated with cancer.

C. Viruses Cause Diseases in Plants

- Viruses infect plant cells, then spread via plasmodesmata.

7.9 Drugs and Vaccines Help Fight Viral Infections

- Antiviral drugs and **vaccines** combat some viral infections.
- Antibiotics that kill bacteria are ineffective against viruses.

7.10 Viroids and Proteins Are Other Noncellular Infectious Agents

- **Viroids** are naked RNA molecules that infect plants.
- A **prion** protein can take multiple shapes, at least one of which can cause mad cow disease. Treatments that destroy bacteria and viruses have no effect on prions.

7.11 Investigating Life: Clues to the Origin of Language

- A family with a language disorder led researchers to discover a gene that is involved in the acquisition of language.
- The gene apparently began evolving rapidly soon after humans arose. Modern humans and Neandertals share the same mutations in the gene.

Multiple Choice Questions

1. Choose the mRNA sequence that is complementary to the gene sequence GGACTTACG.
   a. CCTGAATGC
   b. AACUGGCUA
   c. GGTCAATCG
   d. CCUGAAUGC
2. What might happen if you changed one nucleotide in a codon?
   a. The protein would stop being made.
   b. The protein would have the wrong amino acid sequence.
   c. There would be no effect on the protein.
   d. All of the above are possible.
3. What is the job of tRNA during translation?
   a. It carries amino acids to the mRNA.
   b. It triggers the formation of a covalent bond between amino acids.
   c. It binds to the small ribosomal subunit.
   d. It triggers the termination of the protein.
4. What could cause the *lac* operon to shut off after it has been activated?
   a. The binding of the sugar lactose to the promoter
   b. The inactivation of RNA polymerase by the addition of a modified sugar
   c. The binding of the repressor to the operator after all the lactose is degraded
   d. The binding of the repressor to the promoter
5. Are mutations bad?
   a. Yes, because the DNA is damaged.
   b. No, because changes in the DNA result in better alleles.
   c. Yes, because mutated proteins don't function.
   d. It depends on how the mutation affects the protein's function.
6. Which of the following is NOT a feature associated with viruses?
   a. Cytoplasm
   b. Genetic information
   c. Protein coat
   d. Envelope
7. Which of the following is physically the largest?
   a. HIV
   b. RNA molecule
   c. *E. coli* cell
   d. Human T cell
8. At which stage in viral replication does viral genetic information enter the host cell?
   a. Penetration
   b. Synthesis
   c. Assembly
   d. Release
9. What occurs during a lysogenic infection?
   a. Viral particles attach to but do not penetrate a host cell.
   b. Viral particles fill a host cell and cause it to burst.
   c. Viral genetic material replicates in a host cell but does not cause symptoms.
   d. The viral prophage DNA is packaged into a protein coat.
10. What is a prion?
    a. A highly wound circle of RNA
    b. A virus that has not yet acquired its envelope
    c. A protein that can alter the shape of a second protein
    d. The protein associated with a latent virus

Write It Out

1. Describe the three-dimensional structure of DNA.
2. What is the function of DNA?
3. Arrange the following objects in order from smallest to largest: nucleotide, nitrogenous base, gene, nucleus, cell, codon, chromosome.
4. List the three major types of RNA and their functions.
5. List the differences between RNA and DNA.
6. Define and distinguish between transcription and translation.
7. Where in a eukaryotic cell do transcription and translation occur?
8. Write the sequence of the mRNA molecule transcribed from the following template DNA sequence:
   G G A A T A C G T C T A G C T A G C A
9. Given the following mRNA sequence, reconstruct the corresponding DNA template sequence:
   A G G A A A A C C C C U C U U A U U A U A G A U
10. What is the minimum size of a gene encoding a protein that is 1259 amino acids long?
11. If a cell's genome is analogous to a cookbook and a gene is analogous to a recipe, what is an analogy for a genetic mutation? How could you incorporate viruses into this cookbook analogy?
12. How can a mutation alter the sequence of DNA bases in a gene but not produce a noticeable change in the gene's polypeptide product? How can a mutation alter the amino acid sequence of a polypeptide yet not noticeably alter the organism?
13. Parkinson disease causes rigidity, tremors, and other motor symptoms. Only 2% of cases are inherited, and these tend to have an early onset of symptoms. Some inherited cases result from mutations in a gene that encodes the protein parkin, which has 12 exons. Indicate whether each of the following mutations in the parkin gene would result in a smaller protein, a larger protein, or not change the size of the protein.
    a. Deletion of exon 3
    b. Deletion of six consecutive nucleotides in exon 1
    c. Duplication of exon 5
    d. Disruption of the splice site between exon 8 and intron 8
    e. Deletion of intron 2
14. Consult the genetic code to write codon changes that could account for the following changes in amino acid sequence:
    a. Tryptophan to arginine
    b. Glycine to valine
    c. Tyrosine to histidine
15. What are some ways that cells regulate gene expression?
16. What events occur in each of the five stages of viral replication?
17. Distinguish between lytic and lysogenic infections.
18. Your biology lab instructor gives you a Petri dish of agar covered with visible colonies. Your lab partner says the colonies are viruses, but you disagree. How do you know the colonies are bacteria?
19. With a diameter of about 600 nm, mimiviruses are enormous compared with other viruses. The mimivirus genome consists of about 1.2 million base pairs and encodes more than 1000 genes—more than some bacteria.

If you encountered a mimivirus-like object in your research, what sorts of studies could you carry out to determine whether the object was a virus or a bacterium?

20. Imagine a hybrid virus with the protein coat of virus X and the DNA of virus Y. Will a host cell infected with this hybrid virus produce virus X, virus Y, a mix of virus X and Y, or hybrid viruses? Explain your answer.
21. Why do antibiotics such as penicillin kill bacteria but leave viruses unharmed?
22. Several anti-HIV drugs are already on the market. List some reasons that we might need even more new drugs to fight HIV in the future.
23. How is a biological virus similar to and different from a computer virus?
24. The National Center for Biotechnology Information maintains an online list of viruses for which genome sequence data are available. Choose one and describe some discoveries that have come from research on this virus.

Pull It Together

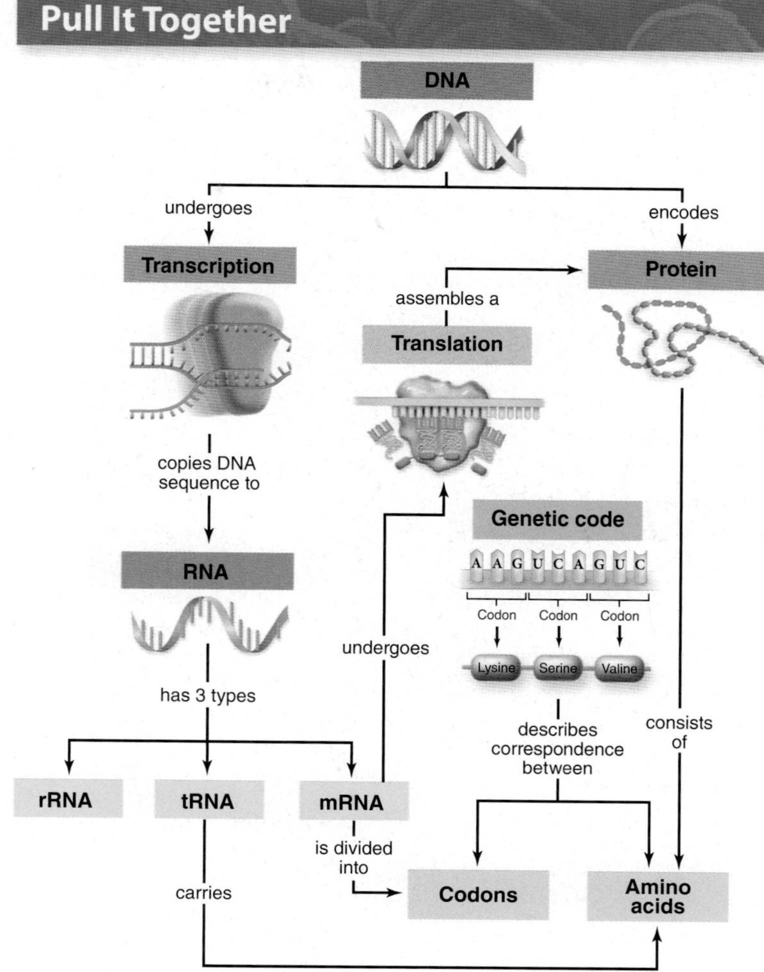

1. Why is protein production essential to cell function?
2. Where do promoters, terminators, stop codons, transcription factors, and RNA polymerase fit into this concept map?
3. How would viruses fit into this concept map?
4. Use the concept map to explain why a mutation in DNA sometimes causes protein function to change.

8 DNA Replication and Cell Division

Learning Outline

Growth. Cell division accounts for the growth of a seedling, a child, and every other multicellular organism.

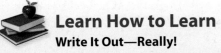

Learn How to Learn

Write It Out—Really!

Get out a pen and a piece of scratch paper, and answer the open-ended "Write It Out" questions at the end of each chapter. This tip applies even if the exams in your class are multiple choice. Putting pen to paper (as opposed to just saying the answer in your head) forces you to organize your thoughts and helps you discover the difference between what you know and what you only THINK you know.

What's the Point?

SEM (false color) 5 µm

Without a doubt, DNA is an amazing molecule. In chapter 7, you learned about DNA's main function: to specify the "recipes" for all of the proteins in a cell. The production of proteins is essential to life, so it stands to reason that every cell needs a complete set of DNA instructions. Where does this DNA come from?

The scientists who discovered the structure of DNA surmised the answer: a cell can copy its own DNA. This process of DNA replication must occur before a cell's nucleus and cytoplasm can split in two. This chapter describes how and when eukaryotic cells divide to reproduce, grow, or repair injuries. Cell division is under tight control. As you will see, an organism that fails to keep cell division in check risks deadly consequences.

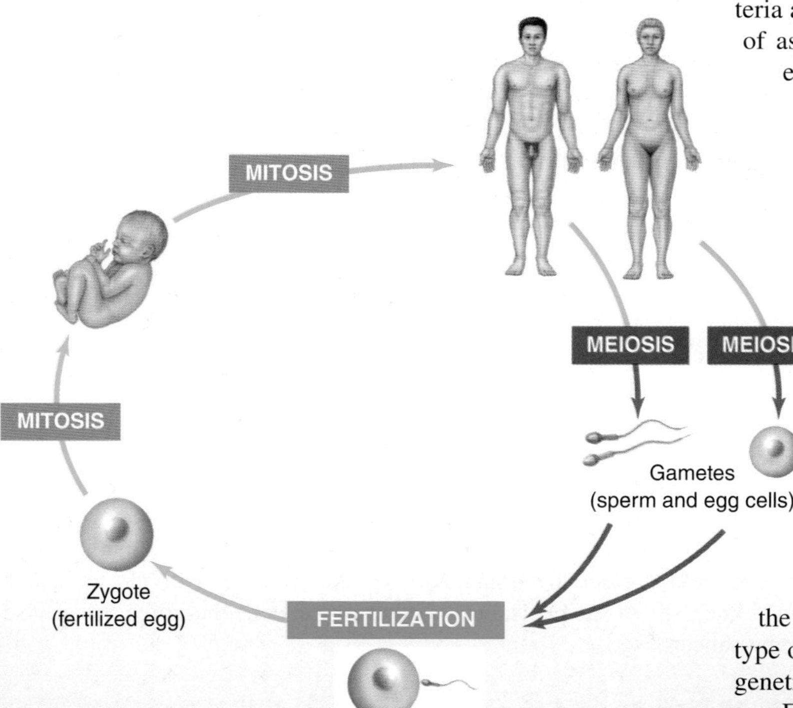

Figure 8.1 **Sexual Reproduction.** In the life cycle of humans and many other organisms, adults produce gametes by meiosis. Fertilization unites sperm and egg, forming a zygote. Mitotic cell division accounts for the growth of the new offspring.

8.1 Cells Divide, and Cells Die

Your cells are too small to see without a microscope, so it is hard to appreciate just how many you lose as you sleep, work, and play. Each minute, for example, you shed tens of thousands of dead skin cells. If you did not have a way to replace these building blocks, your body would literally wear away. Instead, cells in your deep skin layers divide and replace the ones you lose. Each new cell lives an average of about 35 days, so you will gradually replace your entire skin in the next month or so—without even noticing!

Cell division produces a continuous supply of replacement cells, both in your skin and elsewhere in your body. But cell division has other functions as well. No living organism can reproduce without cell division, and the growth and development of a multicellular organism also require the production of new cells.

This chapter explores the opposing but coordinated forces of cell division and cell death. We begin by exploring cell division's role in reproduction, growth, and development.

A. Sexual Life Cycles Include Mitosis, Meiosis, and Fertilization

Organisms must reproduce—generate other individuals like themselves—for a species to persist. The most straightforward and ancient way for a single-celled organism to reproduce is **asexually,** by replicating its genetic material and splitting the contents of one cell into two. Except for the occasional mutation, asexual reproduction generates genetically identical offspring. Most bacteria and archaea, for example, reproduce by binary fission, the simplest type of asexual cell division (see section 8.3). Many protists and multicellular eukaryotes also reproduce asexually.

Sexual reproduction, in contrast, is the production of offspring whose genetic makeup comes from two parents. Each parent contributes a sex cell, and the fusion of these cells signals the start of the next generation. Because sexual reproduction mixes up and recombines traits, the offspring are genetically different from one another.

Figure 8.1 illustrates how two types of cell division, meiosis and mitosis, interact in the sexual life cycle. In humans and many other species, the male parent provides sperm cells, and a female produces egg cells. **Meiosis,** described in chapter 9, is the specialized type of cell division that gives rise to these sex cells (collectively called **gametes**). Meiosis produces cells that are genetically different from one another, which explains why the offspring of two parents generally look different, except for identical twins.

Fertilization is the union of the sperm and the egg cell, producing the first cell of the new offspring. Immediately after fertilization, the other type of cell division—mitotic—takes over. **Mitosis** divides a eukaryotic cell's genetic information into two identical daughter cells.

Each of the trillions of cells in your body therefore retains the genetic information that was present in the fertilized egg. Inspired by the astonishing precision with which this occurs, geneticist Herman J. Müller wrote in 1947:

> *In a sense we contain ourselves, wrapped up within ourselves, trillions of times repeated.*

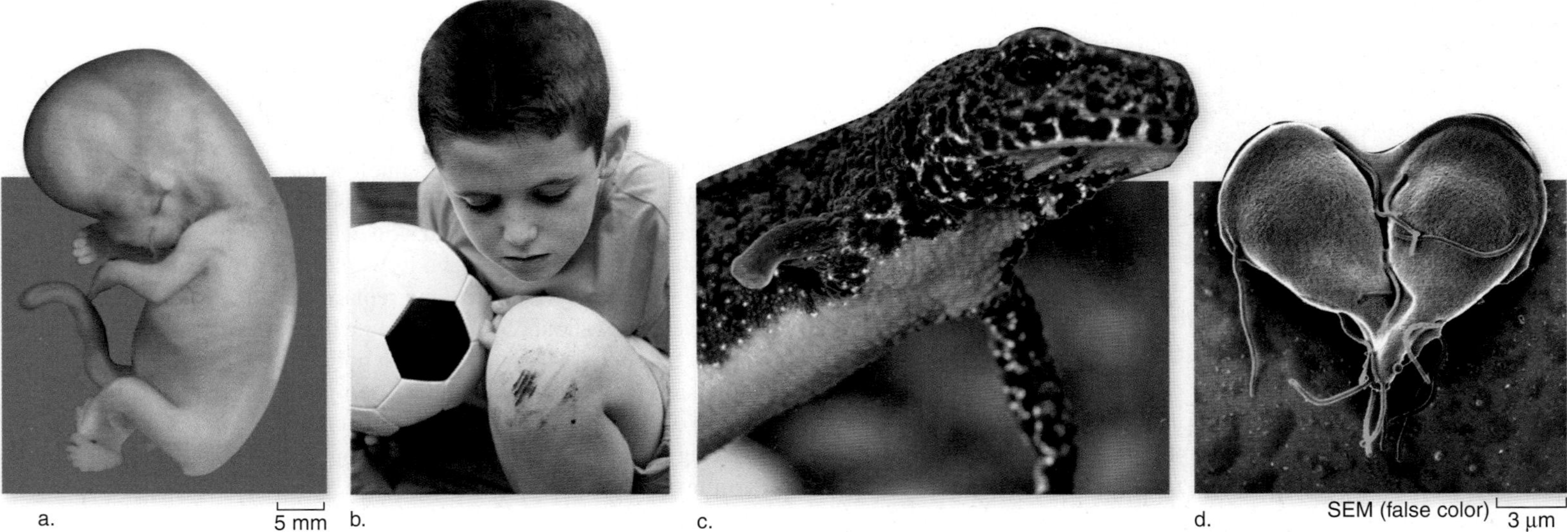

Figure 8.2 Functions of Cell Division. Cells divide mitotically as a eukaryotic organism (a) grows and (b) repairs damaged tissues. (c) Some species can regenerate lost body parts; this newt is regrowing a forelimb. (d) Other organisms, such as this protist, reproduce asexually by mitotic cell division.

This quotation eloquently expresses the powerful idea that every cell in the body results from countless rounds of cell division, each time forming two genetically identical cells from one.

Mitotic cell division explains how you grew from a single cell into an adult, how you repair damage after an injury, and how you replace the cells that you lose every day (figure 8.2). Likewise, mitotic cell division accounts for the growth and development of plants, mushrooms, and other multicellular eukaryotes and for asexual reproduction in protists and many other eukaryotes.

B. Cell Death Is Part of Life

The development of a multicellular organism requires more than just cell division. Cells also die in predictable ways, carving distinctive structures. **Apoptosis** is cell death that is a normal part of development. Like cell division, it is a precise, tightly regulated sequence of events. Apoptosis is therefore also called "programmed cell death."

During early development, both cell division and apoptosis shape new structures. For example, the feet of chickens and ducks start out as webbed paddles. The webs of tissue remain in the duck's foot throughout life. In the chicken, however, individual toes form as cells between the digits die (figure 8.3). Likewise, cells in the tail of a tadpole die as the young frog develops into an adult.

Throughout an animal's life, cell division and cell death are in balance, so tissue neither overgrows nor shrinks. Cell division compensates for the death of skin and blood cells, a little like adding new snow (cell division) to a snowman that is melting (apoptosis). Both cell division and apoptosis also help protect the organism. For example, cells divide to heal a scraped knee; apoptosis peels away sunburnt skin cells that might otherwise become cancerous.

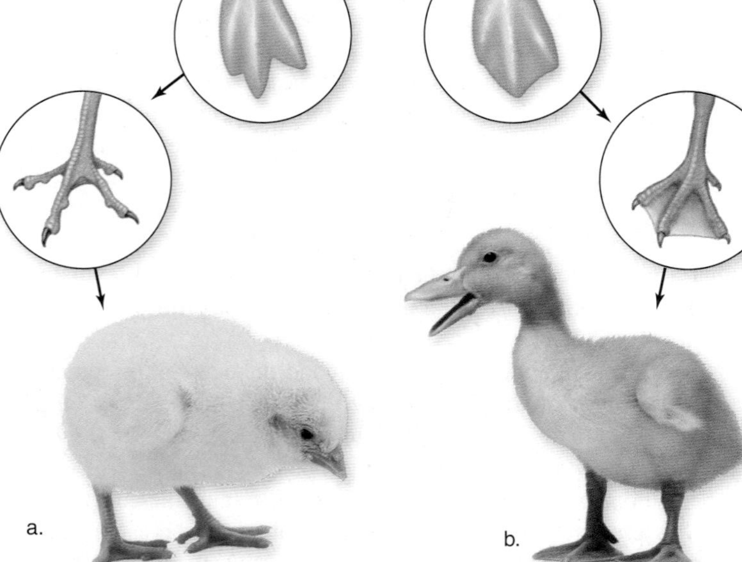

Figure 8.3 Apoptosis Carves Toes. (a) A developing chicken foot undergoes extensive apoptosis. The toes take shape as selected cells die. (b) A duck's foot retains webbing between the digits.

8.1 Mastering Concepts

1. Explain the roles of mitotic cell division, meiosis, and fertilization in the human life cycle.
2. Why are both cell division and apoptosis necessary for the development of an organism?

8.2 DNA Replication Precedes Cell Division

When a cell divides, it must first duplicate its entire **genome,** which consists of all of its genetic material. The genome may consist of just one **chromosome,** which is a single molecule of DNA and associated proteins. A bacterial genome, for example, consists of one circular chromosome. Alternatively, the genome may be divided among multiple chromosomes. A human cell, for example, usually contains 46 chromosomes.

Whatever the number of chromosomes, a cell's DNA contains the instructions for the proteins that sustain life. As the cell splits in two, it must therefore ensure that each new "daughter" cell receives a full set of DNA. If any genetic material is missing, the new cells may die.

Clues to the process of DNA replication came from Watson and Crick's report on DNA's chemical structure. The paper ends with the tantalizing statement, "It has not escaped our notice that the specific pairing we have postulated immediately suggests a possible copying mechanism for the genetic material." They envisioned DNA unwinding, exposing unpaired bases that would attract their complements, and neatly knitting two double helices from one. This route to replication turned out to be essentially correct; each DNA double helix conserves half of the original molecule (figure 8.4a).

Replication

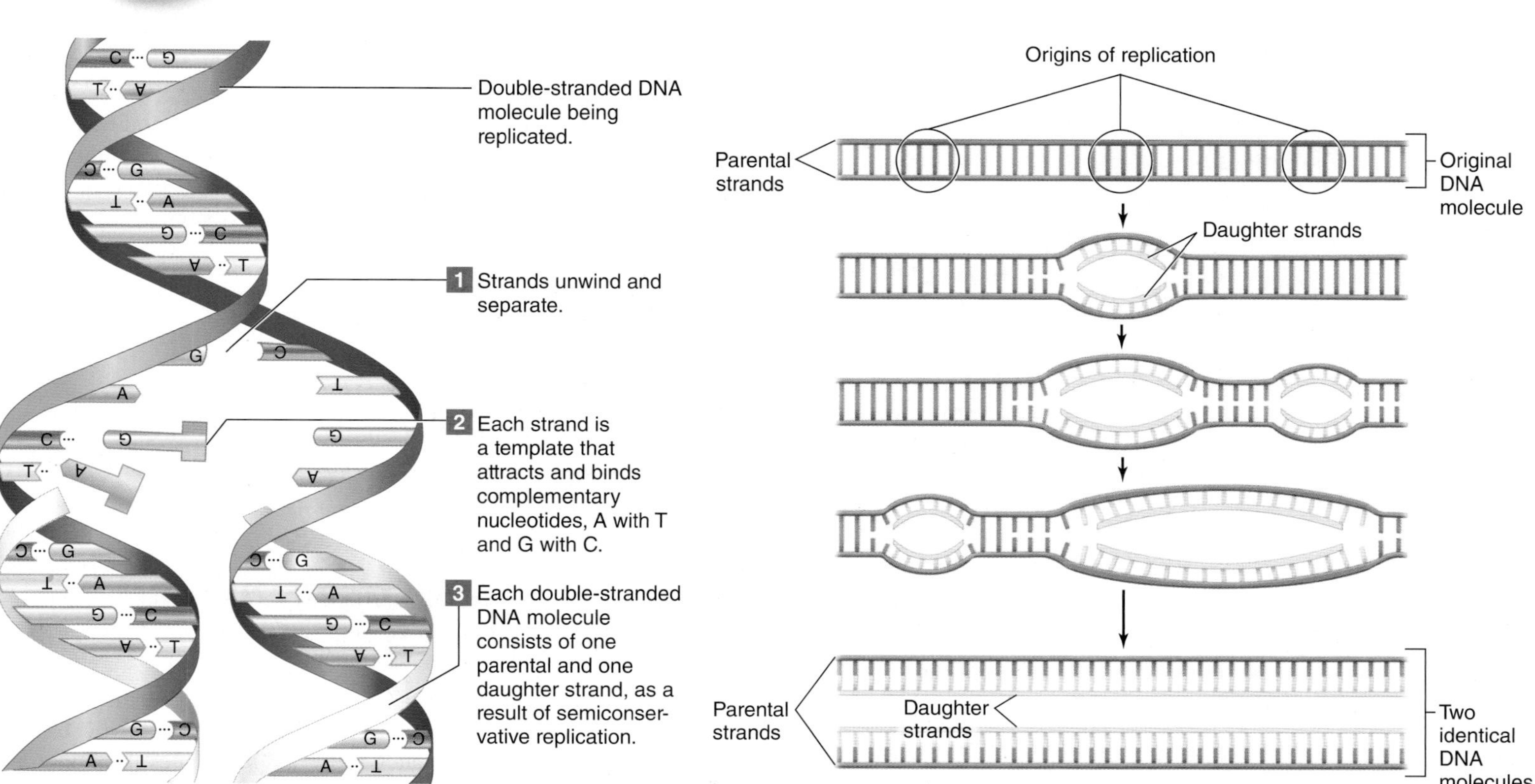
Double-stranded DNA molecule being replicated.
1 Strands unwind and separate.
2 Each strand is a template that attracts and binds complementary nucleotides, A with T and G with C.
3 Each double-stranded DNA molecule consists of one parental and one daughter strand, as a result of semiconservative replication.
a.
Origins of replication
Parental strands
Original DNA molecule
Daughter strands
Parental strands
Daughter strands
Two identical DNA molecules
b.

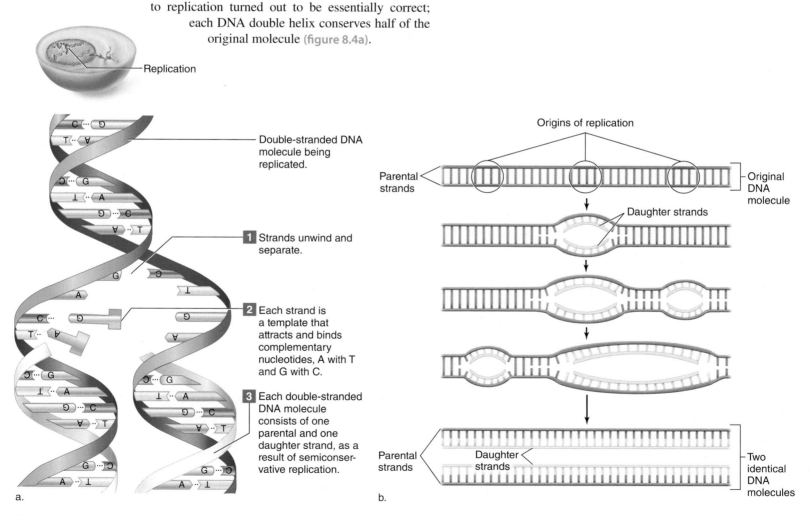

Figure 8.4 DNA Replication: A Simplified View. (a) In the first step of replication, DNA strands unwind and separate. New nucleotides are free to form complementary base pairs with each exposed strand. The process ends with two identical double-stranded DNA molecules. Note that the enzymes that participate in DNA replication are not shown. (b) DNA replication occurs simultaneously at many points along the chromosome.

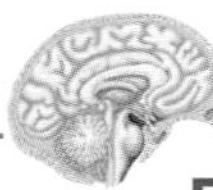

Figure It Out

Write the complementary strand for the following DNA sequence: TCAATACCGATTAT.

Answer: AGTTATGGCTAATA

An army of enzymes copies DNA. Enzymes called helicases unwind and hold apart replicating DNA so that other enzymes can guide the assembly of new DNA strands. Another enzyme breaks the hydrogen bonds that connect a base pair. **DNA polymerase** is the enzyme that adds new DNA nucleotides complementary to the bases on the exposed strand. As each new DNA strand grows, hydrogen bonds form between the complementary bases.

Enzymes copy DNA simultaneously at hundreds of points, called origins of replication, on a long DNA molecule (figure 8.4b). Replication proceeds in both directions at once from each origin of replication. Enzymes called **ligases** form covalent bonds between adjacent DNA segments.

Of course, none of this occurs for free. DNA replication requires a great deal of energy because a large, organized molecule contains much more potential energy than do many individual nucleotides. Energy is required to synthesize nucleotides and to create the covalent bonds that join them together in the new strands of DNA. Many of the enzymes that participate in DNA replication also require energy to catalyze their reactions.

DNA replication is incredibly accurate. DNA polymerase "proofreads" as it goes, discarding mismatched nucleotides and inserting correct ones. After proofreading, only about 1 in a billion nucleotides are incorrect. Other repair enzymes help improve the accuracy of DNA replication by cutting out and replacing incorrect nucleotides. Nevertheless, mistakes occasionally remain. The result is a **mutation,** which is any change in a cell's DNA sequence. In addition to DNA replication errors, mutations can also occur after exposure to radiation or harmful chemicals. If repair enzymes do not fix the damaged DNA, a dividing cell can pass the error to its descendants. ▸ mutations, p. 123

A mutation in a gene sometimes changes the amino acid sequence of its encoded protein so much that the protein can no longer do its job. Inherited diseases, including cystic fibrosis and sickle cell anemia, stem from such DNA sequence changes. In other cases, mutations either do not affect the encoded proteins at all, or they may even improve their function.

Some of the most harmful mutations affect the genes encoding the proteins that repair DNA. If these enzymes cannot fix damaged DNA, then additional mutations begin to accumulate. The cell may die or become cancerous (see section 8.6). Precise DNA replication is therefore essential to cell survival.

8.2 Mastering Concepts

1. Why does DNA replicate?
2. What are the steps of DNA replication?
3. What is a mutation, and why are mutations important?
4. Why is DNA repair necessary?

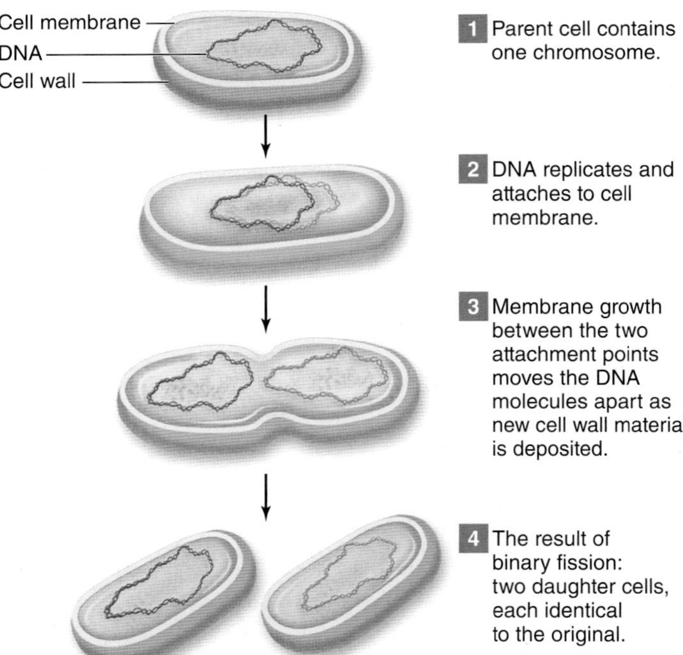
Cell membrane
DNA
Cell wall
1 Parent cell contains one chromosome.
2 DNA replicates and attaches to cell membrane.
3 Membrane growth between the two attachment points moves the DNA molecules apart as new cell wall material is deposited.
4 The result of binary fission: two daughter cells, each identical to the original.

Figure 8.5 Binary Fission. A dividing prokaryotic cell grows while its DNA replicates, and then the cell splits into two.

8.3 Bacteria and Archaea Divide by Binary Fission

Like all organisms, bacteria and archaea transmit DNA from generation to generation as they reproduce. In prokaryotes, reproduction occurs by **binary fission,** an asexual process that replicates DNA and distributes it (along with other cell parts) into two daughter cells (figure 8.5).

As the prokaryotic cell prepares to divide, the DNA replicates. The circular chromosome and its duplicate are attached to the inner surface of the cell. The cell membrane grows between the two DNA molecules, separating them. Then the cell membrane dips inward, pinching in half to form two daughter cells from the original one. Formation of cell walls completes the binary fission process.

In optimal conditions, some bacterial cells can divide every 20 minutes. This rapid reproduction explains how the oral microbes that survive your nightly tooth-brushing regimen produce countless descendants (and the notoriously unpleasant "morning breath") as you sleep.

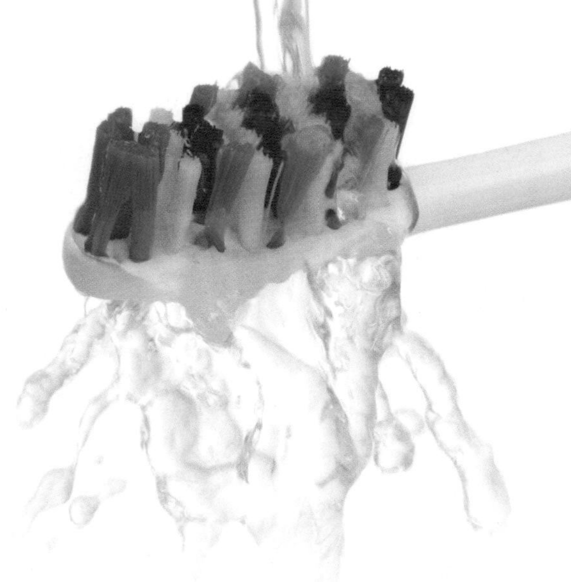

Binary fission is a form of asexual reproduction. In eukaryotes that reproduce asexually, genetic diversity usually arises only from random mutations in a cell's DNA. Bacteria and archaea undergo mutations as well, but they can also acquire new genetic material from other sources. For example, one cell may transfer a copy of some of its DNA to another cell through an appendage called a sex pilus. Alternatively, a cell may absorb stray bits of DNA that are released after another cell dies. Gene transfer among bacterial cells has profound implications in many fields, including medicine. As bacteria continue to swap antibiotic-resistance genes, for example, many once-curable diseases are becoming impossible to treat. ▸ antibiotic resistance, p. 233

8.3 Mastering Concepts

1. What are the events of binary fission?
2. What are the sources of genetic variation in bacteria and archaea?

8.4 Replicated Chromosomes Condense as a Cell Prepares to Divide

In bacterial cells, the genome consists of a single circular DNA molecule, so cell division is relatively simple. In a eukaryotic cell, however, distributing the DNA into daughter cells is a bit more complicated because the genetic information inside the cell's nucleus is divided among multiple chromosomes. Each species has a characteristic number of chromosomes in each cell. A mosquito cell has six chromosomes; grasshoppers, rice plants, and pine trees have 24; humans have 46; a dog and a chicken have 78; a carp has 104.

With so many chromosomes, every eukaryotic cell must balance two needs. On the one hand, to produce the proteins it requires, the cell must have access to the information in its DNA. On the other hand, if the cell is to divide, it must package its DNA into a portable form that can easily move into the two daughter cells (figure 8.6). To understand how cells maintain this balance, we must take a closer look at the structure of the eukaryotic chromosome.

Figure 8.6 Two Views of DNA. In the cell on the left, DNA is loosely packed in the nucleus and available for DNA replication and protein synthesis. Before a cell divides, however, the DNA winds into the compact, portable chromosomes visible in the cell on the right.

LM 30 μm

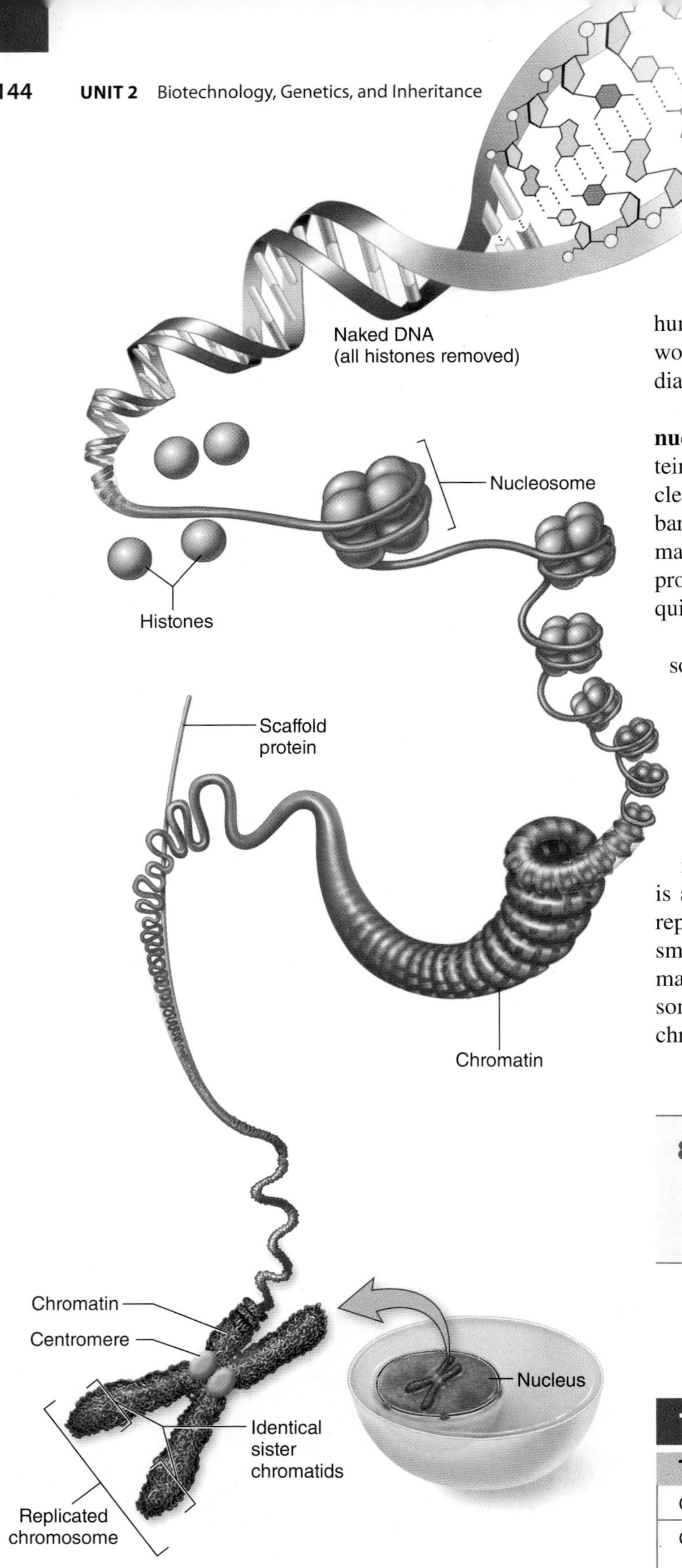

Eukaryotic chromosomes consist of **chromatin,** which is a collective term for DNA and its associated proteins in the nucleus. Among other functions, the proteins help to pack the DNA efficiently inside the cell. Stretched end to end, the DNA in one human cell would form a thread some 2 meters long. If the DNA bases of all 46 human chromosomes were typed as A, C, T, and G, the several billion letters would fill 4000 books of 500 pages each! How can a cell only 100 microns in diameter contain so much material?

The explanation is that chromatin is organized into units called **nucleosomes,** each consisting of a stretch of DNA wrapped around eight proteins called histones (figure 8.7). A continuous thread of DNA connects nucleosomes like beads on a string. When the cell is not dividing, chromatin is barely visible because the nucleosomes are loosely packed together. The information in the DNA is available for the cell to produce the enzymes and other proteins that it needs. Copying DNA in preparation for cell division also requires that the cell's DNA be unwound.

After DNA replication, but shortly before cell division occurs, the nucleosomes begin to fold into progressively larger structures, eventually forming discrete chromosomes that become visible in the microscope. DNA packing is somewhat similar to winding a very long piece of yarn into a compact ball. A ball of yarn occupies less space and is easier to carry than a tangled pile of loose yarn. Likewise, condensed DNA is much easier for the cell to move than is unwound chromatin.

Once condensed, a chromosome has distinct parts (see figure 8.7). A replicated chromosome consists of two identical **chromatids,** each of which is a complete, double-stranded molecule of DNA. The two chromatids of a replicated chromosome are called "sister chromatids." The **centromere** is the small section of DNA and associated proteins that attaches the two sister chromatids to each other. It often appears as a constriction in a replicated chromosome. As a cell's nucleus divides, the centromere splits, and the sister chromatids separate from each other to become individual chromosomes.

Table 8.1 reviews the terminology of chromosome structure.

Figure 8.7 Parts of a Chromosome. After DNA replication, the chromatin condenses into a more compact form by winding around histones and scaffold proteins. Once condensed, the chromosome appears X-shaped because two identical chromatids are attached side-by-side at the centromere.

8.4 Mastering Concepts

1. How do chromatin and histones interact?
2. Sketch and label the main parts of a duplicated chromosome.

TABLE 8.1 Miniglossary of Chromosome Terms

Term	Definition
Chromatin	DNA and associated proteins in the nucleus
Chromosome	A single continuous molecule of DNA wrapped around protein. Eukaryotic cells contain multiple linear chromosomes, whereas prokaryotic cells each contain one circular chromosome.
Chromatid	One of two identical attached copies of a replicated chromosome
Centromere	A small region of a chromosome where sister chromatids attach to each other

8.5 In Eukaryotes, Mitotic Cell Division Generates Exact Copies

Suppose you scrape your leg while sliding into second base during a softball game. At first, the wound bleeds, but the blood soon clots and forms a scab. Underneath the dried crust, cells of the immune system clear away trapped dirt and dead cells. At the same time, undamaged skin cells near the wound begin to divide repeatedly, producing fresh, new daughter cells that eventually fill the damaged area.

Those actively dividing skin cells illustrate the **cell cycle,** which describes the events that occur in one complete round of cell division. Biologists divide the cell cycle into stages (figure 8.8). During **interphase,** the cell replicates its DNA and carries out many functions unrelated to cell division. **Mitosis** is the division of the nucleus, and **cytokinesis** is the splitting of the cell itself. The products of cell division are two daughter cells. Each cell receives complete, identical genetic instructions, plus the cytoplasm, organelles, enzymes, and other substances needed to jump-start its own metabolism.

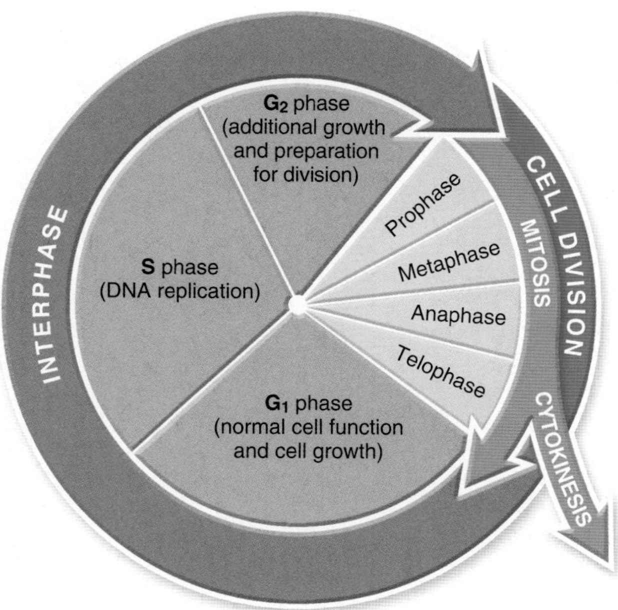

Figure 8.8 The Cell Cycle. Interphase includes gap phases (G_1 and G_2), when the cell grows and some organelles duplicate. During the synthesis (S) phase of interphase, DNA replicates. Mitosis divides the replicated genetic material between two nuclei. Cytokinesis then splits the cytoplasm in two, producing two identical daughter cells.

A. DNA Is Copied During Interphase

Biologists once mistakenly described interphase as a time when the cell is at rest. The cell appears inactive because the chromatin is unwound and therefore barely visible. However, interphase is actually a very active time in the life of a cell. All of the cell's functions continue, and the cell replicates its genetic material. A typical cell actually spends most of its time in interphase.

Interphase is divided into two "gap" phases (designated G_1 and G_2), separated by a "synthesis" (S) phase. During **G_1 phase,** the cell carries out its basic functions, grows, and produces the molecules it needs to build new organelles. The cell also synthesizes the proteins it will require if it divides.

During **S phase,** enzymes replicate the genetic material and repair damaged DNA. In most human cells, assembling billions of DNA nucleotides takes 8 to 10 hours. The cell also produces histone proteins during S phase. By the end of S phase, each chromosome consists of two attached sister chromatids, although they are not yet visible with a light microscope.

In **G_2 phase,** the cell prepares to divide, producing the proteins that will coordinate the movements of the chromosomes during mitosis. The DNA winds more tightly around its associated proteins, and this start of chromosome condensation signals the end of interphase.

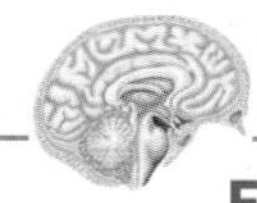

Figure It Out

A cell that has completed interphase contains __ times as much DNA as a cell at the start of interphase.

Answer: Two

Burning Questions

What are the galls that form on plants?

Most organisms tightly control the cell cycle, and cells usually do not divide unless they are supposed to. But some parasites can induce cell division, especially in plants. The result is a gall, an abnormal growth that often forms on the leaves and stems of plants. The growths may be smooth and perfectly round, as in the stem galls shown here. They may also cause grotesque deformities on stems, leaves, flowers, roots, and other plant parts.

Many organisms cause plants to form galls, including fungi, bacteria, and even parasitic plants. The most common galls, however, are traced to a distinctive group of wasps. A female gall wasp lays an egg in the vein of a stem or leaf of a tree. When the egg hatches and develops into a larva, it secretes chemicals that stimulate the plant's cells to divide. The resulting gall does not usually hurt or help the tree, but it does form a protective shell that houses and feeds the young wasp until adulthood.

Submit your burning question to:
marielle_hoefnagels@mcgraw-hill.com

B. Chromosomes Divide During Mitosis

In mitosis, the cell separates the genetic material that replicated during S phase into two identical nuclei (figure 8.9). Biologists divide mitosis into four main stages; note, however, that the process does not actually stop at each stage.

During **prophase,** DNA coils very tightly around its histone "spools," shortening and thickening the chromosomes. As they condense, the chromosomes become visible when stained and viewed under a microscope. At this stage, the chromosomes are still randomly distributed throughout the nucleus.

The **mitotic spindle** is a portion of the cytoskeleton that attaches to the chromosomes and moves them within a dividing cell. Two structures called **centrosomes** organize the microtubule proteins that make up the spindle. In many animal cells, each centrosome includes a pair of barrel-shaped centrioles. (Plant cells and many cells of animal embryos lack centrioles.) During prophase, the centrosomes migrate toward opposite ends of the cell, and the spindle begins to form.

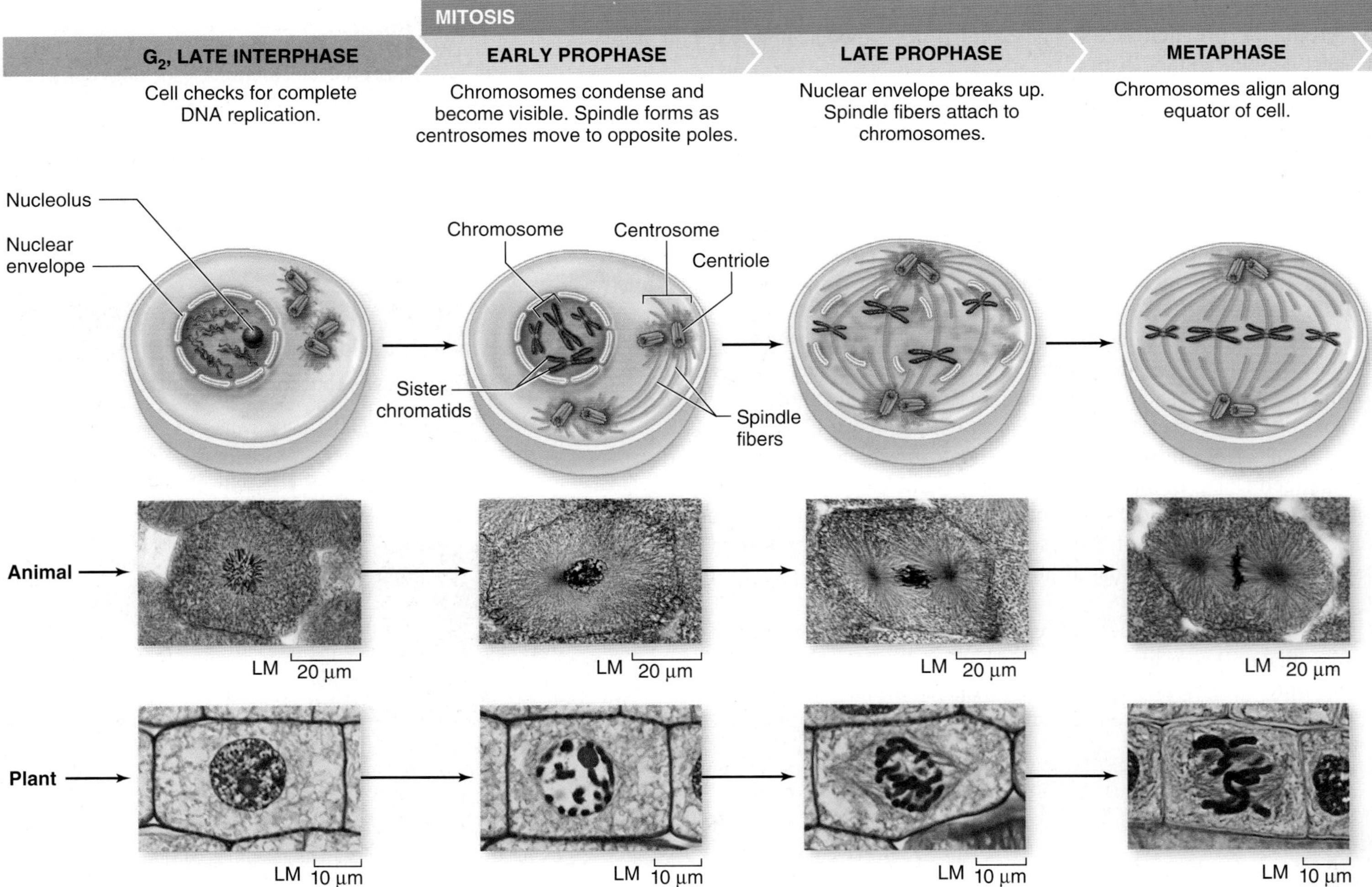

Figure 8.9 Stages of Mitosis. Mitotic cell division includes similar stages in all eukaryotes, including animals and plants.

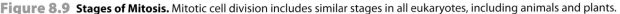

Other events of prophase include the disappearance of the nucleolus, the darkened area in the nucleus. The nuclear envelope breaks into small pieces, as does the surrounding endoplasmic reticulum. The spindle fibers are now free to attach to the chromosomes.

As **metaphase** begins, the mitotic spindle aligns the chromosomes down the center, or equator, of the cell. This alignment ensures that when cell division is complete, each resulting cell will contain one chromatid from each duplicated chromosome.

In **anaphase,** the centromeres split as the mitotic spindle pulls one chromatid from each pair to opposite poles of the cell. As the chromatids separate, some microtubules in the spindle lengthen in a way that moves the poles farther apart, stretching the dividing cell.

In **telophase,** the final stage of mitosis, the mitotic spindle disassembles and chromosomes begin to unwind. A nucleolus and nuclear envelope form at each end of the stretched-out cell. After telophase, division of the genetic material is complete, and the cell contains two nuclei—but not for long.

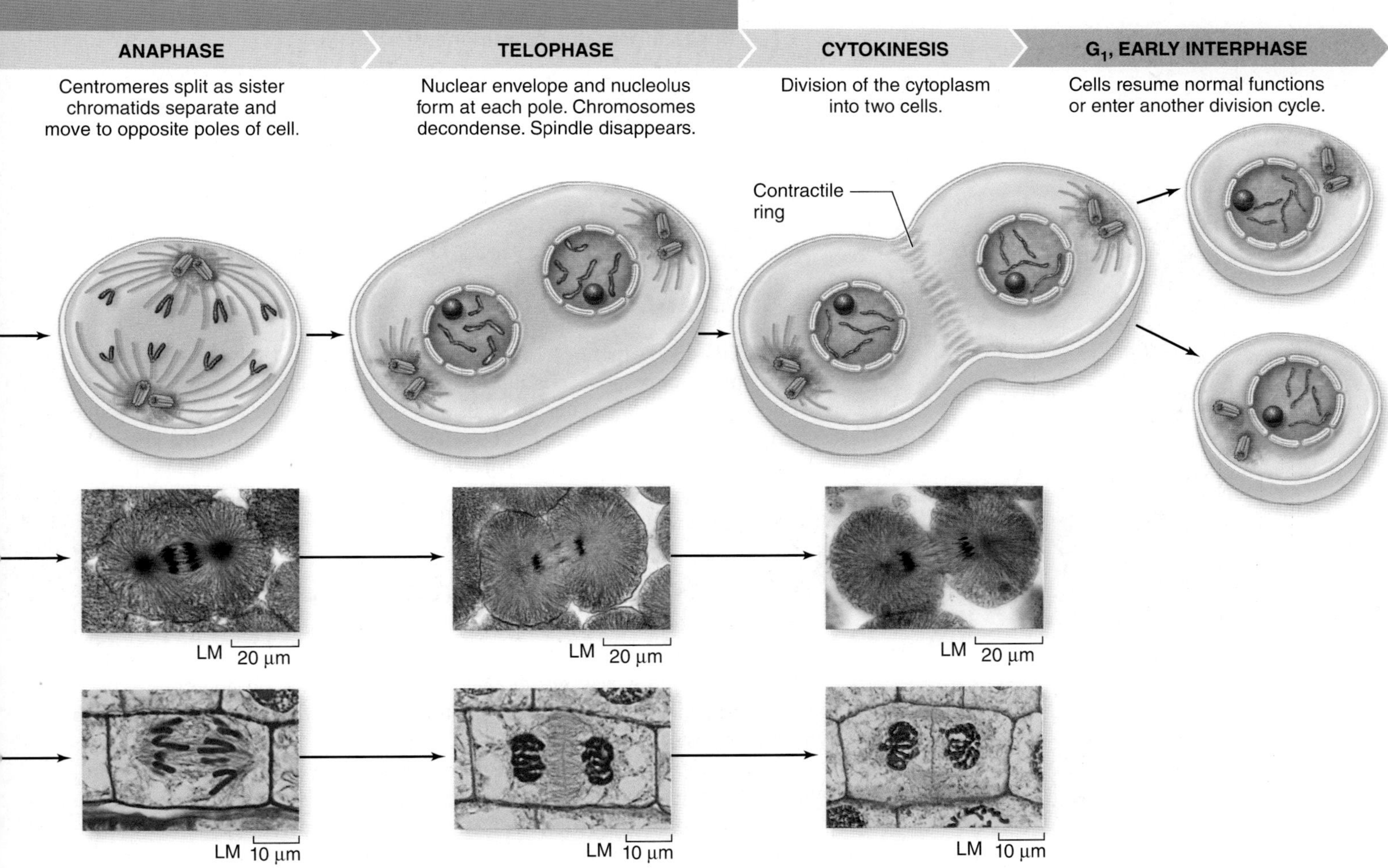
ANAPHASE
Centromeres split as sister chromatids separate and move to opposite poles of cell.
TELOPHASE
Nuclear envelope and nucleolus form at each pole. Chromosomes decondense. Spindle disappears.
CYTOKINESIS
Division of the cytoplasm into two cells.
G1, EARLY INTERPHASE
Cells resume normal functions or enter another division cycle.
Contractile ring
LM 20 μm
LM 20 μm
LM 20 μm
LM 10 μm
LM 10 μm
LM 10 μm

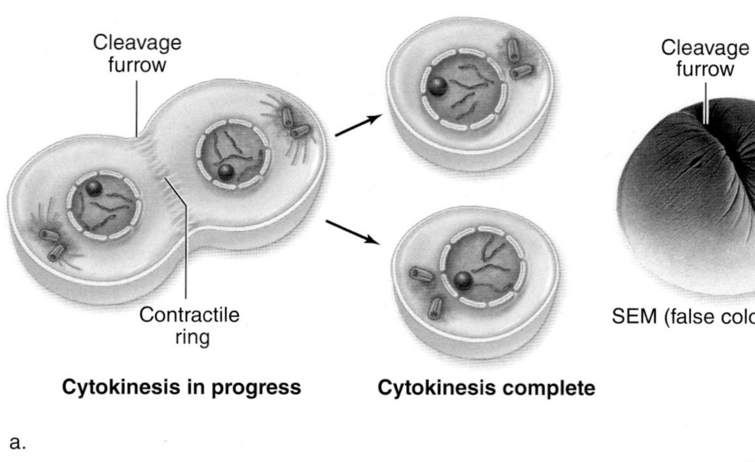

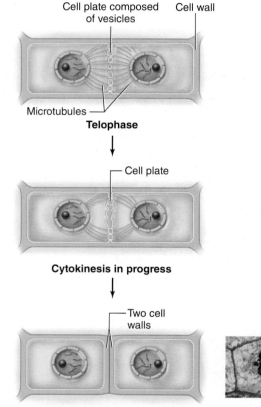

Figure 8.10 Cytokinesis. (a) In an animal cell, the cleavage furrow is formed by a ring of protein filaments. As the proteins contract, the cell divides in two. (b) In plant cells, the cell plate is the first stage in the formation of a new cell wall.

C. The Cytoplasm Splits in Cytokinesis

During cytokinesis, the cell's cytoplasm and two nuclei are distributed into two daughter cells, which then physically separate. After cytokinesis is complete, the daughter cells enter interphase, and the cell cycle begins again.

In an animal cell, the first sign of cytokinesis is the **cleavage furrow,** a slight indentation around the cell's equator (figure 8.10a). A ring of proteins beneath the cell membrane contracts like a drawstring, separating the daughter cells.

Unlike animal cells, plant cells construct a new cell wall that separates the two daughter cells (figure 8.10b). In plants, the first sign of cell wall construction is the **cell plate,** a line separating the forming cells. Vesicles from the Golgi apparatus deliver cellulose, other polysaccharides, and proteins. The layer of cellulose fibers embedded in surrounding material makes a strong, rigid wall that gives plant cells their rectangular shapes. ▸ cell wall, p. 63

8.5 Mastering Concepts

1. What happens during interphase?
2. How does the mitotic spindle form, and what is its function?
3. What happens during each stage of mitosis?
4. Distinguish between mitosis and cytokinesis.

8.6 Cancer Arises When Cells Divide Out of Control

Some cells divide more or less constantly. The cells at the tips of a plant's roots, for example, may continue to divide throughout the growing season, exploring the soil for water and nutrients. Likewise, stem cells in your bone marrow constantly produce new blood cells. On the other hand, the skin cells bordering a wound quit dividing once healing is complete, and the brain's neurons simply do not divide at all once they are mature. How do any of these cells "know" what to do?

A. Chemical Signals Regulate the Cell Cycle

Regulation of mitosis involves several mechanisms that chemically "tell" a cell to divide or to cease dividing. Precise timing is essential. Too little cell division, and an injury may go unrepaired; too much, and an abnormal growth forms. An understanding of these signals has helped reveal how diseases such as cancer arise.

Signals to divide usually come from outside the cell. Proteins that stimulate cell division bind to receptors on a receiving cell's membrane, and then a cascade of chemical reactions inside the cell initiates cell division. At a wound site, for example, a protein called epidermal growth factor stimulates cells to divide and produce new skin underneath a scab.

Inside the cell, several "checkpoints" control the cell cycle, ensuring that a cell does not enter the next stage of the cell cycle until the previous stage is complete. These checkpoints are somewhat like the guards that check passports and other documents at border crossings. Some of the checkpoints screen for damaged DNA. If the genetic material is damaged beyond repair, a signaling protein may trigger apoptosis.

B. Cancer Cells Lose Control of the Cell Cycle

What happens when the body loses control over cell division? Sometimes, a **tumor**—an abnormal mass of tissue—forms. Biologists classify tumors into two groups (figure 8.11). **Benign tumors** are usually slow-growing and harmless, unless they become large enough to disrupt nearby tissues or organs. A tough capsule surrounding the tumor prevents it from invading nearby tissues or spreading to other parts of the body. Warts and moles are examples of benign tumors of the skin.

In contrast, a **malignant tumor** invades adjacent tissue. Because it lacks a surrounding capsule, a malignant tumor is likely to **metastasize,** meaning that its cells can break away from the original mass and travel in the bloodstream or lymphatic system to colonize other areas of the body. **Cancer** is a class of diseases characterized by malignant cells.

Cancer begins with a single cell that breaks through the cell cycle control mechanisms. The cell continues to divide, and it grows into a malignant tumor. Each cancerous cell passes its loss of cell cycle control to its daughter cells. With enough nutrients and space, cancer cells can divide uncontrollably and eternally. As they do so, they may crush vital organs, block the body's passageways, and divert nutrients from other body cells.

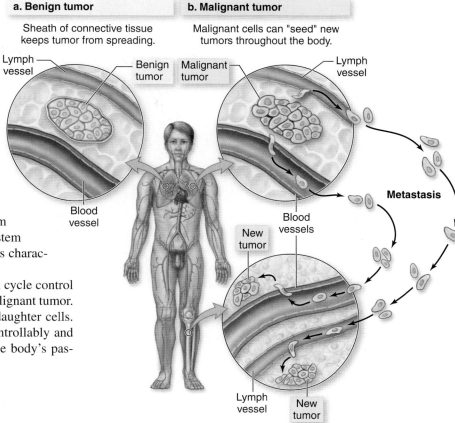

Lymph vessel
Metastasis
Blood vessels
New tumor
Lymph vessel
New tumor

Figure 8.11 Benign and Malignant Tumors. (a) A capsule of connective tissue keeps a benign tumor from invading adjacent tissues. (b) A malignant tumor lacks a capsule and therefore can spread throughout the body in blood and lymph.

C. Genes and Environment Both Can Increase Cancer Risk

Genes encode proteins, and proteins control both the cell cycle and apoptosis. Mutated genes therefore play a key role in causing cancer. Where do the cancer-causing mutations come from? Sometimes, a person inherits mutated versions of the genes from one or both parents. The parent may also have had cancer, or the mutations may have arisen spontaneously in sperm- or egg-producing cells. Often, however, people develop cancer after exposure to harmful chemicals, radiation, and viruses, all of which may alter their genes (see the Why We Care box on page 150). Poor diet and exercise habits, sun exposure, and cigarette smoking also raise cancer risks (figure 8.12).

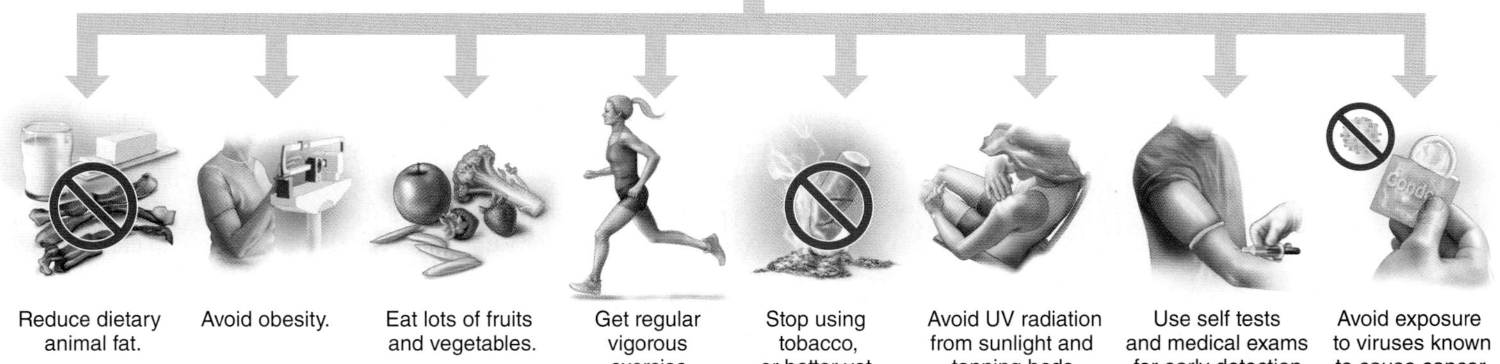

Sheath of connective tissue keeps tumor from spreading.
Lymph vessel

Blood vessel
b. Malignant tumor
Malignant cells can "seed" new tumors throughout the body.

To avoid or reduce the risk of cancer
Reduce dietary animal fat.
Avoid obesity.
Eat lots of fruits and vegetables.
Get regular vigorous exercise.
Stop using tobacco, or better yet, never start.
Avoid UV radiation from sunlight and tanning beds.
Use self tests and medical exams for early detection.
Avoid exposure to viruses known to cause cancer.

Figure 8.12 Cancer Risk. Many aspects of a person's lifestyle influence the risk of cancer.

Why We Care | Skin Cancer

Cancer has many forms, some inherited and others caused by radiation or harmful chemicals. Exposure to ultraviolet radiation from the sun or from tanning beds, for example, increases the risk of skin cancer because UV radiation damages DNA. If mutations occur in genes encoding proteins that control the pace of cell division, cells may begin dividing out of control, forming a malignant tumor on the skin.

How might a person determine whether a mole, sore, or growth on the skin is cancerous? The abnormal skin may vary widely in appearance, and only a physician can tell for sure. Nevertheless, most skin cancers have a few features in common. "ABCD" is a shortcut for remembering these four characteristics:

Asymmetry: Each half of the area looks different from the other.

Borders: The borders are irregular, not smooth.

Color: The color varies within a patch of skin, from tan to dark brown to black. Other colors, including red, may also appear.

Diameter: The diameter of a cancerous area is usually greater than 6 mm, which is about equal to the size of a pencil eraser.

D. Cancer Treatments Remove or Kill Abnormal Cells

Traditional cancer treatments include surgical removal of a tumor and surrounding tissues, drugs (chemotherapy), and radiation. Chemotherapy drugs, usually delivered intravenously, are designed to stop cancer cells throughout the body from dividing. Radiation therapy uses directed streams of energy from radioactive isotopes to kill tumor cells in limited areas. ▸ isotopes, p. 23

Chemotherapy and radiation are relatively "blunt tools" that target rapidly dividing cells, both cancerous and healthy. The death of healthy cells in the digestive tract, hair follicles, and bone marrow causes the most common side effects from cancer treatments: fatigue, nausea, hair loss, and a weakened immune system. Fortunately, the healthy cells usually return after the treatments end.

The success of any cancer treatment depends on many factors, including the type of cancer and the stage in which it is detected. Surgery can cure cancers that have not spread. Once cancer metastasizes, however, it becomes more difficult to treat because mutations accumulate as cancer cells colonize new areas of the body. Treatments that shrank the original tumor may have no effect on this new, changed growth. Also, a treatment that kills 99.9% of a tumor's cells can still leave millions of cells to divide and regrow (see section 8.7).

8.6 Mastering Concepts

1. What keeps cells from dividing when they are not supposed to?
2. What is the relationship between genetic mutations and cancer?
3. List and describe the three most common cancer treatments.

Investigating Life

8.7 Cutting Off a Tumor's Supply Lines in the War on Cancer

The Question: When Charles Darwin proposed natural selection as a mechanism of evolutionary change, he envisioned selective forces operating on tortoises, flowering plants, and other whole organisms. But the power of natural selection extends to a much smaller scale, including the individual cells that make up a tumor. The advance, retreat, resurgence, and death of these renegade cells command dramatic headlines in the war on cancer.

Our weapons against cancer include powerful chemotherapy drugs. Unfortunately, rapidly dividing tumor cells often develop resistance to drugs; frequent cell division produces abundant opportunities for mutations. An alternative cancer-fighting strategy, therefore, might be to launch an indirect attack on a tumor's slow-growing support tissues instead.

Any tumor larger than 1 or 2 mm needs a blood supply to carry nutrients, oxygen, and wastes. Blood travels in vessels lined with endothelial tissue. For a blood vessel to grow, its endothelial cells must divide, which happens rarely in healthy adults. Cancer cells, however, secrete molecules that stimulate blood vessels to sprout new "supply lines," which grow toward the tumor.

Fortunately, biologists have discovered a class of drugs that stop blood vessel growth. One such drug, called endostatin, keeps endothelial cells from dividing but does not kill resting endothelial cells or other cells in the body. It should therefore choke off a tumor's supply lines without toxic side effects. But do cancer cells develop resistance to endostatin?

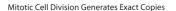

The Approach: Cancer researchers Thomas Boehm, Judah Folkman, and their colleagues at the Dana Farber Cancer Center and Harvard Medical School tested endostatin in mice. The researchers first induced cancer in mice by injecting each animal with one of three types of cancer cells. After tumors developed, the researchers injected the mice with endostatin. Injections continued for several days, until the tumors in endostatin-treated mice were barely detectable. When the tumors regrew, the researchers repeated the injections.

The Conclusion: For each of the three cancer types, the tumors never developed resistance to endostatin (figure 8.13a). Moreover, after multiple treatments with endostatin, the tumors never grew back. For all three cancer types, the endostatin-treated mice remained healthy and gained weight normally. On the other hand, standard chemotherapy drugs temporarily delayed tumor development, but resistant cells soon took over (figure 8.13b).

What does endostatin have to do with evolution? The logic behind endostatin's use as an anticancer drug relies on basic concepts of natural selection. Because DNA may mutate every time it replicates, rapidly dividing cancer cells are genetically slightly different from one another. A conventional drug may kill most cancer cells in a tumor, but a few survive, divide, and give rise to a new, much more resistant tumor. Endostatin, however, does not target the tumor itself; instead, it affects a blood vessel's endothelial cells. These cells rarely divide and therefore accumulate mutations very slowly, so the chance that they will become resistant to endostatin is small.

This may seem comforting, but evolution will not stand still for our convenience. New mutations in tumor cells may still defeat endostatin. Understanding natural selection will help researchers know what to look for—and perhaps even launch new offensives in the war on cancer.

Boehm, Thomas, Judah Folkman, Timothy Browder, and Michael S. O'Reilly. November 27, 1997. Antiangiogenic therapy of experimental cancer does not induce acquired drug resistance. *Nature,* vol. 390, pages 404–407.

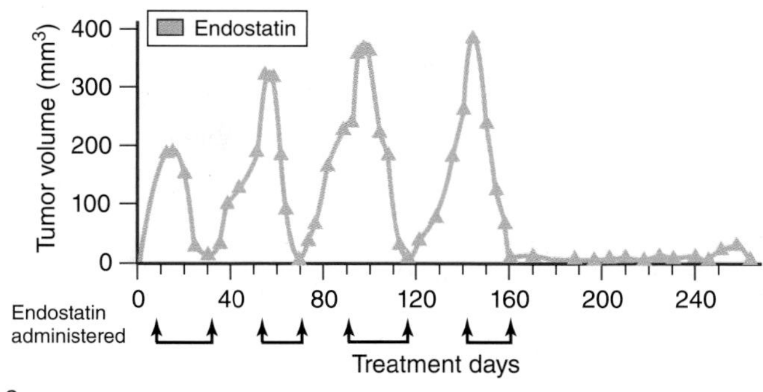

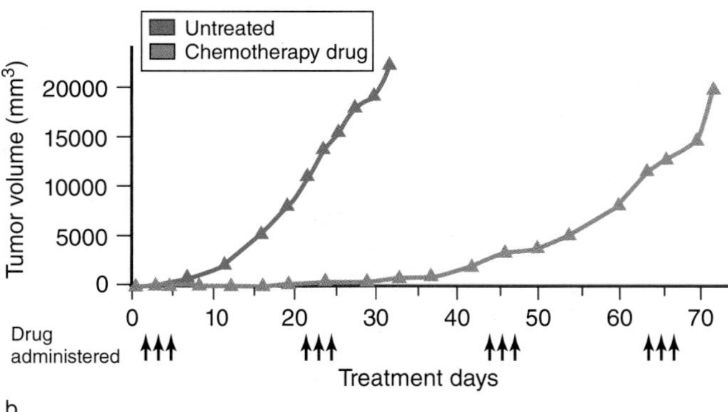

Figure 8.13 No Resistance. (a) Endostatin repeatedly shrank tumors in mice, and the tumors never developed resistance to the drug. (b) In contrast, a traditional chemotherapy drug delayed but did not prevent tumor growth in mice.

8.7 Mastering Concepts

1. Why are traditional chemotherapy drugs often most effective during the first few treatments?
2. Why doesn't endostatin select for drug-resistant cancer cells?

Chapter Summary

8.1 Cells Divide, and Cells Die

A. Sexual Life Cycles Include Mitosis, Meiosis, and Fertilization

- **Asexual reproduction** generates virtually identical copies of an organism, whereas **sexual reproduction** mixes traits from two parents.
- The key events in sexual life cycles are **meiosis,** which creates genetically different **gametes; fertilization,** which occurs when gametes fuse; and **mitosis,** which produces exact copies of eukaryotic cells.

B. Cell Death Is Part of Life

- Cell division produces identical copies of cells, whereas **apoptosis** is programmed cell death. Both processes occur during the normal development of a multicellular organism.

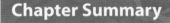

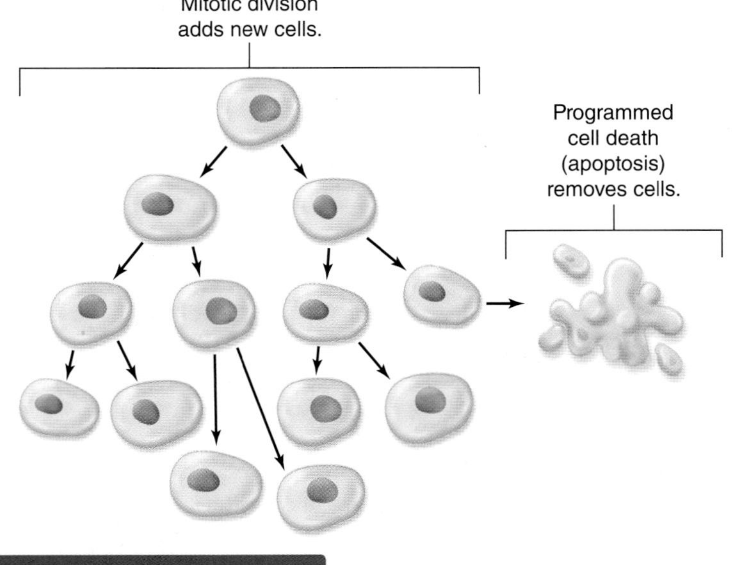

8.2 DNA Replication Precedes Cell Division

- A dividing cell must first duplicate its **genome,** which may consist of one or more **chromosomes.** Most human cells contain 46 chromosomes.
- To replicate, DNA unwinds, and the hydrogen bonds between strands break. **DNA polymerase** adds DNA nucleotides, and **ligase** forms covalent bonds between adjacent segments of the newly created DNA strands.
- Enzymes repair damaged DNA and fix mistakes made during replication.
- **Mutations** are changes in a cell's DNA sequence.

8.3 Bacteria and Archaea Divide by Binary Fission

- Cell division is asexual and occurs by **binary fission** in prokaryotes.
- After DNA replication, the circular chromosome separates from its copy. The cell then divides into two identical daughter cells.

8.4 Replicated Chromosomes Condense as a Cell Prepares to Divide

- A chromosome consists of **chromatin** (DNA plus protein). In eukaryotic cells, chromatin is organized into **nucleosomes,** which enable the cell to pack a lot of DNA into a small space.
- Once replicated, a chromosome consists of two identical **chromatids** attached at a section of DNA called a **centromere.**

8.5 In Eukaryotes, Mitotic Cell Division Generates Exact Copies

- The **cell cycle** is a sequence of events in which a cell prepares to divide (interphase), divides its DNA (mitosis), and divides its cytoplasm (cytokinesis).

A. DNA Is Copied During Interphase

- **Interphase** includes two gap periods, G_1 and G_2, when the cell carries out its normal functions and produces the molecules required to divide. Between G_1 and G_2 is the synthesis (**S**) phase, when the cell replicates its DNA.

B. Chromosomes Divide During Mitosis

- Microtubules make up the **mitotic spindle,** which arises from **centrosomes.**
- **Mitosis** occurs in stages. In **prophase,** the chromosomes condense, the nucleolus disassembles, the nuclear envelope breaks up, and spindle fibers attach to the chromosomes. In **metaphase,** spindle fibers align the chromosomes down the cell's equator. In **anaphase,** the sister chromatids of each chromosome separate; each sister chromatid is now a chromosome in its own right. In **telophase,** the chromosomes arrive at each end of the cell, the spindle breaks down, and nuclear envelopes form.

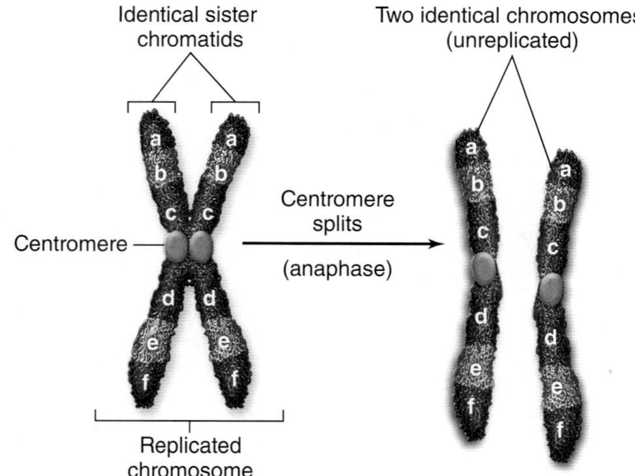

C. The Cytoplasm Splits in Cytokinesis

- **Cytokinesis** is the physical separation of the two daughter cells. When an animal cell undergoes cytokinesis, a **cleavage furrow** forms, and a contractile ring pinches the two cells apart. In a plant cell, a **cell plate** separates the daughter cells, marking the site where a new cell wall will form.

8.6 Cancer Arises When Cells Divide Out of Control

A. Chemical Signals Regulate the Cell Cycle

- External molecular signals normally stimulate cell division.
- Cell cycle control checkpoints allow the cell to ensure that each stage of the cell cycle is complete before the next begins.

B. Cancer Cells Lose Control of the Cell Cycle

- **Tumors** can result from excess cell division. Unlike a **benign tumor,** a **malignant tumor** invades nearby tissues and **metastasizes** if it migrates to other parts of the body in blood or lymph.

C. Genes and Environment Both Can Increase Cancer Risk

- Cancer can result from mutations in genes encoding the proteins that normally regulate the cell cycle. These mutations may be inherited or induced by environmental triggers.

D. Cancer Treatments Remove or Kill Abnormal Cells

- Surgery, chemotherapy, and radiation are common cancer treatments. Success depends on the type of cancer and whether it has spread.

8.7 Investigating Life: Cutting Off a Tumor's Supply Lines in the War on Cancer

- Natural selection occurs inside tumors. Chemotherapy drugs kill susceptible cells, but resistant ones survive. As these cells divide, the tumor regrows.
- Endostatin starves tumors by stopping the growth of blood vessels. Because endothelial cells in blood vessels divide much more slowly than tumor cells, they are much less likely to become resistant to endostatin.

Multiple Choice Questions

1. What is the role of fertilization in the sexual life cycle?
   a. It combines the DNA from two parents.
   b. It produces gametes.
   c. It prevents mutations during DNA replication.
   d. It reverses the effects of mitosis.
2. A chromosome is made of
   a. DNA.
   b. histones.
   c. chromatin.
   d. All of the above are correct.
3. Which of the following best explains why binary fission can occur without a spindle like that found in mitotic cells?
   a. The cell is small, so there is less material to divide.
   b. There is only one chromosome, and it attaches to the membrane.
   c. The prokaryotic DNA does not need to replicate.
   d. The DNA is transferred through the sex pilus.
4. Why is a chromosome sometimes composed of *two* chromatids?
   a. Because the nucleosomes are folded
   b. Because the chromosome contains the entire genome of a cell
   c. Because the DNA has replicated
   d. Because the cell is diploid
5. When is DNA polymerase most likely to be active?
   a. Cytokinesis
   b. Interphase
   c. Anaphase
   d. Prophase
6. Which stage of mitosis occurs immediately *after* the stage in which the chromosomes become visible?
   a. Prophase
   b. Metaphase
   c. Anaphase
   d. Telophase

7. The effects of a drug that disrupts the formation of the mitotic spindle would first become evident during
   a. prophase.
   b. anaphase.
   c. interphase.
   d. cytokinesis.
8. What would happen to an animal cell if interphase and mitosis occurred in the absence of cytokinesis?
   a. The number of nuclei in the cell would increase over time.
   b. The amount of DNA in the cell would decrease over time.
   c. The cell would enter S phase.
   d. The cell would not form a new cell wall.
9. Why are cell cycle control checkpoints so important?
   a. Because they determine how quickly a cell's DNA gets copied
   b. Because they ensure that cytokinesis only occurs once
   c. Because they help prevent damaged cells from dividing
   d. Because they ensure that mitosis occurs continuously in all body cells
10. What is metastasis?
    a. The "programmed death" of an abnormal cell
    b. The abnormal condition in which a cell gets stuck in metaphase
    c. The invasion of new tissues by a malignant tumor
    d. The formation of the mitotic spindle by the centrosomes

Write It Out

1. How would your body look if cells divided but apoptosis never occurred?
2. Use words and diagrams to describe how DNA is copied in a cell.
3. If a cell contains all the genetic material it needs to synthesize protein, why must the DNA also replicate?
4. Sketch and describe the events that occur when a bacterial cell divides.
5. List the ways that binary fission is similar to and different from mitosis.
6. Explain the relationships among chromatin, chromosome, chromatid, and centromere.
7. Biologists once thought interphase is a time of cellular rest, but it is not. What happens during interphase?
8. Which contains the most DNA, a cell in G_1 or a cell in G_2 phase?
9. Describe what happens to a cell if interphase occurs but mitosis does not.
10. In the early 1900s, scientists began to experiment with radiation as a cancer treatment. Many physicians who administered the treatment subsequently died of cancer. Why?
11. Why might combining traditional chemotherapy with a drug that inhibits new blood vessel growth be more effective than either treatment alone?
12. Do an Internet search for the phrase *cancer risk assessment tool.* Choose one for a type of cancer that interests you. Which risk factors mentioned in the tool are under your control? Which are not? Can you think of risk factors that are not mentioned in the assessment tool?

Pull It Together

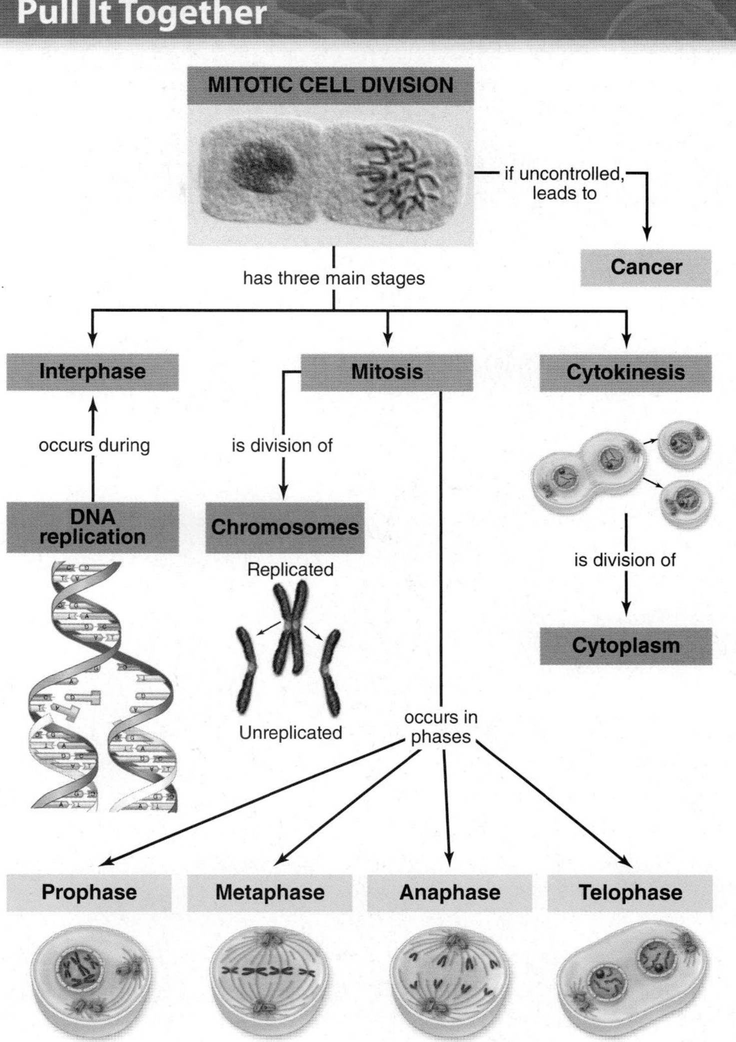

1. Add *DNA polymerase, nucleotides,* and *complementary base pairing* to this concept map.
2. What sort of molecule is DNA polymerase?
3. Describe the events that take place in each phase of mitosis.
4. How do mitotic cell division and meiosis fit into the human life cycle?
5. Which types of cells undergo mitotic cell division?
6. What is the relationship between mitotic cell division and apoptosis?
7. What can cause a cell to lose control over mitotic cell division?

9 Sexual Reproduction and Meiosis

Pollinator. As a bumble bee searches for nectar in a sunflower, pollen covers its body. Inside these tiny yellow particles are the sunflower's sperm nuclei. The bee collects nectar from many neighboring plants as well, and some of the sperm-toting pollen grains stick to the female parts of other flowers. Insects and other pollinators are therefore crucial to sexual reproduction in many flowering plants.

Learning Outline

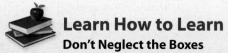

Learn How to Learn

Don't Neglect the Boxes

You may be tempted to skip the boxed readings in a chapter because they're not "required." Read them anyway. The contents should help you remember and visualize the material you are trying to learn. And who knows? You may even find them interesting.

What's the Point?

Humans reproduce sexually, as do the pet dogs, cats, birds, gerbils, and fish that share our lives. But did you know that most plants also use sexual reproduction, as does the mold that grows on your stale bread? Sex occurs in almost all species of multicellular life.

Sexual reproduction requires the production of sperm and egg cells. We already know, from chapter 8, how cells use mitosis to make virtually identical copies of themselves. This chapter explains meiosis, which resembles mitosis in some ways. But whereas mitosis makes identical copies, meiosis does something different: it generates sperm and egg cells, each of which is genetically unique. These specialized cells lie at the heart of sexual reproduction.

9.1 Why Sex?

Humans are so familiar with our way of reproducing that it can be hard to remember that there is any other way to make offspring. In fact, however, reproduction occurs in two main forms: asexual and sexual (figure 9.1). In **asexual reproduction,** an organism replicates its DNA and splits the contents of one cell into two. Except for the occasional mutation, asexual reproduction generates genetically identical offspring. Bacteria and archaea reproduce in this straightforward and ancient way, as do single-celled eukaryotes such as the amoeba in figure 9.1a. Many plants, fungi, and animals also reproduce asexually. ▸ mutations, p. 123

Although bacteria reproduce asexually, they can still acquire new genetic information from their neighbors. In a process called conjugation, for example, one bacterial cell uses a structure called a sex pilus to transfer genetic material to another bacterium. Sharing genes is one way that disease-causing bacteria acquire resistance to antibiotics. The one-celled eukaryote *Paramecium* uses a variation on this theme, exchanging entire nuclei via a bridge of cytoplasm.

In contrast to asexual reproduction, which requires only one parent, **sexual reproduction** is the production of offspring whose DNA comes from two parents. A female parent contributes an egg, and the male produces sperm. The next generation begins when these two cells fuse. As you will learn in this chapter, sexual reproduction mixes up and recombines traits, so the offspring are genetically different from each other and from their parents (see figure 9.1b).

Attracting mates takes a lot of energy, as does producing and dispersing sperm and egg cells. Yet the persistence of sexual reproduction over billions of years and in many species attests to its success. Why does such a costly method of reproducing persist, and why is asexual reproduction comparatively rare?

One answer to this question may be that the mass production of identical offspring makes sense in an unchanging environment, but environmental conditions rarely remain constant in the real world. Faced with a drastic environmental change, poorly suited individuals will die, but others might have a combination of traits that allows them to survive and reproduce. Asexual reproduction cannot create or maintain this diversity, but sexual reproduction can.

9.1 Mastering Concepts

1. How do asexual and sexual reproduction differ?
2. How can asexually reproducing organisms acquire new genetic information?
3. What circumstances select for asexual and sexual reproduction?

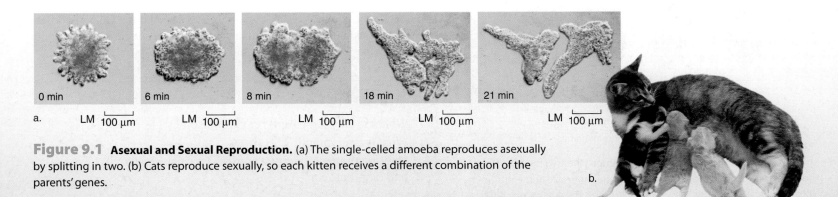

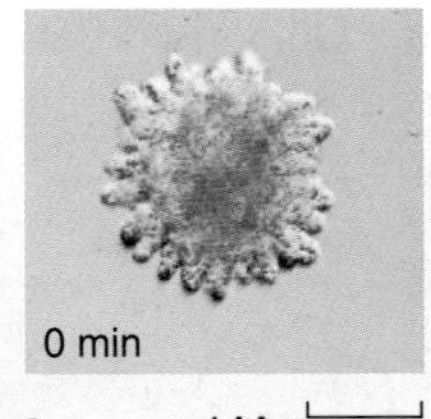

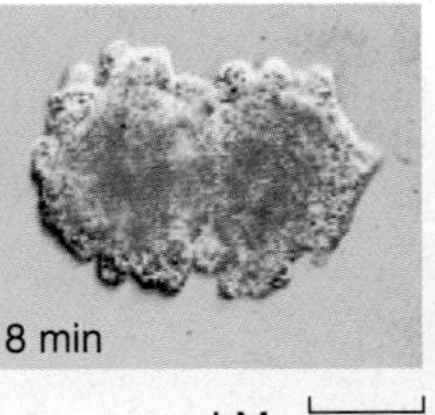

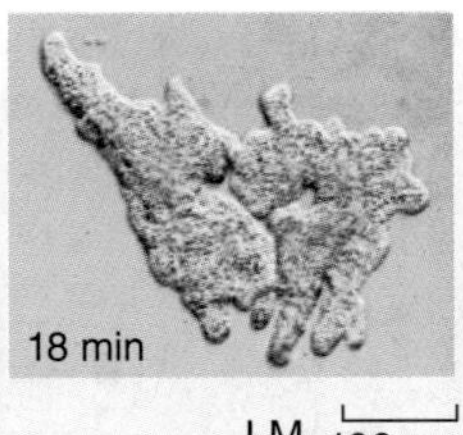

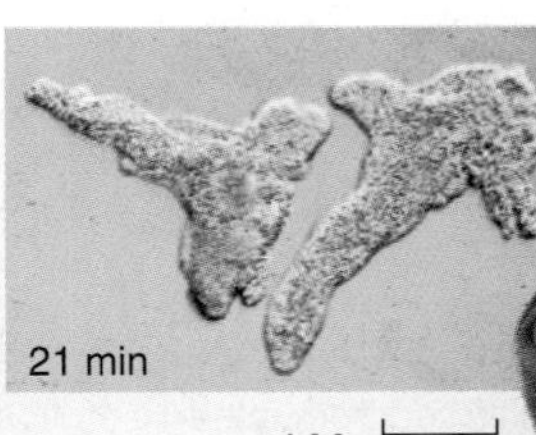

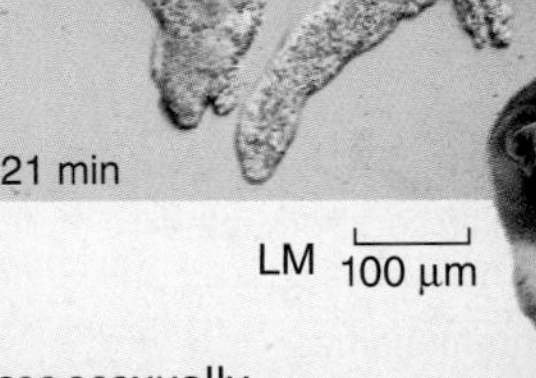

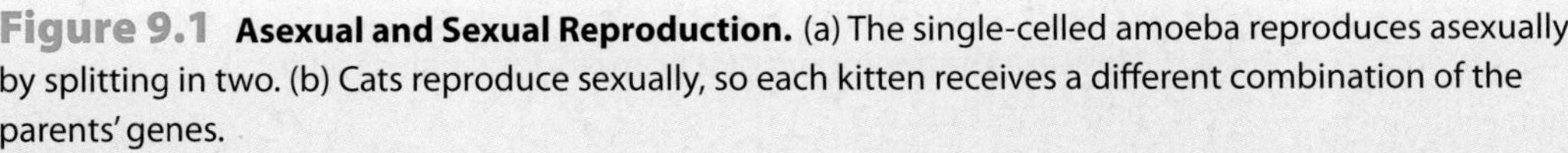
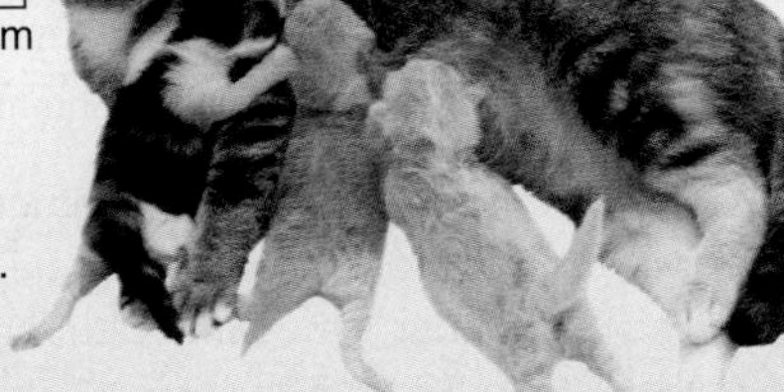

Figure 9.1 Asexual and Sexual Reproduction. (a) The single-celled amoeba reproduces asexually by splitting in two. (b) Cats reproduce sexually, so each kitten receives a different combination of the parents' genes.

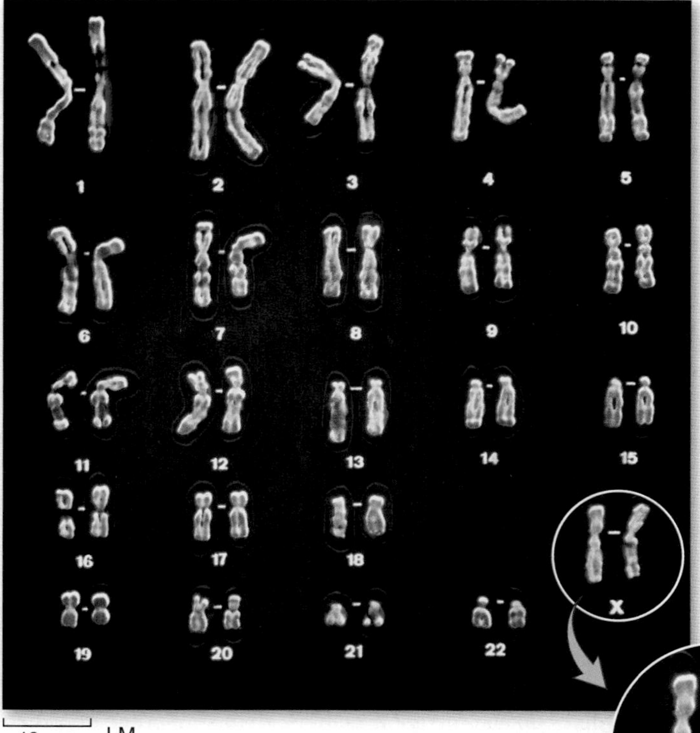

Figure 9.2 Human Chromosomes. A karyotype is a photo of all of a cell's chromosomes, arranged in order of size. Shown here are the 22 pairs of autosomes, plus the sex chromosomes: XX for a female and XY for a male.

9.2 Diploid Cells Contain Two Homologous Sets of Chromosomes

Before exploring sexual reproduction further, a quick look at a human cell's chromosomes is in order. Recall from chapters 7 and 8 that a **chromosome** is a single molecule of DNA and its associated proteins.

A sexually reproducing organism consists mostly of **diploid cells** (abbreviated $2n$), which contain two full sets of chromosomes; one set is inherited from each parent. Each diploid human cell, for example, contains 46 chromosomes (figure 9.2). The photo in figure 9.2 illustrates a **karyotype,** a size-ordered chart of all of the chromosomes in a cell. Notice that the 46 chromosomes are arranged in 23 pairs; your mother and your father each contributed one member of each pair.

Of the 23 chromosome pairs in a human cell, 22 pairs are **autosomes;** they are the same for both sexes, and they do not determine whether an individual is male or female. The two **sex chromosomes** carry genes that determine an individual's sex. A person with two X chromosomes is female, whereas a male has one X and one Y chromosome.

The two members of most chromosome pairs are homologous to each other. A **homologous pair** of chromosomes is a matching pair of chromosomes that look alike and carry the same sequence of genes for the same traits. (The word *homologous* means "having the same basic structure.") The physical similarities between any two homologous chromosomes are evident in figure 9.2 and figure 9.3. For example, the members of a homologous pair share the same size and centromere position.

Homologous chromosomes also carry the same genes in the same order. As described in chapter 7, a gene is a sequence of DNA that encodes a protein. Each gene may have multiple **alleles,** which are alternative versions of the same gene. With the exception of identical twins, each of us inherits a unique combination of alleles for all of the genes in the human genome. Some of this variation is insignificant. For example, two alleles of one gene determine whether a person has a straight hairline or a widow's peak—a minor difference in appearance. At the opposite extreme, however, one or more alleles of another gene may specify faulty proteins that cause serious diseases such as cystic fibrosis or Huntington disease.

If you think of a gene as a "recipe" for a protein, then a chromosome is like a cookbook—that is, a collection of recipes. Inheriting a set of chromosomes from each parent is like acquiring two complete sets of cookbooks, each containing slightly different recipes for the same foods.

Unlike the autosome pairs, X and Y chromosomes are not homologous to each other. X is much larger than Y, and the genes are completely different. (To continue with the cookbook analogy, it is as if males inherit 22 slightly different pairs of "cookbooks" plus one unmatched pair.) Nevertheless, in males, the sex chromosomes behave as homologous chromosomes during meiosis.

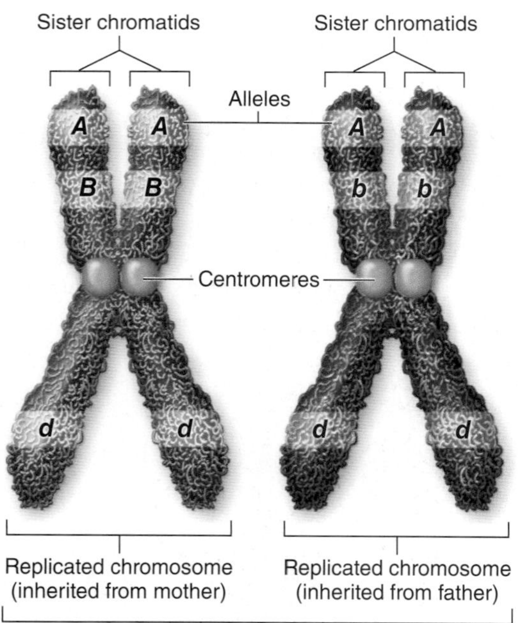

Figure 9.3 Homologous Chromosomes. The two members of a homologous pair of chromosomes have the same size and centromere location. The gene order is the same, although the alleles may differ.

9.2 Mastering Concepts

1. What are autosomes and sex chromosomes?
2. What is a karyotype?
3. How are the members of a homologous pair similar and different?

9.3 Meiosis Is Essential in Sexual Reproduction

Sexually reproducing species range from humans to the mold that grows on bread. This section describes some features that all sexual life cycles share.

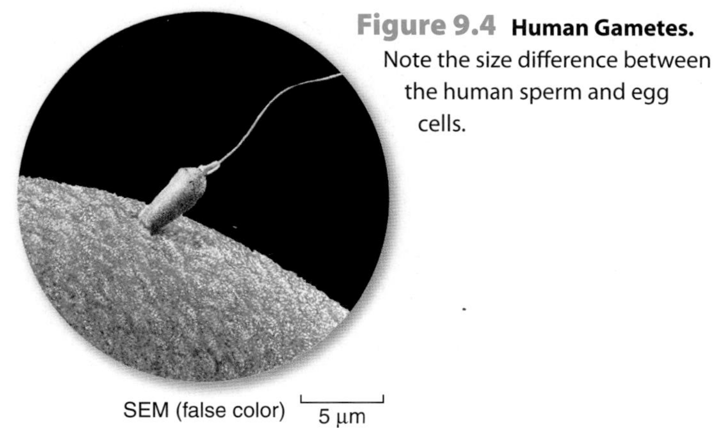

Figure 9.4 Human Gametes. Note the size difference between the human sperm and egg cells.

A. Gametes Are Haploid Sex Cells

Sexual reproduction poses a practical problem: maintaining the correct chromosome number. We have already seen that most cells in the human body contain 46 chromosomes. If a baby arises from the union of a man's sperm and a woman's egg, then why does a human baby not have 92 chromosomes per cell (46 from each parent)? And if that offspring later reproduced, wouldn't cells in the next generation have 184 chromosomes?

In fact, the normal chromosome number does not double with each generation. The explanation is that the special cells required for sexual reproduction, sperm cells and egg cells, are not diploid. Rather, they are **haploid cells** (abbreviated n); that is, they contain only one full set of genetic information instead of two.

These haploid cells, called **gametes,** are sex cells that combine to form a new offspring (figure 9.4). **Fertilization** merges the gametes from two parents and creates the diploid **zygote,** which is the first cell of the new organism. The zygote has two full sets of chromosomes, one set from each parent. In most species, the zygote begins dividing mitotically shortly after fertilization.

Thus, the life of a sexually reproducing, multicellular organism requires two ways to package DNA into daughter cells. **Mitosis,** described in chapter 8, divides a eukaryotic cell's chromosomes into two identical daughter cells. Mitotic cell division produces the cells needed for growth, development, and tissue repair. **Meiosis,** the subject of this chapter, forms genetically variable gametes that each contain half the number of chromosomes as the organism's diploid cells.

B. Specialized Germ Cells Undergo Meiosis

Only some cells can undergo meiosis and produce gametes. In humans and other animals, these specialized diploid cells, called **germ cells,** occur only in the ovaries and testes. Plants don't have the same reproductive organs as animals, but they do have specialized gamete-producing cells in flowers and other reproductive parts.

The rest of the body's diploid cells, called **somatic cells,** do not participate directly in reproduction. Leaf cells, root cells, skin cells, muscle cells, and neurons are examples of somatic cells. Most somatic cells can divide mitotically, but they do not undergo meiosis.

To make sense of this, consider your own life (figure 9.5). It began when a small, swimming sperm cell carrying 23 chromosomes from your father wriggled toward your mother's comparatively enormous egg cell, also containing 23 chromosomes. You were conceived when the sperm fertilized the egg cell. At that moment, you were a one-celled zygote, with 46 chromosomes. That first cell then began dividing, generating identical copies of itself to form an embryo, then a fetus, infant, child, and eventually an adult. Once you reached reproductive maturity, germ cells in your testes or ovaries produced haploid gametes of your own, perpetuating the cycle.

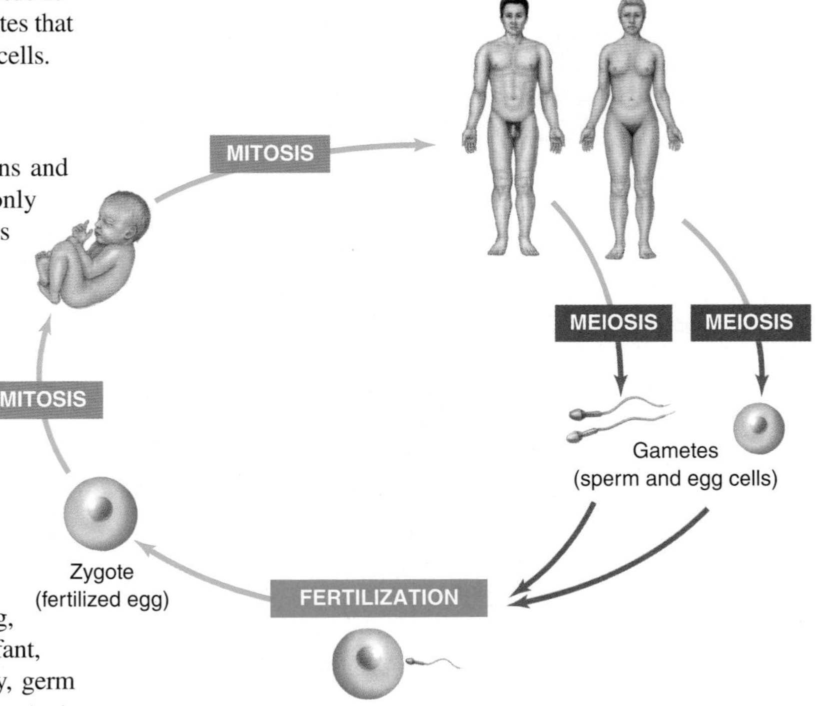

Figure 9.5 The Human Life Cycle. Adults produce sperm and egg cells by meiosis. Fertilization restores the diploid number, and then mitotic cell division enables the zygote to grow and develop into an adult.

The human life cycle is of course most familiar to us, and many animals reproduce in essentially the same way. Gametes are the only haploid cells in our life cycle; all other cells are diploid. Sexual reproduction, however, can take many other forms as well. In some organisms, including plants, both the haploid and the diploid stages are multicellular. Chapters 16, 17, and 30 describe the life cycles of plants and animals in more detail.

9.3 Mastering Concepts

1. How do haploid and diploid nuclei differ?
2. What are the roles of meiosis, gamete formation, and fertilization in sexual life cycles?
3. What is a zygote?
4. What is the difference between somatic cells and germ cells?

9.4 In Meiosis, DNA Replicates Once, but the Nucleus Divides Twice

The mitotic cell cycle described in chapter 8 includes three main parts: interphase, mitosis, and cytokinesis. During interphase, the cell grows, synthesizes molecules, carries out its functions, and replicates its DNA. During mitosis and cytokinesis, the nucleus and cytoplasm split into two. Mitotic cell division creates identical copies by replicating a cell's DNA once and then dividing once.

Meiosis is closely related to mitosis. Interphase also occurs just before meiosis, and the names of the meiotic phases are similar to those in mitosis. One major difference is that meiosis includes two divisions, not just one. The first division is meiosis I, and it reduces the number of chromosomes by half: in

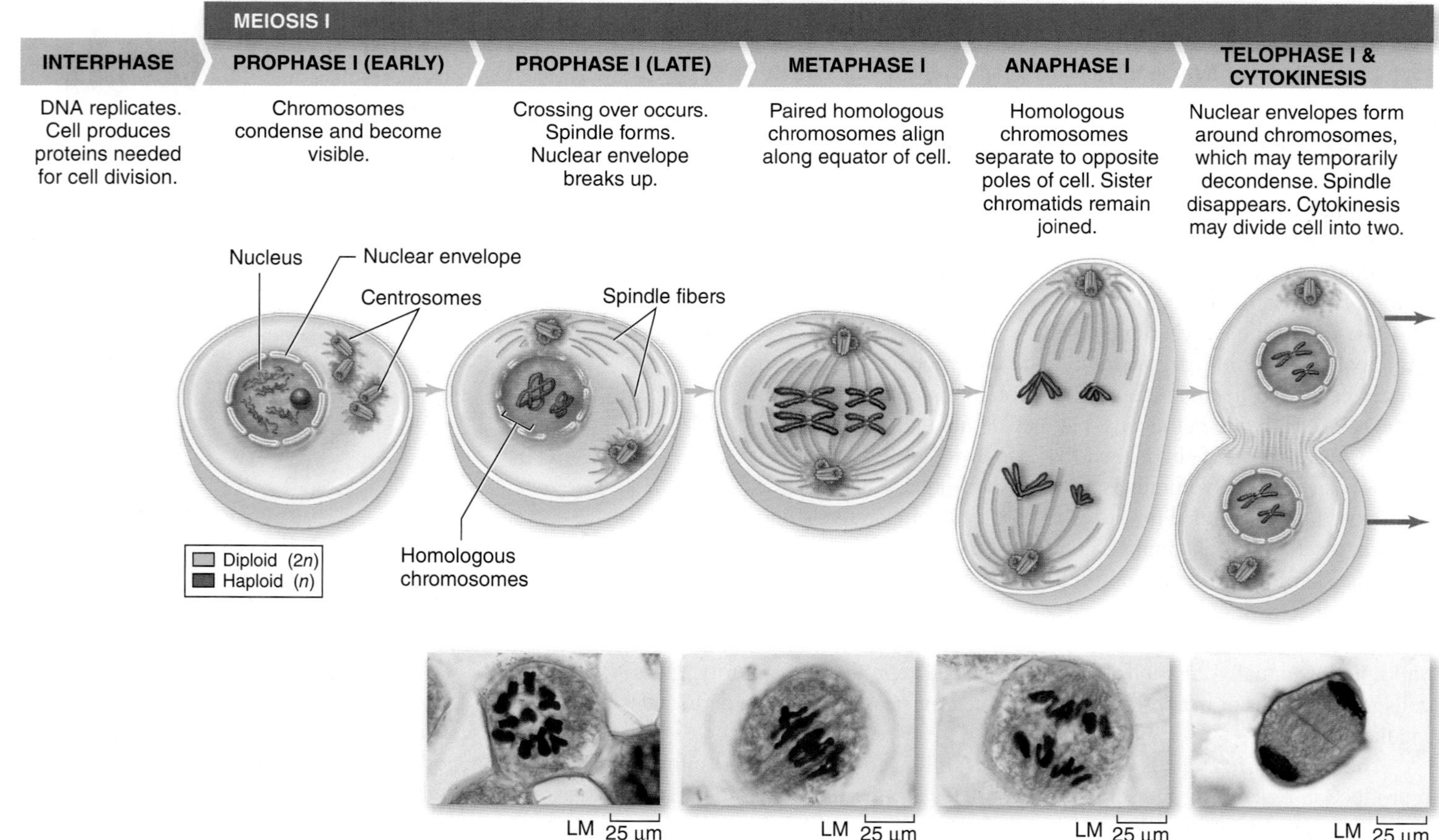

MEIOSIS I
INTERPHASE
DNA replicates. Cell produces proteins needed for cell division.
PROPHASE I (EARLY)
Chromosomes condense and become visible.
PROPHASE I (LATE)
Crossing over occurs. Spindle forms. Nuclear envelope breaks up.
METAPHASE I
Paired homologous chromosomes align along equator of cell.
ANAPHASE I
Homologous chromosomes separate to opposite poles of cell. Sister chromatids remain joined.
TELOPHASE I & CYTOKINESIS
Nuclear envelopes form around chromosomes, which may temporarily decondense. Spindle disappears. Cytokinesis may divide cell into two.
Nucleus
Nuclear envelope
Centrosomes
Spindle fibers
Homologous chromosomes
Diploid (2n)
Haploid (n)
LM 25 μm
LM 25 μm
LM 25 μm
LM 25 μm

humans, from 46 to 23. The second division, meiosis II, produces four haploid nuclei from the two formed in meiosis I. The other major difference is that meiosis I shuffles genetic information (see section 9.5), setting the stage for each haploid nucleus to receive a unique mixture of alleles.

For meiosis to work, a human germ cell must first duplicate all 46 chromosomes, then make sure that each haploid nucleus gets exactly 23. As you shall see, the unique arrangement of the cell's chromosomes during meiosis I makes this feat possible. Before the first meiotic division, every chromosome duplicates and then pairs up with its homologous counterpart. (Mules are typically sterile because their germ cells cannot complete this stage, as described in the Burning Question on page 160.) The homologous pairs split up during meiosis I, then meiosis II partitions one chromatid into each haploid nucleus.

The key to understanding meiosis is therefore to pay careful attention to the movements of the homologous chromosome pairs. Figure 9.6 diagrams the process.

A. In Meiosis I, Homologous Chromosomes Pair Up and Separate

The **interphase** that comes before meiosis is similar to interphase in the mitotic cell cycle. The cell grows during G_1 phase and produces the molecules necessary for division. DNA replicates during S phase, and the cell produces enzymes and other proteins necessary to divide the cell. Afterward, each of the cell's chromosomes consists of two identical sister chromatids attached at a centromere. Finally, in G_2, chromatin begins to condense, and the cell produces the microtubule proteins that will become the spindle.

Figure 9.6 **The Stages of Meiosis.** In meiosis, a diploid nucleus gives rise to four, genetically different, haploid nuclei.

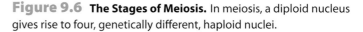

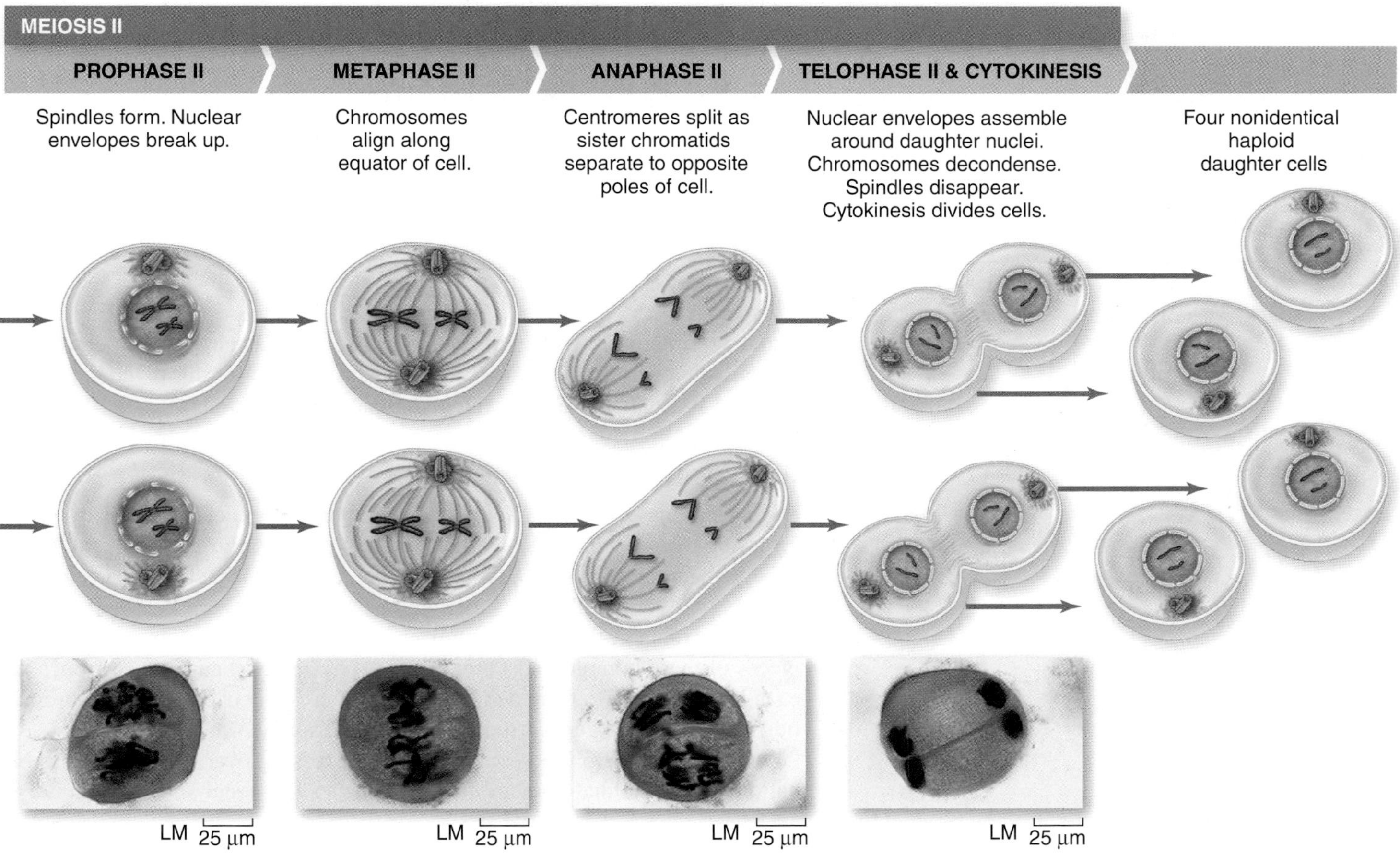
MEIOSIS II
PROPHASE II
METAPHASE II
ANAPHASE II
TELOPHASE II & CYTOKINESIS
Spindles form. Nuclear envelopes break up.
Chromosomes align along equator of cell.
Centromeres split as sister chromatids separate to opposite poles of cell.
Nuclear envelopes assemble around daughter nuclei. Chromosomes decondense. Spindles disappear. Cytokinesis divides cells.
Four nonidentical haploid daughter cells
LM 25 μm
LM 25 μm
LM 25 μm
LM 25 μm

Burning Questions

If mules are sterile, then how are they produced?

A mule is the hybrid offspring of a male donkey and a female horse. The opposite cross (female donkey with male horse) yields a hybrid called a hinny. Mules and hinnies are usually sterile. Why?

A peek at the parents' chromosomes reveals the answer. Donkeys have 31 pairs of chromosomes, whereas horses have 32 pairs. When gametes from horse and donkey unite, the resulting hybrid zygote has 63 chromosomes (31 + 32). The zygote divides mitotically to yield the cells that make up the mule or hinny.

These hybrid cells cannot undergo meiosis for two reasons. First, they have an odd number of chromosomes, which disrupts meiosis because at least one chromosome lacks a homologous partner. Second, donkeys and horses have slightly different chromosome structures, so the hybrid's parental chromosomes cannot align properly during prophase I. The result: an inability to produce sperm and egg cells. The only way to produce another mule or hinny is to again mate a horse with a donkey.

Submit your burning question to:
marielle_hoefnagels@mcgraw-hill.com

During **prophase I** of meiosis, the replicated chromosomes condense. The homologous chromosomes, or homologs, line up next to one another, gene by gene. Section 9.5 describes how this arrangement allows for a gene-shuffling mechanism called crossing over. A spindle begins to form from microtubules, spindle attachment points grow on each centromere, and the nuclear membrane breaks up.

In **metaphase I,** the paired homologs align down the center of the cell. Each member of a homologous pair attaches to a spindle fiber stretching to one pole. The stage is set for the homologous pairs to separate in **anaphase I,** and the chromosomes complete their movement to opposite poles in **telophase I.** In most species, **cytokinesis** occurs after telophase I to produce two haploid cells.

B. In Meiosis II, Sister Chromatids Separate

A second interphase precedes meiosis II in many species, although the DNA does not replicate a second time. Instead, during this time, the chromosomes unfold into very thin threads, allowing the cell to produce proteins.

Prophase II marks the start of the second meiotic division, which closely resembles the events of mitosis. The chromosomes again condense and become visible. In **metaphase II,** the chromosomes align down the center of the cell. In **anaphase II,** the centromeres part, and the separated sister chromatids move to opposite poles. In **telophase II,** nuclear envelopes form, and cytokinesis then separates the nuclei into individual cells.

9.4 Mastering Concepts

1. What happens during interphase of meiosis?
2. How do the events of meiosis I and meiosis II produce four haploid cells from one diploid cell?

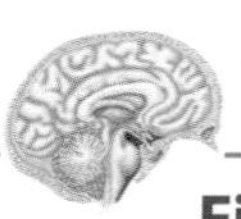

Figure It Out

A cell that is entering prophase I contains __ times as much DNA as one daughter cell at the end of meiosis.

Answer: Four

9.5 Meiosis Generates Enormous Variability

Thanks to meiosis, two parents can give rise to an astounding variety of genetically unique offspring. Three mechanisms account for this diversity: crossing over, independent assortment, and random fertilization.

A. Crossing Over Shuffles Genes

During prophase I, the homologs align themselves precisely, gene by gene. **Crossing over** is a process in which two homologous chromosomes exchange genetic material (figure 9.7). As an example, consider what takes place in your own diploid germ cells. You inherited one member of each homologous pair from your mother; the other came from your father. Crossing over means that pieces of these homologous chromosomes physically change places. Because each homolog comes from a different parent, crossing over produces chromatids that have some genes from the mother and some from the father.

Consider a simplified example of how crossing over mixes trait combinations. Suppose that one chromosome carries the genes for hair color, eye

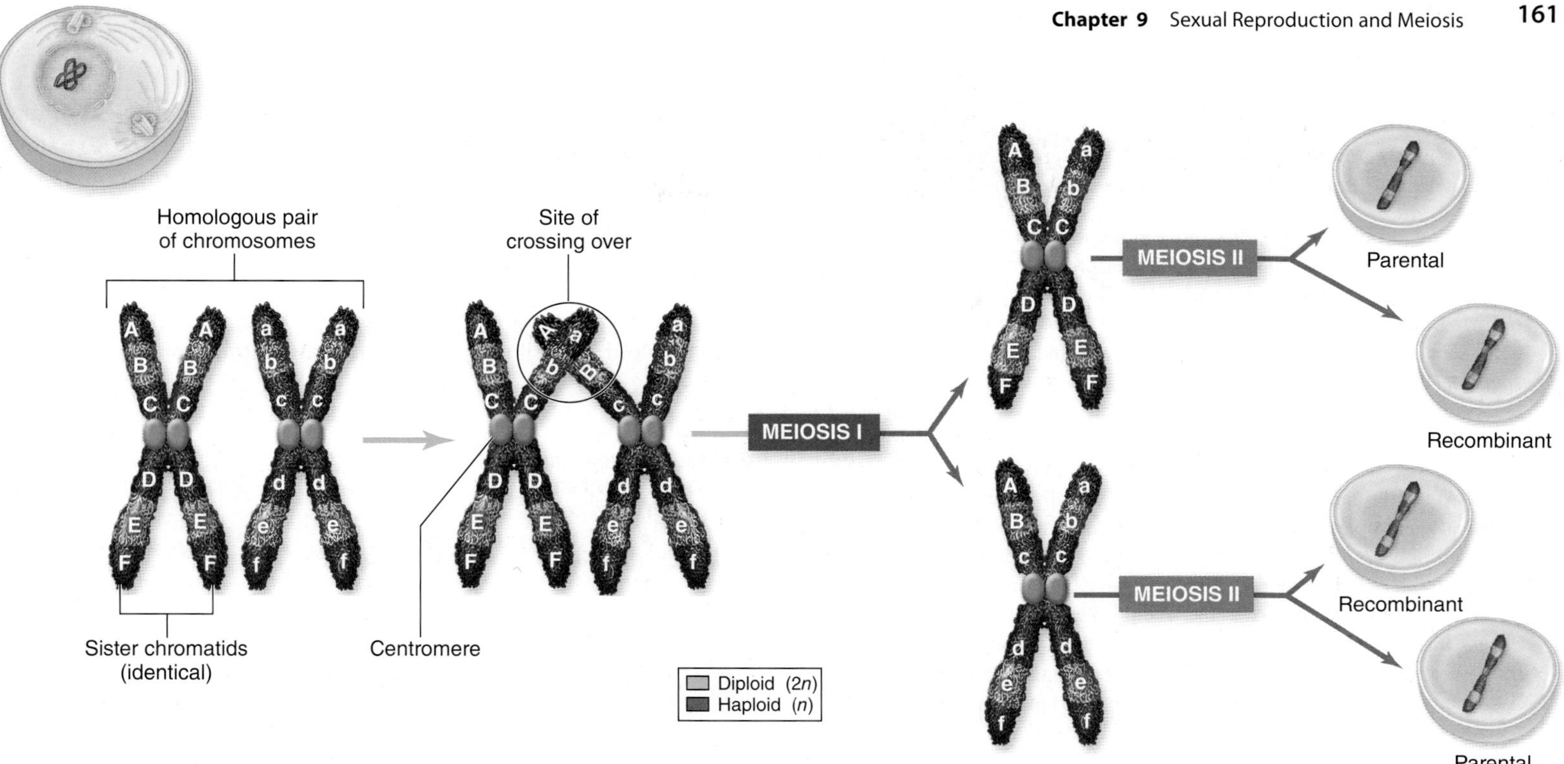

Figure 9.7 Crossing Over. In crossing over, portions of homologous chromosomes swap places. The resulting chromatids may have allele combinations not found in either parent.

color, and finger length. One of the homologs (perhaps the one that came from the father) has alleles that specify blond hair, blue eyes, and short fingers. The homolog from the mother may have different alleles for the same genes, perhaps dictating black hair, brown eyes, and long fingers. Now, suppose that crossing over occurs between the homologous chromosomes. Afterward, one chromatid might bear alleles for blond hair, brown eyes, and long fingers; the other would have the alleles for black hair, blue eyes, and short fingers.

The two chromatids that did not participate, however, remain unchanged. The result: four genetically different chromatids in place of two pairs of identical chromatids. As meiosis continues after crossing over, each chromatid will end up in a separate haploid cell. Thus, crossing over ensures that each haploid cell will be genetically different from the others.

B. Chromosome Pairs Align Randomly During Metaphase I

A look at figure 9.6 reveals a second way that meiosis creates genetic variability. At metaphase I, the homologous chromosome pairs are lined up at the cell's center, with each red chromosome from one parent attached to its blue homolog from the other parent. Examine the orientation of these chromosomes. Notice that the blue chromosome is "on top" in the pair on the left, whereas the red chromosome occupies that position in the pair on the right. In anaphase I, the pairs separate, and the resulting nuclei have a mixture of paternal and maternal genetic material.

The next time a germ cell in the same individual undergoes meiosis, the orientation of the chromosomes may be the same. But it probably will not be, because the alignment of chromosomes at metaphase I occurs at random. The number of possible unique gametes is related to the number of chromosomes.

Why We Care | Multiple Births

Triplets, quadruplets, and higher-order multiple births have become more common since the 1980s. How do they arise?

Triplets come about in several ways. The least common route is for a single embryo to split and develop into three genetically identical babies (monozygotic triplets). Alternatively, if three sperm fertilize three separate egg cells, the triplets will be fraternal (trizygotic). Most commonly, however, an embryo splits and forms two identical babies, and a separate embryo develops into an additional, nonidentical baby. Higher-order multiples likewise usually include combinations of identical and fraternal siblings. Identical quadruplets are exceedingly rare, occurring perhaps once in 11 million deliveries. Monozygotic quintuplets are even more unusual, with only one set ever known to have been born.

Two trends account for the rising incidence of multiple births. First, older women are more likely than younger women to have multiple births, and childbearing among older women has become more common. Second, couples have increasingly sought treatment for infertility. Some fertility drugs stimulate a woman to release one or more egg cells. If sperm fertilize all of them, a multiple birth could result. Another infertility therapy is *in vitro* fertilization, in which sperm fertilize egg cells harvested from a woman's ovaries in the lab. One or more embryos judged most likely to result in a live birth are then implanted into the woman's uterus. Multiple births often result.

For two pairs of homologs, four (2^2) different gametes are possible. For three pairs of homologs, eight (2^3) different gametes can occur (figure 9.8). Extending this formula to humans, with 23 chromosome pairs, there are 8,388,608 (2^{23}) possible genetically unique gametes—all equally likely.

C. Random Fertilization Multiplies the Diversity

We have just seen that every human germ cell undergoing meiosis is likely to produce haploid nuclei with different combinations of chromosomes.

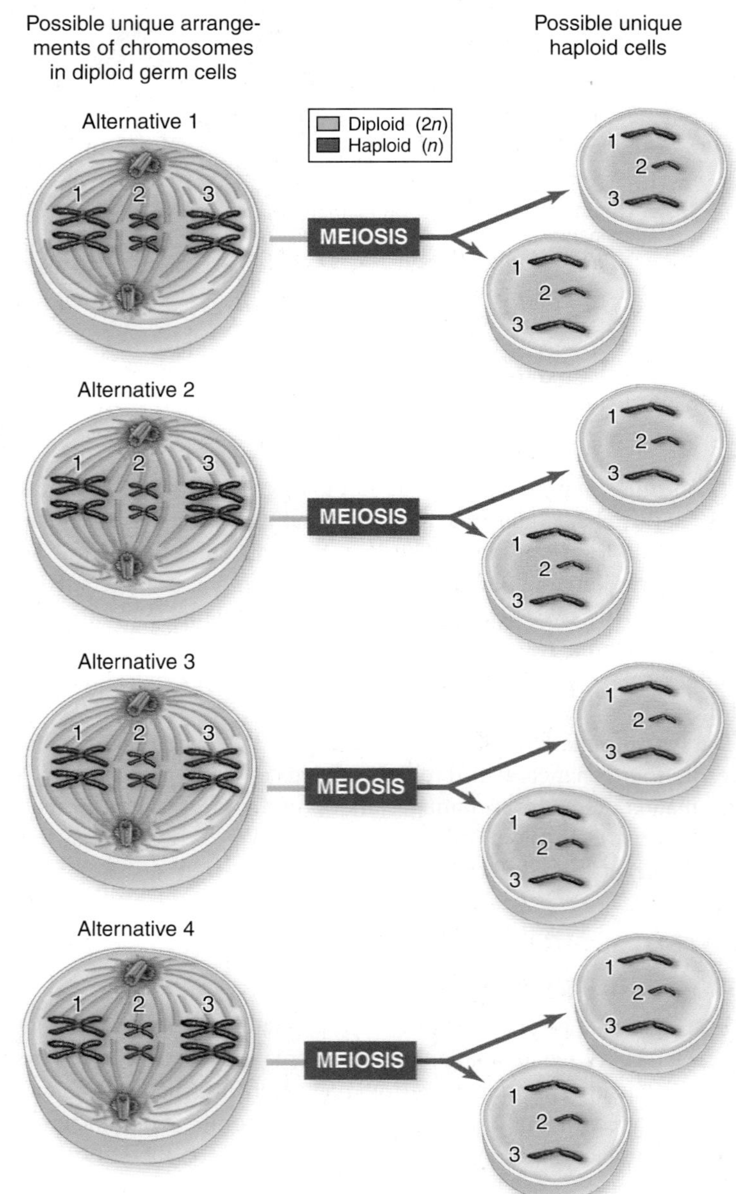

Figure 9.8 Independent Assortment. A germ cell containing three homologous pairs of chromosomes can generate eight genetically different gametes. The number of unique gametes skyrockets when one considers all 23 chromosome pairs (in humans), plus the effects of crossing over.

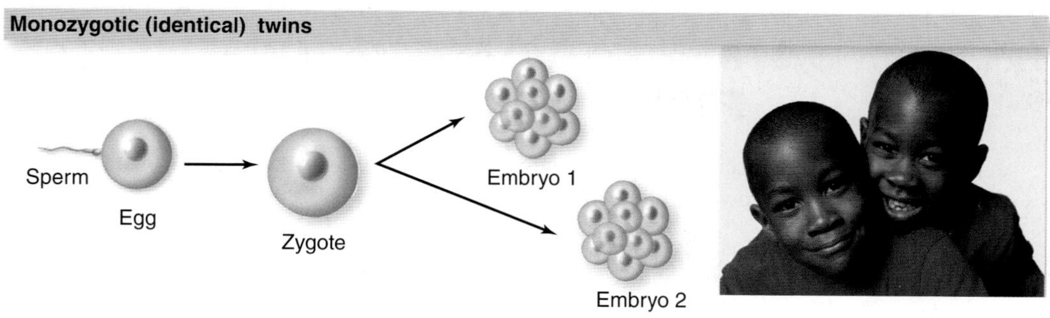

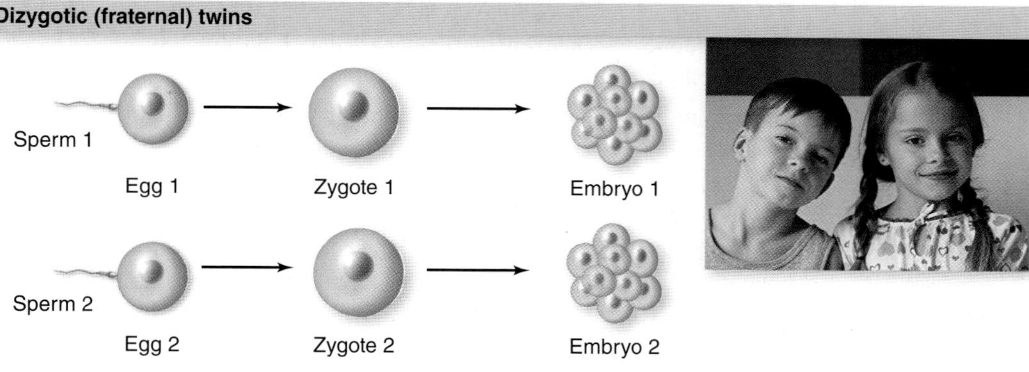

Figure 9.9 Two Ways to Make Twins. Monozygotic twins are genetically identical because they come from the same zygote. Dizygotic (fraternal) twins are not identical because they start as two different zygotes.

Furthermore, it takes two to reproduce. In one mating, any of a woman's 8,388,608 possible egg cells can combine with any of the 8,388,608 possible sperm cells of a partner. One couple could therefore theoretically create more than 70 trillion ($8{,}388{,}608^2$) genetically unique individuals! The number rises even higher when the potential genetic diversity from crossing over is also considered.

With so much potential variability, the chance of two parents producing genetically identical offspring seems exceedingly small. How do the parents of identical twins defy the odds? The answer is that identical twins result from just one fertilization event. Identical twins are called "monozygotic" because they derive from one zygote or embryo that splits in two, resulting in separate, identical babies (figure 9.9). When the embryos fail to separate completely, the twins remain conjoined, or physically attached to one another.

In contrast, nonidentical (fraternal) twins occur when two sperm cells fertilize two separate egg cells. The twins are therefore called "dizygotic." Triplets and higher-order multiple births occur when three or more babies develop at the same time (see this chapter's Why We Care box).

9.5 Mastering Concepts

1. How does crossing over shuffle genes?
2. Explain how different chromosome alignments during metaphase I can result in over 8 million genetically different gametes in a human.
3. How are identical twins different from fraternal twins?

9.6 Mitosis and Meiosis Have Different Functions: A Summary

Mitosis and meiosis are two types of cell division with many events in common. However, there are also many differences (figure 9.10):

- Mitosis occurs in somatic cells throughout the life cycle, whereas meiosis occurs only in germ cells and only at some stages of life.
- In mitotic cell division, cytokinesis occurs once for every DNA replication event, yielding two daughter cells. In meiosis, the DNA replicates once, but cytokinesis occurs twice. As a result, one cell yields four daughter cells.
- After mitosis, the chromosome number in the two daughter cells is the same as in the parent cell. Depending on the species, either haploid or diploid cells can divide mitotically. In contrast, only diploid cells divide by meiosis, producing four haploid daughter cells.
- Mitosis does not require that homologous chromosomes align with one another, whereas meiosis does. This alignment allows for crossing over, which occurs only in meiosis.

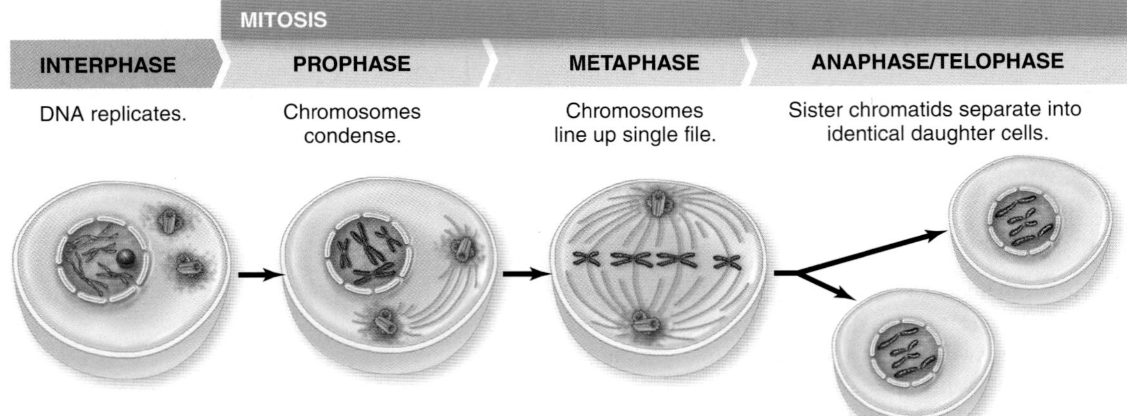
MITOSIS
INTERPHASE
PROPHASE
METAPHASE
ANAPHASE/TELOPHASE
DNA replicates.
Chromosomes condense.
Chromosomes line up single file.
Sister chromatids separate into identical daughter cells.

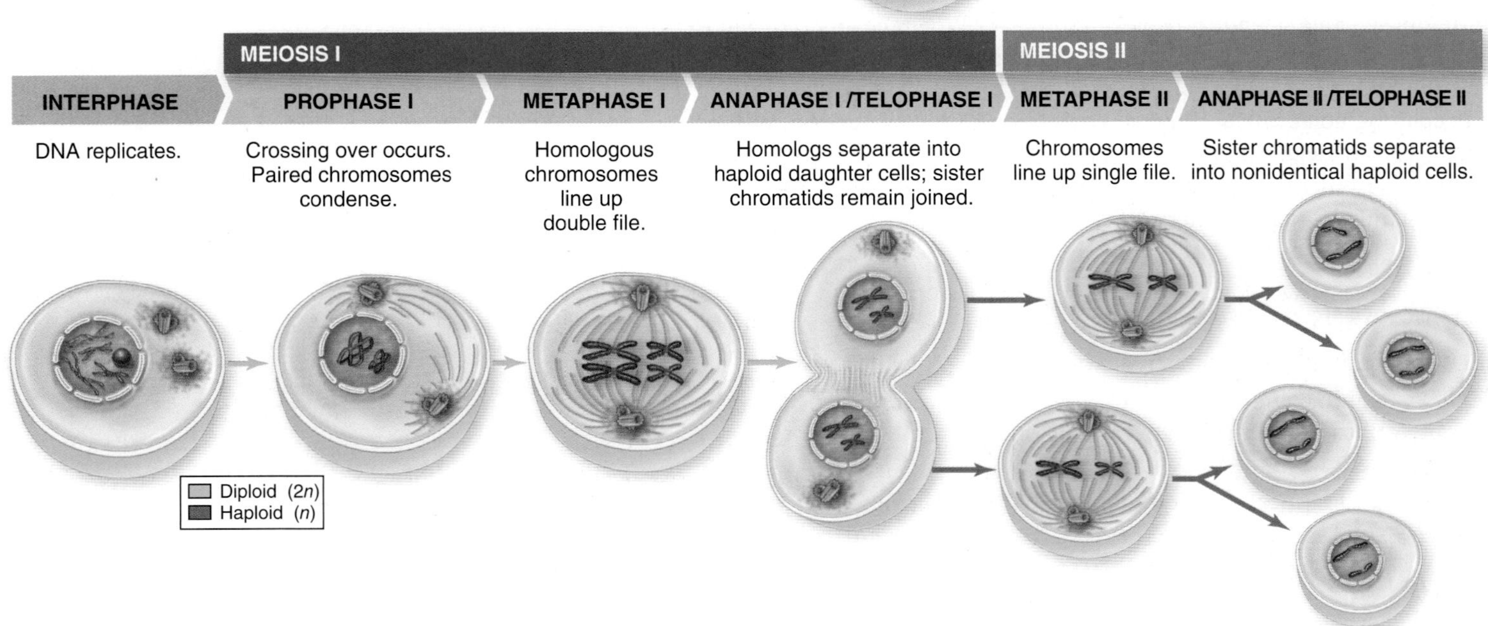
MEIOSIS I
MEIOSIS II
INTERPHASE
PROPHASE I
METAPHASE I
ANAPHASE I /TELOPHASE I
METAPHASE II
ANAPHASE II /TELOPHASE II
DNA replicates.
Crossing over occurs. Paired chromosomes condense.
Homologous chromosomes line up double file.
Homologs separate into haploid daughter cells; sister chromatids remain joined.
Chromosomes line up single file.
Sister chromatids separate into nonidentical haploid cells.
Diploid (2n)
Haploid (n)

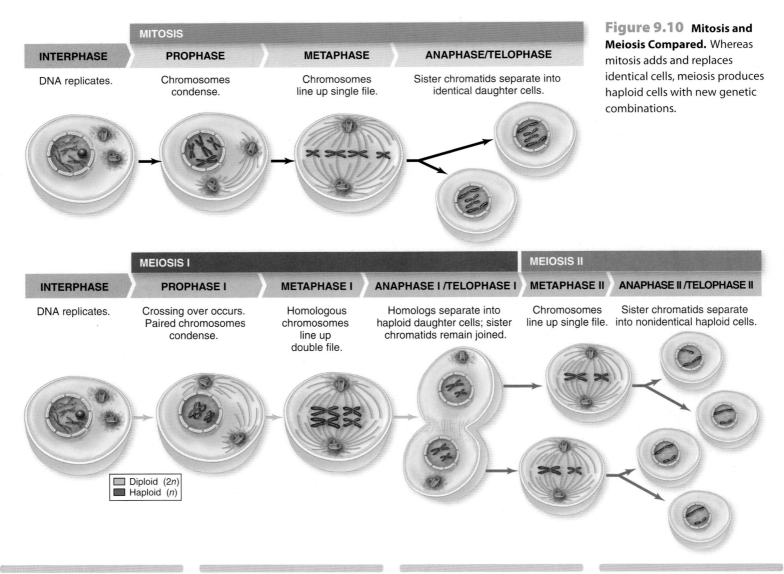

Figure 9.10 Mitosis and Meiosis Compared. Whereas mitosis adds and replaces identical cells, meiosis produces haploid cells with new genetic combinations.

- Mitosis yields identical daughter cells for growth, repair, and asexual reproduction. On the other hand, meiotic division generates genetically variable daughter cells used in sexual reproduction.

9.6 Mastering Concepts

1. In what ways are mitosis and meiosis similar?
2. In what ways are mitosis and meiosis different?

9.7 Errors Sometimes Occur in Meiosis

Considering the number of separate events that take place in meiosis, it is not surprising that things occasionally take a wrong turn. The result can be gametes with extra or missing chromosomes. Even small chromosomal abnormalities can have devastating effects on health.

A. Polyploidy Means Extra Chromosome Sets

An error in meiosis can produce a **polyploid** gamete with one or more complete sets of extra chromosomes (polyploid means "many sets"). For example, if a sperm with the normal 23 chromosomes fertilizes an abnormal egg cell with two full sets (46), the resulting zygote will have three copies of each chromosome (69 total), a type of polyploidy called triploidy. Most human polyploids cease developing as embryos or fetuses.

In contrast to humans, about 30% of flowering plant species tolerate polyploidy well, and many crop plants are polyploids. The durum wheat in pasta is tetraploid (it has four sets of seven chromosomes), and the wheat species in bread is a hexaploid, with six sets of seven chromosomes. Polyploidy is an important force in plant evolution, as section 9.8 describes.

B. Nondisjunction Results in Extra or Missing Chromosomes

Some gametes have just one extra or missing chromosome. The cause of the abnormality is an error called **nondisjunction,** which occurs when chromosomes fail to separate at either the first or the second meiotic division (figure 9.11). The result is a sperm or egg cell with two copies of a particular chromosome or none at all, rather than the normal one copy. When such a gamete fuses with another at fertilization, the resulting zygote has either 45 or 47 chromosomes instead of the normal 46.

Most embryos with incorrect chromosome numbers cease developing before birth; they account for about half of all spontaneous abortions (miscarriages) that occur early in a pregnancy. Extra genetic material, however, causes fewer problems than missing material. This is why most children with the wrong number of chromosomes have an extra one—a trisomy—rather than a missing one.

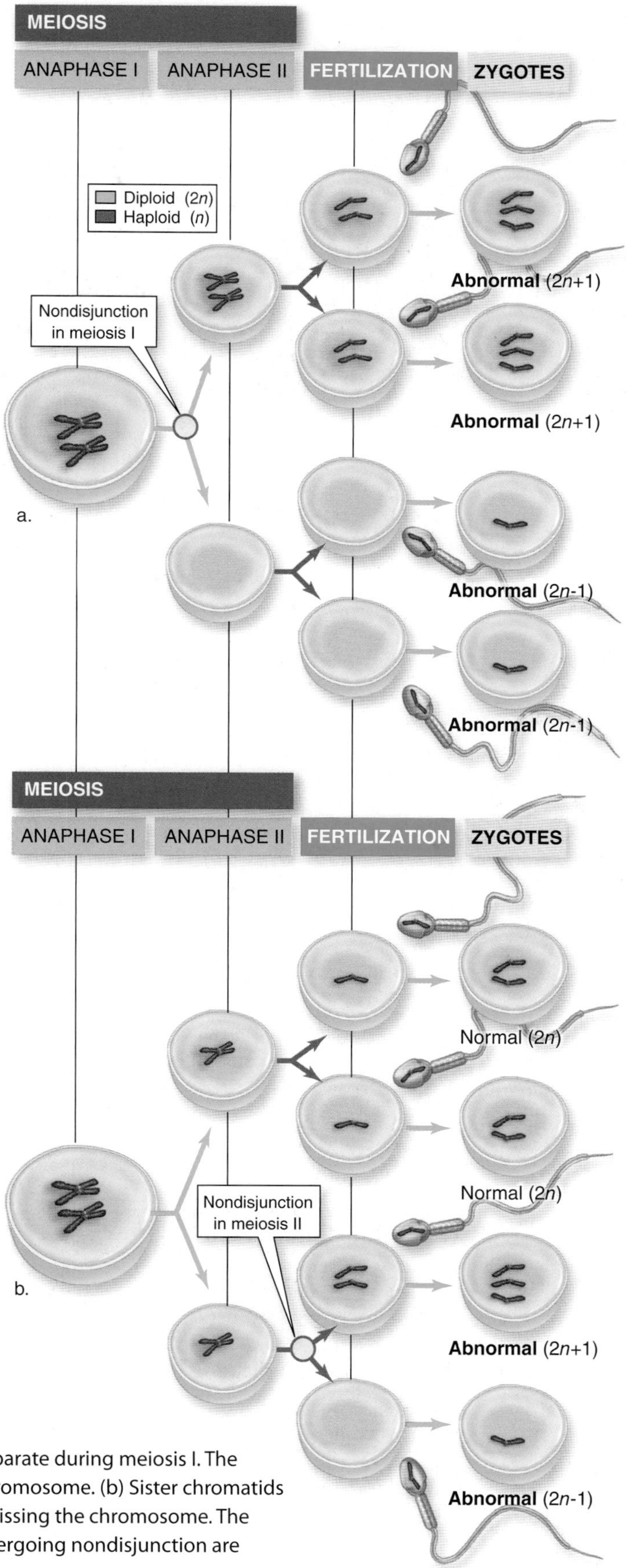

Figure 9.11 Nondisjunction. (a) A homologous pair of chromosomes fails to separate during meiosis I. The result: two nuclei with two copies of the chromosome and two nuclei that lack the chromosome. (b) Sister chromatids fail to separate during meiosis II. One nucleus has an extra chromosome, and one is missing the chromosome. The other two nuclei are unaffected. (Note that all chromosomes other than the ones undergoing nondisjunction are omitted for clarity.)

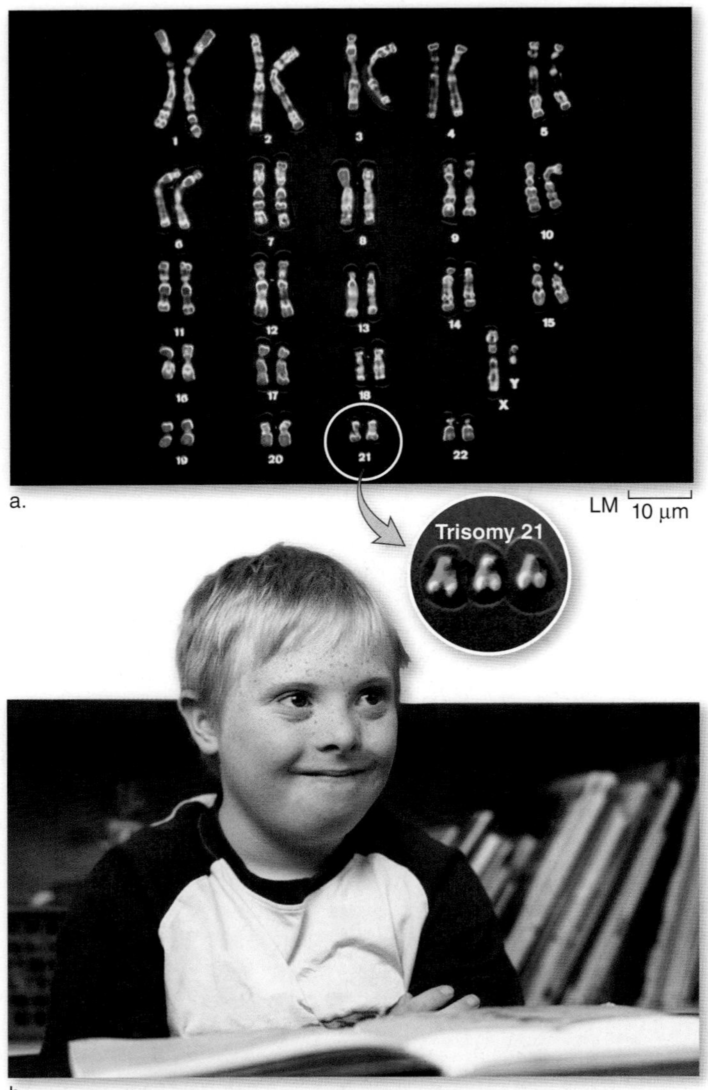

Figure 9.12 **Trisomy 21.** A normal human karyotype reveals 46 chromosomes, but a child born with three copies of chromosome 21 has Down syndrome.

TABLE 9.1 Sex Chromosome Abnormalities

Chromosomes	Name of Condition	Incidence
XXX	Triplo-X	1 in every 1000 to 2000 females
XXY	Klinefelter or XXY syndrome	1 in every 500 to 1000 males
XYY	Jacobs or XYY syndrome	One in every 1000 males
XO	Turner syndrome	1 in every 2000 females

Extra Autosomes The most common cause of Down syndrome is trisomy 21, in which a child inherits three copies of chromosome 21 (figure 9.12). An affected person has distinctive facial features and a unique pattern of hand creases. Intelligence varies greatly; some children have profound mental impairment, whereas others learn well. Many affected children die before their first birthdays, often because of congenital heart defects. People with Down syndrome also have an above average risk for leukemia and Alzheimer disease.

The likelihood of giving birth to a child with trisomy 21 increases dramatically as a woman ages. For women younger than 30, the chance of having a child with the syndrome is 1 in 3000. For a 48-year-old woman, the incidence jumps to 1 in 9. An increased likelihood of nondisjunction apparently accounts for this age association.

Trisomy 21 is the most common autosomal trisomy, but only because the fetus is most likely to be viable. Trisomies 18 and 13 are the next most common; few children with these genetic abnormalities survive infancy. Trisomies undoubtedly occur with other chromosomes, but the embryos fail to develop at all.

Extra or Missing Sex Chromosomes Nondisjunction can produce a gamete that contains two copies of the X or Y chromosome instead of only one. Fertilization then produces a zygote with too many sex chromosomes: XXX, XXY, or XYY (table 9.1). A gamete may also lack a sex chromosome altogether. If one gamete contains an X chromosome and the other gamete has neither X nor Y, the resulting zygote is XO. Interestingly, medical researchers have never reported a person with one Y and no X chromosome. When a zygote lacks an X chromosome, so much genetic material is missing that it probably cannot sustain more than a few cell divisions.

9.7 Mastering Concepts

1. What is polyploidy?
2. How can nondisjunction during meiosis lead to gametes with extra or missing chromosomes?

Investigating Life

9.8 A New Species Is Born, but Who's the Daddy?

Most species on Earth formed long ago, so details about their origin remain lost to history. Sometimes, however, science catches a lucky break, as in the case of a flowering plant called goat's beard, or *Tragopogon*. Europeans introduced three *Tragopogon* species to North America in the 1900s. Since that time, the plants have spread widely across the continent. The most common of the three introduced plants is *T. dubius,* whereas two rarer species are *T. pratensis* and *T. porrifolius*.

A brief lesson on plant reproduction will help clarify why *Tragopogon* is so important. Plants in the three introduced species are diploid, and each individual has two parents, just as you do. Pollen carries haploid sperm nuclei to a female flower part containing an egg cell. After fertilization, the diploid zygote develops into an embryo, which is packaged into a seed. Errors occasionally occur during gamete production, however, and a plant may produce sex cells containing two full sets of chromosomes instead of just one. If a diploid sperm nucleus fertilizes a diploid egg cell, the resulting zygote has four sets of chromosomes; in other words, it is tetraploid.

Biologists have known since the 1950s that the union of diploid gametes gave rise to two brand-new tetraploid species, named *T. miscellus* and *T. mirus* (figure 9.13). These tetraploid plants are considered full-fledged species because they can mate among themselves but not with the "parental" diploid plants. Because *Tragopogon* did not exist in North America before the 1900s, *T. miscellus* and *T. mirus* must have arisen in just half a century.

The Question: This relatively short history makes it possible to trace the ancestry of *T. miscellus* and *T. mirus*. Specifically, Washington State University biologists Douglas and Pamela Soltis wanted to answer this question: Which diploid species was the father and which was the mother of each tetraploid species?

The Approach: To learn more about how the two species formed, the Soltises collected seeds from 39 natural populations of all five *Tragopogon* species. They germinated the seeds in trays of soil, then extracted the chloroplast DNA from each plant's leaves. The researchers were interested in these organelles because each plant inherits chloroplast DNA from just one parent, the female. The egg contributes cytoplasm, containing mitochondria and chloroplasts, to the zygote. The tiny sperm nucleus, on the other hand, contains no organelles.

The researchers digested the chloroplast DNA from each plant with 18 restriction enzymes, each of which cut the DNA at a different sequence. Electrophoresis separated the fragments, and stains made the bands of DNA visible. Different patterns of DNA fragments reflect underlying differences in chloroplast DNA sequences. These unique sequences, in turn, should reveal the maternal heritage of each species.

The Conclusion: As expected, the study revealed a unique fragment pattern for each diploid *Tragopogon* species. When the Soltises compared these genetic "fingerprints" to those of the tetraploid hybrids, it was clear that *T. porrifolius* was the female parent of *T. mirus*. Figure 9.14 shows the results for the other tetraploid species, *T. miscellus*. The DNA patterns revealed that *T. pratensis* was the female parent of most populations of this species, but two samples of *T. miscellus* had chloroplast DNA like that of *T. dubius*. The hybrid *T. miscellus* species has therefore arisen more than once.

The story of goat's beard is important because it shows that new species do not always arise gradually; instead, a sudden genetic change can instantly separate a brand new species from its parents. The observation that this process has occurred more than once in 50 years, at least for *Tragopogon*, is tantalizing. How many times has it happened in life's history? We will probably never know.

Soltis, Douglas E., and Pamela S. Soltis. 1989. Allopolyploid speciation in *Tragopogon:* Insights from chloroplast DNA. *American Journal of Botany*, vol. 76, pages 1119–1124.

Species	Diploid or tetraploid	Number of chromosomes	Parents
T. dubius	Diploid	12	*T. dubius* (both)
T. pratensis	Diploid	12	*T. pratensis* (both)
T. porrifolius	Diploid	12	*T. porrifolius* (both)
T. mirus	Tetraploid	24	*T. dubius* and *T. porrifolius*
T. miscellus	Tetraploid	24	*T. dubius* and *T. pratensis*

Figure 9.13 ***Tragopogon* Species Origins.** Genetic studies have revealed which "parents" hybridized to produce the two tetraploid species. But which species contributed the pollen and which contributed the egg?

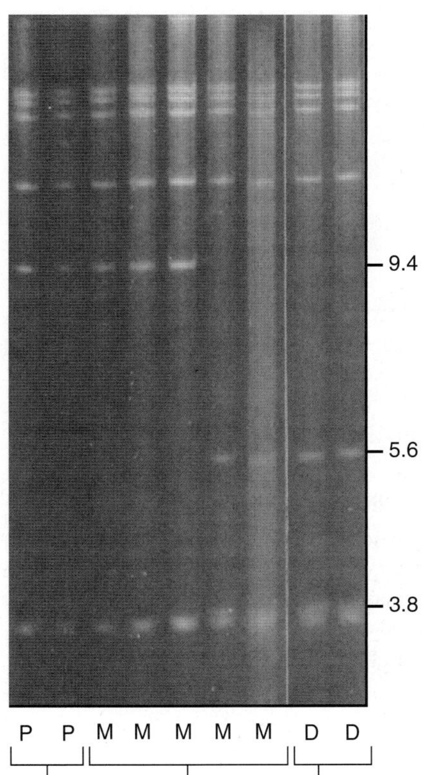

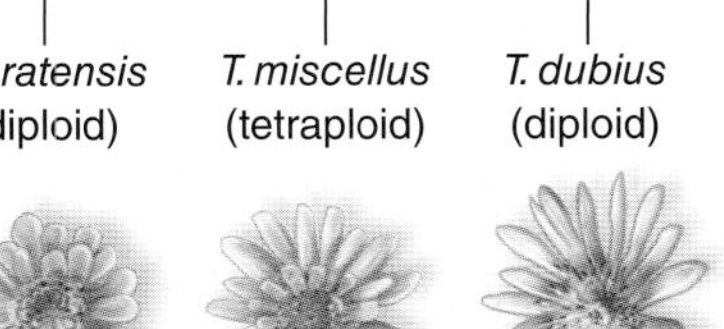

Figure 9.14 **Chloroplast DNA.** The Soltises purified DNA from chloroplasts of *T. pratensis, T. miscellus,* and *T. dubius*. Because chloroplast DNA comes from only the egg, a matching pattern on the electrophoresis gel reveals the identity of the mother. The bands at positions 3.8, 5.6, and 9.4 reveal that the tetraploid species *T. miscellus* may have either *T. pratensis* or *T. dubius* as a maternal parent. This hybrid has therefore arisen more than once.

9.8 Mastering Concepts

1. How did the researchers use chloroplast DNA to learn about the evolutionary history of tetraploid *Tragopogon* species?
2. The Soltises suggest that because *T. dubius* is so much more common than the other two diploid species, its pollen is also the most abundant. How would you test the hypothesis that the most common plant is most likely to be the father of a tetraploid hybrid?

Chapter Summary

9.1 Why Sex?

- **Asexual reproduction** generates virtually identical copies of an organism, whereas **sexual reproduction** mixes traits from two parents.
- Asexual reproduction can be successful in a stable environment, but a changing environment selects for sexual reproduction.

9.2 Diploid Cells Contain Two Homologous Sets of Chromosomes

- **Diploid cells** have two full sets of **chromosomes,** one from each parent. A **karyotype** is a chart that displays all of the chromosomes from one cell.
- In humans, the **sex chromosomes** (X and Y) determine whether an individual is male or female. The 22 **homologous pairs** of **autosomes** do not differ between the sexes.
- Homologous chromosomes share the same size, centromere position, and gene order. A homologous pair may or may not carry the same **alleles** for each gene.

9.3 Meiosis Is Essential in Sexual Reproduction

A. Gametes Are Haploid Sex Cells

- **Gametes** contain one set of chromosomes and are therefore **haploid cells.**
- Three key events in sexual life cycles are **meiosis,** which halves the genetic material; gamete formation; and **fertilization,** which occurs when gametes fuse and form the diploid **zygote.** In most species, the zygote divides by **mitosis** as the new organism develops.

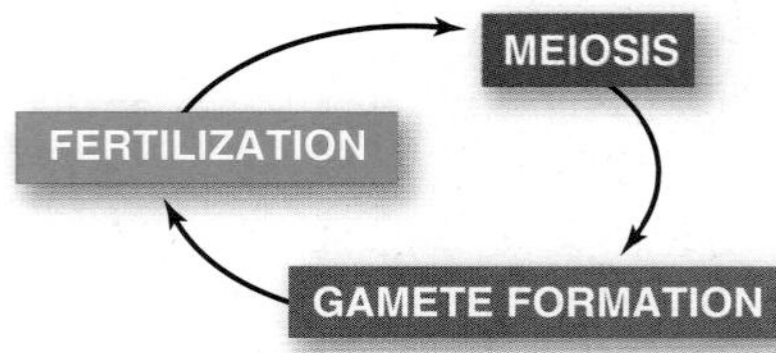

B. Specialized Germ Cells Undergo Meiosis

- **Somatic** cells do not participate in reproduction, but diploid **germ cells** produce gametes by meiosis.

9.4 In Meiosis, DNA Replicates Once, but the Nucleus Divides Twice

A. In Meiosis I, Homologous Chromosomes Pair Up and Separate

- **Interphase** happens before meiosis. Homologous pairs of chromosomes align during **prophase I,** line up double-file at the cell's center during **metaphase I,** then split apart during **anaphase I.** The chromosomes arrive at the poles in **telophase I,** and the cell often divides **(cytokinesis).**

B. In Meiosis II, Sister Chromatids Separate

- The two products of meiosis I divide once more to yield four haploid cells. The chromosomes condense during **prophase II.** During **metaphase II,** they line up single-file at the cell's equator. The sister chromatids are separated in **anaphase II,** and the chromosomes arrive at the poles in **telophase II.** Cytokinesis then occurs once more.

9.5 Meiosis Generates Enormous Variability

A. Crossing Over Shuffles Genes

- **Crossing over,** which occurs in prophase I, produces variability when portions of homologous chromosomes switch places. After crossing over, the chromatids carry new combinations of parental alleles.

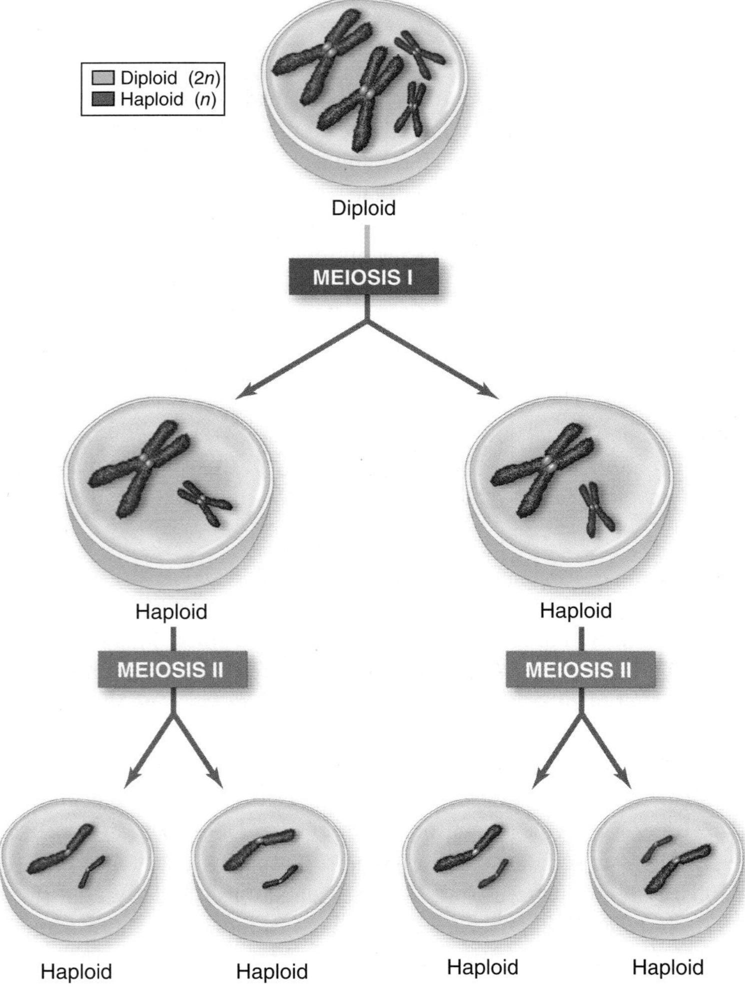

B. Chromosome Pairs Align Randomly During Metaphase I

- Every possible orientation of homologous pairs of chromosomes at metaphase I is equally likely. As a result, one person can produce over 8 million genetically different gametes.

C. Random Fertilization Multiplies the Diversity

- Because any sperm can fertilize any egg cell, a human couple can produce over 70 trillion genetically different offspring.
- Identical (monozygotic) twins arise when a zygote splits into two embryos.

9.6 Mitosis and Meiosis Have Different Functions: A Summary

- Mitotic division produces identical copies of a cell and occurs throughout life.
- Meiosis produces genetically different haploid cells. It occurs only in specialized cells and only during some parts of the life cycle.

9.7 Errors Sometimes Occur In Meiosis

A. Polyploidy Means Extra Chromosome Sets

- **Polyploid** cells have one or more extra sets of chromosomes.

B. Nondisjunction Results in Extra or Missing Chromosomes

- **Nondisjunction** is the failure of chromosomes to separate in meiosis, and it causes gametes to have incorrect chromosome numbers. Sex chromosome abnormalities are typically less severe than an incorrect number of autosomes.

9.8 Investigating Life: A New Species Is Born, but Who's the Daddy?

- Analysis of chloroplast DNA has revealed the parental origin of two species of *Tragopogon* plants that have arisen since the 1950s.

Multiple Choice Questions

1. The unique feature of sex is
   a. the ability of a cell to divide.
   b. the production of offspring.
   c. the ability to generate new genetic combinations.
   d. Each of the above is unique to sexual reproduction.
2. A __ cell is ___ and a gamete is ___.
   a. sperm; diploid; haploid
   b. somatic; diploid; haploid
   c. germ; haploid; diploid
   d. somatic; haploid; diploid
3. Fertilization results in the formation of a
   a. diploid zygote.
   b. haploid gamete.
   c. diploid somatic cell.
   d. haploid zygote.
4. What is the relationship between two homologous chromosomes?
   a. They are exact copies.
   b. They carry the same genes but in different order.
   c. They came from a single parent.
   d. They carry different versions of the same genes.
5. Which of the following events may occur in BOTH meiosis I and meiosis II?
   a. Homologous chromosomes pair up.
   b. Homologous chromosomes move apart from each other.
   c. DNA replicates.
   d. Cytokinesis occurs.
6. Crossing over occurs during which phase of meiosis?
   a. Prophase I
   b. Metaphase I
   c. Metaphase II
   d. Anaphase II
7. Which of the following is *not* a mechanism that contributes to diversity?
   a. Random fertilization
   b. Crossing over
   c. Cytokinesis
   d. Independent assortment
8. Which of the following best describes what happens when identical twins are conceived?
   a. One sperm cell fertilizes one egg cell.
   b. One sperm cell fertilizes two egg cells.
   c. Two sperm cells fertilize one egg cell.
   d. Two sperm cells fertilize two egg cells.
9. Nondisjunction results from an error at which stage of meiosis?
   a. Prophase II
   b. Metaphase I or II
   c. Anaphase I or II
   d. Telophase I
10. Down syndrome results from which of the following?
    a. An extra chromosome 21
    b. An extra X chromosome
    c. The absence of a Y chromosome
    d. The absence of chromosome 18

Write It Out

1. Distinguish between asexual reproduction and sexual reproduction.
2. Some fungi reproduce asexually if nutrients are abundant but switch to sexual reproduction when conditions are not as good. Explain this observation.
3. Sketch the relationships among mitosis, meiosis, and fertilization in a sexual life cycle.
4. What is the difference between haploid and diploid cells? Are your skin cells haploid or diploid? What about gametes?
5. Define the following terms: *crossing over, gamete, diploid, haploid, autosome, homologous pair.*
6. How are mitosis and meiosis different?
7. Draw all possible metaphase I chromosomal arrangements for a cell with a diploid number of 8.
8. A dog has 39 pairs of chromosomes. Considering only the orientation of homologous chromosomes during metaphase I, how many genetically different puppies are possible from the mating of two dogs? Is this number an underestimate or an overestimate? Why?
9. What is the difference between monozygotic and dizygotic twins?
10. Is it possible for a boy–girl pair of twins to be genetically identical? Why or why not?
11. Many male veterans of the Vietnam War claim that their children born years later have birth defects caused by a contaminant in the herbicide Agent Orange used as a defoliant in the conflict. What types of cells would the chemical have to have affected in these men to cause birth defects years later? Explain your answer.

Pull It Together

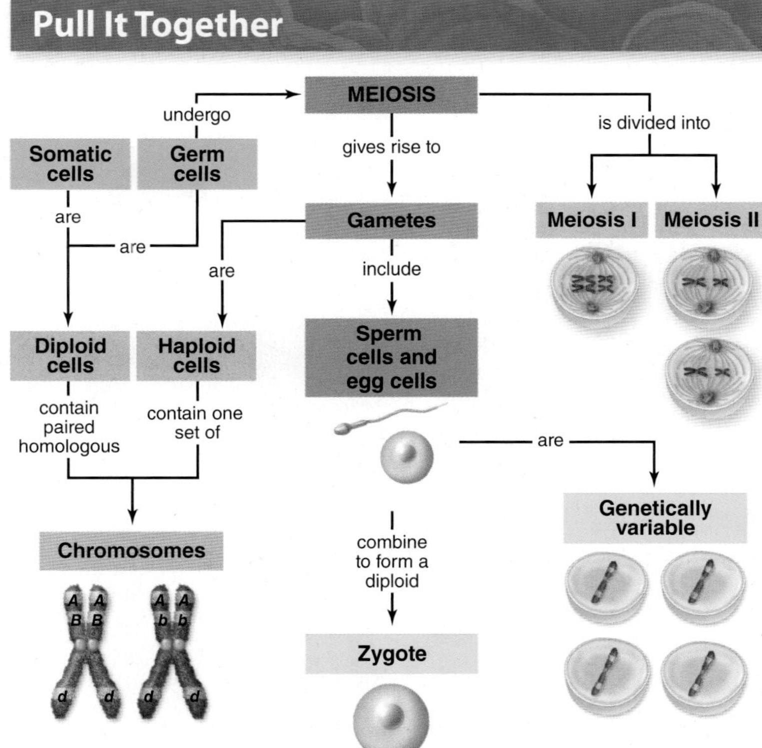

1. Fit the following terms into this concept map: *chromatid, centromere, nondisjunction, fertilization, zygote,* and *mitosis.*
2. What happens in meiosis I and meiosis II?
3. What two processes in meiosis I generate genetic variation among gametes?
4. Why must diploid organisms produce haploid gametes?
5. Where do the members of each pair of homologous chromosomes in a diploid cell come from?

Enhance your study of this chapter with practice quizzes, animations and videos, answer keys, and downloadable study tools.
www.mhhe.com/hoefnagels

10 Patterns of Inheritance

Human Diversity. Everyone inherits a unique combination of DNA sequences from his or her parents. Combined with environmental influences, these genetic sequences determine not only our appearance but many other traits as well.

Learning Outline

Learn How to Learn
Be a Good Problem Solver

This chapter is about the principles of inheritance, and you will find many genetics problems among its pages. The guide at the end of this chapter shows a systematic, step-by-step approach to solving three of the most common types of genetics problems. Keep using the guide until you feel comfortable solving any problem type.

What's the Point?

Interest in heredity is probably as old as humankind itself. People throughout time have wondered at their similarities, and they have used their intuition about inheritance to select for superior varieties of everything from poodles to wheat. But the *systematic* study of inheritance began with a nineteenth-century Austrian monk named Gregor Mendel; subsequent efforts to learn the basic principles of genetics and inheritance continued well into the twentieth century.

Today, genetics and DNA are familiar to nearly everyone, and the entire set of genetic instructions to build a person—the human genome—has been deciphered. Even so, when a family meets with a genetic counselor or physician to learn about an inherited illness, they encounter the same principles of heredity that Mendel derived in his early experiments with peas. Our look at genetics begins the traditional way, with Mendel, but we can appreciate his genius in light of what we now know about DNA.

10.1 Chromosomes Are Packets of Genetic Information: A Review

A healthy young couple, both with family histories of cystic fibrosis, visits a genetic counselor before deciding whether to have children. The counselor suggests genetic tests, which reveal that both the man and the woman are carriers of cystic fibrosis. The counselor tells the couple that each of their future children has a 25% chance of inheriting this serious illness. How does the counselor arrive at that one-in-four chance? This chapter will explain the answer. ▸ genetic testing, p. 211

First, however, it may be useful to review some concepts from previous chapters in this unit. Chapter 7 explained that cells contain DNA, a molecule that encodes all of the information needed to sustain life. Human DNA includes about 25,000 genes. A **gene** is a portion of DNA whose sequence of nucleotides (A, C, G, and T) encodes a protein. When a gene's nucleotide sequence mutates, the encoded protein may also change. Each gene can therefore exist as one or more **alleles,** or alternative forms, each arising from a different mutation.

The DNA in the nucleus of a eukaryotic cell is divided among multiple **chromosomes,** which are long strands of DNA associated with proteins. Recall that a **diploid cell** contains two sets of chromosomes, with one set inherited from each parent. The human genome consists of 23 pairs of chromosomes (figure 10.1a). Of these, 22 pairs are **autosomes,** which are the chromosomes that are the same for both sexes. The single pair of **sex chromosomes**

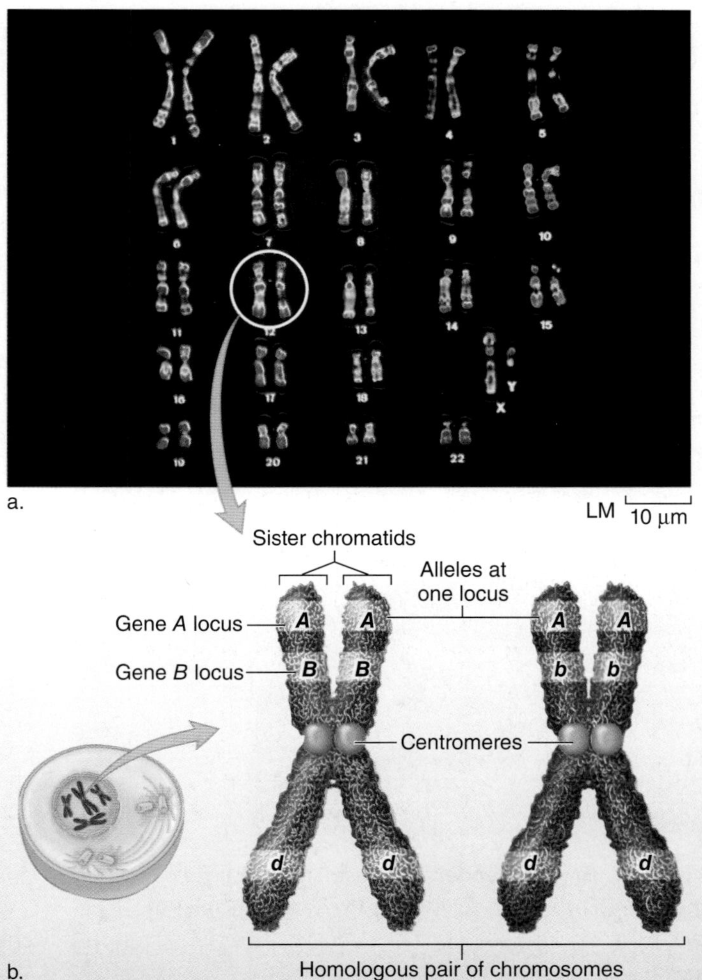

Figure 10.1 Homologous Chromosomes. (a) A human diploid cell contains 23 pairs of chromosomes. (b) Each chromosome has one allele for every gene. For the homologous chromosome pair in this figure, both alleles for gene *A* are identical; the same is true for gene *D*. However, the two chromosomes carry different alleles for gene *B*.

determines whether a person is male or female: a person with two X chromosomes is female, whereas a male has one X and one Y.

With the exception of X and Y, the chromosome pairs are homologous (figure 10.1b). Recall from chapter 9 that the two members of a **homologous pair** of chromosomes look alike and have the same sequence of genes in the same positions. (A gene's "locus" is its physical place on the chromosome.) But the two homologs may or may not carry the same alleles. Since each homolog comes from a different parent, each person inherits two alleles for each gene in the human genome.

The following analogy should help clarify the relationships among these terms. Suppose that each chromosome is like a cookbook; the human genome is a "library" that consists of 46 such volumes, arranged in 23 pairs of similar books. The entire cookbook library includes about 25,000 recipes, each analogous to one gene.

The two alleles for each gene, then, are comparable to two of the many ways to prepare brownies; some recipes include nuts, for example, whereas others use different types of chocolate. The two "brownie recipes" in a cell may be exactly the same, slightly different, or very different from each other. Furthermore, with the exception of identical twins, everyone inherits a unique combination of alleles for all of the genes in the human genome. For example, you may have black hair and brown eyes, whereas your best friend has brown hair and green eyes. The two of you do not look alike because you have different alleles for the hair and eye color genes.

Another important idea to review from chapter 9 is the role of meiosis and fertilization in a sexual life cycle (see figure 9.5). **Meiosis** is a specialized form of cell division that occurs in diploid germ cells and gives rise to **haploid cells,** each containing just one set of chromosomes. In humans, these haploid cells are **gametes**—sperm or egg cells. **Fertilization** unites the gametes from two parents, producing the first cell of the next generation. Gametes are the cells that convey chromosomes from one generation to the next, so they play a critical part in the study of inheritance.

No one can examine a gamete and say for sure which allele it carries for every gene. As we shall see in this chapter, however, for some traits, we can use knowledge of a person's characteristics and family history to say that a gamete has a 100% chance, 50% chance, or 0% chance of carrying a specific allele. With this information for both parents, it is simple to calculate the probability that a child will inherit the allele.

10.1 Mastering Concepts

1. How are chromosomes, DNA, genes, and alleles related?
2. How do meiosis, fertilization, diploid cells, and haploid cells interact in a sexual life cycle?

10.2 Mendel's Experiments Uncovered Basic Laws of Inheritance

Of all the people who have studied inheritance, one nineteenth-century investigator, Gregor Mendel, made the most lasting impression on what would become the science of genetics (figure 10.2). Mendel was born in 1822 and spent his early childhood in a small village in what is now the Czech Republic, where he learned early how to tend fruit trees. After finishing school ahead of schedule, Mendel became a priest at a monastery, where he could teach and do research in natural science.

The young man eagerly learned how to artificially pollinate crop plants to control their breeding. The monastery sent him to earn a college degree at the

Figure 10.2 Gregor Mendel. This Austrian monk used experiments with pea plants to discover the basic principles of inheritance.

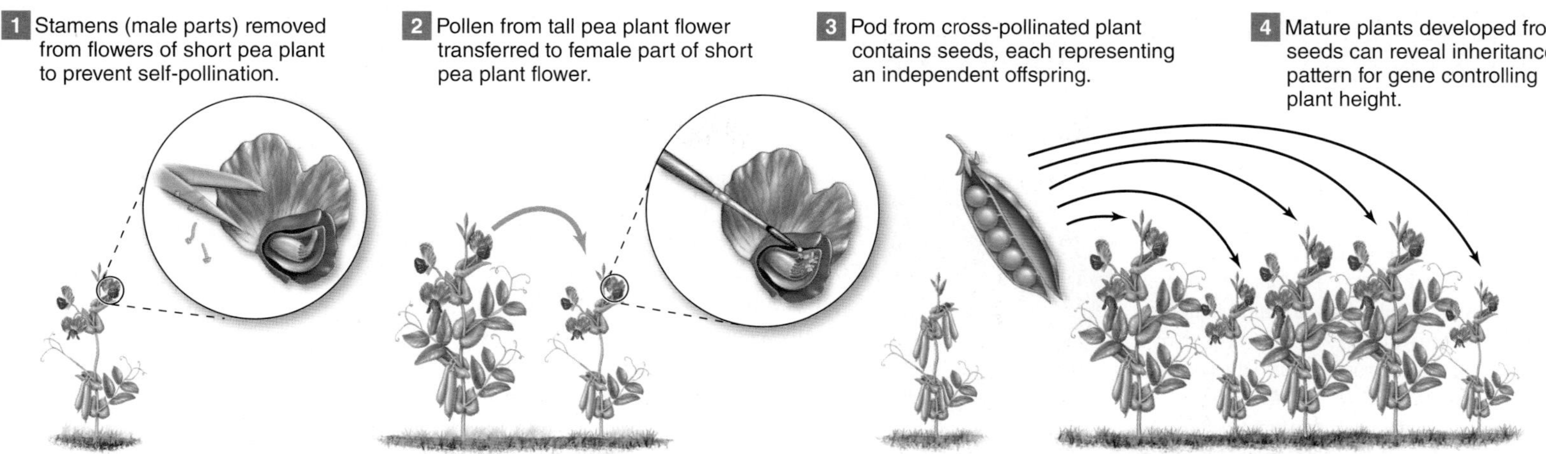

1 Stamens (male parts) removed from flowers of short pea plant to prevent self-pollination.
2 Pollen from tall pea plant flower transferred to female part of short pea plant flower.
3 Pod from cross-pollinated plant contains seeds, each representing an independent offspring.
4 Mature plants developed from seeds can reveal inheritance pattern for gene controlling plant height.

Figure 10.3 Breeding Peas. By hand-pollinating pea plants, an investigator can easily control which plants breed with which.

University of Vienna, where courses in the sciences and statistics fueled his interest in plant breeding. Mendel began to think about experiments to address a compelling question that had confounded other plant breeders: Why did some traits disappear, only to reappear a generation later?

The pea plant *(Pisum sativum)* was Mendel's choice for studying heredity. This species offered many advantages: It is easy to grow, develops quickly, and produces abundant offspring. Also, it has many traits that appear in two easily distinguishable forms. For example, seeds may be yellow or green, pods may be inflated or constricted, and stems may be tall or short.

Pea plants also have another advantage for studies of inheritance: it is easy to control which plants mate with which (figure 10.3). An investigator can take pollen from the male flower parts of one plant and apply it to the female part of another plant, then allow the offspring (seeds) to develop. The investigator can observe the traits that each one inherited, either by examining the seeds directly or by letting them grow into new plants.

A. Mendel Called Each Trait Either Dominant or Recessive

From 1857 to 1863, Mendel crossed and cataloged some 24,034 plants through several generations. He observed consistent ratios of traits in the offspring and deduced that the plants transmitted distinct units, or "elementen" (now called genes).

Mendel's first experiments dealt with single traits that have two expressions, such as yellow and green seed colors. He set up all possible combinations of crosses: yellow with yellow, green with green, and yellow with green (figure 10.4).

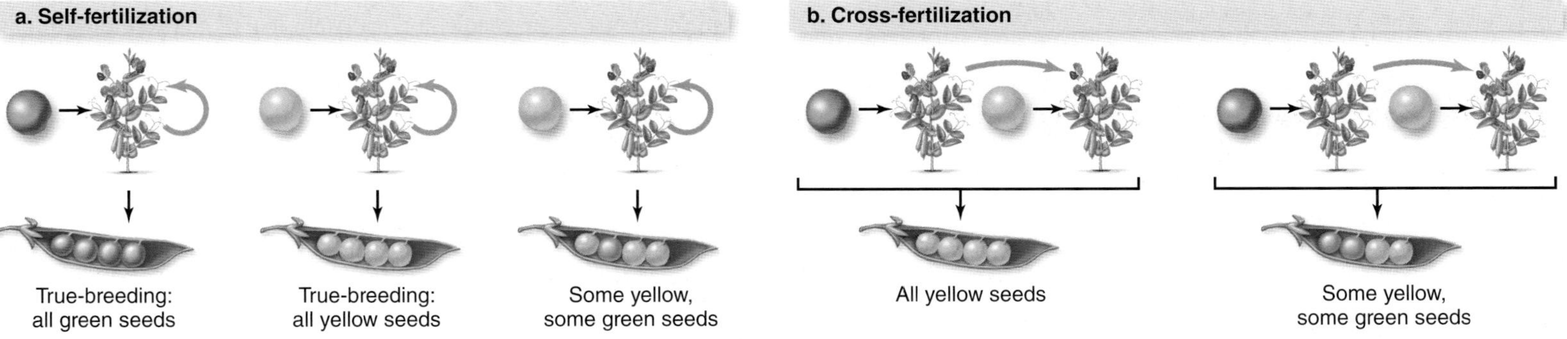

Figure 10.4 All Possible Crosses. Mendel grew plants from green and yellow seeds. He then self- and cross-fertilized the plants in every possible combination. The results enabled him to deduce the principles of inheritance.

Burning Questions

What does "recessive" really mean?

How can a recessive allele seem to hide when a dominant allele is present, then emerge from its hiding place if the dominant allele is absent? How does it "know" what to do? The answer is that a recessive allele does not hide, emerge, or know anything. It remains a part of a cell's DNA, regardless of the presence of a dominant allele. It only seems to hide because it codes for a nonfunctional protein.

For example, consider the disorder phenylketonuria (abbreviated PKU). In most people, an enzyme converts the amino acid phenylalanine into another amino acid. A mutated allele of the gene encoding this enzyme, however, results in the production of an abnormal, nonfunctional protein. People who have just one copy of the recessive allele are healthy because the cell has enough of the normal protein, thanks to the dominant allele. Because heterozygotes have a normal phenotype, the recessive allele seems to "vanish." Individuals who inherit two copies of the recessive allele, however, cannot produce the normal enzyme. Disease symptoms appear when phenylalanine accumulates to toxic levels, causing mental retardation and other problems. Foods containing the artificial sweetener aspartame carry a warning to people with phenylketonuria because aspartame contains phenylalanine.

INGREDIENTS: DEXTROSE WITH MALTODEXTRIN, ASPARTAME
PHENYLKETONURICS: CONTAINS PHENYLALANINE

Submit your burning question to:
marielle_hoefnagels@mcgraw-hill.com

Mendel noted that some plants, when crossed with one another, were always **true-breeding;** that is, they always produced offspring identical to themselves. Plants derived from green seeds, for example, always produced green seeds when self-fertilized. But crosses involving yellow-seeded plants were more variable. Sometimes these plants were true-breeding, but in other cases, the offspring included a mix of yellow and green seeds. Sometimes the green trait vanished in one generation, only to reappear in the next.

Mendel noticed a similar mode of inheritance when he studied other pea plant characteristics: one trait seemed to obscure the other. Mendel called the masking trait *dominant;* the trait being masked was called *recessive*. The yellow-seed trait, for example, was dominant to the green trait.

Although Mendel referred to *traits* as dominant or recessive, today's biologists reserve these terms for *alleles*. A **dominant** allele is one that exerts its effects whenever it is present; a **recessive** allele is one whose effect is masked if a dominant allele is also present. When a gene has two alleles, it is common to symbolize the dominant allele with a capital letter (such as *Y* for yellow) and the recessive allele with the corresponding lowercase letter (*y* for green).

The "dominance" of an allele may seem to imply that it "dominates" in the population as a whole. The dominant allele, however, is not always the most common one. In humans, the allele that causes a form of dwarfism called achondroplasia is dominant, but it is very rare—as is the dominant allele that causes Huntington disease. In contrast, blue eyes are the norm in people of northern European origin, even though the alleles that produce this eye color are recessive.

B. For Each Gene, a Cell's Two Alleles May Be Identical or Different

Mendel chose traits encoded by genes with only two possible alleles, but some genes have hundreds of forms. Regardless of the number of possibilities, however, a diploid cell can have only two alleles for each gene. After all, each diploid individual has inherited one set of chromosomes from each parent, and each chromosome carries only one allele per gene.

For a given gene, a diploid cell's two alleles may be identical or different. The **genotype** expresses the genetic makeup of an individual, and it is written as a pair of letters representing the alleles. An individual that is **homozygous** for a particular gene has two identical alleles, meaning that both parents contributed the same gene version. If both alleles are dominant, the individual is homozygous dominant (written as *YY*, for example); if both are recessive, the individual is homozygous recessive (*yy*). An individual with a **heterozygous** genotype, on the other hand, has two different alleles for the gene (*Yy*); that is, the two parents each contributed different genetic information.

The organism's genotype is distinct from its **phenotype,** or observable characteristics. Flower color, seed color, and stem length are examples of pea plant phenotypes that Mendel studied. Your own phenotype includes not only your height, eye color, shoe size, number of fingers and toes, skin color, and hair texture but also other characteristics that are not readily visible, such as your blood type or the specific shape of your hemoglobin proteins.

A pea plant derived from a green seed always has a homozygous recessive genotype, written *yy* for the two recessive alleles in each diploid cell. Because *Y* is dominant, however, a yellow seed can be either homozygous dominant (*YY*) or heterozygous (*Yy*) for the seed color gene (figure 10.5). The Burning Question on this page explains why recessive alleles "vanish" in heterozygotes.

Mendel's observation that only some yellow-seeded plants were true-breeding arises from the two possible genotypes for the yellow phenotype. All homozygous plants are true-breeding because all of their gametes contain the

Genotype	Phenotype
Homozygous dominant (*YY*)	Yellow
Heterozygous (*Yy*)	Yellow
Homozygous recessive (*yy*)	Green

Figure 10.5 Genotypes and Phenotypes Compared. A pea's genotype for the "seed color" gene consists of the two alleles that the seed inherited from its parents. Its phenotype is its outward appearance: yellow or green.

same allele. Heterozygous plants, however, are not true-breeding because they may pass on either the dominant or the recessive allele.

Today, biologists use additional terms to describe organisms. A **wild-type** allele, genotype, or phenotype is the most common form or expression of a gene in a population. Wild-type fruit flies, for example, have one pair of wings and two antennae. A **mutant** allele or phenotype is a variant that arises when a gene undergoes a mutation. Mutant phenotypes for fruit flies include having multiple pairs of wings or having legs instead of antennae growing out of the head (see figure 7.14).

Table 10.1 summarizes the important terms encountered so far. The remainder of the chapter uses this basic vocabulary to integrate Mendel's findings with what biologists now know about chromosomes and reproduction.

TABLE 10.1 Miniglossary of Genetic Terms

Term	Definition
Chromosomes and genes	
Chromosome	A dark-staining body that consists of a continuous double helix of DNA plus associated proteins; each chromosome carries many genes.
Gene	A sequence of DNA that encodes a protein
Allele	One of the alternative forms of a gene
Dominant and recessive	
Dominant allele	An allele that masks the expression of another allele
Recessive allele	An allele whose expression is masked by another allele
Identical or different alleles	
Homozygous	Possessing identical alleles of one gene
Heterozygous	Possessing different alleles of one gene
Genotypes and phenotypes	
Genotype	The allele combination in an individual
Phenotype	The observable expression of an allele combination
Wild-type	The most common phenotype or allele for a gene in a population
Mutant	A phenotype or allele resulting from a change (mutation) in a gene
True-breeding	Homozygous; always producing offspring identical to self for a given trait

10.2 Mastering Concepts

1. Why did Gregor Mendel choose pea plants as his experimental organism?
2. Distinguish between dominant and recessive; heterozygous and homozygous; phenotype and genotype; wild-type and mutant.

10.3 The Two Alleles of Each Gene End Up in Different Gametes

Part of Mendel's genius was that he kept careful tallies of the offspring from countless crosses. This approach required a systematic accounting of multiple generations of plants. Standardized names for these generations help biologists keep track of inheritance patterns. The purebred **P generation** (for "parental") is the first set of individuals being mated; the **F_1 generation,** or first filial generation, is the offspring from the P generation (*filial* derives from the Latin word for "child"). The **F_2 generation** is the offspring of the F_1 plants, and so on. (Although these terms are applicable only to lab crosses, they are analogous to human family relationships. If you consider your grandparents the P generation, your parents are the F_1 generation, and you and your siblings are the F_2 generation.)

A. Monohybrid Crosses Track the Inheritance of One Gene

Mendel used a systematic series of crosses to deduce the rules of inheritance. He began with a P generation consisting of true-breeding plants derived from yellow seeds (*YY*) and true-breeding plants grown from green seeds (*yy*). The F_1 offspring from this cross had yellow seeds (genotype *Yy*). The green trait therefore seemed to disappear in the F_1 generation.

Next, he used the F_1 plants to set up a **monohybrid cross:** a mating between two individuals that are both heterozygous for one gene. The resulting F_2 generation had both yellow and green phenotypes, in a ratio of 3:1; that is, for every three yellow seeds, Mendel observed one green seed.

A diagram called a **Punnett square** uses the genotypes of the parents to reveal which alleles the offspring may inherit. The Punnett square in figure 10.6, for example, shows how the green phenotype reappeared in the F_2 generation. In a monohybrid cross, both parents are heterozygous (*Yy*) for the seed color gene. Each therefore produces some gametes carrying the *Y* allele and some gametes carrying *y*. All three possible genotypes may therefore appear in the F_2 generation,

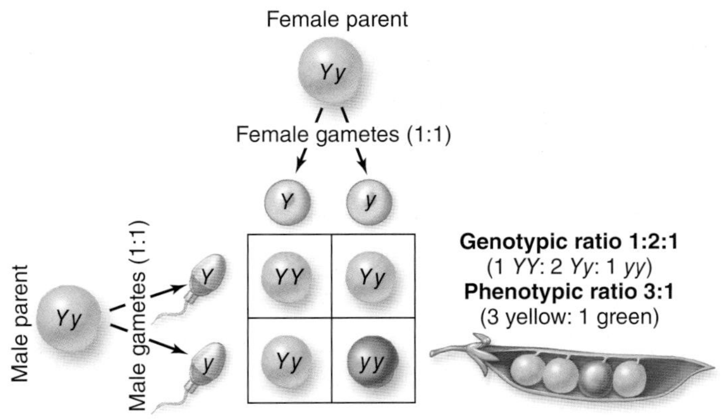

Figure 10.6 Punnett Square. This diagram depicts Mendel's monohybrid cross of two heterozygous yellow-seeded (*Yy*) pea plants. The two possible types of female gametes are listed along the top of the square; the two possible male gametes are listed on the left-hand side. Each compartment within the square contains the genotype and phenotype that results when the corresponding gametes join.

Trait	Dominant allele	Recessive allele
Seed color	Yellow (*Y*)	Green (*y*)
Seed form	Round (*R*)	Wrinkled (*r*)
Pod color	Green (*G*)	Yellow (*g*)
Pod form	Inflated (*V*)	Constricted (*v*)
Flower color	Purple (*P*)	White (*p*)
Flower position	Axial (*A*)	Terminal (*a*)
Stem length	Tall (*L*)	Short (*l*)

Figure 10.7 **Pea Traits.** Mendel's breeding studies deduced the inheritance patterns of these seven pea plant characteristics.

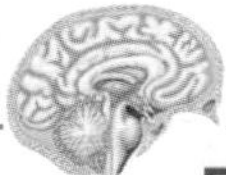

Figure It Out

Holstein cattle suffer from the condition citrullinemia, in which homozygous recessive calves die within a week of birth because they cannot break down ammonia that is produced when amino acids are metabolized. If a cow that is heterozygous for the citrullinemia gene is inseminated by a bull that is homozygous dominant, what is the probability that a calf inherits citrullinemia?

Answer: 0%

in the ratio 1 *YY*: 2 *Yy*: 1 *yy*. The corresponding phenotypic ratio is three yellow seeds to one green seed, or 3:1. Mendel saw similar results for all seven traits that he studied (figure 10.7).

Mendel could tally the number of plants with each phenotype, but he also needed to keep track of each genotype. He knew that green-seeded plants were always homozygous recessive (*yy*). But what was the genotype of each yellow seed, *YY* or *Yy*? He had no way to tell just by looking, so he set up breeding experiments called test crosses to distinguish between the two possibilities. A **test cross** is a mating between an individual of unknown genotype and a homozygous recessive individual (figure 10.8). If a yellow-seeded plant crossed with a *yy* plant produced only yellow seeds, Mendel knew the unknown genotype was *YY*; if the cross produced seeds of both colors, he knew it must be *Yy*.

B. Meiosis Explains Mendel's Law of Segregation

All of Mendel's breeding experiments and calculations added up to a brilliant description of basic genetic principles. Without any knowledge of chromosomes or genes, Mendel used his data to conclude that genes occur in alternative versions (what we now call alleles). He further determined that each individual inherits two alleles for each gene and that these alleles may be the same or different. Finally, he deduced his **law of segregation,** which states

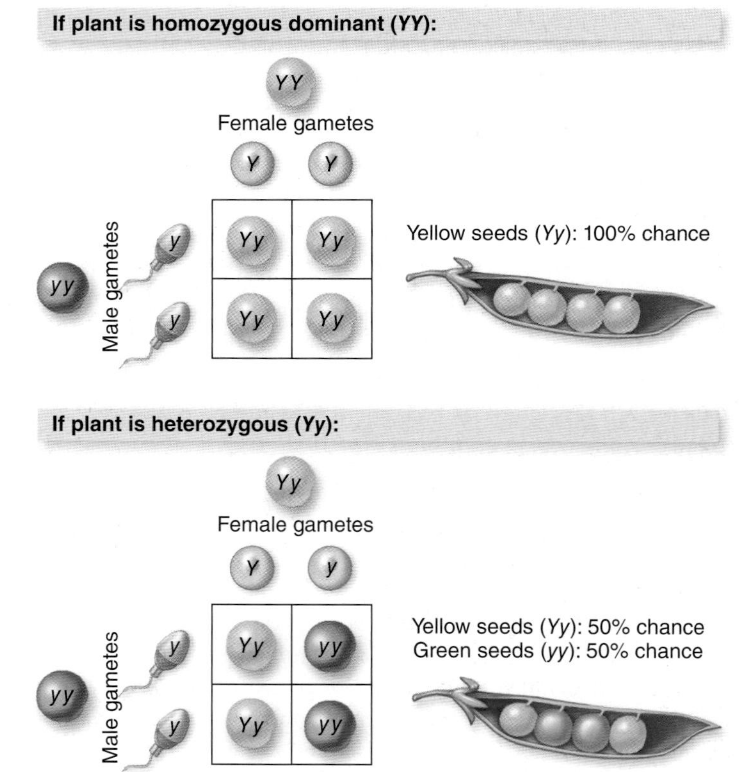

Figure 10.8 **Test Cross.** A yellow-seeded pea plant may be homozygous dominant (*YY*) or heterozygous (*Yy*). To determine the genotype, the plant is mated with a homozygous recessive (*yy*) plant. If the unknown plant is *YY*, all offspring of the test cross will share its phenotype; if the unknown plant is *Yy*, about half the offspring are likely to produce green seeds.

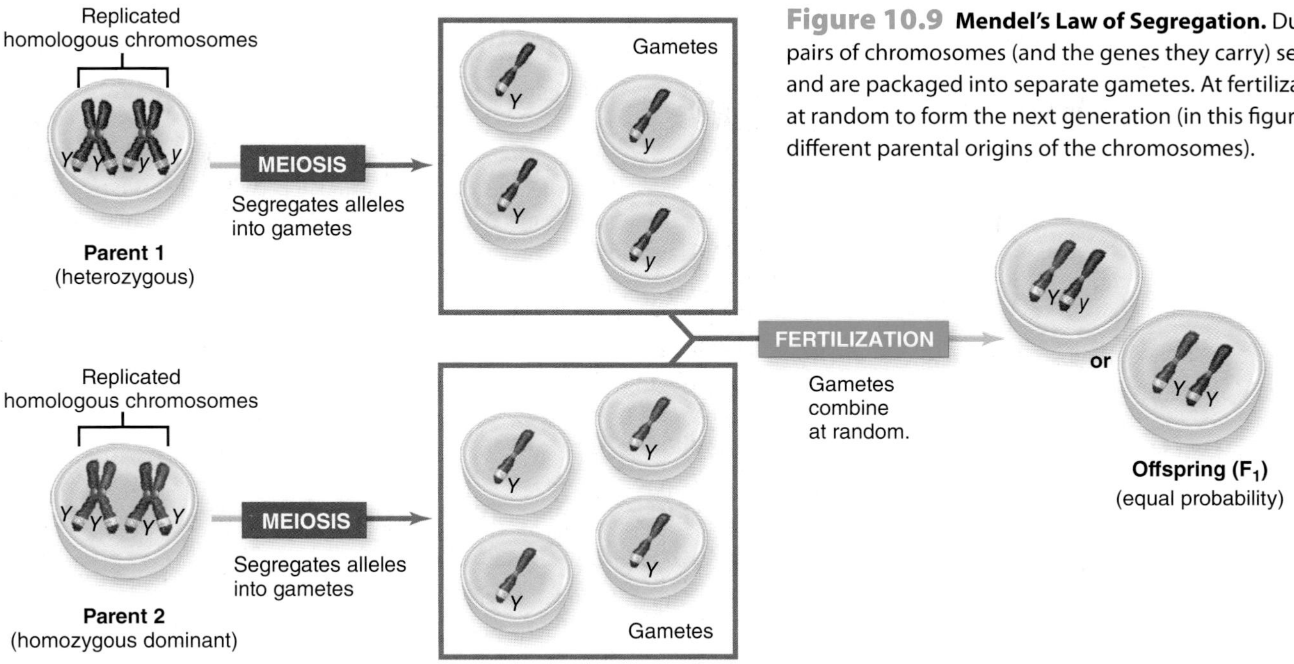

Figure 10.9 Mendel's Law of Segregation. During meiosis, homologous pairs of chromosomes (and the genes they carry) segregate from each other and are packaged into separate gametes. At fertilization, gametes combine at random to form the next generation (in this figure, red and blue denote different parental origins of the chromosomes).

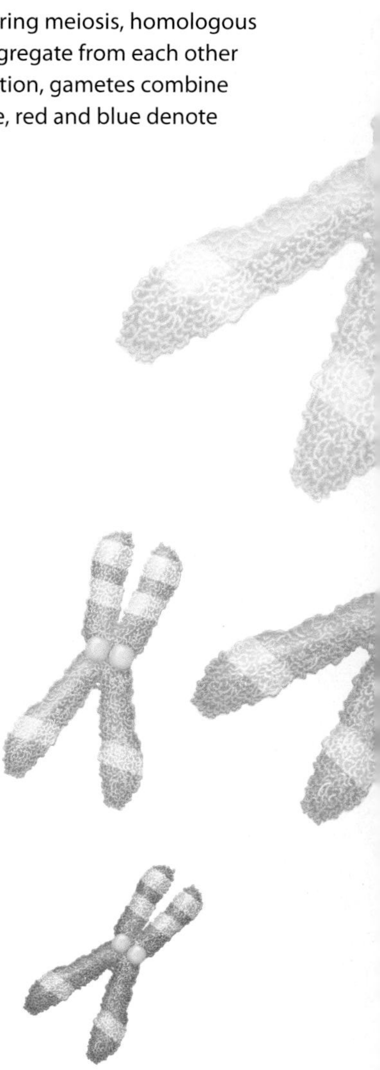

that the two alleles of each gene are packaged into separate gametes; that is, they "segregate," or move apart from each other, during gamete formation.

Mendel's law of segregation makes perfect sense in light of what we now know about meiosis. A plant of genotype *Yy* produces equal numbers of gametes carrying *Y* or *y*, whereas a *YY* plant produces only *Y* gametes (figure 10.9). When two gametes combine randomly at fertilization, both carry *Y* about 50% of the time; the other 50% of the time, one contributes *Y* and the other, *y*.

This basic principle of inheritance applies to all diploid species, including humans. Return for a moment to the couple and their genetic counselor introduced in section 10.1. Cystic fibrosis arises when a person has two recessive alleles for a particular gene on chromosome 7. Genetic testing revealed that the man and the woman are both carriers. In genetic terms, this means that although neither has the disease, both are heterozygous for the gene that causes cystic fibrosis. Just as in Mendel's monohybrid crosses, each of their children has a 25% chance of inheriting two recessive alleles (figure 10.10).

Note that all Punnett squares, including the one in figure 10.10, show the *probabilities* that apply to each offspring. That is, if the couple has four children, there will not necessarily be exactly one with genotype *FF*, two with *Ff*, and one with *ff*. Similarly, the chance of tossing a fair coin and seeing "heads" is 50%, but two tosses will not necessarily yield one head and one tail. If you toss the coin 1000 times, however, you will likely approach the expected 1:1 ratio of heads to tails. As Mendel discovered, pea plants are ideal for genetics studies in part because they produce many offspring in each generation.

Mother: healthy carrier
Female gametes

Father: healthy carrier / Male gametes	*F*	*f*
F	*FF* Healthy non-carrier	*Ff* Healthy carrier
f	*Ff* Healthy carrier	*ff* Affected

Healthy noncarrier (*FF*): 25% chance
Healthy carrier (*Ff*): 50% chance
Affected (*ff*): 25% chance

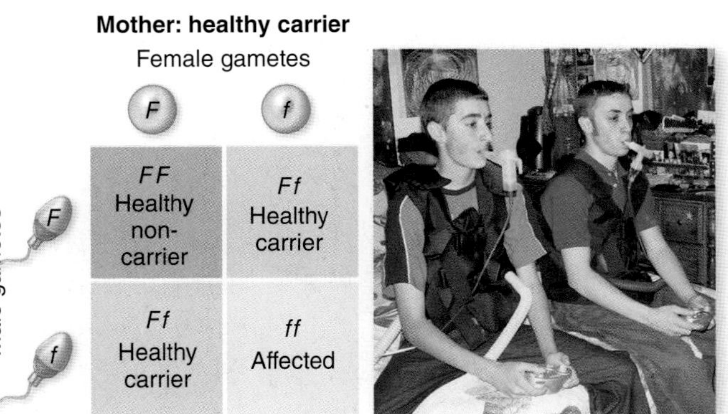

Figure 10.10 Mendel's Law Applied to Humans. This Punnett square shows the possible results of a mating of two carriers of cystic fibrosis. The two brothers in the photo have cystic fibrosis; they are undergoing treatment to reduce the buildup of sticky mucus in their lungs.

10.3 Mastering Concepts

1. What is a monohybrid cross, and what are the genotypic and phenotypic ratios expected in the offspring of the cross?
2. What is a test cross, and why is it useful?
3. How does the law of segregation reflect the events of meiosis?

10.4 Genes on Different Chromosomes Are Inherited Independently

Mendel's law of segregation arose from his studies of the inheritance of single traits. He next asked himself whether the same law would apply if he followed two different characters at the same time. Would one trait influence the inheritance of the other, or would each trait follow its own independent inheritance pattern?

Mendel therefore began another set of breeding experiments in which he simultaneously examined the inheritance of two characteristics of peas: shape and color. A pea's shape may be round or wrinkled (determined by the *R* gene, with the dominant allele specifying round shape). At the same time, its color may be yellow or green (determined by the *Y* gene, with the dominant allele specifying yellow).

A. Dihybrid Crosses Track the Inheritance of Two Genes at Once

As he did before, Mendel began with a P generation consisting of true-breeding parents (figure 10.11a). He crossed plants grown from round, yellow seeds (homozygous dominant for genes *R* and *Y*, denoted *RR YY*) with plants derived from wrinkled, green seeds (homozygous recessive for both genes, *rr yy*). All F_1 plants were heterozygous for both genes (*Rr Yy*) and therefore had round, yellow seeds.

Next, Mendel crossed the F_1 plants with each other (figure 10.11b). A **dihybrid cross** is a mating between two individuals that are each heterozygous for two genes. Each *Rr Yy* individual in the F_1 generation produced equal numbers of gametes of four different types: *R Y, R y, r Y,* and *r y.* After Mendel

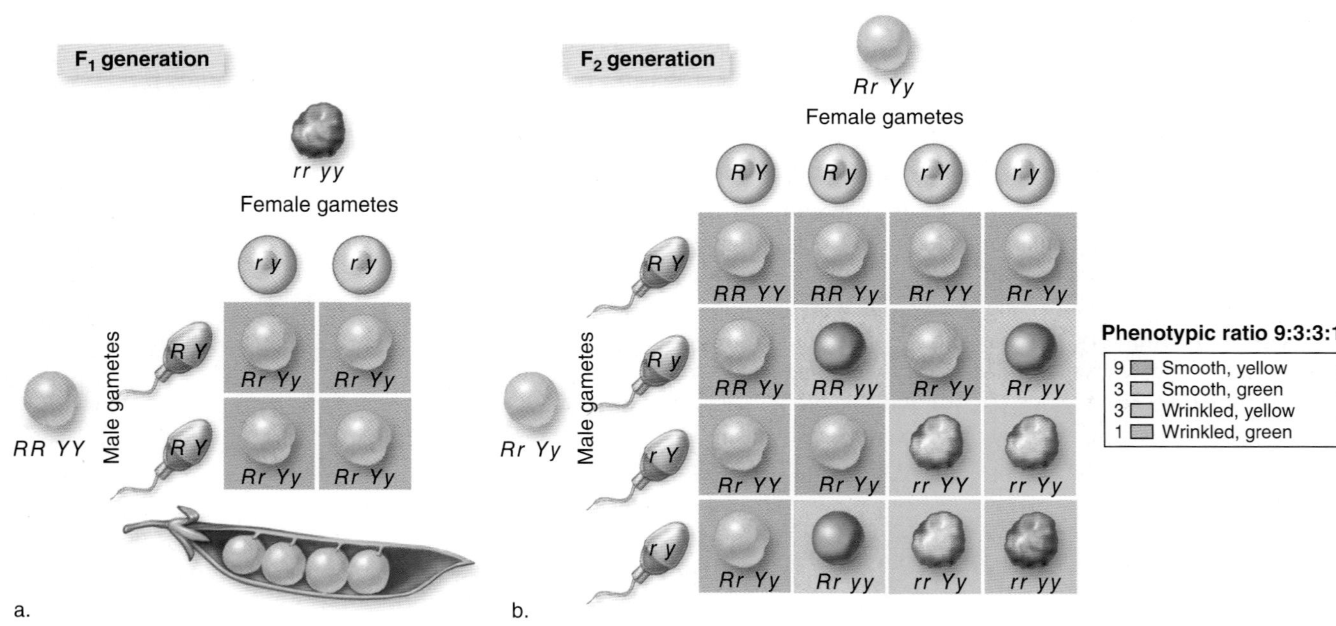

Figure 10.11 Plotting a Dihybrid Cross. (a) In the parental generation, one parent is homozygous dominant for both genes, and the other is homozygous recessive. The F_1 generation is therefore heterozygous for both genes. (B) When plants from the F_1 generation are self-fertilized, the phenotypes of the offspring occur in a distinctive ratio in the F_2 generation.

completed the crosses, he found four phenotypes in the F_2 generation, reflecting all possible combinations of seed shape and color. The Punnett square predicts that the four phenotypes will occur in a ratio of 9:3:3:1. That is, nine of 16 offspring should be round, yellow seeds; three should be round, green seeds; three should be wrinkled, yellow seeds; and just one should be a wrinkled, green seed. This prediction almost exactly matches Mendel's results.

B. Meiosis Explains Mendel's Law of Independent Assortment

Based on the results of the dihybrid cross, Mendel proposed what we now know as the **law of independent assortment.** It states that during gamete formation, the segregation of the alleles for one gene does not influence the segregation of the alleles for another gene. That is, alleles for two different genes are randomly packaged into gametes with respect to each other. With this second set of experiments, Mendel had again inferred a principle of inheritance based on meiosis (figure 10.12).

Interestingly, Mendel found some trait combinations for which a dihybrid cross did not yield the expected phenotypic ratio. Mendel could not explain this result. No one could, until Thomas Hunt Morgan's work led to the chromosomal theory of inheritance. As you will see in section 10.5, the law of independent assortment does not apply to genes that are close together on the same chromosome.

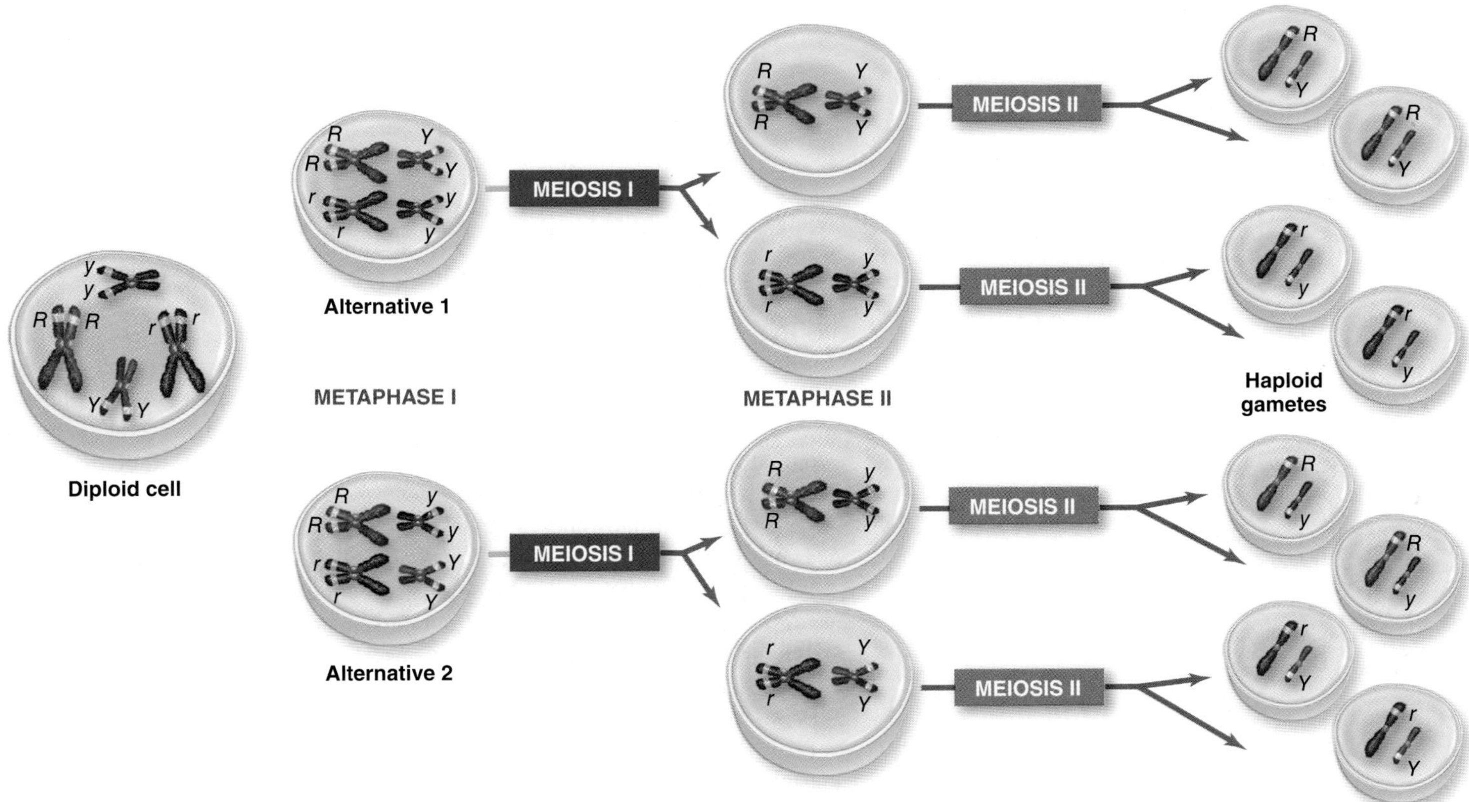

Figure 10.12 Mendel's Law of Independent Assortment. Homologous chromosome pairs align at random during metaphase I of meiosis. The exact allele combination in a gamete depends on which chromosomes happen to be packaged together. An individual of genotype *Rr Yy* therefore produces approximately equal numbers of four types of gametes: *R Y*, *r y*, *R y*, and *r Y*.

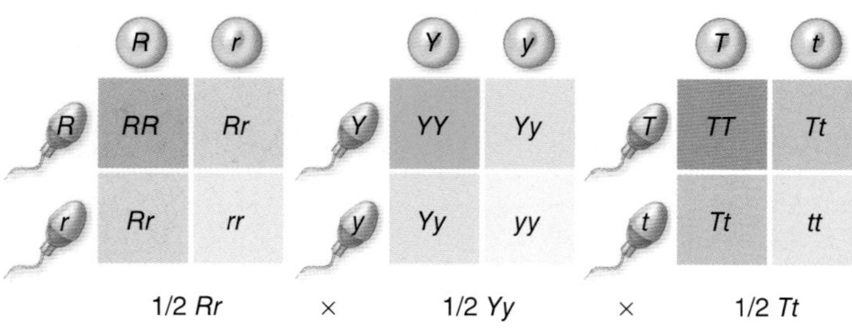

Figure 10.13 The Product Rule. What is the chance that two parents that are heterozygous for three genes (*Rr Yy Tt*) will give rise to an offspring with that same genotype? To find out, multiply the individual probabilities for each gene.

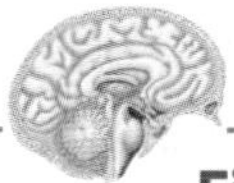

Figure It Out

A man and a woman each have dark eyes, dark hair, and freckles. The genes for these traits are on separate chromosomes. The woman is heterozygous for each of these genes, but the man is homozygous. The dominance relationships of the alleles are as follows:

B = dark eyes; b = blue eyes
H = dark hair; h = blond hair
F = freckles; f = no freckles

Use the product rule to determine the probability that a child will share the genotype of each parent.

Answer: ½ x ½ x ½ = ⅛ chance for each parent

C. The Product Rule Replaces Complex Punnett Squares

Punnett squares become cumbersome when analyzing more than two genes. A Punnett square for three genes has 64 boxes; for four genes, 256 boxes. An easier way to predict genotypes and phenotypes is to use the rules of probability on which Punnett squares are based. The **product rule** states that the chance that two independent events will both occur (for example, an offspring inheriting two particular alleles) equals the product of the individual chances that each event will occur.

The product rule is an easy way to predict the chance of obtaining wrinkled, green seeds (*rr yy*) from dihybrid (*Rr Yy*) parents. The probability that two *Rr* plants will produce *rr* offspring is 25%, or ¼, and the chance of two *Yy* plants producing a *yy* individual is ¼. According to the product rule, the chance of dihybrid parents (*Rr Yy*) producing homozygous recessive (*rr yy*) offspring is therefore ¼ multiplied by ¼, or 1/16. Now consult the 16-box Punnett square for Mendel's dihybrid cross (see figure 10.11). As expected, only one of the 16 boxes contains *rr yy*. Figure 10.13 applies the product rule to three traits.

10.4 Mastering Concepts

1. What is a dihybrid cross, and what is the phenotypic ratio expected in the offspring of the cross?
2. How does the law of independent assortment reflect the events of meiosis?
3. How can the product rule be used to predict the results of crosses in which multiple genes are studied simultaneously?

10.5 Studies of Linked Genes Have Yielded Chromosome Maps

Biologists at the time did not appreciate the significance of Mendel's findings, but his careful observations of pea plants laid the foundation for modern genetics. In 1900, three botanists working independently each rediscovered the principles of inheritance. They eventually found Mendel's paper at about the same time that advances in microscopy were allowing scientists to observe and describe chromosomes for the first time.

Once chromosomes were described, it became apparent that what Mendel called "elementen" (later renamed "genes") and chromosomes had much in common. Both genes and chromosomes, for example, come in pairs. In addition, alleles of a gene are packaged into separate gametes, as are the members of a homologous pair of chromosomes. Finally, both genes and chromosomes are inherited in random combinations.

As biologists cataloged traits and the chromosomes that transmit them in several species, it soon became clear that the number of traits far exceeded the number of chromosomes. Fruit flies, for example, have four pairs of chromosomes, but dozens of different bristle patterns, body colors, eye colors, wing shapes, and other characteristics. How might a few chromosomes control so many traits? The answer: each chromosome carries many genes.

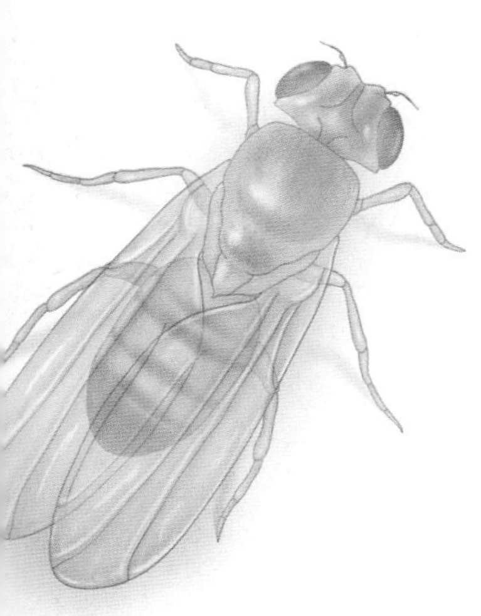

A. Genes on the Same Chromosome Are Linked

Linked genes are carried on the same chromosome; they are therefore inherited together. Unlike genes on different chromosomes, they do not assort independently during meiosis. The seven traits that Mendel followed in his pea plants all happened to be transmitted on separate chromosomes. Had the same chromosome carried these genes, Mendel would have generated markedly different results in his dihybrid crosses.

The inheritance pattern of linked genes was first noticed in the early 1900s. For example, Thomas Hunt Morgan at Columbia University bred the fruit fly *Drosophila melanogaster*. Morgan and his colleagues observed offspring ratios in fruit flies that were different from the ratios predicted by Mendel's laws. Two groups of F_2 flies—those with the same phenotypes as the P generation—were more abundant than predicted. The other two classes of offspring, with a mix of parental phenotypes, were less common than expected. The scientists hypothesized that this pattern reflected two genes on the same chromosome.

If the two genes were on the same chromosome, why did the researchers ever see offspring with trait combinations not seen in either parent? These offspring classes arise because of another event, crossing over (figure 10.14). Recall from chapter 9 that **crossing over** is an exchange of genetic material between homologous chromosomes during meiosis. After crossing over, no two chromatids are identical. **Recombinant chromosomes** have a mix of maternal and paternal alleles, whereas **parental chromosomes** retain the allele combinations from each parent.

As Morgan studied the inheritance of many pairs of fruit fly traits, the data began to indicate four **linkage groups,** collections of genes that tended to be inherited together. Within each linkage group, dihybrid crosses did not produce the proportions of offspring that Mendel's law of independent assortment predicts. Because the number of linkage groups was the same as the number of homologous pairs of chromosomes, scientists eventually realized that each linkage group was simply a set of genes transmitted together on the same chromosome.

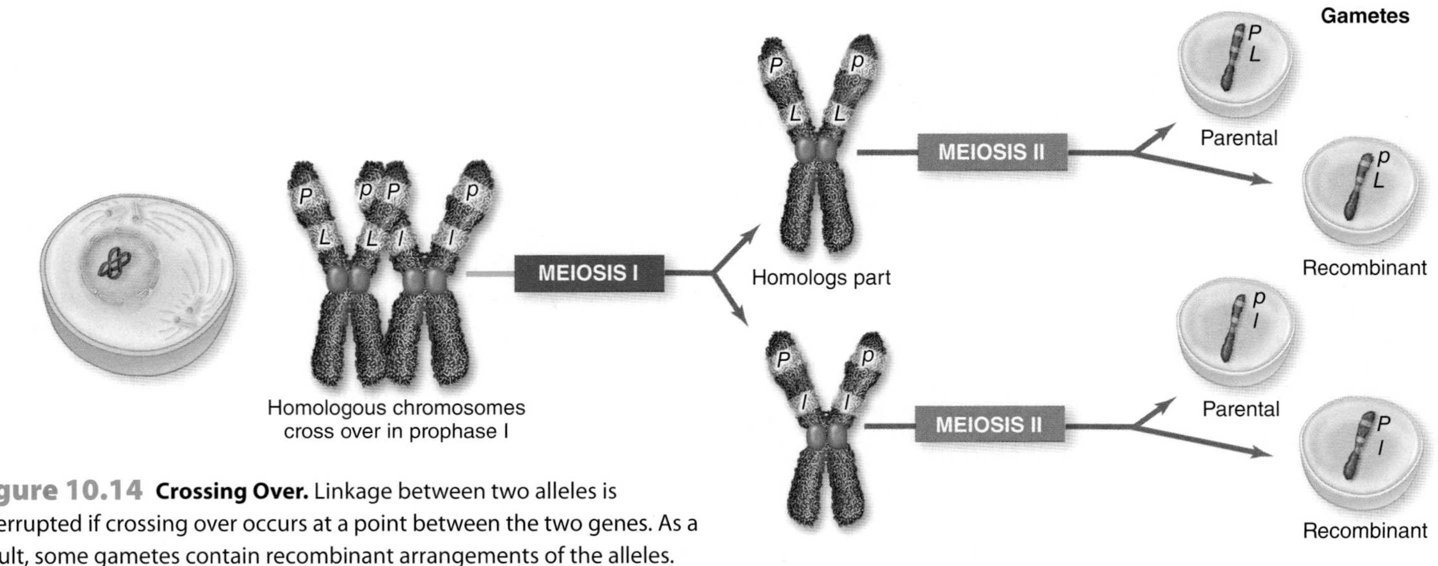

Figure 10.14 Crossing Over. Linkage between two alleles is interrupted if crossing over occurs at a point between the two genes. As a result, some gametes contain recombinant arrangements of the alleles.

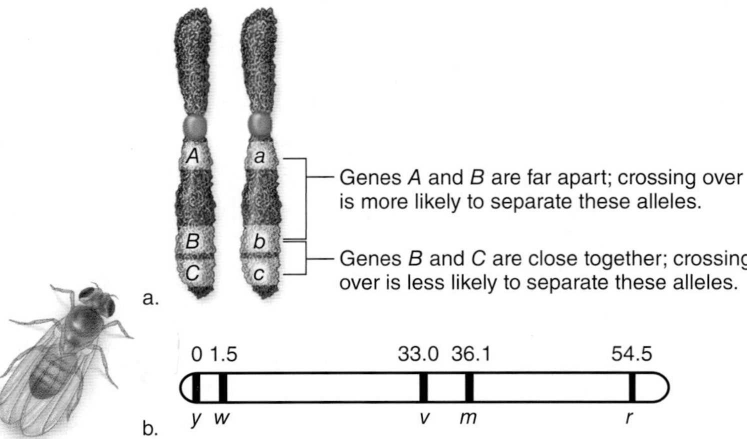

Figure 10.15 Linkage Map. (a) Crossing over is more likely to separate the alleles of genes *A* and *B* (or *A* and *C*) than to separate the alleles of genes *B* and *C*. (b) A linkage map of a fruit fly chromosome, showing the locations of five genes. The numbers represent crossover frequencies relative to the leftmost gene, *y*.

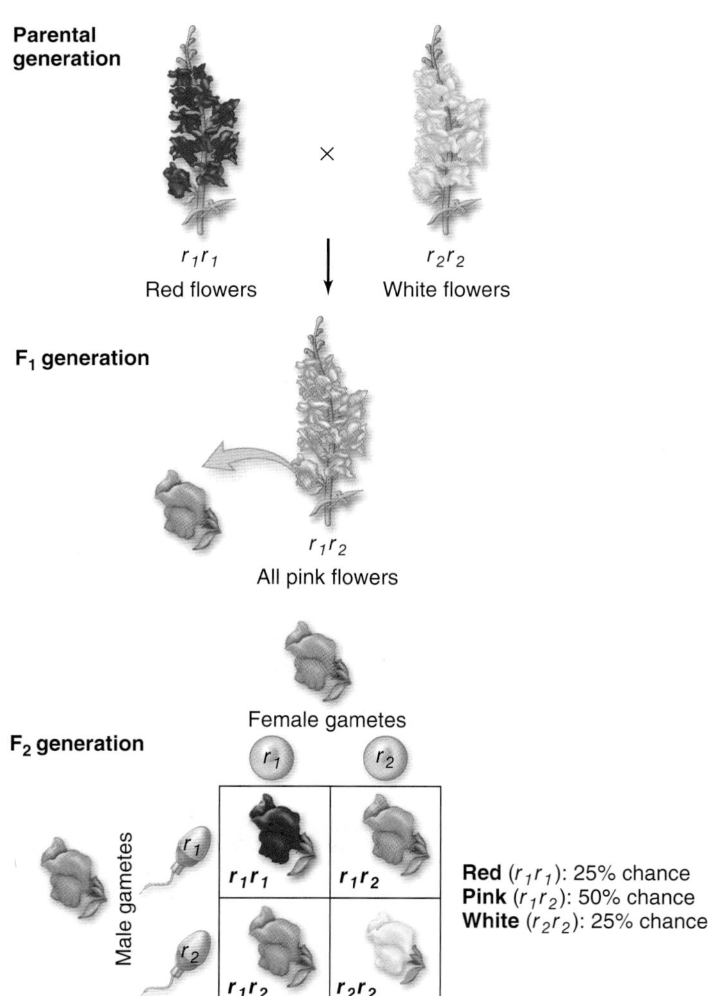

Figure 10.16 Incomplete Dominance. In snapdragons, a cross between a plant with red flowers (r_1r_1) and a plant with white flowers (r_2r_2) produces a heterozygous plant with pink flowers (r_1r_2). The red and white phenotypes reappear in the F_2 generation.

B. Linkage Maps Derive from Crossover Frequencies

If linked genes occur on the same chromosome, why do some crosses produce a higher proportion of recombinant offspring than others? Alfred Sturtevant, Morgan's student, proposed that the differences reflect the physical relationships among the genes on the chromosome. That is, the farther apart two alleles are on the same chromosome, the more likely crossing over is to separate them.

Sturtevant's idea became the basis for mapping genes on chromosomes (figure 10.15). By determining the percentage of recombinant offspring, investigators can infer how far apart the genes are on one chromosome. Crossing over frequently separates alleles on opposite ends of the same chromosome, so recombinant offspring occur frequently. In contrast, a crossover would rarely separate alleles lying very close together on the chromosome, and the proportion of recombinant offspring would be small. Geneticists use this correlation between crossover frequency and the distance between genes to construct **linkage maps,** which are diagrams of gene order and spacing on chromosomes.

In 1913, Sturtevant published the first genetic linkage map, depicting the order of five genes on the X chromosome of the fruit fly (see figure 10.15b). Researchers rapidly mapped genes on all four fruit fly chromosomes, and linkage maps for the human chromosomes followed over the next half century.

10.5 Mastering Concepts

1. How do linked genes complicate patterns of inheritance?
2. How do recombinant and parental chromatids arise?
3. Explain how to use crossover frequencies to make a linkage map.

10.6 Gene Expression Can Appear to Alter Mendelian Ratios

We have just seen that when genes are linked on the same chromosome, offspring traits do not occur in the proportions that Punnett squares predict. Other circumstances may also appear to alter inheritance patterns; the remainder of this chapter describes some of them.

A. Incomplete Dominance and Codominance Add Phenotype Classes

For the traits Mendel studied, one allele is completely dominant, and the other is completely recessive. The phenotype of a heterozygote is therefore identical to that of a homozygous dominant individual. For many genes, however, heterozygous offspring do not share the phenotype of either parent. As you will see, for these genes we cannot simply designate one allele with a capital letter and the other in lower case, because neither allele is dominant over the other.

When a gene shows **incomplete dominance,** the heterozygote has a third phenotype that is intermediate between those of the two homozygotes. For example, a red-flowered snapdragon plant of genotype r_1r_1 crossed with a white-flowered r_2r_2 plant gives rise to an r_1r_2 plant with pink flowers (figure 10.16). The single copy of allele r_1 in the pink heterozygote directs less pigment production than the two copies in a red-flowered r_1r_1 plant.

In **codominance,** two different alleles are expressed together in the phenotype. For example, a person's ABO blood type is determined by the *I* gene, which has three possible alleles: I^A, I^B, and *i* (figure 10.17). The *I* gene encodes enzymes that insert either an "A" or a "B" molecule onto the surfaces of red blood cells. Allele *i* is recessive, so a person with genotype *ii* produces neither molecule A nor molecule B and therefore has type O blood. A person who produces only molecule A (genotype I^AI^A or I^Ai) has type A blood; likewise, someone with only molecule B (genotype I^BI^B or I^Bi) has type B blood. Finally, genotype I^AI^B yields type AB blood. The I^A and I^B alleles are codominant because both are equally expressed when both are present.

What is the difference between the recessive *i* allele and the codominant I^A and I^B alleles? The *i* allele encodes a nonfunctional protein, whereas alleles I^A and I^B code for functional proteins. People with genotype I^AI^B therefore have both molecule A and molecule B on the surfaces of their red blood cells.

The blood type example also illustrates another condition that can alter phenotypic ratios: a gene with three or more alleles can yield many phenotypes. In the ABO blood type system, two codominant alleles (I^A and I^B) and one recessive allele (*i*) produce six possible genotypes and four phenotypes.

Genotypes	Phenotypes	
	Surface molecules	ABO blood type
I^AI^A I^Ai	Only A	Type A
I^BI^B I^Bi	Only B	Type B
I^AI^B	Both A and B	Type AB
ii	None	Type O

Figure 10.17 Codominance. The I^A and I^B alleles of the *I* gene are codominant, meaning that both are expressed in a heterozygote. Allele *i* is recessive to both.

B. Inheritance Patterns Are Often Complicated

Some conditions are especially difficult to trace through families. For example, one gene may influence the phenotype in many ways; conversely, multiple genes may contribute to one phenotype. Although the basic rules of inheritance apply to each gene, the patterns of phenotypes that appear in grandparents, parents, and siblings may be hard to interpret.

In **pleiotropy,** one gene has multiple effects on the phenotype. Pleiotropy arises when one protein is important in different biochemical pathways or affects more than one body part or process. For example, a single faulty connective tissue protein causes Marfan syndrome. Symptoms including long limbs, spindly fingers, a caved-in chest, a weakened aorta, and lens dislocation. Pleiotropy complicates the study of inheritance because individuals with the same genotype may exhibit different symptoms and therefore may appear to have different disorders. ▸ connective tissue, p. 469

Another situation that can complicate the interpretation of inheritance patterns is that different genes can produce similar phenotypes. For example, blood clot formation requires 11 chemical reactions. A different gene encodes each enzyme in the pathway, and clotting disorders may result from mutations in any of these genes. The phenotypes are the same, but the genotypes differ.

One gene may also influence the expression of another. As a simple example, male pattern baldness (a genetic condition) hides the effects of the allele for a "widow's peak" hairline. Likewise, gene interactions account for some apparent inconsistencies in the blood types of parents and their children. Most people with alleles I^A or I^B have blood type A, B, or AB. However, another molecule must physically link the A and B molecules to the cell surface. If a gene called *H* is mutated, part of that molecule is missing, so A and B cannot attach. A person with the extremely rare genotype *hh* therefore has blood that always tests as type O, even though he or she may have a genotype indicating type A, B, or AB blood.

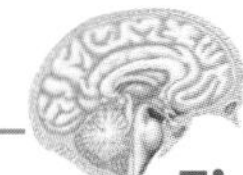

Figure It Out

A woman with type AB blood has children with a man who has type O blood. What is the chance that they have a child with type A blood? Type B? AB? O?

Answer: Type A = 50%; type B = 50%; type O or type AB = 0%

10.6 Mastering Concepts

1. How do incomplete dominance and codominance increase the number of phenotypes?
2. What is pleiotropy?
3. How can the same phenotype stem from many different genotypes?
4. How can gene interactions reduce the number of phenotypes?

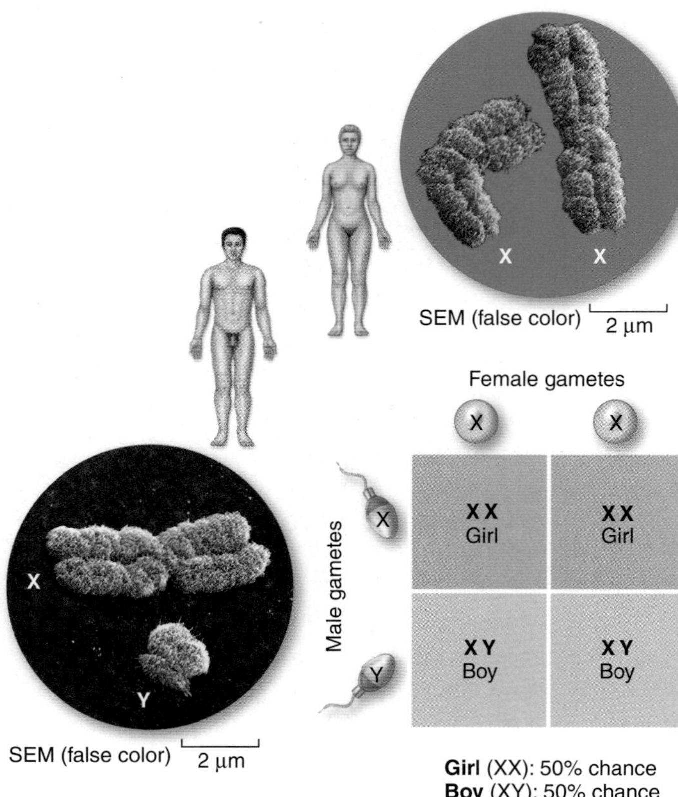

Figure 10.18 The Sperm Determines the Sex of the Baby. In humans, each egg contains 23 chromosomes, including an X chromosome. A sperm cell's 23 chromosomes include either an X or a Y chromosome. If a Y-bearing sperm cell fertilizes an egg, the baby will be a male (XY). If an X-bearing sperm cell fertilizes an egg, the baby will be a female (XX).

10.7 Sex-Linked Genes Have Unique Inheritance Patterns

In many species, including humans, the sexes have equal numbers of autosomes but differ in the sex chromosomes they have. Females have two X chromosomes, whereas males have one X and one Y chromosome (figure 10.18). Because the mother can pass on only the X chromosome, the sex chromosome carried by the sperm (X or Y) determines the sex of the baby.

The human X chromosome carries more than 1000 protein-encoding genes, most of which have nothing to do with sex determination. The Y chromosome is much smaller than the X and carries fewer than 100 genes. As the Why We Care box on page 186 describes, people who seek to increase the odds of conceiving a boy or a girl can exploit the size difference between X and Y chromosomes.

The Y chromosome plays the largest role in human sex determination. All human embryos start with rudimentary female structures, but an embryo having a working copy of a particular gene on the Y chromosome develops into a male (see figure 30.17). This sex-determining gene encodes a protein that switches on other genes; these genes, in turn, direct the undeveloped testes to secrete the male sex hormone testosterone. Cascades of other gene activities follow, promoting the development of male sex organs while the embryonic female structures break down.

A. X-Linked Recessive Disorders Affect More Males Than Females

Huntington disease, cystic fibrosis, and other diseases are caused by genes that are on autosomes; both sexes are therefore equally affected. A few conditions, including red–green color blindness and hemophilia, however, occur much more frequently in males than females. These phenotypes are **sex-linked;** that is, the alleles controlling them are on the X or Y chromosome.

Since only males have a Y chromosome, it is easy to jump to the conclusion that the genes controlling sex-linked disorders must be on the Y chromosome. The human Y chromosome, however, has few genes. Scientists therefore know of very few Y-linked disorders; most involve defects in sperm production, not traits such as blood clotting or color vision.

Because the X chromosome has many more genes than the Y, most human sex-linked traits are **X-linked**; that is, they are controlled by genes on the X chromosome. The alleles that cause most X-linked disorders are recessive, although a few are associated with dominant alleles (table 10.2).

Recessive X-linked traits have unusual inheritance patterns. A male expresses every allele on his X chromosome (whether dominant or recessive) because he lacks a second allele that could mask the expression of recessive alleles. A female, in contrast, exhibits an X-linked recessive disorder only if she inherits the recessive allele from both parents.

Figure 10.19 shows the inheritance of hemophilia A, a disorder with an X-linked recessive mode of inheritance. In hemophilia, a protein called a clotting factor is missing or defective. Blood therefore clots very slowly, and bleeding is excessive. Most people with hemophilia are male. Females rarely have hemophilia, although many are heterozygous "carriers" for the disease-causing allele. The heterozygous woman in the Punnett square, for example, does not exhibit symptoms because her dominant allele encodes a functional

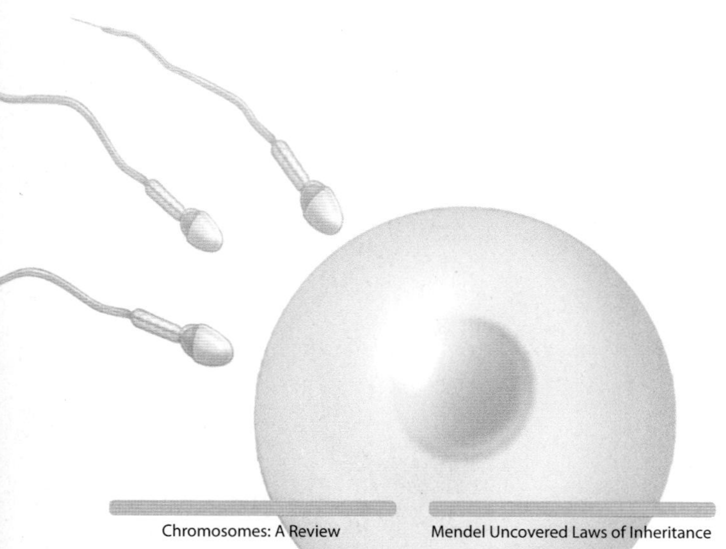

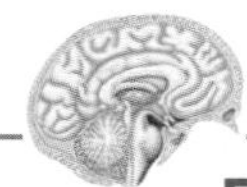

Figure It Out

What is the chance of a daughter expressing a recessive X-linked disease if her mother is a symptomless carrier and her father has the disease?

Answer: 50%

blood-clotting protein. When she has children with a normal male, however, each son has a 50% chance of being affected, and each daughter has a 50% chance of being a carrier.

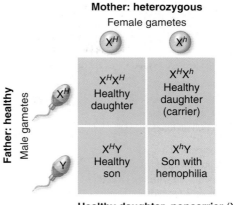

Mother: heterozygous
Female gametes

Father: healthy (Male gametes)	X^H	X^h
X^H	X^HX^H Healthy daughter	X^HX^h Healthy daughter (carrier)
Y	X^HY Healthy son	X^hY Son with hemophilia

Healthy daughter, noncarrier (X^HX^H): 25% chance
Healthy daughter, carrier (X^HX^h): 25% chance
Healthy son (X^HY): 25% chance
Affected son (X^hY): 25% chance

Figure 10.19 Hemophilia A. This Punnett square depicts a cross between a heterozygous woman (a "carrier" for hemophilia A) and a normal male, the most common way to transmit any X-linked recessive allele.

B. X Inactivation Prevents "Double Dosing" of Gene Products

Relative to males, female mammals have a "double dose" of every gene on the X chromosome. Cells balance this inequality by **X inactivation**, in which a cell shuts off all but one X chromosome in each cell. This process happens early in the embryonic development of a mammal.

Which X chromosome becomes inactivated—the one inherited from the father or the one from the mother—is a random event. As a result, a female expresses the paternal X chromosome alleles in some cells and the maternal alleles in others. Moreover, when a cell with an inactivated X chromosome divides mitotically, all of the daughter cells have the same X chromosome inactivated.

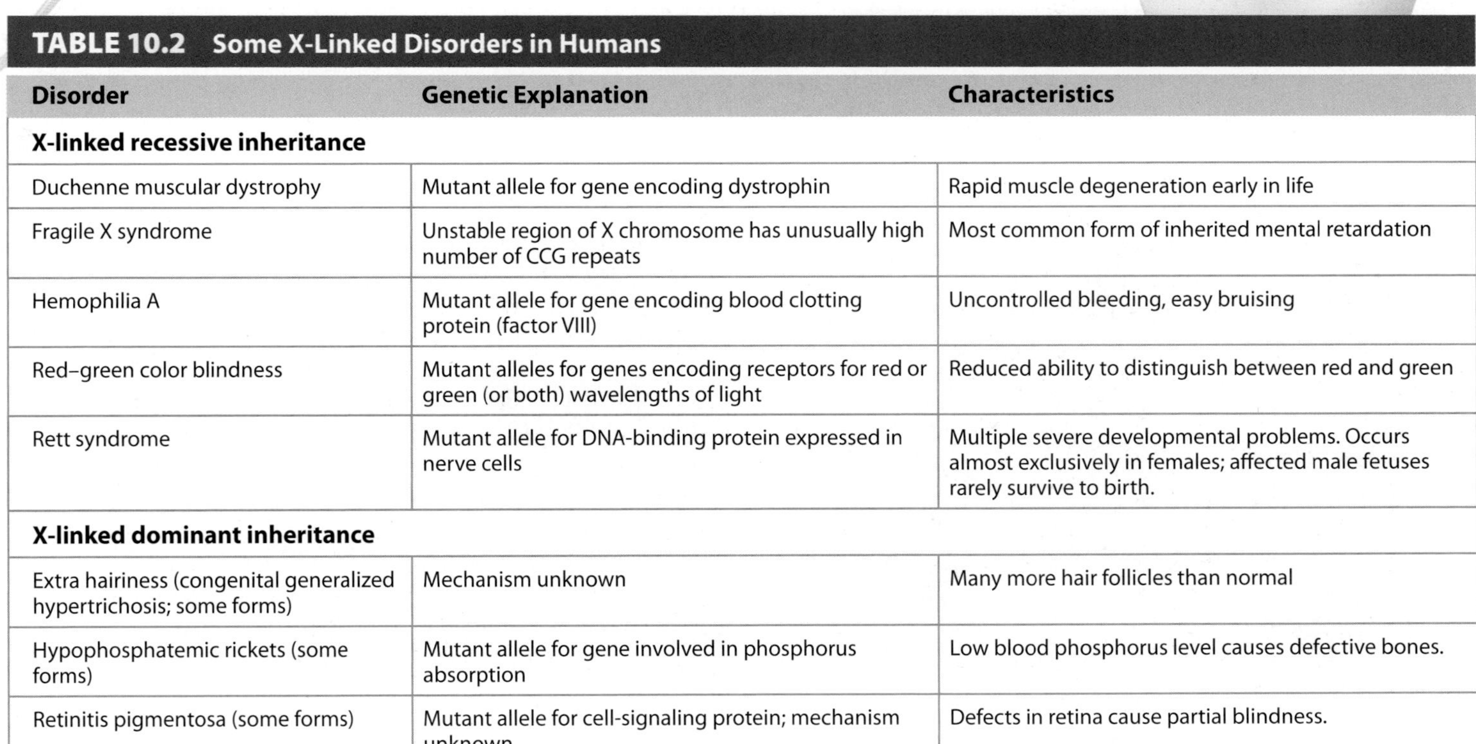

TABLE 10.2 Some X-Linked Disorders in Humans

Disorder	Genetic Explanation	Characteristics
X-linked recessive inheritance		
Duchenne muscular dystrophy	Mutant allele for gene encoding dystrophin	Rapid muscle degeneration early in life
Fragile X syndrome	Unstable region of X chromosome has unusually high number of CCG repeats	Most common form of inherited mental retardation
Hemophilia A	Mutant allele for gene encoding blood clotting protein (factor VIII)	Uncontrolled bleeding, easy bruising
Red–green color blindness	Mutant alleles for genes encoding receptors for red or green (or both) wavelengths of light	Reduced ability to distinguish between red and green
Rett syndrome	Mutant allele for DNA-binding protein expressed in nerve cells	Multiple severe developmental problems. Occurs almost exclusively in females; affected male fetuses rarely survive to birth.
X-linked dominant inheritance		
Extra hairiness (congenital generalized hypertrichosis; some forms)	Mechanism unknown	Many more hair follicles than normal
Hypophosphatemic rickets (some forms)	Mutant allele for gene involved in phosphorus absorption	Low blood phosphorus level causes defective bones.
Retinitis pigmentosa (some forms)	Mutant allele for cell-signaling protein; mechanism unknown	Defects in retina cause partial blindness.

Why We Care | Choosing the Sex of Your Baby

Scientists have used the size difference between the X and Y chromosomes to develop technologies that may help people choose the sex of their babies. Technologies for sex selection include:

- **MicroSort:** Chromosomes in a sperm sample are stained with a fluorescent dye. A sperm cell with an X chromosome absorbs more dye and therefore glows more brightly than one with a Y chromosome.
- **Ericsson method:** Sperm swim through a container holding a thick fluid. The lighter, Y-carrying sperm reach the bottom of the container faster than their heavier, slower counterparts.
- **Spin method:** A sperm sample is placed in a test tube, which is placed into a centrifuge. The centrifuge spins the test tube so that the heavier X-containing sperm fall to the bottom, whereas the lighter sperm remain near the top.

After Y-carrying sperm are separated from X-carrying sperm, the woman is inseminated with the desired fraction of the sperm. Alternatively, if a woman is using *in vitro* fertilization, the egg is fertilized in the laboratory with the sperm most likely to give a baby of the desired sex. None of the methods, however, works all the time; at best, the sperm samples are enriched in sperm that favor one sex over the other.

Because the inactivation occurs early in development, females have patches of tissue that differ in their expression of X-linked alleles. Figure 10.20 shows how X inactivation of either of two alleles of a coat color gene causes the distinctive appearance of calico and tortoiseshell cats, which are always female (except for rare XXY males). The earlier X inactivation occurs in the development of the embryonic cat, the larger the orange and black patches.

X chromosome inactivation also explains another interesting observation: X-linked dominant disorders are typically less severe in females than in males. Thanks to X chromosome inactivation, a female who is heterozygous for an X-linked gene will express a dominant disease-causing allele in only some of her cells. As a result, the female experiences less severe symptoms than an affected male, who expresses the dominant allele in every cell. One example is Rett syndrome, an X-linked disease of the nervous system that occurs almost exclusively in females. A male fetus with the Rett allele usually does not complete development or dies shortly after birth. Thanks to X inactivation, however, a female who inherits one X chromosome with the Rett allele may have symptoms that range from mild to severe, depending on how many of her cells express the disease-causing allele.

10.7 Mastering Concepts

1. What is the role of the Y chromosome in human sex determination?
2. Why do males and females express recessive X-linked alleles differently?
3. How does X inactivation in mammals equalize the contributions of X-linked genes between the sexes?

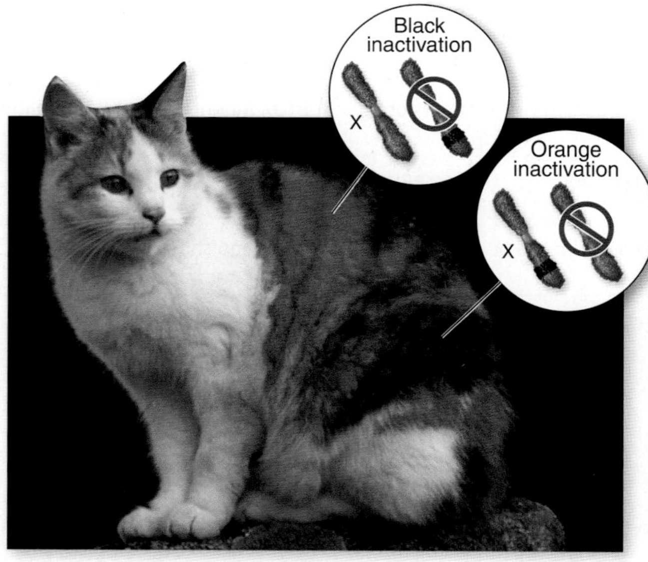

Figure 10.20 X Inactivation. In cats, the X chromosome carries a coat color gene with alleles for black or orange coloration. Calico and tortoiseshell cats are heterozygous for this gene; one of the two X chromosomes is inactivated in each colored patch. (a) X inactivation happened early in the development of this cat, producing large patches of cells with the same color. (A different gene accounts for the white background.) (b) X inactivation occurred later in this cat, producing smaller patches. Can you see why calico cat clones do not share identical fur color patterns?

10.8 Pedigrees Show Modes of Inheritance

Although Gregor Mendel did not study human genetics, our species nevertheless has "Mendelian traits": those determined by single genes with alleles that are either dominant or recessive. Several thousand phenotypes fit these criteria, and most of the corresponding genes are on autosomes. Because both sexes have two copies of each autosome, genes on those chromosomes affect both sexes equally.

Genes on autosomes exhibit two modes of inheritance: autosomal dominant and autosomal recessive (table 10.3). To inherit an **autosomal dominant** disorder, a person can receive the disease-causing allele from either parent. The Burning Question on this page describes a common example of an autosomal dominant condition—male pattern baldness. In contrast, a person with an **autosomal recessive** disorder must have received a disease-causing allele from both parents. Each parent may be homozygous recessive (and therefore also have the disease) or be heterozygous. A person who is heterozygous is called a carrier because he or she is unaffected by the disorder but still has a 50% chance of passing the disease-causing allele to the next generation.

To determine a disorder's mode of inheritance, researchers track its incidence over multiple generations, much as Mendel did with his pea plants more than a century ago. **Pedigree** charts depicting family relationships and phenotypes are useful tools in this research (figure 10.21). In a pedigree chart, squares indicate males, and circles denote females. Horizontal lines connect parents. Siblings connect to their parents by vertical lines and to each other by an elevated horizontal line.

Burning Questions

Is male baldness really from the female side of the family?

Male pattern baldness is the distinctive hair loss that many men (and some women) experience as they enter their 20s, 30s, and 40s. The baldness spreads outward from the temples and crown of the head in a characteristic pattern.

Two conditions are required for male pattern baldness to develop. First, hormones called androgens must be present in high concentrations. Testosterone and dihydrotestosterone (DHT) are androgens; they bind to and enter hair follicle cells, interacting with the DNA to stop growth of the hair follicle. Second, the individual must have a genetic predisposition for the condition. The gene(s) controlling this trait reside on autosomes, not on the sex chromosomes. Therefore, either parent can pass the baldness allele(s) to a child.

Why don't women suffer from baldness as often as males? The answer is that pattern baldness is a so-called "sex-influenced" condition in which males and females can carry the same pair of alleles yet express them differently. In this case, the amount of testosterone is the deciding factor. The higher the concentration of testosterone, the stronger the influence of the "baldness allele." Men typically have more of this sex hormone than women—hence the name, *male* pattern baldness.

Submit your burning question to:
marielle_hoefnagels@mcgraw-hill.com

TABLE 10.3 Some Autosomal Dominant and Autosomal Recessive Disorders in Humans

Disorder	Genetic Explanation	Characteristics
Autosomal recessive inheritance		
Albinism	Mutant allele on chromosome 11 encodes faulty gene required for pigment production.	Lack of pigmentation in skin, hair, and eyes
Cystic fibrosis	Mutant allele on chromosome 7 encodes faulty chloride channel protein.	Lung infections and congestion, poor fat digestion, infertility, poor weight gain, salty sweat
Phenylketonuria (PKU)	Mutant allele on chromosome 12 causes enzyme deficiency in pathway that breaks down the amino acid phenylalanine.	Buildup of metabolic byproducts causes mental retardation.
Tay-Sachs disease	Mutant allele on chromosome 15 causes deficiency of lysosome enzyme.	Buildup of byproducts causes nervous system degeneration.
Autosomal dominant inheritance		
Achondroplasia	Mutant allele on chromosome 4 causes deficiency of receptor protein for growth factor.	Dwarfism with short limbs, normal-size head and trunk
Familial hypercholesterolemia	Mutant allele on chromosome 2 encodes faulty cholesterol-binding protein.	High cholesterol, heart disease
Huntington disease	Mutant allele on chromosome 4 encodes protein that misfolds and forms clumps in brain cells.	Progressive uncontrollable movements and personality changes, beginning in middle age
Marfan syndrome	Mutant allele on chromosome 15 causes connective tissue disorder.	Long limbs, sunken chest, lens dislocation, spindly fingers, weakened aorta

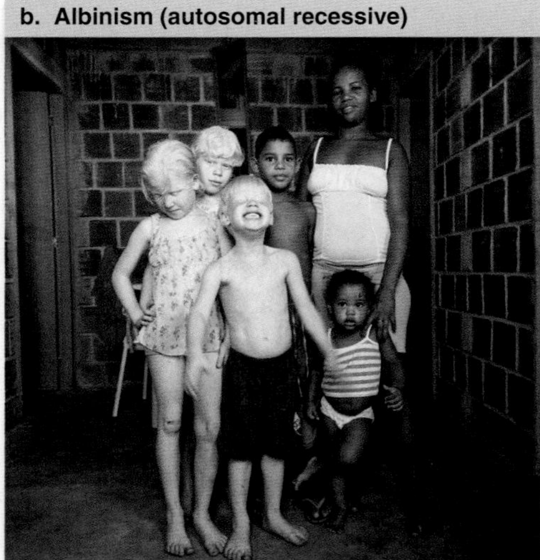

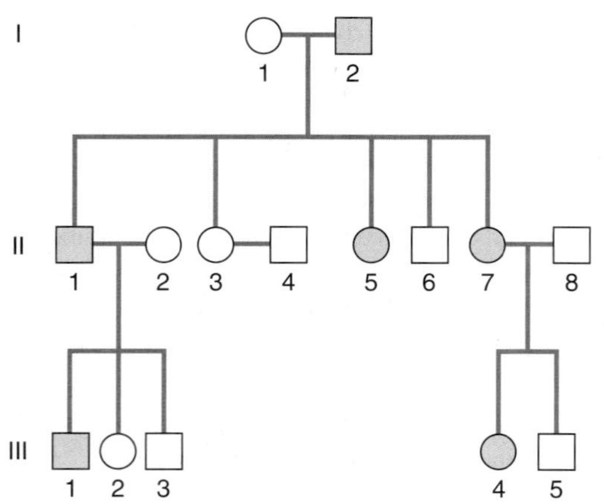

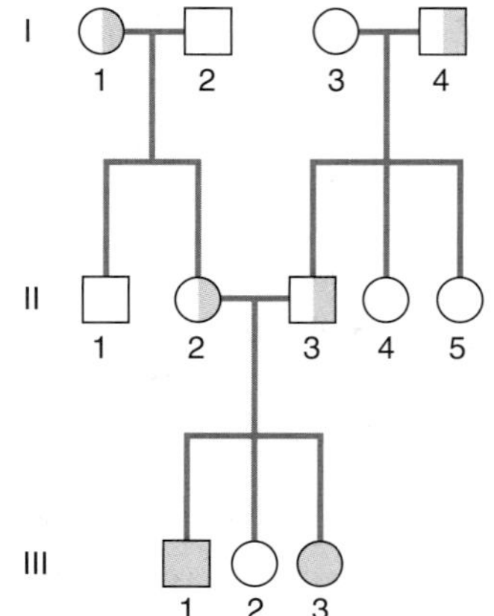

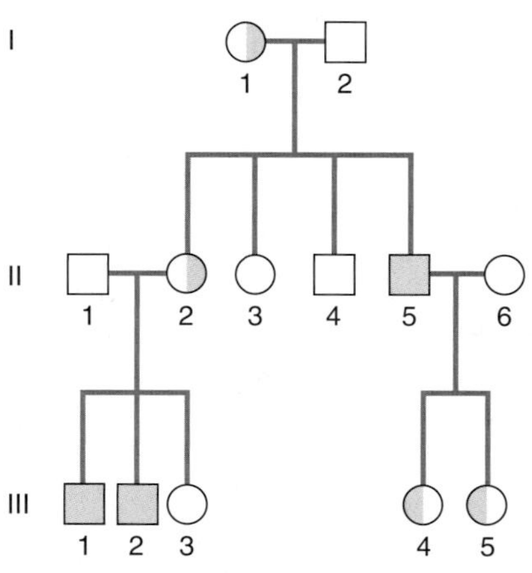

	Normal	Carrier	Affected
Female	○	◐	●
Male	□	◧	■

Figure 10.21 **Pedigrees.** (a) A pedigree for achondroplasia, a type of dwarfism with an autosomal dominant mode of inheritance. (b) A pedigree for albinism, which has an autosomal recessive mode of inheritance. (c) A pedigree for red–green color blindness, a disorder with an X-linked recessive mode of inheritance.

As you can see from figure 10.21, each mode of inheritance has a characteristic pedigree pattern. Autosomal dominant disorders such as achondroplasia (a form of dwarfism) typically appear in every generation. Autosomal recessive conditions such as albinism, however, may seem to disappear in one generation, only to reappear in the next. In X-linked recessive disorders, most or all affected family members are males; females are often unaffected carriers.

10.8 Mastering Concepts

1. What is the difference between autosomal dominant and autosomal recessive modes of inheritance?
2. How are pedigrees helpful in determining a disorder's mode of inheritance?

10.9 Most Traits Are Influenced by the Environment and Multiple Genes

Mendel's data were clear enough for him to infer principles of inheritance because he observed characteristics determined by single genes with two easily distinguished alleles. Moreover, the traits he selected are unaffected by environmental conditions. A genetic counselor can likewise be confident in telling two cystic fibrosis carriers that each of their children has a 25% probability of getting the disease. But the counselor cannot calculate the probability that the child will be an alcoholic, have depression, be a genius, or wear size 9 shoes. The reason is that multiple genes and the environment control these and most other traits.

A. The Environment Can Alter the Phenotype

The environment often affects gene expression; that is, a gene may be active in one circumstance but inactive in another. As a simple example, temperature influences the quantity of pigment molecules in the fur of some animals. Siamese cats and Himalayan rabbits have dark ears, noses, feet, and tails because these parts are colder than the animals' abdomens (figure 10.22).

Likewise, personal circumstances ranging from hormone levels to childhood experiences to diet influence a person's susceptibility to depression, alcoholism, and type II diabetes. These three diseases have a genetic component as well, but sorting out the relative contributions of "nature" and "nurture" is difficult. Studies of twins are often helpful, as are careful observations of everything from family composition to brain structures.

Even human diseases with simple, single-gene inheritance patterns can have an environmental component. Cystic fibrosis, for example, is a single-gene disorder. Because cystic fibrosis patients are very susceptible to infection, however, the course of the illness depends on which infectious agents a person encounters.

Figure 10.22 Environment Affects Phenotype. In Siamese cats, the gene encoding an enzyme required for pigment production is mutated. The heat-sensitive enzyme is active in cool areas, such as the paws, ears, snout, and tail. But the enzyme is inactive at body temperature, so the cat's fur remains light-colored where the skin is warmer.

B. Polygenic Traits Depend on More Than One Gene

Unlike cystic fibrosis, most inherited traits are **polygenic;** that is, the phenotype reflects the activities of more than one gene. Eye color is an example of a polygenic trait because multiple enzymes, encoded by multiple genes, influence the production and distribution of the pigment melanin in the eye's iris. Eye color is among the few traits unaffected by external conditions.

To complicate matters, the environment often profoundly affects the expression of both single-gene and polygenic traits. For example, in plants, polygenic traits typically include flower color, the density of leaf pores (stomata), and crop yield. But these traits do not remain static throughout a plant's life. Soil pH can affect flower color, CO_2 concentration can change the number of stomata, and nutrient and water availability greatly influence crop production. ▸ stomata, p. 432

When the frequencies of all the phenotypes associated with a polygenic trait are plotted on a graph, they form a characteristic bell-shaped curve. Human height, for example, ranges from very tall to very short, with the vast majority somewhere in between. Each person's height reflects not only genetics but also

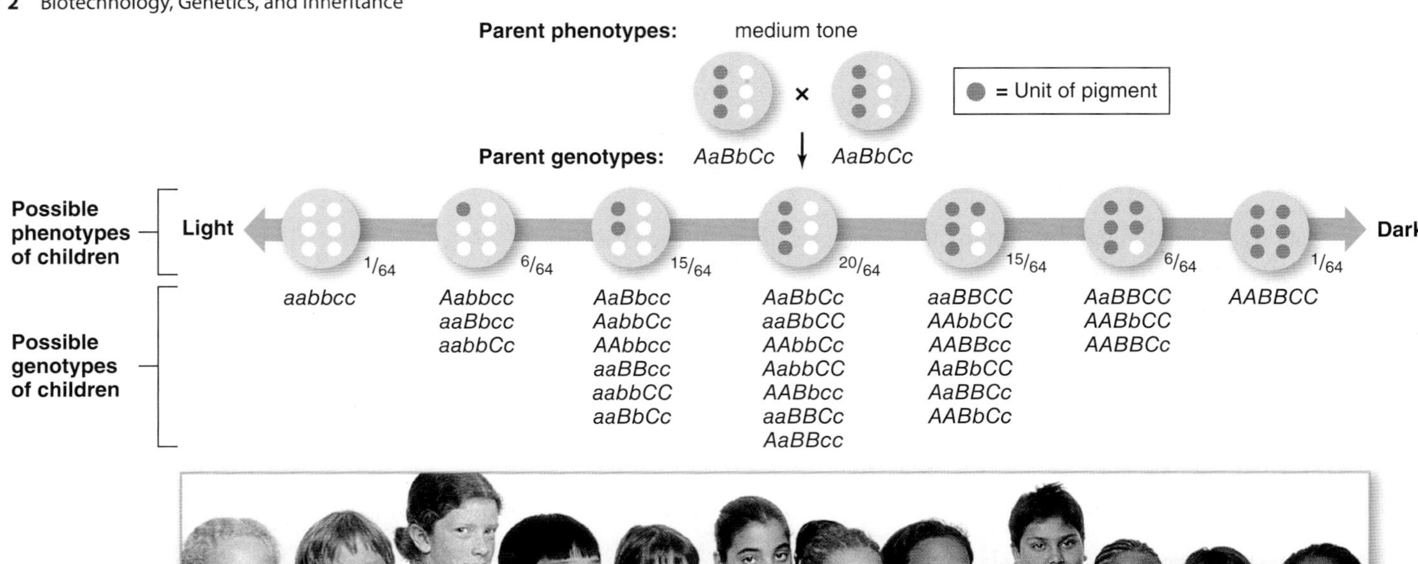

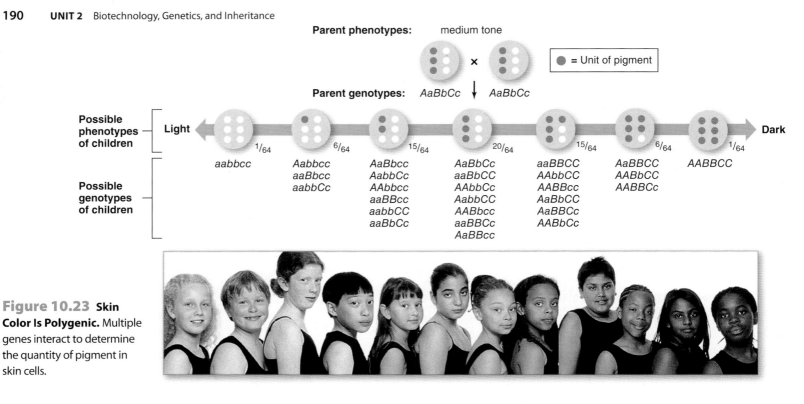

Figure 10.23 Skin Color Is Polygenic. Multiple genes interact to determine the quantity of pigment in skin cells.

childhood nutrition and health care. Figure 10.23 shows a continuum of gene expression for skin color, another trait affected by genes and the environment—in this case, exposure to sunlight. Body weight and intelligence are other traits that are both polygenic and influenced by the environment.

10.9 Mastering Concepts

1. How can the environment affect a phenotype?
2. What is a polygenic trait?

Investigating Life

10.10 Heredity and the Hungry Hordes

The Question: Agriculture provides a steady food supply, but not just to humans. Hungry insects and other animals can devastate crops by eating the leaves, roots, seeds, and fruits of the plants we grow for food or fiber. Farmers continually seek new ways to kill these competitors, but each tactic selects for new adaptations in the insects. It is a long-standing, and seemingly unavoidable, evolutionary arms race.

The larvae of butterflies and moths are particularly voracious. A good example is the pink bollworm (figure 10.24). The adults of this species are moths that lay eggs on cotton bolls. When the eggs hatch, the pink caterpillars tunnel into the boll and eat the seeds, damaging the cotton fibers.

Figure 10.24 Hungry Caterpillar. Pink bollworms cost cotton producers tens of millions of dollars each year.

One tool that keeps bollworms and other caterpillars at bay is a soil bacterium called *Bacillus thuringiensis,* abbreviated Bt. This microbe produces a toxic protein that pokes holes in a caterpillar's intestinal tract, leaving the animal vulnerable to infection and unable to digest food. Bt does not affect humans, because we lack the specific molecule to which the toxin binds. Bt is among the few insecticides that organic farmers can spray on their plants.

In the 1990s, scientists inserted the bacterial gene for the Bt toxin into plant cells (see section 11.2A). Every cell in these so-called Bt plants produces the toxin. When Bt was available only as a spray, insect populations rarely encountered it. But genetically modified Bt crops produce the toxin throughout their lives, so caterpillars are exposed from the moment they begin feeding. Large fields of Bt plants therefore strongly select against susceptible individuals, leaving resistant caterpillars to produce the next generation.

To combat this selective pressure, farmers growing Bt crops must agree to surround each field with a buffer strip planted with a conventional (non-Bt) variety of the same crop—a refuge. If the strip is large enough, a resistant moth has a good chance of encountering a susceptible mate from the buffer strip. Assuming that resistance is conferred by a recessive allele, all of the heterozygous offspring will die if they eat the Bt plants. A ready pool of susceptible mates from the refuge should therefore keep the resistance allele rare. But how can scientists test whether refuges really do keep recessive alleles rare in the real world?

The Approach: One solution is to find a way to measure a bollworm's genotype directly. Biologists Shai Morin, Bruce Tabashnik, and their colleagues at the University of Arizona tackled this problem by studying Bt resistance in several populations of pink bollworms. One population, reared for decades in a lab without exposure to Bt, was susceptible. Other groups, originally collected in Arizona and Texas, were artificially selected for resistance by feeding them Bt-laced meals and allowing the survivors to reproduce. ▸ artificial selection, p. 223

Laboratory experiments confirmed that alleles conferring Bt resistance are recessive (figure 10.25). In addition, from previous studies, the researchers knew that Bt resistance comes from changes in a protein called cadherin, the target molecule to which the toxin binds. They also knew the DNA sequence of the gene that encodes cadherin. They extracted DNA from resistant pink bollworms, determined the cadherin gene sequence for each, and compared it with the gene from susceptible insects.

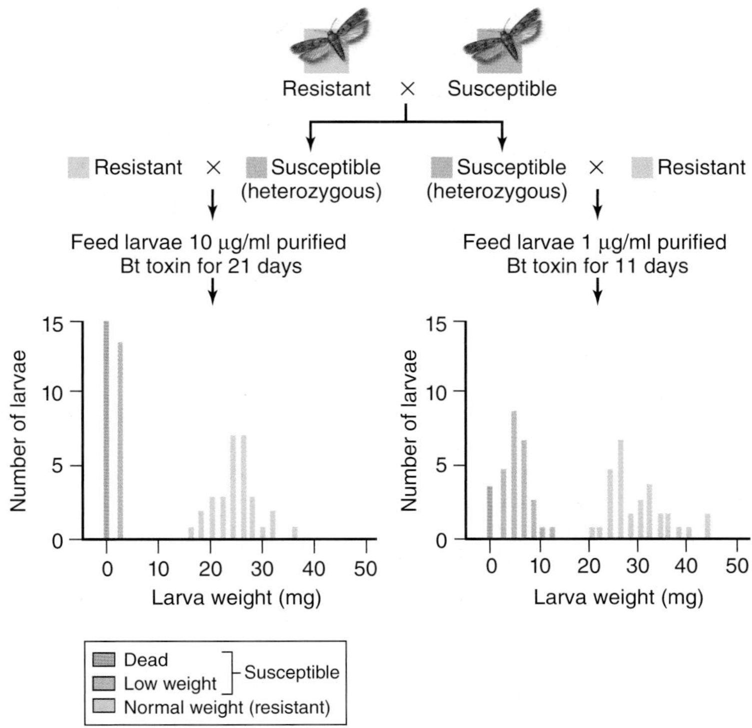

Figure 10.25 Bt Resistance Is Recessive. When a heterozygous susceptible insect is bred with a resistant mate, half the offspring should be resistant and half should be susceptible. Tests with Bt toxin show that this is indeed the case: half of the insects thrived in the presence of Bt toxin, while the susceptible ones died or were very small.

The Conclusion: The results suggested that bollworm populations harbor three unique resistance alleles, each encoding a different variation on the cadherin protein's shape. An insect with two such resistance alleles is immune to the toxin. Furthermore, the researchers developed a method for testing an insect's DNA for the presence of one or more of the recessive alleles. As a result, we can now spy on the pink bollworm's evolution as it happens.

The stakes are high. If the resistance alleles become very common, Bt may become useless as a control measure, forcing growers to switch back to broad-spectrum pesticides that kill many beneficial insects. Careful monitoring will be crucial as we continue to wage war against the insects that will forever compete for our crops.

Morin, Shai, Robert W. Biggs, Mark S. Sisterson, and 10 other authors (including Bruce E. Tabashnik). April 29, 2003. Three cadherin alleles associated with resistance to *Bacillus thuringiensis* in pink bollworm. *Proceedings of the National Academy of Sciences*, vol. 100, pages 5004–5009.

10.10 Mastering Concepts

1. Explain the logic of planting non-Bt crop buffer strips around fields planted with Bt crops.
2. How did the researchers use a feeding experiment to show that Bt resistance alleles in pink bollworms are recessive?
3. If farmers stop planting buffer strips, how will the incidence of resistance alleles in pink bollworm populations change?

Chapter Summary

10.1 Chromosomes Are Packets of Genetic Information: A Review

- Each **gene** encodes a protein; mutations in genes create new **alleles.**
- A **chromosome** is a continuous molecule of DNA with associated proteins. A **diploid** human cell contains 22 **homologous pairs** of **autosomes** and one pair of **sex chromosomes.**
- **Meiosis** is a type of cell division that gives rise to **haploid gametes. Fertilization** unites gametes and restores the diploid number.

10.2 Mendel's Experiments Uncovered Basic Laws of Inheritance

- Gregor Mendel studied inheritance patterns in pea plants because they are easy to grow, develop quickly, and produce abundant offspring. The genes for the traits he studied had only two alleles. It is also easy to control crosses between pea plants.

A. Mendel Called Each Trait Either Dominant or Recessive

- Mendel started each breeding experiment with **true-breeding** parents and followed the inheritance of each trait over multiple generations.
- An allele whose expression masks another is **dominant;** an allele whose expression is masked by a dominant allele is **recessive.** Dominant does not necessarily mean "most common."

B. For Each Gene, a Cell's Two Alleles May Be Identical or Different

- A **heterozygote** has two different alleles of a gene. A **homozygous** recessive individual has two recessive alleles. A homozygous dominant individual has two dominant alleles.
- The combination of alleles for a gene is the individual's **genotype,** and the observable expression of a genotype is the organism's **phenotype.** A **wild-type** allele is the most common in a population. A change in a gene is a **mutation** and may result in a **mutant** phenotype.

10.3 The Two Alleles of Each Gene End Up in Different Gametes

- In genetic crosses, the purebred parental generation is designated **P;** the next generation is the first filial generation, or $\mathbf{F_1}$**;** and the next is the second filial generation, or $\mathbf{F_2}$.

A. Monohybrid Crosses Track the Inheritance of One Gene

- A **monohybrid cross** between two heterozygotes yields a genotypic ratio of 1:2:1 and a phenotypic ratio of 3:1.
- **Punnett squares** are useful for calculating the probability of each possible outcome in a genetic cross.
- A **test cross** reveals an unknown genotype by breeding the individual with a homozygous recessive individual.

B. Meiosis Explains Mendel's Law of Segregation

- Mendel's **law of segregation** states that the two alleles of the same gene separate into different gametes. Each individual receives one allele of each gene from each parent.

10.4 Genes on Different Chromosomes Are Inherited Independently

A. Dihybrid Crosses Track the Inheritance of Two Genes at Once

- A **dihybrid cross** between individuals heterozygous for two genes yields a 9:3:3:1 phenotypic ratio if the genes are on different chromosomes.

B. Meiosis Explains Mendel's Law of Independent Assortment

- According to Mendel's **law of independent assortment,** the inheritance of one gene does not affect the inheritance of another gene on a different chromosome. This law reflects meiosis, in which homologous pairs of chromosomes (and the genes they carry) align randomly during metaphase I.

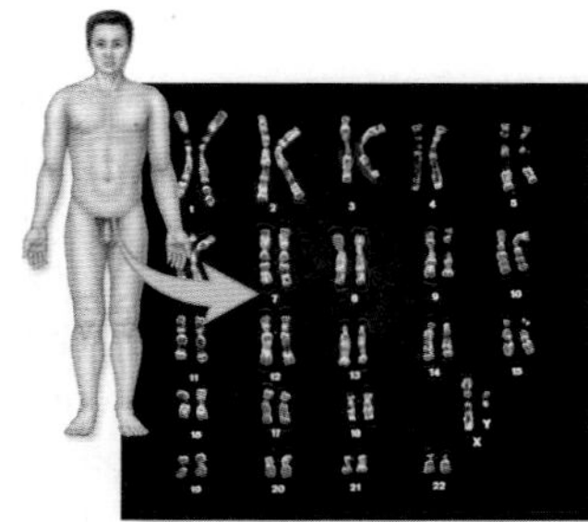

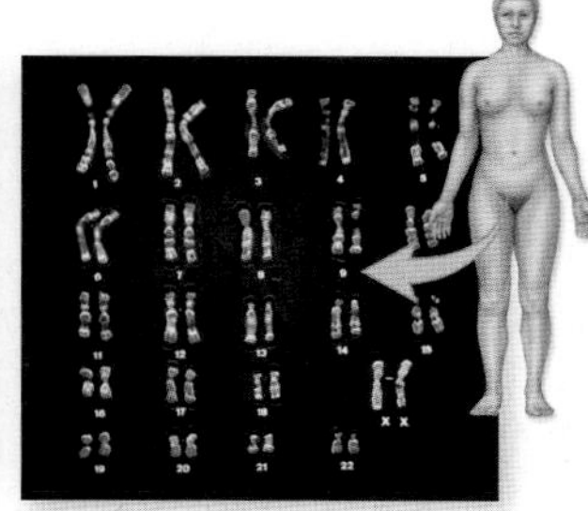

Germ cells contain 46 chromosomes

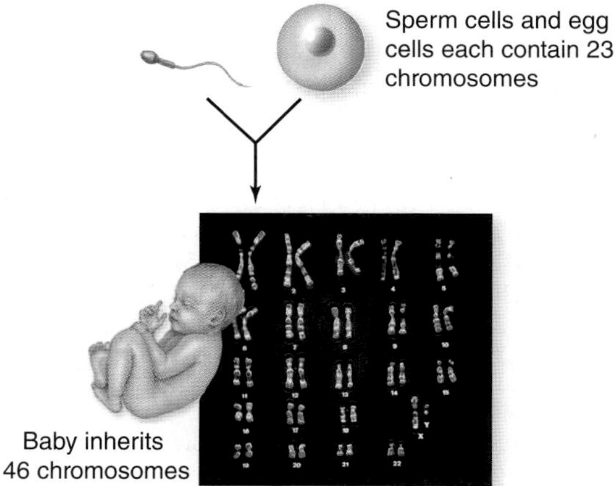

If the parents are both carriers of Tay-Sachs disease (*Tt*), the probability that the baby inherits the disease is 25%:

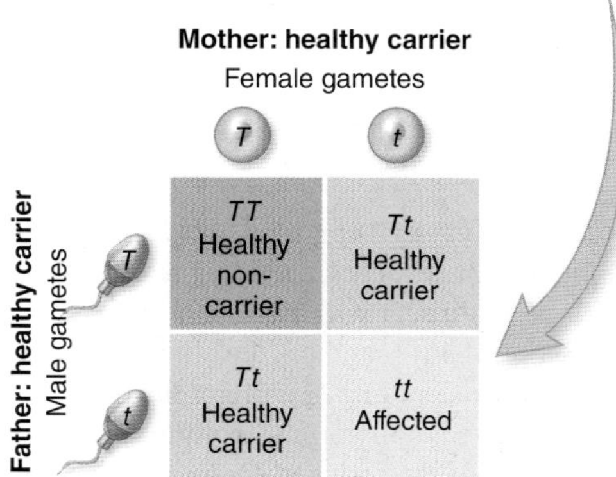

C. The Product Rule Replaces Complex Punnett Squares

- The **product rule** is an alternative to Punnett squares for following inheritance of two or more traits at a time.

10.5 Studies of Linked Genes Have Yielded Chromosome Maps

A. Genes on the Same Chromosome Are Linked

- Dihybrid crosses for pairs of **linked genes** produce more offspring with **parental chromosomes** than with **recombinant chromosomes.**
- **Linkage groups** are collections of genes that are often inherited together because they are on the same chromosome.

B. Linkage Maps Derive from Crossover Frequencies

- The farther apart two genes are on a chromosome, the more likely **crossing over** is to separate their alleles. Breeding studies reveal the crossover frequencies used to create **linkage maps**—diagrams that show the order of genes on a chromosome.

10.6 Gene Expression Can Appear to Alter Mendelian Ratios

- In some crosses, the ratio of offspring phenotypes does not seem to follow Mendel's principles.

A. Incomplete Dominance and Codominance Add Phenotype Classes

- Heterozygotes of **incompletely dominant** alleles have phenotypes intermediate between those of the two homozygotes. **Codominant** alleles are both expressed in a heterozygote.

B. Inheritance Patterns Are Often Complicated

- A **pleiotropic** gene has multiple effects on the body and therefore produces many different phenotypes.
- Many biochemical reactions require multiple proteins. Mutated genes encoding any of the proteins can stop the pathway, producing the same phenotype.
- The activity of one gene may mask the effect of another.

10.7 Sex-Linked Genes Have Unique Inheritance Patterns

- Genes controlling **sex-linked** traits are located on the X or Y chromosomes.

A. X-Linked Recessive Disorders Affect More Males Than Females

- An **X-linked** gene passes from mother to son because the male inherits his X chromosome from his mother and his Y chromosome from his father. Scientists know of many more X-linked disorders than Y-linked disorders.

B. X Inactivation Prevents "Double Dosing" of Gene Products

- **X inactivation** shuts off all but one X chromosome in the cells of female mammals, equalizing the number of active X-linked genes in each sex. A female is a "mosaic" for X-linked genes because the maternal or paternal X chromosome is inactivated at random in each cell.

10.8 Pedigrees Show Modes of Inheritance

- An **autosomal dominant** disorder affects both sexes and is inherited from one affected parent. An **autosomal recessive** disorder can also appear in either sex, is passed from parents who are either carriers or are affected, and can skip generations.
- **Pedigrees** trace phenotypes in families and reveal the mode of inheritance.

10.9 Most Traits Are Influenced by the Environment and Multiple Genes

A. The Environment Can Alter the Phenotype

- Unlike the traits that Mendel studied, many traits have environmental as well as genetic influences.

B. Polygenic Traits Depend on More Than One Gene

- A **polygenic trait** varies continuously in its expression, and the frequencies of the phenotypes form a bell-shaped curve.

10.10 Investigating Life: Heredity and the Hungry Hordes

- Researchers have developed a way to test for the presence of recessive alleles in insect pests of cotton. This genetic test allows researchers to monitor caterpillars for resistance to Bt, a toxin in genetically modified cotton.

Multiple Choice Questions

1. Which of the following is a difference between an autosome and a sex chromosome?
   a. An autosome has more DNA.
   b. A sex chromosome is present only in germ cells.
   c. Only autosomes can be diploid.
   d. There are more autosomes than sex chromosomes in a cell.
2. According to Mendel, if an individual is *heterozygous* for a gene, the phenotype will correspond to that of
   a. the recessive allele.
   b. the dominant allele.
   c. a blend of the dominant and recessive alleles.
   d. a wild-type allele.
3. If an individual is *homozygous* for a gene, then the genotype will contain
   a. only the recessive allele.
   b. only the dominant allele.
   c. both a dominant and a recessive allele.
   d. Either a or b could be true.
4. What can you conclude if the offspring of a test cross all show the phenotype associated with the dominant allele?
   a. One parent was homozygous dominant.
   b. One parent was heterozygous.
   c. The offspring are all homozygous dominant.
   d. Both b and c are correct.
5. Which of the following is a possible gamete for an individual with the genotype *PP rr*?
   a. *PP*
   b. *P r*
   c. *p r*
   d. *rr*
6. Use the product rule to determine the chance of obtaining an offspring with the genotype *Rr Yy* from a dihybrid cross between parents with the genotype *Rr Yy*.
   a. ½
   b. ¼
   c. ⅛
   d. 1⁄16
7. Recombination is most likely to occur between
   a. closely linked genes.
   b. genes on nonhomologous chromosomes.
   c. linked genes that are far apart.
   d. parental chromosomes.
8. How does incomplete dominance affect the phenotype of a heterozygote?
   a. It results in a blend of the dominant and recessive phenotypes.
   b. It results in the expression of only the recessive phenotype.
   c. The dominant phenotype is still expressed, but only in patches.
   d. The trait is not observed in the individual.
9. Suppose a woman is a symptomless carrier of a recessive X-linked disease. If her husband has the disease, what is the chance that they have a girl who also has the disease?
   a. 100%
   b. 50%
   c. 25%
   d. 0%
10. How does X inactivation contribute to an organism's phenotype?
    a. It controls the number and kind of genes expressed on an X chromosome.
    b. It determines which X chromosome is expressed in a male.
    c. It allows for expression of either the maternal or paternal X in different cells.
    d. It enhances expression of Y-linked genes in males.
11. What is a polygenic trait?
    a. A trait that reflects expression of both dominant and recessive alleles
    b. A trait that reflects the influence of the environment
    c. A trait that reflects the expression of many alleles of the same gene
    d. A trait that reflects the expression of many different genes

Write It Out

1. What advantages do pea plants have for studies of inheritance? Why aren't humans equally suitable?
2. Some people compare a homologous pair of chromosomes to a pair of shoes. Explain the similarity. How would you extend the analogy to the sex chromosomes for females and for males?
3. In an attempt to breed winter barley that is resistant to barley mild mosaic virus, agricultural researchers cross a susceptible domesticated strain with a resistant wild strain. The F_1 plants are all susceptible, but when the F_1 plants are crossed with each other, some of the F_2 individuals are resistant. Is the resistance allele recessive or dominant? How do you know?
4. Given the relationship between genes, alleles, and proteins, how can a recessive allele appear to "hide" in a heterozygote?
5. Many plants are polyploid (see chapter 9); that is, they have more than two sets of chromosomes. How would having four (rather than two) copies of a chromosome more effectively mask expression of a recessive allele?
6. Springer spaniels often suffer from canine phosphofructokinase (PFK) deficiency. The dogs lack an enzyme that is crucial in extracting energy from glucose molecules. Affected pups have extremely weak muscles and die within weeks. A DNA test is available to identify male and female dogs that are carriers. Why would breeders wish to identify carriers if these dogs are not affected?
7. How did Mendel use evidence from monohybrid and dihybrid crosses to deduce his laws of segregation and independent assortment? How do these laws relate to meiosis?
8. In a dihybrid cross, the predicted phenotype ratio is 9:3:3:1; the "9" represents the proportion of plants expressing at least one dominant allele for both traits. How would you use test crosses to determine whether these plants are homozygous dominant or heterozygous for one or both genes?
9. A white woman with fair skin, blond hair, and blue eyes and a black man with dark brown skin, dark hair, and brown eyes have fraternal twins. One twin has blond hair, brown eyes, and light skin, and the other has dark hair, brown eyes, and dark skin. What Mendelian law does this real-life case illustrate?
10. The radish has nine groups of traits. Within each group, dihybrid crosses do not yield a 9:3:3:1 phenotypic ratio. Instead, such crosses yield an overabundance of phenotypes like those of the parents. What does this information reveal about the chromosomes of this plant?
11. How does gene linkage interfere with Mendel's law of independent assortment? Why doesn't the inheritance pattern of linked genes disprove Mendel's law?
12. How does crossing over "unlink" genes?
13. If two different but linked genes are located very far apart on a chromosome, how may the inheritance pattern create the appearance of independent assortment?
14. Explain how each of the following appears to disrupt Mendelian ratios: incomplete dominance, codominance, pleiotropy.
15. Suppose a single trait is controlled by a gene with four codominant alleles. A person can inherit any combination of two of the four alleles. How many phenotypes are possible for this trait?
16. What is the role of the Y chromosome in human sex determination?
17. Do you agree with the statement that all alleles on the Y chromosome are dominant? Why or why not?
18. Suppose a fetus has X and Y chromosomes but lacks receptors for the protein encoded by Y chromosome's sex-determining gene. Will the fetus develop as a male or as a female? Explain your answer.
19. How are X-linked genes inherited differently in male and female humans?
20. What does X inactivation accomplish?
21. Rett syndrome is a severe X-linked recessive disorder that affects mostly female children. How does X inactivation explain this observation?
22. A family has an X-linked dominant form of congenital generalized hypertrichosis (excessive hairiness). Although the allele is dominant, males are more severely affected than females. Moreover, the women in the family often have asymmetrical, hairy patches on their bodies. How does X chromosome inactivation explain this observation?
23. Why are male calico cats rare?
24. Study the following pedigree. Is the disorder's mode of inheritance autosomal dominant, autosomal recessive, or X-linked recessive? Explain your reasoning.

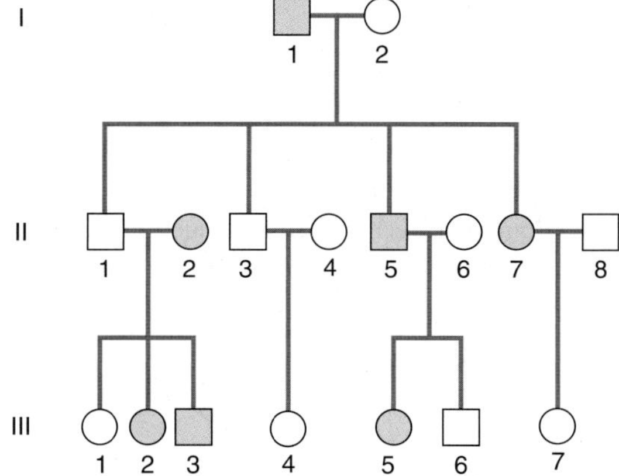

25. Pedigree charts can sometimes be difficult to construct and interpret. People may refuse to supply information, and adoption or serial marriages can produce blended families. Artificial insemination may involve anonymous sperm donors. Many traits are strongly influenced by the environment. How does each of these factors complicate the use of pedigrees?
26. Explain the following "equation":

    Genotype + Environment = Phenotype
27. Mitochondria and chloroplasts contain DNA that encodes some proteins essential to life. These organelles are inherited via the female parent's egg. Do you expect these genes to follow Mendelian laws of inheritance? Explain your answer.

Genetics Problems

See pages 196 and 197 for step-by-step guides to solving genetics problems.

1. Wild-type canaries are yellow. A dominant mutant allele of the color gene, designated W, causes white feathers. Inheriting two dominant alleles is lethal to the embryo. If a yellow canary is crossed to a white canary, what is the probability that an offspring will be yellow? What is the probability that it will be white?
2. In humans, more than 100 forms of deafness are inherited as recessive alleles on many different chromosomes. Suppose that a woman who is heterozygous for a deafness gene on one chromosome has a child with a man who is heterozygous for a deafness gene on a different chromosome. Does the child face the general population risk of inheriting either form of deafness or the 25% chance that Mendelian ratios predict for a monohybrid cross? Explain your answer.
3. A man and a woman each have dark eyes, dark hair, and freckles. The genes for these traits are on separate chromosomes. The woman is

heterozygous for each of these genes, but the man is homozygous. The dominance relationships of the alleles are as follows:

B = dark eyes; b = blue eyes
H = dark hair; h = blond hair
F = freckles; f = no freckles

a. What is the probability that their child will share the parents' phenotype?

b. What is the probability that the child will share the same genotype as the mother? As the father?

Use the product rule or a Punnett square to obtain your answers. Which method do you think is easier?

4. Genes *J, K,* and *L* are on the same chromosome. The crossover frequency between *J* and *K* is 19%, the crossover frequency between *K* and *L* is 2%, and the crossover frequency between *J* and *L* is 21%. Use this information to create a linkage map for the chromosome.
5. A particular gene in dogs contributes to coat color. The two alleles exhibit incomplete dominance. Dogs with genotype *mm* have normal pigmentation; genotype *Mm* leads to "dilute" pigmentation; genotype *MM* produces an all-white dog. If a breeder mates a normal dog with a white dog, what will be the genotypes and phenotypes of the puppies? If two *Mm* dogs are mated, what is the probability that a puppy will be all white?
6. Three babies are born in the hospital on the same day. Baby X has type AB blood; Baby Y has type B blood; Baby Z has type O blood. Use the information in the table below to determine which baby belongs to which couple. (Assume that all individuals are homozygous dominant for the *H* gene.)

Couple	Mother	Blood type	Father	Blood type
1	Abby	B	Seth	AB
2	Carol	A	Sam	A
3	Nancy	AB	Bill	O

7. Consider a woman whose brother has hemophilia A but whose parents are healthy. What is the chance that she has inherited the hemophilia allele? What is the chance that the woman will conceive a son with hemophilia?
8. New parents Gloria and Michael were startled when their son Will's diapers turned blue when he urinated. Fortunately, this occurred for the first time in the hospital, where tests determined that the newborn had inherited "blue diaper syndrome." Because of abnormal transport of the amino acid tryptophan across the small intestinal lining, urine contains a compound that turns blue on contact with the air. Gloria's sister Edith was pregnant at the time of Will's diagnosis and became concerned that her child might inherit the disorder. The family doctor assured Gloria and her sister that this wasn't possible because each parent had to be a carrier. However, Edith and Archie's son Aaron also was born with blue diaper syndrome. Draw a pedigree for this family and describe how this disorder is most likely inherited. How was the doctor's explanation incorrect?

Pull It Together

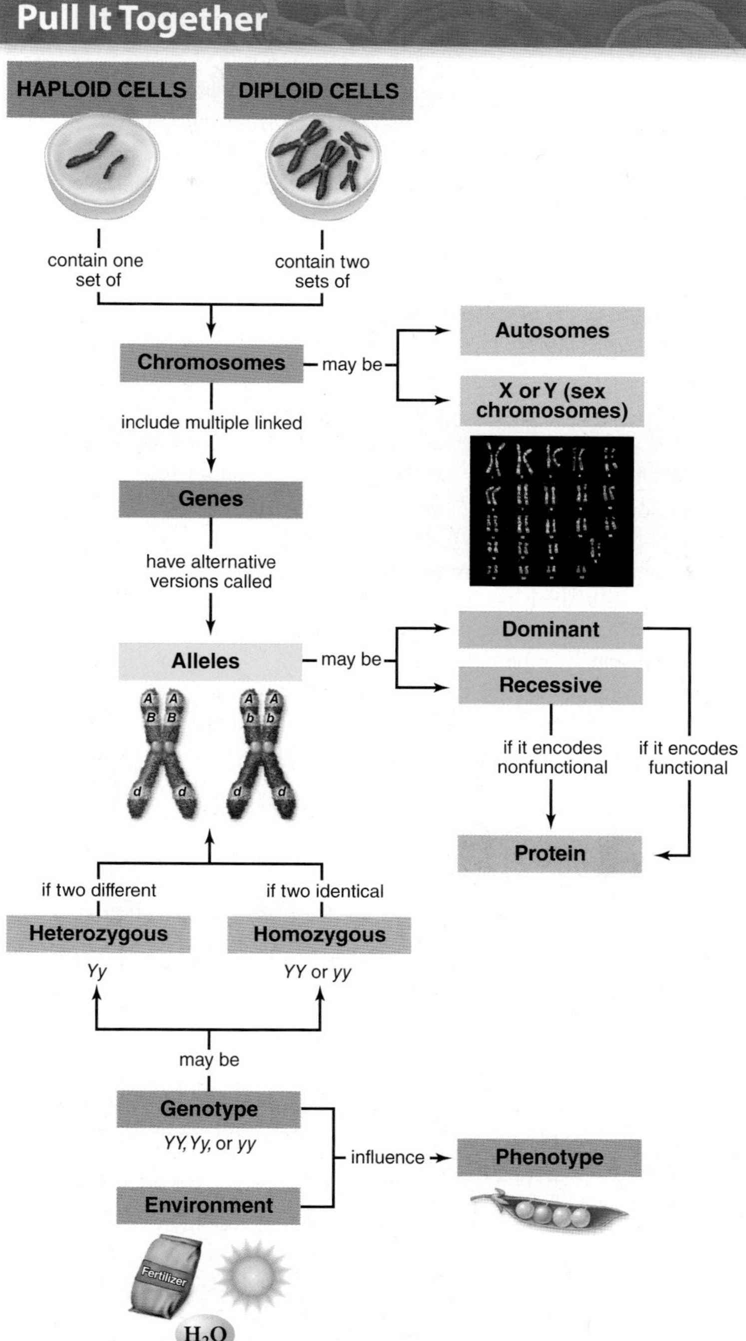

1. Which cells in the human body are haploid? Which cells are diploid?
2. What is the difference between genotype and phenotype?
3. Add *meiosis, gametes, mutations, incomplete dominance, codominance,* and *pleiotropy* to this concept map.

How to Solve a Genetics Problem: One Gene

Sample problem: Phenylketonuria (PKU) is an autosomal recessive disorder. If a man with PKU marries a woman who is a symptomless carrier, what is the probability that their first child will be born with PKU?

1. **Write a key.** Pick ONE letter to represent the gene in your problem. Use the capital form of your letter to symbolize the dominant allele; use the lowercase letter to symbolize the recessive allele.

   Sample: The dominant allele is *K;* the recessive allele is *k*.

2. **Summarize the problem's information.** Make a table listing the phenotypes and genotypes of both parents.

   Sample:

	Male	Female
Phenotype	Has PKU	No PKU (carrier)
Genotype	*kk*	*Kk*

3. **Sketch the parental chromosomes and gametes.** Use the genotypes in your table to draw the alleles onto chromosomes. Then draw short arrows to show the homologous chromosomes moving into separate gametes for each parent.

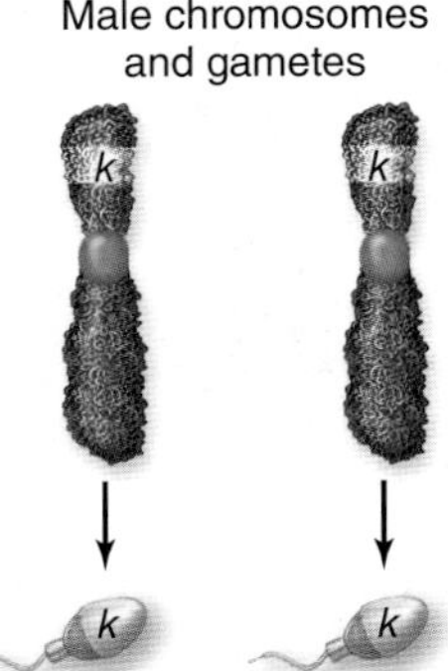

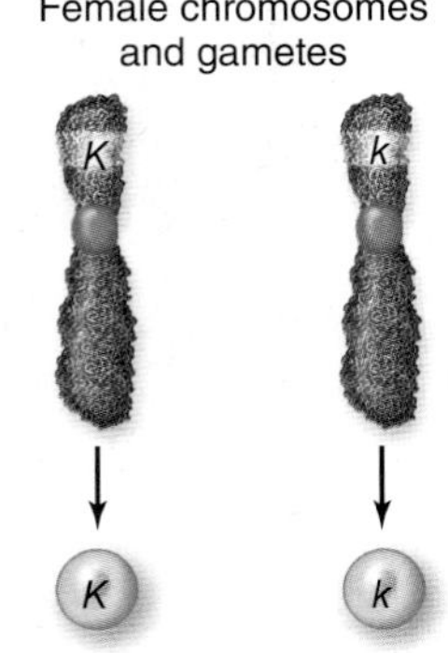

4. **Make a Punnett square.** Arrange the gametes you sketched in step #3 along the edges of the square, and fill in the genotypes of the offspring.

5. **Calculate the genotypic ratio.** Count the number of squares that contain each offspring genotype.

   Sample: 2 *Kk;* 2 *kk*

6. **Calculate the phenotypic ratio.** Count the number of squares that contain each offspring phenotype.

   Sample: 2 PKU carriers; 2 PKU sufferers

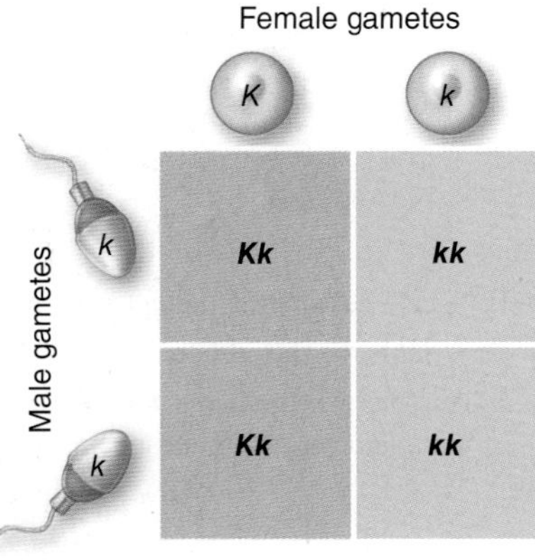

7. **Calculate the probability of each phenotype.** Divide each number in step #6 by 4 (the total number of squares) and multiply by 100.

   Sample: 50% probability that a child will be a carrier; 50% probability that a child will have PKU

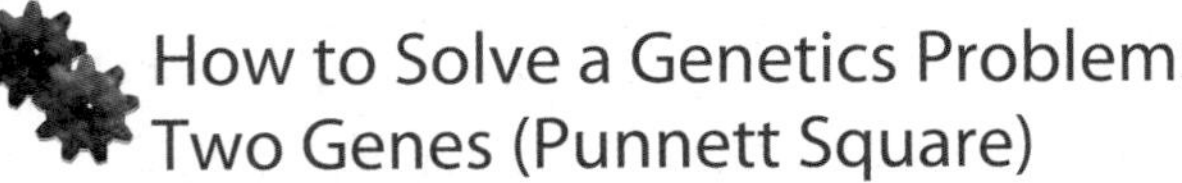

How to Solve a Genetics Problem: Two Genes (Punnett Square)

Sample problem: A student collects pollen (male sex cells) from a pea plant that is homozygous recessive for the genes controlling seed form and seed color. She uses the pollen to fertilize a plant that is heterozygous for both genes. What is the probability that an offspring plant has the same genotype and phenotype as the male parent? Assume the genes are not linked.

1. **Write a key.** Pick ONE letter to represent each of the genes in your problem. Use the capital form of your letter to symbolize the dominant allele; use the lowercase letter to symbolize the recessive allele.

   Sample: For seed form, the dominant allele (round) is *R;* the recessive allele (wrinkled) is *r;* for seed color, the dominant allele (yellow) is *Y;* the recessive allele (green) is *y*.

2. **Summarize the problem's information.** Make a table listing the phenotypes and genotypes of both parents.

   Sample:

	Male	Female
Phenotype	Wrinkled, green	Round, yellow
Genotype	*rr yy*	*Rr Yy*

3. **Sketch the parental chromosomes and gametes.** Use the genotypes in your table to draw the alleles onto two sets of chromosomes, one for each parent. The law of independent assortment means that you need to draw all possible configurations. So redraw the chromosomes, this time switching the order of the alleles in one pair. Then draw short arrows to show the chromosomes separating, and sketch the four possible gametes for each parent. Depending on the parents' genotypes, some of the gametes produced by a parent may have the same genotype.

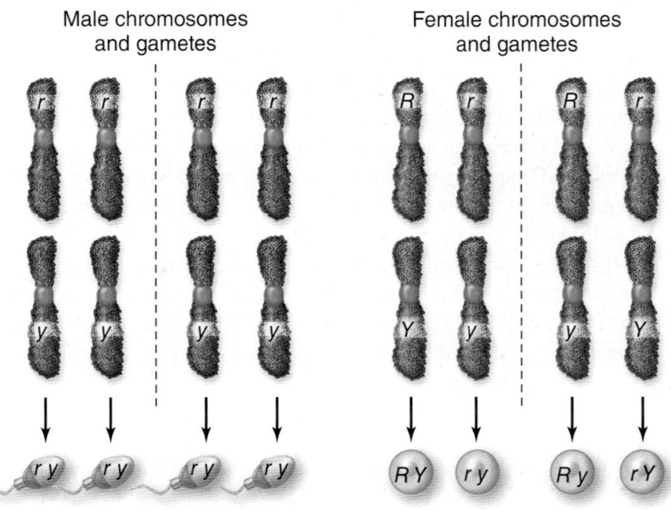

4. **Make a Punnett square.** Arrange the gametes you sketched in step #3 along the edges of the square, and fill in the genotypes of the offspring.

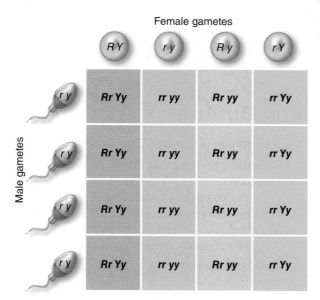

Male gametes \ Female gametes	R Y	r y	R y	r Y
r y	**Rr Yy**	**rr yy**	**Rr yy**	**rr Yy**
r y	**Rr Yy**	**rr yy**	**Rr yy**	**rr Yy**
r y	**Rr Yy**	**rr yy**	**Rr yy**	**rr Yy**
r y	**Rr Yy**	**rr yy**	**Rr yy**	**rr Yy**

5. **Calculate the genotypic ratio.** Count the number of squares that contain each offspring genotype.

   Sample: 4 *Rr Yy,* 4 *rr yy,* 4 *Rr yy,* 4 *rr Yy*

6. **Calculate the phenotypic ratio.** Count the number of squares that correspond to each possible phenotype combination.

   Sample: 4 round, yellow; 4 wrinkled, green; 4 round, green; 4 wrinkled, yellow

7. **Calculate the probability of each phenotype.** Divide each number in step #6 by 16 (the total number of squares) and multiply by 100.

   Sample: 25% probability that an offspring has the same genotype and phenotype as the male parent.

How to Solve a Genetics Problem: Two Genes (Product Rule)

NOTE: The product rule is a simpler way to solve the same problem and eliminates the need for a large Punnett square. To use the product rule in this case, first calculate the probability that the parents (*rr* × *Rr*) produce an offspring with genotype *rr* (½, or 50%). Then calculate the chance that *yy* × *Yy* parents produce a *yy* offspring (½, or 50%). Multiply the two probabilities to calculate the probability that both events occur simultaneously: ½ × ½ = ¼, or 25%. See section 10.4 for more on the product rule.

How to Solve a Genetics Problem: X-Linked Gene

Sample problem: Hemophilia is caused by an X-linked recessive allele. If a man who has hemophilia marries a healthy woman who is not a carrier, what is the chance that their child will have hemophilia?

1. **Write a key.** Pick ONE letter to represent the gene in your problem. Use the capital form of your letter to symbolize the dominant allele; use the lowercase letter to symbolize the recessive allele.

   Sample: The dominant allele is *H;* the recessive allele is *h*. Because these alleles are on the X chromosome, inheritance will differ between males and females. It is therefore best to designate the chromosomes and alleles together as X^H and X^h.

2. **Summarize the problem's information.** Make a table listing the phenotypes and genotypes of both parents.

   Sample:

	Male	Female
Phenotype	Has hemophilia	Healthy
Genotype	X^h Y	$X^H X^H$

3. **Sketch the parental chromosomes and gametes.** Use the genotypes in your table to draw the alleles onto chromosomes. Then draw short arrows to show the chromosomes moving into separate gametes for each parent.

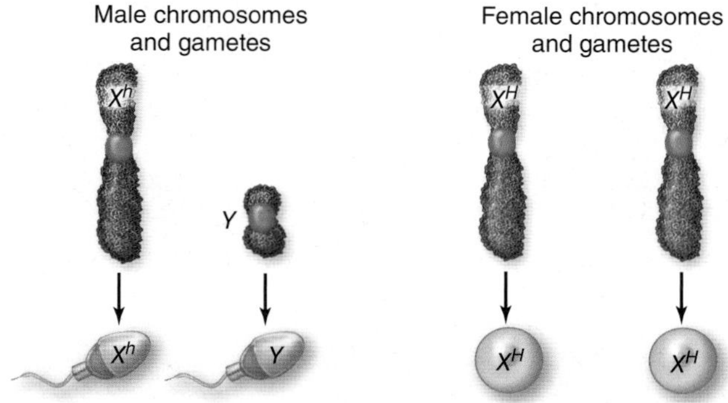

4. **Make a Punnett square.** Arrange the gametes you sketched in step #3 along the edges of the square; fill in the genotypes of the offspring.

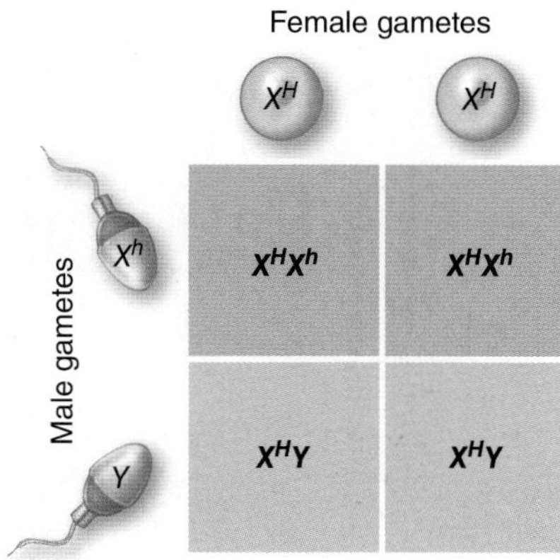

5. **Calculate the genotypic ratio.** Count the number of squares that contain each offspring genotype.

   Sample: 2 $X^H X^h$; 2 X^H Y

6. **Calculate the phenotypic ratio.** Count the number of squares that correspond to each possible phenotype.

   Sample: 2 female carriers; 2 healthy males

7. **Calculate the probability of each phenotype.** Divide each number in step #6 by 4 (the total number of squares) and multiply by 100.

   Sample: 50% probability that a child will be a female carrier; 50% probability that a child will be a healthy male. No child, male or female, will have hemophilia.

11 DNA Technology

Learning Outline

Carbon Copies. Tabouli, left, plays with her sibling, Baba Ganoush. A private company produced the identical kittens by cloning a 1-year-old cat.

Learn How to Learn

Write Your Own Test Questions

Have you ever tried putting yourself in your instructor's place by writing your own multiple-choice test questions? It's a great way to pull the pieces of a chapter together. The easiest questions to write are based on definitions and vocabulary, but those will not always be the most useful. Try to think of questions that integrate multiple ideas or that apply the concepts in a chapter. Write 10 questions, and then let a classmate answer them. You'll probably both learn something new.

What's the Point?

Thanks to more than a century of scientific research, we now understand DNA's structure and function, and we know how DNA passes from generation to generation. We can also manipulate DNA in many ways: we can copy it, figure out its sequence of nucleotides, switch it on and off, and search for specific pieces of it inside a living cell. We can also cut and paste it, transferring genes from one species to another.

The application of these DNA technology tools can produce outcomes that some might consider frivolous, such as the creation of a glow-in-the-dark pet fish. This animal contains a gene, originally isolated from a sea anemone, that encodes a fluorescent protein. But other applications of DNA technology are anything but silly. As you will learn in this chapter, the ability to manipulate DNA can help us solve crimes, save lives, and learn more about our place in the tree of life, among many other worthy goals.

11.1 DNA Technology Is Changing the World

The title of this section is not an exaggeration: DNA-based technologies have affected nearly every imaginable facet of society. **DNA technology** is a broad term that usually means the manipulation of genes for some practical purpose. This chapter describes some of the ways in which DNA technology has become a powerful tool in research, medicine, agriculture, criminal justice, and many other fields.

DNA technology became possible only after biologists discovered the structure and function of DNA. Recall from chapter 7 that the DNA double helix is composed of nucleotides and that the function of DNA is to provide the "recipes" for the cell's proteins (figure 11.1). As described in chapter 8, enzymes copy these recipes as a cell prepares to divide, so that nearly every cell in a multicellular organism carries the same DNA sequence.

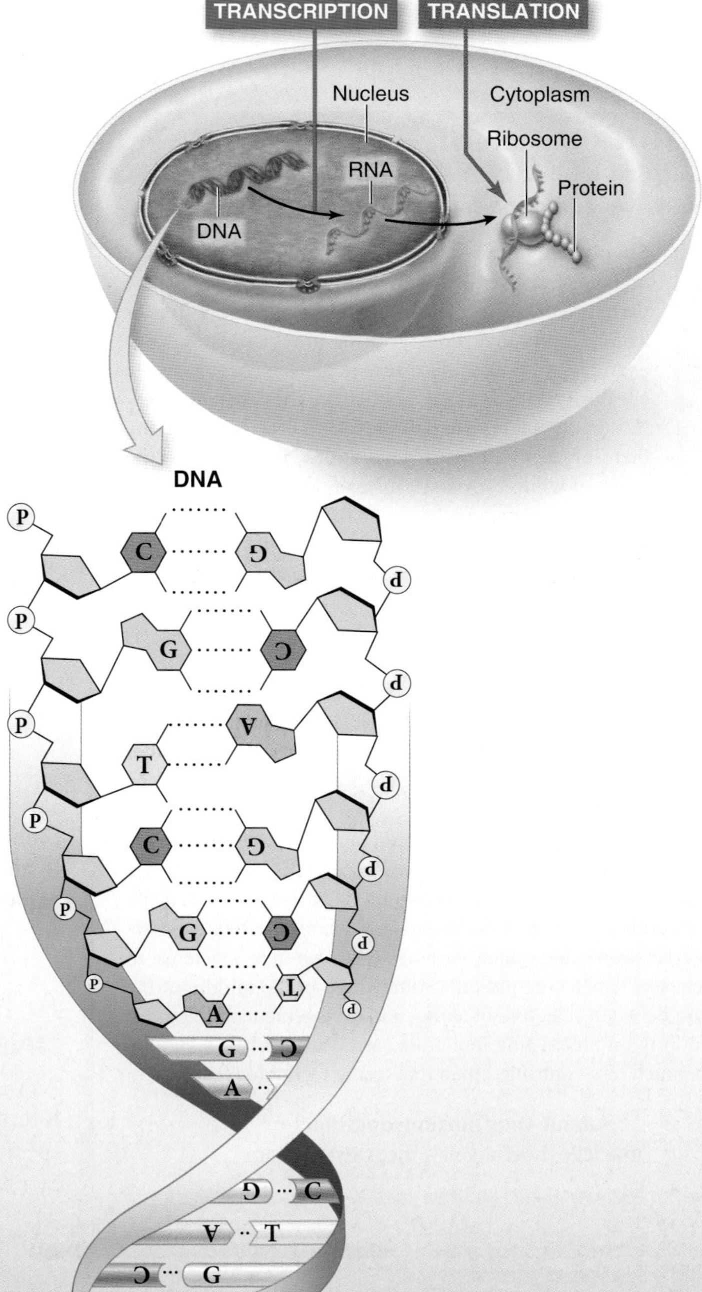

Figure 11.1 DNA Structure and Function. The DNA double helix specifies which proteins a cell can make. Thanks to the tools of DNA technology, biologists can add new DNA to a cell, determine DNA's sequence, copy it, or use it to identify an individual.

We have also learned that each person inherits a unique DNA sequence from his or her parents. As a result, with the exception of identical twins, each person is genetically different. Yet chapter 10 showed how we can trace the inheritance of particular alleles from child to parent to grandparent, and so on. Using this same logic, it is easy to see the power of DNA as a tool for tracing evolutionary history. Throughout the billions of years of life's history, descent with modification has produced countless unique species, each with its own adaptations but still displaying its relationship to the others in its DNA.

DNA technology applies these facts (and many more) to open entirely new ways to learn about life's history, to prevent and relieve human suffering, to protect the environment, and to enforce the law. As you will see, many of the more familiar applications of DNA technology are in medicine. For example, technicians can test a person's DNA for many alleles associated with inherited illnesses, marking a huge advance in disease screening and diagnosis. Stem cells often make headlines as well, especially because the ability to manipulate gene expression in these cells may offer treatments for diseases that presently have no cure.

Many people also know that genetically modified organisms (often abbreviated GMOs) have made their way into the human food supply, mostly in the form of herbicide- and insect-resistant crop plants. Another familiar use of DNA technology is DNA profiling, which has become a powerful tool in convicting murderers, rapists, and other violent criminals. The same technology has also proved the innocence of more than 250 people who were wrongfully convicted and served time in prison for crimes they did not commit.

As helpful as DNA technology can be, the ability to manipulate DNA also carries both risks and ethical questions. This chapter describes not only some of the tools and applications but also some of the downsides of DNA technology.

Burning Questions

Is selective breeding the same as genetic engineering?

Simply put, the answer to this question is no. Selective breeding, also called artificial selection, yields new varieties of plants and animals by selecting for or against traits that already occur in a population. For example, suppose that researchers want to create carrots lacking orange pigments. They would allow those rare plants with pale carrots to breed only among themselves. Over many generations, the result will be a line of white carrots. If, instead, only the most darkly pigmented plants are bred, the offspring might include red or purple carrots. Breeders used these selective breeding strategies to develop the rainbow of carrot colors shown at left.

Introducing new DNA—genetic engineering—is a totally different way to create new plant and animal varieties. We have already seen, for instance, that Bt corn plants contain genes that were originally isolated from bacteria (see section 10.10). Likewise, some transgenic bacteria produce insulin and other human proteins, thanks to our ability to transfer DNA from one species to another.

A third technique for developing new varieties of plants and animals is random mutagenesis. Researchers use chemicals or radiation to induce genetic mutations in an organism's DNA, which sometimes causes interesting new characteristics to arise. Figure 7.16 shows three plant varieties that owe their existence to mutagenesis. This technique falls somewhere in the middle of the spectrum between selective breeding and transgenic technology. It does not rely on preexisting mutations, as does selective breeding, but it is much less controlled than transgenic technology.

Submit your burning question to:
marielle_hoefnagels@mcgraw-hill.com

11.1 Mastering Concepts

1. What is DNA technology?
2. In what fields is DNA technology useful?

11.2 DNA Technology's Tools Apply to Individual Genes or Entire Genomes

Some applications of DNA technology require moving one gene from one cell to another; others require comparisons among multiple genomes. This section explores a few of the tools that biologists use to manipulate everything from short stretches of DNA to the entire genetic makeup of a cell.

A. Transgenic Organisms Contain DNA from Other Species

As we saw in chapter 7, virtually all species use the same genetic code. It therefore makes sense that one type of organism can express a gene from another species, even if the two are distantly related. Biologists take advantage of this fact by coaxing cells to take up **recombinant DNA,** which is genetic material that has been spliced together from multiple types of organisms. A **transgenic organism** is an individual that receives recombinant DNA.

Scientists first accomplished this feat of "genetic engineering" in *Escherichia coli* bacteria in the 1970s, but many microbes, plants, and animals have since been genetically modified. When cells containing the recombinant DNA divide, all of their daughter cells also harbor the new genes. These transgenic organisms express their new genes just as they do their own, producing the desired protein along with all of the others that they normally make. (Note that new varieties of animals and plants may also come from selective breeding. These organisms, however, are not transgenic, as described in this chapter's Burning Question.)

Transgenic Bacteria and Yeasts How do scientists create a transgenic organism? The first step is to obtain DNA from a donor cell—usually a bacterium, plant, or animal (figure 11.2). The next step is to insert this source DNA into a **plasmid,** a small circle of double-stranded DNA.

To create the recombinant plasmid, the researchers use **restriction enzymes,** which are proteins that cut double-stranded DNA at a specific base sequence. Some restriction enzymes generate single-stranded ends that stick to each other by complementary base pairing. When plasmid and donor DNA are cut with the same restriction enzyme and the fragments are mixed, the single-stranded ends of some plasmids stick to the ends of the donor DNA.

The last step is to move the recombinant plasmid into a recipient cell. Zapping a bacterial cell with electricity opens temporary holes through which the DNA can enter. Alternatively, "gene guns" shoot DNA-coated pellets directly into cells. Plasmids can also be packaged inside a fatty bubble that fuses with the recipient cell's membrane, or they can be loaded into a virus that then infects the recipient cell. ▸ viruses, p. 125

In the pharmaceutical industry, transgenic bacteria produce many types of drugs, including human insulin to treat diabetes, blood clotting factors to treat hemophilia, immune system biochemicals, and fertility hormones. Other genetically modified bacteria produce the amino acid phenylalanine, which is part of the artificial sweetener aspartame. Still others degrade petroleum, pesticides, and other soil pollutants. Transgenic yeast cells produce a milk-curdling enzyme called chymosin used by many U.S. cheese producers. ▸ artificial sweeteners, p. 36

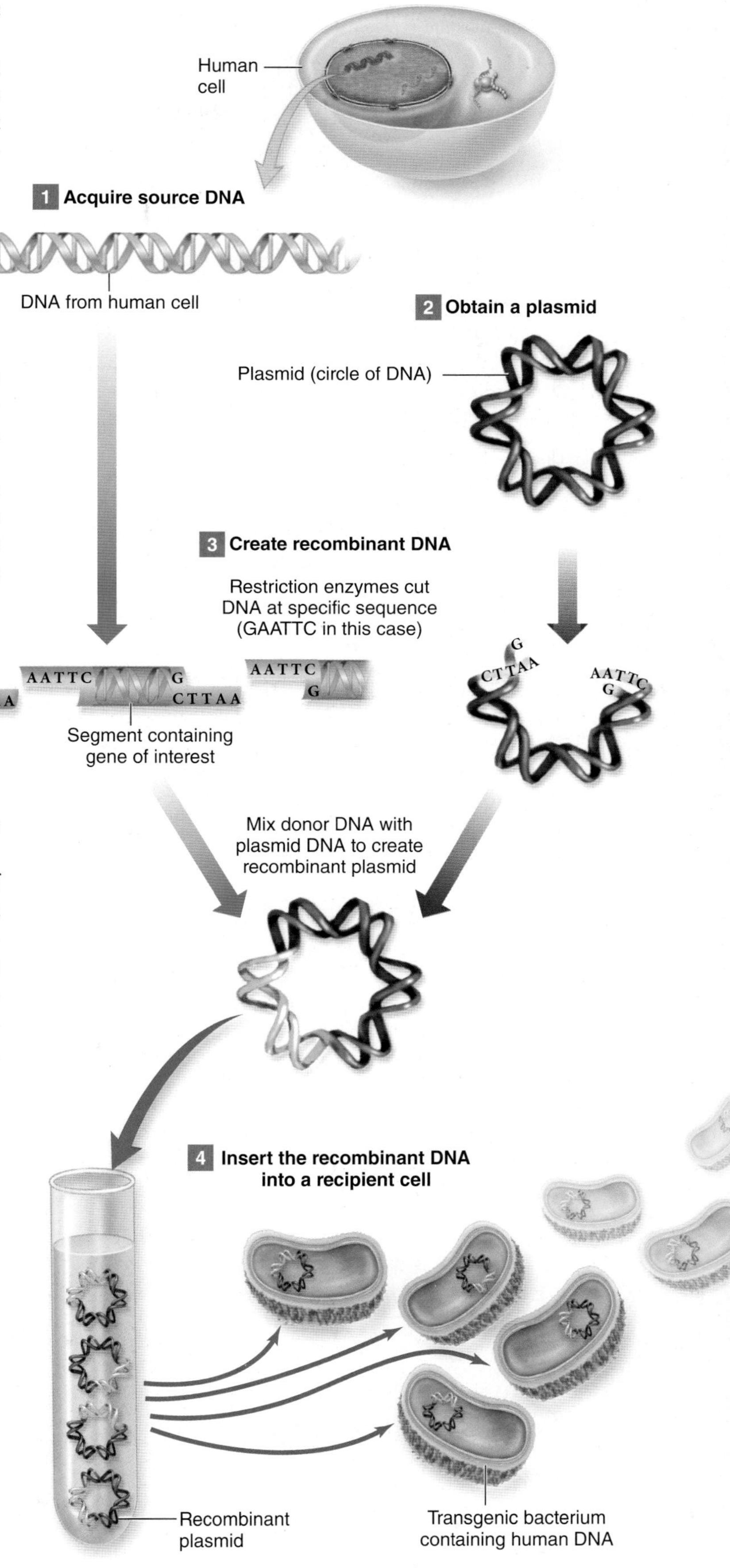
Human cell
1 Acquire source DNA
DNA from human cell
2 Obtain a plasmid
Plasmid (circle of DNA)
3 Create recombinant DNA
Restriction enzymes cut DNA at specific sequence (GAATTC in this case)
G
CTTAA
AATTC
G
CTTAA
AATTC
G
Segment containing gene of interest
Mix donor DNA with plasmid DNA to create recombinant plasmid
4 Insert the recombinant DNA into a recipient cell
Recombinant plasmid
Transgenic bacterium containing human DNA

Figure 11.2 Transgenic Bacteria. The first steps in creating a transgenic bacterium are to [1] isolate source DNA and [2] obtain a plasmid. [3] Researchers then use the same restriction enzyme to cut DNA from the donor cell and the plasmid. When the pieces are mixed, the "sticky ends" of the DNA fragments join, forming recombinant plasmids. [4] After the plasmid is delivered into a bacterium, it is mass-produced as the bacterium divides.

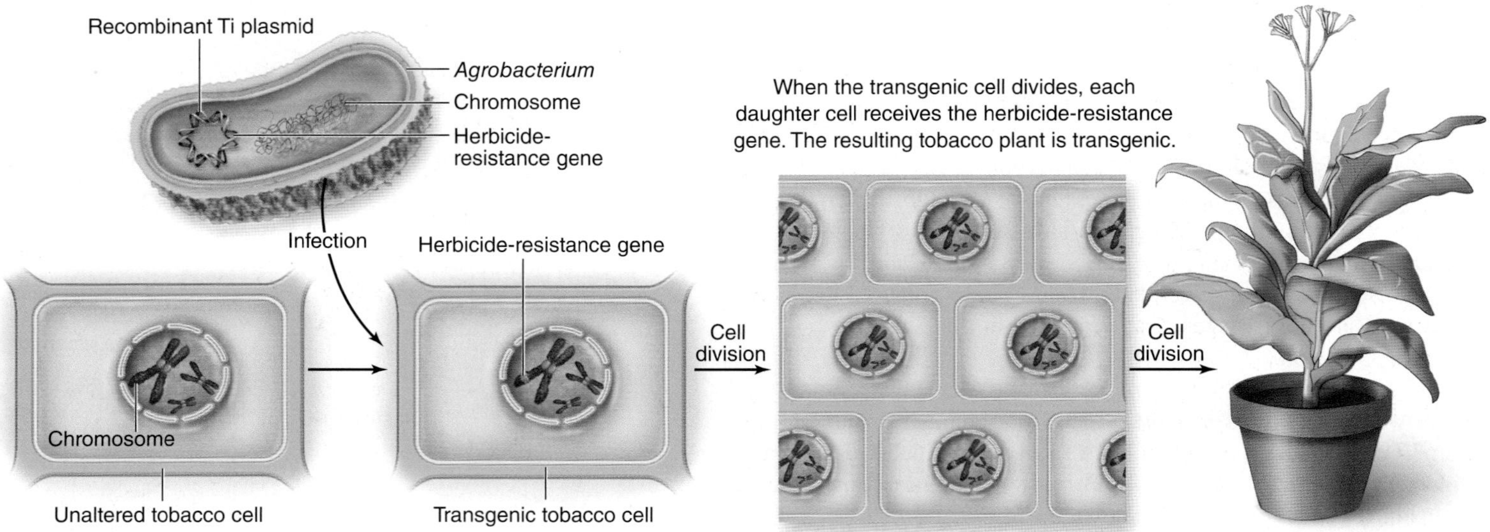

Figure 11.3 Transgenic Plant. This genetically modified *Agrobacterium* cell contains a recombinant Ti plasmid encoding a gene that confers herbicide resistance. The bacterium infects a tobacco plant cell, inserting the Ti plasmid into the plant cell's DNA. The transgenic plant cells can be grown into tobacco plants that express the herbicide resistance gene in every cell.

Transgenic Plants One tool for introducing new genes into plant cells is a bacterium called *Agrobacterium tumefaciens* (figure 11.3). In nature, these bacteria enter a plant at a wound and inject a plasmid into the host's cells. The plasmid normally encodes genes that stimulate the infected plant cells to divide rapidly, producing a tumorlike gall that produces food and habitat for the bacteria. (The name of the plasmid, Ti, stands for "tumor inducing.")

Scientists can replace some of the plasmid's own genes with other DNA, such as a gene encoding a protein that confers herbicide resistance. They allow the transgenic *Agrobacterium* to inject these recombinant plasmids into plant cells. All plants derived from the infected cells should express the new herbicide-resistance gene. The farmer who plants the crop can therefore spray the field with herbicides, killing weeds without harming the genetically modified plants.

Biologists have used a similar technique to produce corn and cotton varieties that produce their own insecticides (see section 10.10). The insect-killing protein originated in a bacterium called *Bacillus thuringiensis,* abbreviated Bt. Any insect that nibbles on a plant expressing the Bt protein dies. These genetically modified Bt crops save farmers time and money because they greatly reduce the need for sprayed insecticides.

Besides tolerating herbicides or producing insecticides, transgenic crop plants may also resist viral infections, survive harsh environmental conditions, or contain nutrients that they otherwise wouldn't. "Golden Rice," for example, is a genetically engineered rice plant containing DNA from petunias and bacteria. These genes enable it to produce beta-carotene (a vitamin A precursor) and extra iron, making the rice grains more nutritious—and gold in color.

Transgenic Animals So far, we have described the use of DNA technology to genetically modify bacteria and plants. Biologists use a different technique to create transgenic mice and other animals. Typically, they pack recombinant DNA into viruses that can infect a gamete or fertilized egg. As the transgenic animal develops, it carries the foreign genes in every cell.

Transgenic animals have many applications. A glow-in-the-dark fish was the first genetically modified house pet (see the photo on page 199). On a more practical note, a transgenic mouse "model" for a human gene can reveal how a

Figure 11.4 Determining the Sequence of DNA. In the Sanger method of DNA sequencing, complementary copies of an unknown DNA sequence are terminated early because of the addition of chemically modified "terminator" nucleotides. Sorting the fragments by size reveals the sequence.

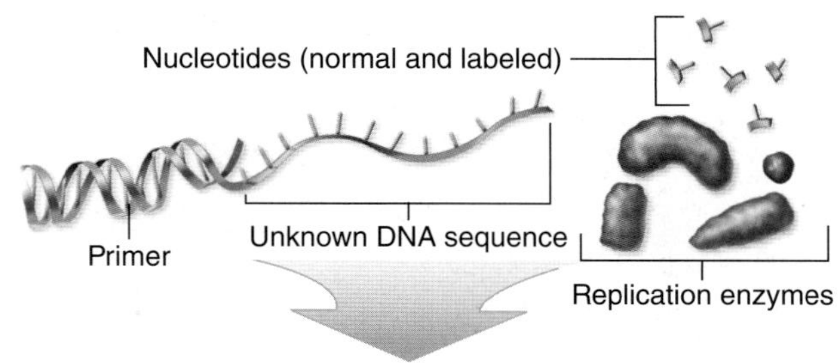
Nucleotides (normal and labeled)
Primer
Unknown DNA sequence
Replication enzymes

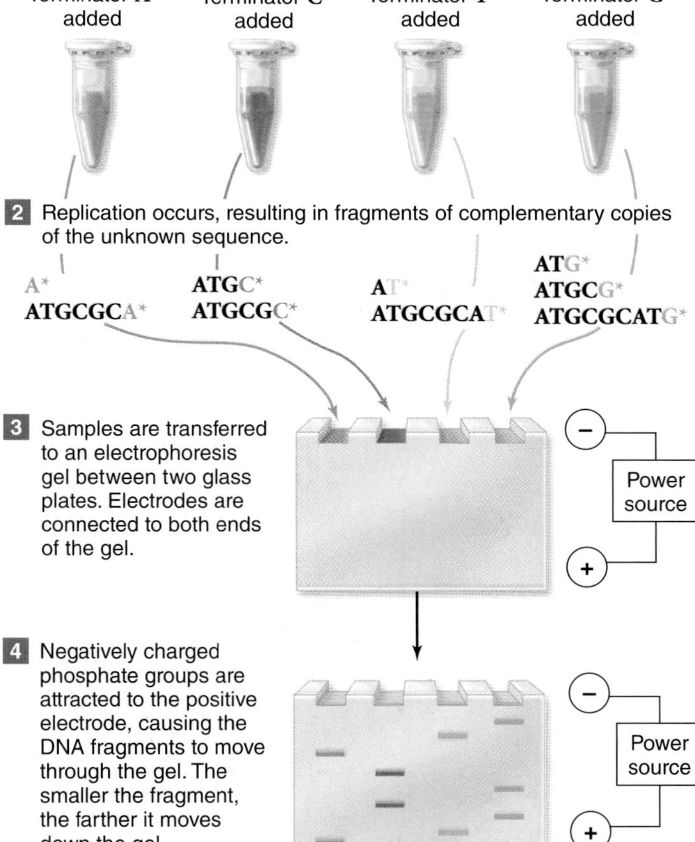
1 Four solutions contain unknown DNA sequence, primers, normal nucleotides (A, C, G, and T), labeled nucleotides, replication enzymes, and a small amount of "terminator" nucleotide.
Terminator A added
Terminator C added
Terminator T added
Terminator G added
2 Replication occurs, resulting in fragments of complementary copies of the unknown sequence.
A*
ATGCGCA*
ATGC*
ATGCGC*
AT*
ATGCGCAT*
ATG*
ATGCG*
ATGCGCATG*
3 Samples are transferred to an electrophoresis gel between two glass plates. Electrodes are connected to both ends of the gel.
Power source
4 Negatively charged phosphate groups are attracted to the positive electrode, causing the DNA fragments to move through the gel. The smaller the fragment, the farther it moves down the gel.
Power source
5 The fragments are read off by size, and the original sequence can be deduced.

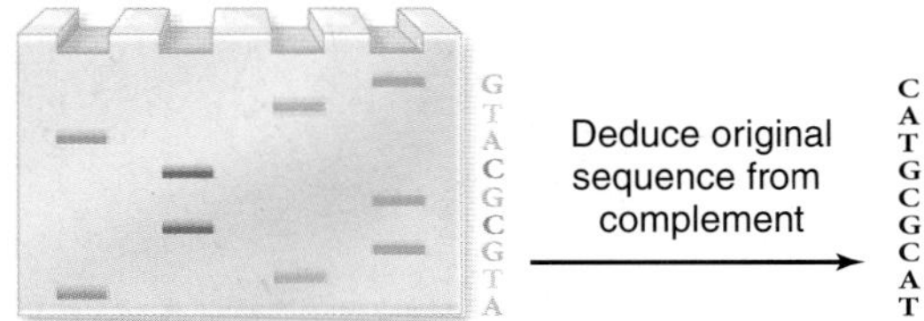
G
T
A
C
G
C
G
T
A
Deduce original sequence from complement
C
A
T
G
C
G
C
A
T

disease begins, enabling researchers to develop drugs that treat the disease in its early stages. Transgenic farm animals can secrete human proteins in their milk or semen, producing abundant supplies of otherwise rare substances that are useful as drugs.

Ethical Issues Although transgenic organisms have many practical uses, some people question whether their benefits outweigh their potential dangers. Some fear that ecological disaster could result if genetically modified organisms outcompete or cross-breed with other species in the wild. Others worry that unfamiliar protein combinations in genetically modified crops could trigger food allergies. Still others object to the "unnatural" practice of combining genes from organisms that would never breed in nature.

B. DNA Sequencing Reveals the Order of Bases

Scientists often want to know the nucleotide sequences of genes, chromosomes, or entire genomes. Researchers can use DNA sequence information to predict protein sequences, as described in chapter 7, or they can compare DNA sequences among species to determine evolutionary relationships. How do investigators get the DNA sequence information they need?

Modern DNA sequencing instruments use a highly automated version of a basic technique Frederick Sanger developed in 1977 (figure 11.4). This process uses the DNA polymerase enzyme to generate a series of DNA fragments that are complementary to the DNA being sequenced. The primers in the reaction mixes are necessary because DNA polymerase can only attach nucleotides to an existing strand. Also included are low concentrations of specially modified nucleotides. Each time DNA polymerase incorporates one of these modified nucleotides, the new DNA chain stops growing. The result is a group of fragments that differ in length by one end base. Once a collection of such pieces is generated, a technique called **electrophoresis** separates the fragments by size.

Sanger used radioactive labels to visualize the DNA, but researchers today use fluorescent labels, one for each of the four base types. The data appear as a sequential readout of the wavelengths of the fluorescence from the labels (figure 11.5).

The most famous application of DNA sequencing technology has been the Human Genome Project. This worldwide effort was aimed at sequencing all 3.2 billion base pairs in the human genome. The sequence, which was completed in 2003, revealed unexpected complexities. For example, it soon became clear that only about 1.5% of the human genome sequence actually encodes protein.

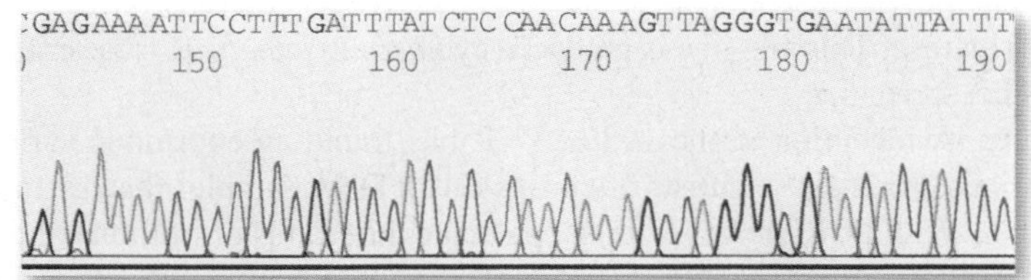
GAGAAAATTCCTTTGATTTATCTCCAACAAAGTTAGGGTGAATATTATTT
150 160 170 180 190

Figure 11.5 Another Way to Read DNA. A computerized readout of a DNA sequence, made possible by fluorescent labels.

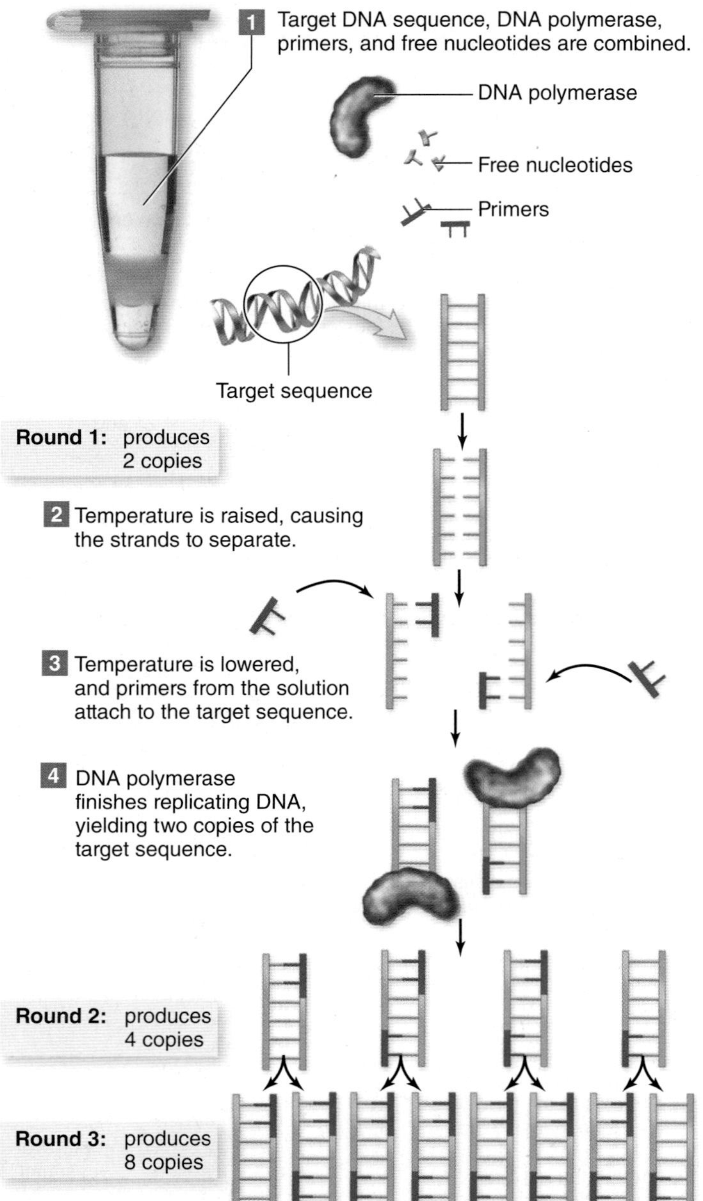
1 Target DNA sequence, DNA polymerase, primers, and free nucleotides are combined.
DNA polymerase
Free nucleotides
Primers
Target sequence
Round 1: produces 2 copies
2 Temperature is raised, causing the strands to separate.
3 Temperature is lowered, and primers from the solution attach to the target sequence.
4 DNA polymerase finishes replicating DNA, yielding two copies of the target sequence.
Round 2: produces 4 copies
Round 3: produces 8 copies

Figure 11.6 Polymerase Chain Reaction. In PCR, primers bracket a DNA sequence of interest. A heat-stable DNA polymerase uses these primers, and plenty of nucleotides, to build up millions of copies of the target sequence.

What does the other 98.5% of the human genome do? This question has several answers. Some of the DNA encodes rRNA, tRNA, and the regulatory sequences that control gene expression. Human chromosomes also contain many pseudogenes. These DNA sequences are very similar to protein-encoding genes and they are transcribed, but the mRNA is not translated into protein. Pseudogenes may be remnants of old genes that once functioned in our nonhuman ancestors but that mutated too much to encode a working protein.

The human genome is also riddled with highly repetitive sequences that have no known function. The most abundant type of repeat is a transposable element, or transposon for short, a DNA sequence that can "jump" within the genome. Transposons make up about 45% of human DNA. The genome also contains many tandem repeats (or "satellite DNAs"), sequences of one or more bases repeated many times without interruption, such as CACACA or ATTCGATTCG. As described in section 11.2D, DNA profiling technology measures variation in these areas.

Researchers are comparing the human genome to the DNA sequences of dozens of other species, from bacteria and archaea to protists, fungi, plants, and other animals. The similarities and differences have yielded unprecedented insights into the genes that unite all life and those that make each species unique. The Investigating Life essay in section 11.5 highlights one example of what biologists can learn by comparing the human genome with that of the chimpanzee, our closest living relative.

C. PCR Replicates DNA in a Test Tube

An extremely powerful and useful tool, the **polymerase chain reaction (PCR),** taps into the cell's DNA copying machinery to produce millions of copies of a DNA sequence of interest. PCR is useful whenever only a small amount of DNA is available. Thanks to this tool, a single hair or a few skin cells left at a crime scene can yield enough genetic material to reveal a person's unique DNA profile.

PCR rapidly replicates a selected sequence of DNA in a test tube. As illustrated at the top of figure 11.6, a PCR reaction tube includes the target DNA to be replicated, DNA polymerase enzymes, free DNA nucleotides, and two types of short, laboratory-made primers that are complementary to opposite ends of the target sequence.

PCR occurs in an automated device called a thermal cycler that controls key temperature changes. In the first step of PCR, heat separates the two strands of the target DNA. Next, the temperature is lowered, and the short primers attach to the separated target strands by complementary base pairing. DNA polymerase adds nucleotides to the primers and builds sequences complementary to the target sequence. The new strands then act as templates in the next round of replication, which is initiated immediately by raising the temperature to separate the strands once more. The number of pieces of DNA doubles with every round of PCR.

The double-stranded DNA molecules become "unzipped" at about 95°C, which is nearly the boiling point of water. This temperature would denature most DNA polymerase enzymes, but PCR uses a heat-tolerant variety such as *Taq* polymerase. This enzyme is produced by *Thermus aquaticus,* a bacterium that inhabits hot springs.

Since its invention in the 1980s, PCR has found an enormous variety of applications. Forensic scientists often work with DNA samples that are too tiny to analyze. With PCR, however, they can make thousands or millions of copies of a particular sequence. Once amplified, the DNA can easily be examined to help establish family relationships, identify human remains, convict criminals, and exonerate the falsely accused. When used to amplify the DNA of microorganisms, viruses, and other parasites, PCR is important in agriculture, veterinary medicine, environmental science, and human health care. In genetics, PCR is both a crucial basic research tool and a way to identify disease-causing genes.

PCR's greatest weakness, ironically, is its exquisite sensitivity. A sample contaminated by leftover DNA from a previous PCR reaction or by a stray eyelash dropped from the technician running the reaction can yield a false result.

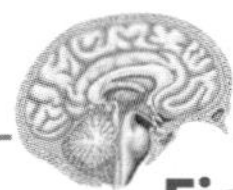

Figure It Out

Suppose a researcher needs a million copies of a viral gene. She decides to use PCR on a sample of fluid containing one copy of the gene. If one round of PCR takes 2 minutes, how long will it take the researcher to obtain her million-fold amplification?

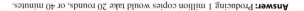

Answer: Producing 1 million copies would take 20 rounds, or 40 minutes.

D. DNA Profiling Detects Genetic Differences

Rather than sequencing and comparing entire genomes, **DNA profiling** uses just the most variable parts of the genome to detect genetic differences between individuals. Applications range from settling paternity claims to solving crimes to identifying the remains of long-dead soldiers.

The most common approach to DNA profiling is to examine **short tandem repeats (STRs),** which are sequences of four to five nucleotides that are repeated in noncoding regions of DNA. These sites tend to vary in a population (figure 11.7). That is, for a given STR site, one individual might have five instances of the repeated nucleotides, whereas another person might have six or seven.

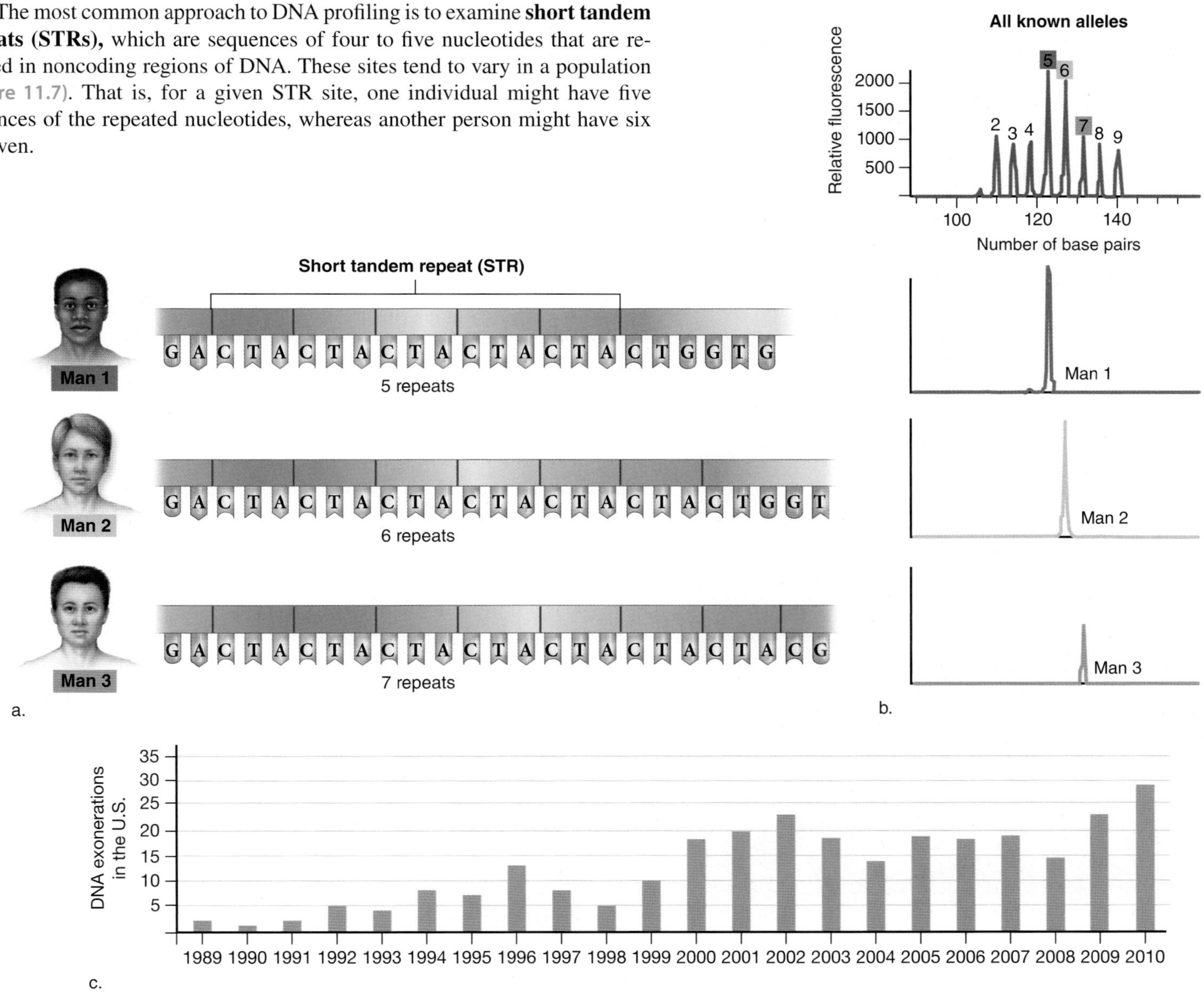

Figure 11.7 DNA Profiling. (a) Modern DNA profiling techniques detect differences in the number of short tandem repeats (STRs) in parts of the human genome that are known to be genetically variable. (b) Results for one STR site for each of three men. (c) In the United States, DNA evidence has exonerated more than 250 prisoners who were serving time for crimes they did not commit.

To generate a DNA profile, a technician extracts DNA from a person's cells and uses PCR to amplify the DNA at each of 13 STR sites, leaving the rest of the DNA alone. A fluorescent label is incorporated into the DNA at the STR sites during the PCR reaction. The technician can then use electrophoresis and a fluorescence imaging system to determine the number of repeats at each site.

Statistical analysis plays a large role in DNA profiling. For example, suppose that DNA extracted from a hair found on a murder victim's body matches DNA from a suspect's white blood cells at all 13 STR sites. What is the probability that the two matching DNA patterns come from the same person—the suspect—rather than from two individuals who happen to share the same DNA sequences? To find out, investigators consult databases that compile the frequency of each STR variant in the population. The statistical analysis suggests that the probability that any two individuals have the same 13 markers is one in 250 trillion.

In addition to STRs in nuclear DNA, analysis of mitochondrial DNA is also sometimes useful. Mitochondrial DNA is typically only about 16,500 base pairs long, far shorter than the billions of nucleotides in nuclear DNA. But because each cell contains multiple mitochondria, each of which contains many DNA molecules, mitochondria can often yield useful information even when nuclear DNA is badly degraded. Investigators extract mitochondrial DNA from hair, bones, and teeth, then use PCR to amplify the variable regions for sequencing.

Because everyone inherits mitochondria only from his or her mother, this technique cannot discriminate between siblings. It is very useful, however, for verifying the relationship between woman and child. For example, children who were kidnapped during infancy can be matched to their biological mothers or grandmothers. The study of human evolution also has benefited from mitochondrial DNA analysis. ▸ human evolution, p. 347

11.2 Mastering Concepts

1. What are some uses for transgenic organisms?
2. What are the steps in creating a transgenic organism?
3. How do researchers determine a sequence of DNA?
4. What is the function of the 98.5% of the human genome that does not encode protein?
5. How does PCR work, and why is it useful?
6. How are short tandem repeats used in DNA profiling?
7. Why do nuclear DNA and mitochondrial DNA provide different information?

a.

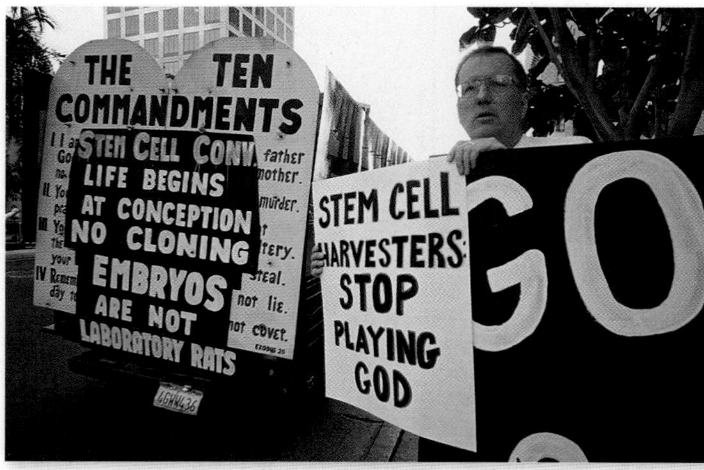

b.

Figure 11.8 Stem Cell Controversy. Debates over stem cells often pit (a) people such as actor Michael J. Fox who advocate the use of embryonic stem cells in medicine against (b) people with moral objections.

11.3 Stem Cells and Cloning Add New Ways to Copy Cells and Organisms

The public debate over stem cells and cloning combines science, philosophy, religion, and politics in ways that few other modern issues do (figure 11.8). What is the biology behind the headlines?

A. Stem Cells Divide to Form Multiple Cell Types

A human develops from a single fertilized egg into an embryo and then a fetus—and eventually into an infant, child, and adult—thanks to mitotic cell division. As development continues, more and more cells become permanently specialized into muscle, skin, liver, brain, and other cell types. All contain the same DNA, but some genes become irreversibly "turned off" in specialized cells. Once committed to a fate, a mature cell rarely reverts to another type. ▸ regulation of gene expression, p. 121

Animal development therefore relies on stem cells. In general, a stem cell is any undifferentiated cell that can give rise to specialized cell types. When a stem cell divides mitotically to yield two daughter cells, one remains a stem cell, able to divide again. The other specializes.

Animals have two general categories of stem cells: embryonic and adult (figure 11.9). **Embryonic stem cells** give rise to all cell types in the body (including adult stem cells) and are therefore called "totipotent"; *toti-* comes from the Latin word for "entire." **Adult stem cells** are more differentiated and produce a limited subset of cell types. For example, stem cells in the skin replace cells lost through wear and tear, and stem cells in the bone marrow produce all of the cell types that make up blood. Adult stem cells are "pluripotent"; *pluri-* means "many" in Latin.

Stem cells are important in biological and medical research. With the correct combination of chemical signals, medical researchers should theoretically be able to coax stem cells to divide in the laboratory and produce blood cells, neurons, or any other cell type. Many people believe that stem cells hold special promise as treatments for neurological disorders such as Parkinson disease and spinal cord injuries, since neurons ordinarily do not divide to replace injured or diseased tissue. Stem cell therapies may also conquer diabetes, heart disease, and many other illnesses that are currently incurable.

The practical benefits would extend beyond treating illness. Currently, pharmaceutical companies test new drugs primarily on whole organisms, such as mice and rats. The ability to test on just kidney or brain cells, for example, would allow researchers to better predict the likely side effects of a new drug. It might also reduce the need for laboratory animals.

Both embryonic and adult stem cells have advantages and disadvantages for medical use. Embryonic stem cells are extremely versatile, but a patient's immune system would probably reject tissues derived from another individual's cells. In addition, research on embryonic stem cells is controversial because of their origin. In fertility clinics, technicians fertilize eggs *in vitro,* and only a few of the resulting embryos are ever implanted into a woman's uterus. Researchers destroy some of the "spare" embryos at about 5 days old to harvest the stem cells. (The other embryos are either stored for possible later implantation or discarded.) Many people consider it unethical to use human embryos in medical research, even if those embryos would otherwise have been thrown away.

Biologists are also investigating adult stem cells in skin, bone marrow, the lining of the small intestine, and other locations in the body. A patient's immune system would not reject tissues derived from his or her own adult stem cells. These stem cells are less abundant than embryonic stem cells, however, and they usually give rise to only some cell types.

New laboratory techniques may eliminate some of these drawbacks. Researchers have discovered how to induce adult cells to behave like embryonic stem cells. This technique could allow differentiated cells taken from an adult to be turned into stem cells, which could then be coaxed to develop into any other cell type. Time will tell how useful these so-called "induced pluripotent stem cells" will be or whether they will match the medical potential of embryonic stem cells.

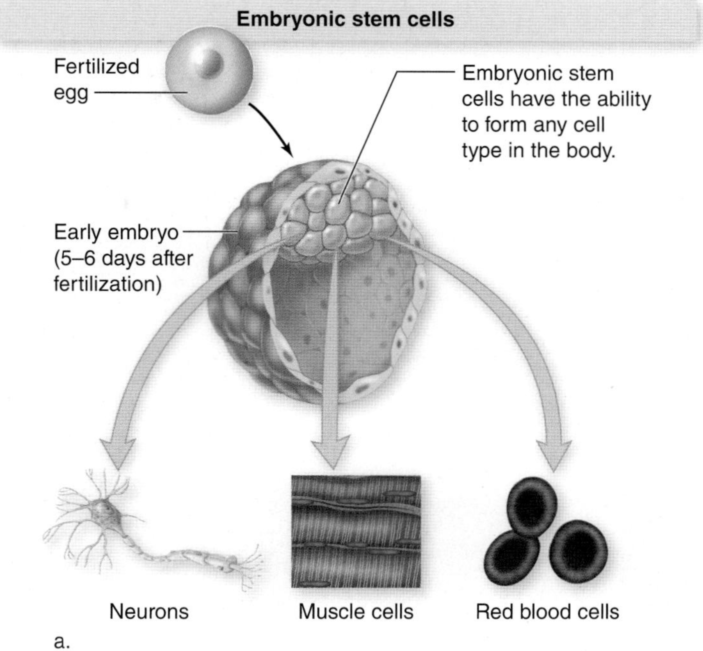

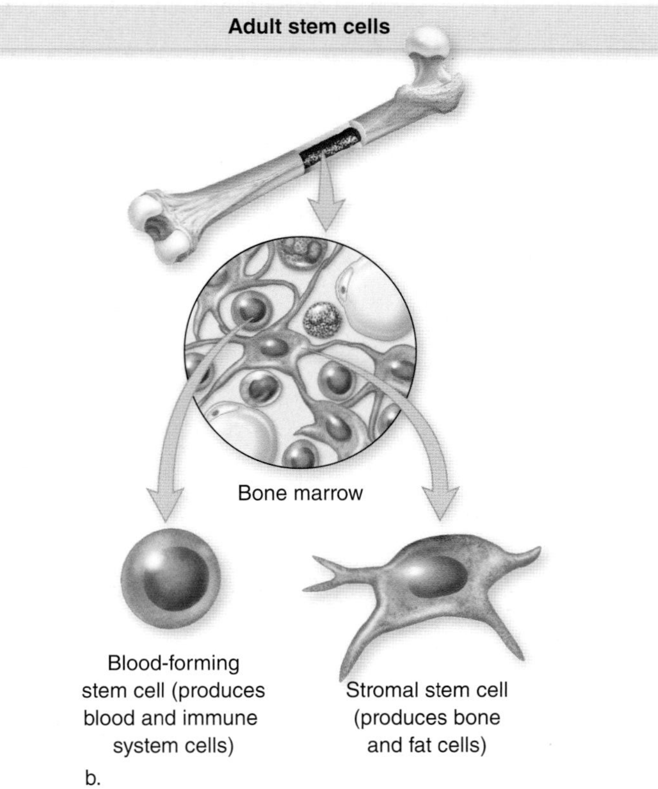

Figure 11.9 **Stem Cells.** (a) Human embryonic stem cells are derived from a ball of cells that forms several days after fertilization. These stem cells give rise to all of the body's cell types. (b) The adult body also contains stem cells, but they may not have the potential to develop into as many different cell types as do embryonic stem cells.

Figure 11.10 Cloning in a Dish. When plant tissue is cultured with the correct combination of hormones and nutrients, it gives rise to genetically identical plantlets.

B. Cloning Creates Identical Copies of an Organism

Imagine being able to grow a new individual, genetically identical to yourself, from a bit of skin or the root of a hair. Although humans cannot reproduce in this way, many organisms do the equivalent. They develop parts of themselves into genetically identical individuals—clones—that then detach and live independently.

Cloning, or asexual reproduction, has been a part of life since the first cell arose billions of years ago. Long before sex evolved, each individual simply reproduced by itself, without a partner to contribute half the offspring's genetic information.

In its simplest form, asexual reproduction consists of the division of a single cell. In bacteria, archaea, and single-celled eukaryotes such as *Amoeba,* the cell's DNA replicates, and then the cell splits into two identical, individual organisms. Although the details of cell division differ between prokaryotes and eukaryotes, the result is the same: one individual becomes two.

Most plants, fungi, and animals reproduce sexually, but at least some organisms in each kingdom also use asexual reproduction. This strategy is especially common in plants and fungi. Hobbyists and commercial plant growers clone everything from fruit trees to African violets in petri dishes (figure 11.10); cuttings from stems, leaves, and roots also can yield new plants. Many fungi produce countless microscopic spores on bread, cheese, and every other imaginable food supply (see section 15.5). Asexual reproduction is much less common in animals, but sponges, coral animals, hydra, and jellyfishes all can "bud" new individuals that break away from the parent.

Unlike many other organisms, mammals do not naturally clone themselves. In 1996, however, researcher Ian Wilmut and his colleagues in Scotland used a new procedure to create Dolly the sheep, the first clone of an adult mammal. The researchers used a technique called **somatic cell nuclear transfer** (figure 11.11). First, they obtained the nucleus from a cell removed from a donor sheep's mammary gland. (The name of the cloning technique derives in part from the fact that mammary glands consist of *somatic* cells, which are body cells that do not give rise to sperm or eggs.) They then transferred this "donor" nucleus to a sheep's egg cell whose own nucleus had been removed. The resulting cell divided mitotically to form an embryo, which the researchers implanted in a surrogate mother's uterus. The embryo then developed into a lamb, named Dolly (after country singer Dolly Parton).

Scientifically, this achievement was remarkable because it showed that the DNA from a differentiated somatic cell (in this case, from a mammary gland) could "turn back the clock" and revert to an undifferentiated state. Mitotic cell division then produced every cell in Dolly's body.

Dolly appeared normal, and she gave birth to six healthy lambs via sexual reproduction. But she had arthritis in her hind legs, and she died of lung disease in 2003 at age six. Normally, sheep of Dolly's breed live 11 or 12 years, and her early death fueled speculation that clones will inevitably have an abnormally brief lifespan.

Since Dolly's birth, researchers have used somatic cell nuclear transfer to clone other mammals as well, including dogs, cats, mice, bulls, and a champion horse that had been castrated (and therefore could not reproduce). Cloning may even help rescue endangered species or recover extinct species. For

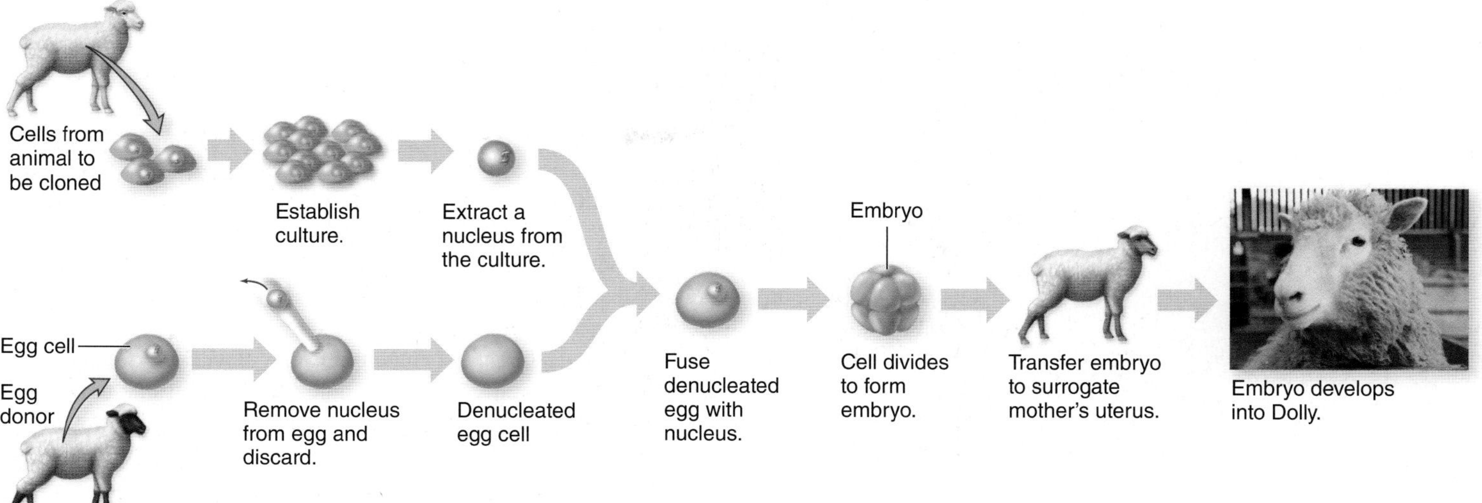

Figure 11.11 Creating Dolly. Biologists cloned an adult female sheep by obtaining a nucleus from a cell of the ewe's udder. They also removed the nucleus from an egg cell. Placing the adult cell's nucleus into the egg yielded a new cell genetically identical to the DNA donor. After being implanted into a surrogate mother sheep, the resulting embryo developed into Dolly.

example, an extinct mountain goat was cloned from preserved DNA, but the animal died shortly after birth.

Many people wonder whether humans can and should be cloned. Reproductive cloning, as achieved with Dolly, could help infertile couples have children. Scientists could also use cloned human embryos as a source of stem cells, which could be used to grow "customized" artificial organs that the patient's immune system would not reject. This application of cloning is called therapeutic cloning.

Despite the potential benefits, however, human cloning carries unresolved ethical questions. For example, most clones die early in development, presumably because the gene regulation mechanisms in an adult cell's nucleus are somehow incompatible with those in the egg cell. Even the tiny percentage of clones that make it to birth often have abnormalities. This difficulty emphasizes the ethical issues surrounding human reproductive cloning. In addition, therapeutic cloning still requires the destruction of an embryo to harvest the stem cells. As we have already seen, many people question the practice of creating human embryos only to destroy them. Finally, both reproductive and therapeutic cloning require unfertilized human eggs. The removal of eggs from a woman's ovaries is costly and poses medical risks.

11.3 Mastering Concepts

1. Describe the differences between embryonic, adult, and induced pluripotent stem cells.
2. What are the potential medical benefits of stem cells?
3. Summarize the steps scientists use to clone an adult mammal.
4. Why is the cloning technique called somatic cell nuclear transfer?

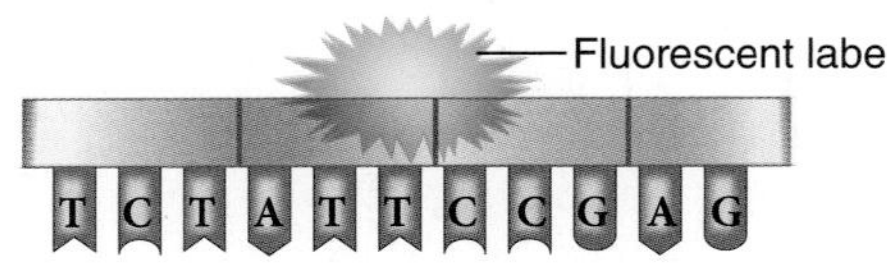

Sequence #1 (complementary to probe)

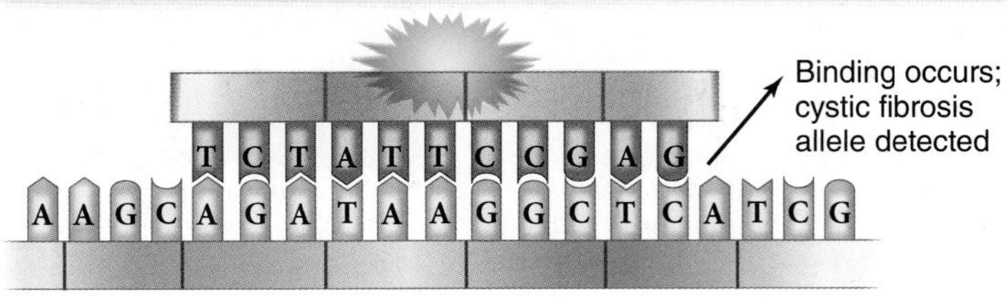

Sequence #2 (not complementary to probe)

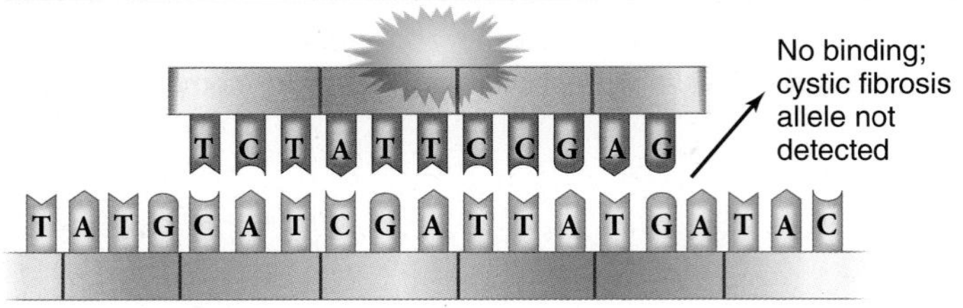

Figure 11.12 **Gene Probe.** Single-stranded DNA labeled with radioactive isotopes or fluorescent compounds helps reveal the presence of complementary single-stranded DNA.

11.4 Many Medical Tests and Procedures Use DNA Technology

The list of human illnesses is long. The top five causes of death include heart disease, stroke, infection, and cancer (see table 18.2); all of these diseases have environmental and genetic components. But some ailments, including cystic fibrosis, hemophilia, Tay-Sachs syndrome, sickle cell disease, and dozens of others, are entirely caused by mutated alleles of single genes. This section describes how the use of DNA technology can help prevent, detect, and treat genetic diseases. Although we use cystic fibrosis as an example, the same techniques are applicable (at least in theory) to any illness associated with a single gene.

A. DNA Probes Detect Specific Sequences

The ability to detect the alleles that cause cystic fibrosis and other genetic illnesses is crucial to the medical applications of DNA technology. At first glance, however, all DNA looks alike: a sequence of A, C, G, and T. With billions of nucleotides in a single cell, how can biologists search through an entire genome to find just the piece they need to "see"?

The answer is a **DNA probe,** a single-stranded sequence of nucleotides that is complementary to a particular known region of DNA (figure 11.12). A typical probe is a short, synthetic strand of DNA that is labeled with either a radioactive isotope or a fluorescent tag. For example, a researcher can construct a probe that is complementary to part of an allele known to be associated with cystic fibrosis. If a region of single-stranded DNA contains a nucleotide sequence that is complementary to the probe, then the probe binds to that region. The radioactivity or wavelength emitted by the probe reveals the presence of the cystic fibrosis allele.

B. Preimplantation Genetic Diagnosis Can Help Prevent Some Diseases

Imagine a young couple that wants a child. Both of the prospective parents know they are symptomless carriers of cystic fibrosis. Can DNA technology help the couple ensure that their baby is free of the disease? The answer is that no one can guarantee a cystic fibrosis-free baby, but a technique called **preimplantation genetic diagnosis (PGD)** can greatly reduce the odds of having an affected child.

The process begins with *in vitro* fertilization (literally, fertilization "in glass"), in which the man's sperm fertilize several of the woman's eggs in a laboratory dish. The resulting zygotes develop into embryos, each consisting of eight genetically identical cells. A technician then selects an embryo for PGD. He or she removes one cell from the embryo (figure 11.13); the loss of this cell will not affect the embryo's subsequent development. DNA extracted from that single cell undergoes PCR, amplifying the region of DNA where the cystic fibrosis gene is located. A DNA probe specific for one or more cystic fibrosis alleles can then determine whether the embryo's cells contain the disease-causing DNA sequences.

If the allele is detected, the embryo can be discarded, and others can be tested. Any embryo that lacks the disease-causing allele is a good candidate to be placed into the woman's body. If the embryo implants into the uterus and develops into a baby, the child is very likely to be born without cystic fibrosis.

There is a small chance, however, that the baby may be born with the disease despite PGD. Human error is one possible explanation. By amplifying

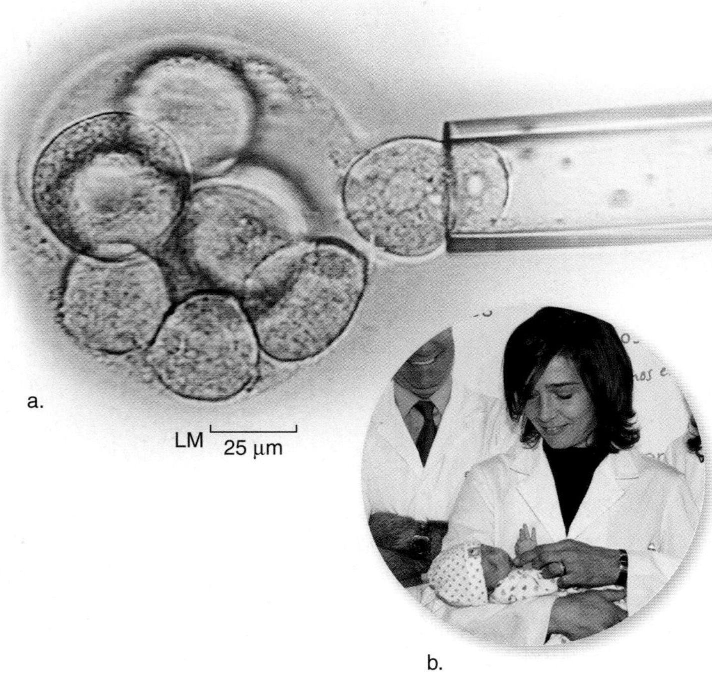

Figure 11.13 **Preimplantation Genetic Diagnosis.** (a) A single cell is removed from a human embryo. (b) A member of a medical team admires a healthy child born after PGD was used to screen for a type of muscular dystrophy that runs in the baby's family.

DNA sequences that occur in just one or two copies from a single cell, PGD pushes PCR to its limits. As we have already seen, PCR is extremely sensitive to contamination; stray DNA that is accidentally amplified can lead to a false result. A second explanation relates to the fact that researchers have identified hundreds of mutations that can cause cystic fibrosis. PGD tests for the most common disease-causing alleles, but the baby may have inherited rare variants that the test cannot detect.

C. Genetic Testing Can Detect Existing Diseases

The same genetic tests used in PGD are also useful for testing fetuses, newborns, older children, and adults for disease-causing alleles. Instead of searching the DNA from an embryonic cell, however, the tests detect the alleles in DNA from cells taken from blood, saliva, or body tissues.

For example, newborns are routinely screened for a genetic disorder called phenylketonuria (PKU). Cells from unborn children can also be tested for disease-causing alleles; the parents can use the information to decide whether to terminate the pregnancy or to prepare for life with a special needs child.

Genetic testing has many applications in adults as well. People who suspect they may be heterozygous carriers of cystic fibrosis might choose to be tested for the disease-causing allele before deciding whether to have children. Likewise, a woman with a family history of breast cancer might be tested for damage to a gene called *BRCA1*, which is strongly associated with susceptibility to that disease. A positive test for the mutant allele might prompt the woman to have her breasts surgically removed to prevent the cancer from ever arising. And patients who already have breast cancer often have DNA from their tumors screened for genes encoding estrogen receptors. The results can indicate which treatments might be most promising.

D. Gene Therapy Treats Disease by Replacing Faulty Genes

Cystic fibrosis and most other genetic illnesses currently have no cure, but **gene therapy** may someday provide new treatment options by replacing a faulty gene in a person's cells (figure 11.14).

Gene therapy shares some similarities with creating transgenic organisms (see section 11.2A) in that new DNA is introduced into existing cells. But the two techniques are also different in key ways. First, the healthy gene replacing the faulty one is from humans, not another species. Second, a typical transgenic organism can theoretically pass the foreign genes to the next generation. A gene therapy patient would only receive new genes in the cell type that needs correction. Other cell types, including the germline cells that produce sperm and egg cells, would be left alone.

Gene therapy is challenging for several reasons. The new gene must be delivered directly to only those cells that express the faulty allele. Viruses may be ideal for carrying DNA into target cells, because they typically infect only a limited range of cells. But for gene therapy to be safe, the viruses must not trigger an immune reaction, and the new DNA must not induce mutations that cause cancer. In addition, the gene therapy patient must express the repaired genes long enough for his or her health to improve.

Gene therapy trials in humans have proceeded slowly since 1999, when 18-year-old Jesse Gelsinger received a massive infusion of viruses carrying a

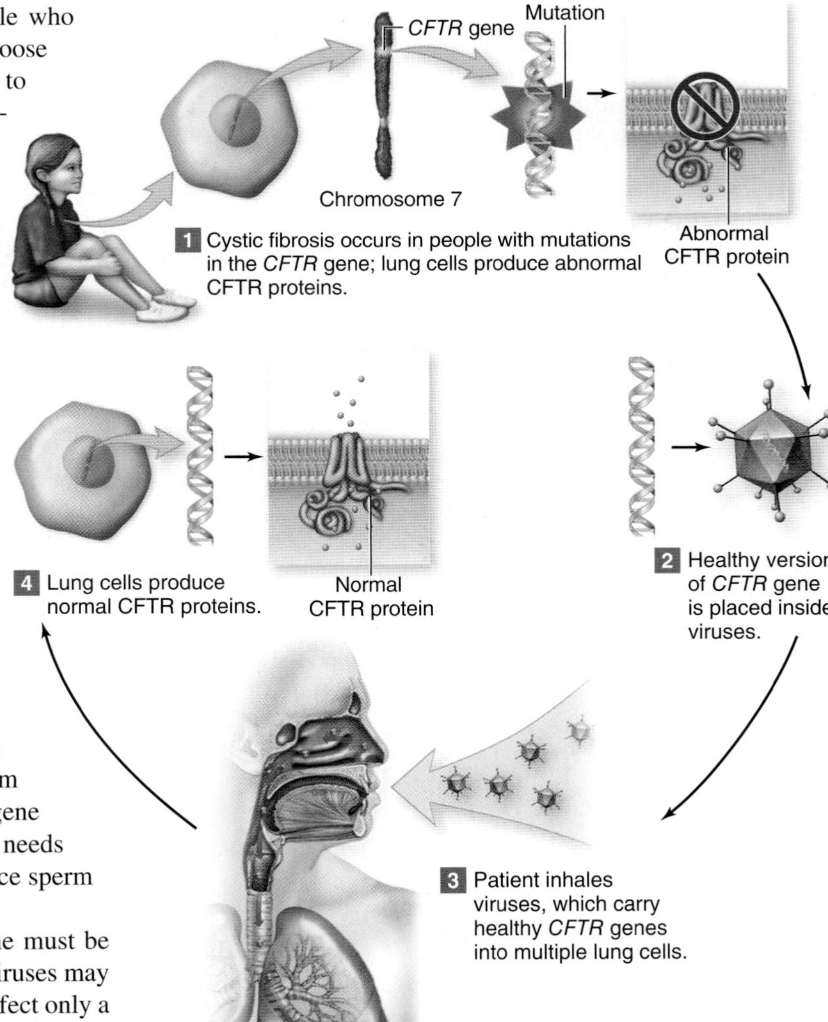
CFTR gene
Mutation
Chromosome 7
Abnormal CFTR protein
1 Cystic fibrosis occurs in people with mutations in the CFTR gene; lung cells produce abnormal CFTR proteins.
2 Healthy version of CFTR gene is placed inside viruses.
3 Patient inhales viruses, which carry healthy CFTR genes into multiple lung cells.
4 Lung cells produce normal CFTR proteins.
Normal CFTR protein

Figure 11.14 Gene Therapy. The overall goal of gene therapy is to replace a faulty gene with a normal, healthy version. In this example, a genetically modified virus delivers a healthy *CFTR* gene to the lungs of a person with cystic fibrosis.

Why We Care | Gene Doping

If we can use genes to cure diseases, it must also be possible to use DNA to make a healthy person even "better." For example, it should be possible to inject genes that make an athlete stronger, faster, or better able to withstand the physical stress of competition.

"Gene doping" is the use of DNA to enhance the function of a healthy person. The techniques would be essentially the same as those used in gene therapy: new genes would be introduced into existing cells, and the proteins encoded by those genes would change the cells' function. The difference is that rather than curing a disease, the goal of gene doping is to give an athlete a competitive edge. An introduced gene might induce the growth of extra muscle, for example. Alternatively, an endurance athlete might use gene doping to boost the production of erythropoietin (EPO), a protein that stimulates red blood cell formation.

In some ways, gene doping might seem like a more attractive option than using anabolic steroids or other performance-enhancing drugs. After all, the altered cells are simply making more of the same proteins that they can already produce. But this view ignores the immense challenges and risks that gene doping entails.

Both gene doping and gene therapy share the same difficulties. One problem is getting the genes into the right cells without triggering an immune reaction; another is activating the DNA once it is in the target cells. The dangers are the same, too. For example, if a newly introduced gene inserts itself into the wrong part of a chromosome, it might cause a mutation that triggers cancer. The gene might also have unwanted side effects. Too much EPO, for example, could be life-threatening if it causes the blood to become too thick to flow in arteries and veins. And if something does go wrong, no one knows how to reverse the gene doping process; getting the introduced gene back out is impossible.

For now, these technical difficulties and risks have kept gene doping from developing into a practical option for athletes seeking an edge. As the process improves, however, gene doping may become common. That prospect has led many sports organizations to simultaneously ban the practice and seek improved detection methods.

gene to correct an inborn error of metabolism. He died in days from an overwhelming immune system reaction. Gelsinger's death prompted a temporary halt to several gene therapy studies and led to stricter rules for conducting experiments. Nevertheless, gene therapy research and clinical trials continue, with promising results for diseases including cystic fibrosis, sickle cell disease, and some forms of inherited blindness and immune disorders.

E. Medical Uses of DNA Technology Raise Many Ethical Issues

The use of DNA technology in medicine can prevent or reduce human suffering in many ways: by improving the chance of having healthy children, by detecting diseases early if they do occur, and by offering the prospect of new treatments for illnesses that currently have no cure.

But these techniques also present ethical dilemmas. A thorough treatment of ethics is beyond the scope of this book, but the rest of this section offers a small sampling of some questions that accompany the use of DNA technology in medicine.

In vitro fertilization and preimplantation genetic diagnosis, for example, are costly. Should these techniques be available only to the wealthy? And consider the diagnosis of a genetic disease in an unborn child. A woman who is pregnant with a fetus that carries a genetic abnormality may decide to end the pregnancy rather than carrying the child to term. Does the morality of her decision depend on the severity of the illness? In other words, should we reserve fetal screening for life-threatening illnesses, or is it morally permissible to use it for milder conditions as well? What about using genetic tests to select for or against embryos with traits that do not affect health at all, such as sex or eye color?

Genetic testing in older children and adults may also lead to sticky questions. For example, a genetic test that reveals a high risk for cancer may be beneficial if it leads to lifestyle changes that promote a longer, healthier life. On the other hand, the same test results may lead to depression or anxiety without improving the chance of treatment or a cure. The potential loss of health insurance coverage may also prevent people from seeking genetic testing, even if they might benefit from knowing the results.

Gene therapy also comes with its share of dilemmas. This new form of treatment currently carries so many risks that its use is extremely limited. Once the technology is perfected, however, how should it be used? Only for debilitating diseases, or for less serious conditions as well? Is it right to use the techniques of gene therapy to enhance a person's appearance or athletic performance, as described in this chapter's Why We Care box? What about using DNA technology to alter the DNA in a person's germline, so that future generations contain the new gene? The answer to this question is not trivial, as it could affect the future evolution of our species.

11.4 Mastering Concepts

1. Explain how and why a researcher might use a DNA probe.
2. Compare and contrast preimplantation genetic diagnosis and genetic testing.
3. What is gene therapy?
4. What are some examples of ethical questions raised by the medical use of DNA technology?

Investigating Life

11.5 What Makes Us Human?

The Question: Perhaps no scientific issue is more tantalizing and entangled with philosophy than the question of what makes us human. One way to look for answers is to study the similarities and differences between humans and chimpanzees, our closest living relatives (figure 11.15). A team of scientists has sequenced the 3 billion or so DNA nucleotides that make up the chimpanzee genome and has begun comparing it with our own.

The Approach: The story begins with the Chimpanzee Sequencing and Analysis Consortium, a group of 67 researchers in the United States, Europe, and Israel who collaborated to determine the genetic sequence of one chimpanzee. The scientists isolated DNA from the chimp's blood cells, broke the genetic material into many small fragments, and inserted each fragment into a separate plasmid. Each plasmid that carried chimp DNA was placed into a different bacterial cell. The researchers allowed all of the bacteria to replicate, producing many copies of each plasmid. Then, when it was a fragment's "turn" to be processed, a technician retrieved a sample of the bacteria, extracted the plasmid, and determined the nucleotide sequence (see section 11.2B). Finally, powerful computers assembled the sequences from tens of millions of fragments.

Figure 11.15 Close Relatives. Humans share 99% of our protein-encoding genes with chimpanzees. What are the differences that make us human?

The Conclusion . . . and Remaining Questions: Long before this project began, the startling genetic similarities between humans and chimps were well known. The chromosomes of the two species, for example, are extremely similar (figure 11.16). Although chimpanzees do have one more pair of chromosomes than do humans, a close look at figure 11.16 reveals why: our chromosome 2 formed when two smaller chromosomes fused some time after the human and chimpanzee lineages split.

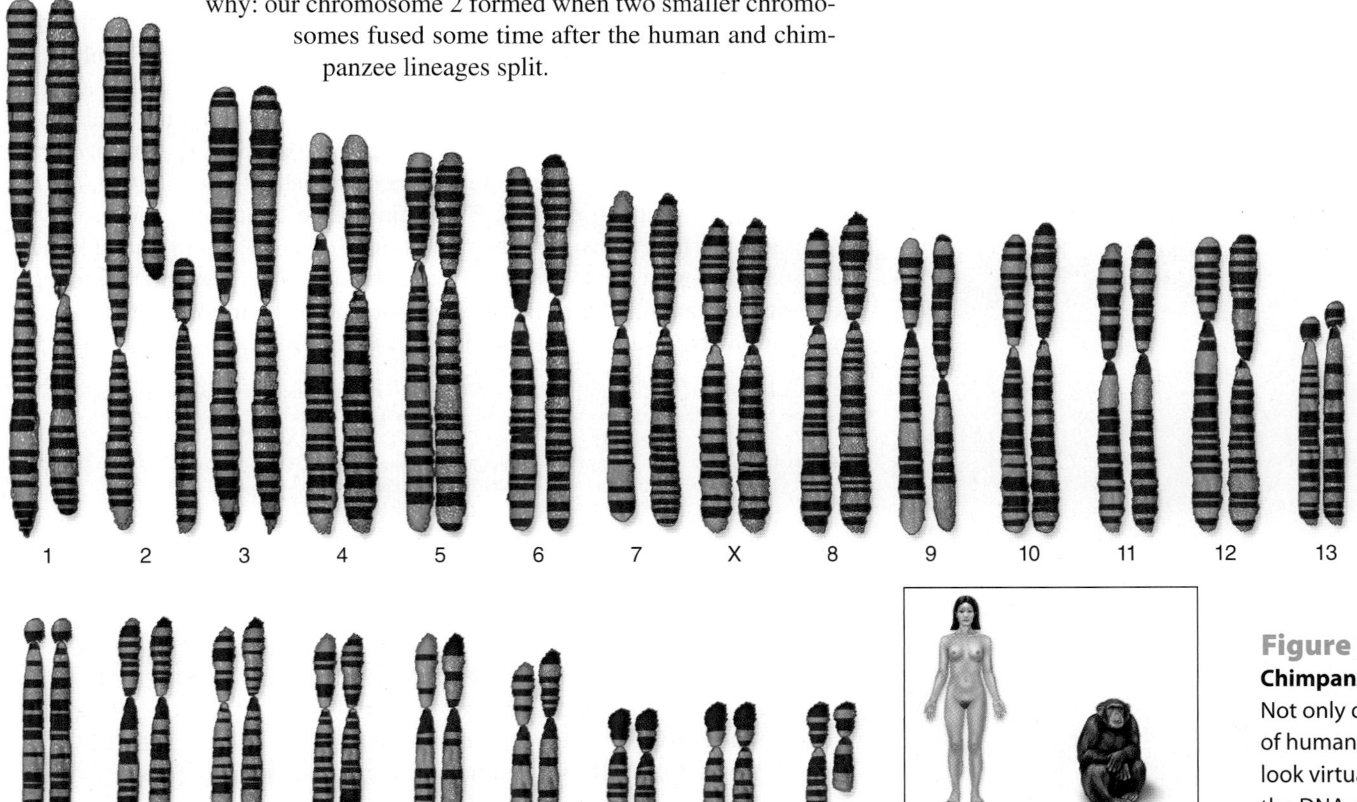

Figure 11.16 Human and Chimpanzee Chromosomes. Not only do the chromosomes of humans and chimpanzees look virtually identical, but the DNA sequences are also extremely similar.

The complete DNA sequences for both species, however, reveal exactly how much we have in common: The two genomes are 96% alike, with the differences concentrated in the noncoding regions. The coding regions (the sequences that specify proteins) are 99% alike.

Scientists must still scrutinize both genomes to identify the 25,000 or so coding regions. They must also sequence the genomes of additional individuals to locate the variable regions, and they must learn which alleles confer which traits. The result will be an unprecedented view of human biology and evolution. Here is a sampling of questions we may soon be able to answer:

• **Which genes define humans?** Previously, scientists could only compare the human genome with those of bacteria, plants, nematodes, fruit flies, and mice. Those comparisons revealed many traits that are common to all animals, all eukaryotes, or all cells. With the chimp genome complete, however, scientists can now search for regions that have changed since humans and chimps last shared a common ancestor. These are the sequences that define humans.

• **What accounts for our uniquely human features?** Considering how genetically similar humans and chimps are, we have strikingly different phenotypes. At least two hypotheses could explain this curious observation. Some scientists suggest that human and chimp proteins are essentially the same but that we express those proteins at different times. For example, section 7.11 illustrates how a small change in just one transcription factor can affect a person's ability to use language. A competing hypothesis is that after humans and chimps diverged, mutations in human DNA made some genes stop working (see, for example, section 26.7, which describes how mutations in one gene may have caused human jaw muscles to weaken). Such "degenerate" genes may make us less muscular than chimpanzees. Comparing the chimp and human genotypes will help biologists test these hypotheses.

• **Why do humans and chimps have different diseases?** A surprising number of diseases affect humans but not chimps, including Alzheimer disease and carcinomas (a type of cancer). Similarly, HIV progresses to AIDS in humans but not in chimps. At least some of these differences will certainly lie in our genes, and their discovery may yield new disease cures.

Whatever the source of our humanity, it is revealed partly in our ability to make reasoned decisions and in our compassion for others. Chimpanzees are endangered in the wild, where they succumb to habitat loss, hunting, the pet trade, and biomedical research. The Chimpanzee Sequencing and Analysis Consortium's paper advocates the protection of chimpanzees in the wild, and it ends with this statement: "We hope that elaborating how few differences separate our species will broaden recognition of our duty to these extraordinary primates that stand as our siblings in the family of life."

Chimpanzee Sequencing and Analysis Consortium. September 1, 2005. Initial sequence of the chimpanzee genome and comparison with the human genome. *Nature*, vol. 437, pages 69–87.

Additional reference: Olson, Maynard V., and Ajit Varki. January 2003. Sequencing the chimpanzee genome: insights into human evolution and disease. *Nature Reviews Genetics*, vol. 4, pages 20–28.

11.5 Mastering Concepts

1. What information can researchers gain by comparing the human and chimpanzee genome sequences?
2. Comparing the chimpanzee and human genomes does not reveal which species has the "ancestral" form of each gene (the version present in the last common ancestor of both species). How could DNA from orangutans or gorillas help scientists resolve which gene variants are ancestral?

Chapter Summary

11.1 DNA Technology Is Changing the World

- Many disciplines benefit from **DNA technology,** the practical application of knowledge about DNA.

11.2 DNA Technology's Tools Apply to Individual Genes or Entire Genomes

A. Transgenic Organisms Contain DNA from Other Species

- **Transgenic organisms** are important in industry, research, and agriculture.
- **Restriction enzymes** and **plasmids** are tools that help researchers create **recombinant DNA** and introduce it to recipient cells.

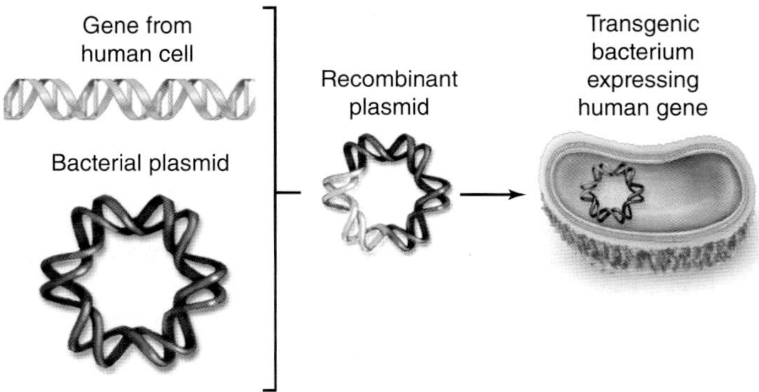

B. DNA Sequencing Reveals the Order of Bases

- The Sanger method uses modified nucleotides to generate DNA fragments of various lengths. Using **electrophoresis** to sort the fragments by size reveals the DNA sequence.
- Only 1.5% of the 3.2 billion base pairs of the human genome encode protein. The remaining 98.5% of the human genome encodes RNA, regulatory sequences, pseudogenes, transposable elements, and other repeats.

C. PCR Replicates DNA in a Test Tube

- In the **polymerase chain reaction (PCR),** DNA separates into two strands, and DNA polymerase adds complementary nucleotides to each strand. Repeated cycles of heating and cooling allow for rapid amplification of the target DNA sequence.
- PCR finds many applications in research, forensics, medicine, agriculture, and other fields.

D. DNA Profiling Detects Genetic Differences

- Individuals vary genetically in single bases and **short tandem repeats (STRs). DNA profiling** detects these differences.
- Investigators can use known frequencies of alleles in the population to calculate the probability that two DNA samples match.
- Analysis of mitochondrial DNA can verify maternal relationships.

11.3 Stem Cells and Cloning Add New Ways to Copy Cells and Organisms

A. Stem Cells Divide to Form Multiple Cell Types

- **Embryonic stem cells** give rise to all cells in the body; **adult stem cells** produce only a limited subset of cell types.
- Induced pluripotent stem cells may eliminate some of the ethical issues associated with embryonic stem cells.

B. Cloning Creates Identical Copies of an Organism

- Researchers use a technique called **somatic cell nuclear transfer** to clone adult mammals.
- Human reproductive and therapeutic cloning have potential medical applications, but they also involve ethical dilemmas.

11.4 Many Medical Tests and Procedures Use DNA Technology

A. DNA Probes Detect Specific Sequences

- A **DNA probe** is a single-stranded fragment of DNA that is labeled. The probe binds to any complementary DNA, revealing its location.

B. Preimplantation Genetic Diagnosis Can Help Prevent Some Diseases

- In **preimplantation genetic diagnosis (PGD),** a human embryo can be tested for a variety of diseases before being implanted into a woman's uterus.

C. Genetic Testing Can Detect Existing Diseases

- With the help of gene probes, DNA extracted from cells of a fetus, child, or adult can be tested for the presence of disease-causing alleles.

D. Gene Therapy Treats Disease by Replacing Faulty Genes

- **Gene therapy** places a functional gene into cells that are expressing a faulty gene.

E. Medical Uses of DNA Technology Raise Many Ethical Issues

- Because of its risks, high expense, and potential to alter human life, DNA technology raises a number of ethical questions.

11.5 Investigating Life: What Makes Us Human?

- Scientists completed the chimpanzee genome project in 2005. Comparing the chimp and human genomes will lead to unprecedented insight into the genes, phenotypes, and diseases that are unique to humans.

Multiple Choice Questions

1. If a restriction enzyme cuts between the G and the A whenever it encounters the sequence GAATTC, how many fragments will be produced when the enzyme is digested with DNA with the following sequence?
TGAGAATTCAACTGAATTCAAATTCGAATTCTTAGC
   a. Two
   b. Three
   c. Four
   d. Five
2. Which of the following is transgenic?
   a. A yeast cell that expresses a gene from a fish
   b. A human patient who receives gene therapy to repair a faulty cystic fibrosis gene
   c. A human embryo being tested for disease-causing alleles
   d. All of the above are transgenic.
3. The noncoding DNA inside your cells
   a. acts as "recipes" for the cell's proteins.
   b. is identical to that of your mother if you are female or your father if you are male.
   c. consists partly of transposons and repeated sequences.
   d. has no function and therefore can safely be removed.
4. Why is PCR useful?
   a. Because it replicates all the DNA in a cell
   b. Because it can create large amounts of DNA from small amounts
   c. Because it produces a heat-tolerant DNA polymerase
   d. Because it occurs in an automated device

5. In 1920, a woman claiming to be a surviving member of the royal family of Tsar Nicholas II of Russia appeared in Europe. What modern method of DNA profiling would you use to verify this person's claims?
   a. Somatic cell nuclear transfer
   b. Analysis of the sequence of the woman's entire genome
   c. Analysis of mitochondrial DNA sequences
   d. Comparison of STR site frequencies to population databases
6. What is an induced pluripotent stem cell?
   a. A cell from which the nucleus has been removed
   b. A cell extracted from an early embryo
   c. A specially treated somatic cell that can develop into any cell type
   d. A specially treated embryonic stem cell that develops into one specialized cell type
7. Tabouli, one of the kittens on page 198, is a clone produced by a similar method as Dolly the sheep. Tabouli is genetically identical to the cat that
   a. gave birth to her.
   b. donated the egg that developed into her.
   c. donated her chromosomes.
   d. Tabouli is equally similar to all of these cats.
8. A gene probe with sequence TCAGGCTTCAG would bind most strongly to which of the following DNA fragments?
   a. AGTCCGAAGTC
   b. TCAGGCTTCAG
   c. GACTTCGGACT
   d. UGAGGCUUGAG
9. Preimplantation genetic diagnosis would be least useful in detecting a ___ disease-causing allele.
   a. dominant
   b. recessive
   c. common
   d. rare
10. What is the role of a virus in gene therapy?
   a. It causes the disease being cured.
   b. It carries the healthy DNA into the patient's cells.
   c. It carries the faulty DNA out of the patient's cells.
   d. It reveals which cells carry the DNA causing the disease.

Write It Out

1. What techniques might researchers use to create transgenic bacteria that produce human growth hormone (a drug used to treat extremely short stature)?
2. Transgenic crops often require fewer herbicides and insecticides than conventional crops. In that respect, they could be considered environmentally friendly. Use the Internet to research the question of why some environmental groups oppose transgenic technology.
3. Genome sequencing projects are complete or in progress for many organisms other than humans and chimpanzees. Use the Internet to choose one of these species, and describe some new discoveries that have come from research on this organism.
4. Explain how the ingredients in a PCR reaction tube replicate DNA.
5. Compare and contrast the use of the DNA polymerase enzyme in DNA sequencing and PCR.
6. Why does DNA profiling require an understanding of probability?
7. Make a chart that lists the advantages and disadvantages of embryonic stem cells, adult stem cells, and induced pluripotent stem cells.
8. Unneeded genes in an adult animal cell are permanently inactivated, making it impossible for most specialized cells to turn into any other cell type. How does this arrangement save energy inside a cell? Why does the ability to clone an adult mammal depend on techniques for reactivating these "dormant" genes?
9. Search the Internet for examples of mammals that have been cloned (other than sheep). What ethical issues should people consider in deciding whether to clone plants, nonhuman animals, and humans?
10. This chapter's Why We Care box (see page 212) describes some potential applications of gene doping. What are some examples of ethical issues that gene doping presents? What might the prospect of gene doping mean for the future of sports?
11. Describe gene therapy and explain the ethical issues that gene therapy presents.
12. If a cell's genome is analogous to a cookbook and a gene is analogous to a recipe, what is an analogy for preimplantation genetic diagnosis? For gene testing? For gene therapy?

Pull It Together

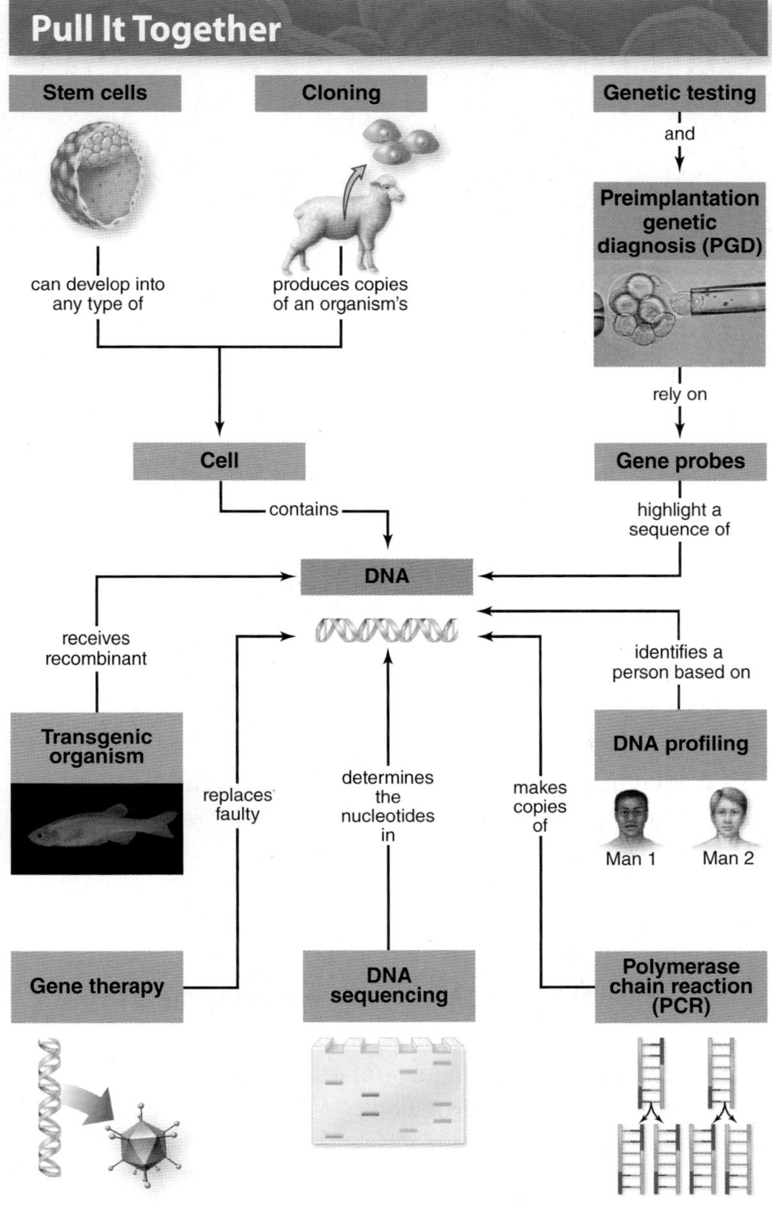

1. What is recombinant DNA?
2. Add the terms *restriction enzyme, plasmid, virus, DNA polymerase,* and *short tandem repeat* to this concept map.
3. How is a patient who receives gene therapy similar to and different from a transgenic organism?

UNIT 3 Evolution and Diversity

12 Forces of Evolutionary Change

Reaching for Food. The giraffe can nibble on leaves high in the treetops, thanks to its long neck. How did this animal acquire its signature trait? Natural selection—the most familiar mechanism of evolution—provides the answer.

Learning Outline

Learn How to Learn

Take the Best Possible Notes

Some students take notes only on what they consider "important" during a lecture. Others write down words but not diagrams. Both strategies risk losing vital information and connections between ideas that could help in later learning. Instead, write down as much as you can during each lecture, including sketches of the diagrams. It will be much easier to study later if you have a complete picture of what happened in every class.

What's the Point?

As the chapters in this unit will repeatedly demonstrate, evolution occurs everywhere and is obvious in many ways. Evolution explains the giraffe's extraordinary neck, the unusual shape of the bleeding heart flower, and countless features of other species from microbes to humans.

Evolution serves as an enormously compelling conceptual framework for many observations about life. In fact, geneticist Theodosius Dobzhansky gave this title to a much-quoted article he wrote: "Nothing in Biology Makes Sense Except in the Light of Evolution." This chapter explains how this powerful process works.

Evolution does not, however, answer one question that fascinates many people: how did life begin in the first place? Because little evidence remains from life's ancient origin, this question is difficult to answer scientifically; chapter 15 describes some of what we do know.

12.1 Evolution Acts on Populations

Scientific reasoning has profoundly changed human thinking about our own origins. Just 250 years ago, most people believed Earth was about 6000 years old. A century later, scientists accepted evidence that Earth is much older (millions of years old or more) but still believed that a creator made all life on Earth in its present form. Contemporary scientists, using evidence from many fields of research, now accept evolution as the best explanation for life's diversity.

But what *is* evolution? A simple definition of **evolution** is descent with modification. "Descent" implies inheritance; "modification" refers to changes in heritable traits from generation to generation. For example, we see evolution at work in the many types of cats—large and small, striped and spotted—that have descended from an ancestral cat species.

Evolution has another, more specific, definition as well. Recall from unit 2 that each gene can have several different versions, or alleles, in a population. We have also seen that a **population** consists of interbreeding members of the same species; see figure 1.2. Biologists say that evolution occurs in a population when some alleles become more common, and others less common, from one generation to the next. A more precise definition of evolution, then, is genetic change in a population over multiple generations.

According to this definition, evolution is detectable by examining a population's **gene pool**—its entire collection of genes and their alleles. Evolution is a change in **allele frequencies;** one allele's frequency is calculated as the number of copies of that allele, divided by the total number of alleles in the population. Suppose, for example, that a gene has two possible alleles, A and a. In a population of 100 individuals, the gene has 200 alleles (assuming the individuals are diploid). If 160 of those alleles are a, then the frequency of a is 160/200, or 0.8. In the next generation, however, a may become either more or less common. Because an individual's alleles do not change, *evolution can occur in populations but not in individuals.*

The allele frequencies for each gene determine the characteristics of a population (figure 12.1). Many people in Sweden, for example, have alleles

Figure 12.1 Same Genes, Different Alleles. Human populations originating in different regions of the world have unique allele frequencies. Blond hair and blue eyes are typical of people from northern European countries, whereas people originating on the Asian continent usually have darker coloration.

conferring blond hair and blue eyes; a population of Asians would have very few, if any, such alleles. Instead, their gene pool would contain mostly alleles conferring darker hair and eyes. If Swedes migrate to Asia and interbreed with the locals (or vice versa), allele frequencies change.

Microevolution consists of the relatively short-term genetic changes within a population or species. Biological evolution also includes "macroevolutionary" events such as the appearance of new species, which usually occurs over much longer periods. It is remarkable to consider that small, generation-by-generation changes occurring in every species account for both short- and long-term changes in the history of life on Earth. This chapter describes the most common ways that such changes occur.

12.1 Mastering Concepts

1. What are two ways to define evolution?
2. Why can evolution act only on populations and not on individuals?

12.2 Evolutionary Thought Has Evolved for Centuries

Although Charles Darwin typically receives credit for developing the theory of evolution, people began pondering life's diversity well before his birth. This section offers a brief glimpse into the history of evolutionary thought.

A. Many Explanations Have Been Proposed for Life's Diversity

People have tried to explain the diversity of life for a very long time (figure 12.2). In ancient Greece, Aristotle recognized that all organisms are related in a hierarchy of simple to complex forms, but he believed that all members of a species were created identical to one another. This idea influenced scientific thinking for nearly 2000 years.

Several other ideas were also considered fundamental principles of science well into the 1800s. Among them was the concept of a "special creation,"

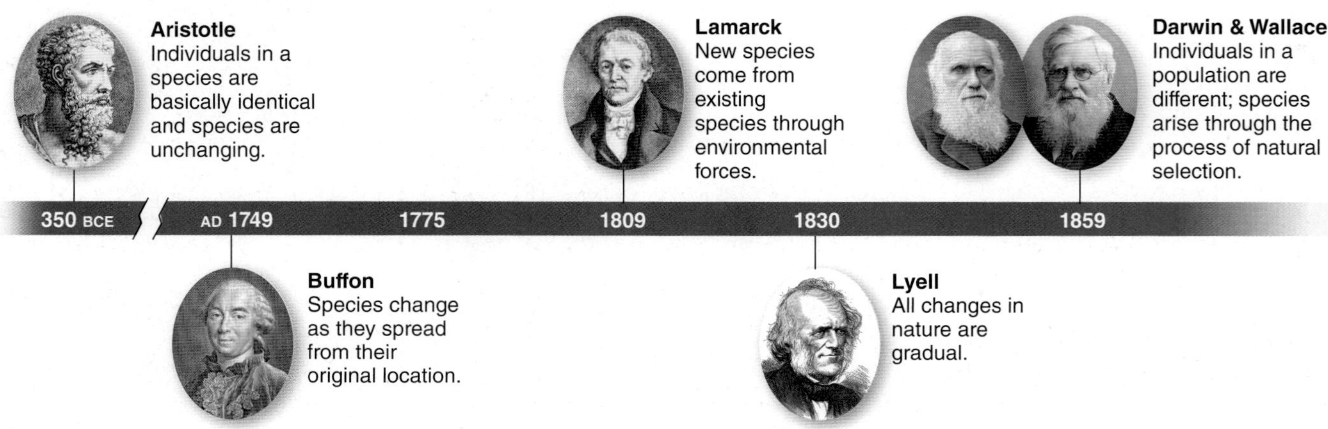
Aristotle
Individuals in a species are basically identical and species are unchanging.
Lamarck
New species come from existing species through environmental forces.
Darwin & Wallace
Individuals in a population are different; species arise through the process of natural selection.
350 BCE
AD 1749
1775
1809
1830
1859
Buffon
Species change as they spread from their original location.
Lyell
All changes in nature are gradual.

Figure 12.2 Evolutionary Thought Before Darwin. Many scientists built the foundation that Charles Darwin used to develop his famous idea: natural selection as the mechanism for evolution. This figure shows a few of the most significant contributors.

the sudden appearance of organisms on Earth. People believed that this creative event was planned and purposeful, that species were fixed and unchangeable, and that Earth was relatively young.

Scientists struggled to reconcile these beliefs with compelling evidence that species could in fact change. Fossils, which had been discovered at least as early as 500 BCE, were at first thought to be oddly shaped crystals or faulty attempts at life that arose spontaneously in rocks. But by the mid-1700s, the increasingly obvious connection between living organisms and fossils argued against these ideas.

To explain the existence of fossils without denying the role of a creator, scientists suggested that fossils represented organisms killed during the biblical flood. Yet some of the fossils depicted organisms not seen before. Because people believed that species created by God could not become extinct, these fossils presented a paradox. The conflict between ideology and observation widened as geologists discovered that different rock layers revealed different groups of fossilized organisms, many of them now extinct (figure 12.3).

Figure 12.3 Rock Layers Reveal Earth's History. Layers of sedimentary rock, such as these in the Grand Canyon, formed from sand, mud, and gravel that were deposited in ancient seas. The rock layers on the bottom are older than those on top. Many layers contain fossils of organisms that lived (and died) when the layer was formed, providing clues about when the organism existed.

In 1749, French naturalist Georges-Louis Buffon became one of the first to openly suggest that closely related species arose from a common ancestor and were changing—a radical idea at the time. By moving the discussion into the public arena, he made possible a new consideration of evolution and its causes from a scientific point of view. Still, no one had proposed how species might change.

Then, in 1809, French taxonomist Jean Baptiste de Lamarck proposed the first scientifically testable evolutionary theory. He reasoned that organisms that used one part of their body repeatedly would increase their abilities, very much like weight lifters developing strong arms. Conversely, disuse would weaken an organ until it disappeared. Lamarck surmised (incorrectly) that these changes would pass to future generations.

B. Charles Darwin's Voyage Provided a Wealth of Evidence

With these new theories and ideas, people were beginning to accept the concept of evolution but did not yet understand how it could result in the formation of new species. Ultimately, Charles Darwin (1809–1882) became the first to solve this puzzle.

Young Charles Darwin attended Cambridge University in England and, at the urging of his family, completed studies to enter the clergy. Meanwhile, he also followed his own interests. He joined geological field trips and met several eminent geology professors.

Eventually, Darwin was offered a position as ship's naturalist aboard the HMS *Beagle*. Before the ship set sail for its 5-year voyage in 1831 (figure 12.4), the botany professor who had arranged Darwin's position gave the young man the first volume of Charles Lyell's *Principles of Geology*. Darwin picked up the second and third volumes in South America. By the time he finished reading these works, Darwin was an avid proponent of Lyell's idea that natural processes are slow and steady, and that Earth is much older than 6000 years—perhaps millions or hundreds of millions of years old.

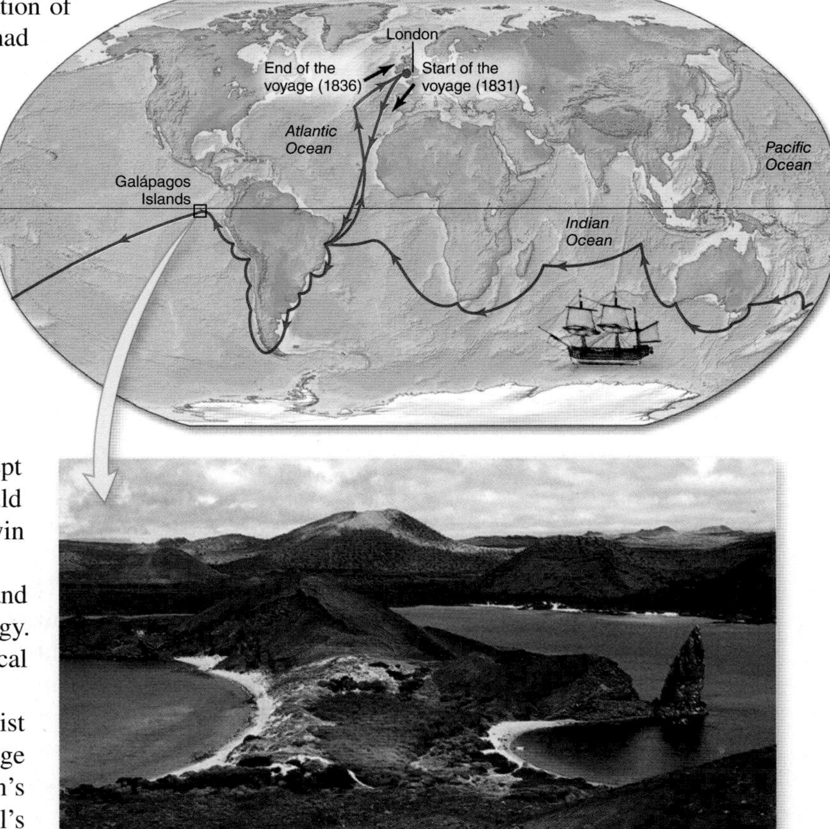

Figure 12.4 The Voyage of the *Beagle*. Darwin observed life and geology throughout the world during the journey of the HMS *Beagle*. Many of Darwin's ideas about natural selection and evolution had their origins in the observations he made on the Galápagos Islands.

Darwin recorded his observations as the ship journeyed around the coast of South America. He noted forces that uplifted new land, such as earthquakes and volcanoes, and the constant erosion that wore it down. He marveled at forest plant fossils mixed with sea sediments and at shell fossils in a mountain cave. Darwin tried to reconstruct the past from contemporary observations and wondered how each fossil had arrived where he found it.

In the fourth year of the voyage, the HMS *Beagle* spent a month in the Galápagos Islands, off the coast of Ecuador. The notes and samples Darwin brought back would form the seed of his theory of evolution by natural selection.

C. *On the Origin of Species* Proposed Natural Selection as an Evolutionary Mechanism

Toward the end of the voyage, Darwin began to assimilate all he had seen and recorded. Pondering the great variety of organisms in South America and their relationships to fossils and geology, he began to think that these were clues to how new species originate.

Descent with Modification Darwin returned to England in 1836, and by 1837 he began assembling his notes in earnest. In March 1837, Darwin consulted ornithologist (bird expert) John Gould about the finches that the *Beagle* brought back from the Galápagos Islands. Gould could tell from bill structures that some of the birds ate small seeds, whereas others ate large seeds, fruits, or insects. In all, he described 14 distinct types of finch, each different from the birds on the mainland yet sharing some features.

Darwin thought that the different varieties of finch on the Galápagos had probably descended from a single ancestral type of finch that had flown to the islands and, finding a relatively unoccupied new habitat, flourished. Over the next 3 million years, the finch population gradually branched in several directions. Different groups ate insects, fruits, and seeds of different sizes, depending on the resources each island offered. Darwin also noted similar changes in the length of the Galápagos tortoise's neck. He coined the phrase "descent with modification" to describe this gradual change from an ancestral type.

Malthus's Ideas on Populations In September 1838, Darwin read a work that helped him further understand the diversity of finches on the Galápagos Islands. Economist and theologian Thomas Malthus's *Essay on the Principle of Population,* written 40 years earlier, stated that food availability, disease, and war limit the size of a human population. Wouldn't other organisms face similar limitations? If so, then individuals that could not obtain essential resources would die.

The insight Malthus provided was that individual members of a population were not all the same, as Aristotle had taught. Instead, individuals better able to obtain resources were more likely to survive and reproduce. This would explain the observation that more individuals are produced in a generation than survive; they do not all obtain enough vital resources to live. Over time, environmental challenges would "select" out the more poorly equipped variants, and gradually, the population would change.

The Concept of Natural Selection Darwin used the term *natural selection* to describe "this preservation of favourable variations and the rejection of injurious variations." Biologists later modified the definition to add modern genetics terminology. We now say that **natural selection** occurs when environmental factors cause the differential reproductive success of individuals with particular genotypes.

Darwin got the idea of natural selection from thinking about artificial selection (also called selective breeding). In **artificial selection,** a human chooses one or a few desired traits, such as the size of a plant's buds or leaves, and then allows only the individuals that best express those qualities to reproduce (figure 12.5). Artificial selection is responsible not only for agriculturally important varieties of plants and animals but also for the many breeds of domesticated cats and dogs. Darwin himself raised pigeons and developed several new breeds by artificial selection.

How did this new idea of natural selection apply to the diversity of finch species on the Galápagos? Most likely, some finches flew from the mainland to one island long ago. Eventually, the finch population outgrew the supply of small seeds, and those that could eat nothing else starved. But birds that could eat other foods, perhaps because of an inherited difference in bill structure, survived and reproduced. Since their food was plentiful, these once-unusual birds gradually came to make up more of the population.

Darwin further realized that he could extend this idea to multiple islands, each of which had a slightly different habitat and therefore selected for different varieties of finches. A new species might arise when a population adapted to so many new conditions that its members could no longer breed with the original group (see chapter 14). In a similar way, new species have evolved throughout the history of life as populations adapted to different resources. All species are therefore ultimately united by common ancestry.

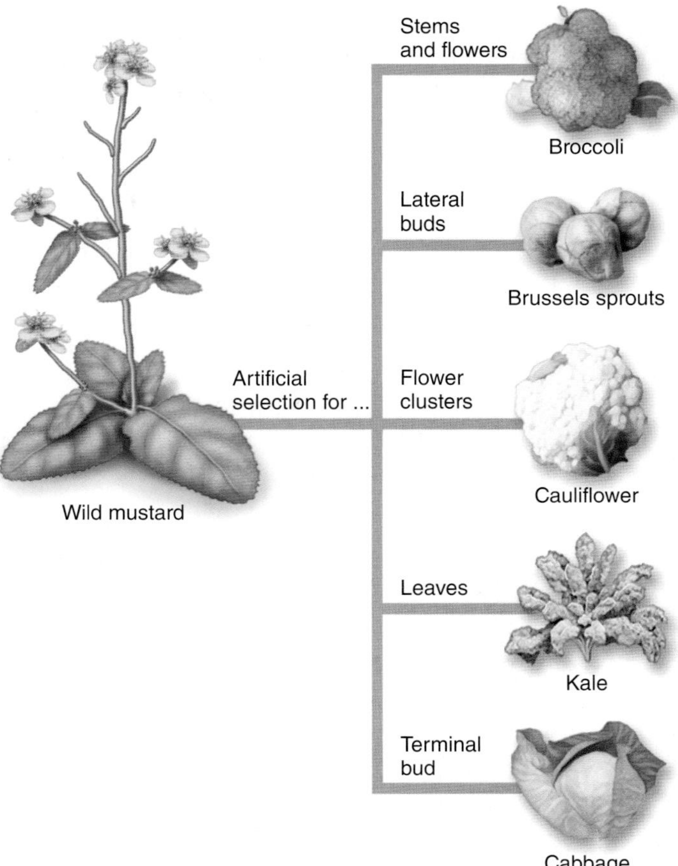

Figure 12.5 Artificial Selection. Plant breeders selected for different traits in wild mustard to create these five vegetable varieties, all of which belong to the same species.

Publication of *On the Origin of Species* Darwin continued to work on his ideas until 1858, when he received a manuscript from Alfred Russel Wallace, a British naturalist. Wallace had observed the diverse insects, birds, and mammals of South America and southeast Asia, and his manuscript independently proposed that natural selection was the driving force of evolution.

Darwin submitted his own paper, along with Wallace's, to a scientific conference later that year. In 1859, Darwin finally published the 490-page *On the Origin of Species by Means of Natural Selection, or Preservation of Favoured Races in the Struggle for Life.* It would form the underpinning of modern life science.

Table 12.1 summarizes Darwin's main arguments in support of natural selection. He observed that individuals in a species are different from one another and that at least some of this variation is heritable. If more individuals are born than can survive, then competition will determine which ones live long enough to reproduce. Darwin realized that those with the most adaptive traits would be most likely to "win" the competition, reproduce, and pass those favorable traits to the next generation. Over many generations, natural selection coupled with environmental change or a new habitat could change a population's characteristics or even give rise to new species. Darwin's own observations of ants, pigeons, orchids, and many other organisms provided abundant support for his ideas.

Some members of the scientific community happily embraced Darwin's efforts. Upon reading *On the Origin of Species,* his friend Thomas Henry Huxley remarked, "How stupid of me not to have thought of that." Others, however, were less appreciative. People in some religious denominations perceived a clash with their beliefs that all life arose from separate special creations, that species did not change, and that nature is harmonious and purposeful. Perhaps most disturbing to many people was the idea that humans were just one more species competing for resources.

TABLE 12.1 The Logic of Natural Selection: A Summary

Observations of Nature
1. **Genetic variation:** Within a species, no two individuals are exactly alike. Some of this variation is heritable.
2. **Limited resources:** Every habitat contains limited supplies of the resources required for survival.
3. **Overproduction of offspring:** More individuals are born than survive to reproduce.
Inferences from Observations
1. **Struggle for existence:** Individuals compete for the limited resources that enable them to survive.
2. **Unequal reproductive success (natural selection):** The inherited characteristics of some individuals make them more likely to obtain resources, survive, and reproduce.
3. **Descent with modification:** Over many generations, natural selection can change the characteristics of populations, even giving rise to new species.

D. Evolutionary Theory Continues to Expand

Although Charles Darwin's arguments were fundamentally sound, he could not explain all that he saw. For instance, he did not understand the source of variation within a population, nor did he know how heritable traits were passed from generation to generation. Ironically, Austrian monk Gregor Mendel was solving the puzzle of inheritance at the same time that Darwin was pondering natural selection (see chapter 10). Mendel's work, however, remained obscure until after Darwin's death.

Since Darwin's time, scientists have learned much more about genes, chromosomes, and the origin and inheritance of genetic variation (figure 12.6). In the 1930s, scientists finally recognized the connection between natural selection and genetics. They unified these ideas into the **modern evolutionary synthesis,** which suggests that genetic mutations create heritable variation and that this variation is the raw material upon which natural selection acts.

After the discovery of DNA's structure in the 1950s, the picture became even clearer. We now know that mutations are changes in DNA sequence (see chapter 7) and that mutations occur at random in all organisms. Sexual reproduction amplifies this variability by shuffling and reshuffling parental alleles to produce genetically different offspring (see chapter 9).

Today, overwhelming evidence supports the theory of evolution by natural selection; chapter 13 describes some of the data in detail. Contemporary biologists therefore accept evolution as the best explanation for the fact that diverse organisms use the same genetic code, the same chemical reactions to extract energy from nutrients, and many of the same (or very similar) enzymes and other proteins. Descent from a common ancestor explains both this great unity of life and the spectacular diversity of organisms today. Coupled with a wide variety of changing habitats and enormous amounts of time, the result of natural selection is a planet packed with millions of variations of the same underlying biochemical theme.

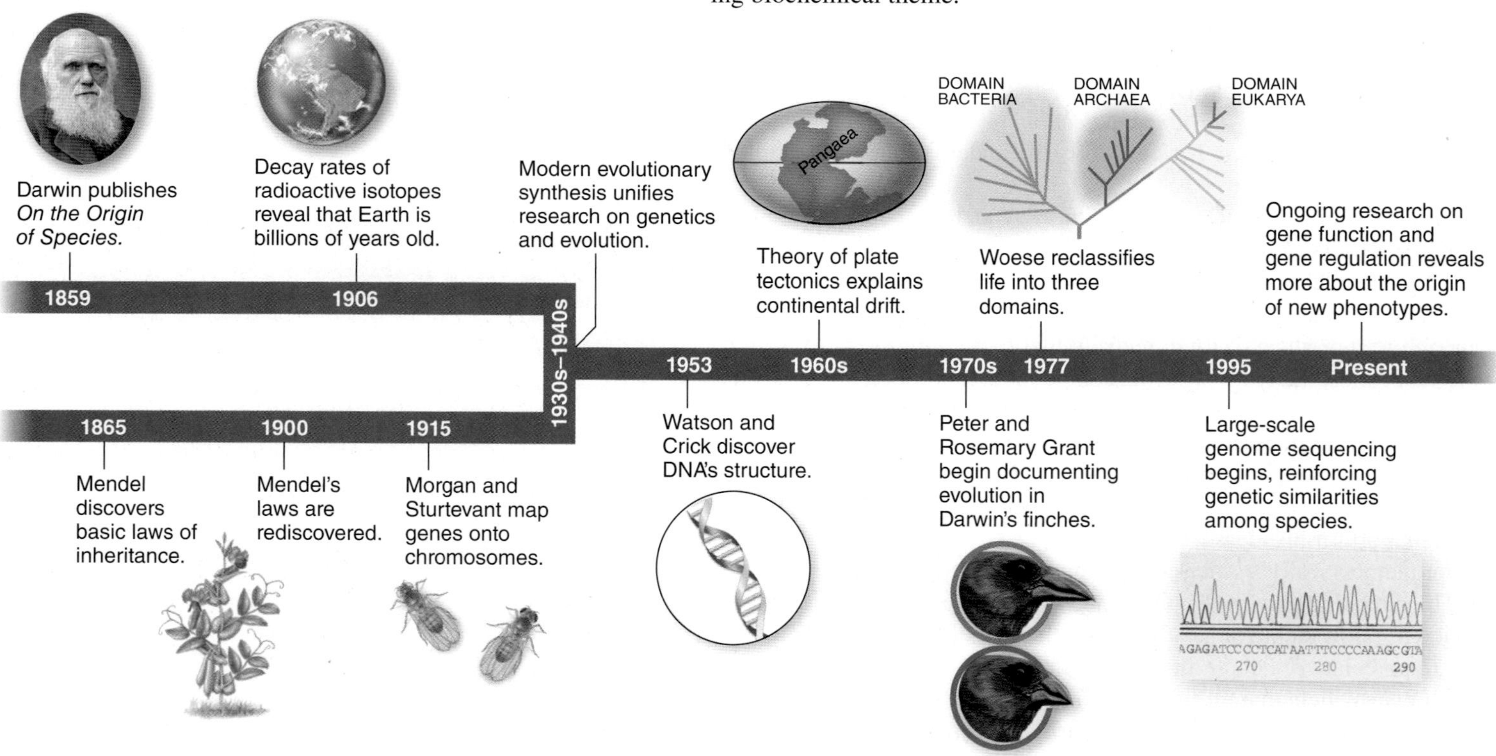

Figure 12.6 Evolutionary Theory Since Darwin. Charles Darwin and Gregor Mendel laid a foundation for evolutionary theory, but many scientists since that time have added to our understanding of how evolution works.

12.2 Mastering Concepts

1. How did people think that species arose and diversified before Darwin published his theory of evolution by natural selection?
2. What did Darwin observe that led him to develop his ideas about the origin of species?
3. How is artificial selection different from natural selection?
4. What is the modern evolutionary synthesis?

12.3 Natural Selection Molds Evolution

Natural selection is the most famous, and often the most important, mechanism of microevolution. This section explains the basic requirements for natural selection to occur. The rest of the chapter describes natural selection and several others forces of evolutionary change in more detail.

A. Adaptations Enhance Reproductive Success

As Darwin knew, organisms of the same species are different from one another, and every population produces more individuals than resources can support (figure 12.7). Some members of any population will not survive to reproduce. A struggle for existence is therefore inevitable.

The variation inherent in each species means that some individuals in a population are better than others at obtaining nutrients and water, avoiding predators, tolerating temperature changes, attracting mates, and reproducing. The heritable traits conferring these advantages are **adaptations**—features that provide a selective advantage because they improve an organism's ability to survive and reproduce.

The word *adaptation* can be confusing because it has multiple meanings. For example, a student might say, "I have adapted well to college life," but

a. Genetic variation

b. Overproduction of offspring

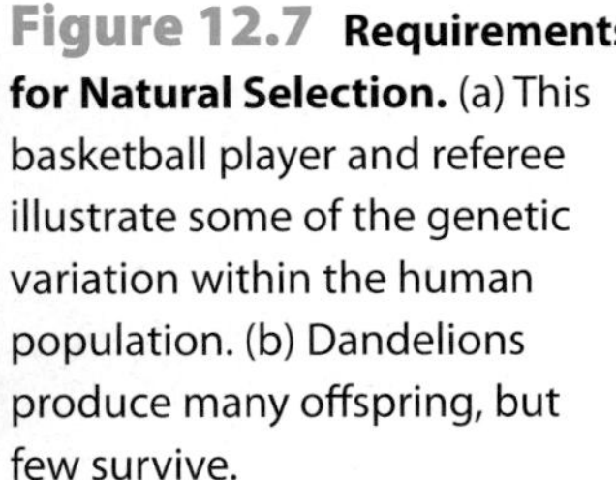

Figure 12.7 Requirements for Natural Selection. (a) This basketball player and referee illustrate some of the genetic variation within the human population. (b) Dandelions produce many offspring, but few survive.

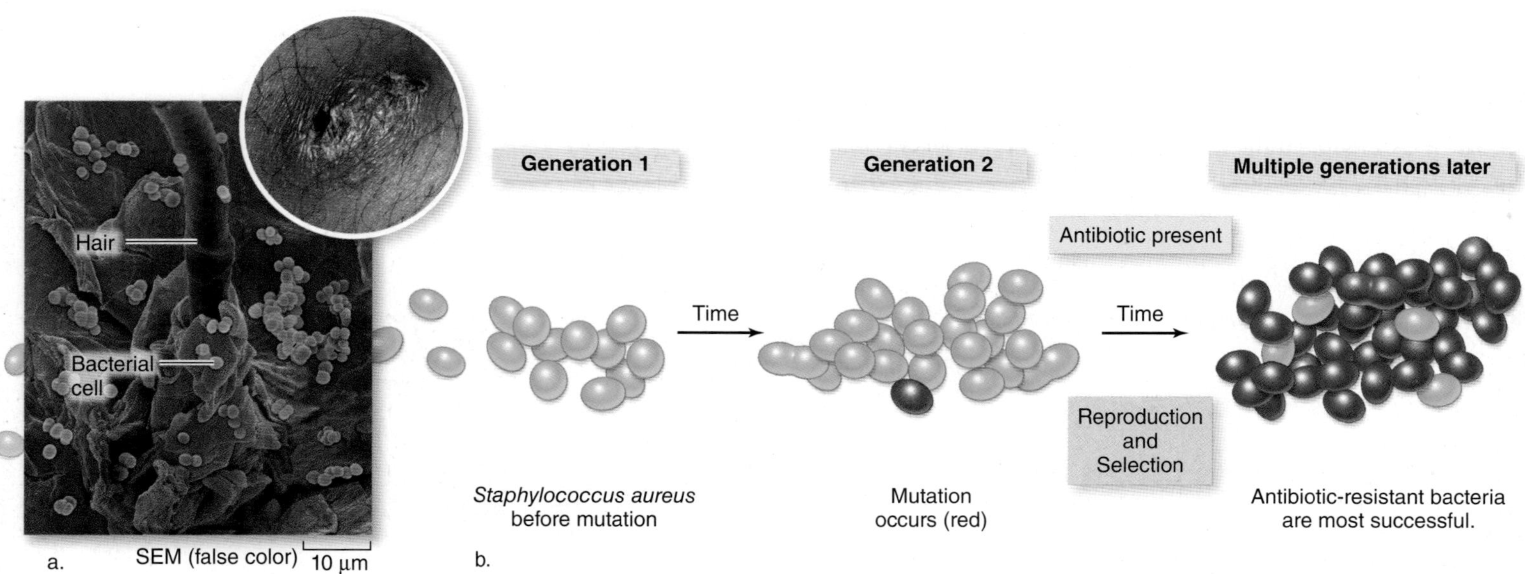

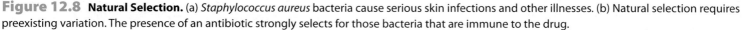

Figure 12.8 **Natural Selection.** (a) *Staphylococcus aureus* bacteria cause serious skin infections and other illnesses. (b) Natural selection requires preexisting variation. The presence of an antibiotic strongly selects for those bacteria that are immune to the drug.

short-term changes in an individual do not constitute evolution. Adaptations in the evolutionary sense include only those structures, behaviors, or physiological processes that are heritable and that contribute to reproductive success.

In any population, individuals with the best adaptations are most likely to reproduce and pass their advantage to their offspring. Because of this "differential reproductive success," a population changes over time, with the best available adaptations to the existing environment becoming more common with each generation (figure 12.8).

Natural selection requires preexisting genetic diversity. Ultimately, this diversity arises largely by chance. Nevertheless, it is important to realize that natural selection itself is not a random process. Instead, it selectively eliminates the individuals that are least able to compete for resources or cope with the prevailing environment.

B. Natural Selection Eliminates Phenotypes

Recall from chapter 10 that an individual's phenotype is its observable properties, most of which arise from a combination of environmental influences and the action of multiple genes. By "weeding out" individuals with poorly adapted phenotypes, natural selection indirectly changes allele frequencies in a population (figure 12.9).

Environmental conditions constantly change, so evolution never really stops. After all, the phenotype that is "best" depends entirely on the time and place; a trait that is adaptive in one set of circumstances may become a liability in another. Some orchids, for example, produce flowers that are pollinated by only one or a few species of wasp (figure 12.10). The orchids release chemicals that mimic a female wasp's pheromones. When a male wasp visits the flower, seeking a mate, pollen from the orchid sticks to its body. The insect later deposits the pollen on another orchid. As long as wasps are present, this exclusive relationship benefits the plants; they do not waste energy by attracting animals that are unlikely to visit another flower of the same species. But if the wasps went extinct, the orchids could no longer reproduce. In that case, having an exclusive relationship with one or a few pollinator species would doom the orchids.

Figure 12.9 **Struggle to Survive.** Newly hatched green sea turtles scurry toward the water. The tiny hatchlings are defenseless against shorebirds, crabs, and other predators; fewer than 1% will survive to maturity. On average, those with the most adaptive combination of traits have the greatest chance of survival.

C. Natural Selection Does Not Have a Goal

Because species complexity has increased over life's long evolutionary history, many people erroneously believe that natural selection leads to ever more "perfect" organisms or that evolution works toward some long-term goal. Explanations that use the words *need* or *in order to* typically reflect this misconception. For example, a person might say, "The orchids started producing pheromones because they needed to attract wasps" or "The orchids make pheromones in order to trick the male wasps into visiting the flowers."

Evolution, however, does not have a goal. How could it? No known mechanism allows the environment to tell DNA how to mutate and generate the alleles needed to confront future conditions. Nor does natural selection strive for perfection; if it did, the vast majority of species in life's history would still exist. Instead, most are extinct.

Several factors combine to prevent natural selection from producing all of the traits that a species might find useful. First, every genome has limited potential, imposed by its evolutionary history. The human skeleton, for example, will not sprout wheels, no matter how useful they might be on paved roads. Second, no population contains every allele needed to confront every possible change in the environment. If the right alleles aren't available at the right time, an environmental change may quickly wipe out a species (figure 12.11). Third, disasters such as floods and volcanic eruptions can indiscriminately wipe out the best allele combinations, simply by chance (see section 12.7). And finally, some harmful genetic traits are out of natural selection's reach; one example is Huntington disease, a severe genetic illness that typically appears after reproductive age.

Figure 12.10 Extremely Specialized. The intimate relationship between this hammer orchid and its pollinator (a wasp) is efficient for the plant. But if the insect goes extinct, the orchid pays the price too.

D. What Does "Survival of the Fittest" Mean?

Natural selection is often called "survival of the fittest," but this phrase is not entirely accurate or complete. In everyday language, the "fittest" individual is the one in the best physical shape: the strongest, fastest, or biggest. Physical fitness, however, is not the key to natural selection (although it may play a part).

Rather, in an evolutionary sense, **fitness** refers to an organism's reproductive contribution to the next generation. A large, quick, burly elk scores zero on the evolutionary fitness scale if poor eyesight makes it vulnerable to an early

a.

b.

Figure 12.11 Extinction. (a) Sea scorpions once thrived worldwide but became extinct some 250 million years ago. (b) These petrified trees in the Arizona desert are from a plant family that is now extinct in the northern hemisphere.

Burning Questions

Why doesn't natural selection produce one superorganism?

Natural selection cannot produce one "perfect" organism that is supremely adapted to every possible habitat on Earth. The simple reason is that the adaptations that seem "perfect" in one habitat would be completely wrong in another. To take an extreme example, a trout's gills and its other adaptations to a cold mountain stream are useless in the sands of the Sahara. The variety of habitats on Earth—from oceans, to freshwater, to the tundra, prairie, desert, and forests—is just too great for one species to be able to thrive everywhere.

Some people believe that evolution actually has produced a superorganism: humans. True, we have the intelligence, dexterity, and cultural background to live on every continent on Earth. But humans can only visit Earth's waters and the highest mountains, areas where other organisms thrive, for brief periods. And few organisms can live in the extreme heat of Earth's interior.

Nevertheless, organisms that can thrive in a wide variety of habitats may threaten Earth's ecosystems. Weeds such as cheat grass and dandelions, along with animal pests such as cockroaches and rats, crowd out native species and appear to be able to live anywhere. Yet even they can't survive where the weather is too hot, too cold, too dry, or too wet. Because different habitats have such different conditions, it seems unlikely that any organism will ever evolve with the combination of traits that would enable it to live everywhere.

Submit your burning question to:
marielle_hoefnagels@mcgraw-hill.com

death in the jaws of a wolf. On the other hand, a mayfly that dies in the act of producing thousands of offspring is highly fit.

Paradoxically, natural selection promotes any trait that increases fitness, even if the trait virtually guarantees an individual's death. For example, a male praying mantis does not resist if the female begins to eat his head during copulation. The male's passive behavior is adaptive because the extra food the female obtains in this way will enhance the chance of survival for their young. Likewise, a male Australian redback spider somersaults his abdomen into the jaws of his mate during copulation. The male's suicidal behavior prolongs copulation, so he sires the most possible offspring. As in the case of the mantis, the male spider does not survive—but his alleles will.

These examples illustrate an important point: *by itself, survival is not enough.* Because successful reproduction is the only way for an organism to perpetuate its genes, fitness depends on the ability to survive just long enough to reproduce. Plants that germinate, flower, produce seeds, and die within a few weeks may have fitness equal to a redwood tree that lives for centuries.

Many adaptations contribute to fitness. If an organism can overcome poor weather conditions, defeat parasites and other disease-causing organisms, evade predators, and compete for resources, it has a good chance of reaching reproductive age. At that point, the ability to attract mates (or pollinators, in the case of many flowering plants) affects the number of offspring an organism produces.

Some people wonder whether evolution will ever produce one species that can thrive and reproduce in every habitat on Earth, outcompeting other species across the globe. This chapter's Burning Question discusses this possibility.

12.3 Mastering Concepts

1. What is an adaptation?
2. What is the role of genetic variation in natural selection?
3. How can natural selection favor different phenotypes at different times?
4. What is "fitness" in the context of evolution?

12.4 Evolution Is Inevitable in Real Populations

Shifting allele frequencies in populations are the small steps of change that collectively drive evolution. Given the large number of genes in any organism and the many factors that can alter allele frequencies (including but not limited to natural selection), evolution is not only possible but unavoidable. This section explains why.

A. At Hardy–Weinberg Equilibrium, Allele Frequencies Do Not Change

The study of population genetics relies on the intimate relationship between allele frequencies and **genotype frequencies.** Each genotype's frequency is the number of individuals with that genotype, divided by the total size of the population. For example, if 64 of the 100 individuals in a population are homozygous recessive, then the frequency of that genotype is 64/100, or 0.64.

Hardy–Weinberg equilibrium is the highly unlikely situation in which allele frequencies and genotype frequencies do not change from one generation to the next. It occurs only in populations that meet the following assumptions: (1) natural selection does not occur; (2) mutations do not occur, so no new alleles arise; (3) the population is infinitely large, or at least large enough to eliminate random changes in allele frequencies; (4) individuals mate at random; and (5) individuals do not migrate into or out of the population.

Two simple equations represent the relationship between allele frequencies and genotype frequencies. Begin by assuming that a gene has only two possible alleles, with frequencies p and q. The first equation, then, is the following expression:

$$p+q=1$$

This equation represents the frequencies of both alleles in the population. For example, suppose that in a population of ferrets, the frequency of the dark fur allele *(D)* is 0.6; the frequency of the tan fur allele *(d)* is 0.4 (figure 12.12). The two frequencies add up to 1 because the two alleles represent all the possibilities in the population.

At Hardy–Weinberg equilibrium, we can use allele frequencies to calculate genotype frequencies, according to the second equation in figure 12.12:

$$p^2 + 2pq + q^2 = 1$$

In this equation, the proportion of the population with genotype *DD* equals p^2, and the proportion of population members with genotype *dd* equals q^2. To calculate the frequency of the heterozygous class, multiply pq by 2. Since the homozygotes and the heterozygotes account for all possible genotypes in the population, the sum of their frequencies must add up to 1.

When the conditions of Hardy–Weinberg equilibrium are met, allele and genotype frequencies will not change in future generations, and evolution will not occur. Conversely, if we observe that genotype frequencies have changed from one generation to the next, we can conclude that the population has evolved.

Besides providing a framework for determining whether evolution has occurred, these two equations are useful because they allow us to infer characteristics of a population based on limited information. One application is the use of known allele frequencies to estimate genotype frequencies in a population. DNA profiling, for example, relies on population databases that contain the known frequencies of each allele at 13 sites in the human genome. Forensic analysts can use this information to calculate the probability that two people share the same genotype across all 13 sites. ▸ DNA profiling, p. 205

Usually, however, we do not know the exact frequency of every allele in a population. In that case, we can use the Hardy–Weinberg equations to estimate allele frequencies based on the known frequency of one genotype. But how do we get that information? Recall from chapter 10 that a distinctive phenotype is often associated with a homozygous recessive genotype. As a result, determining q^2 for some genes is relatively easy. Knowing q, in turn, makes it possible to calculate p. The values of p and q can then be plugged into the second equation to estimate the frequencies of homozygous dominant and heterozygous genotypes. For an example based on a genetic disease called cystic fibrosis, answer the Figure It Out question on this page.

Allele frequencies

p = frequency of D (dominant allele) = dark fur = 0.6
q = frequency of d (recessive allele) = tan fur = 0.4
$p + q = 1$

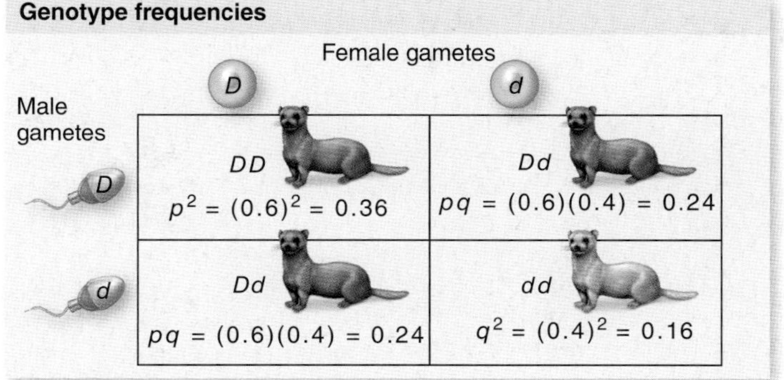

Genotype frequencies
Female gametes
D
d
Male gametes
D
d
DD
$p^2 = (0.6)^2 = 0.36$
Dd
$pq = (0.6)(0.4) = 0.24$
Dd
$pq = (0.6)(0.4) = 0.24$
dd
$q^2 = (0.4)^2 = 0.16$

$p^2 + 2pq + q^2 = 1$

Figure 12.12 Hardy–Weinberg Equilibrium. Two simple equations make it possible to calculate the allele and genotype frequencies of a hypothetical ferret population, assuming that the conditions of Hardy–Weinberg equilibrium are met.

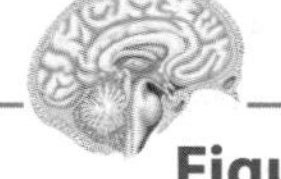

Figure It Out

Assume that one in 3000 Caucasian babies in the United States is born with cystic fibrosis, a disease caused by a recessive allele. The value of q^2 is therefore 1/3000 = 0.0003; q is the square root of 0.0003, or 0.018. Use this information to estimate the frequency of heterozygotes (symptomless carriers) in the American Caucasian population.

Answer: If $q = 0.018$, then $p = 0.982$; the frequency of heterozygotes is $2 \times 0.982 \times 0.018 = 0.035$, or 3.5%.

B. In Reality, Allele Frequencies Always Change

A population at Hardy–Weinberg equilibrium does not evolve. A real population, however, violates some or all of the assumptions of Hardy–Weinberg equilibrium. Allele frequencies change when any of the following occurs:

- some phenotypes are better adapted to the environment than others (natural selection);
- mutations introduce new alleles;
- allele frequencies change due to chance (genetic drift);
- individuals remain in closed groups, mating among themselves rather than with the larger population (nonrandom mating); and
- individuals migrate among populations.

All of these events are common. If you think about the human population, for example, we can sometimes counter natural selection by medically correcting phenotypes that would otherwise prevent some of us from having children. But natural selection still acts to reduce the frequency of alleles that cause deadly childhood illnesses. Moreover, genetic mutations can and do occur. The large size of the human population usually minimizes the chance of random changes in allele frequencies, but they occasionally occur (see section 12.7B). Finally, we do not choose our mates at random, and migration alters allele frequencies as we move and mix.

These forces act on populations of other species as well, so allele frequencies always change over multiple generations. In other words, evolution is inevitable. Even though its assumptions do not apply to real populations, the concept of Hardy–Weinberg equilibrium does serve as a basis of comparison to reveal when microevolution is occurring. Additional studies can then reveal which mechanism of evolution is acting on the population. Sections 12.5 through 12.7 describe these mechanisms of microevolution in more detail.

12.4 Mastering Concepts

1. What five conditions are required for Hardy–Weinberg equilibrium?
2. Explain the components and meaning of the equations $p + q = 1$ and $p^2 + 2pq + q^2 = 1$.
3. Why doesn't Hardy–Weinberg equilibrium occur in real populations?

12.5 Natural Selection Can Shape Populations in Many Ways

Of all the mechanisms by which a population can evolve, natural selection is probably the most important. Natural selection changes the genetic makeup of a population by favoring the alleles that contribute to reproductive success and selecting against those that are harmful.

Natural selection, however, does not eliminate alleles directly. Instead, individuals with the "best" phenotypes are most likely to pass their alleles to the next generation; those with poorly suited phenotypes are less likely to survive long enough to reproduce. Three modes of natural selection—directional, disruptive, and stabilizing—are distinguished by their effects on the phenotypes in a population (figure 12.13).

In **directional selection,** one extreme phenotype is fittest, and the environment selects against the others. In figure 12.13a, for example, a dark brown habitat selects against light-colored moths. The rise of antibiotic resistance among bacteria also reflects directional selection, as described in the Why We Care box on page 233; so does the recent increase in pesticide-resistant insects (see section 10.10). The fittest phenotype may initially be rare, but its frequency increases over multiple generations as the environment changes—for example, after exposure to the antibiotic or insecticide.

In **disruptive selection**, two or more extreme phenotypes are fitter than the intermediate phenotype (see figure 12.13b). Consider, for example, a population of marine snails that live among tan rocks encrusted with white barnacles. The white snails near the barnacles are camouflaged, and the tan ones on the bare rocks likewise blend in. The snails that are not white or tan, or that lie against the oppositely colored background, are more often seen and eaten by predatory shorebirds.

In a third form of natural selection, called **stabilizing selection,** extreme phenotypes are less fit than the intermediate phenotype. Human birth weight illustrates this tendency to stabilize (see figure 12.13c). Very small or very large newborns are less likely to survive than are babies of intermediate weight. By eliminating all but the individuals with the optimal phenotype, stabilizing selection tends to reduce the variation in a population. It is therefore most common in stable, unchanging environments.

These three models of natural selection might seem to suggest that for each trait, only one or a few beneficial alleles ought to persist in the population. The harmful alleles should gradually become less common until they disappear, while the others become "fixed" in the population. For some genes, however, natural selection maintains multiple alleles indefinitely in the population at more or less constant frequencies—even harmful alleles. This situation seems contrary to natural selection; how can it occur?

One circumstance that can maintain harmful alleles occurs when an individual with two different alleles for a gene (a heterozygote) has greater fitness than those whose two alleles are identical (homozygotes). Heterozygotes can maintain a harmful recessive allele in a population, even if homozygous recessive individuals have greatly reduced fitness.

The best documented example is sickle cell disease. The disease-causing allele encodes an abnormal form of hemoglobin. The misshapen hemoglobin proteins do not fold properly; instead, they form chains that bend a red blood cell into a characteristic sickle shape (see figure 7.15). In a person who is homozygous recessive for the sickle cell allele, all the red blood cells are affected. Symptoms include anemia, joint pain, a swollen spleen, and frequent, severe infections; the person may not live long enough to reproduce. On the other hand, a person who is heterozygous for the sickle cell allele is only mildly affected. Some of his or her red blood cells may take abnormal shapes, but the resulting mild anemia is not usually harmful.

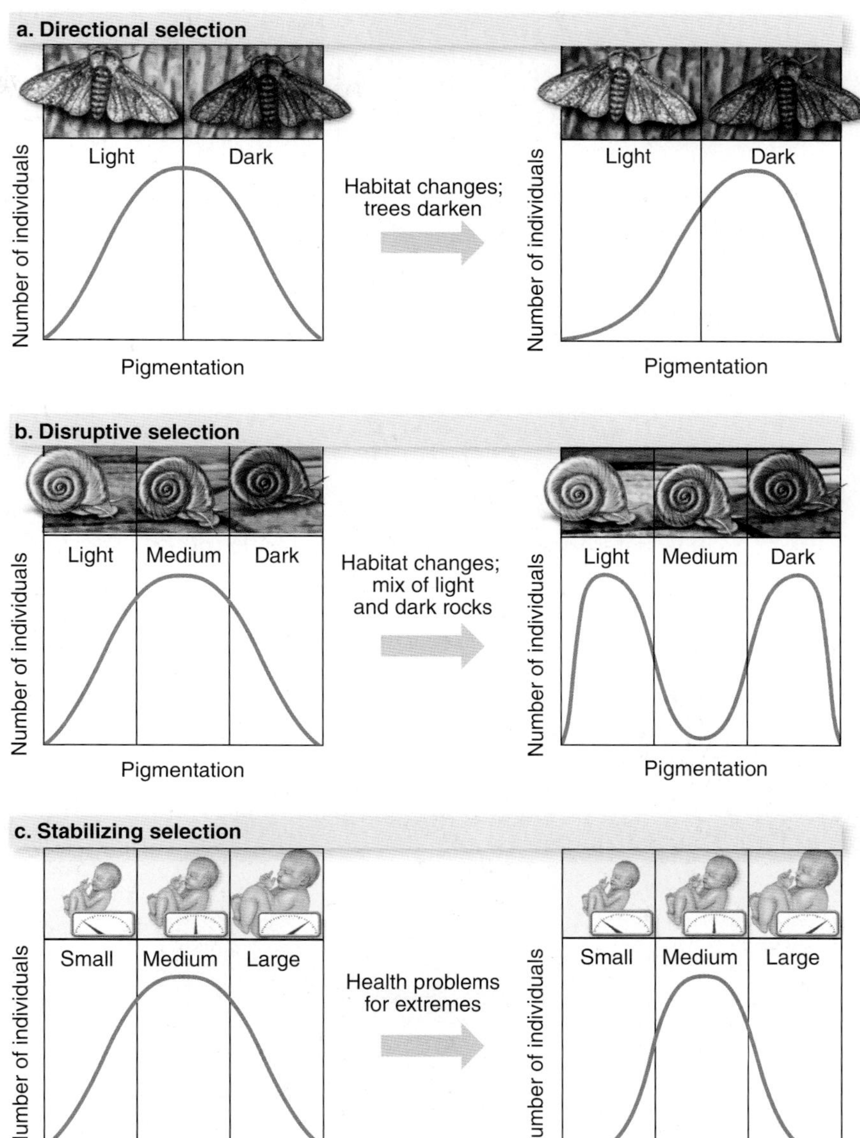

Figure 12.13 Types of Natural Selection. (a) Directional selection results from selection against one extreme phenotype. (b) In disruptive selection, two extreme phenotypes each confer a selective advantage over the intermediate phenotype. (c) Stabilizing selection maintains an intermediate expression of a trait by selecting against extreme variants.

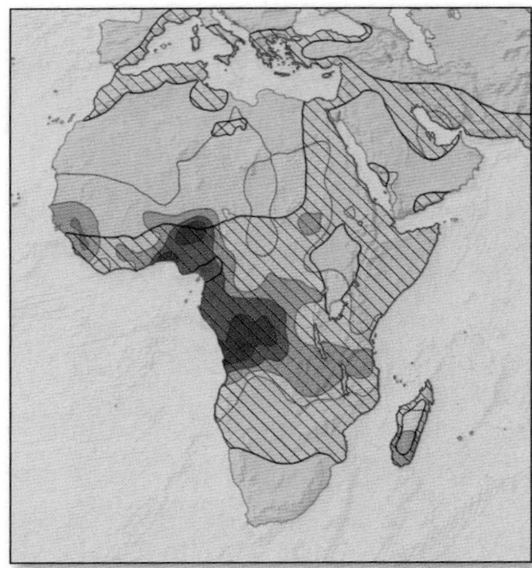

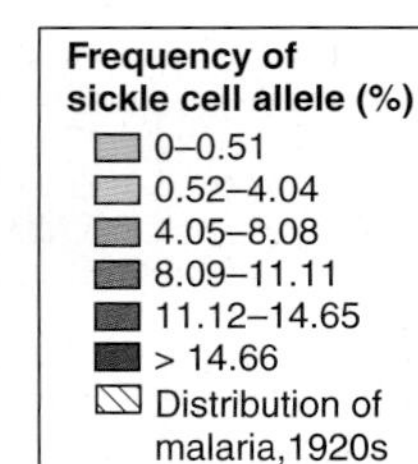

Figure 12.14 Heterozygote Advantage. The distribution of people with the sickle cell allele overlaps closely with the areas where malaria is prevalent. Sickle cell anemia and malaria are opposing selective forces that maintain both alleles of the hemoglobin gene.

Still, why doesn't natural selection eliminate the sickle cell allele from the population? The answer is that heterozygotes also have a reproductive edge over people who are homozygous for the *normal* hemoglobin allele. Specifically, heterozygotes are resistant to a severe infectious disease, malaria. When a mosquito carrying cells of a protist called *Plasmodium* feeds on a human with normal hemoglobin, the parasite enters the red blood cells. Eventually, infected blood cells burst, and the parasite travels throughout the body. But the sickled red blood cells of an infected carrier halt the parasite's spread. ▸ malaria, p. 295

The frequency of the sickle cell allele varies regionally (figure 12.14). In malaria-free areas, anemia is the predominant selective force, and heterozygotes have no advantage. The sickle cell allele is therefore rare. Wherever malaria rages, however, two opposing selective forces are in play—anemia and malaria. In these areas, sickle cell carriers remain healthiest; they are resistant to malaria but not sick from sickle cell disease. The frequency of the sickle cell allele remains high because carriers have higher fitness than people who are homozygous for either allele.

Unfortunately, as described in chapter 10, two carriers have a 25% chance of producing a child who is homozygous for the sickle cell allele. These children pay the evolutionary price for the genetic protection against malaria.

12.5 Mastering Concepts

1. Distinguish among directional, disruptive, and stabilizing selection.
2. How can natural selection maintain harmful alleles in a population?

12.6 Sexual Selection Directly Influences Reproductive Success

In many species, the sexes look alike. The difference between a male and a female house cat, for example, is not immediately obvious. In some species, however, natural selection can maintain a **sexual dimorphism,** which is a difference in appearance between males and females. One sex may be much larger or more colorful than the other, or one sex may have distinctive structures such as horns or antlers.

Some of these sexually dimorphic features may seem to violate natural selection. For example, the vivid red feathers of a male cardinal make the bird extremely obvious to predators, and the extravagant tail of a peacock is both brightly colored and too long to permit extensive flight. How can natural selection allow for traits that apparently reduce survival?

The answer is that a special form of natural selection is at work. **Sexual selection** is a type of natural selection resulting from variation in the ability to obtain mates (figure 12.15). If female cardinals prefer bright red males, then showy plumage increases a male's chance of reproducing. Because the brightest males get the most opportunities to mate, alleles that confer red plumage are common in the population.

Sexual selection has two forms. The members of one sex may compete among themselves for access to the opposite sex; mate choice plays no part in deciding the winner. Male bighorn sheep, for example, use their horns to battle

Figure 12.15 Examples of Sexual Selection. (a) Male weaver birds build nests, then females select mates based on nest quality. (b) The male bird-of-paradise displays bright plumes in his quest to attract females. (c) Two bighorn sheep prepare to butt heads in the Rocky Mountains.

Why We Care | The Rise of Antibiotic Resistance

Biologists discovered antibiotics in the early 1900s, but it took decades for chemists to figure out how to mass-produce them. Once that occurred, antibiotics revolutionized medical care in the twentieth century and enabled people to survive many once-deadly bacterial infections.

Unfortunately, the miracle of antibiotics is under threat, and many infections that once were easily treated are reemerging as killers. Ironically, the overuse and misuse of antibiotics is partly responsible for the problem. Physicians sometimes prescribe antibiotics for viral infections, even though the drugs kill only bacteria; moreover, many patients fail to take the drugs as directed. Agricultural practices contribute to the problem as well. Producers of cattle, chickens, and other animals use antibiotics to treat and prevent disease, even adding small amounts to the animals' feed to promote growth. Farmers also spray antibiotics on fruit and vegetable-producing plants to treat bacterial infections.

By saturating the environment with antibiotics, we have profoundly affected the evolution of bacteria. Microbes that can defeat the drugs are now common, and the explanation is simple. Antibiotics kill susceptible bacteria and leave the resistant ones alone. The survivors multiply, producing a new generation of antibiotic-resistant bacteria. This is an example of natural selection in action, and the public health consequences are both widespread and severe.

Antibiotic-resistant bacteria appeared just four years after these drugs entered medical practice in the late 1940s, and researchers responded by discovering new drugs. But the microbes kept pace. Today, 40% of hospital *Staphylococcus* infections resist all antibiotics but one. These so-called "superbugs" are called MRSA, which is short for methicillin-resistant *Staphylococcus aureus*. Worse, some laboratory strains are resistant to all antibiotics. Researchers fear that the discovery of new antibiotics will not keep up with the rate at which resistant strains evolve and spread around the world (figure 12.A).

Figure 12.A Close Quarters. Extreme crowding in this Russian prison promotes the spread of antibiotic-resistant tuberculosis and other infectious diseases.

for the right to mate with multiple females. The strongest rams are therefore the most likely to pass on their alleles. In the other type of sexual selection, the members of one sex (usually female) choose their mates from among multiple individuals of the opposite sex. The brightest red cardinals and the peacocks with the showiest tails win their respective competitions for female attention.

Why are males typically competing for females, and not the other way around? In most (but not all) animal species, females spend more time and energy rearing offspring than do males. Because of this high investment in reproduction, females tend to be selective about their mates. Males that must compete for access to females show the greatest effects of sexual selection.

The evolutionary origin of the males' elaborate ornaments remains an open question. One possibility is that long tail feathers and bright colors are costly to produce and maintain; they are therefore indirect advertisements of good health or disease resistance. Likewise, the ability to win fights with competing males is also an indicator of good genes. A female who instinctively chooses a high-quality male will increase not only his fitness but also her own.

12.6 Mastering Concepts

1. How does sexual selection promote traits that would seem to decrease fitness?
2. Describe two ways that competition for access to mates can lead to sexual selection.

12.7 Evolution Occurs in Several Additional Ways

Natural selection is responsible for adaptations that enhance survival and reproduction, but it is not the only mechanism of evolution. This section describes four more ways that a population can evolve: mutation, genetic drift, nonrandom mating, and migration. All occur frequently, and each can, by itself, disrupt Hardy–Weinberg equilibrium. The changes in allele frequencies that constitute microevolution therefore occur nearly all the time.

A. Mutation Fuels Evolution

A change in an organism's DNA sequence introduces a new allele to a population. The new variant may be harmful, neutral, or beneficial, depending on its effect on the sequence of the encoded protein. Mutations are the raw material for evolution because genes contribute to phenotypes. As we have already seen, natural selection "weeds out" harmful phenotypes and selects for those that promote reproductive success. ▸ mutations, p. 123

For example, random mutations in bacterial DNA may change the shapes of key proteins in the cell wall. Exposure to antibiotics selects for some of the new phenotypes if they happen to make the cell resistant to the drug. In that case, the mutations will pass to the next generation.

A common misconception is that a mutation produces a novel adaptation precisely when a population "needs" it to confront a new environmental challenge. For example, many people mistakenly believe that antibiotics *create* resistance; that is, that resistance originates in bacteria *in response* to exposure to the drugs.

In reality, genes do not "know" when to mutate. Instead, antibiotic resistance arises when exposure to the drug selects for those bacteria that already happen to have the mutation that confers resistance. The drug simply creates a situation in which these variants can flourish. That trait will then become more common within the population by natural selection. Conversely, if no bacteria are resistant upon exposure to the drug, the entire population may die.

A mutation affects evolution only if subsequent generations can inherit it. In asexually reproducing organisms such as bacteria, each mutated cell gives rise to mutant offspring (if the mutation does not prevent reproduction). In a multicellular organism, however, a mutation can pass to the next generation only if it arises in a germ cell (i.e., one that will give rise to gametes; see chapter 9). For example, a cigarette smoker with lung cancer will not pass any smoking-induced mutations to her children, because her egg cells will not contain the altered DNA.

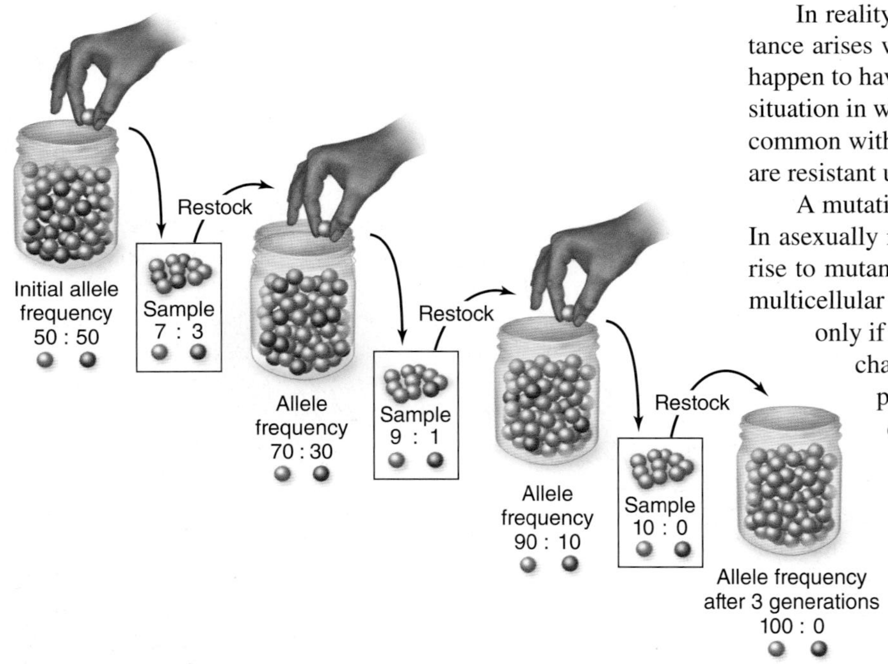

Figure 12.16 Sampling Error. Ten marbles are drawn at random from the jar on the left. Even though 50% of the marbles in the jar are blue, the random sample contains only 30% blue marbles. In the next "generation," 30% of the marbles are blue, but the random sample contains just one blue marble. The third sample contains no blue marbles and therefore eliminates the blue "allele" from the population, purely by chance.

B. Genetic Drift Occurs by Chance

Genetic drift is a change in allele frequencies that occurs purely by chance. Unlike mutation, which increases diversity, genetic drift tends to eliminate alleles from a population.

Genetic drift is rooted in sampling error, which occurs when a sample does not match the larger group from which it is drawn (figure 12.16). Such sampling errors are most likely to affect small populations. Suppose, for example, that one allele of a gene occurs at a very low frequency in a small population. If, by chance, none of the individuals carrying the rare allele happens to reproduce, that variant will disappear from the population. Even if some do reproduce, the allele still might not pass to the next generation. After all, the events of meiosis ensure that each allele has only a 50% chance of passing to each offspring. A rare allele can therefore vanish from a population—not because it reduces fitness but simply by chance.

Two examples of circumstances that illustrate genetic drift are the founder effect and the bottleneck effect.

The Founder Effect The **founder effect** occurs when a small group of individuals separates from its home population and establishes a new, isolated settlement (figure 12.17). The small group's "allele sample" may not represent the allele frequencies of the original population. Some traits that were rare in the original population may therefore be more frequent in the new population. Other traits will be less common or may even disappear.

The Amish people of Pennsylvania provide a famous example of the founder effect. About 200 followers of the Amish denomination immigrated to North America from Switzerland in the 1700s. One couple, who immigrated in 1744, happened to carry the recessive allele associated with Ellis–van Creveld syndrome. This allele is extremely rare in the population at large. Intermarriage among the Amish, however, has kept the disease's incidence high in this subgroup for centuries after the original immigrants arrived.

The Bottleneck Effect Genetic drift also may result from a population **bottleneck,** which occurs when a population drops rapidly over a short period. This bottleneck causes the loss of many alleles that were present in the larger ancestral population (figure 12.18). Even if the few remaining individuals reproduce and restore the population's numbers, the loss of genetic diversity is permanent.

Cheetahs are currently undergoing a population bottleneck. These cats were common in many areas until about 10,000 years ago. Today, just two isolated populations live in South and East Africa, numbering only a few thousand animals. Inbreeding has made the South African cheetahs so genetically alike that even unrelated animals can accept skin grafts from each other. At least two bottlenecks account for this genetic uniformity. One occurred at the end of the most recent ice age, when habitats changed drastically. Another occurred when humans slaughtered many cheetahs during the nineteenth century.

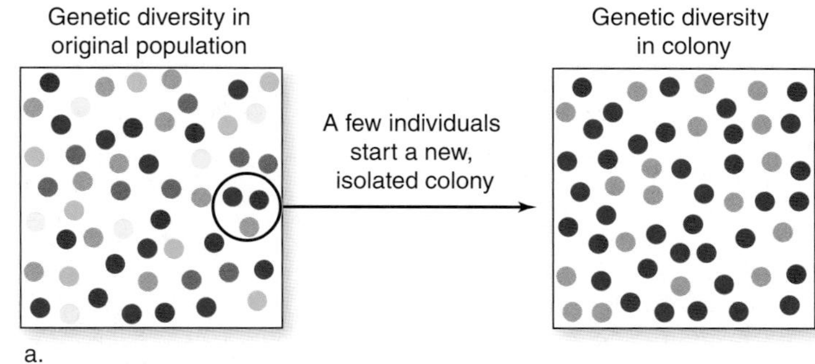
Genetic diversity in original population
A few individuals start a new, isolated colony
Genetic diversity in colony
a.

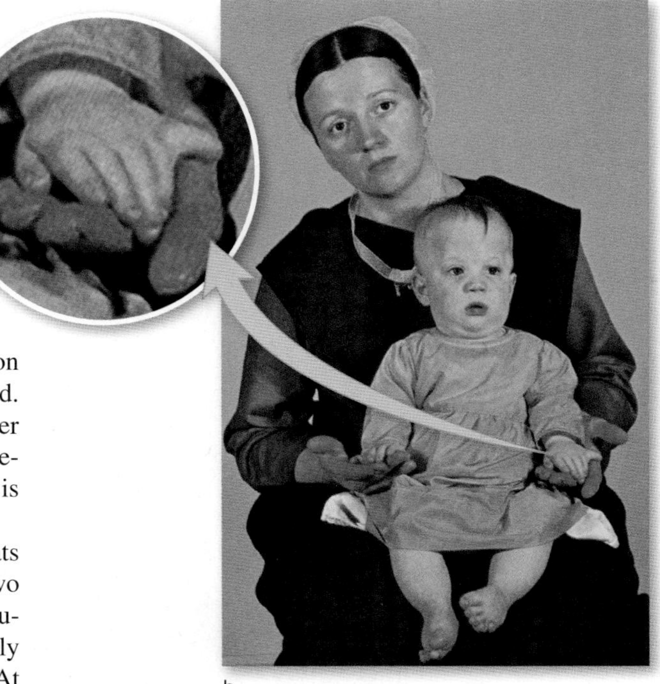
b.

Figure 12.17 **The Founder Effect.** (a) A few individuals leave one population and begin an isolated colony, which contains only some of the original population's diversity. (b) This child from Lancaster County, Pennsylvania, has inherited Ellis–van Creveld syndrome, a condition characterized by short-limbed dwarfism, extra fingers, and other symptoms. This autosomal recessive disorder occurs in 7% of the people of this Amish community but is extremely rare elsewhere.

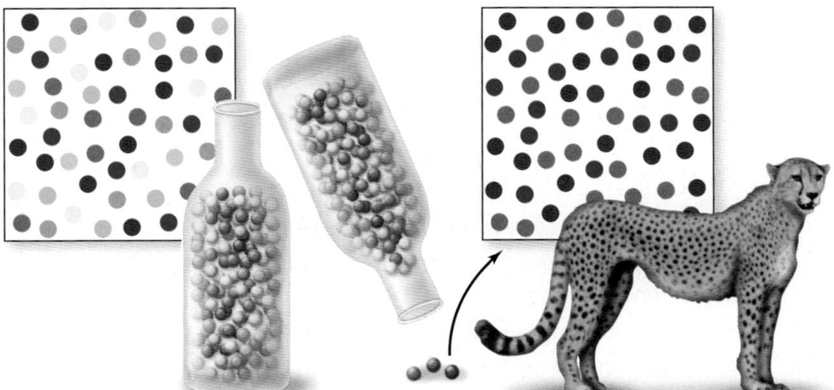
Original cheetah population contains 25 different alleles of a particular gene.
Cheetah population is drastically reduced.
Repopulation occurs. Only three different alleles remain.

Figure 12.18 **The Bottleneck Effect.** A population bottleneck occurs when the size of a population drastically falls, eliminating some alleles at random. Even if the population rebuilds, some genetic diversity is lost forever.

North American species have undergone severe bottlenecks as well. Bison, for example, nearly went extinct because of overhunting in the 1800s. And habitat loss has caused the population of greater prairie chickens to plummet from about 100 million in 1900 to several hundred today. The loss of genetic diversity in cheetahs, bison, and prairie chickens invites disaster: a single change in the environment might doom them all.

C. Mate Selection Leads to Nonrandom Mating

In a population with completely random mating, every individual has an equal chance of mating with any other member of the population. Wind-pollinated plants illustrate random mating, as do sponges and other aquatic animals that cannot move; these animals simply release their sperm into the open water.

In most species, however, mating is rarely random. Most animals exhibit some form of preference in mate choice, including sexual selection. Individuals with the "preferred" traits therefore leave the most offspring. Humans in particular give great consideration to choosing mates; it is hardly a random process. For many people, cultural factors such as social position and religion are especially important in choosing partners.

The practice of artificial selection reduces random mating as well. Humans select those animals or plants that have a desired trait and then prevent them from mating with those lacking that trait. The result is a wide variety of subpopulations (such as different breeds of dogs) that humans maintain by selective breeding.

Figure 12.19 Migration. Immigration is one way for new alleles to enter a population.

D. Migration Moves Alleles Between Populations

Migration is the movement of individuals into or out of a population. Departing members of a population take their alleles with them. Likewise, new members entering and interbreeding with an existing population may add new alleles (figure 12.19).

Consider the human population of a large city such as New York City, the product of multiple waves of immigration. The original Dutch settlers of the 1600s had the alleles typical of northern Europeans. Immigrants from other parts of Europe, Africa, Central and South America, and Asia subsequently introduced many of the alleles present in today's metropolis.

Migration can counteract the effects of both natural selection and genetic drift. At one time, isolated European populations had different frequencies of many genetic diseases. Geographical barriers, such as mountain ranges and large bodies of water, historically restricted migration and kept the gene pools separate. Highways, trains, and airplanes, however, have eliminated physical barriers to migration. Eventually, migration will probably make these regional differences disappear.

12.7 Mastering Concepts

1. How do mutations affect an organism's phenotype?
2. Under what conditions does a mutation in one organism pass to subsequent generations?
3. How does sampling error cause genetic drift?
4. What is the difference between the founder effect and a population bottleneck?
5. How do nonrandom mating and migration result in evolutionary change?

Investigating Life

12.8 Size Matters in Fishing Frenzy

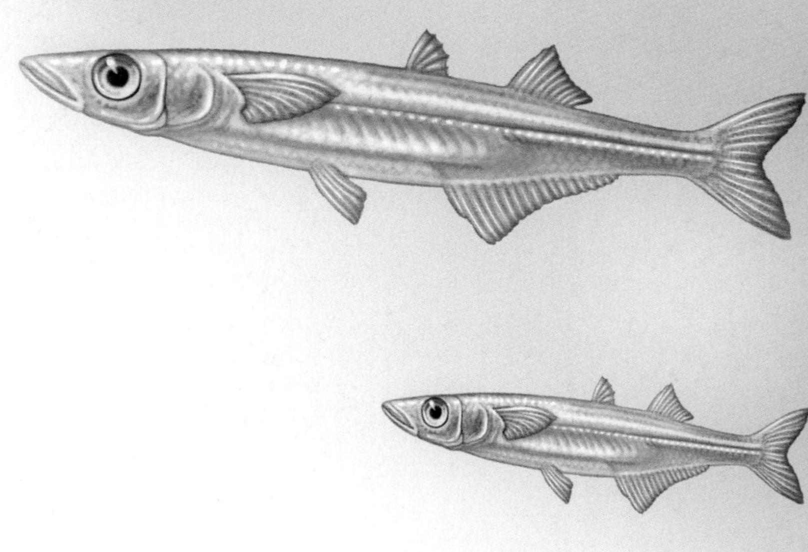

Studying the mechanisms of evolution helps us to understand life's history, but it also has practical consequences. A good example of natural selection is unfolding in fisheries worldwide. The selective force stems from a surprisingly mundane source—fishing regulations—but it affects everything from restaurant menus, to coastal economies, to the future of the ocean ecosystem.

The past several decades have seen devastating declines in the numbers of large predatory fishes such as swordfish, marlin, and sharks, as well as smaller animals including tuna, cod, and flounder. From a biological point of view, the reason for the fisheries decline is simple: the animals' death rate exceeds their reproductive rate. Since the 1950s, industrial-scale fishing fleets have employed larger ships and improved technologies in pursuit of their prey.

The Question: Fishing regulations usually allow the harvest of only those fish that exceed some minimum size. This strategy is logical, because the smallest fish are most likely to be juveniles. Protecting the youngsters should permit the population to recover from the harvest of adult fish. But these regulations may also have evolutionary side effects. That is, if humans selectively harvest the largest individuals, fish that are small at maturity are the most likely to reproduce. Large fish may become more scarce over many generations. The same policy should also select for slow-growing fish, since they would be last to exceed the minimum allowed size. Do current fishing regulations really have the undesirable effect of selecting for small, slow-growing fish?

The Approach: Fish ecologists David Conover and Stephan Munch of the State University of New York tested these predictions on a small coastal fish called the Atlantic silverside *(Menidia menidia).* Conover and Munch set up their experiment by randomly dividing a large, captive population of Atlantic silversides into six tanks, each containing about 1100 juvenile fish. After about 6 months, the researchers assigned two tanks to each of the following treatments:

- **Large harvested:** Remove the largest 90% of the fish from two of the tanks, leaving the smallest 10% to reproduce. This treatment simulated fishing policies that protect all fish below a minimum size.
- **Small harvested:** Remove the smallest 90% of the silversides.
- **Random harvested (control):** Remove 90% of the fish, without size bias.

After the harvests, the 100 or so survivors in each tank reproduced, and their descendants were reared in identical conditions until it was again time to harvest 90% of each population. The researchers repeated the treatments over four generations of fish.

The Conclusion: Predictably, both the total harvest weight and the weight of the average caught fish were initially highest for the large-harvested fish. Over four generations of size-biased fish removal, however, the small-harvested treatment favored both large size and rapid growth; the opposite was true in the large-harvested population (figure 12.20). The researchers concluded that the three treatments imposed different selective forces that changed the genetic structure of the populations.

Conover and Munch's experiment is more than a straightforward demonstration of natural selection in action; it also has economic and ecological applications. Revised regulations that protect the smallest and the largest fish

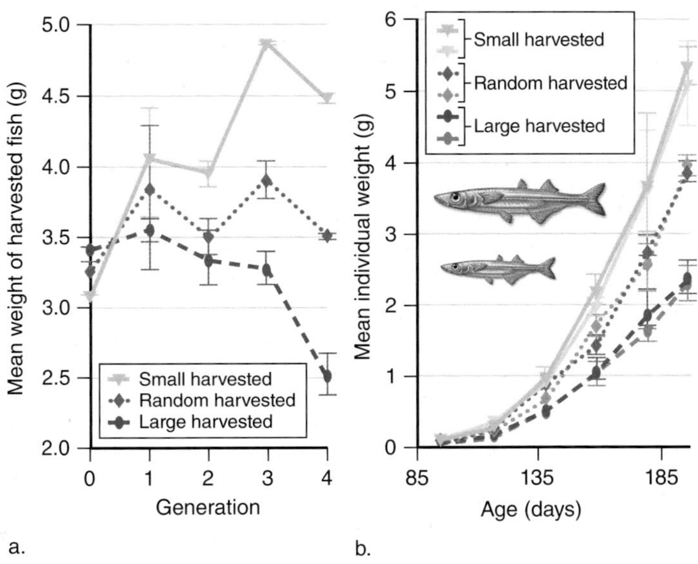

Figure 12.20 Size Matters in Fish Harvests. (a) Over four generations, the average per-fish weight in the large-harvested population was much less than the average for the small-harvested population. (b) Small-harvested fish grew faster than large-harvested fish.

would spare the juveniles that are critical to a species' future reproduction while also selecting for fast-growing fish. Imposing a maximum size limit would also have ecological benefits, restoring the feeding patterns and other "ecosystem services" of the largest fish. This wide range of implications beautifully illustrates the powerful ideas that spring from understanding one fundamental idea: natural selection.

Conover, David O., and Stephan B. Munch. 2002. Sustaining fisheries yields over evolutionary time scales. *Science,* vol. 297, pages 94–96.

12.8 Mastering Concepts

1. What hypothesis did Conover and Munch test?
2. How is a population reared in a tank different from a population in the "real world"?
3. The heritability of a trait is the extent to which it is genetically determined. Heritability ranges from 0 (entirely under environmental control) to 1.0 (100% controlled by genes). In Atlantic silversides, the heritability of body size is about 0.2. How would the results of this experiment differ if heritability of body size were higher? What if it approached zero?

Chapter Summary

12.1 Evolution Acts on Populations

- Biological **evolution** is descent with modification. One way to detect evolution is to look for a shift in the **gene pool** of a **population; allele frequencies** change from one generation to the next when evolution occurs.
- **Microevolution** is the small-scale genetic changes within a species. Over the long term, microevolutionary changes also explain macroevolutionary events.

12.2 Evolutionary Thought Has Evolved for Centuries

A. Many Explanations Have Been Proposed for Life's Diversity

- Early attempts to explain life's diversity relied on belief in a creator.
- Geology laid the groundwork for evolutionary thought. Lower rock layers are older than those above, suggesting a time frame for fossils within them.
- Lamarck was the first to propose a testable mechanism of evolution, but it was erroneously based on inheritance of acquired characteristics.

B. Charles Darwin's Voyage Provided a Wealth of Evidence

- During the voyage of the HMS *Beagle,* Darwin observed the distribution of organisms in diverse habitats and their relationships to geological formations. After much thought and consideration of input from other scientists, he developed his theory of the origin of species by means of natural selection.

C. *On the Origin of Species* Proposed Natural Selection as an Evolutionary Mechanism

- **Natural selection** is based on the observations that individuals vary for inherited traits; that many more offspring are born than survive; and that life is a struggle for use of limited resources.
- **Artificial selection** is based on similar requirements, except that a human breeder takes the place of the environment.
- *On the Origin of Species* offered abundant evidence for the idea of descent with modification. However, people who believed that Earth is young and that humans are unique had difficulty accepting Darwin's ideas.

D. Evolutionary Theory Continues to Expand

- The **modern evolutionary synthesis** unifies ideas about DNA, mutations, inheritance, and natural selection.

12.3 Natural Selection Molds Evolution

A. Adaptations Enhance Reproductive Success

- Individuals with the best **adaptations** to the current environment are most likely to leave fertile offspring, and therefore their alleles become more common in the population over time.
- Natural selection requires variation, which arises ultimately from random mutations.

B. Natural Selection Eliminates Phenotypes

- Natural selection weeds out some phenotypes, causing changes in allele frequencies over multiple generations.

C. Natural Selection Does Not Have a Goal

- Natural selection does not work toward an objective, nor can it achieve perfectly adapted organisms.

D. What Does "Survival of the Fittest" Mean?

- Organisms with the highest evolutionary **fitness** are the ones that have the greatest reproductive success. Many traits contribute to an organism's fitness.

12.4 Evolution Is Inevitable in Real Populations

A. At Hardy–Weinberg Equilibrium, Allele Frequencies Do Not Change

- Calculations of allele frequencies and **genotype frequencies** allow biologists to detect whether evolution has occurred.
- The frequencies of the two alleles for a gene add up to one: $p + q = 1$.

- At **Hardy–Weinberg equilibrium,** we can calculate the frequency of each genotype in a population by inserting known allele frequencies into the following equation: $p^2 + 2pq + q^2 = 1$.
- If a population meets all assumptions of Hardy–Weinberg equilibrium, evolution does not occur because allele frequencies do not change from generation to generation.

B. In Reality, Allele Frequencies Always Change

- The conditions for Hardy–Weinberg equilibrium do not occur together in natural populations, suggesting that allele frequencies always change.

12.5 Natural Selection Can Shape Populations in Many Ways

- In **directional selection,** one extreme phenotype becomes more prevalent in a population.
- In **disruptive selection,** two (or more) extreme phenotypes survive at the expense of intermediate forms.
- In **stabilizing selection,** an intermediate phenotype has an advantage over individuals with extreme phenotypes.
- Harmful recessive alleles may persist in populations where heterozygous carriers have a reproductive advantage over homozygotes.

12.6 Sexual Selection Directly Influences Reproductive Success

- **Sexual dimorphisms** differentiate the sexes. They result from **sexual selection,** a form of natural selection in which inherited traits—even those that seem nonadaptive—make an individual more likely to mate.
- The competition that promotes sexual selection may or may not involve mate choice by members of the opposite sex.

12.7 Evolution Occurs in Several Additional Ways

A. Mutation Fuels Evolution

- Mutation alters allele frequencies by changing one allele into another, sometimes providing new phenotypes for natural selection to act on.

B. Genetic Drift Occurs by Chance

- In **genetic drift,** allele frequencies change purely by chance events, especially in small populations. The **founder effect** and population **bottlenecks** are forms of genetic drift.

C. Mate Selection Leads to Nonrandom Mating

- On average, individuals with traits that are preferred by the opposite sex leave the most offspring.

D. Migration Moves Alleles Between Populations

- As individuals migrate, they can carry new alleles into existing populations, altering allele frequencies.

12.8 Investigating Life: Size Matters in Fishing Frenzy

- Fishing regulations that spare only the smallest fish in a population select for small, slow-growing individuals. Studies of Atlantic silversides suggest that protecting the largest fish as well would increase fishery productivity in the long run.

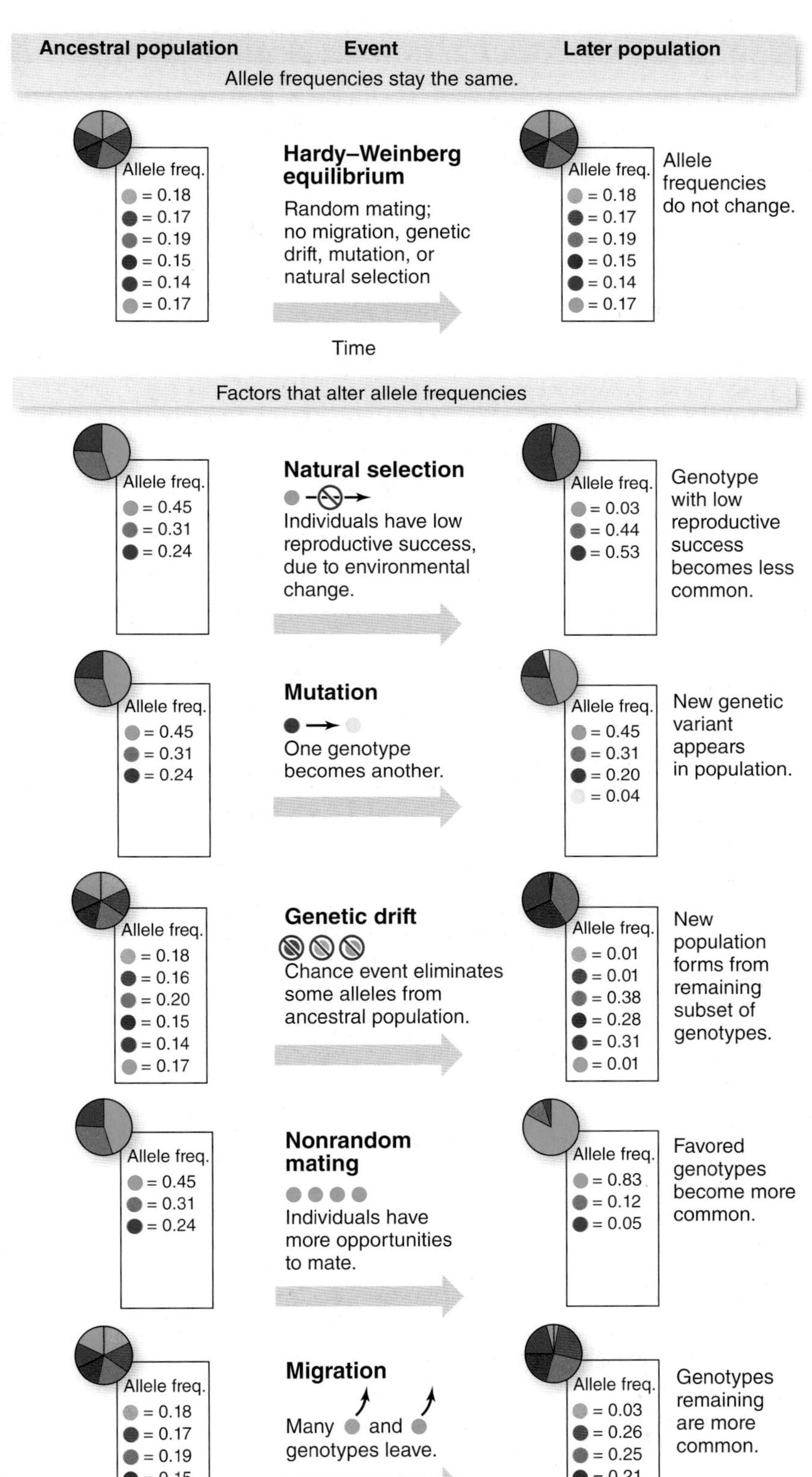

Multiple Choice Questions

1. Microevolution applies to changes that occur
   a. only within small populations of organisms.
   b. in small regions of DNA.
   c. in the allele frequencies of a population or species.
   d. in small cells such as bacteria.
2. How are artificial selection and natural selection similar?
   a. They both rely on human intervention.
   b. They both work toward a predetermined goal.
   c. They both select for specific traits within a population.
   d. They both are processes that only affect animals.
3. How does natural selection influence a gene pool?
   a. It selects for alleles that will be useful in the future.
   b. It triggers mutations, leading to increased diversity.
   c. It alters the frequency of alleles within an individual.
   d. It alters the frequency of alleles within a population.
4. Which of the following is the best definition of evolutionary fitness?
   a. The ability to increase the number of alleles in a gene pool
   b. The ability to survive for a long time
   c. The ability of an individual to adapt to a changing environment
   d. The ability to produce many offspring
5. Selection that favors two or more extreme phenotypes is called
   a. directional selection.
   b. stabilizing selection.
   c. disruptive selection.
   d. normalizing selection.
6. Huntington disease is caused by a lethal dominant allele that usually affects individuals late in life. How can natural selection explain why the disease-causing allele remains in the human population?
   a. The heterozygous individual might have some advantage.
   b. The disease does not interfere with the ability to reproduce.
   c. New mutations generate the allele.
   d. Both a and b are correct.
7. Assume a population is 36% homozygous dominant and 16% homozygous recessive. What percentage of the population is heterozygous, based on Hardy–Weinberg equilibrium?
   a. 64%
   b. 52%
   c. 48%
   d. 26%
8. Sexual selection
   a. typically occurs after mating has already taken place.
   b. is one type of artificial selection.
   c. results in sexual dimorphism.
   d. explains why sexual reproduction occurs in so many species.
9. Darwin observed that different types of organisms were found on either side of a geographic barrier. The barrier was preventing
   a. migration.
   b. genetic drift.
   c. sexual selection.
   d. mutation.
10. Which of the following processes is nonrandom?
    a. A population bottleneck
    b. Natural selection
    c. The founder effect
    d. Mutation

Write It Out

1. List and describe five mechanisms of evolution.
2. How did the work of other scientists influence Charles Darwin's thinking?
3. Your boss is a plant breeder who asks you to develop a sweeter variety of apple. How would you use artificial selection to achieve this goal? How might natural selection produce the same result? Which would occur faster, artificial selection or natural selection?
4. How does variation arise in an asexually reproducing population? A sexually reproducing population?
5. What happens to a population if conditions change and no individuals have the allele combinations required to survive and produce offspring?
6. Many articles about the rise of antibiotic-resistant bacteria claim that overuse of antibiotics creates resistant strains. How is this incorrect?
7. Explain how harmful recessive alleles can persist in populations, even though they prevent homozygous individuals from reproducing.
8. Fraggles are mythical, mouselike creatures that live underground beneath a large vegetable garden. Of the 100 Fraggles in this population, 84 have green fur, and 16 have gray fur. A dominant allele *F* confers green fur, and a recessive allele *f* confers gray fur. Assuming Hardy–Weinberg equilibrium is operating, answer the following questions. (a) What is the frequency of the gray allele *f*? (b) What is the frequency of the green allele *F*? (c) How many Fraggles are heterozygotes (*Ff*)? (d) How many Fraggles are homozygous recessive (*ff*)? (e) How many Fraggles are homozygous dominant (*FF*)?
9. One spring, a dust storm blankets the usually green garden of the Fraggles in gray. The green Fraggles therefore become visible to the Gorgs, who tend the gardens and try to kill the Fraggles to protect their crops. The gray Fraggles, however, blend easily into the dusty background. How might this event affect microevolution in the Fraggles? What mode of natural selection does this represent?
10. Describe examples of directional, disruptive, and stabilizing selection other than those mentioned in the chapter.
11. A male cardinal is bright red; his mate is a drab brown. How does sexual selection explain this difference?
12. Many American farmers routinely use an herbicide called glyphosate to keep their fields weed-free. They are now reporting the emergence and spread of glyphosate-resistant species of "superweeds." Use natural selection to explain this situation. What might farmers do to minimize the problem?
13. The giraffe in the chapter opening photo has a long neck. Use natural selection to explain how a long-necked species could evolve from an ancestral population with short necks. How does your explanation compare to how Lamarck might have explained it?

Pull It Together

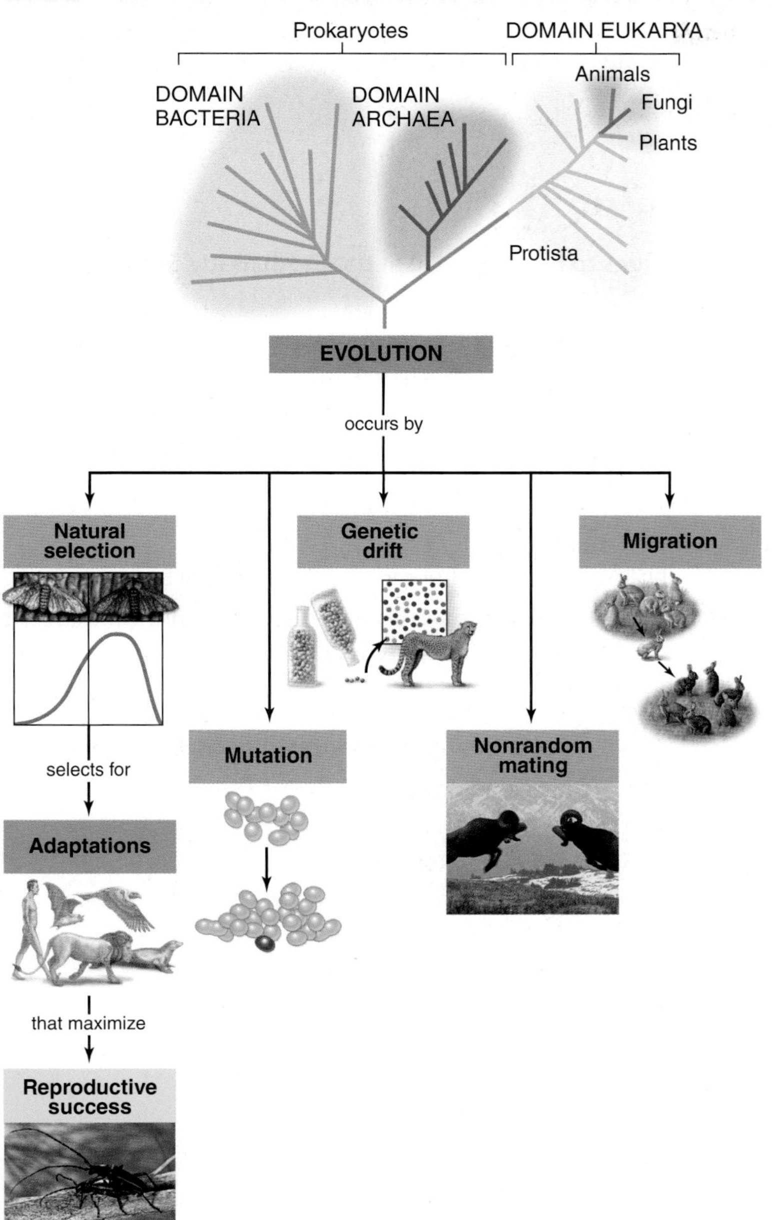

1. What is the biological definition of evolution?
2. Add the terms *genotype, phenotype, allele frequencies, founder effect, bottleneck effect,* and *sexual selection* to this concept map.
3. How does each mechanism of evolution change allele frequencies in a population?
4. Describe the three modes of natural selection.

13 Evidence of Evolution

Feathery Dinosaur. The dinosaur *Protarchaeopteryx* lived about 145 million years ago in China. It had feathers, revealing a close evolutionary relationship to birds. The model (inset) shows what the animal might have looked like.

Learning Outline

Learn How to Learn
Why Rewrite Your Notes?

Your notes are your record of what happened in class, so why should you rewrite them after a lecture is over? One answer is that the abbreviations and shorthand that make perfect sense while you take notes will become increasingly mysterious as time goes by. Rewriting the information in complete sentences not only reinforces learning but also makes your notes much easier to study before an exam.

What's the Point?

Some people believe that evolution cannot be tested because it happened in the past. Although no experiment can recreate the conditions that led to today's diversity of life, evolution is testable. In fact, its validity has been verified repeatedly over the past 150 years.

A mountain of evidence supports the idea of common descent. Extinct organisms have left traces of their existence, both as fossils and as the genetic legacy that all organisms have inherited. The distribution of life on Earth offers other clues, as does the study of everything from anatomical structures to protein sequences. Laboratory experiments and field observations of natural populations likewise support the case for evolution and suggest likely mechanisms for evolutionary change. No other scientifically testable hypothesis explains and unifies all of these observations as well as common descent.

13.1 Clues to Evolution Lie in the Earth, Body Structures, and Molecules

The millions of species alive today did not just pop into existence all at once; they are the products of evolutionary change. This process, which continues today, started with organisms that lived billions of years ago. Many types of clues enable us to hypothesize about how modern species evolved from extinct ancestors and to understand the relationships among organisms that live today.

Traditionally, evidence for evolution came mostly from **paleontology,** the study of fossil remains or other clues to past life (figure 13.1). The discovery of many new types of fossils in the early 1800s created the climate that allowed Charles Darwin to make his tremendous breakthrough (see chapter 12). As people recognized that fossils must represent snapshots from the history of life, scientists developed theories to explain that history. The geographical locations of fossils and modern species provided additional clues.

At Darwin's time, some scientists suspected that Earth was hundreds of millions of years old, but no one knew the exact age. We now know that Earth's history is about 4.6 billion years long, a duration that most people find nearly unimaginable. Scientists describe the events along life's long evolutionary path in the context of the **geologic timescale,** which divides Earth's history into a series of eras defined by major geological or biological events such as mass extinctions (see figure 13.2 on page 244). ▸ mass extinctions, p. 267

Fossils and biogeographical studies provided the original evidence for evolution, revealing when species most likely diverged from common ancestors in the context of other events happening on Earth. Comparisons of embryonic development and anatomical structures provided additional supporting data. An entirely new type of evidence emerged in the 1960s and 1970s, when

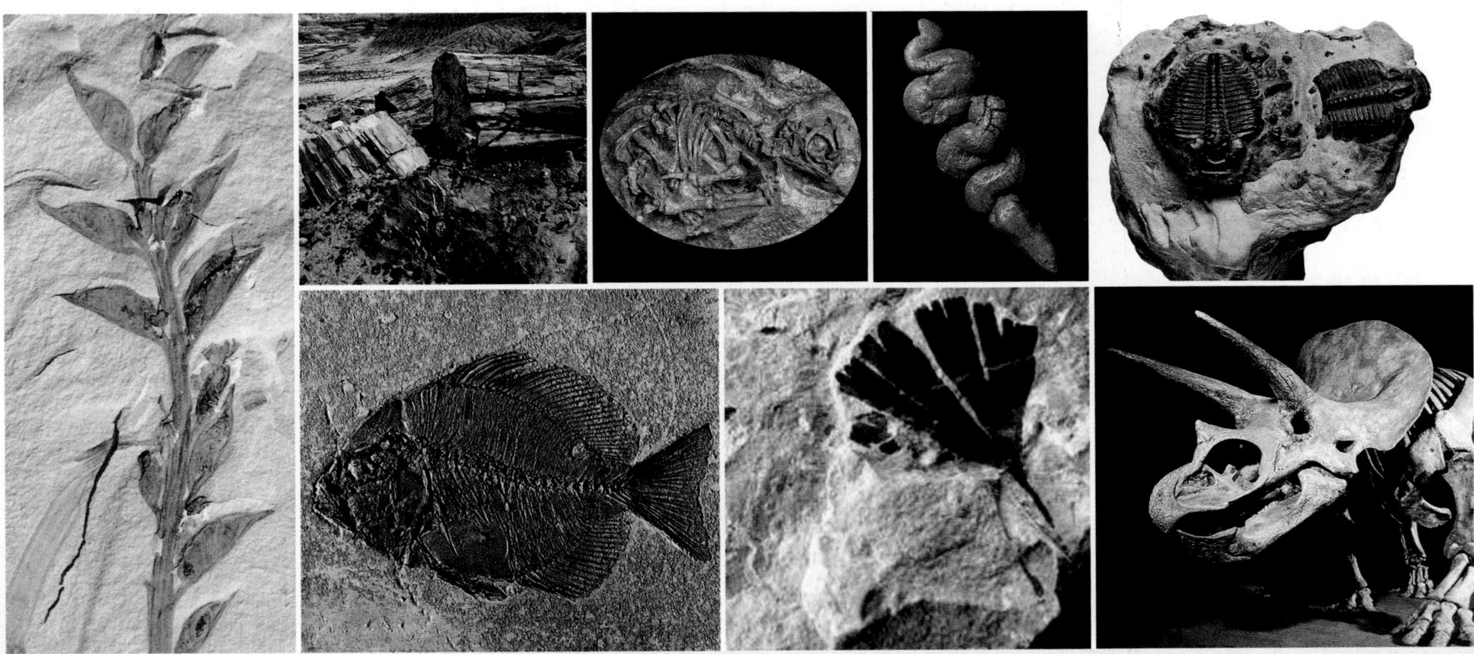

Figure 13.1 Fossil Evidence Is Diverse. Plants and animals have left a rich fossil record. Clockwise from left: An early flowering plant that lived in China 138 million years ago; petrified wood from Arizona; a 190-million-year-old dinosaur egg; fossilized feces of a turtle; extinct arthropods called trilobites; a skull of *Triceratops* (a dinosaur that lived in North America until 65 million years ago); a *Ginkgo* leaf; an exceptionally well-preserved fish.

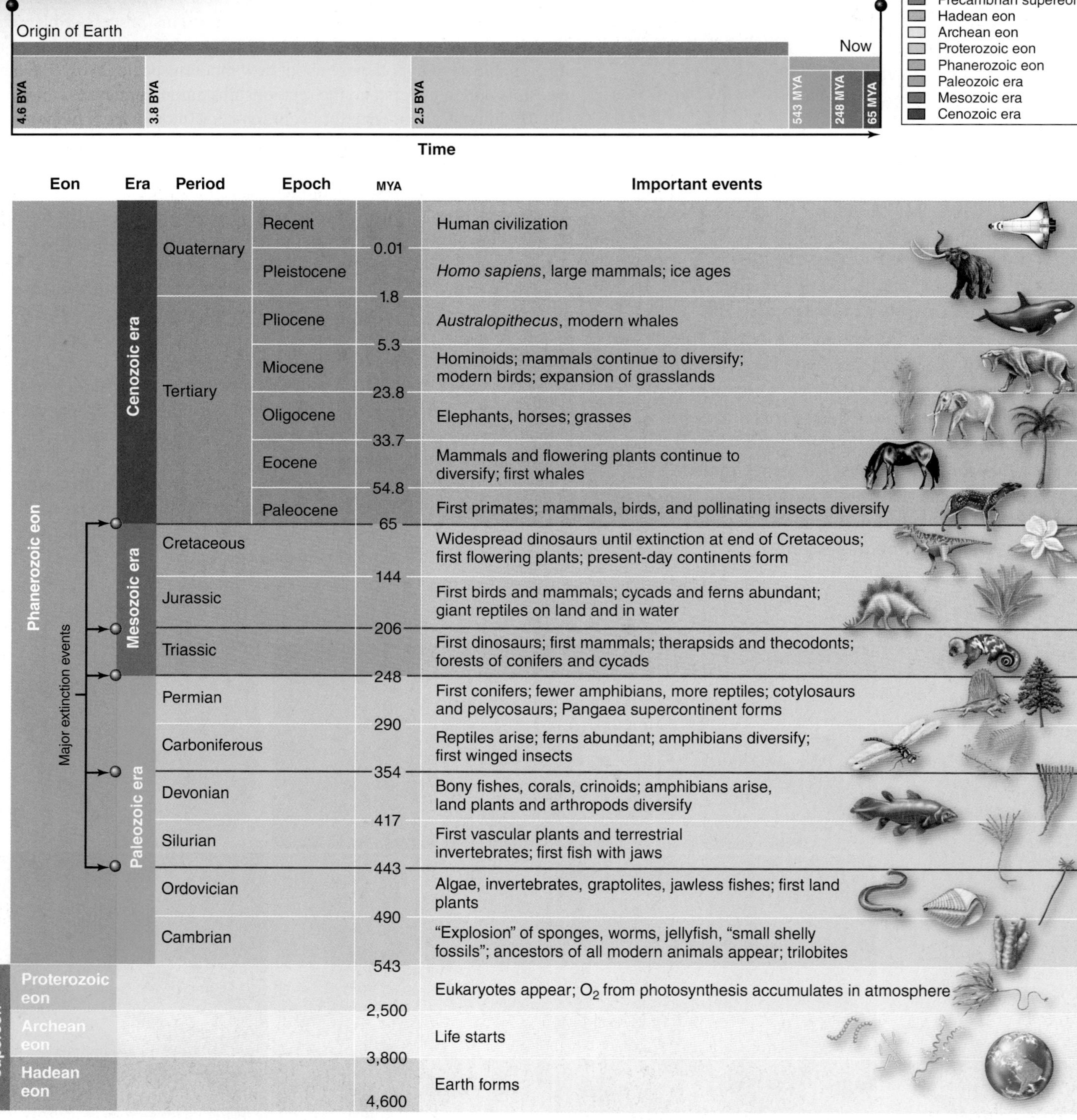

Origin of Earth
Now
4.6 BYA
3.8 BYA
2.5 BYA
543 MYA
248 MYA
65 MYA
Time
Precambrian supereon
Hadean eon
Archean eon
Proterozoic eon
Phanerozoic eon
Paleozoic era
Mesozoic era
Cenozoic era
Eon
Era
Period
Epoch
MYA
Important events
Phanerozoic eon
Cenozoic era
Mesozoic era
Paleozoic era
Major extinction events
Quaternary
Recent
Human civilization
0.01
Pleistocene
Homo sapiens, large mammals; ice ages
1.8
Tertiary
Pliocene
Australopithecus, modern whales
5.3
Miocene
Hominoids; mammals continue to diversify; modern birds; expansion of grasslands
23.8
Oligocene
Elephants, horses; grasses
33.7
Eocene
Mammals and flowering plants continue to diversify; first whales
54.8
Paleocene
First primates; mammals, birds, and pollinating insects diversify
65
Cretaceous
Widespread dinosaurs until extinction at end of Cretaceous; first flowering plants; present-day continents form
144
Jurassic
First birds and mammals; cycads and ferns abundant; giant reptiles on land and in water
206
Triassic
First dinosaurs; first mammals; therapsids and thecodonts; forests of conifers and cycads
248
Permian
First conifers; fewer amphibians, more reptiles; cotylosaurs and pelycosaurs; Pangaea supercontinent forms
290
Carboniferous
Reptiles arise; ferns abundant; amphibians diversify; first winged insects
354
Devonian
Bony fishes, corals, crinoids; amphibians arise, land plants and arthropods diversify
417
Silurian
First vascular plants and terrestrial invertebrates; first fish with jaws
443
Ordovician
Algae, invertebrates, graptolites, jawless fishes; first land plants
490
Cambrian
"Explosion" of sponges, worms, jellyfish, "small shelly fossils"; ancestors of all modern animals appear; trilobites
543
Precambrian supereon
Proterozoic eon
Eukaryotes appear; O_2 from photosynthesis accumulates in atmosphere
2,500
Archean eon
Life starts
3,800
Hadean eon
Earth forms
4,600

Figure 13.2 **The Geologic Timescale.** Scientists divide Earth's 4.6-billion-year history into eons, eras, periods, and epochs. The top panel shows the relative lengths of each eon and era; the bottom panel emphasizes the events of the past 500 million years. (BYA = billion years ago; MYA = million years ago)

scientists began analyzing the sequences of DNA, proteins, and other biological molecules. Since then, the explosion of molecular data has revealed in unprecedented detail how species are related to one another.

Chapter 12 explained how natural selection and other mechanisms of evolution account for changes within species. This chapter examines the different approaches to studying evolution in both living and extinct species. Chapter 14 explains how new species form and become extinct, ending with a description of how scientists assemble diverse clues into hypotheses of the relationships among species. Chapters 15, 16, and 17 continue on this theme by offering a closer look at the history and diversity of life on Earth.

13.1 Mastering Concepts

1. What is the geologic timescale?
2. What types of information provide the clues that scientists use in investigating evolutionary relationships?

13.2 Fossils Record Evolution

A **fossil** is any evidence of an organism from more than 10,000 years ago. Fossils come in all sizes, documenting the evolutionary history of everything from microorganisms to dinosaurs to humans. These remains give us our only direct evidence of organisms that preceded human history. They occur all over the world and represent all major groups of organisms, revealing much about the geological past. For example, fossil hunters in Oklahoma often find abundant remains of extinct marine animals called ammonites (large mollusks similar to the chambered nautilus). These fossils indicate that a vast, shallow ocean once submerged what is now the central United States (figure 13.3).

Fossils do more than simply provide a collection of ancient remains of plants, animals, and microbes. They also allow researchers to test predictions about evolution. Section 17.13 describes an excellent example: the discovery of *Tiktaalik,* an extinct animal with characteristics of both fishes and amphibians. Based on many lines of evidence showing the close relationship between these two groups, biologists had long predicted the existence of such an animal. *Tiktaalik* finally provided direct fossil evidence of the connection.

A. The Fossil Record Is Often Incomplete

Researchers sometimes assemble groups of fossils that document, step-by-step, the evolution of one species into another (see the Burning Question on this page). Usually, however, the fossil record is incomplete, meaning that some of the features marking the transition from one group to another are not recorded in fossils.

Several explanations account for this partial history. First, the vast majority of organisms never leave a fossil trace. Soft-bodied organisms, for example, are much less likely to be preserved than are those with teeth, bones, or shells. Organisms that decompose or are eaten after death, rather than being buried in sediments, are also unlikely to fossilize. Second, erosion or the movements of Earth's continental plates have destroyed many fossils that did form. Third, scientists are unlikely to ever discover the many fossils that must be buried deep in the Earth or submerged under water.

Burning Questions

Does the fossil record include transitional forms?

For some lineages, the fossil record is extraordinarily complete. For example, fossils document the transition from fishes to amphibians, from dinosaurs to birds, from reptiles to mammals, and from terrestrial mammals to whales. In general, the fossil record is most complete for groups that evolved recently and that have bones, teeth, or other hard parts that fossilize readily.

Undoubtedly, the fossil record does contain many gaps. Perhaps the most famous example dates back several hundred million years to an event called the "Cambrian explosion." Despite its name, this phrase refers not to a cataclysmic event but rather to a time during which many new groups of animals first appeared in the ocean.

It is easy to imagine why the fossil record will never be complete. The remains of extinct organisms may never have fossilized in the first place, the fossils may have been destroyed, or paleontologists simply haven't found them yet. Each new find, however, fills another gap in the jigsaw puzzle of life's history.

Submit your burning question to:
marielle_hoefnagels@mcgraw-hill.com

Figure 13.3 Big Change. Ammonite fossils such as these are common in land-locked Oklahoma, indicating that what is now the central United States was once covered by an ocean.

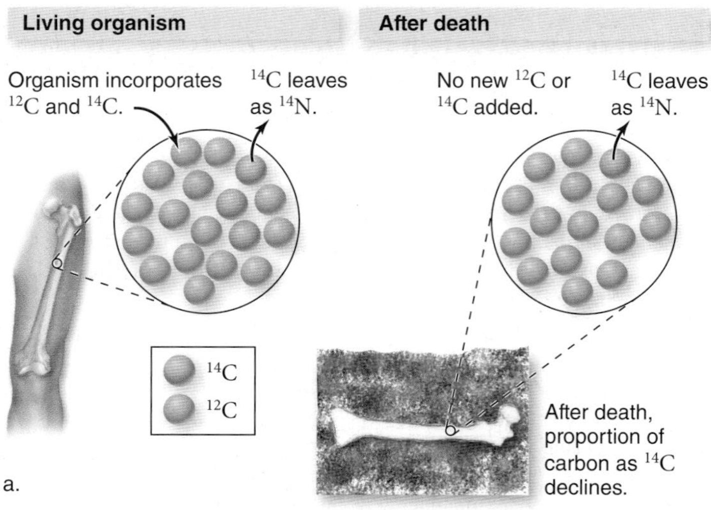
Living organism
After death
Organism incorporates ^{12}C and ^{14}C.
^{14}C leaves as ^{14}N.
No new ^{12}C or ^{14}C added.
^{14}C leaves as ^{14}N.
^{14}C
^{12}C
After death, proportion of carbon as ^{14}C declines.
a.

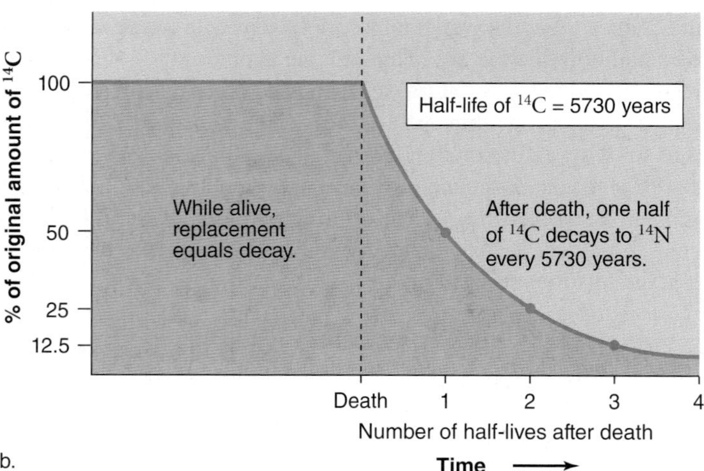
% of original amount of ^{14}C
100
50
25
12.5
Half-life of ^{14}C = 5730 years
While alive, replacement equals decay.
After death, one half of ^{14}C decays to ^{14}N every 5730 years.
Death
1
2
3
4
Number of half-lives after death
Time
b.

c.

Figure 13.4 Carbon-14 Dating. (a) Living organisms accumulate radioactive carbon-14 (^{14}C) by photosynthesis or eating other organisms. During life, ^{14}C is replaced as fast as it decays to nitrogen-14 (^{14}N). After death, no new ^{14}C enters the body, so the proportion of ^{14}C to ^{12}C declines. (b) During one half-life, 50% of the remaining radioactive atoms in a sample decay. (c) Measuring the proportion of ^{14}C to ^{12}C allows scientists to determine how long ago a fossilized organism—such as this woolly mammoth—died.

B. The Age of a Fossil Can Be Estimated in Two Ways

Scientists use two general approaches to estimate when a fossilized organism lived: relative dating and absolute dating.

Relative Dating **Relative dating** places a fossil into a sequence of events without assigning it a specific age. It is usually based on the presumption that lower rock strata are older than higher layers (see figure 12.3). The farther down a fossil is, therefore, the longer ago the organism lived—a little like a memo at the bottom of a pile of papers on a desk being older than one nearer the top. Relative dating therefore places fossils in order from "oldest" to "most recent."

Absolute Dating and Radioactive Decay Researchers use **absolute dating** to assign an age to a fossil by testing the fossil itself or the sediments above and below the fossil. Either way, the dates usually are expressed in relation to the present. For example, scientists studying the dinosaur in the chapter opening photo showed that this animal lived about 145 million years ago (MYA).

Radiometric dating is a type of absolute dating that uses radioactive isotopes as a "clock." Recall from chapter 2 that each isotope of an element has a different number of neutrons. Some isotopes are naturally unstable, which causes them to emit radiation as they radioactively decay. Each radioactive isotope decays at a characteristic and unchangeable rate, called its half-life. The **half-life** is the time it takes for half of the atoms in a sample of a radioactive substance to decay. If an isotope's half-life is 1 year, for example, 50% of the radioactive atoms in a sample will have decayed in a year. In another year, half of the remaining radioactive atoms will decay, leaving 25%, and so on. If we measure the amount of a radioactive isotope in a sample, we can use the isotope's known half-life to deduce when the fossil formed. ▸ isotopes, p. 23

One radioactive isotope often used to assign dates to fossils is carbon-14 (^{14}C; figure 13.4). Carbon-14 has a half-life of 5730 years; it decays to the more stable nitrogen-14 (^{14}N). Organisms accumulate ^{14}C during photosynthesis or by eating organic matter. One in every trillion carbon atoms present in living tissue is ^{14}C; most of the rest are ^{12}C, a nonradioactive (stable) isotope. When an organism dies, however, its intake of carbon, including ^{14}C, stops. As the body's ^{14}C decays without being replenished, the ratio of ^{14}C to ^{12}C decreases. This ratio is then used to determine when death occurred, up to about 40,000 years ago.

For example, radioactive carbon dating determined the age of fossils of vultures that once lived in the Grand Canyon. The birds' remains have about one fourth the ^{14}C-to-^{12}C ratio of a living organism. Therefore, about two half-lives, or about 11,460 years, passed since the animals died. It took 5730 years for half of the ^{14}C to decay, and another 5730 years for half of what was left to decay.

Another widely used radioactive isotope, potassium-40 (^{40}K), decays to argon-40 (^{40}Ar) with a half-life of 1.3 billion years, so it is valuable in dating very old rocks. Chemical analyses can detect the accumulation of ^{40}Ar in amounts corresponding to fossils that are about 300,000 years old or older.

One limitation of ^{14}C and potassium–argon dating is that they leave a gap, resulting from the different half-lives of the radioactive isotopes. To cover the missing years, researchers use isotopes with intermediate half-lives or turn to other techniques.

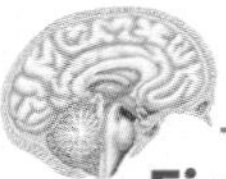

Figure It Out

Kennewick Man is a human whose remains were found in Washington state. Radiometric dating of a bone fragment suggests that he lived about 9300 years ago. About what percentage of the original amount of ^{14}C remains in his bones?

Answer: Approximately 30%

13.2 Mastering Concepts

1. Why will the fossil record always be incomplete?
2. Distinguish between relative and absolute dating of fossils.
3. How does radiometric dating work?

13.3 Biogeography Considers Species' Geographical Locations

Geographical barriers greatly influence the origin of species (see chapter 14). It is therefore not surprising that the studies of geography and biology overlap in a field called **biogeography,** the study of the distribution of species across the planet.

A. The Theory of Plate Tectonics Explains Earth's Shifting Continents

Earth's geological history has been extremely eventful. Fossils tell the story of ancient seafloors rising all the way to Earth's "ceiling": the Himalayan Mountains. Littering the mountains of Nepal are countless fossilized ammonites. How did fossils of marine animals end up more than 3600 meters above sea level?

The answer is that Earth's continents are in motion, an idea called "continental drift" (figure 13.5). According to the theory of **plate tectonics,** Earth's surface consists of several rigid layers, called tectonic plates, that move in response to forces acting deep within the planet. In some areas where plates collide, mountain ranges form as the plates become crumpled and distorted. Long ago, the plate that carries the Indian subcontinent moved slowly north and collided with the Eurasian plate. The mighty Himalayas—once an ancient seafloor—rose at the boundary, lifting the marine fossils toward the sky.

In other places, one plate dives beneath another and forms a deep trench. Meanwhile, new plate material forms at areas where plates move apart and molten rock seeps to Earth's surface at the seam. As a result, wide oceans now separate continents that were once joined together. This slow-motion dance of the continental plates has dramatically affected life's history as oceans shifted, land bridges formed and disappeared, and mountain ranges emerged.

It may seem hard to imagine that Earth's continents have not always been located where they are now. But a wealth of evidence, including the

280–200 MYA

All continents are joined into one supercontinent, Pangaea.

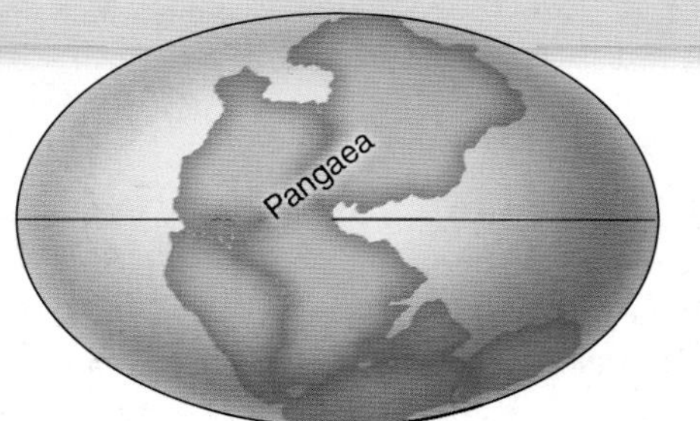

181–135 MYA

Two major continents form.

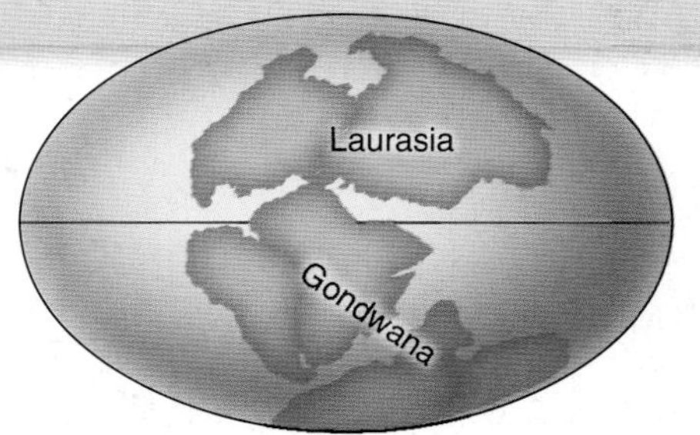

100–65 MYA

Present-day continents form and begin to drift apart.

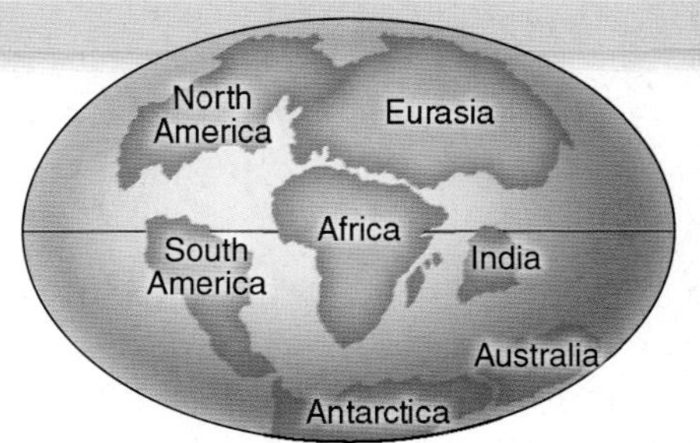

Today

Continents continue to drift apart.

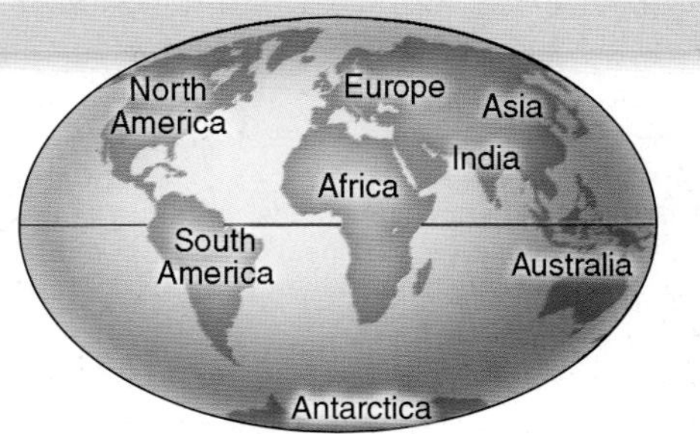

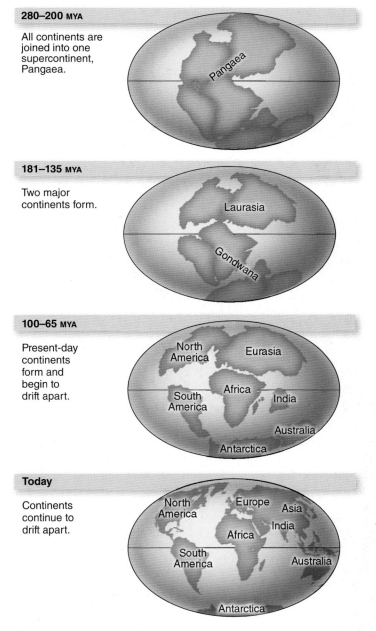

Figure 13.5 A Changing World. The distribution of continents on Earth has changed with time, due to shifting tectonic plates.

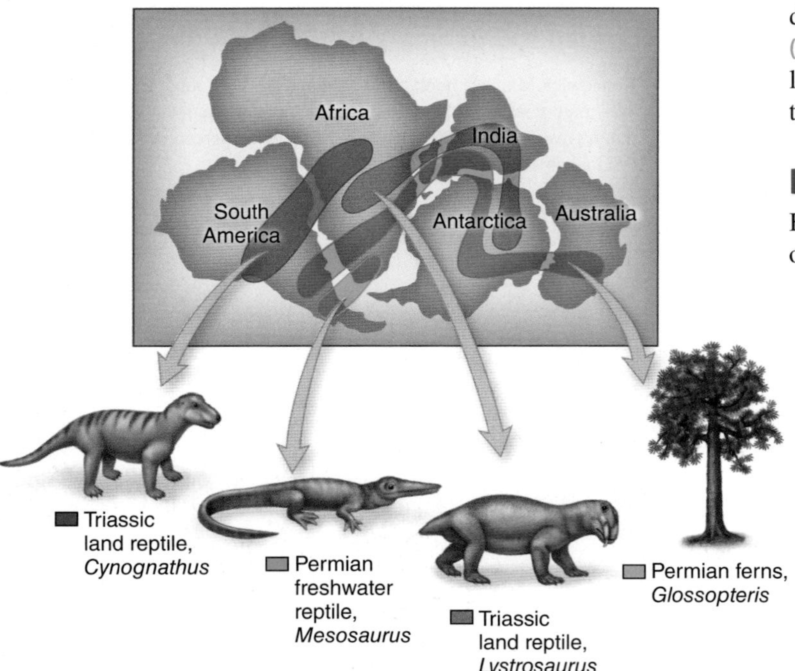

Figure 13.6 Fossils Tell the Tale. Continental drift explains the modern-day distributions of fossils representing life at the time of Pangaea.

distribution of some key fossils, indicates that the continents were once united (figure 13.6). Deep-sea probes that measure seafloor spreading, along with the locations of the world's earthquake-prone and volcanic "hot spots," reveal that the continents continue to move today.

B. Species Distributions Reveal Evolutionary Events

Biogeographical studies have shed light on past evolutionary events. The rest of this section describes two examples.

The Rise and Fall of the Marsupials Marsupials are pouched mammals such as kangaroos, koalas, and sugar gliders. The young are born tiny, hairless, blind, and helpless. As soon as they are born, they crawl along the mother's fur to tiny, milk-secreting nipples inside her pouch.

Marsupials were once the most widespread land mammals on Earth. By about 110 MYA, however, a second group, the placental mammals, had evolved. The young of placental mammals develop within the female's body, nourished in the uterus by the placenta. Baby placental mammals are born more fully developed than are marsupials, giving them a better chance of survival after birth. Because of this reproductive advantage, placental mammals soon displaced marsupials on most continents, including North America. ▶ mammals, p. 346

Nevertheless, fossil evidence suggests that marsupials were diverse and abundant in South America until about 1 or 2 MYA, long after their counterparts on most other continents had disappeared. The reason is that water separated South America from North America until about 3 MYA. But sediments that eroded from both continents eventually created a new land bridge, the isthmus of Panama, which permitted migration between North and South America. The resulting invasion of the placental mammals eventually spelled extinction for most South American marsupials.

Australia's marsupials remained isolated from competition from placental mammals for much longer. Until about 140 MYA, Antarctica and Australia were part of Gondwana (see figure 13.5). Then, about 60 or 70 MYA, Australia separated from Antarctica and began drifting toward Eurasia. The isolation from the other continents meant marsupials remained free of competition from placentals. In fact, Australia remains unique in that most of its native mammals are still marsupials.

Wallace's Line Biogeography figured prominently in the early history of evolutionary thought. Alfred Russel Wallace, the British naturalist who independently discovered natural selection along with Charles Darwin, had noticed unique assemblages of birds and mammals on either side of an imaginary line in the Malay Archipelago (figure 13.7). The explanation for what came to be called "Wallace's line" turned out to be a deep-water trench that has separated the islands on either side of the line, even as sea levels rose and fell over tens of millions of years. The watery barrier prevented the migration of most species, so evolution produced a unique variety of organisms on each side of Wallace's line.

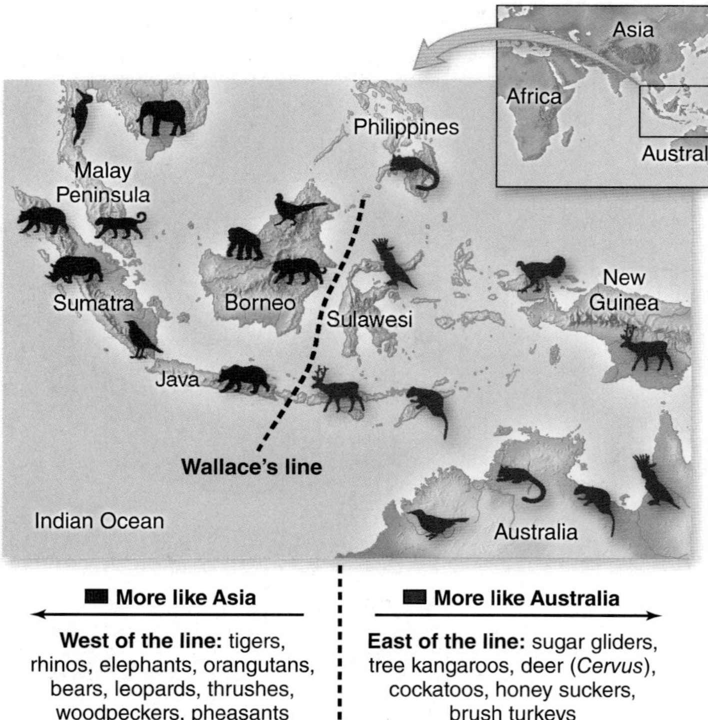

Figure 13.7 Wallace's Line. As Alfred Russel Wallace traveled around the Malay archipelago, he noticed distinct patterns of animal life on either side of an imaginary boundary, which eventually came to be called Wallace's line.

13.3 Mastering Concepts

1. How have the positions of Earth's continents changed over the past 200 million years?
2. How do biogeographical observations help biologists interpret evolutionary history?

13.4 Anatomical Comparisons May Reveal Common Descent

Many clues to the past come from the present. As Unit 1 explains, all life is made of cells, and eukaryotic cells are very similar in the structure and function of their membranes and organelles. On a molecular scale, cells share many similarities in their enzymes and metabolic pathways. Unit 2 describes another set of common features: the relationship between DNA and proteins, and the mechanisms of inheritance. We now turn to the whole-body scale, where comparisons of anatomy and physiology reveal still more commonalities among modern species.

Figure 13.8 Homologous Limbs. Although their forelimbs have different functions, all of these vertebrates have skeletons that are similarly organized and composed of the same type of tissue.

A. Homologous Structures Have a Shared Evolutionary Origin

Two structures are termed **homologous** if the similarities between them reflect common ancestry. (Recall from chapter 9 that two chromosomes are homologous if they have the same genes, though not necessarily the same alleles, arranged in the same order.) Genes can be homologous, as can anatomical structures or other features that are similar in their configuration or developmental path.

The organization of the vertebrate skeleton illustrates homology. All vertebrate skeletons support the body, are made of the same materials, and consist of many of the same parts. Amphibians, birds and other reptiles, and mammals typically have four limbs, and the numbers and positions of the bones that make up those appendages are strikingly similar (figure 13.8). The simplest explanation is that modern vertebrates descended from a common ancestor that had this skeletal organization. Each group gradually modified the skeleton as species adapted to different environments.

Note that homologous structures share a common evolutionary origin, but they may not have the same function. The middle ear bones of mammals, for example, originated as bones that supported the jaws of primitive fishes, and they still exist as such in some vertebrates. These bones are homologous and reveal our shared ancestry with fishes. Likewise, each forelimb pictured in figure 13.8 has a different function.

Homology is a powerful tool for discovering evolutionary relationships. For example, as described in section 13.6, a newly sequenced gene or genome can be compared with homologous genes from other species to infer how closely related any two species are. In addition, fossilized structures are often compared with homologous parts in known species. Comparative studies can also provide clues to why humans have some of the features we do (see the Why We Care box on page 250).

Figure 13.9 Vestigial Structures. (a) Some snakes have tiny hind leg bones that are vestigial but (b) detectable only in the skeleton. (c) Some whales likewise have a vestigial pelvis and hind limbs.

B. Vestigial Structures Have Lost Their Functions

As environmental changes select against some structures, others persist even if they are not used. A **vestigial** structure has no apparent function in one species, yet it is homologous to a functional organ in another. (Darwin compared vestigial structures to silent letters in a word, such as the "g" in *night;* they are not pronounced, but they offer clues to the word's origin.) In some whales and snakes, tiny leg bones are vestigial, retained from vertebrate ancestors that used legs to walk on land (figure 13.9).

Humans have several vestigial organs. The tiny muscles that make hairs stand on end helped our furry ancestors conserve heat or show aggression; in us, they apparently serve only as the basis of goose bumps. Human embryos have tails, which usually disintegrate long before birth; in other vertebrates, tails persist into adulthood. We also retain a trio of muscles that help other mammals move

Why We Care | Hiccups Are an Accident of Evolution

A hiccup is an involuntary muscle spasm that causes the diaphragm to contract. At the same time, a flap of tissue called the epiglottis blocks the airway to the lungs. The result is a sharp intake of air, accompanied by the familiar "hic" sound. This quick inhalation doesn't prevent or solve any known problem. So why do we get the hiccups at all?

One clue is in our anatomy. Hiccups begin when the nerves that trigger contraction of the diaphragm become irritated. These nerves emerge from the spinal cord near the neck and extend all the way down the chest cavity to the diaphragm, below the lungs. A more practical arrangement—that is, an arrangement less prone to irritation and hiccups—would be for the nerves that control breathing to emerge from the spinal cord nearer the diaphragm. But we inherited these nerves from our fishy ancestors, which breathed using gills located near the base of the skull.

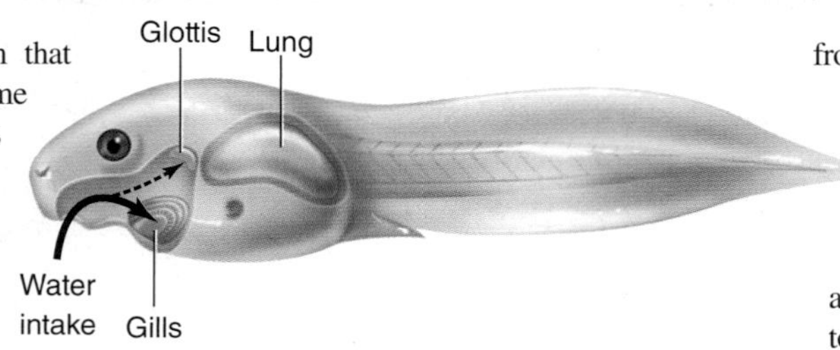

Figure 13.A Hiccup Origins. Amphibian tadpoles may help explain why humans get the hiccups.

A second clue to the origin of hiccups comes from a close examination of young amphibians (figure 13.A). Tadpoles have two ways to breathe: lungs that gulp air, and gills that extract oxygen from water. When a tadpole pumps a mouthful of water across its gills, the glottis closes to keep water out of its lungs. This breathing action almost exactly matches what happens in a human hiccup.

Taken together, both lines of anatomical evidence suggest that the hiccup is an accident of evolution—a remnant of the anatomy we share with the vertebrates that came before us.

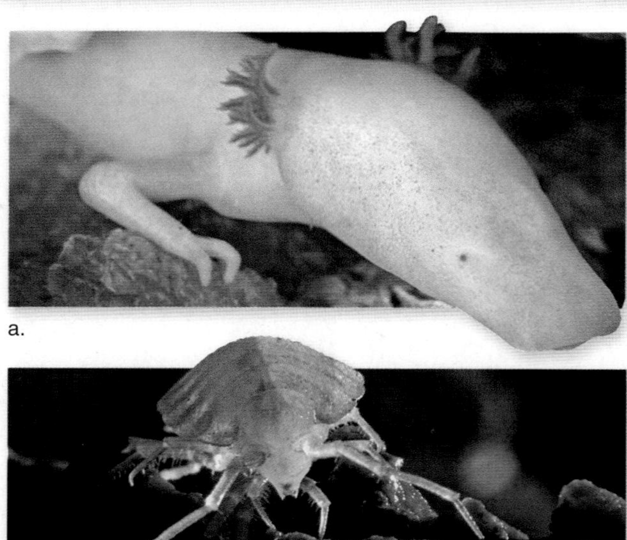

a.

b.

c.

Figure 13.10 Convergent Evolution. (a) The blind cave salamander and (b) the blind cave isopod occur in Slovenia. (c) This cave crayfish from Florida lacks eyes and pigment.

their ears in a way that improves hearing (most of us can't use these muscles). Each vestigial structure links us to other animals that still use these features.

C. Convergent Evolution Produces Superficial Similarities

Some anatomical parts have similar functions and appear superficially similar among different species, but they are not homologous. Rather, they are **analogous,** meaning that the structures evolved independently. Flight, for example, evolved independently in birds and in insects. The bird's wing is a modification of vertebrate limb bones, whereas the insect's wing is an outgrowth of the exoskeleton that covers its body. The wings have the same function—flight—and enhance fitness in the face of similar environmental challenges. The differences in structure, however, indicate they do not have a common developmental pathway. They are analogous, not homologous.

Analogous structures may be the product of **convergent evolution,** which produces similar adaptations in organisms that do not share the same evolutionary lineage. The loss of pigmentation and eyes in cave animals provides a striking example of convergent evolution (figure 13.10). Likewise, the similarities between sharks and dolphins illustrate the power of selective forces in shaping organisms. A shark is a fish, whereas a dolphin is a mammal that evolved from terrestrial ancestors. The two animals are not closely related. Nevertheless, their marine habitat and predatory lifestyle have selected for many shared adaptations, including the streamlined body and the shape and locations of the fins or flippers.

13.4 Mastering Concepts

1. What can homologies reveal about evolution?
2. What is a vestigial structure? What are some examples of vestigial structures in humans and other animals?
3. What is convergent evolution?

13.5 Embryonic Development Patterns Provide Evolutionary Clues

Because related organisms share many physical traits, they must also share the processes that produce those traits. Developmental biologists study how the adult body takes shape from its single-celled beginning. Careful comparisons of developing body parts can be enlightening. As just one example, figure 13.11 shows that skulls can develop in different ways, depending on how each part grows in proportion to the others.

Developmental biologists have also photographed embryos and fetuses of a variety of vertebrate species throughout development (figure 13.12). The data show striking similarities in embryonic structures, supporting the concept of common ancestry.

More recently, the discovery of genes that contribute to development has spawned the field of evolutionary developmental biology (or "evo-devo" for short). Recall from chapter 7 that a gene is a region of DNA that encodes a protein. Some genes encode proteins that dictate how an organism will develop. One goal of researchers in evolutionary developmental biology is to identify these genes and determine how mutations can give rise to new body forms.

A basic question in developmental biology, for example, is how a clump of identical cells transforms into a body with a distinct head, tail, segments, and limbs. One way to learn more about this process is to study genes encoding proteins that regulate development. Mutations in these genes can produce dramatic new phenotypes—see, for example, the fruit fly with legs growing out of its head in figure 7.14.

Homeotic is a general term describing any gene that, when mutated, leads to organisms with structures in abnormal or unusual places. Homeotic genes occur in all animal phyla studied to date, as well as in plants and fungi, and they provide important clues about development. Consider, for example, a pair

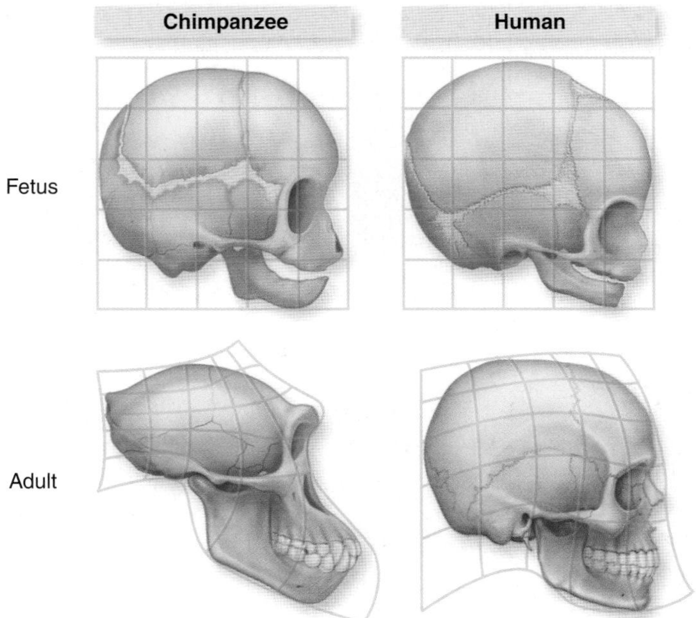

Figure 13.11 Same Parts, Different Proportions. The fetuses of humans and chimpanzees have very similar skulls, but the two species follow different developmental pathways. The grids superimposed on each image show that in an adult human, the brain is larger and the jaw is smaller than in chimpanzees.

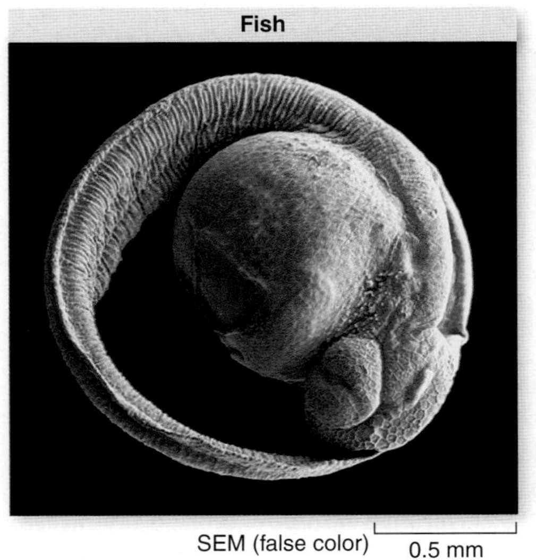

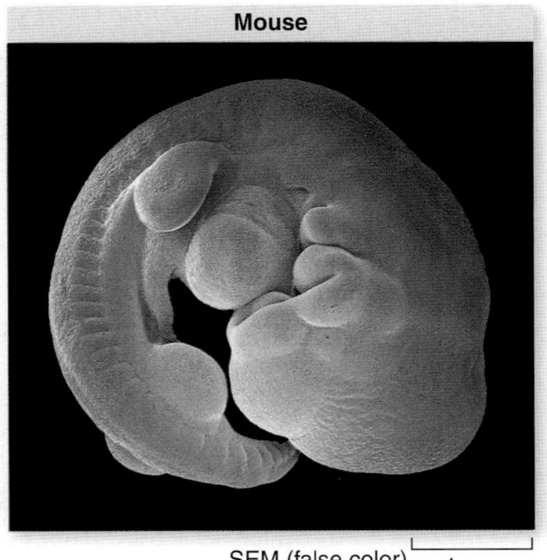

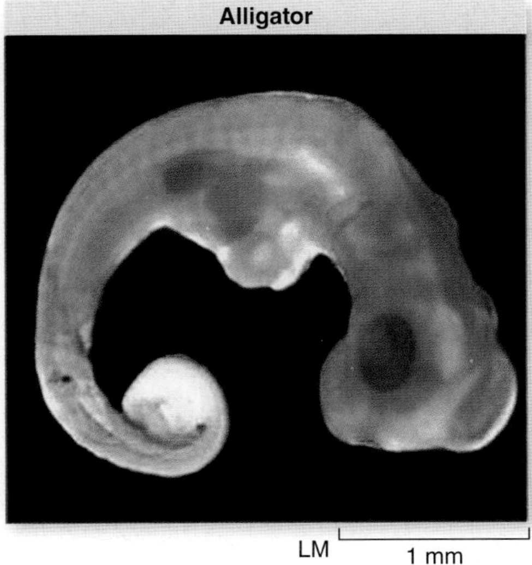

Figure 13.12 Embryo Resemblances. Vertebrate embryos appear alike early in development, reflecting similar basic processes as cells divide and specialize. As development continues, parts grow at different rates in different species, and the embryos do not look as similar.
Source: Fish © Dr. Richard Kessel/Visuals Unlimited

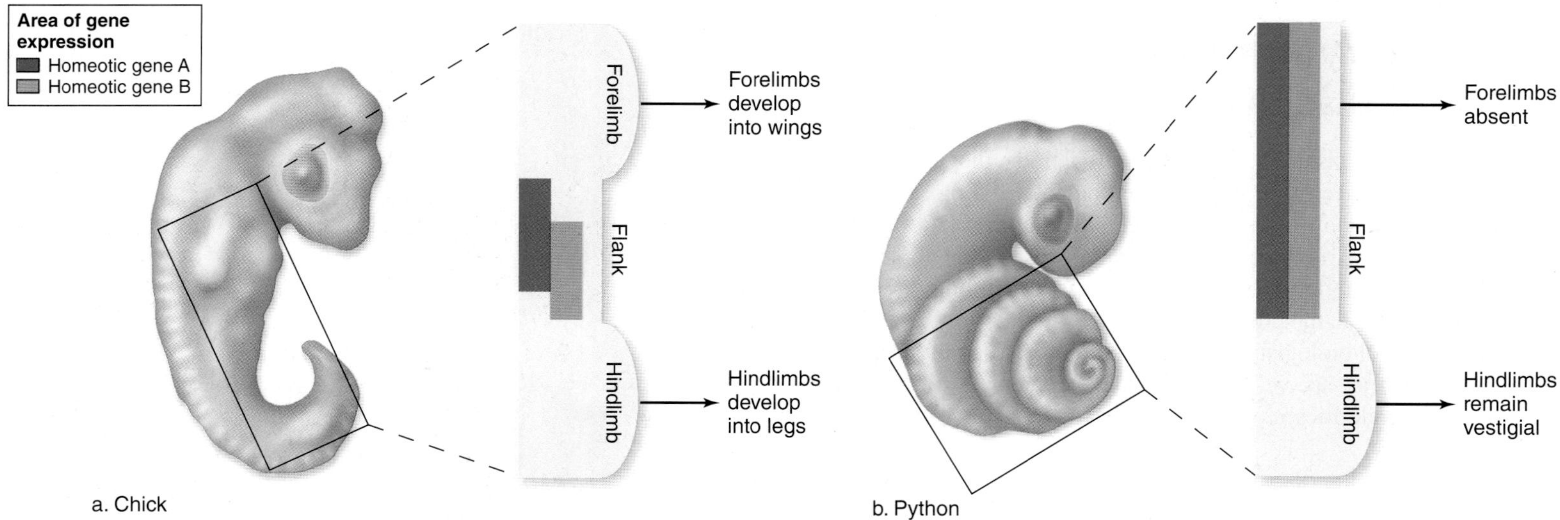

Figure 13.13 Homeotic Genes. (a) Two homeotic genes are expressed unequally along the length of a chicken embryo. Where both genes are expressed, no limbs form. (b) The same pair of homeotic genes prevents the development of forelimbs in a python embryo.

of homeotic genes that influence limb formation in vertebrates (figure 13.13). In the chick embryo in figure 13.13a, the gene labeled A prompts wing development, whereas the gene labeled B stimulates formation of the legs. No limbs occur where both genes are expressed, such as in the midsection of the body. Now compare the chick with the pattern of gene expression in the python (figure 13.13b). The same two genes are expressed along most of the snake's body; as a result, the animal never develops forelimbs at all. (Another gene prevents the development of the python's vestigial hindlimbs.)

These examples only scratch the surface of the types of information about evolution that biologists can learn by studying development. The relatively new field of evolutionary developmental biology is sure to yield much more insight into evolution in the future.

13.5 Mastering Concepts

1. How does the study of embryonic development reveal clues to a shared evolutionary history?
2. Why are evolutionary biologists interested in how genes influence development?

13.6 Molecules Reveal Relatedness

The evidence for evolution described so far in this chapter is compelling, but it is only the beginning. Since the 1970s, biologists have compiled a wealth of additional data by comparing the molecules inside the cells of diverse organisms. The results have not only confirmed many previous studies but have also added unprecedented detail to our ability to detect and measure the pace of evolutionary change.

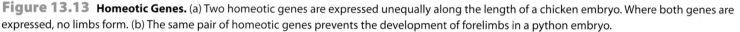

The molecules that are most useful to evolutionary biologists are DNA and proteins. As described in chapter 2, DNA is a long chain of subunits called nucleotides, whereas proteins are composed of amino acids. Cells use the information in DNA to produce proteins.

This intimate relationship between nucleic acids and proteins is itself a powerful argument for common ancestry. All species use the same genetic code in making proteins, and cells use the same 20 amino acids. The fact that biologists can move DNA among species to create transgenic organisms is a practical reminder of the universal genetic code. ▸ transgenic organisms, p. 200

A. Comparing DNA and Protein Sequences May Reveal Close Relationships

To study molecular evolution, biologists compare nucleotide and amino acid sequences among species. It is highly unlikely that two unrelated species would evolve precisely the same DNA and protein sequences by chance. It is more likely that the similarities were inherited from a common ancestor and that differences arose by mutation after the species diverged from the ancestral type.

DNA The ability to rapidly sequence DNA has led to an explosion of information. The human genome project has called attention to whole-genome comparisons among species. But DNA differences can also be assessed for just a few bases, for a single gene, and for families of genes with related structures or functions. Biologists routinely locate a gene in one organism, then scan huge databases to study its function in other species. ▸ DNA sequencing, p. 203

The recent explosion of information about gene sequences has also helped explain how evolution works. We now know that cells can add new functions by acquiring DNA from other organisms and by duplicating entire genes. And we have already seen that the study of gene regulation is especially fruitful in showing how the timing and location of gene expression can differ among closely related species (see figure 13.13). The list of additional applications is endless, ranging from learning which species inhabited ancient ecosystems (see section 16.6) to monitoring the evolution of pesticide-resistant insects (see section 10.10).

Proteins Like DNA, protein sequences also often support fossil and anatomical evidence of evolutionary relationships. One study, for example, found seven of 20 proteins to be identical in humans and chimps, our closest relatives. Many other proteins have only minor sequence differences from one species to another. One example is the keratin of sheep's wool, which is virtually identical to that of human hair. The similarity reflects the shared evolutionary history of all mammals.

Keratin is useful in studies of mammals, but other species lack this protein. To study broader groups of organisms, biologists use proteins that are present in all species. One example is cytochrome *c*, which is part of the electron transport chain in mitochondria (see section 6.5C). Figure 13.14 shows that the more closely related two species are, the more alike is their cytochrome *c* amino acid sequence.

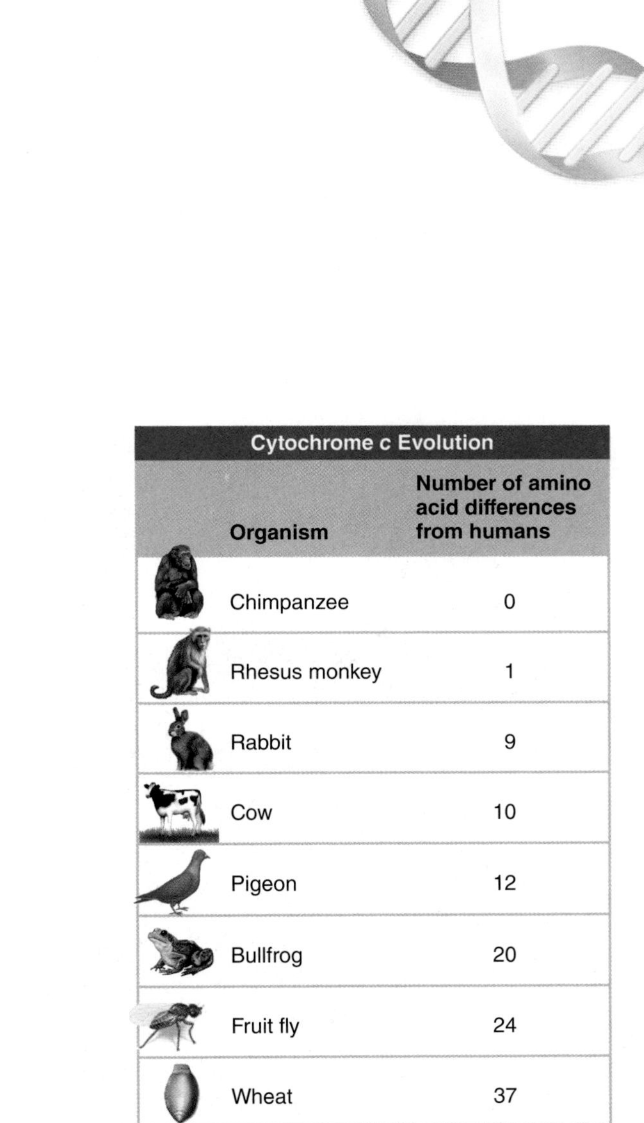

Cytochrome c Evolution	
Organism	Number of amino acid differences from humans
Chimpanzee	0
Rhesus monkey	1
Rabbit	9
Cow	10
Pigeon	12
Bullfrog	20
Fruit fly	24
Wheat	37
Yeast	42

Figure 13.14 Cytochrome *c* Comparison. The more recent the shared ancestor with humans, the fewer the differences in the amino acid sequence for the respiratory protein cytochrome *c*.

B. Molecular Clocks Help Assign Dates to Evolutionary Events

A biological molecule such as DNA can act as a "clock." If biologists know the mutation rate for a gene, plus the number of differences in the DNA sequences for that gene in two species, they can use the DNA as a **molecular clock**

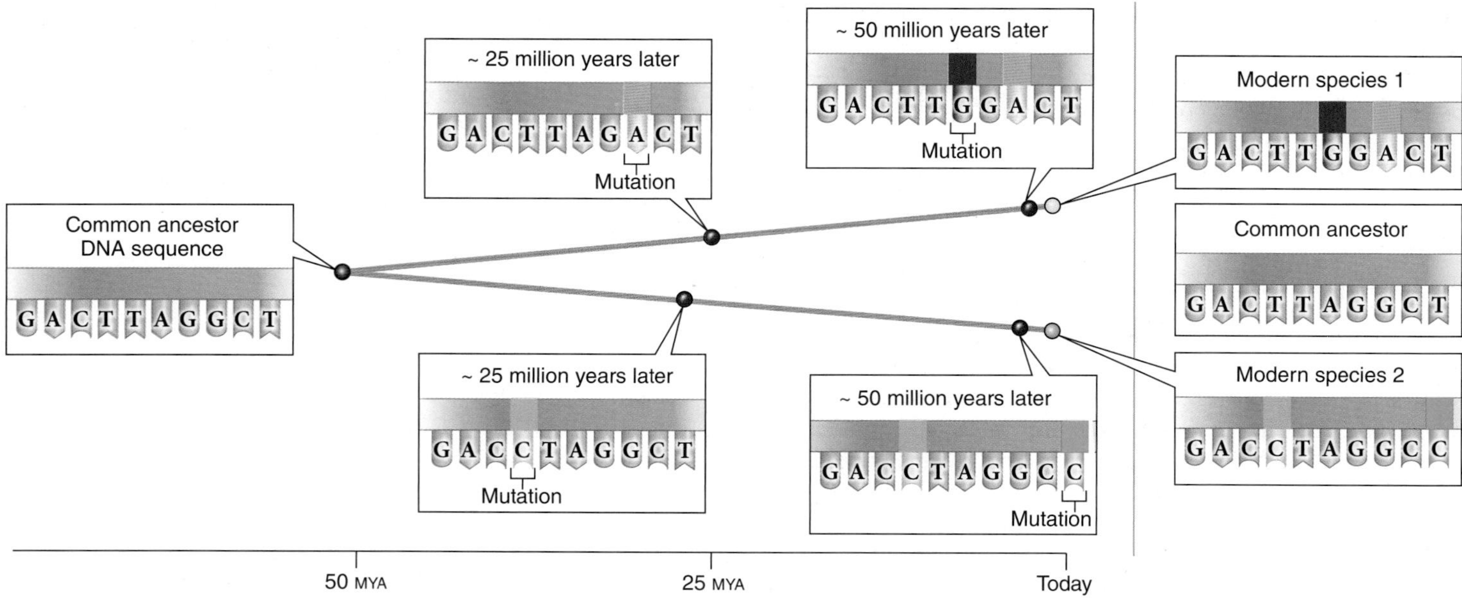

Figure 13.15 Molecular Clock. If a sequence of DNA accumulates mutations at a regular rate, then the number of sequence changes can act as a "clock" that tells how much time has passed since two species last shared a common ancestor.

to estimate the time when the organisms diverged from a common ancestor (figure 13.15).

For example, many human and chimpanzee genes differ in about 4% to 6% of their nucleotides, and substitutions occur at an estimated rate of 1% per 1 million years. Therefore, about 4 million to 6 million years have passed since the two species diverged.

Molecular clock studies are not quite as straightforward as glancing at a wristwatch, in part because DNA replication errors occur in different regions of a chromosome at different rates. Therefore, to make a large-scale tree that incorporates all life, researchers consider DNA sequences that are common to all organisms and that are slow to evolve. The genes encoding ribosomal RNA fit the bill. Carl Woese used these genes to deduce the existence of the three domains (Archaea, Bacteria, and Eukarya; see figure 1.8).

13.6 Mastering Concepts

1. How does analysis of DNA and proteins support other evidence for evolution?
2. How can molecular clocks help determine when two species diverged from a common ancestor?

Investigating Life

13.7 Evolving Backwards

Evolution sometimes seems to run in reverse, such as when species lose features that their ancestors had. Snakes provide a notable example. These animals lack the limbs that characterize most other vertebrate species. Evidently a smooth, elongated body is adaptive in animals that tunnel underground. And the absence of legs does not seem to hurt the snakes' ability to move or find food. These animals can slither along the ground, swim, and even climb trees. Without legs, they can easily slide into small spaces as they hunt for rodents and other prey.

Biologists know quite a bit about the evolution of snakes. Anatomical information, including vestigial hind legs in some snakes (see figure 13.9), clearly indicates that snakes evolved from lizards with four legs. Additional fossil evidence confirms that the forelimbs disappeared before the hindlimbs. That is, paleontologists have discovered fossil snakes with hindlimbs but no forelimbs, but the reverse is not true. And the molecular part of the equation became clearer when researchers reported how the expression of two homeotic genes prevents forelimb formation in pythons (see figure 13.13b).

The Question: Although some events in snake evolution are clear, for a long time no one knew the answer to this puzzle: *Where* in the world did snakes lose their limbs? Scientists have proposed two competing ideas. Noting that snakes resemble two existing groups of burrowing lizards, some scientists suggested that snakes evolved on land. Opposing scientists, citing skull and jaw similarities, contend that snakes descend from mosasaurs, extinct marine lizards that thrived during the Cretaceous period.

The Approach: Fossils have offered a breakthrough in the debate over snake origins. Argentinian paleontologist Sebastián Apesteguía, along with Brazilian colleague Hussam Zaher, added a critical clue when they reported finding three fossilized snakes in the Patagonia region of Argentina (figure 13.16). The snakes, which they named *Najash rionegrina,* lived during the Upper Cretaceous period, about 90 MYA.

Najash was the first snake ever found to have not only functional legs and a pelvis but also a sacrum—a bone connecting the pelvis to the spine. (In other fossil snakes with limbs, the pelvis is "free floating" and not connected to the backbone.) This observation is important because lizards and other tetrapods have the same bone, providing evidence that *Najash* is more primitive than any snake ever found (see figure 13.16b). Moreover, both the fossil's features and the rock where it was found suggest that it was terrestrial, not marine.

The Conclusion: Taken together, these two pieces of evidence seem to settle the matter: snakes originated on land. These animals apparently lost their limbs as they adapted to a burrowing lifestyle. Since that time, snakes have diversified into thousands of species. The existence of so many snake species provides evidence that in evolution, going backwards can sometimes be a good thing.

Apesteguía, Sebastián, and Hussam Zaher. April 20, 2006. A Cretaceous terrestrial snake with robust hindlimbs and a sacrum. *Nature*, vol. 440, pages 1037–1040.

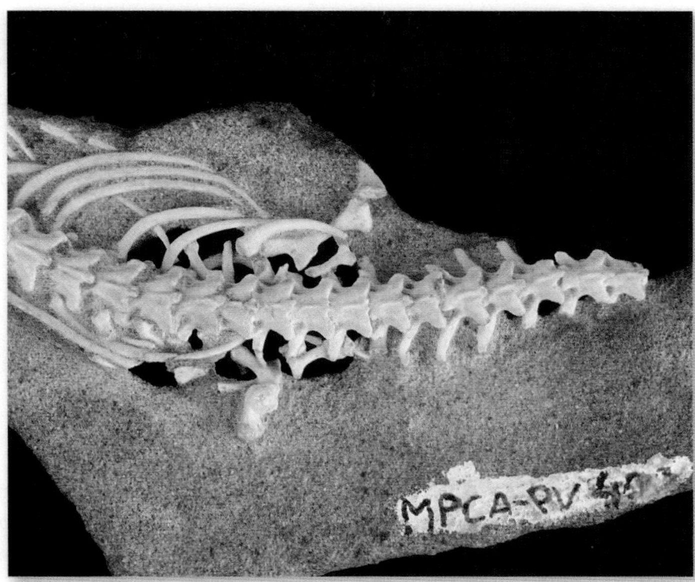

a.

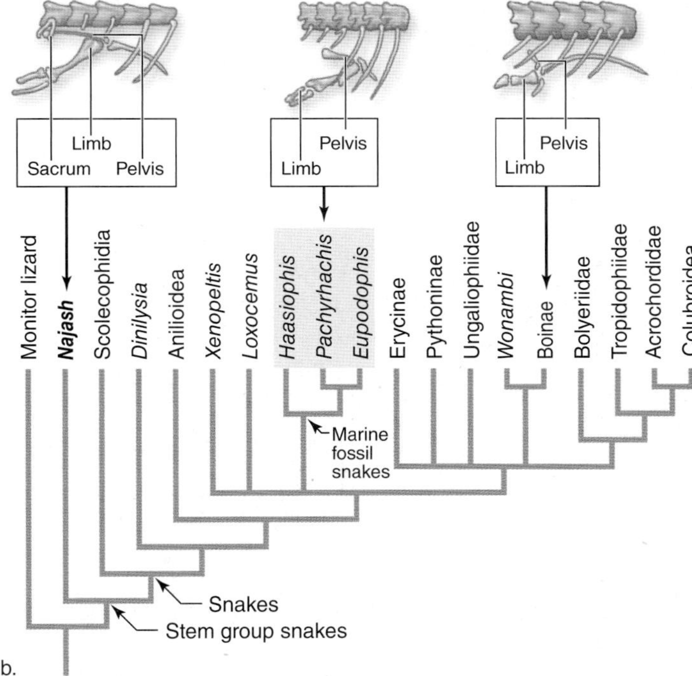

b.

Figure 13.16 ***Najash*, the Fossil Snake.** (a) *Najash* had hindlimbs, a pelvis, and a sacrum. (b) This phylogenetic tree places *Najash,* which lived on land, as one of the most primitive snakes. In contrast, the three marine fossil snakes with legs (highlighted) belong to a more derived group. This result supports the hypothesis that snakes evolved on land, not in the sea.

13.7 Mastering Concepts

1. How might the loss of limbs enhance the fitness of a burrowing animal such as a snake?
2. Why was *Najash* a significant discovery?

Chapter Summary

13.1 Clues to Evolution Lie in the Earth, Body Structures, and Molecules

- The **geologic timescale** divides Earth's history into eras defined by major events such as mass extinctions.
- Evidence for evolutionary relationships comes from **paleontology** (the study of past life) and comparing anatomical and biochemical characteristics of species.

13.2 Fossils Record Evolution

- **Fossils** are the remains of ancient organisms.

A. The Fossil Record Is Often Incomplete

- Many organisms that lived in the past have not left fossil evidence.

B. The Age of a Fossil Can Be Estimated in Two Ways

- The position of a fossil in the context of others provides a **relative date.**
- The ratio of a radioactive isotope to its breakdown product gives an **absolute date,** which is a range of time when an organism lived. Radioactive isotopes with different **half-lives** are useful for **radiometric dating** of different-aged fossils.

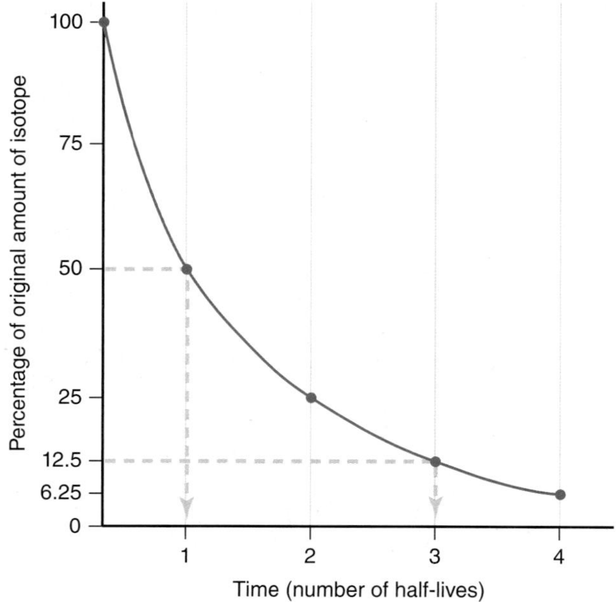

13.3 Biogeography Considers Species' Geographical Locations

- **Biogeography** is the study of the distribution of species on Earth.

A. The Theory of Plate Tectonics Explains Earth's Shifting Continents

- The **plate tectonics** theory indicates that forces deep inside Earth have moved the continents throughout much of life's history, creating and eliminating geographical barriers.

B. Species Distributions Reveal Evolutionary Events

- Biogeography provides evidence of large- and small-scale evolutionary events.

13.4 Anatomical Comparisons May Reveal Common Descent

A. Homologous Structures Have a Shared Evolutionary Origin

- **Homologous** anatomical structures and molecules have similarities that indicate they were inherited from a shared ancestor, although they may differ in function.

B. Vestigial Structures Have Lost Their Functions

- **Vestigial** structures have no function in an organism but are homologous to functioning structures in related species.

C. Convergent Evolution Produces Superficial Similarities

- **Analogous** structures are similar in function but do not reflect shared ancestry. **Convergent evolution** can produce analogous features, such as the loss of pigmentation and eyes in cave-dwelling animals.

13.5 Embryonic Development Patterns Provide Evolutionary Clues

- Embryos of different species reflect genes retained from ancestors.
- Evolutionary developmental biology combines the study of development with the study of DNA sequences. Many genes, including **homeotic genes,** influence the development of new phenotypes.

13.6 Molecules Reveal Relatedness

A. Comparing DNA and Protein Sequences May Reveal Close Relationships

- Molecular sequences contain so much information that similarities probably did not occur by chance; descent from a shared ancestor is more likely.
- DNA sequence comparisons provide an indication of the relationship between species, as can the amino acid sequences of proteins.

B. Molecular Clocks Help Assign Dates to Evolutionary Events

- A **molecular clock** compares DNA sequences to estimate the time when two species diverged from a common ancestor.

13.7 Investigating Life: Evolving Backwards

- Fossils have lent support to the hypothesis that snakes evolved on land from four-legged ancestors.

Multiple Choice Questions

1. You are living in which of the following geological eras?
   a. Archean
   b. Mesozoic
   c. Paleozoic
   d. Cenozoic
2. Why is the fossil record incomplete?
   a. Because many organisms with soft body parts never fossilize
   b. Because many fossils are destroyed by geological events
   c. Because many fossils are buried where no one will ever find them
   d. All of the above are correct.
3. Suppose a fossilized lizard bone contains one eighth of the amount of ^{14}C present in the atmosphere. How long ago did the lizard die?
   a. 5730 years ago
   b. 11,460 years ago
   c. 17,190 years ago
   d. 22,920 years ago
4. The study of biogeography is most concerned with the
   a. correct placement of species on the evolutionary tree.
   b. precise rock layer in which a fossil is found.
   c. current and past distribution of species on Earth.
   d. predicted locations of future extinction "hot spots."
5. The wing of a bird and the wing of a fly are
   a. homologous structures.
   b. vestigial structures.
   c. analogous structures.
   d. convergent structures.
6. What term is used to describe the tiny, nonfunctional eyes of a cave fish?
   a. homeotic
   b. vestigial
   c. analogous
   d. fossilized

7. As described in chapter 7, a genetic mutation does not necessarily change the amino acid sequence of a protein. For a given gene, which molecule would you expect to change the most over evolutionary time?
   a. The DNA sequence should change more than the protein sequence.
   b. The protein sequence should change more than the DNA sequence.
   c. The two should have exactly the same number of changes.
   d. The answer depends on the gene.
8. How does the activity of a homeotic gene relate to evolution?
   a. Homeotic genes serve as a marker for convergent evolution.
   b. Organisms with similar homeotic genes have the same vestigial structures.
   c. Mutations in homeotic genes can produce new body plans.
   d. The presence of homeotic genes helps to identify a fossil as that of an animal.
9. Which of the following would be most useful for comparing ALL known groups of organisms?
   a. DNA encoding ribosomal RNA
   b. DNA encoding the keratin protein
   c. Mitochondrial DNA
   d. Y chromosome DNA

Write It Out

1. What types of information are used to determine how species are related to one another by descent from shared ancestors? Give an example of how multiple types of evidence can support one another.
2. Why is the fossil record useful, even if it doesn't represent every type of organism that ever lived?
3. Index fossils represent organisms that were widespread but lived during relatively short periods of time. How are index fossils useful in relative dating?
4. How do molecular sequences provide different information than relative and absolute dating?
5. How have geological events such as continental movements influenced the history of life on Earth?
6. Why is it important for evolutionary biologists to be able to distinguish between homologous and analogous anatomical structures?
7. How did the discovery of homeotic genes help launch the field called "evo-devo"?
8. Suggest a type of genetic change that could have a drastic effect on the evolution of a species.
9. How do biologists use sequences of proteins and genes to infer evolutionary relationships?
10. Some genes are more alike between human and chimp than other genes are from person to person. Does this mean that chimps are humans or that humans with different alleles are different species? What other explanation fits the facts?
11. Search the Internet to learn about the evidence suggesting that birds and dinosaurs are closely related. If scientists could extract DNA from dinosaur fossils, how could they use the sequence to learn more about the origin of birds?
12. Why are molecular clocks useful, and what are their limitations?
13. Genetic anthropology combines the study of DNA with physical evidence such as fossils to reveal the history of the human species. Use the Internet to research the goals and methods of the Genographic Project, HapMap, or the Human Genome Diversity Project. What are the benefits of these projects? What ethical issues arise from this type of research?

Pull It Together

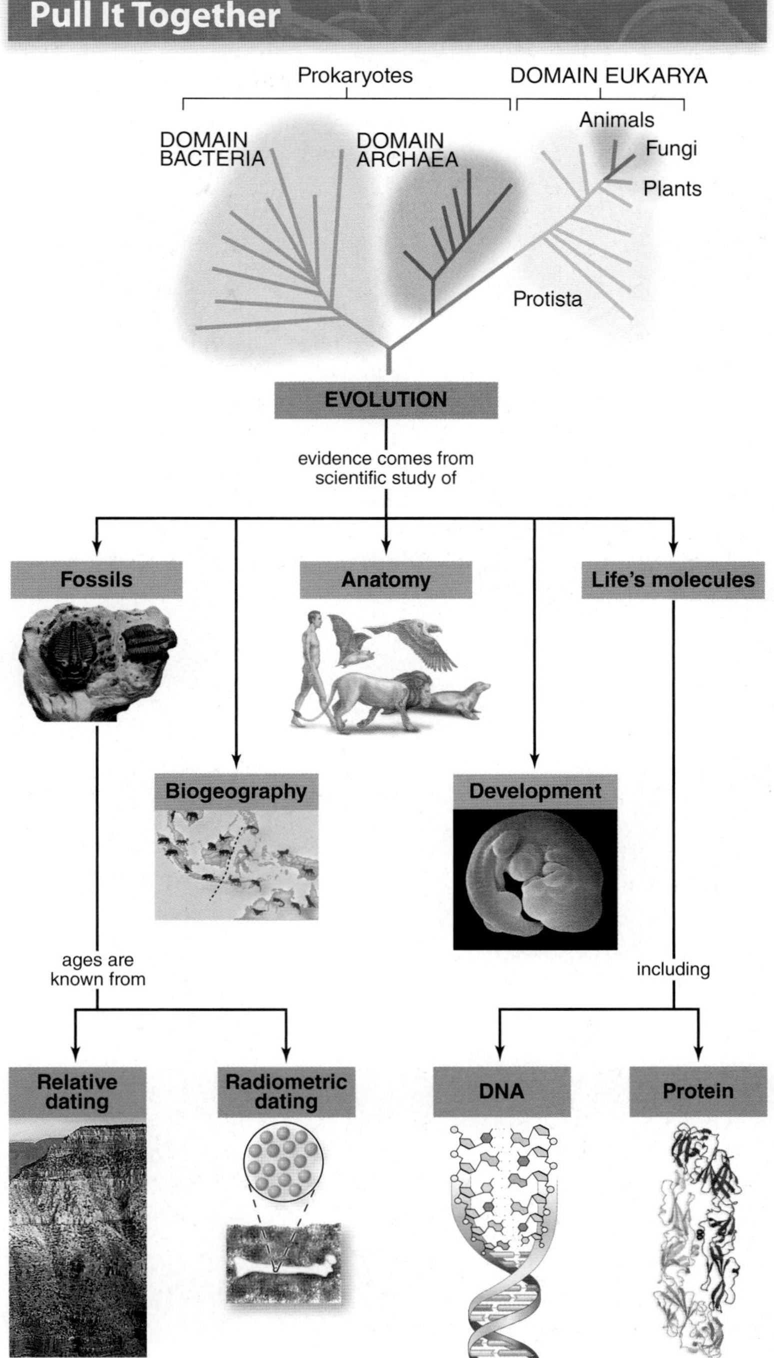

1. What are some examples of each line of evidence for evolution?
2. Add the following terms to this concept map: *homologous structures, vestigial structures, homeotic genes,* and *molecular clock.*

14 Speciation and Extinction

Endangered Eagle. The Philippine eagle is one of many species in danger of extinction, thanks to the destruction of its forest habitat.

Learning Outline

14.1 What Is a Species?
- A. Every Species Has a Two-Word Name
- B. Species Can Be Defined Based on the Potential to Interbreed

14.2 Reproductive Barriers Cause Species to Diverge
- A. Prezygotic Barriers Prevent Fertilization
- B. Postzygotic Barriers Prevent Development of a Fertile Offspring

14.3 Spatial Patterns Define Two Types of Speciation
- A. Allopatric Speciation Reflects a Geographic Barrier
- B. Sympatric Speciation Occurs in a Shared Habitat
- C. Determining the Type of Speciation May Be Difficult

14.4 Speciation May Be Gradual or Occur in Bursts

14.5 Extinction Marks the End of the Line

14.6 Biological Classification Systems Are Based on Common Descent
- A. The Taxonomic Hierarchy Organizes Species into Groups
- B. A Cladistics Approach Is Based on Shared Derived Traits
- C. Cladograms Depict Hypothesized Evolutionary Relationships
- D. Many Traditional Groups Are Not Clades

14.7 Investigating Life: Birds Do It, Bees Do It

Learn How to Learn

Take Notes on Your Reading

Taking notes as you read should help you not only retain information but also identify what you don't understand. Before you take notes, read through the assigned pages once; otherwise, you may have trouble distinguishing between main points and minor details. Then read it again. This time, pause after each section and write the most important ideas in your own words. What if you can't remember it or don't understand it well enough to summarize the passage? Read it again, and if that doesn't work, ask for help with the points that aren't clear.

What's the Point?

Over billions of years, many new species have appeared on Earth. Most do not suddenly pop into existence. Instead, populations slowly become isolated into subgroups that cannot interbreed. This chapter describes how small evolutionary changes can lead to the development of entirely new species.

Yet most species that have ever lived are now extinct. Over billions of years, many species have vanished following global disasters. Dinosaurs, which died out 65 million years ago, are the most famous examples. More recently, the explosive growth of the human population has doomed countless species. The dodo, which was exterminated by 1681, was the first of many extinctions caused by human activities.

The opposing, ongoing processes of species formation and extinction have likely been a part of evolution since life began. This chapter explains how these processes occur.

14.1 What Is a Species?

Throughout the history of life, the types of organisms have changed: new species have appeared, and existing ones have gone extinct. The term **macroevolution** describes these large, complex changes in life's panorama. Macroevolutionary events tend to span very long periods, whereas the microevolutionary processes described in chapter 12 happen so rapidly that we can sometimes observe them over just a few years (see the Burning Question on page 262). Nevertheless, the many small changes that accumulate in a population by microevolution eventually lead to large-scale macroevolution.

Evolution has produced an obvious diversity of life. A bacterium, for example, is clearly distinct from a tree or a bird (figure 14.1). At the same time, some organisms are more closely related to one another than they are to other groups; the bird in figure 14.1 is more similar to a chicken than it is to a tree. To make sense of these observations, biologists recognize the importance of grouping similar individuals into **species**—that is, distinct types of organisms. This task requires agreement on what the word *species* means. Perhaps surprisingly, the definition has changed considerably over time and is still the topic of vigorous debate among biologists.

A. Every Species Has a Two-Word Name

Swedish botanist Carolus Linnaeus (1707–1778) was not the first to ponder what constitutes a species, but his contributions last to this day. Linnaeus defined species as "all examples of creatures that were alike in minute detail of body structure." Importantly, he was the first investigator to give every species a two-word biological name. Each species's name combines the broader classification *genus* (plural: genera) with the term *species*. The scientific name for humans, for example, is *Homo sapiens*.

Linnaeus's classifications began to organize the great diversity of life and helped scientists communicate with one another. His system did not, however, consider the role of evolutionary relationships. Linnaeus thought that each species was created separately and could not change. Therefore, species could not appear or disappear, nor were they related to one another.

Charles Darwin (1809–1882) finally connected species diversity to evolution, writing that "our classifications will come to be, as far as they can be so made, genealogies." As the theory of evolution by natural selection became widely accepted in the nineteenth and twentieth centuries, scientists no longer viewed classifications merely as ways to organize life. They considered them to be hypotheses about evolutionary history. We return to this topic in section 14.6.

Figure 14.1 Distinctive Species. Bacteria, trees, and birds are about as dissimilar as three types of organisms can be.

B. Species Can Be Defined Based on the Potential to Interbreed

In the 1940s, biologists incorporated reproduction and genetics into the question of what constitutes a species. According to the **biological species concept,** a species is a population, or group of populations, whose members can interbreed and produce fertile offspring. **Speciation,** the formation of new species, occurs when some individuals can no longer successfully interbreed with the rest of the group.

Figure 14.2 How Many Species? Linnaeus would have categorized these butterflies based on their physical appearance. The biological species definition, however, provides an objective rule for determining whether each group really is a separate species.

How might this happen? A new species can form if a population somehow becomes divided. Recall from chapter 12 that a population's **gene pool** is its entire collection of genes and their alleles. An intact, interbreeding population shares a common gene pool. After a population splits in two, however, microevolutionary changes such as mutations, natural selection, and genetic drift can lead to genetic divergence between the groups. With the accumulation of enough differences in their separate gene pools, the two groups can no longer produce fertile offspring even if they come into contact once again. In this way, microevolution becomes macroevolution.

The biological species definition does not rely on physical appearance, so it is much less subjective than Linnaeus's observations. Under the system of Linnaeus, it would be impossible to determine whether two similar-looking butterflies belong to different species (figure 14.2). Using the biological species concept, however, we can say that they belong to one species if the two groups can produce fertile offspring together.

Nevertheless, the biological species concept raises several difficulties. First, it cannot apply to asexually reproducing organisms, such as bacteria, archaea, and many fungi and protists. Second, it is impossible to apply the biological species definition to extinct organisms known only from fossils. Third, some types of organisms have the *potential* to interbreed in captivity, but they do not do so in nature. Fourth, for some species, reproductive isolation is not absolute. Many closely related species of plants, for example, occasionally produce fertile offspring together even though their gene pools usually remain separate.

As a result, the biological species concept does not provide a perfect way to determine the "boundaries" of each species. DNA sequence analysis has helped to fill in some of these gaps. Biologists working with bacteria and archaea, for example, use a stretch of DNA that encodes ribosomal RNA to define species. If the DNA sequences of two specimens are more than 97% identical, they are considered to be the same species. These genetic sequences, however, still present some ambiguity because they cannot reveal whether genetically similar organisms currently share a gene pool.

Despite these difficulties, reproductive isolation is the most common criterion used to define species. The rest of this chapter therefore uses the biological species concept to describe how speciation occurs.

14.1 Mastering Concepts

1. What is the relationship between macroevolution and microevolution?
2. How does the biological species concept differ from Linnaeus's definition of the term *species?*
3. What are some of the challenges in defining species?

14.2 Reproductive Barriers Cause Species to Diverge

In keeping with the biological species concept, a new species forms when one portion of a population can no longer breed and produce fertile offspring with the rest of the population. That is, the two separate groups no longer share a common gene pool. Each subpopulation then follows its own, independent evolutionary path.

Two parts of a population can become reproductively isolated in many ways, because successful reproduction requires so many complex events. Any interruption in courtship, fertilization, embryo formation, or offspring development can be a reproductive barrier.

Biologists divide the many mechanisms of reproductive isolation into two broad groups: prezygotic and postzygotic. **Prezygotic reproductive barriers** occur before the formation of the zygote, or fertilized egg; **postzygotic reproductive barriers** reduce the fitness of a hybrid offspring. (A hybrid, in this context, is the offspring of individuals from two different species.) Figure 14.3 summarizes the reproductive barriers, which are described in more detail on page 262.

Barrier	Description	Example	Illustration
PREZYGOTIC REPRODUCTIVE ISOLATION			
Habitat isolation	Different environments	Ladybugs feed on different plants.	
Temporal isolation	Active or fertile at different times	Field crickets mature at different rates.	
Behavioral isolation	Different courtship activities	Frog mating calls differ.	
Mechanical isolation	Mating organs or pollinators incompatible	Sage species use different pollinators.	
Gametic isolation	Gametes cannot unite.	Sea urchin gametes are incompatible.	
POSTZYGOTIC REPRODUCTIVE ISOLATION			
Hybrid inviability	Hybrid offspring fail to reach maturity.	Hybrid eucalyptus seeds and seedlings are not viable.	
Hybrid infertility (sterility)	Hybrid offspring unable to reproduce	Lion-tiger cross (liger) is infertile.	
Hybrid breakdown	Second-generation hybrid offspring have reduced fitness.	Offspring of hybrid mosquitoes have abnormal genitalia.	

Figure 14.3 Reproductive Barriers: A Summary. Any one of these barriers can prevent two related species from interbreeding.

Burning Questions

Can people watch evolution and speciation in action?

Microevolution is ongoing in every species, so it is not surprising that biologists have documented many instances of evolution "in action." Medicine provides the most familiar context. One example is the discovery that HIV evolved from a virus that occurs in chimpanzees; another is the rise of antibiotic resistance among the bacteria that cause staph infections and tuberculosis.

The use of pesticides has provided ample examples as well. Many people know that populations of DDT-resistant insects skyrocketed shortly after people began using DDT to kill mosquito larvae. Likewise, section 10.10 describes the selection for moth larvae that are resistant to Bt, an insecticidal protein.

Speciation is observable as well. Mosquito populations that have been isolated for more than 100 years in the tunnels of the London Underground, for example, can no longer breed with their aboveground counterparts. Scientists have also witnessed the birth of new plant species in western North America over several decades (see section 9.8).

Submit your burning question to:
marielle_hoefnagels@mcgraw-hill.com

A. Prezygotic Barriers Prevent Fertilization

Mechanisms of prezygotic reproductive isolation affect the ability of two species to combine gametes. As you can see in figure 14.3, two of the prezygotic barriers keep members of two different species from ever encountering each other. The populations may live in different places (habitat isolation) or be active at different times of the day or year (temporal isolation).

Even if individuals from two species do encounter each other, prezygotic barriers may still prevent breeding. The two species may use such different mating rituals that they are not attracted to each other (behavioral isolation). For example, mate selection in many birds is based on intricate courtship dances. Any variation in the ritual from one group to another could prevent them from mating.

Prezygotic barriers may apply even if the members of two species attempt to mate. In animals, the male and female parts of two related species may not match; in plants, the pollinator of one species may be unable to fit into the flower of another. Both scenarios illustrate a reproductive barrier called mechanical isolation, which prevents male and female gametes from meeting even if mating does occur.

The final prezygotic barrier is gametic isolation. Even if sperm and egg cells from two different species meet, the gametes have unique surface molecules that enable an egg cell to recognize sperm of the same species. In the absence of a "match," fertilization will not occur, and the gene pools will remain separate. Gametic isolation explains why no one can create a dog-cat hybrid in a laboratory by mixing sperm from a dog with egg cells from a cat. The gametes are simply incompatible.

B. Postzygotic Barriers Prevent Development of a Fertile Offspring

Individuals of two different species may bypass all of the prezygotic barriers and produce a hybrid zygote. Even then, three types of postzygotic barriers may keep the species separate by selecting against the hybrid offspring (see figure 14.3).

One type of postzygotic reproductive barrier is hybrid inviability. In this case, a hybrid embryo dies before reaching reproductive maturity, typically because the genes of its parents are incompatible. Alternatively, the hybrid offspring may develop to adulthood but be unable to produce offspring of its own (hybrid infertility). The most familiar example of this postzygotic barrier is a mule, which is the hybrid offspring of a female horse and a male donkey. Meiosis does not occur in the mule's germ cells because the two parents contribute different numbers of chromosomes. As a result, the mule cannot produce gametes. Similarly, a liger is the hybrid offspring of a male lion and a female tiger. Like mules, ligers are usually sterile. ▸▸ homologous chromosomes, p. 156; mules, p. 160

Some species produce hybrid offspring that are fertile. When the hybrids reproduce, however, their offspring may have abnormalities that reduce their fitness. Some second-generation hybrid offspring of two mosquito species, for example, have abnormal genitalia that make mating difficult. This last type of postzygotic reproductive barrier is called hybrid breakdown.

14.2 Mastering Concepts

1. How do reproductive barriers lead to speciation?
2. Name five modes of prezygotic reproductive isolation.
3. What are three ways that postzygotic reproductive isolation may occur?

14.3 Spatial Patterns Define Two Types of Speciation

Reproductive barriers keep related species apart, but how do these barriers arise in the first place? More specifically, how could two populations of the same species evolve along different pathways, eventually yielding two species?

The most obvious way is to physically separate the populations so that they do not exchange genes. Eventually, the genetic differences between the populations would give rise to one or more reproductive barriers. Yet speciation can also occur between populations that have physical contact with each other. Biologists recognize these different circumstances by dividing the geographic setting of speciation into two categories: allopatric and sympatric (figure 14.4).

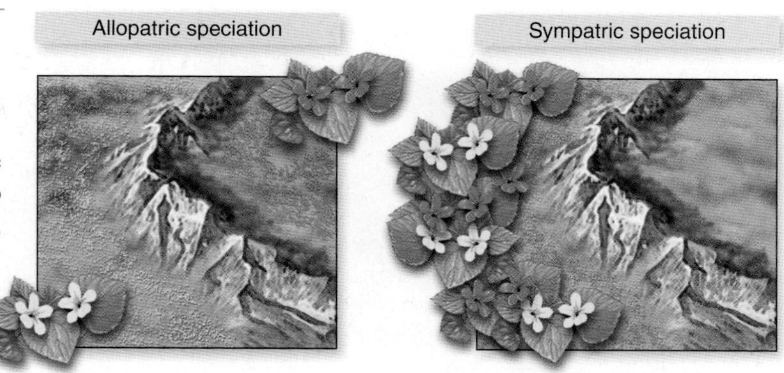

Figure 14.4 Speciation and Geography. Allopatric and sympatric speciation are distinguished based on whether populations are separated by a physical barrier or mingle within a shared area.

A. Allopatric Speciation Reflects a Geographic Barrier

In **allopatric speciation,** a barrier physically separates a population into two groups that cannot interbreed (*allo-* means "other," and *patria* means "fatherland"). The isolation may result from rivers, deserts, glaciers, changes in sea level, the formation of mountains or bodies of water, or the appearance of any other physical barrier to gene exchange.

If the two groups cannot contact each other, gene exchange between them stops. Natural selection and genetic drift would then act independently in each group. The result may be one or more reproductive barriers. Once the descendants of the two isolated populations cannot interbreed, one species has become two.

Allopatric speciation explains the clusters of closely related species on island groups. For example, 11 subspecies of tortoise occupy the Galápagos islands (figure 14.5). According to DNA analysis, a few newcomers from the South

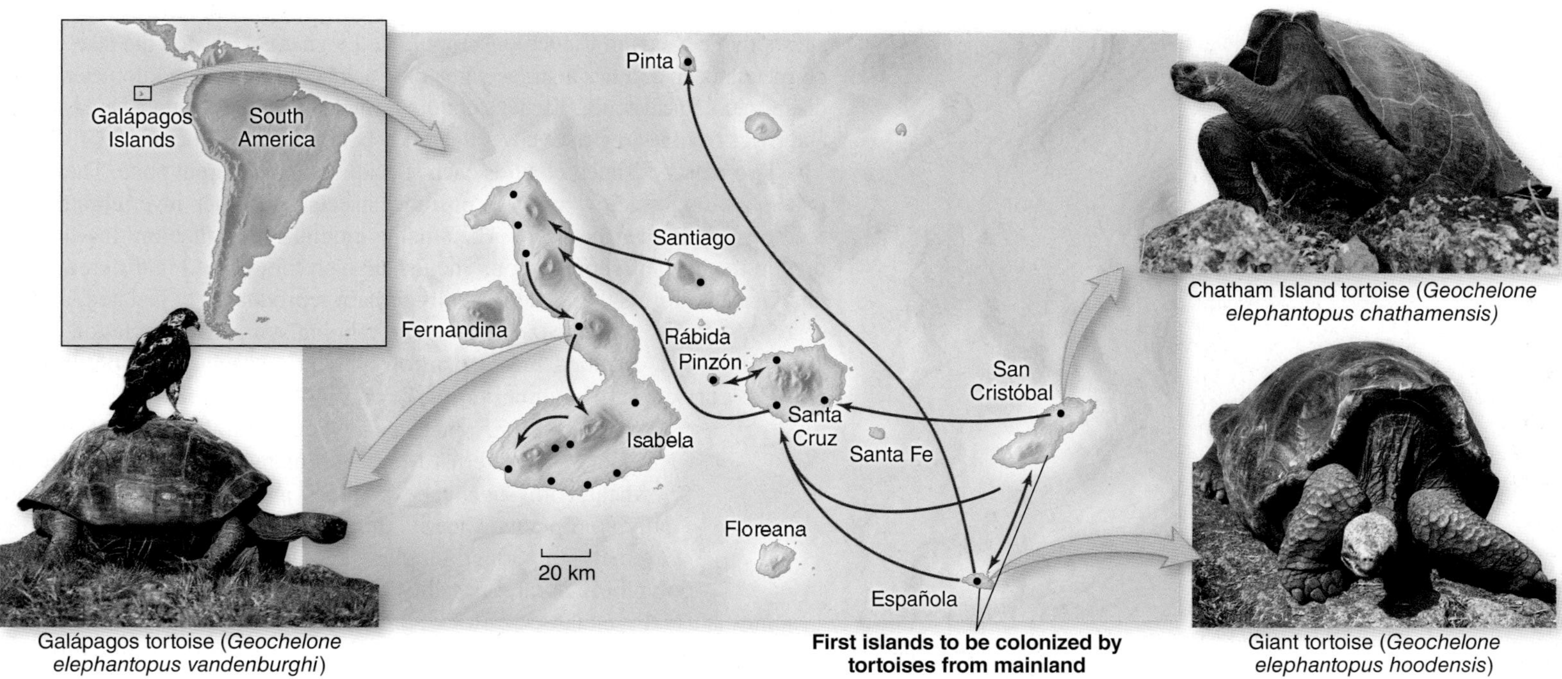

Figure 14.5 Allopatric Speciation in Tortoises. Descendants of the first tortoises to arrive on the Galápagos have colonized most of the islands, evolving into many subspecies. Unique habitats have selected for different sets of adaptations in the tortoises.

Figure 14.6 **Allopatric Speciation in Pupfish.** Devil's Hole is a pool in a limestone cavern east of Death Valley National Park. The pupfish species that lives there is a product of allopatric speciation.

American mainland first colonized either San Cristóbal or Española a couple of million years ago. As the population grew, the tortoises migrated to nearby islands, where they encountered new habitats that selected for different adaptations, especially in shell shape. Dry islands with sparse vegetation have selected for notched shells that enable the tortoises to reach for higher food sources. On islands with lush, low-growing vegetation, the tortoises have domed shells.

Although many of the subspecies look distinctly different from one another, the tortoises can interbreed. They are not yet separate species, but the genetic similarities among tortoises on each island suggest that migration from island to island was historically rare. The Galápagos tortoises illustrate an ongoing process of allopatric speciation.

In addition to island groups, isolated springs also offer opportunities for allopatric speciation. The Devil's Hole pupfish, which inhabits a warm spring at the base of a mountain near Death Valley, California, provides one example (figure 14.6). The spring was isolated from other bodies of water about 50,000 years ago, preventing genetic exchange between the fish trapped in the spring and those in the original population. Since that time, the gene pool has shifted sufficiently so that a Devil's Hole pupfish cannot mate with fish from another spring. It has become a distinct species.

B. Sympatric Speciation Occurs in a Shared Habitat

In **sympatric speciation,** populations diverge genetically while living in the same physical area (*sym-* means "together"). Among evolutionary biologists, the idea of sympatric speciation can be controversial. After all, how can a new species arise in the midst of an existing population?

Often sympatric speciation reflects the fact that a habitat that appears uniform actually consists of many microenvironments. Fishes called cichlids, for example, have diversified into many species within the same lakes in Africa. Figure 14.7 shows two cichlids in Cameroon's tiny Lake Ejagham. Although the lake is only 18 meters deep and has a surface area of less than half a square kilometer, it has distinct ecological zones. The lake bottom is muddy near the center, whereas leaves and twigs from nearby trees cover the sandy bottom near the shore.

Two closely related cichlids each specialize in a different zone. The larger fish inhabiting shallow waters consume insects and other invertebrates that feed on leaves near the shore. The smaller cichlids specialize on tiny floating prey in the deep offshore region. The fish also prefer to breed in different habitats. The two forms therefore typically remain reproductively isolated, and researchers surmise that the cichlids are undergoing sympatric speciation.

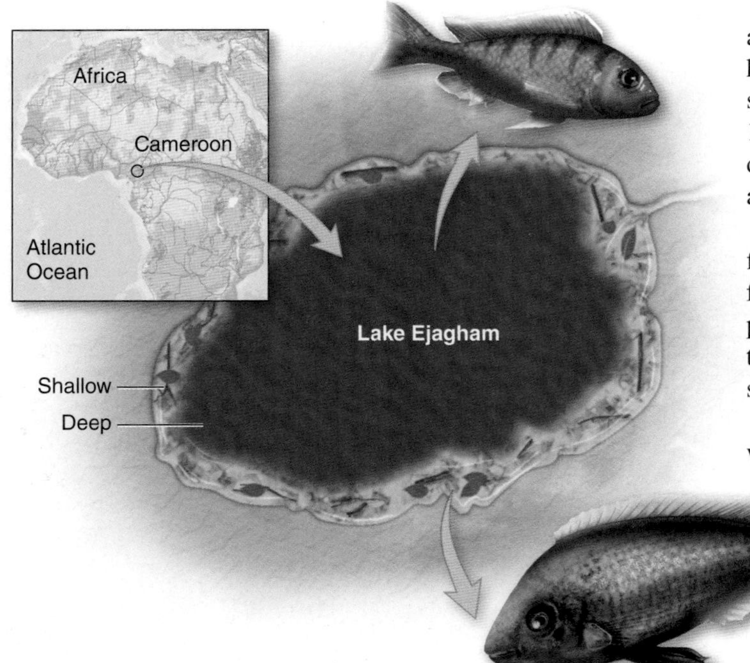

Figure 14.7 **Sympatric Speciation.** Cichlids live throughout Cameroon's Lake Ejagham, but those living in shallow waters (bottom) have larger bodies than do deep-water fish (top).

In plants, a common mechanism of sympatric speciation is **polyploidy,** which occurs when the number of sets of chromosomes increases. Nearly half of all flowering plant species are natural polyploids, as are about 95% of ferns. Moreover, many major crops, including wheat, corn, sugar cane, potatoes, and coffee, are derived from polyploid plants. Clearly, this form of reproductive isolation is extremely important in plant evolution. In animals, however, polyploidy is rare, possibly because the extra "dose" of chromosomes is usually fatal. ▸ polyploidy, p. 165

Polyploid organisms sometimes arise when gametes from two different species fuse. For example, section 9.8 describes how new polyploid species of *Tragopogon* wildflowers arose after plants in this genus were introduced to Washington state in the 1950s. Cotton plants provide another example. An Old

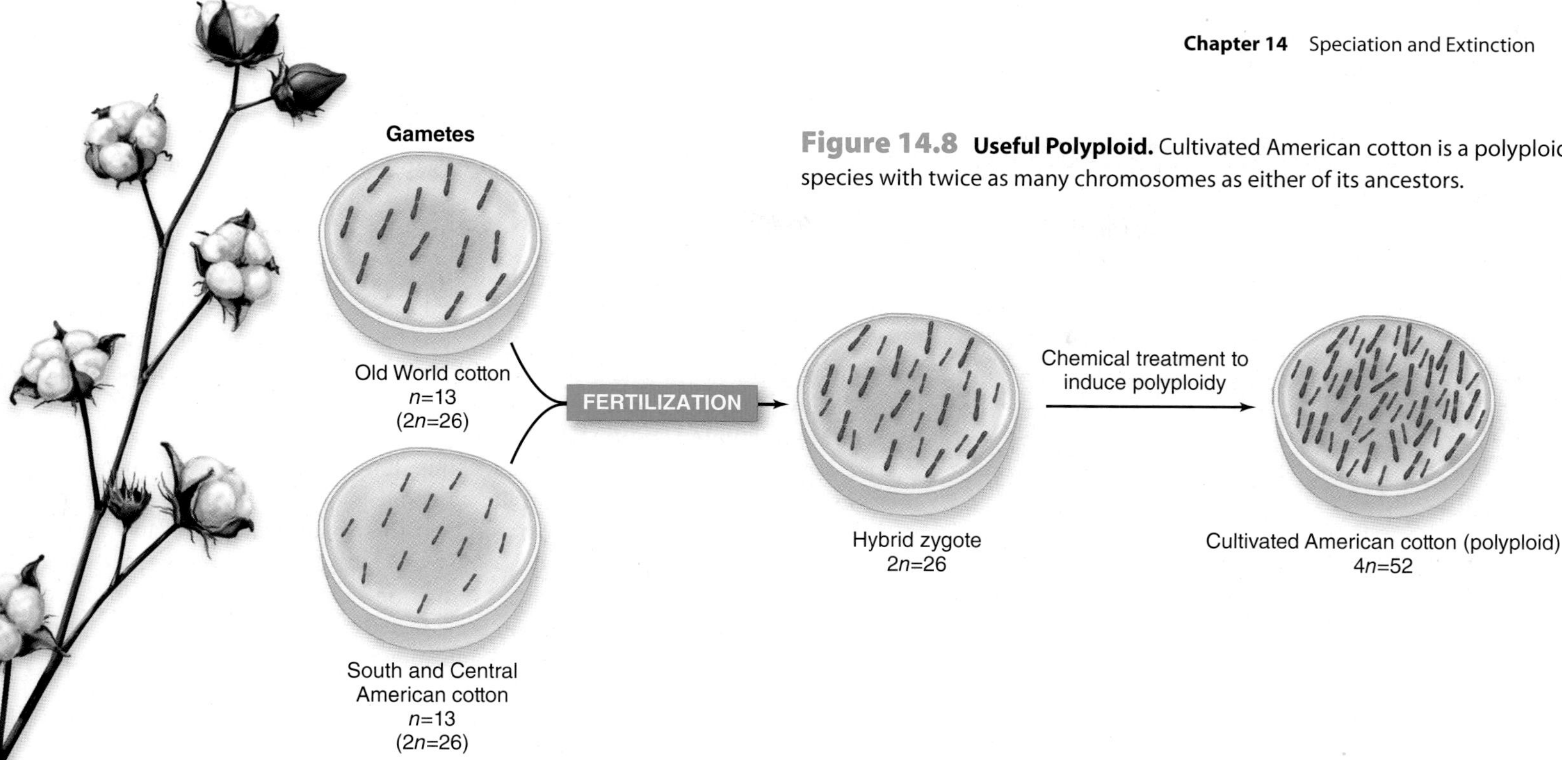

Figure 14.8 Useful Polyploid. Cultivated American cotton is a polyploid species with twice as many chromosomes as either of its ancestors.

World species of wild cotton has 26 large chromosomes, whereas one from Central and South America has 26 small chromosomes (figure 14.8). Plant breeders crossed haploid cells from the two species to create a hybrid with 26 chromosomes, then applied a chemical that caused the chromosome number to double. The resulting cotton plant is a polyploid with 52 chromosomes: 26 large and 26 small. Farmers around the world cultivate this species to harvest cotton for cloth.

C. Determining the Type of Speciation May Be Difficult

Biologists sometimes debate whether a speciation event is allopatric or sympatric. One reason for the disagreements is that we may not be able to detect the barriers that are important to other species. Is an apparently uniform patch of forest a potential setting for sympatric speciation? Our perspective may differ from that of a soil-dwelling insect, whose habitat differs greatly from the environment in the treetops.

The problem of perspective also leads to debate over the size of the geographic barrier needed to separate two populations, which depends on the distance over which a species can spread its gametes. A plant with windblown pollen or a fungus producing lightweight spores encounters few barriers to gene exchange; pollen and spores can travel thousands of miles in the upper atmosphere. On the other hand, a desert pupfish cannot migrate out of its spring, so the isolation of its habitat instantly creates an insurmountable geographic barrier. The same circumstance would not deter gene exchange in species that walk or fly between pools.

14.3 Mastering Concepts

1. Distinguish between allopatric and sympatric speciation, and provide examples of each.
2. How can polyploidy contribute to sympatric speciation?
3. Why is it sometimes difficult to determine whether speciation is allopatric or sympatric?

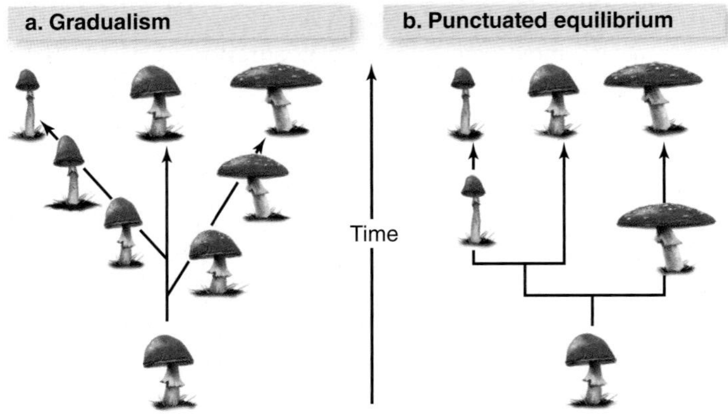

Figure 14.9 Evolution—Both Gradual and in Bursts. (a) In gradualism, multiple species arise from one ancestor by way of small, incremental steps. (b) Punctuated equilibrium produces the same result, except that the new species arise in rapid bursts followed by periods of little change.

Figure 14.10 Speciation Following a Mass Extinction. Many ecological niches were vacated when nonavian dinosaurs went extinct. Mammals diversified and flourished in the aftermath.

14.4 Speciation May Be Gradual or Occur in Bursts

Darwin envisioned one species gradually transforming into another through a series of intermediate stages. The pace as he saw it was slow, although not necessarily constant. This idea, which became known as **gradualism,** held that evolution proceeds in small, incremental changes over many generations. In 1972, however, paleontologists Stephen Jay Gould and Niles Eldredge coined the term **punctuated equilibrium** to describe the opposite situation: relatively brief bursts of rapid evolution interrupting long periods of little change. Figure 14.9 compares and contrasts these two ideas.

If the gradualism model is correct, then fossils should reveal "slow and steady" evolutionary change. Much of the fossil record, however, suggests the opposite. That is, many steps in species formation did not leave fossil evidence, and so we often cannot observe the intermediate forms between species.

What accounts for the "missing" transitional forms? One explanation is that the fossil record is incomplete, for many reasons: poor preservation of biological material, natural forces that destroyed fossils, and the simple fact that we haven't discovered every fossil on Earth. Chapter 13 explores these reasons in more detail.

Punctuated equilibrium provides another explanation for the absence of some predicted transitional forms: the "missing links" may have been too rare to leave many fossils. After all, periods of rapid biological changes would not leave much fossil evidence of any single intermediate form. The fossil record lacks some transitional forms because they never existed in a particular location or because there were simply too few organisms to leave fossils.

What could account for the alternating "fast and slow" pace of punctuated equilibrium? A rapid bout of speciation may occur when some members of a population inherit a key adaptation that gives them an advantage. The oldest flowering plant fossil, for example, is about 125 million years old. The descendants of the first flowering plants diversified rapidly, and all of today's major lineages were already in place 100 million years ago. Hundreds of thousands of flowering plant species now inhabit Earth. The new adaptation—the flower—unleashed an entirely new set of options for reproduction, prompting rapid diversification.

Rapid speciation may also occur when some members of a population inherit adaptations that enable them to survive a major environmental change. After the poorly suited organisms perish, the survivors diversify as they exploit the new resources in the changed environment. Mammals, for example, underwent a burst of speciation after the extinction of the nonavian dinosaurs opened up many new habitats about 65 million years ago (figure 14.10).

The fossil record supports both punctuated equilibrium and gradualism. Microscopic protists such as foraminiferans and diatoms, for example, have evolved gradually. On the other hand, the fossils of diverse animals such as bryozoans, mollusks, and mammals all reveal many examples of rapid evolution followed by periods of stability.

14.4 Mastering Concepts

1. Describe the theories of gradualism and punctuated equilibrium.
2. How can the fossil record support both gradualism and punctuated equilibrium?

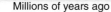

14.5 Extinction Marks the End of the Line

A species goes **extinct** when all of its members have died. Many factors can cause extinction, but all amount to a failure to adapt to environmental change. Any species will vanish if its gene pool does not contain the "right" alleles necessary for individuals to produce fertile offspring and sustain the population; genetic diversity is therefore essential in a changing environment. The change that wipes out a species may be habitat loss, new predators, or new diseases. Extinction may also be a matter of bad luck: sometimes no individual of a species survives a volcanic eruption or asteroid impact.

Biologists distinguish between two different types of extinction events (figure 14.11). Most extinctions overall occur as part of the **background extinction rate,** which results from the gradual loss of species as populations shrink in the face of new challenges. Paleontologists have used the fossil record to calculate that the background rate is roughly 0.1 to 1.0 extinctions per year per million species. But Earth has also witnessed several periods of **mass extinctions,** when a great number of species disappeared over relatively short expanses of time. Mass extinctions have had a great influence on Earth's history because they have periodically opened vast new habitats for surviving species to diversify (see figure 14.10).

Paleontologists study clues in Earth's sediments to understand the catastrophic events that contribute to mass extinctions. For example, the **impact theory** suggests that meteorites or comets have occasionally crashed to Earth, sending dust, soot, and other debris into the sky. These particles blocked sunlight and set into motion a deadly chain reaction. Without sunlight, plants died. The animals that ate plants, and the animals that ate those animals, then perished. Such an event apparently caused the mass extinction that doomed the dinosaurs 65 million years ago. Evidence includes layers of rock that are rich in iridium, an element rare on Earth but common in meteorites (figure 14.12).

Movements of Earth's crust may also explain some mass extinctions. The crust, or uppermost layer of the planet's surface, is divided into many pieces, called tectonic plates. During Earth's history, these plates have drifted apart and come back together. Climates changed as continents moved toward or away from the poles, while oceans mixed and separated. Colliding continents also altered shorelines, causing shallow coastal areas packed with life to disappear. The overall result was dramatic environmental change that profoundly affected life.
▸ plate tectonics, p. 247

The role of *Homo sapiens* in causing extinctions is evident today. Ecologists are documenting an alarming increase in background extinction rates, now estimated at 20 to 200 extinctions per million species per year. Habitat loss and habitat fragmentation, pollution, introduced species, and overharvesting combine to imperil many species (see chapter 20). This chapter's Why We Care box, on page 268, lists a few of the many vertebrate species that have recently become extinct.

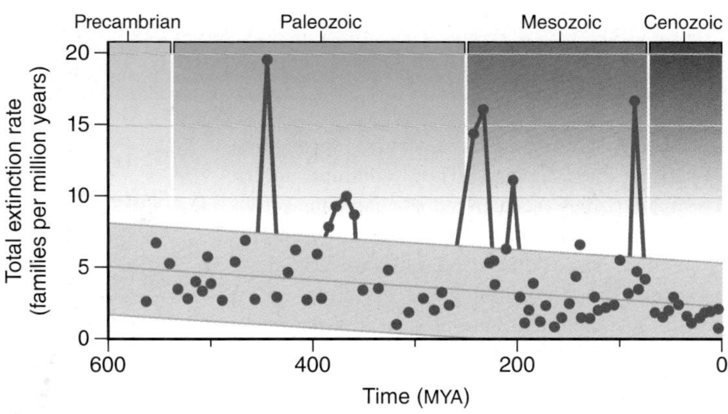

Figure 14.11 Extinctions at Sea. This graph shows extinction rates for marine animal families over the past 600 million years. The shaded area near the bottom of the graph estimates the background extinction rate; peaks show five mass extinctions.

Figure 14.12 Impact Theory Evidence. This distinctive layer of rock (inset) marks the cataclysmic end of the Cretaceous period.

14.5 Mastering Concepts

1. What factors can cause or hasten extinction?
2. Distinguish between background extinction and mass extinctions.
3. How have humans influenced extinctions?

Why We Care | Recent Species Extinctions

Species extinctions have occurred throughout life's long history. They continue today, many times accelerated by human activities. Overharvesting contributes to species extinctions, as does habitat loss to agriculture, urbanization, damming, or pollution. Introduced plants and animals can deplete native species by competing with or preying on them. Many biologists estimate that we are currently experiencing a sixth global mass extinction; global climate change may make the effects even worse (see chapter 20).

This box lists a few species of vertebrate animals that have disappeared during the past few centuries. This list is far from complete; many more species of animals (both vertebrate and invertebrate) and plants have become extinct during the same time. Countless others are threatened or endangered, meaning that they are at risk for extinction.

Name	Cause of Extinction	Former Location
Fishes:		
Chinese paddlefish (*Psephurus gladius*)	Habitat destruction	China
Las Vegas dace (*Rhinichthys deaconi*)	Habitat destruction	North America
Amphibians:		
Palestinian painted frog (*Discoglossus nigriventer*)	Habitat destruction	Israel
Southern day frog (*Taudactylus diurnus*)	Undetermined	Australia
Reptiles:		
Yunnan box turtle (*Cuora yunnanensis*)	Habitat destruction, overharvesting	China
Martinique lizard (*Leiocephalus herminieri*)	Undetermined	Martinique
Birds:		
Dodo (*Raphus cucullatus*)	Habitat destruction, overharvesting	Mauritius
Moa (*Megalapteryx diderius*)	Overharvesting	New Zealand
Laysan honeycreeper (*Himatione sanguinea*)	Habitat destruction	Hawaii
Black mamo (*Drepanis funerea*)	Habitat destruction, introduced predators	Hawaii
Passenger pigeon (*Ectopistes migratorius*)	Overharvesting	North America
Great auk (*Alca impennis*)	Overharvesting	North Atlantic
Mammals:		
Quagga (*Equus quagga quagga*)	Overharvesting	South Africa
Steller's sea cow (*Hydrodamalis gigas*)	Overharvesting	Bering Sea
Bali tiger (*Panthera tigris balica*)	Habitat destruction, overharvesting	Indonesia
Javan tiger (*Panthera tigris sondaica*)	Habitat destruction, overharvesting	Indonesia
Caspian tiger (*Panthera tigris virgata*)	Habitat destruction, overharvesting	Central Asia

14.6 Biological Classification Systems Are Based on Common Descent

Darwin proposed that evolution occurs in a branched fashion, with each species giving rise to other species as populations occupy and adapt to new habitats. As described in chapter 13, ample evidence has since shown him to be correct.

The goal of modern classification systems is to reflect this shared evolutionary history. **Systematics,** the study of classification, therefore incorporates two interrelated specialties: taxonomy and phylogenetics. **Taxonomy** is the science of describing, naming, and classifying species; **phylogenetics** is the study of evolutionary relationships among species. This section describes how biologists apply the evidence for evolution to the monumental task of organizing life's diversity into groups.

A. The Taxonomic Hierarchy Organizes Species into Groups

Carolus Linnaeus, the sixteenth-century biologist introduced at the start of this chapter, made a lasting contribution to systematics. He devised a way to organize life into a hierarchical classification scheme. He grouped similar genera into orders, classes, and kingdoms; his system also assigned a consistent, scientific name to each type of organism.

Linnaeus's idea is the basis of the taxonomic hierarchy used today. Biologists organize life into nested groups of taxonomic levels, based on similarities (figure 14.13). The three domains—Archaea, Bacteria, and Eukarya—are the most inclusive levels. Each domain is divided into kingdoms, which in turn are divided into phyla, then classes, orders, families, genera, and species. A **taxon** (plural: taxa) is a group at any rank; that is, domain Eukarya is a taxon, as is the order Liliales and the species *Aloe vera*.

The more features two organisms have in common, the more taxonomic levels they share. A human, a squid, and a fly are all members of the animal kingdom, but their many differences place them in separate phyla. A human, a rat, and a pig are more closely related—all belong to the same kingdom, phylum, and class (Mammalia). A human, an orangutan, and a chimpanzee are even more closely related, sharing the same kingdom, phylum, class, order, and family (Order Primates, Family Hominidae). As humans, our full classification is Eukarya-Animalia-Chordata-Mammalia-Primates-Hominidae-*Homo*-*Homo sapiens*.

This taxonomic hierarchy is useful, but it has a flaw. The system includes eight main levels, ranging from domain to species, which might give the incorrect impression that evolution took eight "steps" to produce each modern species. In fact, however, the taxonomic ranks are not equivalent across kingdoms. As just one example, the family Felidae contains 37 species of cats, whereas the family Orchidaceae contains about 22,000 species of orchids. The "family" level therefore does not reflect the same species diversity in plants as it does in animals. The Linnaean system is an imperfect reflection of evolutionary history, but it remains in widespread use because biologists have not agreed on a better approach.

B. A Cladistics Approach Is Based on Shared Derived Traits

Biologists illustrate life's diversity in the form of phylogenetic trees that depict species's evolutionary relationships based on descent from shared ancestors. Multiple lines of evidence are used to construct these trees. Anatomical features of fossils and existing organisms are useful, as are behaviors, physiological adaptations, and DNA or protein sequences.

In the past, systematists constructed phylogenetic tree diagrams by comparing as many characteristics as possible among species. Those organisms with the most characteristics in common would be neighbors on the tree's branches.

Basing a tree entirely on similarities, however, can be misleading. As just one example, many types of cave animals are eyeless and unpigmented (see figure 13.10). But these resemblances do not mean that the species that occupy caves are closely related to one another; instead, they are the product of convergent evolution. If the goal of a classification system is to group related organisms together, then simply attending to similarities might therefore lead to an incorrect classification.

A cladistics approach solves this problem. Widely adopted beginning in the 1990s, **cladistics** is a phylogenetic system that defines groups by distinguishing between ancestral and derived characters. **Ancestral characters** are inherited attributes that resemble those of the ancestor of a group; an organism with **derived characters** has features not found in the group's ancestor.

Taxonomic group	*Aloe vera* plant found in:	Number of species
Domain	Eukarya	Several million
Kingdom	Plantae	~375,000
Phylum	Anthophyta	~235,000
Class	Liliopsida	~65,000
Order	Liliales	~1200
Family	Asphodelaceae	785
Genus	*Aloe*	500
Species	*Aloe vera*	1

Figure 14.13 Taxonomic Hierarchy. Similar species are grouped into genera, genera are grouped into families, and so on. This diagram shows the complete classification for the plant *Aloe vera*.

Cladistics therefore builds on the concept of homology, described in chapter 13. Homologous structures, such as the forelimbs of birds and mammals (see figure 13.8), are inherited from a common ancestor. We have already seen that natural selection can modify homologous structures (and genes) into a wide variety of new forms. In a cladistics analysis, an ancestral character has changed little from its state in a group's ancestor; a derived character, on the other hand, has changed more.

How do researchers know which characters are ancestral and which are derived? They choose an **outgroup** consisting of comparator organisms that are not part of the group being studied. For example, in a cladistic analysis of land vertebrates, an appropriate outgroup might be lungfishes. Features that are present in lungfishes and land vertebrates are assumed to be ancestral; a segmented backbone and two eyes are therefore ancestral features. Derived features in land vertebrates would include four limbs, feathers, fur, or other characteristics that do not appear in lungfish.

In a cladistics approach, biologists use shared derived characters to define groups. A **clade** is a group of organisms consisting of a common ancestor and all of its descendants; in other words, it is a group of species united by a single evolutionary pathway. For example, modern birds form a clade because they all descended from the same group of reptiles. A clade may contain any number of species, as long as all of its members share an ancestor that organisms outside the clade do not share.

C. Cladograms Depict Hypothesized Evolutionary Relationships

The result of a cladistics analysis is a **cladogram,** a treelike diagram built using shared derived characteristics (figure 14.14). The emphasis in a cladogram is not physical similarities but rather historical relationships. To emphasize this point, imagine a lizard, a crocodile, and a chicken. Which resembles the lizard more closely: the crocodile or the chicken? Clearly, the most *similar* animals are the lizard and the crocodile. But these resemblances are only superficial. The shared derived characters tell a more complete story of

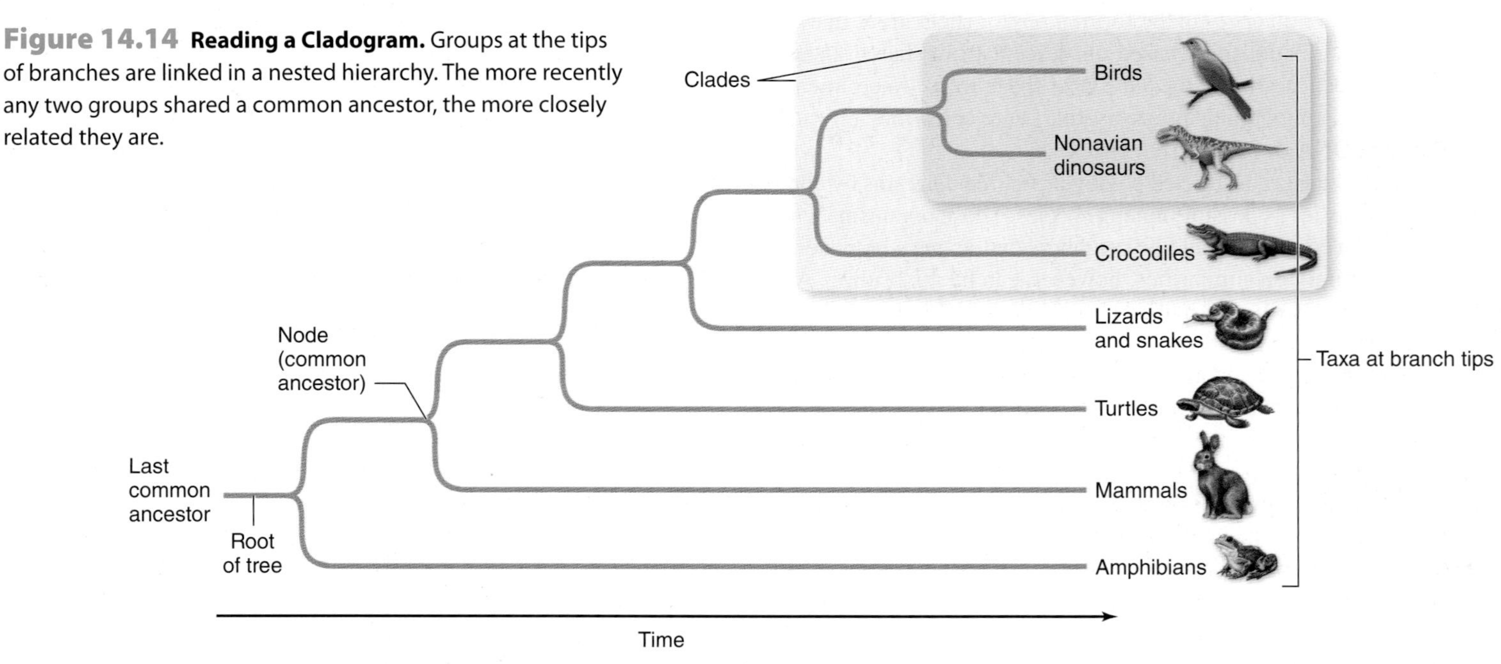

Figure 14.14 Reading a Cladogram. Groups at the tips of branches are linked in a nested hierarchy. The more recently any two groups shared a common ancestor, the more closely related they are.

evolutionary history. According to this evidence, crocodiles are more closely related to birds than they are to lizards.

All cladograms have features in common. The tips of the branches represent the taxa in the group being studied. Existing species, such as birds and turtles, are at the tips of longer branches in figure 14.14; the nonavian dinosaurs are extinct and therefore occupy a shorter branch. Each node in a cladogram indicates where two groups arose from a common ancestor. A branching pattern of lines therefore represents populations that diverge genetically, splitting off to form a new species.

A common mistake in interpreting cladograms is to incorrectly assume that a taxon must be closely related to both groups that appear next to it on the tree. In figure 14.14, for example, mammals are adjacent to both turtles and amphibians. Does this mean that rabbits are as closely related to frogs as they are to turtles? To find out, look at the relative amount of time that has passed since mammals last shared a common ancestor with each group. Because the common ancestor of mammals and turtles existed more recently, these groups are more closely related than are mammals and amphibians.

All phylogenetic trees are based on limited and sometimes ambiguous information. They are therefore not peeks into the past but rather tools that researchers can use to construct hypotheses about the relationships among different types of organisms. These investigators can then add other approaches to test the hypotheses.

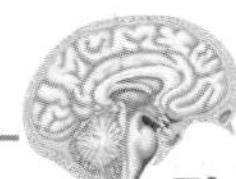

Figure It Out

How many clades are represented in the phylogenetic tree in figure 14.14?

Answer: 6

D. Many Traditional Groups Are Not Clades

Contemporary scientists using a cladistics approach typically assign names only to clades and not to groups that reflect incomplete clades or that combine portions of multiple clades. Many familiar groups of species, however, are not clades.

For example, according to the traditional Linnaean classification system, class Reptilia includes turtles, lizards, snakes, crocodiles, and the extinct dinosaurs, but it excludes birds. The cladogram in figure 14.14, however, places birds in the same clade with the reptiles based on their many shared derived characteristics. Most biologists therefore now consider birds to be reptiles, so they make a distinction between birds and "nonavian" dinosaurs.

Nor does the kingdom Protista form a clade. Protists include mostly single-celled eukaryotes that do not fit into any of the three eukaryotic kingdoms (plants, fungi, and animals). Yet all three of these groups share a common eukaryotic ancestor with the protists. Biologists are currently struggling to divide kingdom Protista into clades, an immense task (see figure 1.8).

As yet another example, a group consisting of endothermic (formerly called "warm-blooded") animals would include only birds and mammals. This group is not a clade because it excludes the most recent common ancestor of birds and mammals, which was an ectotherm (formerly called "cold-blooded"). Likewise, the term *algae* reflects a grouping of many unrelated species of aquatic organisms that carry out photosynthesis.

Table 14.1 summarizes some of the language of systematics.

TABLE 14.1 Miniglossary of Systematics Terms

Term	Definition
Ancestral characters	Features present in the common ancestor of a clade
Clade	Group of organisms consisting of a common ancestor and all of its descendants
Cladistics	Phylogenetic system that groups organisms by characteristics that best indicate shared ancestry
Cladogram	Phylogenetic tree built on shared derived characteristics
Derived characters	Features of an organism that are not found in a clade's ancestors
Outgroup	Comparator organism outside the group being studied; useful for identifying ancestral traits
Phylogenetic tree	Diagram depicting hypothesized evolutionary relationships
Systematics	The combined study of taxonomy and evolutionary relationships among organisms

14.6 Mastering Concepts

1. Describe the taxonomic hierarchy.
2. What is the advantage of a cladistics approach over a more traditional approach to phylogeny?
3. Distinguish between ancestral and derived characters.
4. List some examples of familiar groups of organisms that are not clades.

Figure 14.15 Wild-Type and Selectively Bred *Mimulus*. With the help of selective breeding, researchers created *Mimulus* plants that resembled their wild-type counterparts in every respect—except flower color. They used the wild-type and selectively bred plants to test hypotheses about reproductive barriers in *Mimulus*.

TABLE 14.2 Wild-Type Monkeyflower Characteristics

Species	Flower Color	Genotype at Flower Color Locus	Pollinator
Purple monkey-flower, *Mimulus lewisii*	Pink-purple	*YUP/YUP* or *YUP/yup*	Bumblebee
Scarlet monkey-flower, *Mimulus cardinalis*	Red	*yup/yup*	Hummingbird

Investigating Life

14.7 Birds Do It, Bees Do It

The Question: According to the biological species concept, the formation of a reproductive barrier is the event that signals the birth of a new species. It is easy to understand how mountains, glaciers, and other physical obstacles can divide a population and prevent interbreeding. But how can a new reproductive barrier arise within a single population, creating two species from one?

Plants offer an ideal opportunity to answer this question. Many species of flowering plants depend on animals such as birds or bees as pollen carriers. Closely related plant species may employ different pollinators, thus creating a reproductive barrier. Consider two species of wildflowers native to the western United States (figure 14.15): the purple monkeyflower *(Mimulus lewisii)* and the scarlet monkeyflower *(Mimulus cardinalis)*. Bumblebees pollinate *M. lewisii*, whereas hummingbirds prefer the red-flowered *M. cardinalis*. If, by chance, a hummingbird carries *M. cardinalis* pollen to *M. lewisii*, the resulting hybrid offspring are viable. Such cross-breeding rarely happens in the wild, however, thanks to the more-or-less exclusive relationship between each plant and its pollinators.

Because the two monkeyflowers are so closely related, it is reasonable to suppose that, in the past, one ancestral *Mimulus* species gave rise to both types. The reproductive barrier that separates them may have arisen after the slow, constant buildup of mutations in many genes. Alternatively, a mutation in one or a few "major" genes (those that control flower form or color, for example) may have had the same effect. We know that a single mutation can dramatically alter an organism's appearance (see the flies with homeotic mutations in figure 7.14). Can one genetic change in a plant species create a reproductive barrier by attracting a new pollinator?

The Approach: Biologist H. D. "Toby" Bradshaw, of the University of Washington, and Michigan State University's Douglas Schemske studied the two *Mimulus* species to find out. They considered a gene called *YUP*. In the wild-type purple monkeyflower, the dominant *YUP* allele confers the pinkish-purple petal color. Wild-type scarlet monkeyflowers have two copies of the recessive *yup* allele, so the flowers are red (table 14.2).

Bradshaw and Schemske used selective breeding to create two new lineages of plants that mimicked the effect of a mutation in the *YUP* gene. Each was 97% identical to its parent strain, but with one obvious difference—the flower colors (see figure 14.15). That is, the researchers had created *M. lewisii* plants with orange flowers and *M. cardinalis* plants with dark pink flowers.

All four *Mimulus* varieties (the two wild-type species and their selectively bred siblings) were planted at a California location where both species normally occur. For about a week and a half, the researchers observed the plants from dawn until evening, recording the animal species that visited each flower.

The Conclusion: Bradshaw and Schemske found that the new flower colors did indeed alter pollinator preferences (table 14.3). The orange *M. lewisii* flowers attracted fewer bees but more hummingbirds than did their wild-type purple counterparts. *M. cardinalis* drew far more bumblebee visits with its new dark pink petals than did the wild-type red plants, while hummingbird visits stayed about the same.

This experiment supports the hypothesis that a change in just one gene may have jump-started speciation in *Mimulus*. Additional mutations, coupled with natural selection, eventually sculpted the unique flower shapes and petal positions that also help to define the purple and scarlet monkeyflower species.

It is tempting to extend this finding to other species. Can a single mutation modify an animal's mating ritual just enough to create a new reproductive barrier? Or cause a flower to open its petals at a different time of day? Or enable an animal to exploit a new food source, extending its habitat? This experiment cannot answer these questions. Every now and then, however, small genetic changes may fuel the birth of an entirely new species.

Bradshaw, H. D., Jr., and Douglas W. Schemske. November 13, 2003. Allele substitution at a flower colour locus produces a pollinator shift in monkeyflowers. *Nature*, vol. 426, pages 176–178.

TABLE 14.3 Pollinator Visits

	Number of visits (10^{-3} visits/flower/hour) Bumblebees	Hummingbirds
M. lewisii		
Wild-type (pink-purple)	15.4	0.0212
Selectively bred (yellow-orange)	2.63	1.44
M. cardinalis		
Wild-type (red)	0.148	189
Selectively bred (dark pink)	10.9	168

14.7 Mastering Concepts

1. What hypothesis were the investigators testing, and why did they choose these two plant species as experimental subjects?
2. If biologists could mutate the gene that controls petal color, they could generate pairs of plants that differ only in that one gene, improving on the 97% similarity achieved in this study. Explain why this improvement would help the researchers test their hypothesis.

Chapter Summary

14.1 What Is a Species?

- **Macroevolution** refers to large-scale changes in life's diversity, including the appearance of new **species** and higher taxonomic levels.

A. Every Species Has a Two-Word Name

- Linnaeus's species designations and classifications helped scientists communicate. Darwin added evolutionary meaning.

B. Species Can Be Defined Based on the Potential to Interbreed

- Reproductive isolation defines a **biological species.**
- **Speciation** is the formation of a new species, which occurs when a population's **gene pool** is divided and each part takes its own evolutionary course.

14.2 Reproductive Barriers Cause Species to Diverge

A. Prezygotic Barriers Prevent Fertilization

- **Prezygotic reproductive isolation** occurs before or during fertilization. It includes obstacles to mating such as space, time, and behavior; mechanical mismatches between male and female; and molecular mismatches between gametes.

B. Postzygotic Barriers Prevent Development of a Fertile Offspring

- **Postzygotic reproductive isolation** results in offspring that die early in development, are infertile, or produce a second generation of offspring with abnormalities.

14.3 Spatial Patterns Define Two Types of Speciation

A. Allopatric Speciation Reflects a Geographic Barrier

- **Allopatric speciation** occurs when a geographic barrier separates a population. The two populations then diverge genetically to the

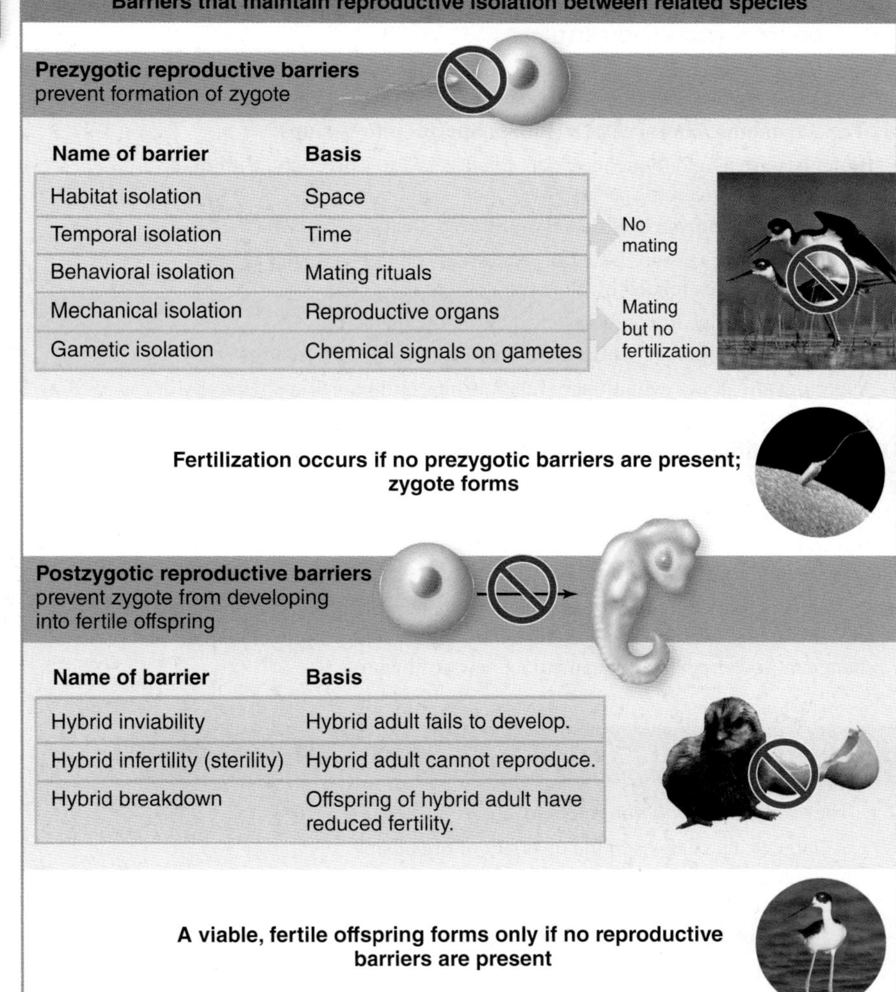

Barriers that maintain reproductive isolation between related species
Prezygotic reproductive barriers prevent formation of zygote
Name of barrier | Basis
Habitat isolation | Space
Temporal isolation | Time
Behavioral isolation | Mating rituals
Mechanical isolation | Reproductive organs
Gametic isolation | Chemical signals on gametes
No mating
Mating but no fertilization
Fertilization occurs if no prezygotic barriers are present; zygote forms
Postzygotic reproductive barriers prevent zygote from developing into fertile offspring
Name of barrier | Basis
Hybrid inviability | Hybrid adult fails to develop.
Hybrid infertility (sterility) | Hybrid adult cannot reproduce.
Hybrid breakdown | Offspring of hybrid adult have reduced fertility.
A viable, fertile offspring forms only if no reproductive barriers are present

point that their members can no longer produce fertile offspring together.

B. Sympatric Speciation Occurs in a Shared Habitat

- **Sympatric speciation** enables populations that occupy the same area to diverge, often via major genetic changes such as **polyploidy.**

C. Determining the Type of Speciation May Be Difficult

- The distinction between allopatric and sympatric speciation is not always straightforward, partly because it is difficult to define the size and significance of a geographic barrier.

14.4 Speciation May Be Gradual or Occur in Bursts

- Evolutionary change occurs at many rates, from slow and steady **gradualism** to the periodic bursts that characterize **punctuated equilibrium.**

14.5 Extinction Marks the End of the Line

- **Extinction** is the disappearance of a species.
- The **background extinction rate** reflects ongoing losses of species on a local scale.
- Historically, **mass extinctions** have resulted from global changes such as continental drift. The **impact theory** suggests that a meteorite or comet changed Earth's climate and caused a mass extinction at the end of the Cretaceous period.
- Human activities are increasing the extinction rate.

14.6 Biological Classification Systems Are Based on Common Descent

- The study of **systematics** includes **taxonomy** (the science of classification) and **phylogenetics** (the study of species relationships).

A. The Taxonomic Hierarchy Organizes Species into Groups

- Biologists use a taxonomic hierarchy to classify life's diversity, with **taxa** ranging from domain to species.

B. A Cladistics Approach Is Based on Shared Derived Traits

- **Cladistics** defines groups based on **ancestral** and **derived characters.** A group of species related by common descent is a **clade.**
- An **outgroup** helps researchers detect ancestral characters.

C. Cladograms Depict Hypothesized Evolutionary Relationships

- A **cladogram** shows evolutionary relationships as a branching hierarchy of shared derived characters.

D. Many Traditional Groups Are Not Clades

- Group names such as "protist" and "algae" remain in common usage, but they do not reflect evolutionary relationships.

14.7 Investigating Life: Birds Do It, Bees Do It

- Researchers have studied *Mimulus* plants to determine how the reproductive barrier that separates two species may have arisen. They discovered that a change in flower petal color can attract new pollinators.

Multiple Choice Questions

1. The term *macroevolution* refers to
   a. large-scale changes in the diversity of organisms.
   b. large-scale changes in the DNA of organisms.
   c. evolutionary changes that affect larger organisms.
   d. evolutionary changes that can be observed.
2. The biological species concept defines species based on
   a. external appearance.
   b. the number of adaptations to the same habitat.
   c. ability to interbreed.
   d. DNA and protein sequences.
3. Which reproductive barrier applies to two species that cannot interbreed because they are active at different times of day?
   a. Temporal isolation
   b. Gametic isolation
   c. Mechanical isolation
   d. Ecological isolation
4. How can infertility occur in a hybrid whose parents have different numbers of chromosomes?
   a. The difference prevents mitotic cell division.
   b. The cells of the hybrid cannot grow, so the embryo dies.
   c. Meiosis is blocked, so gametes cannot form.
   d. Mitosis is altered, so the gametes are not viable.
5. Agriculture and urban development often divide wildlife habitat into isolated fragments. What type of speciation might occur as a result of this human activity?
   a. Sympatric speciation
   b. Allopatric speciation
   c. Postzygotic speciation
   d. Cladistic speciation
6. Why might speciation occur at an unusually rapid pace?
   a. A new phenotype adapts a population especially well to its environment.
   b. The environment changes relatively rapidly, selecting for new phenotypes.
   c. A dominant group of organisms goes extinct, paving the way for the evolution of new species.
   d. All of the above are possibilities.
7. In general, why might a species with a small population be more likely than a large population to become extinct?
   a. Because they cannot produce enough offspring
   b. Because genetic diversity is likely to be lower in a small population
   c. Because the individuals are isolated from one another
   d. Because they take too long to produce offspring
8. All organisms within a clade
   a. belong to the same species.
   b. share DNA and protein sequences with a common ancestor.
   c. share one or more characteristics derived through evolution from a common ancestor.
   d. share a common developmental pathway.
9. How can DNA sequences contribute to our understanding of phylogenies?
   a. They allow scientists to determine whether speciation was allopatric or sympatric.
   b. They can be used as characters in a cladistic analysis.
   c. They demonstrate whether gradualism or punctuated equilibrium occurred.
   d. They identify extinctions.
10. Which of the groups in figure 1.8 represents a clade?
   a. The prokaryotes
   b. Domain Eukarya
   c. Kingdom Protista
   d. None of the above is a clade.

Write It Out

1. How has the meaning of the term *species* changed since the time of Linnaeus?
2. What type of reproductive barrier applies to each of these scenarios?
   a. Humans introduced apple trees to North America in the 1800s. Insects called hawthorn flies, which feed and mate on hawthorn plants, quickly discovered the new fruits. Some flies preferred the taste of apples to their native host plants. Because these flies mate where they eat, this difference in food preference quickly led to a reproductive barrier.
   b. Water buffalo and cattle can mate, but the embryos die early in development.
   c. Eastern and western meadowlarks are difficult to distinguish based on size, shape, and color. Yet their calls are distinct, a difference that presumably helps the birds identify potential mates.
   d. The shells of two species of snails in the genus *Bradybaena* spiral in different directions. The snails' genital openings are therefore not aligned, so they cannot mate.
   e. A fish species inhabiting a sunny stream rarely encounters a closely related fish species that lives in caves.
3. If the apple-feeding flies from question 2a form a different species from their hawthorn-feeding relatives, which type of speciation has occurred?
4. Examine the tortoises in figure 14.5. How could each of these subspecies have arisen from a common ancestor?
5. How does natural selection predict a gradualistic mode of evolution? Does the presence of fossils that are consistent with punctuated equilibrium mean that natural selection does not occur?
6. Why do species become extinct? Choose a species that has recently become extinct and describe some possible evolutionary consequences to other species that interacted with that species before its extinction.
7. What information would you need to determine the background extinction rate hundreds of millions of years ago? How might you determine the current extinction rate?
8. Examine the following cladogram, which shows the relationships among a fossilized tree *(Hymenaea protera),* three living relatives, and six other organisms:

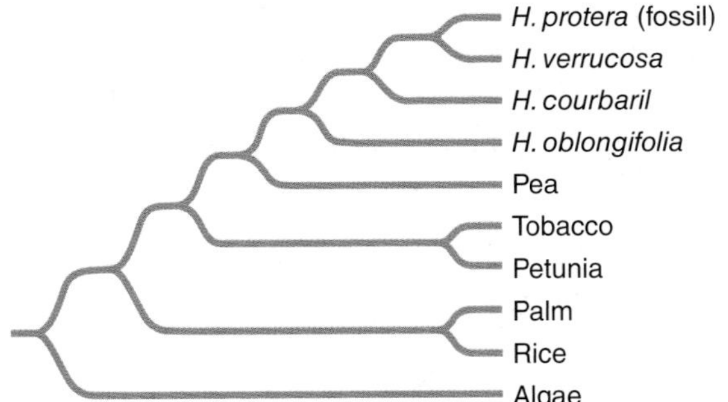

   a. Which organism is *H. protera*'s closest relative?
   b. Is *H. protera* more closely related to tobacco or to palm?
   c. Which organism depicted is ancestral to all the others?
   d. Redraw the tree so that *H. protera* is next to tobacco without changing the evolutionary relationships among any of the species.
9. Figure 16.3 summarizes the hypothesized evolutionary relationships among living plants. Do the gymnosperms form a clade? Explain your answer.
10. Figure 17.3 shows a phylogenetic tree for animals. How many clades are depicted in the figure?

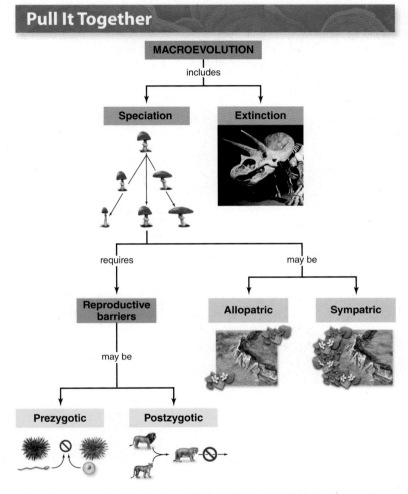

Pull It Together

MACROEVOLUTION
includes
Speciation
Extinction
requires
may be
Reproductive barriers
Allopatric
Sympatric
may be
Prezygotic
Postzygotic

1. How do reproductive barriers relate to the biological species concept?
2. Distinguish between pre- and postzygotic reproductive barriers.
3. Describe allopatric and sympatric speciation and give an example of each.
4. Add *gradualism* and *punctuated equilibrium* to this concept map.
5. How do species become extinct?

15 Evolution and Diversity of Microbial Life

Heat Lovers. Colorful microbes thrive in hot water from one of Yellowstone National Park's geysers. These organisms tolerate heat that would kill most other life.

Learning Outline

Learn How to Learn

Use All Your Resources

Textbooks come with online quizzes, animations, and other resources that can help you learn biology. After you have studied the material in a chapter, test yourself by taking an online quiz. Take note of the questions for which you are unsure of the answers, and remember to go back to study those topics again. Also, check for animations that take you through complex processes one step at a time. Sometimes, the motion of an animation can help you understand what's happening more easily than studying a static image.

What's the Point?

When it comes to biodiversity, most people think about plants and animals. But the microbes that inhabit Earth are just as important.

We can't see most microbes with the unaided eye, yet they profoundly influence human life. Most obviously, some types of microbes cause deadly illnesses, not only in humans but also in other animals and in plants. Most people also know that microbes play a role in the production of cheese, beer, wine, bread, and other household items.

Microbes also have played most of the starring roles in the history of life on Earth; plants, animals, and even fungi are newcomers compared with the bacteria and archaea. Even today, ecosystems would grind to a halt without the photosynthesis and decomposition services that microbes provide.

This chapter introduces the tiny world of microbiology. It combines the bacteria, archaea, protists, and fungi based on just one shared feature: some or all of their members are microscopic. As you will see, these distantly related organisms are as diverse as they are vital to life on Earth.

15.1 Life's Origin Remains Mysterious

Reconstructing life's start is like reading all the chapters of a novel except the first. A reader can get some idea of the events and setting of the opening chapter from clues throughout the novel. Similarly, scattered clues from life through the ages reflect events that may have led to the origin of life.

Scientists describe the history of life in the context of the **geologic timescale,** which divides time into eons, eras, periods, and epochs defined by major geological or biological events. Figure 15.1 shows a simplified version of the geologic timescale; a more complete one appears in figure 13.2.

The study of life's origin begins with astronomy and geology. Earth and the solar system's other planets formed about 4.6 billion years ago (BYA) as solid matter condensed out of a vast expanse of dust and gas swirling around the early Sun. The red-hot ball that became Earth cooled enough to form a crust by about 4.2 to 4.1 BYA, when the surface temperature ranged from 500°C to 1,000°C and atmospheric pressure was 10 times what it is now.

The geological evidence paints a chaotic picture of this Hadean eon, including volcanic eruptions, earthquakes, and ultraviolet radiation. Analysis of craters on other objects in the solar system suggest that comets, meteorites, and possibly asteroids bombarded Earth's surface during its first 500 to 600 million years. These impacts repeatedly boiled off the seas and vaporized rocks to carve the features of the fledgling world.

Still, organic molecules could probably interact in protected pockets of the environment. At some point, probably during the Archean eon, an entity arose that could survive, thrive, reproduce, and diversify. The clues from geology and paleontology suggest that from 4.2 to 3.85 BYA, simple cells (or their precursors) arose.

Unfortunately, direct evidence of the first life is likely gone because most of Earth's initial crust has been destroyed. Erosion tears rocks and minerals into particles, only to be built up again into sediments, heated and compressed. Seafloor is dragged into Earth's interior at deep-sea trenches, where it is melted and recycled. The oldest rocks that remain today date to about 3.85 BYA. ▸ plate tectonics, p. 247

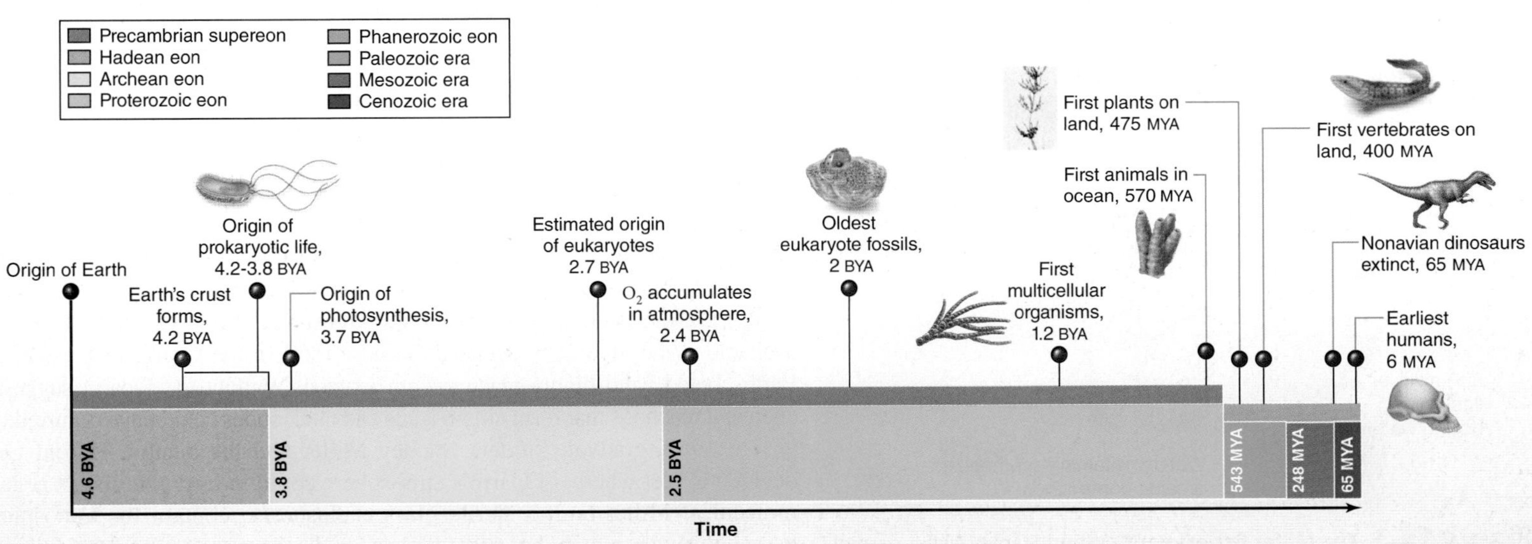

Figure 15.1 Highlights in Life's History. In this simplified geologic timescale, the size of each eon and era is proportional to its length in years. (BYA = billion years ago; MYA = million years ago)

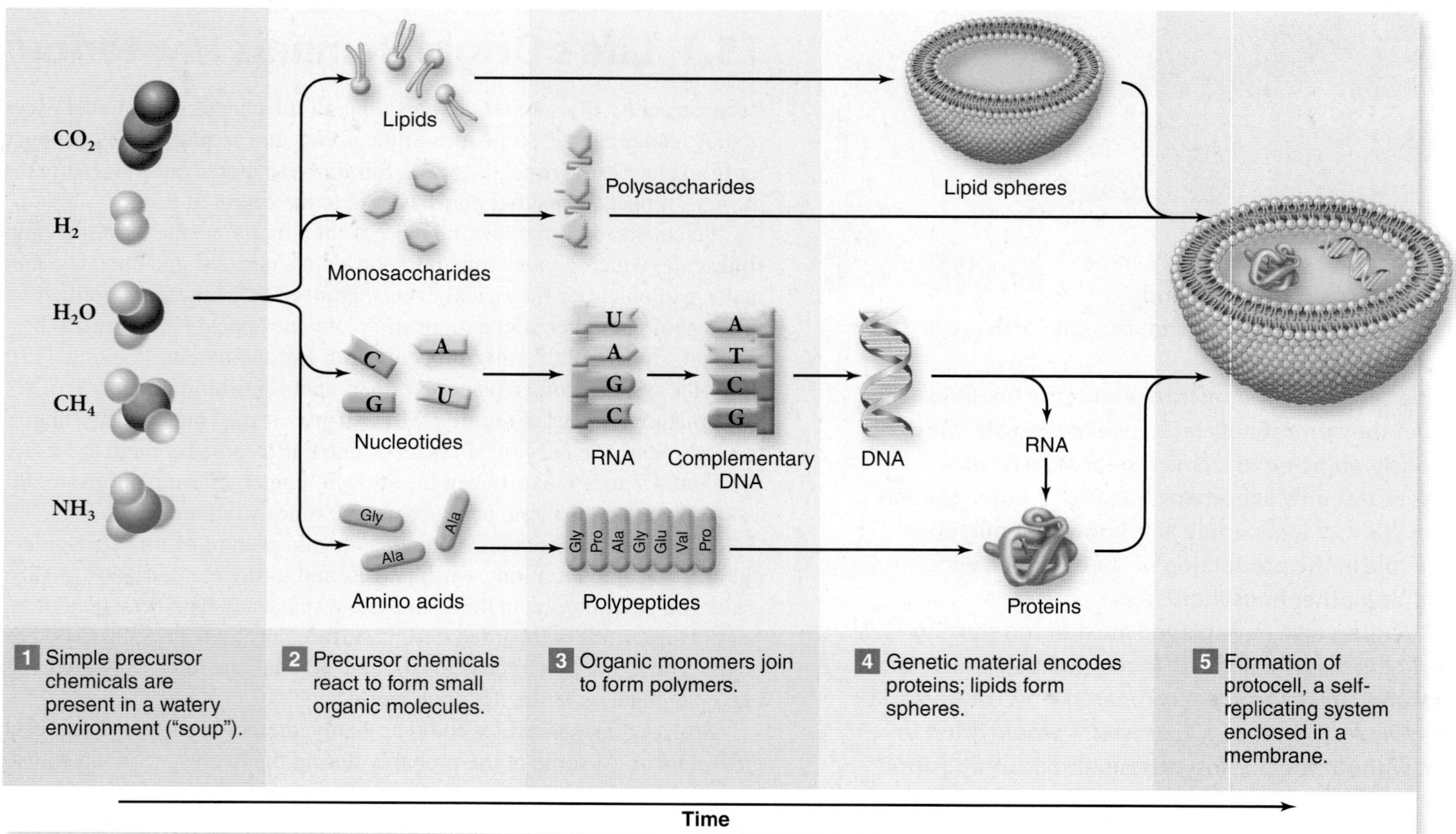

Figure 15.2 Pathway to a Cell. The steps leading to the origin of life on Earth may have started with the formation of organic molecules from simple precursors. However it originated, the first cell would have contained self-replicating molecules enclosed in a phospholipid bilayer membrane.

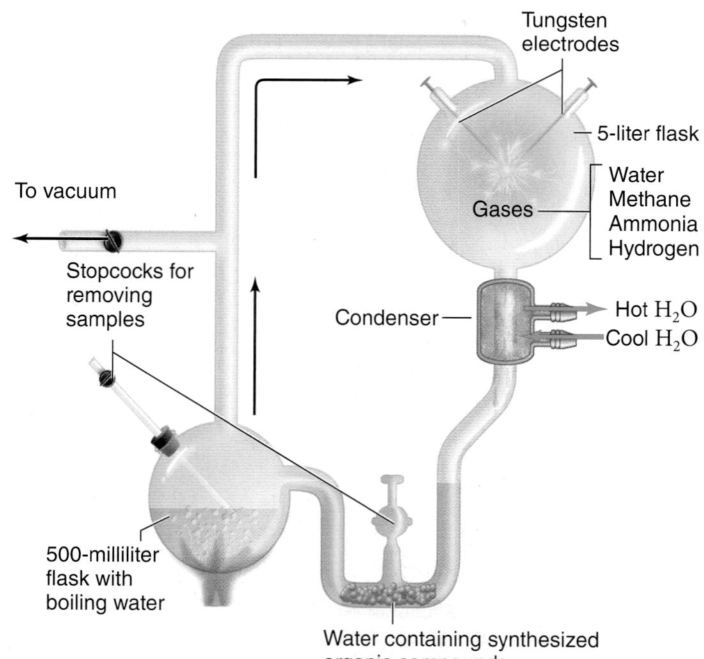

Figure 15.3 The Miller Experiment. When Stanley Miller passed an electrical spark through heated gases, the mixture generated amino acids and other organic molecules.

This section describes some of the major steps in the chemical evolution that eventually led to the first cell; figure 15.2 summarizes one possible version of the process. (Today, however, new life is unlikely to originate from nonliving matter; the Burning Question on page 280 explains why.)

A. Simple Organic Molecules May Have Formed in a Chemical "Soup"

Early Earth was not only different geologically from today's planet, but it was also different chemically. The atmosphere today is rich in nitrogen (N_2), oxygen (O_2), carbon dioxide (CO_2), and water (H_2O). What might it have been like 4 BYA?

Russian chemist Alex I. Oparin hypothesized in a 1938 book, *The Origin of Life,* that Earth's atmosphere included abundant methane (CH_4), ammonia (NH_3), water, and hydrogen (H_2), similar to the atmospheres of the outer planets today. These simple chemicals appear in step 1 of figure 15.2. Note the absence of oxygen gas (O_2), a major component of today's atmosphere. Little O_2 would have been available at the time life originated, because most of the chemicals present after Earth cooled were highly reactive with oxygen. Without O_2, Oparin suggested, chemical reactions that form amino acids and nucleotides could have occurred.

In 1953, graduate student Stanley Miller and his mentor, Harold Urey, decided to test whether Oparin's atmosphere could indeed give rise to organic molecules. Miller built a sterile glass enclosure to contain the atmospheric gases, through which he passed electric discharges to simulate lightning (figure 15.3). He condensed the gases in a narrow tube and passed them over an electric heater, a laboratory version of a volcano. ▸ organic molecules, p. 33

After a few failures and adjustments, Miller saw the condensed liquid turn yellowish, then varying shades of red, pink, and yellow-brown. Chemical analysis revealed a variety of amino acids, some found in life. A prestigious journal published the work, and the 25-year-old Miller made headlines reporting (incorrectly) that he had created "life in a test tube."

Life is far more than just a few amino acids, but "the Miller experiment" went down in history as the first attempt to re-create chemical conditions on Earth before life arose. Miller and many others later extended his results by altering conditions or using different starting materials. For example, methane and ammonia could form clouds of hydrogen cyanide (HCN), which produced amino acids in the presence of ultraviolet light and water. "Soups" that included phosphates yielded nucleotides, including the biological energy molecule ATP. Other experiments produced carbohydrates and phospholipids similar to those in biological membranes.

The experiment has survived criticisms that Earth's early atmosphere actually contained abundant CO_2, a gas not present in Miller's original setup. Organic molecules still form, even with an adjusted gas mixture.

B. Clays May Have Helped Monomers Form Polymers

Once the organic building blocks (monomers) of macromolecules were present, they had to have linked into chains (polymers). This process, depicted in step 3 of figure 15.2, may have happened on hot clays or other minerals that provided ample, dry surfaces.

Clays may have played an important role in early organic chemistry. Clay minerals can form templates on which chemical building blocks could have linked to build larger molecules. Some minerals in clay can release electrons, providing energy to form chemical bonds. These minerals, including iron pyrite ("fool's gold"), may also have acted as catalysts to speed chemical reactions.

For example, the first RNA molecules could have formed on clay surfaces (figure 15.4). Not only do the positive charges on clay's surface attract and hold negatively charged RNA nucleotides, but clays also promote formation of the covalent bonds that link the nucleotides into chains. They even attract other nucleotides to form a complementary strand. About 4 BYA, clays might have been fringed with an ever-increasing variety of growing polymers. Some of these might have become the macromolecules that would eventually build cells.

The origin of RNA is especially important because life requires an informational molecule. That molecule may have been RNA, or something like it, because RNA is the most versatile molecule that we know of. RNA not only stores genetic information and uses it to manufacture proteins, but it can also catalyze chemical reactions and duplicate on its own.

The term **RNA world** has come to describe how self-replicating RNA may have been an essential precursor to life on Earth. Perhaps pieces of RNA on clay surfaces continued to form and accumulate, growing longer, becoming more complex in sequence, and changing as replication errors led to mutations. Some members of this accumulating community of molecules would have been more stable than others, leading to an early form of natural selection.

At some point, RNA might have begun encoding proteins, just short chains of amino acids at first. An RNA molecule may eventually have grown long enough to encode the enzyme reverse transcriptase, which copies RNA to DNA. With DNA, the chemical blueprints of life found a much more stable home. Protein enzymes eventually took over some of the functions of catalytic RNAs. Step 4 in figure 15.2 shows this stage in life's origin.

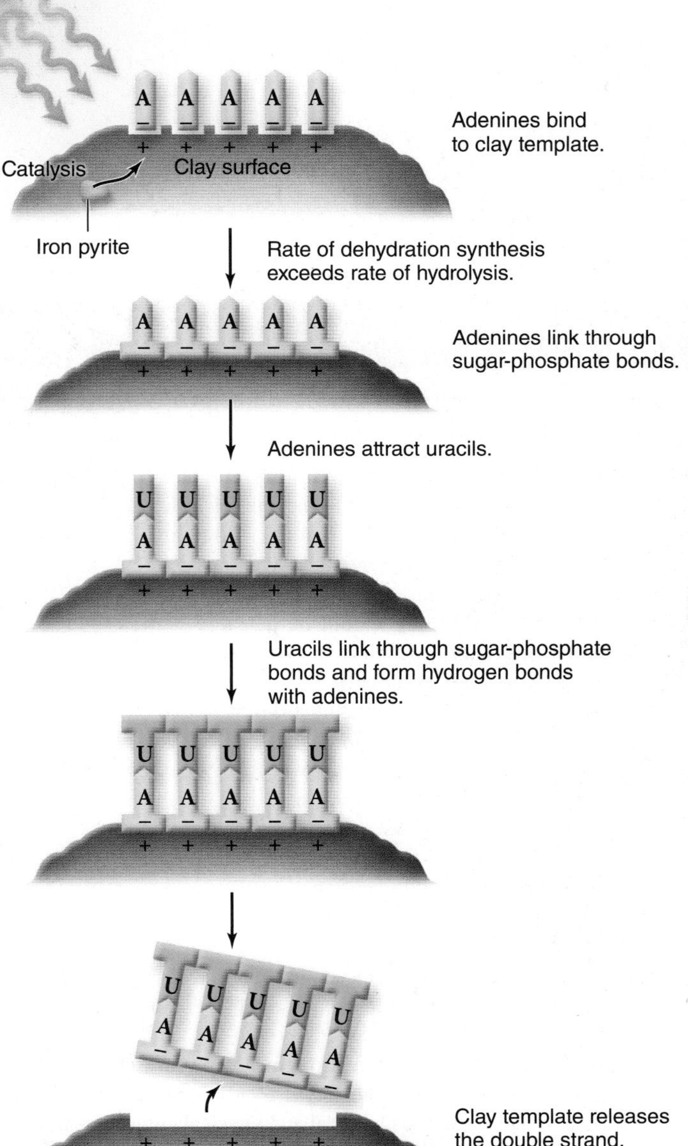

Figure 15.4 A Possible Role for Clay. Chains of nucleotides may have formed on clay templates. In this hypothesized scenario, iron pyrite ("fool's gold") was the catalyst for polymer formation, and sunlight provided the energy.

C. Membranes Enclosed the First Protocells

Meanwhile, lipids would have been entering the picture. Under the right temperature and pH conditions, phospholipids could have formed membrane-like structures, some of which left evidence in ancient sediments. Laboratory experiments show that pieces of membrane can indeed grow on structural supports and break free, forming a bubble. ▸ phospholipids, p. 54

Perhaps an ancient membrane bubble enclosed a collection of nucleic acids and proteins to form a cell-like assemblage, or protocell (see figure 15.2, step 5). These hypothetical, ancient aggregates of RNA, DNA, proteins, and lipids were precursors of cells, but not nearly as complex. The capacity of nucleic acids to mutate, however, may have enabled protocells to become increasingly self-sufficient, giving rise eventually to the reaction pathways of metabolism.

D. Early Life Changed Earth Forever

Stanley Miller once said, "The origin of life is the origin of evolution, which requires replication, mutation, and selection. Replication is the hard part. Once a genetic material could replicate, life would have just taken off." Several types of early cells probably prevailed for millions of years, competing for resources and sharing genetic material. Eventually, however, a type of cell arose that was the last shared ancestor of all life on Earth today.

The first cells lived in the absence of O_2 and probably used organic molecules as a source of both carbon and energy. Another source of carbon, however, was the CO_2 in the atmosphere. Photosynthetic organisms eventually evolved that could use light for energy and atmospheric CO_2 as a carbon source (see chapter 5). These cells no longer relied on organic compounds in their surroundings for food.

Photosynthesis probably originated in cells that used hydrogen sulfide (H_2S) instead of water as an electron donor. These first photosynthetic microorganisms would have released sulfur, rather than O_2, into the environment. Eventually, changes in pigment molecules enabled some of these organisms to use H_2O instead of H_2S as an electron donor. Cells using this new form of photosynthesis released O_2 as a waste product.

Some of the oldest fossils are from 3.7 billion-year-old rock in Warrawoona, Australia, and Swaziland, South Africa. The fossils strongly resemble large formations of cyanobacteria called stromatolites (figure 15.5). Ancient cyanobacteria, along with many others, would have changed the composition of Earth's atmosphere by consuming CO_2 and releasing O_2 over millions of years during the Archean and Proterozoic eons.

Extensive iron deposits dating to about 2 billion years ago provide evidence of the changing atmosphere. As O_2 from photosynthesis built up in the oceans, iron that was previously dissolved in seawater reacted with the O_2 and sank to the bottom of the sea, producing distinctive layers of iron-rich sediments.

The evolution of photosynthesis forever altered life on Earth. Photosynthetic organisms formed the base of new food chains. In addition, natural selection began to favor organisms that could use O_2 in aerobic metabolism. Anaerobic species persisted, but only in pockets of the environment that lacked oxygen. Ozone (O_3) also formed from O_2 high in the atmosphere, blocking the sun's damaging ultraviolet radiation. The overall result was an explosion of new life that eventually gave rise to today's microbes, plants, fungi, and animals.

The remaining sections in this chapter offer a taste of the diversity in the microbial world, beginning with a tour of prokaryotic cells. A sampling of protists comes next, and the chapter ends by describing the fungi.

Burning Questions

Does new life spring from simple molecules now, as it did in the past?

It is intriguing to think of the possibility that new life could be forming from nonliving matter now, just as it did long ago in Earth's history. Although theoretically possible, scientists have never seen life emerging from a collection of simple chemicals. Such a finding would be a major blow to the cell theory, which says that cells come only from preexisting cells.

The emergence of new life from simple molecules seems improbable today. Why? Because conditions now are very different than they were in the past. When Earth was young, no life existed, so the first simple cells encountered no competition. Now, however, life thrives nearly everywhere on Earth. Perhaps new life *is* forming, but before it has a chance to become established, a hungry microbe gobbles it up. Such an event would be extremely difficult to detect.

So does the ancient chemical origin for life on Earth violate the cell theory? The answer is no, because the cell theory applies to today's circumstances. The chemical and physical environment on the young Earth was nothing like that of today's world. Scientists have never observed the formation of life from nonliving matter—but that does not mean that it did not happen in the distant past.

Submit your burning question to:
marielle_hoefnagels@mcgraw-hill.com

15.1 Mastering Concepts

1. How were conditions on Earth before life began different from current conditions?
2. What types of information can simulations of early Earth provide?
3. Why is RNA likely to have been pivotal in life's beginnings?
4. What is a protocell?
5. About when did the first cells probably originate?
6. How did early life change Earth?

15.2 Prokaryotes Are a Biological Success Story

Figure 15.5 Stromatolites. These mounds in Shark Bay, Western Australia, are stromatolites consisting of sediments and cyanobacteria. Some of the world's oldest fossils resemble stromatolites.

The microscopic world of life may be invisible to the naked eye, but its importance is immense. The earliest known fossils closely resemble today's bacteria, suggesting that the first cells were prokaryotic. As we have already seen, ancient photosynthetic microbes changed Earth's chemistry by contributing O_2 to the atmosphere. Along the road of evolution, bacteria probably gave rise to the chloroplasts and mitochondria of eukaryotic cells (see section 15.3). ▸ aerobic respiration, p. 99

The reign of the prokaryotes continues today. Virtually no place on Earth is free of bacteria and archaea; their cells live within rocks and ice, high in the atmosphere, far below the ocean's surface, in thermal vents, nuclear reactors, hot springs, animal intestines, plant roots, and practically everywhere else. Many species prefer hot, cold, acidic, alkaline, or salty habitats that humans consider "extreme." This section describes the diversity and importance of prokaryotic life.

A. What Is a Prokaryote?

A **prokaryote** is a single-celled organism that lacks a nucleus and membrane-bounded organelles. DNA sequences and other lines of evidence suggest the existence of two prokaryotic domains: **Bacteria** and **Archaea** (figure 15.6).

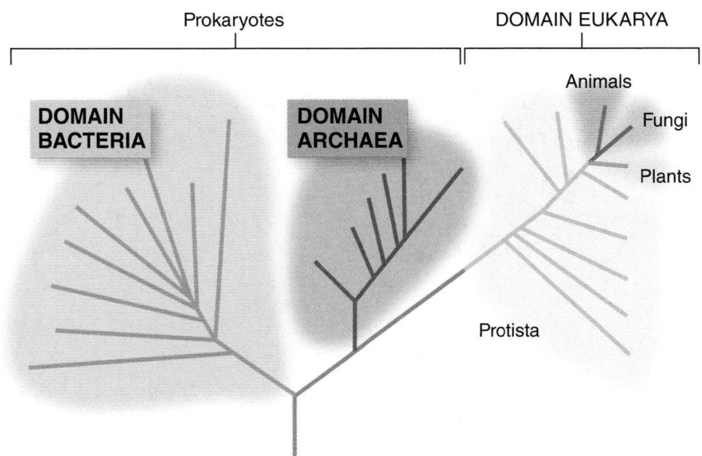

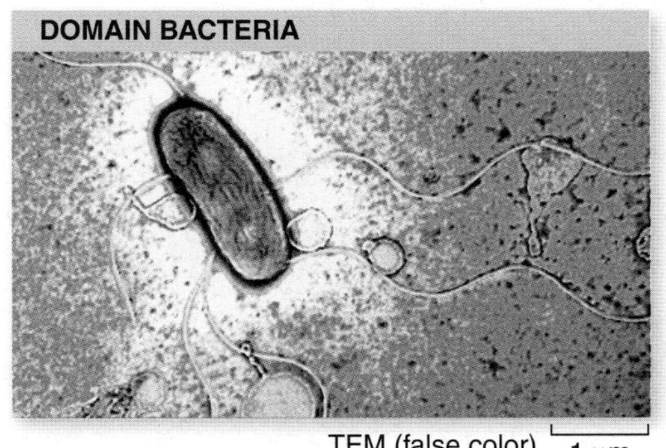

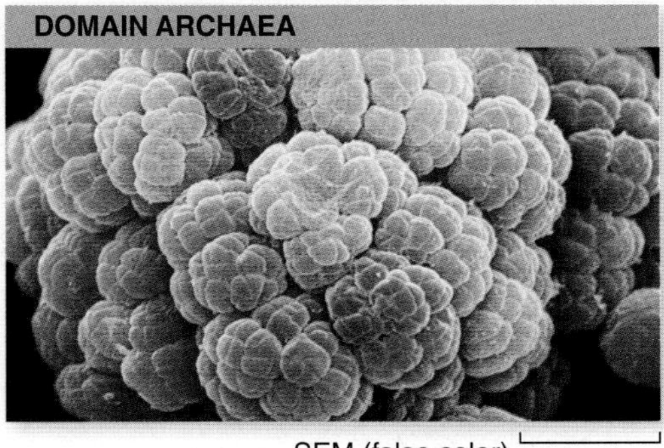

Figure 15.6 Diversity of Prokaryotic Life. Domains Bacteria and Archaea form two of the three main branches of life.

Microbiologists have probably discovered just a tiny fraction of prokaryotic life on Earth; new microbes turn up every time biologists examine a spoonful of soil or a milliliter of water. The total number of species in both domains may be anywhere between 100,000 and 10,000,000; no one knows.

Before embarking on a tour of prokaryote biology and ecology, it is worth noting that the term *prokaryote* has become somewhat controversial among microbiologists. The reason is that the word falsely implies a close evolutionary relationship between bacteria and archaea, despite strong evidence that archaea are actually more closely related to eukaryotes. Nevertheless, many biologists continue to use the term as a handy shortcut for describing all cells that lack nuclei.

B. Prokaryote Classification Traditionally Relies on Visible Features

Bacteria and archaea differ in the details of their chemical composition (see figure 3.4), but under the microscope they look similar. At about 1 to 10 μm long, a typical prokaryotic cell is 10 to 100 times smaller than most eukaryotic cells (see figure 3.1). Bacteria and archaea also lack the membrane-bounded organelles that characterize eukaryotic cells.

How do microbiologists classify the diversity of life within these two domains, given the tiny cell sizes and scarcity of distinctive internal structures? The answer to that question has evolved over time. For hundreds of years, biologists classified microbes based on close scrutiny of their cells and metabolism. More recent studies of DNA sequences have revealed that the traditional classification criteria almost certainly group together organisms that are only distantly related to one another. The "old" criteria remain useful, however, because they are based on characteristics that are relatively easy to observe using a microscope and well-defined laboratory tests.

Internal Cell Structures Like the cells of other organisms, all bacteria and archaea are bounded by a cell membrane that encloses cytoplasm, DNA, and ribosomes (figure 15.7). A prokaryotic cell's DNA typically consists of one circular chromosome. The **nucleoid** is the region where this DNA is located, along with some RNA and a few proteins. Unlike the nucleus of a eukaryotic cell, a membranous envelope does not surround the nucleoid.

The cells of many bacteria and archaea also contain one or more **plasmids,** circles of DNA apart from the chromosome. Because cells can easily copy and exchange these small rings of DNA, the traits encoded on plasmids can spread rapidly within a population of prokaryotic cells. The exchange of plasmids encoding antibiotic-resistance genes, for example, partly explains the increasing numbers of bacterial infections that cannot be treated with antibiotics.

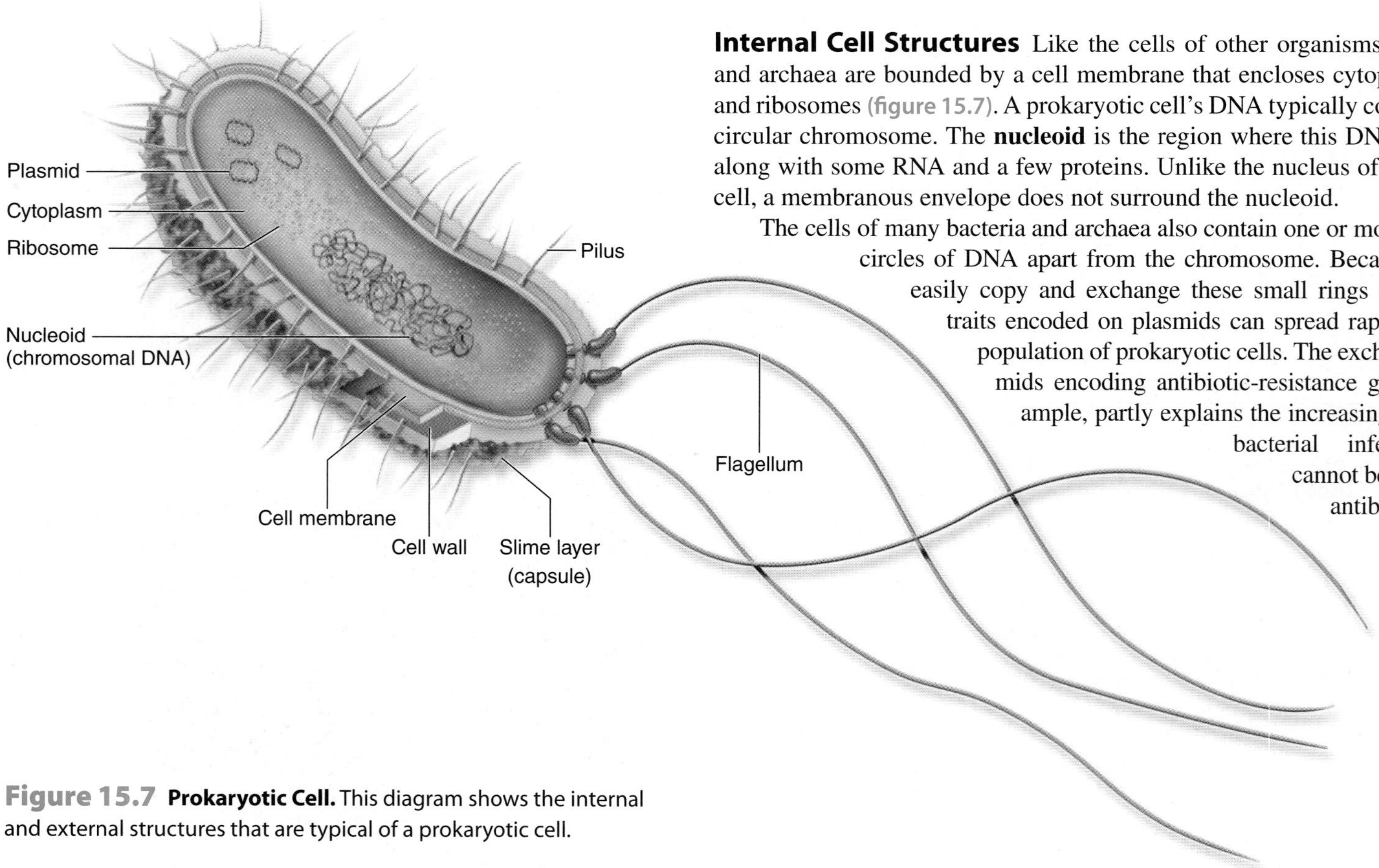

Figure 15.7 Prokaryotic Cell. This diagram shows the internal and external structures that are typical of a prokaryotic cell.

The **ribosomes** are structures where proteins are assembled, a process described in chapter 7. Bacterial, archaean, and eukaryotic ribosomes are all structurally different from one another. Some antibiotics, such as streptomycin, kill bacteria without harming eukaryotic host cells by exploiting this difference. The Why We Care box on page 286 describes more examples of how antibiotics work.

External Cell Structures The **cell wall** is a rigid barrier that surrounds the cells of most bacteria and archaea. Bacterial cell walls contain **peptidoglycan,** a complex polysaccharide that does not occur in the cell walls of archaea. The wall gives the cell its shape (figure 15.8). Three of the most common forms are **coccus** (spherical), **bacillus** (rod-shaped), and **spirillum** (spiral- or corkscrew-shaped). In addition, the arrangement of the cells in pairs, clusters (*staphylo-*), or chains (*strepto-*) is sometimes important in classification. The disease-causing bacterium *Staphylococcus,* for example, forms grapelike clusters of spherical cells.

Outside the cell wall, some bacteria have an outer membrane consisting of lipid, polysaccharide, and protein. Parts of this outer layer trigger a strong immune response, including fever and inflammation (see chapter 29). The outer membrane also causes the toxic effects of many disease-causing bacteria, a subject we return to in section 15.2C.

Many prokaryotic cells have other distinctive structures outside the cell wall (see figure 15.7). A slime layer (or capsule) is a sticky layer of proteins or polysaccharides that may surround the cell wall. The slime layer has many functions, including attachment to surfaces, resistance to drying, and protection from immune system cells.

Some cells have **pili** (singular: pilus), which are short, hairlike projections made of protein. Attachment pili enable cells to adhere to objects. The bacterium that causes cholera, for example, uses pili to attach to a human's intestinal wall. Other projections, called sex pili, aid in the transfer of DNA from cell to cell.

Not all prokaryotes can move, but many can do so. For example, cells may move toward or away from an external stimulus such as food, toxins, oxygen, or light. Cells that can move have a **flagellum,** which is a whiplike extension that rotates like a propeller. The bacterium in figure 15.7 has multiple flagella; other cells have one or none at all. (Some eukaryotic cells also have flagella, but they are not homologous to those on bacterial or archaean cells.)

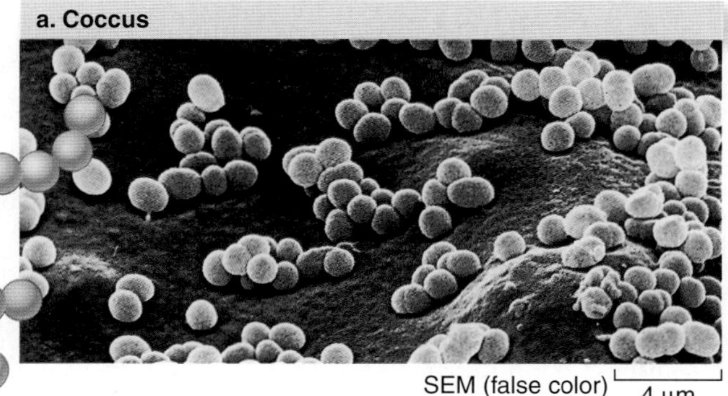

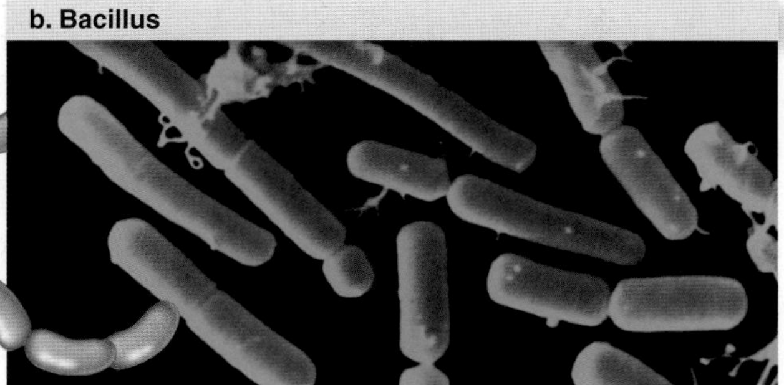

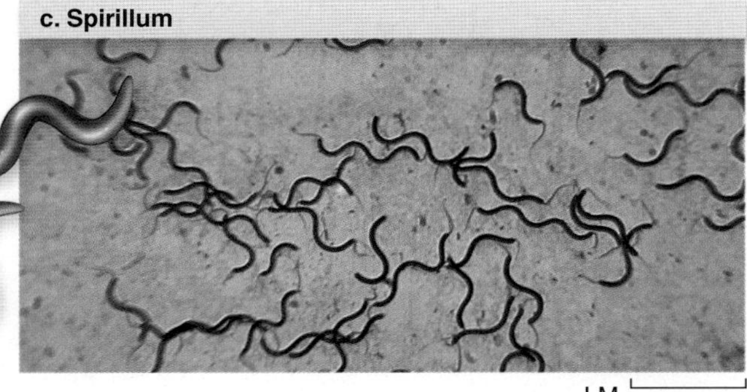

Figure 15.8 Cell Shapes. (a) Cocci such as these *Micrococcus* cells are spherical. (b) A bacillus is rod-shaped; *Bacillus megaterium* is an example. (c) A spirillum is spiral-shaped. This is *Spirillum volutans,* which is among the largest types of bacteria.

Endospores Two genera of bacteria produce **endospores,** which are dormant, thick-walled structures that can survive harsh conditions (figure 15.9). An endospore can withstand boiling, drying, ultraviolet radiation, and disinfectants. Once environmental conditions improve, the endospore germinates and develops into a normal cell.

One spore-forming soil bacterium is *Clostridium botulinum.* Food canning processes typically include a high-pressure heat sterilization treatment to destroy endospores of this species. If any endospores survive, they may germinate inside the can, producing cells that thrive in the absence of oxygen. The cells produce a toxin that causes botulism, a severe (and sometimes deadly) form of food poisoning. Green beans, corn, and other vegetables that are improperly home-canned are the most frequent sources of foodborne botulism.

Another spore-forming bacterium is *Bacillus anthracis.* This organism, ordinarily found in soil, can cause a deadly disease called anthrax when inhaled. Cultures of *B. anthracis* can be dried to induce formation of endospores, then ground into a fine powder that remains infectious for decades. This property

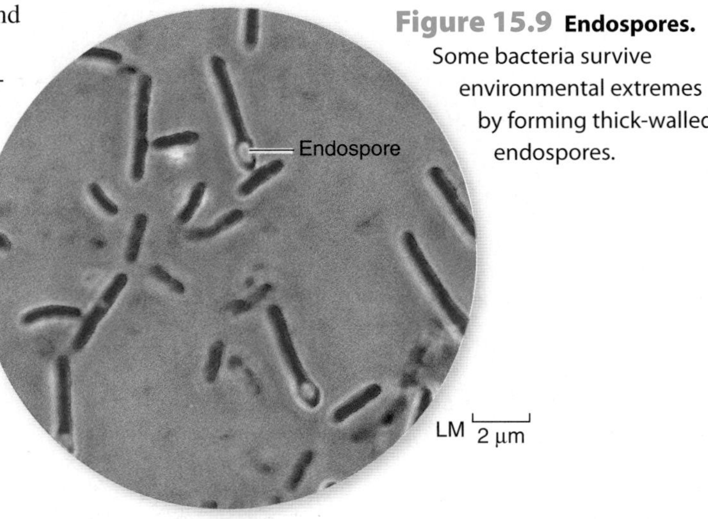

Figure 15.9 Endospores. Some bacteria survive environmental extremes by forming thick-walled endospores.

TABLE 15.1 Metabolic Strategies: A Summary

		Carbon Source	
		Inorganic source such as CO_2 (auto-)	Organic source such as glucose (hetero-)
Energy Source	Light (photo-)	Photoautotroph	Photoheterotroph
	Inorganic or organic chemicals (chemo-)	Chemoautotroph	Chemoheterotroph

makes anthrax a potential biological weapon. In late 2001, anthrax-tainted mail killed five people in the United States. The case remained unsolved until 2008, when distinctive DNA sequences in the powder implicated a military scientist in the crime.

Metabolic Diversity Over billions of years, bacteria and archaea have developed a tremendous variety of chemical reactions that allow them to metabolize everything from organic matter to metal. One way to group microorganisms is to examine some of these key metabolic pathways.

The methods by which organisms acquire carbon and energy form one basis for classification (table 15.1). **Autotrophs,** for example, acquire carbon from inorganic sources such as carbon dioxide (CO_2); plants and algae are the most familiar autotrophs. **Heterotrophs,** on the other hand, get carbon by consuming organic molecules produced by other organisms. *Escherichia coli,* a notorious intestinal bacterium, is a heterotroph. Energy sources also vary. **Phototrophs** derive energy from the sun; **chemotrophs** gain energy by oxidizing inorganic or organic chemicals.

By combining these terms for carbon and energy sources, a biologist can describe how a microbe fits into the environment. Plants and cyanobacteria, for example, are photoautotrophs; they use sunlight (*photo-*) for energy and CO_2 (*auto-*) for carbon, as described in chapter 5. Many disease-causing bacteria are chemoheterotrophs because they use organic molecules from their hosts as sources of both carbon and energy. Humans are also chemoheterotrophs, as are all other animals.

In addition, oxygen requirements are often important in classification. **Obligate aerobes** require O_2 for generating ATP in respiration (see chapter 6). For **obligate anaerobes,** O_2 is toxic, and they live in habitats that lack it. *Clostridium tetani,* the bacterium that causes tetanus, is one example. **Facultative anaerobes,** which include the intestinal microbes *E. coli* and *Salmonella,* can live either with or without O_2.

C. Prokaryotes Include Two Domains with Enormous Diversity

For many decades, the tendency to lump together all prokaryotic organisms hid much of the diversity in the microbial world. We now know of so many species of bacteria and archaea in so many habitats that it would take many books to describe them all—and many more species remain undiscovered. This section contains a small sampling of this extraordinary diversity.

Domain Bacteria Scientists have identified 23 phyla within domain Bacteria, but the evolutionary relationships among them remain unclear. Figure 15.10 illustrates two examples.

Proteobacteria exemplify the overall diversity within the domain. Some carry out photosynthesis. Others play important roles in nitrogen or sulfur cycling, whereas still others form a medically important group that includes enteric bacteria and vibrios. *Helicobacter,* a bacterium that causes ulcers in humans, is a proteobacterium, as are the intestinal bacteria *E. coli* and *Salmonella.*

Cyanobacteria form another lineage of bacteria. Billions of years ago, these autotrophs were the first to produce O_2 as a byproduct of photosynthesis. They also gave rise to the chloroplasts inside the cells of land plants and green algae (see section 15.3A). Cyanobacteria remain important in ecosystems, forming the base of aquatic food chains and participating in symbiotic relationships with fungi on land (see section 15.5C).

Spirochaetes are spiral-shaped organisms such as *Borrelia burgdorferi,* a bacterium that can cause Lyme disease when transmitted to humans in a tick's bite. *Treponema pallidum* is a spirochaete that causes the sexually transmitted disease syphilis.

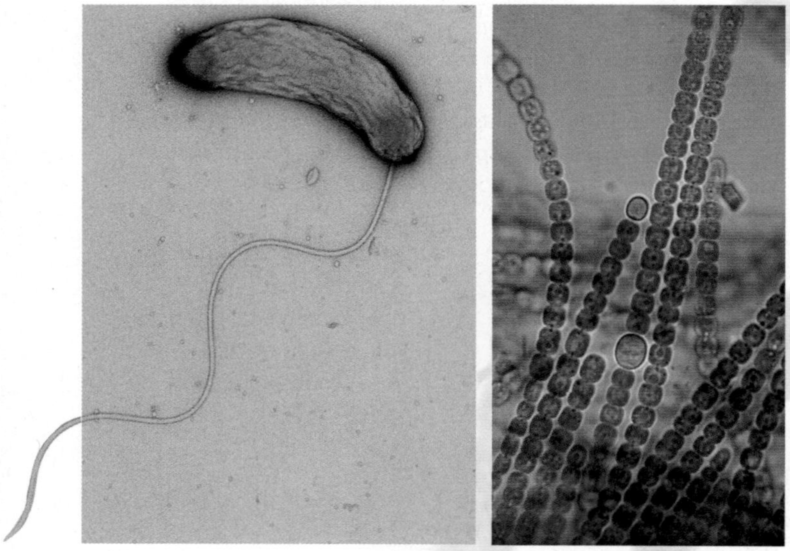

a. TEM (false color) 0.5 μm b. LM 7 μm

Figure 15.10 Two Types of Bacteria. (a) *Vibrio cholera,* a proteobacterium. (b) Filaments of *Anabaena,* a cyanobacterium.

Many other bacteria are medically important as well. As we have already seen, *Bacillus anthracis* causes anthrax; another endospore-former, *Clostridium tetani*, causes tetanus. Other disease-causing bacteria include *Staphylococcus* and *Streptococcus*. But bacteria can also be our allies in medicine. For example, actinobacteria are filamentous, soil-dwelling microbes that produce infection-fighting antibiotics such as streptomycin.

Domain Archaea Archaea are often collectively described as "extremophiles" because scientists originally found them in places that lacked oxygen or that were extremely salty, acidic, or hot (figure 15.11). At first, the organisms were informally divided into groups based on habitat. The thermophiles, for example, live in habitats such as boiling hot springs and hydrothermal vents, whereas the halophiles prefer salt concentrations of up to 30%, and the acidophiles tolerate pH as low as 1.0. Methanogens live in stagnant waters and the anaerobic intestinal tracts of many animals, generating huge quantities of methane gas. As more archaea are discovered in moderate environments such as soil or the open ocean, however, formal classification is becoming more important. This process is ongoing; in fact, scientists do not yet agree on how many phyla of archaea exist, let alone the number of species.

The importance of archaea in ecosystems is slowly becoming clearer as scientists decipher more about their roles in global carbon, nitrogen, and sulfur cycles. Many live in ocean waters and sediments, a hard-to-explore habitat in which the role of archaea is particularly poorly understood. Their immense numbers, however, suggest that archaea are critical players in ocean ecology.

Figure 15.11 Extremophiles. Archaea such as *Sulfolobus* thrive in boiling mud pools. This is Krafla caldera in Iceland.

D. Bacteria and Archaea Are Essential to All Life

Many people think of microbes as harmful "germs" that cause disease. Indeed, most of the familiar examples of bacteria listed in the previous section are pathogens (disease-causing organisms). Some bacteria do make people sick, but most microbes do not harm us at all. This section describes some of the many ways that bacteria and archaea affect our lives.

Vital Links in Ecosystems Although it may seem hard to believe that one-celled organisms can be essential, the truth is that all other species would die without bacteria and archaea. For example, microbes play essential roles in the global carbon cycle. They decompose organic matter in soil and water, releasing CO_2. Other microorganisms absorb CO_2 in photosynthesis. And all kinds of microbes, both heterotrophs and autotrophs, are eaten by countless organisms in every imaginable habitat. Chapter 19 explains these community interactions in more detail. ▸ carbon cycle, p. 400

Another essential process is **nitrogen fixation,** the chemical reactions in which prokaryotes convert atmospheric nitrogen gas (N_2) to ammonia (NH_3). The element nitrogen is a component of protein, DNA, and many other organic molecules. The only organisms that can use N_2 directly are a few species of bacteria and archaea. Ultimately, most of Earth's nitrogen would be locked in the atmosphere if not for nitrogen-fixers releasing NH_3 that plants and other organisms can absorb. The nitrogen cycle—and therefore all life—would eventually cease without these crucial microbes. ▸ nitrogen cycle, p. 401

Some nitrogen-fixing bacteria live in soil or water. Others, such as those in the genus *Rhizobium,* induce the formation of nodules in the roots of clover and other plants in the legume family (figure 15.12). Inside the nodules, *Rhizobium* cells share the nitrogen that they fix with their hosts; in exchange, the bacteria receive nutrients and protection.

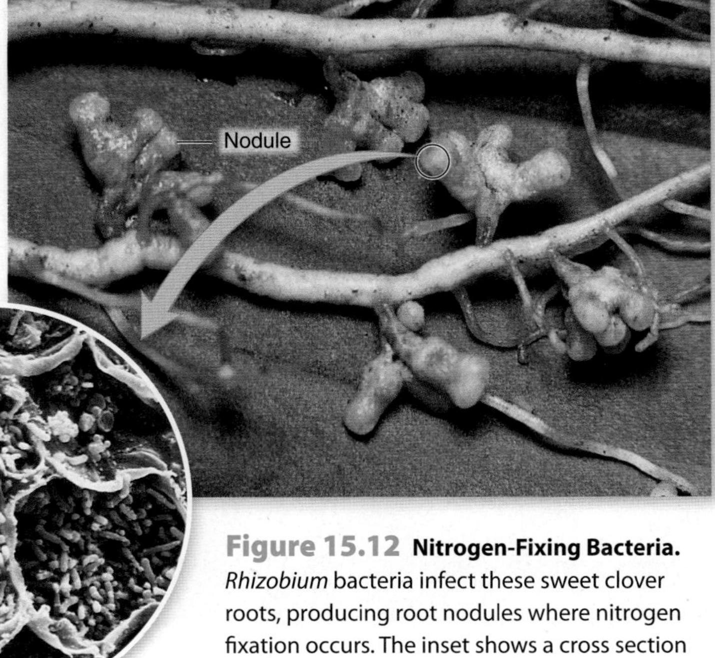

Figure 15.12 Nitrogen-Fixing Bacteria. *Rhizobium* bacteria infect these sweet clover roots, producing root nodules where nitrogen fixation occurs. The inset shows a cross section of a root nodule, revealing bacteria inside the plant's cells.

Why We Care | Antibiotics and Other Germ Killers

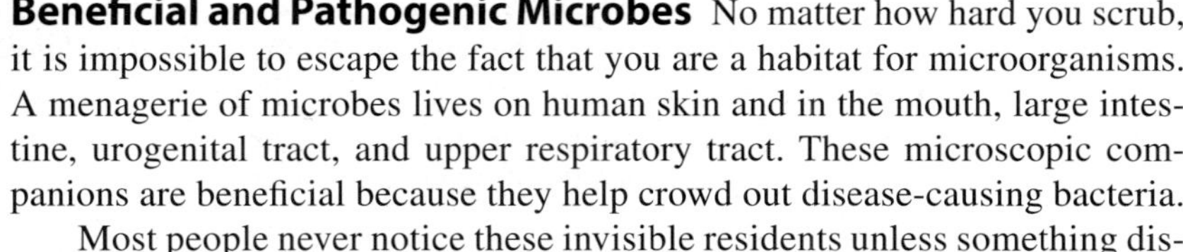

When a person develops a bacterial infection, a physician may prescribe antibiotics. These drugs typically inhibit structures and functions present in bacterial, but not host, cells. Some mechanisms of action include:

- **Inhibiting cell wall synthesis:** Penicillin is an antibiotic that interferes with cell wall formation. A bacterium that cannot make a rigid cell wall will burst and die.
- **Disrupting cell membranes:** Polymyxin antibiotics exploit differences between bacterial and eukaryotic cell membranes. ▸ membranes, p. 54
- **Inhibiting transcription:** Rifamycin antibiotics prevent RNA synthesis in bacteria by binding to a bacterial form of RNA polymerase. ▸ transcription, p. 114
- **Inhibiting protein assembly:** The antibiotics streptomycin, chloramphenicol, and erythromycin bind to bacterial ribosomes, killing bacteria without harming us. ▸ ribosomes, p. 50
- **Inhibiting enzymes:** Theoretically, antibiotics could block any bacterial metabolic pathway that does not occur in host cells. Sulfanilamide, for example, interferes with a bacterial enzyme that participates in an essential chain of chemical reactions. ▸ enzymes, p. 74

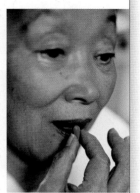

Beneficial and Pathogenic Microbes No matter how hard you scrub, it is impossible to escape the fact that you are a habitat for microorganisms. A menagerie of microbes lives on human skin and in the mouth, large intestine, urogenital tract, and upper respiratory tract. These microscopic companions are beneficial because they help crowd out disease-causing bacteria.

Most people never notice these invisible residents unless something disrupts their personal microbial community. Suppose, for example, that your cat scratches your leg and the wound becomes infected. If you take antibiotics to fight the infection, the drug will probably also kill off some of the resident microbes in your body. As they die, harmful ones can take their place. The resulting microbial imbalance in the intestines or genital tract causes unpleasant side effects such as diarrhea or a vaginal yeast infection. These problems subside in time as the normal microbes divide and restore their populations.

Although most bacteria in and on the human body are harmless, some cause disease. (So far, no archaea are linked to human illnesses.) To cause an infection, bacteria must first enter the body. Animal bites transmit some bacteria, as can sexual activity. A person can also inhale air containing respiratory droplets from a sick coworker or ingest bacteria in contaminated food or water. Bacteria can also enter the body through open wounds.

Once inside the host, pili or slime capsules attach the pathogens to host cells. As the invaders multiply, disease may develop. Some symptoms result from damage caused by the bacteria themselves. The cells may produce enzymes that break down host tissues, for example, or they may release toxins that harm the host's circulatory, digestive, or nervous system. ▸ enzymes, p. 74

Microbiologists divide bacterial toxins into two categories: exotoxins and endotoxins. Exotoxins are toxic proteins that diffuse out of a bacterial cell. *Staphylococcus aureus* and *Clostridium botulinum* are two examples of bacteria that produce exotoxins; *S. aureus* causes toxic shock syndrome, and *C. botulinum* causes botulism.

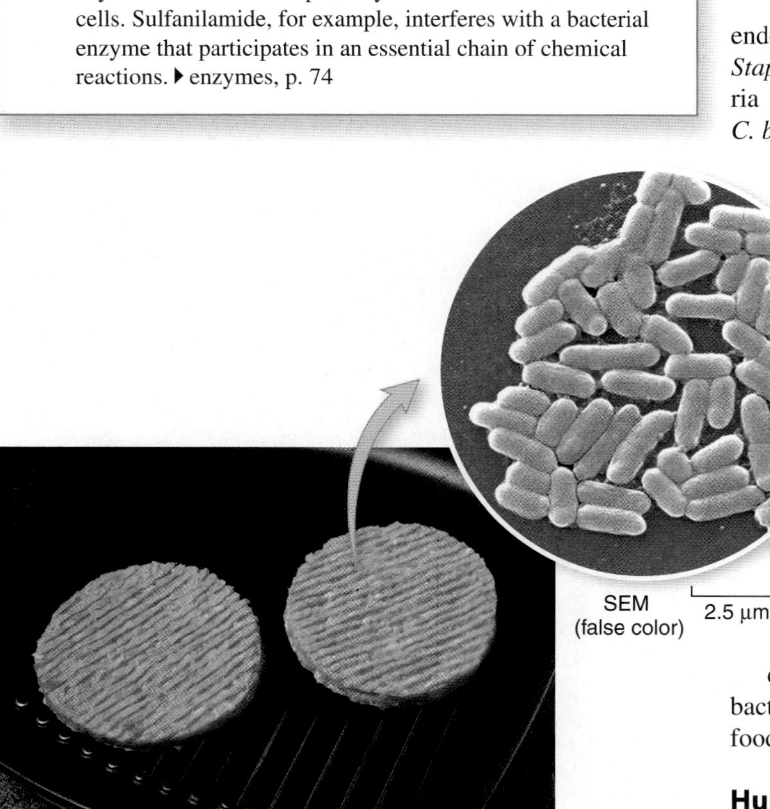

Figure 15.13 Cook with Care. Undercooked hamburger meat is a common source of *E. coli* strain O157:H7.

Rather than diffusing out of a bacterial cell, endotoxins form a component of the cell itself—specifically, the outer membrane that surrounds some bacterial cell walls. Consider, for example, *E. coli,* a normal inhabitant of animal intestines. Sometimes, cattle manure containing *E. coli* contaminates water, milk, raw fruits and vegetables, hamburger, and other foods (figure 15.13). Most cells of *E. coli* are harmless, but strain O157:H7 multiplies inside the body. Its endotoxin can cause belly pain, bloody diarrhea, and, in some cases, life-threatening kidney failure. Outbreaks of *E. coli* strain O157:H7 have led to widely publicized recalls of everything from raw spinach to ground beef to unpasteurized apple juice. Raw eggs and other foods contaminated with animal feces also may contain *Salmonella,* a close relative of *E. coli.*

E. coli and *Salmonella* are two examples of microbes that thrive in foods that have been improperly refrigerated or inadequately cooked. The toxins they produce in the food—not infection with the bacteria themselves—produce the vomiting and diarrhea associated with food poisoning.

Human Uses of Prokaryotes Humans have exploited the metabolic talents of microbes for centuries, long before we could see their cells under a microscope (figure 15.14). For instance, many foods are the products of bacterial metabolism. Vinegar, sauerkraut, sourdough bread, pickles, olives, yogurt,

a.

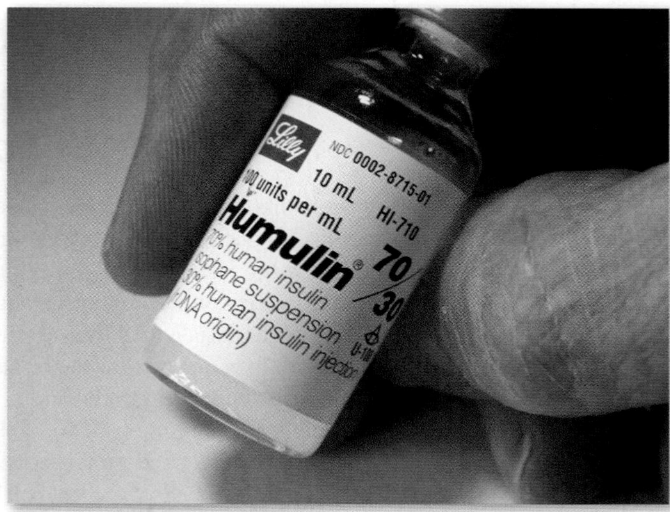

b.

c.

Figure 15.14 Bacteria at Work. (a) Bacteria that ferment milk participate in the manufacture of cheddar cheese. (b) Transgenic bacteria produce many drugs, including human insulin. (c) Raw sewage is sprayed on a trickling filter at a municipal wastewater treatment plant. Bacterial biofilms on the filter degrade the organic matter in the sewage.

and cheese are just a few examples; organic acids released in fermentation produce the tart flavors of these foods. ▸ fermentation, p. 108

Scientists continue to invent new ways to use the microbial world. Bacteria help produce enormous quantities of vitamins and useful chemicals such as ethanol and acetone. Transgenic bacteria also mass-produce human proteins, including insulin and blood-clotting factors. In addition, heat-, acid-, and salt-tolerant enzymes isolated from microbes have found their way into dishwashing detergents and other household products. A heat-tolerant enzyme also transformed modern biology by improving the efficiency of PCR, the polymerase chain reaction. ▸ polymerase chain reaction, p. 204

Water and waste treatment also use bacteria and archaea. Sewage treatment plants in most communities, for example, rely on slimy biofilms consisting of countless microbes that degrade organic wastes. And a technique called bioremediation uses microorganisms to metabolize and detoxify pollutants such as petroleum spills, polychlorinated biphenyls (PCBs), and mercury.

15.2 Mastering Concepts

1. What are two domains that contain prokaryotes?
2. Without looking at figure 15.7, sketch the internal and external features of a typical prokaryotic cell. What are the functions of each structure?
3. What terms do microbiologists use to describe carbon sources, energy sources, and oxygen requirements?
4. In what ways are bacteria and archaea important to eukaryotic life in general and to human life in particular?
5. What adaptations enable pathogenic bacteria to enter the body and cause disease?

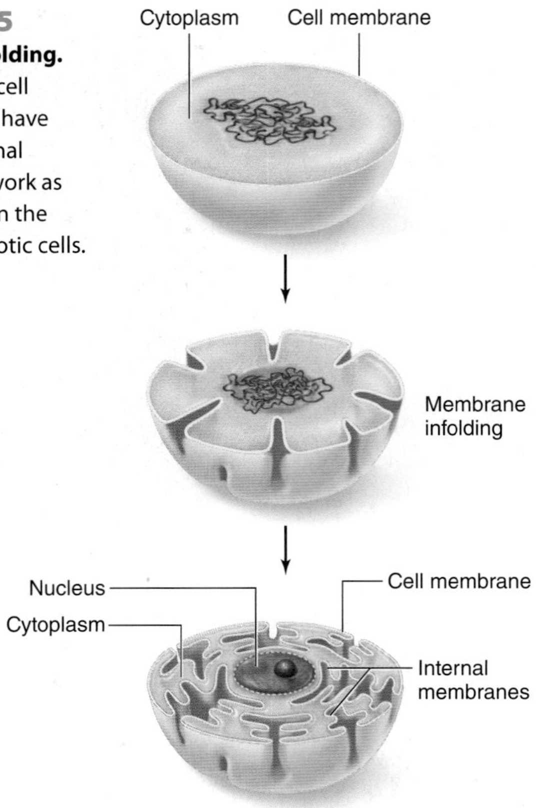

Figure 15.15 **Membrane Infolding.** A highly folded cell membrane may have formed an internal membrane network as a possible step in the origin of eukaryotic cells.

15.3 Eukaryotic Cells and Multicellularity Arose More Than a Billion Years Ago

Until this point, we have considered the origin and diversity of prokaryotic cells. About 2.7 billion years ago, however, the prokaryotes gave rise to a new, more complex cell type: the eukaryote. In contrast to a prokaryote, a **eukaryotic cell** has a nucleus and other membrane-bounded organelles, such as mitochondria and chloroplasts.

We may never know the origin of the membranes that make up the nuclear envelope, endoplasmic reticulum, Golgi apparatus, and some other organelles within the eukaryotic cell. We do know, however, that these membranes consist of phospholipids and proteins, as does the cell's outer membrane. Perhaps the outer membrane of an ancient cell folded in on itself, over and over, until a complex internal network formed (figure 15.15). Unfortunately, that hypothesis is difficult or impossible to test, so we can only speculate about that aspect of eukaryotic cell evolution.

A. Endosymbiosis Explains the Origin of Mitochondria and Chloroplasts

The origin of two types of organelles, however, is much clearer. The **endosymbiont theory** proposes that mitochondria and chloroplasts originated as free-living bacteria that were engulfed by other prokaryotic cells (figure 15.16). The term *endosymbiont* derives from *endo-*, meaning "inside," and *symbiont,* meaning "to live together."

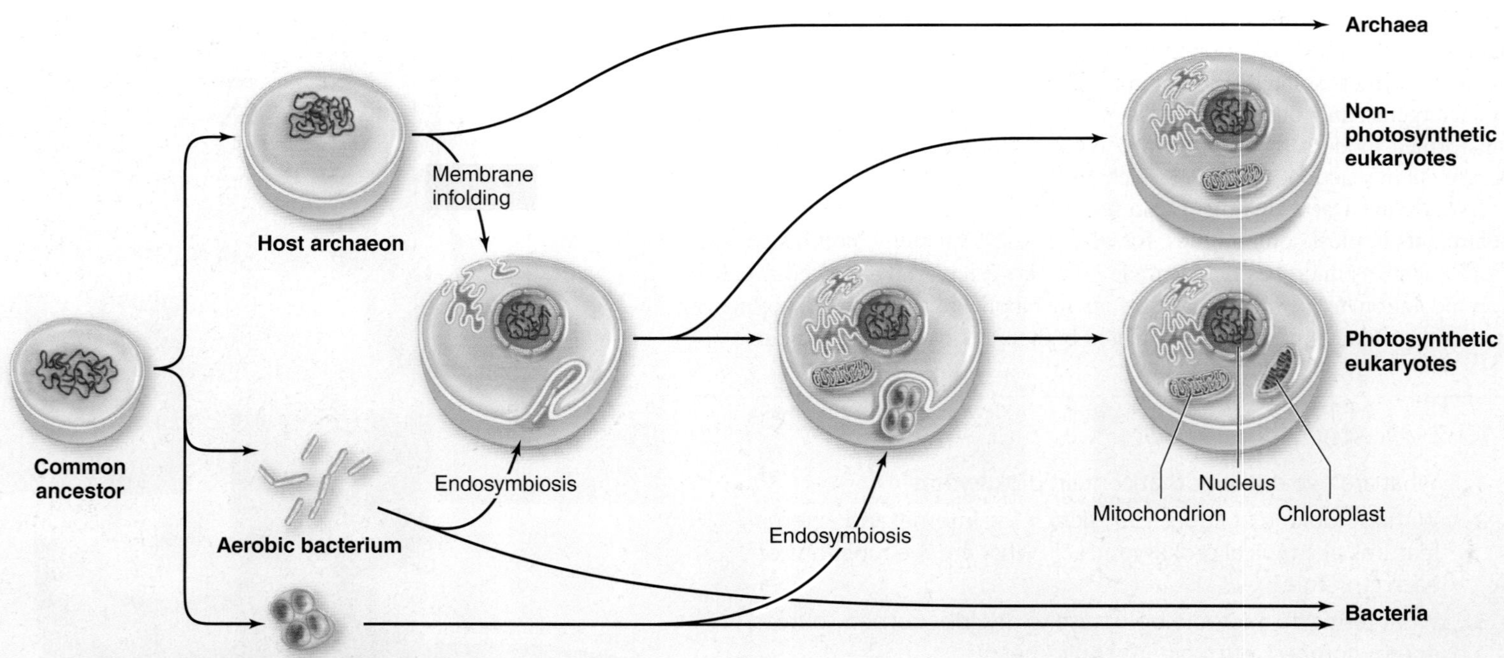

Figure 15.16 **The Endosymbiont Theory.** Mitochondria and chloroplasts may have originated from an ancient union of bacterial cells with archaean cells.

The evidence supporting the idea that mitochondria and chloroplasts originated as independent organisms includes:

- similarities in size, shape, and membrane structure between the organelles and some types of bacteria;
- the double membrane surrounding mitochondria and chloroplasts, a presumed relic of the original engulfing event;
- the observation that mitochondria and chloroplasts are not assembled in cells but instead reproduce by binary fission, as do bacterial cells;
- the similarity between the photosynthetic pigments in chloroplasts and those in cyanobacteria;
- the observation that mitochondria and chloroplasts contain DNA, RNA, and ribosomes, which are similar to those in bacterial cells; and
- DNA sequence analysis, which shows a close relationship between mitochondria and aerobic bacteria, and between chloroplasts and cyanobacteria.

After the ancient endosymbiosis events, many genes moved from the DNA of the organelles to the nuclei of the host cells. These genetic changes made the captured microorganisms unable to live on their own outside their hosts. Over time, they came to depend on one another for survival. The result of this biological interdependency, according to the endosymbiont theory, is the compartmentalized cells of modern eukaryotes.

Mitochondria must have come first, because virtually all eukaryotes have these organelles. Chloroplasts came later, in the lineages that eventually gave rise to photosynthetic protists and plants. In fact, the chloroplasts of some types of photosynthetic protists apparently derive from a secondary endosymbiosis—that is, of a eukaryotic cell engulfing another eukaryote (figure 15.17). In these species, three or four membranes surround the chloroplasts; some of their cells even retain remnants of the engulfed cell's nucleus. No one knows exactly how many times, or when, these endosymbiosis events happened. Biologists are just beginning to unravel the events surrounding the origins of all the different types of chloroplasts.

B. Multicellularity May Also Have Its Origin in Cooperation

Another important milestone in eukaryote history is the origin of multicellularity, an event that occurred about 1.2 BYA. No one knows how eukaryotes came to adopt a multicellular lifestyle. The fossil record is essentially silent on the matter, mostly because the first multicellular organisms lacked hard parts that fossilize readily. We do know, however, that multicellularity arose independently in multiple lineages. After all, genetic evidence clearly suggests that plants, fungi, and animals arose from different lineages of unicellular protists.

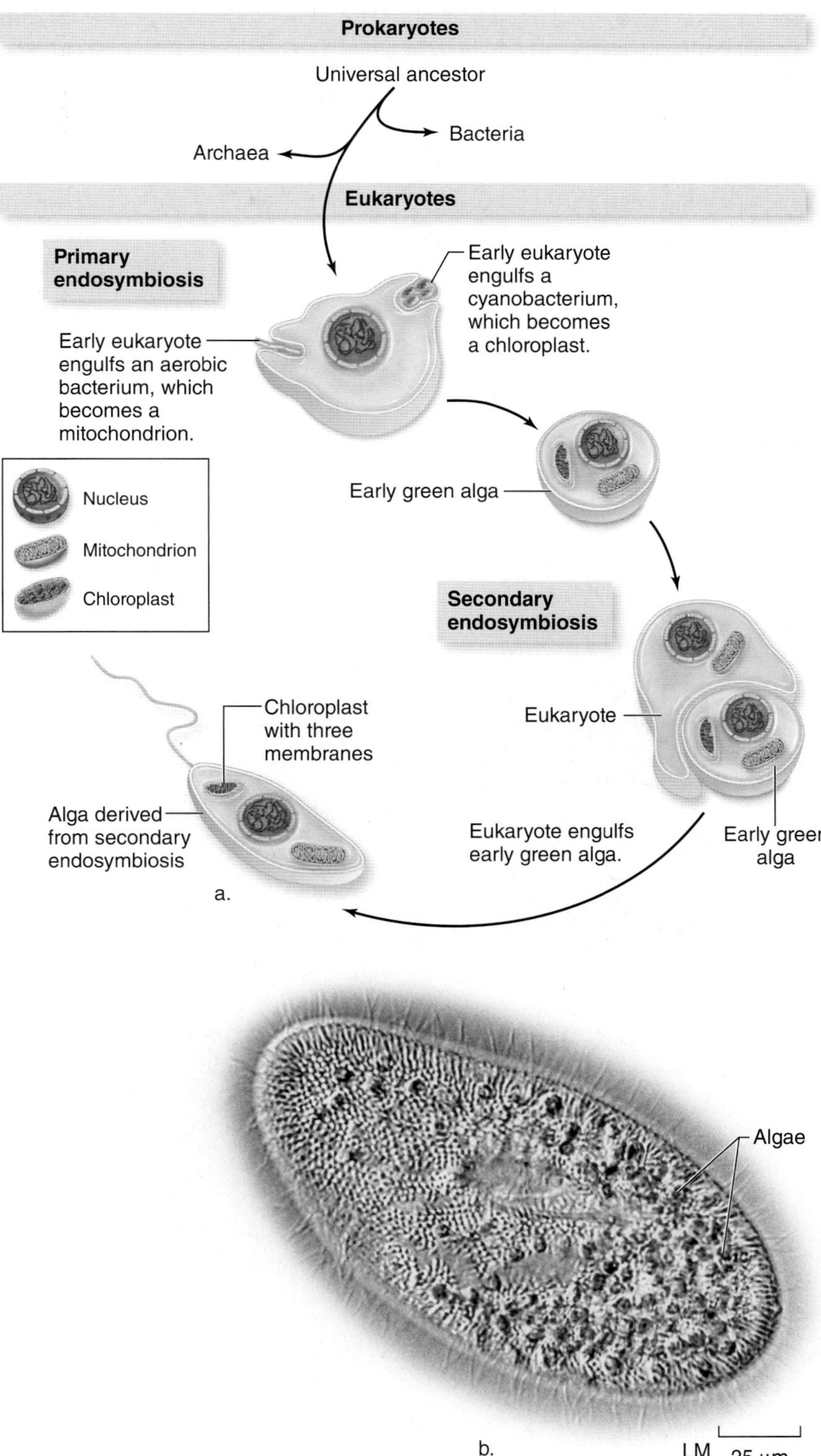

Figure 15.17 Secondary Endosymbiosis. (a) Many photosynthetic eukaryotes acquired chloroplasts by engulfing existing eukaryotic cells. (b) This protist, *Paramecium bursaria*, has engulfed eukaryotic algae, which live inside its cytoplasm. This dual organism (and many others in similar partnerships) provide evidence for the endosymbiont theory.

Perhaps many individual cells came together, joined, and took on specialized tasks to form a multicellular organism. The life cycle of modern-day protists called cellular slime molds illustrates how this may have occurred (see figure 15.25). Alternatively, a single-celled organism may have divided, and the daughter cells may have remained stuck together rather than separating. After many rounds of cell division, these cells may have begun expressing different subsets of their DNA. The result would be a multicellular organism with specialized cells—similar to the way in which modern animals and plants develop from a single fertilized egg cell.

No matter how it happened, the origin of multicellularity and specialized cells allowed for new features such as attachment to a surface or an upright orientation. The resulting explosion in the variety of body sizes and forms introduced new evolutionary possibilities and opened new habitats for other organisms.

15.3 Mastering Concepts

1. When did eukaryotic cells first appear?
2. How might the endoplasmic reticulum, nuclear envelope, and other internal membranes have arisen in eukaryotic cells?
3. What is the evidence that mitochondria and chloroplasts descend from simpler cells engulfed long ago?
4. What are two ways that multicellular organisms may have originated?
5. How is multicellularity adaptive?

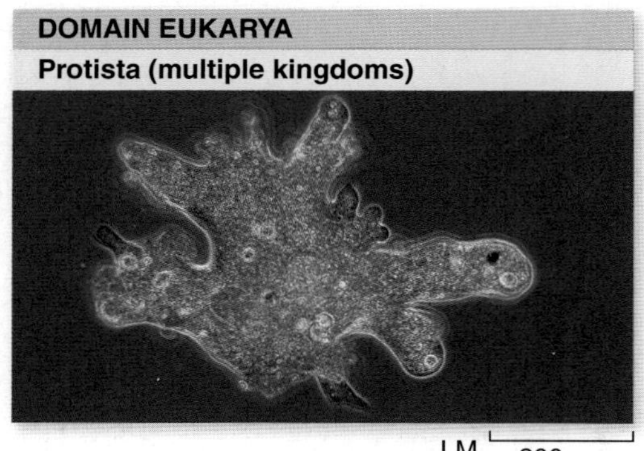

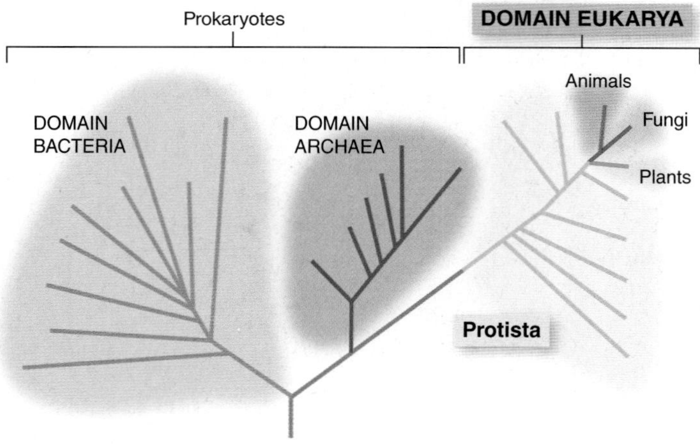

Figure 15.18 Protists at the Crossroads. "Kingdom" Protista consists of many lineages, each of which may eventually be considered its own kingdom. Plants, fungi, and animals trace their ancestry to protists, living or extinct.

15.4 Protists Are the Simplest Eukaryotes

We now embark on a tour of the protists, the simplest eukaryotes. As you will see, the metabolic diversity among protists means they have an astonishingly wide variety of functions and roles in human life.

A. What Is a Protist?

Until recently, biologists recognized four eukaryotic kingdoms: Protista, Plantae, Fungi, and Animalia. The plants, fungi, and animals are distinguished based on their characteristics. Loosely defined, plants are multicellular eukaryotes that carry out photosynthesis; fungi are mostly multicellular eukaryotes that obtain food by external digestion; and animals are multicellular eukaryotes that obtain food by ingestion.

Kingdom Protista, in contrast, was defined by *exclusion*. An organism was designated a **protist** if it was a eukaryote that did not fit the description of a plant, fungus, or animal. Kingdom Protista was, in effect, a convenient but artificial "none of the above" category (figure 15.18). Not surprisingly, the nearly 100,000 named species of protists are extremely diverse, displaying great variety in size, nutrition, locomotion, reproduction, and cell surfaces.

Textbooks and taxonomists have traditionally considered the protists in terms of the more familiar organisms that they resemble: the plantlike algae, funguslike slime molds, and animal-like protozoa. Modern systematists, however, try to group organisms based on evolutionary relationships. Based on DNA sequence data, the former Kingdom Protista has shattered into dozens of groups whose relationships to one another remain uncertain. Whether those groups become full-fledged kingdoms, subkingdom "supergroups," phyla, or some other taxonomic designation remains to be seen. ▸ systematics, p. 268

Because the classification of protists is in transition and many of the new groupings are not universally accepted, this chapter uses the traditional approach to classification. Protistan classification will continue to evolve as research reveals new molecular sequences, but it will likely remain a work in progress for years to come.

Burning Questions

Why and how do algae form?

Algae are common aquatic organisms, but they are often inconspicuous. Sometimes, however, their populations grow so large that they seem to take over; ponds and poorly maintained swimming pools can turn bright green with algal overgrowth. This population explosion, also called an algal bloom, occurs whenever nutrients and sunlight are abundant.

Algal blooms are normal in some ecosystems, such as in many ponds. A bloom where water is normally clear, however, usually indicates that nutrients from sewage, fertilizer, or animal waste are polluting the waterway. The use of lawn fertilizers, for example, is a common cause of algal blooms in ponds in residential settings. ▸ eutrophication, p. 412

Submit your burning question to:
marielle_hoefnagels@mcgraw-hill.com

B. Algae Are Photosynthetic Protists

Most people probably think of algae as pond scum, but **algae** is a general term that refers to any photosynthetic protist that lives in water. (Although the cyanobacteria were traditionally called "blue-green algae," most biologists now reserve the term *algae* for eukaryotes.) The cells of algae contain chloroplasts that house yellow, gold, brown, red, or green photosynthetic pigments.

These organisms produce much of the O_2 in Earth's atmosphere and support food webs in oceans, lakes, rivers, and ponds. In addition, algae living among the threads of fungi on rocks and tree bark form lichens, which play a crucial role in building soil from bare rock (see section 15.5C). This section describes some major types of algae. ▸ food webs, p. 394

Dinoflagellates The marine protists known as **dinoflagellates** have two flagella that propel the cell with a whirling motion (the Greek *dinein* means "to whirl"). In addition, many dinoflagellates have cell walls that consist of overlapping cellulose plates (figure 15.19).

A red tide is a sudden population explosion, or "bloom," of dinoflagellates that turn the water red, orange, or brown. Because some dinoflagellates are colorless, however, many biologists now prefer the term *harmful algal bloom* over *red tide.* Usually these blooms occur in response to a boost in the nutrient content of the water, as described in this section's Burning Question.

A bloom of dinoflagellates is harmful because their cells can release deadly toxins. A person who eats clams, oysters, scallops, or mussels tainted with dinoflagellate toxins may develop paralytic shellfish poisoning. In this context, the recommendation to "never eat shellfish in a month without an R" makes sense, because toxic algae blooms are most frequent in May, June, July, and August. In reality, however, most commercially harvested shellfish are tested for toxins and are therefore safe to eat year-round.

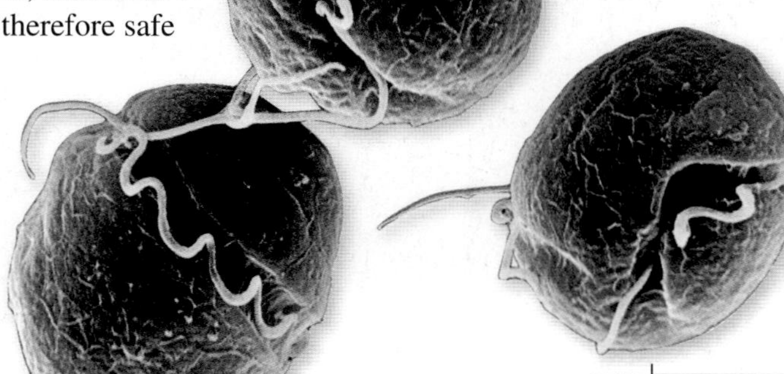

Figure 15.19 **Dinoflagellates.** *Gymnodinium* sp. exhibits classic dinoflagellate structure. Note the two flagella and the cellulose plates that make up the cell wall.

Diatoms and Brown Algae The diatoms and brown algae contain a yellowish photosynthetic pigment that gives these organisms a golden, olive green, or brown color. **Diatoms** are unicellular algae with ornate, two-part silica cell walls that fit together like a shoebox

Figure 15.20 Diatoms. The "glass houses" (silica cell walls) of these photosynthetic protists exhibit a dazzling variety of forms.

and its lid (figure 15.20). These protists occupy just about every moist habitat on Earth, but most live in oceans. Their cells can reach huge densities, and they are an important food source for zooplankton.

Over millions of years, the glassy shells of diatoms have accumulated on the ocean floor. The abrasive shells mined from these deposits are used in swimming pool filters, polishes, and toothpaste. Diatoms also impart the reflective quality of paints used in roadway signs and license plates.

The **brown algae** are the most complex and largest protists. These multicellular algae live in marine habitats all over the world. The kelps, which are the largest of the brown algae, produce enormous underwater forests that provide food and habitat for many animals (figure 15.21).

Humans consume several species of kelp. *Laminaria digitata,* for example, is an ingredient in many Asian dishes. Algin, a chemical extracted from the cell walls of brown algae, is used as an emulsifying, thickening, and stabilizing agent in products including ice cream, candies, chocolate, salad dressings, sauces, soft drinks, beer, cough syrup, toothpaste, cosmetics, polishes, latex paint, and paper.

Red Algae Most **red algae** are relatively large (figure 15.22), although some are microscopic. These marine organisms can live in water exceeding 200 meters in depth, thanks to reddish and bluish photosynthetic pigments that absorb wavelengths of light that chlorophyll *a* cannot capture.

Humans use red algae in many ways. Agar, for example, is a polysaccharide in the cell walls of some species. This jellylike substance is used as a culture medium for microorganisms and as a thickener in ice cream. Another useful product is carrageenan, a polysaccharide that emulsifies fats in chocolate bars and stabilizes paints, cosmetics, and creamy foods.

Figure 15.21 Giant Kelp. These brown algae form huge underwater forests near coastlines. Each individual may be dozens of meters long.

Figure 15.22 Red Algae. *Bossiella* is a coralline red alga that secretes calcium carbonate and helps build coral reefs.

Green Algae Evolutionary biologists are especially interested in the **green algae,** which share many chemical and genetic similarities with the land plants. These organisms may be unicellular, filamentous, colonial, or multicellular (figure 15.23). The multicellular species may have rootlike and stemlike structures, but their bodies are far less specialized than plants.

One well-studied green alga is *Chlamydomonas,* a unicellular organism that reproduces asexually and sexually; scientists study these algae to learn about the evolution of sex. A classroom favorite is the colonial green alga, *Volvox.* Hundreds to thousands of *Volvox* cells form hollow balls; the cells move their flagella in coordinated waves to move the sphere. New colonies remain within the parental ball of cells until they burst free. *Volvox* has been important in studies of the evolution of multicellularity.

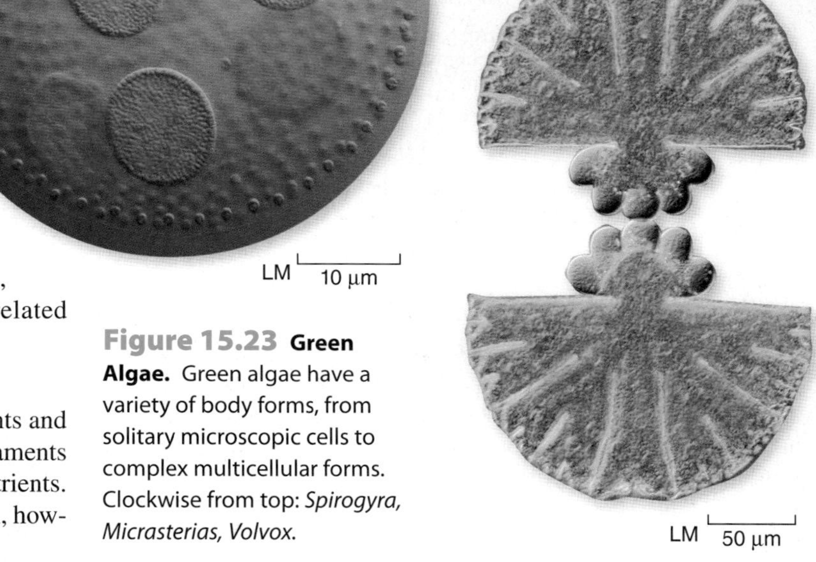

Figure 15.23 Green Algae. Green algae have a variety of body forms, from solitary microscopic cells to complex multicellular forms. Clockwise from top: *Spirogyra, Micrasterias, Volvox.*

C. Some Heterotrophic Protists Were Once Classified as Fungi

Water molds and slime molds are protists that resemble fungi in some ways: they are heterotrophic, and some produce filamentous feeding structures similar to those in fungi. Nevertheless, molecular evidence clearly indicates that neither group is closely related to fungi.

Water Molds The **water molds** are decomposers or parasites of plants and animals in moist environments. Like fungi, these protists produce filaments that secrete digestive enzymes into their surroundings and absorb the nutrients. Swimming spores help them disperse in water and wet soil. Unlike fungi, however the cell walls of water molds contain cellulose.

The best-known water molds are those that ruin crops, causing such diseases as downy mildew of grapes and lettuce. The water mold *Phytophthora infestans,* which means "plant destroyer," causes late blight of potatoes (figure 15.24). This disease caused the devastating Irish potato famine from 1845 to 1847, during which more than a million people starved and millions more emigrated from Ireland.

Figure 15.24 Water Mold. *Phytophthora infestans* is a water mold that causes late blight of potatoes. This disease was responsible for the Irish potato famine in the mid-1840s.

Slime Molds Slime molds live in damp habitats such as forest floors, engulfing bacteria and other microbes on decaying vegetation. Their life cycles are extremely unusual: they can exist either as single cells or as large masses that behave as one multicellular organism.

The feeding stage of a **plasmodial slime mold** consists of a huge cell: a mass of thousands of nuclei enclosed by a single cell membrane. This conspicuous, slimy, bright yellow or orange mass may be up to 25 cm in diameter. It migrates along the forest floor, engulfing its food. In times of drought or starvation, the gigantic cell halts and forms fruiting bodies, which produce thick-walled reproductive cells called spores. When favorable conditions return, the spores germinate and form new cells that resume feeding.

In contrast to the plasmodial slime molds, individual cells of a **cellular slime mold** retain their membranes throughout the life cycle. The cells exist as haploid feeding amoebae. When food becomes scarce, the amoebae secrete chemical signals that stimulate the neighboring cells to aggregate into a

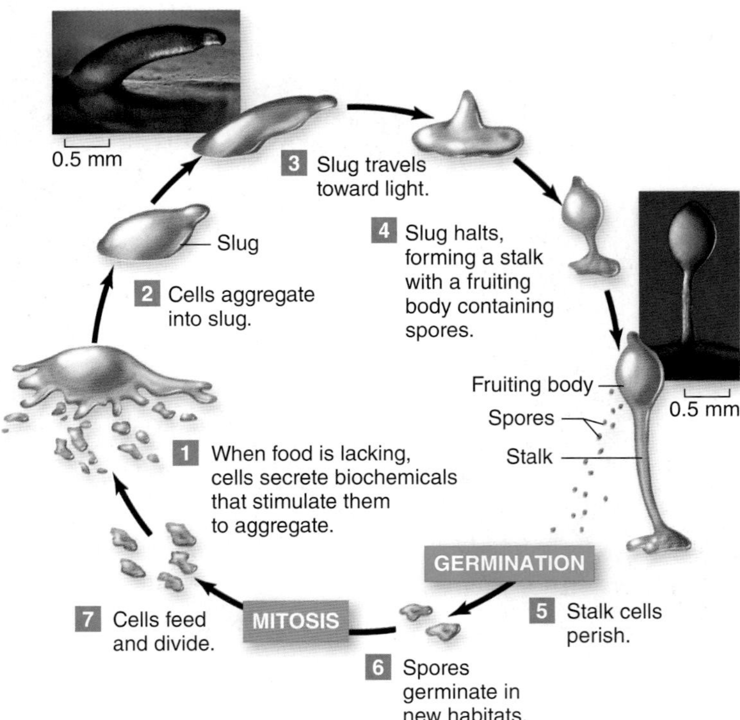

Figure 15.25 Life Cycle of a Cellular Slime Mold. The individual cells of a cellular slime mold feed on bacteria. Starvation stimulates the cells to aggregate into a multicellular "slug," which crawls to a new habitat. Eventually the slug forms a fruiting body that releases spores, which germinate to start the life cycle anew.

sluglike structure (figure 15.25). The "slug" moves toward light, stops, and forms a stalk topped by a fruiting body that produces spores. The cells of the stalk perish, but the spores survive; wind, water, soil-dwelling animals, or birds carry them to new habitats. The spores then germinate, and the cycle begins anew.

D. Protozoa Are Diverse Heterotrophic Protists

Finding a list of characteristics that unite the diverse **protozoa** is difficult. Most are unicellular, and the vast majority are heterotrophs, but several autotrophic species exist. Some can swim, but others cannot. Some are free-living, but others are parasites. Most are asexual, but sexual reproduction occurs in many species.

This section describes four groups of distantly related protozoa that are defined by locomotion and morphology. New molecular techniques are redefining the protozoa, but until the newer system of classification is better defined and more widely accepted, these four groups remain practical for general biology, education, and medicine.

Flagellated Protozoa The **flagellated protozoa** are unicellular organisms with one or more flagella (figure 15.26). Most are free-living in fresh water, the ocean, and soil, but a few parasitic species harm humans.

For example, *Trichomonas vaginalis* resides in the urogenital tracts of both men and women. It is sexually transmitted and causes a form of vaginitis in females. *Giardia intestinalis* (also known as *Giardia lamblia*) causes "hiker's diarrhea," or giardiasis. People ingest the cysts of the organism in contaminated water. Another group of disease-causing flagellates are the trypanosomes, whip-shaped parasites that invade the bloodstream and brain. Insects transmit trypanosomes to humans, causing illnesses such as African sleeping sickness and Chagas disease.

Amoeboid Protozoa The **amoeboid protozoa** produce cytoplasmic extensions called pseudopodia (Latin, meaning "false feet"), which are important in locomotion and capturing food. The most studied species is *Amoeba proteus,* a common freshwater microbe that engulfs bacteria, algae, and other protists in its pseudopodia (see figure 15.18).

The **foraminiferans,** or forams, are an ancient group of mostly marine amoeboid protozoa. Forams and their close relatives have complex shells made of durable minerals (figure 15.27). Their populations are immense: about one

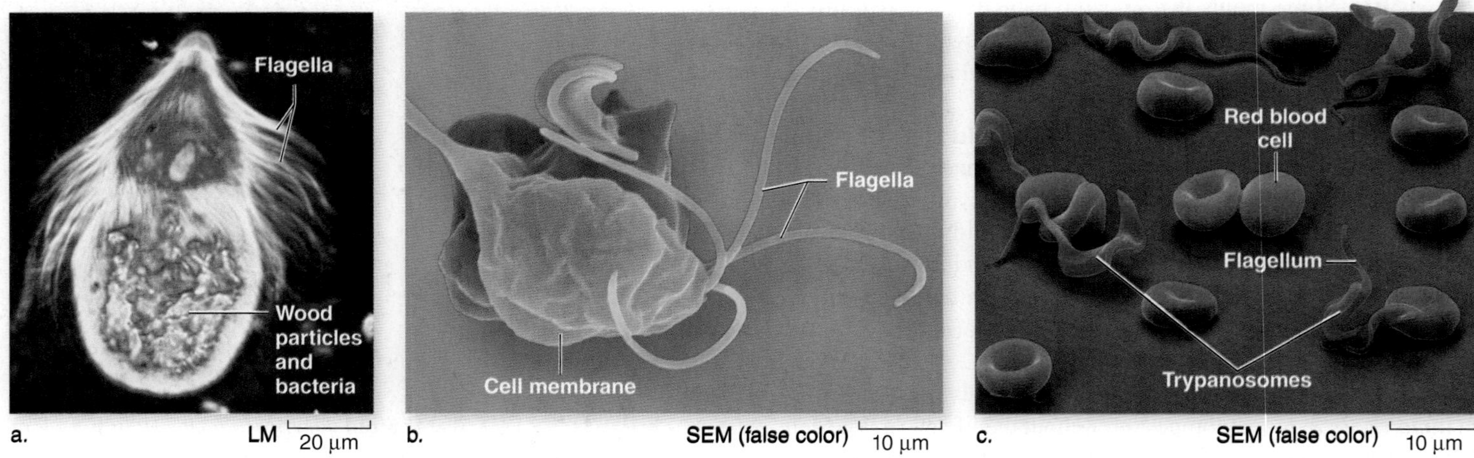

Figure 15.26 Flagellated Protozoa. (a) *Trichonympha* is a protist that lives in termites. Note the fringe of flagella. (b) *Trichomonas vaginalis* causes the sexually transmitted disease trichomoniasis. (c) *Trypanosoma brucei* is a trypanosome that causes African sleeping sickness.

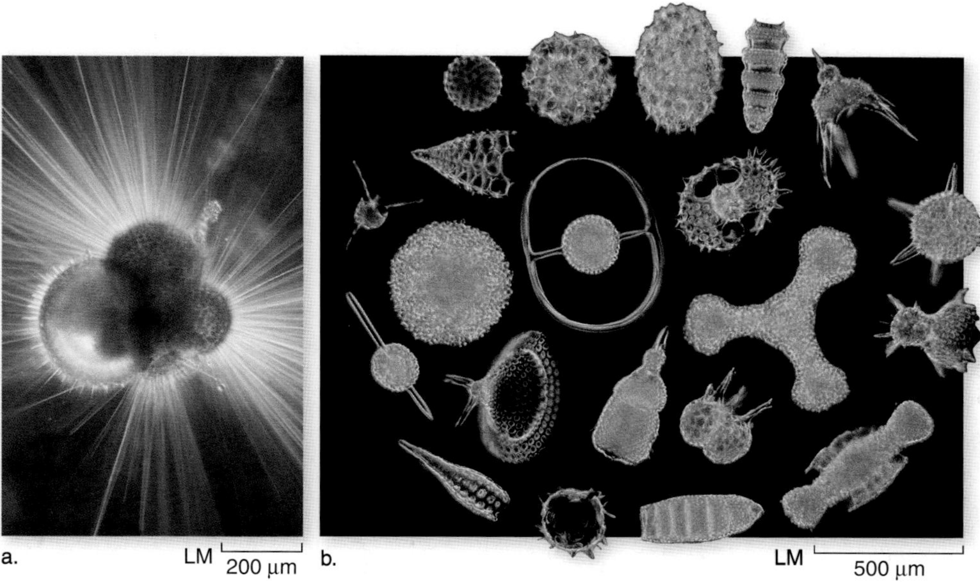

Figure 15.27 Foraminiferans and Kin. (a) Thin threads of cytoplasm extend from the calcium-rich shell of this foram. (b) These protists, called radiolarians, are close relatives of the forams. Their silica shells come in a wide variety of shapes and sizes.

third of the ocean floor is made of the shells of the marine foram *Globigerina.* Paleontologists studying extinct forams have learned which species correlate with oil and gas deposits. The shells are also useful in dating rock strata.

Ciliates The **ciliates** are complex, mostly unicellular protists characterized by abundant hairlike cilia (figure 15.28). Waves of moving cilia propel the organism through the water. Cilia also sweep bacteria, algae, and other ciliates into the cell's gullet. ▸ cilia, p. 63

Most ciliates are free-living, motile cells such as *Paramecium.* Nearly one third of ciliates, however, live in the bodies of crustaceans, mollusks, and vertebrates. Some inhabit the stomachs of cattle, where they house bacteria that break down the cellulose in grass. Others are parasites. The ciliate *Ichthyophthirius multifilis,* for example, causes a common epidermal disease called "ich" in freshwater fish.

Apicomplexans The **apicomplexans** are nonmotile, spore-forming, internal parasites of animals. The name *apicomplexa* comes from the apical complex, a cluster of microtubules and organelles at one end of the cell. This structure, visible only with an electron microscope, apparently helps the parasite attach to and invade host cells.

Apicomplexans include several organisms that cause illness. The Why We Care box on page 297 describes *Cryptosporidium,* a genus containing several species that cause waterborne disease. Another example is *Toxoplasma gondii,* a protist that infects cats and other mammals. A person who handles feces from infected cats can accidentally ingest *Toxoplasma* cysts. The infection can pass to a fetus, which is why pregnant women should avoid cat litter boxes.

Malaria is another example of an illness caused by an apicomplexan. Four species of *Plasmodium* cause mosquito-borne malaria in humans. Despite decades of research, malaria continues to be the world's most significant infectious disease. No effective vaccine exists, and *Plasmodium* continues to develop resistance to drugs that were effective in the past. Malaria prevention efforts therefore focus on repelling and killing mosquitoes.

Not everyone is equally susceptible to malaria. People with one copy of the recessive sickle cell allele are much less likely to contract malaria than are people with two dominant alleles. In areas of the world where malaria is endemic, human populations have a relatively high incidence of the

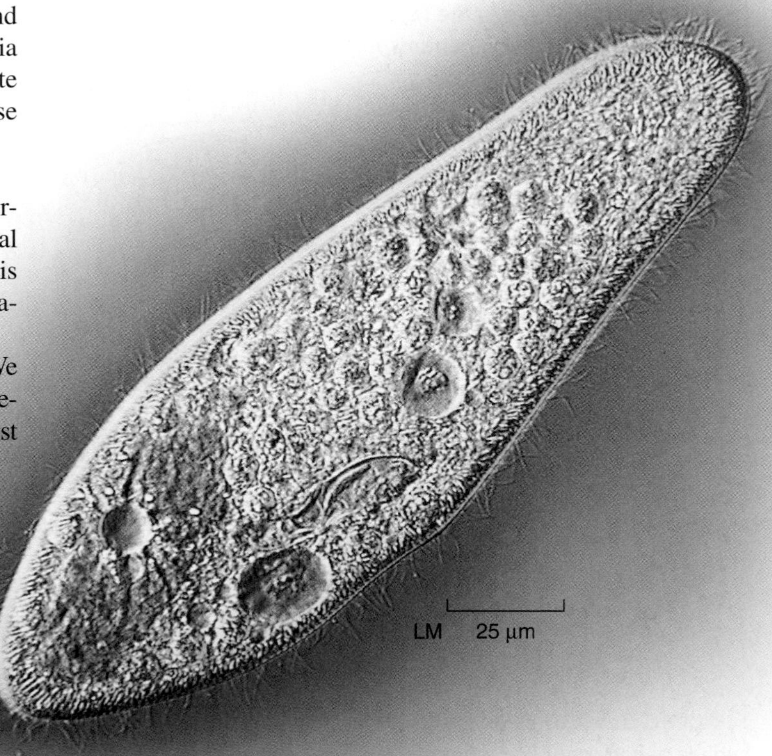

Figure 15.28 The Ciliate *Paramecium.* Numerous hairlike cilia on the cell's exterior give these protozoans their name.

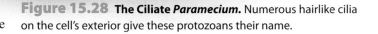

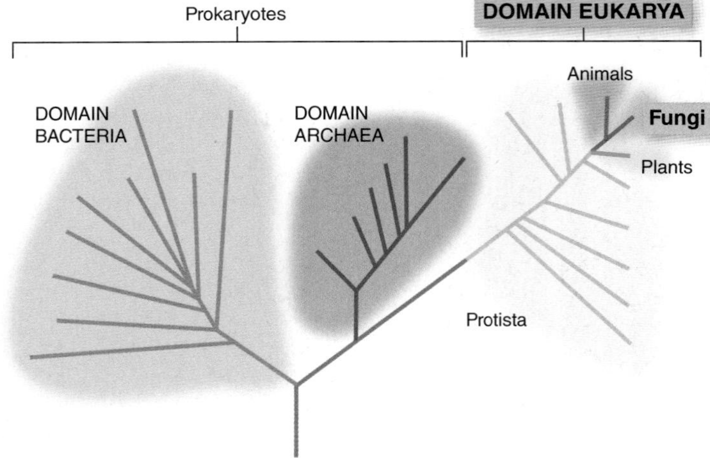

Figure 15.29 Fungi in the Tree of Life. Kingdom Fungi contains many types of eukaryotic organisms, including mushrooms.

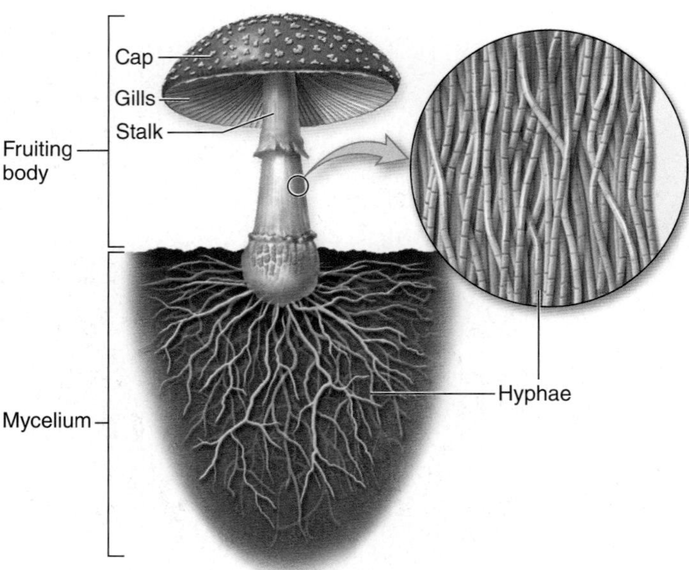

Figure 15.30 The Fungal Body. A mushroom arises from hyphae penetrating the fungus's food source. The mushroom itself is composed of hyphae that are tightly aligned to form a solid structure.

sickle cell allele (see figure 12.14). In malaria-free areas, the sickle cell allele is much rarer. This pattern illustrates the selective force that malaria exerts on the human population. ▸ sickle cell mutation, p. 124

15.4 Mastering Concepts

1. What features define the protists?
2. Describe examples illustrating why protists are important.
3. What mode of nutrition do the algae, slime molds, water molds, and protozoa use?
4. List and describe the characteristics of the major groups of algae.
5. Compare and contrast the plasmodial slime molds, cellular slime molds, and water molds.
6. Describe each of the major groups of protozoa.

15.5 Fungi Are Essential Decomposers

The members of kingdom **Fungi** live nearly everywhere—in soil, in and on plants and animals, in water, even in animal dung. Microscopic fungi infect the cells of protists, while massive fungi extend enormous distances. For example, a single underground fungus occupies about 9 square kilometers in an Oregon forest. Mycologists (biologists who study fungi) have identified about 80,000 species of fungi, but 1.5 million or so are thought to exist.

A. What Is a Fungus?

Fungi are more closely related to animals than to plants (figure 15.29). This finding may surprise those who notice the superficial similarities between plants and fungi. Unlike plants, however, fungi cannot carry out photosynthesis. Moreover, fungi share many chemical and metabolic features with animals.

Fungi have a unique combination of characteristics:

- The cells of fungi are eukaryotic.
- Fungi are heterotrophs, as are animals, but these two groups acquire food in different ways. Animals ingest their food and digest it internally; fungi secrete enzymes that break down organic matter outside their bodies. The fungus then absorbs the nutrients.
- Fungal cell walls are composed primarily of the modified carbohydrate chitin. This tough, flexible molecule also forms the exoskeletons of some animals. ▸ carbohydrates, p. 34
- The storage carbohydrate of fungi is glycogen, the same as for animals (see figure 2.16).
- Most fungi are multicellular, although **yeasts** are unicellular.

The body of a fungus is much more extensive than just a mushroom or the visible fuzz on a moldy piece of food (figure 15.30). Instead, fungi usually consist of an enormous number of microscopic, threadlike filaments called **hyphae** (singular: hypha). These filaments branch rapidly within a food source, growing and absorbing nutrients at their tips. A **mycelium** is a mass of aggregated hyphae that may form visible strands in soil or decaying wood.

While the feeding hyphae remain hidden in the food, the reproductive structures emerge at the surface. Most fungi produce abundant **spores,** which are microscopic reproductive cells. Spores can be asexually or sexually produced. Either way, spores that land on a suitable habitat can germinate and give rise to feeding hyphae, starting a new colony.

B. Fungal Classification Is Based on Reproductive Structures

Mycologists classify fungi into five phyla based on the presence and types of sexual structures (figure 15.31). The **chytridiomycetes** (phylum Chytridiomycota), or chytrids, produce sexual and asexual spores with flagella. **Zygomycetes** (phylum Zygomycota) produce thick-walled sexual spores called zygospores. **Glomeromycetes** (phylum Glomeromycota) do not reproduce sexually at all; instead, they have large, distinctive asexual spores, the largest of which are visible with the unaided eye.

The remaining two phyla, the **ascomycetes** (phylum Ascomycota) and the **basidiomycetes** (phylum Basidiomycota), are the most complex fungi. Their hyphae aggregate to form a **fruiting body,** a large, specialized, sexual spore-producing organ such as a mushroom, morel, puffball, or truffle. The two phyla differ, however, in the ways they produce sexual spores. Ascomycetes produce sexual spores in characteristic sacs, and basidiomycetes release sexual spores from club-shaped structures.

Why We Care — Don't Drink That Water

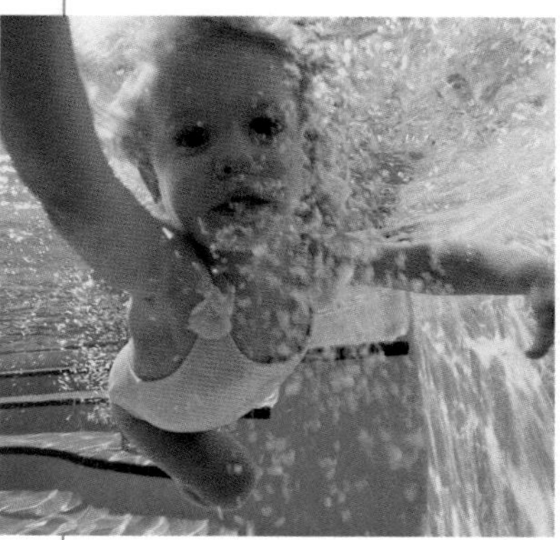

Cryptosporidium, or "crypto," is one example of a contagious microorganism that spreads easily in water. This apicomplexan protist lives in the intestinal tracts of infected humans, entering the body through the mouth and exiting in feces. It produces tough-walled cysts that can survive for days in the chlorinated water of public pools, water parks, splash pads, and other places where people gather to play in the water. Even tiny amounts of feces, invisible to the unaided eye, can contaminate water with *Cryptosporidium* cysts, triggering an outbreak.

Swimmers who accidentally swallow the tainted water typically become ill within a week, as cells released from the cysts invade the lining of the digestive tract. Symptoms include diarrhea, cramps, fever, vomiting, and dehydration.

Outbreaks occasionally occur in pools and other recreational water venues, where the victims are often young children who ingest the water. Simple preventive measures include keeping children with diarrhea out of the water, washing hands thoroughly after using the toilet or changing diapers, and showering before entering a pool.

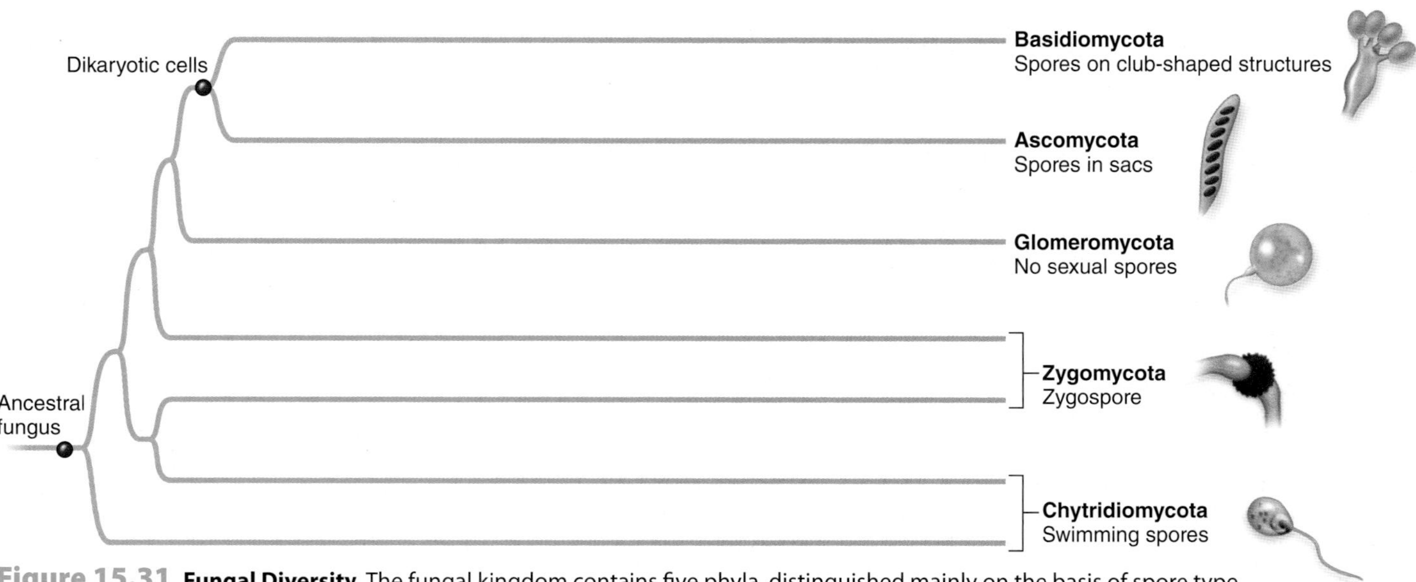

Figure 15.31 Fungal Diversity. The fungal kingdom contains five phyla, distinguished mainly on the basis of spore type.

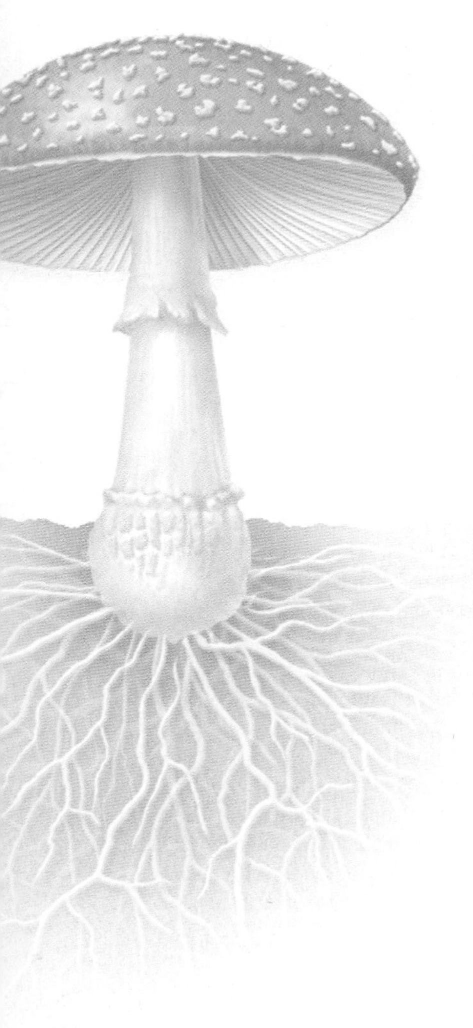

Figure 15.32 shows how the fruiting body fits into the basidiomycete life cycle. In step 1 of the life cycle, the fusion of two haploid hyphae creates a dikaryotic mycelium. The term *dikaryotic* means "two nuclei," and it refers to the fact that the nuclei from the two fused hyphae remain separate. This mycelium typically grows unseen within its food source. When environmental conditions are favorable, however, one or more mushrooms emerge (step 2).

Step 3 of the life cycle shows that numerous dikaryotic, club-shaped cells line the mushroom's gills. Inside each one, the haploid nuclei fuse, giving rise to a diploid zygote (step 4). The zygote immediately undergoes meiosis, yielding four haploid nuclei (step 5). Each nucleus migrates into a spore, which germinates after dispersal by wind or water (step 6). A new colony begins to grow.

Sometimes, a circle of mushrooms emerges from the ground all at once. The growth pattern of the underground mycelium explains this phenomenon. Hyphae extend outward in all directions from a colony's center. Mushrooms poke up at the margins of the mycelium, creating the "fairy rings" of folklore.

C. Fungi Interact with Other Organisms

Many people know that fungi can cause disease and turn foods moldy, so these organisms have a rather unsavory reputation. But this reputation is undeserved.

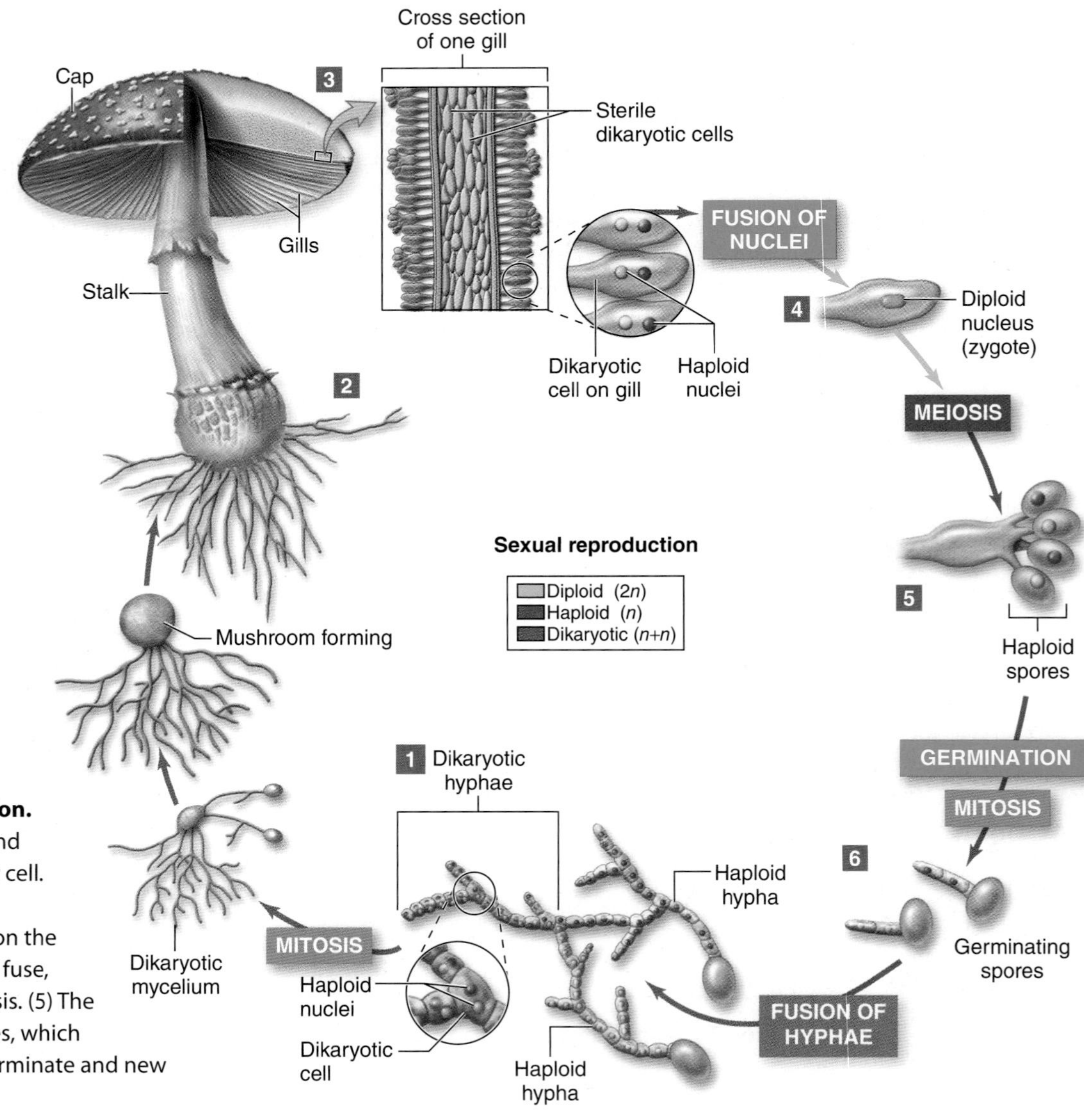

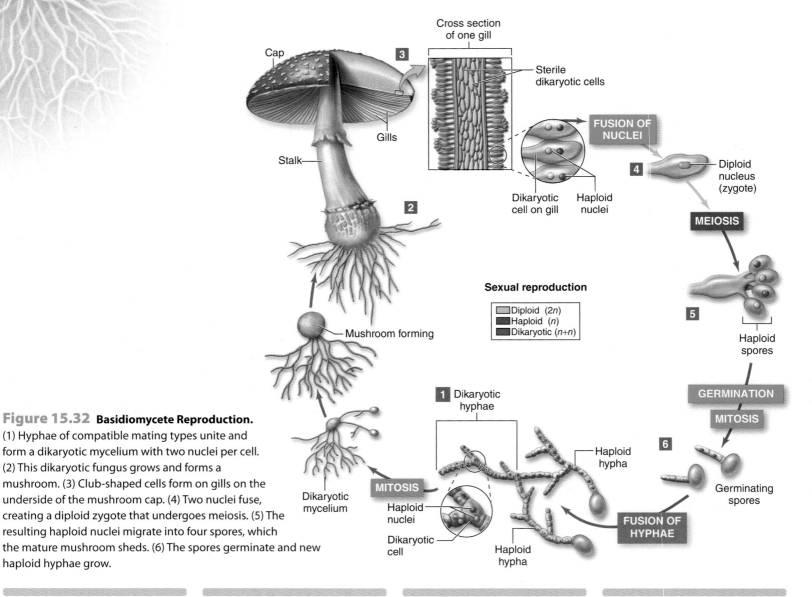

Figure 15.32 Basidiomycete Reproduction. (1) Hyphae of compatible mating types unite and form a dikaryotic mycelium with two nuclei per cell. (2) This dikaryotic fungus grows and forms a mushroom. (3) Club-shaped cells form on gills on the underside of the mushroom cap. (4) Two nuclei fuse, creating a diploid zygote that undergoes meiosis. (5) The resulting haploid nuclei migrate into four spores, which the mature mushroom sheds. (6) The spores germinate and new haploid hyphae grow.

Although some fungi do harm people, many others are beneficial. Here we profile a few interesting examples of fungi that affect our world.

Decomposers Many fungi secrete digestive enzymes that break down dead plants and animals, releasing inorganic nutrients and recycling them to plants. These decomposers are, in a sense, the garbage processors of the planet.

In forests, fungi that decay wood play a vital role in Earth's carbon cycle. Unfortunately, their talent for degrading the cellulose and lignin in fallen logs also makes them serious pests in another context: they cause dry rot in wooden wall studs and other building materials.

Likewise, most molds become obvious only when they are decaying our own foods and possessions. The general term *mold* includes many types of fungi. For example, a zygomycete called *Rhizopus stolonifer* forms a black fuzz on bread, fruits, and vegetables. Many of the common molds that ravage flood-damaged homes, however, are ascomycetes.

Figure 15.33 **Mushrooms Galore.** This man is picking mushrooms in a commercial "grow room."

Food and Medicine Commercial mushroom growers cultivate many edible fungi (figure 15.33). The white "button mushroom" is most familiar, but shiitakes, oyster mushrooms, and other basidiomycete species are commercially available as well. Ascomycetes called truffles and morels also are prized for their delicious flavors.

Fungi also find their way into the human diet in less obvious ways. For example, a species of the ascomycete *Penicillium* lends its sharp flavors to Roquefort cheese. Fermentation by yeasts such as *Saccharomyces* is essential for baking bread, brewing beer, and making wine. *Aspergillus oryzae,* another ascomycete, ferments soybean pulp to produce soy sauce. ▸ fermentation, p. 108

Other species of *Penicillium* are famous as well: they secrete penicillin, the first antibiotic discovered. Cyclosporine, a drug that suppresses the immune systems of organ transplant recipients, also comes from an ascomycete.

Plant and Animal Health Fungi cause a wide variety of diseases in plants and animals (figure 15.34). Figure 15.34a, for example, shows an ascomycete called a powdery mildew fungus, which causes a common disease of garden plants. Ascomycetes also cause most other fungal diseases of plants, including Dutch elm disease and chestnut blight.

Animals also suffer from fungal diseases. The dead moth in figure 15.34b is infected with an ascomycete called *Cordyceps.* The eerie yellow spikes protruding from the moth release the fungal spores, which may go on to infect another victim.

Infections with chytrids are contributing to the ongoing worldwide decline in amphibian populations (figure 15.34c). The fungus feeds on keratin in the frog's skin and coats the host's legs and undersides, impairing the frog's ability to breathe through its skin. The fungus spreads to new hosts by releasing swimming spores into the water. ▸ amphibians, p. 344

A few fungi threaten human health by causing mild to fatal infections, allergic reactions, or poisonings. For example, fungi can infect our skin, hair, and nails, causing ringworm, athlete's foot, and other irritating diseases. Some fungi, such as *Candida albicans,* inhabit the mucous membranes of the mouth, intestines, and vagina. Normally these fungi are harmless, but they can cause yeast infections under some conditions. Mold spores can trigger allergies. Moreover, some fungi are deadly poisonous, and others are hallucinogenic.

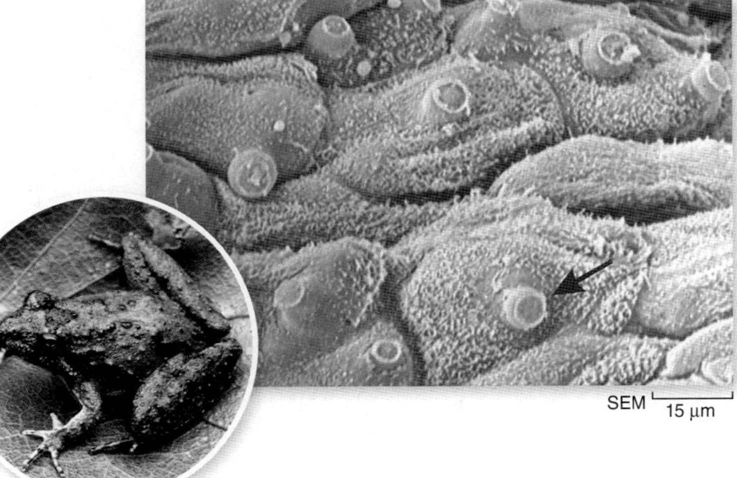

Figure 15.34 **Pathogenic Fungi.** (a) Powdery mildew fungi produce tiny reproductive structures (inset) on leaves. (b) *Cordyceps* fungi killed this moth. (c) Chytrids infect frog skin. The chytrid's swimming spores exit infected skin cells through small tubes (arrow).

Fungi Are Essential Decomposers

The Battle for Position in Cacao Tree Leaves

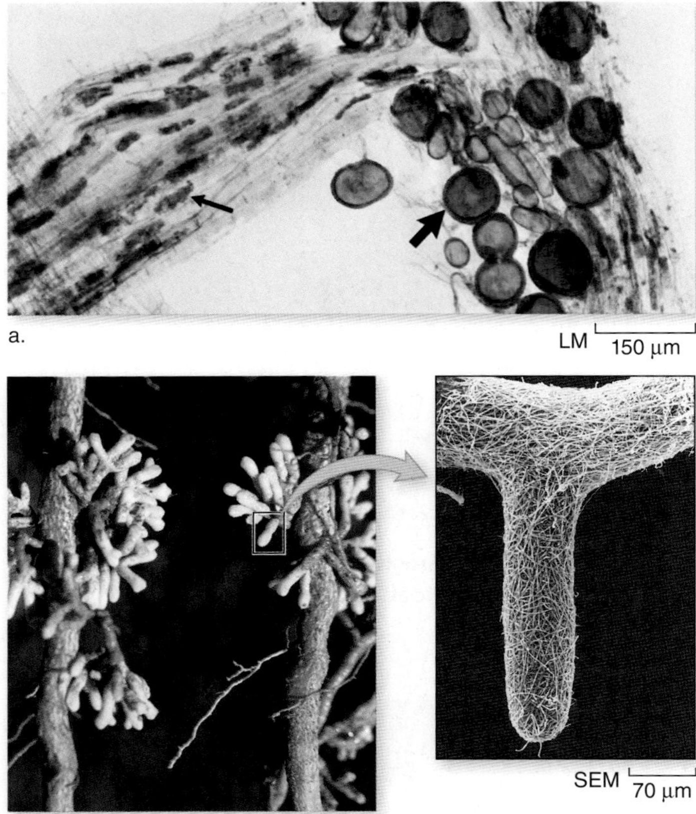

Figure 15.35 Mycorrhizae. (a) The arbuscules (small arrow) and spores (large arrow) of a glomeromycete fill this root. (b) The creamy white root tips of this buckthorn tree are colonized by a mycorrhizal fungus. Microscopic hyphae wrap around each root tip.

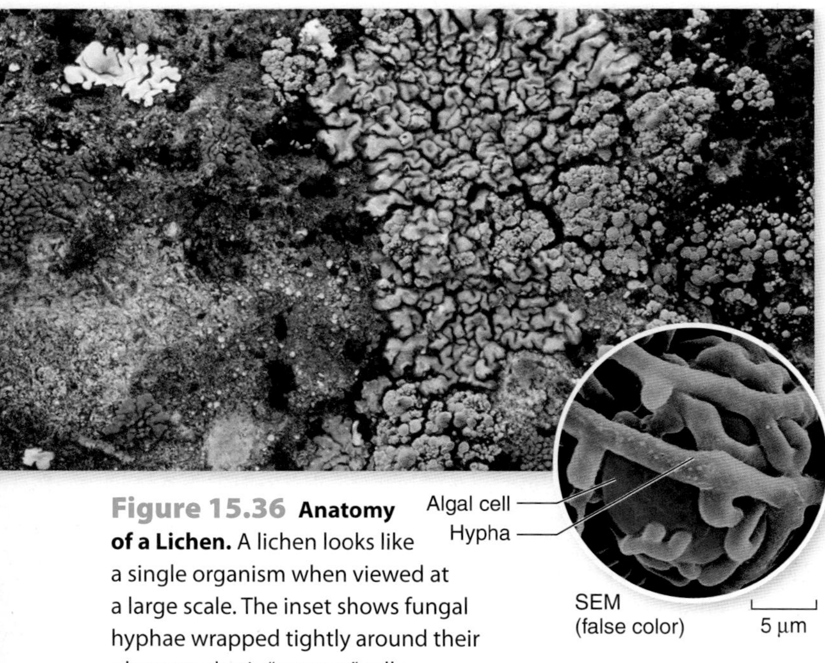

Figure 15.36 Anatomy of a Lichen. A lichen looks like a single organism when viewed at a large scale. The inset shows fungal hyphae wrapped tightly around their photosynthetic "partner" cells.

Endophytes and Mycorrhizae Not all fungi that colonize plant tissues are harmful. **Endophytes,** for example, are fungi that live among the cells of a plant's leaves and stems without triggering disease symptoms (*endo-* means inside, and *-phyte* means plant). Every known plant, from mosses to angiosperms, harbors endophytes. The ubiquity of endophytes has led some researchers to comment that "all plants are part fungi." Section 15.6 describes research showing that endophytes can help defend plants against disease.

Other plant-fungal partnerships occur belowground (figure 15.35). In a **mycorrhiza** (literally, "fungus-root"), fungal hyphae colonize plant roots in a way that benefits both partners. The hyphae extend into the soil, absorbing water and minerals that the fungus shares with the plant; in return, the fungus gains carbohydrates that the plant produces in photosynthesis. Some of the oldest known plant fossils show evidence of mycorrhizae, indicating that plants and fungi moved onto land together hundreds of millions of years ago.

Glomeromycetes form a type of mycorrhiza in which the exchange of materials occurs at structures called arbuscules; the fungus produces the arbuscules inside the root cells (figure 15.35a). Basidiomycetes and ascomycetes form a different type of mycorrhiza. In ectomycorrhizae, the fungal hyphae wrap around root tips (figure 15.35b).

Many edible fungi depend on their mycorrhizal relationships with live tree roots; these mushrooms are therefore difficult to cultivate commercially. The popularity and high price of these wild delicacies have lured many mushroom pickers into the woods. Scientists are debating whether the wild mushroom trade will harm populations of fungi—and the trees that rely on them—in the long term.

Lichens A **lichen** forms when a fungus, either an ascomycete or a basidiomycete, harbors green algae or cyanobacteria among its hyphae (figure 15.36). The photosynthetic partner contributes carbohydrates; the fungus absorbs water and essential minerals from the environment.

Lichens are sometimes called "dual organisms" because the two species—the fungus and its autotrophic partner—appear to be one individual when viewed with the unaided eye. The body forms can vary widely. Many lichens are colorful, flattened crusts, but others form upright structures that resemble mosses or miniature shrubs. Still others are long, scraggly growths that dangle from tree branches.

Just about any stable surface, from tree bark to boulders to soil, can support lichens. Polluted habitats, however, are hostile to lichens. Lichens absorb toxins but cannot excrete them. Toxin buildup hampers photosynthesis, and the lichen dies. Disappearance of native lichens is a sign that pollution is disturbing the environment; scientists therefore use lichens to monitor air quality.

15.5 Mastering Concepts

1. What combination of characteristics defines the fungi?
2. Describe how fungi acquire food.
3. Which features distinguish the five phyla of fungi?
4. Describe the life cycle of basidiomycetes.
5. How do fungi benefit humans?
6. In what ways are fungi important in ecosystems?
7. Compare and contrast endophytes, mycorrhizae, and lichens.

Investigating Life

15.6 The Battle for Position in Cacao Tree Leaves

Chocolate has many friends; its delectable flavor and healthful antioxidants make it a favorite food. But chocolate also has its enemies. Most of its adversaries are microbial pathogens of the cacao tree, *Theobroma cacao,* which is the source of cocoa (figure 15.37). Diseases such as frosty pod and witches' broom, for example, are the work of protists and fungi.

The Question: Plants deploy many defenses and weapons as they fight the never-ending battle against pathogens. Waxy leaf coverings and noxious chemicals, for example, deter many enemies. Nevertheless, endophytic fungi thrive in leaves without triggering the plant's defenses (see section 15.5).

What does the tree gain from allowing plant-eating fungi to thrive in its tissues? University of Arizona biologist A. Elizabeth Arnold, along with a research team at the Smithsonian Tropical Research Institute in Panama, hypothesized that the endophytes help protect cacao trees from disease.

The Approach: The team began by raising endophyte-free cacao plants in a greenhouse. Next, they sprayed a mixture of spores from several species of endophyte fungi on some of the leaves, so each tree had some treated leaves and some that remained free of the fungi.

A couple of weeks later, once the endophytes were thriving in the sprayed leaves, the researchers were ready to test their hypothesis. They inoculated both endophyte-treated and control leaves with spores of a water mold called *Phytophthora,* which causes black pod disease of cacao. After 15 days, Arnold and her team counted the number of dead leaves on each tree and measured the *Phytophthora*-damaged area on surviving leaves.

The Conclusion: Plant parts without endophytes lost twice as much leaf area as those with the resident fungi (figure 15.38). This finding provided evidence in support of the "bodyguard" hypothesis that Arnold and her colleagues had proposed.

Scientists are now trying to develop some of these cooperative endophytes into biological control agents that might prevent disease in cacao plants without the use of harmful chemicals. Our fungal allies are already living quietly in the stems and leaves of our crop plants. Perhaps one day farmers will enlist these friendly fungi in a more aggressive fight to preserve our chocolate fix.

Arnold, A. Elizabeth, Luis Carlos Mejia, Damond Kyllo, et al. December 23, 2003. Fungal endophytes limit pathogen damage in a tropical tree. *Proceedings of the National Academy of Sciences,* U.S.A., vol. 100, pages 15649–15654.

15.6 Mastering Concepts

1. How did the researchers test their hypothesis that endophytes help prevent plant disease?
2. This study used a mix of endophyte species. How would you design an experiment to determine whether one species of endophyte or some combination of multiple species protects the leaves against pathogens?
3. Endophytes were associated with a small but statistically significant reduction in cacao leaf disease. In what ways might this seemingly small difference be important to the plant?

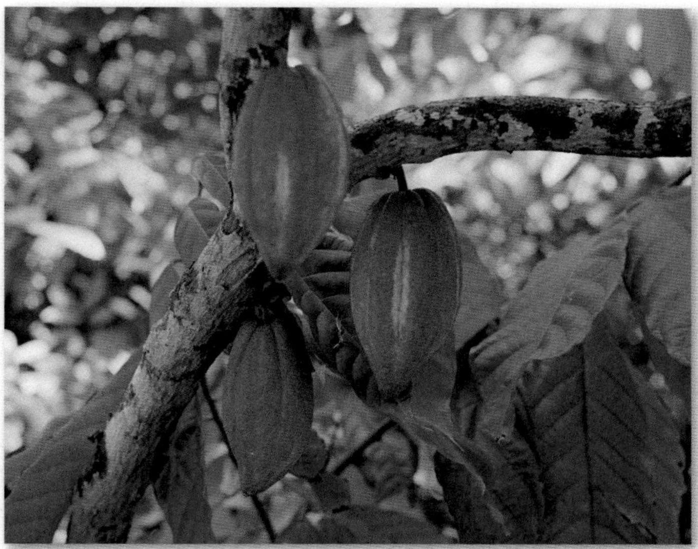

Figure 15.37 The Cacao Tree. The pods of *Theobroma cacao* are the source of chocolate.

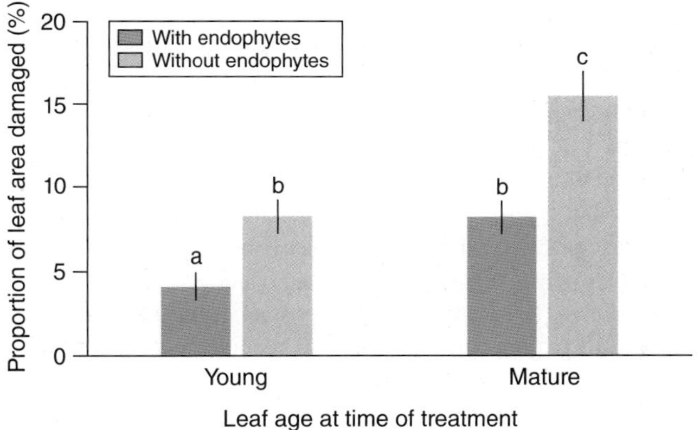

Figure 15.38 Helpful Partners. Endophytic fungi protected young and mature cacao leaves from damage by the pathogen *Phytophthora.*

Chapter Summary

15.1 Life's Origin Remains Mysterious

- Earth and the rest of the solar system formed about 4.6 BYA, and the oldest fossils occur in rocks from about 3.7 BYA. The **geologic timescale** describes these and other events in life's history.

A. Simple Organic Molecules May Have Formed in a Chemical "Soup"

- On early Earth, simple precursor chemicals may have combined to form life's organic building blocks.

B. Clays May Have Helped Monomers Form Polymers

- Amino acids and nucleotides may have formed proteins and nucleic acids on hot clay surfaces. The **RNA world** theory proposes that RNA preceded formation of the first cells.

C. Membranes Enclosed the First Protocells

- Phospholipids may have formed bubbles around proteins and nucleic acids, forming cell precursors (protocells).

D. Early Life Changed Earth Forever

- Early organisms permanently changed the physical and chemical conditions in which life continued to evolve.

15.2 Prokaryotes Are a Biological Success Story

A. What Is a Prokaryote?

- **Prokaryotes** (domains **Bacteria** and **Archaea**) have cells that lack nuclei.

B. Prokaryote Classification Traditionally Relies on Visible Features

- Prokaryotic cells contain DNA and **ribosomes,** and they are bounded by a cell membrane. The chromosome is in an area called the **nucleoid. Plasmids** are circles of DNA apart from the chromosome.
- Most prokaryotes have a **cell wall** made of **peptidoglycan.** The wall gives the cell its shape: a spherical **coccus,** rod-shaped **bacillus,** or spiral-shaped **spirillum.**
- External cell structures may include a carbohydrate-rich slime layer (or capsule), short projections called **pili,** and **flagella** that provide movement.
- Some bacteria survive harsh conditions by forming protective **endospores.**
- Prokaryotes may acquire carbon from inorganic sources **(autotrophs)** or organic sources **(heterotrophs);** energy sources include light **(phototrophs)** or chemicals **(chemotrophs).** Cells may require oxygen **(obligate aerobes),** die if oxygen is present **(obligate anaerobes),** or live in either condition **(facultative anaerobes).**

C. Prokaryotes Include Two Domains with Enormous Diversity

- Groups in domain Bacteria include proteobacteria, cyanobacteria, spirochaetes, and actinobacteria; domain Archaea contains methanogens, halophiles, thermophiles, and organisms that live in moderate conditions.

D. Bacteria and Archaea Are Essential to All Life

- All life depends on the bacteria and archaea that recycle organic matter and **fix nitrogen.** Humans harbor and use many beneficial microbes.

15.3 Eukaryotic Cells and Multicellularity Arose More Than a Billion Years Ago

- The internal membranes of **eukaryotic cells** may have formed when the outer membrane folded in on itself repeatedly.

A. Endosymbiosis Explains the Origin of Mitochondria and Chloroplasts

- The **endosymbiont theory** proposes that chloroplasts and mitochondria originated as bacteria that were engulfed by larger cells.

B. Multicellularity May Also Have Its Origin in Cooperation

- Multicellularity evolved multiple times in life's history.

15.4 Protists Are the Simplest Eukaryotes

A. What Is a Protist?

- **Protists** are eukaryotes that are not plants, fungi, or animals. Classification of protists is changing as molecular sequence data are considered.

B. Algae Are Photosynthetic Protists

- Photosynthesis by **algae** supports food webs and releases oxygen. The many lineages of algae include **dinoflagellates, diatoms, brown algae, red algae,** and **green algae.**

C. Some Heterotrophic Protists Were Once Classified as Fungi

- **Plasmodial slime molds, cellular slime molds,** and **water molds** are funguslike in some ways, but none is closely related to the fungi.

D. Protozoa Are Diverse Heterotrophic Protists

- Most **protozoa** are heterotrophs, and most have motile cells. Groups include **flagellated protozoa, amoeboid protozoa,** (including amoebae and the **foraminiferans), ciliates,** and **apicomplexans.**

15.5 Fungi Are Essential Decomposers

A. What Is a Fungus?

- **Fungi** are heterotrophs that produce chitin cell walls and glycogen.
- A fungal body includes a **mycelium** built of threads called **hyphae,** which may form a **fruiting body.**
- Fungi reproduce using asexual and sexual **spores.**

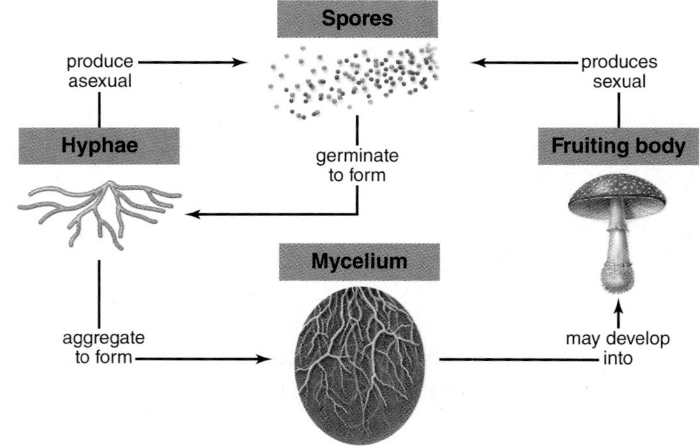

B. Fungal Classification Is Based on Reproductive Structures

- The five main groups of fungi are **chytridiomycetes, zygomycetes, glomeromycetes, ascomycetes,** and **basidiomycetes.** Each produces distinctive types of spores.

C. Fungi Interact with Other Organisms

- Many foods and antibiotics derive from fungi. Fungi have essential roles in ecosystems as decomposers. Most plant pathogens are fungi.
- Many fungal species form partnerships with photosynthetic organisms. **Endophytes** colonize plant leaves and stems without triggering disease symptoms; **mycorrhizae** are associations between fungi and roots; a **lichen** consists of a fungus that harbors cyanobacteria or green algae among its hyphae.

15.6 Investigating Life: The Battle for Position in Cacao Tree Leaves

- Experimental evidence indicates that endophytes protect cacao tree leaves from *Phytophthora* pathogens.

Multiple Choice Questions

1. Which of the following reflects the likely order of events in the origin of life?
   a. Endosymbiosis; RNA world; prokaryotic cells; multicellularity
   b. Prokaryotic cells; multicellularity; endosymbiosis; RNA world
   c. Endosymbiosis; prokaryotic cells; multicellularity; RNA world
   d. RNA world; prokaryotic cells; endosymbiosis; multicellularity
2. A *prokaryotic* cell is one that
   a. lacks DNA.
   b. has membrane-bounded organelles.
   c. lacks a nucleus.
   d. lacks a plasma membrane.
3. Which of the following processes occurs ONLY in prokaryotes?
   a. Nitrogen fixation
   b. Photosynthesis
   c. Asexual reproduction
   d. All of the above are correct.
4. Fungi are considered ______ because they get their carbon and energy from ______.
   a. photoautotrophs; photosynthesis
   b. chemoautotrophs; organic matter
   c. chemoheterotrophs; organic matter
   d. photoheterotrophs; photosynthesis
5. What is a lichen?
   a. A type of photosynthetic fungus
   b. A combination of a fungus and an alga or cyanobacterium
   c. A combination of two phyla of fungi
   d. A combination of a fungus and a root

Write It Out

1. Suppose someone hands you a microscope and a slide on which you can see single-celled organisms. Create a flowchart that you could use to identify the specimens as bacteria, algae, or yeasts.
2. Distinguish between the following pairs of terms: (a) phototroph and chemotroph; (b) autotroph and heterotroph; (c) obligate anaerobe and facultative anaerobe; (d) yeast and mycelium; and (e) mycorrhiza and lichen.
3. What adaptations in pathogenic bacteria enable them to cause disease?
4. How have humans harnessed the metabolic diversity of bacteria and archaea for practical purposes?
5. Use the Internet to learn how the federal government investigates outbreaks of foodborne illnesses such as *E. coli* O157:H7 and *Salmonella.* What can you do to protect yourself from food poisoning?
6. Describe the relationship between nutrient pollution and harmful algal blooms. Why might harmful algal blooms be more frequent in summer? What steps could coastal communities take to prevent nutrient pollution?
7. Explain why the fossil record for diatoms is much more complete than that of other protists, such as amoebas and slime molds.
8. Give examples of fungi that are important economically, ecologically, and as food for humans.
9. Hyphae are highly branched structures. How does their extensive surface area contribute to their functions?
10. Use the Internet to find examples of fungi that cause diseases in plants or animals. How does each fungus infect a host and spread to new hosts? What can humans do to fight each disease? What are the costs and benefits of doing so?

Pull It Together

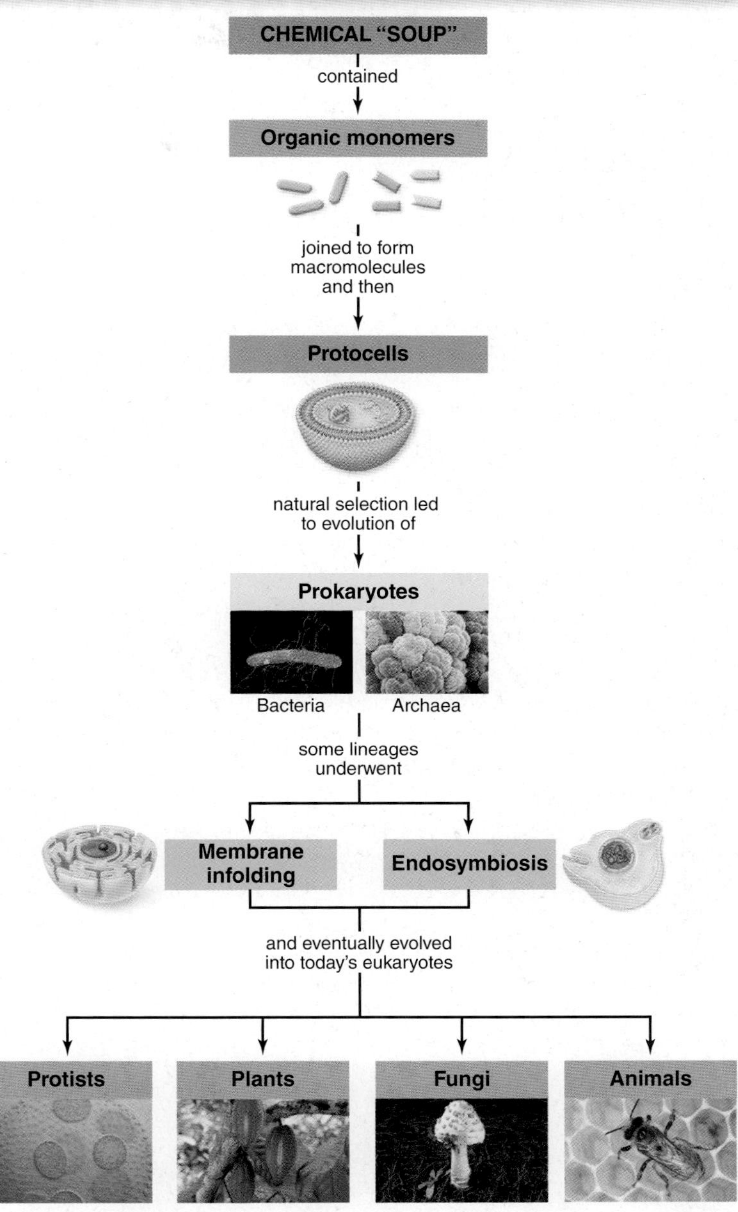

1. Review the structures of nucleic acids and proteins in chapter 2. Which chemical elements had to have been in the chemical "soup" to generate these organic molecules on early Earth?
2. List the evidence that supports the endosymbiont theory.
3. Which organisms in this concept map are heterotrophs, and which are autotrophs? Which groups contain both autotrophs and heterotrophs?
4. Add labeled arrows to this concept map that depict the relationships that connect (a) leaves and endophytes; (b) roots and mycorrhizal fungi; and (c) the fungal and photosynthetic partners in a lichen.

16 Evolution and Diversity of Plants

Peat Bog. *Sphagnum*, or peat moss, is a plant that grows in bogs. This man is cutting peat for fuel.

Learning Outline

16.1 Plants Have Changed the World
- A. Green Algae Are the Closest Relatives of Plants
- B. Plants Are Adapted to Life on Land

16.2 Bryophytes Are the Simplest Plants

16.3 Seedless Vascular Plants Have Xylem and Phloem but No Seeds

16.4 Gymnosperms Are "Naked Seed" Plants

16.5 Angiosperms Produce Seeds in Fruits

16.6 Investigating Life: Genetic Messages from Ancient Ecosystems

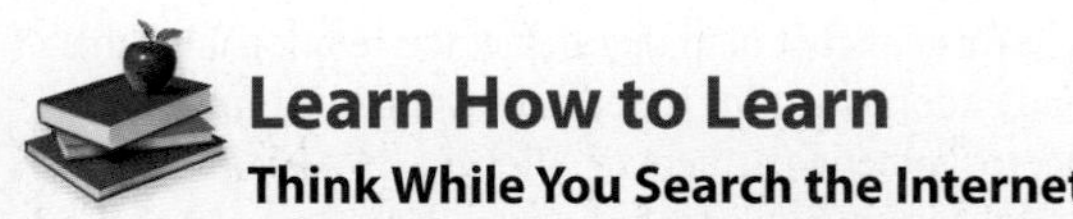

Learn How to Learn

Think While You Search the Internet

Your instructor may give you assignments that require you to find news or information on the Internet. You can use a search engine, but how do you know if the sites you find are credible? The Internet is full of misinformation, so you must evaluate every site you visit. Collaborative online encyclopedias such as Wikipedia may be unreliable because anyone can change any article. For other sites, ask the following questions. Are you looking at someone's personal page? Is there an educational, governmental, nonprofit, or commercial sponsor? Is the author reputable? Is the information up-to-date? Does the page contain facts or opinions? Are the facts backed up with documentation? Taking the time to find the answers to these questions will help ensure that the information you find is valid.

What's the Point?

Most people know that plants are essential to animal life. Vegetation provides the food and habitat that support nearly every ecosystem on land, and photosynthesis produces oxygen.

Yet plants serve us in many unexpected ways as well. Peat moss is an essential component of potting mix, the bark of a tree called the Pacific yew contains a cancer-fighting chemical, and cotton provides the fibers that make up T-shirts and towels. In the landscape and indoors, plants provide a beautiful variety of forms and textures. On a more utilitarian level, the roots of plants bind soil particles, preventing erosion and water pollution. Some plants even clean the soil by absorbing toxic wastes.

Plants are also useful in science. To name just one example, plants carry out many of the same chemical processes that occur in your own cells, including respiration. Plants, however, are much easier to grow and study in the laboratory than are animals. Biologists have therefore studied everything from inheritance to immunity to Alzheimer disease by observing the cells of plants.

LM 2 mm

Figure 16.1 Charophyte. This green alga, called *Chara*, may resemble the ancestors of land plants.

16.1 Plants Have Changed the World

If you glance at your surroundings in almost any outdoor setting, the first thing you see is plants: grasses, trees, shrubs, ferns, or mosses exist nearly everywhere, at least on land. Members of kingdom **Plantae** dominate habitats from moist bogs to parched deserts. They are so familiar that it is difficult to imagine a world without plants.

Today's plants transform the landscape, but their effect on the evolution of life has been even more dramatic. Plants are autotrophs: they use sunlight as an energy source to assemble CO_2 and H_2O into sugars (chapter 5 describes the reactions of photosynthesis). The sugars, in turn, provide the energy and raw materials that maintain and build a plant's body. Moreover, the chemical reactions of photosynthesis release oxygen gas, O_2, as a waste product. Animals and other organisms that use aerobic respiration need this gas; in addition, O_2 in the atmosphere helps form the ozone layer that protects life from the sun's harmful ultraviolet radiation.

Plants emerged onto land hundreds of millions of years ago. As they gradually expanded from the water's edge to the world's driest habitats, they formed the bases of intricate food webs, providing diverse habitats for many types of animals, fungi, and microbes. Herbivores consume living leaves, stems, roots, seeds, and fruits. Dead leaves accumulating on the soil surface feed countless soil microorganisms, insects, and worms. When washed into streams and rivers, this leaf litter supports a spectacular assortment of fishes and other aquatic animals.

From a human perspective, farms and forests provide the foods we eat, the paper we read, the lumber we use to build our homes, many of the clothes we wear, and some of the fuel we burn. (The Burning Question on page 308 introduces biofuels derived from plants.) The list goes on and on. It is amazing to think that plants do so much with such modest raw materials: sunlight, water, minerals, and CO_2.

A. Green Algae Are the Closest Relatives of Plants

All plants, from mosses to maple trees, are multicellular organisms with eukaryotic cells. With the exception of a few parasitic species, plants are autotrophs. A careful reading of section 15.4B, however, will reveal that some algae have the same combination of traits. Which of the many algal lineages, then, gave rise to plants?

The answer is that green algae and plants apparently share the most recent common ancestor. About 475 million years ago, during the Paleozoic era, one group of green algae related to today's **charophytes** likely gave rise to plants (figure 16.1). Evidence for this evolutionary connection includes chemical and structural similarities. For example, the chloroplasts of plants and green algae contain the same photosynthetic pigments (chlorophyll *a* and *b*). In addition, like green algae, plants have cellulose-rich cell walls and use starch as a nutrient reserve. Similar DNA sequences offer additional evidence of a close relationship. ▸▸ green algae, p. 293; polysaccharides, p. 34

Nevertheless, the body forms of algae are quite different from those of plants. Light, water, minerals, and dissolved gases surround the whole body of a submerged green alga, and the buoyancy of water provides physical support. In sexual reproduction, an alga simply releases gametes into the water, and the current carries the sex cells to another individual.

Now consider the selective forces on land, which are far different from those in water. On land, the water and minerals essential for plant growth are in the soil, and only the aboveground part of the plant is exposed to light. Air

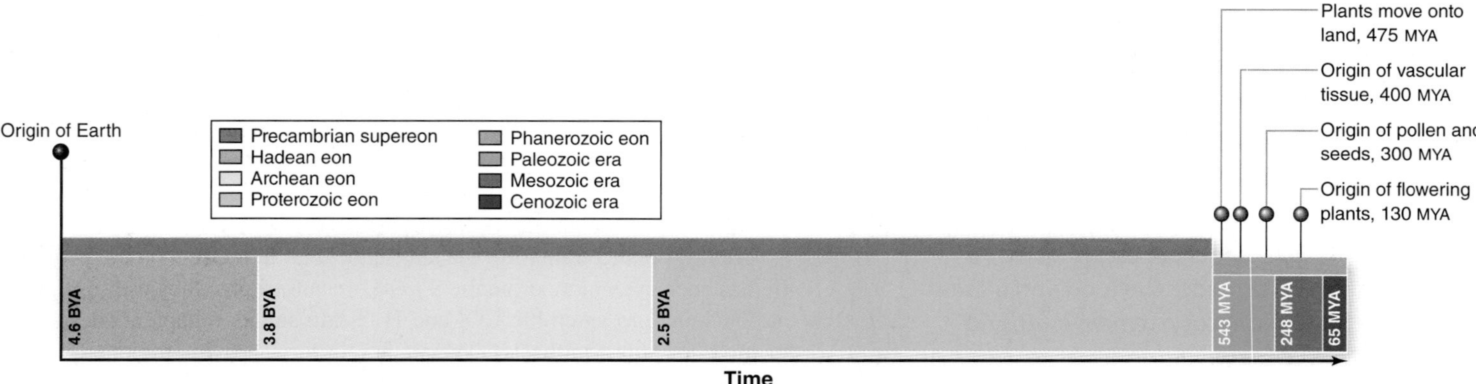

Figure 16.2 Highlights in the History of Plants. Plants moved onto land about 475 million years ago. Over time, some of their descendants acquired adaptations such as vascular tissue, pollen, seeds, and flowers. Each of these adaptations increased survival and reproductive success on dry land.

not only provides much less physical support than does water, but it also dries out the plant's aboveground tissues. Furthermore, the dispersal of gametes for sexual reproduction becomes more complicated on dry land.

These conditions gradually selected for unique adaptations in the body forms and reproductive strategies of plants (figure 16.2). As described in the rest of this section, biologists use some of these features to organize land plants into four main groups (figure 16.3): the bryophytes, seedless vascular plants, gymnosperms, and angiosperms.

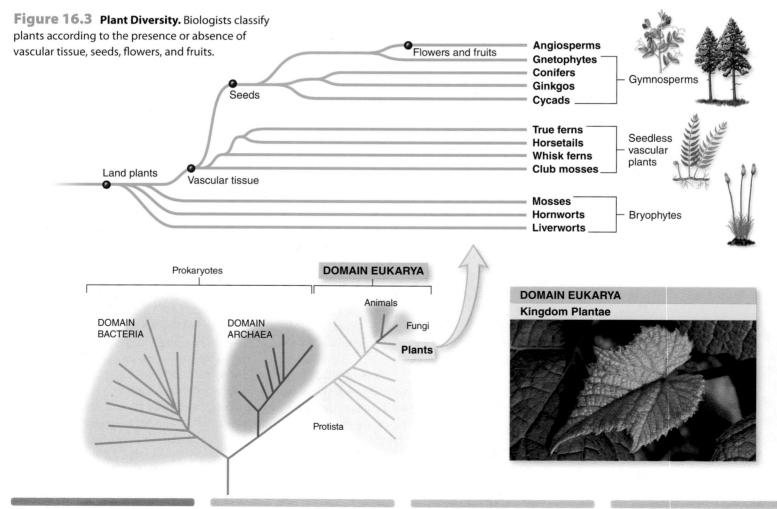

Figure 16.3 Plant Diversity. Biologists classify plants according to the presence or absence of vascular tissue, seeds, flowers, and fruits.

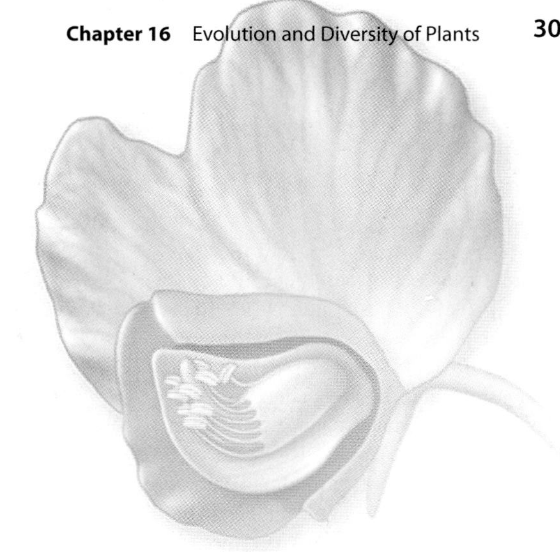

B. Plants Are Adapted to Life on Land

Figure 16.4 illustrates many of the adaptations that enable plants to grow upright, retain moisture, survive, and reproduce without being immersed in water. Refer to this figure frequently while reading the rest of this section.

Obtaining Resources A suite of adaptations enables plants to acquire light, CO_2, water, and minerals. Most plants, for example, have aboveground stems that support multiple leaves. The extensive surface area of the leaves maximizes exposure to sunlight and CO_2. Below the ground surface, highly branched root systems not only anchor the plant in the soil but also absorb water and minerals.

Water can also be scarce on land, and a plant that dries out will not survive. One water-conserving adaptation is the **cuticle,** a waxy coating that minimizes water loss from the aboveground parts of a plant. Dry habitats such as deserts select for extra-thick cuticles; plants in moist habitats typically have thin cuticles.

The waxy cuticle is impermeable not only to water but also to gases such as CO_2 and O_2. How do plants exchange these gases with the atmosphere? The answer is that the cuticle is interrupted by many **stomata,** which are pores in the epidermis of stems and leaves. Two guard cells surround each stoma and control whether the pore is open or closed. As gases diffuse through open stomata, water also escapes from the plant's tissues. Plants close the stomata in dry weather, minimizing water loss. ▸ plant epidermis, p. 432

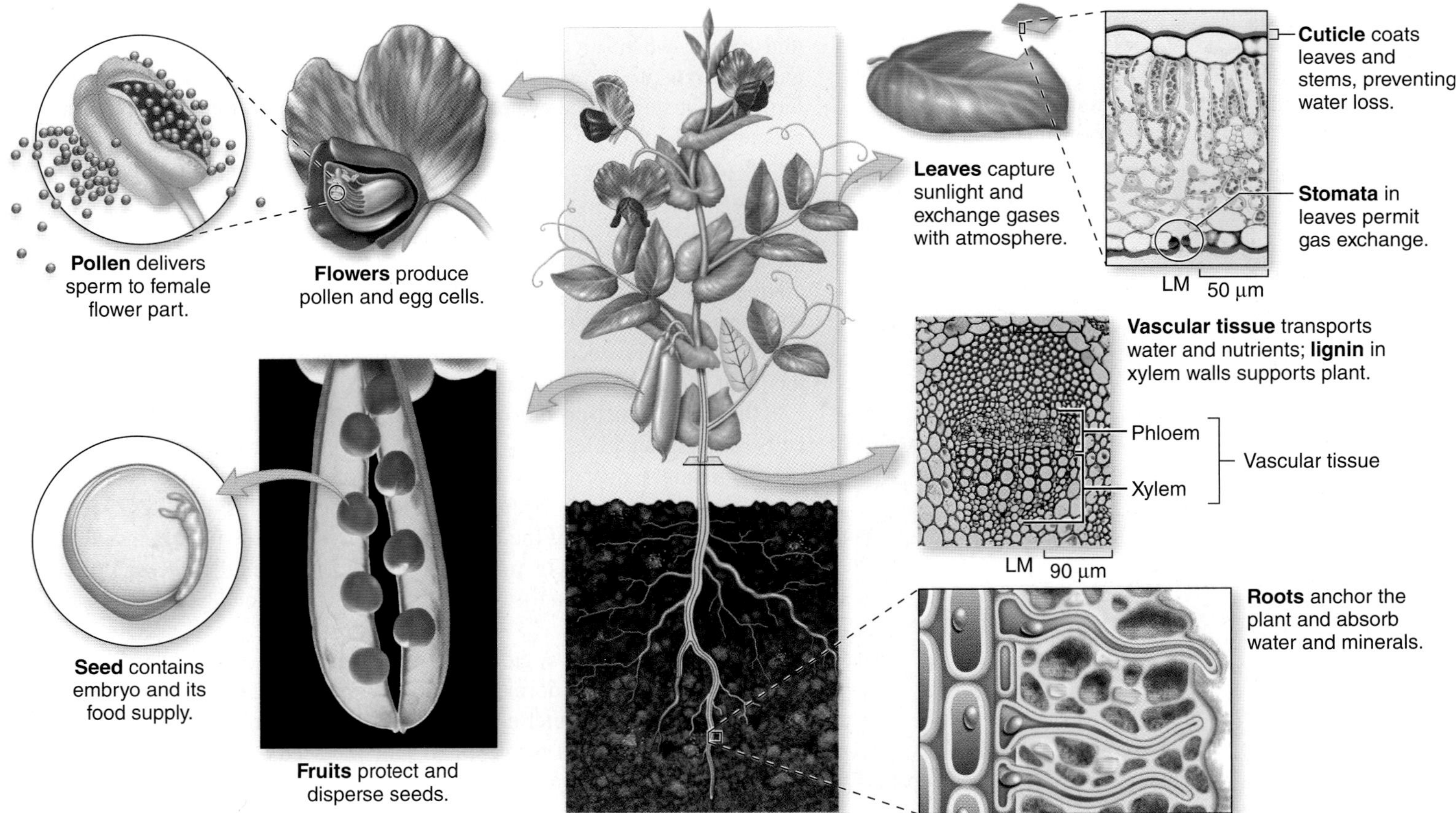

Pollen delivers sperm to female flower part.
Flowers produce pollen and egg cells.
Leaves capture sunlight and exchange gases with atmosphere.
Cuticle coats leaves and stems, preventing water loss.
Stomata in leaves permit gas exchange.
LM 50 µm
Vascular tissue transports water and nutrients; lignin in xylem walls supports plant.
Phloem
Xylem
Vascular tissue
LM 90 µm
Seed contains embryo and its food supply.
Fruits protect and disperse seeds.
Roots anchor the plant and absorb water and minerals.

Figure 16.4 Plant Adaptations. Pea plants have many features that support life on land.

Burning Questions

What are biofuels?

Biofuels are plant-based substitutes for fossil fuels. These alternative fuels can help decrease reliance on foreign petroleum and should help reduce CO_2 emissions and the associated problem of global climate change. ▶ global climate change, p. 415

Two types of biofuels are biodiesel and ethanol. As the name suggests, biodiesel is a diesel fuel substitute. Currently, most biodiesel comes from oil extracted from crushed soybeans or canola seeds. Ethanol, the other main biofuel, is a gasoline substitute. Corn kernels and sugarcane are the main sources of ethanol in the United States and Brazil.

To avoid driving up the price of food crops, researchers are looking for economical, nonfood sources of biofuels. The inedible stems of corn or of prairie grasses such as switchgrass would be ideal; bacterial and fungal enzymes easily break the cellulose in the plant cell walls into simple sugars to use in ethanol production. One problem, however, is that the stems also contain lignin, a complex molecule that interferes with cellulose extraction. So far, the heat and acid treatment needed to eliminate the lignin is too costly and inefficient to make cellulose-derived ethanol economical.

Biofuels are promising, but it is important to realize that they are not exactly "carbon-neutral." Most plants used in biofuel production require fertilizers and pesticides—both of which come from fossil fuels.

Submit your burning question to:
marielle_hoefnagels@mcgraw-hill.com

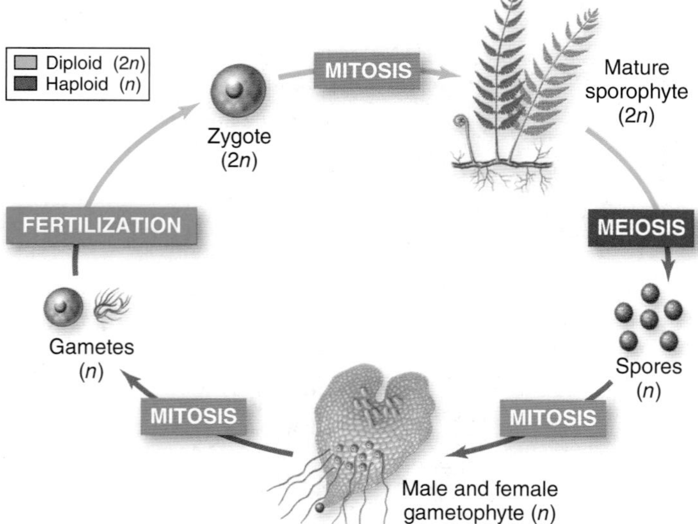

Figure 16.5 Alternation of Generations. Plants have multicellular haploid and diploid generations. Note the relationships among the diploid sporophyte, the spores, the haploid gametophyte, and the gametes.

Internal Transportation and Support The division of labor in a plant poses a problem: roots and other nonphotosynthetic parts need the food produced at the leaves. The leaves, in turn, need water and minerals from soil. In the simplest plants, the bryophytes, cell-to-cell diffusion meets these needs. Other plants, however, have **vascular tissue,** a collection of tubes that transport sugar, water, and minerals throughout the plant. Fossil evidence suggests that the earliest species of vascular plants originated in the Devonian period, about 400 million years ago (see figure 13.2).

The two types of vascular tissue are xylem and phloem. **Xylem** (pronounced "zy-lem") is composed of dead, empty cells that conduct water and dissolved minerals from roots to leaves. **Phloem** (pronounced "flow-um") consists of live cells that transport sugars produced in photosynthesis to the roots and other nongreen parts of the plant. This internal transportation system has supported the evolution of specialized roots, stems, and leaves, many of which have adaptations that enable plants to exploit extremely dry habitats.

In addition, xylem is rich in **lignin,** a complex polymer that strengthens cell walls. The additional support from lignin means that vascular plants can grow tall and form branches. This increase in size was adaptive because taller plants have the edge over their shorter neighbors in the competition for sunlight. Larger plants, including trees, also triggered evolutionary changes in other organisms by providing new habitats and more diverse food sources for arthropods, vertebrates, and other land animals.

Reproduction Plants and green algae have a life cycle called **alternation of generations,** in which a multicellular diploid stage alternates with a multicellular haploid stage (figure 16.5). The **sporophyte** (diploid) generation develops from a zygote that forms when gametes come together at fertilization. In a mature sporophyte, some cells undergo meiosis and produce haploid spores, which divide mitotically to form the gametophyte. The haploid **gametophyte** produces gametes by mitotic cell division; these sex cells fuse at fertilization, starting the cycle anew. (Read more about mitosis and meiosis in chapters 8 and 9.)

A prominent trend among land plants is a change in the relative sizes and independence of the gametophyte and sporophyte generations (figure 16.6). In a bryophyte such as a moss, for example, the brown sporophyte depends on the green gametophyte for nutrition. In more complex plants, the sporophyte generation is photosynthetic and much larger than the gametophytes. Ferns, pines, and flowering plants have gametophytes that range from microscopic to barely visible with the unaided eye. Keep this evolutionary trend in mind as you study the plant life cycles in this chapter.

Plant reproduction has other variations as well. The swimming sperm cells of mosses and ferns require a film of free water to reach an egg, limiting the distance over which gametes can spread. Gymnosperms and angiosperms can reproduce over far greater distances, thanks to pollen (see figure 16.4). **Pollen** consists of the male gametophytes of seed plants; each pollen grain produces sperm. In **pollination,** wind or animals deliver pollen directly to female plant parts, eliminating the need for free water in sexual reproduction.

Gymnosperms and angiosperms also share another reproductive adaptation: seeds. A **seed** is a dormant plant embryo packaged together with a food supply inside a tough outer coat that prevents moisture loss. The food supply sustains the young plant between the time the seed germinates and when the seedling begins photosynthesis.

The origin of pollen and seeds occurred about 300 million years ago, during the Permian period (see figure 13.2). This was a significant event

	Bryophytes	Seedless vascular plants	Gymnosperms	Angiosperms
GAMETOPHYTE				
Size relative to sporophyte?	Varies	Small	Microscopic	Microscopic
Depends on sporophyte for nutrition?	No	No	Yes	Yes
SPOROPHYTE				
Size relative to gametophyte?	Varies	Large	Large	Large
Depends on gametophyte for nutrition?	Yes	No	No	No

Figure 16.6 Changes in the Generations. As plants became more complex, the gametophyte generation was reduced to just a few cells that depend on the sporophyte for nutrition.

in the evolution of plants. The spores of mosses and ferns—the seedless plants—take little energy to produce, but they are short-lived and tend to remain relatively close to the parent plant. The gymnosperms and angiosperms, in contrast, can disperse their gametes and seeds over long distances and in dry conditions. Moreover, seeds can remain dormant for years, germinating when conditions are favorable. Pollen and seeds therefore give gymnosperms and angiosperms a competitive edge over seedless plants in many habitats.

Two additional reproductive adaptations occur only in the angiosperms: flowers and fruits. **Flowers** are reproductive structures that produce pollen and egg cells. After fertilization, parts of the flower develop into a **fruit** that contains the seeds. Flowers and fruits help angiosperms protect and disperse both their pollen and their offspring.

Fossil evidence places the origin of angiosperms in the early Cretaceous period, at least 130 million years ago. Their adaptations were spectacularly successful. Angiosperms now far outpace all other plants, both in numbers and in species diversity.

16.1 Mastering Concepts

1. How have plants changed the landscape, and how are they vital to life today?
2. What evidence suggests that plants evolved from green algae?
3. What are the functions of the cuticle and stomata?
4. How does vascular tissue adapt plants to land?
5. Describe the reproductive adaptations of plants.
6. What features differentiate the four major groups of plants?

16.2 Bryophytes Are the Simplest Plants

Bryophytes are seedless plants that lack vascular tissue. Without vascular tissue and lignin, bryophytes lack the physical support to grow very large. Bryophytes are therefore small, compact plants in which each cell absorbs minerals and water directly from its surroundings. Materials move from cell to cell within the plant by diffusion and osmosis, not within specialized transport tissues.

Although bryophytes lack true leaves and roots, many have structures that are similar to these organs. For example, photosynthesis occurs at flattened leaflike areas. In addition, hairlike extensions called rhizoids cover a bryophyte's lower surface, anchoring the plant to its substrate. These rhizoids, however, cannot tap distant sources of water when conditions turn dry. Many species are therefore restricted to moist, shady habitats that are unlikely to dry out. Others tolerate periods of drought by entering dormancy until moisture returns.

Biologists classify the 24,000 or so species of bryophytes into three phyla (figure 16.7):

- **Liverworts** (phylum Marchantiophyta) have flattened leaflike gametophytes. The diverse liverworts may be the bryophytes most closely related to ancestral land plants.
- **Hornworts** (phylum Anthocerotophyta) are named for their sporophytes, which are shaped like tapered horns.
- **Mosses** (phylum Bryophyta) are the closest living relatives to the vascular plants. The gametophytes resemble short "stems" with many "leaves." The brown or green sporophyte looks nothing like the gametophyte.

Figure 16.8 shows the life cycle of a moss. The sporophyte is a stalk attached to the leafy gametophyte. At the tip of the stalk, specialized cells inside a sporangium undergo meiosis and produce haploid spores. After the spores are released, they germinate, giving rise to new haploid gametophytes. Gametes form by mitosis in separate sperm- and egg-producing structures on the gametophyte. Sperm swim to the egg cell in water that coats the plants. The sporophyte generation begins at fertilization, with the formation of the diploid zygote. This cell divides mitotically, producing the sporophyte's stalk.

Bryophytes play important roles in ecosystems. For example, mosses can survive on bare rock or in a very thin layer of soil. As their tissues die, they

Figure 16.7 A Gallery of Bryophytes. (a) The gametophyte of this liverwort resembles small leaves. The umbrella-shaped structures produce sperm and egg cells. (b) In the hornwort *Anthoceros,* the tapered hornlike structures are sporophytes, below which the flat gametophytes are visible. (c) Short sporophytes, topped with dark capsules, peek above the gametophytes of *Sphagnum* moss.

a.

b.

c.

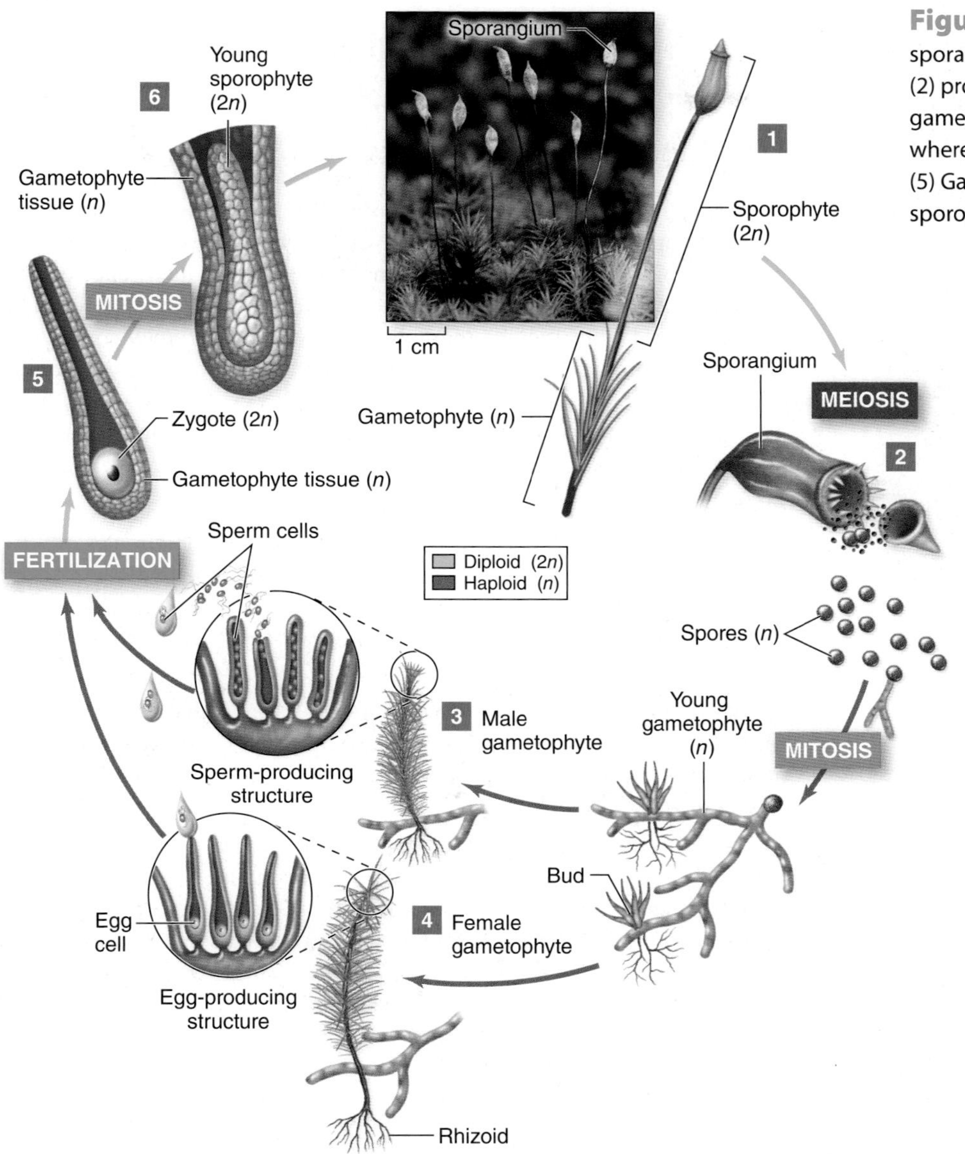

Figure 16.8 Sexual Reproduction in a Bryophyte. (1) In the sporangium at the tip of a sporophyte, cells undergo meiosis and (2) produce haploid spores that generate the male and female gametophytes. (3) Male gametophytes produce swimming sperm, whereas (4) egg cells are produced at the female gametophyte tip. (5) Gametes join and form a zygote, which (6) develops into a new sporophyte.

contribute organic matter that helps build soil. Larger plants subsequently colonize the soil, triggering other changes in the ecosystem. A similar process occurs in forest canopies, where bryophytes living on tree limbs help build an organic soil that sustains entire communities of tree-dwelling organisms.

Mosses also find many human uses. Gardeners and houseplant lovers recognize peat moss as a major ingredient in potting mixes. Peat comes from partially decomposed sphagnum moss harvested from enormous bogs (see the chapter opening photo). The dried moss is unusually spongy, absorbing 20 times its weight in water. When mixed with soil, peat slowly releases water to plant roots. People also burn peat as cooking fuel or to generate electricity.

16.2 Mastering Concepts

1. Describe the three main groups of bryophytes.
2. Name two reasons mosses usually live in moist, shady habitats.
3. How do bryophytes reproduce?

a. b.

c. d. e.

Figure 16.9 A Gallery of Seedless Vascular Plants. (a) The club moss *Lycopodium obscurum* produces upright stems. (b) The spike moss *Selaginella martensii* has scalelike foliage. (c) Yellowish spore-producing structures are visible on this whisk fern, *Psilotum nudum.* (d) *Equisetum telmateia* is a horsetail. (e) The long beech fern *(Thelypteris phegopteris)* is a true fern.

16.3 Seedless Vascular Plants Have Xylem and Phloem but No Seeds

The 12,000 or so species of **seedless vascular plants** have xylem and phloem but do not produce seeds. Unlike the bryophytes, the seedless vascular plants typically have true roots, stems, and leaves. In many species, the leaves and roots arise from underground stems called rhizomes (not to be confused with the rhizoids of bryophytes). Rhizomes sometimes also store carbohydrates that provide energy for the growth of new leaves and roots.

The seedless vascular plants include four main lineages, divided among two phyla (figure 16.9):

- **Club mosses** (phylum Lycopodiophyta) are small plants in genus *Lycopodium.* These plants have simple leaves that resemble scales or needles, and the name reflects their club-shaped reproductive structures. Their close relatives are the spike mosses *(Selaginella).* Collectively, club mosses and spike mosses are sometimes called lycopods.
- **Whisk ferns** (phylum Pteridophyta) are simple plants that have rhizomes but not roots. Most species have no obvious leaves. Their name comes from the highly branched stems of *Psilotum,* which resemble whisk brooms.
- **Horsetails** (phylum Pteridophyta) grow along streams or at the borders of forests. The only living genus of horsetails, *Equisetum,* includes plants with branched rhizomes that give rise to green stems bearing spores at their tips. Horsetails are also called scouring rushes because their stems and leaves contain abrasive silica particles. Native Americans used horsetails to polish bows and arrows, and early colonists and pioneers used them to scrub pots and pans.
- **True ferns** (phylum Pteridophyta) make up the largest group of seedless vascular plants, with about 11,000 species. The fronds, or leaves, of ferns are their most obvious feature; some species are popular as ornamental plants. Ferns were especially widespread and abundant during the Carboniferous period, when their huge fronds dominated warm, moist forests. Their remains form most coal deposits.

Figure 16.10 illustrates the life cycle of a fern. The sporophyte produces haploid spores by meiosis in collections of sporangia on the underside of each frond. Once shed, the spores germinate and develop into tiny, heart-shaped gametophytes that produce gametes by mitotic cell division. The swimming sperm require a film of free water to reach the egg cell. The gametes fuse, forming a zygote. This diploid cell divides mitotically and forms the sporophyte, which quickly dwarfs the gametophyte.

Many seedless vascular plants live in shady, moist habitats. Like bryophytes, these plants cannot reproduce sexually in the absence of free water. Most live on land, where their roots and rhizomes help stabilize soil and prevent erosion. But not all species are terrestrial. The tiny fern *Azolla* lives in water, where its leaves house cyanobacteria that fix nitrogen. In Asia, rice farmers cultivate *Azolla* to help fertilize their crops. ▸ nitrogen fixation, p. 401

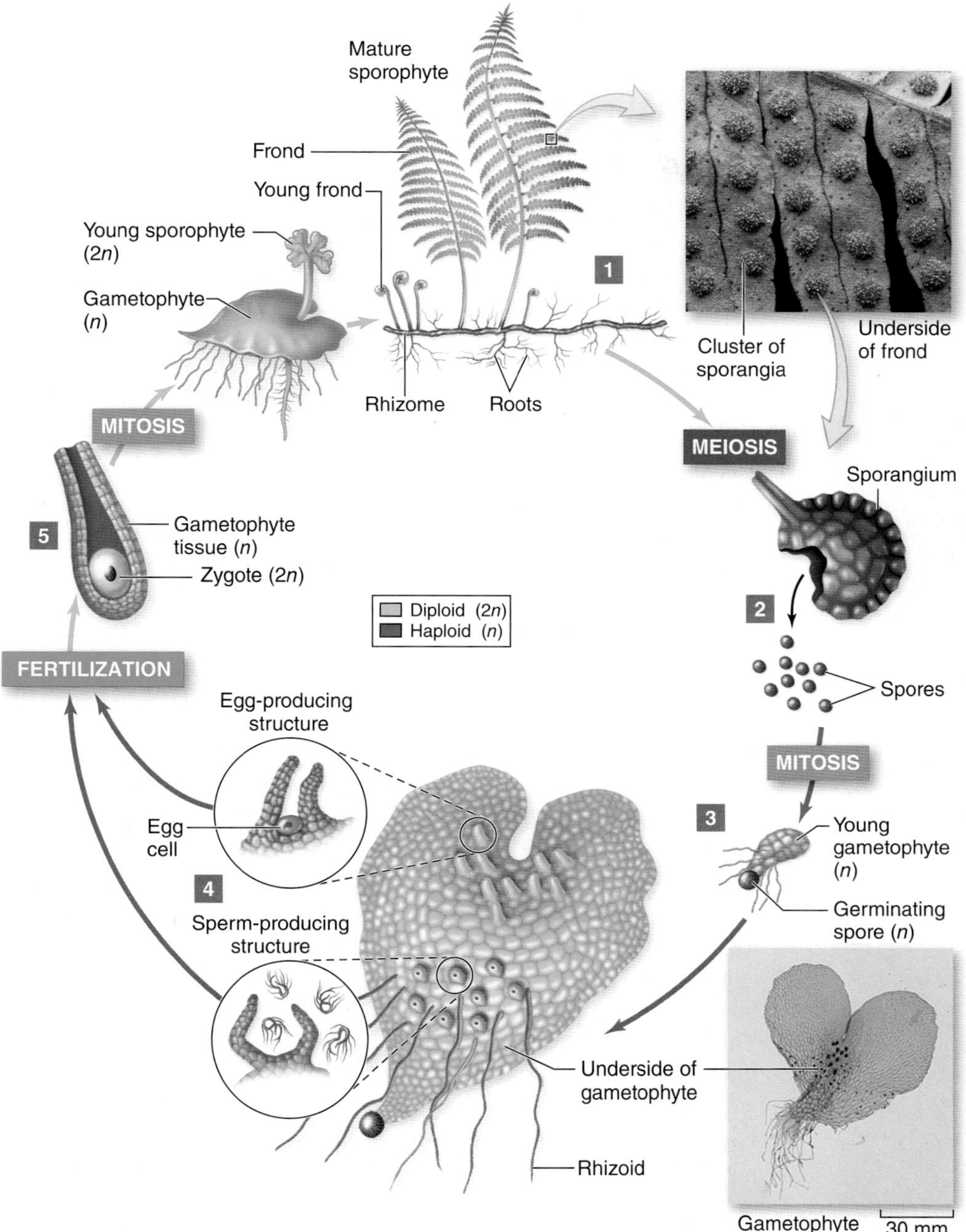

Figure 16.10 **Sexual Reproduction in a True Fern.** (1) Sporangia on sporophyte fronds house cells that (2) produce spores through meiosis. (3) A haploid spore develops into a gametophyte, which (4) produces egg cells and swimming sperm. (5) These gametes join and produce a zygote, which develops into the sporophyte.

16.3 Mastering Concepts

1. Describe the four groups of seedless vascular plants.
2. How do seedless vascular plants reproduce?
3. How are seedless vascular plants similar to and different from bryophytes?

16.4 Gymnosperms Are "Naked Seed" Plants

The first seed plants were gymnosperms. The term **gymnosperm** derives from the Greek words *gymnos,* meaning "naked," and *sperma,* meaning "seed." The seeds of these plants are "naked" because they are not enclosed in fruits.

Living gymnosperms are remarkably diverse in reproductive structures and leaf types. The sporophytes of most gymnosperms are woody trees or shrubs, although a few species are more vinelike. Leaf shapes range from tiny reduced scales to needles, flat blades, and large fernlike leaves. The 800 or so species of gymnosperms group into four phyla (figure 16.11):

- **Cycads** (phylum Cycadophyta) live primarily in tropical and subtropical regions. They have palmlike leaves, and they produce large cones. Many cycads are planted as ornamentals, but only two species are native to the United States. Cycads dominated Mesozoic era landscapes. Today, many species are near extinction because of their slow growth, low reproductive rates, and shrinking habitats.
- The **ginkgo** (phylum Ginkgophyta), also called the maidenhair tree, has distinctive, fan-shaped leaves. Only one species exists: *Ginkgo biloba.* It no longer grows wild in nature, but it is a popular cultivated tree. Ginkgos have male and female organs on separate plants; landscapers avoid planting female ginkgo trees because the fleshy seeds produce a foul odor. Although clinical trials have not conclusively supported its medical benefits, some people believe that extracts of *Ginkgo biloba* leaves may improve memory and concentration.
- **Conifers** (phylum Pinophyta) are by far the most familiar gymnosperms. These plants often have needlelike or scalelike leaves, and they produce egg cells and pollen in cones. Conifers are commonly called "evergreens" because most retain their leaves all year, unlike deciduous trees. This term is somewhat misleading, however, because conifers do shed their needles. They just do it a few needles at a time, turning over their entire needle supply every few years.
- **Gnetophytes** (phylum Gnetophyta) include some of the most distinctive (if not bizarre) of all seed plants. Botanists have struggled with the classification of these plants. Some details of their life history have led to speculation that gnetophytes are closely related to the flowering plants. Molecular evidence, however, places these puzzling plants with the conifers. *Ephedra* is a gnetophyte, as is *Welwitschia,* a slow-growing plant that lives in African deserts. Mature *Welwitschia* plants have a single pair of large, strap-shaped leaves that persist throughout the life of the plant.

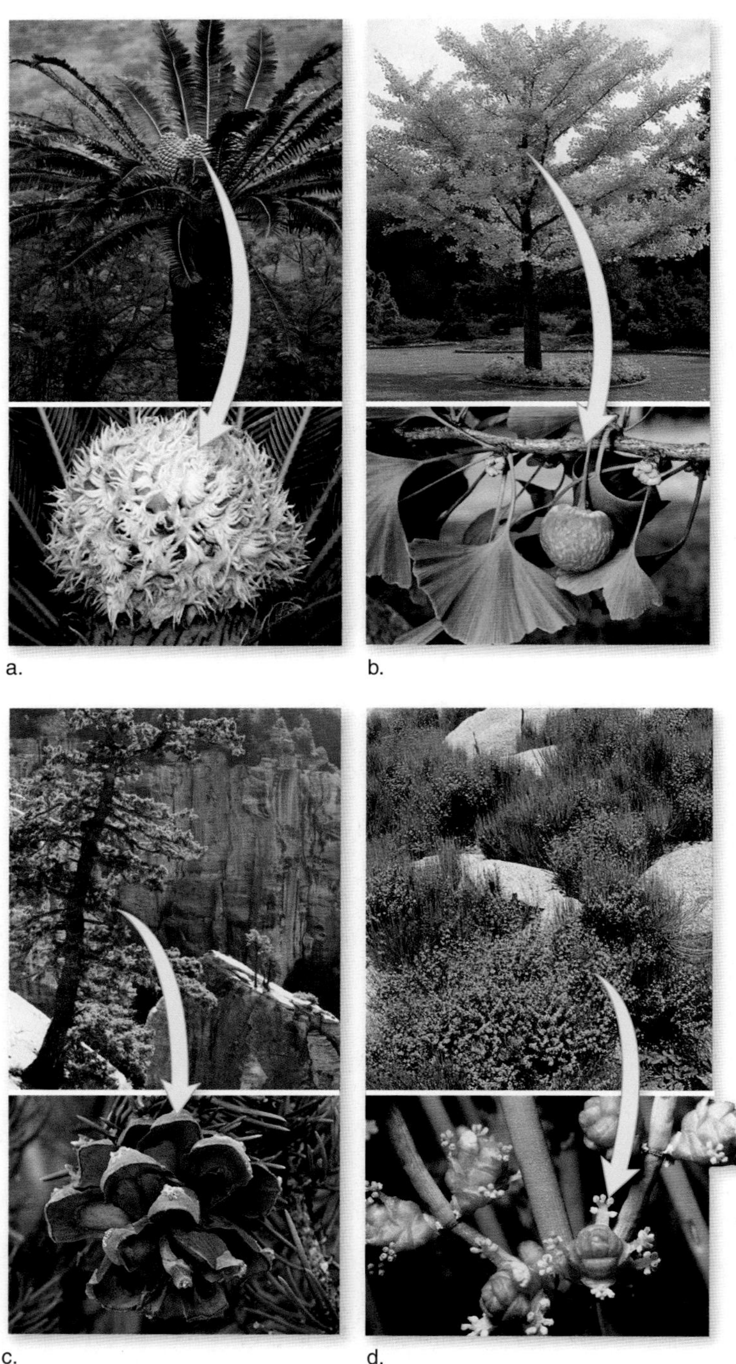

Figure 16.11 A Gallery of Gymnosperms. (a) Cycads are ancient seed plants with cones that form in the center of a crown of large leaves. A seed cone is shown here. (b) The leaves of *Ginkgo biloba* turn yellow in the fall. The lower photo shows the fleshy seed. (c) This pinyon pine is an example of a conifer. The seed cone has woody scales. (d) *Ephedra* is a gnetophyte with cones that resemble tiny flowers.

Pines illustrate the gymnosperm life cycle (figure 16.12). In these plants, **cones** are the organs that bear the reproductive structures. Large female cones bear two sporangia, called **ovules,** on the upper surface of each scale. Through meiosis, each ovule produces four haploid structures called megaspores, only one of which develops into a female gametophyte. Over many months, the female gametophyte undergoes mitosis and gives rise to two to six egg cells. At the same time, small male cones bear sporangia on thin, delicate scales. These sporangia undergo meiosis and produce microspores, which eventually become wind-blown pollen grains (immature male gametophytes). Pollination occurs when pollen grains settle between the scales of female cones and adhere to drops of a sticky secretion.

The pollen grain then germinates, giving rise to a pollen tube that grows through the ovule toward the egg cell. Two haploid sperm nuclei develop inside the pollen

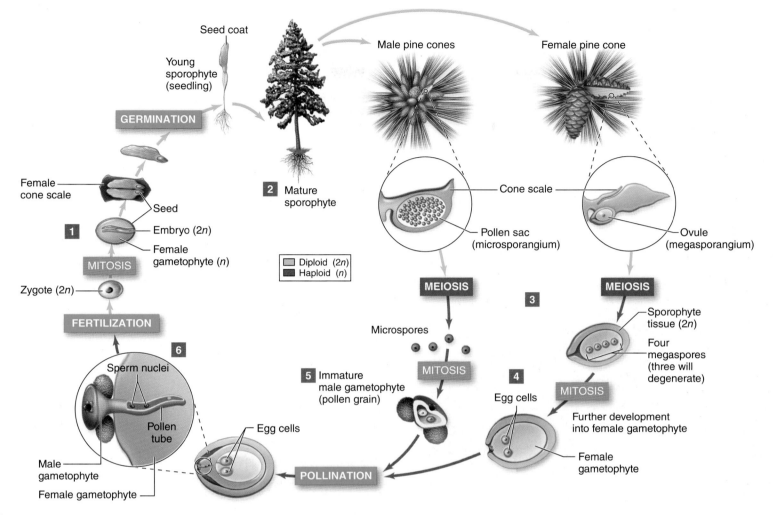

Figure 16.12 Sexual Reproduction in Pines. (1) A pine tree's seed contains the embryo, or young diploid sporophyte. (2) The seed germinates, and the sporophyte grows into a mature, cone-producing tree. (3) Cells in the male and female cone scales undergo meiosis, producing spores that develop into haploid gametophytes consisting of just a few cells each. (4) On the female cones, each scale has two ovules (only one is shown), each of which yields an egg-producing gametophyte. (5) The male cones produce pollen, the male gametophytes. (6) A pollen grain delivers a sperm nucleus to an egg cell via a pollen tube. More than a year later, each fertilized egg (zygote) completes its development into a seed.

tube; one sperm nucleus fertilizes the haploid egg cell, and the other disintegrates. The resulting zygote is the first cell of the sporophyte generation. The whole process is so slow that fertilization occurs about 15 months after pollination.

Within the ovule, the haploid tissue of the female gametophyte nourishes the developing diploid embryo. The embryo soon becomes dormant, and the ovule develops a tough, protective seed coat. The seed may remain in the cone for another year. Eventually, however, the seed is shed and dispersed by wind or animals. If conditions are favorable, the seed germinates, giving rise to a new tree.

16.4 Mastering Concepts

1. What are the characteristics of gymnosperms?
2. What are the four groups of gymnosperms?
3. What is the role of cones in conifer reproduction?
4. What happens during and after pollination in gymnosperms?

16.5 Angiosperms Produce Seeds in Fruits

The **angiosperms,** or flowering plants (phylum Magnoliophyta), make up 95% of all modern plant species. Examples include apple trees, corn, roses, petunias, lilies, grasses, and many other familiar plants, including those we grow for our food.

Many people think of flowers only as decorations for the human habitat. Although many ornamental plants are the products of selective breeding for their spectacular blooms, not all flowers are showy, sweet-smelling beauties (figure 16.13). The flowers of wind-pollinated plants such as grasses, for example, are plain and easily overlooked.

Biologists are still working to sort out the evolutionary relationships among the angiosperms. The two largest groups are the eudicots and the monocots, which together account for about 97% of all flowering plants. The **eudicots** have two cotyledons (the first leaf structures to arise in the embryo), and their pollen grains feature three or more pores. About 175,000 species exist. The diverse eudicots include roses, daisies, sunflowers, oaks, tomatoes, beans, and many others.

Monocots are named for their single cotyledon; in addition, their pollen grains have just one pore. (Monocots and eudicots also differ by other characteristics, further described in chapter 21.) Examples of the 70,000 species of monocots are orchids, lilies, grasses, bananas, and ginger. The grasses include not only lawn plants but also sugarcane and grains such as rice, wheat, barley, and corn (see the Why We Care box on page 318).

The angiosperm life cycle is similar to that of gymnosperms in some ways (figure 16.14). For example, the sporophyte is the only conspicuous generation, and both types of plants produce pollen and seeds. Yet the life cycles differ in important ways. Most obviously, the reproductive organs in angiosperms are flowers, not cones. Another difference is that angiosperm seeds develop inside the flower's ovary following fertilization; other floral parts develop into a fruit that houses the seeds. Thus, an angiosperm's seeds are not "naked" like those of gymnosperms.

Pollination is at the heart of angiosperm sexual reproduction, and many species rely on animal "couriers" that unwittingly carry pollen from flower to flower. Of course, animals do not pollinate plants as an act of charity; they usually visit flowers in search of food. Bright colors and alluring scents signal the availability of a sweet reward such as nectar.

One other unique feature of the angiosperm life cycle is **double fertilization.** Each pollen grain produces two sperm nuclei, one of which fertilizes an egg. The fertilized egg, or zygote, will develop into the embryo. The other sperm nucleus fertilizes a pair of polar nuclei in the female gametophyte. The resulting triploid nucleus develops into the **endosperm,** a tissue that supplies nutrients to the germinating seedling.

In many angiosperms, the main food storage molecule in the seed is starch. For example, the endosperm of wheat and other grains is starchy; bakers grind these seeds into flour to make bread and other baked goods. In other species, the endosperm is rich in oil. Coconuts and castor seeds are two sources of useful oils derived from endosperm.

The embryo and endosperm, together with a seed coat, make up the seed; one or more seeds develop inside each fruit. The main functions of the fruit are to protect and disperse the seeds. Some fruits, such as those of dandelions, have "parachutes" that promote wind dispersal. Others, however, spread only with

Figure 16.13 A Gallery of Angiosperms. The angiosperms exhibit an astonishing variety of flowers and fruits. (a) Cattails *(Typha latifolia)* are familiar wetland plants. The brown cylindrical "tails" are actually spikes of tiny brown flowers. (b) In bananas (genus *Musa*), flowers occur in clusters. Pale yellow flowers and green developing fruits are visible in this photograph. (c) Passion vines are tropical plants with very showy flowers. (d) Red maple *(Acer rubrum)* produces small, bright red flowers that develop into winged fruits after fertilization.

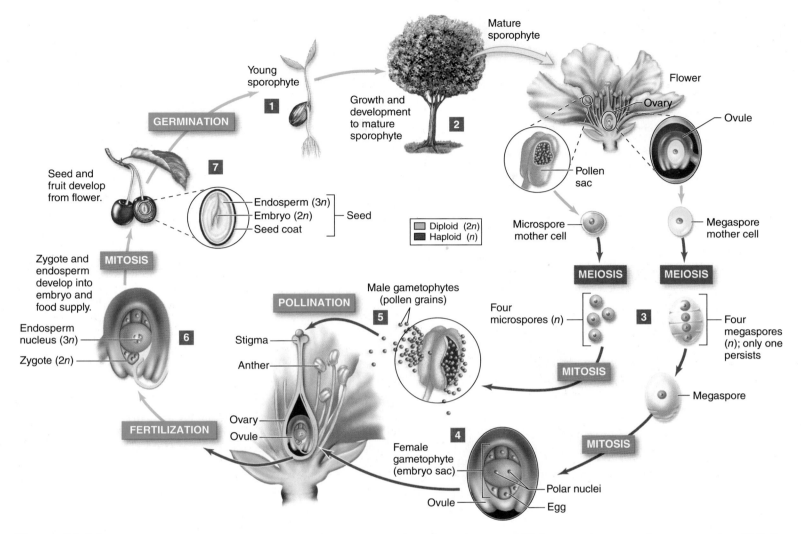

Figure 16.14 **Sexual Reproduction in Angiosperms.** (1) An angiosperm's seed germinates, and (2) the sporophyte grows into a mature tree. (3) Cells in the pollen sac and ovary undergo meiosis, producing spores that develop into haploid male and female gametophytes. (4) Inside the ovary, the female gametophyte includes one egg cell and two polar nuclei. (5) The pollen sac produces pollen, the male gametophytes. (6) A pollen grain delivers two sperm nuclei. One fertilizes the egg. The other fertilizes the polar nuclei, forming triploid tissue that develops into the endosperm. (7) The fruit, which contains the seeds, develops from the ovary wall.

the help of animals. Some have burrs that cling to animal fur. Others are sweet and fleshy, attracting animals that eat the fruits and later spit out the seeds or discard them with their feces. ▸ seed dispersal, p. 455

16.5 Mastering Concepts

1. What are the two largest groups of angiosperms?
2. In what ways are the life cycles of angiosperms similar to and different from those of conifers?
3. What is the relationship between flowers and fruits?
4. Describe two ways that animals participate in angiosperm reproduction and dispersal.

Why We Care | Corn, Corn, Everywhere

Even if you don't eat the kernels off the cob, you likely have much more corn in your diet than you imagine. Besides fresh corn, frozen corn, canned corn, corn meal, corn oil, and corn starch, some of the many unexpected fates of corn include:

- baking powder and confectioners ("powdered") sugar, which often contain corn starch.
- corn syrup, a liquid sugar derived from corn starch, that sweetens soft drinks, ketchup, and many other foods.
- vanilla extract, which is often made with corn syrup.
- dextrin and maltodextrins, polysaccharides that thicken syrups and provide texture to low-fat foods (among many other uses). These food additives are produced by the partial hydrolysis of corn starch. ▸ hydrolysis, p. 33
- the simple sugars dextrose (glucose) and fructose.
- margarine, which often contains corn oil.
- the grain alcohol in bourbon whiskey. Ethanol from corn is also a biofuel (see this chapter's Burning Question).
- animal feed. Chickens, hogs, and cattle on many commercial farms are fed corn, effectively converting the nutrients in corn into meat.

Figure 16.15 Core Sample. Cores of frozen sediment taken from permafrost may contain ancient DNA.

Investigating Life

16.6 Genetic Messages from Ancient Ecosystems

Psychics claim to be able to communicate with the spirits of the dead. Although scientists do not assert the same spiritual connection, they can bring back the genetic remnants of species that lived and died long ago.

When an organism dies, its DNA usually degrades rapidly. But in some special cases, the genetic material remains intact indefinitely. Freezing is one way to preserve DNA. An ideal source of ancient DNA is therefore a landscape that once teemed with life but has since become permanently frozen.

One such example is a land bridge called Beringia, which once connected present-day northeastern Siberia to Alaska. Long ago, giant mammals such as mammoth, bear, bison, and large cats roamed the Beringian landscape. But climates shift, and much of Beringia is now permanently frozen land in Siberia, Alaska, and the Yukon.

The Question: Can DNA preserved in frozen Siberian soil reveal which plants supported ecosystems hundreds of thousands—or even millions—of years ago?

The Approach: Danish researchers Eske Willerslev, Anders Hansen, and their colleagues drove metal cylinders deep into the permafrost and removed long, thin rods (called "cores") of ice, soil, and organic material (figure 16.15). The deepest holes yield the oldest deposits, because new sediments accumulate over old ones. Radiometric dating, pollen analysis, and other techniques helped them estimate the age of each layer of material in the cores. ▸ radiometric dating, p. 246

The scientists tried to extract DNA from eight sediment samples ranging in age from modern to about 2 million years old. Wherever DNA was present, they searched for two sets of genes. One target was part of the gene encoding the protein rubisco, which is essential for photosynthesis (see chapter 5). The presence of this gene indicates plant material. The other targets were fragments of genes found only in the mitochondria of vertebrate animals such as mammals. The researchers sequenced all of the chloroplast and mitochondrial genes they found.

The Conclusion: Sediments from 300,000 to 400,000 years old contained plant DNA, including a tremendous diversity of mosses, herbs (grasses and other nonwoody plants), shrubs, and trees. On the other hand, the oldest mitochondrial DNA from vertebrates was only about 20,000 to 30,000 years old. Some came from grazers that still exist today, such as the horse, lemming, hare, musk ox, and reindeer, but the researchers also found genes from extinct mammoth and bison. The presence of genes from animals that vanished long ago suggests that the sediment DNA was authentic and not simply a modern contaminant.

These gene fragments can help scientists reconstruct ancient ecosystems. The chloroplast DNA, for example, reveals that herbs dominated the Beringian landscape 300,000 or so years ago but lost ground to shrubs over time (figure 16.16). The most dramatic decline of grasses occurred in the past 10,000 years, a time that coincided with the extinction of the mammoth and bison. Did one event cause the other? Or did the end of the last ice age cause both? What role did increasing human populations play? These questions remain unanswered for now.

Willerslev's team hopes their work will inspire others to extract DNA from ancient sediments around the world. The resulting patchwork of gene fragments, pieced together, will reveal valuable information about the changes that shaped ancient ecosystems—without the help of a psychic.

Willerslev, E., A. J. Hansen, J. Binladen, et al. May 2, 2003. Diverse plant and animal genetic records from Holocene and Pleistocene sediments. *Science,* vol. 300, pages 791–795.

16.6 Mastering Concepts

1. Why do researchers collect DNA from permafrost?
2. What are some hypotheses for why the researchers failed to recover any DNA from sediments that were more than 300,000 to 400,000 years old? How would you test your hypotheses?

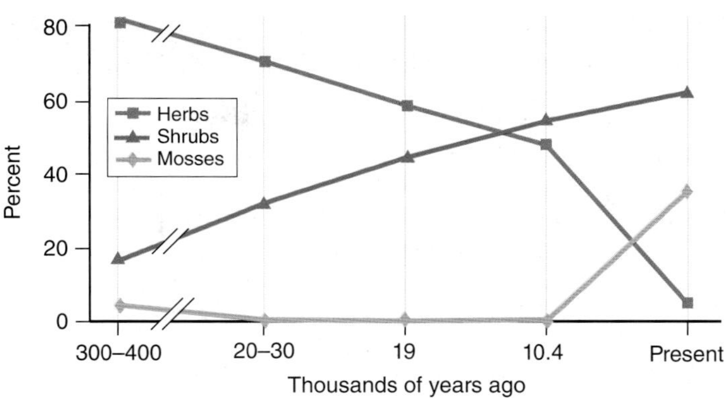

Figure 16.16 Communities Change. Chloroplast DNA isolated from sediment samples reveals changes in the Siberian plant community over the past 400,000 years. Grasses and other herbs have become much less common, whereas shrubs and mosses have become more common.

Plant Characteristics: A Summary

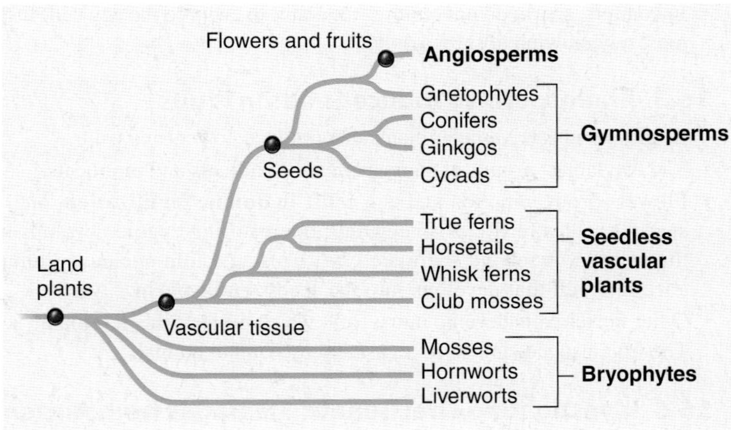

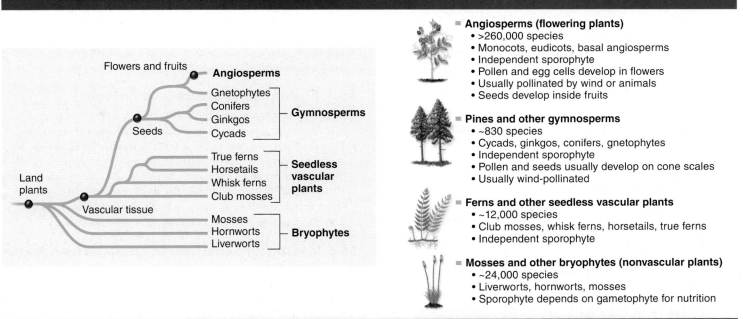

Angiosperms (flowering plants)
- >260,000 species
- Monocots, eudicots, basal angiosperms
- Independent sporophyte
- Pollen and egg cells develop in flowers
- Usually pollinated by wind or animals
- Seeds develop inside fruits

Pines and other gymnosperms
- ~830 species
- Cycads, ginkgos, conifers, gnetophytes
- Independent sporophyte
- Pollen and seeds usually develop on cone scales
- Usually wind-pollinated

Ferns and other seedless vascular plants
- ~12,000 species
- Club mosses, whisk ferns, horsetails, true ferns
- Independent sporophyte

Mosses and other bryophytes (nonvascular plants)
- ~24,000 species
- Liverworts, hornworts, mosses
- Sporophyte depends on gametophyte for nutrition

Group	Swimming sperm	Vascular tissue	Pollen	Seeds	Flowers	Fruits
Bryophytes	Yes	No	No	No	No	No
Seedless vascular plants	Yes	Yes	No	No	No	No
Gymnosperms	No	Yes	Yes	Yes	No	No
Angiosperms	No	Yes	Yes	Yes	Yes	Yes

Chapter Summary

16.1 Plants Have Changed the World

- Members of kingdom **Plantae** provide food and habitat for other organisms, remove CO_2 from the atmosphere, and produce O_2. Humans rely on plants for food, lumber, clothing, paper, and many other resources.

A. Green Algae Are the Closest Relatives of Plants

- Plants evolved about 475 million years ago from green algae closely related to today's **charophytes.**
- Like many green algae, plants are multicellular, eukaryotic autotrophs that have cellulose cell walls and use starch as a carbohydrate reserve. Green algae and plants also use the same photosynthetic pigments.

B. Plants Are Adapted to Life on Land

- Adaptations that enable plants to obtain and conserve resources include roots, leaves, a waterproof **cuticle,** and **stomata.**
- **Vascular tissue** (**xylem** and **phloem**) transports water, minerals, food, and other substances within a plant body. **Lignin** strengthens cell walls, providing physical support.
- Plant life cycles have an **alternation of generations,** with multicellular **sporophyte** (diploid) and **gametophyte** (haploid) phases. The sporophyte produces haploid spores by meiosis; the gametophyte produces haploid sperm and egg cells by mitosis. Fertilization restores the diploid number.

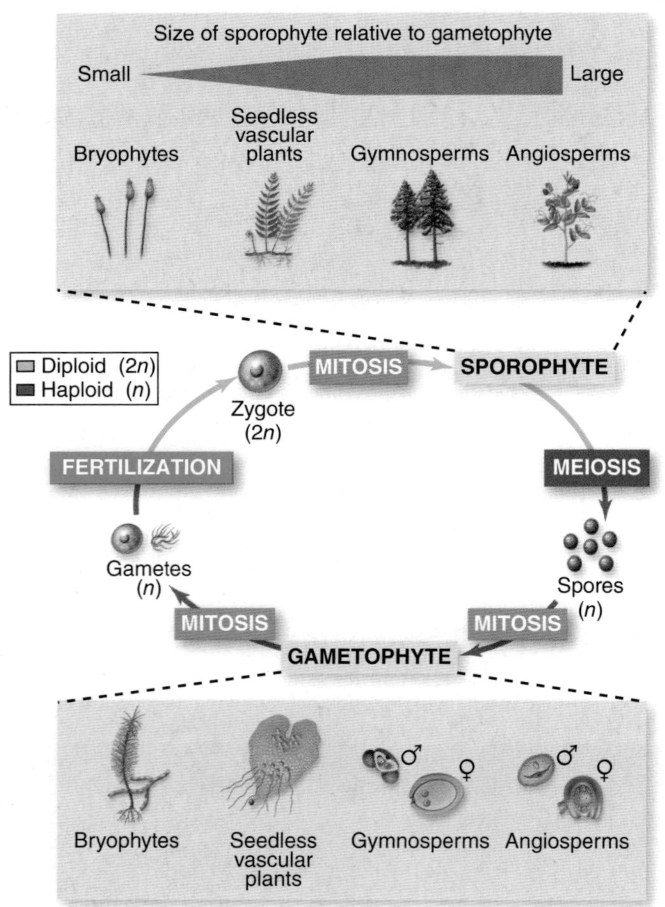

- In the simplest plants, the gametophyte generation is most prominent; in more complex plants, the sporophyte dominates.
- In gymnosperms and angiosperms, reproductive adaptations include **pollen** and **seeds. Pollination** delivers sperm to egg. The resulting zygote develops into an embryo, which is packaged along with a food supply into a seed. Angiosperms also produce **flowers** and **fruits.**
- Plants are classified by the presence or absence of vascular tissue, seeds, flowers, and fruits.

16.2 Bryophytes Are the Simplest Plants

- **Bryophytes** are small green plants lacking vascular tissue, leaves, roots, and stems. The three groups of bryophytes are **liverworts, hornworts,** and **mosses.**
- In bryophytes, the gametophyte stage is dominant. Sperm require free water to swim to egg cells.

16.3 Seedless Vascular Plants Have Xylem and Phloem but No Seeds

- **Seedless vascular plants** have vascular tissue but lack seeds. This group includes **club mosses, whisk ferns, horsetails,** and **true ferns.**
- The sporophyte generation is the most obvious stage of a fern life cycle; the gametophyte forms a tiny separate plant.
- In the sexual life cycle of ferns, meiosis occurs in the sporangia and yields haploid spores, which germinate and develop into gametophytes. The gametophytes produce egg cells and swimming sperm.

16.4 Gymnosperms Are "Naked Seed" Plants

- **Gymnosperms** are vascular plants with seeds that are not enclosed in fruits. The four groups of gymnosperms are **cycads, ginkgos, conifers,** and **gnetophytes.**
- **Cones** house the reproductive structures. Male cones release pollen, and female cones produce egg cells inside **ovules.** Pollen germination yields a pollen tube, through which a sperm nucleus travels to fertilize the egg cell. The resulting embryo remains dormant in a seed until germination.
- In conifers, sperm do not require free water to swim to the egg cell. Instead, most rely on wind to spread pollen.

16.5 Angiosperms Produce Seeds in Fruits

- **Angiosperms** are vascular plants that produce flowers and fruits.
- The two largest groups of angiosperms are **eudicots** and **monocots.**
- Flowers produce pollen and egg cells. In **double fertilization**, one sperm nucleus fertilizes an egg cell; the resulting zygote develops into the embryo. A second sperm cell fertilizes a diploid nucleus, producing a triploid cell that develops into the seed's **endosperm.**
- Other flower parts develop into a fruit, which protects the developing seeds. The fruit also aids in dispersal, usually by wind or animals.

16.6 Investigating Life: Genetic Messages from Ancient Ecosystems

- Researchers have extracted DNA from plants and animals buried long ago in frozen sediments. These studies reveal changes in the landscape over hundreds of thousands of years.

Multiple Choice Questions

1. Which of the following is NOT a property common to both land plants and green algae?
   a. Photosynthesis
   b. Starch as a form of stored energy
   c. Cellulose cell walls
   d. The presence of a cuticle and stomata

2. In the alternation of generations in plants, the gametophyte is _______ and produces gametes by _______.
   a. haploid; mitosis
   b. diploid; mitosis
   c. haploid; meiosis
   d. diploid; meiosis
3. A moss spore develops into a
   a. sperm cell.
   b. gametophyte.
   c. sporophyte.
   d. frond.
4. How does the presence of vascular tissue (xylem and phloem) affect a plant?
   a. It reduces the plant's dependence on a moist environment.
   b. It allows specialization of roots, leaves, and stems.
   c. It allows for the growth of larger plants.
   d. All of the above are correct.
5. Why do many ferns require a shady, moist habitat?
   a. They lack vascular tissue.
   b. They use swimming sperm for sexual reproduction.
   c. They lack a water-retaining cuticle layer.
   d. The production of spores within the sporangium requires moisture.
6. Reproduction in a pine tree is associated with
   a. male and female cones.
   b. windblown pollen.
   c. the formation of pollen tubes.
   d. All of the above are correct.
7. What is a key adaptation that is unique to the angiosperms?
   a. Dominant gametophyte generation
   b. Pollen grains that use pollen tubes to fertilize egg cells
   c. The use of flowers as reproductive structures
   d. Both a and b are correct.
8. In comparing the life cycle of an angiosperm to that of a human, pollination is analogous to ___ and the seed is analogous to the __.
   a. childbirth; growth of the child
   b. sexual intercourse; baby
   c. production of egg cells; mother
   d. production of sperm; uterus

Write It Out

1. What characteristics do all land plants have in common?
2. How are terrestrial habitats different from aquatic habitats? List the adaptations that enable plants to obtain resources, transport materials, and reproduce; explain how each adaptation contributes to reproductive success on land.
3. Give at least two explanations for the observation that bryophytes are much smaller than most vascular plants. How can increased height be adaptive? In what circumstances is small size adaptive?
4. How do the adaptations of gymnosperms and angiosperms enable them to live in drier habitats than bryophytes and seedless vascular plants?
5. How do angiosperms differ from gymnosperms? How are the two groups of plants similar?
6. Compare and contrast the life cycles of the four groups of plants. How does each group represent a variation on the theme of alternation of generations?

Pull It Together

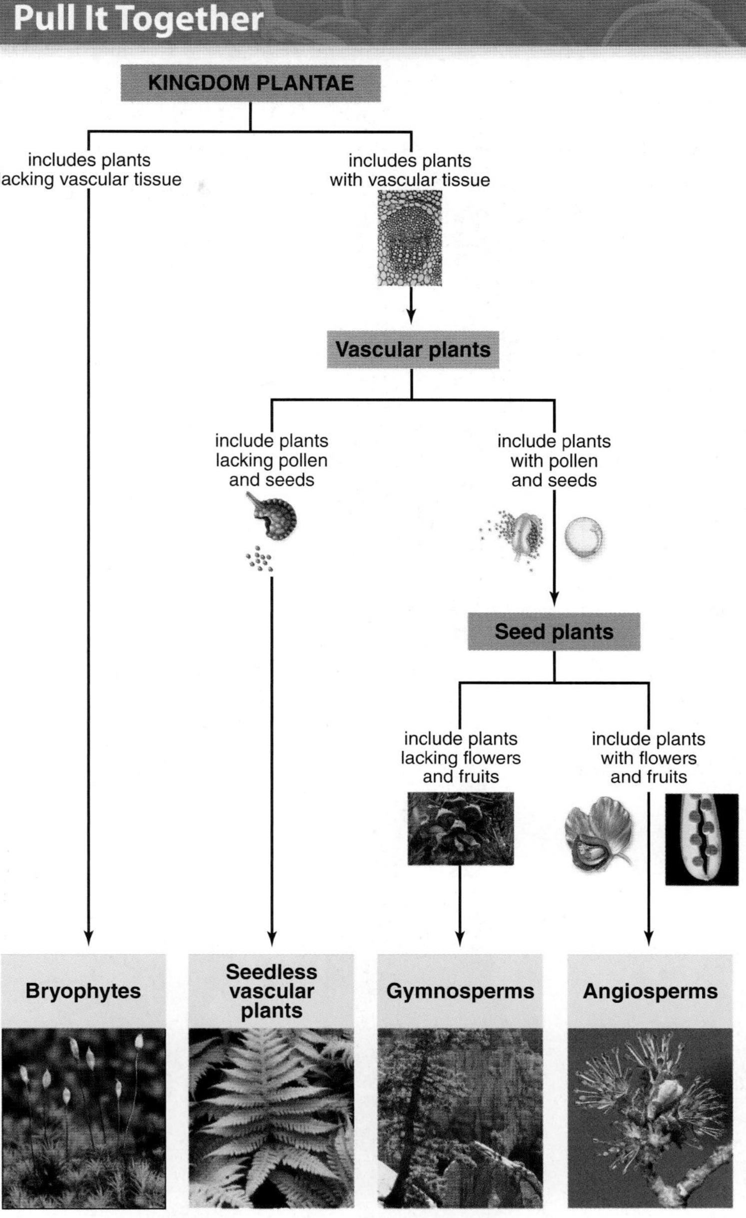

1. What are the main groups of plants within the bryophytes, seedless vascular plants, gymnosperms, and angiosperms?
2. For each of the four main groups of plants, describe the gametophyte and sporophyte generations.
3. How do bryophytes and seedless vascular plants reproduce if they lack pollen and seeds?
4. Describe the relationship between pollen and seeds.

17 Evolution and Diversity of Animals

Colorful Beetles. This photo shows a few representatives of the amazingly diverse beetles. Biologists have described over 350,000 species of beetles, more than any other type of animal.

Learning Outline

Learn How to Learn
Flashcard Excellence

While making flashcards, you may be tempted to focus on definitions. For example, after reading this chapter, you might make a flashcard with "amnion" on one side and "membrane surrounding an embryo" on the other. This description is correct, but it won't help you understand the bigger picture. Instead, your flashcards should include realistic questions that cover both the big picture and the small details. Try making flashcards that pose a question, such as "Which animals are amniotes?" or "How are amniotes adapted for life on land?" Write the full answer on the other side, then practice writing the answers on scratch paper until you are sure you have them right.

What's the Point?

Think of any animal. There's a good chance that the example that popped into your head was a mammal such as a dog, cat, horse, or cow. Although it makes sense that we think first of our most familiar companions, the mammals represent only a tiny subset of organisms in kingdom Animalia.

Biologists have described about 1,200,000 animal species, and their diversity is astonishing. More than 1 million of the described animal species are insects. Only about 57,000 animal species are vertebrates, and most of those are fishes. Mammals make up a paltry 5,800 or so species.

Why are animals important? Pets provide companionship, whereas other animals provide food in the form of milk, cheese, meat, and eggs. Animals also play important roles in ecosystems. They graze on vegetation, scavenge dead organic matter, till the earth, control the populations of other animals, pollinate flowers, and carry seeds to new habitats.

It is almost impossible to describe the beauty, diversity, and importance of animals in just one textbook chapter. The pages that follow provide a small sampling of the fascinating organisms that make up kingdom Animalia.

17.1 Animals Live Nearly Everywhere

The diversity of animals is astonishing. Animals live in us, on us, and around us. They are extremely diverse in size, habitat, body form, and intelligence. Whales are immense; roundworms can be microscopic. Bighorn sheep scale mountaintops; crabs scuttle on the deep ocean floor. Earthworms are squishy; clams surround themselves in heavy armor. Sponges are witless; humans, chimps, and dolphins are clever.

This chapter explores some of this amazing variety, describing nine of the 37 phyla of animals in detail. The vast majority of animals are **invertebrates** (animals without backbones). The phylum Arthropoda alone, for example, includes more than 1 million identified species of invertebrates such as insects, crustaceans, and spiders. Only about 57,000 known animal species are **vertebrates** (animals with backbones) such as mammals and birds.

A. What Is an Animal?

All animals share a combination of features. First, they are multicellular organisms with eukaryotic cells, as are plants, fungi, and some protists. Unlike the cells of plants and fungi, however, animal cells lack cell walls. ▸ animal cell, p. 53

Second, all animals are heterotrophs, obtaining both carbon and energy from organic compounds produced by other organisms. Most animals ingest their food, break it down in a digestive tract, absorb the nutrients, and eliminate the indigestible wastes.

Third, animal development is unlike that of any other type of organism. After fertilization, the diploid zygote (the first cell of the new organism) divides rapidly. The early animal embryo begins as a solid ball of cells that quickly hollows out to form a **blastula,** a sphere of cells surrounding a fluid-filled cavity. No other organisms besides animals go through a blastula stage of development.

Fourth, animal cells secrete and bind to a nonliving substance called the extracellular matrix. This complex mixture of proteins and other substances enables some cells to move, others to assemble into sheets, and yet others to embed in supportive surroundings, such as bone or shell.

B. Animal Life Began in the Water

All of today's animals have their origins in aquatic ancestors (figure 17.1). The first animals, which arose about 570 million years ago (MYA), may have been related to aquatic protists called choanoflagellates. Although no one knows exactly what the first animal looked like, the Ediacaran organisms that thrived

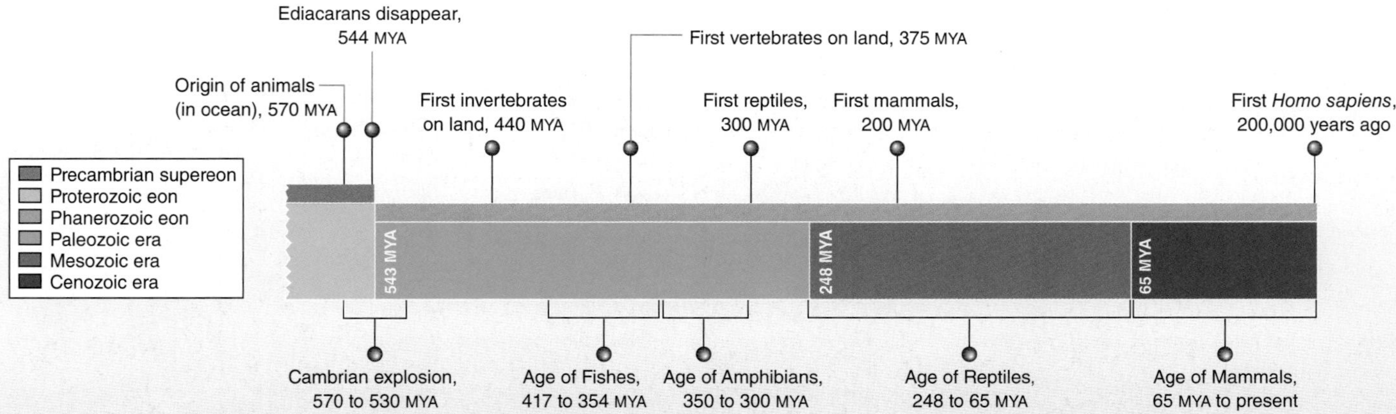

Figure 17.1 Highlights in the History of Animals. Animal life started in the oceans about 570 million years ago. About 440 MYA, some animals began to move from water onto land. Today, animals are abundant both on land and in water.

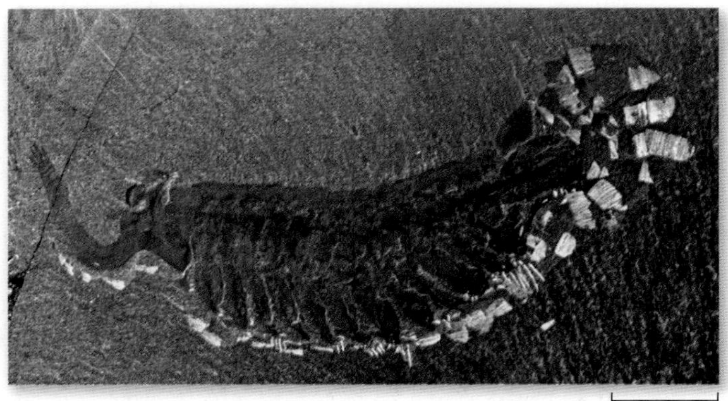

Figure 17.2 **Cambrian Life.** *Opabinia* is one of many strange animals whose fossils have been discovered in the Burgess Shale. Its body was segmented, and its head sported stalked eyes and a long, flexible snout.

during the Precambrian may provide some clues. These organisms vanished from the fossil record about 544 MYA and left no known modern descendants.

Fossils of all major phyla of animals appeared in the Cambrian seas during a period that lasted about 40 million years, a spectacular diversification sometimes called the "Cambrian explosion." Most of today's phyla of animals, including sponges, jellyfishes, arthropods, mollusks, and many types of worms, originated during the Cambrian, which lasted from about 543 to 490 MYA. The Burgess Shale from the Canadian province of British Columbia preserves a glimpse of life from this time (figure 17.2).

Aquatic animals were therefore already diverse by the time plants and fungi colonized the land about 475 MYA. Arthropods, vertebrates, and other animals soon followed, diversifying further as they adapted to new food sources and habitats.

C. Biologists Classify Animals Based on Organization, Morphology, and Development

Figure 17.3 compiles the nine animal phyla described in this chapter into a phylogenetic tree. This section explains the features that biologists use to construct the tree. Section 17.1D lists additional traits that are sometimes important in describing animals but that do not represent branching points on the tree.

Figure 17.3 **Animal Diversity.** Biologists classify animals based on body form, developmental characteristics, and DNA sequences.

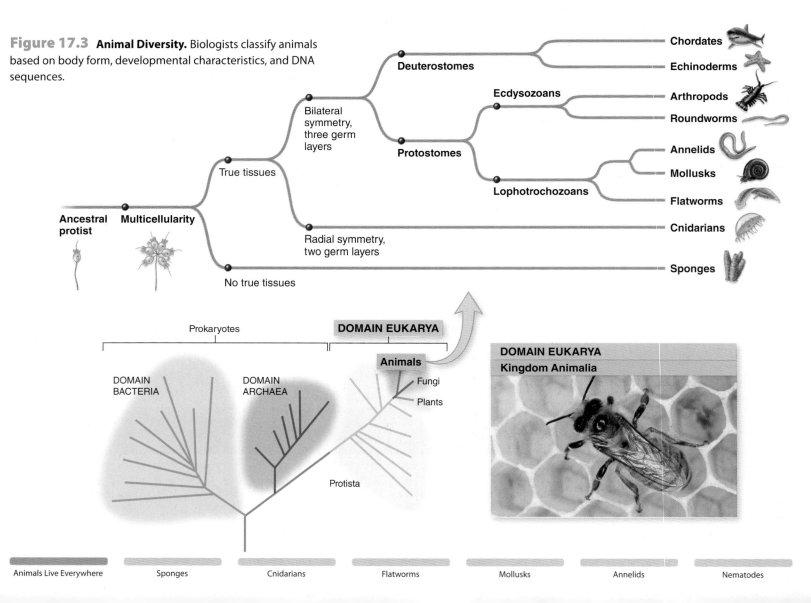

Ancestral protist
Multicellularity
No true tissues
True tissues
Radial symmetry, two germ layers
Bilateral symmetry, three germ layers
Deuterostomes
Protostomes
Ecdysozoans
Lophotrochozoans
Chordates
Echinoderms
Arthropods
Roundworms
Annelids
Mollusks
Flatworms
Cnidarians
Sponges

Prokaryotes
DOMAIN EUKARYA
DOMAIN BACTERIA
DOMAIN ARCHAEA
Animals
Fungi
Plants
Protista

DOMAIN EUKARYA
Kingdom Animalia

Cell and Tissue Organization The first major branching point separates animals into two clades. The simplest animals, the sponges, have several specialized cell types, but the cells do not interact to provide specific functions as they would in a true tissue. The other clade contains animals with true tissues. In complex animals, multiple tissue types interact to form organs, which work together to circulate and distribute blood, dispose of wastes, and carry out other functions.

Body Symmetry and Cephalization Body symmetry is another major criterion used in animal classification (figure 17.4). Many sponges are asymmetrical; that is, they lack symmetry. Other sponges, hydras, jellyfishes, adult sea stars, and their close relatives have **radial symmetry,** in which any plane passing through the body from the mouth to the opposite end divides the body into mirror images. The remaining animals have **bilateral symmetry,** in which only one plane can divide the animal into mirror images. Bilaterally symmetrical animals such as crayfish and horses have head (anterior) and tail (posterior) ends, and they typically move through their environment head first. This behavior is correlated with **cephalization,** the tendency to concentrate sensory organs and a brain at the head end of the animal.

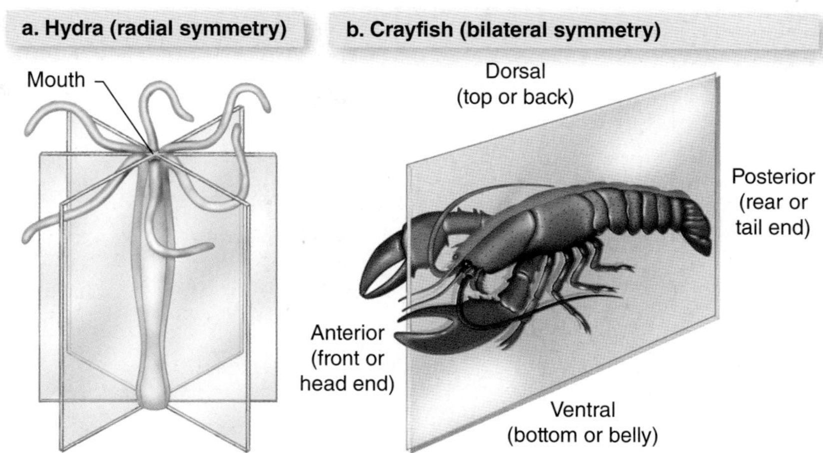

Figure 17.4 **Types of Symmetry.** (a) A hydra has radial symmetry. (b) Animals with bilateral symmetry, such as this crayfish, have a front (anterior) and rear (posterior) end, and a dorsal (back or top) and ventral (bottom or belly) side.

Embryonic Development: Two or Three Germ Layers Early embryos give other clues to evolutionary relationships (figure 17.5). In animals with true tissues, the blastula folds in on itself to generate the **gastrula,** which is composed of two or three tissue layers called primary germ layers. The gastrulas of jellyfishes and their relatives have two germ layers: **ectoderm** to the outside, and **endoderm** to the inside. All other animals with true tissues have a third germ layer, **mesoderm,** that forms between the ectoderm and endoderm.

These germ layers give rise to all of the body's tissues and organs. Ectoderm develops into the skin and nervous system, whereas endoderm becomes the digestive tract and the organs derived from it. Mesoderm gives rise to the muscles, the reproductive system, and many other specialized structures.

Embryonic Development: Protostomes and Deuterostomes Biologists traditionally divide bilaterally symmetrical animals into two clades, based in part on events that occur after the embryo has begun to fold into a gastrula. As development proceeds, the inner cell layer of the gastrula fuses with the opposite side of the embryo, forming a tube with two openings. This cylinder of endoderm will develop into the animal's digestive tract.

In most **protostomes,** the first indentation to form develops into the mouth, and the anus develops from the second opening. (*Protostome* literally means "mouth first.") In **deuterostomes,** such as echinoderms and chordates, the first indentation becomes the anus, and the mouth develops from the second opening. (*Deuterostome* means "mouth second.") We now know that some animals classified as protostomes do not conform to the "mouth first" pattern. Nevertheless, DNA sequences support their placement in the protostome clade.

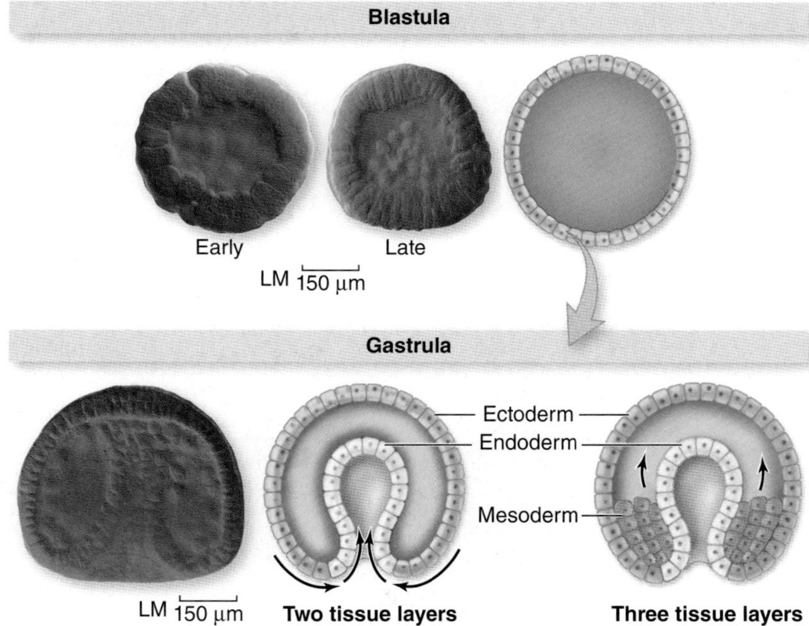

Figure 17.5 **Blastula and Gastrula.** A blastula is a fluid-filled sphere of cells that forms early in development. This ball soon folds in on itself and forms the gastrula. (The photos show a sea star's blastula and gastrula.) Animals with two primary germ layers have an outer ectoderm and an inner endoderm layer. In other animals, mesoderm forms between the ectoderm and endoderm.

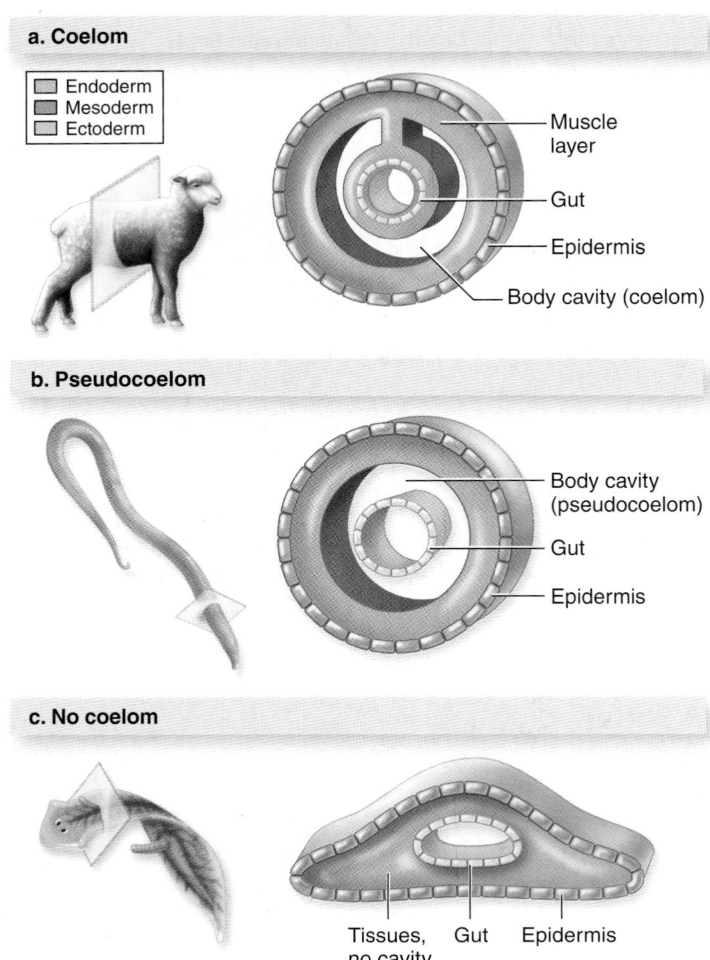

Figure 17.6 Body Cavities. (a) Like many other animals, a sheep has a coelom. The internal organs grow into the coelom, greatly distorting the cavity's shape. (b) A roundworm has a pseudocoelom. (c) A flatworm lacks a coelom.

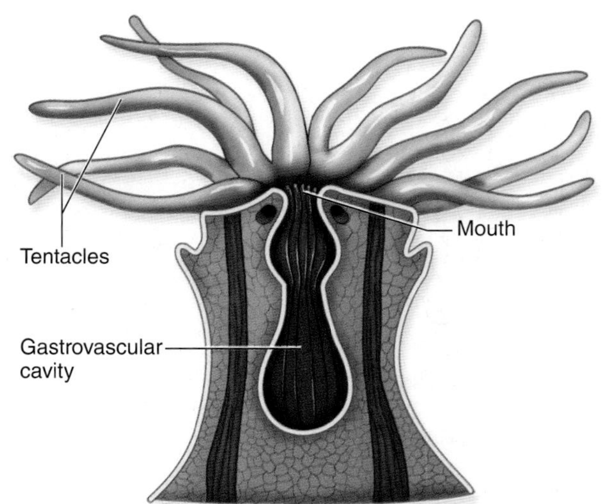

Figure 17.7 Incomplete Digestive Tract. In sea anemones and other animals with an incomplete digestive tract, the mouth takes in food and ejects undigested wastes.

D. Biologists Also Consider Additional Characteristics

Other features that describe animals include the body cavity, the organization of the digestive tract, and segmentation.

Body Cavity (Coelom) Biologists once classified bilaterally symmetrical animals based on the presence or absence of a coelom (figure 17.6). The **coelom** is a fluid-filled body cavity that forms completely within the mesoderm. Animals that have a coelom include earthworms, snails, insects, sea stars, and chordates. In contrast, roundworms have a body cavity called a **pseudocoelom** ("false coelom") that is lined partly with mesoderm and partly with endoderm. Flatworms lack a coelom, although evidence suggests their ancestors did have body cavities.

The coelom's chief advantage is flexibility. As internal organs such as the heart, lungs, liver, and intestines develop, they push into the coelom. The fluid of the coelom cushions the organs, protects them, and enables them to shift as the animal bends and moves.

In many animals, the coelom or pseudocoelom serves as a hydrostatic skeleton that provides support and movement. In a **hydrostatic skeleton,** muscles push against a constrained fluid. An earthworm, for example, burrows through soil by alternately contracting and relaxing muscles surrounding its coelom. Jellyfishes, flatworms, and other invertebrates lacking a coelom or pseudocoelom also have hydrostatic skeletons. In these animals, muscles act on other fluid-filled compartments in the body.

Digestive Tract A sponge lacks a digestive tract; instead, the animal has a central cavity with a single large opening through which filtered water leaves the body. In other animals, the digestive tract may be incomplete or complete. Cnidarians and flatworms have an **incomplete digestive tract,** in which the mouth both takes in food and ejects wastes (figure 17.7). In these animals, digestion occurs in the **gastrovascular cavity,** which secretes digestive enzymes and distributes nutrients to all parts of the animal's body.

In humans and other animals with a **complete digestive tract,** food passes in one direction from mouth to anus (see chapter 28). A complete digestive tract allows for increased efficiency and specialization. Cells near the mouth can secrete digestive enzymes into the tract, "downstream" cells can absorb nutrients, and those near the anus can help eject wastes.

Segmentation **Segmentation** is the division of an animal body into repeated parts. In centipedes, millipedes, and earthworms, the segments are clearly visible. Insects and chordates also have segmented bodies, although the subdivisions may be less obvious. Segmentation adds to the body's flexibility, and it enormously increases the potential for the development of specialized body parts. Activating different combinations of genes in each segment can create regions with unique functions. Antennae can form on an insect's head, for example, while wings or legs sprout from other segments.

17.1 Mastering Concepts

1. What characteristics do all animals share?
2. When and in what habitat did animals likely originate?
3. What features were used to build the animal phylogenetic tree?
4. Distinguish between a coelom and a pseudocoelom.
5. What are the two main types of digestive tract?
6. What advantages does segmentation confer?

17.2 Sponges Are Simple Animals That Lack Differentiated Tissues

The **sponges** belong to phylum Porifera, which means "pore-bearers"—an apt description of these simple animals that lack true tissues and organs (figure 17.8).

Habitat: Aquatic. Most are marine, although some live in fresh water.

Body Structure: Sponges have hollow, porous bodies that are typically asymmetrical, although some have radial symmetry. The body wall has an outer layer of flattened cells and an inner layer of flagellated "collar cells." (These cells strongly resemble choanoflagellates, the protists that may be the closest relatives to animals.) Sandwiched between the two layers is a noncellular, jellylike matrix that gives the sponge body its shape. Embedded in the matrix are many types of cells, including amoebocytes that digest food, store and transport nutrients, divide, or secrete skeletal components.

Feeding: Sponges are filter feeders. Movement of flagella on the collar cells produces a current of water, which flows through the body wall and into the sponge's central cavity. (Contractile cells in the body wall can close the pores when the water contains too much sediment.) Cells lining the central cavity trap and partially digest bacteria and particles of organic matter. The food particles then pass to amoebocytes, which distribute the food to other cells. Water and wastes exit the sponge through a large hole at the top.

Support and Movement: Protein fibers and sharp slivers (spicules) of silica or calcium carbonate provide support. Although some sponges can move very slowly, these animals are generally considered sessile, meaning they remain anchored to their substrate.

Reproduction: Sponges are hermaphrodites; each animal releases sperm into water currents and retains eggs. After fertilization, the zygote develops into a blastula, which is released and may drift for some time before settling into a new habitat. Sponges also commonly reproduce asexually by budding or fragmentation.

Defense: Spicules and toxic chemicals help sponges deter predators.

Effects on Humans: Some people use natural sponges in bathing. Also, the chemicals that protect sponges from predators may yield useful anticancer and antimicrobial drugs. Collecting sponges, however, can harm ecosystems.

17.2 Mastering Concepts

1. How is a sponge's body different from that of other animals?
2. How do sponges feed?
3. What are two of the cell types in a sponge?
4. What is the function of spicules?
5. How do sponges reproduce sexually and asexually?
6. In what ways are sponges important?

Phylogeny

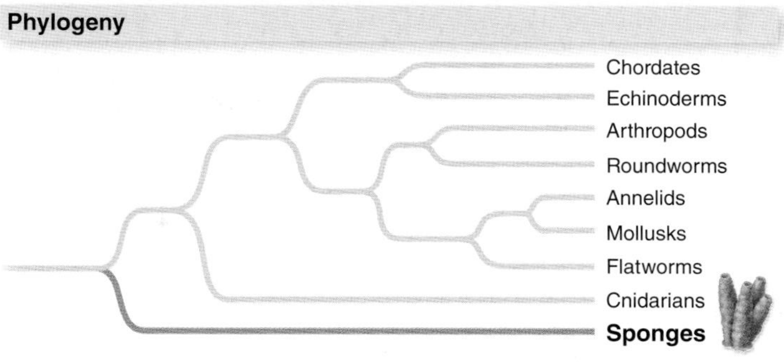

Characteristics

Sponges	
Level of organization	Cellular
Symmetry	Asymmetrical (usually) or radial
Cephalization	Absent
Coelom	Absent
Type of digestive tract	Absent
Segmentation	Absent
Other features	Porous bodies; filter feeders

Diversity

Anatomy

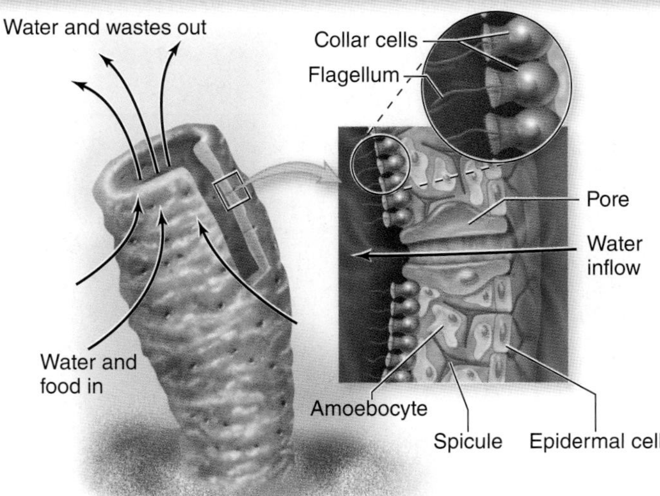

Figure 17.8 **Sponges (Phylum Porifera).**

Phylogeny

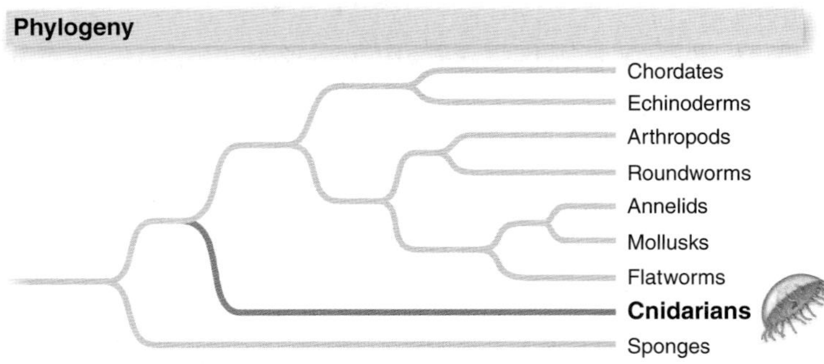

Characteristics

Cnidarians	
Level of organization	Tissue
Symmetry	Radial
Cephalization	Absent
Coelom	Absent
Type of digestive tract	Incomplete
Segmentation	Absent
Other features	Stinging cells

Diversity

Anatomy

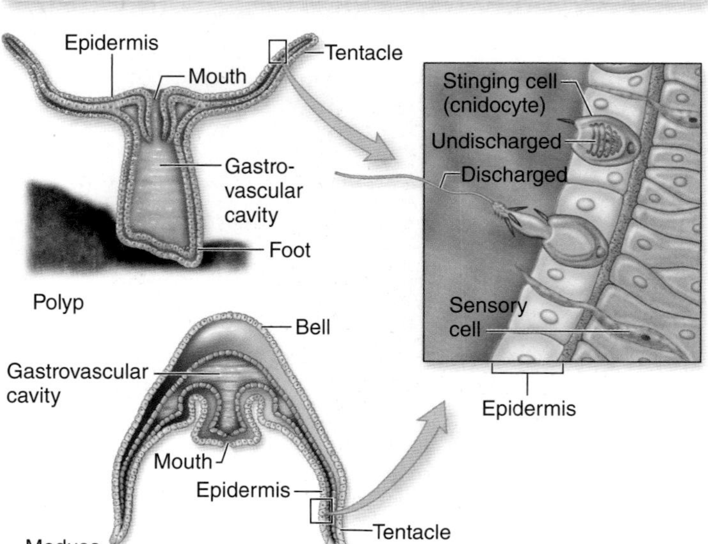

Figure 17.9 Cnidarians (Phylum Cnidaria).

17.3 Cnidarians Are Radially Symmetrical, Aquatic Animals

Phylum Cnidaria takes its name from the Greek word for "nettle," a stinging plant. The **cnidarians** all share the ability to sting predators and prey (figure 17.9).

Habitat: Aquatic (mostly marine).

Body Structure: Cnidarians are radially symmetrical, and their bodies can take either of two forms. A **polyp** is a sessile stalk with tentacles on one end, whereas a **medusa** is a free-swimming, bell-shaped body form typical of jelly-fishes. One opening, the mouth, leads to the dead-end gastrovascular cavity. Tentacles surrounding the mouth house **cnidocytes,** which act as tiny harpoons that either inject venom or entangle the prey.

Diversity: Corals and sea anemones belong to a clade of cnidarians that exist exclusively as sessile polyps. A second clade contains hydras and the jellyfishes.

Feeding: Cnidarians are carnivores that use their tentacles to grab and sting passing prey, which they stuff into the gastrovascular cavity. Cells lining the digestive tract secrete enzymes that digest the food. After absorbing the nutrients, the animal ejects indigestible matter through the mouth.

Support and Movement: In all cnidarians, the body wall acts as a hydrostatic skeleton. These animals can swim and move their tentacles, thanks to specialized nerve and muscle cells. Groups of linked neurons, called nerve nets, coordinate the contraction of muscle cells. As the cells contract, they force water out of the bell of a jellyfish, propelling the animal through the water. The same mechanism enables a sea anemone to stuff food into its gastrovascular cavity.

Some cnidarians also secrete calcium carbonate exoskeletons. Over many generations, the exoskeletons secreted by countless coral animals have built magnificent coral reefs. ▸ coral reefs, p. 386

Reproduction: Cnidarians reproduce sexually and asexually.

Defense: Stinging cnidocytes are the main defense against predators.

Effects on Humans: Huge swarms of jellyfish are becoming increasingly common, presenting a nuisance for tourist destinations and fisheries. Jellyfish stings may cause skin irritation or cramps; a few species have toxins that can be lethal on contact. On the positive side, coral reefs house many commercially important species of fishes and other animals, and they protect coastlines from erosion. As they build their calcium carbonate reefs, corals play an important role in the carbon cycle. A molecule originally isolated from corals (but now produced in the laboratory) is being developed into a sunscreen for human use.

17.3 Mastering Concepts

1. What features do all cnidarians share?
2. What are some examples of cnidarians?
3. How do cnidarians move and defend themselves?
4. In what ways are cnidarians important?

17.4 Flatworms Have Bilateral Symmetry and Incomplete Digestive Tracts

Phylum Platyhelminthes includes the **flatworms** (*platy* means "flat," like a plate; *helminth* means "worm"). Some of these animals are surprisingly beautiful, whereas others look downright scary (figure 17.10).

Habitat: Free-living (usually aquatic) or parasitic on other animals.

Body Structure: Flatworms lack a coelom. Thanks to their flattened bodies, each cell can exchange materials with the environment. These animals have bilateral symmetry.

Diversity: This phylum includes **free-living flatworms** (such as a marine flatworm and a planarian), **flukes,** and **tapeworms.**

Feeding: Free-living flatworms usually are predators or scavengers. A muscular, tubelike pharynx takes in food and ejects wastes from the highly branched gut. A fluke feeds on blood and other host tissues, using its pharynx to pull food into the gastrovascular cavity. A tapeworm lacks a mouth and digestive system entirely; instead, it attaches to the host's intestine and absorbs food through its body wall.

Circulation and Respiration: Flatworms lack specialized circulatory and respiratory systems. CO_2 and O_2 simply diffuse through the body wall.

Excretion: Specialized structures maintain internal water balance and excrete nitrogenous wastes through pores on the body surface.

Nervous System: Some flatworms have nerve cords and clusters of nerve cells at the head end, forming a simple brain; others have a nerve net.

Support and Movement: Flatworms have a hydrostatic skeleton and may creep or swim by contracting muscles in a rolling motion.

Reproduction: Many flatworms reproduce asexually. Free-living species, for example, may simply pinch in half and regenerate the missing parts. Tapeworms have a different strategy. The posterior end of a tapeworm's body consists of repeated reproductive organs. Portions containing fertilized eggs break off and leave the host in feces. When a new host swallows the reproductive structures in contaminated water, the eggs hatch into larvae that colonize and mature in the host's body.

Defense: When inside the host, parasitic flatworms are safe from predators; free-living forms secrete a protective mucus.

Effects on Humans: Worldwide, infections with blood flukes, lung flukes, liver flukes, and tapeworms affect hundreds of millions of people and countless domesticated and wild animals.

17.4 Mastering Concepts

1. What features do all flatworms share?
2. How does the body shape of a flatworm enhance gas exchange?
3. How do flatworms eat, move, and reproduce?
4. In what ways are flatworms important?

Phylogeny

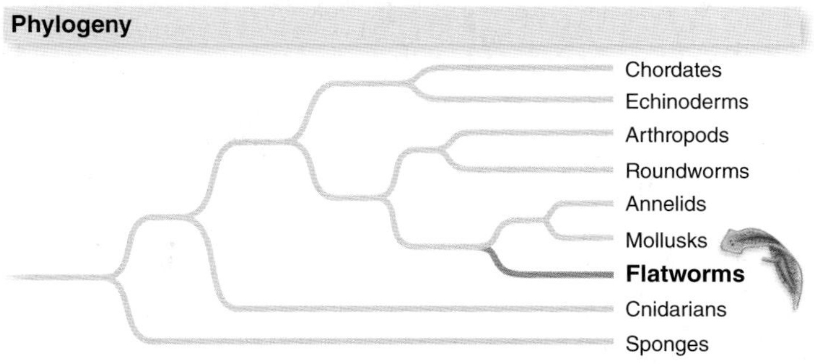

Characteristics

Flatworms	
Level of organization	Organ system
Symmetry	Bilateral
Cephalization	Present
Coelom	Absent
Type of digestive tract	Incomplete (when present)
Segmentation	Absent

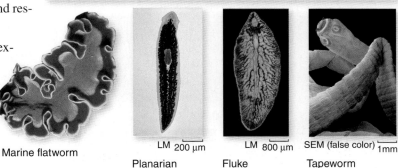

Diversity

Marine flatworm

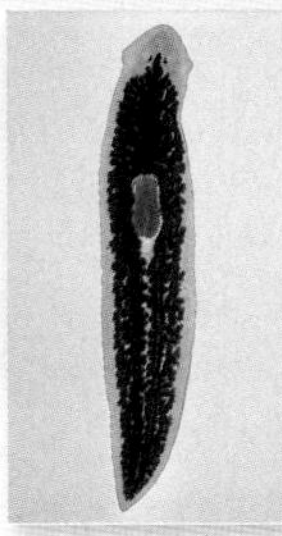

Planarian

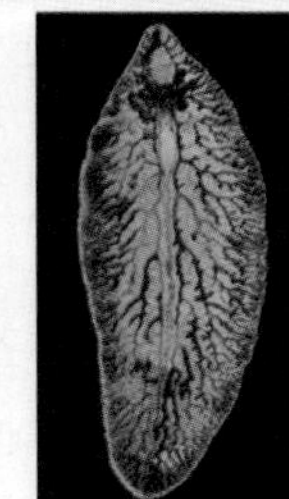

Fluke

Tapeworm

Anatomy

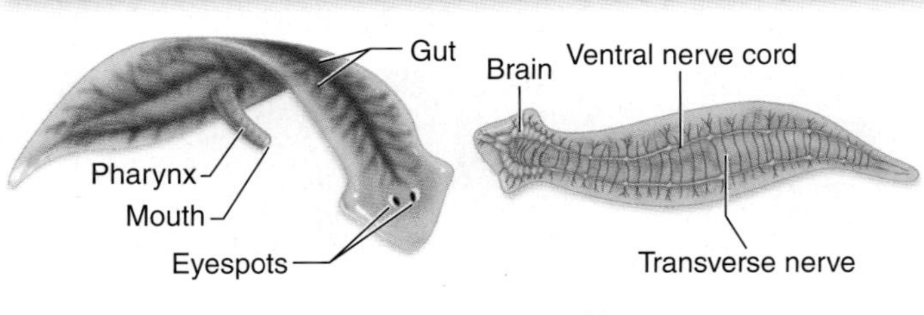

Figure 17.10 Flatworms (Phylum Platyhelminthes).

Phylogeny

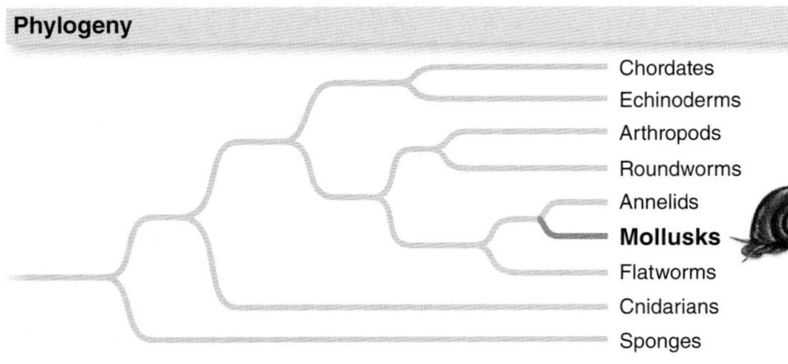

Characteristics

Mollusks	
Level of organization	Organ system
Symmetry	Bilateral
Cephalization	Usually
Coelom	Present
Type of digestive tract	Complete
Segmentation	Absent
Other features	Mantle, shell, foot, visceral mass, radula

Diversity

Anatomy

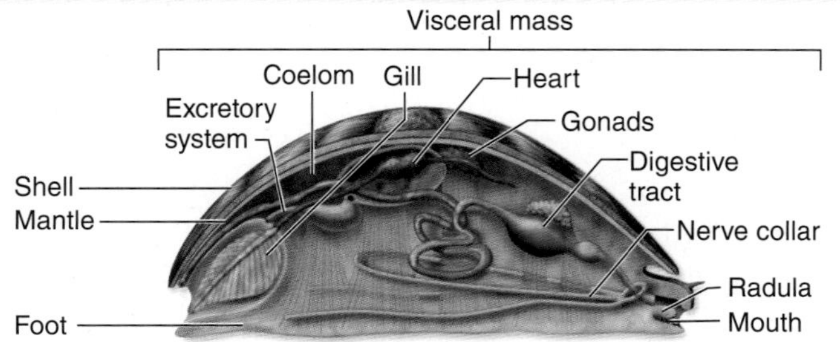

Figure 17.11 **Mollusks (Phylum Mollusca).**

17.5 Mollusks Are Soft, Unsegmented Animals

Mollusks include many familiar animals (figure 17.11). The word *mollusk* comes from the Latin word for "soft," reflecting the fleshy bodies in this phylum.

Habitat: Terrestrial, marine, and freshwater.

Body Structure: The **mantle** is a fold of tissue that secretes a shell in most species. A muscular **foot** provides movement, and an area called the **visceral mass** contains the digestive and reproductive organs. Many mollusks have a **radula,** a tonguelike strap with teeth made of chitin (a tough polysaccharide). They use the radula to scrape food into their mouths.

Diversity: **Chitons** are marine animals with eight flat shells that overlap like shingles. **Bivalves,** such as clams and scallops, have two-part, hinged shells. **Gastropods** ("stomach-foot") include snails and slugs. The **cephalopods** ("head-foot") are marine animals such as octopuses and squids.

Feeding: Chitons scrape algae off rocks; bivalves filter food particles out of water; most gastropods are herbivores; and cephalopods are predators.

Circulatory System: Most mollusks have an open circulatory system in which a heart pumps blood to tissues throughout the body cavity instead of within vessels. Cephalopods, however, have a closed circulatory system, with blood confined to vessels.

Respiratory System: Aquatic mollusks have gills; terrestrial snails and slugs have a lung derived from a space called the mantle cavity.

Excretory System: An excretory organ filters blood and produces urine.

Nervous System: The nervous system varies from simple and ladderlike to complex and cephalized. An octopus's nervous system includes a brain, a highly developed visual system, and an excellent sense of touch.

Support and Movement: All mollusks have a hydrostatic skeleton, and most have a supportive internal or external shell.

Reproduction: In sexual reproduction, fertilization may be external (in bivalves) or internal (in gastropods and cephalopods).

Defense: The hard shells of bivalves and snails protect against many predators. Cephalopods have other defenses. Squids and octopuses, for example, can change their color and shape to match their background. When alarmed, cephalopods can squirt "ink" that cloaks their escape.

Effects on Humans: We harvest pearls from oysters, and we eat clams, mussels, oysters, snails, squids, and octopuses. However, bivalves can be poisonous if they accumulate pollutants or toxins. Snails and slugs are voracious consumers of garden plants, and invasive zebra mussels have disrupted aquatic ecosystems in the central United States. ▸ invasive species, p. 417

17.5 Mastering Concepts

1. What adaptations do mollusks have in common?
2. How do mollusks feed, move, and protect themselves?
3. In what ways are mollusks important?

17.6 Annelids Are Segmented Worms

Earthworms and other segmented worms are **annelids.** The name of the phylum, Annelida, derives from the Latin word *annulus* ("little ring"), a reference to the segmented bodies of these animals (figure 17.12).

Habitat: Terrestrial, freshwater, and marine.

Body Structure: The most obvious characteristic of annelids is segmentation. They also have a complete digestive tract. A coelom separates the gut from the body wall and acts as a hydrostatic skeleton.

Diversity: Biologists recognize two main classes of annelids. One class contains the **leeches** and the **oligochaetes,** such as earthworms. The other class, the **polychaetes,** contains the marine segmented worms.

Feeding: Earthworms ingest soil, digest the organic matter, and eliminate the indigestible particles. Some leeches suck blood from vertebrates, but most eat small prey such as arthropods, snails, or other annelids. Polychaetes are often filter feeders or deposit feeders, although some are predators.

Circulatory System: All except leeches have a closed circulatory system.

Respiratory System: Some polychaetes have feathery gills, but oligochaetes and leeches exchange gases by diffusion through the body wall. They must therefore remain moist.

Excretory System: The excretory system draws in fluid from the coelom, returns some ions and other substances to the blood, and discharges the waste-laden fluid outside the body through a pore.

Nervous System: The simple "brain" consists of a mass of nerve cells at the head end of the animal. These cells connect around the digestive tract to a ventral nerve cord, with lateral nerves running through each segment.

Support and Movement: Circular and longitudinal muscles push against the coelom as the worm crawls, burrows, or swims. Leeches crawl, inchworm-style, by using the suckers at each end of the body. Polychaetes have paddlelike structures that help them walk, swim, and dig.

Reproduction: Leeches and oligochaetes are hermaphrodites, which means that each individual has the reproductive organs of both sexes. In contrast, polychaetes have separate sexes.

Defense: Many annelids avoid predation by burrowing underground or in sediments. Polychaetes called tubeworms construct stationary tubes of chitin into which they can retract, and some also have powerful jaws.

Effects on Humans: Earthworms aerate and fertilize soil. Worm farms raise oligochaetes for sale as fishing bait or as soil conditioners. A blood-thinning chemical from leeches can stimulate circulation in surgically reattached digits and ears, and physicians sometimes apply leeches to remove blood that accumulates after damage to the nervous system.

17.6 Mastering Concepts

1. What features do all annelids share?
2. List examples of animals in each of the two classes of annelids.
3. How do annelids feed, exchange gases, and move?

Phylogeny

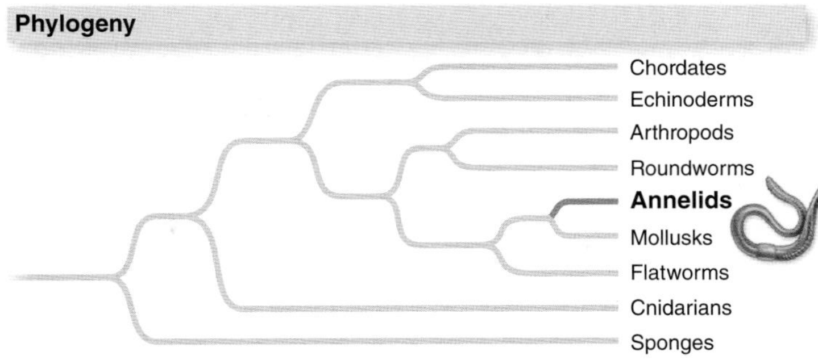

Characteristics

Annelids	
Level of organization	Organ system
Symmetry	Bilateral
Cephalization	Present
Coelom	Present
Type of digestive tract	Complete
Segmentation	Present

Diversity

Anatomy

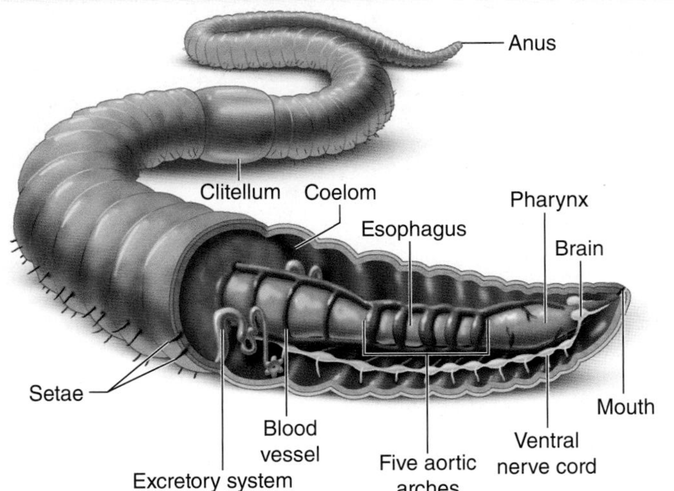

Figure 17.12 Annelids (Phylum Annelida).

17.7 Nematodes Are Unsegmented, Cylindrical Worms

Most **roundworms** (phylum Nematoda) are barely visible to the unaided eye, but they are extremely abundant in every habitat (figure 17.13).

Habitat: Some nematodes parasitize plants or animals, but most are free-living in soil or in the sediments of aquatic ecosystems.

Body Structure: Nematodes are unsegmented worms with tapered ends and a complete digestive tract. An external layer of tissue secretes a tough cuticle, which is periodically molted.

Diversity: No one knows how many species of nematodes exist. According to one estimate, 80,000 species have been discovered, but hundreds of thousands more may remain undescribed.

Feeding: Free-living nematodes eat insect larvae, fungi, bacteria, or plants. Parasitic nematodes may suck blood or consume food in the host's intestines.

Circulation and Respiration: Nematodes lack specialized circulatory or respiratory organs. Instead, fluid in the pseudocoelom distributes nutrients, O_2, and CO_2 throughout the body.

Excretory System: Specialized cells maintain salt balance and eliminate nitrogenous wastes through an excretory pore.

Nervous System: Nematodes have a brain, which is connected to two nerve cords that run along the length of the body. Bristles and other sensory structures on the body surface enable the worms to detect touch and chemicals.

Support and Movement: The pseudocoelom acts as a hydrostatic skeleton. Nematodes are limited to back-and-forth, thrashing motions because only longitudinal (lengthwise) muscles act on the pseudocoelom. As a result, a nematode can neither crawl nor lift its body above its substrate.

Reproduction: Most species have separate sexes. Females produce tough eggs that survive drying and exposure to damaging chemicals.

Defense: The cuticle may be protective. Parasitic roundworms are protected from predators while inside their hosts. Many nematodes can survive extreme heat, cold, or drying by entering a state of suspended animation.

Effects on Humans: The most familiar nematodes are parasites such as pinworms, hookworms, heartworms, and the *Trichinella* worms that are transmitted by eating undercooked pork. Nematodes also profoundly affect agriculture. Some are plant pathogens that cause diseases in and spread viruses among important food crops; others aid farmers by attacking insect pests. Finally, biologists use the nematode *Caenorhabditis elegans* in scientific research.

17.7 Mastering Concepts

1. What features do all roundworms share?
2. Contrast the bodies of roundworms, flatworms, and annelids.
3. How do nematodes feed and move?
4. How are roundworms important?

Phylogeny

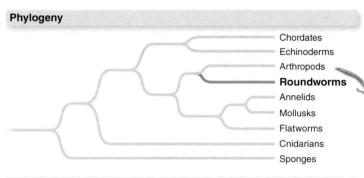

Chordates
Echinoderms
Arthropods
Roundworms
Annelids
Mollusks
Flatworms
Cnidarians
Sponges

Characteristics

Roundworms	
Level of organization	Organ system
Symmetry	Bilateral
Cephalization	Present
Coelom	Pseudocoelom
Type of digestive tract	Complete
Segmentation	Absent
Other features	Molting

Diversity

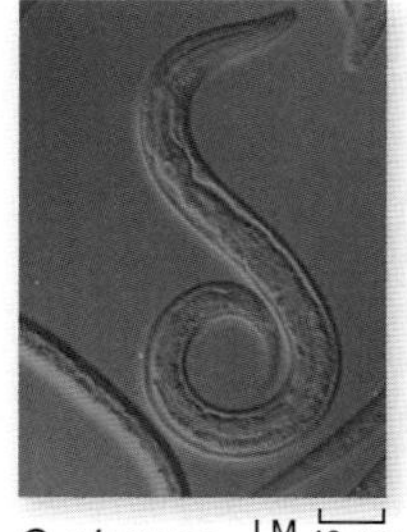

C. elegans

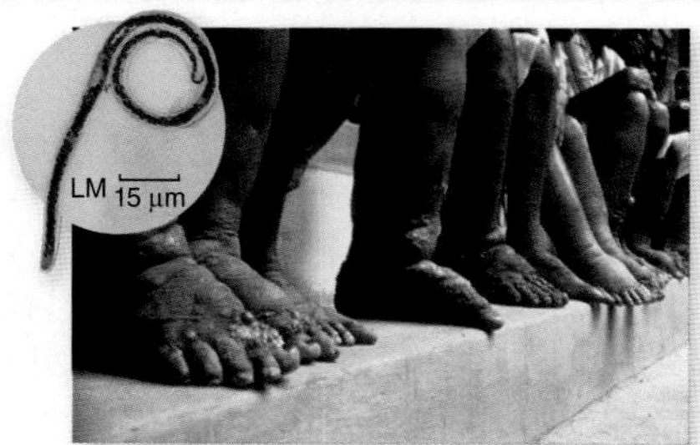

Elephantiasis, caused by a roundworm

Anatomy

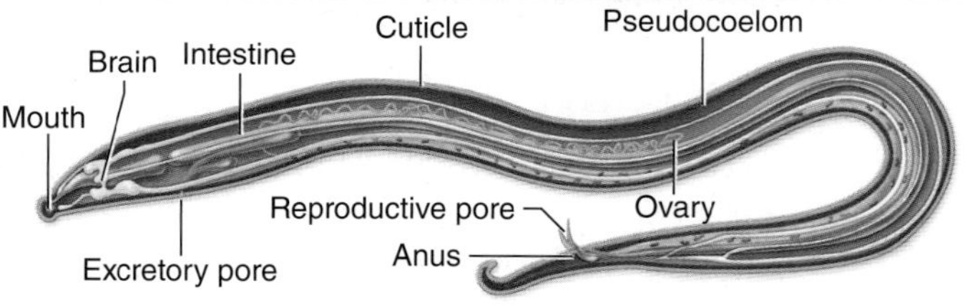

Figure 17.13 Roundworms (Phylum Nematoda).

17.8 Arthropods Have Exoskeletons and Jointed Appendages

If diversity and sheer numbers are the measure of biological success, then the phylum Arthropoda certainly is the most successful group of animals. More than 1,000,000 species of **arthropods** have been recorded already, and biologists speculate that twice this many species may exist. The number of individuals is also astonishing: according to some estimates, arthropods outnumber humans by more than 200 million to one.

Arthropoda means "jointed foot," a reference to the most distinctive feature of this phylum: their jointed appendages (figure 17.14). These appendages include not only feet but also legs, mouthparts, wings, antennae, copulatory organs, ornaments, and weapons.

In addition, all arthropods have a versatile, lightweight **exoskeleton** made mostly of chitin, protein, and (sometimes) calcium salts. Thin, flexible areas create moveable joints between body segments and within appendages. An exoskeleton has a drawback, though—to grow, an animal must molt and secrete a bigger one, leaving the animal vulnerable while its new exoskeleton is still soft. Molting is one feature that arthropods share with nematodes, another extraordinarily successful group.

A. Arthropods Have Complex Organ Systems

Habitat: Terrestrial, freshwater, and marine.

Body Structure: In addition to the distinctive exoskeleton and jointed appendages, arthropod bodies are segmented. In many arthropods, the segments group into three major body regions: head, thorax, and abdomen. The coelom is reduced to small fluid-filled cavities surrounding the reproductive and excretory organs.

Feeding: Depending on the species, arthropods can eat almost anything, including dead organic matter, plant parts, and other animals.

Circulatory System: Arthropods have open circulatory systems. A heart propels the blood, which circulates freely around the animal's organs.

Respiratory System: In most land arthropods, the body wall is perforated with holes that open into a series of branching tubes called tracheae, transporting oxygen and carbon dioxide to and from tissues. In contrast, aquatic arthropods have gills, and spiders and scorpions have stacked plates called book lungs.

Excretory System: Insects, spiders, and other terrestrial arthropods have organs called Malpighian tubules that collect and remove nitrogenous wastes while reabsorbing water. (The "green gland" in crayfish and lobsters has a similar function.) The tubules deposit dry, nitrogen-rich waste into the posterior end of the digestive tract. The animal ejects the waste, together with undigested food, through its anus.

Nervous System: Thanks to a nervous system with a brain and ventral nerve cords, many arthropods are active, fast, and sensitive to their environment. Consider, for example, the speed with which a fly can detect and react to a swatter. Their sensory systems can detect light, sound, touch, vibrations, air currents, and chemical signals. All of these clues help arthropods find food, identify mates, and escape predation.

Phylogeny

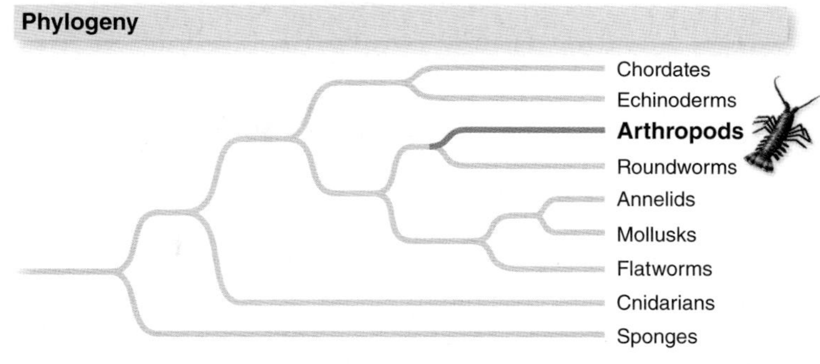

Characteristics

Arthropods	
Level of organization	Organ system
Symmetry	Bilateral
Cephalization	Present
Coelom	Present
Type of digestive tract	Complete
Segmentation	Present
Other features	Jointed appendages; exoskeleton; molting

Anatomy

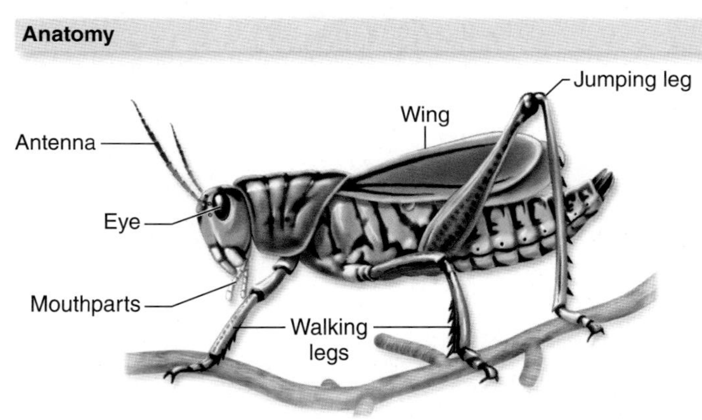

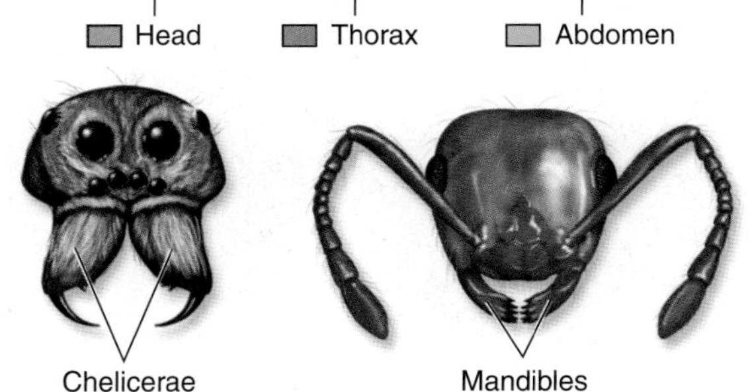

Arthropod mouthparts

Figure 17.14 Arthropods (Phylum Arthropoda).

Support and Movement: The tough exoskeleton protects the animal and gives it its shape. Internal muscles span the joints between body segments and within appendages. This arrangement generates precise, forceful movements as the animal crawls, jumps, swims, or flies.

Reproduction: Most arthropods have separate sexes. The male commonly produces a packet of sperm, which the female takes into her genital opening. The sperm fertilize her eggs internally. In most species, the female then lays the fertilized eggs, although mites and scorpions bear live young. Ants and bees tend their young, but in most other arthropods, parental care is minimal.

In some insects, such as butterflies and moths, the body changes dramatically as the animal develops. The hatched egg develops into a larva, which is an immature stage that does not resemble the adult of the species. Caterpillars are examples of larvae. The larvae eventually undergo **metamorphosis,** in which their bodies change greatly as they mature into adults. Larvae often live in different habitats and eat different foods from the adults, an adaptation that may help reduce competition between the generations. Mosquitoes and flies also undergo metamorphosis during development. Other insects, such as crickets, have young that resemble the adults; these animals change only gradually from molt to molt.

Defense: Besides the protective exoskeleton, many arthropods can bite, sting, pinch, make noises, or emit foul odors or toxins that deter predators. Some have excellent camouflage that enables them to blend into their surroundings. Others have defensive behaviors; they may jump, run, roll into a ball, dig into soil, or fly away when threatened. Some moths unfurl wings with dramatic eyespots that startle or confuse predators.

Effects on Humans: Arthropods intersect with human society in about every way imaginable. Mosquitoes, flies, fleas, and ticks transmit infectious diseases as they consume human blood. Bees and scorpions sting, termites chew wood in our homes, and many insect larvae destroy crops. Yet entire industries rely on arthropods—consider beeswax, honey, silk, and delicacies such as shrimp, crabs, and lobsters. Insects pollinate many plants, and spiders eat crop pests. The fruit fly, *Drosophila melanogaster,* is important in biological research. On a much smaller scale, dust mites eat flakes of skin that we shed as we move about our homes, while follicle mites inhabit our pores (see the Why We Care box on page 337).

Figure 17.15 Trilobites. These extinct marine arthropods have three distinct body regions along the length of the body: a long central lobe plus flanking right and left lobes.

B. Arthropods Are the Most Diverse Animals

Phylum Arthropoda is divided into five subphyla. One contains the 17,000 species of extinct **trilobites** (figure 17.15). The other four subphyla are classified based on mouthpart shape (see figure 17.14). Spiders, scorpions, and other **chelicerates** have grasping, clawlike mouthparts called chelicerae. The three subphyla of **mandibulates** have chewing, jawlike mouthparts termed mandibles.

Chelicerates: Spiders and Their Relatives

Habitat: Terrestrial and aquatic.

Body Structure: Most chelicerates have two major body regions: an abdomen and a fused head and thorax. They also have chelicerae and four or more pairs of walking legs.

Diversity: The two most familiar groups of chelicerates are horseshoe crabs and arachnids (figure 17.16). **Horseshoe crabs** are primitive-looking animals whose name refers to the hard, horseshoe-shaped exoskeleton, which

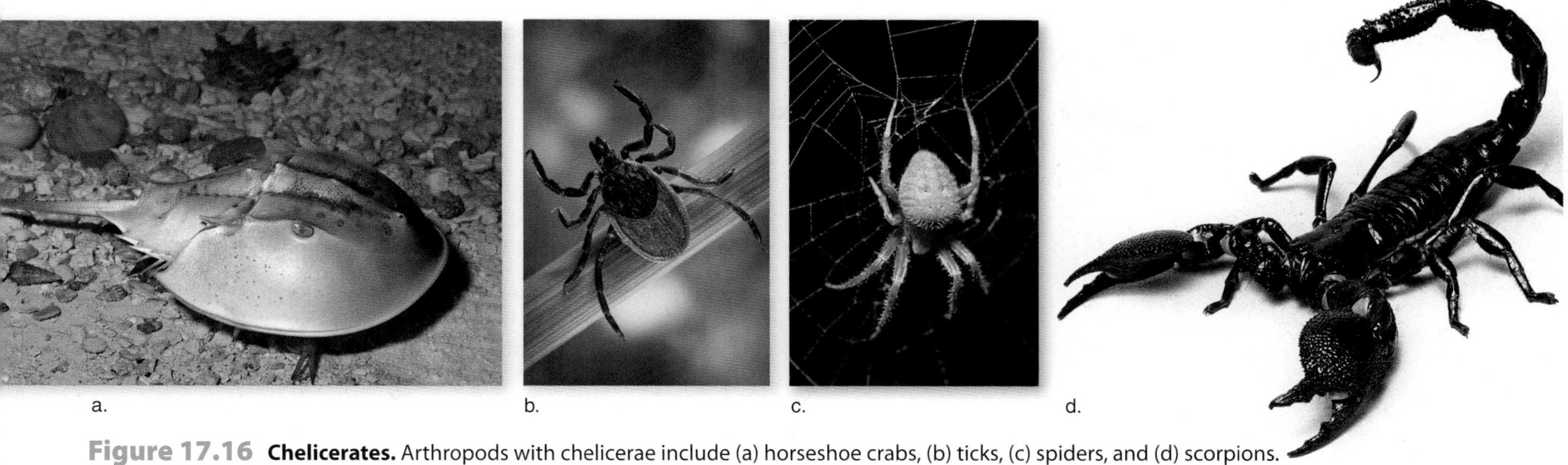

a. b. c. d.

Figure 17.16 Chelicerates. Arthropods with chelicerae include (a) horseshoe crabs, (b) ticks, (c) spiders, and (d) scorpions.

covers a wide abdomen and a long tailpiece. The four species of horseshoe crabs are not true crabs, which are crustaceans. The more than 100,000 species of **arachnids** are eight-legged arthropods, including mites and ticks; spiders; harvestmen ("daddy longlegs"); and scorpions. The first terrestrial animals to leave fossils resembled scorpions, which may have preyed upon other small animals exploring the land during the Silurian period, some 440 million years ago.

Special Features: Technicians use a compound extracted from the blood of horseshoe crabs to test medical supplies for bacteria. Spiders make "silk" and use it to produce webs, tunnels, egg cases, and spiderling nurseries. Some spiderlings use silk driftlines to float to a new habitat.

Mandibulates: Millipedes and Centipedes

About 13,000 species of **millipedes** and **centipedes** make up a group called the myriapods (figure 17.17).

Habitat: Terrestrial.

Body Structure: The head features mandibles and one pair of antennae. The rest of the body is divided into repeating subunits, each with one or two pairs of appendages.

a.

b.

Figure 17.17 Myriapods. (a) A millipede has two pairs of legs per body segment. (b) This centipede has strong mandibles and venomous claws.

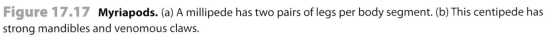

Special Features: Centipedes subdue their prey with venom; the sting of a centipede can therefore be very painful.

Mandibulates: Crustaceans

Habitat: Mostly aquatic.

Body Structure: **Crustaceans** have mandibles, two pairs of antennae, two or three major body segments, and branched appendages (figure 17.18).

Diversity: This group of about 52,000 species contains many familiar animals, including crabs, shrimp, and lobsters. Smaller crustaceans include brine shrimp, water fleas *(Daphnia),* copepods, and barnacles. Isopods, commonly known as pill bugs or "roly-polies," are the only terrestrial crustaceans.

Mandibulates: Insects

Insects colonized land shortly after plants, about 475 MYA, and they diversified rapidly. Scientists know of well over 1 million species, with many more awaiting formal description. Why did so many species of insects evolve? Biologists surmise that the answer relates to the high reproductive rates of insects. In addition, mutations in homeotic genes can modify the body segments of insects into seemingly unlimited variations; some biologists liken the insect body plan to the versatility of a Swiss army knife. ▸ homeotic genes, p. 125

Habitat: Most insects are terrestrial, but many live or reproduce in fresh water. Oceans, high altitudes, and extremely cold habitats are about the only places that are nearly devoid of insects.

Body Structure: All members of this group have mandibles and one pair of antennae. The body is divided into a head, thorax, and abdomen. Insects have six legs and usually two pairs of wings.

Diversity: Insect diversity almost defies description (figure 17.19 and table 17.1). They range in size from wingless soil-dwellers less than 1 mm long to fist-sized beetles and moths with 30-cm wingspans. Some extinct dragonflies were even larger—one had a wingspan of about 75 cm, about as long as an adult human's arm!

Special Features: The evolution of flight was an important event in life's history. Insects were the first animals to fly, using their wings to disperse to new habitats,

Figure 17.18 Crustaceans. (a) The lobster is a familiar crustacean, as is (b) this crab.

a.

b.
c.

Figure 17.19 Insects. (a) This molting cicada is an insect, as is (b) this dragonfly and (c) this beetle.

escape predators, court mates, and find food. Moreover, many of today's flowering plants evolved in conjunction with flying insects, trading nectar for rapid, efficient pollination services. ▸ pollination, p. 452

17.8 Mastering Concepts

1. What features distinguish the arthropods?
2. What are the main body regions of an arthropod?
3. How do arthropods use their jointed appendages?
4. Describe how arthropods feed, respire, excrete metabolic wastes, sense their environment, move, reproduce, and defend themselves.
5. What is the function of the exoskeleton?
6. In what ways are arthropods important?
7. How are chelicerates different from mandibulates?
8. Give an example of an animal in each subphylum of arthropods.

Why We Care | Your Tiny Companions

Even when you think you are alone, you aren't; your body may host a diverse assortment of arthropods. Head lice and body lice are biting insects that cause skin irritation. Ticks latch onto the skin and suck your blood, sometimes transmitting the bacteria that cause Lyme disease. The tiny larvae of chigger mites produce saliva that digests small areas of skin tissue, causing intense itching.

Lice, ticks, and chiggers are hard to ignore, but you may never notice one inconspicuous companion: the follicle mite, *Demodex* (figure 17.A). This arachnid, which is less than half a millimeter long, lives in hair follicles and nearby oil glands, where it eats skin secretions and dead skin cells. *Demodex* mites are by no means rare. Nearly everyone has them, and each follicle may house up to 25 of the tiny animals. (If you would like to see your own follicle mites, carefully remove an eyebrow hair or eyelash and examine it with a compound microscope.) Luckily, the infestation is typically symptomless, although occasionally the mites may cause a rash.

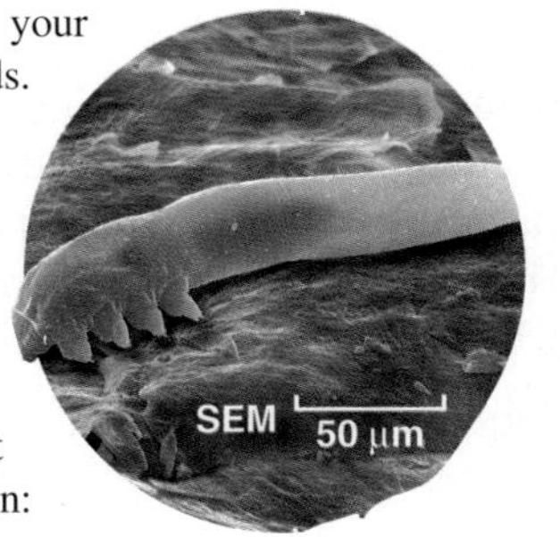

Figure 17.A Follicle Mites. Tiny *Demodex* mites live in skin pores and hair follicles.

TABLE 17.1 Some Major Orders of Insects

Order	Examples
Thysanura	Silverfish
Ephemeroptera	Mayflies
Odonata	Dragonflies and damselflies
Orthoptera	Roaches, crickets, grasshoppers
Phthiraptera	Lice
Hemiptera	Cicadas, aphids
Coleoptera	Beetles
Hymenoptera	Ants, wasps, bees
Lepidoptera	Moths, butterflies
Diptera	True flies
Siphonaptera	Fleas

17.9 Echinoderm Adults Have Five-Part, Radial Symmetry

The **echinoderms** (phylum Echinodermata) include some of the most colorful and distinctive sea animals (figure 17.20). Their name means "spiny skin."

Habitat: Marine.

Body Structure: Adult echinoderms have radial symmetry, with the body divided into five parts. Another unique feature of echinoderms is the **water vascular system,** a series of enclosed, water-filled canals that end in hollow tube feet. Coordinated muscle contractions extend and retract each foot, bending it from side to side or creating a suction-cup effect when applied to a hard surface.

Diversity: The most familiar echinoderms are sea stars, sea urchins, sand dollars, and sea cucumbers.

Feeding: Some echinoderms, such as sea stars, are predators. Sea cucumbers eat dead organic matter; sea urchins scrape algae from rocks.

Circulatory and Respiratory Systems: Tube feet absorb oxygen from water. Respiration may also occur by means of tiny skin gills (in sea stars) or by a network of passageways called a respiratory tree (in sea cucumbers).

Excretory System: The water vascular system helps flush metabolic wastes from echinoderm bodies.

Nervous System: Echinoderms lack heads and brains. Nerves extending down the arms and tentacles connect with a central nerve ring surrounding the gut. Some tube feet detect touch or chemicals.

Support and Movement: Tube feet allow echinoderms to glide slowly while maintaining a firm grip on the substrate. Sand dollars and some sea cucumbers burrow into soft sediments, and some brittle stars can swim by using their appendages as oars.

Reproduction: Echinoderms usually reproduce sexually. The larvae start out with bilateral symmetry, but then a group of cells assembles into a five-sided disc that turns inside out and consumes the remainder of the larva. The animal, now a tiny replica of the adult form, continues to grow to its mature size.

Defense: Besides spines, the skin of echinoderms may also be equipped with small pincers that deter predators. In addition, sea stars have internal skeletal plates; in sea urchins and sand dollars, these plates fuse into a protective shell. The soft-bodied sea cucumbers often produce poisonous chemicals, and many echinoderms can regenerate severed body parts.

Effects on Humans: People harvest some species of sea urchins for their reproductive organs, an edible delicacy called *uni*. Parts of some sea cucumbers are also edible. On the other hand, the crown-of-thorns sea star can cause painful wounds in humans who touch them. These animals eat corals and have wiped out large areas of Australia's Great Barrier Reef.

17.9 Mastering Concepts

1. What characteristics distinguish the echinoderms?
2. What are some examples of echinoderms?
3. In what ways are echinoderms important?

Phylogeny

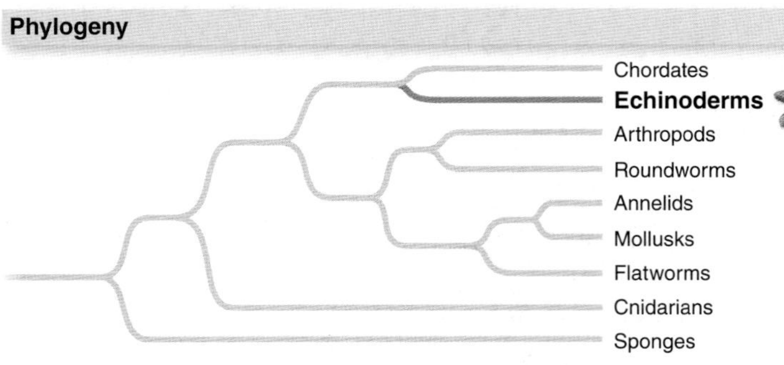

Characteristics

Echinoderms	
Level of organization	Organ system
Symmetry	Bilateral larvae; radial adults
Cephalization	Absent
Coelom	Present
Type of digestive tract	Complete
Segmentation	Absent

Larva LM 500 μm

Adult

Diversity

Anatomy

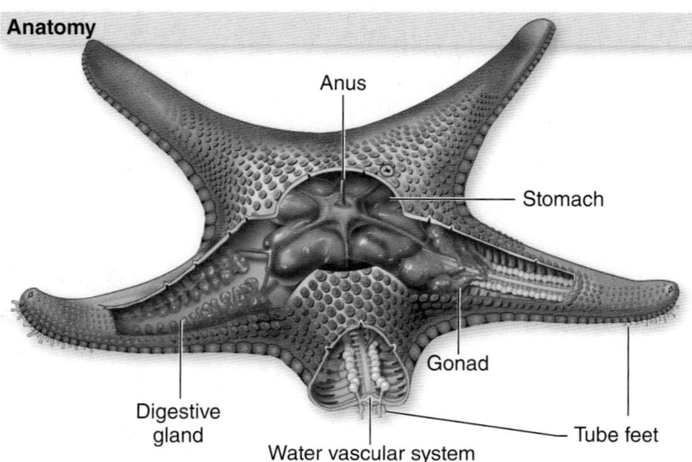

Figure 17.20 Echinoderms (Phylum Echinodermata).

17.10 Most Chordates Are Vertebrates

Many people find phylum Chordata to be the most interesting of all, at least in part because it contains humans and many of the animals that we eat, keep as pets, and enjoy observing in zoos and in the wild. The **chordates** are a diverse group of at least 60,000 species. From the tiniest tadpole to fearsome sharks and lumbering elephants, chordates are dazzling in their variety of forms.

Every chordate has the following four features at some point during its life (figure 17.21):

1. **Notochord:** The notochord is a flexible rod that extends dorsally (along the back) down the length of a chordate's body. In most vertebrates, the notochord does not persist into adulthood but rather is replaced by the backbone that surrounds the spinal cord.
2. **Dorsal, hollow nerve cord:** The dorsal, hollow nerve cord is parallel to the notochord. In many chordates, the nerve cord develops into the spinal cord and enlarges at the head end, forming a brain.
3. **Pharyngeal pouches or slits:** In most chordate embryos, pouches or slits form in the pharynx, the muscular tube that begins at the back of the mouth.
4. **Postanal tail:** A muscular tail extends past the anus in all chordate embryos. In humans, chimpanzees, and gorillas, the tail normally withers away before birth, leaving only the tailbone as a vestige. In fishes, salamanders, lizards, cats, and many other species, adults retain the tail.

Figure 17.22 on page 340 depicts the evolutionary relationships within phylum Chordata. One of the earliest branching points denotes the evolution of the bony or cartilage-rich **cranium,** which surrounds and protects the brain. The next branching point shows the appearance of vertebrates, which are chordates that have a backbone composed of cartilage or bone. **Vertebrae** protect the spinal cord and provide attachment points for muscles, giving the animal a greater range of movement.

Jaws are the bones that frame the entrance to the mouth. The development of hinged jaws from gill supports greatly expanded the ways that animals could feed. New food sources, in turn, selected for a more complex brain that could develop a hunting strategy or plan an escape. In many vertebrate species, teeth or a beak are attached to the jaw. These features enhance the ability of the animal to grasp prey or gather small food items.

Lungs were another important evolutionary milestone. Most fishes have gills that exchange O_2 and CO_2 with water. In contrast, most air-breathing vertebrates have internal saclike **lungs** as the organs of respiration. Lungs are homologous to the gas bladders of bony fishes. Originally, these sacs allowed fishes to gulp air; in the ancestors of terrestrial vertebrates, however, they developed into air-breathing lungs.

The evolution of limbs came next. **Tetrapods** are vertebrates with two pairs of limbs that enable the animals to walk on land (*tetrapod* means "four legs"). Amphibians, reptiles (including birds), and mammals are all tetrapods. Some animals classified as tetrapods, however, have fewer than four limbs. Snakes, for example, lack limbs entirely. The limbs of whales, dolphins, and sea lions are either modified into flippers or are too small to project from the body. Anatomical and molecular evidence, however, clearly links all of these animals to tetrapod ancestors.

Another important event in the evolution of terrestrial chordates was the evolution of the watertight egg. The eggs of fishes and amphibians must remain moist, or the embryos inside will die. In contrast, reptiles (including

Phylogeny

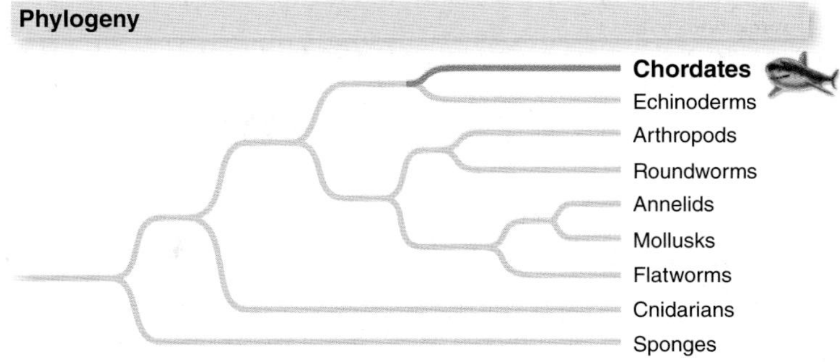

Characteristics

Chordates	
Level of organization	Organ system
Symmetry	Bilateral
Cephalization	Present
Coelom	Present
Type of digestive tract	Complete
Segmentation	Present (except in tunicates)
Other features	Notochord; dorsal, hollow nerve cord; pharyngeal pouches or slits; postanal tail

Anatomy

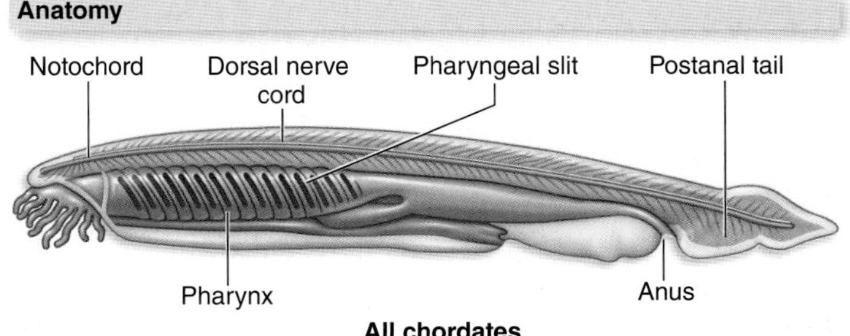

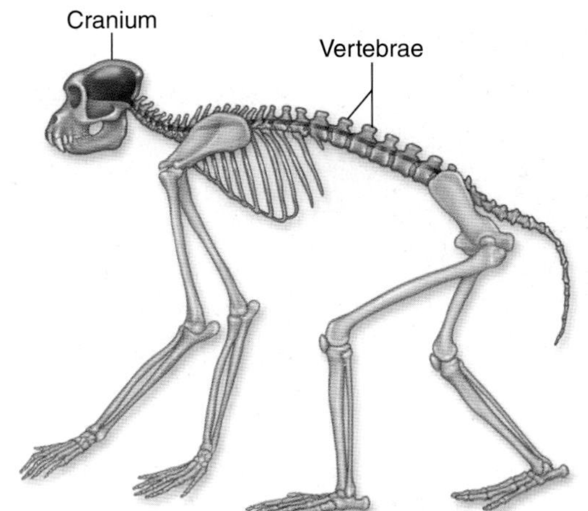

Figure 17.21 Chordates (Phylum Chordata).

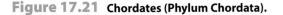

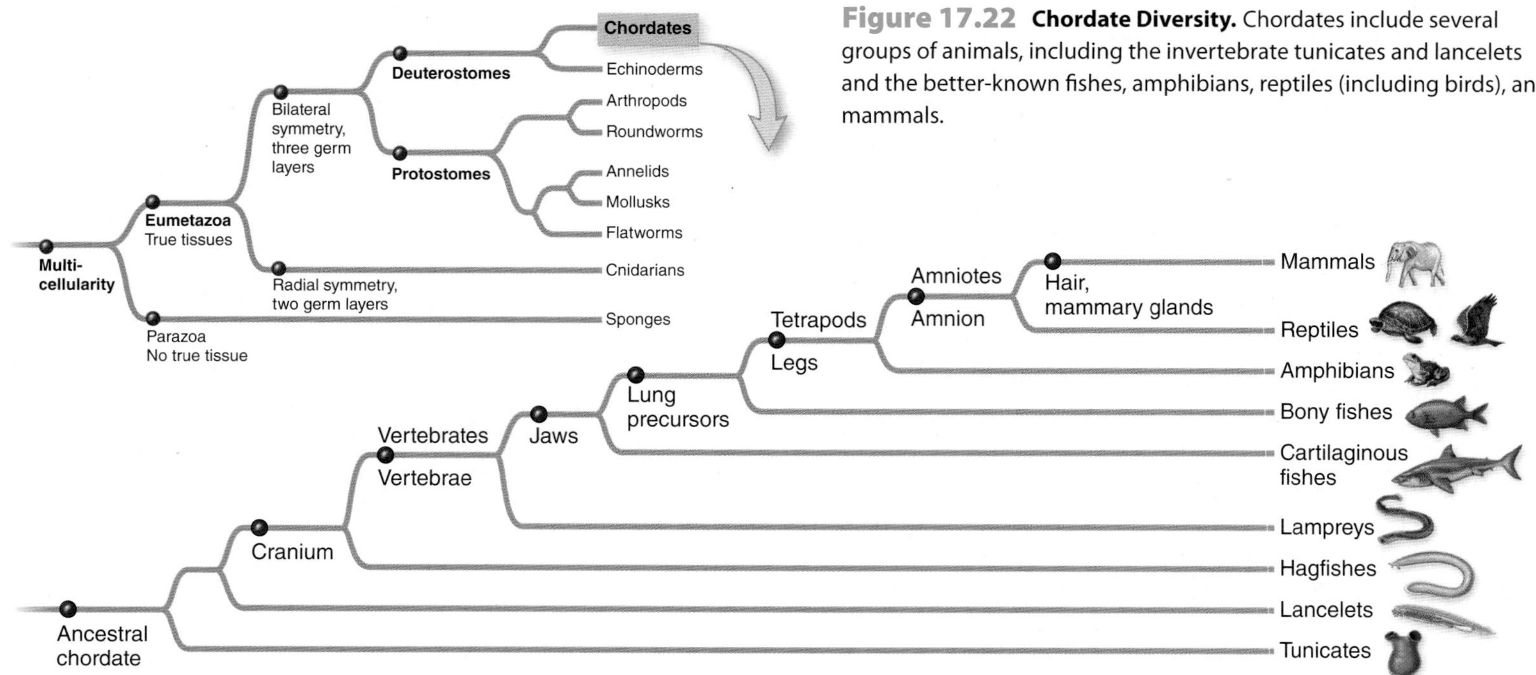

Figure 17.22 Chordate Diversity. Chordates include several groups of animals, including the invertebrate tunicates and lancelets and the better-known fishes, amphibians, reptiles (including birds), and mammals.

birds) and mammals form a clade of **amniotes** that can breed in dry habitats, in part because of the evolution of the **amniotic egg** (figure 17.23). Its leathery or hard outer layer surrounds a yolk that nourishes the developing embryo and enables it to survive outside of water. Also inside the egg are several membranes (the amnion, chorion, and allantois) that cushion the embryo, provide for gas exchange, and store metabolic wastes. These membranes are homologous to the protective structures that surround a developing fetus in the uterus of a female mammal.

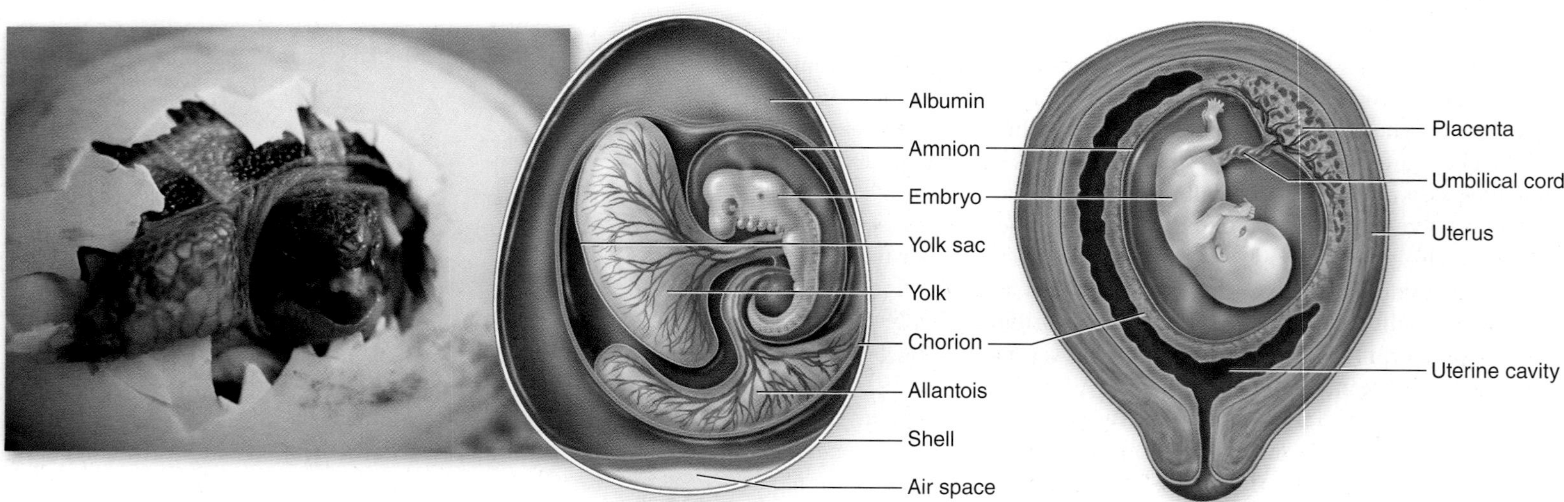

Figure 17.23 The Amnion. The amnion is a sac that encloses the developing embryo of a reptile or mammal. In an amniotic egg, the embryo is encased in a hard, protective shell, and it is supported internally by the amnion, allantois, and chorion. Placental mammals have the same structures (the allantois, which is not shown for the mammal, becomes part of the umbilical cord).

The regulation of body temperature is an additional characteristic that is important in animal biology. The body temperature of an **ectotherm** tends to fluctuate with the environment; these animals have no internal mechanism keeping their temperature within a narrow range. Invertebrates, fishes, amphibians, and nonavian reptiles are ectotherms. Many behaviors, such as basking in the sun or burrowing into the ground during the hottest part of the day, help an ectotherm adjust its temperature. In contrast, birds and mammals are **endotherms,** which means they maintain a more-or-less constant body temperature by using heat generated from their own metabolism. Endothermy requires an enormous amount of energy, which explains why birds and mammals must eat so much more food than ectotherms of the same size. Fur and feathers help retain heat in these animals.

17.10 Mastering Concepts

1. What are the four defining characteristics of chordates?
2. Which chordates have a cranium, and which are also vertebrates?
3. How did the origin of jaws, lungs, limbs, and the amnion affect the course of vertebrate evolution?
4. What is the difference between an ectotherm and an endotherm?

17.11 Chordate Diversity Extends from Water to Land to Sky

The first part of this chapter explored differences among internal organ systems, highlighting the dramatic transitions between the simplest animals and the most complex. The rest of this chapter takes a slightly different approach. Most chordates have complex respiratory, digestive, excretory, and nervous systems. We therefore focus here on the evolutionary transitions between the main groups of chordates and on the diversity of animals within the phylum.

A. Tunicates and Lancelets Have Neither Cranium nor Backbone

Tunicates and lancelets form two subphyla of invertebrates that probably resemble the ancestral chordates (figure 17.24). **Tunicates** are sessile marine animals that resemble a bag with two siphons. Cilia pull water in through one siphon. The animal extracts oxygen and food particles, and the water exits through the other siphon. Only the free-swimming tunicate larva, which resembles a tadpole, has all four chordate characteristics.

Lancelets resemble small, eyeless fishes with translucent bodies. They live in shallow seas, with their tails buried in sediment. Their mouths filter food particles out of the water. These animals clearly display all four major chordate characteristics, as well as inklings of the muscular and nervous systems that appear in the vertebrates.

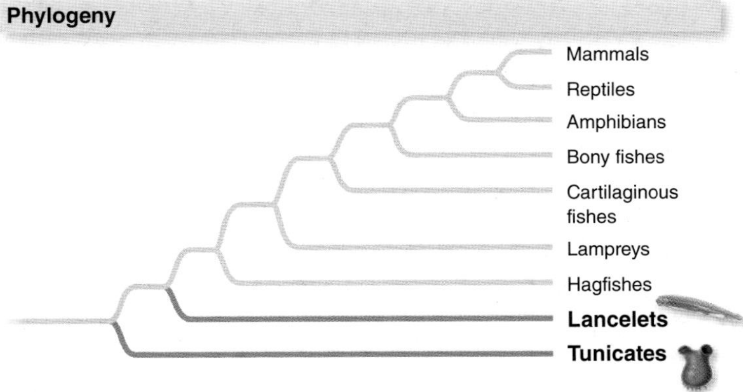

Characteristics

Tunicates and lancelets	
Cranium	Absent
Vertebrae	Absent
Jaws	Absent
Skeletal composition	Does not apply
Lungs	Absent
Limbs	Absent
Amnion	Absent
Body temperature regulation	Ectotherm

Diversity

Figure 17.24 Tunicates and Lancelets.

Phylogeny

Characteristics

Hagfishes	
Cranium	Present
Vertebrae	Absent
Jaws	Absent
Skeletal composition	Cartilage
Lungs	Absent
Limbs	Absent
Amnion	Absent
Body temperature regulation	Ectotherm
Other features	Slime production

Diversity

Figure 17.25 Hagfishes.

B. Hagfishes Have a Cranium but Lack a Backbone

The long, slender **hagfish** looks something like an eel (figure 17.25). Even though hagfish skin is marketed as "eel skin" in boots and wallets, hagfishes are not eels. In a hagfish, cartilage makes up the cranium and notochord. But because vertebrae do not surround the nerve cord, hagfishes are not vertebrates. On the other hand, an eel is a true fish—a vertebrate.

Hagfishes live in cold ocean waters, eating marine invertebrates such as shrimp and worms or using their tongues to scavenge the soft tissues of dead or near-dead animals. These animals have some unusual abilities. They can slide their flexible bodies in and out of knots to escape predation or clean themselves. Hagfishes are also called "slime hags," in recognition of the glands that release copious amounts of a sticky slime when the animal is disturbed.

C. Fishes Are Aquatic Vertebrates with Gills and Fins

Fishes are the most diverse and abundant of the vertebrates, with more than 30,000 known species that vary greatly in size, shape, and color (figure 17.26). They occupy nearly all types of water, from fresh to salty, from clear to murky, and from frigid to warm, although they cannot tolerate hot springs.

Fishes play important roles in their aquatic habitats. They graze on algae, scavenge dead organic matter, or prey on other animals, eating everything from mosquito larvae and other small invertebrates to one another. Tuna and many other fish species are also an important source of dietary protein for people (and their pets) on every continent. Angling for trout, bass, salmon, and other fishes remains a popular sport. Fishes also inspire a wide range of emotions, from an intense fear of sharks to the tranquility that comes from watching tropical fish in a home aquarium.

Fishes originated some 500 MYA. Segmented backbones and jaws arose in this group, as did two of the adaptations that enabled vertebrates to thrive on land: lungs and limbs. Lungs developed in a few species of fishes, and the air-breathing descendants of these animals eventually colonized the land. No fish has true limbs, but some fishes have fins with stronger bones and more flesh than the delicate, swimming fins of other fishes. These robust fins may have enabled tetrapod ancestors to move along the sediments of their shallow-water homes. Whatever their original selective advantage, those fins eventually evolved into the limbs that define the tetrapods.

Modern fishes include the jawless **lampreys**. Lampreys are the simplest organisms to have cartilage around the nerve cord, so they are most like the first true vertebrates. The adults feed on small invertebrates, although some species use their suckers to consume the blood of fish. Over the past century, some lampreys have ventured beyond their natural Lake Ontario range into the other Great Lakes, where they have been largely responsible for the decline in populations of lake trout and whitefish. ▸ invasive species, p. 417

Unlike lampreys, the vast majority of fishes have jaws. Biologists divide the jawed fishes into two major groups, the cartilaginous fishes and the bony fishes. The **cartilaginous fishes** include sharks, skates, and rays. This clade arose some 450 MYA. As the name implies, their skeletons are made of cartilage. Although some sharks feed on plankton, the carnivorous species are notorious for their ability to detect blood in the water. Cartilaginous fishes also have a **lateral line,** which is a sense organ extending along both sides of the fish. The lateral line is a series of canals that detect vibration in nearby water, helping the animal to find prey and escape predation. Some species of cartilaginous fishes must swim continuously to keep water flowing over their gills.

The **bony fishes** form a clade that includes 96% of existing fish species. They have skeletons of bony tissue reinforced with mineral deposits of calcium phosphate. Like sharks, bony fishes have a lateral line system. Unlike cartilaginous fishes, however, the bony fishes have a hinged gill covering that can direct water over the gills, eliminating the need for constant swimming. In addition, most bony fishes have a gas bladder that helps the animal adjust its buoyancy.

Bony fishes are divided into two classes:

- The **ray-finned fishes** include nearly all familiar fishes: eels, minnows, catfish, trout, tuna, salmon, and many others. Their diversity and abundance reflect their superb adaptations to a watery world.
- The **lobe-finned fishes** are the bony fishes most closely related to the tetrapods, based on the anatomical structure of their fleshy paired fins. This group includes the lungfishes and the coelacanths. **Lungfishes** have lungs that are homologous to those of tetrapods. During droughts, a lungfish burrows into the mud beneath stagnant water, gulping air and temporarily slowing their metabolism. **Coelacanths** are called "living fossils"; they originated during the Devonian period and remain the oldest existing lineage of vertebrates with jaws.

Phylogeny

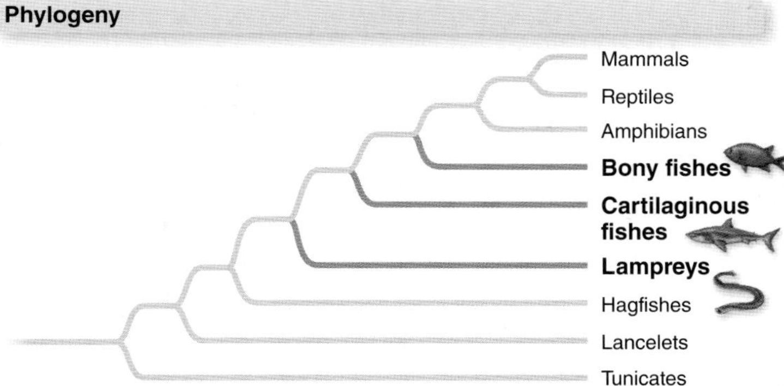

Characteristics

Fishes	
Cranium	Present
Vertebrae	Present
Jaws	Present (except in lampreys)
Skeletal composition	Cartilage or bone
Lungs	Absent (except in lungfishes)
Limbs	Absent
Amnion	Absent
Body temperature regulation	Ectotherm

Diversity

Lamprey

Figure 17.26 The Fishes.

Stingray (cartilaginous fish)

Shark (cartilaginous fish)

Ray-finned fish (bony fish)

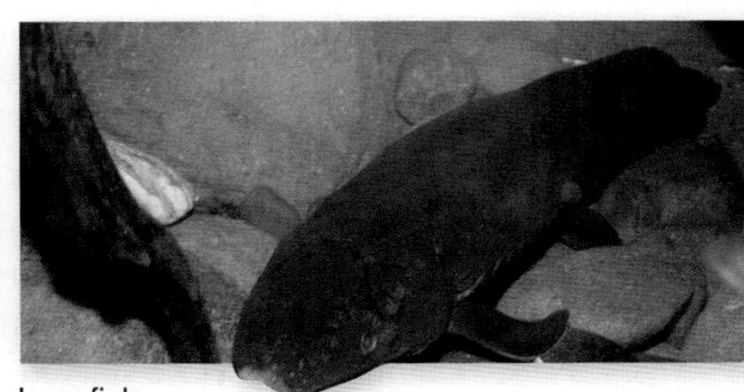

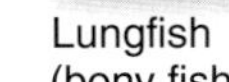

Lungfish (bony fish)

Coelacanth (bony fish)

Phylogeny

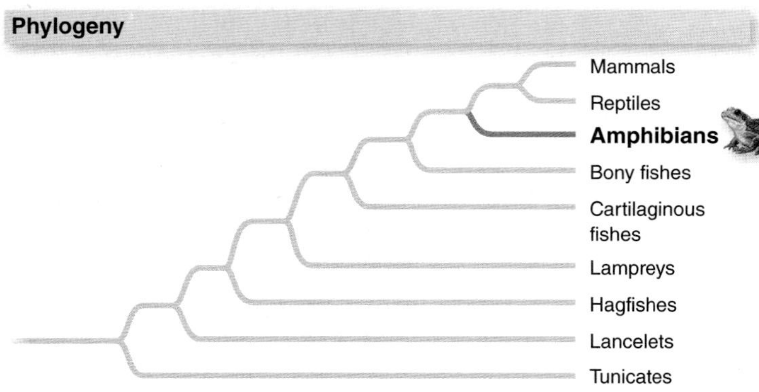

Characteristics

Amphibians	
Cranium	Present
Vertebrae	Present
Jaws	Present
Skeletal composition	Bone
Lungs	Present
Limbs	Present
Amnion	Absent
Body temperature regulation	Ectotherm
Other features	Breathe through skin; require water for reproduction

Diversity

Frog

Caecilian

Salamander

Figure 17.27 The Amphibians.

D. Amphibians Live on Land and in Water

The word **amphibian** comes from the Greek words for "double-life," referring to the ability of these tetrapod vertebrates to live in fresh water and on land (figure 17.27). Amphibians are probably the least familiar vertebrates because most people do not eat them or keep them as pets. Nevertheless, they are important in ecosystems, controlling algae and populations of insects that transmit human disease. Scientists are also studying toxins in amphibian skin as possible painkilling drugs.

When the ancestors of today's amphibians moved to land, they encountered plentiful hiding places, food, and oxygen. But the terrestrial habitat also presented new challenges. The animals faced wider swings in temperature, and their delicate gills collapsed without the buoyancy of water. As a result of these new selective pressures, lungs improved, and circulatory systems grew more complex and powerful. The skeleton became denser and better able to withstand gravity. Natural selection also favored acute hearing and sight, with tear glands and eyelids keeping eyes moist.

Yet amphibians retain a strong link to the water. Amphibian eggs, which lack protective shells and membranes, will die if they dry out. Also, the larvae (tadpoles) respire through external gills, which require water. Although most adults have lungs, many supplement oxygen intake by gas exchange through their skin, which must therefore remain moist.

Today's amphibians include three main lineages: frogs and toads; salamanders and newts; and caecilians. Most amphibian species are **frogs** or toads. In most species, the young start out as legless, aquatic tadpoles. As they mature, tadpoles typically undergo a dramatic change in body form—a metamorphosis. They develop legs and lungs, lose the tail, and acquire carnivorous tastes. **Salamanders** and newts have tails and four legs, so they resemble lizards. Both adults and young are carnivores, eating arthropods, worms, snails, fish, and other salamanders. The limbless **caecilians,** on the other hand, resemble giant earthworms. Most species burrow under the soil in tropical forests, but a few inhabit shallow freshwater ponds. Caecilians are carnivores, eating insects and worms.

E. Reptiles Were the First Vertebrates to Thrive on Dry Land

The changeability of scientific knowledge is evident in any modern discussion of **reptiles** and **birds** (figure 17.28). The word *reptile* traditionally referred only to snakes, lizards, crocodiles, and other amniotes with dry, scaly skin. Birds had feathery body coverings and were considered a separate lineage. But that point of view has changed. We now know that birds form one of several clades of reptiles. Modern use of the term *reptile* therefore includes both the nonavian reptiles and the birds.

Reptiles evolved from amphibians between 363 and 290 MYA. They dominated animal life during the Mesozoic era, until their decline beginning 65 MYA. Although many reptile species survived to the present day, many others are known only from fossils. The extinct groups include the marine ichthyosaurs and plesiosaurs, the flying pterosaurs, and the terrestrial dinosaurs (see the Burning Question in section 17.12). We do not know what caused the mass extinction that ended the Mesozoic era, but it coincides with an asteroid impact near the Yucatán peninsula. Biologists estimate that photosynthesis was almost nonexistent for years, as debris from the impact circulated in the atmosphere and blocked the sunlight. With the base of the food chain gone, many animals must have starved.

Most reptiles have adaptations that enable them to live and reproduce on dry land. Tough scales cover the skin, and the kidneys excrete only small amounts of water. In addition, internal fertilization meant that reptiles no longer deposited sperm in water. Their amniotic eggs are adapted to dry conditions. Finally, well-developed lungs increased their respiratory capacity beyond that of their aquatic ancestors.

Nonavian Reptiles The orders of nonavian reptiles include turtles and tortoises; lizards and snakes; and crocodilians. Like fishes and amphibians, all of the nonavian reptiles are ectothermic.

Movies depict snakes, alligators, and crocodiles as terrifying killers, but most reptiles are inconspicuous animals that cannot harm people. Yet they are an important link in ecosystems, controlling populations of rodents and insects while providing food for owls and other predatory birds. In addition, some people keep snakes, lizards, or turtles as pets. In some parts of the world, reptiles have an even greater economic effect; the skins of farm-raised snakes and crocodiles are the raw material for boots, belts, and wallets, and some restaurants serve alligator meat.

Almost 95% of nonavian reptile species are **snakes** or **lizards.** These animals are similar to each other; the main difference is that lizards usually have legs and snakes do not. The **crocodilians** (crocodiles, alligators, and their relatives) all live in or near water. Their horizontally held heads have eyes on top and nostrils at the end of the elongated snout. Heavy scales cover their bodies; four legs project from the sides. These reptiles look somewhat primitive, yet they have acute senses and complex behaviors. For example, like birds, crocodilians lay eggs in nests, which the adults guard. The adults also care for the hatchlings, which stay with their mothers while they are young and call to the adults when they are in danger.

Birds The behavioral similarities between crocodilians and birds are unsurprising in light of evolutionary history. Birds, dinosaurs, and crocodilians all belonged to a reptilian group called archosaurs, of which only the birds and crocodilians survive today.

Of course, birds have unique features that set them apart from other reptiles. Like mammals and unlike all other reptiles, birds are endothermic. Also, most birds can fly, although ostriches and some other species are flightless. Anatomical adaptations to flight include a tapered body with a streamlined profile. Their lightweight bones are hollow, with internal struts that add support. The powerful heart and unique lungs supply the oxygen that supports the high metabolic demands of flight. Wings provide lift, while highly developed muscles power flight.

Birds are the only modern animals that have **feathers,** which provide insulation and enable birds to fly. Feathers are also important in mating behavior, as anyone who has watched a peacock show off his plumage can attest. Like a snake's scales, a feather is built of the protein keratin.

Today, birds are a part of everyday human life. U.S. consumers eat hundreds of millions of chickens and turkeys every year, along with countless chicken eggs. We keep caged birds as pets, and we use feathers in everything from hats to down blankets. Songbirds enrich the lives of many birdwatchers, and hunters pursue wild turkeys, doves, and ducks. Birds are important in ecosystems as well. Some pollinate plants and disperse fruits and seeds, whereas others eat rodents, insects, and other vermin. But birds can also be pests. Starlings and pigeons are a nuisance in cities, fouling buildings and sidewalks with their droppings and speeding the rusting of bridges. Moreover, ducks and other domesticated birds transmit bird flu and other diseases to humans.

Phylogeny

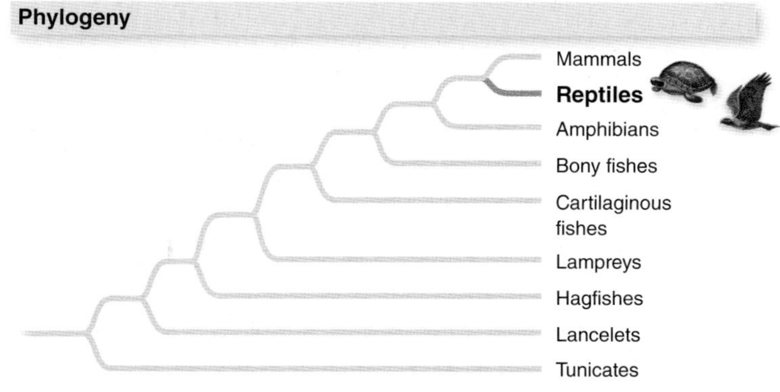

Characteristics

Reptiles	
Cranium	Present
Vertebrae	Present
Jaws	Present
Skeletal composition	Bone
Lungs	Present
Limbs	Present
Amnion	Present
Body temperature regulation	Ectotherm (nonavian reptiles); endotherm (birds)
Other features	Nonavian reptiles have dry, scaly skin; birds have feathers and hollow bones

Diversity

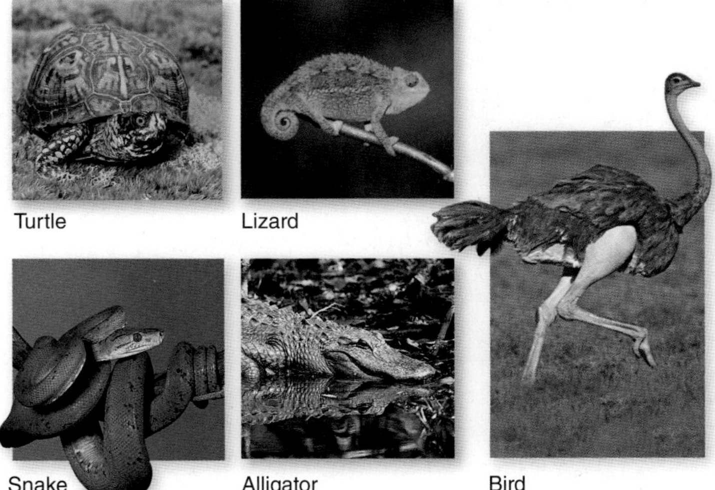

Figure 17.28 The Reptiles.

F. Mammals Are Warm, Furry Milk-Drinkers

Mammals are the most familiar vertebrates, not only because we are them but also because we surround ourselves with them (figure 17.29). We keep dogs and cats as pets. Farmers raise cows, pigs, and goats for their meat or milk. Sheep provide meat and wool, and leather from cows makes up everything from upholstery to shoes. Horses, oxen, mules, and dogs are important work animals. Many people hunt or trap mammals for food, sport, or fur.

Mammals also play important roles in ecosystems. Coyotes, wolves, and foxes keep populations of herbivorous deer and small mammals in check. Some bats eat insects, and others pollinate plants. On the other hand, pests such as rats, mice, and skunks thrive alongside human populations. Some transmit diseases, including hantavirus, rabies, and plague.

Mammals arose before the end of the Triassic period (about 200 MYA). Most were small until after the mass extinction that occurred 65 MYA. The loss of so many reptile species paved the way for the rapid diversification of many larger species of mammals. At the same time, the rise of flowering plants provided new food sources and habitats for mammals and for the arthropods that many mammals eat.

The word *mammal* derives from the Latin *mammae* for "breast" and refers to the milk-secreting **mammary glands** of the female. Infant mammals are nourished by their mother's milk. Mammals are also distinguished from other vertebrates by hair, which is composed of keratin and helps conserve body heat. Even whales and dolphins have hair at birth, but they lose it as they mature into their streamlined shapes.

Biologists divide mammals into two subclasses, one containing egg-laying mammals and the other containing live-bearing mammals. The **monotremes** are mammals that lay eggs, such as the duck-billed platypus and echidnas of Australia and New Guinea. The live-bearing mammals are further subdivided into two clades, the marsupials and the placental mammals. **Marsupials,** such as kangaroos and opossums, give birth to tiny, immature young about 4 to 5 weeks after conception. In many marsupials, the babies crawl from the mother's vagina to a pouch, where they suckle milk and continue developing. Some species, however, have poorly developed pouches or none at all. In these marsupials, the nipples are exposed, and only the mother's body protects the suckling young.

The **placental mammals** are the most diverse of the three groups. Placental mammals have much longer pregnancies than do marsupials. Females carry their young inside the uterus, where a **placenta** connects the maternal and fetal circulatory systems (see figure 17.23). Bats, rodents, cetaceans (whales and dolphins), carnivores (dogs and cats), hoofed mammals, elephants, and many other mammals are placental mammals, as are humans. We belong to an order, Primates, that arose some 60 MYA. Section 17.12 describes how this group gave rise to the characteristics and abilities that distinguish our own species.

Phylogeny

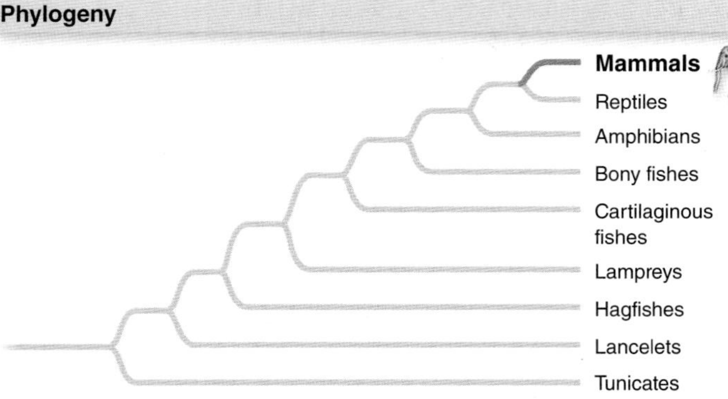

Characteristics

Mammals	
Cranium	Present
Vertebrae	Present
Jaws	Present
Skeletal composition	Bone
Lungs	Present
Limbs	Present
Amnion	Present
Body temperature regulation	Endotherm
Other features	Hair or fur; mammary glands

Diversity

Monotremes

Marsupials

Placental mammals

Figure 17.29 The Mammals.

17.11 Mastering Concepts

1. What are tunicates and lancelets?
2. Make a table comparing the features of each vertebrate group.
3. Describe the adaptations that mark the transition from fishes to amphibians, reptiles, and mammals.
4. What characteristics place the birds within the reptiles, and how are birds different from other reptiles?

17.12 Fossils and DNA Tell the Human Evolution Story

Figure 17.30 **Two Types of Primates.** The behavioral similarities between baboons and humans are evident in many ways, including parental care.

In many ways, humans are Earth's dominant species. We are not the most numerous—more microbes occupy one person's intestinal tract than there are people on Earth. In the short time of human existence, however, we have colonized most continents, altered Earth's surface, eliminated many species, and changed many others to fit our needs. Where did we come from?

A. Humans Are Primates

If you watch the monkeys or apes in a zoo for a few minutes, it is almost impossible to ignore how similar they seem to humans (figure 17.30). Young ones scramble about and play. They sniff and handle food. Babies cling to their mothers. Adults gather in small groups or sit quietly, snoozing or staring into space.

It is no surprise that we see ourselves reflected in the behaviors of monkeys and apes. All **primates,** including monkeys, apes, and humans, share a suite of physical characteristics. First, primates have grasping hands with opposable thumbs that can bend inward to touch the pads of the fingers. Some primates also have grasping feet with opposable big toes. Second, a primate's fingers and toes have flat nails instead of claws. Third, eyes set in the front of the skull give primates binocular vision with overlapping fields of sight that produce excellent depth perception. Fourth, the primate brain is large by comparison with body size.

Compared with many other groups of mammals, primate anatomy is unusually versatile. For instance, bat wings are useful for flight but not much else; likewise, horse hooves are best for fast running. In contrast, primates have multipurpose fingers and toes that are useful not only for locomotion but also for grasping and manipulating small objects. Primate limbs are similarly versatile.

The primate lineage contains three main groups: prosimians, simians, and hominoids (figure 17.31). **Prosimian** is an informal umbrella term for

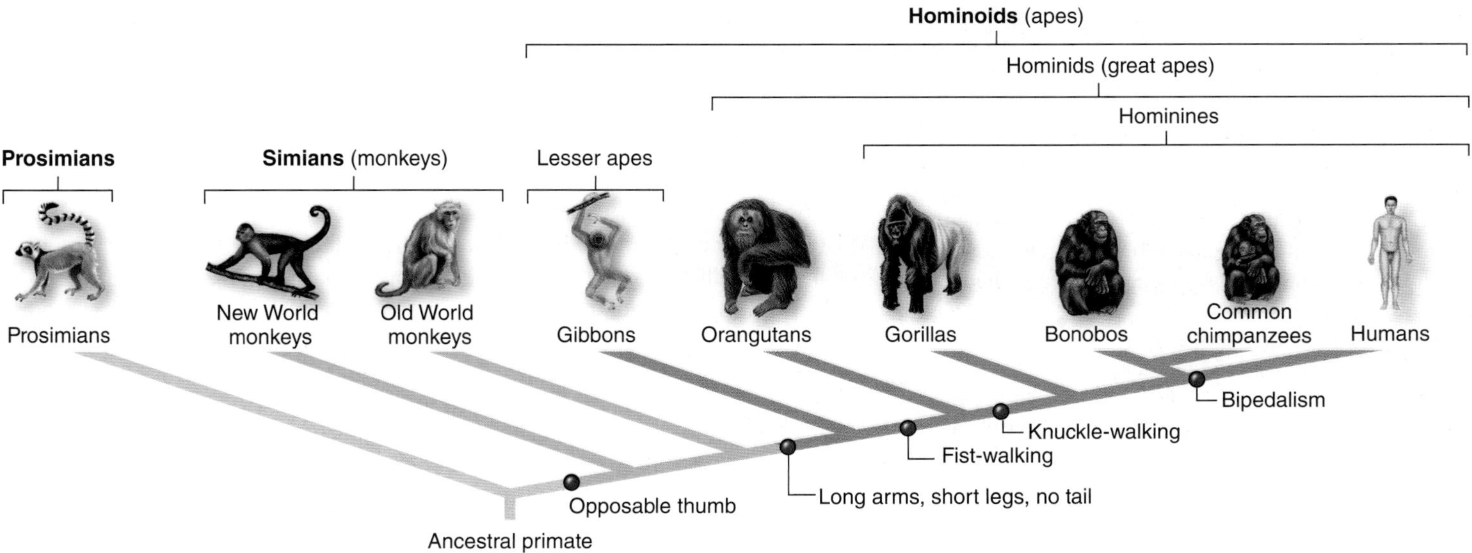

Figure 17.31 **Primate Lineages.** This evolutionary tree shows the physical traits that differentiate the three main groups of primates: prosimians, simians, and hominoids. Molecular data support this hypothesis of the evolutionary relationships among primates.

lemurs, aye-ayes, lorises, tarsiers, and bush babies. **Simian** is the corresponding term for monkeys, both Old World (native to Africa and Asia) and New World (native to South and Central America). The **hominoids** are apes, including humans.

Hominoids are further divided into two groups. One contains the gibbons, or "lesser apes." The other, the **hominids,** contains all of the "great apes": orangutans, gorillas, chimpanzees (including bonobos), and humans. Orangutans, however, are not as closely related to the other great apes. **Hominines** include only gorillas, chimpanzees, and humans.

As you examine figure 17.31, keep in mind two important concepts. First, note that humans are not descended from other groups of modern apes. Instead, all living humans and chimpanzees share a common ancestor and diverged from that ancestor perhaps 4.5 MYA. Second, note that gibbons, orangutans, gorillas, and chimpanzees are not "less evolved" than humans. All living species are on an equal evolutionary footing, although some may belong to older lineages.

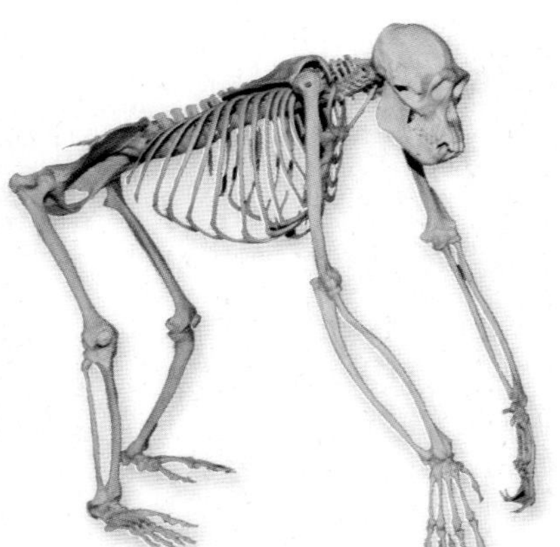

Figure 17.32 Clues from Bones. The skeleton on the left, from a chimpanzee, shares many similarities with the human skeleton on the right.

B. Anatomical and Molecular Evidence Documents Primate Relationships

By examining the physical characteristics of skeletons, paleontologists have learned much about the evolutionary relationships among primates (figure 17.32). Most human fossils consist of bones and teeth. Comparing these remains with existing primates reveals surprisingly detailed information about locomotion and diet. For this reason, knowledge of primate skeletal anatomy is essential to interpreting human fossils.

Locomotion Adaptations related to locomotion are among the most important characteristics in hominoid skeletons. Brachiation, for example, is swinging from one arm to the other while the body dangles below. Many hominoids move through the treetops in this way; in contrast, monkeys run on all fours along the tops of branches. Orangutans spend most of their lives in trees and move by brachiation when they are in treetops. Gibbons, the most superbly acrobatic hominoids, have long arms and hands. The size and opposability of the thumb are reduced, but their arms connect to the shoulders by ball-and-socket joints that allow free movement of the arms in 360 degrees. In addition, a long collarbone acts as a brace and keeps the shoulder from collapsing toward the chest.

Heavier bodied chimpanzees and gorillas don't brachiate as much as gibbons and orangutans, but they can do so. Humans seldom brachiate, with the exception of small, light-bodied children playing on schoolyard "monkey bars." Adult human arms are typically too weak to support their heavy legs.

Chimpanzees and gorillas move by knuckle-walking, a behavioral modification that allows an animal to run rapidly on the ground on all fours, with their weight resting on the knuckles. The proportionately longer arms of chimps and gorillas are an adaptation to knuckle-walking.

One important feature distinguishes humans from the other great apes: bipedalism, or the ability to walk upright on two legs. Adaptations to bipedalism include relatively short arms and longer, stronger leg bones. Foot bones form firm supports for walking, with the big toe fixed in place and not opposable. The bowl-shaped pelvis supports most of the weight of the body, and the vertebrae in the lower back add flexibility that eases walking.

Burning Questions

Did humans and dinosaurs ever coexist?

To answer this question, it is important to first understand what dinosaurs were—and what they were not. Dinosaurs were terrestrial reptiles that lived during the Mesozoic era, between 245 and 65 MYA. They ranged in stature from chicken-sized to truly gargantuan—the largest could have peeked into the sixth story of a modern-day building.

Many people mistakenly believe that all reptiles (or even all mammals) that lived during the Mesozoic era were dinosaurs. In reality, lizards, snakes, crocodiles, and other terrestrial reptiles lived alongside the dinosaurs. The Mesozoic also saw marine reptiles such as plesiosaurs and flying reptiles such as pterodactyls, but they were not dinosaurs either; all dinosaurs were terrestrial. Nor did all dinosaurs live at the same time. As some species appeared, others went extinct throughout the Mesozoic.

Although several comic strips, cartoons, and feature films suggest the contrary, humans and dinosaurs never coexisted. The last of the dinosaurs were gone by the time our own mammalian lineage—the primates—was just getting started. Tens of millions of years later, humans finally roamed the Earth and found the fossils that prove that these huge reptiles once existed.

Submit your burning question to:
marielle_hoefnagels@mcgraw-hill.com

Bipedalism is also reflected in the bones of the head (figure 17.33). The foramen magnum is the large hole in the skull where the spinal cord leaves the brain. In modern humans, this hole is tucked beneath the skull. In gorillas and chimps, the foramen magnum is located nearer the rear of the skull; in animals that run on all fours, such as horses and dogs, the foramen magnum is at the rear of the skull.

Diet Other skeletal characteristics, including the size and shape of the teeth, are related to diet. Upper and lower molar teeth have ridges that fit together, much as the teeth of gears intermesh. Food caught between these surfaces is ground, crushed, and mashed. The size of these teeth is an adaptation that reflects the toughness of the diet.

As you examine the photos in figure 17.33, note that the chimpanzee skull features a sagittal crest. This bony ridge runs lengthwise along the top of the skull. The sagittal crest is an attachment point for muscles, and its presence signals particularly strong jaws, another clue to an animal's diet. Humans lack a sagittal crest.

Other important features in primate skulls include the size of jaw bones, the prominence of the ridge of bone above the eye, the degree to which the jaw protrudes, and the shape of the curve of the tooth row. All of these characteristics allow paleoanthropologists, the scientists who study human fossils, to identify hominid species.

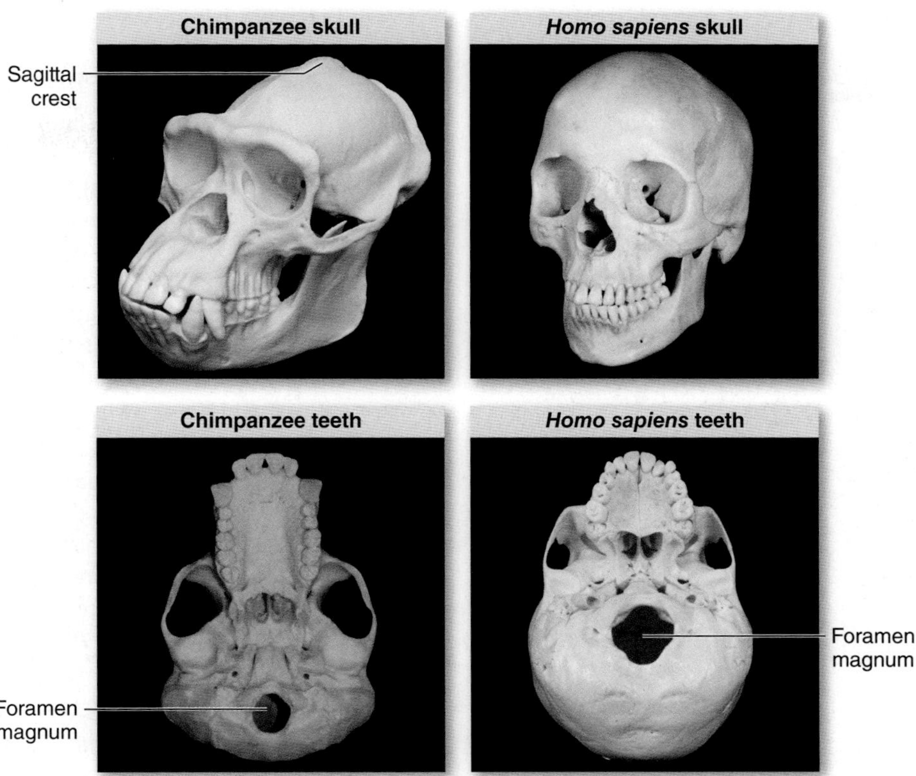

Figure 17.33 Skulls and Teeth. The skulls and teeth of a chimpanzee and a human reveal details about posture, diet, and jaw strength. Biologists compare fossils of extinct species to bones of existing primates to learn how our ancestors lived.

Molecular Data Fossil evidence and anatomical similarities were once the only lines of evidence that paleoanthropologists could analyze in tracing the course of human evolution. Around 1960, however, scientists began to use molecular sequences to investigate relationships among primates. Studies of blood proteins and DNA presented a new picture of primate evolution, as it became clear that humans are a species of great ape. One of the astounding findings of these molecular studies was that the genes of humans and chimpanzees are 99% identical. The evolutionary tree in figure 17.31 takes into account both the anatomical characteristics and the molecular data.

Other research has further eroded the distinctions between humans and other great apes. Previously, humans had been placed in a separate group, supposedly characterized by upright walking, tool-making, and language. Then, in the 1970s, chimpanzees and wild gorillas were observed to use tools, and captive great apes learned to use sign language to communicate with their trainers. The only characteristic that now remains unique to *Homo* is bipedal locomotion.

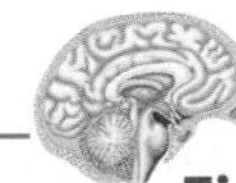

Figure It Out

Suppose that a 100-meter track represents Earth's 4.6 billion-year history. Primates originated about 60 million years ago. How close to the end of the track would you mark the origin of primates?

Answer: 1.3 m

C. Human Evolution Is Partially Recorded in Fossils

Even though DNA and proteins provide overwhelming evidence of the relationships between living primates, these molecules deteriorate with time. Scientists therefore cannot usually use molecular data to establish relationships of prehistoric hominines. For this, we must turn to studies of fossilized remains.

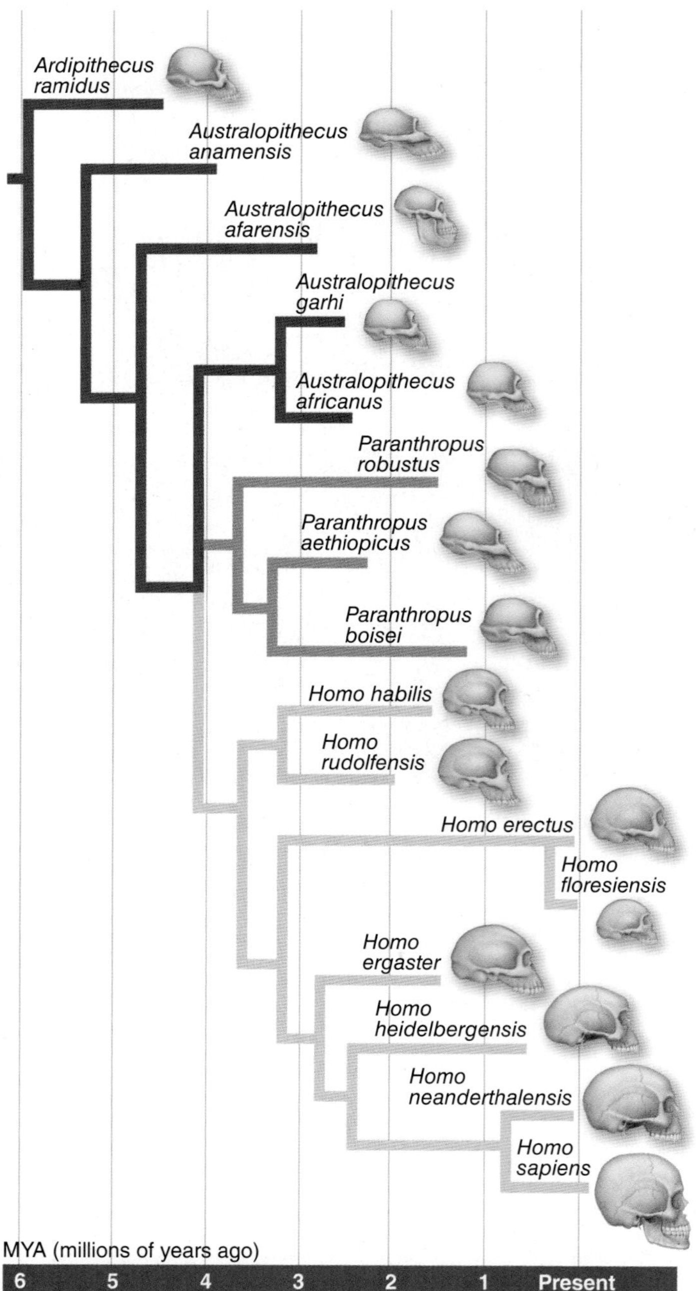

Figure 17.34 Human Family Tree. Fossilized remains place our close relatives into three main groups: australopiths, *Paranthropus*, and *Homo.* Skull sizes are approximately to scale and range from about 400 cm^3 for *Australopithecus afarensis* to about 1450 cm^3 for modern humans. The evolutionary relationships in this tree are hypothesized.

To interpret fossils from the human family tree, paleoanthropologists compare details of the ancient skeletal features with modern primates and try to reconstruct as much information about diet and lifestyle as they can. So far, fossil hominines in the human family tree have fallen into three groups (figure 17.34):

- **Australopiths.** Fossils of several species of extinct small apes have been assigned to the genus *Australopithecus,* meaning "Southern ape-man." The downward position of the foramen magnum indicates that these apes walked upright. A remarkable trail of fossilized footprints is additional evidence of their hominine heritage (figure 17.35). *Australopithecus afarensis* (including the famous "Lucy" fossil) and *A. africanus* are members of this group, which dates from about 4 to 2.5 MYA.
- ***Paranthropus.*** This extinct group, whose name literally means "beside humans," is characterized by extremely large teeth, protruding jaws, and skulls that have a sagittal crest. All of these specializations probably relate to the large jaw muscles needed to crush tough plants or crack nuts. Most researchers hypothesize that *Paranthropus* descended from *Australopithecus*. *Paranthropus aethiopicus, P. boisei,* and *P. robustus* are members of this group, which dates from about 3 to 1.5 MYA. *Paranthropus* seems to be an evolutionary dead end that gave rise to no other group.
- ***Homo.*** Fossils in this group are associated with stone tools. *Homo* species tend to have larger bodies and larger brains than do australopiths. All members of genus *Homo* are considered humans, and *Homo habilis, H. ergaster,* and *H. erectus* belong to the group of extinct species that are called "early *Homo*." These species lived from about 2.5 MYA to about 1 MYA and gave rise to "recent *Homo*." Recent species of *Homo* have smaller teeth, lighter and less protruding jaws, larger braincases, and lighter brow ridges. Their fossils are associated with evidence of culture. Recent *Homo* species include *H. heidelbergensis, H. neanderthalensis, H. floresiensis* (the hobbitlike humans whose bones were discovered in Indonesia in 2003), and *H. sapiens*. The only human species alive today is *Homo sapiens*.

One interesting trend in human evolution has been a rapid diversification of species, followed by extinctions. Fossil evidence shows that about 1.8 MYA, as many as five species of hominines lived together in Africa. About 200,000 years ago, three species of recent *Homo* coexisted in Europe. Today, however, all except *Homo sapiens* are extinct.

What happened to the other *Homo* species? No one knows, but many anthropologists wonder whether *H. sapiens* contributed to their extinction. Scientists had speculated that Neandertals disappeared after interbreeding with *H. sapiens,* a hypothesis called "extinction through absorption." But an analysis of Neandertal DNA has led most scientists to reject that hypothesis.

D. Environmental Changes Have Spurred Human Evolution

What provoked the hominid ancestors of humans to abandon brachiation in favor of bipedal, upright walking? What allowed the large brains that are characteristic of recent *Homo* to develop? To find these answers, we have to consider a related question: Where did hominids evolve?

Charles Darwin was one of the first to speculate that humans evolved in Africa. About 12 MYA, tectonic movements caused a period of great mountain building. The continental plates beneath India and the Himalayan region collided and ground together, heaving up the Himalayas. The resulting climatic shift had enormous ecological consequences. Cooler temperatures reduced the thick tropical forests that had covered much of Europe, India, the Middle East, and East Africa. Open plains appeared, bringing new opportunities for species that could live there. These included less competition for food in the treetops, a new assortment of foods, and a different group of predators. Experts speculate that one small ape, perhaps *Australopithecus* or an as-yet-unidentified hominine, moved out of the trees and began life on the African savannas.

Perhaps at first this species alternated between running on all fours and bipedal walking. On open plains, however, there are advantages to bipedal walking, especially the elevated vantage point for sensing danger and spotting food and friends. This environment would have selected for apes with the best skeletal adaptations to bipedalism, and the trait would have been preserved and honed in the plains. Bipedalism also freed hominine hands to carry objects and use the tools that are so characteristic of *Homo* species.

No one knows what might have spurred the evolution of the large brain that characterizes humans. Some experts relate the development of a large brain to tool use; others relate it to language and life in social groups.

Figure 17.35 Fossil Footprints. The so-called Laetoli footprints, which date to about 3.7 are preserved in volcanic ash. They were discovered in Tanzania in 1978.

E. Migration and Culture Have Changed *Homo sapiens*

Mitochondrial DNA sampled from people around the world has revealed a compelling portrait of human migration out of Africa (figure 17.36). Asia, Australia, and Europe all were colonized at least 40,000 years ago, but it took somewhat longer for humans to reach the Americas.

As humans spread throughout the world, new habitats selected for different adaptations. Near the equator, for example, sunlight is much more intense than at higher latitudes. One component of sunlight is ultraviolet (UV) radiation, which is both harmful and beneficial. On the one hand, UV radiation destroys folic acid (vitamin B_9), damages DNA, and causes skin cancer. On the other hand, some UV wavelengths help the skin produce vitamin D, which is essential to bone development and overall health (see section 23.6).

These two counteracting selective pressures help explain why skin pigmentation is strongly correlated with the amount of ultraviolet radiation striking the Earth. One pigment that contributes to skin color, melanin, blocks UV radiation.

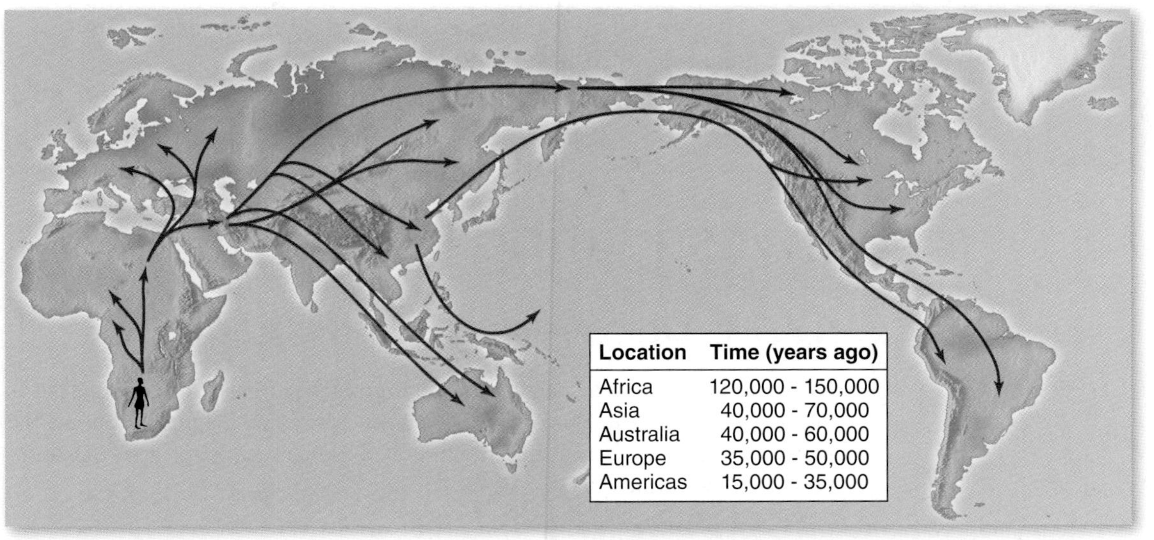

Location	Time (years ago)
Africa	120,000 - 150,000
Asia	40,000 - 70,000
Australia	40,000 - 60,000
Europe	35,000 - 50,000
Americas	15,000 - 35,000

Figure 17.36 Out of Africa. Researchers used mitochondrial DNA sequences to deduce approximately when humans originally settled each continent after migrating out of Africa.

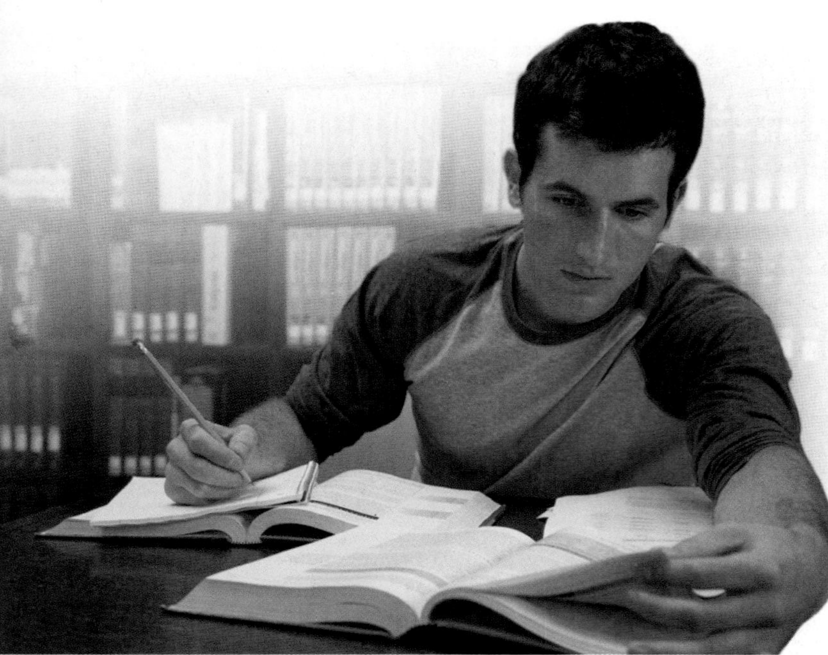

Figure 17.37 Learning from the Past. Thanks to our ability to store and retrieve information, humans can continuously build on the knowledge that previous generations have accumulated.

Intense UV radiation selects for alleles that confer abundant melanin. People whose ancestry is near the equator, such as in Africa and Australia, therefore tend to have very dark brown skin. In northern Europe and other areas with weak sunlight, however, heavily pigmented skin would block so much UV light that indigenous people would suffer from vitamin D deficiency. These conditions are correlated with a high frequency of alleles conferring pale, pinkish skin.

No matter where people roamed, one byproduct of the large human brain was **culture:** the knowledge, beliefs, and behaviors that we transmit from generation to generation. Among the earliest signs of culture is cave art from about 30,000 years ago, which indicates that our ancestors had developed fine hand coordination and could use symbols.

By 10,000 years ago, depending on which native plants and animals were available for early farmers to domesticate, agriculture began to replace a hunter–gatherer lifestyle in many places. Agriculture meant increased food production, which profoundly changed societies. Freed from the necessity of producing their own food, specialized groups of political leaders, soldiers, weapon-makers, religious leaders, scientists, engineers, artists, writers, and many other types of workers arose. These new occupations meant improved transportation and communication, better technologies, and the ability to explore the world for new lands and new resources.

Undoubtedly, humans are a special species. We can modify the environment much more than, for example, a slime mold or an earthworm can. We can also alter natural selection, in our own species and in others. Finally, culture allows each generation to build on information accumulated in the past (figure 17.37). The knowledge, beliefs, and behaviors that shape each culture are constantly modified within a person's lifetime, in stark contrast to the millions of years required for biological evolution. Our species is therefore extremely responsive to short-term changes.

Despite our unique set of features, however, we are a species, descended from ancestors with whom we share many characteristics. It is intriguing to think about where the human species is headed, which species will vanish, and how life will continue to diversify in the next 500 million years.

17.12 Mastering Concepts

1. Name and describe the three groups of contemporary primates. To which group do humans belong?
2. What can skeletal anatomy and DNA sequences in existing primates tell us about human evolution?
3. What are the three groups of hominines in the human family tree, and which still exist today?
4. Which conditions may have contributed to the evolution of humans?

Investigating Life

17.13 Discovering the "Fishapod"

Every now and then, a spectacular fossil grabs headlines worldwide. That is exactly what happened in April 2006, when fossils shed light on one of the most important questions in vertebrate evolutionary biology: how did tetrapods gain their limbs?

The idea that early amphibians crawled onto land some 375 MYA is intriguing, especially since the descendants of those early colonists are today's amphibians, reptiles, and mammals. Fossils discovered over the past half-century, including *Acanthostega* and *Ichthyostega,* have clarified the fish-amphibian transition (figure 17.38). Still, some details of this fascinating event remain poorly understood.

Scientists Edward B. (Ted) Daeschler of Philadelphia's Academy of Natural Sciences, Neil Shubin of the University of Chicago, and Harvard University's Farish Jenkins added new insights when they published back-to-back papers in the journal *Nature* in April 2006. The articles described fossils of an extinct animal, *Tiktaalik roseae,* that the researchers had unearthed in Arctic Canada (figure 17.39). *Tiktaalik* either crawled or paddled in shallow tropical streams during the late Devonian period, about 380 MYA. (Although today's Canada is anything but tropical, the entire North American continent was near the equator during the Devonian.)

a. *Acanthostega*

b. *Ichthyostega*

Figure 17.38 From Water to a Land. (a) *Acanthostega* stayed mostly in the water but had legs and other adaptations that permitted it to spend short periods on land. (b) *Ichthyostega* could spend longer periods on land because its rib cage was stronger. It retained the skull shape and finned tail of its ancestors.

Scientists jokingly call the animal a "fishapod" because of its uncanny mix of fish and tetrapod characteristics. Like a fish, *Tiktaalik* had scales and gills. Like a tetrapod, it had lungs, and its ribs were robust enough to support its body. But the appendages got the most attention. *Tiktaalik* had moveable wrist bones that were sturdy enough to support the animal in shallow water or on short excursions to land. Although the bones were clearly limblike, the "limbs" were fringed with fins, not toes.

The *Tiktaalik* fossils caught the world's eye because they were extraordinarily complete and exquisitely preserved. Scientifically, *Tiktaalik* is important for two reasons. First, it adds to our knowledge about tetrapod evolution. Second, it highlights the predictive power of evolutionary biology. The researchers did not stumble on *Tiktaalik* by accident. Instead, they were looking for a fossil representing the fish–amphibian transition, based on previous knowledge of how and when vertebrates moved onto land. Finding *Tiktaalik* confirmed the prediction.

Spectacular fossils such as *Tiktaalik* spark a flurry of excitement that obscures the countless hours of tedious, labor-intensive work needed to interpret fossils. Researchers scrutinize the limbs, skull, vertebrae, and other parts of each new find to glean every possible piece of information about the animal and how it lived. In this way, fossils contribute immeasurably to our understanding of life's long history.

Daeschler, Edward B., Neil H. Shubin, and Farish A. Jenkins, Jr. April 6, 2006. A Devonian tetrapod-like fish and the evolution of the tetrapod body plan. *Nature,* vol. 440, pages 757–763.

Shubin, Neil H., Edward B. Daeschler, and Farish A. Jenkins, Jr. April 6, 2006. A pectoral fin of *Tiktaalik roseae* and the origin of the tetrapod limb. *Nature,* vol. 440, pages 764–771.

a.

b.

Figure 17.39 Fossil "Fishapod." (a) This photo shows the *Tiktaalik* fossil discovered in 2006. (b) *Tiktaalik's* limbs clearly contained bones, yet they were fringed with fins—one clue to the animal's aquatic heritage.

17.13 Mastering Concepts

1. Explain why *Tiktaalik* is called a "fishapod."
2. How might the ability to crawl on land for short periods have enhanced the fitness of *Tiktaalik*?

Animal Characteristics: A Summary

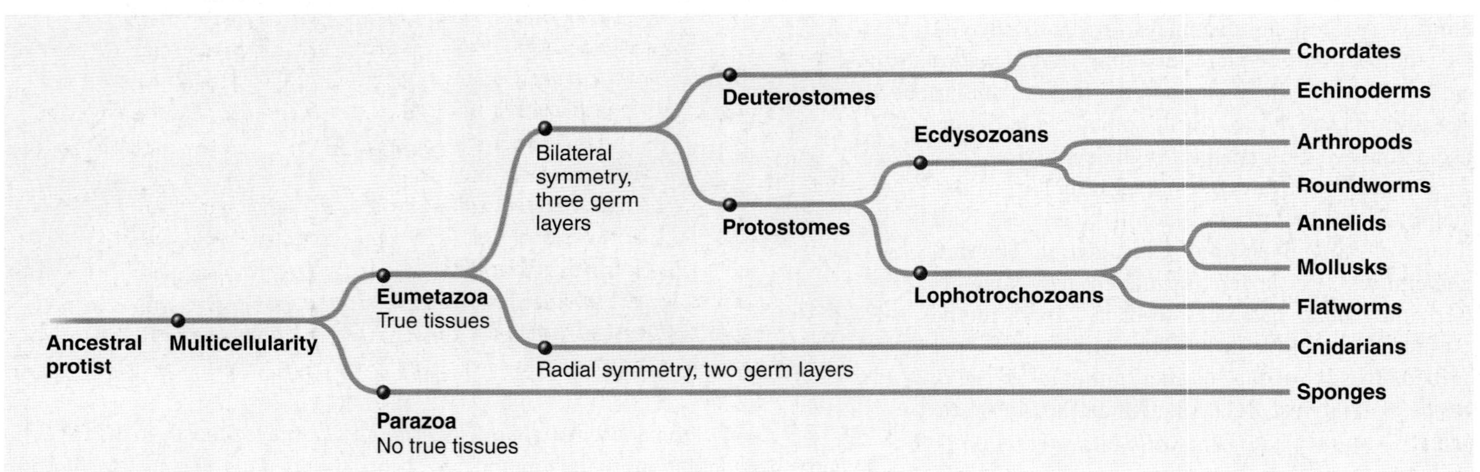

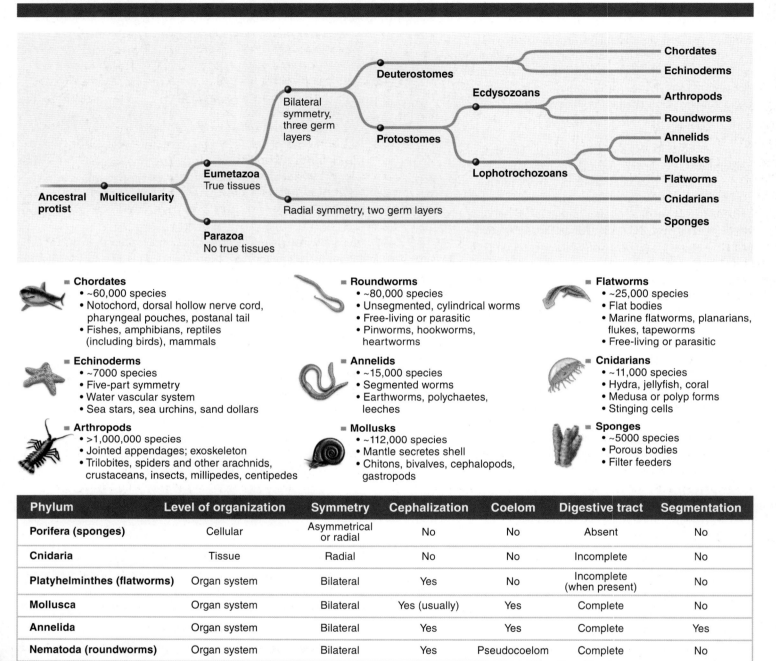

- **Chordates**
  - ~60,000 species
  - Notochord, dorsal hollow nerve cord, pharyngeal pouches, postanal tail
  - Fishes, amphibians, reptiles (including birds), mammals

- **Echinoderms**
  - ~7000 species
  - Five-part symmetry
  - Water vascular system
  - Sea stars, sea urchins, sand dollars

- **Arthropods**
  - >1,000,000 species
  - Jointed appendages; exoskeleton
  - Trilobites, spiders and other arachnids, crustaceans, insects, millipedes, centipedes

- **Roundworms**
  - ~80,000 species
  - Unsegmented, cylindrical worms
  - Free-living or parasitic
  - Pinworms, hookworms, heartworms

- **Annelids**
  - ~15,000 species
  - Segmented worms
  - Earthworms, polychaetes, leeches

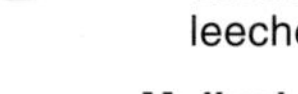

- **Mollusks**
  - ~112,000 species
  - Mantle secretes shell
  - Chitons, bivalves, cephalopods, gastropods

- **Flatworms**
  - ~25,000 species
  - Flat bodies
  - Marine flatworms, planarians, flukes, tapeworms
  - Free-living or parasitic

- **Cnidarians**
  - ~11,000 species
  - Hydra, jellyfish, coral
  - Medusa or polyp forms
  - Stinging cells

- **Sponges**
  - ~5000 species
  - Porous bodies
  - Filter feeders

Phylum	Level of organization	Symmetry	Cephalization	Coelom	Digestive tract	Segmentation
Porifera (sponges)	Cellular	Asymmetrical or radial	No	No	Absent	No
Cnidaria	Tissue	Radial	No	No	Incomplete	No
Platyhelminthes (flatworms)	Organ system	Bilateral	Yes	No	Incomplete (when present)	No
Mollusca	Organ system	Bilateral	Yes (usually)	Yes	Complete	No
Annelida	Organ system	Bilateral	Yes	Yes	Complete	Yes
Nematoda (roundworms)	Organ system	Bilateral	Yes	Pseudocoelom	Complete	No
Arthropoda	Organ system	Bilateral	Yes	Yes	Complete	Yes
Echinodermata	Organ system	Bilateral larvae; radial adults	No	Yes	Complete	No
Chordata	Organ system	Bilateral	Yes	Yes	Complete	Yes (usually)

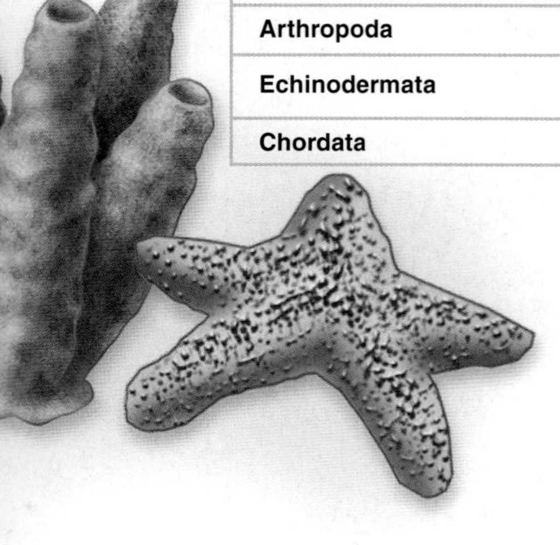

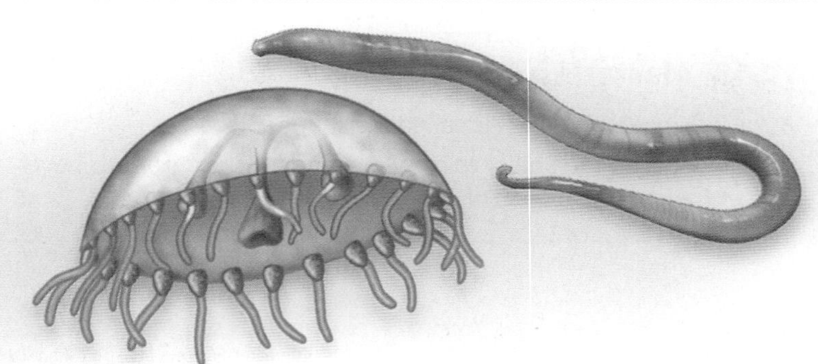

Chordate Characteristics: A Summary

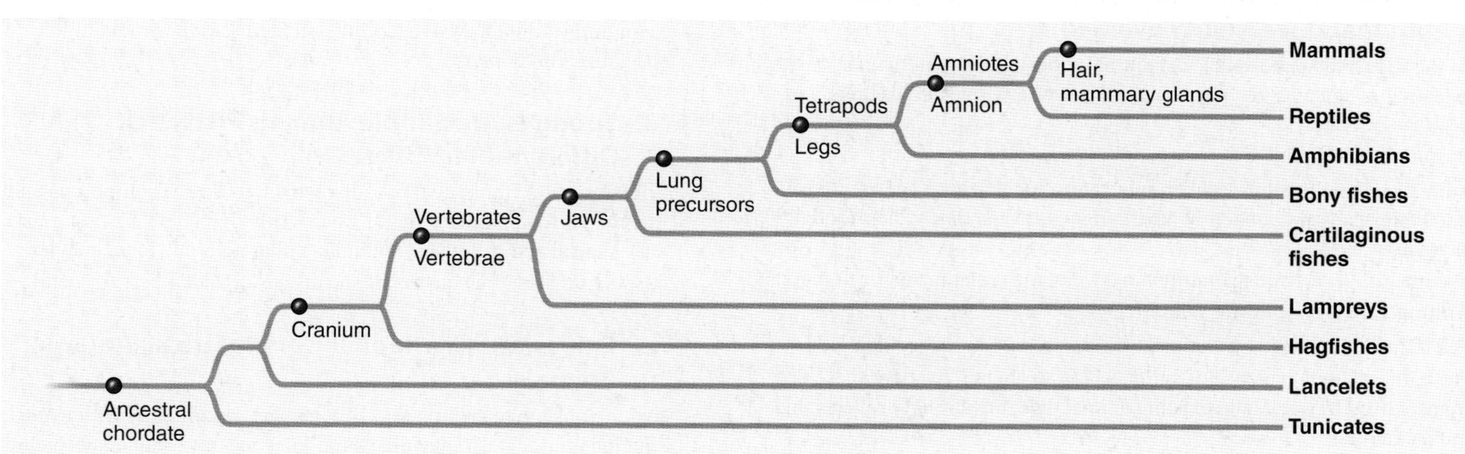

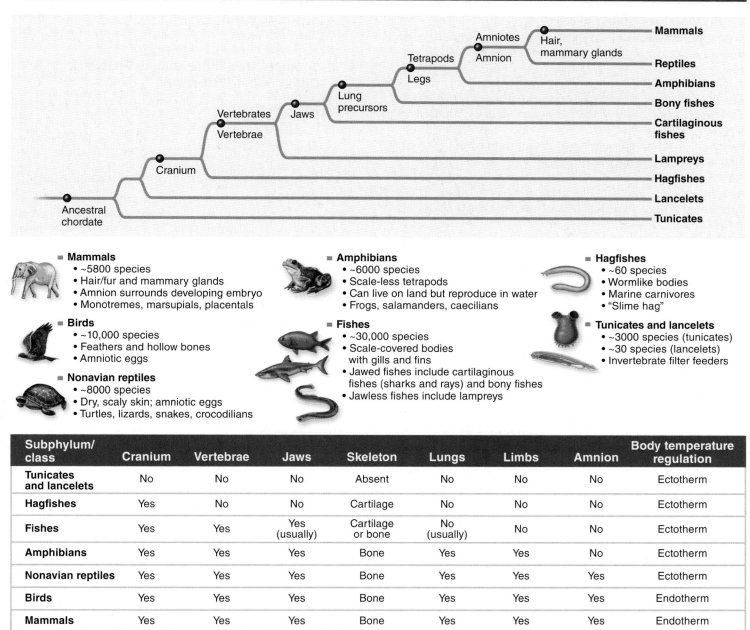

- **Mammals**
  - ~5800 species
  - Hair/fur and mammary glands
  - Amnion surrounds developing embryo
  - Monotremes, marsupials, placentals

- **Birds**
  - ~10,000 species
  - Feathers and hollow bones
  - Amniotic eggs

- **Nonavian reptiles**
  - ~8000 species
  - Dry, scaly skin; amniotic eggs
  - Turtles, lizards, snakes, crocodilians

- **Amphibians**
  - ~6000 species
  - Scale-less tetrapods
  - Can live on land but reproduce in water
  - Frogs, salamanders, caecilians

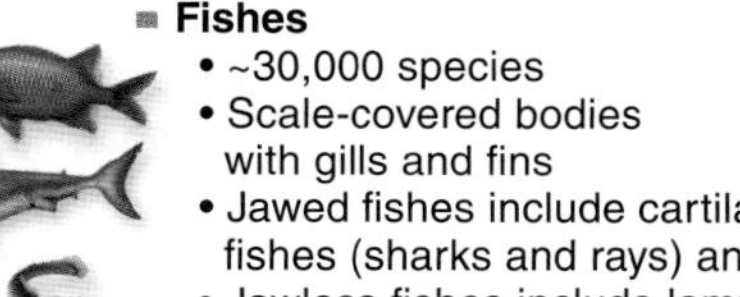

- **Fishes**
  - ~30,000 species
  - Scale-covered bodies with gills and fins
  - Jawed fishes include cartilaginous fishes (sharks and rays) and bony fishes
  - Jawless fishes include lampreys

- **Hagfishes**
  - ~60 species
  - Wormlike bodies
  - Marine carnivores
  - "Slime hag"

- **Tunicates and lancelets**
  - ~3000 species (tunicates)
  - ~30 species (lancelets)
  - Invertebrate filter feeders

Subphylum/ class	Cranium	Vertebrae	Jaws	Skeleton	Lungs	Limbs	Amnion	Body temperature regulation
Tunicates and lancelets	No	No	No	Absent	No	No	No	Ectotherm
Hagfishes	Yes	No	No	Cartilage	No	No	No	Ectotherm
Fishes	Yes	Yes	Yes (usually)	Cartilage or bone	No (usually)	No	No	Ectotherm
Amphibians	Yes	Yes	Yes	Bone	Yes	Yes	No	Ectotherm
Nonavian reptiles	Yes	Yes	Yes	Bone	Yes	Yes	Yes	Ectotherm
Birds	Yes	Yes	Yes	Bone	Yes	Yes	Yes	Endotherm
Mammals	Yes	Yes	Yes	Bone	Yes	Yes	Yes	Endotherm

Chapter Summary

17.1 Animals Live Nearly Everywhere

- Of the 1,200,000 or so species of animals, most are **invertebrates;** only one phylum contains **vertebrates,** which have a segmented backbone of cartilage or bone.

A. What Is an Animal?

- Animals are multicellular, eukaryotic heterotrophs whose cells secrete extracellular matrix but do not have cell walls. Most digest their food internally.
- The **blastula** is a stage in embryonic development that is unique to animals.

B. Animal Life Began in the Water

- The immediate ancestor of animals was likely a choanoflagellate.
- The earliest fossil evidence of animals is from about 570 MYA. These first animals lived in water, and existing animal diversity strongly reflects this aquatic heritage.
- The Ediacarans were soft, flat organisms that lived in the late Precambrian and early Cambrian periods.
- The Cambrian explosion introduced many species.

C. Biologists Classify Animals Based on Organization, Morphology, and Development

- Differences in development account for major groupings of animal phyla.
- All animals except sponges have true tissues.
- In most phyla, body symmetry is **radial** or **bilateral. Cephalization** is correlated with bilateral symmetry.
- An animal zygote divides mitotically to form a blastula and then usually a **gastrula.** In some animals, the gastrula has two tissue layers (**ectoderm** and **endoderm**). In others, a third layer (**mesoderm**) forms between the other two.
- Bilaterally symmetrical animals are **protostomes** if the gastrula's first indentation forms into the mouth. In **deuterostomes,** the first indentation develops into the anus.

D. Biologists Also Consider Additional Characteristics

- Biologists also describe animals based on the presence or absence of a body cavity (**coelom** or **pseudocoelom**).

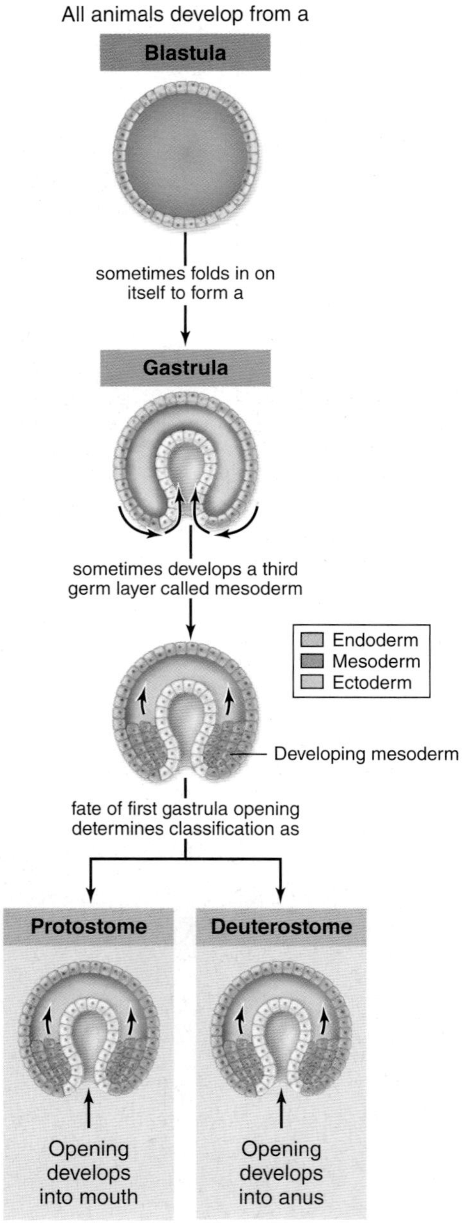

The body cavity can act as a **hydrostatic skeleton.**

- Digestive tracts are **incomplete** or **complete;** a **gastrovascular cavity** is an incomplete digestive tract.
- **Segmentation** improves flexibility and increases the potential for specialized body parts.

17.2 Sponges Are Simple Animals That Lack Differentiated Tissues

- **Sponges** are asymmetrical or radially symmetrical. Their porous bodies filter small food particles out of water. Although they lack tissues, sponges have specialized cell types, including collar cells and amoebocytes.
- A sponge's skeleton consists of spicules or organic fibers (or both).

17.3 Cnidarians Are Radially Symmetrical, Aquatic Animals

- **Cnidarians** are mostly marine animals that capture prey with tentacles and stinging **cnidocytes.** They digest food in a gastrovascular cavity. Cnidarians move by contracting muscle cells that act on a hydrostatic skeleton.
- A cnidarian body form is a **polyp** or a **medusa.**
- Examples of cnidarians include corals, hydras, and jellyfishes.

17.4 Flatworms Have Bilateral Symmetry and Incomplete Digestive Tracts

- **Flatworms** are unsegmented animals that lack a coelom. The flat shape allows individual cells to exchange gases with their environment.
- These animals include **free-living flatworms** such as planarians; **flukes** and **tapeworms** are parasitic.
- Flatworms lack circulatory and respiratory systems, but specialized structures maintain water balance. They have simple nervous systems and hydrostatic skeletons.

17.5 Mollusks Are Soft, Unsegmented Animals

- **Mollusks** have bilateral symmetry and a complete digestive tract. The main groups of mollusks are **chitons, bivalves, gastropods,** and **cephalopods.**
- The mollusk body includes a **mantle,** a muscular **foot,** and a **visceral mass.** Most mollusks have a shell, and many have a tonguelike **radula.** They are filter feeders, herbivores, or predators.
- Cephalopods such as octopuses have complex sensory and nervous systems.

17.6 Annelids Are Segmented Worms

- **Annelid** bodies consist of repeated segments. Annelids include **oligochaetes, leeches,** and **polychaetes,** and they feed in diverse ways.
- Organ systems include a complete digestive tract, a closed circulatory system, and respiratory, excretory, and nervous systems. The coelom acts as a hydrostatic skeleton.

17.7 Nematodes Are Unsegmented, Cylindrical Worms

- **Roundworms** are unsegmented worms that molt periodically. They include parasitic and free-living species in soil and aquatic sediments.
- Nematodes have diverse diets and complete digestive tracts. The pseudocoelom is a hydrostatic skeleton.

17.8 Arthropods Have Exoskeletons and Jointed Appendages

- **Arthropods** are segmented animals with jointed appendages and a chitin-rich **exoskeleton.**

A. Arthropods Have Complex Organ Systems

- Arthropods exhibit great diversity in feeding, respiratory systems, excretory systems, nervous systems, and reproduction. They have open circulatory systems.

B. Arthropods Are the Most Diverse Animals

- The extinct **trilobites** were arthropods, as are the **chelicerates** (**horseshoe crabs** and **arachnids**). **Mandibulate** arthropods include **centipedes** and **millipedes; crustaceans;** and **insects.**
- Insects are by far the most diverse arthropods.

17.9 Echinoderm Adults Have Five-Part, Radial Symmetry

- **Echinoderms** are spiny-skinned marine animals whose adults have radial symmetry. Echinoderms are deuterostomes, as are the chordates.
- Echinoderms move by using tube feet, which are part of the **water vascular system.** This network of canals also aids in circulation and gas exchange.
- The bilaterally symmetrical larvae of echinoderms look very different from the radially symmetrical adults.

17.10 Most Chordates Are Vertebrates

- **Chordates** share four characteristics: a **notochord,** a **dorsal hollow nerve cord, pharyngeal pouches** or slits in the pharynx, and a **postanal tail.**
- Most chordates also have a **cranium** that protects the brain.
- Other features that distinguish chordates from one another include **vertebrae, jaws, lungs,** and the presence of limbs in **tetrapods.**
- Reptiles and mammals are **amniotes;** in these animals, the **amniotic egg** or amnion protects the developing embryo.
- **Ectotherms** allow their body temperature to fluctuate with the environment, whereas **endotherms** maintain a relatively constant body temperature.

Key Vertebrate Adaptations

Adaptation	Adaptive significance	Animals with adaptation
Vertebrae	Expand range of motion	Lampreys, fishes, amphibians, reptiles, mammals
Jaws	Increase feeding versatility	Fishes, amphibians, reptiles, mammals
Lungs	Enable animal to breathe air	Bony fishes (a few species), amphibians, reptiles, mammals
Limbs	Allow for locomotion on land	Amphibians, reptiles, mammals
Amnion	Enables reproduction away from water	Reptiles, mammals

17.11 Chordate Diversity Extends from Water to Land to Sky

A. Tunicates and Lancelets Have Neither Cranium nor Backbone

- **Tunicates** obtain food and oxygen with a siphon system. The tunicate larva has all four chordate characteristics, but adults retain only the pharyngeal slits.
- **Lancelets** resemble eyeless fishes; adults have all four chordate characteristics.

B. Hagfishes Have a Cranium but Lack a Backbone

- **Hagfishes** have a cranium, but these animals are not vertebrates. Special features include the ability to secrete slime and the absence of jaws.

C. Fishes Are Aquatic Vertebrates with Gills and Fins

- **Fishes** are abundant and diverse vertebrates.
- Adaptations in fishes that allowed vertebrates to move onto land include lungs and fleshy, paired fins that were later modified as limbs. Jaws and a vertebral column also originated in fishes.
- Jawless fishes include the **lampreys.**
- The **cartilaginous fishes** include skates, rays, and sharks. Sharks detect vibrations from prey with a **lateral line** system.
- The **bony fishes** account for 96% of existing fish species. Bony fishes have lateral line systems and gas bladders, which enable them to control their buoyancy. The two groups of bony fishes are the **ray-finned fishes** and **lobe-finned fishes,** which are further subdivided into **lungfishes** and **coelacanths.**

D. Amphibians Live on Land and in Water

- **Amphibians** breed in water and must keep their skin moist to breathe. Adaptations to life on land include a sturdy skeleton, lungs, and limbs.
- Amphibians include **frogs** and toads; **salamanders** and newts; and **caecilians.**

E. Reptiles Were the First Vertebrates to Thrive on Dry Land

- **Reptiles** (including **birds**) have efficient excretory, respiratory, and circulatory systems. Internal fertilization and amniotic eggs permit reproduction on dry land.
- Nonavian reptiles include **turtles** and tortoises; **lizards** and **snakes;** and **crocodilians.**
- Birds retain scales and egg-laying from reptilian ancestors. Honeycombed bones, streamlined bodies, and **feathers** are adaptations that enable flight.
- Unlike nonavian reptiles, birds are endothermic.

F. Mammals Are Warm, Furry Milk-Drinkers

- **Mammals** have fur, secrete milk from **mammary glands,** and have distinctive teeth and highly developed brains.
- **Monotremes** are mammals that hatch from an amniotic egg. The young of **marsupial** mammals are born after a short pregnancy and often develop inside the mother's pouch. **Placental mammals** have longer pregnancies; the young are nourished by the **placenta** in the mother's uterus.

17.12 Fossils and DNA Tell the Human Evolution Story

A. Humans Are Primates

- **Primates** have grasping hands, opposable thumbs, binocular vision, large brains, and flat nails. The three groups are **prosimians, simians,** and **hominoids.**
- **Hominids** are the "great apes," whereas **hominines** are gorillas, chimpanzees, and humans.

B. Anatomical and Molecular Evidence Documents Primate Relationships

- Fossil bones and teeth reveal how extinct species moved and what they ate.
- Protein and DNA analysis has altered how scientists draw the primate family tree.

C. Human Evolution Is Partially Recorded in Fossils

- Three groups of hominines are australopiths, *Paranthropus,* and *Homo.*

D. Environmental Changes Have Spurred Human Evolution

- Millions of years ago, new mountain ranges arose, causing climate shifts. Savannas replaced tropical forests, and apes—the ancestors of humans—moved from the trees to the savanna.

E. Migration and Culture Have Changed *Homo sapiens*

- After migrating out of Africa, humans encountered new habitats that selected for new allele combinations.
- Humans owe our success to language and **culture.**

17.13 Investigating Life: Discovering the "Fishapod"

- *Tiktaalik roseae* is an extinct "fishapod." Its fossils clearly reflect the transition between fishes and amphibians, which occurred about 375 MYA.

Multiple Choice Questions

1. Which animal phylum has bilateral symmetry but an incomplete digestive tract?
   a. Porifera c. Nematoda
   b. Platyhelminthes d. Cnidaria
2. Nematodes and arthropods are grouped together in the same clade because they
   a. have a radula. c. have a pseudocoelom.
   b. molt. d. have only two germ layers.
3. What is a key characteristic of all arthropods?
   a. Six legs c. Hydrostatic skeleton
   b. Pseudocoelom d. Exoskeleton
4. How is the body structure of an annelid different from an arthropod?
   a. Annelids lack jointed appendages.
   b. Annelids have a complete digestive tract.
   c. Annelids have cephalization.
   d. Annelids are bilateral.
5. When an earthworm is moving through the soil, its muscles are pushing against its
   a. digestive tract. c. bony skeleton.
   b. coelom. d. cnidocytes.
6. Arthropods molt because
   a. they undergo metamorphosis.
   b. the exoskeleton becomes damaged over time.
   c. the exoskeleton prevents the organism from growing.
   d. they have an open circulatory system.
7. Which of the following characteristics is associated with echinoderms?
   a. Protostome
   b. Only two germ layers (ectoderm and endoderm)
   c. Bilaterally symmetrical larvae
   d. All of the above are correct.
8. What is a *water vascular system*?
   a. A network of canals that enables echinoderms to move
   b. The circulatory system of an echinoderm
   c. The excretory system of an echinoderm
   d. All of the above are correct.
9. What is a notochord?
   a. The spine of a chordate animal
   b. One segment in the vertebrate backbone
   c. A type of germ layer
   d. A fibrous rod that runs down the back of a chordate
10. Since a tunicate is considered to be a chordate, it must have a
    a. cranium. c. amniotic egg.
    b. notochord. d. lung.
11. Why is it important for amphibians to live in a moist habitat?
    a. To protect their scales
    b. To maintain their eggs
    c. To maintain their buoyancy
    d. Both a and b are correct.
12. How do reptiles and mammals differ from amphibians?
    a. Only reptiles and mammals are amniotes.
    b. Only reptiles and mammals are tetrapods.
    c. Only reptiles and mammals have lungs.
    d. All of the above are correct.
13. What is the evolutionary link between birds and crocodilians?
    a. Amnion c. Scales
    b. Egg laying d. All of the above are correct.
14. Since a whale is a mammal, it must
    a. have scales. c. produce milk.
    b. have gills. d. All of the above are correct.
15. Which of the following represents the correct order of appearance, from earliest to most recent?
    a. Fishes, reptiles, Ediacarans, primates
    b. Ediacarans, fishes, reptiles, primates
    c. Ediacarans, primates, fishes, reptiles
    d. Primates, reptiles, fishes, Ediacarans
16. Primates share all of the following characteristics except
    a. opposable thumbs. c. bipedalism.
    b. excellent depth perception. d. flat fingernails.
17. Which group of hominines is the oldest?
    a. Australopiths c. *Homo*
    b. *Paranthropus* d. Simians

Write It Out

1. Compare the nine major animal phyla in the order in which the chapter presents them, listing the new features for each group.
2. You are visiting the aquarium, and your companion points at an animal in a tank. None of the signs shows a picture of the animal or its name. What criteria would you use to assign the animal to a phylum?
3. List the criteria used to distinguish: (a) animals from other organisms; (b) vertebrates from invertebrates; (c) protostomes from deuterostomes; (d) ectotherms from endotherms; (e) a tapeworm, a nematode, a slug, an earthworm, a snake, and a caecilian.
4. Distinguish between: (a) radial and bilateral symmetry; (b) blastula and gastrula; (c) complete and incomplete digestive tract; (d) coelom and pseudocoelom.
5. Segmented animals occur in multiple phyla. How might segmentation benefit an animal? If segmentation is adaptive, why do unsegmented animals still exist?
6. What is the evidence for the surprisingly close relationship between echinoderms and chordates?
7. What are the four distinguishing characteristics of chordates?
8. How do tunicates and lancelets differ from fishes and tetrapods?
9. Draw from memory a phylogenetic tree that traces the evolutionary history of vertebrates. Include the features that mark each branching point in your tree.
10. Tunicates look much different than other chordates. Why are they classified in this phylum?

11. If you found an eel-like animal in the ocean, what features would you look for in deciding whether you had a hagfish or an eel (a true fish)?
12. List three adaptations that enable fishes to live in water, amphibians to live on land, snakes to live in the desert, and birds to fly.
13. How does the changing placement of birds in the vertebrate family tree illustrate the scientific process? Why does this type of research matter?
14. How are fishes, amphibians, nonavian reptiles, birds, and mammals important to humans? How are they important in ecosystems?
15. Among plants and vertebrates, some species are well-adapted to dry land, whereas others require moisture to reproduce. Compare and contrast the adaptations in plants and vertebrates that have allowed each group to breed in increasingly dry habitats.
16. Give three examples of interactions between animals classified in different phyla.
17. Explain how a sessile or slow-moving lifestyle, such as that of sponges, sea cucumbers, and tunicates, might select for bright colors and an arsenal of toxic chemicals.
18. Biologists have speculated that the first feathered dinosaurs may have used feathers in mating displays, to conserve body heat, or in flight. How might you use fossils, living species, or both to test each hypothesis?
19. Invasive animal species are disrupting ecosystems around the world. Search the Internet for a list of invasive animal species. Which phyla are represented in the list? What harm do invasive species do? How important is it to try to eradicate invasive species?
20. What can scientists learn by comparing the fossilized skeletons of extinct primates with the bones of modern species?
21. The foramen magnum in *Australopithecus africanus* is closer to the front of the skull than in gorillas. What does this observation indicate about *A. africanus*?
22. Use the Internet to learn about National Geographic's Genographic Project. What are the main objectives and components of the project, and how are researchers using the information they gather to learn more about human evolution?
23. In what ways has culture been an important factor in human evolution?
24. At one time, several species of *Homo* existed at the same time. Propose at least two hypotheses that might explain why only *Homo sapiens* remains.
25. How do you predict a scientist would respond to a question about whether humans "evolved from monkeys"?

Pull It Together

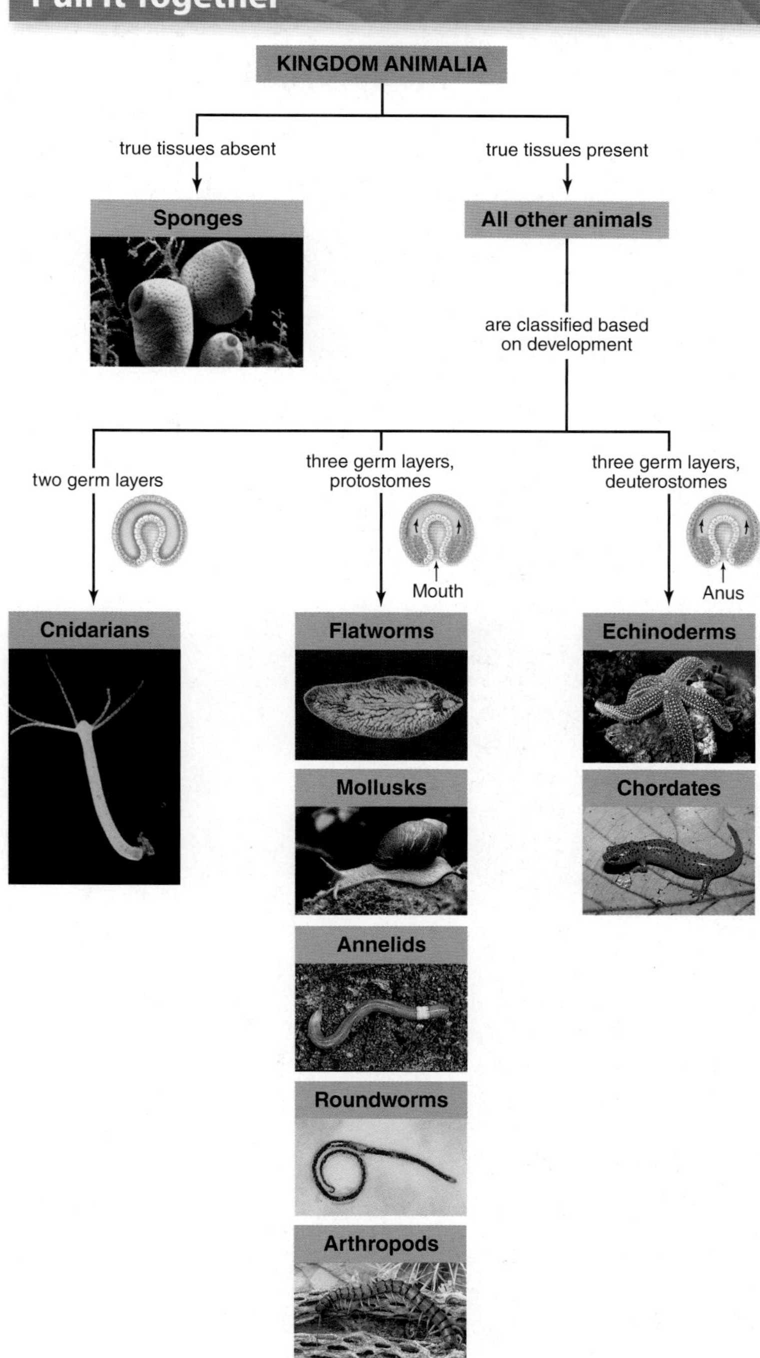

1. Which animals are cephalized?
2. Which animals have an incomplete digestive tract?
3. Which animals have segmented bodies?
4. Which animals have a coelom or pseudocoelom?
5. Add tunicates, hagfishes, birds, monotremes, vertebrates, marsupials, and placental mammals to this concept map.
6. Which animals are aquatic and which are terrestrial? What advantages were gained by the first organisms to leave the water?
7. Other than the ones pictured, give an example of a species in each phylum.

UNIT 4 Ecology

18 Population Ecology

Close Quarters. A destructive earthquake in 2010 forced thousands of Haitians into overpopulated tent cities, where diseases easily spread.

Learning Outline

Learn How to Learn

Use Those Office Hours

Most instructors maintain office hours. Do not be afraid to use this valuable resource! Besides letting you get help with course materials, using office hours gives you an opportunity to know your professors personally. After all, at some point you may need a letter of recommendation; a letter from a professor who knows you well can carry a lot of weight. If you do decide to visit during office hours, be prepared with specific questions. And if you request a separate appointment, it is polite to confirm that you intend to come at the time you have arranged.

What's the Point?

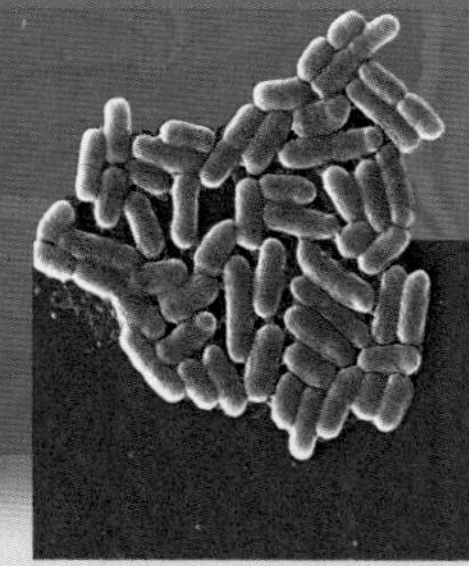
SEM (false color) 3 μm

The photo on the facing page shows the aftermath of a terrible tragedy: the earthquake that devastated Haiti in early 2010. Hundreds of thousands of Haitians died, and countless survivors sought shelter in crowded tent cities. Close quarters and poor sanitation fostered the spread of infectious disease that claimed many more lives.

The sad story of the Haitian earthquake illustrates some of the lessons of population ecology. A population ecologist is a scientist who studies the factors—including disasters and exposure to disease-causing organisms—that determine whether a population grows, shrinks, or stays the same size.

But the study of population ecology extends well beyond the human population. Land management, the protection of endangered species, and many other fields rely on population ecology as well. Typical questions that population ecologists might ask include: "Which weather conditions favor the spread of invasive species?" "How many deer should hunters cull to keep the herd healthy?" "How many humans can Earth support?" Scientists begin to answer these and many other important questions by using the principles described in this chapter.

18.1 Ecology Is the Study of Interactions

Take a moment to think of all the ways you have interacted with the world today. You have certainly breathed air, and you have probably sipped a beverage, eaten one or more meals, put on some clothes, and greeted other people. You may have stepped on the grass or driven a car or played with a pet. Such interactions are part of the science of **ecology,** the study of the relationships among organisms and the environment.

Ecologists classify these relationships at several levels (figure 18.1). A **population** is a group of interbreeding organisms of one species occupying a geographic location at the same time. Humans form a population, as do the acacia trees in figure 18.1. Population ecology is the topic of this chapter.

A **community** includes all of the populations, representing multiple species, that interact in a given area. All of the species in a backyard or park, for example, form a community. Figure 18.1 shows how acacia trees share the landscape with other members of the same community, such as grasses and large grazing animals. Community ecologists study the **biotic** interactions among these species, such as competition and herbivory. On a still broader scale, an **ecosystem** is a community plus its **abiotic,** or nonliving, environment.

Figure 18.1 From Organism to Biosphere. Individual organisms make up populations, which in turn make up communities. An ecosystem includes interactions between a community and its nonliving environment, and the biosphere includes all ecosystems on Earth.

ECOSYSTEM
The living and nonliving components of an area.
Example: The savanna

These nonliving components include light, air, water, minerals, and fire. Chapter 19 describes community- and ecosystem-level processes.

The science of ecology is global because life exists almost everywhere on Earth, even in places once thought to be much too harsh to support it. Scientists have discovered life in Arctic ice, salt flats, hot springs, hydrothermal vents, and mines that plunge miles below Earth's surface. All of these areas are part of the **biosphere,** the portion of Earth where life exists. Thanks to the global circulation of energy, nutrients, and water, the biosphere forms one huge, interconnected ecosystem.

Within the biosphere are prairies, seashores, deserts, jungles, mountain tops, and a patchwork of other unique landscapes, each with its own set of conditions. Fire regularly ravages the prairie but not the beach; water is scarce in the desert but not in the jungle. The species that are native to each location have adaptations that correspond to these conditions. The same basic evolutionary process—natural selection—has produced unique populations and communities of organisms in nearly every possible habitat. As we shall see in this unit, both biotic and abiotic interactions shape the adaptations that contribute to the survival and reproductive success of each species.

18.1 Mastering Concepts

1. Distinguish among ecosystems, communities, and populations.
2. Name some abiotic and biotic components of your environment.
3. What is the biosphere?

Figure 18.2 Portraits of Two Populations. (a) These penguins form a dense breeding colony. (b) Clumps of palms grow in the sand dunes of Tunisia.

18.2 A Population Consists of Individuals of One Species

The organisms that make up a population occupy a **habitat,** which is the physical location where the members of a population normally live. The ocean, desert, or rain forest are typical examples, but an organism's habitat might even be another organism. Your body, for example, is home to billions of microbes. ▸ beneficial microbes, p. 286

Population density is the number of individuals of a species per unit area or unit volume of habitat. Density varies greatly among species. Figure 18.2, for example, shows a densely packed penguin colony and widely spaced clumps of palm trees. Bacteria often live in extremely dense populations, with billions of bacteria occupying a spoonful of soil. At the opposite extreme, redwood trees may live at densities of one trunk per 100 or more square meters. Because a tiny individual generally requires fewer resources than a large one, it is not surprising that the smallest organisms tend to live at the highest densities.

Collecting long-term data on plant and animal population sizes can help scientists learn which species are healthy and which are threatened with extinction. Population data can also help ecologists measure the effects of catastrophes such as fires or oil spills. Hunting, trapping, and fishing regulations are based on population estimates, as are decisions on where to build (or not to build) houses, dams, bridges, and pipelines. But how do researchers know how many individuals of each species inhabit an area?

Simple counts are occasionally possible. For example, aerial photos can reveal the number of seals on an island or caribou in a herd. Unless a species is extremely rare or restricted to a limited range, however, it is usually impossible to count each individual. Instead, most population estimates rely on sampling techniques. One common way to estimate the size of a plant population is to count the number of stems in randomly selected locations, such as within a 1-meter square or along a 50-meter line. As another example, a soil ecologist might count the insects or spiders that stumble into a pitfall trap.

A widely used technique to estimate animal populations is called mark–recapture. Suppose researchers want to know how many squirrels inhabit a park. They begin their investigation by placing baited nest boxes in trees. After a day or two, the researchers record the weight, sex, age, and health status of each captured squirrel. Each squirrel also receives a unique tattoo or other identifying mark before being released. The proportion of marked squirrels that are subsequently recaptured can help the biologists estimate the population size.

Population density measurements provide static "snapshots" of a population at one time. By repeatedly using the same method to measure a population's size over weeks, months, or years, ecologists can determine whether the population is growing, shrinking, or stable. Section 18.3 explains the factors that determine the population's fate.

18.2 Mastering Concepts

1. What is population density?
2. What are some ways to measure a population's density?

18.3 Births and Deaths Help Determine Population Size

Some populations grow, whereas others remain stable and still others decline. Table 18.1 summarizes the factors that influence these changes in a population's size.

Births and deaths are the most obvious ways to add to and subtract from a population. If a population adds more individuals than are subtracted, the population grows. If the opposite happens, the population shrinks (and may even become extinct). The population size remains unchanged if additions exactly balance subtractions.

Regionally, dispersal to new habitats can also increase or decrease a population. For example, immigration has tremendously increased the human population in the United States. Most Americans are either immigrants or descended from immigrants, and today migration accounts for over 30% of population growth in this country. Likewise, nonhuman species disperse to new habitats. They may swim, fly, or walk under their own power; alternatively, wind or water currents may move individuals into or out of a population.

A. Births Add Individuals to a Population

A population's **birth rate** is the number of new individuals produced per individual in a defined time period. For example, the human birth rate worldwide is about 20 per 1000 people per year.

The number of offspring an individual produces over its lifetime depends on many variables. The number of times it reproduces and the number of offspring per reproductive episode are important, as is the age at first reproduction.

TABLE 18.1 Factors Affecting Population Growth: A Summary

Factor	Affected by ...
Additions	
Births	• Number of reproductive episodes per lifetime • Number of offspring per reproductive episode • Age at first reproduction • Population age structure
Migration into the population	• Availability of dispersal mechanism • Availability of suitable habitat
Subtractions	
Deaths	• Accidents • Genetic/infectious disease • Predation • Nutrient availability
Migration out of the population	• Availability of dispersal mechanism

All other things being equal, the earlier reproduction begins, the faster the population will grow.

A population's **age structure,** or distribution of age classes, helps determine whether a population is growing, stable, or declining (figure 18.3). A population with a large fraction of prereproductive individuals will grow. As these individuals enter their reproductive years and produce offspring, the prereproductive age classes swell further, building a foundation that ensures future growth. Conversely, a population that consists mainly of older individuals will be stable or may even decline. This situation can doom a population of endangered plants if, for example, habitat destruction makes it impossible for seedlings to establish themselves. With few individuals of reproductive age, the population may go extinct.

B. Survivorship Curves Show the Probability of Dying at a Given Age

A population's **death rate** is the number of deaths per unit time, scaled by the population size. The causes of death may include accidents, disease, predation, and competition for scarce resources. In the human population, for example, the overall death rate is approximately 8 per 1000 people per year; section 18.6 describes human mortality in more detail.

Each individual in a population will eventually die; the only question is when. But species vary tremendously in their patterns of survivorship. In species that invest little energy or care in each individual offspring, for example, the probability of dying before reaching reproductive age is very high. In other species, heavy parental investment in a small number of offspring means that most individuals survive long enough to reproduce.

To help interpret which pattern might apply to a particular species, population biologists developed the **life table,** a chart that shows the probability of surviving to any given age. (Life insurance companies use life tables to compute premiums for clients of different ages.) Figure 18.4a, for example, shows a life table for yellow-eyed penguins. The values in the life table account for predation, disease, food availability, and all other factors that prevent an individual from reaching its theoretical life span.

The values in a life table are often plotted onto a **survivorship curve,** a graph of the proportion of surviving individuals at each age. Figure 18.4b

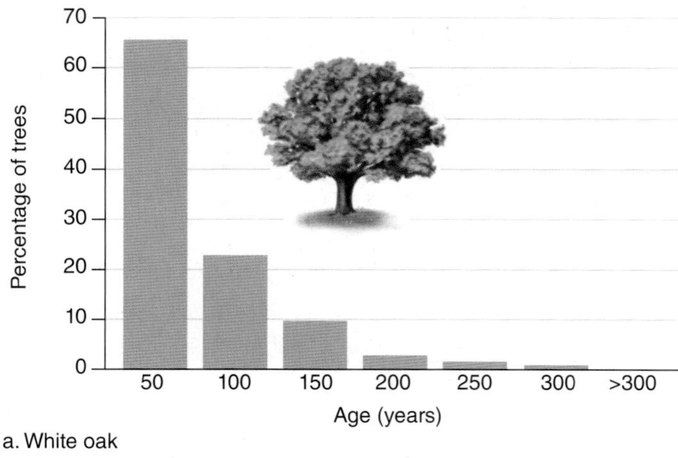

a. White oak

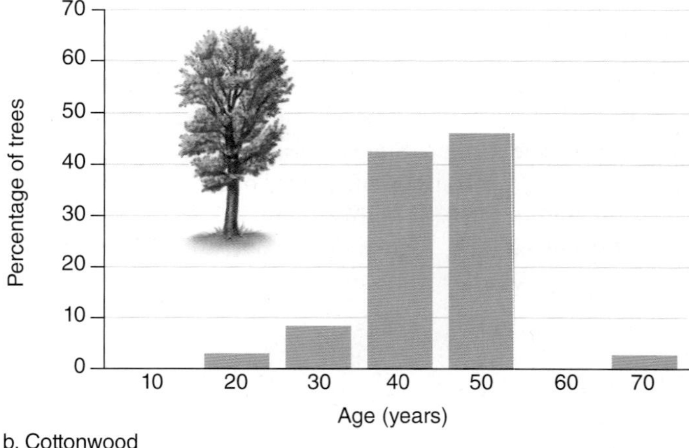

b. Cottonwood

Figure 18.3 Age Structures. (a) This white oak population is dominated by younger individuals, indicating high potential for future growth. (b) This population of cottonwoods has few individuals in the youngest age classes. Lacking young trees, the population may not survive.

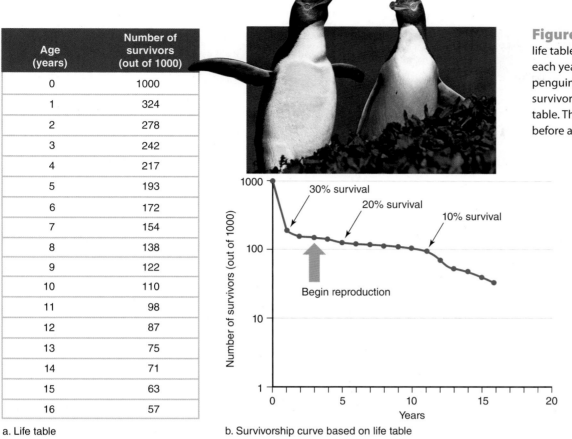

Age (years)	Number of survivors (out of 1000)
0	1000
1	324
2	278
3	242
4	217
5	193
6	172
7	154
8	138
9	122
10	110
11	98
12	87
13	75
14	71
15	63
16	57

a. Life table

b. Survivorship curve based on life table

Figure 18.4 Penguin Survivorship. (a) This life table lists the number of survivors remaining each year out of a group of 1000 yellow-eyed penguins that hatch at the same time. (b) A survivorship curve is a graph of the data in a life table. The curve reveals that most penguins die before age 1, after which mortality levels off.

shows a graph of the values from the penguin life table. Note that the *y*-axis data are plotted on a logarithmic scale, not a linear one. The log scale makes it easier to see trends along the entire range of values, from 0 to 1000.

The survivorship curves of many species follow one of three general patterns (figure 18.5). Type I species, such as humans and elephants, invest a great deal of energy and time in each offspring. Most individuals live long enough to reproduce, and the mortality rate is highest as individuals approach the maximum life span. Type II species, including many birds and mammals, have an approximately equal probability of dying at any age. Type III species, such as many fishes and most invertebrates and plants, may produce many offspring but invest little in each one. Most offspring of type III species therefore die at a very young age. Section 18.5 looks more closely at the evolutionary trade-offs that these survivorship curves reflect.

Of course, these generalized examples do not describe all populations. Many species have survivorship curves that fall between two patterns. The yellow-eyed penguin, for example, has a survivorship curve that has features of both type I and type II curves.

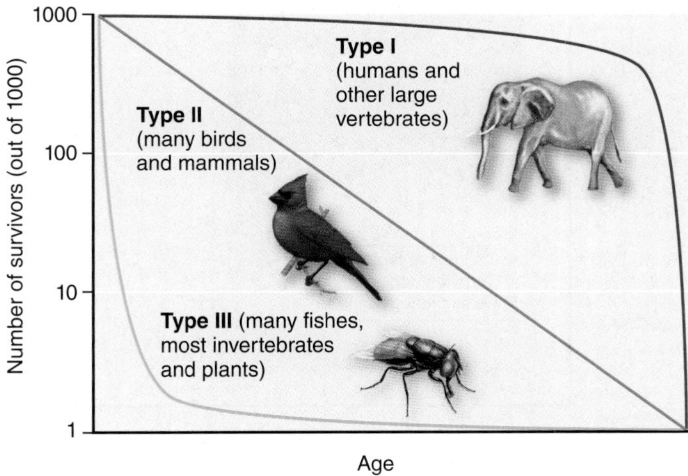

Figure 18.5 Three Survivorship Curves. In type I species, most individuals survive to old age, whereas in type III species, most individuals die young. Type II species are in between, with constant survivorship throughout the lifespan.

18.3 Mastering Concepts

1. Under what conditions will a population grow?
2. What factors determine birth and death rates in a population?
3. How does a life table relate to a survivorship curve?
4. Describe three patterns of survivorship curves.

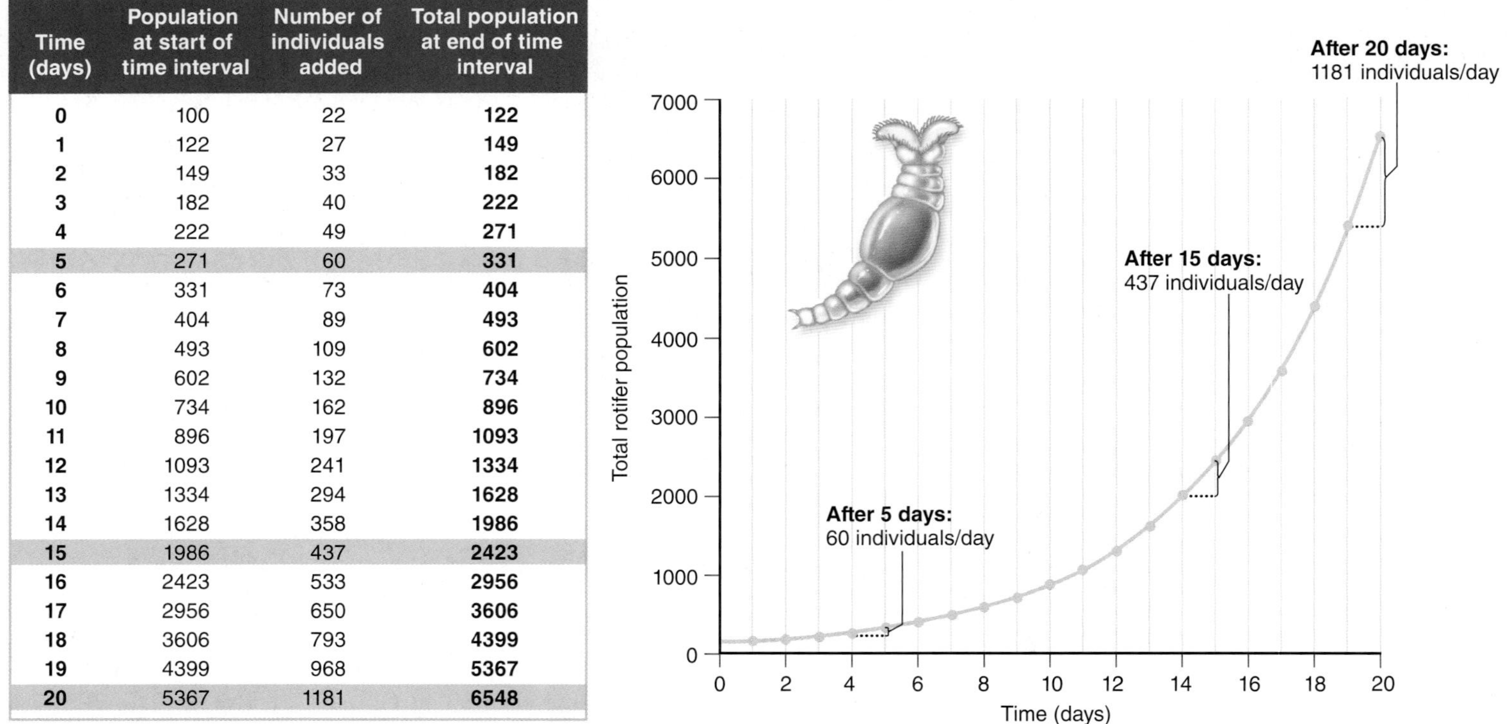

Time (days)	Population at start of time interval	Number of individuals added	Total population at end of time interval
0	100	22	**122**
1	122	27	**149**
2	149	33	**182**
3	182	40	**222**
4	222	49	**271**
5	271	60	**331**
6	331	73	**404**
7	404	89	**493**
8	493	109	**602**
9	602	132	**734**
10	734	162	**896**
11	896	197	**1093**
12	1093	241	**1334**
13	1334	294	**1628**
14	1628	358	**1986**
15	1986	437	**2423**
16	2423	533	**2956**
17	2956	650	**3606**
18	3606	793	**4399**
19	4399	968	**5367**
20	5367	1181	**6548**

Figure 18.6 Exponential Population Growth. For a population of rotifers with unlimited resources, the number of individuals added per day increases with each generation. Colored bars in the table represent time points that are labeled in the graph.

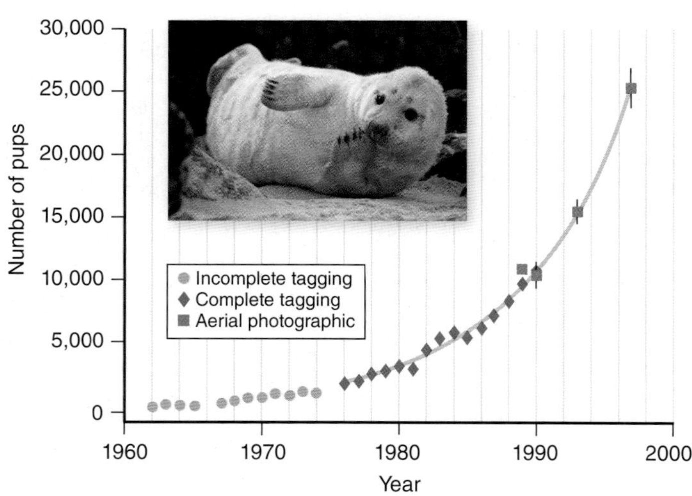

Figure 18.7 Seal Pup Population. Forty years of tagging and aerial surveys of the grey seal pups on Sable Island, Nova Scotia, reveal a consistent pattern of exponential population growth.

18.4 Population Growth May Be Exponential or Logistic

Any population will grow if the number of individuals added exceeds the number removed. But how fast will it grow, and how large can the population become? Two mathematical models, called exponential and logistic growth, illustrate two simple patterns of population growth.

A. Growth Is Exponential When Resources Are Unlimited

In the simplest model of population growth, **exponential growth**, the number of new individuals is proportional to the size of the population. For example, suppose that 100 aquatic animals called rotifers are placed in a tank under ideal growth conditions. How many new rotifers are produced each day? The answer depends on the size of the population: the more rotifers in the tank, the larger the capacity to add offspring. Figure 18.6 shows the size of each generation and plots the running total on a graph.

As figure 18.6 shows, a **J-shaped curve** emerges when exponential growth is plotted over time. Growth resulting from repeated doubling (1, 2, 4, 8, 16, 32, . . .), such as in bacteria, is exponential. Species introduced to an area where they are not native may also proliferate exponentially for a time, since they often have no natural population controls. Figure 18.7 shows another example

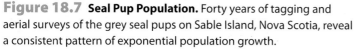

Time (days)	Population at start of time interval	Number of individuals added	Total population at end of time interval
0-5	100	202	**302**
5-10	302	366	**668**
10-15	668	529	**1197**
15-20	1197	454	**1651**
20-25	1651	230	**1881**
25-30	1881	83	**1964**
30-35	1964	26	**1990**
35-40	1990	7	**1997**

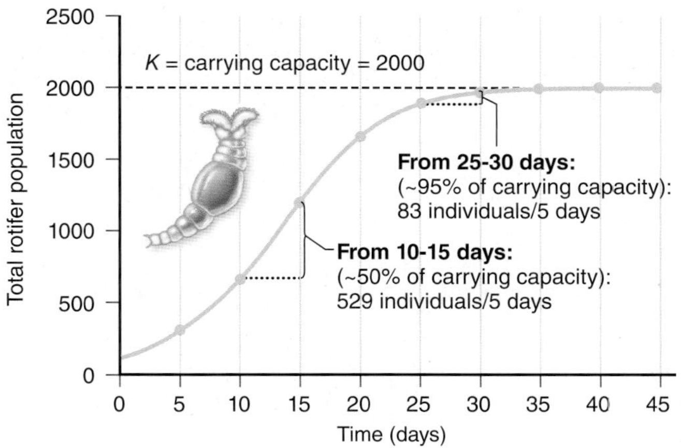

Figure 18.8 Logistic Population Growth. When resources are limited, the number of individuals added each day declines as the carrying capacity approaches. Colored bars in the table represent time intervals that are labeled in the graph.

of exponential growth: the production of grey seal pups on Sable Island, Nova Scotia. If growth were to continue at this rate for another 75 years, the seal pup population would exceed 1 billion!

B. Population Growth Eventually Slows

Exponential growth may continue for a short time, but it cannot continue indefinitely because some resource is eventually depleted. Competition, predation, and anything else that reduces birth rates or increases mortality all can keep a population from reaching its maximum growth rate. (Section 19.4 describes these factors in more detail.)

Every habitat has a **carrying capacity,** which is the maximum number of individuals that the habitat can support indefinitely. This carrying capacity imposes an upper limit on a population's size. How does this limit affect the population's growth rate? According to the **logistic growth** model, the early growth of a population may be exponential, but growth slows as the population approaches the habitat's carrying capacity (figure 18.8). The resulting **S-shaped curve** depicts the leveling off of the population.

The carrying capacity of a habitat typically is not fixed. A drought that lasts for a decade may be followed by a year of exceptionally heavy rainfall, causing a flush of new plant growth and a sudden increase in food availability for animals. Alternatively, the food on which a species relies may disappear, or a catastrophic flood can drastically reduce the carrying capacity as habitat is destroyed.

In studying population growth, it is important to understand that some species do not fit neatly into either the exponential or logistic models. In collared lemmings, for example, the population fluctuates on a 4-year cycle (figure 18.9). The origin of such boom-and-bust cycles remains mysterious, but predation by stoats (a type of weasel) appears to be one of the main factors maintaining the ups and downs of the lemming population.

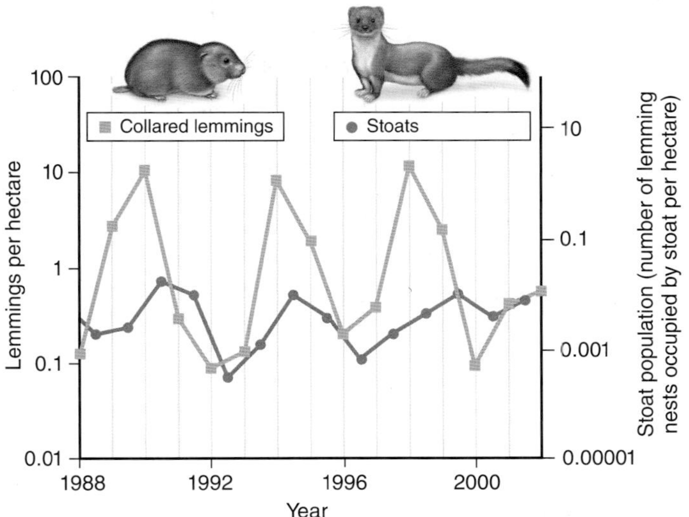

Figure 18.9 Population Cycle. The population of collared lemmings fluctuates regularly over a 4-year period. Research suggests that a major influence on the lemming population is the number of stoats, a type of weasel that preys on the lemmings.

C. Many Conditions Limit Population Size

A combination of factors regulates the size of most populations. Consider the population of songbirds in your town. Some lose their lives to cold weather or food shortages, whereas others succumb to infectious disease or the jaws of a

a.

b.

Figure 18.10 Factors Limiting Populations. (a) Density-dependent factors become more important as the habitat becomes crowded. These lesser flamingoes are feeding on a mud flat. (b) Density-independent factors such as forest fires limit populations at all densities.

cat. These and other limits on the growth of the bird population fall into two general categories: density-dependent and density-independent (figure 18.10).

Density-dependent factors are conditions whose effects increase as a population grows. Most density-dependent limits result from interactions with living organisms. Within a population, competition for space, nutrients, sunlight, food, mates, and breeding sites is density-dependent. When many individuals share limited resources, few may be able to reproduce, and population growth slows or even crashes.

Other species can also exert density-dependent limits on a population's growth. Multiple species often compete fiercely for the same nutrients and space. Infectious disease also takes a toll. Many viruses, bacteria, fungi, and protists spread by direct contact between infected individuals and new hosts. The higher the host population density, the more opportunity for these disease-causing organisms to spread. Likewise, a higher population density may lead to a higher probability of death by predation (see this chapter's Why We Care box).

Density-independent factors exert effects that are unrelated to population density. Natural disasters such as fires, earthquakes, floods, volcanic eruptions, and severe weather are typical density-independent factors. The high winds of a hurricane, for example, may destroy 50% of the bird nests in a forest, without regard to the density of the bird population. Likewise, a lava flow kills everything in its path. The effects of oil spills and other industrial accidents are density-independent, too. In addition, as described in chapter 20, habitat destruction related to human activities is a density-independent factor that is pushing many species to the brink of extinction.

No matter what combination of factors controls a population's size, it is worth remembering the importance of these limits in natural selection and evolution. Many individuals do not survive long enough to reproduce. Those that do manage to breed have the adaptations that allow them to escape the biotic and abiotic challenges that claim the lives of many of their counterparts. As these "fittest" individuals pass their genes on, the next generation contains a higher proportion of offspring with those same adaptations.

18.4 Mastering Concepts

1. What conditions support exponential population growth?
2. How does logistic growth differ from exponential growth?
3. Distinguish between density-dependent and density-independent factors that limit population size, and give three examples of each.

18.5 Natural Selection Influences Life Histories

As we have already seen, a population's size depends in part on birth and death rates. Species differ widely, however, in the timing of these events. Population ecologists therefore find it useful to document a species' **life history,** which includes all events of an organism's life from conception through death. The main focus of life history analysis is the adaptations that influence reproductive success.

Population life tables and growth curves, described in sections 18.3 and 18.4, document two elements of an organism's life history. Other aspects include the life span, developmental rate, reproductive timing, social behaviors, mate selection, number and size of offspring, number of reproductive events, and amount of parental care. This section explores how natural selection shapes some of these life history traits.

A. Organisms Balance Reproduction Against Other Requirements

A species' life history reflects a series of evolutionary trade-offs; after all, supplies of time, energy, and resources are always limited. Just as an investor allocates money among stocks, bonds, and real estate, a juvenile organism divides its efforts among growth, maintenance, and survival. After reaching maturity, another competing demand—reproduction—joins the list.

Reproduction is extremely costly. Many animals, for example, devote time and energy to attracting mates, building and defending nests, and incubating or gestating offspring. Once the young are hatched or born, the parents may feed and protect them. All of these activities limit a parent's ability to feed itself, defend itself, or reproduce again. In plants, the reproductive investment is also substantial. Flowers, fruits, and defensive chemicals cost energy to produce and may take away from a plant's photosynthetic area, reducing the ability to capture sunlight.

Besides the total effort allocated to reproduction, the timing is also critical. An organism that delays reproduction for too long may die before producing any offspring at all. On the other hand, reproducing too early diverts energy away from the growth and maintenance that may be crucial to survival.

The solutions to these trade-offs vary tremendously among species. A bacterial cell, for example, may grow for just 20 minutes before dividing asexually. A female winter moth mates once and lays hundreds of fertilized eggs just before she dies. A pigweed plant sheds 100,000 seeds in the one summer of its life. These and many other organisms mature early, produce many offspring in a single reproductive burst, and die. Humans, elephants, and century plants, on the other hand, mature late and produce only a few offspring throughout their long lives.

B. Opportunistic and Equilibrium Species Differ in the Trade-Off Between Quantity and Quality

Although each species is unique, ecologists have discovered that life histories fall into patterns shaped by natural selection. One prominent trade-off is the balance between offspring quality and quantity.

At one extreme are **opportunistic species**, in which individuals tend to be short-lived, reproduce at an early age, and have many offspring that receive little care (figure 18.11). The population's growth rate can be very high if

Why We Care | An Ecological View of Backyard Bird Feeders

Many people love to watch the songbirds that visit backyard feeders and bird baths. A well-stocked feeding station provides seeds, fruits, and suet cakes that are packed with carbohydrates, protein, and fat. Bird baths supply fresh water for drinking; in addition, a brief splash in the water helps clean and maintain feathers.

What do bird feeders and bird baths have to do with population ecology? One answer is that providing food and water should help boost songbird populations. After all, the extra nutrients may enable an adult bird to survive a harsh winter or help a breeding pair feed their young in spring and summer.

A second answer, however, takes a more ominous view. Feeders and bird baths may attract large flocks that actually increase the effect of two density-dependent limits on bird populations. Crowded conditions promote the spread of infectious disease as droppings accumulate near feeders and in the water. The birds also attract predators such as hawks and cats, which kill large numbers of songbirds.

a.

b.

Figure 18.11 Opportunistic Species. (a) Grasses such as rice plants and (b) insects such as sawflies produce many small offspring and invest little in each one.

a.

b.

Figure 18.12 Equilibrium Species. (a) Coconut trees produce large fruits that each represent a relatively large investment of energy. (b) Grizzly bears devote extensive time and resources to rearing a small number of young.

conditions are optimal. In general, however, each offspring has a very low probability of surviving to reproduce; this pattern is typical of species with type III survivorship curves (see figure 18.5).

Weeds, insects, and many other invertebrates are opportunistic. Their populations can skyrocket when conditions are favorable, but density-independent factors such as frost or drought soon limit their growth.

At the other extreme are **equilibrium species,** in which individuals tend to be long-lived, to be late-maturing, and to produce a small number of offspring that receive extended parental care (figure 18.12). High parental investment in each offspring means that most live long enough to reproduce. Density-dependent factors such as competition keep these populations close to the carrying capacity. Many birds and large mammals (organisms with survivorship curves that approximate type I or type II) live in equilibrial populations.

It is important to realize that species vary widely in their life histories; strict adherence to an opportunistic or equilibrial life history is the exception, not the rule. For example, even populations of large animals with equilibrium life histories fluctuate greatly in response to changes in their environments. Nevertheless, these two strategies illustrate the important point that natural selection shapes a species' life history characteristics, which reflect the competing demands of reproduction and survival.

C. Guppies Illustrate the Importance of Natural Selection

Experiments show that natural selection directly influences the details of a life history, including age at maturity and the number of offspring per reproductive event. For example, section 12.8 described how changes in fishing regulations can alter the life histories of commercially fished species.

Caribbean fish called guppies offer another well-studied example. These fish live in rivers and streams on the South American mainland and on the islands of Trinidad and Tobago. The guppies in some streams face high predation intensity; that is, they share the water with other fish species that eat many adult guppies. Other streams contain predators that eat fewer guppies and therefore exert only moderate predation intensity on the guppy population. In a third set of streams, the guppies do not face significant predation at all.

The researchers hypothesized that predation would be a selective force influencing the guppies' life histories. For example, they predicted that guppies from streams with high predation intensity would reach reproductive maturity at a younger age and devote more energy to reproduction than guppies from other streams. To test their hypothesis, they collected guppies from streams with high, medium, and low predation intensity. They dissected each female fish and weighed any offspring she carried inside her, and they measured the mature males and females from each stream to estimate the age at maturity.

Guppies from the high-predation streams had the smallest offspring (figure 18.13). They also matured earlier, reproduced more frequently, and had more offspring. Other studies confirmed that these differences were genetic and therefore were subject to natural selection. The investigators also used field and laboratory experiments to confirm that the predation intensity (not some other condition in the streams) was responsible for these life history differences.

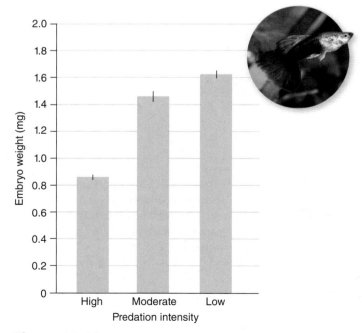

Figure 18.13 Guppy Life History. Guppies are brightly colored fish that are popular subjects for studies of population ecology. In this study, high predation intensity was correlated with the production of small offspring, along with other life history changes.

18.5 Mastering Concepts

1. Distinguish between opportunistic and equilibrium species.
2. How have studies with guppies shown that natural selection shapes life histories?

18.6 The Human Population Continues to Grow

The human population has grown exponentially in the last 2000 years (figure 18.14). So far, humans have found ways to escape many of the forces that limit the growth of other animal species, but exponential growth will not continue indefinitely. This section describes how the principles of population growth apply to the human population.

A. Birth and Death Rates Vary Worldwide

By late 2011, the world's human population was around 7 billion. Since Earth's land area is about 150 million square kilometers, the average population density is about 47 people per square kilometer of land area. But the distribution is far from random. For the most part, the highest population densities worldwide occur along coastlines and in the valleys of major rivers; very few people live on high mountains, in the middle of the world's major deserts, or on Antarctica. Two countries—China and India—account for one third of all humans.

Overall, the human population growth rate is about 1.2% per year and declining. Demographers project that zero population growth may happen between the years 2050 and 2100, but no one is certain. Nor do we know how many people will inhabit Earth when that occurs (see this chapter's Burning Question).

Burning Questions

What will happen to the human population?

No one knows exactly how growth rates will change in the future, so it is impossible to predict when or at what level the human population will stabilize. In 2008, the United Nations issued three projections for the world's population, assuming high, medium, and low growth rates. The highest projection says the Earth's population will be around 10.5 billion (and still growing) in 2050. The medium estimate shows the population leveling off at around 9.1 billion in 2050. The low estimate predicts that the population will peak at just over 8 billion in 2042, then decline to just under 8 billion by 2050.

These projections are only as good as their assumptions. Will fertility in developing countries continue to decline? If so, by how much, and how fast will it happen? Will fertility decline by the same amount in all countries? Will more-developed countries be willing and able to provide family planning services even as the rural populations of less-developed countries continue to grow? The answers to these questions will determine the future of Earth's human population.

Submit your burning question to:
marielle_hoefnagels@mcgraw-hill.com

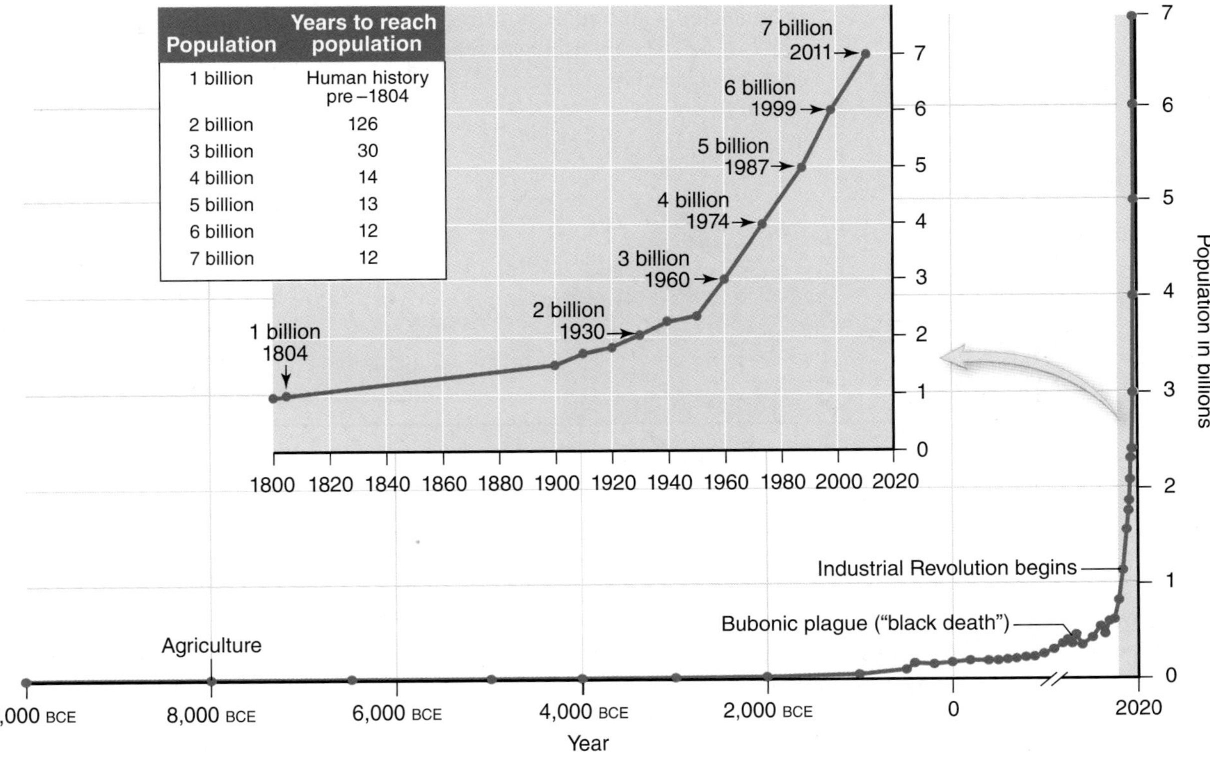

Population	Years to reach population
1 billion	Human history pre–1804
2 billion	126
3 billion	30
4 billion	14
5 billion	13
6 billion	12
7 billion	12

Figure 18.14 Historical Growth of the Human Population. The J-shaped curve indicates exponential growth, with the most rapid population growth occurring in the past 200 years *(inset)*. (Data from U.S. Census Bureau.)

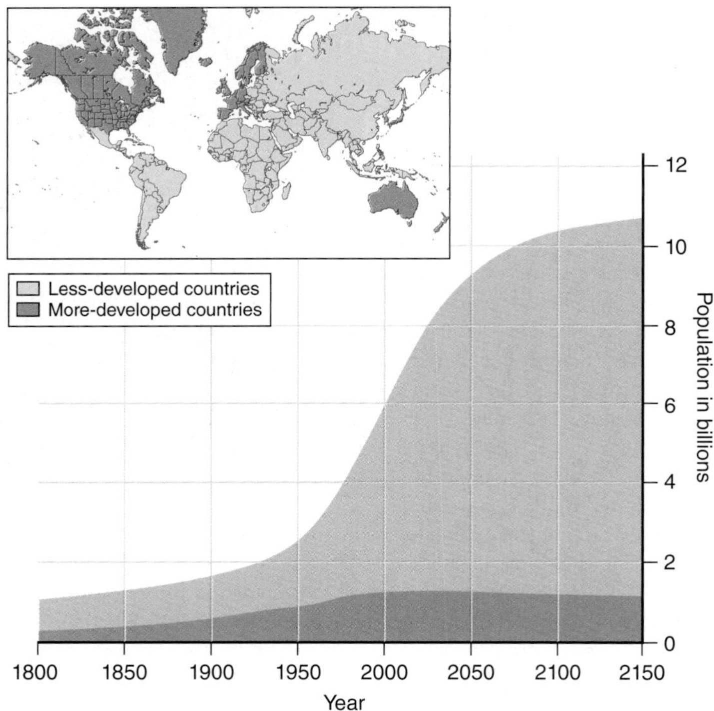

Figure 18.15 Projected Human Population Growth. Future population growth will continue to be concentrated in less-developed countries.

Clearly, however, less-developed countries are growing at much faster rates than are more-developed countries (figure 18.15). Why the difference? The answer is that each country's economic development influences its birth and death rates. Early in human history, population growth was minimal because both birth and death rates were high. Then, in the next stage of the so-called "demographic transition," improved living conditions lower the death rate, but birth rates remain high. This transitional period therefore sees the rapid population growth typical of the world's less-developed countries. Eventually, however, birth rates fall, and the population's growth rate slows once more. The world's more-developed countries have entered this stage; a few even have declining populations because death rates exceed birth rates.

Factors Affecting Birth Rates As described in section 18.3, a population's age structure helps predict its future birth rate. Figure 18.16 shows the age structures for the world's three most populous countries. In India and many other less-developed countries, a large fraction of the population is entering its reproductive years, suggesting a high potential for future growth (see figure 18.16a). In the United States, as in many other developed countries, the population consists mainly of older individuals (see figure 18.16b). Such populations are stable.

As recently as 1990, China's age structure resembled that of present-day India. But China's population now shows a decline in the youngest age classes, so its future growth rate should be lower (see figure 18.16c). The Chinese government has controlled runaway population growth with drastic measures, rewarding one-child families and revoking the first child's benefits if a second child is born. Although China remains the world's most populous nation, demographers expect India to take the lead by 2025.

A close look at China's age structure diagram also reveals another consequence of that country's childbirth policy. Although the numbers of older males and females are approximately equal, the diagram reveals a bias toward male children in younger age classes. According to cultural tradition in China, parents prefer male children. Couples who are allowed just one child may end pregnancies with female fetuses in hopes of conceiving a male later. Population biologists are closely studying the social and demographic consequences of this gender shift.

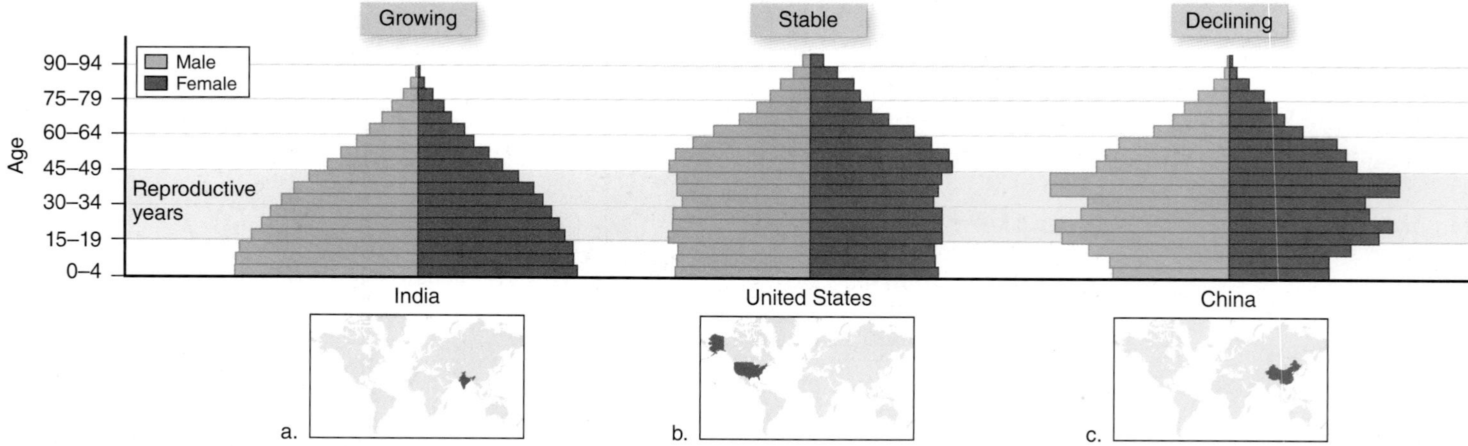

Figure 18.16 Age Structures for Three Human Populations. In age structure diagrams, the width of each bar is proportional to the percent of individuals in that age class. (a) India's population is likely to continue to grow because a high proportion of individuals are in prereproductive age classes. (b) The population of the United States is stable, with roughly equal numbers of people in each age group. (c) China's future growth rate should decline because most of its members are in reproductive or postreproductive age classes. (Data from U.S. Census Bureau, International Data Base.)

Overall, why do birth rates tend to decline as economic development progresses? One explanation for this trend is the availability of family planning programs, which are relatively inexpensive and have immediate results. Social and economic factors play an important role as well. Educated women are most likely to learn about and use family planning services, have more opportunities outside the home, and may delay marriage and childbearing until after they enter the work force. Delayed childbearing often means fewer children and therefore slows population growth.

Factors Affecting Mortality Besides birth rate, mortality is the other major factor influencing population growth rates. Overall, average life expectancy has increased steadily throughout history, from 22 during the Roman Empire to 33 in the Middle Ages. Today, average life expectancy is about 75 in the most-developed countries and about 50 in the least-developed countries, reflecting a substantial difference in mortality rates.

Table 18.2 shows the top five causes of death in developed and developing countries. Heart disease, stroke, lung cancer, and other lung problems top the list in the developed world. Infectious diseases rank relatively low, thanks in large part to sanitation, antibiotics, and vaccines. In contrast, deadly infectious diseases such as diarrhea, pneumonia, and HIV/AIDS are more prominent in developing countries. Crowded conditions facilitate the spread of disease, especially in areas with limited access to clean drinking water. AIDS has taken an especially high toll in sub-Saharan Africa, where the epidemic has significantly increased mortality rates. ▸ HIV, p. 130

TABLE 18.2 Top Five Causes of Death in High- and Low-Income Countries

Rank	High-Income Countries	Low-Income Countries
1	Heart disease (coronary artery blockage)	Lower respiratory infection (pneumonia, acute bronchitis)
2	Stroke	Heart disease (coronary artery blockage)
3	Lung cancer	Diarrhea (e.g., cholera, rotavirus)
4	Lower respiratory infection (pneumonia, acute bronchitis)	HIV/AIDS
5	Chronic obstructive pulmonary disease (chronic bronchitis, emphysema)	Stroke

Source: World Health Organization Fact Sheet, "The 10 Leading Causes of Death by Broad Income Group."

B. The Ecological Footprint Is an Estimate of Resource Use

The human population cannot continue to grow exponentially because living space and other resources are finite. Worldwide, increasing numbers of people will mean greater pressure on land, water, air, and fossil fuels as people demand more resources and generate more waste.

Ecologists summarize each country's demands on the planet by calculating an ecological footprint. Just as an actual footprint shows the area that a shoe occupies with each step, an **ecological footprint** measures the amount of land area needed to support a country's overall lifestyle. The calculation includes energy consumption and the land area used to grow crops for food and fiber, produce timber, and raise cattle and other animals. The area occupied by streets, buildings, and other infrastructure is also part of the ecological footprint, as is land used for waste disposal. Not surprisingly, the world's wealthiest and most populous countries have the largest ecological footprints (figure 18.17).

Energy consumption accounts for about half of the ecological footprint. The wealthiest countries make up less than 20% of the world's population yet consume more than half of the energy. Less-developed countries, however, will take a larger share of energy supplies as their populations grow and their economies become more industrialized. Since the vast majority of the energy comes from oil, coal, and natural gas, the result will be increased air pollution, acid rain, and carbon dioxide buildup in the atmosphere. The accumulation of CO_2 and other greenhouse gases is implicated in global climate change.

Food production is another significant element of the ecological footprint. Overall, agricultural productivity rises each year. However, increased demand for food, coupled with competition for corn and soybeans from the biofuels and animal feed markets, has pushed food prices beyond the reach of many of the world's poor. To boost food production, people often expand their farms into forests, destroying habitat and threatening biodiversity. ▸ biofuels, p. 308

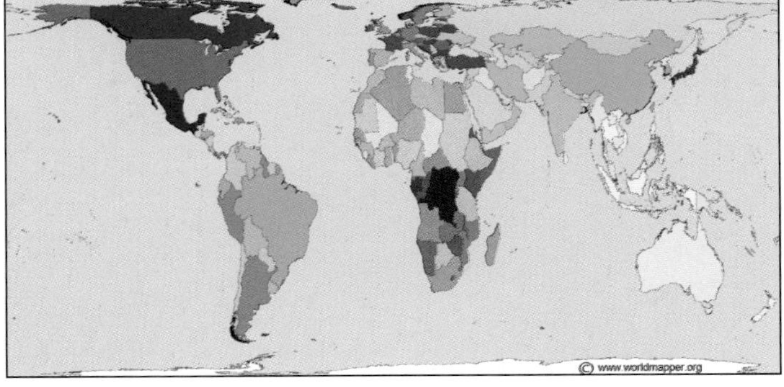

a.

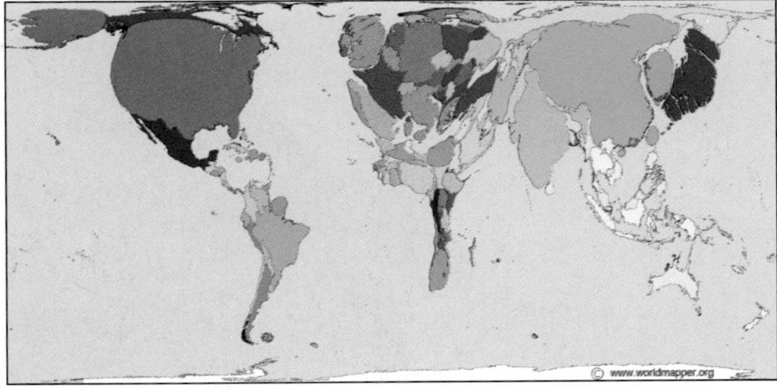

b.

Figure 18.17 Ecological Footprint. (a) In a traditional world map, each country's size reflects its land area. (b) In this map, each country's size is proportional to its ecological footprint. The 12 geographic regions in each map are ordered in a rainbow scale ranging from dark red (poorest) to deep violet (richest).

Because the ecological footprint focuses on land area, it does not include water consumption. Nevertheless, the availability of fresh water has declined worldwide as people have demanded more water for agriculture, industry, and household use. In many poor countries, less than half the population has access to safe water for drinking and cooking. As a result, waterborne diseases such as cholera periodically surge through the dense populations of India and many African and South American countries.

Chapter 20 further explores deforestation, species extinctions, increased fuel consumption, global climate change, and other environmental problems related to the expanding human population.

18.6 Mastering Concepts

1. Which parts of the world have the highest and lowest rates of human population growth?
2. What factors affect birth and mortality rates worldwide?
3. What are some of the environmental consequences of human population growth?

Investigating Life

18.7 Let Your Love Light Shine

In sexually reproducing organisms, the production of new individuals—the foundation of population growth—requires that sperm find their way to egg cells. The life histories of many species include elaborate games of seduction in which the spoils of mating go to those who play their cards just right. But why does the game exist in the first place? What prompts a ram to butt heads with a rival, a frog to croak, or a peacock to flourish his magnificent tail? The answer is that these actions draw the attention of choosy mates. Individuals with the most mating opportunities, in turn, usually leave the most offspring. ▸ sexual selection, p. 232

A female's reproductive success—that is, her fitness—depends in part on a mate that offers the best provisions for the next generation. Clearly, there is strong selective pressure on females to choose mates based on honest signals. Yet every male conveys many possible signals, including his strength, color, calls, and movements. Sorting out which features are key to the female's choice is a challenge for biologists.

Tufts University biologists Christopher Cratsley and Sara Lewis sought to unravel the mystery of the sexual dialogue in the firefly *Photinus ignitus*. The consummate act in firefly mating is the transfer of a protein-rich sperm packet, called a spermatophore, from the male to the female's reproductive tract. The spermatophore contains not only sperm but also nutritious amino acids for the developing offspring.

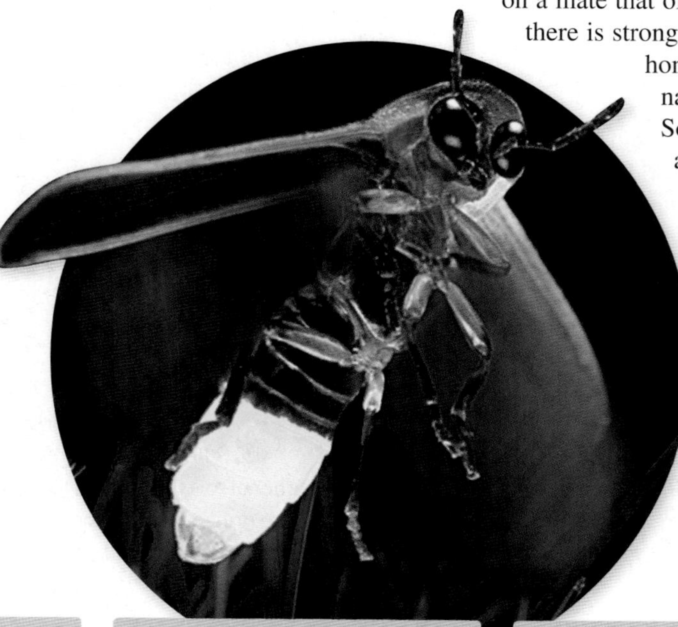

The Question: Cratsley and Lewis figured that a fitness advantage should go to females that choose males with larger spermatophores. The larger the packet, the more protein available for the offspring and the greater the female's reproductive success. But how would a female know which male packed the largest spermatophore? The researchers hypothesized that male fireflies might code this information in flashes of light.

The Approach: To test their hypothesis, the researchers watched 36 male fireflies copulate with females in the laboratory. They dissected the females immediately after spermatophore transfer and weighed each packet of sperm and protein. The spermatophore weights were analyzed against male flash duration, body mass, lantern width, and lantern area. Of these, flash duration carried the most reliable information: the longer the flash, the heavier the spermatophore (figure 18.18a).

Next, the team let female fireflies tell them what they liked about the males. Would they prefer the long flashes that signal a large spermatophore? One way to answer this question would have been to let the females choose between males with different flash durations. However, because males differ in other ways as well, it would have been difficult to conclude that the female preference was for flash duration and not some other variable that the researchers never thought to measure.

The researchers therefore created artificial males. In a series of clever experiments, they flashed a yellow light-emitting diode, and the females responded to the artificial males by giving a return flash if they liked what they saw. The researchers tested the females against three flash durations: 80 milliseconds (the average for males of the species); 108 milliseconds (near the upper limit of male flash duration); and 132 milliseconds (longer than those the males can produce).

They found that females preferred long flashes, but only up to a limit (figure 18.18b). Apparently, extremely long flashes resemble those of predatory fireflies. Furthermore, wasting time and energy responding to flashes from the wrong species would reduce the female's reproductive success.

The Conclusion: Cratsley and Lewis' experiments support the notion that males use light to advertise the size of their spermatophore gifts; females respond when the size and flash duration are right. In some ways, these advertisements are similar to commercial messages on TV. Manufacturers of everything from deodorant to dishwashing detergent clamor for your attention, each claiming that their products are best. If you are dissatisfied with your purchase, the worst that can happen is that you buy another brand on your next trip to the store. In the mating game, however, the consequence of a "wrong" decision may make or break an individual's contribution to the next generation.

Cratsley, Christopher K., and Sara M. Lewis. 2003. Female preferences for male courtship flashes in *Photinus ignitus* fireflies. *Behavioral Ecology*, vol. 14, pages 135–140.

18.7 Mastering Concepts

1. How did researchers test the hypothesis that a firefly's flash duration is correlated with spermatophore mass?
2. A male firefly with a small spermatophore could "lie" by using a long flash. What might be the consequence in the short term? In the long term, what would happen to the reliability of the flash duration signal if many males "cheated" in this way?

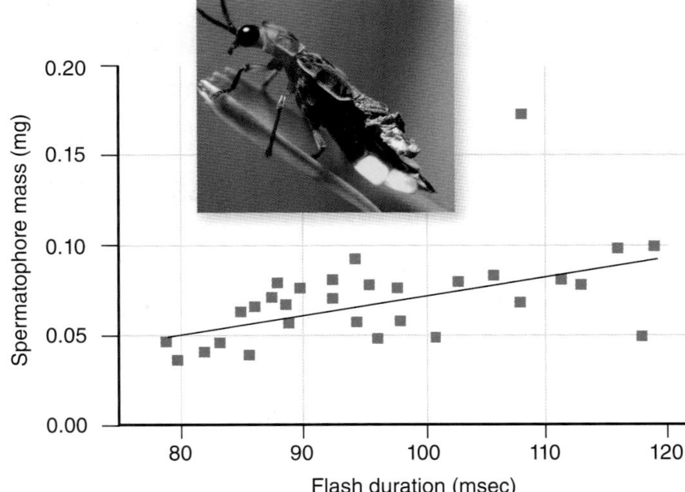

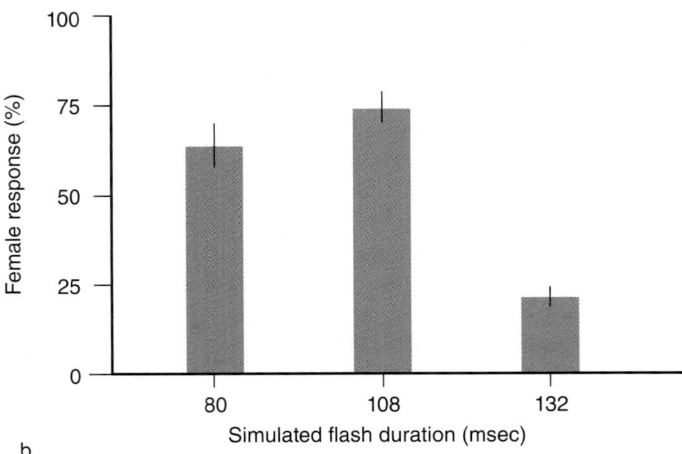

Figure 18.18 The Firefly Flash: An Honest Signal. (a) Flash duration is positively correlated with the mass of a male firefly's spermatophore, which contains both sperm and nutrition for the future offspring. (b) Female fireflies responded the most to flashes that were long—but not too long.

Chapter Summary

18.1 Ecology Is the Study of Interactions

- **Ecology** considers interrelationships between organisms and the environment.
- In general, **biotic** interactions occur among living organisms. **Population**-level interactions involve members of the same species, whereas **community**-level interactions involve multiple species. **Ecosystem**-level interactions include a community's exchanges of materials and energy with the **abiotic** (nonliving) environment.
- The **biosphere,** which includes all areas where life exists, is one interconnected ecosystem.

18.2 A Population Consists of Individuals of One Species

- A **habitat** is the location where an individual normally lives.
- **Population density** is a measure of the number of individuals per unit area of habitat.

18.3 Births and Deaths Help Determine Population Size

A. Births Add Individuals to a Population

- A population grows when new individuals are added through birth or migration into the population.
- The **birth rate** is the number of individuals produced per capita in a defined time period. A population's birth rate depends on many factors, including the **age structure.**

B. Survivorship Curves Show the Probability of Dying at a Given Age

- The **death rate** reflects the number of deaths per unit time.
- A **life table** shows the number of survivors remaining in a population at each age. **Survivorship curves** fall into three patterns, reflecting the balance between number of offspring and the amount of parental investment in each.

18.4 Population Growth May Be Exponential or Logistic

A. Growth Is Exponential When Resources Are Unlimited

- Population growth that is proportional to the size of the population is **exponential** and produces a **J-shaped curve.**

B. Population Growth Eventually Slows

- In response to competition, predation, and other factors that reduce birth rates and increase death rates, the population may stabilize indefinitely at the habitat's **carrying capacity.** A plot of the resulting **logistic growth** produces a characteristic **S-shaped curve.**

C. Many Conditions Limit Population Size

- **Density-dependent factors** such as infectious disease, predation, and competition have the greatest effect on crowded populations.
- **Density-independent factors,** such as natural disasters, kill the same fraction of the population regardless of the population's density.

18.4 Natural Selection Influences Life Histories

- The **life history** of a species includes all events from birth to death but typically emphasizes the factors that affect reproduction.

A. Organisms Balance Reproduction Against Other Requirements

- Organisms must allocate limited time, energy, and resources among growth, maintenance, survival, and reproduction.

B. Opportunistic and Equilibrium Species Differ in the Trade-Off Between Quantity and Quality

- **Opportunistic species** produce many offspring but expend little energy on each, whereas **equilibrium species** invest heavily in rearing relatively few young.

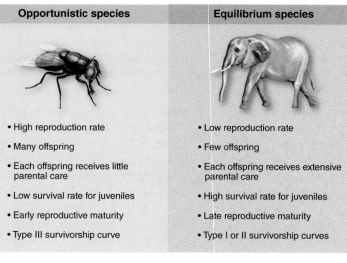

Opportunistic species	Equilibrium species
• High reproduction rate	• Low reproduction rate
• Many offspring	• Few offspring
• Each offspring receives little parental care	• Each offspring receives extensive parental care
• Low survival rate for juveniles	• High survival rate for juveniles
• Early reproductive maturity	• Late reproductive maturity
• Type III survivorship curve	• Type I or II survivorship curves

C. Guppies Illustrate the Importance of Natural Selection

- Natural selection influences a population's life history characteristics.

18.6 The Human Population Continues to Grow

A. Birth and Death Rates Vary Worldwide

- In less-developed countries, birth rates are high and death rates are low, producing rapid population growth. As economic development increases, birth rates decline and population growth slows.
- Education, contraception, and government policies affect birth rates.
- The top causes of death vary around the world. Although sanitation and medical advances have increased life expectancy overall, HIV/AIDS is reducing life expectancy in some parts of the world.

B. The Ecological Footprint Is an Estimate of Resource Use

- Countries differ in their **ecological footprint,** a measure of the amount of land required to support a country's lifestyle. Sustained population growth will continue to strain supplies of natural resources.

18.7 Investigating Life: Let Your Love Light Shine

- Female fireflies prefer males that generate long flashes of light, a signal that is positively correlated with the size of the male's spermatophore. The larger the spermatophore, the more nutrition available to the pair's offspring.

Multiple Choice Questions

1. Which of the following is arranged from least inclusive to most inclusive?
   a. Community < biosphere < population < ecosystem
   b. Ecosystem < population < biosphere < community
   c. Biosphere < ecosystem < community < population
   d. Population < community < ecosystem < biosphere
2. A declining growth rate can be attributed to a large percentage of a population in its
   a. postreproductive years.
   b. reproductive years.
   c. prereproductive years.
   d. Both b and c are correct.
3. A population that has a consistent survivorship rate is a ______ species.
   a. Type I
   b. Type II
   c. Type III
   d. Type IV
4. What happens to a population as it approaches the carrying capacity?
   a. The death rate exceeds the birth rate.
   b. The birth rate increases.
   c. The carrying capacity increases.
   d. Fewer new individuals are added with each generation.

5. As a habitat becomes more crowded, which of the following is likely to increase?
   a. Predation
   b. Disease
   c. Competition for food
   d. All of the above are correct.
6. A juvenile organism must balance all of the following demands EXCEPT
   a. survival.
   b. maintenance.
   c. reproduction.
   d. growth.
7. An opportunistic species emphasizes
   a. large offspring size.
   b. high offspring quantity.
   c. late reproduction.
   d. type I survivorship.
8. Which of the following is typical of developed countries such as the United States?
   a. Smaller ecological footprint than less-developed countries
   b. Sustained exponential growth
   c. Low birth rates and low death rates
   d. A shift from opportunistic to equilibrium life history

Write It Out

1. Rats, mustangs, koalas, and deer are overpopulated in at least some parts of the world. Use the Internet to learn about proposed strategies for addressing each overpopulation problem. Is each strategy aimed at increasing death rates, reducing birth rates, or changing distribution patterns?
2. Population biologists often tag animals with radio collars equipped with Geographic Positioning System units. What type of useful information might ecologists gain by learning more about animal movements?
3. Decades of overfishing led to the collapse of the cod fishing industry off the coast of North America in the 1980s and 1990s. Given the effect of birth rates, death rates, and age structure on a population, propose an explanation for the decline of the cod population. What sorts of policies might protect the cod from extinction?
4. Why does a population's age structure help predict the population's future?
5. Give three examples of how a habitat's carrying capacity might change over time.
6. What prevents predators from eliminating prey populations?
7. Cite three recent environmental upheavals that may have had a density-independent influence on wildlife populations.
8. The grey seal population on Sable Island cannot continue its exponential growth forever. What are three examples of density-dependent factors that might eventually limit population growth for these marine mammals?
9. Some animal behaviors seem at odds with survival and reproduction. For example, when food is scarce, a female scorpion may consume her offspring. Explain this behavior in terms of evolutionary trade-offs.
10. Describe the trends for human birth and death rates in more- and less-developed countries.
11. What is the relationship between the human population and the ecological footprint? Why does the ecological footprint vary around the world? Overall, humans are using many resources at a faster rate than they can be replenished. What actions would be necessary to reduce humanity's ecological footprint to a sustainable level?

Pull It Together

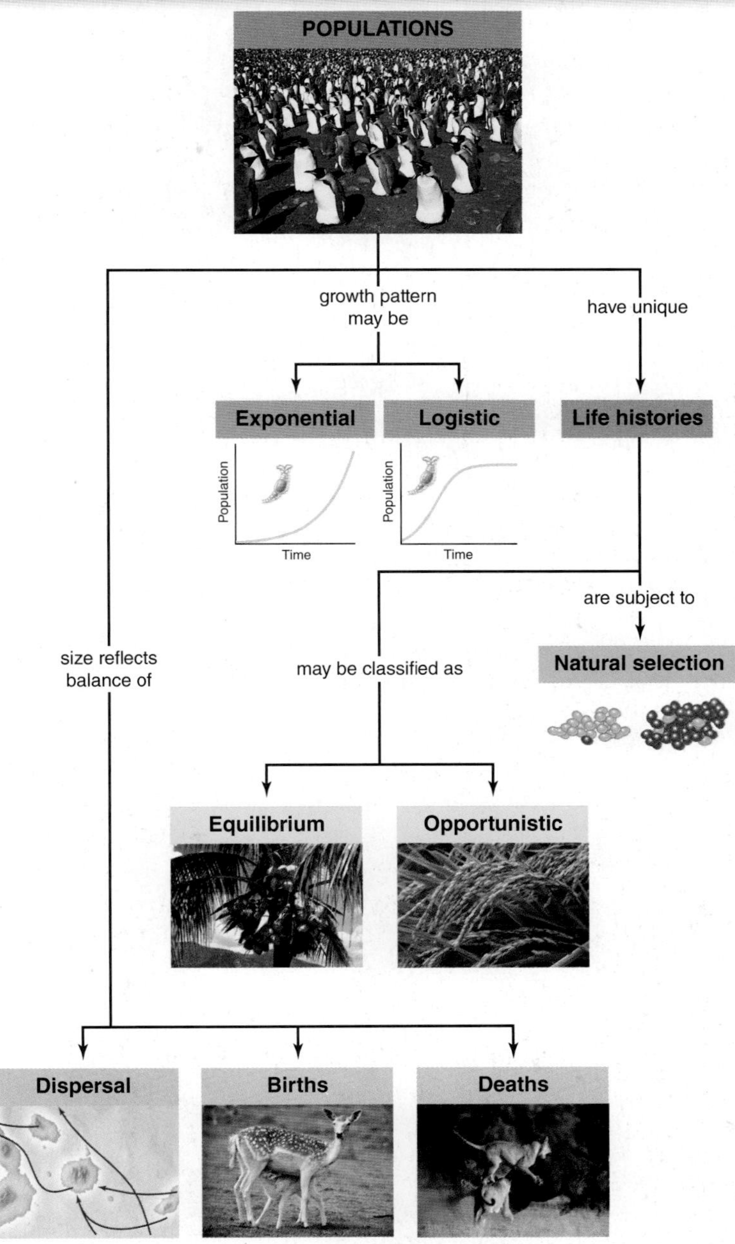

1. What are the additions to and subtractions from a population?
2. Add the following terms to this concept map: *density-dependent, density-independent, carrying capacity,* and *age structure.*
3. What conditions result in exponential growth? Logistic growth?

19 Communities and Ecosystems

Unbalanced Ecosystem. Chickens and other farm animals may have little interaction with other species or with the outdoors.

Learn How to Learn

Don't Throw That Exam Away!

Whether or not you were satisfied with your last exam, take the time to learn from your mistakes. Mark the questions that you missed and the ones that you got right but were unsure about. Then figure out what went wrong for each question. For example, did you neglect to study the information, thinking it wouldn't be on the test? Did you memorize a term's definition without understanding how it fits with other material? Did you misread the question? After you have finished your analysis, look for patterns and think about what you could have done differently. Then revise your study plan so that you can avoid making the same mistakes in the future.

Learning Outline

19.1 Organisms Interact Within Communities and Ecosystems

19.2 Earth Has Diverse Climates

19.3 Biomes Are Ecosystems with Distinctive Communities of Life

- A. The Physical Environment Dictates Where Each Species Can Live
- B. Terrestrial Biomes Range from the Lush Tropics to the Frozen Poles
- C. Aquatic Biomes Include Fresh Water and the Oceans

19.4 Community Interactions Occur Within Each Biome

- A. Many Species Compete for the Same Resources
- B. Symbiotic Interactions Can Benefit or Harm a Species
- C. Herbivory and Predation Link Species in Feeding Relationships
- D. Closely Interacting Species May Coevolve
- E. A Keystone Species Has a Pivotal Role in the Community

19.5 A Community's Diversity and Species Composition May Change Over Time

19.6 Ecosystems Require Continuous Energy Input

- A. Food Webs Depict the Transfer of Energy and Atoms
- B. Every Trophic Level Loses Energy
- C. In Biomagnification, Harmful Chemicals Accumulate in the Highest Trophic Levels

19.7 Chemicals Cycle Within Ecosystems

- A. Water Circulates Between the Land and the Atmosphere
- B. Autotrophs Obtain Carbon as CO_2
- C. The Nitrogen Cycle Relies on Bacteria
- D. The Phosphorus Cycle Begins with the Weathering of Rocks
- E. Terrestrial and Aquatic Ecosystems Are Linked in Surprising Ways

19.8 Investigating Life: Two Kingdoms and a Virus Team Up to Beat the Heat

What's the Point?

The photo on the facing page shows a confined animal feeding operation, or CAFO. Much of the chicken, turkey, pork, and beef consumed in the United States comes from operations such as this one.

What does a CAFO have to do with a chapter on communities and ecosystems? As you will see, ecosystems rely on interactions among multiple species (the community) and the nonliving environment. A typical ecosystem on land includes plants that absorb inorganic nutrients and harvest energy from the sun. Animals eat the plants, and decomposers return inorganic nutrients to the soil. As the photo shows, however, a CAFO has an extremely high density of animals, and plants are nowhere in sight.

The CAFO ecosystem is therefore "subsidized" with food brought from outside. Moreover, the animals release immense volumes of organic wastes—too much for the local decomposers to handle. Spreading the wastes on nearby land can cause nutrient overloads, throwing those ecosystems out of balance as well. Solving these and other environmental problems requires an understanding of both community and ecosystem ecology.

19.1 Organisms Interact Within Communities and Ecosystems

Chapter 18 explored the ecology of **populations,** which consist of members of the same species that inhabit the same area. Douglas fir trees, for example, form a population in the forests of the Pacific Northwest. But no population lives in isolation; this chapter therefore extends the study of ecology to communities and ecosystems.

A **community** is a group of interacting populations. Figure 19.1 illustrates three distinctly different examples: the kelp and damselfish that live in the Pacific Ocean; the trees and mushrooms of a coniferous forest; and the cacti and other plants of a scorching desert. **Biotic** interactions are those that occur among the living species in a community. Moreover, each community exists within the context of its physical and chemical surroundings. The **ecosystem** includes the community plus the **abiotic,** or nonliving, environment.

Each species in a community has a characteristic home and way of life. Recall from chapter 18 that a **habitat** is the physical place where members of a population typically live, such as the Pacific coastline or the forest floor. The habitat is one part of the **niche,** which includes all the resources a species requires for its survival, growth, and reproduction. In addition to the physical habitat, the niche includes the salinity, temperature, light, water availability, and other abiotic conditions where the species lives. Biotic interactions, such as an organism's place in the food chain, are part of the niche as well.

This chapter describes the interactions that characterize both communities and ecosystems. We begin at the broadest possible scale, by explaining why climates differ across the planet. Next, the chapter describes the major ecosystems on Earth, with a focus on how climate and other features of the physical environment select for a unique community of organisms. The species that occupy each habitat are interconnected, setting the stage for a discussion of community-level interactions. Finally, the chapter returns its focus to ecosystems and the ways that communities exchange materials and energy with the physical environment.

a.

b.

c.

Figure 19.1 Distinctive Communities. (a) A kelp bed along the coast of southern California is home to a damselfish. (b) The forest floor community includes plants, fungi, and many unseen animals and microbes. (c) A saguaro cactus is one of many plant species in this Arizona desert community.

In studying these topics, keep in mind that community- and ecosystem-level interactions are among the selective forces that shape the evolution of each species. Plants, animals, and every other organism must defend themselves and acquire resources for growth, maintenance, and reproduction. The adaptations that characterize each species—such as the ability to produce thorns or live in salt water or catch a gazelle—ultimately trace their origins to genetic mutations. But these features persist because they enhance reproductive success in a dangerous and competitive world.

19.1 Mastering Concepts

1. Distinguish between ecosystems, communities, and populations.
2. Which abiotic conditions influence the distribution of species in the biosphere?
3. What is the relationship between an organism's habitat and its niche?

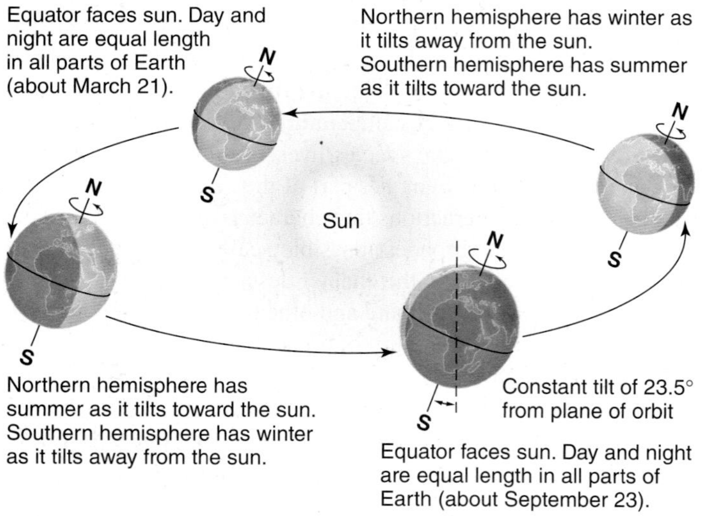

19.2 Earth Has Diverse Climates

Earth has a wide variety of climates, from the year-round warmth and moisture of the tropics to the perpetually chilly poles. Why does each part of the planet have a different climate? The answer relates to Earth's spherical shape and to the tilt of its axis as it orbits the sun (figure 19.2).

Equator faces sun. Day and night are equal length in all parts of Earth (about March 21).

Northern hemisphere has winter as it tilts away from the sun. Southern hemisphere has summer as it tilts toward the sun.

Sun

N

S

Northern hemisphere has summer as it tilts toward the sun. Southern hemisphere has winter as it tilts away from the sun.

Constant tilt of 23.5° from plane of orbit

Equator faces sun. Day and night are equal length in all parts of Earth (about September 23).

Figure 19.2 Earth's Seasons. The tilt of Earth's axis produces distinct seasons in the northern and southern hemispheres as Earth travels around the sun.

At the equator, the sun is overhead (or nearly so) all year; equatorial regions therefore receive the most intense sunlight, and the temperature is warm year-round. Thanks to Earth's curvature, however, sunlight hits other parts of the surface at more oblique angles. The average temperature falls with distance from the equator because the same amount of light is distributed over a larger area. Figure 19.3 shows the resulting broad temperature bands from the equator to the poles.

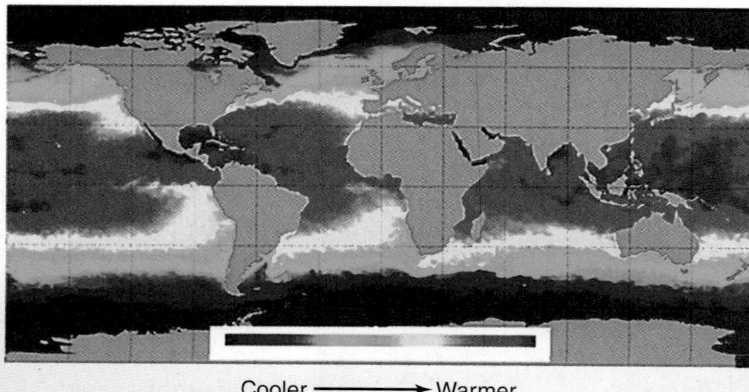

Figure 19.3 From Warm to Cold. Earth's surface temperature ranges from the year-round warmth of the tropics to the bitter cold of the poles.

The tilt of Earth's axis accounts for seasonal temperature changes in non-equatorial regions. From March through September, the northern hemisphere tilts toward the sun and experiences the warmth of spring and summer. During the rest of the year, cooler temperatures prevail as the northern hemisphere tilts away from the sun. The seasons are the opposite in the southern hemisphere.

Equatorial regions receive not only the most light but also the most precipitation. When sunlight heats the air over the equator, the air rises, expands, and cools. Because cool air does not hold as much moisture as warm air, the excess water vapor condenses, forming clouds that pour rain over the tropics.

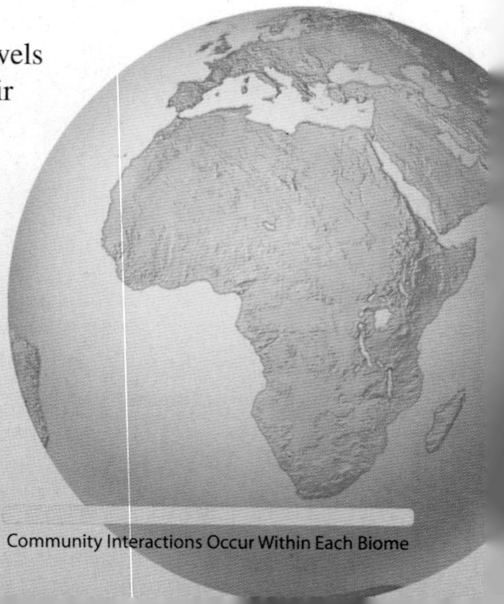

Air that rises near the equator also travels north and south (figure 19.4). As the air cools at higher latitudes, its density increases, and it sinks back down to Earth at about 30° North and South latitude. Here the warming air absorbs moisture from the land, creating the vast deserts of Asia, Africa, the Americas, and Australia. Some of the air continues toward the poles, rising and cooling at about 60° North and South latitude, bringing the rains that support temperate (midlatitude) forests in these areas. The air rises, and some again continues toward the poles, where precipitation is quite low. The rest returns to the equator, where the air heats up again, and the cycle begins anew.

A cycle of heating and cooling, rising and falling air is called a convection cell. The planet has three such convection cells north of the equator and three south. As figure 19.4 illustrates, Earth's major winds correspond to these convection cells. (From Earth, the winds appear deflected toward the east and west because the planet rotates beneath them.) These winds power major ocean currents, including the Gulf Stream along the east coast of North America (figure 19.5).

Ocean currents, in turn, influence coastal climates, in part because they transport warm and cold water around the globe. Figure 19.3, for example, shows bands of cold water along the western coasts of North America and South America. In addition, large water bodies heat up and cool down much more slowly than does the land. Coastal regions therefore often have milder climates than do inland areas at the same latitude. On a hot summer day, beachgoers notice this effect as they enjoy cooling breezes from the sea. Conversely, during the winter, the ocean releases stored heat.

Mountain ranges also influence climate, in two ways. First, the top of a mountain is generally cooler than its base. Second, mountains often

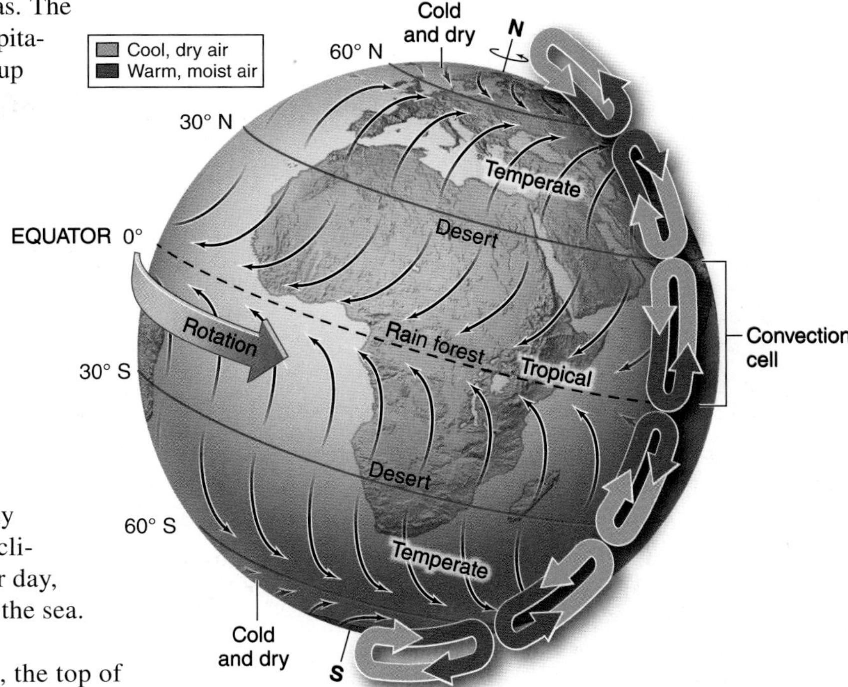

Figure 19.4 Patterns of Air Circulation and Moisture. In each of Earth's six convection cells, air cools as it rises and releases its moisture as rain. Conversely, descending air masses pick up warmth and absorb moisture from the land. From Earth, the prevailing winds appear to come from the east or west because the planet rotates beneath the convection cells.

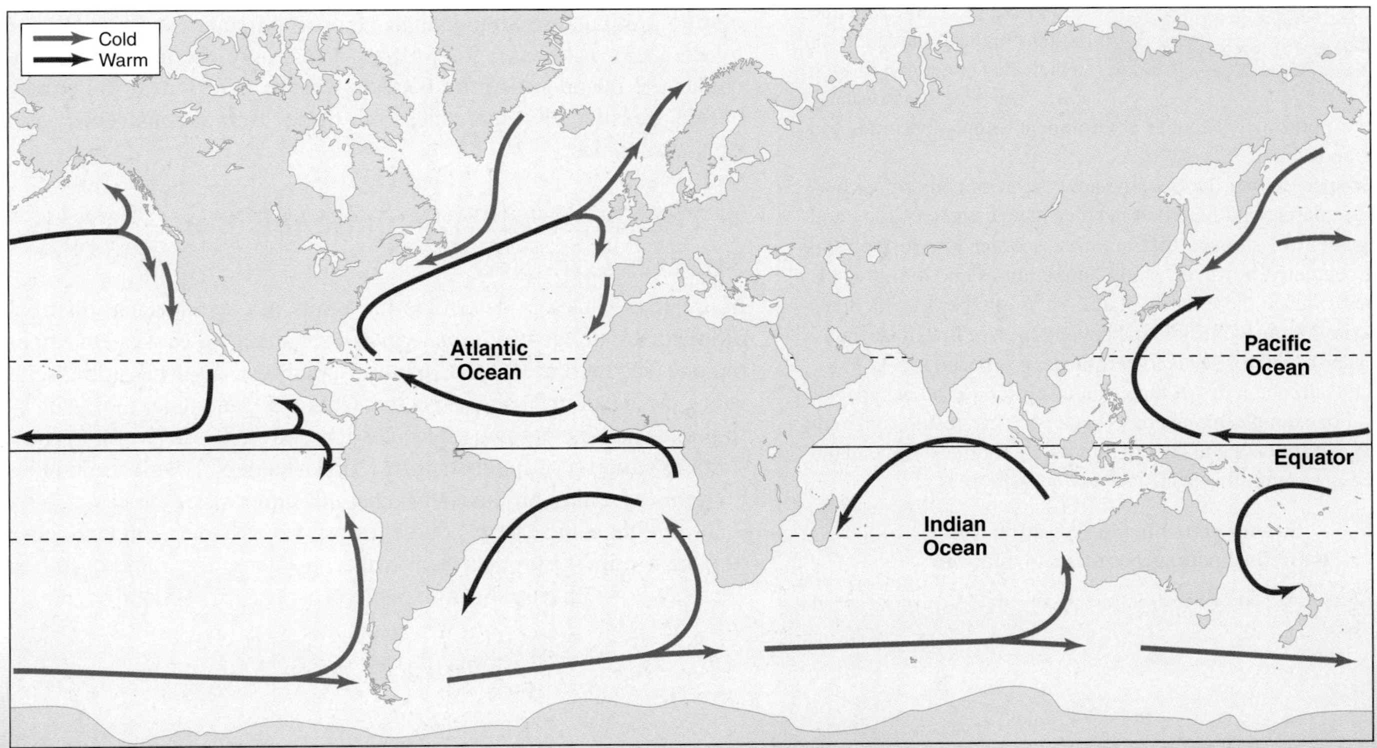

Figure 19.5 Ocean Currents. Earth's prevailing winds produce the major ocean currents, which redistribute water and nutrients throughout the oceans.

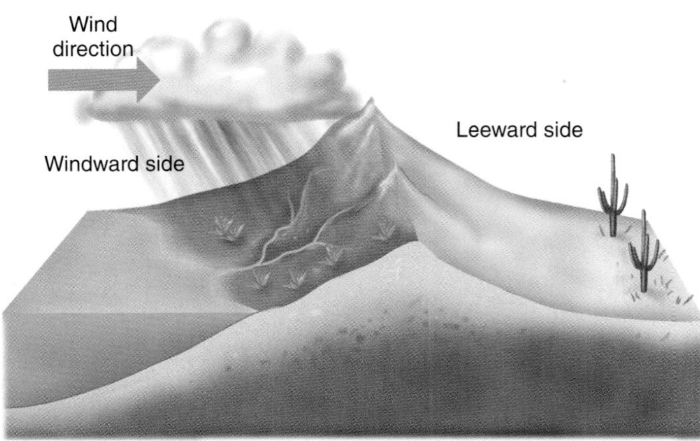

Figure 19.6 Rain Shadow. Precipitation falls on the windward side of the mountain, leaving the leeward side with a dry climate.

Burning Questions

Why is there a "tree line" above which trees won't grow?

The tree line, or timberline, is an edge beyond which trees will not grow. The Arctic and Antarctic tree lines are the farthest points north and south, respectively, that trees can grow; the alpine tree line is the highest elevation at which they can grow. In each case, the tree line usually defines the point at which the environment simply becomes too cold to support trees.

Most species near the tree line are evergreen conifers such as pine, spruce, larch, and fir. Their needles have a waxy coating and an arrangement of stomata that minimizes water loss in the thin, dry air. Eventually, however, chilly temperatures and biting winds get the best of even these hardy plants. At the timberline, the trees shorten to low, stunted bushes, and beyond the tree line, it is simply too cold year-round for seeds to germinate. ▸ stomata, p. 432

Wind, salt, and a dry climate can also produce other types of tree lines. For example, along coasts, a tree line can result from high winds and salt spray that make life impossible for trees. Beyond the desert tree line, rainfall is insufficient to support trees.

Submit your burning question to:
marielle_hoefnagels@mcgraw-hill.com

block wind and moisture-laden clouds on their upwind side. The resulting **rain shadow** on the downwind side of the mountain has a much drier climate (figure 19.6).

19.2 Mastering Concepts

1. Explain why average temperature declines with distance from the equator.
2. How do prevailing winds, ocean currents, and mountain ranges affect climate?

19.3 Biomes Are Ecosystems with Distinctive Communities of Life

Ecologists divide the biosphere into **biomes,** which are the major types of ecosystems. Forests, deserts, and grasslands are examples of terrestrial biomes. Lakes, streams, and oceans are water-based ecosystems. Each biome is characterized by a distinctive group of species. Although it is convenient to classify each ecosystem as belonging to one biome or another, keep in mind that no ecosystem exists in isolation. Water, air, sediments, and organisms can travel freely from one part of the biosphere to another.

This section explains the distribution of the main biomes on land and in water. As you read this material, remember that the biomes we see today have not been in place forever. Over hundreds of millions of years, the continents have moved, and sea levels have risen and fallen. The central United States, for example, was once under the sea, which explains why fossils of marine animals are abundant in landlocked states such as Oklahoma (see figure 13.3). Likewise, 375 million years ago, the land mass that now includes the islands of Arctic Canada was once very near the equator. Long-buried fossils tell the tales of these tremendous ecosystem shifts. ▸ plate tectonics, p. 247

A. The Physical Environment Dictates Where Each Species Can Live

Many abiotic factors determine the limits of each species' distribution. The ultimate abiotic factor is an energy source, since no ecosystem can exist without one (see section 19.6). A **primary producer,** or **autotroph** ("self-feeder"), is any organism that can use energy, CO_2, H_2O, and other inorganic substances to produce all the organic molecules it requires. These primary producers support **consumers,** or **heterotrophs** ("other-feeders"), which obtain energy and nutrients by eating producers or other consumers.

Sunlight is the energy source for most ecosystems. On land, plants are the dominant primary producers. In water, however, most photosynthesis occurs courtesy of **phytoplankton:** microscopic, free-floating, photosynthetic organisms such as cyanobacteria and algae. A few ecosystems, such as deep-sea hydrothermal vents, are based on chemical energy rather than sunlight. There, the producers are microbes that extract energy from hydrogen sulfide and other inorganic chemicals.

Besides sunlight, the major abiotic factors that determine the numbers and types of plants on land are temperature and moisture. All organisms are adapted to a limited temperature range; trees, for example, cannot live where the temperature is too low (see the Burning Question on page 382). In addition, all life requires water. The plants that grow where water is abundant, such as the tropical rain forest, have very different adaptations from the vegetation that characterizes a desert ecosystem.

Nutrient availability is another crucial abiotic factor that often determines an ecosystem's productivity. On land, soil provides essential mineral elements such as nitrogen and phosphorus. In aquatic ecosystems, both nutrients and sunlight are often scarce, especially with increasing depth and distance from the shoreline.

Fire is an essential abiotic condition in some terrestrial biomes. In grasslands, for example, periodic fires kill trees that might otherwise take over. In coniferous forests, many adult trees die in fires, but their cones open only after prolonged exposure to heat. The seeds germinate after the fire, and the young trees thrive with little competition for sunlight or nutrients.

Other abiotic factors may also be important in some ecosystems. In aquatic ecosystems, one notable example is the amount of dissolved oxygen, which influences the types of microbes and animals that can live in the water. Likewise, many organisms are adapted to seawater or salty soils, but others are not.

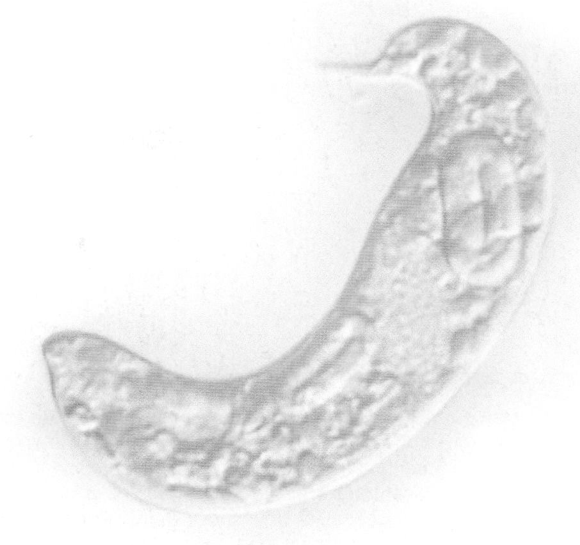

B. Terrestrial Biomes Range from the Lush Tropics to the Frozen Poles

Earth's climatic zones give rise to huge bands of characteristic types of vegetation, which correspond to the terrestrial biomes. Temperature and moisture are the main factors that determine the dominant plants in each location (figure 19.7). The overall pattern of vegetation, in turn, influences which microorganisms and animals can live in a biome.

Soils form the framework of terrestrial biomes, for they directly support plant life. Although soil may seem like "just dirt," it is actually a complex mixture of rock fragments, organic matter, and microbes. Climate influences soil development in many ways. Heavy rain may leach nutrients from surface layers and deposit them in deeper layers, or it may remove them entirely from the soil. In addition, in a warm, moist climate, rapid decomposition may leave little organic material in the soil. At the opposite extreme, undecomposed peat may accumulate in cold, damp soils.

Figure 19.8, which covers pages 384 and 385, describes ten major terrestrial biomes. The map at the center of the figure shows the original range of each biome. It is important to remember, however, that humans have drastically reduced many natural biomes, replacing them with farmland, suburban housing, and cities. In addition, as described in chapter 20, human activities threaten much of the native habitat that remains.

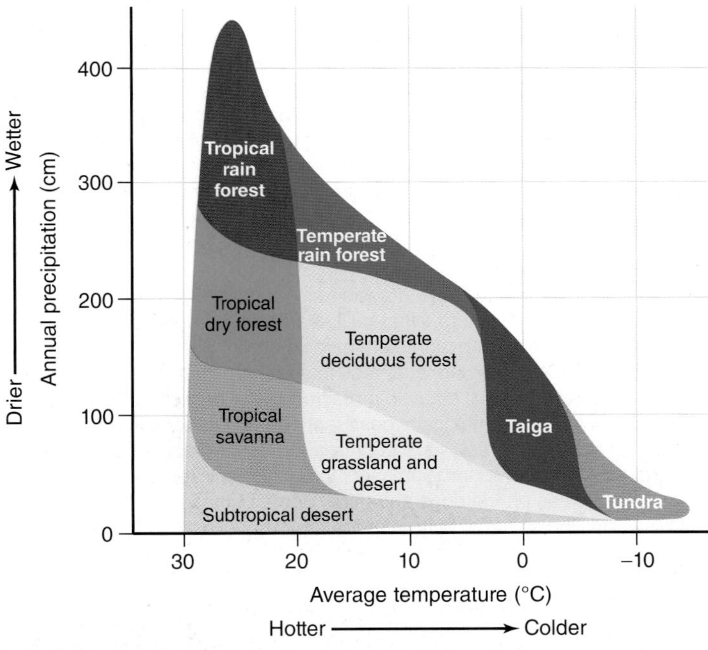

Figure 19.7 Biome Classification. Temperature and precipitation influence the distribution of the major terrestrial biomes.

Figure 19.8 Earth's Major Terrestrial Biomes.

Northern coniferous forest (also called taiga or boreal forest)
The climate is relatively dry, with short summers and long, cold winters. Moisture can be scarce in winter, when water may remain frozen for months. The soils are cold, damp, acidic, and nutrient-poor. Plants adapted to these conditions include conifers such as spruce, fir, and pine. Their evergreen needles resist water loss. Many migratory birds visit during the short growing season, whereas the mammals and birds that live in the taiga year-round have thick layers of insulation that retain body heat. Herbivorous mammals, such as caribou, moose, and snowshoe hares, eat whatever vegetation they can find during the cold winters. Others, such as the black bear, hibernate for the winter. Predatory mammals include lynx, gray wolves, and wolverines.

Temperate coniferous forest (also called temperate rain forest)
Temperate coniferous forests occur in areas with mild winters, cool summers, and abundant rain and fog. Water is plentiful, and plant diversity is high. Most trees are evergreens such as spruce, cedar, Douglas fir, and hemlock, all of which have waxy, needlelike leaves adapted to year-round photosynthesis. Moisture-loving mosses, ferns, and lichens cover nearly every surface. Many fishes, amphibians, birds, small mammals, and deer consume the plants and invertebrates in the forest and its streams. Owls, black bears, and cougars hunt small animals.

Temperate deciduous forest
This biome occurs where summers are warm, winters are cold, and rainfall is approximately constant throughout the year. The cold winters select for plant species such as oak, hickory, and maple trees that shed their foliage in autumn. Shade-tolerant shrubs grow beneath the trees. Below them, small flowering plants grow in early spring, when light penetrates the leafless tree canopy. Many of the animals of the deciduous forest adjust to the seasons by putting on fat in the summer and hibernating in the winter, or they may store seeds and nuts that sustain them when food is scarce. Still others migrate to warmer areas for the winter. Herbivores include seed- and nut-eating mice and birds, whitetail deer, and gray squirrels. Red foxes and snakes are common predators.

Temperate grassland
The climate of the temperate grassland is moderately moist, with hot summers and cold winters. Wind-pollinated grasses dominate this biome, although other flowering plants are also common. Summertime drought, along with fire and grazing, suppress tree growth; grasses survive because their perennial buds lie protected below the soil surface. Bison, elk, and pronghorn antelope, whose teeth and digestive systems are adapted to a grassy diet, were originally the large, grazing herbivores of North America. Other herbivores include prairie chickens, insects, and rodents such as prairie dogs and mice. Some of these small animals burrow into the soil to hide from predators, whereas others have camouflage. Coyotes, bobcats, snakes, and birds of prey feed on the herbivores.

Tropical rain forest
The warm, wet climate near the equator means favorable conditions for plant growth year-round. The main selective forces affecting plant growth are competition for light and nutrients. Broadleaf evergreen trees with tall, straight trunks form the forest canopy. Vegetation in the shade beneath the canopy includes climbing vines and small plants that grow on the surfaces of other plants. In the deep shade of the forest floor, plants often have large leaves that maximize the capture of scarce light. These forests also house an incredible diversity of arthropods, fishes, amphibians, reptiles, and mammals that eat plants or other animals. Many of these animals have similar adaptations to life in the trees: bright colors that maximize visibility, coupled with loud calls that are audible throughout the forest canopy.

Tundra

Snow covers the Arctic and Antarctic tundra during the bitterly cold and dark winter. Temperatures venture above freezing for a few months each year. Below the top layer of soil the ground remains frozen year-round. This layer of permafrost limits rooting depth and prevents the establishment of large plants, but reindeer lichens, mosses, dwarf shrubs, and low-growing perennial plants such as sedges, grasses, and broad-leafed herbs are common. In the summer, migratory birds raise their young and feed on the insects that flourish in the tundra. Year-round inhabitants of the Arctic tundra include caribou, lemmings, hares, foxes, and wolverines, all of which have thick, warm fur. Animal life in the Antarctic tundra is much less diverse.

Mediterranean shrubland (chaparral)

Summers are hot and dry; winters are mild and moist. Chaparral plants such as poison oak, manzanita, and scrub oak have thick bark and small, leathery, evergreen leaves that slow moisture loss during the dry summers. This biome is especially susceptible to fires because the vegetation dries out during the summer. Fire-adapted plants resprout from underground parts or produce seeds that germinate only after the heat of a fire. Herbivores include jackrabbits, deer, and birds and rodents that forage for seeds under the shrub canopy; some of their predators include coyotes, foxes, snakes, and hawks.

Desert

All deserts are dry, receiving less than 20 centimeters of rainfall per year. The temperature can vary dramatically. In a hot desert such as the Sonoran, which spans parts of Arizona and Mexico, the days can be scorchingly hot. In China's cold Gobi desert, in contrast, the average annual temperature is below freezing. Desert plants often have long taproots, quick life cycles that exploit the brief rainy periods, fleshy stems or leaves that store water, and spines or toxins that guard against thirsty herbivores. Most desert animals burrow or seek shelter during the day, then become active when the sun goes down. Standing water is scarce, so most water comes from the animal's food. Desert herbivores include jackrabbits and kangaroo rats, which eat seeds and leaves. Snakes and cougars hunt the herbivores.

Tropical savanna

Tropical savannas are grasslands with scattered trees or shrubs and bands of woody vegetation along streams. The weather is warm year-round, with distinct wet and dry seasons. Perennial grasses dominate the savanna along with scattered patches of drought- and fire-resistant trees and shrubs such as palms, acacias, and baobab trees. These plants have deep roots, thick bark, and trunks that store water. During the dry season, great herds of animals migrate enormous distances in search of water. The Australian savanna is home to many birds and kangaroos, whereas the grassland in Africa features herds of zebra, giraffes, wildebeests, gazelles, and elephants. Lions, cheetahs, wild dogs, birds of prey, and hyenas prey on the herbivores, and vultures and other scavengers eat the leftovers.

Polar ice

Both Antarctica and the Arctic ice cap are extremely cold, dry, and windy year-round. The primary producers in ice and the surrounding ocean are phytoplankton. The light passing through the ice is dim, even in the summer. Yet these phytoplankton support a unique food web consisting of bacteria, archaea, worms, crustaceans, and ice fishes. All of these organisms have antifreeze chemicals that prevent deadly ice crystals from forming in their cells. Larger animals that exploit the Arctic food web include polar bears, seals, whales, and birds. On Antarctica, vertebrates include penguins and seals. Whales and squid inhabit the waters surrounding Antarctica as well.

Freshwater Biomes

Standing water: lakes and ponds

Light penetrates the regions of a lake to differing degrees. The shallow, nutrient-rich shoreline is part of the photic zone, where light is sufficient for photosynthesis. Rooted plants and phytoplankton thrive along the shore, providing food and shelter for invertebrates, fishes, amphibians, and other animals. In open water, phytoplankton are the dominant producers of the photic zone; zooplankton and fishes are typical consumers. But light does not penetrate the deeper water, where scavengers and decomposers such as insect larvae and bacteria rely on organic material from above to supply energy and nutrients.

Running water: rivers

A river carries water and sediment from land toward the ocean, providing moisture and habitat to aquatic and terrestrial organisms. At the headwaters, the water is clear, the stream channel is narrow, and the current may be swift. Turbulence mixes air with water, so the water is rich in oxygen. Algae, mosses, and insects cling to any available surface, such as rocks and logs. The river widens as small streams drain additional land areas and contribute water, sediments, and nutrients. As the land flattens, the current slows. The river is now murky, restricting photosynthesis to the banks and water surface. As a result, the oxygen content is relatively low. Typical animals in a slow-moving river include crayfish, snails, bass, and catfish; worms burrow in the muddy bottom.

Marine Biomes

Open ocean

The oceans, which cover most of Earth's surface, contain 97% of the planet's water. Both light and nutrients are abundant in the shallow waters above the continental shelf, supporting high primary productivity and extensive marine food webs such as the great kelp forests that fringe many cool-water coastal areas. Beyond the continental shelf, the open ocean's photic zone houses phytoplankton and the zooplankton that feed on them; fishes and whales, in turn, scoop up vast quantities of krill and zooplankton. Below the photic zone, light is too dim for photosynthesis, but a continual rain of organic matter supports great numbers of jellyfishes, fishes, whales, dolphins, mollusks, echinoderms, and crustaceans. The communities that occupy hydrothermal vents add biodiversity to the ocean floor.

Estuary

An estuary is an area where the fresh water of a river meets the salty ocean. When the tide is out, the water may not be much saltier than water in the river. The returning tide, however, may make the water nearly as salty as the sea. Organisms that can withstand these extremes receive nutrients from both the river and the tides. Estuaries therefore house some of the world's most productive ecosystems. In the open water, phytoplankton account for most of the productivity, whereas salt-tolerant plants dominate the salt marshes that often occur along the fringes of an estuary. Together, these producers support many species of fish, shellfish, and migratory birds.

Intertidal zone

Along coastlines, the intertidal zone is the area between the high tide and low tide marks. This region is alternately exposed and covered with water as the tide rises and falls. A sandy beach is one familiar example. Constantly shifting sands mean that few producers can take root on the beach, but ocean water delivers a constant supply of organic matter that feeds crabs and shorebirds. In a rocky intertidal zone, seaweeds and mussels attach to rocks, whereas sea anemones, sea urchins, sea stars, and snails occupy the small tidepools.

Coral reef

Coral reefs border tropical coastlines where the water is clear and sediment-free. These vast underwater structures of calcium carbonate are built by coral animals. The tissues of the coral animals house algae that are essential for the coral's—and the ecosystem's—survival. Sunlight penetrates the clear, shallow water, allowing photosynthesis to occur, and constant wave action brings in additional nutrients. The nooks and crannies of the reef provide food and habitat for a huge variety of algae, fishes, sponges, snails, sea stars, sea urchins, sea turtles, and countless microorganisms.

Figure 19.9 **Aquatic Biomes.**

C. Aquatic Biomes Include Fresh Water and the Oceans

Although terrestrial biomes are most familiar to us, the aquatic ecosystems illustrated in figure 19.9 occupy much more space. Water moves continuously among the ocean, atmosphere, land surface, and groundwater, providing vital connections among all biomes. Section 19.7 describes the water cycle in detail.

Biologists divide aquatic biomes into two main categories: freshwater and marine. Lakes and rivers, such as those in figure 19.9, contain only about 0.3% of the freshwater supply; the rest is in groundwater or locked in ice caps and glaciers. Nevertheless, that tiny sliver of the global water "pie" is vital to humans for drinking water and irrigation. Most other terrestrial species rely on this fresh water as well.

At the opposite extreme, the oceans cover 70% of Earth's surface and contain 97% of the planet's water; they therefore form the world's largest biome. Most photosynthesis on Earth occurs in the vast oceans, contributing enormous amounts of oxygen to the atmosphere. Moreover, oceans absorb so much heat from the sun that they help stabilize Earth's climate.

Whether freshwater or marine, aquatic communities need nutrients and sunlight. Supplies of both of these resources—and therefore ecosystem productivity—are highest in the shallow, well-lit waters of the **photic zone.** In deep water away from the shore, however, both energy and nutrients can be scarce. Figure 19.9 explains how each set of conditions selects for a unique community of life.

19.3 Mastering Concepts

1. How do climate and soil composition determine the characteristics of terrestrial biomes?
2. List and describe the climate and inhabitants of each of the major terrestrial biomes.
3. Describe the types of organisms that live in each zone of a lake.
4. How does a river change from its headwaters to its mouth?
5. Describe some of the adaptations that characterize organisms in the open ocean, estuaries, intertidal zones, and coral reefs.

19.4 Community Interactions Occur Within Each Biome

Communities usually include many species. Some are easily visible, whereas others are microscopic. One on one, their interactions may seem simple—a whale eats an otter, or a wasp kills a caterpillar. But an attempt to map all interactions within a community quickly becomes complicated. Individuals of different species compete for limited resources, live in or on one another, eat one another, and try to avoid being eaten. Table 19.1, on page 391, summarizes these interactions.

Figure 19.10 Competition. Battles for limited resources define many community interactions. These two scavengers—a vulture and a stork—are fighting over a wildebeest carcass.

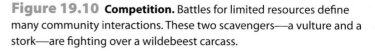

A. Many Species Compete for the Same Resources

Competition occurs when two or more species vie for the same limited resource, such as shelter, nutrients, water, light, or food (figure 19.10). Assuming that neither participant obtains all of the resource, the effects of

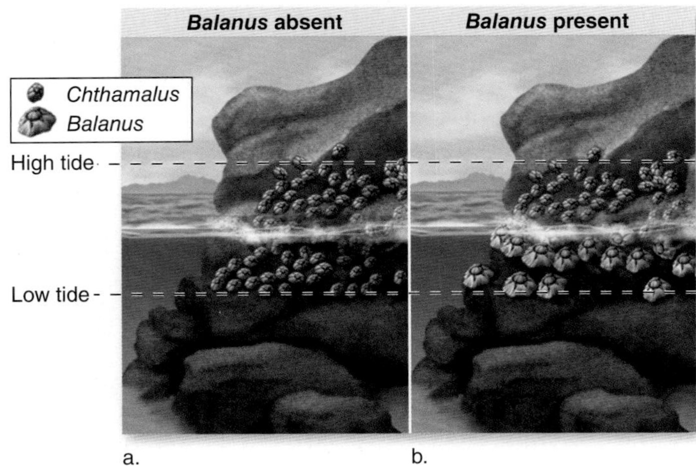

Figure 19.11 Competitive Exclusion. (a) When the barnacle *Balanus* is absent, *Chthamalus* adults occupy the entire intertidal zone. (b) When the faster-growing *Balanus* is present, however, competition for space limits *Chthamalus* to the upper intertidal zone.

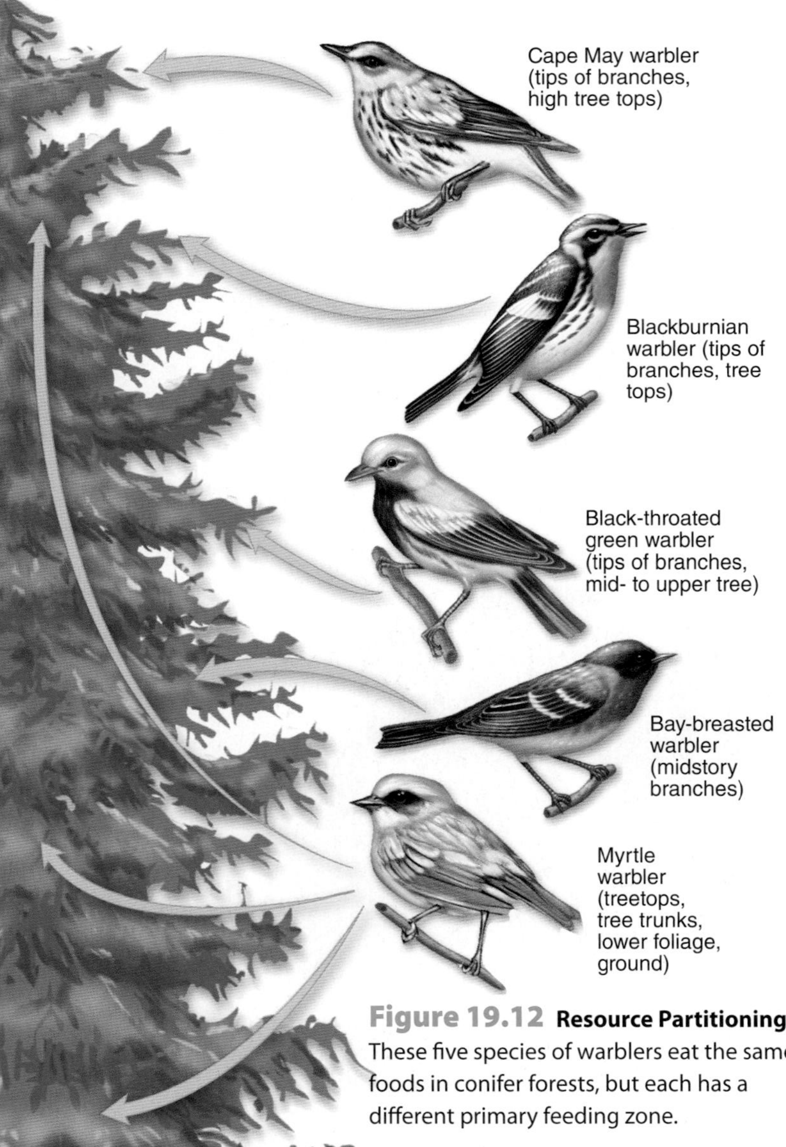

Figure 19.12 Resource Partitioning. These five species of warblers eat the same foods in conifer forests, but each has a different primary feeding zone.

competition are negative for both. As described in the Why We Care box on page 392, invasive species can be powerful competitors that disrupt entire communities.

Even in the absence of invasive species, competition can help shape the species composition of a community. Consider the **competitive exclusion principle,** which states that two species cannot coexist indefinitely in the same niche. The two species will compete for the limited resources that they both require, such as food, nesting sites, or soil nutrients. According to the competitive exclusion principle, the species that acquires more of the resources will eventually "win." The less successful species dies out.

Figure 19.11 illustrates a classic example of competitive exclusion, which affects two species of barnacles living in the intertidal zone along Scotland's shoreline. By itself, either type of barnacle can survive throughout the intertidal zone. But what if both species are present? The faster-growing species *(Balanus)* crowds out its competitor *(Chthamalus)* in the lower intertidal zone. Yet the slower-growing *Chthamalus* better tolerates dehydration while the tide is out. It can therefore more efficiently use the resources of the upper region of the intertidal zone. Each species "wins" in the zone where it competes best.

Competitive exclusion, however, is not inevitable; coexistence in overlapping niches is also possible. After all, if competition between species reduces fitness, then natural selection should favor organisms that avoid competition. Therefore, another possible outcome of competition is **resource partitioning,** in which multiple species use the same resource in a slightly different way or at a different time. For example, five species of warblers coexist in the same trees in New England forests, occupying similar niches: they all appear similar, and they all eat small insects. Careful observations of the birds, however, revealed that the five species feed in different ways and on different parts of the tree (figure 19.12). Their feeding locations and behaviors reduce competition and therefore improve the reproductive success of all five species.

B. Symbiotic Interactions Can Benefit or Harm a Species

In a **symbiosis** (literally, "living together"), one species lives in or on another. The relationship between symbiotic species may take several forms, defined by the effect on each participant.

Mutualistic relationships improve the fitness of both partners. Flowering plants and their reward-seeking pollinators are a classic example, as are mycorrhizal fungi. In the latter case, the fungus acquires nutrients and water that it shares with its host plant; the plant feeds sugars to its live-in partner. Many of the bacteria in our intestines are also mutualistic; they consume some of our food, but these microbes also produce vitamins and defend our bodies against disease. ▸ mycorrhizal fungi, p. 300; beneficial microbes, p. 286

Commensalism is a type of symbiosis in which one species benefits, but the other is not significantly affected. Most humans, for example, never notice the tiny mites that live, eat, and breed in our hair follicles. Similarly, the reproductive success of a tree is neither helped nor harmed by the moss plants and lichens that grow on its trunk and branches (figure 19.13). ▸ tiny companions, p. 337

In **parasitism,** one species benefits at the expense of another. The most familiar parasites are disease-causing bacteria, protists, fungi, and worms. Some of these organisms can suppress their host's immune system, an adaptation that favors long-term colonization of the body (see section 29.6). Plants may also be parasites on one another. Mistletoe, for example, is a parasitic

plant that taps into the water- and nutrient-conducting "pipes" of a host plant.
▸ parasitic plants, p. 442

Figure 19.13 Commensalism. Moss plants and lichens live on the branches and trunks of trees. The relationship is commensal because these small residents benefit from increased sun exposure without harming their hosts.

C. Herbivory and Predation Link Species in Feeding Relationships

All animals must obtain energy and nutrients by eating other organisms, living or dead. An **herbivore** is an animal that consumes plants; a **predator** is an animal that eats other animals, also called **prey.** As in the case of parasitism, the fitness of the herbivore or predator increases at the expense of the organism being consumed. In some cases, predator–prey interactions are directly responsible for fluctuations in an animal's population size (see section 18.4).

Herbivores may eat leaves, roots, stems, flowers, fruits, or seeds (figure 19.14). The loss of leaf and root tissue reduces a plant's ability to carry out photosynthesis; consumption of flowers or immature fruits and seeds compromises the plant's reproductive success. Natural selection therefore favors plant defenses against herbivory. Some plant species produce thorns, a milky sap, or distasteful or poisonous chemicals that deter herbivores. The spicy hot chemicals in chili peppers, for example, discourage attack by both fungi and animals (see section 22.7). At the same time, many herbivores have adaptations that nullify the plant's defenses. The caterpillars of monarch butterflies, for example, tolerate the noxious chemicals in milkweed plants.

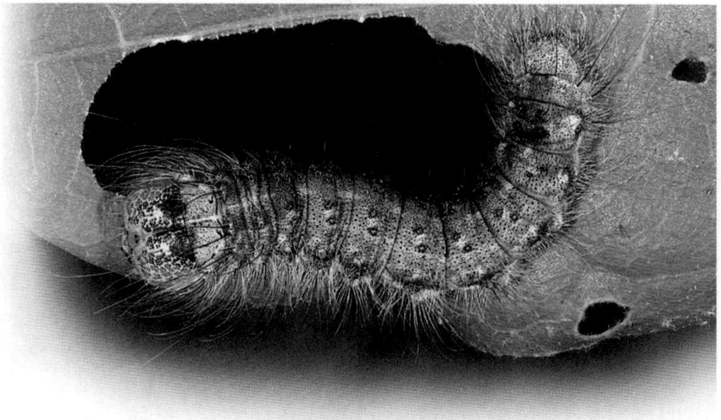

Figure 19.14 Herbivory. A greater oak dagger moth caterpillar munches on an oak leaf.

Likewise, predation exerts strong selective pressure on prey animals, which often have adaptations that help them avoid being eaten (figure 19.15). Camouflage and warning coloration are two examples. An interesting variation on the theme of warning coloration is mimicry, in which different species develop similar appearances. For example, a harmless species of fly may deter predators with yellow and black stripes similar to those of a stinging bee.

Prey species also commonly have weapons and structural defenses. Many animals have hard shells, pincers, stingers, or other defensive adaptations (some of which are also useful in capturing their own prey). Prey animals also display a repertoire of defensive behaviors, including fleeing, fighting, releasing noxious chemicals, or forming a tight group.

Only those predators that can defeat prey defenses will live long enough to reproduce and care for their young. Acute senses, agility, sharp teeth, and claws are common among predators. Camouflage is adaptive in predators as well.

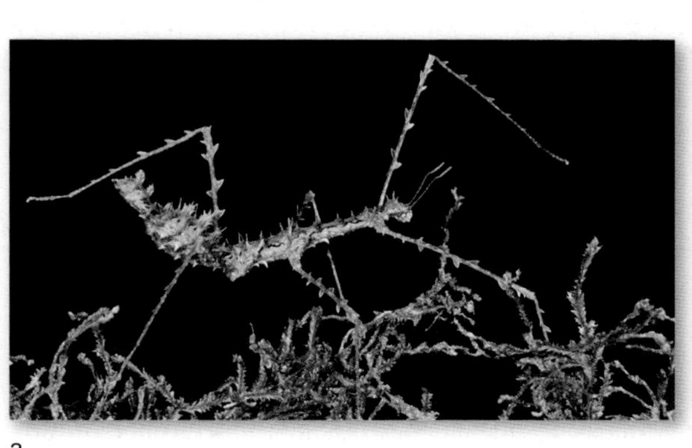

a.

b.

c.

Figure 19.15 Prey Defenses. (a) Camouflage helps prey species hide. This insect from Madagascar resembles the leaves in its habitat. (b) Warning coloration advertises a poison dart frog's defenses. (c) These animals look like ants, but they are actually ant-mimicking jumping spiders. The spiders have none of the weaponry of the ants they resemble.

Figure 19.16 Predator Cooperation. By working together, a pack of lions can bring down prey animals that are much larger than the lions themselves. Sharp teeth and claws aid in prey capture as well.

Figure 19.17 Coevolution of Ants and Plants. Acacias have adaptations, including these nutritious nodules, that suggest they coevolved with ants.

Figure 19.18 Keystone Species. Sea otters are a keystone species in the Pacific Northwest, thanks to their taste for sea urchins.

Tigers and other big cats, for example, have markings that hide their shape against their surroundings, which helps them sneak up on their prey. Hunting in groups is a behavioral adaptation that helps predators capture large prey (figure 19.16).

D. Closely Interacting Species May Coevolve

Some connections are so strong that two species directly influence one another's evolution. In **coevolution,** a genetic change in one species selects for subsequent change in the genome of another species. Of course, all interacting species in a community have the potential to influence one another, and they are all "evolving together." These genetic changes are considered coevolution only if scientists can demonstrate that adaptations specifically result from the interactions between the species.

Consider, for example, garter snakes that eat poisonous newts (a type of amphibian). The newts produce a toxin that binds to sodium channel proteins in a predator's muscle cells, causing paralysis and death. Some newts produce exceedingly high concentrations of the toxin—one newt may contain enough poison to kill several adult humans! Yet many garter snakes can eat super-toxic newts and survive. These snakes have modified sodium channels that are resistant to the poison. Snakes with resistant sodium channels have greater reproductive success than those with wild-type channels; on the other hand, resistant snakes select for newts that produce increasingly potent toxins.

Coevolution also links flowering plants and insects. As described in chapter 22, a plant may rely exclusively on one insect species for pollination, and the insect may eat nothing but nectar from that plant. The plant–insect relationship may also select for specialized structures and behaviors. Some species of ants and acacia trees, for example, have adaptations not found among related species. The acacia produces swollen, hollow thorns in which the ants live, and they provide nectar and nutritious nodules that the ants consume (figure 19.17). These adaptations have, in turn, selected for ant behaviors that defend "their" tree from other herbivores.

E. A Keystone Species Has a Pivotal Role in the Community

Sometimes, many species in a community depend on one type of organism, called a **keystone species,** which makes up a small portion of the community yet has a disproportionate influence on community diversity. Note that *keystone* does not simply mean *essential.* For example, the grasses that underlie the prairie biome are obviously essential to the other species in the grassland, but they are not considered keystone species because they make up the bulk of the community.

One example of a keystone species is the sea otter (figure 19.18), which plays a critical role in the vast underwater kelp forests that fringe the Pacific Northwest coast. Otters eat sea urchins, which devour kelp. In the absence of otters, sea urchin populations explode. The loss of kelp, in turn, eliminates the habitat for many species of marine shrimps, fishes, sea stars, snails, and corals. The otter is a keystone species because it keeps other predators in check.

Many keystone species, including sea otters, are versatile predators. But mutualists may also be keystone species. For example, mycorrhizal fungi help coniferous trees acquire nutrients from soil, and they produce underground fruiting bodies that small rodents eat. Owls and other predators hunt these small mammals. The fungi are considered keystone species because their small biomass is disproportionate to their enormous influence on community structure.

TABLE 19.1 Types of Species Interactions: A Summary

Type	Definition and Fitness Effects	Examples
Competition	Two or more species vie for the same limited resource (–/–)	Two species of barnacles compete for space in intertidal zone
Symbiosis	One species lives in or on another	
Mutualism	Symbiosis in which both partners benefit (+/+)	Algae in coral animals; mycorrhizal fungi in plant roots; animal pollinators of flowering plants
Commensalism	Symbiosis in which one partner benefits with no effect on the other (+/0)	Moss plants on tree bark
Parasitism	Symbiosis in which one partner benefits and the other is harmed (+/–)	Tick on a deer; tapeworm in a human (see chapters 15, 16, and 17 for many examples of disease-causing organisms)
Herbivory	Animal consumes a plant or other photosynthetic organism (+/–)	Cattle grazing on grassland; caterpillar eating tree leaves
Predation	Animal consumes another animal (+/–)	Cat eating birds; bat eating insects

19.4 Mastering Concepts

1. What is the competitive exclusion principle?
2. List three examples of symbiotic relationships.
3. Describe some adaptations that protect against herbivory and predation.
4. Define *coevolution* and describe an example.
5. How are keystone species important in communities?

19.5 A Community's Diversity and Species Composition May Change Over Time

From oceans to mountaintops, many species share each habitat, but these communities vary greatly in diversity. Ecologists use two measures, called species richness and species evenness, to describe these differences (figure 19.19). **Species richness** is simply the total number of species occupying a habitat. A patch of prairie, for instance, may contain about 100 plant species, whereas an equal-sized area of desert might house only six types of plants. In this example, the prairie has greater species richness than the desert.

But two communities with the same species richness may not be equally diverse. **Species evenness,** or relative abundance, describes the proportion of the community that each species occupies. In our patch of prairie, for example, suppose that one type of plant accounts for 90% of the individuals in the community, with 99 species making up the remaining 10%. Because one species has such high relative abundance, that community is less diverse than one in which, say, each of the 100 species makes up 1% of the community.

The numbers and types of species that form each community may appear to remain constant, but that is only because we usually only observe them over a relatively short period. **Succession** is a gradual change in a community's species composition. Ecologists define two major types of succession: primary and secondary. Both types occur when competing organisms, especially plants, modify the physical environment in a way that changes the mixture of other

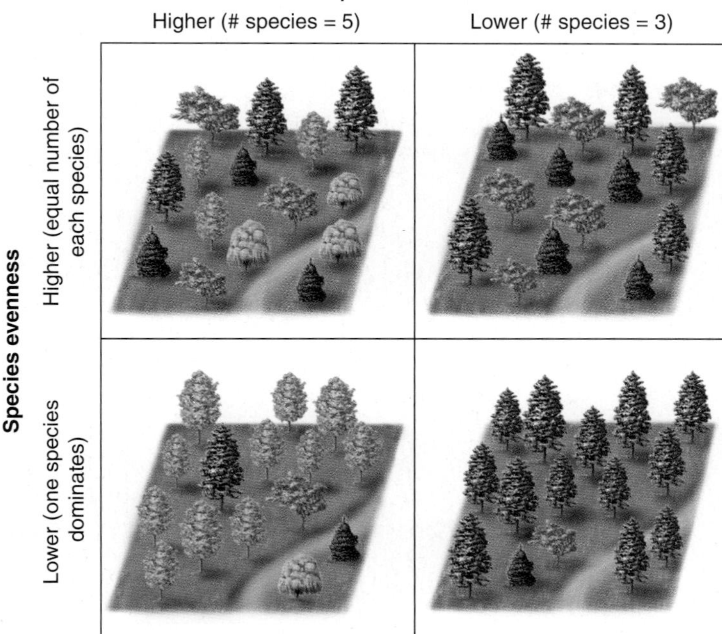

Figure 19.19 Measures of Community Diversity. Species diversity in a community has two components: species richness and species evenness.

Why We Care | Invasion of the Zebra Mussels

Introduced species sometimes displace native species by competitive exclusion. Zebra mussels, for example, are native to the Caspian Sea in Asia. These mollusks were accidentally introduced to the Great Lakes in the 1980s and have since spread to many waterways in the United States and Canada. The tiny filter feeders reproduce rapidly and have crowded out native mussel species, with which they compete for food and oxygen. ▸ invasive species, p. 417

The effects of the zebra mussel invasion have rippled through the rest of the lake community as well. Zebra mussels have greatly increased water clarity, which has changed aquatic plant communities. In turn, the altered plant species composition has triggered changes in the community of fishes.

species that can occupy the habitat. When pine trees invade a site, for example, they simultaneously shade out lower-growing plants while attracting species that grow on or eat pines.

Primary succession occurs in an area where no community previously existed. When a volcano erupts, for example, lava may obliterate existing life, a little like suddenly replacing an intricate painting with a blank canvas. Road cuts and glaciers that scour the landscape also expose virtually lifeless areas on which new communities eventually arise.

A patch of bare rock also provides a clear view of primary succession (figure 19.20). **Pioneer species** are first to colonize the area. These hardy organisms, such as lichens and mosses, can grow on smooth rock. Lichens release organic acids that erode the rock, producing crevices where sand and dust accumulate. Decomposing lichens add organic material, eventually forming a thin covering of soil. Then rooted plants such as herbs and grasses invade. Soil continues to form, and larger plants such as shrubs appear. As these new plants take root, a changing variety of birds, mammals, and other vertebrates joins the community as well. Next come aspens and conifers, such as jack pines or black spruces. Finally, hundreds of years after lichens first colonized bare rock, the soil becomes rich enough to support other deciduous trees, and a stable oak-hickory forest community may develop. ▸ lichens, p. 300

In contrast to primary succession, **secondary succession** occurs where a community is disturbed but not destroyed. Because some soil and life remain, secondary succession occurs faster than primary succession. Fires, hurricanes, and agriculture commonly trigger secondary succession (figure 19.21).

Primary and secondary succession share a common set of processes. First, pioneer species colonize a bare or disturbed site. These hardy species are usually opportunistic, with rapid reproduction and efficient dispersal. The early colonists often alter the physical conditions in ways that enable other species to become established. The new arrivals, in turn, continue to change the

Figure 19.20 Primary Succession. It takes centuries for a mature forest community to develop on a patch of bare rock. The changing plant species attract an ever-changing variety of animals. The example shown here includes plant species typical of New England.

environment. Some early colonists do not survive the new challenges, further altering the community. Later in succession, the dominant species are usually long-lived, late-maturing, equilibrium species that are strong competitors in a stable environment. ▸ opportunistic and equilibrium species, p. 369

A century ago, ecologists hypothesized that primary and secondary succession eventually lead to a so-called **climax community,** which is a community that remains fairly constant. We now know, however, that few (if any) communities ever reach true climax conditions. In the Pacific Northwest, for example, old-growth forests are 500 to 1000 years old, yet they are still changing in their structure and composition. Major disturbances such as fire, disease, and severe storms can leave a mark that lasts for centuries. On a smaller scale, pockets of local disturbance, such as the area affected when a large tree blows over, create a patchy distribution of successional stages across a landscape.

Succession is not limited to land; it occurs in aquatic communities as well. A young lake, for example, is too low in nutrients to support abundant phytoplankton. These lakes are therefore clear and sparkling blue. As a lake ages, however, nutrients accumulate from decaying organisms and sediment. Rich algal growth turns the water green and murky. In time, a lake continues to fill with sediments and transforms into a freshwater wetland, where the soil is permanently or seasonally saturated with water. Wetlands often host spectacularly diverse assemblages of plants and animals that rely on the interface between land and water. Eventually, the wetland fills in completely and becomes dry land.

Figure 19.21 Secondary Succession. A forest fire can devastate an existing community, but it does not take long for seedlings to sprout and take advantage of the nutrients in the ashes. Soon, fresh green foliage will obscure the burned stumps.

19.5 Mastering Concepts

1. How do ecologists measure species diversity in a community?
2. What is succession?
3. Distinguish between primary and secondary succession.
4. What processes contribute to primary and secondary succession?
5. How do disturbances prevent true climax communities from developing?
6. How does succession occur as a lake becomes a wetland?

19.6 Ecosystems Require Continuous Energy Input

Sections 19.4 and 19.5 described the biotic interactions among members of a community. We now turn to the ecosystem-level processes by which communities interact with the nonliving environment.

To understand the interactions in an ecosystem, it is useful to recall from unit 1 that all organisms consist of both matter and energy. One way to remember this is to picture a candy bar's nutrition label, which lists the nutrient and calorie (energy) content of the snack. The food label mirrors the contents of a living cell. Inside each cell are organic molecules such as fats, sugars, and ATP. These molecules consist of carbon, hydrogen, oxygen, nitrogen, and other elements. Moreover, the covalent bonds of organic molecules store potential energy that cells can use to do work. ▸ organic molecules, p. 33

Both energy and nutrients are critical to the two properties shared by all ecosystems on Earth. First, energy flows through ecosystems in one direction only. All ecosystems therefore rely on a continuous supply of energy from some outside source, usually the sun. Second, biogeochemical cycles constantly recycle the atoms that make up every object in an ecosystem. This section and

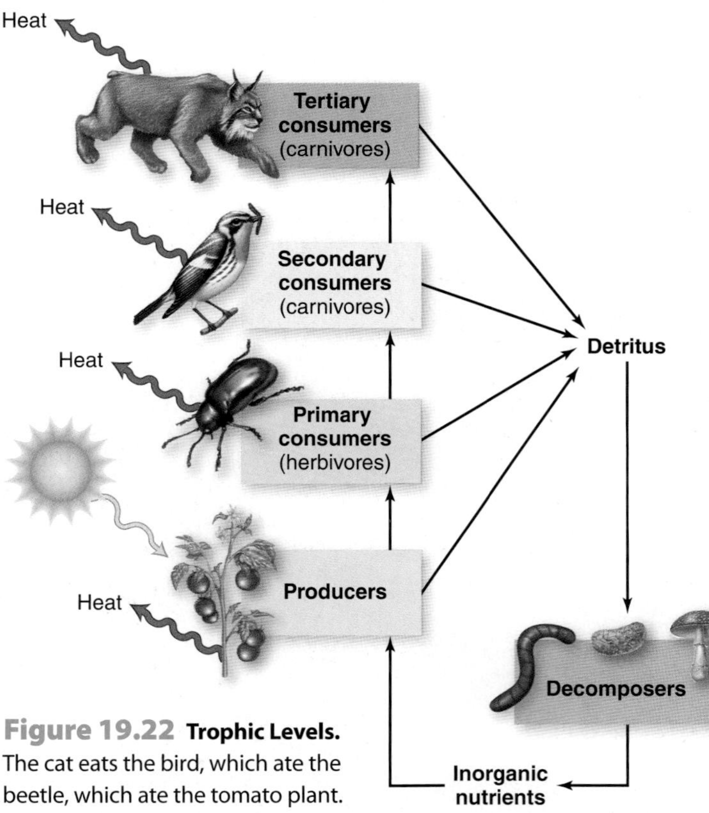

Figure 19.22 Trophic Levels. The cat eats the bird, which ate the beetle, which ate the tomato plant. All organisms contribute organic wastes and dead bodies (detritus) to the ecosystem. Decomposers recycle the detritus back into inorganic nutrients that producers can use.

section 19.7 describe these two properties and their consequences for ecosystem function.

A. Food Webs Depict the Transfer of Energy and Atoms

Many energy and nutrient transfers occur in the context of food chains and food webs. A **food chain** is a series of organisms that successively eat one another (figure 19.22). Each organism's **trophic level** describes its position in the food chain.

Trophic levels are defined relative to the ecosystem's energy source, which is sunlight in figure 19.22. The first trophic level in the food chain is a primary producer, and all of the other trophic levels consist of consumers. For example, the primary consumers in figure 19.22 are herbivores, which eat the primary producers. Secondary consumers are carnivores (meat-eaters) that eat primary consumers, and tertiary consumers eat secondary consumers.

Decomposers, such as fungi, bacteria, insects, and worms, are consumers that break down **detritus** (dead organisms and organic wastes). The Why We Care box on this page describes how we employ decomposers in community wastewater treatment facilities. Without decomposers, dead bodies and organic wastes would tie up all useful nutrients, and ecosystems would grind to a halt.

Autotrophs and decomposers have opposite roles in ecosystems. Whereas autotrophs absorb inorganic nutrients and produce organic molecules, decomposers return the elements in those organic molecules to their inorganic forms. Both roles are critical to ecosystem function.

Of course, feeding relationships in an ecosystem are more complex than a simple food chain might suggest. A **food web** is a network of interconnected food chains, such as the Antarctic web in figure 19.23. Keep in mind that this diagram is highly simplified. Not shown, for example, are the worms, crabs, hagfishes, sharks, and microbes that feed on the carcasses of dead whales that sink to the seafloor.

Careful examination of a food web diagram reveals that even the fiercest top predator, such as a killer whale, relies on other organisms, many of them microscopic. The same principle applies to the food web in which humans participate. Think of everything you have eaten today: in all likelihood, your meals and snacks have included both plant and animal products. Humans have developed an extremely complex global food chain that includes organisms harvested from land and water all over the world. Some of the connections are surprising. For example, pigs and chickens raised on commercial farms eat millions of tons of fish harvested near South America each year.

Why We Care: What Happens After You Flush

Community wastewater treatment plants harness the power of microorganisms to consume the organic matter in sewage before it enters waterways. In trickling filters, for example, sewage-eating bacteria and archaea are given "dream homes"—all the organic matter they can eat, along with plenty of moisture and O_2 (see figure 15.14c). After the microbes have done their job, the treated water contains a very low concentration of organic matter.

The presence of these microscopic workers explains why communities prohibit dumping used motor oil or organic solvents down the drain. Toxic chemicals can poison the bacteria and archaea that degrade sewage, making water treatment impossible.

The most commonly used forms of sewage treatment fail to remove a wide array of household chemicals and pharmaceutical drugs from the waste stream. The antibiotics in soaps and hand sanitizers are especially common, as are hormones excreted by women taking birth control pills. Ecologists are still studying the effects of these chemicals on wildlife. In the meantime, experts recommend against flushing medications—or anything other than human waste—down the toilet.

B. Every Trophic Level Loses Energy

The total amount of energy that is trapped, or "fixed," by all autotrophs in an ecosystem is called gross primary production. Autotrophs use much of this energy to generate ATP for their own growth, maintenance, and reproduction. As they do so, they lose heat energy (section 4.1B explains this loss). The remaining energy in the producer level is called **net primary production;** it is the amount of energy available for consumers to eat.

Primary production varies widely across the globe. Water availability and the prevailing temperature often determine the potential for plant growth on land. Tropical rain forests therefore have among the highest rates of net primary production per square meter; deserts have the lowest. In aquatic ecosystems, the availability of inorganic nutrients such as phosphorus is extremely important: the more nutrients, the more algae.

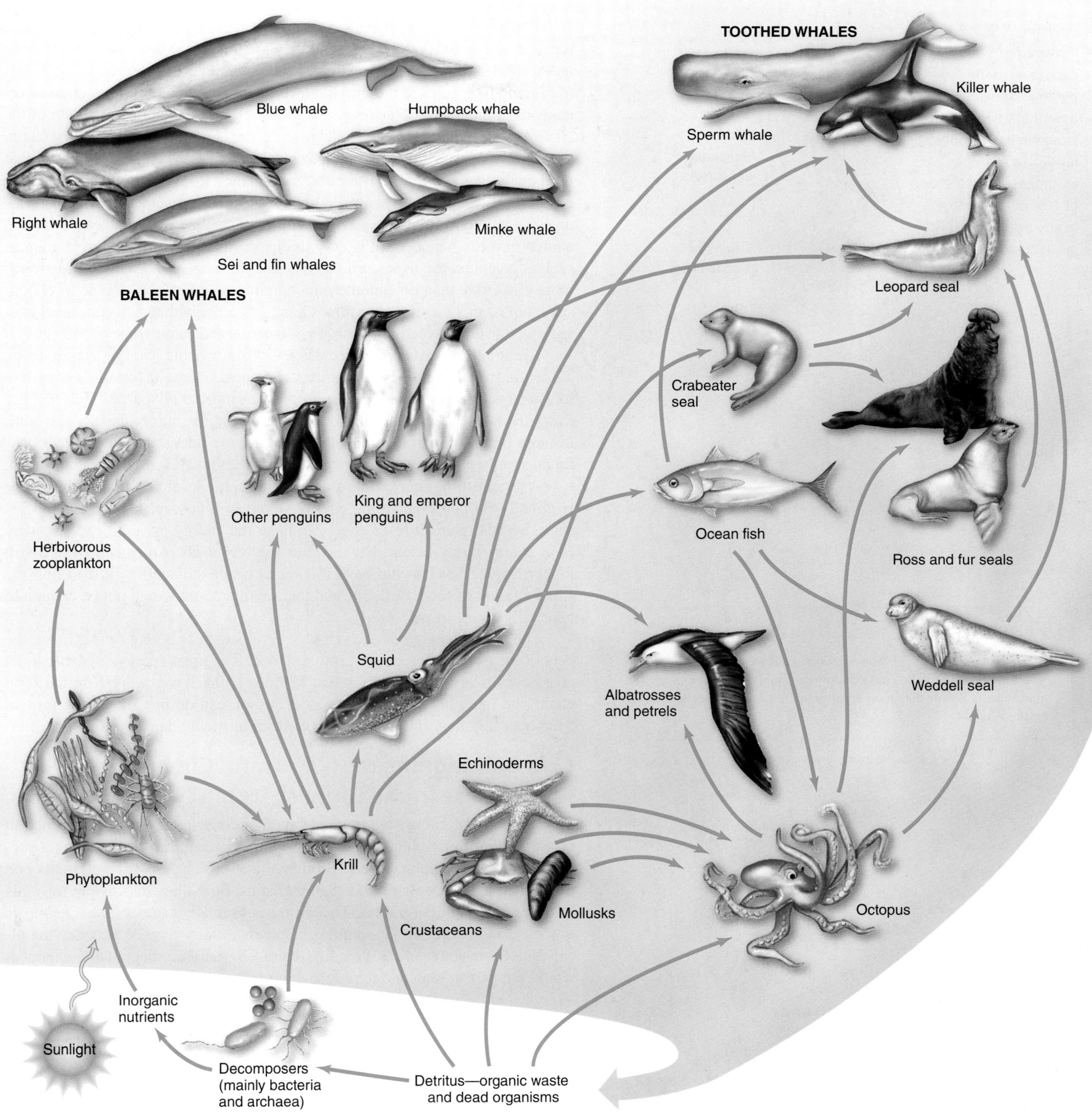

Figure 19.23 The Antarctic Web of Life. The interactions among Antarctic residents form a very complex network. Note that producers, consumers, and scavengers are all present and that decomposers release inorganic nutrients that producers can use. For simplicity, losses to heat are not illustrated.

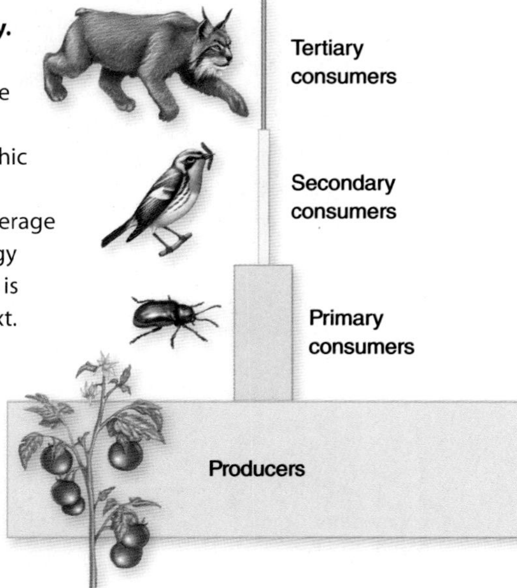

Figure 19.24 Pyramid of Energy. Each level in the pyramid depicts the amount of energy stored in each trophic level. This example assumes that an average of 10% of the energy in any trophic level is available to the next.

Consumers are no better than producers at conserving energy; they cannot digest every bit of food they eat, and they lose energy to heat. Because of these inefficiencies, only a small fraction of the potential energy stored in the bonds of organic molecules at one trophic level fuels growth and reproduction of organisms at the next trophic level. As an overall average, about one tenth of the energy at one trophic level is available to the next highest rank in the food chain.

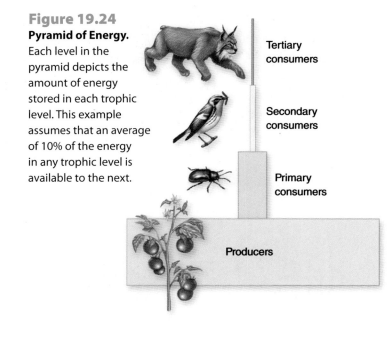

This "10% rule" provides a convenient estimate, but it ignores the fact that food quality varies widely. The transfer efficiency from one trophic level to the next actually ranges from about 2% to 30%. Primary consumers that eat hard-to-digest plants convert only a small percentage of the energy available to them into animal tissue, whereas meat is easy to digest. In addition, ectothermic animals such as invertebrates, fishes, amphibians, and nonavian reptiles use energy much more efficiently than do endothermic mammals and birds. A trophic level consisting of lizards therefore consumes much less energy than a trophic level consisting of an equal weight of birds. ▸ endotherms and ectotherms, p. 566

Eventually, as organic molecules pass from trophic level to trophic level, all of the stored energy is lost as heat. The heat energy leaves the ecosystem forever, because no organism can use heat as its energy source. Thus, energy flows through an ecosystem in one direction: from source (usually the sun), through organisms, to heat. For the ecosystem to persist, it must have a continual supply of energy. If the energy source goes away, so does the ecosystem.

A **pyramid of energy** represents each trophic level as a block whose size is directly proportional to the energy stored in that level (figure 19.24). Because every organism loses energy to heat, the energy pyramid explains why food chains rarely extend beyond four trophic levels. An organism in a still higher trophic level would have to expend tremendous effort just to find the small amount of food available, and that small amount would not be enough to make all that effort pay off.

The loss of energy at each trophic level suggests a way to maximize the benefit we get from crops we grow for food. The most energy available in an ecosystem is at the producer level. Therefore, the lower we eat on the food chain, the more people we can feed. A person can do this by getting protein from beans, grains, and nuts instead of from meat and dairy (figure 19.25).

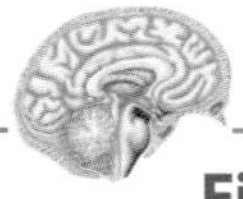

Figure It Out

According to figure 19.23, baleen whales mainly eat herbivorous zooplankton, and sperm whales mainly eat squid. About how much more energy is available in the ecosystem for baleen whales than for sperm whales?

Answer: About 10 times more energy is available for baleen whales.

C. In Biomagnification, Harmful Chemicals Accumulate in the Highest Trophic Levels

The shape of the energy pyramid has another consequence for ecosystems. In **biomagnification,** a chemical becomes more concentrated in organisms at successively higher trophic levels. Biomagnification happens for pollutants and other chemicals that share two characteristics. First, they dissolve in fat. This characteristic is important because animals eliminate water-soluble chemicals in their urine but retain fat-soluble chemicals in fatty tissues. Second, chemicals that biomagnify are not readily degraded. A highly degradable chemical would not persist long enough in the environment to ascend food chains.

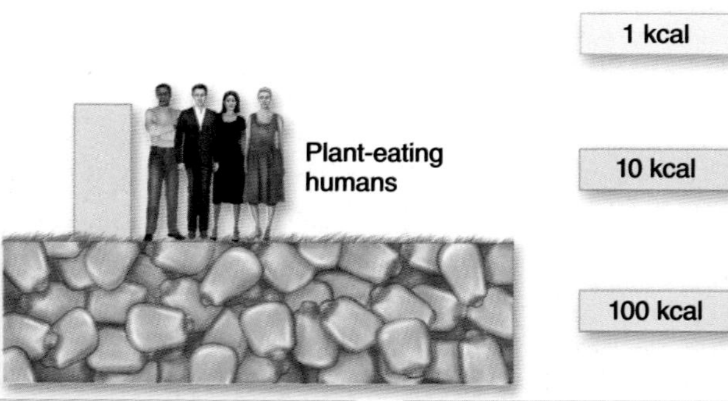

Figure 19.25 The Energetic Cost of Meat. Humans who derive energy by eating meat are getting only a small fraction of the energy originally present in grain.

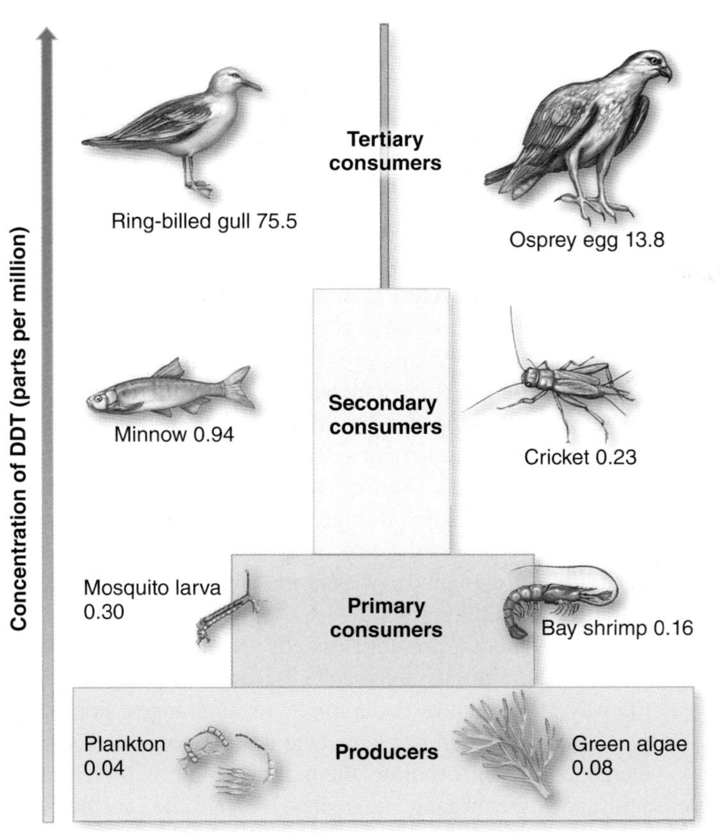

Figure 19.26 **Biomagnification.** (a) Organisms at the top of the food web have the highest concentration of DDT in their bodies. Numbers represent concentrations of DDT per unit of tissue, measured in parts per million (ppm). (b) An osprey with its prey.

DDT is a persistent chemical that illustrates biomagnification (figure 19.26). In the 1950s and 1960s, this insecticide was widely used to kill pests such as mosquitoes and body lice. Researchers soon found that it also harmed other organisms indirectly. Imagine DDT being sprayed over a waterway for mosquito control. Its concentration in the water is low. But DDT is fat-soluble, and once it enters an organism's body, it is not eliminated in urine or other watery wastes. As one animal eats another, all of the DDT stored in the prey ends up in the predator. Each predator eats many prey, so the DDT concentrates in the predator's tissues. In organisms at the fourth level of the food chain, DDT concentrations may be 2000 times greater than in organisms at the base of the food web.

These concentrations do not kill top predators outright, yet the use of DDT corresponded with declining numbers of bald eagles, peregrine falcons, osprey, and other birds of prey. Research eventually showed that high concentrations of DDT caused the birds to produce weak eggshells, which broke when adult birds attempted to incubate the eggs. Few young birds hatched, and populations plummeted. The United States therefore banned use of DDT in 1971. Nevertheless, DDT is still used in other countries, especially to control the mosquitoes that transmit malaria.

19.6 Mastering Concepts

1. Identify the trophic levels in a food chain.
2. What roles do primary producers and decomposers play in ecosystems?
3. How efficient is energy transfer between trophic levels in food webs?
4. Draw an energy pyramid for an ecosystem with three levels of consumers.
5. Explain how biomagnification affects organisms at the top of a food chain.

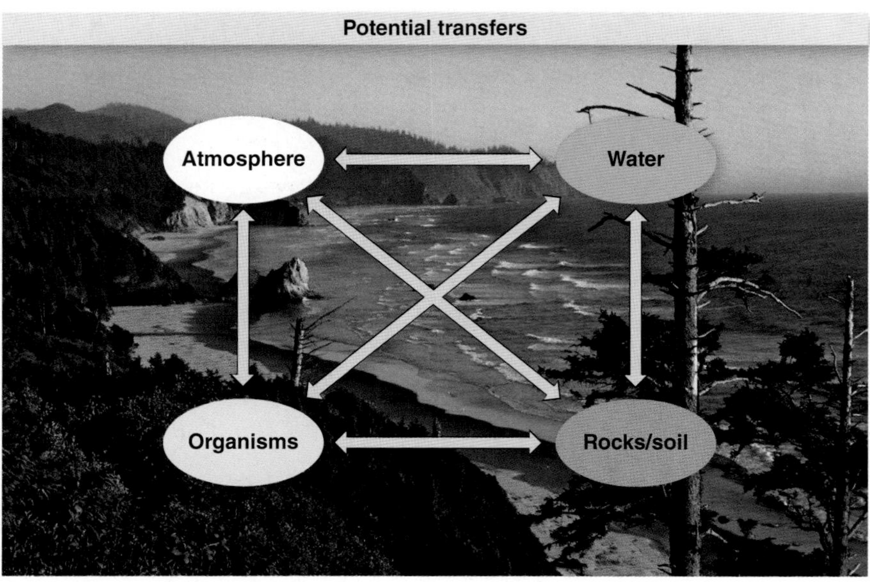

Figure 19.27 Biogeochemical Cycle. Water and inorganic nutrients cycle among four basic storage reservoirs. The photo in the background shows all four.

19.7 Chemicals Cycle Within Ecosystems

Energy flows in one direction, but all life must use the elements that were present when Earth formed. In **biogeochemical cycles,** interactions of organisms and their environment continuously recycle these elements. If not for this worldwide recycling program, supplies of essential elements would have been depleted as they became bound in the bodies of organisms that lived eons ago.

Whatever the element, all biogeochemical cycles have features in common (figure 19.27). Each element is distributed among four major storage reservoirs: organisms, the atmosphere, water, and rocks and soil. Depending on the reservoir, the element may combine with other elements and form a solid, liquid, or gas.

These "pools" are not isolated; instead, transfers among the pools form the basis of each biogeochemical cycle. Along the way, the elements undergo chemical changes. For example, autotrophs such as plants take up the inorganic forms of elements and incorporate them into lipids, carbohydrates, proteins, nucleic acids, and other organic molecules. If an animal eats the plant, the element may become part of the animal's tissue. If a predator eats the herbivore, the element may be incorporated into the predator's body, and so on. Eventually, however, decomposers release the inorganic forms of the elements back into the soil, water, or atmosphere.

This section describes the water, carbon, nitrogen, and phosphorus cycles. All of these substances are essential to life and abundant in cells. As you will see, however, the water cycle is somewhat different from the other three cycles. Most processes in the water cycle are physical, not biological. Its status as a *bio*geochemical cycle is therefore tenuous. Nevertheless, carbon, nitrogen, and phosphorus compounds can dissolve in water, and water movement is important in transporting these elements among the storage pools. Knowledge of the water cycle is therefore essential to understanding the three nutrient cycles.

A. Water Circulates Between the Land and the Atmosphere

Water covers much of Earth's surface, primarily as oceans but also as lakes, rivers, streams, ponds, swamps, snow, and ice (figure 19.28). Water also occurs below the land surface as groundwater.

The main processes that transfer water among these major storage compartments are evaporation, precipitation, runoff, and percolation. The sun's heat evaporates water from land and water surfaces (figure 19.28, step 1). Water vapor rises on warm air currents, then cools and forms clouds (step 2). If the wind carries this moisture higher or over cold water, more cooling occurs, and

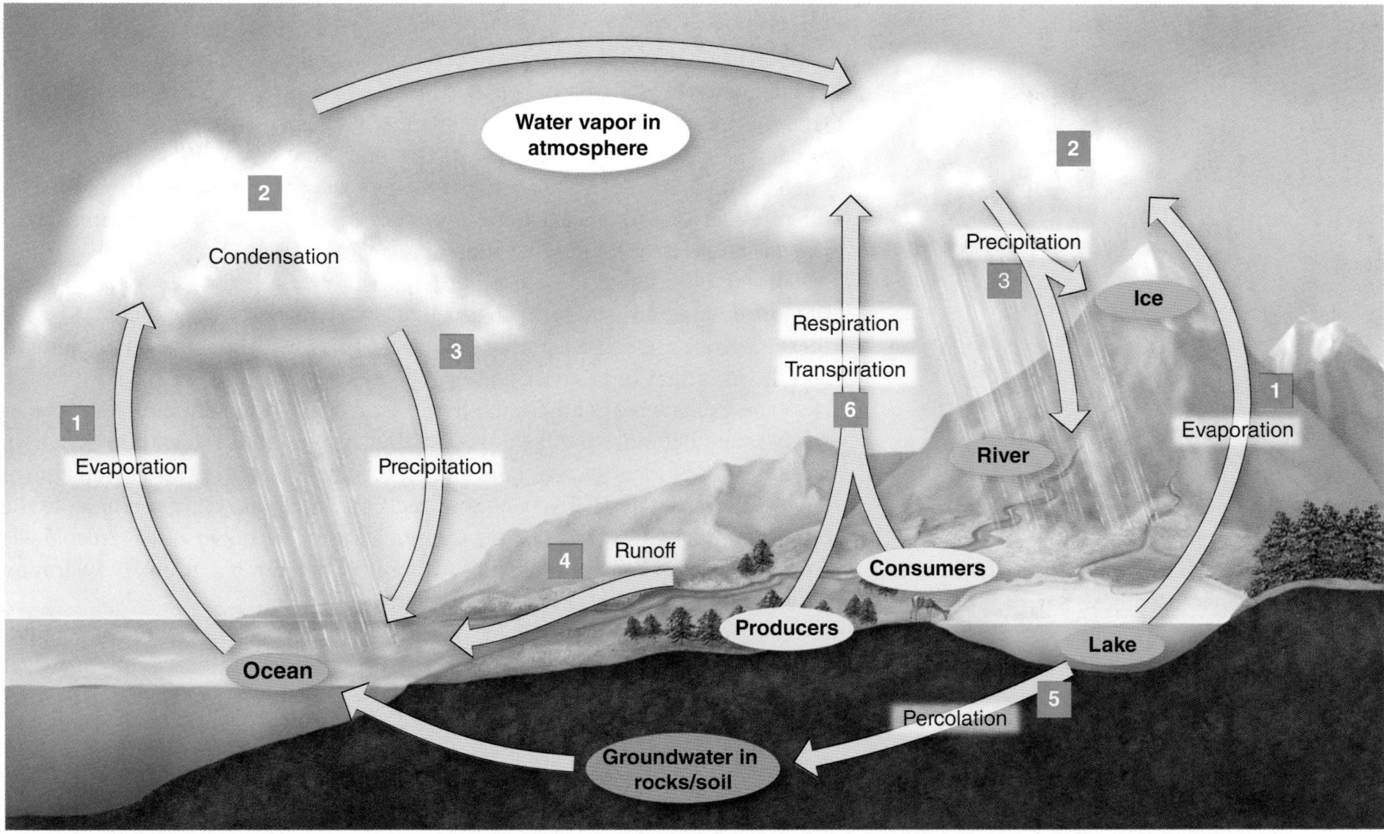

Figure 19.28 **The Water Cycle.** Water falls to Earth as precipitation. Organisms use some water, and the remainder evaporates, runs off into streams and the ocean, or enters the ground. Respiration and transpiration return water to the environment.

the vapor condenses into water droplets that fall as rain, snow, or other precipitation (step 3). Some of this water falls on land, where it may run along the surface. Streams unite into rivers that lead back to the ocean (step 4), where the sun's energy again heats the surface, continuing the cycle.

Rain and snowmelt may also soak (percolate) into the ground, restoring soil moisture and groundwater (step 5). This underground water feeds the springs that support many species. Spring water evaporates or flows into streams, linking groundwater to the overall water cycle.

Although most processes in the water cycle are physical, organisms do participate (step 6); after all, water is essential to life. Animals drink water and return it to the environment through respiration and urination. In addition, plants absorb water from soil and release much of it from their leaves in transpiration. The lush plant life of the tropical rain forests draws huge amounts of water from soil and returns it to the atmosphere. ▸ transpiration, p. 440

B. Autotrophs Obtain Carbon as CO_2

Carbon is a part of all organic molecules, and organisms continually exchange this element with the atmosphere (figure 19.29). Autotrophs absorb atmospheric CO_2 and produce organic compounds that they incorporate into their tissues (step 1). Cellular respiration releases carbon back to the atmosphere as CO_2 (step 2). Dead organisms and excrement deposit organic carbon in soil or water (step 3). Invertebrates, bacteria, and fungi decompose these organic compounds and release CO_2 to the soil, air, and water (step 4).

Some types of archaea also participate in the carbon cycle by consuming organic compounds and releasing methane (CH_4) into the atmosphere. Most of these microbes live in anaerobic habitats such as wetlands, marine sediments, and the intestines of humans, cattle, and other animals.

The exchange of carbon between organisms and the environment is relatively rapid, but more stable pools of carbon also exist in soil and the ocean. In addition, fossil fuels such as coal and oil formed long ago from the remains of dead organisms (step 5). When these fuels burn (step 6), carbon returns to the atmosphere as CO_2. Decades of accumulation of CO_2 and other greenhouse gases in the atmosphere are likely responsible for Earth's gradually warming climate. Chapter 20 describes this topic in more detail.

One of the largest reservoirs of carbon is the ocean. CO_2 from the atmosphere dissolves in ocean water. Most of the dissolved gas reacts with the water to form carbonic acid (H_2CO_3). Some of this carbon reacts with calcium to form

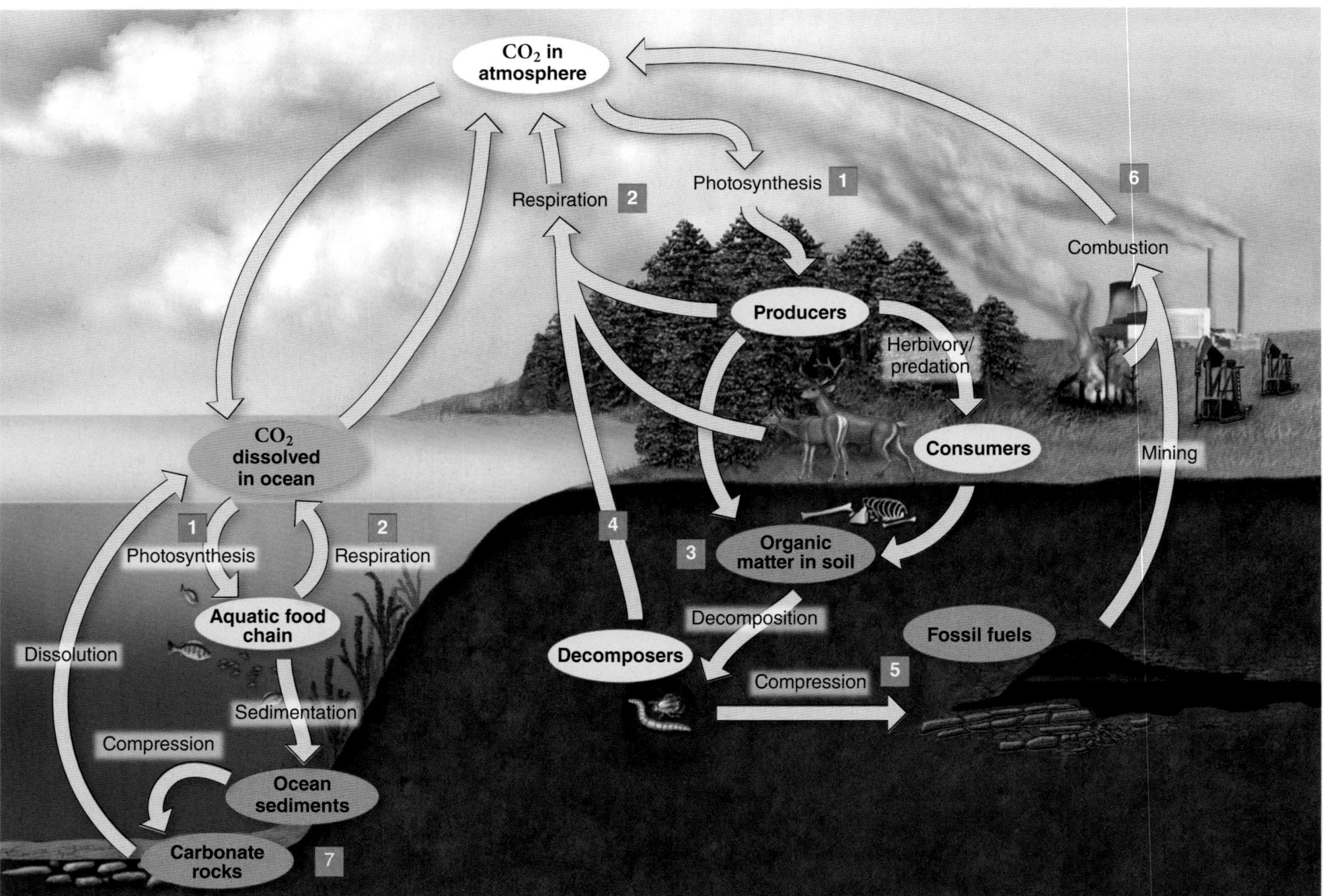

Figure 19.29 The Carbon Cycle. Carbon dioxide in the air and water enters ecosystems through photosynthesis and then passes along food chains. Respiration and combustion return carbon to the abiotic environment. Carbon can be retained for long periods in carbonate rocks and fossil fuels.

calcium carbonate, which precipitates into sediments on the ocean floor (step 7). These sediments are one of the major stable reservoirs of carbon on the planet.

The reaction between CO_2 and water, coupled with the accumulation of CO_2 in the atmosphere, means that the ocean is becoming more acidic. Ocean acidification harms coral reefs by dissolving the calcium carbonate skeletons of coral animals, joining global climate change as another side effect of greenhouse gas buildup. ▸ pH scale, p. 32

C. The Nitrogen Cycle Relies on Bacteria

Nitrogen is an essential component of proteins, nucleic acids, and other biochemicals in living cells. Figure 19.30 depicts the nitrogen cycle.

Although the atmosphere is about 78% nitrogen gas (N_2), most organisms cannot use this form of nitrogen. The nitrogen cycle therefore depends on **nitrogen fixation,** the process by which some bacteria and archaea convert N_2 into ammonium ions, NH_4^+ (step 1). Examples of nitrogen-fixing bacteria include *Rhizobium,* which lives in nodules on the roots of legume plants such as beans, peas, and clover (see figure 15.12 and figure 21.4). In addition, many farmers boost plant growth by applying nitrogen fertilizers to their fields (step 2). Fertilizer production relies on an industrial-scale form of nitrogen fixation.

Nitrogen can also occur in the form of nitrate (NO_3^-). In a process called **nitrification,** bacteria and archaea convert ammonium to nitrate (step 3). In addition, the combustion of fossil fuels such as coal, oil, and natural gas releases

Figure 19.30 The Nitrogen Cycle. Nitrogen-fixing bacteria and archaea convert atmospheric nitrogen gas (N_2) to ammonium ions (NH_4^+), which plants can absorb. Nitrogen returns to the abiotic environment in urine and during the decomposition of organic matter. Bacteria and archaea convert ammonium to nitrate, NO_3^- (another form plants can use). Microbes also convert nitrate to N_2, completing the cycle.

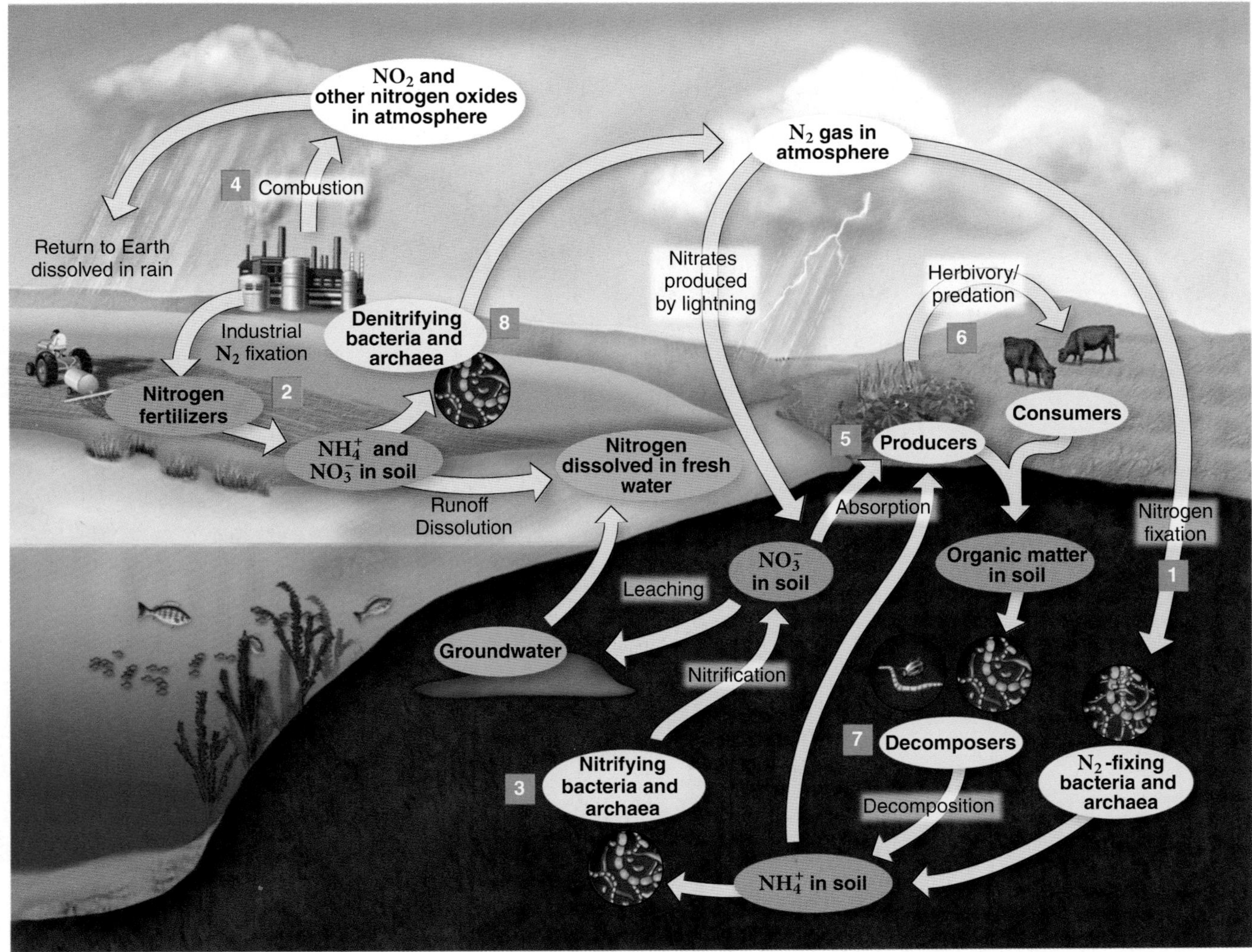

Why We Care | The Nitrogen Cycle in Your Fish Tank

Nitrification and denitrification occur in a fish aquarium, a miniature ecosystem with a nitrogen cycle of its own. Fish eat nitrogen-rich food and then release toxic ammonia as a waste product, which begins to accumulate soon after the animals move into a new aquarium. Given enough time, however, populations of nitrifying bacteria grow on the gravel and in the aquarium's filter. These microbes convert the ammonia to nitrites and nitrates. Other microbes carry out denitrification, eliminating the nitrogen as N_2 gas.

When starting a new aquarium, one way to jump-start this process is to obtain a used filter or some gravel from an established aquarium. The microbes in the transplanted biofilms will give the new tank a head start in establishing a functioning nitrogen cycle.

NO_2^- and other nitrogen oxides into the atmosphere (step 4). These compounds return to Earth in precipitation. Excess nitrogen deposition from the atmosphere may be altering the ecology of some low-nitrogen ecosystems, including the bogs where carnivorous plants thrive. ▸ carnivorous plants, p. 444

Plants and other autotrophs can absorb either ammonium or nitrate and incorporate it into the organic molecules that make up their own bodies (step 5). Consumers then acquire the nitrogen by eating the producers (step 6), and so on up the food chain. Decomposers release some ammonia when they decay the dead bodies and wastes (step 7).

Yet another group of bacteria completes the cycle. In **denitrification,** bacteria return nitrogen to the atmosphere as they convert nitrate to N_2 (step 8). This process occurs where O_2 is scarce, such as wetlands, water-saturated soils, groundwater, and ocean sediments.

D. The Phosphorus Cycle Begins with the Weathering of Rocks

Phosphorus occurs in nucleic acids, ATP, and membrane phospholipids; in vertebrates, this element is also a major component of bones and teeth.

Unlike in the carbon and nitrogen cycles, the atmosphere plays little role in the phosphorus cycle (figure 19.31). Instead, the main storage reservoirs for phosphorus are marine sediments and rocks. As phosphate-rich rocks erode, they gradually release phosphate ions (PO_4^{-3}) into the water (step 1).

Many soils, however, are relatively low in phosphorus; a deficiency of this element often limits plant growth. Humans therefore mine phosphate rocks to produce plant fertilizers (step 2). Animal waste also contains abundant

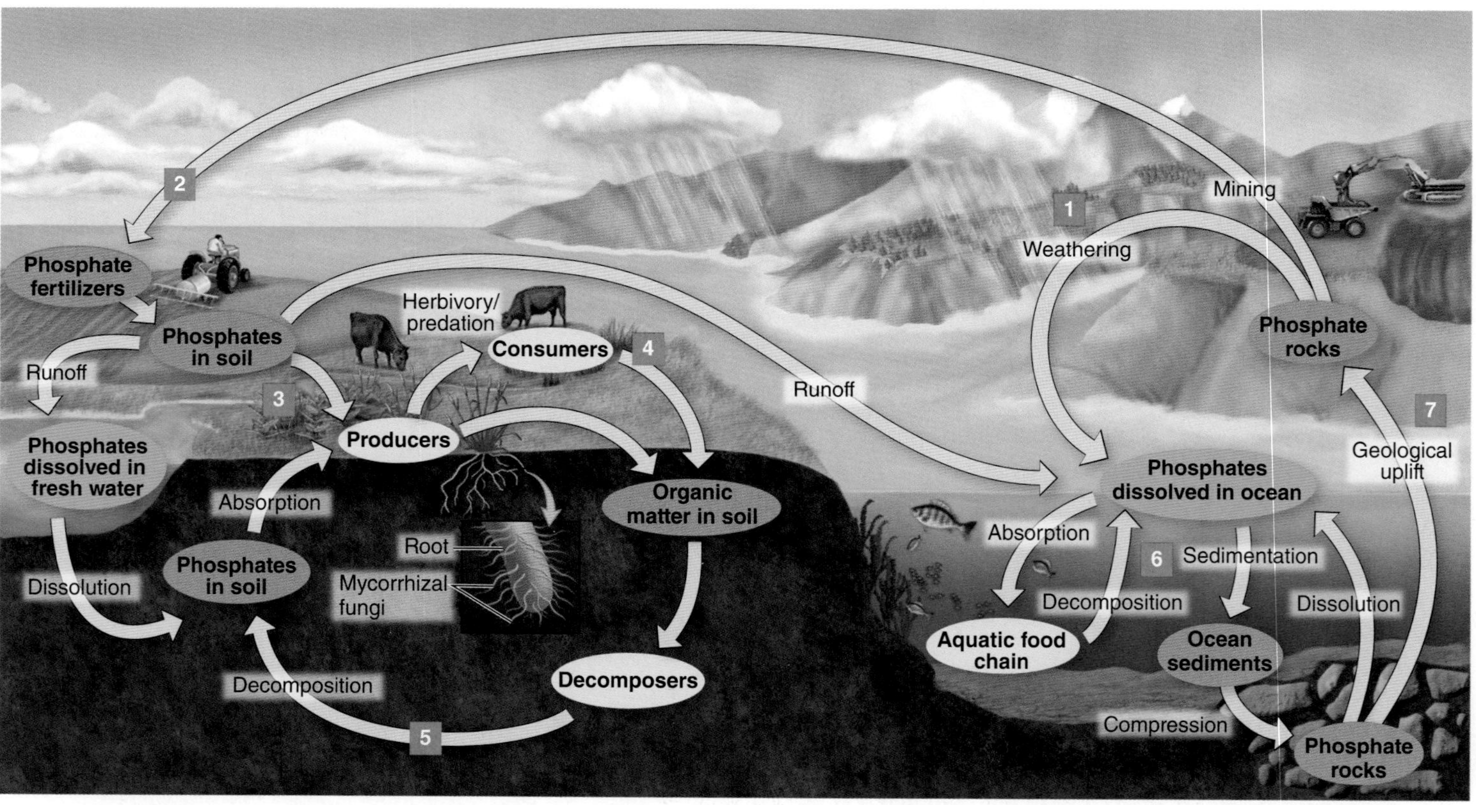

Figure 19.31 The Phosphorus Cycle. As phosphate-rich rocks erode, they release phosphorus that plants can absorb and pass to the rest of the food chain. Decomposers return phosphorus to the abiotic environment. Fertilizers have increased phosphorus availability to both terrestrial and aquatic organisms.

phosphorus; some people harvest the guano (droppings) of birds and bats for use as fertilizer. As described in section 20.3A, however, excess phosphorus in water from detergents and organic wastes can pose environmental problems.

Autotrophs absorb phosphorus, often with the help of mycorrhizal fungi (step 3). Consumers move the element throughout the food web (step 4), and decomposers eventually return inorganic phosphates to soil and water (step 5). Much of the phosphate, however, joins the sediments raining down onto the ocean floor (step 6). After many millions of years, geological uplift returns some of this underwater sedimentary rock to the land (step 7).

E. Terrestrial and Aquatic Ecosystems Are Linked in Surprising Ways

Sometimes, nutrients in an ecosystem can come from unexpected sources. Consider, for example, a mountain stream in Alaska. The eggs of Alaska salmon hatch in the streambed, and over the next year or so, the hatchlings develop into juveniles as they make their way to the mouths of their home rivers. As they transform into adults, their bodies adjust to seawater, and the fish swim into the Pacific Ocean. They spend as many as 4 years in the ocean, eating crustaceans and small fish. During this portion of their life cycle, the salmon (and their prey) rely on nutrients from the ocean.

Eventually, the fully grown salmon readjust to fresh water and swim upstream, back to the same waters where they hatched. As they make their way to their home stream to spawn, their bodies carry nutrients from the ocean to the heart of Alaska. Bears and eagles feast on the salmon (figure 19.32), and decomposers consume the remains. The nutrients they release support the growth of algae, which form the foundation of the stream's food chain. The adult salmon therefore form a link between the biogeochemical cycles of the ocean and the land.

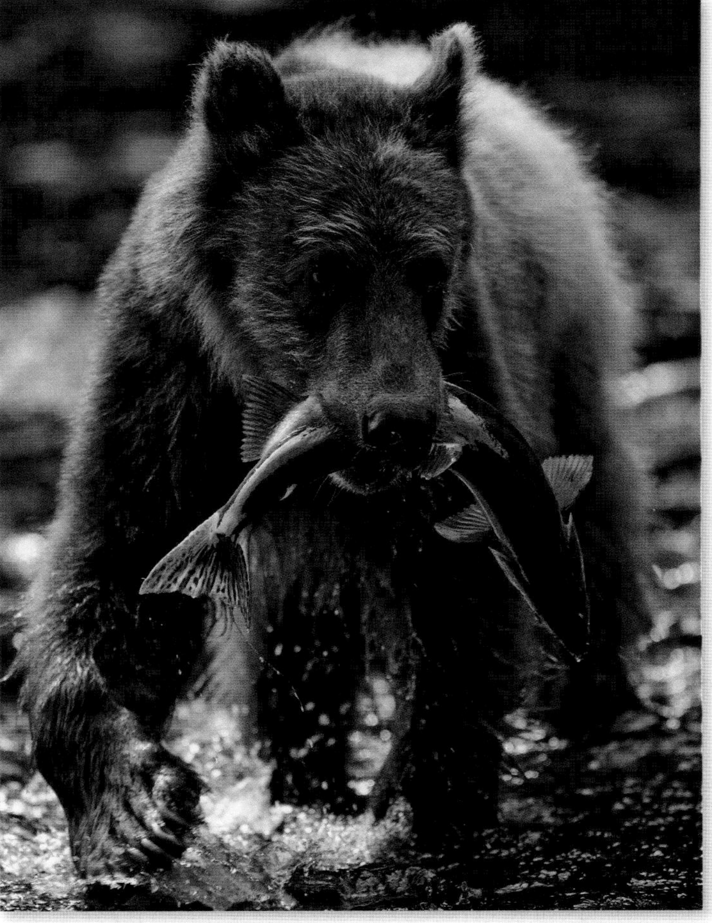

Figure 19.32 Fish Feast. This brown bear is carrying a sockeye salmon, which contains nutrients from the sea.

19.7 Mastering Concepts

1. What features do biogeochemical cycles share?
2. Describe the steps of the water, carbon, nitrogen, and phosphorus cycles.
3. Describe how a terrestrial ecosystem can interact with a faraway aquatic ecosystem.

Investigating Life

19.8 Two Kingdoms and a Virus Team Up to Beat the Heat

In his 1733 poem entitled *On Poetry, a Rhapsody,* Jonathan Swift wrote:

So, naturalists observe, a flea
Has smaller fleas that on him prey;
And these have smaller still to bite 'em;
And so proceed ad infinitum.

Swift's observation, though not literally true, showed amazing insight into the relationships between the merely small and the truly microscopic. We now know that symbiotic arrangements can bind together species from many different groups. Mutualism is a particularly interesting form of symbiosis, in which both species benefit from the deal.

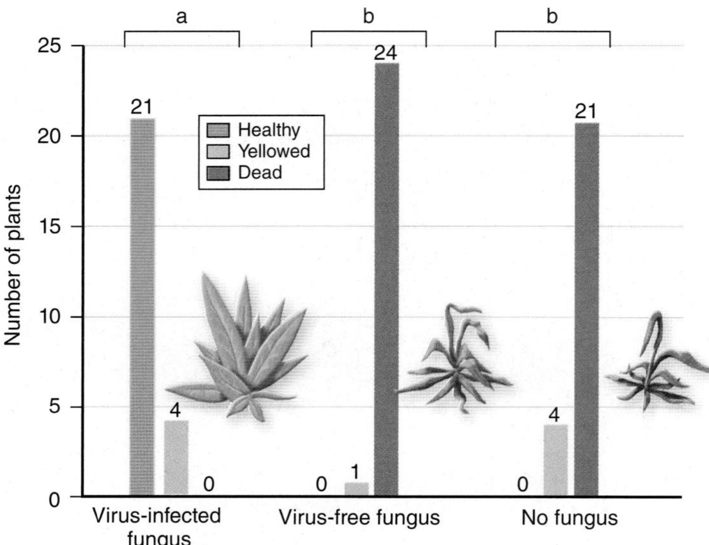

Figure 19.33 The Virus Matters. Plants that were inoculated with the normal virus-infected fungus survived the heat. Not so for plants infected with virus-free fungi or for plants without fungal endophytes. (See Appendix B for a brief discussion of the notation that represents statistically significant differences between treatments.)

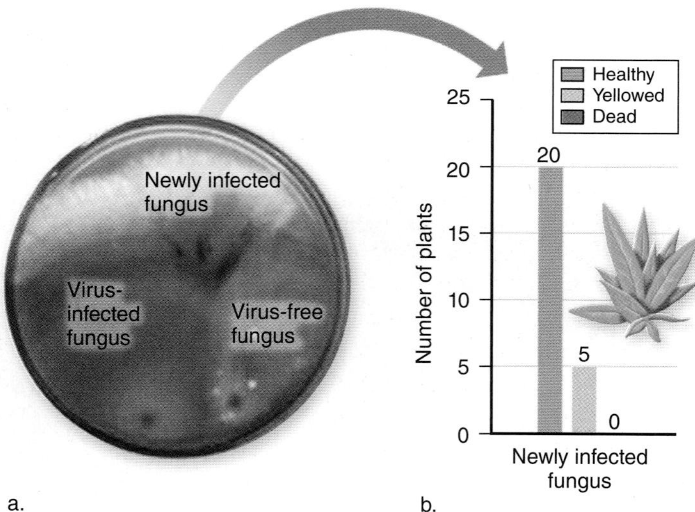

Figure 19.34 Reinfecting a "Cured" Fungus. (a) The researchers grew virus-infected (wild-type) and virus-free fungi on agar in a petri dish. In the zone where the two colonies are growing together, previously virus-free fungi reacquired the virus. (b) Plants that were colonized by the newly infected fungi were heat-tolerant once more.

Researchers at the Noble Foundation in Ardmore, Oklahoma, have discovered an unusual three-way symbiosis and documented its survival benefit to the partners. Biologists Luis Márquez and Marilyn Roossinck knew of a type of panic grass (*Dichanthelium lanuginosum*) that endured the scorching geothermal soils of Yellowstone National Park. Previous studies had shown that the grass benefited from a fungus growing in its tissues. The fungus (*Curvularia protuberate*) is an endophyte, an organism that lives between a plant's cells without causing disease. By itself, neither plant nor fungus could grow at temperatures above 38°C (100°F). The grass–fungus relationship somehow allows the plant to survive in soil temperatures up to 65°C (about 150°F). As long as the grass survives, so does the fungus, but each is doomed without the other.

The Question: By itself, a plant–endophyte relationship is not unusual; section 15.6 described endophytes that help cacao plants fight off diseases. But Márquez and his team dug a bit deeper. They knew that many fungi are themselves infected with viruses. The team wondered whether the fungus within the grass might also have a partnership with a virus.

The Approach: The first thing to do was to see if a virus was present. The viruses that infect fungi usually have genomes made of double-stranded RNA, which is distinctive from the fungus's own double-stranded DNA. The researchers extracted nucleic acids from the fungal cells and found telltale fragments of double-stranded RNA within the fungal tissue. ▸ nucleic acids, p. 42

Next, the team wanted to see if the presence of the virus within the fungal endophytes helped plants survive in hot soils. They found a colony of the fungus that contained very low amounts of viral RNA. By repeatedly drying, freezing, and thawing this fungus in the laboratory, they "cured" the fungus of its virus. The researchers then set up an experiment with three treatment groups: grass with the wild-type (virus-infected) fungus, grass inoculated with virus-free fungus, and grass without any fungus at all. They submitted the three groups of plants to a tough regimen of 65°C soil temperatures for 10 hours a day, followed by 14 hours at 37°C. After 14 days, they checked to see how the plants were doing. The results were clear: only the plants with the virally infected fungus survived the ordeal (figure 19.33).

The results seemed promising, but the team had to be certain it was the virus that did the trick. They therefore grew one of their virus-free fungus samples on a plate next to a fungus that contained the virus (figure 19.34a). They let the two fungi grow across each other so that the previously virus-free fungus picked up the virus. They inoculated grass with this newly infected fungus and turned up the heat. Sure enough, these plants survived, too (figure 19.34b).

The Conclusion: This work illustrates the intricate relationships that bind members of a community together. The grass–fungus–virus partnership apparently allows all of the partners to colonize habitats that were previously unavailable. It is not that each species is advocating the success of the other's genome. Rather, the alliance gives each party a selective advantage in a challenging environment.

Márquez, Luis M., Regina S. Redman, Russell J. Rodriguez, and Marilyn J. Roossinck. 2007. A virus in a fungus in a plant: Three-way symbiosis required for thermal tolerance. *Science,* vol. 315, pages 513–515.

19.8 Mastering Concepts

1. Describe the relationships among the grass, fungus, and virus.
2. List the benefits and drawbacks of inoculating all of our food crop plants with the fungus–virus team. What would you need to know before recommending that strategy?

Chapter Summary

19.1 Organisms Interact Within Communities and Ecosystems

- **Communities** are composed of coexisting **populations** of multiple species.
- An **ecosystem** consists of a **biotic** community plus its **abiotic** environment.
- Each species in a community has a place where it normally lives **(habitat)** and a set of resources necessary for its life activities **(niche).**

19.2 Earth Has Diverse Climates

- Solar radiation is most intense at the equator and least intense at the poles. The resulting uneven heating creates the patterns of precipitation, prevailing winds, and ocean currents that influence climate.
- A mountain range can influence local climate by producing a **rain shadow**.

19.3 Biomes Are Ecosystems with Distinctive Communities of Life

- **Biomes** are major types of ecosystems that occupy large geographic areas and share a characteristic climate and group of species.

A. The Physical Environment Dictates Where Each Species Can Live

- **Autotrophs (primary producers)** directly or indirectly support the **heterotrophs (consumers)** in each biome. On land, the most important primary producers are plants; in water, **phytoplankton** are most important.
- The major abiotic factors that limit a species' distribution include sunlight, temperature, moisture, salinity, and fire.

B. Terrestrial Biomes Range from the Lush Tropics to the Frozen Poles

- Several types of forest biomes extend from the tropics to the temperate zone to the high northern latitudes.
- Grasslands include the tropical savannas and the temperate grasslands. Fire, grazing, and seasonal drought keep trees from dominating these biomes.
- Desert plants have adaptations that help them obtain and store water.
- Mediterranean shrublands have dry summers and fire-adapted plants.
- Tundras have very cold, long winters. A layer of permafrost prevents the growth of trees.
- At the poles, the climate is extremely cold and dry.

C. Aquatic Biomes Include Fresh Water and the Oceans

- In a lake's **photic zone,** light is sufficient for photosynthesis. Rooted plants fringe the shallow shoreline, whereas phytoplankton are the primary producers in the upper layer of open water. Nutrients from the upper layers support life in the deeper zones where light does not penetrate.
- Near the headwaters of a river, the channel is narrow, and the current is swift. As the river accumulates water and sediments, the current slows, and the channel widens.
- The ocean has a productive, nutrient-rich shoreline. Photosynthesis occurs in the photic zone, but life in the deep ocean relies on organic matter from above.
- An estuary is a highly productive area where rivers empty into oceans, and life is adapted to fluctuating salinity. Residents of the rocky intertidal zone are adapted to stay in place as the tide ebbs and flows. In tropical regions, coral reefs support many thousands of species.

19.4 Community Interactions Occur Within Each Ecosystem

A. Many Species Compete for the Same Resources

- Populations that share a habitat often **compete** for limited resources. Competition reduces the fitness of both species.
- According to the **competitive exclusion principle,** two species cannot indefinitely occupy the exact same niche. If multiple species with similar niches share a habitat, competition may restrict each species to only some of the resources available. This process is called **resource partitioning.**

B. Symbiotic Interactions Can Benefit or Harm a Species

- **Symbiotic** relationships include **mutualism** (both species benefit), **commensalism** (one species benefits, whereas the other is unaffected), and **parasitism** (one species benefits, and the other is harmed).

Interaction	Effects
Competition	- / -
Mutualism	+ / +
Commensalism	+ / 0
Parasitism	+ / -
Herbivory	+ / -
Predation	+ / -

C. Herbivory and Predation Link Species in Feeding Relationships

- **Herbivory** is an interaction in which a consumer eats a plant; a **predator** is an animal that eats another animal (its **prey**).
- Plants and prey animals have defenses against herbivores and predators; in addition, animals have adaptations that help them capture food.

D. Closely Interacting Species May Coevolve

- In **coevolution,** the interaction between species is so strong that genetic changes in one population select for genetic changes in the other.

E. A Keystone Species Has a Pivotal Role in the Community

- A **keystone species** makes up a small proportion of a community's biomass but has a large influence on the community's composition.

19.5 A Community's Diversity and Species Composition May Change Over Time

- Ecologists describe the diversity of a community by measuring **species richness** (the number of species) and **species evenness,** which indicates the relative abundance of each species.
- As species interact with one another and their physical habitats, they change the composition of the community. This process is called **succession.**
- **Primary succession** occurs in a previously unoccupied area, beginning with **pioneer species** that allow soil to develop, paving the way for additional organisms to thrive.
- **Secondary succession** is more rapid than primary succession because soil does not have to build anew.
- Succession may lead toward a stable **climax community,** but true long-term stability is rare. Pockets of local disturbance mean that most communities are a patchwork of successional stages.
- Lakes also undergo succession as they age. Young lakes contain few nutrients to support phytoplankton. As nutrients gradually accumulate, algae tint the water green. A continuous influx of sediments from the land eventually transforms the lake into a wetland.

19.6 Ecosystems Require Continuous Energy Input

A. Food Webs Depict the Transfer of Energy and Atoms

- Within a community, each species occupies one or more **trophic levels,** depending on its relationship to the ecosystem's energy source.
- At the base of each **food chain** are primary producers that harness energy from the sun or inorganic chemicals.
- Consumers make up the next trophic levels. Primary consumers (herbivores) eat the primary producers. A secondary consumer may eat the primary consumer, and a tertiary consumer may eat the secondary consumer. **Decomposers** break down **detritus** (nonliving organic material) into inorganic nutrients.
- Interconnected food chains form **food webs.**

B. Every Trophic Level Loses Energy

- Gross primary production is the total amount of energy converted to chemical energy in an ecosystem. After subtracting energy devoted to growth, maintenance, and reproduction, the energy remaining in the producer trophic level is **net primary production.**
- Food chains rarely extend beyond four trophic levels because only a small percentage of the energy in one trophic level transfers to the next level.
- A **pyramid of energy** is a diagram that depicts the amount of energy at each trophic level in a food chain.

C. In Biomagnification, Harmful Chemicals Accumulate in the Highest Trophic Levels

- **Biomagnification** concentrates stable, fat-soluble chemicals in the highest trophic levels because the chemical passes to the next consumer rather than being metabolized or eliminated in urine.

19.7 Chemicals Cycle Within Ecosystems

- **Biogeochemical cycles** are geological and chemical processes that recycle chemicals essential to life.

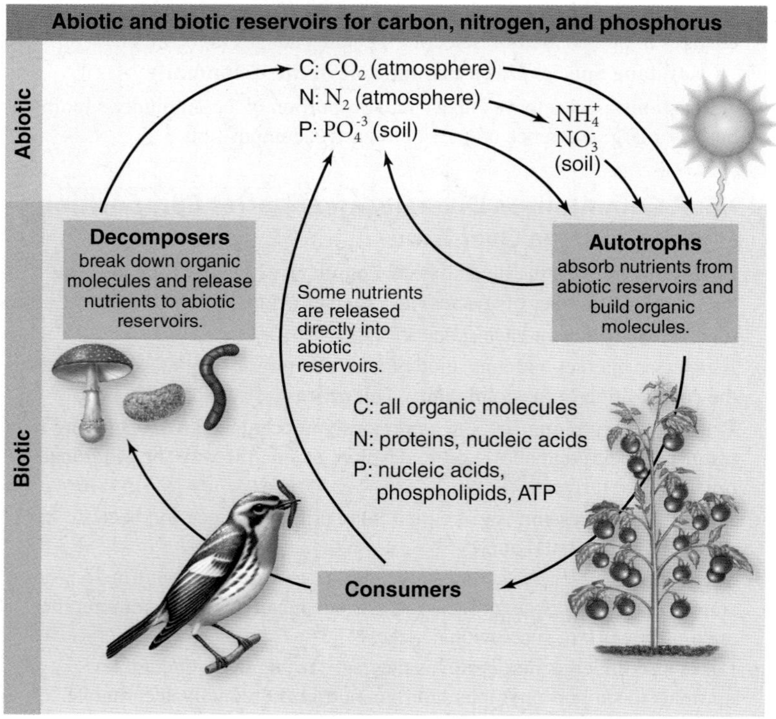

- Each cycle is characterized by transfers among four main storage reservoirs: organisms, the atmosphere, water, and rocks and soil.

A. Water Circulates Between the Land and the Atmosphere

- Water is transferred from the atmosphere to the land or to bodies of water as precipitation. Organisms release water in transpiration, evaporation, or urination.

B. Autotrophs Obtain Carbon as CO_2

- Autotrophs use carbon in CO_2 to produce carbohydrates. Cellular respiration and burning fossil fuels release CO_2. Decomposers release carbon from once-living material.

C. The Nitrogen Cycle Relies on Bacteria

- **Nitrogen-fixing** microbes convert atmospheric nitrogen to ammonium, which plants can incorporate into their tissues. Decomposers convert the nitrogen in dead organisms back to ammonium. **Nitrification** converts the ammonium to nitrites and nitrates, whereas **denitrification** converts these compounds to nitrogen gas.

D. The Phosphorus Cycle Begins with the Weathering of Rocks

- Rocks release phosphorus as they weather. Autotrophs absorb the phosphates and incorporate them into organic molecules; decomposers return inorganic phosphates to the environment.

E. Terrestrial and Aquatic Ecosystems Are Linked in Surprising Ways

- During the salmon life cycle, nutrients are transferred from the ocean to inland ecosystems.

19.8 Investigating Life: Two Kingdoms and a Virus Team Up to Beat the Heat

- Researchers have discovered a three-way symbiosis between a grass plant, a fungus, and a virus that enables plants to survive extremely high temperatures.

Multiple Choice Questions

1. If Earth's axis were not tilted, there would be no
   a. equator.
   b. seasons.
   c. difference in the intensity of solar radiation between the equator and the poles.
   d. precipitation.
2. A biome composed of trees that seasonally shed their leaves is a
   a. chaparral.
   b. tropical rain forest.
   c. temperate deciduous forest.
   d. taiga.
3. Two species of photosynthetic bacteria live in ocean water but use different wavelengths of light in photosynthesis. This example illustrates
   a. competitive exclusion.
   b. commensalism.
   c. resource partitioning.
   d. biomagnification.
4. Which of the following examples illustrates mutualism?
   a. Barnacles attached to a whale's skin neither harm nor help the whale.
   b. Sparrows and chickadees fight for access to the seeds in a homeowner's bird feeder.
   c. A mosquito consumes a person's blood.
   d. Fig wasps help pollinate fig trees and reproduce inside the tree's fruit.
5. A moth that eats plants is a(n) ______, whereas the bat that eats the moth is a ______.
   a. heterotroph; decomposer
   b. secondary consumer; decomposer
   c. primary consumer; secondary consumer
   d. autotroph; secondary consumer
6. Which statement best explains why persistent, fat-soluble chemicals such as DDT accumulate in the highest trophic levels?
   a. Animals at the highest trophic levels eat the lowest-quality food.
   b. The amount of biomass increases in each trophic level, and large organisms accumulate the most DDT.
   c. Large organisms are often herbivores, so they consume DDT directly.
   d. DDT does not leave an animal's body; each predator therefore consumes the DDT contained in many prey.

Write It Out

1. How does a community differ from an ecosystem?
2. How does a habitat differ from a niche? Describe your own habitat and niche.
3. How does the fact that Earth is a sphere tilted on its axis influence the distribution of life?
4. List adaptations that characterize organisms in each of the following biomes: tropical rain forest, savanna, temperate grassland, tundra, desert, taiga, the rocky intertidal zone, the bottom of a lake.
5. Suppose you are exploring the chaparral ecosystem in California. You encounter a shrub species that you think may be fire-adapted, and you wonder whether the plant can reproduce in the absence of fire. Design an experiment that would help answer your question.
6. Describe how and why photosynthetic activity differs in each region of a lake or ocean.
7. Nuisance aquatic plants such as hydrilla can disrupt the ecology of a lake. Two of the most common ways to control nuisance aquatic plants are herbicides (chemicals that kill plants) and biological control (introducing fungi or animals that consume the plants). How might each strategy help or harm the lake ecosystem?
8. How can two species share the same habitat without one driving the other to extinction?
9. Describe and give examples of three types of symbiotic relationships.
10. List examples of adaptations that enable an organism to compete with other species, live inside another species, find food, and avoid herbivory or predation. How does each adaptation contribute to the organism's fitness?
11. What is a keystone species? How do researchers design experiments that help them identify keystone species?
12. Distinguish between primary and secondary succession.
13. How is natural selection apparent in ecological succession?
14. How are decomposers and autotrophs essential to ecosystem function?
15. In the United States, people have reduced or eliminated the populations of top predators such as wolves and coyotes. How might this history relate to the recent explosion of deer populations? Using the ecological principles you have learned in this unit, what are some possible ways to reduce deer populations? What are the pros and cons of each approach?
16. How do organisms return water, carbon, nitrogen, and phosphorus to the abiotic environment?
17. Several sites on the Internet offer water- or carbon-footprint calculators. Use one to compute your footprints. What assumptions go into these calculations? What strategies could you use to reduce either footprint?
18. Review the structures of organic molecules in chapter 2. How do the molecules in living cells create interconnections between the carbon, nitrogen, and phosphorus cycles?

Pull It Together

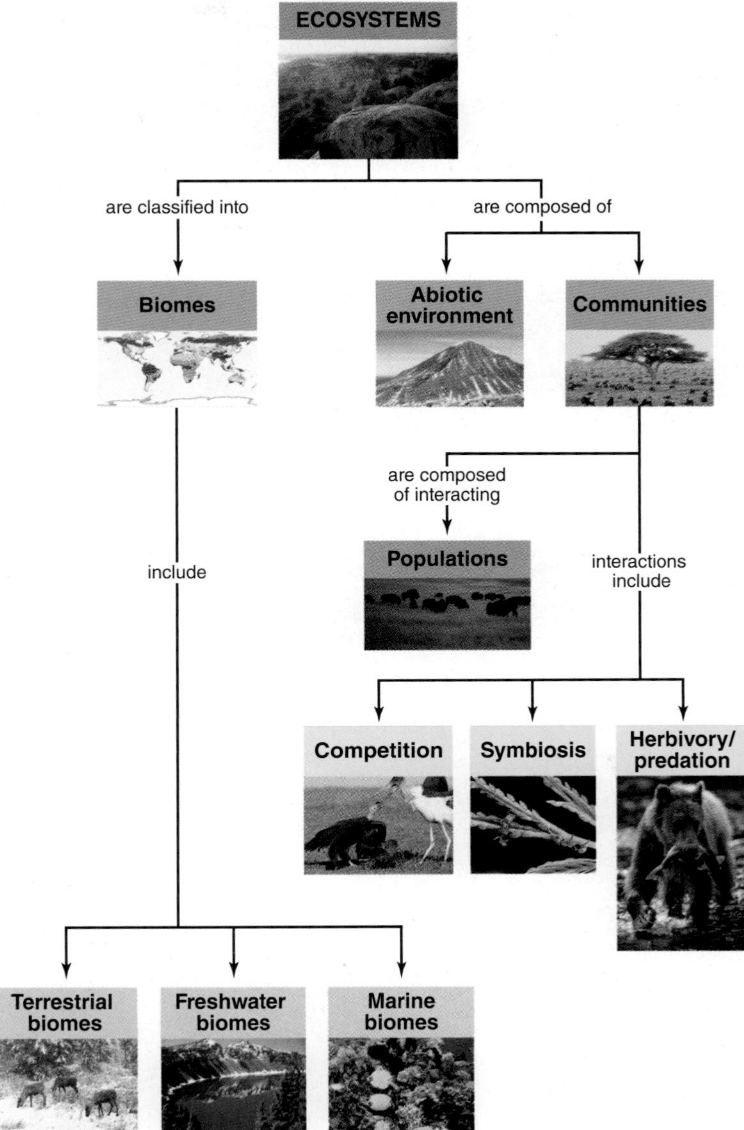

1. What factors determine the location of each biome on Earth?
2. What types of forests occur on Earth, and what combination of conditions favors each type?
3. List examples of coastal ecosystems.
4. List some components of your abiotic environment.
5. Where do mutualism, commensalism, and parasitism fit into this concept map?
6. Where do primary, secondary, and tertiary consumers fit into this concept map?

20 Preserving Biodiversity

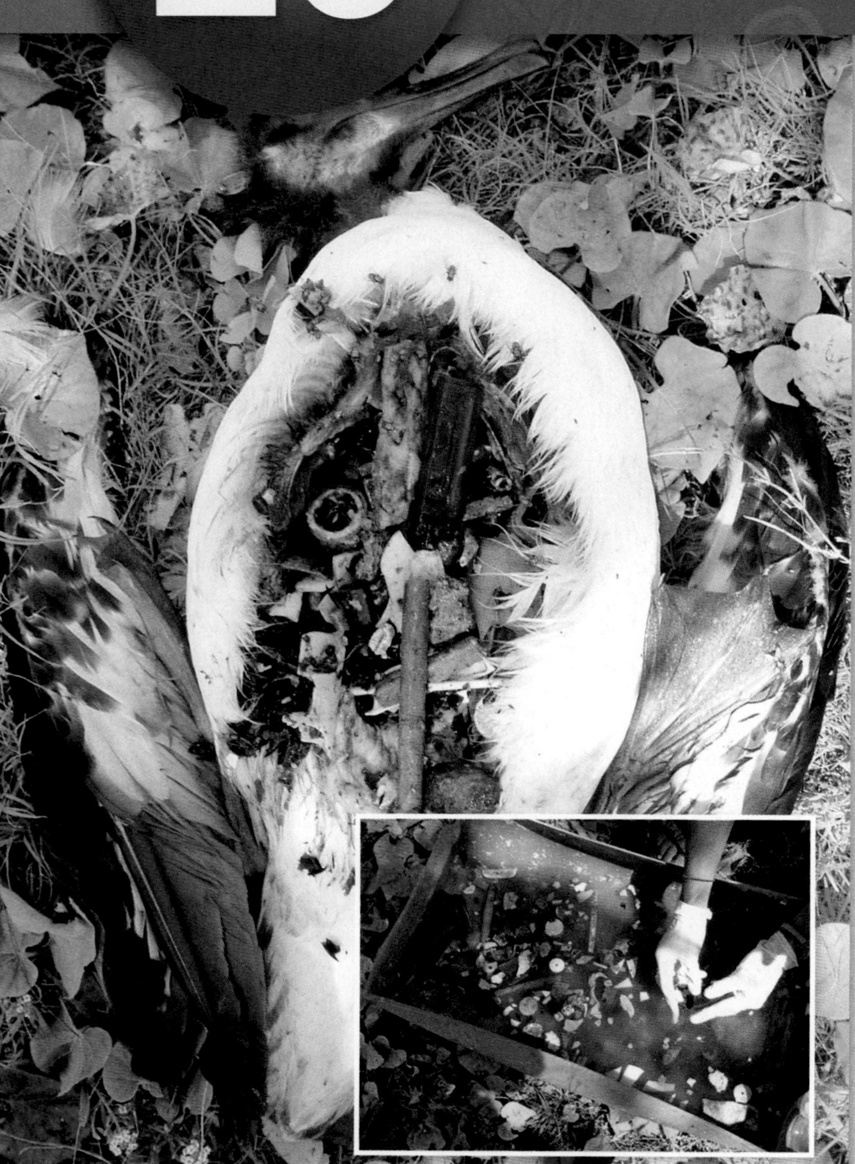

Death by Plastic. This young albatross died after eating plastic garbage that humans threw in the ocean.

Learning Outline

Learn How to Learn

How to Use a Study Guide

Some professors hand out study guides to help students prepare for exams. Used wisely, a study guide can be a valuable tool. One good way to use a study guide is AFTER you have studied the material, when you can go through the guide and make sure you haven't overlooked any important topics. Alternatively, you can cross off topics as you encounter them while you study. No matter which technique you choose, don't just memorize isolated facts. Instead, try to understand how the items on the study guide relate to one another. If you're unclear on the relationships, be sure to ask your instructor.

What's the Point?

Do you think that humans are at the "top of the heap"? That we can go it alone or with just a few carefully selected plant and animal companions? Think again. The truth is that we rely on other species for a huge variety of ecosystem services, many of which are not obvious until the species that provide them are gone.

Chapter 19 described the interactions that unite species in ecosystems; we now turn to the many strands in the web of life that are being torn. You may find this chapter depressing—the list of problems goes on and on because human activities threaten other species in so many ways. The albatross on the facing page is a particularly striking example. It died after consuming plastic garbage that its mother mistook for food floating in the ocean. A photographer captured the evidence in this case, but countless other animals, plants, and other organisms are dying as well.

Given our reliance on other species, the loss of biodiversity is not only sad but also dangerous. But as you will see, humans can undo some of the damage if we are willing to commit the time, effort, and money to preserve the other species that share our planet.

20.1 Earth's Biodiversity Is Dwindling

For more than 3 billion years, evolution has produced an extraordinary diversity of life, both obvious and unseen; unit 3 provided an overview of Earth's inhabitants. Humans simply cannot live without these other species. We use other organisms for food, shelter, energy, clothing, and drugs. Microbes carry out indispensable tasks, from digesting food in our intestines, to decaying organic matter in soil, to producing oxygen (O_2). Plants and microbes absorb carbon dioxide (CO_2) and purify the air, soil, and water. Wetland species reduce the severity of floods. Insects pollinate our crops. The remains of species that lived millions of years ago provide the fossil fuels that sustain our economies. The list goes on and on.

Clearly, our existence as a species depends on **biodiversity**—the variety of life on Earth. Biologists measure biodiversity at three levels: genetic, species, and ecosystem. Genetic diversity is the amount of variation that exists within a species. This aspect of biodiversity is essential for populations to adapt to changing conditions. The next level, species diversity, measures the number of species occupying the biosphere. Finally, ecosystem diversity means the variety of ecosystems on Earth, such as deserts, rain forests, grasslands, and mountaintops. ▸▸ biomes, p. 382; species richness and evenness, p. 391

One way to monitor species biodiversity is to count how many known species are at risk of extinction. **Extinction** means that the last individual of a species has perished. Some species, such as the dodo, are extinct altogether; others, such as a bird called the Guam rail, are extinct in the wild but still exist in captivity. A species that is **endangered** has a high risk of extinction in the near future, and a **vulnerable** species is likely to become extinct in the more distant future. The International Union for Conservation of Nature (IUCN) combines endangered and vulnerable species into one umbrella category ("threatened").

The data suggest that Earth is in the midst of a biodiversity crisis that affects animals, plants, and other organisms (figure 20.1). Vertebrates are going extinct at about 100 to 1000 times the "background" species extinction rate,

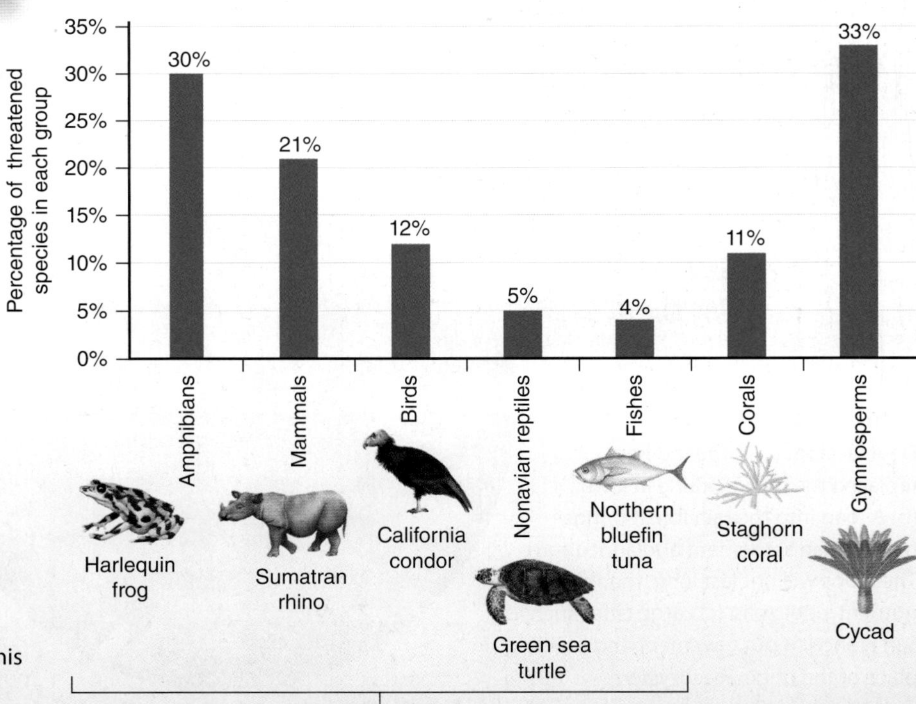

Figure 20.1 Biodiversity Crisis. The International Union for the Conservation of Nature monitors populations of vertebrates, invertebrates, and plants from around the world. Species in all groups are in peril, but some groups are harder hit than others. This graph shows a few examples; in each case, the bar represents the percentage of known species that are considered threatened.

which estimates how quickly species disappeared before human intervention. Overall, the current biodiversity crisis is comparable to that of the five major mass extinctions that have occurred in the past 600 million years (see figure 14.11).

Conservation biologists study the preservation of biodiversity at all levels. These scientists try to determine why species disappear, and they develop strategies for maintaining diversity. This chapter focuses first on the main causes of the loss of biodiversity: habitat destruction and degradation, global climate change, the introduction of nonnative species, and overexploitation. Each of these threats to biodiversity will only become worse as the human population continues to grow. Nevertheless, the chapter ends on a hopeful note, with some ways people can help counteract the biodiversity crisis.

20.1 Mastering Concepts

1. What is the value of biodiversity to humans and to ecosystems as a whole?
2. Describe the three types of biodiversity.
3. Differentiate among extinct, endangered, and vulnerable species.
4. What is conservation biology?

Figure 20.2 Habitat Destruction. (a) Farmland has replaced the native prairie in Iowa. (b) A road into the rain forest brings new human settlement and agriculture. The crops will not last long, thanks to nutrient-poor soils. (c) Large cities such as San Francisco put pavement and buildings in place of the original ecosystem.

20.2 Many Human Activities Destroy Habitats

Habitat destruction is the primary threat to biodiversity (figure 20.2). Humans have altered nearly 50% of the land, replacing prairies, wetlands, and forests with farms, rangeland, and cities. The link to biodiversity is obvious: destroying habitat makes it difficult or impossible for its occupants to survive and reproduce.

Prairies and other temperate grasslands have disappeared as the human population has expanded. The deep, black prairie soils of the North American grasslands are famously fertile and rich in organic matter. Because these soils are ideal for cultivation, only small patches remain of the vast grasslands that once occupied three continents. Fields of corn, soybeans, wheat, and other crops have replaced diverse grasses (see figure 20.2a). Most prairie remnants are too small to sustain the herds of large herbivores that once roamed the plains.

Another form of habitat destruction is **deforestation,** the removal of all tree cover from a forested area. Like all plants, trees absorb CO_2 from the atmosphere and use it in photosynthesis, a process that also releases O_2. The wood of a living tree is an especially important long-term "carbon sink" that helps offset CO_2 released when humans burn fossil fuels. ▸ carbon cycle, p. 400

Forests harbor a tremendous diversity of organisms that supply many of the resources that we use every day: lumber, paper, furniture, and foods such as wild mushrooms and nuts. The trees in the forest also provide wildlife habitat. As plants near extinction, we lose potential medicines along with the ancestors of many of our most important domesticated plants. These older varieties are a valuable resource to plant breeders, who are always searching for disease-resistance genes to breed into modern crop plants.

Trees also play a critical role in the global water cycle. Deforestation reduces the potential for transpiration, an important avenue by which water returns to the atmosphere. This decrease in transpiration may trigger changes in the global water cycle and, by extension, in the global climate. In addition, in an intact forest, rain and melting snow seep slowly through the forest floor and into the soil, helping to recharge groundwater. Forest destruction removes the spongy duff on the forest floor, so rainwater runs off into streams rather than soaking into the soil. The excess runoff hurts both forests and streams. As the forest soil erodes away, waterways become choked with nutrients and sediments. ▸ water cycle, p. 398

All of the world's forest biomes are under threat. Logging, mining, and exploration for oil and gas are rapidly depleting the northern coniferous forest. In addition, nearly all of the world's native temperate forests are already gone. In North America, for example, people have cleared the land to create farmland, obtain fuel, and make room for railroads and cities. Today, although vast areas of managed forests and plantations occupy the region, less than 1% of the original temperate forest survives.

Worldwide, people are logging and burning tropical rain forests to make room for crops and domesticated animals (see figure 20.2b). When the trees burn, they release stored carbon into the atmosphere, contributing to the greenhouse effect (see section 20.4). Ironically, the same soils that support the lush rain forest produce poor crop yields. The tropical climate explains this apparent contradiction. Warm temperatures promote rapid decomposition of organic matter, and heavy rains deplete soil nutrients. Once native plants give way to crops or grazing animals, the nutrient-poor soils harden into a cement-like crust. Species disappear and food webs topple, threatening biodiversity in the entire region.

Grasslands and forests are shrinking worldwide, but deserts are expanding as unsustainable agriculture eats away at forests and savannas. For example, widespread overgrazing by domesticated animals threatens to turn large areas of tropical savanna to desert. But human activities can also destroy native deserts (figure 20.3). Many people are drawn to the warm climate of the southwestern United States. Desert cities such as Phoenix, Las Vegas, and Palm Springs demand huge amounts of water for household use, irrigation, and recreation. The water comes from faraway rivers, changing the desert ecosystem and reducing the river's flow.

Freshwater habitats in general are vulnerable to destruction. Damming for flood control or power generation, for example, completely alters river ecosystems (figure 20.4). Worldwide, the number of large dams (over 15 meters high) is estimated at more than 48,000. How do dams reduce biodiversity? Deep reservoirs replace waterfalls, rapids, and wetlands, where birds and many other species breed. Areas that were once seasonally flooded become dry. Water temperature, oxygen content, and nutrient levels all change, triggering shifts in species diversity and food webs both above and below the dam. Dams also disrupt the migration of fish and other aquatic animals.

Another threat to freshwater biodiversity is alterations to a river's path. Along the banks of the Mississippi River, levees built to prevent flooding alter the pattern of sediment deposition. Channelization increases the water's flow rate, eroding sediments and choking out downstream communities. Nutrients that once spread over the floodplain during periodic floods are now confined to the river channel, which carries them to the Gulf of Mexico. There, the nutrients stimulate the growth of algae, causing additional problems described in section 20.3.

Figure 20.3 **Thirsty Ecosystem.** Water diverted from the Colorado River helps keep this Palm Springs golf course lush.

Figure 20.4 **Big Dam.** The Ataturk Dam on the Euphrates River provides power to Turkey. Dams help control flooding and provide irrigation water, but they also eliminate streamside habitat and disrupt the migration of fishes and other animals.

Coastlines are also suffering from habitat destruction (see figure 20.2c). The world's coasts are a vital source of food, transportation, recreation, and waste disposal. Many fishes and invertebrates spend part of their lives in estuaries, and diverse algae and flowering plants support the food web. Yet humans have drained and filled estuaries for urbanization, housing, tourism, dredging, mining, and agriculture. These activities affect life in the oceans, too. The loss of coastal habitats can threaten populations of commercially important species of marine animals such as bluefin tuna, grouper, and cod. These problems are only expected to get worse. Most of the world's largest cities are located along coastlines, and human populations in those cities will probably continue to rise in the future. ▸ estuaries, p. 386

TABLE 20.1 Examples of Chemical Water Pollutants

Organic	Inorganic
Sewage	Chloride ions
Pharmaceutical drugs	Heavy metals (mercury, lead, chromium, zinc, nickel, copper, cadmium)
Cosmetics	Nitrogen from fertilizer
Antibacterial soaps	Phosphorus from fertilizer and sewage
Detergents	Cyanide
Pesticides	Selenium
Petroleum	
Persistent organic pollutants (PCBs, PAHs)	

20.2 Mastering Concepts

1. Which human activities account for most of the loss of terrestrial habitat?
2. How do dams and channelization alter river ecosystems?
3. Why is damage to estuaries and coastlines especially devastating?

20.3 Pollution Degrades Habitats

Pollution is any chemical, physical, or biological change in the environment that harms living organisms. Pollution lowers the quality of air, water, and soil, threatening biodiversity worldwide.

A. Water Pollution Threatens Aquatic Life

A diverse array of pollutants affects rivers, lakes, and groundwater (table 20.1). For example, mining operations often release inorganic pollutants such as heavy metals or cyanide into the water, whereas shipping accidents cause oil spills.

Raw sewage can also be a major pollutant. In addition to carrying disease-causing organisms, sewage contains organic matter and nutrients such as nitrogen and phosphorus. When released into waterways, organic matter fuels the growth of bacteria, whose respiration depletes the water of oxygen. Fish and other organisms die. Meanwhile, in a process called **eutrophication,** the excess nutrients trigger the explosive growth of algae populations. The resulting algal blooms are unsightly. Moreover, when the algae die, the microbes that decompose their dead bodies further deplete dissolved oxygen in the water. The resulting anaerobic conditions kill many aquatic organisms, including fish.

Fertilizer and animal wastes that enter waterways also cause eutrophication, sometimes on a massive scale. For example, nutrients from croplands and feedlots along the Mississippi River drainage basin find their way into the Gulf of Mexico. There, the nutrients create a huge oxygen-depleted zone each summer near the seafloor off the coast of Louisiana (figure 20.5). The seasonal lack of oxygen in this so-called "dead zone" kills many animals, disrupting not only the Gulf's food web but also its economy: commercially important fish and shrimp cannot live in oxygen-depleted water.

Some pollutants seem deceptively harmless. Sediments, for example, reduce photosynthesis by blocking light penetration into water. Even heat can be a pollutant. Hot water discharged from power plants reduces the ability of a river to carry dissolved oxygen, harming fishes and other aquatic organisms.

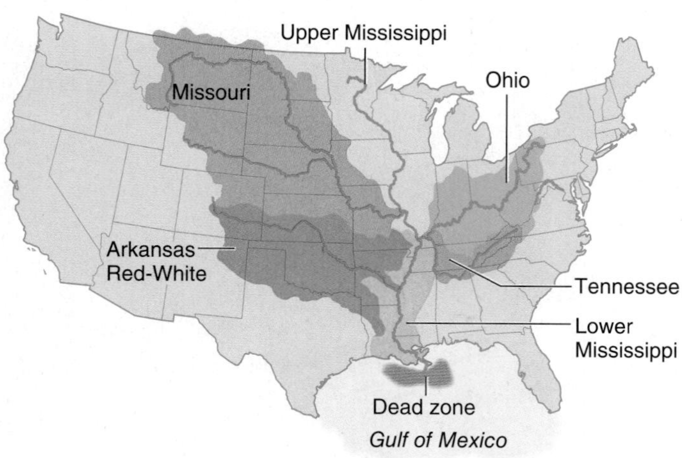

Figure 20.5 "Dead Zone." Nutrient-rich runoff enters the major river systems draining into the Mississippi River, then pours into the Gulf of Mexico. The resulting eutrophication causes a zone of seasonal oxygen depletion off the coast of Louisiana.

Toxic chemicals and trash also pollute the open ocean. For example, ocean currents have concentrated millions of tons of plastic in a huge area dubbed the "Great Pacific Garbage Patch." Floating just below the water surface in the northern Pacific Ocean are tiny pellets, called "nurdles," that form when plastic debris disintegrates. Fishes, sea turtles, and seabirds mistake the plastic for their natural food. The pellets can lodge in intestines and kill the animals outright, as the albatross in the chapter opening photo illustrates.

Alternatively, chemicals from the plastic may accumulate in animal tissues. The chemicals leached from plastic are a small subset of human-made **persistent organic pollutants,** carbon-containing molecules such as polychlorinated biphenyls (PCBs), polycyclic aromatic hydrocarbons (PAHs), and DDT. These substances contaminate ecosystems over long periods. Some of these compounds cause cancer; others are hormone mimics that disrupt reproduction (see chapter 30). Because they are not biodegradable, these fat-soluble chemicals become more concentrated in the highest levels of the food chain. This process, called biomagnification, accounts for the high concentrations of toxic chemicals in the fatty tissues of tunas, polar bears, and other top-level predators. ▸ biomagnification, p. 396

Organisms living in contaminated areas are often exposed to several pollutants at once (figure 20.6). A lake or river may contain not only garbage but also raw sewage, crude oil, gasoline, lead and other heavy metals, pesticides, and countless other toxic substances spilled from nearby factories. The toxic soup threatens not only human health but also the entire aquatic food chain.

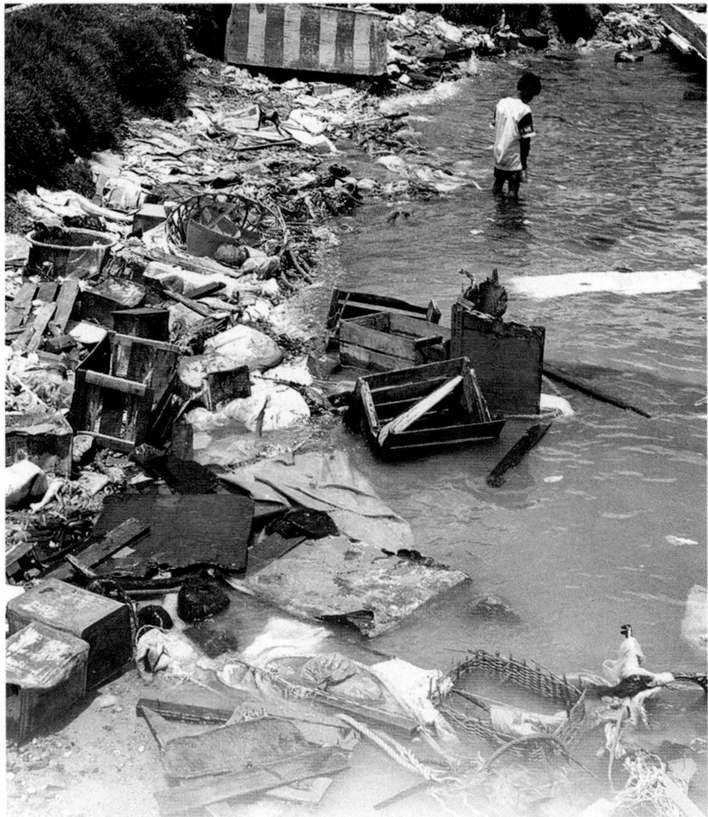

Figure 20.6 Water Pollution. A child wades in garbage-strewn water in Borneo. Heavily polluted waters are likely to be fouled with many contaminants at the same time.

B. Air Pollution Causes Many Types of Damage

Smog is a type of air pollution that forms a visible haze in the lower atmosphere (figure 20.7). Industrial smog occurs wherever power plants, factories, and households burn coal and oil. The resulting smoke and sulfur dioxide (SO_2) may form a dark haze. Photochemical smog forms when nitrogen oxides and emissions from vehicle tailpipes undergo chemical reactions in the presence of light, producing ozone (O_3) and other harmful chemicals that injure plants and cause severe respiratory problems in humans. Warm, sunny areas with heavy automobile traffic have the most photochemical smog, but winds may carry the pollutants to sparsely populated areas.

Other forms of air pollution are less visible but perhaps more harmful than smog. One example is **acid deposition:** acidic rain, snow, fog, dew, or dry particles. Burning fossil fuels release sulfur and nitrogen oxides (SO_2 and NO_2) into the atmosphere, where they mix with water and form sulfuric acid and nitric acid. These acids return to the Earth as acid deposition. ▸ pH scale, p. 32

Coal-burning power plants release the most sulfur and nitrogen oxides, although emissions of these pollutants have declined since the 1980s. In the United States, winds carry airborne acids hundreds of miles east and northeast of the power plants in the Midwest. Rainfall in the eastern United States therefore has an average pH of about 4.6, compared to a normal pH of 5.6. Acid deposition also affects the Pacific Northwest, the Rockies, Canada, Europe, East Asia, and the former Soviet Union.

Acid deposition harms both aquatic and terrestrial ecosystems. In a lake, excess acid can leach toxic metals such as aluminum or mercury from soils and sediments, killing aquatic plants, fish eggs, and other organisms. In a forest, acid deposition releases aluminum ions from soil. Plants that absorb the metals

Figure 20.7 Smog. Air pollution plagues many cities. This is Santiago, Chile.

Figure 20.8 Acid Deposition. Acid rain has severely damaged this fir forest in the Czech Republic.

in their roots may be stunted and unable to resist infection or to survive harsh weather (figure 20.8).

Chemicals that destroy ozone can also be extremely harmful air pollutants. Ozone is an atmospheric molecule with two faces. In photochemical smog at Earth's surface, ozone is harmful. In the upper atmosphere, however, the stratospheric **ozone layer** blocks damaging ultraviolet (UV) radiation from the sun.

In the past several decades, the ozone layer has thinned over parts of Asia, Europe, North America, Australia, and New Zealand; a "hole" in the ozone layer has formed over Antarctica (see the Burning Question on page 416). As the ozone layer thins, UV radiation increases at Earth's surface. In humans, exposure to UV radiation can cause skin cancer or cataracts. Ozone depletion may also indirectly contribute to species extinctions. For example, increasing UV radiation may be one of many factors causing amphibian populations to plummet.

What is causing the ozone hole? The main culprits are persistent, human-made chlorofluorocarbon (CFC) gases. These compounds were once used in refrigerants such as Freon, as propellants in aerosol cans, and to produce foamed plastics. They can persist for decades in the upper atmosphere, catalyzing chemical reactions that break down ozone. An international treaty signed in 1987, the Montreal Protocol, banned the use of CFCs. If all countries comply with the treaty, experts estimate that the ozone layer should recover by 2050.

20.3 Mastering Concepts

1. How do pollutants affect aquatic ecosystems?
2. What are major sources of smog and acid deposition?
3. What effects does the thinning ozone layer have on life?

20.4 Global Climate Change Alters and Shifts Habitats

We now turn to air pollutants with the potential to do the most harm of all: greenhouse gases. In the past, scientists debated whether human activities could actually change something as complex as Earth's overall climate. Now, the scientific consensus is clear: we can and do.

A. Greenhouse Gases Warm Earth's Surface

CO_2 is a colorless, odorless gas present in the atmosphere at a concentration of about 390 parts per million. Although it makes up a tiny fraction of the atmosphere, CO_2 is one of several gases that contribute to the **greenhouse effect,** an increase in surface temperature caused by heat-trapping gases in Earth's atmosphere. As illustrated in figure 20.9, sunlight passes through the atmosphere and reaches Earth's surface. Some of the energy is reflected, but some is absorbed and reradiated as heat. So-called "greenhouse gases" block the escape of this heat from the atmosphere, just as transparent panes of glass trap heat inside a greenhouse.

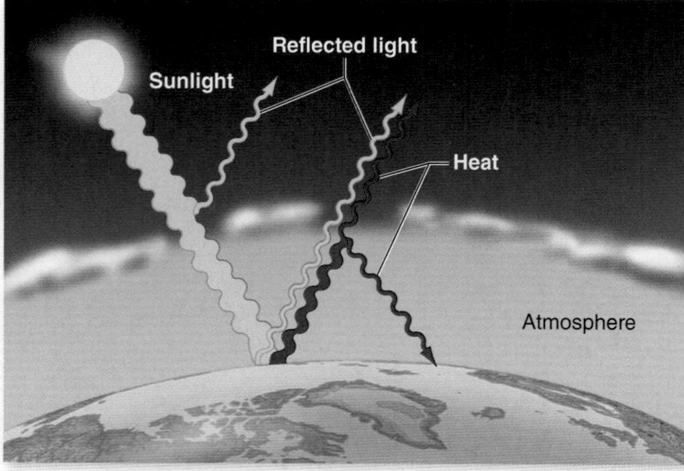

Figure 20.9 The Greenhouse Effect. Solar radiation heats Earth's surface. Some of this heat energy is reradiated to the atmosphere, but some is trapped near the surface by CO_2 and other greenhouse gases.

Carbon dioxide is one greenhouse gas; others include methane, nitrous oxide, and CFCs. These other gases actually trap heat much more efficiently than does CO_2, but because they are less abundant, they contribute only half as much to the greenhouse effect.

In a sense, the greenhouse effect supports life, because Earth's average temperature would be much lower without its blanket of greenhouse gases. But CO_2 has been steadily accumulating in the atmosphere since monitoring began in the 1950s (figure 20.10). The increase in atmospheric concentration of CO_2 is largely caused by burning fossil fuels such as coal, oil, and gas. Tropical deforestation and other combustion activities also add a share. All together, human activities release some 6 million metric tons of CO_2 into the atmosphere each year. Photosynthesis temporarily removes some of this carbon from the atmosphere. Overall, however, more CO_2 is added than is removed. ▸ carbon cycle, p. 400

This accumulation of CO_2—along with climbing levels of other greenhouse gases—was accompanied by an increase in average global temperatures in the twentieth century (see figure 20.10). Computer models predict that these trends will continue. Depending on the future concentration of CO_2 in the atmosphere, the Intergovernmental Panel on Climate Change estimates that the global average surface temperature could increase by anywhere from 1.8 to 4.0°C by the end of the twenty-first century, accompanied by a sea level rise of 18 to 59 centimeters.

Because Earth's average temperature is rising, this phenomenon is often called "global warming." In reality, however, some areas will become warmer and others will become cooler. **Global climate change** is therefore a more accurate term for past and future changes in Earth's weather patterns.

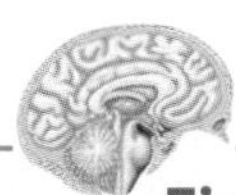

Figure It Out

Using the graph in figure 20.10, calculate the percent increase in atmospheric CO_2 concentration between 1960 and today.

Answer: 390/315 = 1.2; the CO_2 concentration is 20% higher today.

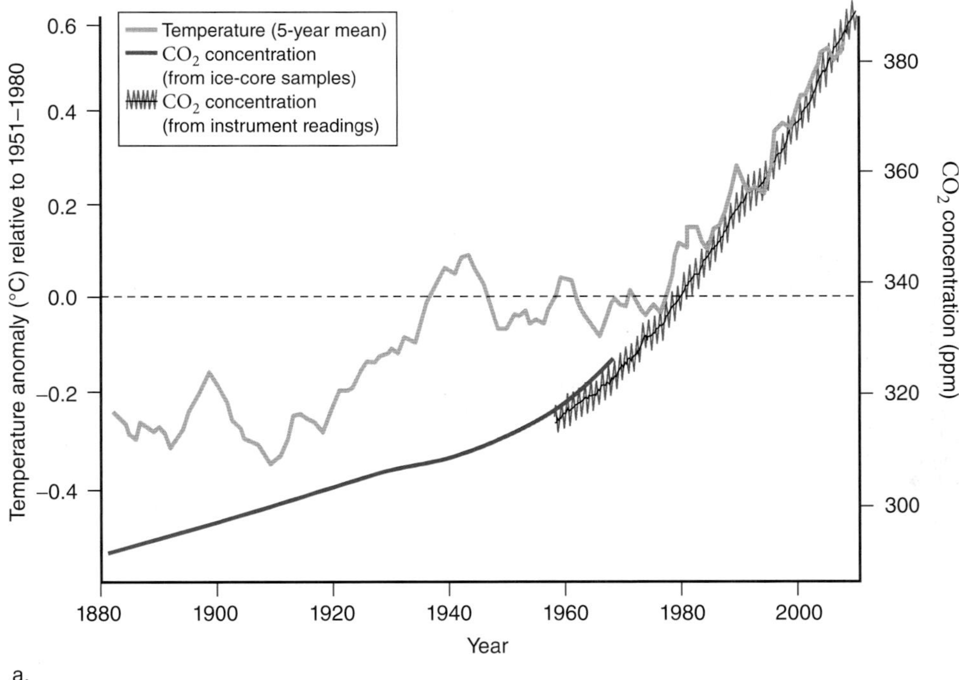

a.

b.

Figure 20.10 **CO_2 and Global Average Temperature.** (a) Measures of CO_2 concentrations from ice cores and instrument readings at Mauna Loa, Hawaii, show that CO_2 continues to accumulate. At the same time, the average global temperature has also increased. (b) Coal-fired power plants are among the main culprits in the rising levels of CO_2.
Sources of data: NOAA Earth System Research Laboratory; NASA Goddard Institute for Space Studies Surface Temperature Analysis.

Burning Questions

What does the ozone hole have to do with global climate change?

The two satellite images to the right show the change in the Antarctic ozone hole over the last three decades. As this hole grows, scientists are recording rising global temperatures. But are these two observations related?

Many people confuse global climate change and the ozone hole. These two problems are largely separate, but they do share two common threads. First, the chlorofluorocarbon gases that deplete the ozone layer are also greenhouse gases, contributing to a warmer atmosphere. Second, the greenhouse effect may cause the hole in the ozone layer to grow. A thick, heat-trapping "blanket" of greenhouse gases in the lowest part of the atmosphere means less heat reaches the stratosphere, where the ozone layer is. A cooler stratosphere, in turn, extends the time that stratospheric clouds blanket the polar regions in winter. These clouds of ice and nitric acid speed the chemical reactions that deplete stratospheric ozone.

Submit your burning question to:
marielle_hoefnagels@mcgraw-hill.com

Figure 20.11 Shrinking Ice. A polar bear breaks through a thin layer of ice in the Arctic Ocean.

B. Global Climate Change Has Severe Consequences

An overall increase of 1.8 to 4.0°C may seem too small to make much difference. Yet the gradual warming that has already occurred has been associated with many measurable effects, including the shrinking of alpine glaciers and polar ice sheets (figure 20.11). When floating sea ice melts, its effect on sea level is minimal (just as ice melting in a full glass of lemonade does not cause the liquid to overflow). However, the loss of ice from Greenland and Antarctica has contributed to a rise in sea level, which could eventually alter the ocean ecosystem, drive rare species to extinction, and flood coastal cities.

Weather conditions in tropical and temperate regions are also changing, thanks in part to a rise in sea surface temperature. In the tropics, warmer water means higher winds and more evaporation, which increases the amount of rainfall in a severe storm. In dry areas, on the other hand, global climate change may mean more intense and longer droughts, fewer cold snaps, and more heat waves.

These changes kill some organisms outright, stress others, or trigger migrations to higher latitudes or higher elevations. Warming in Yosemite National Park, for example, has driven ground squirrels and other small mammals to cooler mountaintop habitats. Elsewhere, the ranges of at least 34 species of butterflies are moving northward. At the southern ends of their ranges, where temperatures are rising, some species have become locally extinct. In addition, scientists are tracking events known to occur at the same time each year. In the United Kingdom, butterflies are emerging and amphibians are mating a few days earlier than usual; in North America, many plants are flowering and birds are migrating earlier.

Continued climate change will affect not only wild organisms but also agriculture and public health. Growing seasons in temperate areas are lengthening, and the southern United States may become too dry to sustain many traditional crops. Drought-related water shortages may affect more than a billion people worldwide. Tropical diseases such as malaria, African sleeping sickness, dengue fever, and river blindness may move into temperate areas.

Ocean life is also vulnerable to CO_2 accumulation and global climate change. One problem is that the buildup of CO_2 causes ocean water to become more acidic. The lowered pH causes the calcium carbonate shells of oysters, clams, and other mollusks to dissolve, along with the exoskeletons of coral animals. At the same time, high sea temperatures threaten coral reefs by triggering coral bleaching.

20.4 Mastering Concepts

1. Why is CO_2 accumulating in Earth's atmosphere?
2. Describe how and why Earth's climate has changed during the past century.
3. How does global climate change threaten biodiversity?

20.5 Exotic Invaders and Overexploitation Devastate Many Species

In addition to habitat destruction, pollution, and global climate change, two other threats to biodiversity are invasive species and overexploitation.

A. Invasive Species Displace Native Organisms

An introduced species (also called a nonnative, alien, or exotic species) is one that humans bring to an area where it did not previously exist. When we move from one location to another, we often bring along our pets, crops, livestock, and ornamental plants. We also unintentionally introduce microorganisms, parasites, and stowaways such as rodents and insects on ships, cars, and planes.

This transport may be harmless. Many introduced species die without damaging anything, and even if they do survive in their new homes, they may not cause problems. For example, the house sparrow was introduced to the United States from Europe in the 1850s. Although it has spread throughout the North American continent, it has not caused obvious ecological problems. In addition, at least 5000 nonnative plant species live in U.S. ecosystems, introduced from agriculture and urbanization. Most have apparently done no harm.

If a nonnative species becomes invasive, however, it can cause immense destruction (figure 20.12). To be considered **invasive,** an introduced species must breed in its new location and spread widely from the original point of introduction. In addition, according to some definitions, the species must harm the environment, human health, or the economy. Of every 100 species introduced, only one persists to take over a niche. Nonetheless, the Global Invasive Species Database lists 498 invasive plants, animals, and microorganisms in the United States alone; many more invasive species occur worldwide.

Examples of invasive species in North America include the following:

- European starlings are birds that were released in New York City's Central Park in 1890. Huge flocks of starlings now reside all across North America, ruining crops and fouling cities with their droppings.
- The marine toad is a voracious omnivore that competes with and consumes native amphibians in Florida.
- Asian carp are large, fast-breeding fish that were originally introduced to catfish ponds in the South but have since spread along the Mississippi River toward the Great Lakes. They eat algae voraciously, outcompeting other plankton-eaters for food.
- Hungry caterpillars of the gypsy moth strip the foliage from hundreds of species of hardwood trees in North America (see figure 20.12a).
- Kudzu is a fast-growing plant that smothers native plants in the southeastern United States (see figure 20.12b).
- Hydrilla is an aquatic plant that alters nutrient cycles, affects aquatic animals, and reduces recreational use of lakes and rivers.

Figure 20.12 Invasive Species. (a) Gypsy moths were introduced to the United States from Europe or Asia in the late 1860s. These gypsy moth caterpillars are eating oak leaves. (b) An invasive population of kudzu in Virginia blankets every surface in sight.

Figure 20.13 Unsustainable Harvest. Customs officials in Lhasa, the capital of Tibet, inspect confiscated tiger, leopard, and otter skins. Trade in these skins is illegal, yet poaching remains one of the main threats to mammal populations in Asia.

- Purple loosestrife is a wetland plant that displaces native plants, threatening the turtles and other animals that would otherwise eat them.
- Introduced fungi have all but eradicated American chestnut and American elm trees.

When an invasion does occur, the harm may be ecological and economic. A nonnative species not only changes the composition of a community but also may carry diseases that spread to native species. The economic costs include everything from the purchase of herbicides that kill invasive weeds, to the loss of grain eaten by hungry birds and rodents, to declining tax revenue when invasive aquatic plants interfere with boating and recreation.

B. Overexploitation Can Drive Species to Extinction

Another cause of species extinction is **overexploitation:** harvesting a species faster than it can reproduce (figure 20.13). The market for exotic pets, for example, is harming populations of many species of mammals, birds, snakes, lizards, amphibians, and fishes.

Many of the most famous examples of species extinctions result from overhunting of terrestrial animals. The dodo, for example, was a flightless bird that once lived on the Indian Ocean island of Mauritius. In the late seventeenth century, humans hunted the dodo for food while introducing other species to the island. The dodo soon went extinct. In the United States, commercial-scale hunting nearly drove the American bison to extinction in the 1800s. The passenger pigeon and Carolina parakeet did go extinct in the 1900s, victims of overhunting and habitat destruction.

The best illustration of widespread overexploitation is the recent collapse of ocean fisheries (see section 12.8). Since the 1950s, some 90% of the world's large, predatory ocean fishes have disappeared, including tuna, flounder, halibut, swordfish, and cod. Superefficient fishing boats harvest the adults faster than the fishes can reproduce. Moreover, fishing pressure has shifted to other species as predatory fishes have vanished. Fishing equipment scrapes and scours the seafloor, destroying habitat for many other species. Meanwhile, many marine mammals, seabirds, sea turtles, and nontarget fish species are killed accidentally as they are caught up in the nets set for the target species (figure 20.14). Even seafood farms may contribute to the problem. Ocean fishes are fed to farmed shrimp and salmon, depleting marine food webs.

Improved management practices can help an overharvested population recover its numbers. Consider, for example, the Chesapeake Bay blue crab. The federal government declared the crab fishery a disaster in 2008. The state of Virginia had already stopped issuing new commercial crabbing licenses in the 1990s, but in 2009, the state began buying back existing licenses as well. The overall goal of this approach, combined with other new regulations, is to reduce pressure on the dwindling number of crabs, which have been depleted not only by overharvesting but also by pollution and habitat loss. Thanks to these new management practices, the blue crab population has begun to rebound.

Figure 20.14 Bycatch. Nontarget animals sometimes get caught in nets meant for other species. Fishermen often discard these "bycatch" animals, dead or alive.

20.5 Mastering Concepts

1. What features characterize an invasive species?
2. How do invasive species disrupt ecosystems?
3. List examples of species declines caused by overexploitation.

20.6 Some Biodiversity May Be Recoverable

As the human population continues to grow, pressure on natural resources will only increase. One key to reversing environmental decline will therefore be to slow the growth of the human population. In addition, although some species are gone forever, humans may have the power to undo some of our past mistakes (see this chapter's Why We Care box). For example, thanks to the Endangered Species Act of 1973, some species that faced extinction, such as the bald eagle, have recovered (figure 20.15).

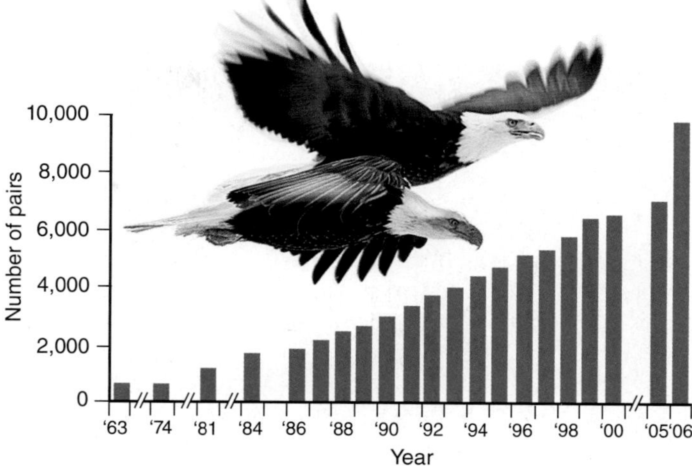

Figure 20.15 Good News for Bald Eagles. After nearing extinction in the 1960s, bald eagles have made a steady recovery. Federal officials removed the bird from the endangered species list in 2007.

A. Protecting and Restoring Habitat Saves Many Species at Once

One important conservation tool is to set aside parks, wildlife refuges, and other natural areas and to protect them from destruction, invasive species, and hunting. Preserving critical habitat is a good conservation tool because it saves not just one endangered species but also the many other species that share its habitat. For example, the red-cockaded woodpecker is native to the southeastern United States, where it builds its nest in a cavity that it excavates high on the trunk of a mature pine tree. Although most of its preferred habitat has been logged, private property owners and the government have cooperated to save some of the remaining habitat. Other animals that use the nesting cavities, including birds, mammals, snakes, amphibians, and insects, also benefit from the woodpecker recovery plan.

Reversing habitat destruction is a second conservation tool. Major restoration projects show that recovery, although costly and difficult, may yet reverse some species declines. For example, human activities have damaged Florida's Everglades region for more than a century. Over many decades, engineers built a massive system of canals, levees, and pumps that direct

Why We Care | Environmental Legislation

Since the creation of the Environmental Protection Agency in 1970, Congress has passed laws to combat some of the worst environmental problems in the United States. Below are a few major pieces of environmental legislation:

- The Endangered Species Act of 1973 requires that the U.S. Secretary of the Interior identify threatened and endangered species. The overall goals are to prevent extinction and to help endangered species recover their numbers. Since the act was implemented, more than 575 species of vertebrate and invertebrate animals and nearly 750 species of plants and lichens have been classified as threatened or endangered. Only a few dozen species have been removed from the list because they have either recovered or become extinct, or because new information revealed that their populations are larger than had been thought.
- The Clean Air Act, passed in 1970 and amended several times since, sets minimum air quality standards for many types of air pollutants. Since 1970, emissions of nitrogen and sulfur oxides, lead, carbon monoxide, and other pollutants have declined, leading to significant improvements in air quality.
- Among other provisions, the Clean Water Act of 1972 required nearly every city to build and maintain a sewage treatment plant, drastically reducing discharge of raw sewage into rivers and lakes. The 1987 Water Quality Act followed up on the Clean Water Act, regulating water pollution from industry, agricultural runoff, overflow from sewage treatment plants during storms, and runoff from city streets. Many of the nation's surface waters have recovered from past unregulated discharge of phosphorus, other nutrients, and toxic chemicals.

water to agricultural and urban areas. These changes have altered the natural course of the rivers and starved the wetlands of fresh water. Dozens of species have become endangered. But an ambitious restoration project is underway. One part of the plan is to gradually restore flow to 69 kilometers of the Kissimmee River's channel and the surrounding floodplain wetlands. Native vegetation, waterfowl, aquatic invertebrates, and fishes have already returned to areas where the project is complete.

On a smaller scale, we can also help species bypass degraded habitats by supplying wildlife corridors through housing developments or building "fish ladders" over dams (figure 20.16).

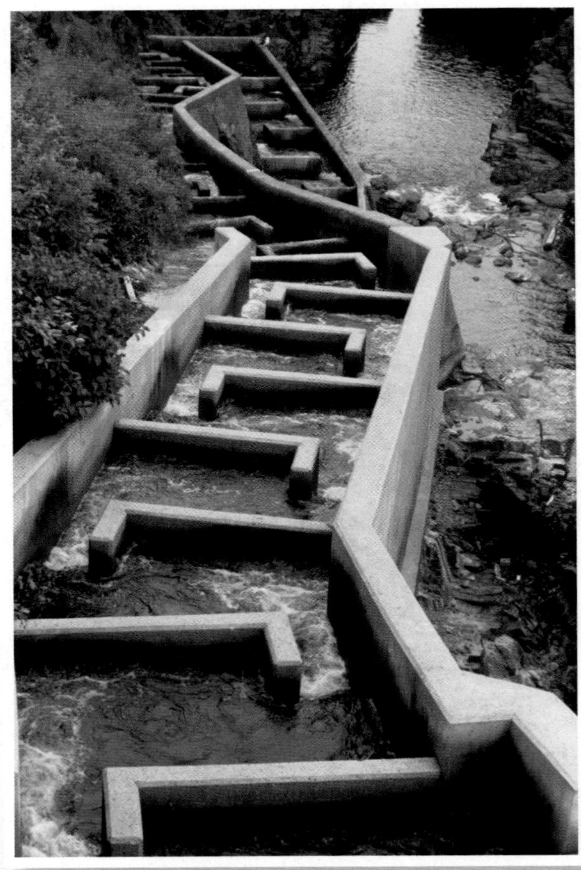

Figure 20.16 Taking the High Road. Fish use "ladders" such as this one to migrate over dams.

B. Some Conservation Tools Target Individual Species

One straightforward way to save a species is to protect its individuals. For example, it is illegal to collect endangered carnivorous plants such as Venus flytraps and pitcher plants in the wild. In the ocean, northern and southern right whales were nearly hunted to extinction for their blubber in the 1800s. They remain endangered, but it is now illegal to kill them. Likewise, the catastrophic decline of Atlantic cod in the past few decades prompted the closure of some fisheries off Newfoundland's coast, along with strict quotas for the overall catch. Whether conservation efforts are on time to save the cod fishery remains to be seen.

Predator control programs can also help. For example, rats, weasels, dogs, and other predators brought by European settlers endanger the great spotted kiwi, a flightless bird native to New Zealand. Removing these predators from nature preserves has made life much easier for the endangered kiwis.

In areas where wildlife poaching is a problem, changing the local economic incentives can be a powerful conservation tool. Poaching is profitable if a dead animal is worth more money than a live one in its natural habitat. But ecotourism can turn this economic calculation on its head. By attracting visitors who pay to see endangered animals, conservation may bring in more money than poaching. A black rhino conservation program in Namibia, for example, hires former poachers as armed guards to protect the animals from hunters. Meanwhile, guides lead tourists, who pay to see rhinos in the wild (figure 20.17).

Protective laws and predator control programs may help halt the decline of a threatened species, but sometimes it is possible to boost reproduction as well. A captive breeding program can be very useful. Biologists can capture adults from the wild, allow them to reproduce in captivity, then nurture and protect

Figure 20.17 Black Rhino. Ecotourism may provide some hope for the survival of the endangered black rhinoceros.

the young until they are old enough to return to their native habitat. The California condor, red wolf, and black-footed ferret are notable examples. But this solution does not work for species whose habitat is gone (submerged after dam construction, for example) or still under the same pressures that threatened the species in the first place.

The biotechnology revolution plays a role in yet another approach to species conservation. In one project, researchers are using DNA to identify bison whose genes are uncontaminated with those of domesticated cattle. The "purest" bison are set aside as the best candidates for reestablishing wild bison herds. In the future, it may even be possible to recover extinct species using DNA extracted from preserved specimens. Scientists who are sequencing DNA from a frozen baby mammoth, for example, may one day be able to recreate a live mammoth by using a cloning technique similar to the one used to make Dolly the sheep. One possible approach would be to replace the DNA in a fertilized elephant egg with mammoth DNA and then implant the resulting embryo into an elephant's uterus. After gestation, a woolly mammoth would be born—some 10,000 years after its species went extinct. ▸ cloning, p. 208

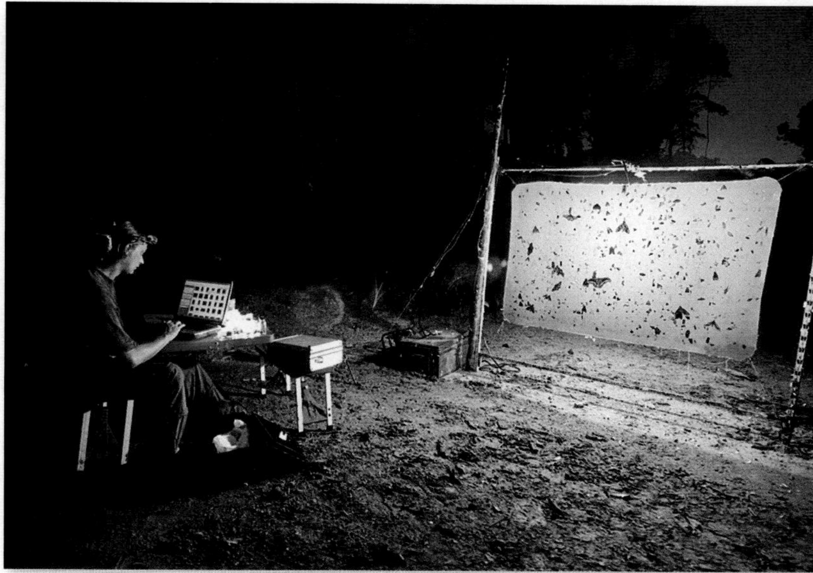

Figure 20.18 Cataloging Insect Diversity. This researcher is using a lamp and a white sheet to attract and study nocturnal insects in a tropical rain forest in French Guiana.

C. Conserving Biodiversity Involves Scientists and Ordinary Citizens

Regardless of which tools are used to preserve biodiversity, all conservation efforts require a scientific approach. To get a true measure of Earth's biodiversity, taxonomists must continue to catalog all organisms, not just vertebrates and plants (figure 20.18). Evolutionary biologists must continue to analyze the relationships among all species. Preserving biodiversity also requires an understanding of which species need help, whether current conservation efforts are working, and the consequences to ecosystems as species disappear.

But not every important question has a scientific answer. Are the only species worth saving the photogenic ones, such as giant pandas? Or do we also commit to saving the worms, algae, bacteria, and fungi so essential to global ecology? How much money should we spend on conservation? Should developed countries help poor nations with their efforts? How do we balance the need for conservation with the need for economic growth? Which of the tangle of threads that tie all life together should we sacrifice to other interests?

It would be very difficult to halt life on Earth completely, short of a global catastrophe such as a meteor collision or a nuclear holocaust. Just the presence of life, however, does not guarantee that the surviving species will have the diversity that humans value. It is safest to try to protect the remaining resources for the future, while maintaining a reasonable standard of living for all people. Scientists and politicians, as well as ordinary citizens, share this heavy burden. Part of the solution lies within you and how you choose to live (see the Burning Question on page 422). Do whatever you can to preserve the diversity of life, for in diversity lies resiliency and the future of life on Earth.

20.6 Mastering Concepts

1. How does human population growth affect conservation biology?
2. List and describe the tools that conservation biologists use to preserve biodiversity.
3. How can scientists, governments, and ordinary citizens work together for conservation?

Burning Questions

What can an ordinary person do to help the environment?

Even ordinary citizens can join forces to clean and preserve the environment. Together, countless small actions can make a big difference. Here are a few ideas:

- Conserve energy. Replace conventional light bulbs with compact fluorescent bulbs, recycle, carpool, drive a fuel-efficient car, ride a bicycle, or turn down the thermostat. Pouring filtered tap water into a reusable bottle rather than buying bottled water not only saves energy but also reduces landfill waste.
- Check with your electric company to see whether you can select renewable energy sources, such as wind or solar energy.
- Buy less stuff. Manufacturing, packaging, transporting, and storing consumer goods use energy and raw materials and produce waste. The less you buy, the fewer resources you consume and the less waste you discard.
- Use what you buy. Energy and raw materials go to waste if you don't end up using the food and consumer goods you buy.
- Choose products that reflect sustainable practices. Buying organic food, for example, reduces the use of pesticides in agriculture. Shade-grown coffee plantations provide habitat for a wide variety of tropical plants and animals. Download a Seafood Watch guide for your area to learn which entrées to choose and which to avoid. Lumber and paper certified by the nonprofit Forest Stewardship Council have been harvested and produced in an environmentally responsible way.
- Eat less meat, dairy, and eggs. Farm animals and their manure emit copious greenhouse gases—especially methane—into the atmosphere. Moreover, eating lower on the food chain is energy-efficient (see section 19.6).
- Buy local. Reduce the transportation and storage costs of food by shopping close to home and by selecting produce that is in season and locally grown.
- Pay attention to what you discard and pour down the drain. Pharmaceutical drugs, petroleum products, and harsh chemicals can end up in waterways and harm ecosystems.
- If you garden, avoid invasive species. Instead, choose native plant species that attract wildlife.
- Don't buy rare or exotic species as pets.
- Donate time or money to groups that save critical habitats.
- Encourage your local government to set aside land for parks.
- Write to state and federal lawmakers to ask them to support legislation that can help protect the environment. The house.gov and senate.gov websites have contact information for your House and Senate representatives.

Submit your burning question to:
marielle_hoefnagels@mcgraw-hill.com

Investigating Life

20.7 The Case of the Missing Frogs: Is Climate the Culprit?

With so many different threats to biodiversity, how can we ever know what drives a species to extinction? It's one thing to document that a species has vanished; it's another thing to explain how it happened. Not knowing what has gone wrong in the past makes it difficult to prevent future extinctions.

The Question: The global decline of amphibians such as frogs and salamanders has been especially difficult to unravel. According to some estimates, populations of about one third of the world's amphibian species have declined. Hundreds of species are critically endangered, and hundreds more have already vanished. Researchers have pointed at pollution, habitat loss, and overhunting as possible culprits. But what causes extinctions in pristine habitats and in species that humans do not hunt for food or medicine? ▸ amphibians, p. 344

The Approach: Harlequin frogs in the genus *Atelopus* offer a chance to start answering this question. Compared with other amphibians, their populations are relatively easy to monitor. Harlequin frogs are brightly colored and active during the day, so they are much easier to observe than animals that either blend in with their surroundings or are active at night.

A multinational research team, led by J. Alan Pounds of the Monteverde Cloud Forest Preserve and Tropical Science Center in Costa Rica, examined a database that cataloged the last reported sightings of more than 100 species of harlequin frogs in mountainous regions of Central and South America. Many had not been observed since the 1980s or 1990s and were apparently extinct. The researchers found that none of the doomed species was from lowland areas (elevation less than 200 meters). Instead, the most vulnerable species occupied the middle elevations, between 1000 and 2400 meters (figure 20.19).

The researchers then focused on extinctions of harlequin frogs in one study area, Costa Rica's Monteverde Cloud Forest Preserve. This area is perpetually shrouded in fog from an elevation of about 1500 meters to about 1850 meters, which closely overlaps the habitats of the amphibians that were most likely to go extinct.

Pounds and his team scrutinized weather station records collected at Monteverde between 1977 and 1997. They learned that days had gotten cooler and nights had gotten warmer during those two decades (figure 20.20). This made sense. Air temperatures and sea surface temperatures were climbing throughout the tropics at that time, causing more evaporation and therefore more clouds. The researchers surmised that the thicker cloud cover blocked the sun during the day but trapped heat close to the surface at night.

How did these changes affect the frogs? According to Pounds and his team, the new conditions made the amphibians more susceptible to a skin disease caused by a type of fungus called a chytrid (see figure 15.34). This fungus has an optimal growth temperature that matches the cooler days and warmer nights at Monteverde. Furthermore, the chytrid dies if the temperature climbs above 30°C. The additional cloud cover may have meant fewer sunny spots where the frogs could raise their skin temperatures enough to kill the fungi. Without this defense, perhaps the chytrids finally gained the advantage over their amphibian hosts, driving many to extinction.

The Conclusion: Overall, the researchers concluded that higher temperatures in the tropics created conditions that favored the spread of skin disease, producing a wave of amphibian extinctions. According to Pounds, "The disease was the bullet killing the frogs, but climate was pulling the trigger." Nevertheless, one critical link in this chain of events is missing: no one knows whether the frogs that vanished in recent decades actually died from the chytrid. Without evidence of a direct cause-and-effect relationship, the meaning of this study remains open to debate.

This research illustrates the difficulty that scientists will face in assessing the biological effects of global climate change. Clearly, Earth's average temperature is rising, local weather patterns are shifting, and habitats are changing. Will it ever be possible to "connect the dots," linking global climate change directly to species extinctions? Scientists around the globe continue to study these issues, knowing that the first step toward preserving biodiversity is to understand what affects it.

Pounds, J. Alan, Martín R. Bustamante, Luis A. Coloma, et al. 2006. Widespread amphibian extinctions from epidemic disease driven by global warming. *Nature,* vol. 439, pages 161–167.

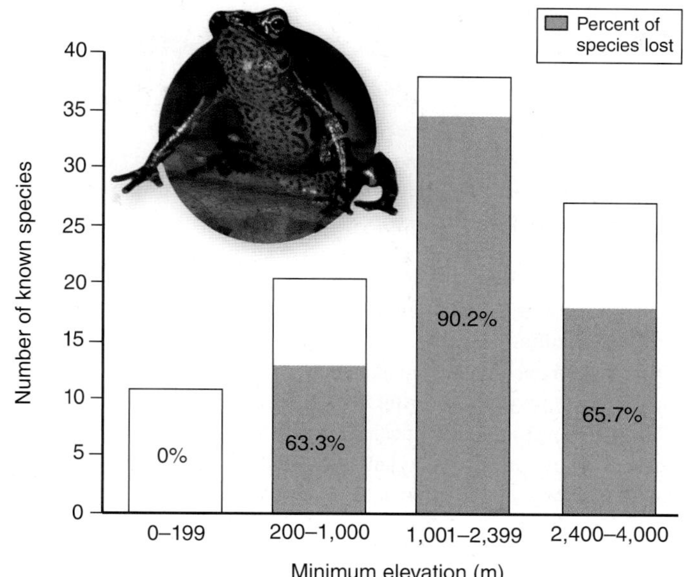

Figure 20.19 Elevation Matters. In Central and South America, the harlequin frogs at middle elevations are at greatest risk of extinction. The inset shows a Pebas stubfoot toad, one of many vulnerable amphibian species.

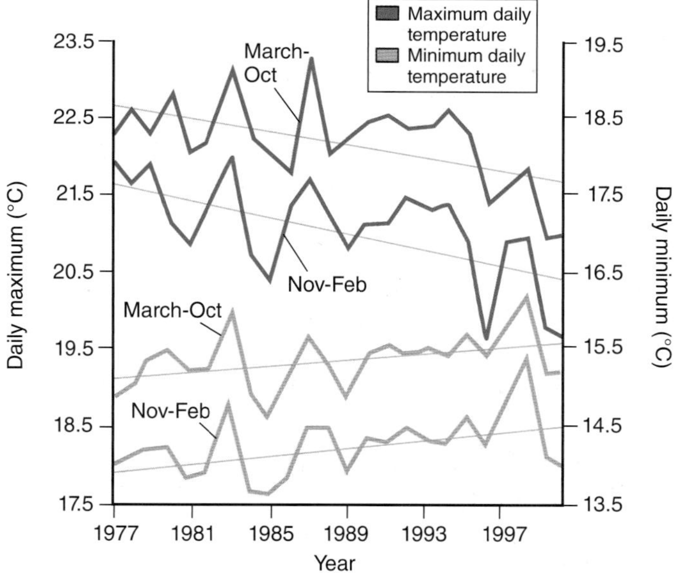

Figure 20.20 Changing Weather. Days are getting cooler and nights are getting warmer at the Monteverde Cloud Forest Preserve in Costa Rica.

20.7 Mastering Concepts

1. Summarize the evidence that climate change is a factor in the extinction of harlequin frogs.
2. Other than climate change, what is an alternative hypothesis that could explain the extinction of harlequin frogs? How would you test your hypothesis?

Chapter Summary

20.1 Earth's Biodiversity Is Dwindling

- **Biodiversity** means the variety of life on Earth.
- Increasing numbers of species are threatened with **extinction** or are **endangered** or **vulnerable. Conservation biologists** study and attempt to preserve biodiversity.

20.2 Many Human Activities Destroy Habitats

- Prairies and other grasslands have been destroyed, usually to make room for crops. Agriculture, logging, and urbanization contribute to **deforestation**.
- Drought and overgrazing are expanding Earth's deserts. At the same time, native desert habitats are being lost to urbanization.
- Dams and levees alter the species that live in and near rivers.
- Preserving estuaries is important because they are breeding grounds for many species.

20.3 Pollution Degrades Habitats

- **Pollution** is any environmental change that harms living organisms.

A. Water Pollution Threatens Aquatic Life

- Excessive nutrient levels cause **eutrophication.** Sediments and heat also pollute aquatic ecosystems.
- Water and sediments can be contaminated by toxic substances such as **persistent organic pollutants,** heavy metals, spilled oil, and plastics.

B. Air Pollution Causes Many Types of Damage

- Air pollutants include heavy metals and emissions from fossil fuel combustion. Some of these pollutants form photochemical **smog.**
- Nitric and sulfuric acids form in the atmosphere and return to Earth as **acid deposition.**
- Use of chlorofluorocarbon compounds (CFCs) has thinned the atmosphere's **ozone layer,** which protects life from damaging ultraviolet radiation.

20.4 Global Climate Change Alters and Shifts Habitats

A. Greenhouse Gases Warm Earth's Surface

- Human activities produce CO_2 and other gases that trap heat near Earth's surface, producing the **greenhouse effect.**
- This accumulation of greenhouse gases is causing Earth's average temperature to rise. The result is **global climate change.**

B. Global Climate Change Has Severe Consequences

- As the temperature increases, polar ice is melting, sea level is rising, coral reefs are declining, and species ranges are shifting.

20.5 Exotic Invaders and Overexploitation Devastate Many Species

A. Invasive Species Displace Native Organisms

- **Invasive** species consume or outcompete native organisms.

B. Overexploitation Can Drive Species to Extinction

- **Overexploitation** means individuals are harvested faster than they can reproduce. High fishing pressure puts global fisheries in danger of collapse.

20.6 Some Biodiversity May Be Recoverable

A. Protecting and Restoring Habitat Saves Many Species at Once

- Protected reserves, habitat restoration, and wildlife corridors are conservation tools that protect multiple species simultaneously.

B. Some Conservation Tools Target Individual Species

- Harvest management, predator exclusion, economic incentives, captive breeding programs, and biotechnology can help save one species at a time.

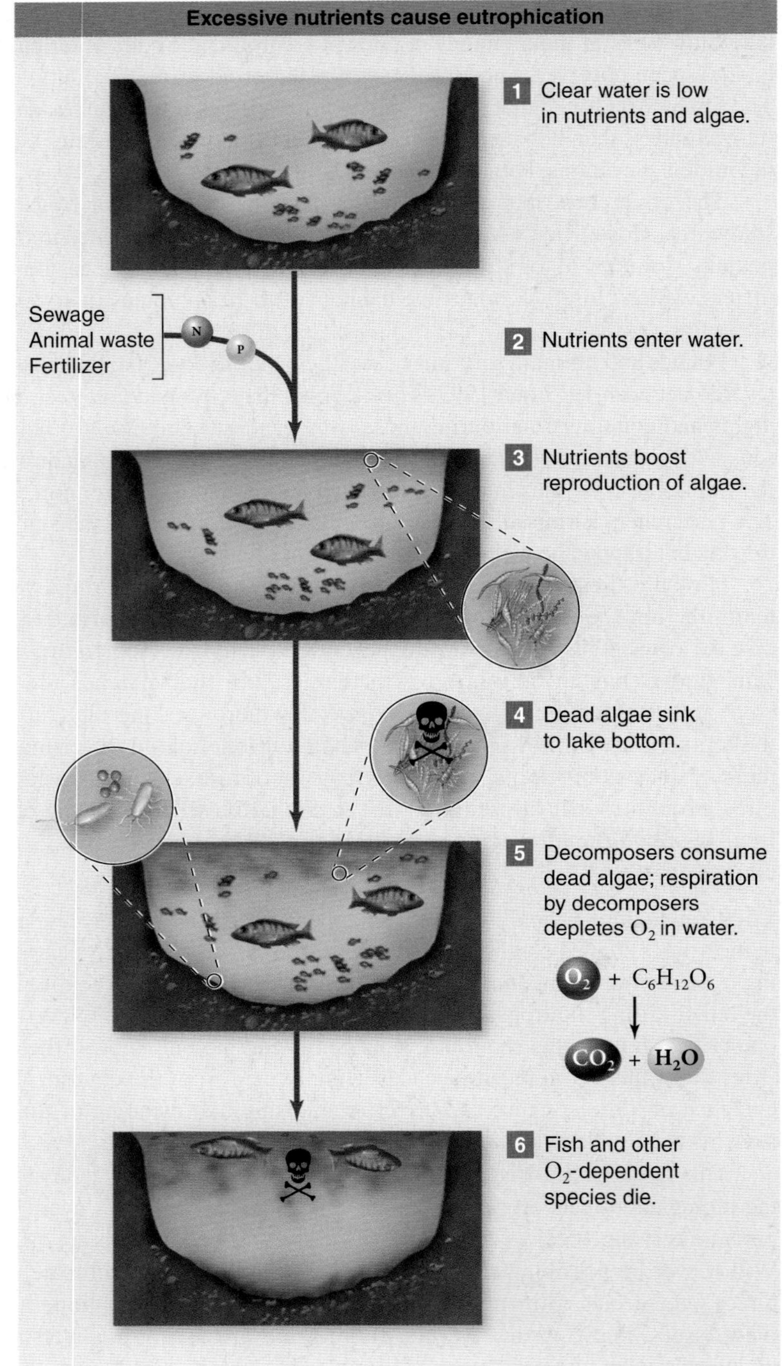
Excessive nutrients cause eutrophication
1 Clear water is low in nutrients and algae.
Sewage
Animal waste
Fertilizer
N
P
2 Nutrients enter water.
3 Nutrients boost reproduction of algae.
4 Dead algae sink to lake bottom.
5 Decomposers consume dead algae; respiration by decomposers depletes O_2 in water.
O_2 + $C_6H_{12}O_6$
CO_2 + H_2O
6 Fish and other O_2-dependent species die.

C. Conserving Biodiversity Involves Scientists and Ordinary Citizens

- Conservation biologists can monitor biodiversity trends and recommend strategies for saving threatened species, but everyone can choose actions that preserve or deplete biodiversity.

20.7 Investigating Life: The Case of the Missing Frogs: Is Climate the Culprit?

- Researchers studying the disappearance of amphibians in Central and South America have suggested a direct link to climate change.
- Increasing cloud cover has altered temperatures in a way that favors the spread of a fungus that infects frogs.

Multiple Choice Questions

1. Which of the following is not one of the main causes of today's biodiversity crisis?
   a. Natural disasters, such as earthquakes
   b. Habitat destruction and degradation
   c. Overexploitation
   d. Introduction of nonnative species
2. What is the connection between agriculture in the midwestern United States and the Gulf of Mexico's "dead zone"?
   a. Pesticides from farmlands are killing ocean life.
   b. Nutrient enrichment causes oxygen depletion in the waters of the Gulf.
   c. River sediments block out the light needed for photosynthesis in the Gulf.
   d. Farmlands use up all of the nitrogen in the water, so the Gulf waters are starved for nutrients.
3. How does destruction of the ozone layer affect life on Earth?
   a. It alters global temperatures.
   b. It leads to DNA damage.
   c. It changes the spectrum of light reaching the surface of the Earth.
   d. It reduces the amount of O_2 in the atmosphere.
4. What is the greenhouse effect?
   a. The filtering of specific wavelengths of light by Earth's atmosphere
   b. The increase in global plant growth due to enhanced photosynthesis
   c. The trapping of heat by gases in the atmosphere
   d. The reduction in the amount of CO_2 in Earth's atmosphere
5. Which conservation tool is likely to save the most species at the same time?
   a. Captive breeding program
   b. Establishing a new national park
   c. Excluding predators from a protected reserve
   d. A law that prohibits removing a rare plant species from its habitat
6. What might limit the effectiveness of a captive breeding program for the restoration of an extremely rare endangered species?
   a. A very rare species has limited genetic diversity.
   b. Captive breeding programs do not preserve the habitat of an organism.
   c. Not all animals will breed in captivity.
   d. All of the above are correct.

Write It Out

1. List the main threats to biodiversity worldwide.
2. Which human activities promote habitat destruction?
3. Visit the waterfootprint.org website to see how much water is required to produce various foods and beverages. Why might it be important for an individual to choose products with a low water footprint?
4. How does the combustion of fossil fuels influence such different phenomena as acid deposition and global climate change?
5. In what ways is the greenhouse effect both beneficial and detrimental?
6. Explain the logic behind planting trees to reduce global climate change.
7. Why are invasive species harmful?
8. List three ways you can alter your lifestyle to promote conservation.
9. Search the Internet for information on the Convention on Biological Diversity and on the international agreement called CITES. How does each approach tackle the biodiversity crisis on a global scale?
10. Give an example of an environmental problem that can immediately reduce biodiversity and one that has a delayed effect.

Pull It Together

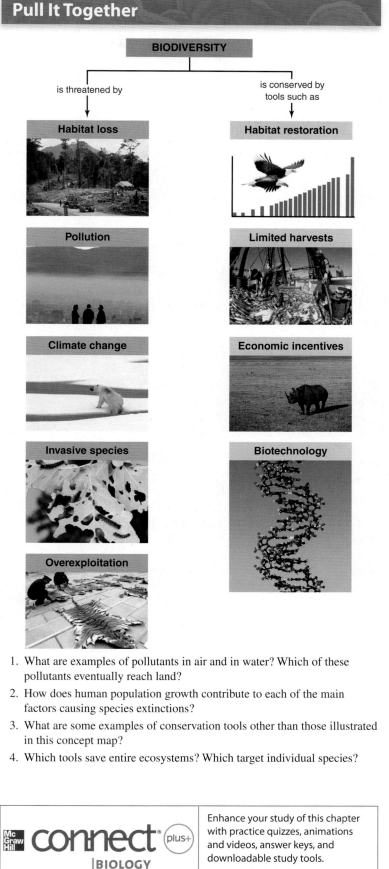

1. What are examples of pollutants in air and in water? Which of these pollutants eventually reach land?
2. How does human population growth contribute to each of the main factors causing species extinctions?
3. What are some examples of conservation tools other than those illustrated in this concept map?
4. Which tools save entire ecosystems? Which target individual species?

UNIT 5 Plant Physiology

21 Plant Form and Function

A Taste for Flies. The leaves of the Venus flytrap can snap shut to catch prey.

Learning Outline

Learn How to Learn

Studying in Groups

Study groups offer a great way to learn from other students, but they can also dissolve into social events that accomplish little real work. Of course, your choice of study partners makes a huge difference, so try to pick people who are at least as serious as you are about learning. To stay focused, plan activities that are well-suited for groups. For example, you can agree on a list of vocabulary words and take turns adding them to a group concept map. You can also write exam questions for your study partners to answer, or you can simply explain the material to each other in your own words. Focus on what you need to learn, and your study sessions should be productive.

What's the Point?

The Venus flytrap and barrel cactus on these pages may look unusual, but they are typical plants in most respects. They are composed of cells that are assembled into tissues, which form organs such as leaves, flowers, stems, and roots. They require the same essential elements. Their roots extract water and nutrients from soil, and their chloroplasts carry out photosynthesis. They produce flowers, fruits, and seeds.

Why do they look so different? Natural selection provides the answer. Nitrogen-poor soil selects for the insect-eating lifestyle, whereas the thorns and fleshy stem of the barrel cactus are water-saving adaptations.

Plants provide us with food, textiles, building materials, fuel, paper, pharmaceutical drugs, and much more. All of these useful items derive their properties from the cells and tissues illustrated in this chapter, which describes the form and function of a plant's nonreproductive parts.

21.1 Vegetative Plant Parts Include Stems, Leaves, and Roots

Imagine a rose bush that produces a bounty of sweet-smelling flowers. Biologists would divide your plant into two sets of parts. The gorgeous flowers, which will eventually give rise to fruits called rose hips, are the reproductive parts of the plant. Chapter 22 describes flowers and fruits in detail. The **vegetative,** or nonreproductive, parts are the roots, stems, and leaves.

This chapter focuses on the **anatomy** (form) and **physiology** (function) of a plant's vegetative organs. As you will see, a plant's **organs** are composed of multiple **tissues,** which are groups of cells that interact to provide a specific function. This section begins our tour of the plant body with an overview of its major organs.

A plant's vegetative organs work together (figure 21.1). The **shoot** is the aboveground part of the plant. The shoot's **stem** supports the **leaves,** which produce carbohydrates such as sucrose by photosynthesis. A large portion of this sugar moves down the stem and nourishes the **roots,** which are usually below ground. Root cells depend completely on the shoots to provide fuel for their metabolism. At the same time, however, roots anchor the plant and absorb water and minerals that move via the stem to the leaves.

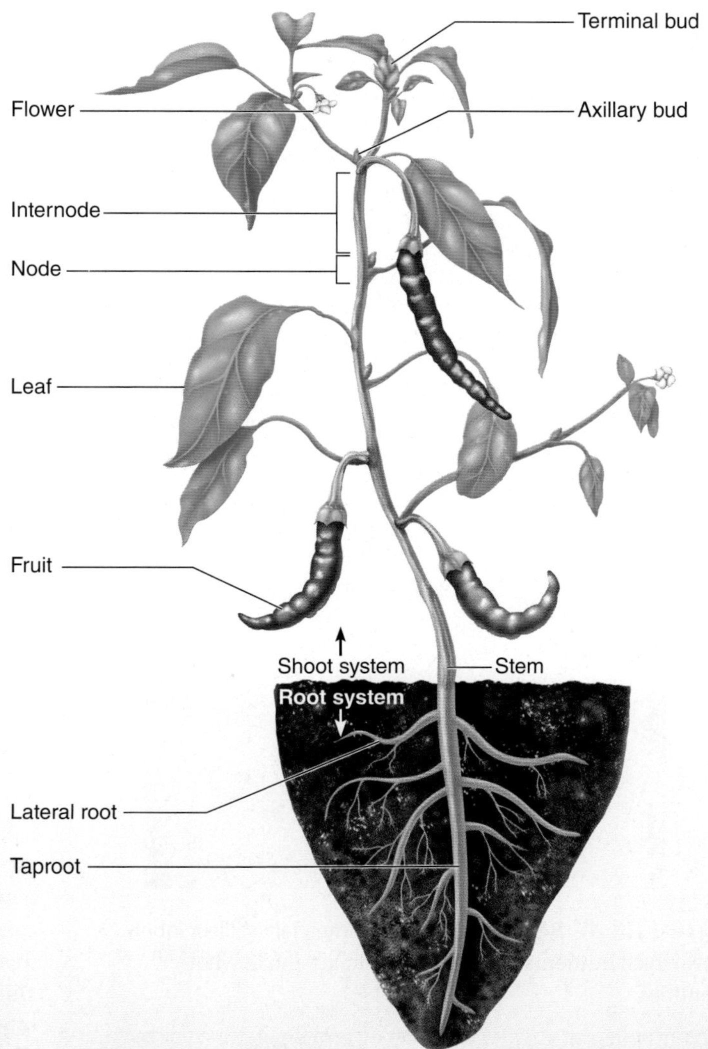

Figure 21.1 Parts of a Flowering Plant. A plant consists of a root system and a shoot system. Roots, stems, and leaves are vegetative organs; flowers and fruits are reproductive structures (see chapter 22).

A close look at a stem reveals that it consists of alternating nodes and internodes (see figure 21.1). A **node** is a point at which one or more leaves attach to the stem. **Internodes** are the stem areas between the nodes. Along with at least one leaf, each node features an **axillary bud,** an undeveloped shoot that forms in the angle between the stem and leaf stalk. Although these buds have the potential to elongate to form a branch or flower, many remain dormant.

Informally, biologists divide plants into two categories based on the characteristics of the stem. A **herbaceous plant** has a green, soft stem at maturity. The chili plant in figure 21.1 is herbaceous; other examples include grasses, daisies, dandelions, and radishes. The stems of **woody plants** such as elm and cedar trees are made of tough wood covered with bark.

Natural selection ensures that roots, stems, and leaves do not always look exactly like those in figure 21.1. Depending on the habitat, plants may contend with everything from hungry animals to extreme drought to continuous flooding to frozen winters. These selective forces have sculpted vegetative plant bodies into a tremendous diversity of forms.

Artificial selection has also modified stems, leaves, roots, flowers, and fruits to suit human needs. We cultivate Brussels sprouts for their axillary buds, spinach plants for their leaves, carrot plants for their roots, and tomato plants for their fruits. Most people divide these foods into two categories: fruits and vegetables. Botanically speaking, any seed-bearing structure produced by a flowering plant is a fruit. Apples, cherries, oranges, peaches, and raspberries are fruits. So are foods that we think of as vegetables, such as tomatoes and bell peppers. The term *vegetable* does not have a botanical definition—just a culinary one. That is, foods that we consider vegetables may come from any part of a plant, but they are typically used in salty or savory dishes, not sweet ones.

21.1 Mastering Concepts

1. How do stems, leaves, and roots support one another?
2. What are the other major parts of the plant body?

21.2 Soil and Air Provide Water and Nutrients

To stay healthy, a person needs water and the right dietary mix of fat, protein, carbohydrates, vitamins, and minerals (see chapter 28). Plants have similar needs, but they do not acquire these raw materials by eating and drinking. Instead, they are autotrophs that use photosynthesis to assemble sugar and other organic molecules from elements absorbed from their surroundings.

This section describes the sources of the elements that plants require. The rest of the chapter focuses on how plants absorb and transport water, minerals, and organic substances within their tissues.

A. Plants Require 16 Essential Elements

Like every organism, a plant requires certain **essential nutrients,** which are chemicals that are vital for metabolism, growth, and reproduction. Biologists have identified at least 16 elements essential to all plants (figure 21.2). Nine are **macronutrients,** meaning that they are needed in fairly large amounts. The macronutrients are carbon (C), oxygen (O), hydrogen (H), nitrogen (N), potassium (K), calcium (Ca), magnesium (Mg), phosphorus (P), and sulfur (S). The others are **micronutrients,** which are required in much smaller amounts.

Why We Care — Boost Plant Growth with Fertilizer

Farmers and gardeners often amend soil with commercial synthetic fertilizers or with nutrient-rich organic matter, such as manure or compost. Plant growth surges if the added material provides a nutrient that was previously scarce.

Commercial fertilizer labels prominently display three numbers that indicate the content of nitrogen, phosphorus, and potassium (figure 21.A). These are the three elements that are most commonly deficient in soils. The label also lists other macro- and micronutrients in the fertilizer.

Chemically, nutrients from inorganic fertilizer (such as the one in figure 21.A) are equivalent to those from manure or compost. So why should a gardener bother adding organic matter to soil? The answer is that organic matter not only contains nutrients but also aerates the soil, increases soil's ability to hold water, and provides food for beneficial microbes and animals. Manure and compost also release nutrients slowly, providing long-lasting results.

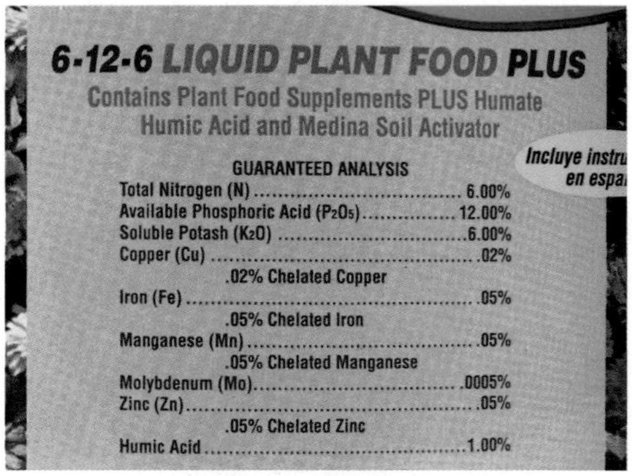

Figure 21.A Read the Label. Commercial fertilizer labels show which nutrients the product contains and in what quantities.

Macronutrients	Form taken up by plants	Percent dry weight	Selected functions
Carbon (C)	CO_2	45	Part of organic compounds
Oxygen (O)	H_2O, O_2, CO_2	45	Part of organic compounds
Hydrogen (H)	H_2O	6	Part of organic compounds
Nitrogen (N)	NO_3^-, NH_4^+	1.5	Part of nucleic acids, amino acids, coenzymes, chlorophyll, ATP
Potassium (K)	K^+	1.0	Controls opening and closing of stomata, activates enzymes
Calcium (Ca)	Ca^{2+}	0.5	Cell wall component, activates enzymes, second messenger in signal transduction, maintains membranes
Magnesium (Mg)	Mg^{2+}	0.2	Part of chlorophyll, activates enzymes, participates in protein synthesis
Phosphorus (P)	$H_2PO_4^-$, HPO_4^{2-}	0.2	Part of nucleic acids, sugar phosphates, ATP, coenzymes, phospholipids
Sulfur (S)	SO_4^{2-}	0.1	Part of cysteine and methionine (amino acids), coenzyme A
Micronutrients	**Form taken up by plants**	**Percent dry weight**	**Selected functions**
Chlorine (Cl)	Cl^-	0.01	Water balance
Iron (Fe)	Fe^{3+}, Fe^{2+}	0.01	Chlorophyll synthesis, cofactor for enzymes, part of electron carriers
Boron (B)	BO_3^-, $B_4O_7^{2-}$	0.002	Growth of pollen tubes, sugar transport, regulates certain enzymes
Zinc (Zn)	Zn^{2+}	0.002	Hormone synthesis, activates enzymes, stabilizes ribosomes
Manganese (Mn)	Mn^{2+}	0.005	Activates enzymes, electron transfer, photosynthesis
Copper (Cu)	Cu^{2+}	0.0006	Part of plastid pigments, lignin synthesis, activates enzymes
Molybdenum (Mo)	MoO_4^{2-}	0.00001	Nitrate reduction

Carbon, oxygen, and hydrogen (96% of dry weight)
Other macronutrients (~3.5%)
Micronutrients (~0.5%)

Figure 21.2 Essential Nutrients for Plants. Nine elements make up about 99.5% of a plant's body; the seven micronutrients occur in much lower concentrations.

Among the essential elements, C, H, and O are by far the most abundant, together accounting for about 96% of the dry weight of a plant. The six other macronutrients account for another 3.5%. Of these, N, P, and K are the most common ingredients in commercial fertilizers (see this chapter's Why We Care box).

Gardeners and farmers use fertilizers to prevent or treat nutrient deficiencies such as those shown in figure 21.3. At the other end of the nutritional spectrum are plants that accumulate unusually high concentrations of some elements, such as zinc or nickel. This "hyperaccumulation" of heavy metals is an adaptation that reduces herbivory.

B. Leaves and Roots Absorb Essential Elements

Plants obtain their three most abundant elements (C, H, and O) from water and the atmosphere. Water (H_2O) enters the plant through the roots, as described in section 21.6. Carbon and oxygen atoms come from the atmosphere in the form of CO_2 gas, which diffuses into the leaf or stem through pores called stomata. All of the other mineral elements listed in figure 21.2 dissolve in the soil's water when rock particles disintegrate or when microbes decompose dead organisms. As roots absorb water, they also take up these minerals. ▸ diffusion, p. 76

In most plant species, roots do not explore the soil alone. Recall from chapter 15 that the roots of most land plants are colonized with mycorrhizal fungi. Fungal filaments inside the root feed on the plant's sugars and extend into the soil, absorbing water and minerals that the plant's roots could not otherwise reach. In particular, phosphorus is poorly soluble in water and does not move easily to roots. Mycorrhizae therefore especially boost phosphorus absorption. ▸ mycorrhizae, p. 300

a.

b.

Figure 21.3 Nutrient Deficiencies. (a) Iron deficiency causes yellowed leaves, but the veins remain green. (b) Phosphorus deficiency causes plants to develop purplish leaves.

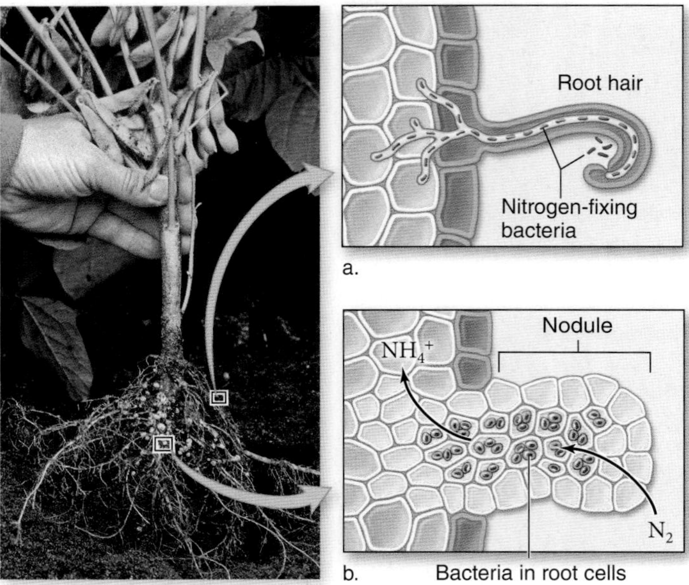

Figure 21.4 Root Nodules. (a) Nitrogen-fixing bacteria enter a root hair and trigger the formation of a root nodule in a soybean plant. (b) The bacteria use N_2 from the atmosphere to produce ammonium (NH_4^+); the plant provides the energy.

The source of nitrogen also deserves special mention. As described in chapter 2, nitrogen atoms occur in proteins, nucleic acids, and chlorophyll. Nitrogen gas (N_2) makes up 78% of the atmosphere, but a strong triple covalent bond holds the two nitrogen atoms together. This bond requires more energy to break than a plant can muster. Instead, roots must take up nitrogen from soil in the form of nitrate (NO_3^-) or ammonium (NH_4^+). These ions can be scarce, so nitrogen availability often limits plant growth.

Fortunately for plants (and ultimately animals), several types of bacteria use **nitrogen-fixing** enzymes to convert N_2 to NH_4^+. Many nitrogen-fixing bacteria are free-living, but others live in growths called **nodules** on the roots of some types of plants (figures 21.4 and 15.12). The bacteria consume sugars that the plant produces by photosynthesis. The plant, in turn, incorporates the nitrogen atoms from NH_4^+ into its own tissues. When the plant dies, decomposers make the nitrogen available to other organisms. Biological nitrogen fixation therefore jump-starts the nitrogen cycle, bringing otherwise inaccessible nitrogen to other organisms (see figure 19.30 for a detailed look at the nitrogen cycle).

The most famous nitrogen-fixing bacteria, in genus *Rhizobium,* stimulate nodule formation on the roots of plants called legumes (clover, beans, peas, peanuts, soybeans, and alfalfa). A farming technique called crop rotation alternates legume crops with nitrogen-hungry plants such as corn or cotton. The legume replenishes the soil's nitrogen, reducing the need for fertilizer.

A few plants acquire nutrients from more unusual sources. For example, carnivorous plants often live in waterlogged, acidic soils where organic matter decays slowly and nutrients are scarce. They obtain nitrogen and phosphorus from their prey (see the chapter opening photo).

21.2 Mastering Concepts

1. Which macro- and micronutrients do all plants require?
2. How do plants acquire C, H, O, N, and P?
3. How do bacteria form a critical link in the nitrogen cycle?

21.3 Plant Cells Build Tissues

A cactus, an elm tree, and a dandelion may seem to have little in common, but a closer look reveals that all consist of the same types of cells and tissues. Before examining these building blocks, it may be helpful to review the structure of the plant cell in figure 3.7 and the cell wall in figure 3.23. Note that in many plant cells, the wall has two layers: a thin, flexible primary one and a thick, rigid secondary one that forms after the cell is fully grown.

A. Plants Have Several Cell Types

Plants consist of multiple types of cells. This section lists the most common ones, which are illustrated in figure 21.5.

Ground Tissue Cells **Ground tissue** makes up the majority of the body of a herbaceous plant. It consists of three main cell types: parenchyma, collenchyma, and sclerenchyma.

Parenchyma cells are the most abundant. These cells are alive at maturity, and they retain the ability to divide, which enables them to differentiate in response to injury or a changing environment. It is parenchyma cells, for example, that divide to produce the roots that emerge from a houseplant cutting placed in water. Parenchyma cells have vital functions, including photosynthesis, respiration, gas exchange, and the storage of starch and other materials.

Collenchyma cells are elongated living cells with thickened primary walls that can stretch as the cells grow. These cells provide elastic support without interfering with the growth of young stems or expanding leaves. Collections of collenchyma cells make up the tough, flexible "strings" in celery stalks.

Sclerenchyma cells provide inelastic support to parts of a plant that are no longer growing. These cells are dead at maturity. They have thick, rigid secondary cell walls that usually contain **lignin,** a tough, complex molecule that adds great strength to the cell walls. Some sclerenchyma cells are elongated fibers; linen, for example, comes from the soft fibers of the stems of the flax plant. Other sclerenchyma cells form hard layers or clusters, such as the small groups of cells that create a pear's gritty texture.

Conducting Cells in Xylem and Phloem

Vascular tissues transport water, minerals, carbohydrates, and other dissolved compounds. Two types of vascular tissue are xylem and phloem.

Xylem transports water and dissolved minerals from the roots to all other parts of the plant. The water-conducting cells of xylem are elongated and have thick, lignin-rich secondary walls. They are dead at maturity, which means that no cytoplasm blocks water flow.

The two kinds of water-conducting cells in the xylem of flowering plants are tracheids and vessel elements. **Tracheids** are long, narrow cells that overlap at their tapered ends. Water moves from tracheid to tracheid through pits, which are thin areas in the cell wall. **Vessel elements** are short, wide, barrel-shaped conducting cells that stack end to end, forming long tubes. Their side walls have pits, but their end walls are either perforated or absent. Water moves much faster in vessels than in tracheids, both because of their greater diameter and because water can pass easily from one vessel element to the next. On the other hand, the narrower tracheids are less vulnerable to air bubble formation.

Phloem transports dissolved organic compounds, primarily sugars produced in photosynthesis. The main conducting cells are **sieve tube elements,** which align end to end to make a single functional unit called a sieve tube. The sieve tube elements are alive, but they lack a nucleus and have little cytoplasm. Adjacent to each sieve tube element is at least one **companion cell,** a specialized parenchyma cell that retains all of its organelles. Companion cells transfer carbohydrates into and out of the sieve tube elements, and they provide energy and proteins to the conducting cells.

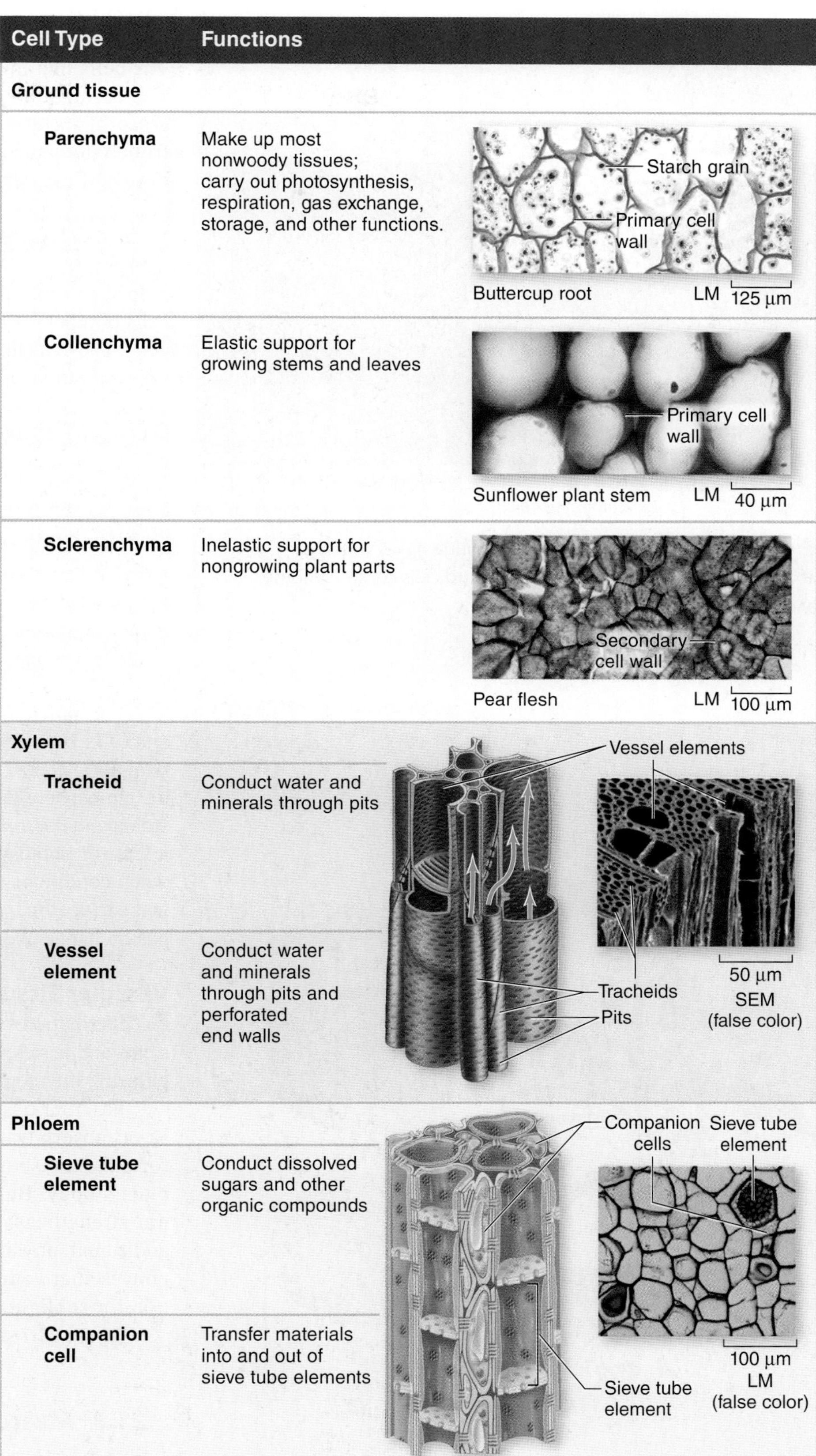

Cell Type	Functions
Ground tissue	
Parenchyma	Make up most nonwoody tissues; carry out photosynthesis, respiration, gas exchange, storage, and other functions.
Collenchyma	Elastic support for growing stems and leaves
Sclerenchyma	Inelastic support for nongrowing plant parts
Xylem	
Tracheid	Conduct water and minerals through pits
Vessel element	Conduct water and minerals through pits and perforated end walls
Phloem	
Sieve tube element	Conduct dissolved sugars and other organic compounds
Companion cell	Transfer materials into and out of sieve tube elements

Figure 21.5 Plant Cell Types: A Summary. Parenchyma, collenchyma, and sclerenchyma cells compose the majority of a herbaceous plant's body; other specialized cell types make up the xylem and phloem that transport materials within the plant.

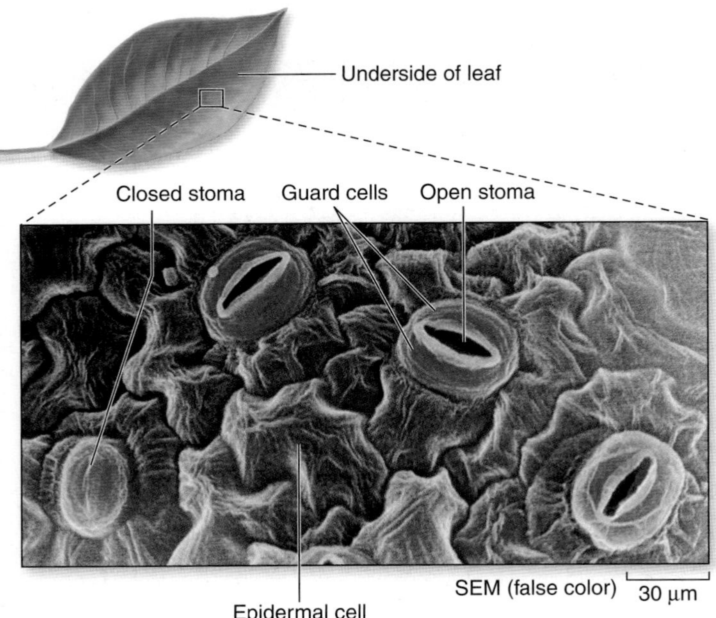

Figure 21.6 Stomata. Plants exchange gases with the atmosphere through open stomata. Guard cells control whether each stoma is open or closed.

B. Plant Cells Form Three Main Tissue Systems

The cells that make up a plant form three main tissue systems: ground tissue, dermal tissue, and vascular tissue. For comparison, animals have four types of tissues (see chapter 23). Each tissue type derives its properties from a unique combination of specialized cells. Together, these cells carry out all of the plant's functions.

Ground Tissue Ground tissue often fills the spaces between more specialized cell types inside roots, stems, leaves, fruits, and seeds. For example, the pulp of an apple, the photosynthetic area inside a leaf, and the starch-containing cells of a potato all consist of ground tissue composed mainly of parenchyma cells. The cells that compose ground tissue are important sites of photosynthesis, respiration, and storage.

Dermal Tissue **Dermal tissue** covers the plant. In a herbaceous plant, dermal tissue consists of the **epidermis,** a single layer of tightly packed, flat, transparent parenchyma cells. In woody plants, tough bark replaces the epidermis in stems and roots (see section 21.5D).

Natural selection has shaped dermal tissue over hundreds of millions of years. When plants first moved onto land, they were at risk for drying out. This threat selected for new water-conserving adaptations. For instance, in land plants, epidermal cells secrete a **cuticle,** a waxy layer that coats the epidermis of the leaves and stem. The cuticle conserves water and protects the plant from predators and fungi.

The cuticle is impermeable not only to water but also to gases such as O_2 and CO_2. How do these gases pass through the cuticle? The answer is **stomata** (singular: stoma), pores through which leaves and stems exchange gases with the atmosphere (figure 21.6). A pair of specialized **guard cells** surrounds each stoma and controls its opening and closing. Open stomata let CO_2 diffuse into a leaf for photosynthesis but also allow water to diffuse out; the pores close when conditions are too dry. Stomata, which occupy about 1% to 2% of the leaf surface area, therefore enable plants to balance the competing demands of gas exchange and water conservation.

Vascular Tissue Vascular tissues—xylem and phloem—form a continuous distribution system embedded in the ground tissue of shoots and roots. In stems and leaves, a **vascular bundle** is a strand of tissue containing xylem and phloem, often together with tough collenchyma or sclerenchyma fibers.

Vascular tissue allows for a division of labor between roots and shoots. Roots absorb water and minerals; shoots produce food. Xylem and phloem form the transportation system that shuttles these materials throughout the plant's body. But vascular tissue also has another function: support. Lignin strengthens the walls of xylem cells and sclerenchyma fibers. This additional physical support enables vascular plants to tower over their nonvascular counterparts, an important adaptation in the intense competition for sunlight.

Figure 21.7 summarizes the locations of the tissue systems in plants.

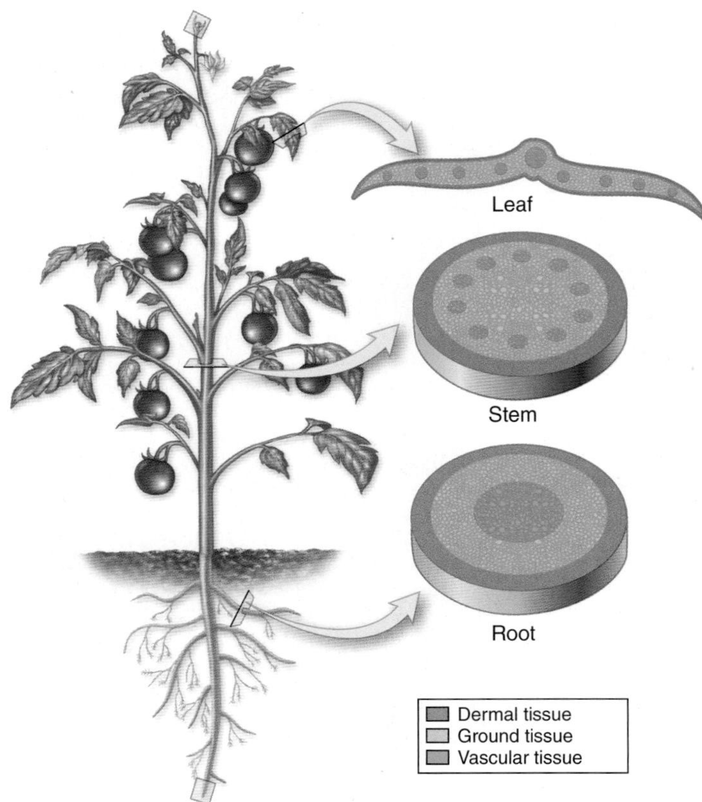

Figure 21.7 Three Tissue Types. Dermal, ground, and vascular tissues make up the leaves, stem, and roots of a plant.

21.3 Mastering Concepts

1. Describe the cell types that make up a plant body.
2. Where in the plant does ground tissue occur?
3. What are the functions of dermal tissue and vascular tissue?

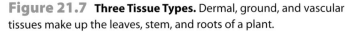

21.4 Tissues Build Stems, Leaves, and Roots

The tissues described in section 21.3 make up the stems, leaves, and roots of vascular plants. We now return to these organs to examine their structures more closely. Note that flowering plants (angiosperms) differ in the internal anatomy of their main vegetative organs. As described in chapter 16, the two largest clades of angiosperms are eudicots and monocots. Eudicots include everything from chili peppers to green beans to sunflowers to elm trees. Examples of monocots are orchids, lawn grasses, corn, rice, wheat, and bamboo. This section describes the structural similarities and differences between these two groups of plants.

A. Stems Support Leaves

Ground tissue occupies most of the volume of the stem of a herbaceous plant. The ground tissue, which consists mostly of parenchyma cells, stores water and starch. The cells are often loosely packed, allowing for gas exchange between the stem interior and the atmosphere.

Vascular bundles are embedded in the stem's ground tissue. The vascular bundles, which typically have phloem to the outside and xylem toward the inside, are arranged differently in monocots and eudicots (figure 21.8). In most monocot stems, vascular bundles are scattered throughout the ground tissue. Most eudicot stems, in contrast, have a single ring of vascular bundles. Ground tissue occupies most of the rest of the eudicot stem: the **cortex** fills the area between the epidermis and vascular tissue, and **pith** occupies the center.

Some stems have specialized functions. The stems of climbing plants may form tendrils that coil around objects, maximizing exposure of the leaves to the sun. The succulent, fleshy stems of cacti stockpile water. Rhizomes are thickened underground stems that produce both shoots and roots; tubers, such as potatoes, are swollen regions of rhizomes that store starch. Still other stems are protective; some types of thorns, such as those on hawthorn plants, are modified branches.

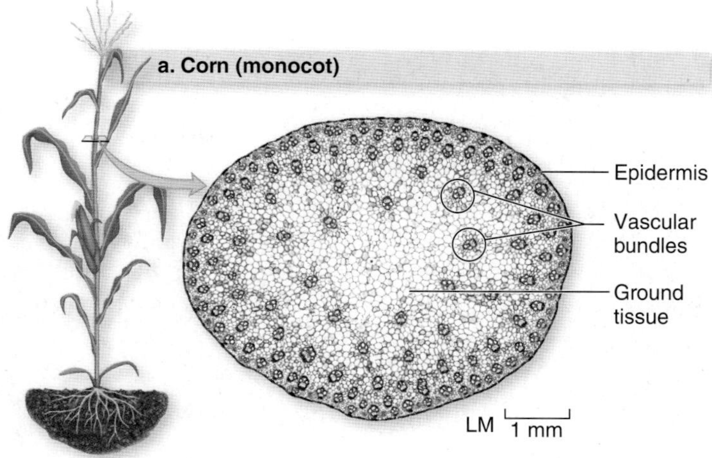

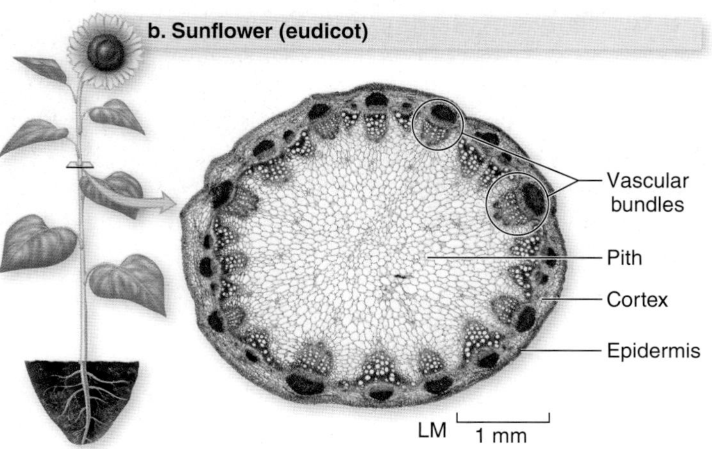

Figure 21.8 Stem Anatomy. (a) The cross section of a monocot stem features vascular bundles scattered in ground tissue. (b) A eudicot stem has a ring of vascular bundles surrounding a central pith.

B. Leaves Are the Primary Organs of Photosynthesis

Most leaves have two main parts: the flattened **blade** and the supporting, stalklike **petiole.** The broad, flat blade maximizes the surface area available to capture solar energy. For example, a large maple tree has approximately 100,000 leaves, with a total surface area that would cover six basketball courts (about 2500 square meters).

Biologists categorize leaves according to their basic forms (figure 21.9). A **simple leaf** has an undivided blade. **Compound leaves** are divided into leaflets, typically either paired along a central line or all attached to one point at

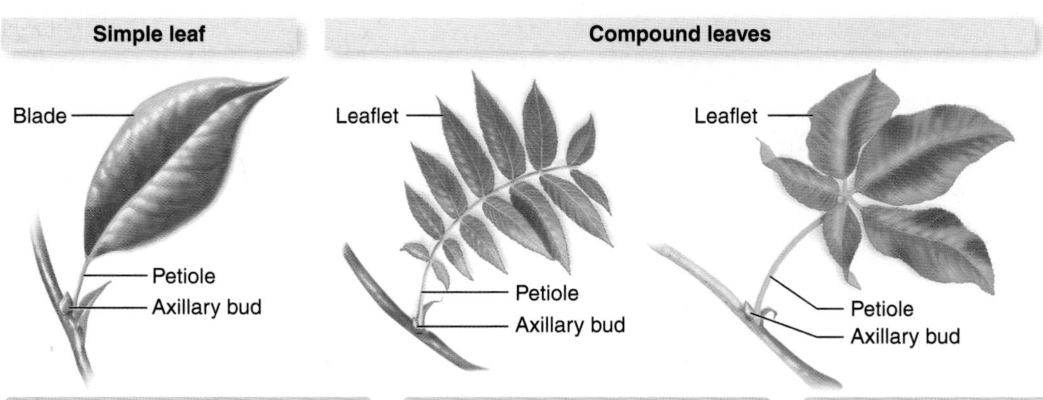

Figure 21.9 Leaf Forms. A simple leaf consists of one undivided blade, whereas compound leaves include multiple leaflets. Two types of compound leaves are illustrated here.

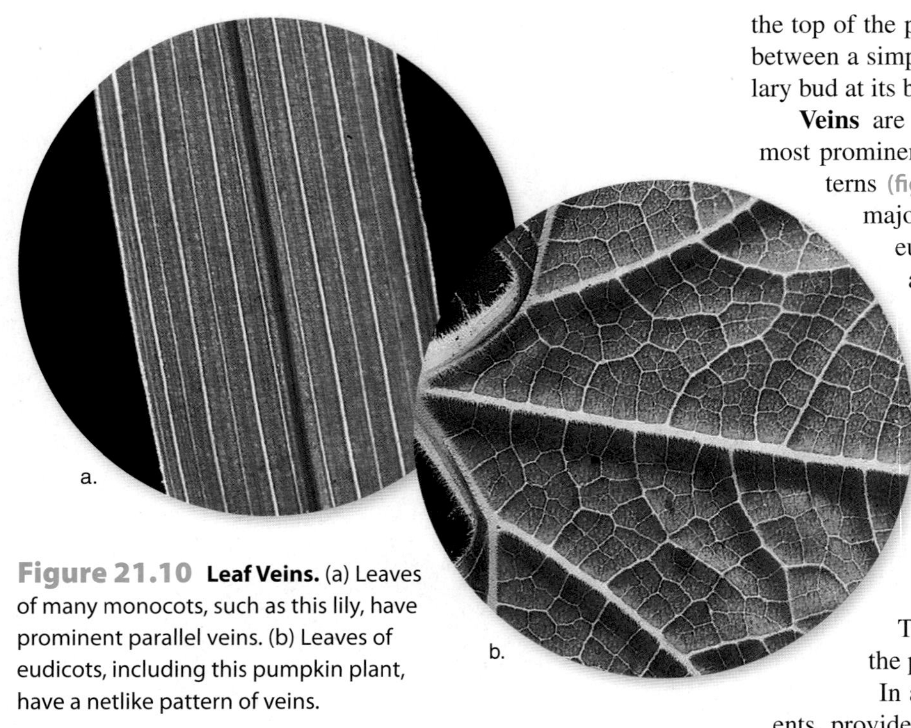

Figure 21.10 Leaf Veins. (a) Leaves of many monocots, such as this lily, have prominent parallel veins. (b) Leaves of eudicots, including this pumpkin plant, have a netlike pattern of veins.

the top of the petiole, like fingers on a hand. How can you tell the difference between a simple leaf and one leaflet of a compound leaf? A leaf has an axillary bud at its base, whereas an individual leaflet does not (see figure 21.9).

Veins are vascular bundles inside leaves, and they are often a leaf's most prominent external feature. Networks of veins occur in two main patterns (figure 21.10). Many monocots have parallel veins, with several major longitudinal veins connected by smaller minor veins. Most eudicots have netted veins. In these leaves, minor veins branch in all directions from large, prominent midveins.

The ground tissue inside a leaf is called **mesophyll,** and it is composed mostly of parenchyma cells (figure 21.11). Most mesophyll cells have abundant chloroplasts and produce sugars by photosynthesis. When the stomata are open, mesophyll cells exchange CO_2 and O_2 directly with the atmosphere.

Mesophyll cells also exchange materials with vascular tissue. Xylem in the tiniest leaf veins delivers water and minerals to nearby mesophyll cells. Meanwhile, sugars produced in photosynthesis move from the mesophyll cells to the phloem's companion cells and then to the sieve tube elements. The sugars, along with other organic compounds, travel within the phloem to the roots and other nonphotosynthetic plant parts.

In addition to carrying out photosynthesis, leaves can store nutrients, provide protection, and even trap animals. Onion bulbs, for example, are collections of the fleshy bases of leaves that store nutrients. Cactus spines are modified leaves that deter predators. Some flower parts, such as petals, are modified leaves. And in carnivorous plants, leaves attract, capture, and digest prey, as shown in the chapter opening photo.

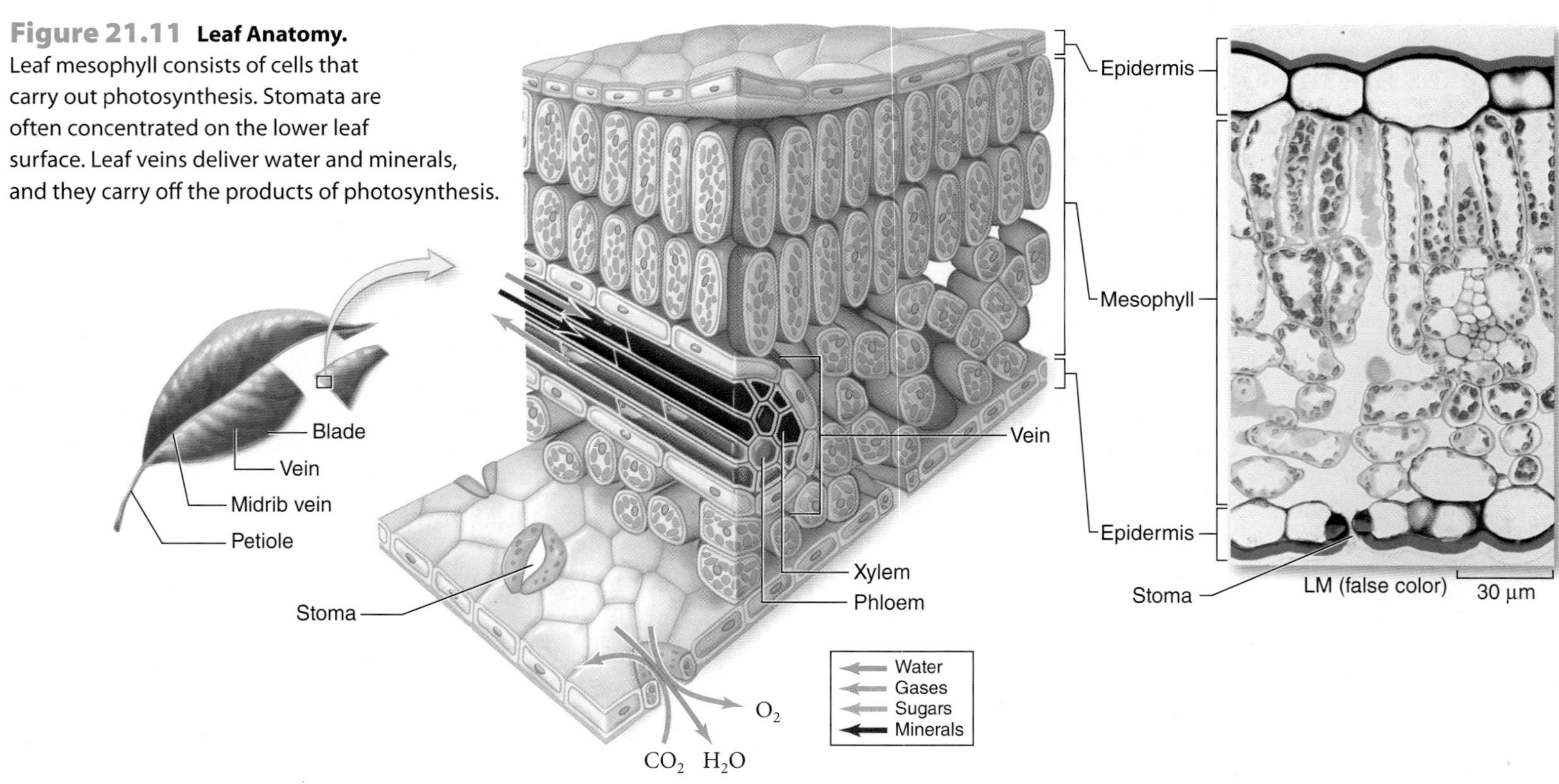

Figure 21.11 Leaf Anatomy. Leaf mesophyll consists of cells that carry out photosynthesis. Stomata are often concentrated on the lower leaf surface. Leaf veins deliver water and minerals, and they carry off the products of photosynthesis.

C. Roots Absorb Water and Minerals, and Anchor the Plant

Roots grow in two main patterns that differ based on the fate of the primary root, which is the first root to develop after a seed germinates (figure 21.12). In a **fibrous root system,** slender roots arise from the base of the stem and replace the short-lived primary root. Grasses and other monocots usually have fibrous root systems. Because they are relatively shallow, these roots rapidly absorb minerals and water near the soil surface and prevent erosion. In a **taproot system,** on the other hand, the primary root enlarges to form a thick root that persists throughout the life of the plant. Lateral branches emerge from this main root. Taproots grow fast and deep, maximizing support and enabling a plant to use minerals and water deep in the soil. Most eudicots develop taproot systems.

Figure 21.12 also reveals that the vascular cylinders of monocot and eudicot roots have different arrangements. In most monocot roots, a ring of vascular tissue surrounds a central core (pith) of parenchyma cells. In most eudicots, the vascular cylinder consists of a solid core of xylem, with ridges that project toward the root's exterior. Phloem strands are generally located between the "arms" of the xylem core.

In both fibrous and taproot systems, countless root tips explore the soil for water and nutrients. The **root cap** protects the growing tip from abrasion. Root cap cells, which slough off and are continually replaced, secrete a slimy substance that lubricates the root as it pushes through the soil. The root cap also plays a role in sensing gravity. ▸ gravitropism, p. 461

The epidermis surrounds the entire root except the root cap. Root hairs are extensions of epidermal cells, maximizing the surface area for absorption of

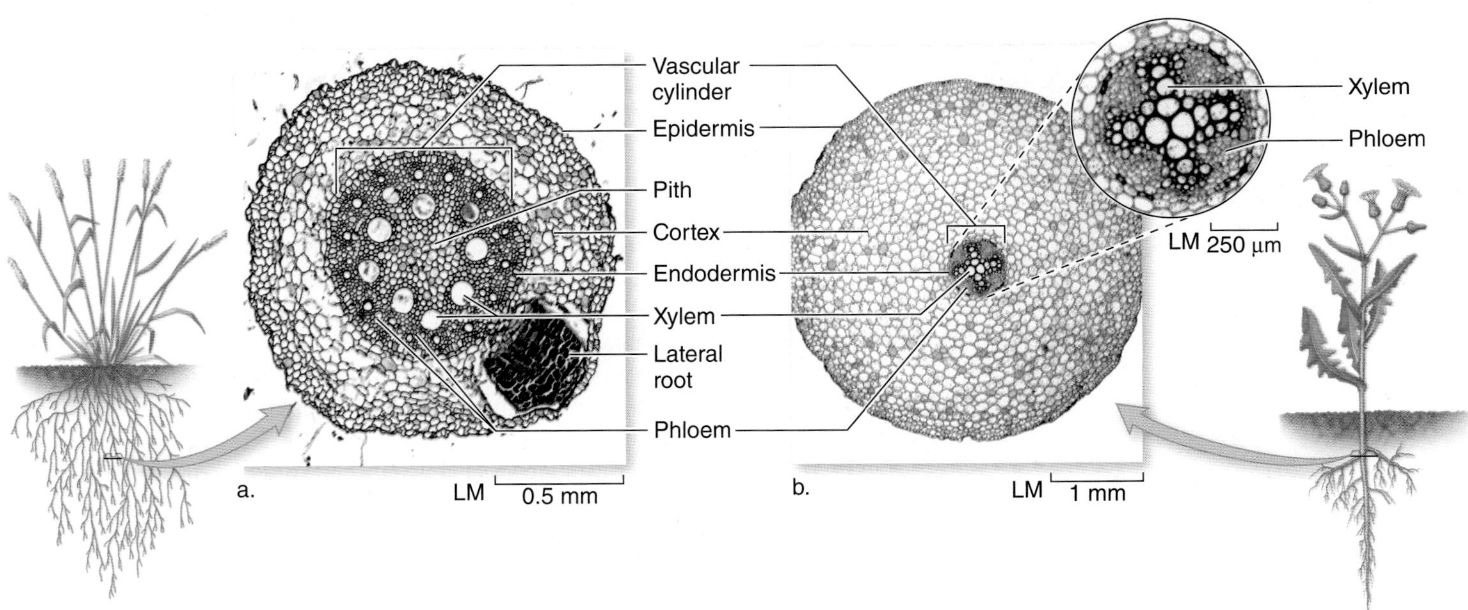

Figure 21.12 Root Anatomy. (a) A fibrous root system, which is typical of monocots, features numerous slender roots. A cross section of a root reveals a ring of vascular tissue surrounding a central pith. (b) A eudicot's taproot system features a central, thick root with large lateral branches. Inside each root, a central cylinder of vascular tissue is surrounded by the cortex.

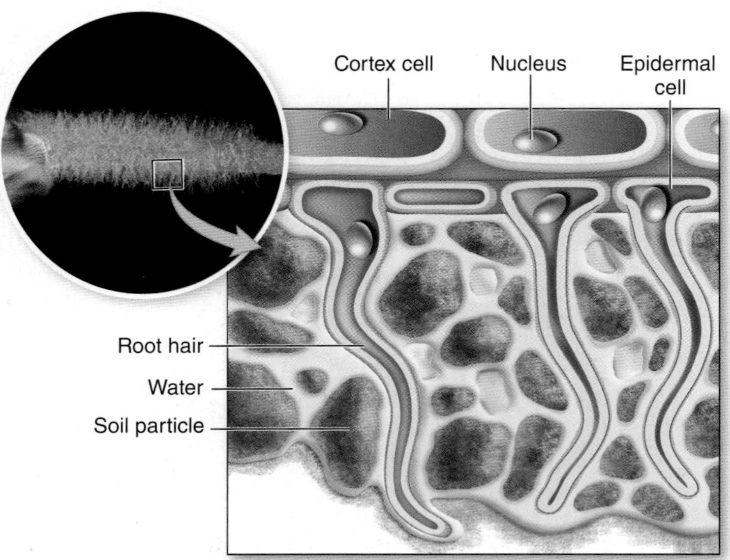

Figure 21.13 **Root Hairs.** These epidermal cell outgrowths greatly increase the surface area of this corn seedling's root.

TABLE 21.1 Apical and Lateral Meristems: A Summary

Type	Locations	Function
Apical	Terminal and axillary buds of shoots; root tips	Produces tissues that lengthen the tips of shoots and roots
Lateral	Internal cylinder along the length of roots and stems of woody plants	Thickens roots and stems

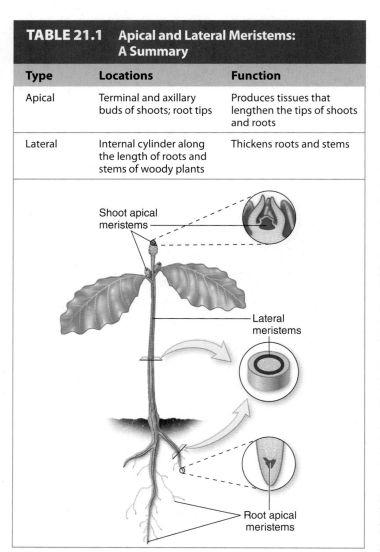

Shoot apical meristems
Lateral meristems
Root apical meristems

water and minerals (figure 21.13). Just internal to the epidermis is the cortex, which consists of loosely packed cells that may store starch or other materials. The spaces between the cells allow for both gas exchange and the free movement of water.

The **endodermis** is the innermost cell layer of the cortex. The walls of its tightly packed cells contain a ribbon of waxy, waterproof material. These deposits form a barrier that blocks the passive diffusion of water and dissolved substances into the xylem. The endodermis therefore acts as a filter, enabling the plant to exclude toxins and control the concentrations of some minerals.

Some roots have functions other than absorption, including storage and gas exchange. Beet and carrot roots stockpile starch, for example, and desert plant roots may store water. In oxygen-poor habitats such as swamps, specialized roots grow up into the air, allowing oxygen to diffuse in.

21.4 Mastering Concepts

1. Name the cell layers that occur in the stem of a monocot and a eudicot, moving from the epidermis to the innermost tissues.
2. List the parts of a simple and a compound leaf.
3. Describe the internal anatomy of a leaf.
4. Compare and contrast the development of fibrous roots and taproots.
5. How do the roots of monocots and eudicots differ?

21.5 Plants Have Flexible Growth Patterns, Thanks to Meristems

Consider the plight of a green plant. Rooted in place, it seems vulnerable and defenseless against drought, flood, wind, fire, and hungry herbivores. Yet plants dominate nearly every habitat on land. How do they do it? In many ways, plants owe their success to modular growth.

A. Plants Grow by Adding New Modules

To understand modular growth, imagine a landowner who plans to build a motel. Money is tight at first, so she starts with just a few rooms. As her business grows, however, she adds more units to the basic plan. Plant growth is similar. Shoots become larger by adding units ("modules") consisting of repeated nodes and internodes.

Some plants, such as dandelions, stop growing after they reach their mature size, a pattern called **determinate growth.** Most plants, however, can grow indefinitely by adding module after module. Such **indeterminate growth** can persist as long as environmental conditions allow it.

Modular growth enhances a plant's ability to respond to the environment. For example, plants produce the most root tips in pockets of soil with the richest nutrients. Likewise, a shrub growing in partial shade can add new branches where it receives the most sunlight, while the shaded limbs remain unchanged.

In addition, modular growth means that the loss of a branch or root does not harm a plant as much as, say, the loss of a leg affects a cat. Neighboring branches can add modules to compensate for a broken tree limb, but the cat's body cannot regenerate a leg. Modular growth is one key feature that distinguishes plants from animals.

B. Plant Growth Occurs at Meristems

All of a plant's new cells come from **meristems,** regions that undergo active mitotic cell division (see chapter 8). Meristems are patches of "immortality" that allow a plant to grow, replace damaged parts, and respond to environmental change.

Most plants have two main types of meristems (table 21.1). **Apical meristems** are small patches of actively dividing cells near the tips of roots and shoots. When cells in the apical meristem divide, they give rise to new cells that differentiate into all of the tissue types described in section 21.3.

Woody plants also have **lateral meristems,** which produce cells that thicken a stem or root. A lateral meristem is usually an internal cylinder of cells extending along most of the length of the plant. When the cells divide, they typically produce tissues both to the inside and to the outside of the meristem.

Figure 21.14 **Shoot Apical Meristem.** The apical meristem at the tip of a growing shoot gives rise to the tissues that make up the aboveground parts of the plant.

C. In Primary Growth, Apical Meristems Lengthen Stems and Roots

Primary growth lengthens the shoot or root tip by adding cells produced by the apical meristems. Figure 21.14 shows how a stem grows and differentiates at its tip. New cells originate at the apical meristem. The daughter cells eventually give rise to ground tissue, the epidermis, and vascular tissue. The stem elongates as the vacuoles of the new cells absorb water, pushing the apical meristem upward. Meanwhile, new leaves originate on the flanks of the meristem.

Remnants of the apical meristem remain in the axillary buds that form at stem nodes. These buds may either remain dormant or "awaken" to form side branches. When a shoot loses its terminal bud, cells in one or more dormant axillary buds begin to divide. The result is a bushy growth form. Gardeners exploit this phenomenon by pinching off the tips of young tomato or basil stems, a practice that promotes the growth of side branches and therefore greatly increases yields. ▸ apical dominance, p. 458

Roots also grow at their tips. Just behind the tip of each actively growing root is an apical meristem (figure 21.15). Some of the cells produced at this meristem differentiate into the root cap. Other cells elongate by absorbing water into their vacuoles. As the cells become larger, the root grows farther into the soil. Beyond this zone of elongation, cells complete their differentiation and mature into the functional tissue systems that make up the root.

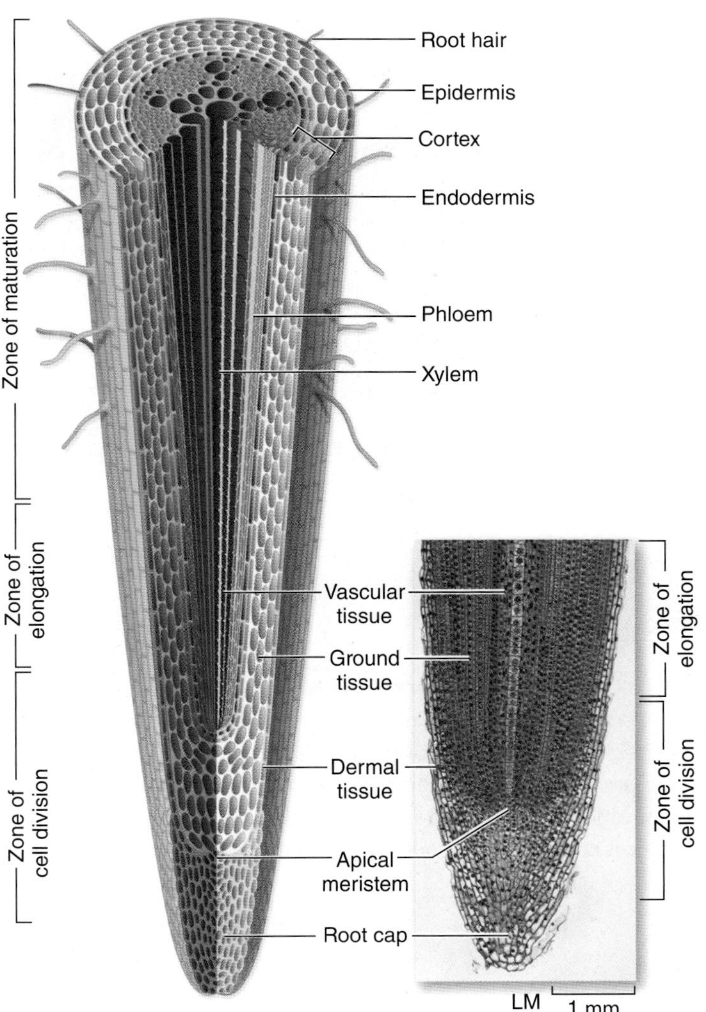

Figure 21.15 **Root Apical Meristem.** The apical meristem at the tip of a growing root produces root cap cells, ground tissue, vascular tissue, and the epidermis.

D. In Secondary Growth, Lateral Meristems Thicken Stems and Roots

In many habitats, plants compete for sunlight. The tallest plants reach the most light, so selection for height has been a powerful force in the evolutionary history of plants. But primary tissue is not strong enough to support a very tall plant. The increasing competition for light therefore selected for additional support, in the form of **secondary growth** that increases the girth of stems and roots in woody plants.

The Origin of Wood and Bark Wood and bark are tissues that arise from secondary growth originating at two types of lateral meristems: vascular

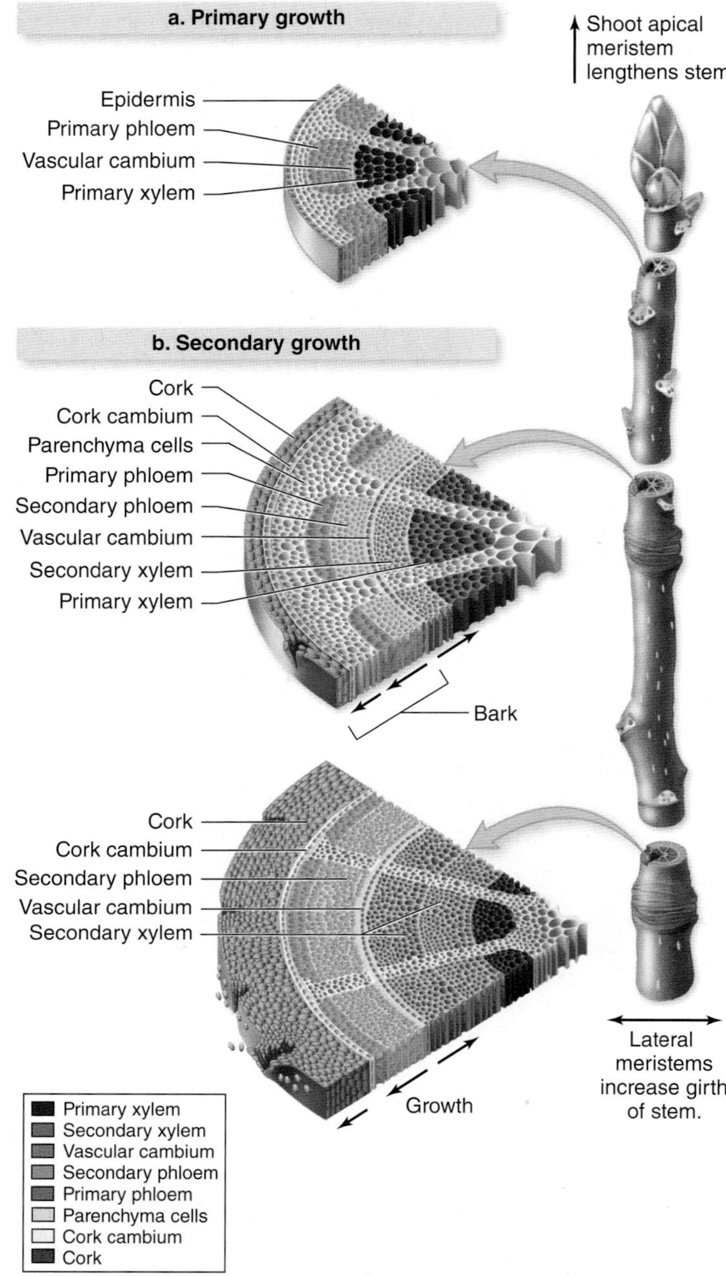

Figure 21.16 Secondary Growth. (a) In a primary shoot, the microscopic vascular cambium has not yet started producing secondary vascular tissue. (b) In secondary growth, the vascular cambium produces secondary xylem toward the inside of the stem and secondary phloem toward the outside. Cork cambium, meanwhile, produces cork cells to the outside and parenchyma to the inside.

cambium and cork cambium (figure 21.16). These meristems occur in gymnosperms (conifers and their relatives) and many eudicots, but not in monocots.

The **vascular cambium** is an internal cylinder of meristem tissue that produces most of the diameter of a woody root or stem. This lateral meristem forms a thin layer between the primary xylem and phloem (see figure 21.16a). When a cell in the vascular cambium divides, it produces two daughter cells, one of which remains a meristem cell. Cells produced to the inside of the cambium become secondary xylem; secondary phloem forms on the outer side (see figure 21.16b).

Secondary xylem, more commonly known as **wood,** can accumulate to massive proportions. For example, a giant sequoia tree in California is 100 meters tall and more than 7 meters in diameter. Secondary phloem occupies much less volume. This tissue forms the live, innermost layer of **bark,** a collective term for all tissues to the outside of the vascular cambium.

The **cork cambium** is a lateral meristem that gives rise to cork to the outside and parenchyma to the inside (see figure 21.16b). Cork consists of layers of densely packed, waxy cells on the surfaces of mature stems and roots. The cells are dead at maturity and form waterproof, insulating layers that protect the plant. The corks used in wine bottles come from oak trees that grow in the Mediterranean region. Every 10 years, harvesters remove much of the cork cambium and cork, which grows back. Cork is also important in the history of biology; in 1665, Robert Hooke became the first person to see cells when he used a primitive microscope to gaze at cork.

A Closer Look at Wood Few plant products are as versatile or economically important as wood. Lumber forms the internal frame that supports many buildings. Firewood provides heat and cooking fuel. Most paper comes from wood. Throughout history, humans have fashioned wood into furniture, pencils, cabinets, boats, baseball bats, serving bowls, roofing shingles, jewelry, picture frames, and countless other items.

Figure 21.17a illustrates the internal anatomy of a tree trunk, including the bark, vascular cambium, and secondary xylem. Nearly all of the trunk consists of secondary xylem, or wood. The cross section in figure 21.17b reveals that the innermost wood is darker than the outer portion. This color difference arises as the tree ages. As the years pass, the oldest secondary xylem gradually becomes unable to conduct water. This darker colored, nonfunctioning region is called **heartwood.** The lighter colored **sapwood,** located nearest the vascular cambium, transports water and dissolved minerals.

Another feature of a trunk's cross section is tree rings. In temperate climates, cells in the vascular cambium are dormant in winter, but they divide to produce wood during the spring and summer. During the moist days of spring, the vascular cambium produces water-conducting cells that are relatively large. During the drier days of summer, new wood has smaller cells. The contrast between the summer wood of one year and the spring wood of the next highlights each annual tree ring (figure 21.17c).

By counting these rings, a forester can estimate a tree's age. Growth rings also provide clues about climate and significant events throughout a tree's life. A thick ring indicates plentiful rainfall and good growing conditions. Narrow tree rings may reflect stress from herbivory, disease, or fierce competition for light or water. A fire leaves behind a charred "burn scar." Geologists have even

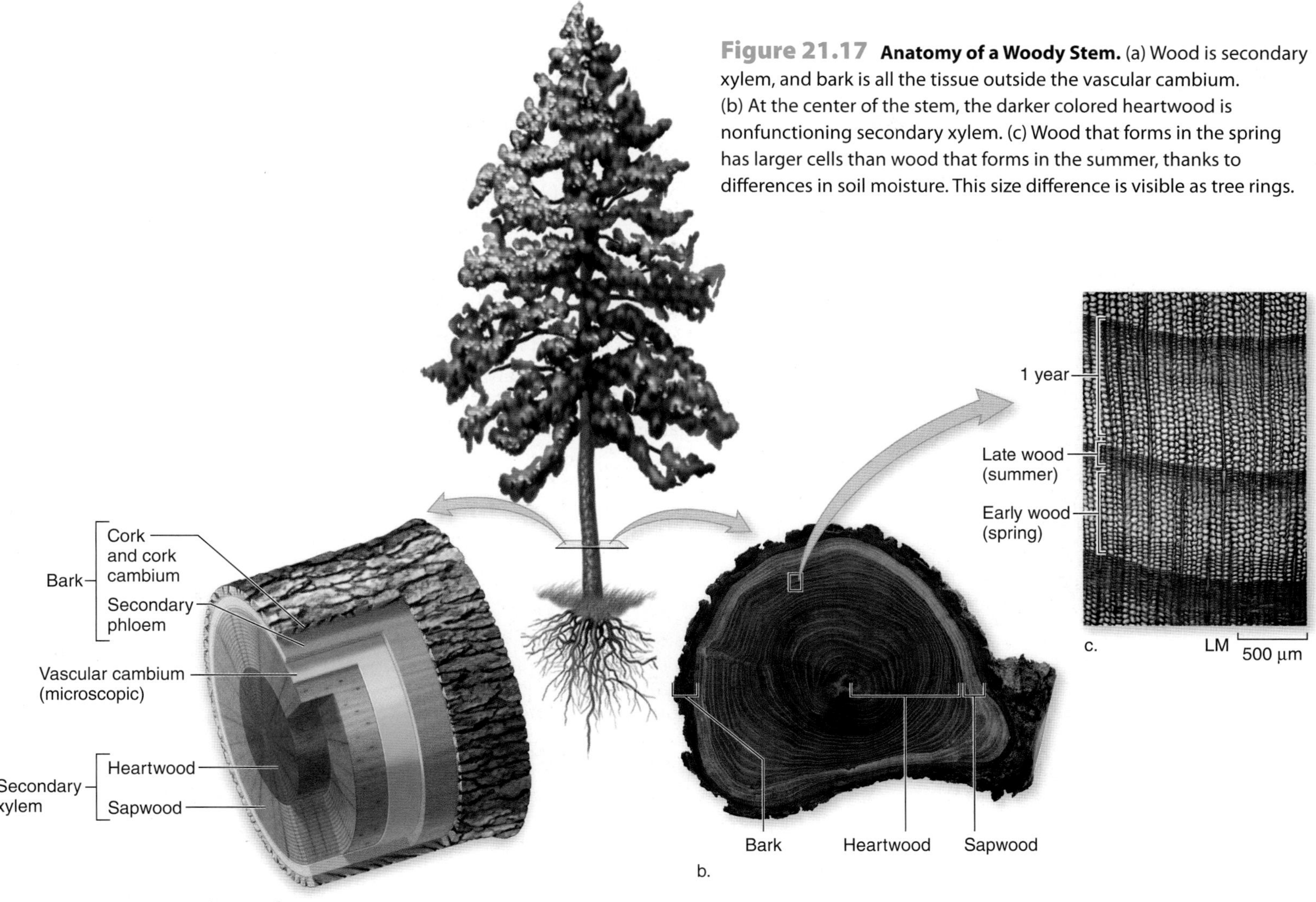

Figure 21.17 Anatomy of a Woody Stem. (a) Wood is secondary xylem, and bark is all the tissue outside the vascular cambium. (b) At the center of the stem, the darker colored heartwood is nonfunctioning secondary xylem. (c) Wood that forms in the spring has larger cells than wood that forms in the summer, thanks to differences in soil moisture. This size difference is visible as tree rings.

used tree rings to infer the dates of earthquakes that occurred before recorded history. Ground shaking can break stems and change water flow patterns on the land, both of which can leave signals in tree ring data.

21.5 Mastering Concepts

1. What is the difference between determinate and indeterminate growth?
2. What are the locations and functions of meristems?
3. What are the two lateral meristems in a woody stem or root, and which tissues does each meristem produce?
4. Explain the origin of tree rings.

21.6 Vascular Tissue Transports Water, Minerals, and Sugar

We turn next to a closer look at the function of vascular tissue, the transportation system that connects the plant's roots, stems, leaves, flowers, and fruits (figure 21.18). This section describes how xylem and phloem interact to move substances throughout the plant.

A. Water and Minerals Are Pulled Up to Leaves in Xylem

Xylem is the vascular tissue that transports **xylem sap,** a dilute solution consisting of water and dissolved minerals absorbed from soil. How do these substances move within the plant?

Vapor Is Lost from Leaves Through Transpiration The easiest way to visualize how plants acquire and transport water is to begin at the end. Plants lose water through **transpiration,** the evaporation of water from a leaf. Heat

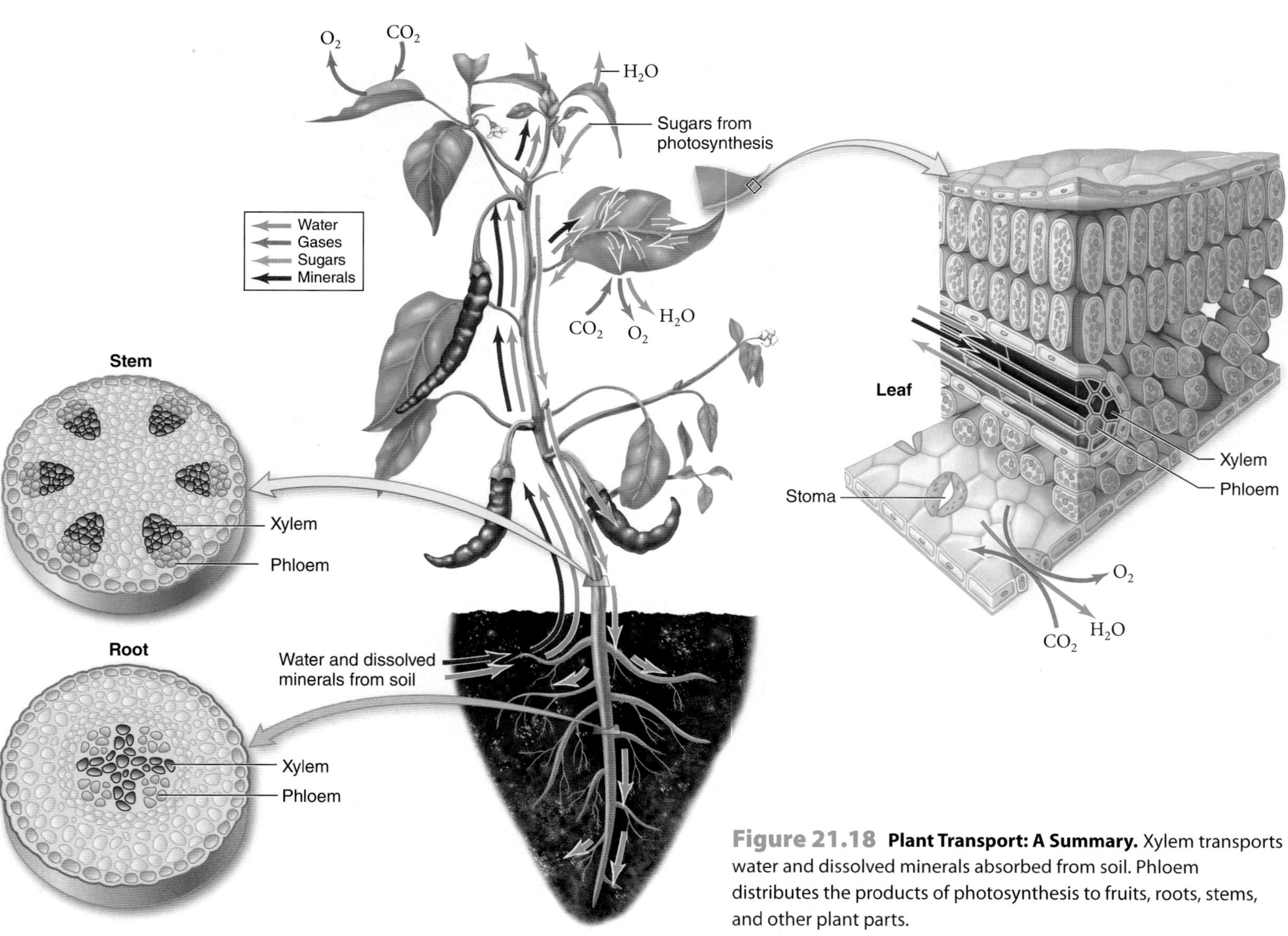

Figure 21.18 Plant Transport: A Summary. Xylem transports water and dissolved minerals absorbed from soil. Phloem distributes the products of photosynthesis to fruits, roots, stems, and other plant parts.

from the sun causes water in the cell walls to evaporate into the spaces between the mesophyll cells. This evaporation establishes a gradient: that is, the concentration of water molecules inside the leaf is higher than in the air surrounding the leaf. Water vapor therefore diffuses from inside the leaf to the outside air. Most transpiration occurs through open stomata (see figure 21.18).

The bigger the concentration gradient between the leaf interior and the surrounding air, the faster the transpiration rate. Low humidity, wind, and high temperatures therefore all cause the transpiration rate to soar. As long as the plant contains enough moisture to replace water lost in transpiration, it will flourish. But if the plant loses too much water, it will wilt—unless it closes its stomata and temporarily shuts down the transpiration stream.

A plant that closes its stomata, however, also cuts off its supply of CO_2 for use in photosynthesis. Most plants therefore conserve water by closing their stomata after dark, when photosynthesis cannot occur anyway. Many plants in dry habitats also use water-saving variations on the photosynthetic pathway. ▸ C_4 and CAM plants, p. 92

Xylem Transport Relies on Cohesion The plant must replace the moisture lost in transpiration by transporting water upward from the roots. The functional cells of the xylem, however, are dead at maturity (see figure 21.5). Metabolic activity in xylem cells therefore cannot drive water transport in a plant. So how does water in the xylem get from the roots to the leaves?

The **cohesion–tension theory** explains how xylem sap moves within a plant (figure 21.19). As its name implies, the cohesion–tension theory hinges on the cohesive properties of water—the tendency for water molecules to form hydrogen bonds and "cling" together. As water molecules evaporate through the stomata, additional water diffuses out of leaf veins and into the mesophyll. Water molecules leaving the vein attract molecules adjacent to them in the xylem, pulling them toward the vein ending. Each water molecule tugs on the one behind it. ▸ cohesion, p. 29

As evaporation from leaf surfaces pulls water up the stem, additional water enters roots from the soil. Just behind each growing root tip, the epidermis is fringed with root hairs (see figure 21.13). The plant's millions of root hairs, coupled with filaments of mycorrhizal fungi, add up to an enormous surface area for water and mineral absorption.

The solution flows among and within the cells that make up the outer portion of the root until it reaches the endodermis. At that point, a waxy barrier forces the materials that had gone around cells to now enter the cells of the endodermis. Water enters by osmosis, because the concentration of solutes in cells is generally higher than in the soil. ▸ osmosis, p. 77

Materials that cross the endodermis continue into the xylem, enter the transpiration stream, and move up the plant. As we have already seen, the water eventually returns to the atmosphere through the open stomata in the leaves and stem; the dissolved nutrients are incorporated into the plant's tissues.

As long as sufficient moisture is available in the soil, the cohesion between water molecules is enough to move continuous, narrow columns of xylem sap upward against the force of gravity. Notice that this mechanism exploits the physical properties of water, so the plant does not spend energy hauling xylem sap from soil to the tips of its leaves.

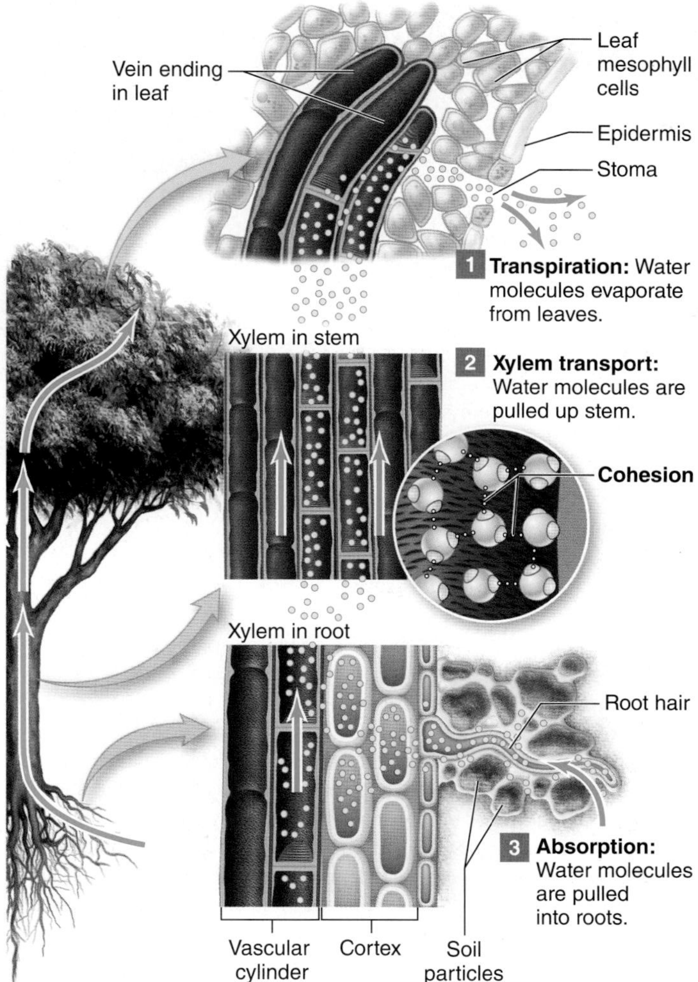

Figure 21.19 Xylem Transport. Transpiration of water from leaves pulls water up a plant's stem from the roots. The cohesiveness of water makes xylem transport possible.

B. Sugars Are Pushed to Nonphotosynthetic Cells in Phloem

With sufficient light, water, and nutrients, a photosynthetic cell will produce sugars that can be transported in phloem to the plant's nonphotosynthetic cells,

Burning Questions

Where does maple syrup come from?

The source of maple syrup is the xylem sap of the sugar maple tree. During the winter and early spring, these trees produce copious amounts of xylem sap. To harvest the sap, collectors drill a hole and insert a spout through the tree's bark and into the xylem. The xylem sap drips off the end of the spout and into a container (figure 21.B). Each tap produces about 40 liters of xylem sap each year, which boils down to about 1 liter of finished syrup.

Figure 21.B Sap Flow. The sugar maple tree produces sweet xylem sap, the precursor to maple syrup.

The upward flow of this sweet fluid was once a bit of a puzzle. After all, during the sap flow period, sugar maples lack leaves, which are required for transpiration. The cohesion–tension theory that explains most water movement in the xylem therefore cannot apply.

Instead, the sap flow apparently results from alternating freezing and thawing of the xylem tissues. During the day, respiring cells in the stem produce CO_2. At night, compressed CO_2 bubbles are trapped in ice that forms in the xylem. When the xylem thaws during the day, the gases expand once more, pushing the sap up the tree.

Submit your burning question to:
marielle_hoefnagels@mcgraw-hill.com

which cannot produce food on their own. The major transport structures of phloem are the microscopic sieve tubes (see figure 21.5). Unlike cells of xylem, the cells that make up sieve tubes are alive.

The organic compounds carried in phloem are dissolved in the **phloem sap,** a solution that also includes water and minerals from the xylem. The carbohydrates in phloem sap are mostly dissolved sugars such as sucrose (see figure 2.16). Phloem sap also contains amino acids, hormones, enzymes, and messenger RNA molecules. (Although phloem sap is the most common vehicle for sugar transport, it is not the only one, as this chapter's Burning Question explains.)

Pressure flow theory explains how transport occurs in phloem. This theory suggests that phloem sap moves under positive pressure from "sources" to "sinks." A **source** is any plant part that produces or releases sugars; a **sink** is any plant part that does not photosynthesize. Examples of sinks include flowers, fruits, shoot apical meristems, roots, and storage organs. If the cells that make up these sinks do not receive enough sugar to generate the ATP they require, the plant may die or fail to reproduce.

Inside a leaf or other sugar source, companion cells load sucrose into sieve tube elements by active transport. Because sucrose becomes so much more concentrated in the sieve tubes than in the adjacent xylem, water moves by osmosis out of the xylem and into the phloem sap. The resulting increased pressure drives phloem sap through the sieve tubes (figure 21.20). ▸ active transport, p. 78

At a root, flower, fruit, or other sink, cells take up the sucrose (and other compounds in the phloem sap) through facilitated diffusion or active transport. As the sucrose is unloaded from the sieve tubes, the concentration of solutes in the phloem sap is reduced. Water therefore moves by osmosis from the sieve tube to the surrounding tissue (often xylem). Movement of water out of the sieve tube relieves the pressure, so the phloem sap in the sieve tube continues to flow toward the sink.

A given organ may act as a sink and a source at different times. For example, a developing potato tuber is a sink, storing the plant's sugars in the form of starch. Later, when the plant uses those stored reserves to fuel the growth of new tissues, that same tuber becomes a source. The starch in the tuber breaks down into simple sugars, which are loaded into phloem sap for transport to other plant parts.

A similar mobilization occurs each spring when a deciduous tree produces new stems and leaves, using carbohydrates stored in roots. Later in the growing season, leaves approach their mature size and produce sugar of their own. The leaves are then sources, and the roots are again sinks.

C. Parasitic Plants Tap into Another Plant's Vascular Tissue

Of the hundreds of thousands of plant species, most are self-sufficient. They produce their own food by photosynthesis, and they absorb their own nutrients and water from soil. Some plant species, however, are parasites that exploit the hard-won resources of other plants.

Parasitic plants acquire water, minerals, and food by tapping into the vascular tissues of their hosts. The story begins with the parasite's seeds, which typically are carried to the host by birds or released explosively from seed pods. Either way, a seed germinates, and the seedling secretes an adhesive that sticks the young plant to its host. The seedling's root pushes through the host's epidermis and connects the parasite's vascular tissues to those of the host.

Figure 21.20 Phloem Transport. According to the pressure flow theory, sugar produced in green "source" organs such as leaves moves under positive pressure to roots, fruits, and other nonphotosynthetic sinks.

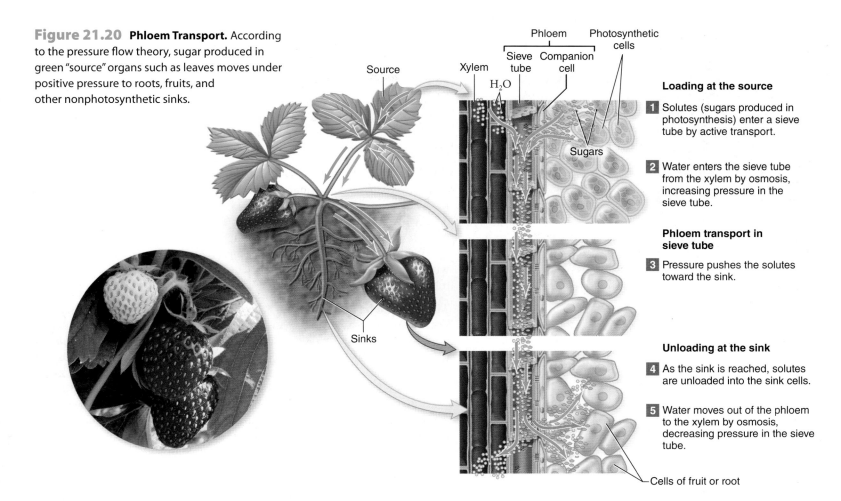

Source
Sinks
Phloem
Sieve tube
Companion cell
Xylem
Photosynthetic cells
H_2O
Sugars

Loading at the source

1 Solutes (sugars produced in photosynthesis) enter a sieve tube by active transport.

2 Water enters the sieve tube from the xylem by osmosis, increasing pressure in the sieve tube.

Phloem transport in sieve tube

3 Pressure pushes the solutes toward the sink.

Unloading at the sink

4 As the sink is reached, solutes are unloaded into the sink cells.

5 Water moves out of the phloem to the xylem by osmosis, decreasing pressure in the sieve tube.

Cells of fruit or root

The most common parasitic plants are the many species of mistletoe. These dark green shrubs live in the branches of host trees throughout the United States (figure 21.21). Most plants infected with mistletoe are weakened but do not die, an observation that makes sense from an evolutionary perspective. The most successful parasites extract enough resources to survive and reproduce—but not so much that the host dies. After all, a dead plant is of no use to a parasite that requires a living host.

Figure 21.21 Mistletoe. This apple tree is heavily infested with parasitic mistletoe plants, which look like green shrubs in the tree's branches.

21.6 Mastering Concepts

1. What are the components of xylem sap?
2. How does transpiration occur?
3. How do stomata help plants conserve water?
4. Summarize the cohesion–tension theory.
5. What are the components of phloem sap?
6. Explain the pressure flow theory of phloem transport.
7. What are some examples of sources and sinks in a plant?
8. How does a parasitic plant infect a host?

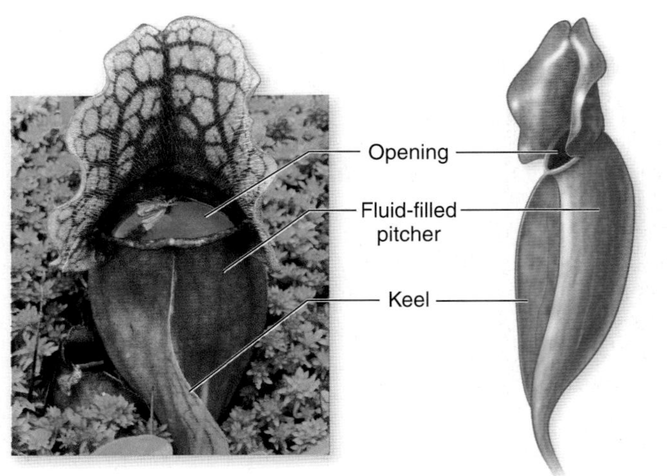

Figure 21.22 Anatomy of a Pitcher. Insects enter the fluid-filled pitcher through a mouthlike opening. The keel is the flap of tissue running the length of the pitcher.

Investigating Life

21.7 The Hidden Cost of Traps

Carnivorous plants seem to have it made: they live in boggy habitats with plentiful water, their invertebrate prey provide nutrients, and they can use energy from sunlight to produce their own food. Yet most plants don't eat bugs.

The Question: Biologists hypothesize that carnivorous plants cannot compete anywhere except sunny, nutrient-poor wetlands because carnivory involves an evolutionary trade-off. To catch an insect, a plant must invest energy in a trap, which takes away from the leaf area available for capturing light. In other words, more traps mean less photosynthesis.

If this hypothetical cost-benefit balance is correct, then a carnivorous plant with sufficient nutrients should invest in photosynthetic leaf area rather than traps. Does this prediction hold true?

The Approach: Aaron Ellison, a biologist at Harvard Forest in Massachusetts, worked with University of Vermont biologist Nicholas Gotelli to test this prediction. They studied the northern pitcher plant, *Sarracenia purpurea* (figure 21.22). The prey-capturing pitchers are modified leaves adorned with a flaplike keel. Once the pitcher fills with rainwater, invertebrates fall in, drown, and decay. The pitchers absorb the nutrients through a thin cuticle.

Ellison and Gotelli manipulated the concentrations of nutrients available to pitcher plants. Ten adult plants each were randomly assigned to one of nine treatments: two controls (distilled water or micronutrients only) and seven solutions containing different amounts of nitrogen and phosphorus. Every two weeks from June through September, the researchers poured 5 milliliters of the assigned solution into every open pitcher of each of the 90 plants. Afterward, they plugged each pitcher to prevent prey capture. The additions continued throughout the growing seasons of three consecutive years.

Every September, the researchers measured all of the pitchers on each study plant (figure 21.23). A normal pitcher has a narrow keel and a wide opening, maximizing the potential for trapping prey. On the other hand, a leaf optimized for photosynthesis has a wide keel and a small pitcher opening. As predicted, the control plants, with low nutrient availability, had prominent pitchers with wide openings and small keels. In contrast, plants that received the most nitrogen had the largest keels and the smallest openings.

The Conclusion: Overall, the study showed that a shortage of nitrogen favored prey capture at the expense of photosynthesis. This experiment has therefore helped shed light on an interesting twist on plant evolution. Carnivory apparently represents a significant trade-off; in most habitats with abundant nutrients, the traps simply cost more energy than they are worth.

Ellison, Aaron M., and Nicholas J. Gotelli. 2002. Nitrogen availability alters the expression of carnivory in the northern pitcher plant, *Sarracenia purpurea*. *Proceedings of the National Academy of Sciences*, vol. 99, no. 7, pages 4409–4412.

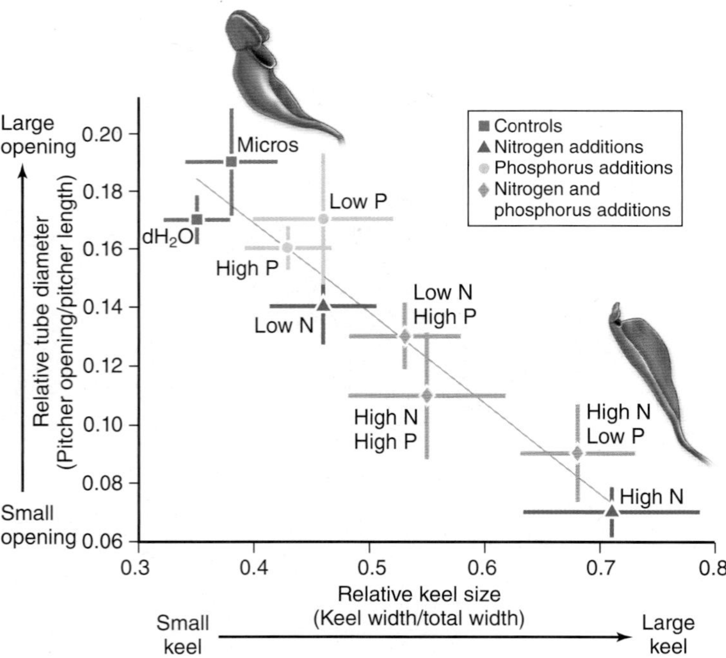

Figure 21.23 Nitrogen Matters. Pitcher plants that received extra nitrogen had much larger keels and smaller pitchers than plants that received little nitrogen, which produced normal pitchers. In this graph, each point represents a treatment average; horizontal and vertical bars represent 95% confidence intervals.

21.7 Mastering Concepts

1. Describe the hypothesis and experimental design in this study.
2. Predict how the graph in figure 21.23 would look if nitrogen did not affect pitcher shape.

Chapter Summary

21.1 Vegetative Plant Parts Include Stems, Leaves, and Roots

- **Anatomy** is the study of an organism's form, and **physiology** is the study of its function. A plant's body consists of **organs** composed of **tissues** that carry out specific functions.
- The **vegetative** plant body consists of a **shoot** and **roots** that depend on each other. Photosynthesis occurs in the shoot, whereas roots absorb water and dissolved minerals.
- The **stem** is the central axis of a shoot and consists of **nodes,** where **leaves** attach, and **internodes** between leaves. An **axillary bud** is located at each node.
- **Herbaceous plants** typically have soft, green stems; **woody plants** have stems and roots strengthened with wood.

21.2 Soil and Air Provide Water and Nutrients

A. Plants Require 16 Essential Elements

- Like all organisms, plants require water and **essential nutrients.**
- In all plants, the nine essential **macronutrients** are C, H, O, P, K, N, S, Ca, and Mg. The seven **micronutrients** are Cl, Fe, B, Mn, Zn, Cu, and Mo.

B. Leaves and Roots Absorb Essential Elements

- Plants obtain CO_2 and O_2 from the atmosphere, and they acquire hydrogen and additional oxygen atoms from H_2O in soil. The other elements also come from soil.
- Mycorrhizal fungi add to the root's surface area for absorbing water and nutrients, especially phosphorus. Several types of bacteria live in root **nodules** and **fix nitrogen,** converting it into forms that plants can use.

21.3 Plant Cells Build Tissues

A. Plants Have Several Cell Types

- **Parenchyma** cells are alive at maturity. They are relatively unspecialized and often function in metabolism or storage.
- **Collenchyma** cells are also alive. Their thick primary cell walls provide elastic support to growing shoots.
- **Sclerenchyma** cells are dead at maturity. Their thick secondary cell walls contain **lignin,** supporting plant parts that are no longer growing.
- Water-conducting cells in **xylem** include long, narrow **tracheids** and barrel-shaped **vessel elements.** Both cell types have thick walls and are dead when functioning. Water moves through pits in tracheids and through the end walls of vessel elements.
- Sugar-conducting cells in **phloem** include **sieve tube elements. Companion cells** help transfer carbohydrates into sieve tubes.

B. Plant Cells Form Three Main Tissue Systems

- Most of the primary plant body consists of **ground tissue,** relatively unspecialized parenchyma cells that fill the space between dermal and vascular tissues.
- **Dermal tissue** includes the **epidermis,** a single cell layer covering the plant. The epidermis secretes a waxy **cuticle** that coats aboveground plant parts. Gas and water exchanges in the shoot occur through **stomata** bounded by **guard cells.**
- **Vascular tissue** is conducting tissue. Xylem transports water and dissolved minerals from roots upward. Phloem transports dissolved carbohydrates and other substances throughout a plant. Xylem and phloem occur together with other tissues to form **vascular bundles.**

21.4 Tissues Build Stems, Leaves, and Roots

A. Stems Support Leaves

- Cells in the shoot apical meristem divide to form the dermal tissue, vascular tissue, and ground tissue in stems and leaves.
- Vascular bundles are scattered in the ground tissue of monocot stems but form a ring in eudicot stems. Between a eudicot stem's epidermis and vascular tissue lies the **cortex,** made of ground tissue. **Pith** is ground tissue in the center of a stem.

B. Leaves Are the Primary Organs of Photosynthesis

- A stalklike **petiole** supports each leaf **blade.** A **simple leaf** has one undivided blade, and a **compound leaf** has multiple leaflets. **Veins** are vascular bundles in leaves; they may be in either netted or parallel formation.

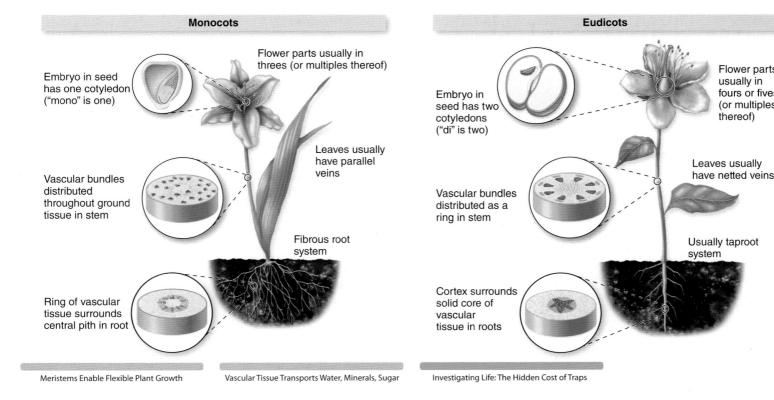

Monocots

Embryo in seed has one cotyledon ("mono" is one)

Flower parts usually in threes (or multiples thereof)

Leaves usually have parallel veins

Vascular bundles distributed throughout ground tissue in stem

Fibrous root system

Ring of vascular tissue surrounds central pith in root

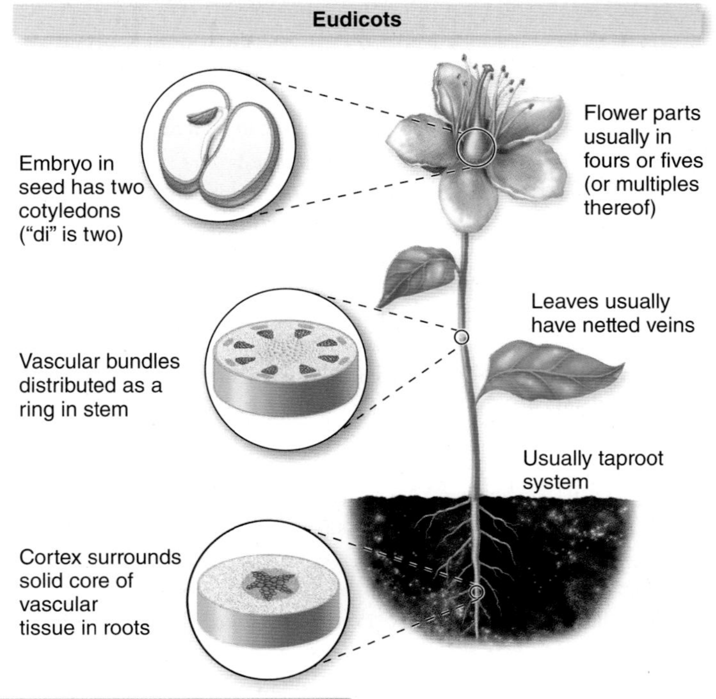
Eudicots
Embryo in seed has two cotyledons ("di" is two)
Flower parts usually in fours or fives (or multiples thereof)
Leaves usually have netted veins
Vascular bundles distributed as a ring in stem
Usually taproot system
Cortex surrounds solid core of vascular tissue in roots

- The cells that make up a leaf's epidermis are tightly packed, transparent, and mostly nonphotosynthetic. Leaf ground tissue includes **mesophyll** cells that carry out photosynthesis. Stomata enable gas exchange.

C. Roots Absorb Water and Minerals, and Anchor the Plant

- **Fibrous root systems** consist of shallow, branched, relatively fine roots, whereas **taproot systems** have a large, persistent major root with small branches emerging from it.
- A **root cap** protects the tip of a growing root. The root cortex consists of storage parenchyma and the **endodermis.** A waxy strip surrounding the cells of the endodermis ensures that the solution entering the root's xylem first passes through the living cells of the endodermis.

21.5 Plants Have Flexible Growth Patterns, Thanks to Meristems

A. Plants Grow by Adding New Modules

- Plants with **determinate growth** stop growing when they reach their mature size; plants with **indeterminate growth** grow indefinitely.

B. Plant Growth Occurs at Meristems

- **Meristems** are localized collections of cells that retain the ability to divide throughout the life of the plant. **Apical meristems** are at the tips of shoots and roots; **lateral meristems** are cylinders of cells at the periphery of a woody stem or root.

C. In Primary Growth, Apical Meristems Lengthen Stems and Roots

- Apical meristems at the root and shoot tips provide **primary growth.** As the tip lengthens, cells arising from the apical meristems differentiate into the three tissue types.

D. In Secondary Growth, Lateral Meristems Thicken Stems and Roots

- **Secondary growth** increases the girth of the stem or root. The **vascular cambium** is a lateral meristem that produces **wood** (secondary xylem) and secondary phloem.
- Another type of lateral meristem, the **cork cambium,** produces parenchyma cells and cork. The cork makes up the majority of a woody plant's **bark.**
- **Heartwood** is the central, dark-colored, nonfunctioning wood in a tree. The light-colored **sapwood** transports water and minerals.
- Tree rings result from seasonal differences in the size of wood's xylem cells.

21.6 Vascular Tissue Transports Water, Minerals, and Sugar

A. Water and Minerals Are Pulled Up to Leaves in Xylem

- **Xylem sap** consists of water and dissolved minerals.
- Leaves lose water by **transpiration** through open stomata.
- According to the **cohesion–tension theory,** water molecules evaporating from leaves are replaced by those pulled up from below, a consequence of the cohesive properties of water.
- Water enters roots by osmosis and moves through the root's epidermis and cortex. The endodermis controls which minerals enter the xylem.

B. Sugars Are Pushed to Nonphotosynthetic Cells in Phloem

- **Phloem sap** includes sugars, hormones, and other organic molecules, along with water and minerals from xylem.
- According to the **pressure flow theory,** phloem sap flows under positive pressure through sieve tubes from a **source** (such as a leaf) to a **sink.**
- Sources are photosynthetic or sugar-storing parts that load carbohydrates into phloem. Water follows by osmosis. The increase in pressure drives phloem sap to nonphotosynthetic sinks such as roots, flowers, and fruits.

C. Parasitic Plants Tap into Another Plant's Vascular Tissue

- Mistletoe and other parasitic plants absorb water, minerals, and sugar from a host plant's xylem and phloem.

21.7 Investigating Life: The Hidden Cost of Traps

- Carnivorous plants produce leaves that reflect a balance between prey capture and photosynthesis. Experiments show that nutrient additions tip the balance in favor of photosynthetic leaf area.

Multiple Choice Questions

1. Which of the following is NOT a vegetative organ in a plant?
   a. Stem c. Flower
   b. Leaf d. Root
2. What is the difference between a macronutrient and a micronutrient?
   a. The size of the atoms
   b. The amount required by the plant
   c. The use by multicellular (macroorganisms) versus microorganisms
   d. The source of the nutrient
3. Which of the following is a living cell type that physically supports the growing plant?
   a. Parenchyma c. Sclerenchyma
   b. Collenchyma d. Both b and c are correct.
4. If you spray herbicide onto a weed, which barrier might prevent the chemical from entering the leaves?
   a. The stomata c. The cuticle
   b. The endodermis d. The pith
5. What is the function of the endodermis?
   a. It allows the root to control which substances enter the xylem.
   b. It is made of meristem cells that produce vascular tissue.
   c. It blocks the movement of water out of the vascular bundle.
   d. It minimizes the loss of water from the leaves of a plant.
6. The ability of a sunflower plant to become taller is directly due to its
   a. apical meristem. c. mesophyll cells.
   b. lateral meristems. d. taproot system.
7. Which tissue type occupies most of the volume of a woody stem?
   a. Secondary xylem c. Bark
   b. Secondary phloem d. Vascular cambium
8. Sugars and other organic compounds travel through ______, whereas water and dissolved minerals travel through ______.
   a. the cytoplasm of xylem cells; sieve cells
   b. tracheids and vessels; companion cells
   c. phloem sieve tubes; companion cells
   d. phloem sieve tubes; tracheids and vessels
9. According to the cohesion–tension theory, transpiration drives xylem sap movement because of
   a. the presence of the endodermis.
   b. hydrogen bond formation between water molecules.
   c. upward pressure from water moving into roots.
   d. the presence of the cuticle.
10. Where do the simple sugars in phloem sap ultimately come from?
    a. The roots c. Photosynthesis
    b. Storage organs such as fruits d. Starch

Write It Out

1. List the vegetative organs of a plant. How does each rely on the others?
2. Biologists often say that "form follows function"; that is, the form of a biological structure facilitates its function. List a function of each organ,

tissue, and cell type described in this chapter, and then list at least one feature that facilitates that function.

3. How do plants obtain carbon and nitrogen?
4. How might DNA technology (see chapter 11) be used to create transgenic plants that can fix their own nitrogen? In what ways would this new feature change agriculture?
5. Apoptosis (programmed cell death) is a normal part of development in both plants and animals. Which plant tissues have cells that are dead at maturity? Why is it advantageous to the plant for these cells to die?
6. Corn is a monocot and sunflower is a eudicot. Make a chart that compares the stems, leaves, and roots of these plants.
7. Many biology labs use slides of root tips to demonstrate the stages of mitosis. Why is a root tip a better choice than a mature leaf?
8. Thorns, spines, and tendrils are so highly modified that it can be difficult to tell whether they derive from leaves or stems. How could a biologist use his or her knowledge of plant anatomy to determine their origin?
9. Describe why and how leaves and roots maximize surface area.
10. Mammals exchange gases in the alveoli of the lungs (see figure 27.17). How do the structures and functions of leaf mesophyll compare with those of alveoli?
11. Explain the evolutionary forces that selected for the cuticle, stomata, vascular tissue, roots, stems, and leaves in land plants.
12. Girdling is cutting away or severing the living bark in a ring around a tree's trunk. Which part of a girdled tree do you expect to die first, the roots or the shoot? Why? Would the tree be harmed as much by a vertical gash? Why or why not?
13. Heartwood often contains chemicals that inhibit microbial growth. How are these chemicals adaptive?
14. Make a chart comparing xylem and phloem transport. Include sap composition, characteristics of the conducting cells, how the sap moves, whether the transport costs energy, and direction of flow within the plant.
15. Trace the path of water and dissolved minerals from soil, into the root's xylem, and up to the leaves.
16. Explain the role of cohesion in xylem transport.
17. Review C_3, C_4, and CAM photosynthesis in chapter 5. Explain how plants that use each pathway conserve water.
18. Distinguish between a source and a sink. How can the same plant part act as both a source and a sink?
19. Peach and nectarine growers remove some flowers and small, immature fruits from trees. Why does this practice yield larger, higher-quality fruit?
20. Suppose that a scientist exposes a leaf to CO_2 labeled with carbon-14 and that the radioactive carbon is incorporated into organic compounds in photosynthetic cells. At various times after exposure, the scientist can determine the location of the radioactive carbon in the plant. In what tissues do you expect to find the radioactive material immediately after exposure to the labeled carbon? What about during transport? When transport is complete, will the radioactive material be in plant parts above the leaf, below the leaf, or both?
21. Pitcher plants are threatened in the wild by habitat destruction and collection for plant trade. Researchers are also concerned that air pollution will deposit additional nitrogen on soil. How would additional nitrogen affect pitcher plants?
22. Some architects specialize in building living roofs covered with plants. What are the benefits and risks of living roofs? What raw materials must be supplied to plants living on a roof? What types of plants would be the best choice? How does your answer depend on where you live?

Pull It Together

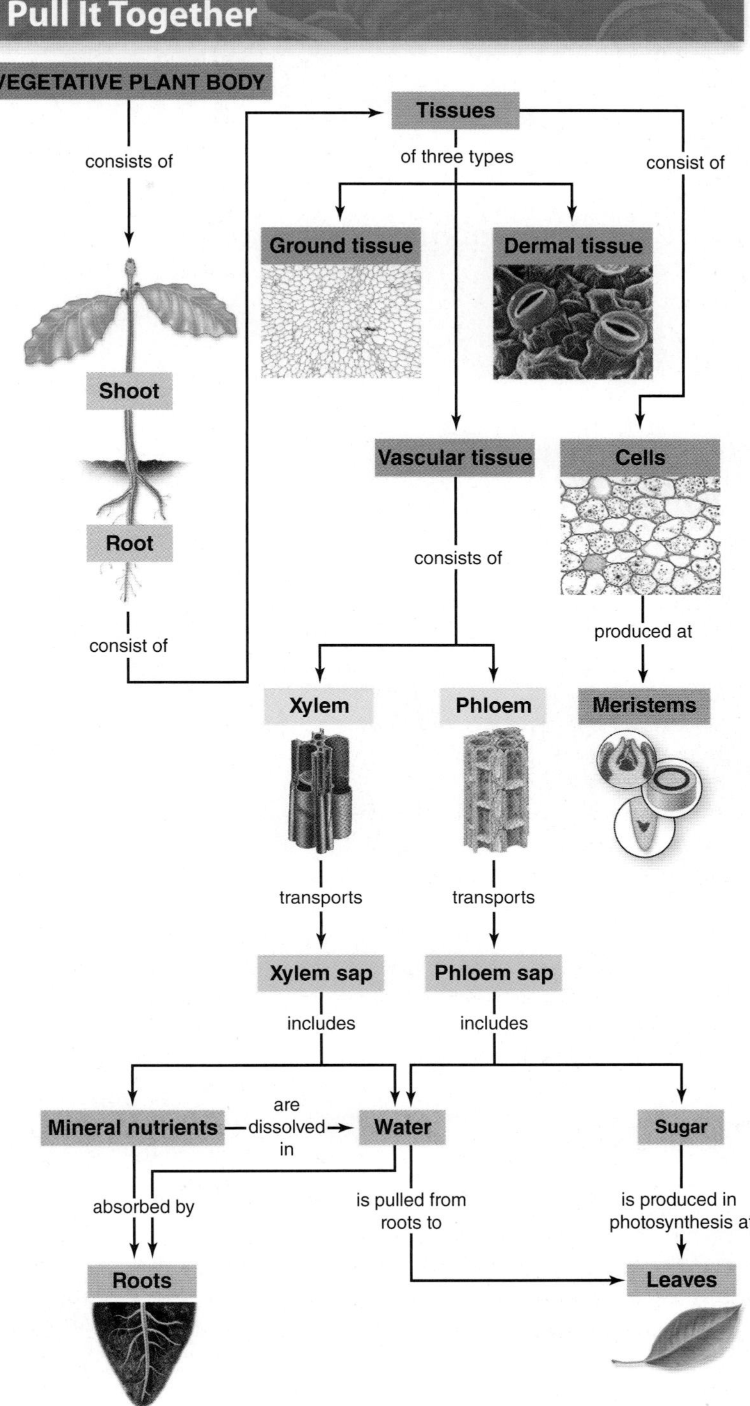

1. Which nutrients come from soil? Which come from the atmosphere?
2. How do parenchyma, collenchyma, and sclerenchyma fit into this map?
3. What are the two types of meristems? How do they differ?
4. Add *soil, source, sink, pressure flow*, and *transpiration* to this map.
5. What role do stomata play in transpiration?

Enhance your study of this chapter with practice quizzes, animations and videos, answer keys, and downloadable study tools.
www.mhhe.com/hoefnagels

22 Reproduction and Development of Flowering Plants

Big Prize. This ant's treasure is a huge seed. But the plant wins too when the ant buries the seed.

Learning Outline

Learn How to Learn

How to Use a Tutor

Your school may provide tutoring sessions for your class, or perhaps you have hired a private tutor. How can you make the most of this resource? First, meet regularly with your tutor for an hour or two each week; don't wait until just before an exam. Second, if possible, tell your tutor what you want to work on before each session, so he or she can prepare. Third, bring your textbook, class notes, and questions to your tutoring session. Fourth, be realistic. Your tutor can discuss difficult concepts and help you practice with the material, but don't expect him or her to simply give you the answers to your homework.

What's the Point?

Flowers, fruits, and seeds enrich all of our lives. Humans depend on plants, so we have a strong interest in understanding plant reproduction and development.

Other animals have a stake in plant reproduction, too. The bee in the above photo is gathering pollen and nectar; on the left, an ant is toting a seed. Each insect is serving its own interests, using plants for food. But at the same time, each is also contributing to a plant's reproductive success. After all, the pollen contains the plant's sperm, which the bee may deliver to another plant's egg. And the ant will store its prize in its underground nest, where the seed may eventually germinate. If the nest is any distance from the seed's source, the ant has benefited the plant by reducing competition between parent and offspring.

The connections between flowering plants and animals are fascinating and intricate. So are the interactions among genes, hormones, and environmental cues that enable a seed to germinate and grow. This chapter assembles some of the pieces of the complex puzzle of plant reproduction and development.

22.1 Angiosperms Reproduce Sexually and Asexually

Flowering plants (angiosperms) dominate many terrestrial landscapes. From grasslands to deciduous forests and from garden plots to large-scale agriculture, angiosperms have been extremely successful. These plants first evolved only about 130 million years ago, yet they subsequently branched into more than 250,000 species, and they occupy nearly every habitat on land.

Angiosperms share the land with three other groups of plants: the mosses and their relatives; the ferns and their relatives; and the conifers and other gymnosperms (see chapter 16). But the flowering plants are by far the most diverse and widespread. Angiosperms owe their success to three adaptations. First, they produce pollen, which enables sperm to fertilize an egg in the absence of free water. In contrast, the sperm cells of mosses and ferns must swim to the egg, so these plants can reproduce sexually only in moist habitats. Second, the seed protects the embryo during dormancy and nourishes the developing seedling. Third, flowers not only promote pollination but also develop into fruits that help disperse the seeds far from the parent plant.

Most angiosperms reproduce sexually. **Sexual reproduction** yields genetically unique offspring with a mix of traits derived from two parents. Scrambling genes in this way is adaptive in a changing environment. After all, a gene combination that is successful today might not work in the future if selective pressures change. Producing variable offspring improves reproductive success in an uncertain world. Section 22.2 describes the sexual life cycle of angiosperms in detail. ▸ why sex?, p. 155

Many species of angiosperms also reproduce asexually, forming new individuals by mitotic cell division. In **asexual reproduction,** a parent organism produces offspring that are genetically identical to it and to each other—they are clones. Asexual reproduction, also called vegetative reproduction, is advantageous when conditions are stable and plants are well adapted to their surroundings, because the clones will be equally suited to the same environment.

Plants often reproduce asexually by forming new plants from portions of their roots, stems, or leaves (figure 22.1). For example, aerial shoots can grow upward from buds on the roots of aspen, cherry, pear, apple, and black locust trees. If these shoots, called "suckers," are cut or broken away from the parent plant, they can become new individuals.

The rest of this chapter begins with a look at sexual reproduction in flowering plants. As you will see, the plant packages its offspring inside a seed. When the seed germinates, the young plant faces a host of challenges. The second half of this chapter explores the hormonal signals and environmental factors that influence the development of the angiosperm throughout its life.

a.

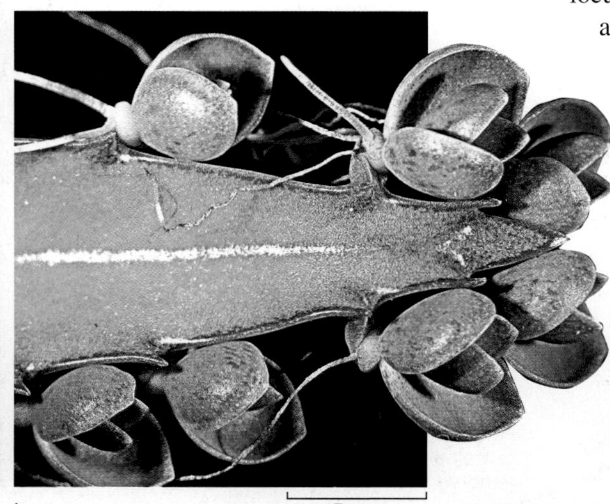

b.

Figure 22.1 Asexual Reproduction. (a) Quaking aspen trees are clones connected by a common root system. (b) The leaf of this kalanchoe plant is producing genetically identical plantlets.

22.1 Mastering Concepts

1. What adaptations contribute to the reproductive success of angiosperms?
2. When are sexual and asexual reproduction each adaptive?
3. What are some examples of asexual reproduction in plants?

22.2 The Angiosperm Life Cycle Includes Flowers, Fruits, and Seeds

When humans reproduce, sexual intercourse brings sperm near an egg cell, and the embryo develops into a fetus. Childbirth separates woman from baby. Clearly, flowering plant sexual reproduction is different from our own. How does the sperm get to the egg in angiosperms? How does the angiosperm embryo develop (along with surrounding tissues) into a seed? How do the seeds separate from the "mother" plant? This section answers these questions as it explains sexual reproduction in flowering plants.

Figure 22.2 summarizes the life cycle of a typical flowering plant; you may find it helpful to refer back to this figure often as you read the rest of this section. The first thing to notice is that the angiosperm life cycle includes an **alternation of generations** with multicellular diploid and haploid stages (see figure 16.5). The **sporophyte,** or diploid generation, produces haploid **spores** by meiosis; in figure 22.2, the sporophyte is the tree at top center. A spore, in turn, divides mitotically to produce a multicellular haploid **gametophyte,** which undergoes mitosis to generate haploid **gametes** (egg cells or sperm).

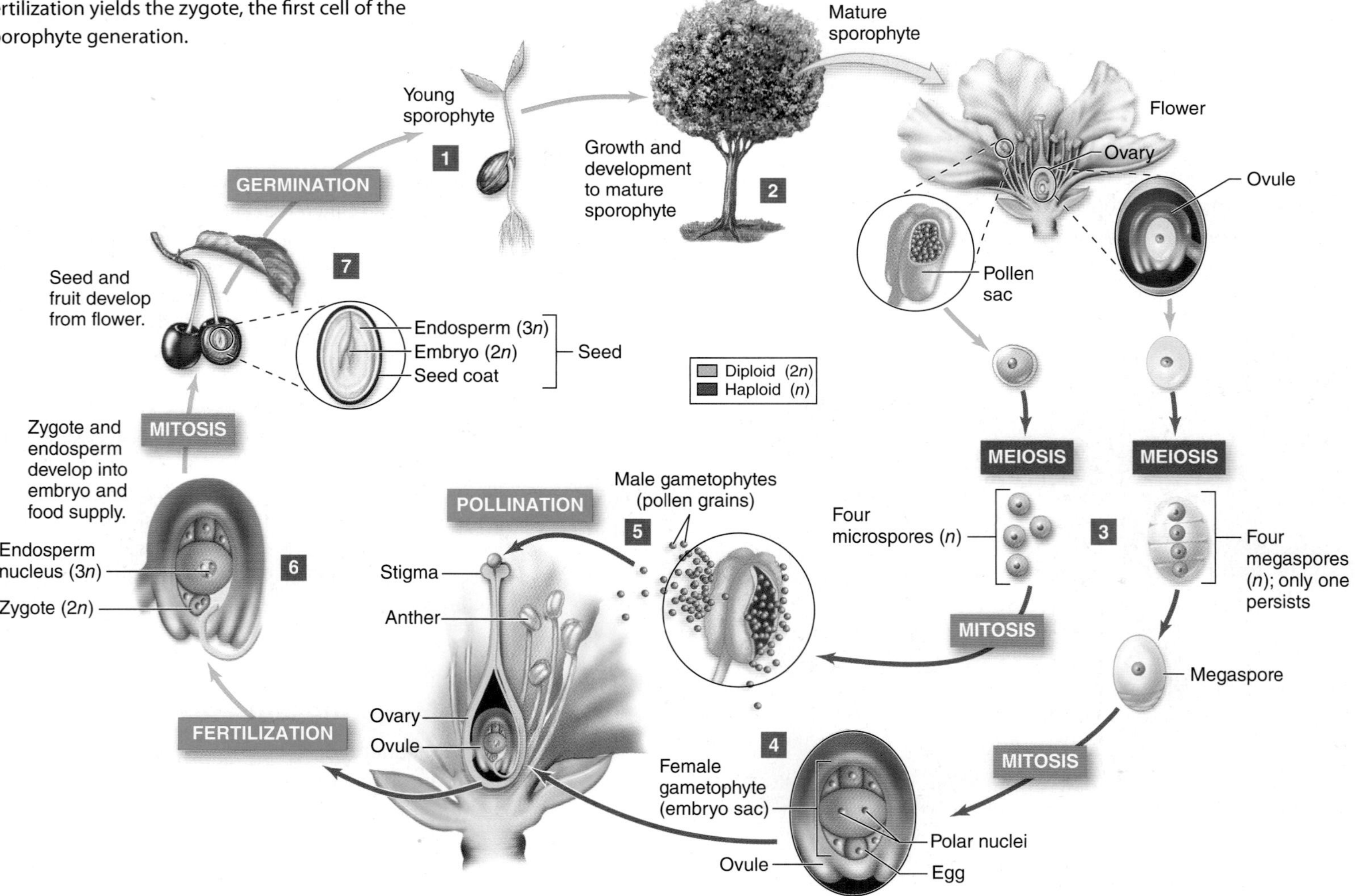

Figure 22.2 Flowering Plant Life Cycle. Cells in the flower undergo meiosis to produce microspores and megaspores, which develop into the gametophytes that produce sperm and egg cells. Fertilization yields the zygote, the first cell of the sporophyte generation.

These gametophytes appear near the bottom of figure 22.2. In **fertilization,** male and female gametes fuse to form a diploid **zygote.** The zygote develops into an embryo as its cells divide mitotically. With additional growth, the embryo becomes a mature sporophyte, and the cycle begins anew.

Notice also that figure 22.2 shows two adaptations that are unique to the angiosperms: flowers and fruits. **Flowers** are reproductive organs that bring together eggs and sperm. Parts of the flower develop into a **fruit,** which protects and disperses the seeds.

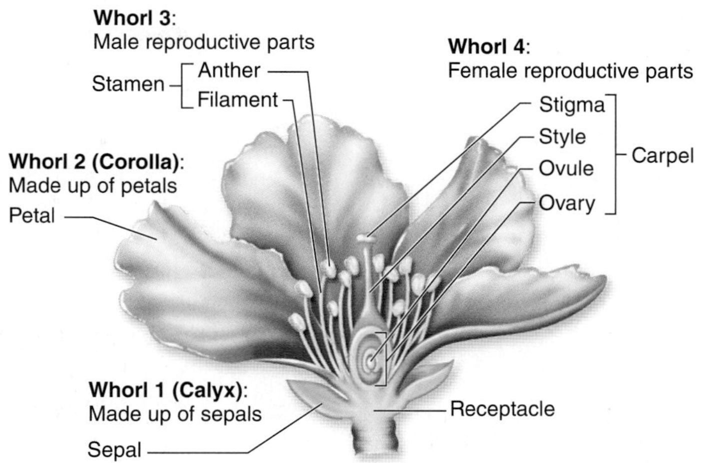

Figure 22.3 Parts of a Flower. A complete flower consists of four whorls: sepals, petals, male reproductive parts, and female reproductive parts.

A. Flowers Are Reproductive Organs

The first step in angiosperm reproduction is the formation of flowers on the mature sporophyte. A part of the floral stalk called the **receptacle** is the attachment point for all flower parts (figure 22.3). A typical flower has four types of structures, all of which are modified leaves. The outermost whorl is called the **calyx**. It consists of **sepals,** which are green, leaflike structures that enclose and protect the inner floral parts. Inside the calyx is the **corolla,** which is a whorl of **petals.** The calyx and corolla do not play a direct role in sexual reproduction, although in many flowers, colorful petals attract pollinators.

The two innermost whorls of a flower are essential for sexual reproduction. The whorl within the corolla consists of the **stamens,** which are filaments that bear pollen-producing bodies called **anthers** at their tips. The whorl at the center of a flower is composed of one or more **carpels,** the structures enclosing the egg-bearing **ovules.** The bases of carpels and their enclosed ovules make up the **ovary.** The upper part of each carpel is a stalklike **style** that bears a structure called a **stigma** at its tip. Stigmas receive pollen.

The flower in figure 22.3 is "complete" because it includes all four whorls, including both male and female parts. In some species, however, the sexes are separate. That is, each flower has either male or female parts but not both. An individual plant may have both types of single-sex flowers, or the plant may produce just one flower type. A holly plant, for example, is either male or female; only the female plants produce the distinctive red berries.

Recall from chapters 16 and 21 that the two largest clades of angiosperms are monocots and eudicots. Flower structure is one feature that distinguishes the two groups. Most monocots, such as lilies and tulips, have petals, stamens, and other flower parts in multiples of three. Most eudicots, on the other hand, have flower parts in multiples of four or five. Buttercups and geraniums are examples of eudicots with five prominent petals on each flower.

B. The Pollen Grain and Embryo Sac Are Gametophytes

Once the flowers have formed, the next step is to produce the microscopic male and female gametophytes (see figure 22.2). Inside the anther's pollen sacs, diploid cells divide by meiosis to produce four haploid **microspores.** Each microspore then divides mitotically and produces a two-celled, thick-walled structure called a **pollen** grain, which is the young male gametophyte. One of the haploid cells inside the pollen grain divides by mitosis to form two sperm nuclei.

Meanwhile, meiosis also occurs in the female flower parts. The ovary may contain one or more ovules, each containing a diploid cell that divides by meiosis to produce four haploid **megaspores.** In many species, three of these cells quickly disintegrate, leaving one large megaspore. The megaspore undergoes three mitotic divisions to form the **embryo sac,** which is the mature female

gametophyte. Each female gametophyte therefore consists of eight haploid nuclei but only seven cells. One of these cells is the egg. In addition, a large, central cell contains two **polar nuclei;** as we shall see, both the egg and the polar nuclei participate in fertilization.

C. Pollination Brings Pollen to the Stigma

Eventually, the pollen sac opens and releases millions of pollen grains. The next step is **pollination:** the transfer of pollen from an anther to a receptive stigma. Usually, pollen is carried by animals or the wind (figure 22.4).

Flower color, shape, and odor attract animal pollinators. For example, hummingbirds are attracted to red, tubular flowers. Butterflies prefer red or purple flowers with wide landing pads. Moths and bats pollinate white or yellow, heavily scented flowers, which are easy to locate at night. Blue or yellow sweet-smelling blooms attract bees. Bee-pollinated flowers often have markings that are visible only at ultraviolet wavelengths of light, which bees can perceive. Beetles visit dull-colored flowers with spicy scents.

Many animals benefit from their association with plants: they obtain food in the form of pollen or sugary nectar, seek shelter among the petals, or use the flower for a mating ground (see section 6.9). The connection between plant and pollinator may be so strong that the partners directly influence each other's evolution. In **coevolution,** a genetic change in one species selects for subsequent change in the genome of another species. Coevolution is likely when a plant has an exclusive relationship with just one pollinator species. For example, some hummingbirds have long, curved bills that fit precisely into the tubular flowers from which they sip nectar. No other species can drink from these tubular flowers.

About 10% of angiosperms (along with most gymnosperms) use wind, not animals, to carry pollen. Wind-pollinated flowers are small and odorless, and their petals are typically reduced or absent; perfume, nectar, and showy flowers are not necessary for wind to disperse pollen. One advantage of wind pollination is that the plant does not spend energy on nectar or other lures. On the other hand, an animal delivers pollen directly to another plant, whereas the wind is "wasteful." That is, wind-blown pollen may land on the ground, on water, or on the wrong plant species. Wind-pollinated plants therefore manufacture abundant pollen, an adaptation that compensates for this inefficiency. The large quantities of pollen produced by oaks, cottonwoods, ragweed, and grasses provoke allergies in many people. ▸ allergies, p. 602

a.

b.

c.

d.

e.

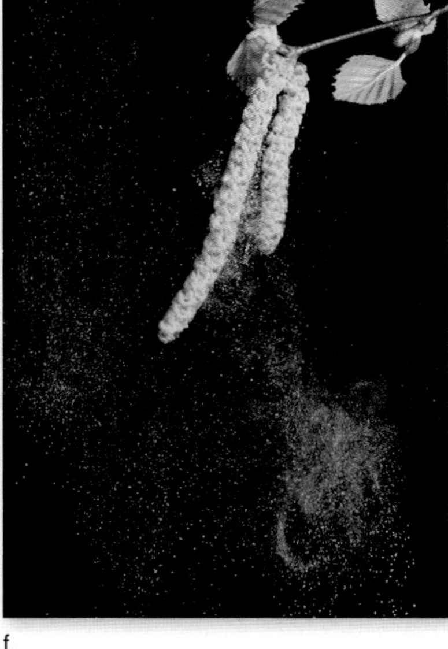
f.

Figure 22.4 Pollination. Animal pollinators include (a) hummingbirds, (b) butterflies, and (c) bats. (d) These yellow petals appear uniform to our eyes, but (e) the flower actually has distinctive markings that attract insects and are visible only in ultraviolet light. (f) The birch tree is wind-pollinated.

D. Double Fertilization Yields Zygote and Endosperm

After a pollen grain lands on a stigma of the correct species, a pollen tube emerges (figure 22.5, step 1). The pollen grain's two haploid sperm nuclei enter the pollen tube as it grows through the tissue of the style toward the ovary (figure 22.5, step 2). When the pollen tube reaches an ovule, it discharges its two sperm nuclei into the embryo sac.

Then, in **double fertilization,** these sperm nuclei fertilize the egg and the two polar nuclei (figure 22.5, step 3). That is, one sperm nucleus fuses with the haploid egg nucleus and forms a diploid zygote, which will develop into the embryo. The second sperm nucleus fuses with the two haploid polar nuclei. The resulting triploid nucleus divides to form a tissue called **endosperm,** which is composed of parenchyma cells that store food for the developing embryo. Familiar endosperms are the "milk" and "meat" of a coconut and the

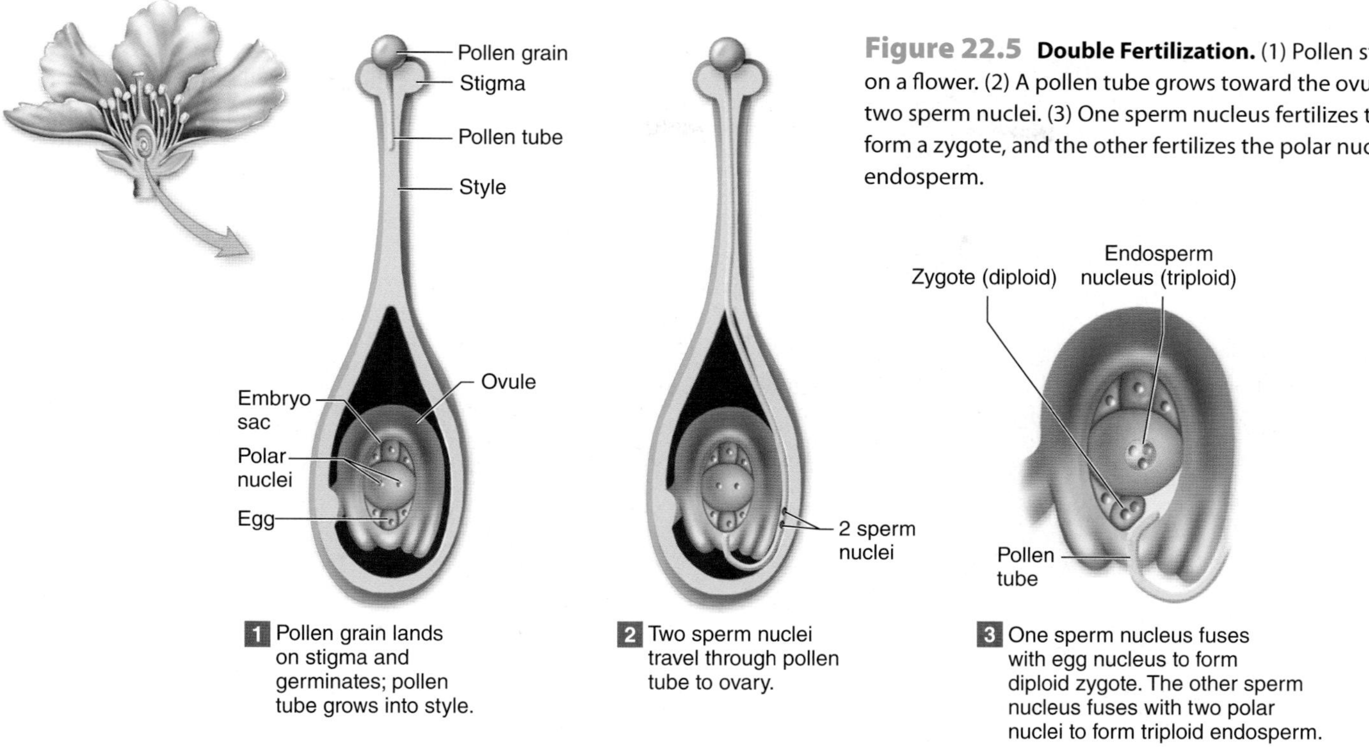
Pollen grain
Stigma
Pollen tube
Style
Ovule
Embryo sac
Polar nuclei
Egg
2 sperm nuclei
Zygote (diploid)
Endosperm nucleus (triploid)
Pollen tube
1 Pollen grain lands on stigma and germinates; pollen tube grows into style.
2 Two sperm nuclei travel through pollen tube to ovary.
3 One sperm nucleus fuses with egg nucleus to form diploid zygote. The other sperm nucleus fuses with two polar nuclei to form triploid endosperm.

Figure 22.5 Double Fertilization. (1) Pollen sticks to a stigma on a flower. (2) A pollen tube grows toward the ovule and transports two sperm nuclei. (3) One sperm nucleus fertilizes the egg to form a zygote, and the other fertilizes the polar nuclei to yield the endosperm.

starchy part of a rice grain. The starchy endosperm of corn is an important food source and a raw material for producing ethanol, a biofuel. ▶ biofuels, p. 308

Double fertilization reduces the energetic cost of reproduction. In gymnosperms, the female gametophyte stockpiles food for the embryo in advance of fertilization. The investment is wasted if no zygote ever forms. In contrast, double fertilization ensures that an angiosperm devotes energy to producing endosperm only if a sperm nucleus actually fertilizes an egg.

E. A Seed Is an Embryo with Its Food Supply Inside a Seed Coat

Immediately after fertilization, the ovule contains an embryo sac with a diploid zygote and a triploid endosperm. The ovule eventually develops into a **seed:** a plant embryo together with its stored food, surrounded by a seed coat. Where do these parts come from?

The zygote divides to form the embryo (figure 22.6). Among the first features of the developing embryo are the **cotyledons,** or seed leaves. Soon, the shoot and root apical meristems form at opposite ends of the embryo. (The cotyledons are called "seed leaves" because in many species they emerge from the soil with the seedling and carry out photosynthesis for a short time. But they are not true leaves, which always form at the shoot apical meristem.)

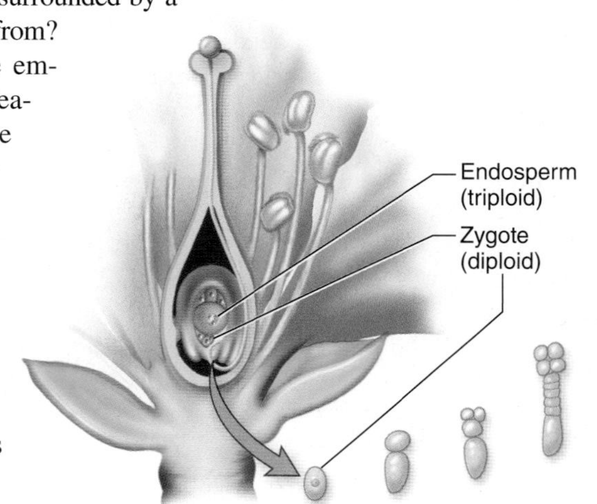
Endosperm (triploid)
Zygote (diploid)

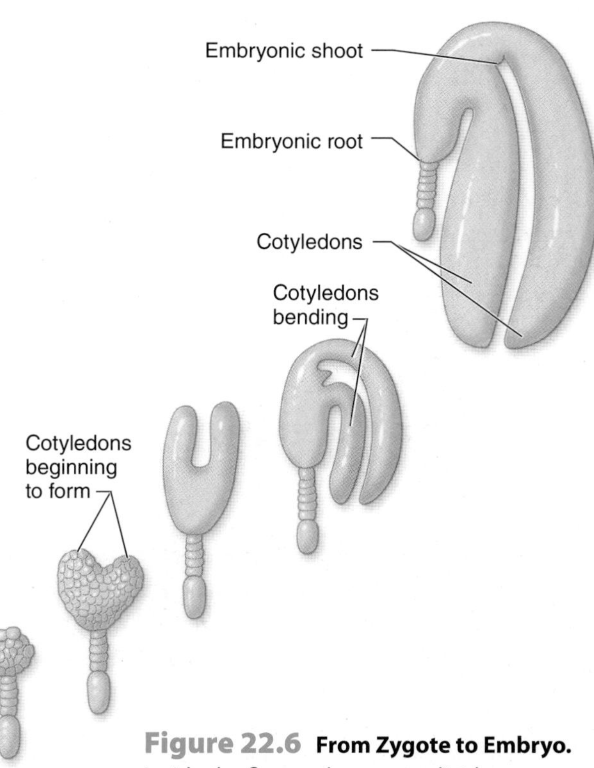
Embryonic shoot
Embryonic root
Cotyledons
Cotyledons bending
Cotyledons beginning to form

Figure 22.6 From Zygote to Embryo. Inside the flower, the zygote divides repeatedly to form the tiny embryonic plant.

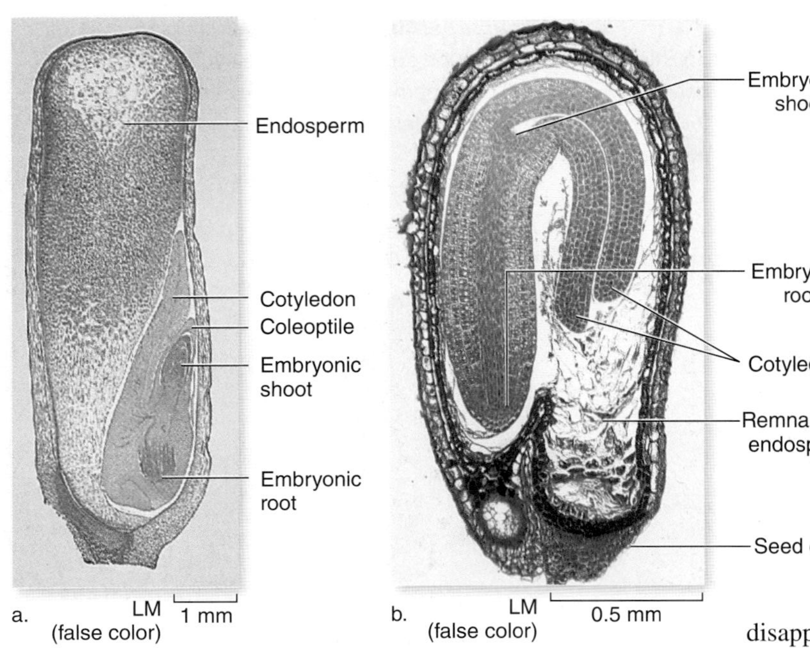

Figure 22.7 Mature Seeds. (a) Corn is a monocot. The seed includes a starchy endosperm and an embryo with one cotyledon. (b) The seeds of eudicots have paired cotyledons, which may absorb much of the endosperm. The photo shows a seed of a plant called shepherd's purse; the diagram shows the corresponding structures in a bean seed.

What about the embryo's food supply? Inside the developing seed, the endosperm cells divide more rapidly than the zygote and thus form a large multicellular mass. This endosperm supplies nutrients to the developing embryo. In monocots, the single cotyledon transfers stored nutrients from the endosperm to the embryo during germination. The paired cotyledons of many eudicots, on the other hand, become thick and fleshy as they absorb the endosperm. Figure 22.7 illustrates these differences between the seeds of monocots and eudicots.

As the embryo and endosperm develop, the seed coat also begins to form. In many species, the **seed coat** is a tough outer layer that protects both the embryo and its food supply from damage, predators, and dehydration. In other plants, including corn, the thin seed coat all but disappears as the seed matures.

At some point in seed development, hormones "tell" cells in the embryo and endosperm to stop dividing, and the seed gradually loses moisture and enters dormancy. The ripe, mature seeds are firm, dry, and ready for dispersal.

Seed dormancy is a crucial adaptation because it ensures that seeds have time to disperse away from the parent plant before germinating. Moreover, dormancy enables seeds to postpone development if the environment is unfavorable, such as during a drought or frost. Favorable conditions trigger embryo growth to resume when young plants are more likely to survive.

Producing seeds is costly: the plant uses precious sugars, lipids, and other organic molecules to produce both the embryo and its stored food supply. The seed continues to consume its parent's resources until it enters dormancy. From that time until the young seedling begins carrying out photosynthesis on its own, however, the only energy available to the embryo is the fuel stored inside the seed.

F. The Fruit Develops from the Ovary

The rest of the flower changes as the seeds develop inside. When a pollen tube begins growing, the stigma produces large amounts of ethylene, a plant hormone discussed in section 22.4. Ethylene stimulates unneeded flower parts such as stamens and petals to wither and fall to the ground. Developing seeds also produce another hormone, auxin, that triggers fruit formation.

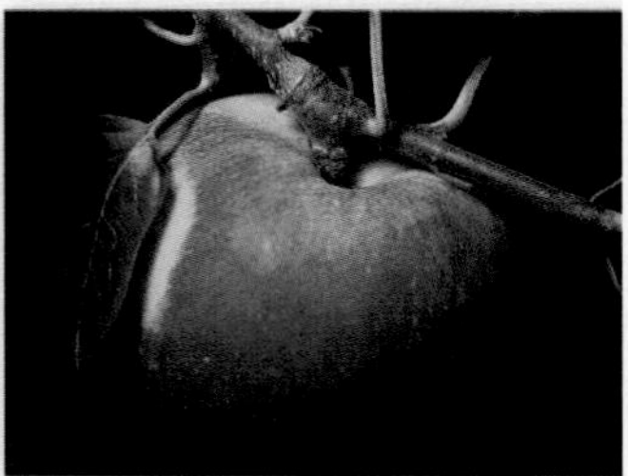

Figure 22.8 Development of a Fruit. After pollination and fertilization, the apple tree's flower begins to develop into a fruit. The fleshy part of an apple develops from the receptacle, which enlarges along with the ovary wall as the fruit develops.

In many angiosperms, the ovary grows rapidly to form the fruit, which may contain one or more seeds. (The Burning Question on page 456 explores how seedless fruits develop.) In some species, additional plant parts also join in fruit development. The pulp of an apple, for example, derives from a cup-shaped region of the receptacle. The apple's core is derived from the carpel walls, which enclose the seeds. Figure 22.8 shows how the parts of an apple flower give rise to the fruit.

Fruits come in many forms (table 22.1). A simple fruit develops from a flower with one carpel. The carpel may have one seed, as in a cherry, or many seeds, as in a tomato. An aggregate fruit develops from one flower with many carpels. Strawberries and raspberries are examples of aggregate fruits. A multiple fruit develops from clusters of flowers that fuse into a single fruit as they mature. Pineapples and figs are multiple fruits.

Only shoots give rise to flowers, so it may seem surprising that some fruits develop underground. The yellow flowers of peanut plants, for example, form on the shoot. After fertilization, the petals wither, and the young fruit produces a peg that turns downward and buries itself in the soil. Three to five months later, farmers dig up the plants to harvest the mature fruits. Each fruit consists of a fibrous shell enclosing one to three peanuts—the seeds.

TABLE 22.1 Types of Fruits: A Summary

Fruit Type	Characteristics	Example(s)
Simple	Derived from one flower with one carpel	Olive, cherry, peach, plum, coconut, grape, tomato, pepper, eggplant, apple, pear
Aggregate	Derived from one flower with many separate carpels	Blackberry, strawberry, raspberry, magnolia
Multiple	Derived from tightly clustered flowers whose ovaries fuse as fruit develops	Pineapple

G. Fruits Protect and Disperse Seeds

Fruits have two main functions, one of which is the protection of the seeds. Many developing fruits contain chemicals that animals find distasteful. Anyone who has ever bitten into an unripe apple, plum, or tomato can testify to the hard texture and intensely sour flavor. Animals avoid these unappealing, unripe fruits, so the immature seeds inside remain safe from herbivory. Once the seeds are mature, however, the fruit changes: it becomes soft, sweet, and appealing to animals.

These changes relate to the second function of fruits: to promote seed dispersal by animals, wind, and water (figure 22.9). Regardless of the transportation mode, the seeds are often deposited far from the parent plant, promoting reproductive success by minimizing competition between parent and offspring.

a.

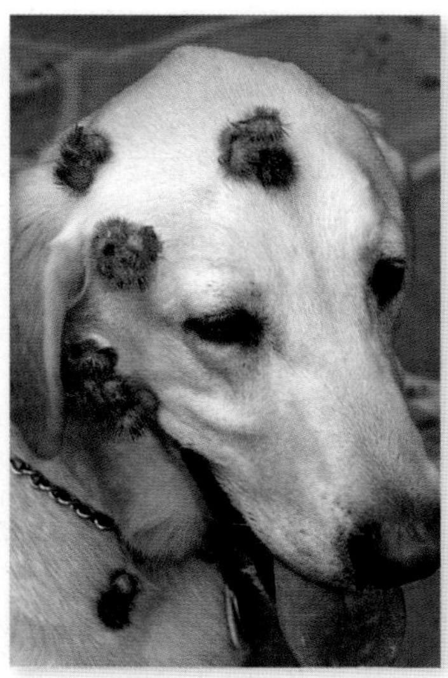
b.

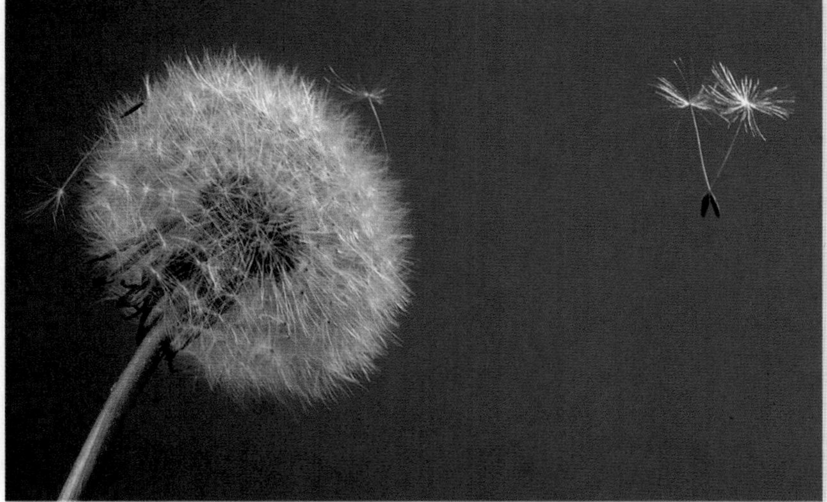
c.

Figure 22.9 Seed Dispersal. (a) This bird, a cedar waxwing, eats winterberry fruits and eliminates the seeds in its droppings. (b) Dogs and other mammals unwittingly disperse prickly fruits, such as these burrs from a burdock plant. (c) Dandelion fruits have fluff that enables them to float on a breeze.

Burning Questions

How can a fruit be seedless?

Given the role of seeds and fruits in plant reproduction, seedless fruits might seem to be a bit of a puzzle. After all, from a plant's point of view, what's the point of producing a fruit without seeds inside? Natural selection clearly would not favor such a trait in the wild! But humans often consider seeds a nuisance and have selected for seedless varieties.

Seedless fruits can form in two ways. Often, the fruit develops in the absence of fertilization. Seedless oranges and watermelons are two examples. Alternatively, if fertilization does occur, the embryos may die during development. Tiny, immature seeds remain inside the fruit, but they do not interfere with eating. Seedless grapes and bananas illustrate this second path to seedlessness.

Since seedless fruits lack seeds, how do farmers grow more of them? Most are produced asexually by grafting or taking cuttings. But, surprisingly, seedless watermelons do come from seeds! To make "seedless watermelon seeds," plant breeders first cross a regular diploid watermelon plant with a tetraploid plant (with four sets of chromosomes). Farmers then sow the triploid seeds arising from this union. The new triploid plants produce flowers, which the grower pollinates with diploid pollen. Pollination stimulates fruit production, but, like a mule, the triploid plant is sterile. The "seeds" that do develop inside seedless watermelons are actually empty, soft hulls that are easy to chew and swallow. ▸ why mules are sterile, p. 160

Submit your burning question to:
marielle_hoefnagels@mcgraw-hill.com

Many animals disperse fruits and seeds. Colored berries attract birds and other animals that carry the ingested seeds to new locations, only to release them in their droppings. Birds and mammals spread seeds when spiny fruits attach to their feathers or fur. Squirrels and other nut-hoarding animals also disperse seeds. Although they later eat many of the seeds they hide, they also forget some of their cache locations. The uneaten seeds may germinate.

Wind and water can also distribute seeds. Wind-dispersed fruits, such as those of dandelions and maples, have wings or other structures that catch air currents. Water-dispersed fruits include gourds. These fruits are native to Asia, but they have drifted across the oceans multiple times and established new populations in South America, Australia, and Africa. Likewise, coconuts are water-dispersed fruits that travel long distances before colonizing distant islands.

22.2 Mastering Concepts

1. What is the function of each part of a flower?
2. Describe the male and female gametophytes in angiosperms.
3. How does pollen move from one flower to another, and why is this process essential for sexual reproduction?
4. Describe the events of double fertilization.
5. How is endosperm important to plants? To humans?
6. What are the components of a seed?
7. Which flower parts develop into a fruit?
8. What are the two main functions of fruits?
9. How do fruits and seeds disperse to new habitats?

22.3 Plant Growth Begins with Seed Germination

If a seed arrives at a favorable habitat, it may germinate, beginning the life of an independent young plant. **Germination** is the resumption of growth and development after a period of seed dormancy. It usually requires water, oxygen, and a favorable temperature. First, the seed absorbs water. The incoming water swells the seed, rupturing the seed coat and exposing the plant embryo to oxygen. Water also may cause the embryo to release hormones that stimulate the production of starch-digesting enzymes (see section 22.4B). The stored starch in the seed breaks down to sugars, providing energy for the now-growing embryo.

Growth and development continue after the embryo bursts out of the seed coat (figure 22.10). Rapidly dividing cells in apical meristems add length to both shoots and roots (see section 21.5). The new cells differentiate into the ground tissue, vascular tissue, and dermal tissue that make up the plant body. ▸ plant tissue types, p. 432

The seedling soon begins to take on its mature form. Young roots grow downward in response to gravity, anchoring the plant in the soil and absorbing water and minerals. The shoot produces leaves as it grows upward toward the light. Initially, the energy source for the seedling's growth is stored food inside the seed. By the time the seedling has depleted its reserves, the new green

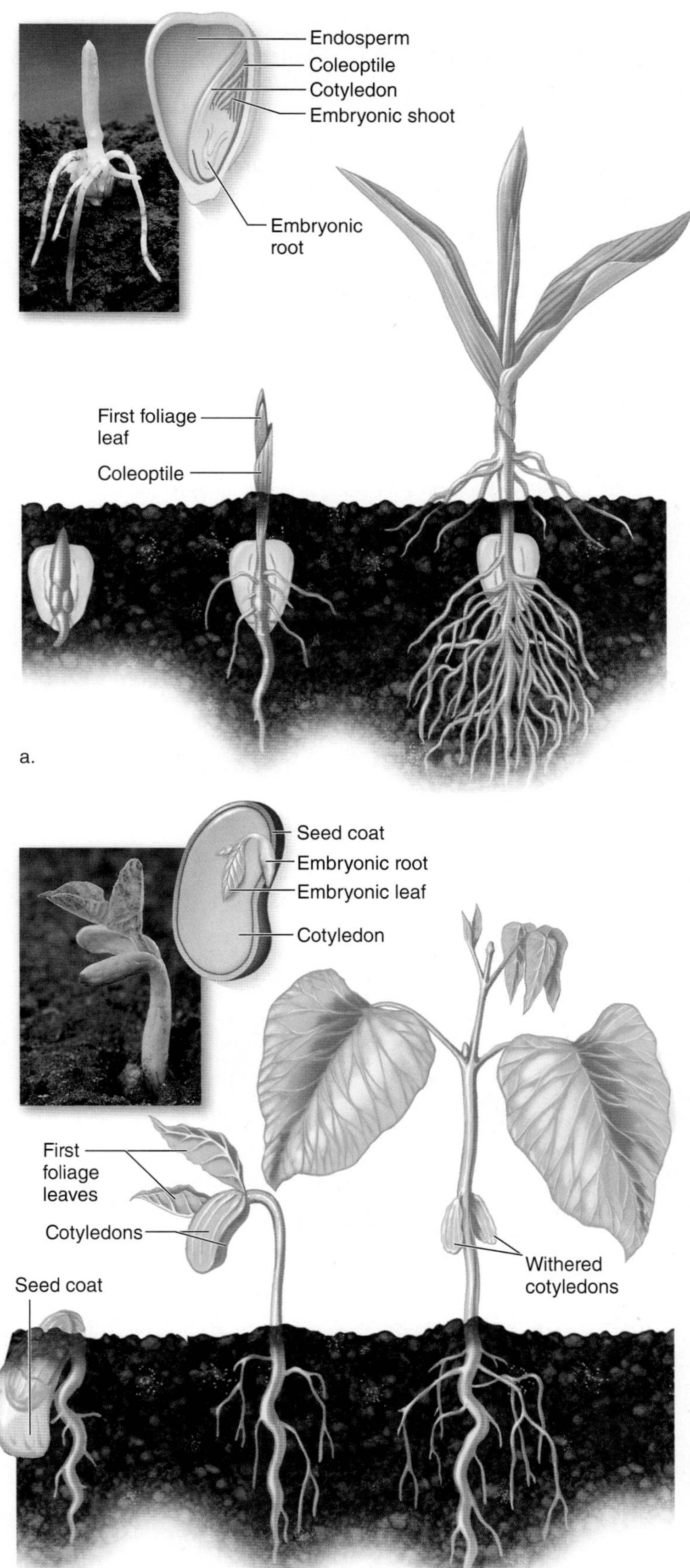

Figure 22.10 Seed Germination and Early Seedling Development. The root emerges first from a germinating seed, and then the shoot begins to elongate. (a) In a monocot such as corn, a sheathlike coleoptile covers the shoot until the first foliage leaves develop. The cotyledon remains belowground. (b) In green beans and some other eudicots, the cotyledons carry out photosynthesis until the first foliage leaves form.

leaves should begin producing food by photosynthesis. But if a seed is buried too deep in the soil, the young plant will never emerge—in effect, it will starve to death before reaching the light.

The size of a plant's seeds reflects an evolutionary trade-off. Large, heavy seeds contain ample nutrient reserves to fuel seedling growth but may not travel far. Small seeds, on the other hand, store limited nutrients but tend to disperse far and wide. Interestingly, the crops that humans cultivate typically have larger seeds than do their wild ancestors. We gather and plant the seeds ourselves, removing the selection pressure favoring small seed size.

Depending on the species, a plant may keep growing for weeks, months, years, decades, or even centuries. When the plant reaches reproductive maturity, it too will develop flowers, seeds, and fruits, continuing the life cycle.

22.3 Mastering Concepts

1. Why must seeds absorb water before germinating?
2. What are the events of early seedling development?
3. How does natural selection influence seed size?

22.4 Hormones Regulate Plant Growth and Development

A plant's responses to environmental stimuli usually seem much more subtle than those of an animal. Plants cannot hide, bite, or flee; instead they must adjust their growth and physiology to external conditions. The rest of this chapter explores some of the ways in which a plant responds to the changing environment as it grows and develops.

The environment affects plant growth in many ways. Shoots grow toward light and against gravity; roots grow down. Many plants leaf out in the spring, produce flowers and fruits, then enter dormancy in autumn—all in response to seasonal changes. Other responses are immediate. When the weather is hot, plants reduce transpiration by closing their stomata. A Venus flytrap snaps shut when a fly wanders across a leaf. Plants may even strengthen their defenses against insects and disease in response to chemical signals from neighboring plants.

Chemicals called **hormones** regulate many aspects of plant growth, flower and fruit development, and responses to environmental change. Hormones move within a plant's body either by diffusing from cell to cell or by

TABLE 22.2 Five Plant Hormones: A Summary

Class	Selected Actions
Auxins	• Stimulate elongation of cells in stem • Control phototropism, gravitropism, thigmotropism • Stimulate growth of roots from stem cuttings • Suppress growth of lateral buds (apical dominance)
Cytokinins	• Stimulate cell division in seeds, roots, young leaves, fruits • Delay shedding of leaves • Stimulate growth of lateral buds
Gibberellins	• Stimulate cell division and elongation in roots, shoots, young leaves • Break seed dormancy
Ethylene	• Hastens fruit ripening • Stimulates shedding of leaves, flowers, and fruits • Participates in thigmotropism
Abscisic acid	• Inhibits shoot growth and maintains bud dormancy • Induces and maintains seed dormancy • Stimulates protein storage in seeds • Stimulates closure of stomata • Stimulates shedding of leaves, flowers, and fruits

Figure 22.11 Apical Dominance. The plant on the right had its shoot tip removed, promoting the growth of lateral buds.

High auxin: lateral buds remain dormant.

Low auxin: cytokinin stimulates growth of lateral shoots.

entering xylem or phloem. When a hormone reaches a target cell, it binds to a receptor protein. This interaction triggers a cascade of chemical reactions that ultimately change the expression of genes in target cells.

The "classic five" plant hormones are auxins, cytokinins, gibberellins, ethylene, and abscisic acid (table 22.2). A plant must produce auxins and cytokinins if it is to develop at all. Both of these hormones occur in all major organs of all plants at all times, and biologists have never found a mutant plant lacking either one. The other hormones are required for normal development, but plants can complete their life cycles without them.

A. Auxins and Cytokinins Are Essential for Plant Growth

Auxins (from the Greek meaning "to grow") are hormones with many effects on plant growth and development. For example, by promoting cell elongation, auxins control plant responses to light and gravity (see sections 22.5 and 22.6). In addition, the embryos inside seeds secrete auxins that stimulate fruit development.

Auxins have commercial uses. These hormones stimulate the formation of roots from cuttings, which is important in the asexual production of plants. A synthetic auxin called 2,4-D (2,4-dichlorophenoxyacetic acid) is a widely used herbicide, although the mechanism by which this compound kills plants is unclear. ▸ weed killers, p. 92

Cytokinins earned their name because they stimulate cytokinesis, or cell division. In flowering plants, most cytokinins affect roots and developing organs such as seeds, fruits, and young leaves. Cytokinins also slow the aging of mature leaves, so these hormones are used to extend the shelf lives of leafy vegetables.

The actions of cytokinins and auxins compete with each other. Cytokinins are more concentrated in the roots, whereas auxins are more concentrated in shoot tips. Cytokinins move upward within the xylem and stimulate lateral bud sprouting. In a counteracting effect called **apical dominance,** the terminal bud of a plant secretes auxins that move downward and suppress the growth of lateral buds. If the shoot tip is removed, the concentration of auxins in lateral buds decreases (figure 22.11). Meristem cells in the buds then begin dividing, thanks to the ever-present cytokinins. Apical dominance explains why gardeners can promote bushier growth by pinching off a plant's tip.

B. Gibberellins, Ethylene, and Abscisic Acid Influence Plant Development in Many Ways

Gibberellins are another class of plant hormone that causes shoot elongation. Young shoots produce gibberellins, which stimulate both cell division and cell elongation. Farmers therefore use these hormones in agriculture to stimulate stem elongation and fruit growth in seedless grapes (figure 22.12). But gibberellins also have other functions. For example, they trigger seed germination by inducing the production of enzymes that digest starch in the seed.

Ethylene is a gaseous hormone that ripens fruit in many species. Ethylene released from one overripe apple can hasten the ripening, and eventual spoiling, of others nearby, leading to the expression "one bad apple spoils the bushel." Exposure to ethylene also ripens immature fruits after harvest (figure 22.13). For example, shipping can damage soft, vine-ripened tomatoes. Farmers therefore pick the fruit while it is still hard and green. Ethylene

Why We Care | Cheating Death

In some ways, ethylene is the enemy of agriculture. This hormone causes flowers to fade and fruits to spoil, greatly reducing the shelf life of perishable plant products. What's a seller to do?

One solution is to interfere with the action of ethylene. A gas sold under the brand names EthylBloc and SmartFresh does just that. The gas binds to ethylene receptor proteins in the cell membranes of the plants. As a result, ethylene cannot bind to the cells, so spoilage is delayed.

Biologists have also learned to tinker with the ethylene receptor directly. The fresh-looking petunia flowers in figure 22.A, for example, are genetically engineered to have mutant ethylene receptor genes. The modified flowers remain fresh because they do not respond to ethylene.

Figure 22.A Ethylene's Effects on Flowers. All four of these petunia flowers were treated with ethylene gas for 18 hours. The normal flowers on the left withered, but the fresh-looking flowers on the right are genetically modified to be insensitive to ethylene.

treatment just before distribution to supermarkets yields ripe-looking (if not good-tasting) tomatoes.

All parts of flowering plants synthesize ethylene, especially the shoot apical meristem, nodes, flowers, and ripening fruits. Like other hormones, ethylene has several effects. In most species, it causes flowers to fade and wither (see this chapter's Why We Care box). In addition, a damaged plant part produces ethylene, which hastens aging; the plant then sheds the affected part before the problem spreads. This effect was noticed in Germany in 1864, when ethylene in a mixture of gases in street lamps caused nearby trees to lose their leaves.

A fifth plant hormone, **abscisic acid** (abbreviated ABA), counters the growth-stimulating effects of many other hormones. The name of this hormone comes from its role in promoting the abscission (shedding) of leaves, flowers, and fruits. Stresses such as drought and frost stimulate the production of ABA. One immediate effect is to trigger stomata to close, which helps plants conserve water. ABA also inhibits seed germination, opposing the effects of gibberellins. Commercial growers apply ABA to inhibit the growth of nursery plants so that shipping is less likely to damage them.

Figure 22.12 Gibberellins and Shoot Elongation. Gibberellins applied to grapes lengthen the stems and increase the size of the fruit. Treated grapes are on the right.

22.4 Mastering Concepts

1. What is a hormone?
2. How does a plant hormone exert its effects?
3. List the major classes of plant hormones and name some of their functions.
4. Give an example of how plant hormones interact.

Figure 22.13 Unripe Fruit. Exposure to ethylene would turn these green tomatoes red.

Figure 22.14 Phototropism. This bean seedling shows strong phototropism when the light is off to the side.

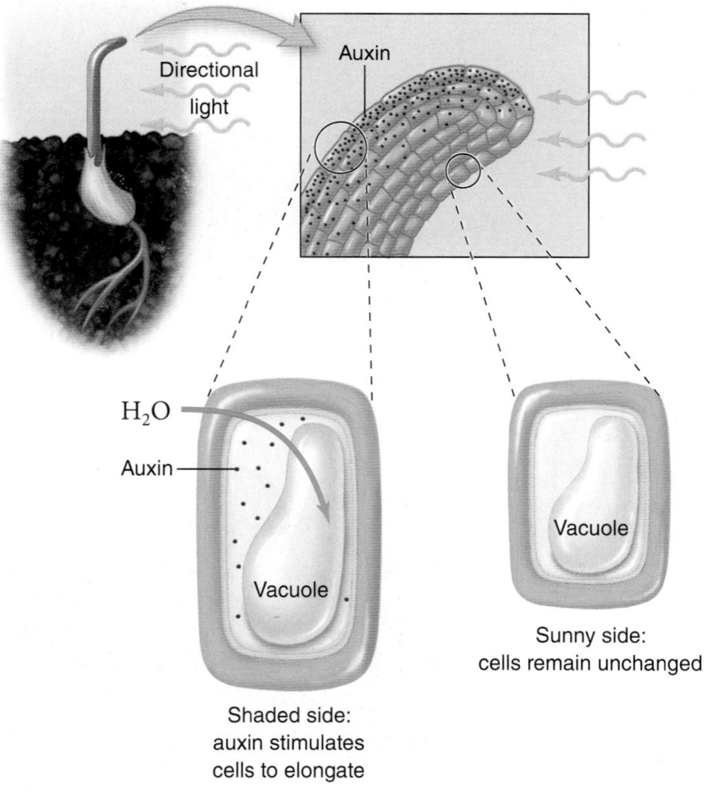

Figure 22.15 Auxin and Stem Elongation. Phototropism occurs because auxins (red dots) move to the shaded side of a shoot, stimulating elongation of the affected cells.

22.5 Light Is a Powerful Influence on Plant Life

Plants are exquisitely attuned to light. Their lives depend on it, because light is their sole energy source for photosynthesis (see chapter 5). This section illustrates how light influences both plant growth and flowering time.

In general, a **tropism** is the orientation of a plant part toward or away from a stimulus such as light, gravity, or touch. All tropisms result from differential growth, in which one side of the responding organ grows faster than the other. One familiar example is **phototropism,** which is growth toward or away from light (figure 22.14). Phototropism occurs when cells on the shaded side of a stem elongate more than cells on the opposite side.

Photoreceptors and auxins participate in phototropism. A **photoreceptor** is a molecule that detects the quality and quantity of light. In phototropism, photoreceptors absorb light, which somehow causes auxins to migrate to the shaded side of the stem. Water follows the auxins into the cells, and the resulting increase in turgor pressure causes the cells to elongate. The stem therefore bends toward the light (figure 22.15).

The plant commonly sold as "lucky bamboo" often has a curled stem, illustrating the effects of phototropism. Farmers grow the plants for a year or more in greenhouses, exposing only one side to light. Periodically rotating each plant directs the stem's growth into a twist.

The timing of light exposure also influences many aspects of a plant's life. For example, plants respond in several ways to the **photoperiod,** or relative length of day and night. Consider the changes that occur in a deciduous forest throughout the year. The short days that accompany the approach of winter are associated with the formation of buds, the loss of leaves, and dormancy. In the spring, as days grow longer, buds resume growth and rapidly transform a barren deciduous forest into a leafy canopy. These seasonal changes illustrate the interactions among environmental signals, hormones, and the plant's genes.

Photoperiod also regulates the production of flowers in some plant species. Traditionally, biologists used the term "long-day plants" for plants that flower when days grow longer than a critical length, usually 9 to 16 hours. These plants typically bloom in the spring or early summer and include lettuce, spinach, beets, clover, and irises. Likewise, "short-day plants" produce flowers when days become shorter than some critical length, usually in late summer or fall. Asters, strawberries, poinsettias, potatoes, soybeans, ragweed, and goldenrods are short-day plants. "Day-neutral plants" such as roses produce flowers when the plants are mature, regardless of day length.

However, experiments eventually confirmed that flowering actually requires a defined period of uninterrupted darkness, rather than a certain day length (figure 22.16). Thus, short-day plants are really long-night plants, because they flower only if their uninterrupted dark period exceeds a critical length. Similarly, long-day plants are really short-night plants.

22.5 Mastering Concepts

1. What is auxin's role in phototropism?
2. How does light help regulate flowering time?

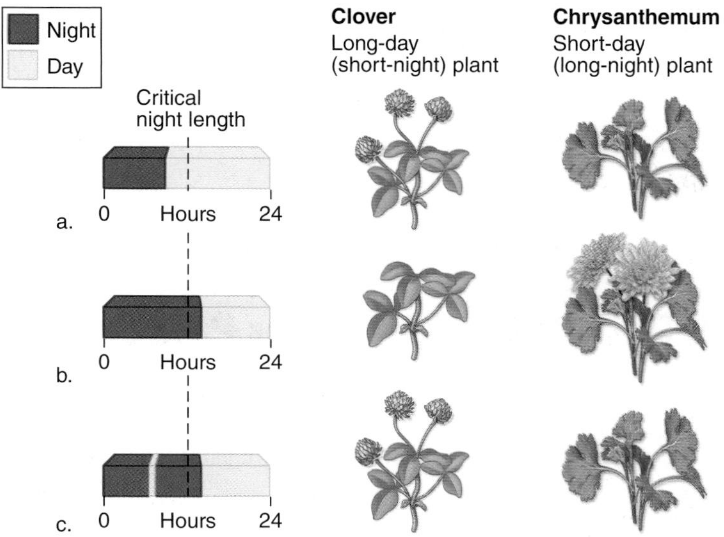

Figure 22.16 Night Length Matters. (a) When nights are shorter than a critical length, long-day (short-night) plants produce flowers. (b) When nights exceed a critical length, short-day (long-night) plants flower. (c) If a long period of darkness is interrupted with a flash of light, the short-night plants flower, but the long-night plants do not.

22.6 Plants Respond to Gravity and Touch

Besides light, a developing plant also responds to countless other environmental cues. For example, the more CO_2 in the atmosphere, the lower the density of stomata on leaves. Likewise, a plant in soil with abundant nitrogen produces fewer lateral roots than in nutrient-poor soil. Plants can also sense temperature; many require a prolonged cold spell before producing buds or flowering. A warm period in December, before temperatures have really plummeted, does not stimulate apple and cherry trees' buds to "break," but a similar warm-up in late February does induce growth.

Gravity is another important environmental cue. **Gravitropism** is directional growth in response to gravity (figure 22.17). As a seed germinates, its shoot points upward toward light, and its root grows downward into the soil. Turn the plant sideways, and the stem and roots bend according to the new direction of gravity.

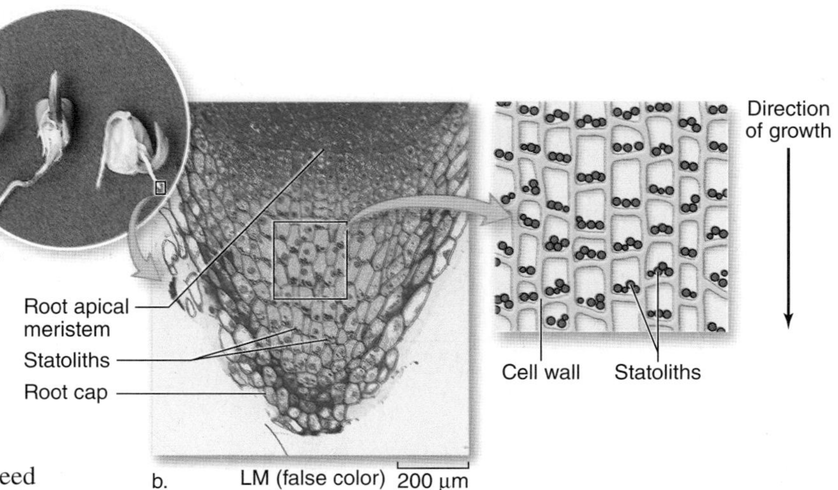

Figure 22.17 Gravitropism. (a) Shoots grow up and roots grow down, whether a seed is oriented sideways (left), rightside up (center), or upside down (right). (b) Starch-filled statoliths in the root cap may help the plant detect gravity.

No one knows exactly how gravitropism works, although it is clear that the root cap must be present for roots to respond to gravity. One hypothesis centers on root cap cells with **statoliths,** starch-containing plastids that function as gravity detectors (see figure 22.17). Statoliths normally sink to the bottoms of the cells, somehow telling the cells which direction is down. Turning a root sideways causes the statoliths to move, redistributing calcium ions and auxins in a way that bends the root. ▸ plastids, p. 60

Besides ever-present gravity, a plant also encounters a changing variety of mechanical stimuli, including contact with wind, rain, animals, and other plants. These stimuli can prompt **thigmotropism,** a directional response to touch. The coiling tendrils of twining plants exhibit thigmotropism (figure 22.18). Specialized epidermal cells detect contact with an object, which stimulates the tendril to bend. In only 5 to 10 minutes, the tendril completely encircles the object. Auxins and ethylene apparently control thigmotropism.

Figure 22.18 Thigmotropism. A tendril's epidermis is sensitive to touch. This tendril of a passion vine wraps around a blackberry stem.

22.6 Mastering Concepts

1. How do auxins participate in gravitropism?
2. What is thigmotropism?

Figure 22.19 Chilies. These fruits of the chili plant can be very spicy.

Investigating Life

22.7 A Red Hot Chili Pepper Paradox

Chili peppers are famous for their hot, spicy taste (figure 22.19). Chilies get their kick from a unique chemical compound called capsaicin. The sensation ranges from the pleasantly mild pimento to the outright painful habanero.

The Question: The pungency of chilies is a bit of a paradox. After all, the main functions of fruits are protection and seed dispersal. Many plants produce chemicals that make their fruits unpalatable until the seeds are mature. Once they are ripe, however, most fruits lose their defensive chemicals. But chilies repel animals, even after the fruit is fully developed. Why?

Biologists Joshua Tewksbury, of the University of Washington, and Gary Nabhan, of the University of Arizona, developed a hypothesis to explain this paradox. Tewksbury and Nabhan realized that some fruit-eating animals disperse seeds intact, but others destroy seeds. Perhaps, they suggested, capsaicin deters the harmful seed-destroyers without affecting the beneficial dispersers.

The Approach: The researchers used field observations and laboratory feeding studies to test their hypothesis. Their study population consisted of wild chiltepin chilies growing in a canyon in southern Arizona. These shrubby plants produce tiny, round chilies. First, Tewksbury and Nabhan wanted to learn which animals consumed the fruits. After videotaping chili plants for a total of 146 daylight hours, they found that birds called curve-billed thrashers were responsible for 72% of fruits removed from the plants. The researchers also had indirect evidence that small mammals, which are active at night, avoided the chili fruits.

A laboratory study settled the question. The team captured five cactus mice, five pack rats, and 10 thrashers from the study site. Each animal was offered three types of fruit: hot chilies from the field sites, nonpungent mutant chilies, and desert hackberries. The birds ate all three fruits; the mice and pack rats consumed the hackberries but avoided the chilies (figure 22.20a).

According to Tewksbury and Nabhan's hypothesis, capsaicin should repel seed-destroying animals without affecting dispersers. Clearly, chilies deter mammals but not birds. Do mammals harm chili seeds more than the thrashers do? The researchers set up another laboratory test to answer that question. They fed nonpungent chilies to thrashers, mice, and pack rats; control chilies remained uneaten. The team then measured the germination rates of the control seeds and the seeds that had passed through an animal's digestive system. Figure 22.20b shows the result. The mice and pack rats destroyed the seeds, which presumably were crushed in the mammals' molars. In contrast, the seeds remained viable after consumption by thrashers.

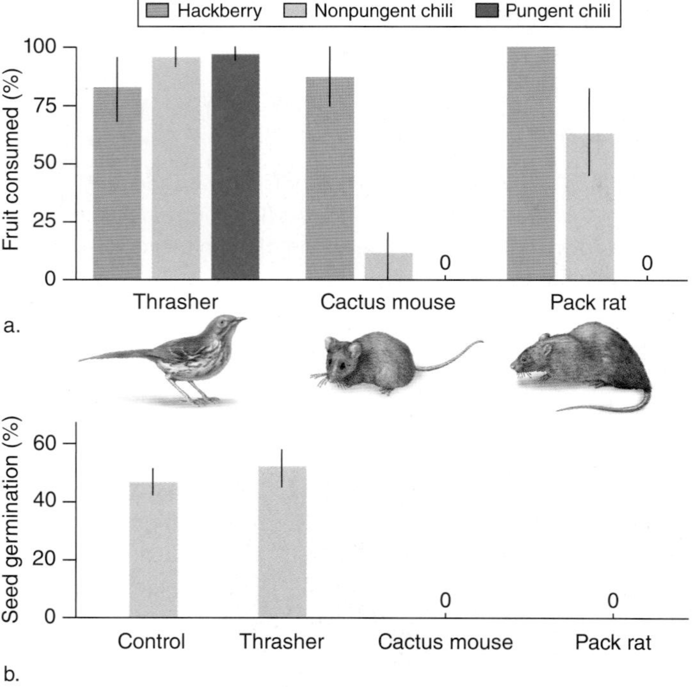

Figure 22.20 Some Like It Hot. (a) In a feeding preference experiment, thrashers readily accepted pungent chilies, but mice and pack rats rejected the spicy fruits. (b) Chili seeds that passed through thrashers remained viable, whereas seeds eaten by mice and pack rats were destroyed.

The Conclusion: These experiments help explain the evolutionary forces that select for capsaicin production in mature chili peppers. Interestingly, thrashers and other birds seem insensitive to capsaicin, while most mammals avoid it. The real paradox is how humans transformed this innate mammalian aversion into a worldwide love affair with the chili pepper.

Tewksbury, Joshua J., and Gary P. Nabhan. 2001. Directed deterrence by capsaicin in chillies. *Nature*, vol. 412, pages 403-404.

22.7 Mastering Concepts

1. What did Tewksbury and Nabhan conclude about the function of capsaicin in mature chili fruits?
2. Summarize the evidence that Tewksbury and Nabhan used to arrive at their conclusion.

Chapter Summary

22.1 Angiosperms Reproduce Sexually and Asexually

- **Sexual reproduction** produces genetically variable offspring, which increases reproductive success in a changing environment.
- In **asexual reproduction,** clones develop from the roots, stems, or leaves of a parent plant. Asexual reproduction is advantageous in a stable environment where plants are well adapted to their surroundings.

22.2 The Angiosperm Life Cycle Includes Flowers, Fruits, and Seeds

- Plant life cycles include **alternation of generations.** The diploid **sporophyte** undergoes meiosis and produces haploid **spores,** which give rise to the haploid **gametophyte** generation. The gametophytes, in turn, produce **gametes. Fertilization** yields the diploid **zygote.**

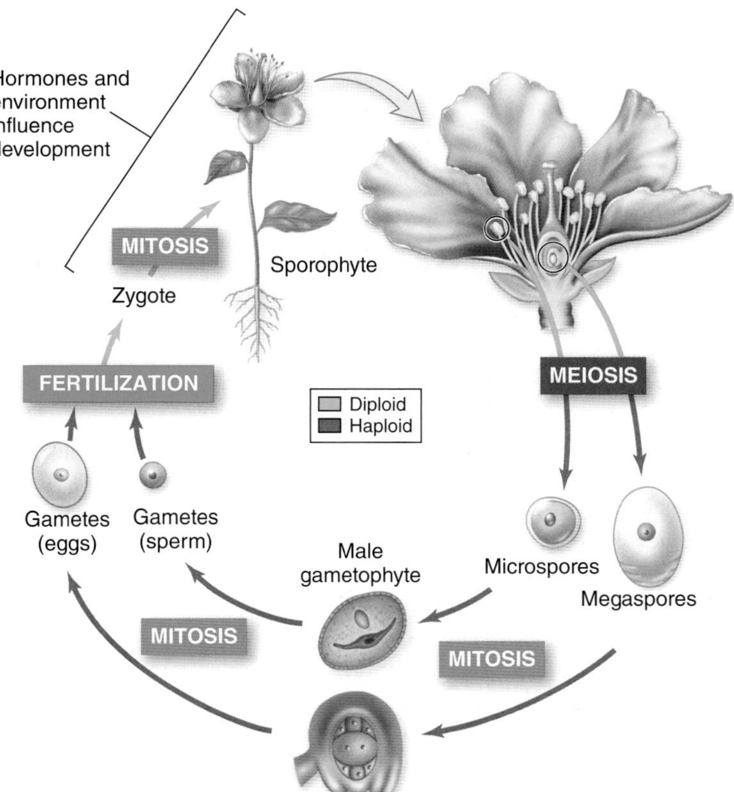

- Two features unique to the angiosperm life cycle are **flowers** and **fruits.**

A. Flowers Are Reproductive Organs

- Flowers are reproductive structures built of whorls of parts attached to a **receptacle.** The **sepals** (collectively called the **calyx**) and **petals** (collectively called the **corolla**) are accessory parts that enclose the **stamens,** which have pollen-containing **anthers** at their tips. **Carpels** occupy the center of the flower. Each carpel's **ovary** contains one or more **ovules.** The **stigma** tops the **style,** which extends from the ovary.

B. The Pollen Grain and Embryo Sac Are Gametophytes

- In the anther, specialized cells divide meiotically, each producing four haploid **microspores**. The microspores divide mitotically to yield haploid cells. The **pollen** grain is the immature male gametophyte; it produces two identical sperm nuclei.
- In ovules, specialized cells divide meiotically to yield four haploid cells, one of which persists as a haploid **megaspore** that divides mitotically three times. The resulting female gametophyte, or **embryo sac,** contains seven cells. One is the egg, and another has two **polar nuclei.**

C. Pollination Brings Pollen to the Stigma

- Animals and wind carry pollen from anthers to a stigma. Flower structures and odors are usually adapted to either animal or wind **pollination.** Animal pollinators and flowers select for changes in one another in **coevolution.**

D. Double Fertilization Yields Zygote and Endosperm

- Once on a stigma, a pollen grain grows a pollen tube, and its two sperm nuclei move through the tube toward the ovary.
- In the embryo sac, one sperm nucleus fertilizes the egg to form the zygote, and the other sperm nucleus fertilizes the polar nuclei to form the **endosperm.** This phenomenon is termed **double fertilization.**

E. A Seed Is an Embryo with Its Food Supply Inside a Seed Coat

- A **seed** is an embryo, endosperm, and **seed coat.** The endosperm nourishes the developing embryo as cells in apical meristems divide to produce the embryonic shoot and root. As the embryo grows, **cotyledons** develop.
- Seeds enter a dormancy period in which the embryo postpones development.

F. The Fruit Develops from the Ovary

- After fertilization, nonessential flower parts fall off, and hormones influence the ovary (and sometimes other plant parts) to develop into a fruit.

G. Fruits Protect and Disperse Seeds

- The fruit protects the seeds and aids in dispersal.
- Animals, wind, and water disperse seeds to new habitats, reducing competition between parent plants and their offspring.

22.3 Plant Growth Begins with Seed Germination

- Seed **germination** requires oxygen, water, and a favorable temperature. When the embryo bursts from the seed coat, the plant's primary growth begins.

22.4 Hormones Regulate Plant Growth and Development

- Plants respond to the environment with changes in growth and movement, mediated by the action of **hormones.**

A. Auxins and Cytokinins Are Essential for Plant Growth

- **Auxins** stimulate cell elongation in shoot tips, embryos, young leaves, flowers, fruits, and pollen. Auxins are most concentrated at the main shoot tip, which blocks growth of lateral buds (**apical dominance**).

- **Cytokinins** stimulate cell division in actively developing plant parts, including lateral buds.

B. Gibberellins, Ethylene, and Abscisic Acid Influence Plant Development in Many Ways

- **Gibberellins** stimulate cell division and elongation, and they help break seed dormancy.
- **Ethylene** is a gas that speeds ripening, aging, and the loss of leaves and petals.
- **Abscisic acid** counters the growth-inducing effects of other hormones by inducing dormancy and inhibiting shoot growth.

22.5 Light Is a Powerful Influence on Plant Life

- A **tropism** is a growth response toward or away from an environmental stimulus. In a tropism, one part of an organ or structure grows faster than the other parts.
- **Photoreceptors** absorb light energy and influence a plant's growth, development, or response to the environment.
- In **phototropism,** light stimulates auxin to move to the shaded side of the stem, which therefore bends toward the light.
- **Photoperiod** is the relative length of night and day. Some plants are day-neutral, but others use photoperiod as a cue to produce flowers. Short-day plants flower only when the duration of uninterrupted darkness is greater than a critical length. Long-day plants require a dark period shorter than a critical length.

22.6 Plants Respond to Gravity and Touch

- **Gravitropism** is growth toward or away from the direction of gravity. Examples are the upward growth of shoots and the downward growth of roots. The positions of starch-rich **statoliths** in cells apparently help plants detect gravity.
- **Thigmotropism** is growth directed toward or away from a mechanical stimulus such as wind or touch.

22.7 Investigating Life: A Red Hot Chili Pepper Paradox

- The capsaicin in chili peppers repels mammals; these animals would otherwise destroy the chili plant's seeds. Capsaicin does not affect birds, which eat chili pepper fruits and disperse the seeds intact.

Multiple Choice Questions

1. The new gene combinations associated with sexual reproduction in plants are the result of
   a. mitosis.
   b. meiosis.
   c. cloning.
   d. Both b and c are correct.
2. Which of the following is NOT a flower structure associated with reproduction?
   a. Anther
   b. Stigma
   c. Sepal
   d. Carpel
3. Where would you find a male gametophyte?
   a. Inside a ripe pollen sac
   b. Inside an ovule
   c. Inside the embryo sac
   d. Both b and c are correct.
4. What are the products of double fertilization?
   a. Two diploid zygotes
   b. A diploid zygote and a triploid endosperm
   c. A haploid sperm and a diploid zygote
   d. A triploid zygote
5. What is the function of a cotyledon?
   a. To support photosynthesis for the embryo before germination
   b. To protect the dormant embryo
   c. To transfer nutrients from the endosperm
   d. To produce more cells for the growth of the embryo
6. Predict what would happen if a plant produced too much auxin.
   a. The plant would be very bushy.
   b. The plant would be very tall.
   c. The plant would have very long roots.
   d. The leaves of the plant would not die.
7. How does auxin cause bending in a plant?
   a. It causes an increase in cell division on one side of the plant.
   b. It suppresses cell division on one side of the plant.
   c. It triggers elongation of cells at the apical meristems of the plant.
   d. It triggers elongation of cells on one side of the plant.
8. Spinach plants are typically compact and leafy, but a change in photoperiod can cause bolting, in which the plant's stem elongates and produces flowers. Which plant hormone is most associated with the rapidly lengthening stalk?
   a. Gibberellins
   b. Abscisic acid
   c. Ethylene
   d. Cytokinins
9. Chrysanthemums are long-night plants that normally flower in the fall. If you could manipulate photoperiod, what would be the simplest way to prevent mums from blooming (without killing the plants)?
   a. Never expose the mums to light at all.
   b. Interrupt each night with a flash of light.
   c. Interrupt each day with a brief period of darkness.
   d. Make sure each uninterrupted night lasts longer than the critical period.
10. Statoliths play a role in a plant's response to
    a. light.
    b. disease.
    c. touch.
    d. gravity.

Write It Out

1. Give an example of asexual reproduction in a plant.
2. Explain how flowers, fruits, and seeds contribute to the reproductive success of angiosperms.
3. Sketch a flower, indicating the location and function of the following parts: sepal, petal, carpel, stamen, stigma, corolla, calyx, style, anther.
4. Name tissues or cells in an angiosperm that are haploid, diploid, and triploid.
5. What happens to the two sperm nuclei that form inside a pollen tube?
6. How does an exclusive relationship between a plant and its pollinator benefit each partner? What are the risks of exclusivity?
7. If fruit production is a measure of fitness, why wouldn't a plant spend all of its energy producing fruits instead of roots and leaves? Why do you think some annual plants die back as they produce fruits?
8. An oak tree may produce thousands of acorns, which squirrels bury or eat. Why does the tree make so many acorns? Why might a plant whose seeds disperse far from the parent have better reproductive success than one whose seeds fall at the base of the parent plant?
9. How does seed dormancy promote reproductive success?
10. List the major plant hormones and describe some of their actions.

11. How does pruning stimulate the growth of new branches on a shrub?
12. Explain why one rotten orange promotes decay of all of the others.
13. What is the function of photoreceptors?
14. Describe three tropisms. Which hormone is common to all three?
15. Develop a hypothesis that explains why it might be adaptive for a plant to flower in response to photoperiod rather than temperature.
16. How is gravitropism adaptive?

Pull It Together

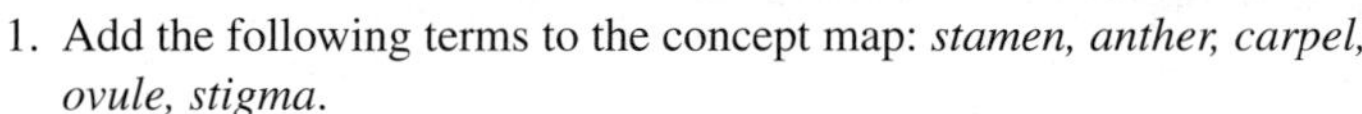

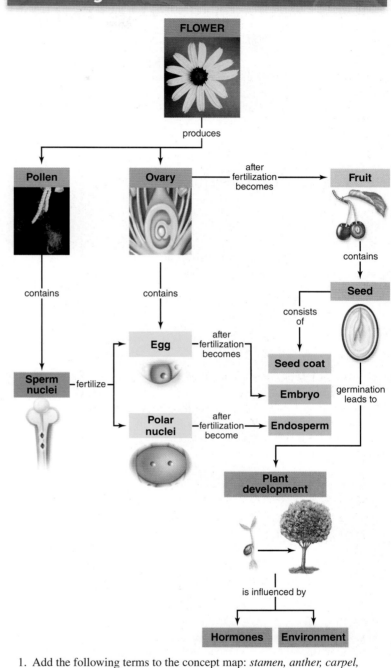

1. Add the following terms to the concept map: *stamen, anther, carpel, ovule, stigma.*
2. What event leads to the formation of the endosperm?
3. What roles do animals play in plant life cycles?
4. What hormones are involved in plant development?
5. List examples of environmental conditions that influence plant development.

UNIT 6 Animal Physiology

23 Animal Tissues and Organ Systems

Bone Recipe. A researcher holds a porous ceramic scaffold and a dish of cultured cells that he can use to build an artificial bone.

Learning Outline

Learn How to Learn

Pay Attention in Class

It happens to everyone occasionally: your mind begins to wander while you are sitting in class, so you doodle or doze off. How can you keep from wasting your class time this way? One strategy is to get plenty of sleep and eat well, so your mind stays active instead of drifting off. Another is to prepare for class in advance, since getting lost can be an excuse for drifting off. When you get to class, sit near the front, listen carefully, and take good notes. Finally, a friendly reminder can't hurt; make a small PAY ATTENTION sign to put on your desk, where you can always see it.

What's the Point?

The two photos on these pages may seem unrelated, but each illustrates an important point about animal life. The image on the facing page shows the ingredients used to produce artificial bone, a medical advance made possible by basic research into the biology of cells, tissues, and organs. This chapter introduces these levels of organization in the animal body; subsequent chapters in this unit explore each organ system in detail.

The other photo shows a penguin, a bird that spends much of its life in cold water. The penguin's organ systems work together to keep its body warm despite the frigid surroundings. This state of internal constancy, which applies not only to temperature but also to other vital conditions in the body, is called homeostasis. We introduce the idea of homeostasis in this chapter, but every other chapter in this unit reinforces the concept with additional examples.

23.1 Specialized Cells Build Animal Bodies

Everywhere we look, form and function are entwined. The broad, flat surface of a plant's leaf maximizes its exposure to light. A neuron's many branches permit the cell-to-cell connections essential to communication in the nervous system. In birds, fluffy down feathers trap pockets of air and conserve warmth.

Anatomy, the study of an organism's structure, describes the parts that compose the body—that is, its form. **Physiology** is a related discipline that considers how those parts work—their function. Unit 5 described the anatomy and physiology of plants; unit 6 turns to animals.

Biologists describe the animal body in terms of an organizational hierarchy (figure 23.1). Most animals have specialized cells organized into **tissues,** which are groups of cells that interact and provide a specific function. Blood is a tissue, as are bone, muscle, and the lining of the stomach. An **organ** consists of two or more tissues that interact and function as a unit. The stomach, for example, is an organ that consists of muscle, blood, nerves, and an inner lining that secretes stomach acid. (Organ donation is the topic of this chapter's Burning Question, on page 475.) Still farther up the organizational hierarchy are **organ systems,** which consist of two or more organs that are physically or functionally joined. The human digestive system, for example, is composed of many organs, including the stomach, small intestine, and large intestine.

Everyone is familiar with the overall form of the human body, from fetus to child to adult. Other animal bodies have wildly different shapes, from the flattened tapeworm to the squishy squid to the armored lobster to the scaly snake. But all of these animals have organs that carry out the same basic functions as our own: they sense their environment, acquire food and oxygen, eliminate wastes, protect themselves from injury and disease, and reproduce. Although this unit describes some notable adaptations in other animals, the focus is mainly on humans.

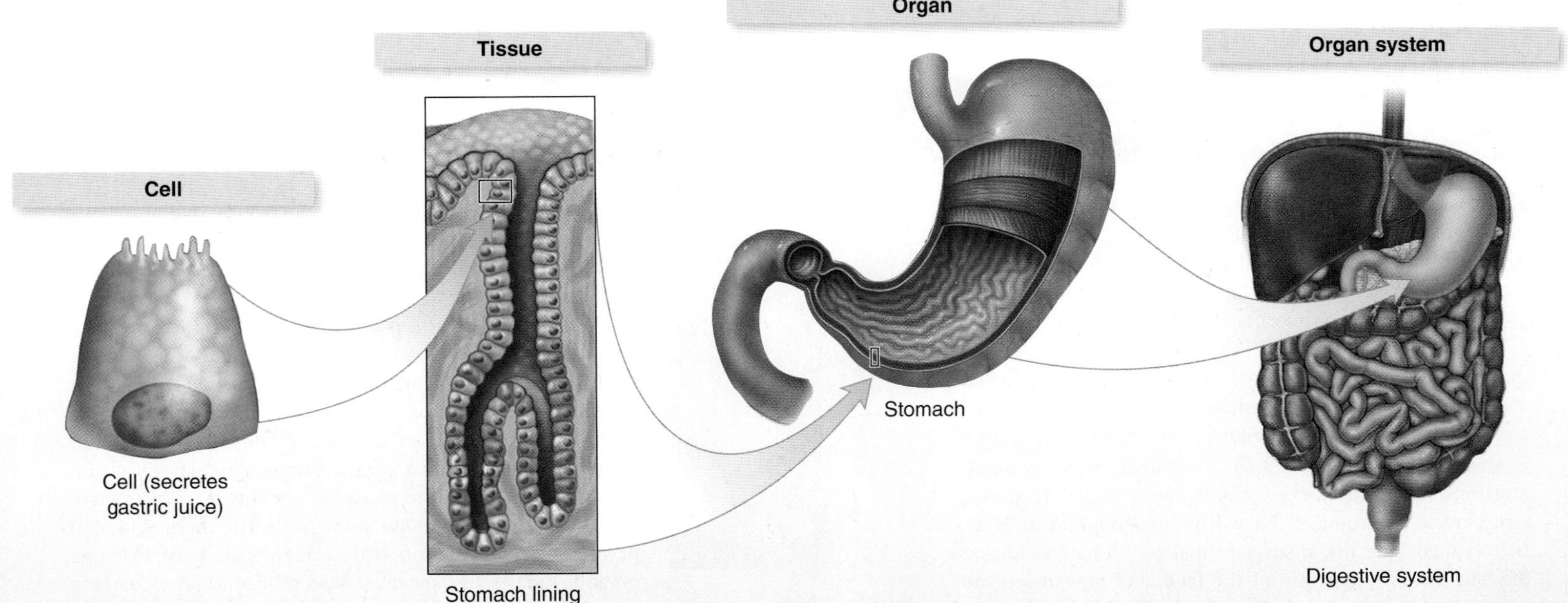

Figure 23.1 Organizational Hierarchy. A cell that secretes gastric juice is just one cell type in the tissue that lines the stomach. This organ, in turn, is one of many that make up the digestive system.

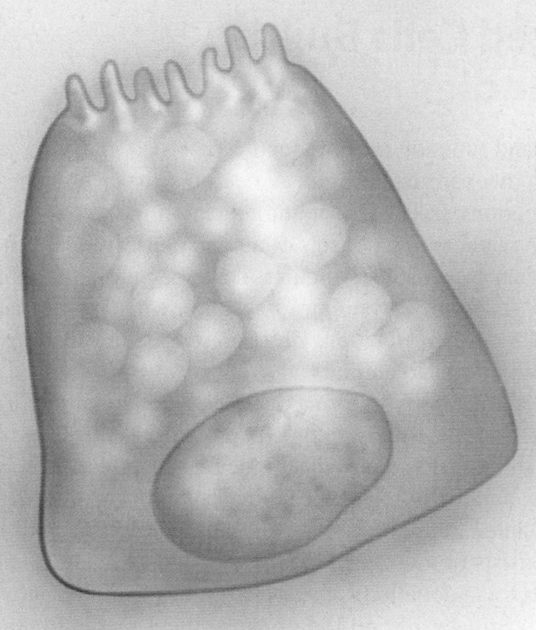

This chapter introduces the basic cells and tissues that build animal bodies. Chapters 24 through 30 then consider the organ systems one at a time.

23.1 Mastering Concepts

1. What is the difference between anatomy and physiology?
2. What is the relationship among cells, tissues, organs, and organ systems?

23.2 Animals Consist of Four Tissue Types

The vertebrate body, including that of humans, has at least 260 cell types. But these cells do not act alone. Instead, some cell types tend to occur in groups and to share common functions. Together, these interacting cells form tissues that fall into four broad categories: epithelial, connective, muscle, and nervous. This section summarizes their characteristics, functions, and locations; the Why We Care box describes how plastic surgeons reposition these tissues to improve a person's appearance or repair damage.

All animal tissues have a feature in common: the cells are embedded in an **extracellular matrix,** which is a mixture of water, carbohydrates, lipids, and (usually) protein fibers such as collagen and elastin. Interestingly, most normal body cells cannot survive or replicate when removed from the extracellular matrix. Somehow, cancer cells escape this "anchorage dependence," breaking away from the extracellular matrix yet retaining the ability to divide. These abnormal cells also often secrete enzymes that destroy the fibers of the extracellular matrix, clearing the way for the cancer cells to invade adjacent tissues. ▸ cancer, p. 148

Why We Care | Two Faces of Plastic Surgery

The "plastic" in "plastic surgery" has nothing to do with the substance that makes up water bottles. Instead, the word derives from the Greek word *plastikos,* which means "to mold." Plastic surgeons "mold" a person's appearance by moving and reshaping tissues such as fat, bone, and cartilage.

Cosmetic surgery is one field of plastic surgery. Among the most common procedures is a "nose job," in which a surgeon removes or repositions some of the cartilage and bone of the nose to create a new shape. Liposuction is also popular (figure 23.A). The surgeon makes small incisions and removes excess fat from the thighs, buttocks, arms, neck, or stomach. Face lifts are common as well. In a typical face lift, a surgeon makes a long incision at the hairline, lifts the skin of the face, and repositions the muscle and connective tissue under the skin. He or she then tightens the skin and trims the excess before reattaching the skin to the face. Other popular procedures include breast augmentation, breast reduction, breast lifts, buttock lifts, tummy tucks, laser skin resurfacing, hair transplants, and collagen injections.

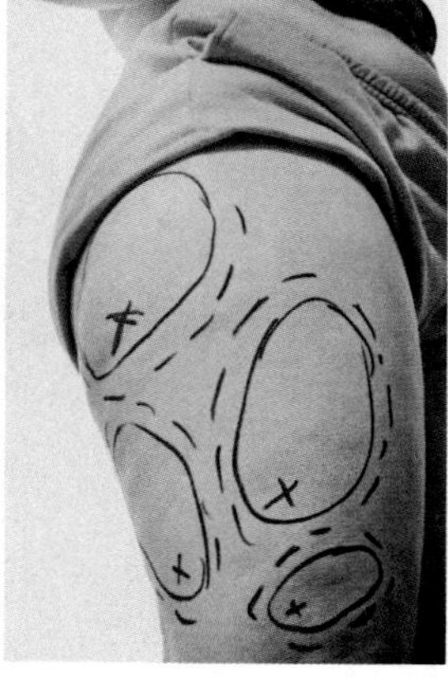

Figure 23.A Liposuction Markings.

Cosmetic surgery may enhance a healthy person's appearance, but reconstructive plastic surgery has another goal: to restore the function of damaged body parts. For example, some children are born with a cleft palate (a gap in the bones between the nose and mouth). To repair a cleft palate, a reconstructive plastic surgeon moves tissue on either side of the gap to close the opening. Reconstructive surgery may also include skin grafts (for burn patients) or breast reconstruction (for women who have lost one or both breasts to cancer). These procedures can make a tremendous, life-changing improvement in a patient's ability to function.

A. Epithelial Tissue Covers Surfaces

Epithelial tissues coat the body's internal and external surfaces with one or more layers of tightly packed cells (figure 23.2). They cover organs and line the inside of hollow organs and body cavities. The diverse functions of epithelial tissues include protection, nutrient absorption along the intestinal tract, and gas diffusion in the lungs. These tissues also form **glands**, organs that secrete substances into ducts or into the bloodstream. Glands release breast milk, sweat, saliva, tears, mucus, hormones, enzymes, and many other important secretions.

Epithelial tissues always have a "free" surface that is exposed either to the outside or to a space within the body. On the opposite side, epithelium is anchored to underlying tissues by a layer of extracellular matrix called the basement membrane. The epithelial cells are often connected to one another, forming leak-proof sheets. The tightly knit structure of epithelial tissue is closely tied to its function as a border between the body's tissues and an open space.

Epithelial tissues are classified partly by the shapes of their cells: squamous (flattened), cuboidal (cube-shaped), or columnar (tall and thin). The number of cell layers is also important. Simple epithelial tissues consist of a single layer of cells, whereas stratified epithelial tissues are made of multiple cell layers.

About 90% of human cancers arise in epithelial tissues. Such a cancer is called a carcinoma. The most common carcinomas include cancers of the skin, breast, lung, prostate, and colon.

B. Most Connective Tissues Bind Other Tissues Together

The most widespread tissue type in a vertebrate's body is **connective tissue,** which consists of cells that are scattered within the extracellular matrix rather than being attached to one another. Connective tissues fill spaces, attach epithelium to other tissues, protect and cushion organs, and provide both flexible and firm structural support. Unlike epithelial tissues, connective tissues never coat any body surface.

Simple squamous epithelial tissue

Composition: Single layer of flattened cells

Functions: Allows substances to pass by diffusion and osmosis

Locations: Lining of blood vessels, alveoli of lungs

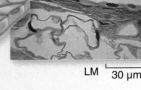

Basement membrane | Cell | LM 30 μm

Simple cuboidal epithelial tissue

Composition: Single layer of cube-shaped cells

Functions: Secretes and absorbs substances

Locations: Glands, lining of kidney tubules

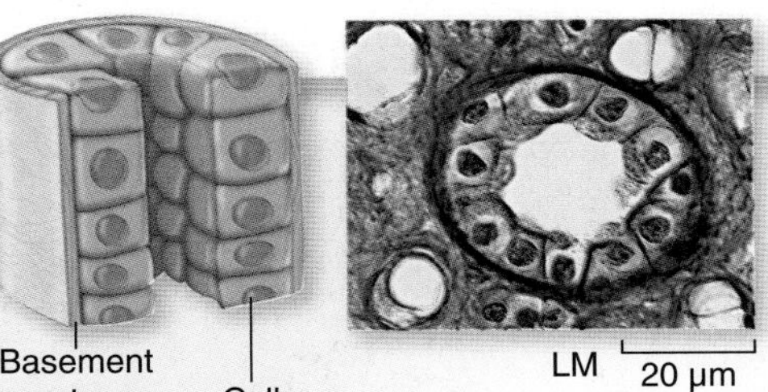

Simple columnar epithelial tissue

Composition: Single layer of column-shaped cells

Functions: Secretes and absorbs substances; sweeps egg/embryo along uterine tube

Locations: Lining of digestive tract, bronchi of lungs, uterine tubes

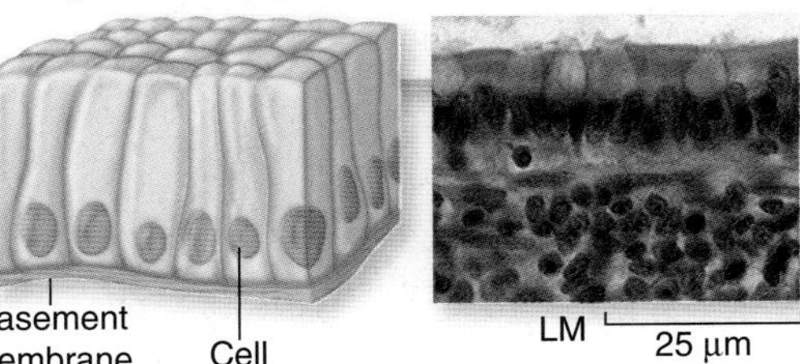

Stratified squamous epithelial tissue

Composition: Multiple layers of flattened cells

Functions: Protects areas subject to abrasion; prevents water loss and infection

Location: Outer layer of skin

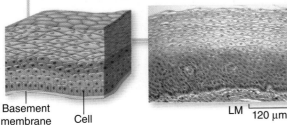

Basement membrane | Cell | LM 120 μm

Figure 23.2 Epithelial Tissues. Epithelial tissues cover body surfaces and line hollow organs and body cavities. These tissues are composed of tightly packed cells in single or multiple layers.

Connective tissues are extremely variable in both structure and function (figure 23.3). Loose connective tissue binds other tissues together and fills the space between organs; dense connective tissue builds ligaments and tendons; and adipose tissue stores energy as fat. Blood is a connective tissue, as are the cartilage and bone that make up the vertebrate skeleton. A close look at figure 23.3 reveals that in all connective tissues except adipose tissue, the extracellular matrix occupies more volume than do the cells.

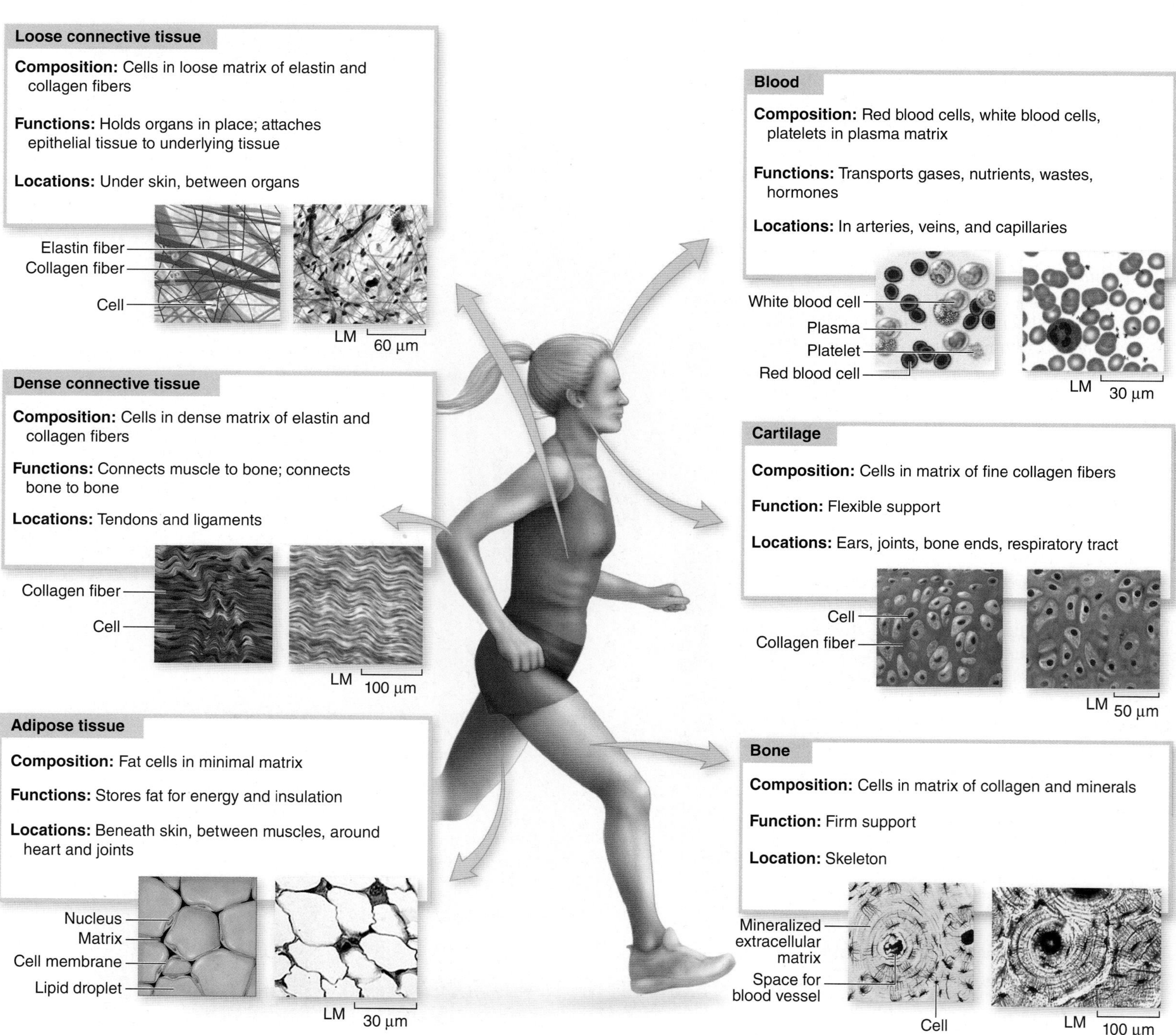

Loose connective tissue
Composition: Cells in loose matrix of elastin and collagen fibers
Functions: Holds organs in place; attaches epithelial tissue to underlying tissue
Locations: Under skin, between organs
Elastin fiber
Collagen fiber
Cell
LM 60 μm
Dense connective tissue
Composition: Cells in dense matrix of elastin and collagen fibers
Functions: Connects muscle to bone; connects bone to bone
Locations: Tendons and ligaments
Collagen fiber
Cell
LM 100 μm
Adipose tissue
Composition: Fat cells in minimal matrix
Functions: Stores fat for energy and insulation
Locations: Beneath skin, between muscles, around heart and joints
Nucleus
Matrix
Cell membrane
Lipid droplet
LM 30 μm
Blood
Composition: Red blood cells, white blood cells, platelets in plasma matrix
Functions: Transports gases, nutrients, wastes, hormones
Locations: In arteries, veins, and capillaries
White blood cell
Plasma
Platelet
Red blood cell
LM 30 μm
Cartilage
Composition: Cells in matrix of fine collagen fibers
Function: Flexible support
Locations: Ears, joints, bone ends, respiratory tract
Cell
Collagen fiber
LM 50 μm
Bone
Composition: Cells in matrix of collagen and minerals
Function: Firm support
Location: Skeleton
Mineralized extracellular matrix
Space for blood vessel
Cell
LM 100 μm

Figure 23.3 Connective Tissues. Connective tissues are extremely diverse in both structure and function. Most connective tissues are dominated by the extracellular matrix, not the cells themselves.

Blood is an unusual tissue because it is a liquid, not a solid. It consists of red blood cells, white blood cells, and cell fragments called platelets, all traveling in a liquid called plasma. The fluid extracellular matrix of blood is also unique in that it lacks protein fibers.

C. Muscle Tissue Provides Movement

Muscle tissue consists of cells that contract (become shorter) when electrically stimulated. Contraction occurs when long, thin protein filaments inside the muscle cells slide past one another. Abundant mitochondria provide the energy for contraction.

The heat generated by muscle contraction is important in body temperature regulation. The most familiar function of muscle tissue, however, is to move other tissues and organs. Muscle cells attach to soft tissue or bone; when the cells contract, the body part moves. Digestion, the elimination of wastes, blood circulation, and the motion of the limbs all rely on muscle contraction.

Animal bodies contain three types of muscle tissue (figure 23.4). Skeletal muscle tissue consists of long cells. When viewed with a microscope, skeletal muscle tissue appears striped, or striated, because the protein filaments that fill the cells align in a repeated pattern. Most skeletal muscle attaches to bone and provides voluntary movements that a person can consciously control. Cardiac muscle tissue, which occurs only in the heart, is also striated, but the cells are shorter, and their control is involuntary. Cardiac muscle cells are electrically coupled with one another, so they contract simultaneously to produce the heartbeat. Smooth muscle tissue is not striated, and its contraction is involuntary. This type of muscle pushes food along the intestinal tract, regulates the diameter of blood vessels, and controls the size of the pupil of the eye.

D. Nervous Tissue Forms a Rapid Communication Network

Nervous tissue uses electrical signals to convey information rapidly within an animal's body. Sensory cells detect stimuli such as the scent of a rose or a prick of its thorn. Other cells then transmit that information along nerves to the central nervous system (brain and spinal cord), which helps you interpret what you experience.

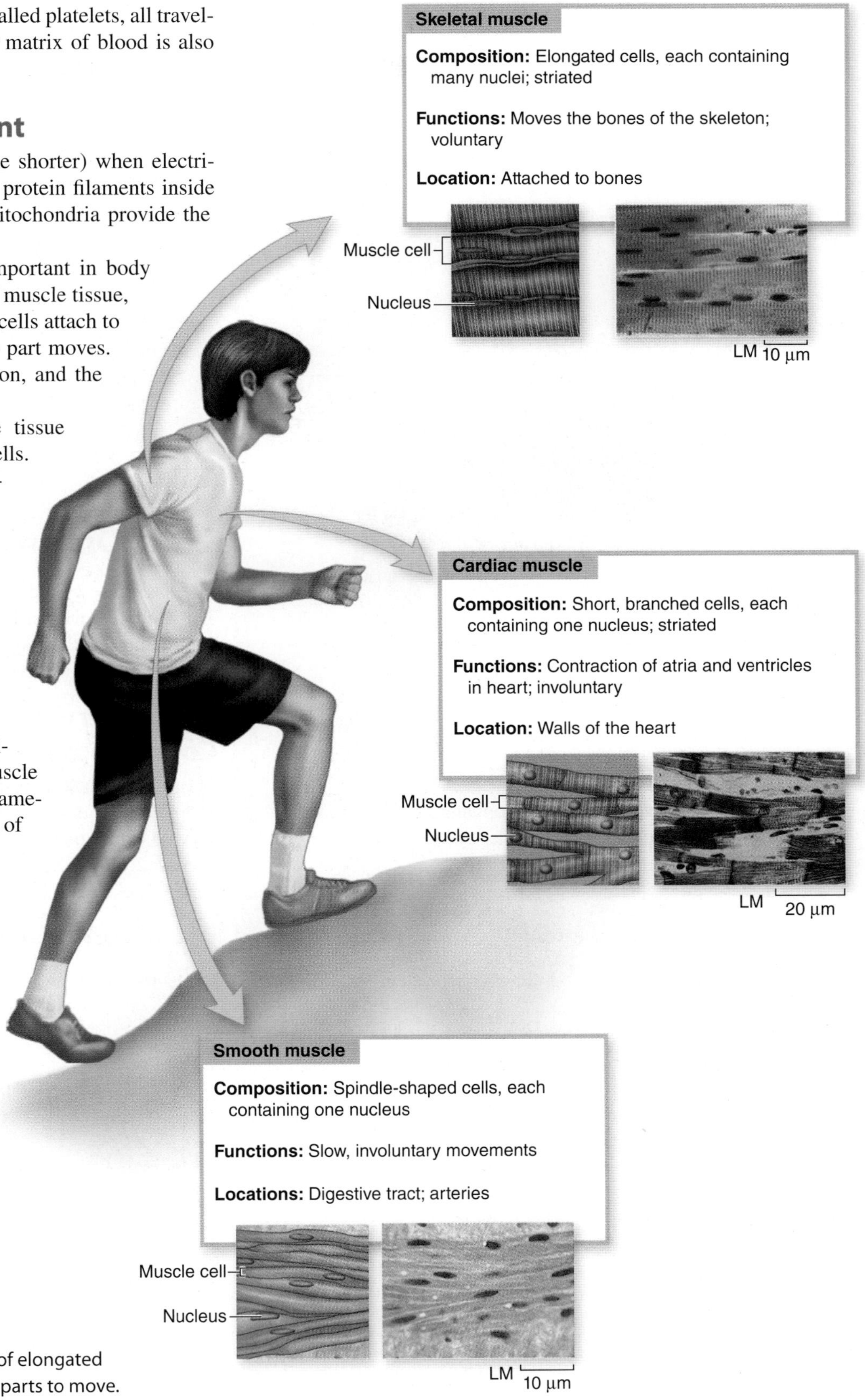

Skeletal muscle

Composition: Elongated cells, each containing many nuclei; striated

Functions: Moves the bones of the skeleton; voluntary

Location: Attached to bones

Muscle cell
Nucleus
LM 10 μm

Cardiac muscle

Composition: Short, branched cells, each containing one nucleus; striated

Functions: Contraction of atria and ventricles in heart; involuntary

Location: Walls of the heart

Muscle cell
Nucleus
LM 20 μm

Smooth muscle

Composition: Spindle-shaped cells, each containing one nucleus

Functions: Slow, involuntary movements

Locations: Digestive tract; arteries

Muscle cell
Nucleus
LM 10 μm

Figure 23.4 **Muscle Tissues.** Muscle tissues consist of elongated cells that can contract. All three types enable other body parts to move.

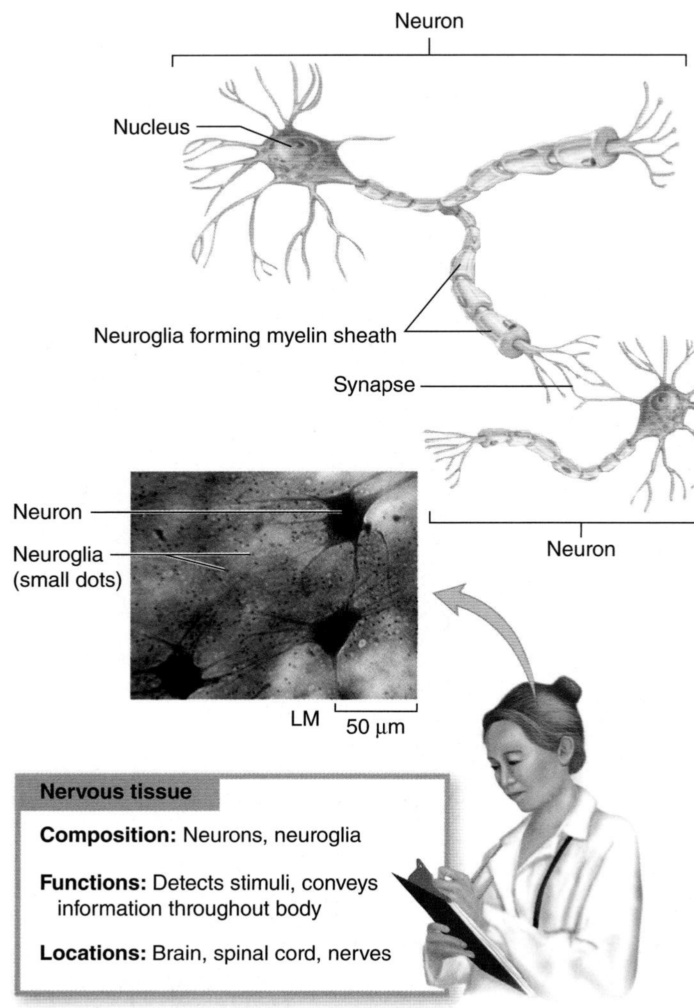

Neuron
Nucleus
Neuroglia forming myelin sheath
Synapse
Neuron
Neuron
Neuroglia
(small dots)
LM 50 μm
Nervous tissue
Composition: Neurons, neuroglia
Functions: Detects stimuli, conveys information throughout body
Locations: Brain, spinal cord, nerves

Figure 23.5 Nervous Tissue. Neurons and several types of neuroglia make up nervous tissue, which specializes in rapid communication.

Two main cell types occur in nervous tissue: neurons and neuroglia (figure 23.5). Neurons form communication networks that receive, process, and transmit information. A neuron may connect to another neuron at a junction called a synapse, or it may stimulate a muscle or gland. Neuroglia are cells that support neurons and assist in their functioning. The drawing in figure 23.5 shows the neuroglia that form insulating sheaths of myelin around parts of a neuron. As explained in chapter 24, the myelin sheath speeds the conduction of electrical impulses. Other types of neuroglia surround and support the neurons in the photo in figure 23.5.

23.2 Mastering Concepts

1. List the four main tissue types in animal bodies.
2. Where do epithelial tissues occur, and how are they named?
3. List and describe six types of connective tissue.
4. Explain the similarities and differences among the three types of muscle tissue.
5. What are the two main cell types in nervous tissue?

23.3 Organ Systems Are Interconnected

The tissues described in section 23.2 build organs, which form organ systems. This section provides a brief overview of human organ systems, organized by their contributions to the body's function (figure 23.6). Each system may seem distinct, but the function of each one relies on extensive interactions with the others.

A. The Nervous and Endocrine Systems Coordinate Communication

The human **nervous system** is a vast network composed of trillions of neurons and neuroglia that specialize in rapid communication. Some neurons are sensory receptors that detect stimuli; others relay the sensory input to the central nervous system. Still other neurons carry impulses from the brain or spinal cord to muscles or glands, which contract or secrete products in response.

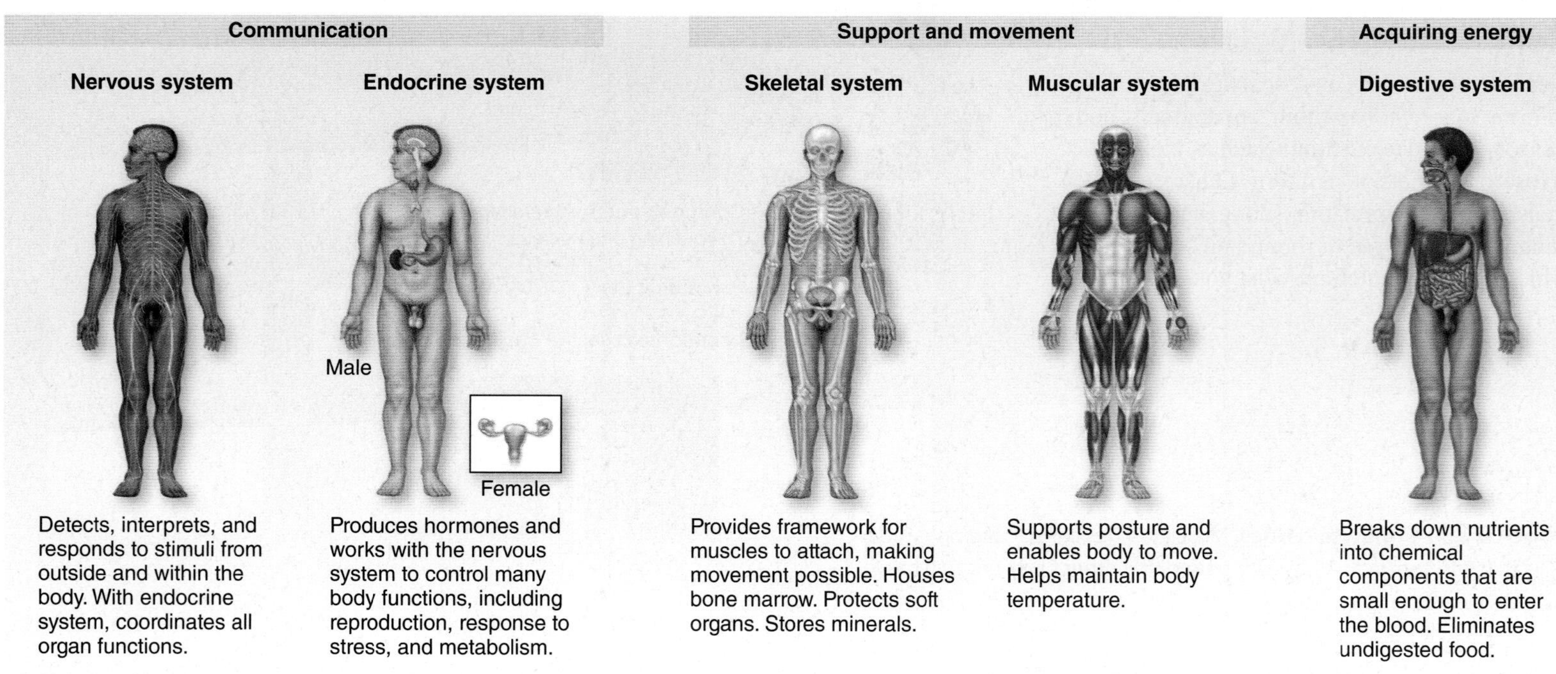

Communication
Nervous system
Endocrine system
Support and movement
Skeletal system
Muscular system
Acquiring energy
Digestive system
Male
Female
Detects, interprets, and responds to stimuli from outside and within the body. With endocrine system, coordinates all organ functions.
Produces hormones and works with the nervous system to control many body functions, including reproduction, response to stress, and metabolism.
Provides framework for muscles to attach, making movement possible. Houses bone marrow. Protects soft organs. Stores minerals.
Supports posture and enables body to move. Helps maintain body temperature.
Breaks down nutrients into chemical components that are small enough to enter the blood. Eliminates undigested food.

The **endocrine system** includes glands that secrete hormones, which are communication molecules that affect development, reproduction, mental health, metabolism, and many other functions. Hormones travel within the circulatory system and stimulate a characteristic response in target organs. Hormones act relatively slowly, but their effects last longer than nerve impulses.

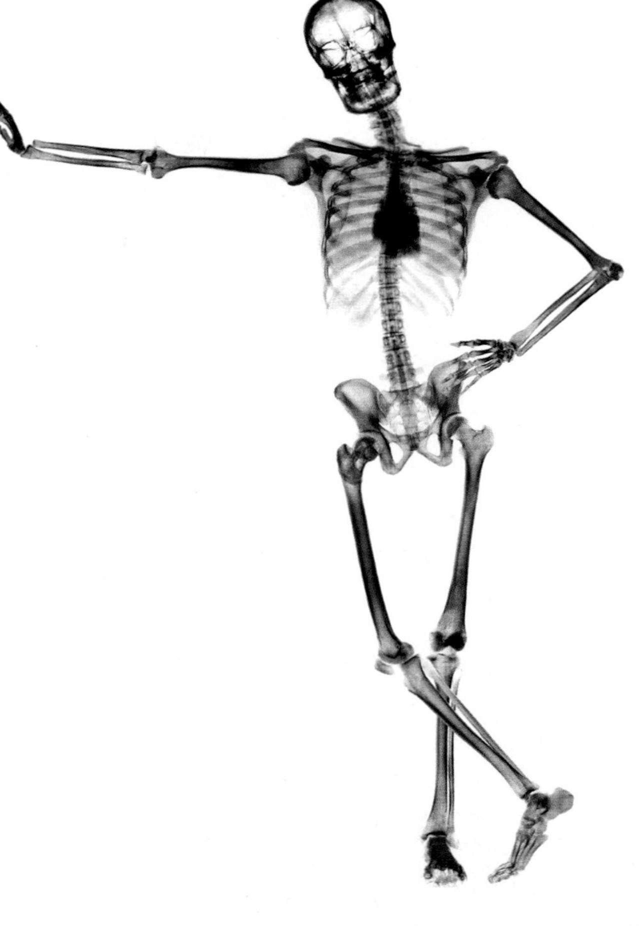

B. The Skeletal and Muscular Systems Support and Move the Body

The **skeletal system** consists of bones, ligaments, and cartilage. Bones protect underlying soft tissues and serve as attachment points for muscles. The marrow within some bones produces the components of blood; bones also store minerals such as calcium.

Individual skeletal muscles are the organs that make up the **muscular system.** When a skeletal muscle contracts, it moves another body part or helps support a person's posture. The heat released by contracting skeletal muscles also helps maintain body temperature.

C. The Digestive, Circulatory, and Respiratory Systems Work Together to Acquire Energy

The organs of the **digestive system** dismantle food into small molecules. The body's cells use the digested food molecules in two ways: to generate energy in cellular respiration and as raw materials in maintenance and growth. Meanwhile, the digestive system eliminates indigestible wastes.

The **circulatory system** transports digested food molecules (and many other substances) throughout the body. Nutrients absorbed by the digestive system enter blood at the intestines. The heart pumps the nutrient-laden blood through blood vessels that extend to all of the body's cells.

The **respiratory system** exchanges gases with the atmosphere. Cellular respiration requires not only food but also oxygen gas (O_2), which diffuses into blood at the lungs. The circulatory system delivers the O_2 throughout the body. Blood also carries a waste product of cellular respiration, carbon dioxide (CO_2), to the lungs to be exhaled.

Figure 23.6 Human Organ Systems.

Vessels carry blood throughout the body, nourishing cells, delivering oxygen, and removing wastes.

Delivers oxygen to blood and removes carbon dioxide.

Manufactures gametes and enables the female to carry and give birth to offspring.

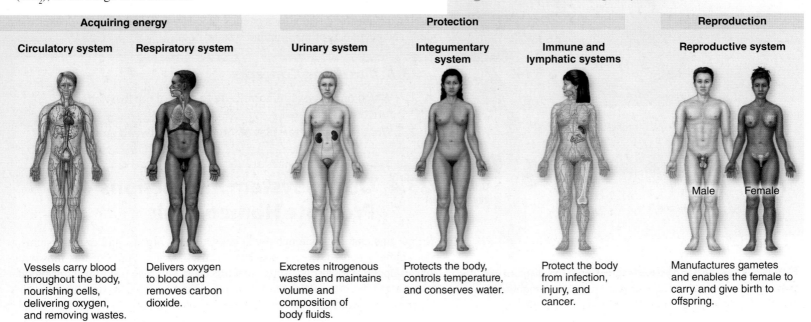

D. The Urinary, Integumentary, Immune, and Lymphatic Systems Protect the Body

Cell metabolism generates many waste products in addition to CO_2. These wastes enter the blood, which circulates through the kidneys. These organs are part of the **urinary system**, the organs that remove water-soluble wastes and other toxins from blood and eliminate them in urine. The kidneys also have other protective functions; they adjust the concentrations of many ions, balance the blood's pH, and regulate blood pressure.

One line of physical protection is the **integumentary system,** which consists of skin, associated glands, hair, and nails. Skin is a waterproof barrier that helps keep the underlying tissues from drying out, blocks the entry of many disease-causing organisms, and helps maintain body temperature.

The body also fights infection and cancer. The **immune system** attacks cancer cells, viruses, microbes, and other foreign substances. Moreover, the immune system quickly neutralizes harmful molecules that it "remembers" from previous infections. Vaccines build upon this memory by "teaching" the immune system about disease-causing agents the body has never actually encountered.

The **lymphatic system** is a bridge between the immune system and the circulatory system. Lymph originates as fluid that leaks out of blood capillaries and fills the spaces around the body's cells. Lymphatic capillaries absorb the excess fluid and pass it through the lymph nodes, where immune system cells destroy foreign substances. The cleansed fluid then returns to the circulatory system.

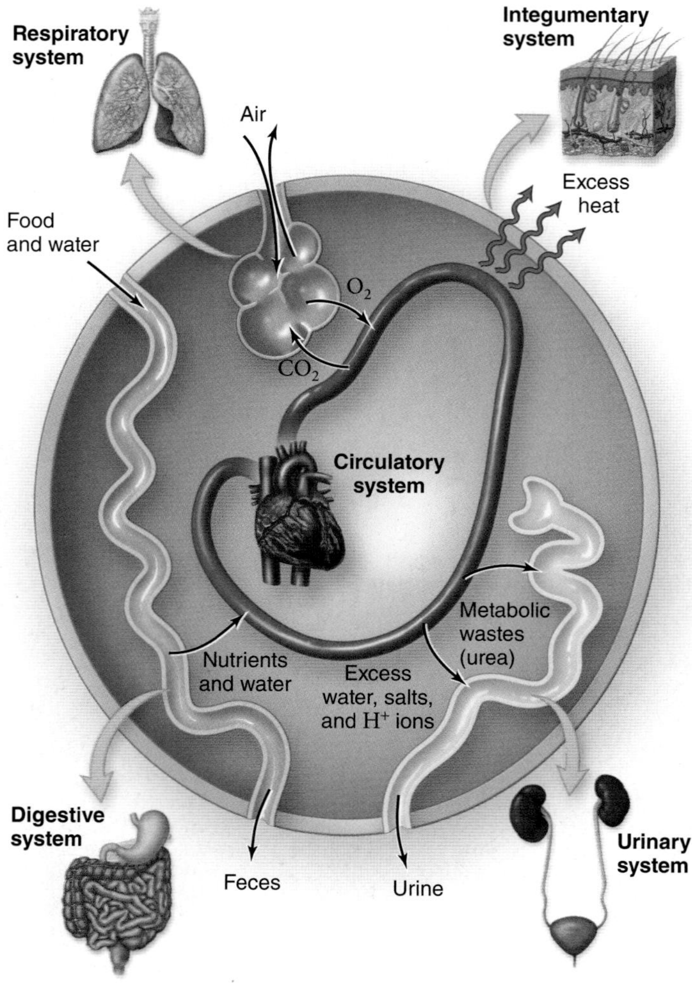

Figure 23.7 Organ System Interactions. This diagram of a "generic" animal illustrates how organ systems work together to maintain body temperature and the concentrations of oxygen, carbon dioxide, nutrients, water, and urea (a metabolic waste).

E. The Reproductive System Produces the Next Generation

The **reproductive system** consists of organs that produce and transport sperm and egg cells. The female body also can nurture developing offspring. Moreover, hormones from reproductive organs promote the development of secondary sex characteristics, such as facial hair in men and breasts in women.

The reproductive system illustrates how the organ systems are, in a sense, not separate at all. Consider the uterus, the pear-shaped sac that houses the embryo and fetus. The majority of the uterus is muscle. It also contains nervous tissue, which is why a woman feels cramps when it contracts. Hormones from the endocrine system stimulate these contractions. The entire system is richly supplied with the circulatory system's blood vessels, which also deliver the cells and chemicals of the immune system.

23.3 Mastering Concepts

1. Which organ systems contribute to each of the five general functions of life?
2. What are some examples of interactions between organ systems?

23.4 Organ System Interactions Promote Homeostasis

So far, this chapter has emphasized cells, tissues, organs, and organ systems. An animal's body, however, consists mostly of water. Some of this moisture makes up the cytoplasmic "soup" that fills every cell. The rest of it forms blood plasma and the **interstitial fluid** that bathes the body's cells. Because interstitial fluid is inside the body but outside the cells, biologists consider it part of the "internal environment." Many organ systems interact to help maintain the correct concentrations of nutrients, salts, hydrogen ions, and dissolved gases in the body's fluids (figure 23.7).

Yet the external environment changes constantly. Temperatures rise and fall; food may be abundant or scarce; water comes and goes. In the midst of this great variability, an animal's body must maintain its internal temperature, its blood pressure, and the chemical composition of its fluids within certain limits. **Homeostasis** is this state of internal constancy.

If a body system cannot maintain homeostasis, it may stop functioning, and the organism may die. As just one example, consider what happens if the lungs fill with water. The body can no longer acquire O_2 or dispose of CO_2, yet cells continue to respire. Soon, all available O_2 is consumed, and CO_2 accumulates to toxic levels. Cells begin to die, and the person will drown unless help arrives quickly.

A common way to maintain homeostasis is by **negative feedback,** which is an action that counters an existing condition. Figure 23.8 illustrates negative feedback in a familiar situation: maintaining room temperature. When the room gets too warm, the heater turns off. When the temperature is low, the thermostat signals the heater to switch back on.

In all negative feedback systems, sensors (such as the thermostat in figure 23.8) monitor changes in some parameter. If the value is too high or too low, the system responds by counteracting the original change. In the body, the "supervisor" that coordinates much of the action is an almond-sized part of the brain called the hypothalamus. If blood pressure rises too high, for example, receptors in the walls of blood vessels signal the hypothalamus to slow the contraction of the heart. The pressure drops. If blood pressure falls too low, the hypothalamus signals the heart to speed up, sending out more blood.

The hypothalamus participates in many negative feedback loops. If the concentration of glucose in the blood is too high, the hypothalamus indirectly signals the pancreas to secrete a hormone called insulin. The insulin, in turn, stimulates body cells to absorb more sugar from blood. If the concentration of salts is too high, hormones from the hypothalamus signal the kidney to release more salt into urine. If oxygen is scarce, the hypothalamus stimulates faster breathing, and so on.

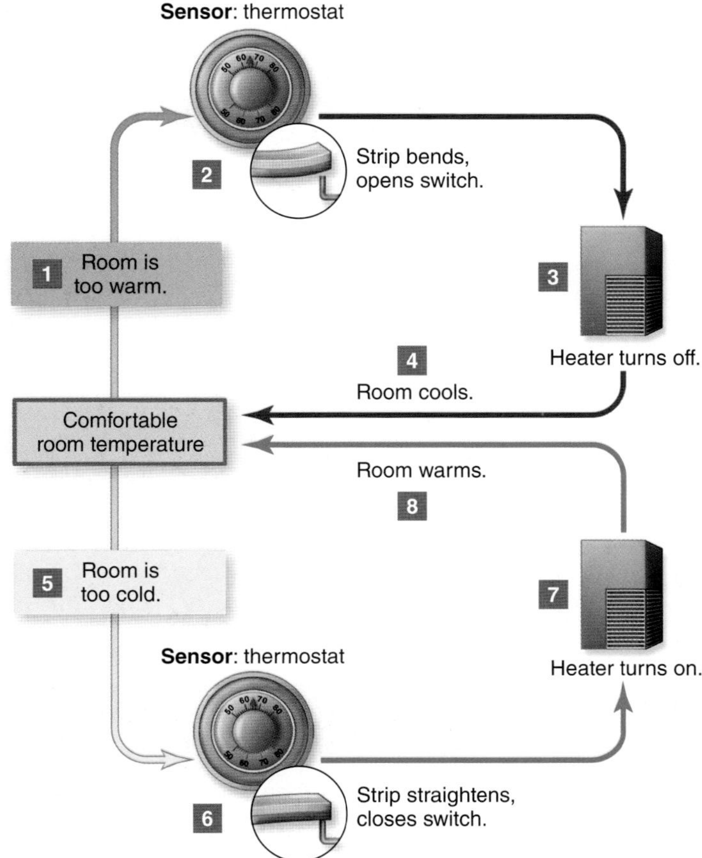

Figure 23.8 Negative Feedback: An Example. A negative feedback system maintains room temperature within comfortable limits. If the room is too warm, the heater shuts off, and the room cools. If the room becomes too cold, the heater switches on, and the temperature rises.

Burning Questions

Which types of organs can be transplanted in humans?

Medical technology can help replace body parts damaged by disease or injury. Transplantable organs include corneas, pancreases, kidneys, skin, livers, lungs, bone marrow, parts of the digestive tract, and hearts. Surgeons have even transplanted entire hands and faces.

One of the challenges in transplanting an organ is to prevent the recipient's immune system from rejecting the foreign tissues. Transplant surgeons minimize rejection by carefully matching organ donors with recipients. In addition, physicians can prescribe drugs that suppress the immune system, but this strategy increases the risk of deadly infection.

Unfortunately, the demand for transplantable organs far exceeds the supply. The chapter opening photo illustrates tissue engineering as one approach to solving this problem. Transplanting tissues and organs from other species into humans is another possible solution. Heart valves from pigs, for example, can replace malfunctioning ones in humans. Rarely, baboon hearts have been transplanted into gravely ill human patients who have no other options (figure 23.B).

But cross-species transplants are risky because they may transmit viruses from the donor animal to the recipient. We do not know what effect these viruses might have on a human body. Moreover, because many viral infections take years to cause symptoms, a new infectious disease in the future could be the trade-off for using nonhuman animal parts today.

Submit your burning question to:
marielle_hoefnagels@mcgraw-hill.com

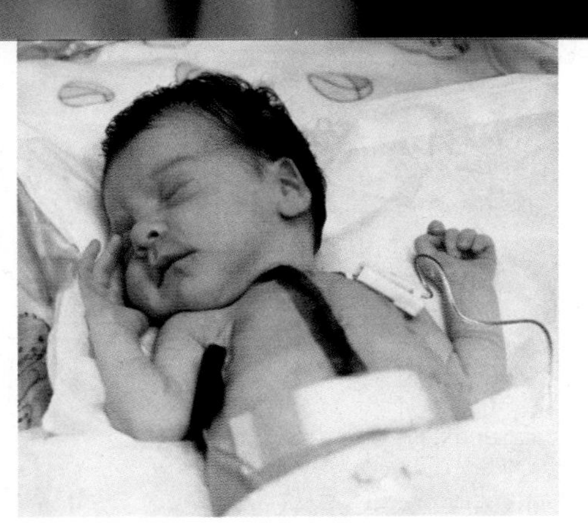

Figure 23.B Xenograft. In 1984, a California newborn, Baby Fae, lived 20 days with a baboon heart. The left half of her own heart was underdeveloped.

Only a few biological functions demonstrate **positive feedback,** in which the body reacts to a change by amplifying it. Blood clotting and milk secretion are examples of positive feedback—once started, they perpetuate their activity. Positive feedback therefore does not maintain homeostasis. Ultimately, however, other controls take over and restore equilibrium.

23.4 Mastering Concepts

1. Which fluids are part of the body's internal environment?
2. What is homeostasis?
3. What happens to an organism that fails to maintain homeostasis?
4. Distinguish between negative and positive feedback.

23.5 The Integumentary System Regulates Temperature and Conserves Moisture

The integumentary system consists mostly of **skin,** the organ that forms the body's outer surface. Hair, nails, and several types of glands complete the system.

This organ system beautifully illustrates the main themes of this chapter. Not only does skin (also called the integument) consist of multiple interacting tissue types, but the integumentary system also helps the body maintain homeostasis in several ways.

The most obvious way that skin helps maintain homeostasis is body temperature regulation. Specialized nerve endings in the skin sense the temperature and convey the information to the hypothalamus, which stimulates the warming or cooling response (see chapter 25).

The integument contributes to homeostasis in other ways as well. For example, skin conserves water. People who suffer extensive burns lose large amounts of skin and may die of dehydration. Moreover, burn patients are especially vulnerable to infection because intact skin is the first defense against disease-causing microorganisms. Skin even plays a role in nutrition, because the initial step in vitamin D synthesis occurs when light strikes the skin.

Human skin has two major layers (figure 23.9): the epidermis and the dermis. The **epidermis,** or outermost layer, consists mostly of stratified squamous epithelium. Active cell division continuously replaces epidermal cells lost to abrasion at the surface. Below the epidermis is the **dermis,** which is composed mostly of collagen but also contains elastic fibers, nerve endings, smooth muscle, blood vessels, and glands. Beneath the dermis lies a layer of loose connective tissue and adipose tissue that is not technically part of the skin.

The epidermis has many protective functions. For example, calluses are thick, scaly accumulations that protect skin from disease-causing organisms and abrasion. The skin's color derives from melanin,

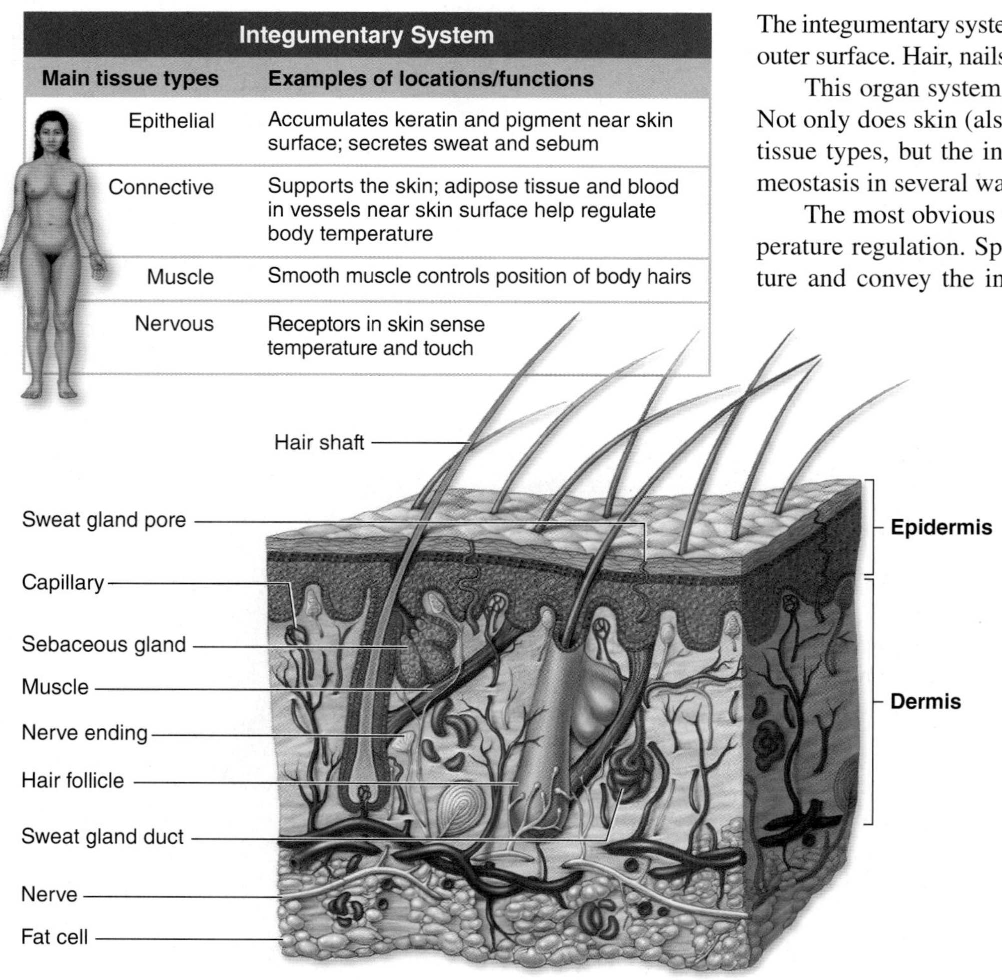

Integumentary System	
Main tissue types	**Examples of locations/functions**
Epithelial	Accumulates keratin and pigment near skin surface; secretes sweat and sebum
Connective	Supports the skin; adipose tissue and blood in vessels near skin surface help regulate body temperature
Muscle	Smooth muscle controls position of body hairs
Nervous	Receptors in skin sense temperature and touch

Figure 23.9 The Integumentary System. Skin is an organ that consists of all four tissue types. The outer layer, the epidermis, is made mostly of epithelial tissue. Sweat glands, blood vessels, small muscles, nerve endings, and other structures are embedded in the dermis.

a pigment that absorbs ultraviolet radiation and therefore protects against some types of skin cancer. ▸ skin cancer, p. 150

The epidermis also produces hair (and fur in other mammals). A hair grows from a group of cells called a hair follicle, which is anchored in the dermis. Hair and fur have many functions. The color of a mammal's fur can provide camouflage, as the white fur of an Arctic fox illustrates. Conversely, the prominent striped fur of a skunk is a warning to other animals. In addition, smooth muscle tissue surrounding each hair follicle can contract and make the hair "stand on end" when skin senses cold—this is the basis of goose bumps. This reaction has no apparent function in humans, but in many other mammals, erect fur provides extra insulation that helps retain body heat.

The dermis has many functions as well. Muscles attached to fibers in the dermis allow us to generate a wide array of facial expressions. Nerve endings in the dermis convey information from sensory receptors to the brain. Sweat glands originating in the dermis produce perspiration. Many mammals, including humans, have sebaceous glands, which secrete an oily substance that softens and helps protect the skin and hair.

Injuries that damage the dermis, such as a cut from broken glass, can leave a scar. As the injury heals, the replacement skin lacks hair follicles and sweat glands. The resulting scar consists of new skin that does not look or work exactly like the old.

A tattoo is an intentional "injury" to the dermis. The ink may look like it is on the surface of the skin (figure 23.10), but if it were, it would quickly disappear as epidermal cells slough off. Instead, a tattoo needle deposits the ink directly into the dermis. The ink remains in place permanently, just beneath the boundary with the epidermis.

Figure 23.10 Tattoo. To create a tattoo, a needle is used to deposit ink into the dermis of the skin.

23.5 Mastering Concepts

1. How does the integumentary system help the body maintain homeostasis?
2. What tissue types occur in each layer of human skin?

Investigating Life

23.6 Vitamins and the Evolution of Human Skin Pigmentation

Human skin color ranges from the deeply pigmented to the very pale (figure 23.11). How did this variation arise?

Scientists have long understood that the darker the skin, the higher the concentration of melanin. Moreover, indigenous people from the tropics (near the equator) tend to have darker skin than their counterparts from higher latitudes (toward the poles). Tropical areas receive more ultraviolet (UV) radiation than do locations farther north and south. High melanin production is therefore correlated with exposure to UV radiation.

The Question: Have these differences in UV radiation selected for variation in pigmentation? The risk of developing skin cancer offers

Figure 23.11 Skin Pigmentation. Melanin is the pigment that produces skin's color: the more melanin, the darker the skin.

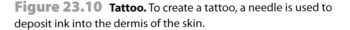

one possible answer. The more melanin in the skin, the less UV radiation penetrates below the epidermis and the lower the risk for cancer. But skin cancer is rarely fatal, and most cases develop after a person's reproductive age. Since skin cancer usually does not interfere with reproductive success, it is probably not a strong selective force in the evolution of skin color.

Oddly enough, nutrition may offer a more convincing explanation for the worldwide distribution of skin pigmentation. The body produces vitamin D when sunlight strikes the skin. This vitamin is crucial to reproductive success; a vitamin D deficiency can cause death or pelvic deformities that make childbirth difficult. One hypothesis that explains the variation in skin pigmentation, then, reflects the body's need for vitamin D. In high latitudes, light skin may maximize the potential to synthesize this essential molecule.

The Approach: Pennsylvania State University anthropologists Nina Jablonski and George Chaplin tested the strength of the association between vitamin D nutrition and UV radiation. They began by mapping satellite measurements of UV radiation striking Earth's surface. The pair also searched the scientific literature for measurements of skin pigmentation in indigenous peoples anywhere in the world. They then superimposed three zones on their map, corresponding to areas where indigenous people have lightly, moderately, and highly pigmented skin (figure 23.12).

Jablonski and Chaplin also looked for scientific papers documenting how much UV radiation is needed to synthesize sufficient vitamin D. They compared the results to their map and found a strong association between skin pigmentation and the potential to produce vitamin D. That is, in high latitudes, UV exposure is insufficient to produce vitamin D in people with dark skin. These regions therefore select for light pigmentation.

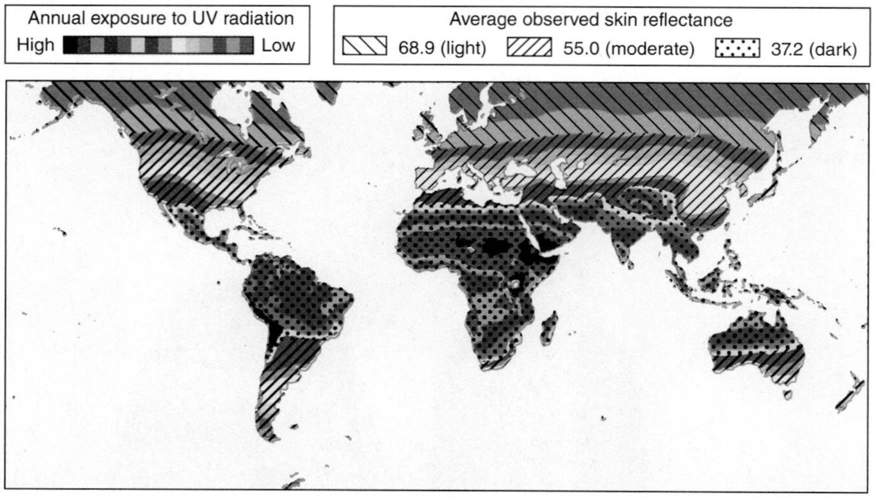

Figure 23.12 UV Radiation and Skin Pigmentation The colors on this map indicate average annual exposure to UV radiation. The map also shows average skin reflectance among indigenous people from each zone. The higher the skin reflectance value, the lighter the pigmentation.

The Conclusion: Jablonski and Chaplin's work supports the hypothesis that vitamin D deficiency becomes an increasingly important selective force at higher latitudes, where sunlight can be scarce.

This result leaves open the question of why areas with high UV exposure are associated with dark skin pigmentation. The answer may relate to another vitamin, B_9 (folic acid). UV radiation destroys folic acid in the skin. In men, insufficient folic acid may cause infertility. If a woman has too little folic acid, her children may be born with serious birth defects.

Skin pigmentation may therefore reflect a nutritional trade-off. In the tropics, abundant UV radiation selects for a high concentration of melanin, which blocks light penetration and therefore minimizes the sun-induced loss of folic acid. In higher latitudes, where people are exposed to less UV radiation than in the tropics, lighter skin pigmentation maximizes the potential to synthesize vitamin D.

This study not only provides insight into an interesting question about human evolution, but it also illustrates two important features of scientific investigation. First, technological advances can offer new ways to test old hypotheses. In this case, satellites enabled Jablonski and Chaplin to peek with unprecedented detail at ultraviolet radiation patterns across the globe. Second, scientists often borrow heavily from the past; dozens of previous studies on skin pigmentation and vitamin D synthesis gave the research team the information they needed to reach their conclusion.

Jablonski, Nina G., and George Chaplin. 2000. The evolution of human skin coloration. *Journal of Human Evolution,* vol. 39, pages 57–106.

23.6 Mastering Concepts

1. Describe how folic acid and vitamin D nutrition might explain the variation in human skin pigmentation.
2. Why do you think people who migrate from the tropics to urban areas in northern latitudes are at high risk for vitamin D deficiency? How might they decrease this risk?
3. Suggest a specific prediction related to folic acid that follows from the nutritional trade-off hypothesis.

Chapter Summary

23.1 Specialized Cells Build Animal Bodies

- **Anatomy** and **physiology** are interacting studies of the structure and function of organisms.
- Specialized cells function together to form **tissues.** Tissues build **organs,** and interacting organs form **organ systems**.

23.2 Animals Consist of Four Tissue Types

- Animal tissues consist of cells within an **extracellular matrix** of water, dissolved substances, and (usually) protein fibers.

A. Epithelial Tissue Covers Surfaces

- **Epithelial tissue** lines organs and forms **glands.** This tissue protects the underlying tissues and secretes substances.
- Epithelium may be simple (one layer) or stratified (more than one layer), and the cells may be flat, cube-shaped, or columnar.

B. Most Connective Tissues Bind Other Tissues Together

- **Connective tissues** have diverse structures and functions. Most consist of scattered cells and a prominent extracellular matrix.
- The six major types of connective tissues are loose connective tissue, dense connective tissue, adipose tissue, cartilage, bone, and blood.

C. Muscle Tissue Provides Movement

- **Muscle tissue** contracts when stimulated by electrical signals.
- Three types of muscle tissue are skeletal, cardiac, and smooth muscle.

D. Nervous Tissue Forms a Rapid Communication Network

- Neurons and neuroglia make up **nervous tissue.**
- A neuron functions in rapid communication; neuroglia support neurons.

23.3 Organ Systems Are Interconnected

A. The Nervous and Endocrine Systems Coordinate Communication

- The **nervous system** and **endocrine system** coordinate all other organ systems.
- Neurons form networks of cells that communicate rapidly, whereas hormones produced by the endocrine system act more slowly.

B. The Skeletal and Muscular Systems Support and Move the Body

- The bones of the **skeletal system** protect and support the body, and they act as a reservoir for calcium and other minerals.
- The **muscular system** enables body parts to move and generates body heat.

C. The Digestive, Circulatory, and Respiratory Systems Work Together to Acquire Energy

- The **digestive system** provides nutrients. The **respiratory system** obtains O_2, and the **circulatory system** delivers nutrients and O_2 to tissues.
- The body's cells use O_2 to extract energy from food molecules, producing waste CO_2. Together, the circulatory and respiratory systems eliminate this gas.

D. The Urinary, Integumentary, Immune, and Lymphatic Systems Protect the Body

- The **urinary system** removes metabolic wastes from the blood and reabsorbs useful substances.

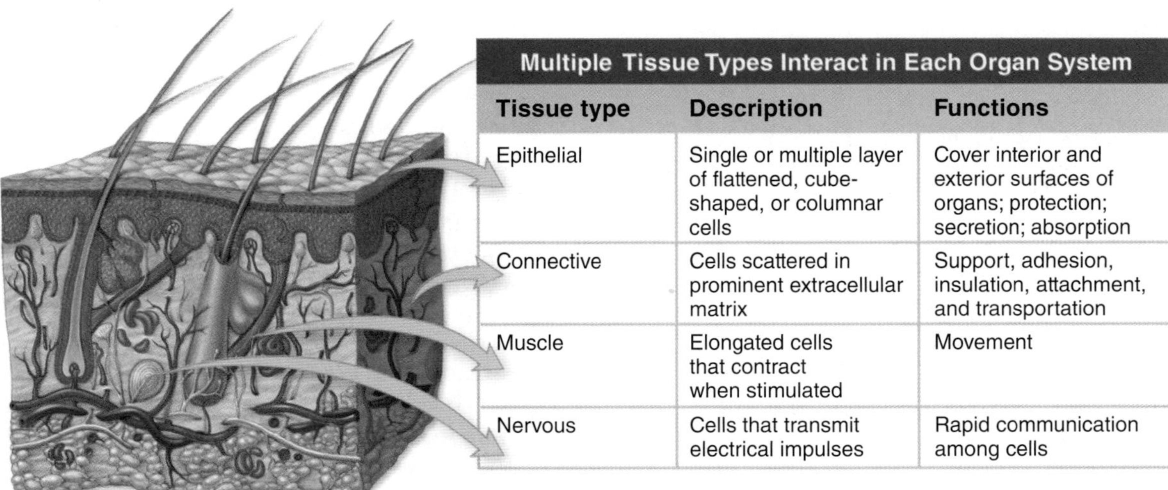

Multiple Tissue Types Interact in Each Organ System

Tissue type	Description	Functions
Epithelial	Single or multiple layer of flattened, cube-shaped, or columnar cells	Cover interior and exterior surfaces of organs; protection; secretion; absorption
Connective	Cells scattered in prominent extracellular matrix	Support, adhesion, insulation, attachment, and transportation
Muscle	Elongated cells that contract when stimulated	Movement
Nervous	Cells that transmit electrical impulses	Rapid communication among cells

- The **integumentary system** provides a physical barrier between the body and its surroundings.
- The **immune system** protects against infection, injury, and cancer.
- The **lymphatic system** connects the circulatory and immune systems, filtering the body's fluids through the lymph nodes.

E. The Reproductive System Produces the Next Generation

- The male and female **reproductive systems** are essential for the production of offspring.

23.4 Organ System Interactions Promote Homeostasis

- **Homeostasis** is the maintenance of a stable internal environment, including regulation of body temperature and the chemical composition of blood plasma and **interstitial fluid.**
- **Negative feedback** restores the level of a parameter to within a normal range. Sensors detect changes in the internal environment and activate responses that counteract the change.
- **Positive feedback** reinforces the effect of a change.

23.5 The Integumentary System Regulates Temperature and Conserves Moisture

- **Skin** helps regulate body temperature, conserves moisture, and contributes to vitamin D production.
- Skin consists of an **epidermis** over a **dermis,** plus specialized structures such as hair follicles and sweat glands.

23.6 Investigating Life: Vitamins and the Evolution of Human Skin Pigmentation

- Variation in exposure to ultraviolet radiation may select for a range of skin pigmentation, reflecting a balance between folic acid and vitamin D nutrition.

Multiple Choice Questions

1. Which of the following represents the correct order of organization of an animal's body?
   a. Cells; organs; organ systems; tissues
   b. Cells; tissues; organ systems; organs
   c. Tissues; cells; organs; organ systems
   d. Cells; tissues; organs; organ systems
2. The cells of epithelial tissue must ______ to function properly.
   a. form a single layer
   b. attach tightly to one another
   c. secrete substances
   d. form multiple layers
3. Which of the following features do all types of connective tissue share?
   a. The formation of a solid connection between two other tissue types
   b. The presence of cells
   c. The presence of an extracellular matrix
   d. Both b and c are correct.
4. Blood is an example of what type of tissue?
   a. Epithelial
   b. Nervous
   c. Connective
   d. Muscle
5. Smooth muscle is *different* from skeletal muscle because
   a. smooth muscle contraction is involuntary.
   b. skeletal muscle is striated (striped).
   c. smooth muscle contains sliding protein filaments.
   d. Both a and b are correct.
6. The digestive system interacts most closely with the ____ system.
   a. urinary
   b. respiratory
   c. circulatory
   d. endocrine
7. Ovaries produce egg cells and hormones; these organs therefore belong to the ________ systems.
   a. immune and integumentary
   b. endocrine and reproductive
   c. circulatory and nervous
   d. urinary and lymphatic
8. Which of the following scenarios does NOT illustrate negative feedback?
   a. In childbirth, contractions stimulate the release of oxytocin, which provokes more contractions.
   b. Body temperature climbs so high that a person begins to sweat, which cools the body.
   c. The salt concentration in blood is too high, so the kidneys eliminate salt in urine.
   d. Eating a meal causes a rise in blood sugar, which stimulates the pancreas to release insulin.
9. The inner layer of skin is composed of _______, whereas the outer layer is ________ .
   a. epithelial tissue; connective tissue
   b. dermis; epidermis
   c. epidermis; epithelial tissue
   d. epithelial tissue; epidermis
10. How does the integumentary system influence homeostasis?
    a. By preventing water loss
    b. By sensing external temperature
    c. By preventing infection
    d. All of the above are correct.

Write It Out

1. Distinguish between:
   a. organs and organ systems.
   b. simple squamous and stratified squamous epithelial tissue.
   c. loose and dense connective tissue.
   d. skeletal and cardiac muscle tissue.
   e. neurons and neuroglia.
   f. negative and positive feedback.
2. Marfan syndrome (see chapter 10) and osteogenesis imperfecta are two heritable disorders of connective tissue. Use the Internet to learn about these two diseases. Why do people with connective tissue disorders have many interrelated symptoms?
3. What is homeostasis, and how is it important?
4. When a person gets cold, he or she may begin to shiver. If the weather is too hot, the heart rate increases and blood vessels dilate, sending more blood to the skin. How does each scenario illustrate homeostasis?
5. Observe what happens to the size of your eye's pupil when you leave a dark room and enter the sunshine. What happens in the opposite situation, when you enter a dark room? How do the opposing reactions of your eye illustrate negative feedback?
6. Which tissues make up skin, the largest organ of the body? How do these tissues interact to provide the functions of skin? Describe one interaction between skin and each of the other organ systems (see figure 23.6).
7. How would you design an experiment to determine whether a new brand of artificial skin is safe for use in humans?
8. Make a chart that compares and contrasts the organization of the animal body with that of a plant (see chapter 21).

Pull It Together

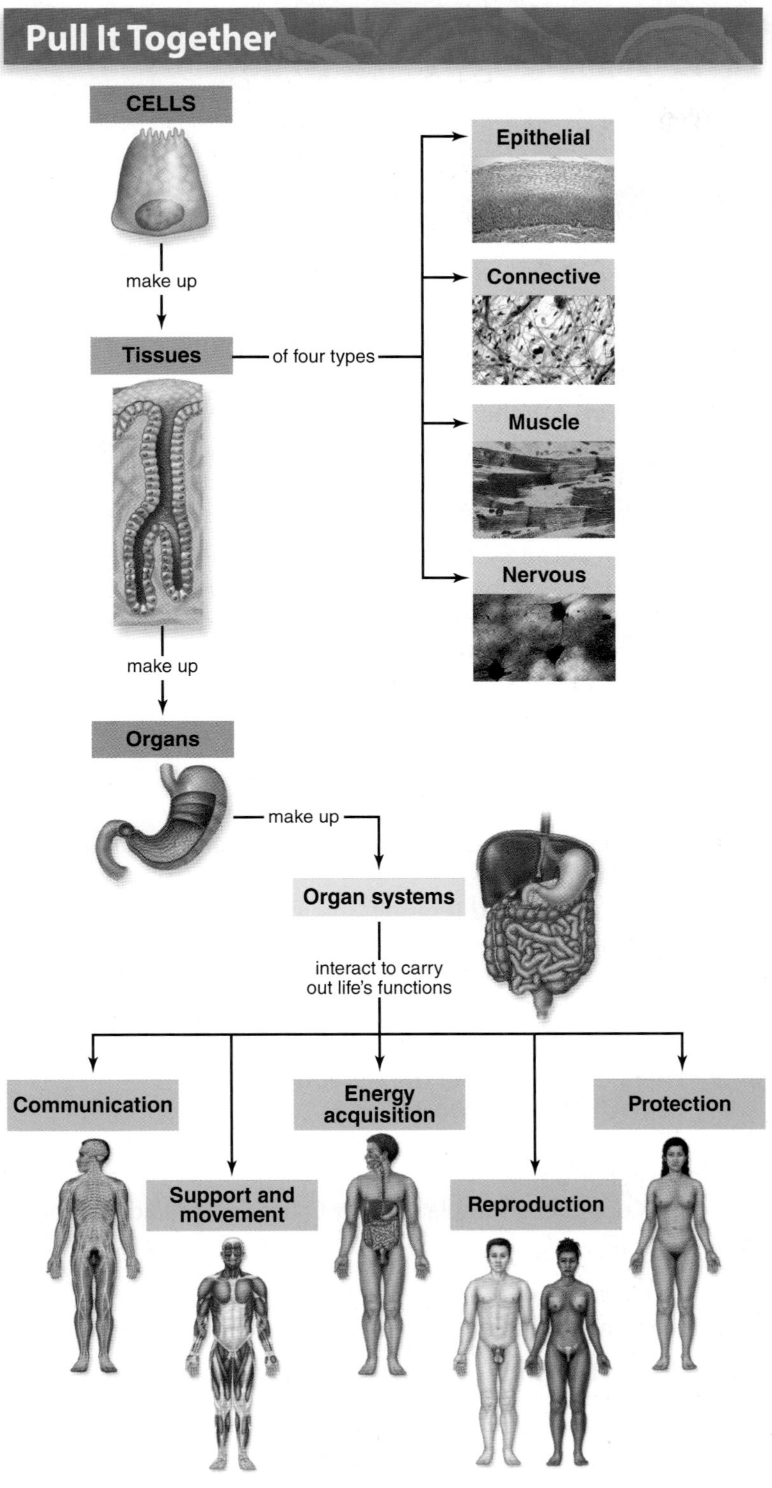

1. What features distinguish the four types of tissue?
2. Add the specific types of epithelial, connective, muscle, and nervous tissue to this concept map.
3. Add the names of the 11 organ systems to this concept map.
4. Describe examples of organ system interactions that maintain homeostasis.

24 The Nervous System and the Senses

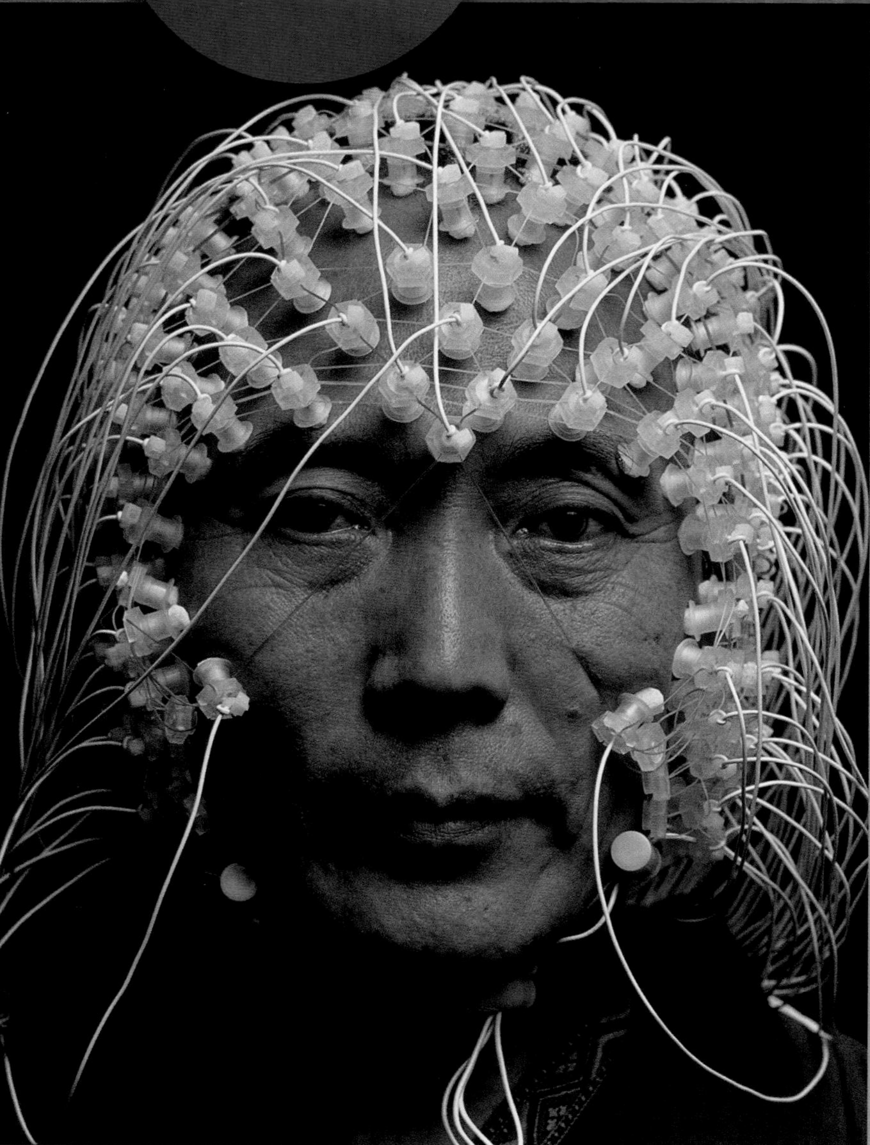

Mapping Brain Activity. Electrodes detect charge fluctuations in this man's neurons as he meditates.

Learning Outline

Learn How to Learn

Find a Good Listener

For many complex topics, it is not easy to know how well you really understand what is going on. One tip is to try explaining what you think you know to somebody else. Choose a subject that takes a few minutes to explain. As you describe the topic in your own words, your partner should ask follow-up questions and note where your explanation is vague. Those insights should help draw your attention to important details that you have overlooked.

What's the Point?

It is almost impossible to conceive of the nervous system's complexity. Intricate connections among 100 billion neurons simultaneously influence everything from wakefulness to muscle contraction to memory.

As complex as the nervous system is, however, the neurons all work on the same basic principles: electrical signals zip from cell to cell, producing instantaneous responses. Some of the effects, such as adjustments to heart rate or hormone production, happen without your awareness. But the nervous system also accounts for entirely conscious decisions such as where to drive your car or what to eat for lunch.

This chapter explores the basic structure and function of the nervous system before focusing on one familiar component: the senses. The eyes, ears, skin, nose, and mouth are our gateways to the outside world. Thanks to the blend of our senses, we experience the world as an exciting, multidimensional place.

24.1 The Nervous System Forms a Rapid Communication Network

Love, happiness, tranquility, sadness, jealousy, rage, fear, and excitement—all of these emotions spring from the cells of the nervous system. So do the ability to understand language, the sensation of warmth, memories of your childhood, and your perception of pain, color, sound, smell, and taste. The muscles that move when you chew, blink, or breathe all are controlled by the nervous system, as is the unseen motion that propels food along your digestive tract.

The nervous system's most critical functions are the "behind the scenes" activities that maintain a state of internal constancy, or homeostasis. The feedback systems that maintain homeostasis require communication between the sensors that detect each condition and the muscles and glands that make adjustments. Together, the **nervous system** and the **endocrine system** provide this essential communication. ▸ homeostasis, p. 475

A major difference between these two organ systems is the speed with which they act. The nervous system's electrical impulses travel so rapidly that their effects are essentially instantaneous. Endocrine glands, on the other hand, secrete chemical messages called hormones that can take hours to exert their effects. (Hormonal signals, however, are much longer-lasting; see chapter 25.)

As described in chapter 23, nervous tissue includes two basic cell types. **Neurons** are interconnected cells that communicate via electrical impulses. **Neuroglia** are cells that provide physical support, help maintain homeostasis in the fluid surrounding the neurons, guide neuron growth, and play many other roles that researchers are just beginning to discover. ▸ nervous tissue, p. 471

These basic building blocks form a wide variety of animal nervous systems, which range from diffuse networks of neurons in jellyfishes to the highly centralized nervous systems of vertebrates. As nervous systems increased in complexity, so too did animals' abilities to detect stimuli, coordinate responses, form memories, solve problems, and communicate. These capabilities are most highly developed in vertebrates.

The vertebrate nervous system has two main divisions: the central and peripheral nervous systems. The **central nervous system** consists of the **brain** (inside the skull) and **spinal cord.** The main function of these two organs is to integrate sensory information and coordinate the body's response. The **peripheral nervous system** carries information between the central nervous system and the rest of the body.

To understand how the nervous system regulates virtually all other organ systems, imagine a lynx hunting a hare (figure 24.1). Sensory neurons in the peripheral nervous system enable the cat to hear, see, and smell its prey. The lynx's central nervous system interprets

Sensory input (ears, eyes, and nose detect prey)

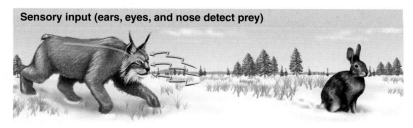

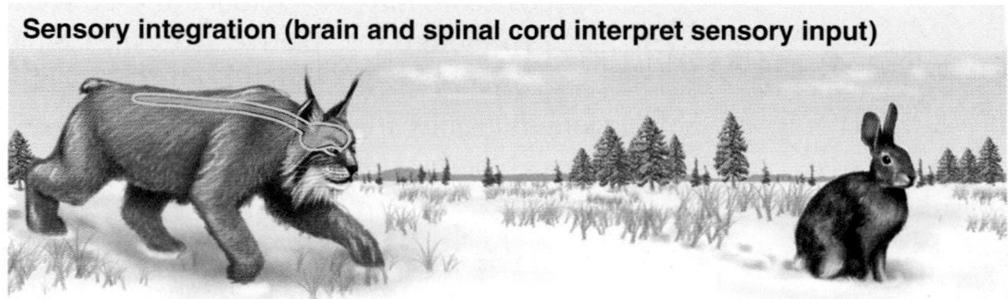

Sensory integration (brain and spinal cord interpret sensory input)

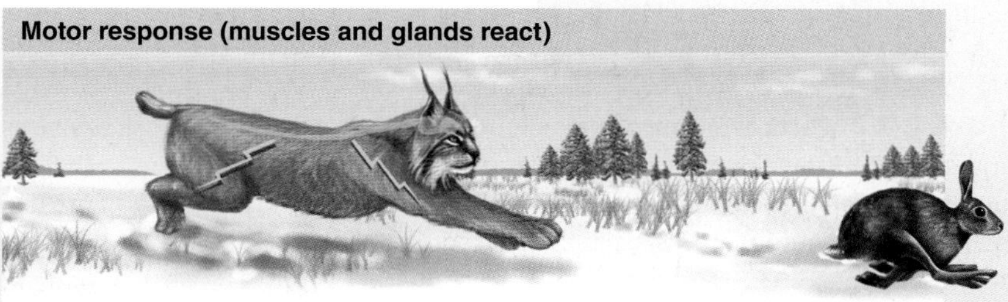

Figure 24.1 Roles of the Nervous System. Sensory organs, such as a lynx's eyes, ears, and nose, receive sensory input. The central nervous system integrates the information and sends signals that initiate appropriate motor responses.

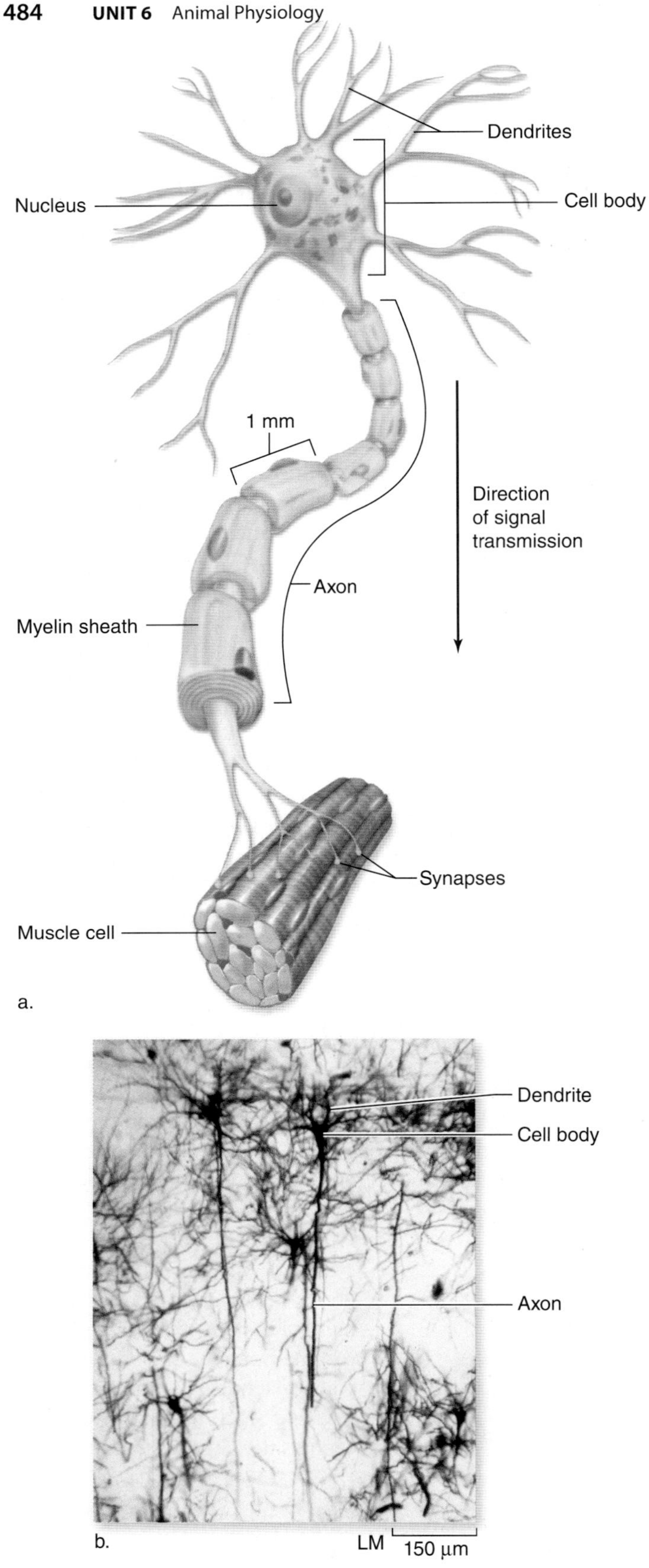

Figure 24.2 **Parts of a Neuron.** (a) A neuron consists of a rounded cell body, one or more dendrites, and an axon. In many neurons, the axon is encased in a myelin sheath interrupted by gaps. (b) Several neurons are visible in this micrograph of the brain's outermost layer.

this sensory input and decides how to act, and then motor neurons coordinate the skeletal muscles that move the lynx into position to catch the hare. Meanwhile, the cat's heart pumps blood, and its lungs inhale and exhale—all under the control of the central and peripheral nervous systems.

24.1 Mastering Concepts

1. How is the nervous system's role in maintaining homeostasis different from that of the endocrine system?
2. What are the roles of neurons and neuroglia?
3. Distinguish between the central and peripheral nervous systems.

24.2 Neurons Are the Functional Units of a Nervous System

The nervous system's function is rapid communication by electrical and chemical signals. Neurons are the cells that do the communicating, both with one another and with muscles and glands. To understand how neurons carry out their function, it helps to first learn about their structure.

A. A Typical Neuron Consists of a Cell Body, Dendrites, and an Axon

All neurons have the same basic parts (figure 24.2). The enlarged, rounded **cell body** contains the nucleus, mitochondria, ribosomes, and other organelles. **Dendrites** are short, branched extensions that transmit information toward the cell body. The number of dendrites may range from one to thousands, and each can receive input from many other neurons. The **axon,** also called the nerve fiber, conducts nerve impulses away from the cell body. An axon is typically a single long extension that is finely branched at its tip. Each tiny terminal extension communicates with another cell at a junction called a synapse.

In many neurons, a **myelin sheath** coats sections of the axon. The myelin sheath is composed of specialized neuroglia that are wrapped tightly around the axon. These neuroglia contain a fatty material that insulates the axon and speeds nerve impulse conduction (see section 24.3C).

To picture the relative sizes of a typical neuron's parts, imagine its cell body is the size of a tennis ball. The axon might then be up to 1.5 kilometers long but only a few centimeters thick. The mass of dendrites extending from the cell body would fill an average-size living room.

B. The Nervous System Includes Three Classes of Neurons

Biologists divide neurons into three classes, based on general function (figure 24.3).

- A **sensory neuron** brings information from the body's organs toward the central nervous system. Sensory neurons respond to light, pressure from sound waves, heat, touch, pain, and chemicals detected as odors or taste. The dendrites, cell body, and most of the axon of each sensory neuron lie in the peripheral nervous system, whereas the axon's endings reside in the central nervous system.

- About 90% of all neurons are **interneurons,** which connect one neuron to another within the spinal cord and brain. Interneurons receive information from sensory neurons, process this information, and generate the messages that the motor neurons carry to muscles and glands.
- A **motor neuron** conducts its message from the central nervous system toward a muscle or gland cell. A motor neuron's cell body and dendrites reside in the central nervous system, but its axon extends into the peripheral nervous system. Thus, motor neurons stimulate muscle cells to contract and glands to secrete. (They are called motor neurons because most lead to muscle cells, not glands.)

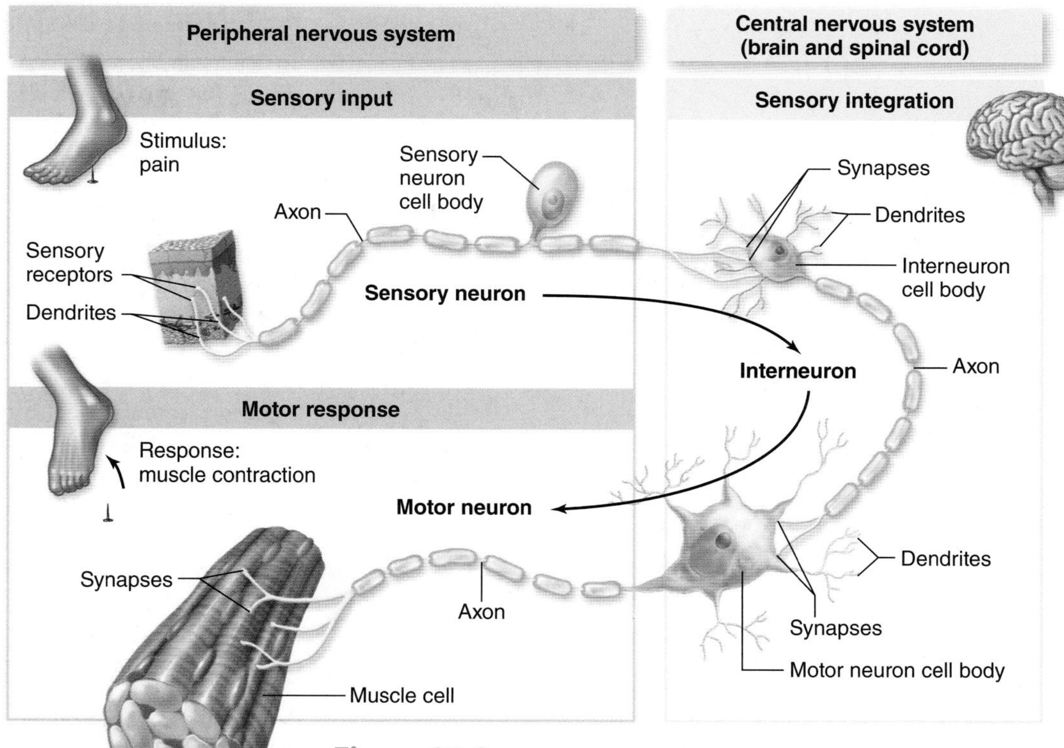

Figure 24.3 Categories of Neurons. Sensory neurons transmit information from sensory receptors to the central nervous system. Interneurons connect sensory neurons to motor neurons, which send information from the central nervous system to muscles or glands.

Figure 24.3 shows a simplified example of how the three types of neurons work together to coordinate the body's reaction to a painful stimulus. The process begins when a person steps on a tack. Sensory neurons whose dendrites are in the skin of the foot convey information about the puncture to the spinal cord. There, the sensory neuron transmits the signal to an interneuron, which relays the information to an area of the brain that interprets the sensation as pain. Another interneuron connects the brain's sensory area with the motor area. The motor area, in turn, relays a command to yet another interneuron, which activates the motor neurons that stimulate muscle contraction in the leg and foot. The signals move so quickly that the foot withdraws at about the same time as the brain perceives the pain.

24.2 Mastering Concepts

1. Describe the parts of a typical neuron.
2. Where is the myelin sheath located?
3. What is the usual direction in which a message moves within a neuron?
4. What are the functions of each of the three classes of neurons?

24.3 Action Potentials Convey Messages

A neuron sends messages by conveying a neural impulse. These signals result from the movement of charged particles (ions) across the cell membrane. This section describes the distribution of ions in neurons, both when the cell is "at rest" and when it is transmitting a neural impulse. ▸ ions, p. 27

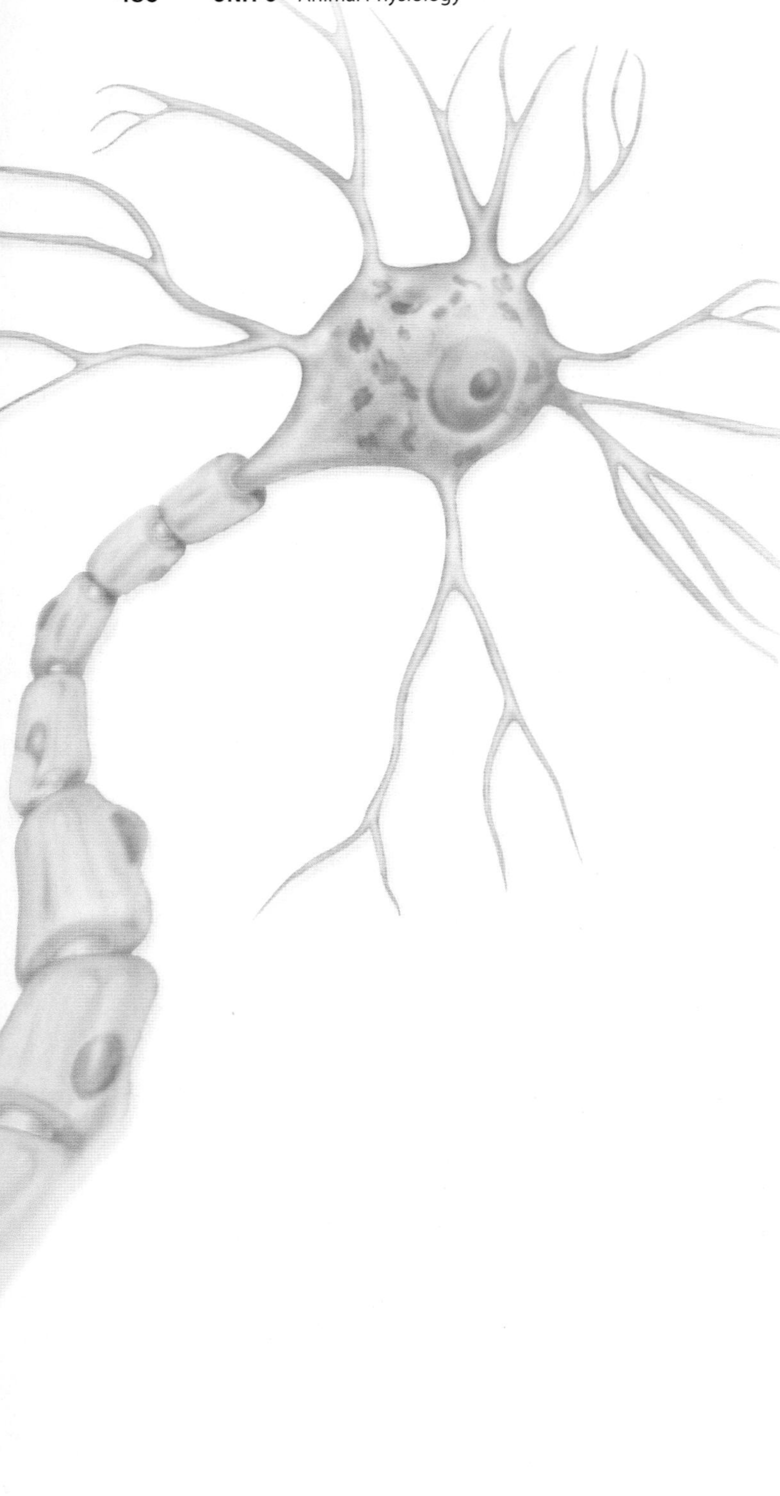

A. A Neuron at Rest Has a Negative Charge

To understand how ions move in a neural impulse, it helps to be familiar with the **resting potential,** which is the charge difference between the inside and outside of a neuron that is not conducting a message. At rest, the inside of a neuron carries a slightly negative electrical charge relative to the outside (figure 24.4, step 1).

A neuron has a resting potential because it maintains an unequal distribution of ions across its membrane. In a neuron at rest, the concentration of potassium (K^+) is much higher inside the cell than outside, while the reverse is true for sodium (Na^+). An ion pump (the sodium–potassium pump) in the axon membrane helps maintain this gradient by simultaneously importing two K^+ for every three Na^+ exported. ▸ active transport, p. 78

The term *resting potential* is a bit misleading because the neuron consumes a tremendous amount of energy while "at rest." In fact, the nervous system devotes about three quarters of its total energy budget to maintaining the resting potential of its neurons. The resulting state of readiness allows the neuron to respond more quickly than it could if it had to generate an ion gradient across the membrane each time it received a stimulus. The neuron's resting potential is therefore analogous to holding back the string on a bow to be constantly ready to shoot an arrow.

B. A Neuron's Membrane Potential Rises and Falls During an Action Potential

A neuron's resting potential keeps it primed to convey messages at any moment. If a stimulus does arrive, action potentials may occur along the neuron's axon. An **action potential** is a brief change in membrane potential that propagates like a wave along the membrane of the nerve fiber. A neural impulse is the spread of action potentials along an axon.

The stimulus that triggers a neuron to "fire" may be a change in pH, a touch, or a signal from another neuron. Whatever the stimulus, some sodium channels in a neuron's membrane open and then immediately close, usually at the dendrites or cell body. A small amount of Na^+ leaks into the cell through the open channels, causing the interior to become less negative. An action potential occurs only if enough Na^+ reaches the axon to exceed the cell's **threshold potential.** When threshold potential is reached, additional sodium channels open (figure 24.4, step 2), and more Na^+ pours into the cell.

The interior of the axon now has a positive charge, but only for an instant. Near the peak of the action potential, sodium channels close, again preventing Na^+ from entering the cell. Repelled by the positively charged ions inside the cell, K^+ diffuses out of the cell, again making the inside of the axon negative relative to the outside (figure 24.4, step 3). Meanwhile, the sodium–potassium pump returns Na^+ to the membrane's exterior. Resting potential is restored (figure 24.4, step 4). The entire process, from the initial influx of Na^+ to the restoration of the resting potential, takes only 1 to 5 milliseconds to complete.

Figure 24.4 shows how an action potential occurs at one small patch of a neuron's membrane. To transmit a neural impulse, however, the electrical signal must move from near the cell body to the end of the axon. How does this occur? During an action potential, some of the Na^+ ions that rush into the cell diffuse along the interior of the cell. As a result of this local influx of Na^+, the neighboring patch of the axon reaches its threshold potential as well, triggering a new influx of Na^+. The resulting chain reaction carries the impulse forward. The impulse does not spread "backward" because the membrane must reestablish its resting potential before another action potential can occur.

A neural impulse is therefore similar to people doing "the wave" in a football stadium, when successive groups of spectators stand and then quickly sit. The participants do not change their locations, yet the wave appears to travel around the stadium.

Figure It Out

If negatively charged chlorine atoms (Cl^-) move into a neuron, is an action potential become more likely or less likely to occur? Why?

Answer: Less likely; the membrane potential becomes more negative.

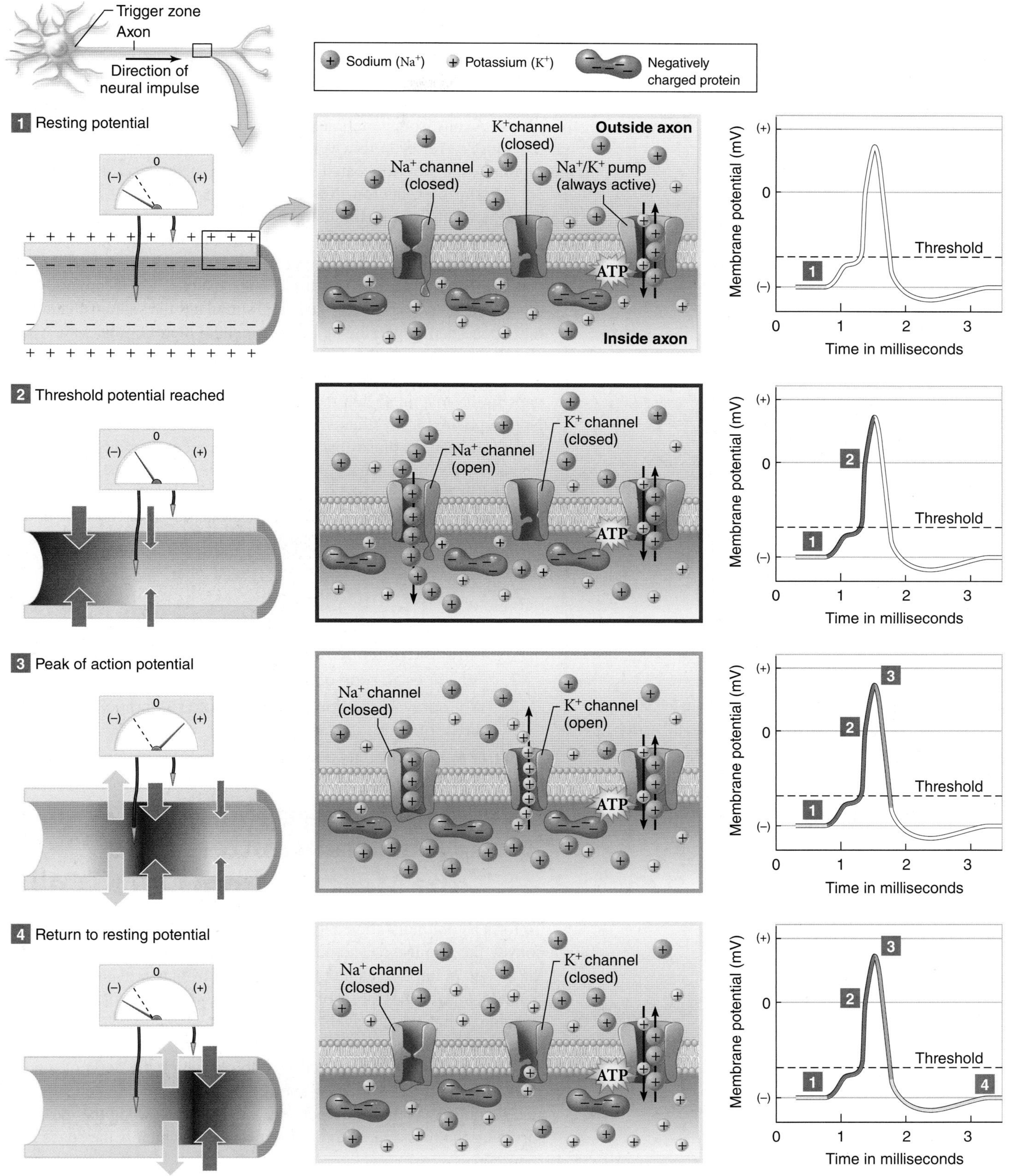

Figure 24.4 The Action Potential. (1) At resting potential, the inside of the neuron has a negative charge relative to the outside. The neuron is ready to fire. (2) A stimulus causes some Na^+ channels to open briefly. Na^+ diffuses into the cell. This local increase in charge causes additional Na^+ channels to open. If enough Na^+ channels open, the cell reaches its threshold potential. (3) An action potential occurs, and the inside of the axon becomes positively charged. After a split second, Na^+ channels close, and K^+ leaves the axon. The inside of the axon becomes negatively charged again. (4) Resting potential is reestablished.

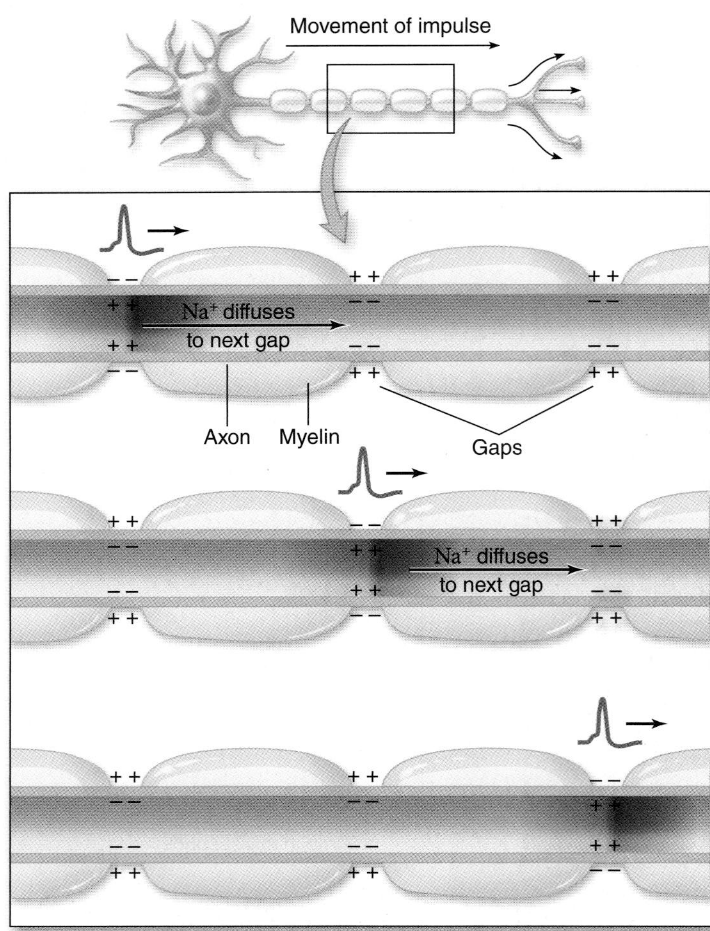

Figure 24.5 The Role of the Myelin Sheath. In myelinated axons, Na^+ channels occur only at the gaps in the myelin sheath. Action potentials appear to "jump" between the gaps, which speeds impulse transmission along the axon.

C. The Myelin Sheath Speeds Communication

The greater the diameter of an axon, the faster it conducts an impulse. A squid's "giant axons" are up to 1 millimeter in diameter. (Much of what biologists know about action potentials comes from studies on these large-diameter nerve fibers.) Axons from vertebrates are a hundredth to a thousandth the diameter of the squid's. Yet even thin vertebrate nerve fibers can conduct impulses very rapidly when they are coated with a myelin sheath (figure 24.5).

Myelin prevents ion flow across the membrane. At first glance, it might therefore seem that myelin should prevent the spread of action potentials. But the entire axon is not coated with myelin. Instead, ions can move across the membrane at the gaps in the myelin sheath. When an action potential happens at one gap, Na^+ entering the axon diffuses to the next gap. The incoming Na^+ makes the membrane potential more positive and stimulates the sodium channels to open at the second gap, triggering an action potential there. In this way, when a neural impulse travels along the axon, it appears to "jump" from gap to gap.

The neural impulse moves up to 100 times faster when it leaps between gaps in the myelin sheath than when it spreads along an unmyelinated axon. Not surprisingly, myelinated fibers occur in neural pathways where speed is essential, such as those that transmit motor commands to skeletal muscles. Thanks to myelin, a sensory message travels from the toe to the spinal cord in less than 1/100 of a second (about one third the speed of sound). Unmyelinated fibers occur in pathways where speed is less important, such as in the neurons that trigger the secretion of stomach acid.

24.3 Mastering Concepts

1. What is the difference between the resting potential, the threshold potential, and an action potential?
2. How does an axon generate and transmit a neural impulse?
3. What prevents action potentials from spreading in both directions along an axon?
4. How does myelin speed neural impulse transmission?

24.4 Neurotransmitters Pass the Message from Cell to Cell

To form a communication network, a neuron conducting action potentials must convey the impulse to another cell. Most neurons do not touch each other, so the electrical impulse cannot travel directly from cell to cell. Instead, an action potential that reaches the tip of an axon causes the release of a **neurotransmitter,** a chemical signal that travels from a "sending" cell to a "receiving" cell across a tiny space.

A **synapse** is a specialized junction at which the axon of a neuron communicates with another cell—another neuron, a muscle cell, or a gland cell. Each synapse has three components: the neuron sending the message, the cell receiving the message, and the **synaptic cleft,** which is the space between the two cells.

A close look at a synapse reveals that the tip of the axon of a sending neuron branches into many **synaptic terminals,** tiny knobs that enlarge at the tips. These knobs contain many small sacs, or vesicles, that hold neurotransmitter molecules. On the receiving cell's membrane, immediately opposite a synaptic terminal, are receptor proteins that can bind to a neurotransmitter.

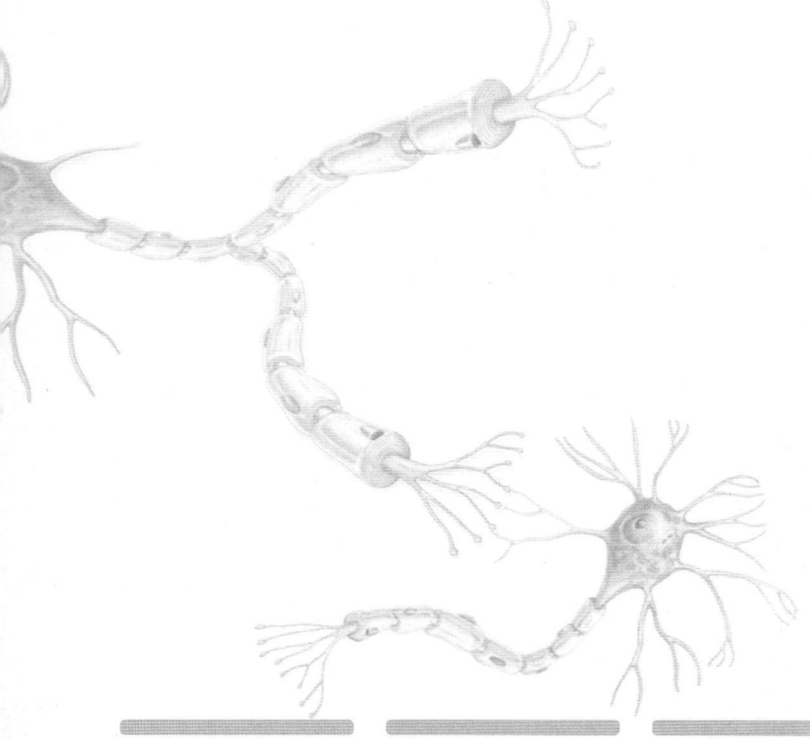

Figure 24.6 shows how a synapse works. Action potentials travel along the membrane of the sending neuron and reach the membrane of a synaptic terminal. Those neural impulses, in turn, stimulate the vesicles inside the synaptic terminal to dump neurotransmitters into the synaptic cleft.

The neurotransmitter molecules released by the sending cell diffuse across the synaptic cleft and attach to receptors on the membrane of the receiving cell. When the neurotransmitter contacts the receptor, ion channels open in the receiving cell's membrane, changing the probability that an action potential will occur. The neurotransmitter then might diffuse away from the synaptic cleft, be destroyed by an enzyme, or be taken back into the sending axon soon after its release, an event called reuptake.

The interaction between a neurotransmitter and the receptor may be excitatory; that is, the membrane of the receiving cell may become more positive, increasing the probability that an action potential will occur. In figure 24.6, the Na^+ ions entering the receiving cell are having this effect. Conversely, the interaction may be inhibitory, making the interior of the cell more negative and reducing the likelihood of an action potential.

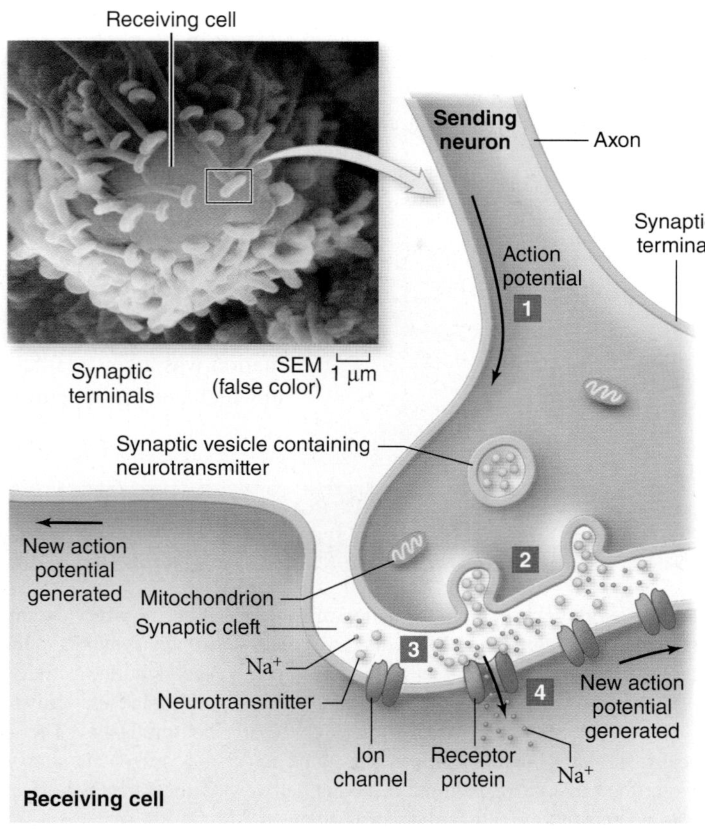

Figure 24.6 The Synapse. An action potential triggers the release of neurotransmitter molecules from a synaptic terminal. The neurotransmitters diffuse across the synaptic cleft and bind with receptors in the receiving cell membrane. Ion channels then open, changing the likelihood of an action potential in the receiving cell. The inset shows synaptic terminals from many neurons converging on the cell body of a neuron.

The human brain uses at least 100 neurotransmitters. The two most common are the amino acids glutamate and GABA (gamma-aminobutyric acid). Other neurotransmitters occur at fewer synapses but still are vital. Serotonin, dopamine, epinephrine, norepinephrine, and acetylcholine are examples.

Too much or too little of a neurotransmitter can cause serious illness; table 24.1 lists a few examples of disorders that are at least partly associated with neurotransmitter imbalances. Moreover, some drugs can alter the

TABLE 24.1 Disorders Associated with Neurotransmitter Imbalances

Condition	Imbalance of Neurotransmitter in Brain	Symptoms
Alzheimer disease	Deficient acetylcholine (caused by death of acetylcholine-producing cells)	Memory loss, depression, disorientation, dementia, hallucinations, death
Epilepsy	Excess GABA leads to excess norepinephrine and dopamine.	Seizures, loss of consciousness
Huntington disease	Deficient GABA	Uncontrollable movements, dementia, behavioral and personality changes, death
Hypersomnia	Excess serotonin	Excessive sleeping
Insomnia	Deficient serotonin	Inability to sleep
Myasthenia gravis	Deficient receptors for acetylcholine at synapse between motor neuron and muscle cell	Progressive muscle weakness
Parkinson disease	Deficient dopamine	Tremors of hands, slowed movements, muscle rigidity
Schizophrenia	Deficient GABA leads to excess dopamine.	Inappropriate emotional responses, hallucinations

functioning of the nervous system by either halting or enhancing the activity of a neurotransmitter. A drug may bind to a receptor on a receiving neuron, blocking a neurotransmitter from binding there. Alternatively, a drug may activate the receptor and trigger an action potential. The Why We Care box on this page illustrates how drugs such as nicotine, cocaine, and heroin tamper with the communication between neurons.

Notice that a synapse is asymmetrical; that is, nerve impulses travel from sending neuron to receiving cell and not in the opposite direction. This one-way traffic of information stands in contrast to the nerve net of a jellyfish, in which nerve impulses travel in all directions. The unidirectional flow of information was a key adaptation that permitted the evolution of dedicated circuits in which one set of neurons communicated with a limited set of receiving cells.

Why We Care | Drugs and Neurotransmitters

Understanding how neurotransmitters work helps explain the action of some mind-altering illicit and pharmaceutical drugs. The following are some examples, organized by the neurotransmitter affected.

Norepinephrine

Amphetamine drugs are chemically similar to norepinephrine; they bind to norepinephrine receptors and trigger the same changes in the receiving cell's membrane. The resulting enhanced norepinephrine activity heightens alertness and mood. Cocaine, which is chemically related to amphetamine, produces a short-lived feeling of euphoria, in part by blocking reuptake of norepinephrine.

Acetylcholine

Nicotine crosses the blood–brain barrier and reaches the brain within seconds of inhaling from a cigarette. An acetylcholine mimic, nicotine binds to acetylcholine receptor proteins in neuron cell membranes. The nicotine-stimulated neurons signal other brain cells to release dopamine, which provides the pleasurable feelings associated with smoking. Nicotine addiction stems from two sources: seeking the dopamine release and avoiding painful withdrawal symptoms.

On the other hand, excess acetylcholine accounts for the deadly effects of poisonous nerve gases and some insecticides. These toxic chemicals prevent acetylcholine from breaking down in the synaptic cleft. The resulting excess acetylcholine activity overstimulates skeletal muscles, causing them to contract continuously. The twitching legs of a cockroach sprayed with insecticide demonstrate the effects.

Serotonin

Norepinephrine and serotonin are associated with some forms of clinical depression. Drugs called selective serotonin reuptake inhibitors (SSRIs) block the reuptake of serotonin at the synaptic cleft. The neurotransmitter therefore accumulates in the synapse, offsetting a deficit that presumably causes the symptoms (figure 24.A).

Endorphins

Humans produce several types of endorphins, molecules that influence mood and perception of pain. Opiate drugs such as morphine, heroin, codeine, and opium are potent painkillers that bind endorphin receptors in the brain. In doing so, they elevate mood and make the pain easier to tolerate.

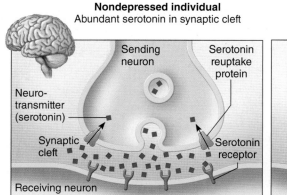

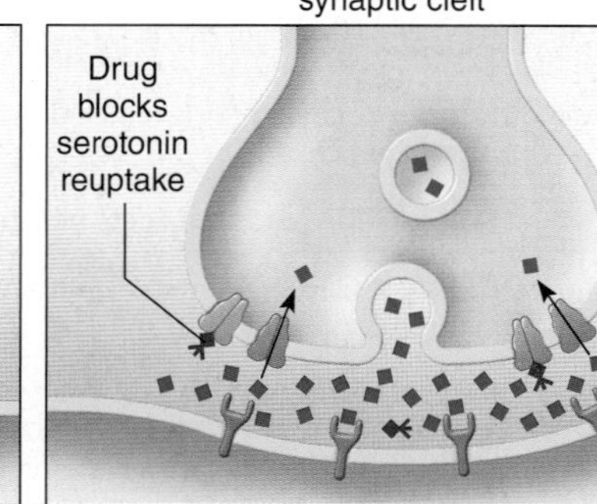

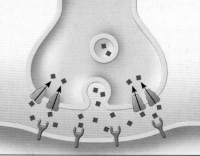

Figure 24.A Anatomy of an Antidepressant. Selective serotonin reuptake inhibitors (SSRIs) block the reuptake of serotonin. As a result, more serotonin is available in the synaptic cleft; compare the untreated and SSRI-treated synapses in the figure. The precise mechanism by which SSRIs relieve the symptoms of depression is not well understood.

Over time, some circuits became associated with specific functions, controlling complex behaviors and forming the specialized sense organs typical of many animals.

24.4 Mastering Concepts

1. Describe the structure of a synapse.
2. What event stimulates a neuron to release neurotransmitters?
3. What happens to a neurotransmitter after its release?

24.5 The Peripheral Nervous System Consists of Nerve Cells Outside the Central Nervous System

We now turn to the structure and function of the human nervous system (figure 24.7). The top half of figure 24.7 illustrates the nervous system's two main divisions: the central and peripheral nervous systems. Section 24.6 describes the central nervous system—the brain and spinal cord—in detail. The peripheral nervous system consists mainly of **nerves,** which are bundles of axons encased in connective tissue. The nerves, in turn, are classified based on where they originate. Cranial nerves emerge directly from the brain; examples include the nerves that transmit information from the eyes and ears to the brain. Spinal nerves emerge from the spinal cord and control many functions from the neck down.

The neurons of the central nervous system interact constantly with those of the peripheral nervous system (see figure 24.7). The sensory pathways of the peripheral nervous system carry signals from sensory receptors to the spinal cord and brain. Motor pathways, on the other hand, convey information from the central nervous system to muscles and glands.

The motor pathways of the peripheral nervous system, in turn, include the somatic (voluntary) nervous system and the autonomic (involuntary) nervous system. The **somatic nervous system** carries signals to voluntary skeletal muscles, such as those that enable you to ride a bicycle, shake hands, or talk. The **autonomic nervous system** transmits impulses to smooth muscle, cardiac muscle, and glands, enabling internal organs to function without conscious awareness.

The autonomic nervous system is further subdivided into the sympathetic and parasympathetic nervous systems. The **sympathetic nervous system** dominates under stress and emergencies, when the body readies itself for "fight or flight." The neurons of the sympathetic nervous system influence many organs: they accelerate heart rate and breathing rate; they divert blood away from the digestive system and toward the heart, brain, and skeletal muscles; and they dilate airways, easing gas exchange. During more relaxed times ("rest and repose"), the **parasympathetic nervous system** returns body systems to normal; heart rate and respiration slow, and digestion resumes.

Despite the "fight or flight" and "rest and repose" nicknames, the autonomic nervous system is always active, no matter what a person is doing. The parasympathetic and sympathetic divisions continuously work together to maintain homeostasis by having

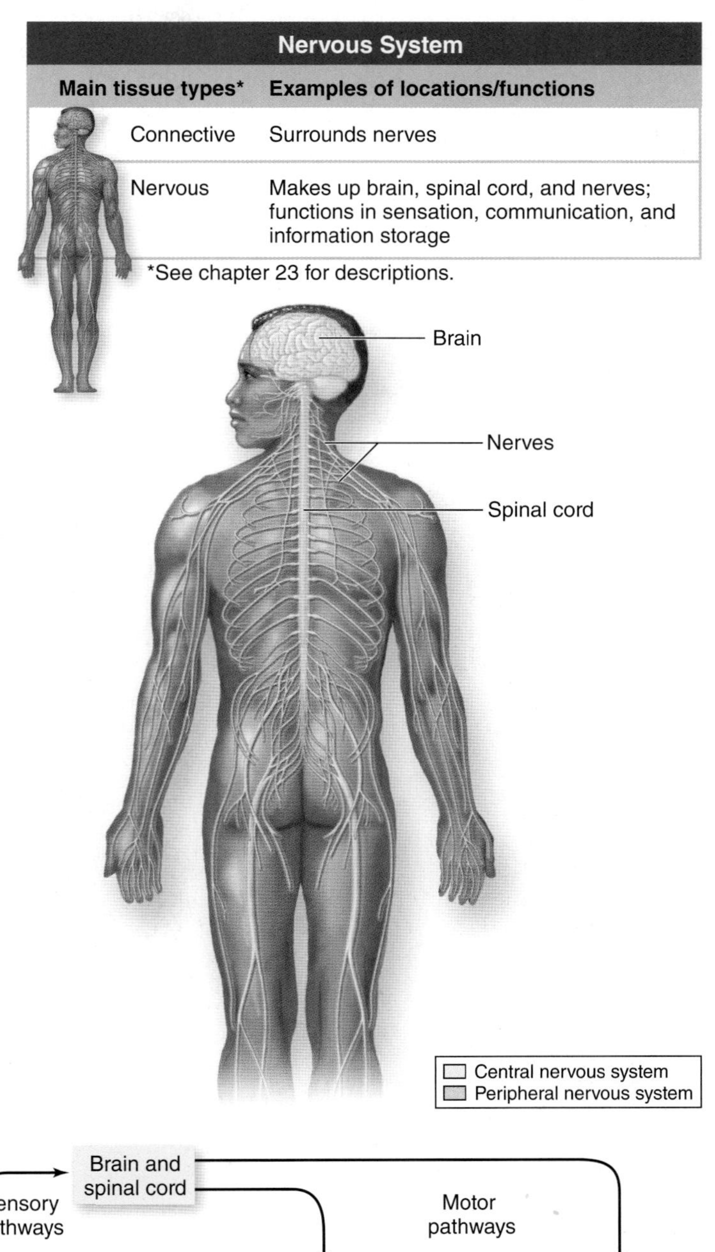

Nervous System	
Main tissue types*	**Examples of locations/functions**
Connective	Surrounds nerves
Nervous	Makes up brain, spinal cord, and nerves; functions in sensation, communication, and information storage

*See chapter 23 for descriptions.

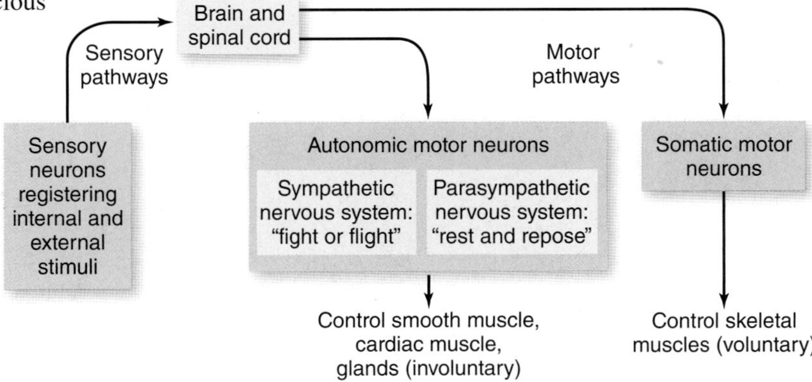

Figure 24.7 Subdivisions of the Nervous System. Sensory pathways of the peripheral nervous system provide input to the central nervous system. The brain and spinal cord, in turn, regulate the motor pathways of the peripheral nervous system.

opposite effects on the same organs. The body's moment-to-moment adjustments in blood pressure, for example, occur whether you are napping, standing up to stretch, rushing to class, or sitting down to dinner. Whatever you are doing, the autonomic nervous system regulates your body's vital functions without conscious thought.

Some illnesses interfere with the function of the peripheral nervous system. In Guillain–Barré syndrome, for example, the immune system attacks and destroys the nerves of the peripheral nervous system. The disease can be life-threatening if it causes paralysis, breathing difficulty, and heart problems. In a person with Bell's palsy, another peripheral nervous system disorder, the cranial nerve that controls the muscles on one side of the face is damaged. The facial paralysis typically strikes suddenly and may either resolve on its own or be permanent. The cause is unknown.

24.5 Mastering Concepts

1. Which structures make up the peripheral nervous system?
2. How do the sensory and motor pathways of the peripheral nervous system differ?
3. Describe the relationships among the motor, somatic, autonomic, sympathetic, and parasympathetic nervous systems.
4. How do the sympathetic and parasympathetic nervous systems maintain homeostasis?

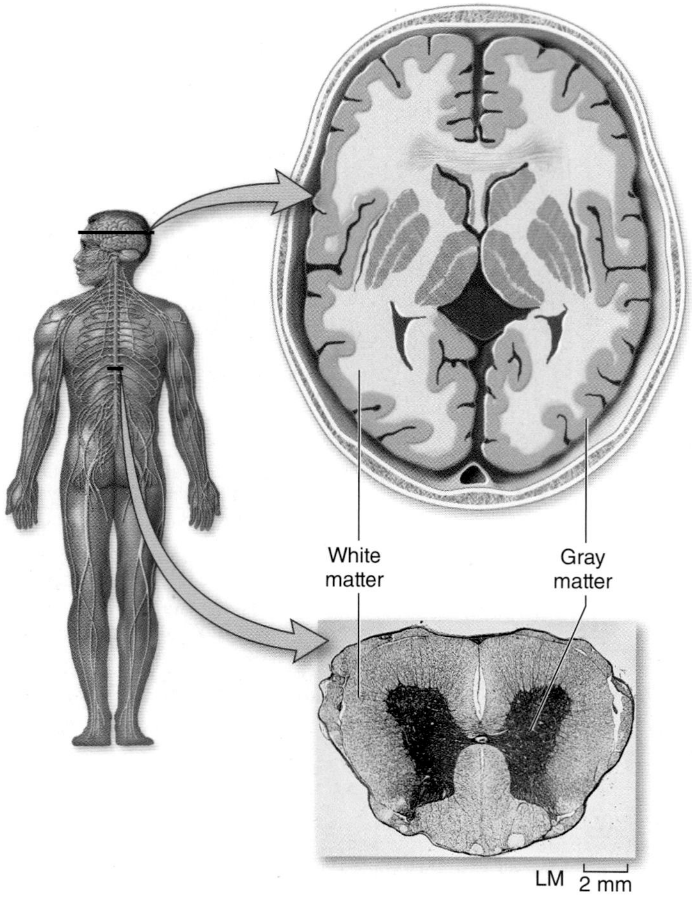

24.6 The Central Nervous System Consists of the Spinal Cord and Brain

The nerves of the peripheral nervous system spread across the body, but the brain and spinal cord form the largest part of the nervous system (figure 24.8). Two types of nervous tissue occur in the central nervous system. **Gray matter** consists of neuron cell bodies and dendrites, along with the synapses by which they communicate with other cells. Information processing occurs in the gray matter. **White matter** consists of myelinated axons transmitting information throughout the central nervous system.

Figure 24.8 Gray Matter and White Matter. Gray matter makes up the exterior of the brain and some internal structures. It also makes up the central core of the spinal cord. Myelin-rich white matter is at the periphery of the spinal cord and forms most of the brain's interior.

A. The Spinal Cord Transmits Information Between Body and Brain

The spinal cord is a tube of neural tissue that emerges from the base of the brain and extends along the back of the body. This critical component of the central nervous system is encased in the bony armor of the vertebral column, or backbone. The backbone protects the delicate nervous tissue and provides points of attachment for muscles.

The spinal cord handles reflexes without interacting with the brain. A **reflex** is a rapid, involuntary response to a stimulus. For example, if a flying insect or a splash of water hits your face, your eyes close immediately, without you being conscious of the need to do so. This response is a reflex because it does not require input from the brain. (Nevertheless, impulses must be relayed to the brain for awareness to occur.)

B. The Brain Is Divided into Several Regions

The human brain weighs, on average, about 1.4 to 1.6 kilograms; it looks and feels like grayish pudding. The brain requires a large and constant energy supply to oversee organ systems and to provide the qualities of "mind"—learning, reasoning, and memory. At any time, brain activity consumes 20% of the body's oxygen and 15% of its blood glucose. Permanent brain damage occurs after just 5 minutes of oxygen deprivation.

The brain has three main subdivisions: the hindbrain, the midbrain, and the forebrain (figure 24.9). The **hindbrain** is located toward the lower back of the skull. The **midbrain** is a narrow region that connects the hindbrain with the forebrain, and the **forebrain** is the front of the brain. All three subdivisions are obvious early in embryonic development, but the forebrain's rapid growth soon obscures the midbrain and much of the hindbrain.

The midbrain and parts of the hindbrain make up the **brainstem,** the stalklike lower portion of the brain. The brainstem regulates essential survival functions such as breathing and heartbeat. In addition, most of the cranial nerves emerge from the brainstem. Among other functions, these nerves control movements of the eyes, face, neck, and mouth along with the senses of taste and hearing.

The brainstem includes two parts of the hindbrain: the medulla oblongata and the pons. The **medulla oblongata** is a continuation of the spinal cord; this region not only regulates breathing, blood pressure, and heart rate, but it also contains reflex centers for vomiting, coughing, sneezing, defecating, swallowing, and hiccupping. The **pons,** which means "bridge," is the area above the medulla. White matter in this oval mass connects the forebrain to the medulla and to another part of the hindbrain, the cerebellum.

The midbrain is also part of the brainstem. Portions of the midbrain help control consciousness and participate in hearing and eye reflexes. In addition, nerve fibers that control voluntary motor function pass from the forebrain through the brainstem. The uncontrollable movements of Parkinson disease result from the death of certain neurons in the midbrain.

Behind the brainstem is the cerebellum, the largest part of the hindbrain. The neurons of the **cerebellum** refine motor messages and coordinate muscle movements subconsciously. Many routine physical skills, including tying your shoes or brushing your teeth, are difficult to learn at first. But with practice, the cerebellum takes over. Once it does, you can complete those activities without thinking about how to do them each time.

By far the largest part of the human brain is the forebrain, which contains structures that participate in complex functions such as learning, memory, language, motivation, and emotion. Three major parts of the forebrain are the thalamus, hypothalamus, and cerebrum.

The **thalamus** is a mass of gray matter that acts as a relay station for sensory input, processing incoming information and sending it to the appropriate part of the brain. The almond-sized **hypothalamus,** which lies below the thalamus, occupies less than 1% of the brain volume, but it plays a unique role in maintaining homeostasis by linking the nervous and endocrine systems. Cells in the hypothalamus are sensitive not only to neural input but also to hormones circulating in the bloodstream. Neural signals from the hypothalamus, in turn, control involuntary muscles and glands. Moreover, hormones produced in the hypothalamus coordinate the production and release of many other hormones (see chapter 25). All together, neural and hormonal signals from the hypothalamus regulate body temperature, heartbeat, water balance, blood pressure, hunger, thirst, sleep, and sexual arousal.

Structure	Selected functions
Hindbrain	
Medulla oblongata	Regulates essential physiological processes such as blood pressure, heartbeat, and breathing
Pons	Connects forebrain with medulla and cerebellum
Cerebellum	Controls posture and balance; coordinates subconscious muscular movements
Midbrain	Relays information about voluntary movements from forebrain to spinal cord
Forebrain	
Thalamus	Processes information and relays it to the cerebrum
Hypothalamus	Homeostatic control of most organs
Cerebrum	
White matter	Transmits information within brain
Gray matter (cerebral cortex)	Sensory, motor, and association areas

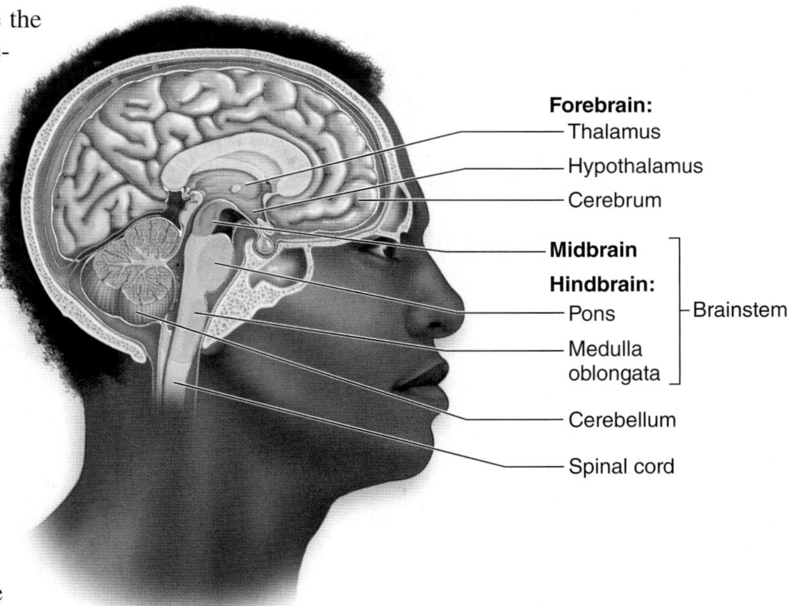

Figure 24.9 The Human Brain. The three major areas of the vertebrate brain are the hindbrain, the midbrain, and the forebrain.

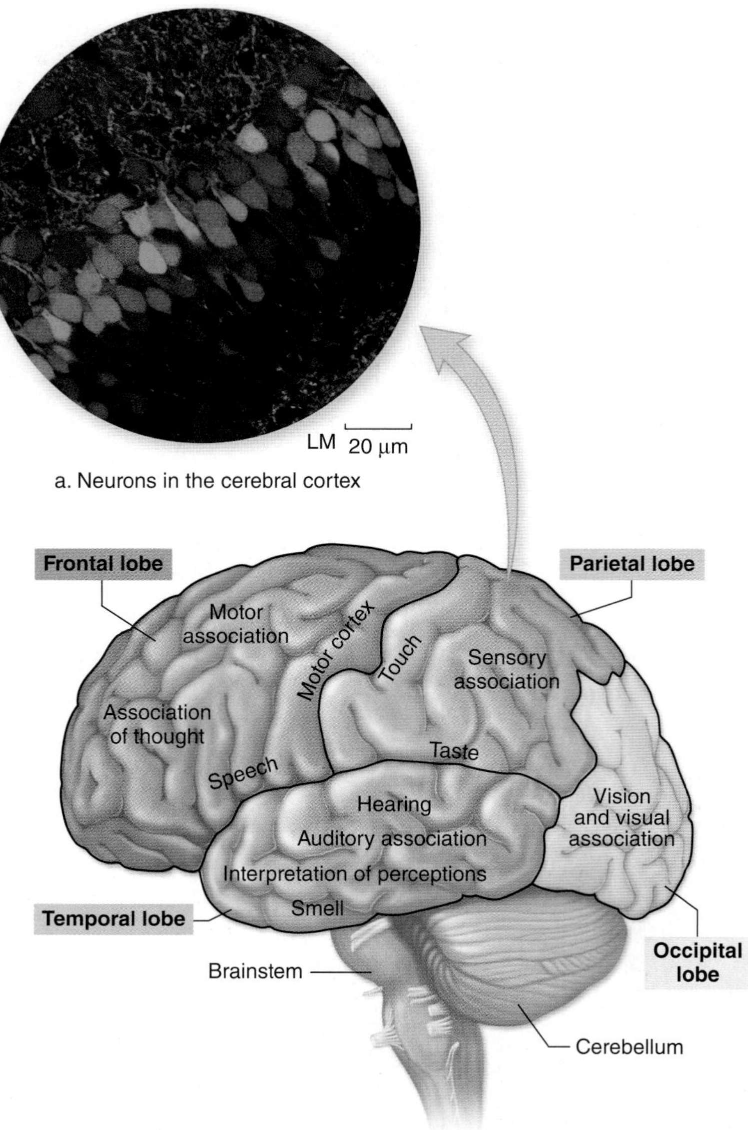

a. Neurons in the cerebral cortex

b. The four lobes of the cerebral cortex (only the left hemisphere is shown)

Division	Function(s)	Brain region(s)
Sensory	Senses of vision, hearing, smell, taste, and touch	Parietal, occipital, and temporal lobes
Motor	Voluntary movements	Frontal lobe
Association	Judgment, analysis, learning, creativity	Frontal lobe and parts of the parietal, occipital, and temporal lobes

c. Functional divisions of the cerebral cortex

Figure 24.10 Major Subdivisions of the Cerebrum. (a) Special labelling techniques reveal the individual neurons that make up the intricate circuits of the cerebral cortex. (b) The surface of each hemisphere of the cerebrum is divided into four lobes. (c) Experiments have revealed which areas are associated with sensory, motor, or association functions.

The other major region of the forebrain is the **cerebrum,** which controls the qualities of what we consider the "mind"—that is, personality, intelligence, learning, perception, and emotion. In humans, the cerebrum occupies 83% of the brain's volume. It is divided into two **hemispheres** that gather and process information simultaneously. The cerebral hemispheres work together, interconnected by a thick band of nerve fibers called the corpus callosum.

Each hemisphere controls the opposite side of the body, so that damage to the left side of the brain affects the right side of the body (and vice versa). In addition, although each side of the brain participates in most brain functions, some specialization does occur. In most people, for example, parts of the left hemisphere are associated with speech, language skills, mathematical ability, and reasoning, whereas the right hemisphere specializes in spatial, intuitive, musical, and artistic abilities.

The cerebrum consists mostly of white matter that transmits information, either within the cerebrum or between the cerebrum and other parts of the brain or spinal cord. But the outer layer of the cerebrum, the **cerebral cortex,** consists of gray matter that processes information. The human cerebral cortex is only a few millimeters thick, but it boasts about 10 billion neurons forming some 60 trillion synapses. In humans and other large mammals, deep folds enhance the surface area of the cerebral cortex.

Anatomically, the cerebral cortex of each hemisphere is divided into four main parts (figure 24.10): the frontal, parietal, temporal, and occipital lobes. The functions of the cerebral cortex, however, overlap across these lobes. Sensory areas receive and interpret messages from sense organs. Motor areas send impulses to skeletal muscles, which produce voluntary movements. Association areas analyze, integrate, and interpret information from many brain areas. These are the seats of judgment, problem-solving, learning, abstract thought, language, and creativity.

The cerebrum's interior houses the emotional center of the brain. The **limbic system** is a loosely defined collection of structures surrounding the corpus callosum. The thalamus and hypothalamus are part of the limbic system. So are two areas at the edges of the temporal lobes: the hippocampus, which participates in long-term memory formation, and the amygdala, which is a center for emotions such as pleasure or fear. The hypothalamus processes information from the amygdala and coordinates the physical sensations associated with strong emotions.

C. Many Brain Regions Participate in Memory

Why is it that you can't remember the name of someone you met a few minutes ago, but you can easily picture your first-grade teacher or your best friend from childhood (figure 24.11)? The answer relates to the difference between short-term and long-term memories. Your brain apparently stored the new acquaintance's name only in **short-term memory,** where it remained available for a few moments before being forgotten. You remember the teacher, however, because you interacted with that person every day for months at a time. This repeated reinforcement meant your brain stored the information in **long-term memory,** which can last a lifetime.

Much of what scientists know about memory comes from research on people with damage to specific parts of the brain. One famous example is a man called Henry Molaison, known in the medical literature by the initials H. M. until his death in 2008. Surgeons removed portions of his temporal lobes and hippocampus in 1953 in an effort to alleviate his severe epilepsy. The surgery had an unintended consequence: H. M. was unable to form new memories. Although he could recall events that occurred before the surgery, he could not remember what he ate for breakfast. Clues from H. M. and other patients suggest that the hippocampus is essential in the formation of long-term memories, but memories are not actually stored there.

No one knows exactly what happens to the brain's neurons and synapses when a new memory forms, but researchers are actively trying to learn more. Practical applications could include drugs that enhance memory in patients with disorders that cause memory loss, including Alzheimer disease. Conversely, pharmaceuticals that selectively erase memories could help people who are struggling in the aftermath of traumatic experiences.

Figure 24.11 **Memories.** A glance at old photos can bring back memories from times past.

D. Damage to the Central Nervous System Can Be Devastating

The central nervous system is well protected. The bones of the skull and vertebral column shield nervous tissue from bumps and blows. **Meninges** are layered membranes that jacket and cushion the central nervous system. The **blood–brain barrier,** formed by specialized brain capillaries, helps protect the brain from extreme chemical fluctuations. The epithelial cells that form these capillaries fit so tightly together that only some chemicals can cross into the **cerebrospinal fluid** that bathes the brain and spinal cord. This fluid further insulates the central nervous system from injury.

Nevertheless, trauma and illness can harm the central nervous system (figure 24.12). An accident can damage the spinal cord and prevent motor impulses from descending from the brain, causing full or partial paralysis. Brain damage can also result from infectious agents, degenerative diseases, or a more subtle killer: stroke. In a stroke, a burst or blocked blood vessel interrupts the flow of blood to part of the brain. Deprived of oxygen, some brain cells die, often so many that the stroke is fatal. In other cases, the patient may suffer from temporary or permanent muscle weakness, paralysis, loss of speech, blindness, or other impairment. Often, only one side of the body is affected.

Whatever its cause, part of the difficulty in reversing nervous system damage is that mature neurons typically do not divide. The nervous system therefore cannot simply heal itself by producing new cells, as your skin does after a minor cut. The neurons that survive the damage can, however, form some new connections that compensate for the loss. Therapy can therefore help restore some function to injured tissues. Moreover, stem cells and gene therapy may one day improve the outlook for patients with brain damage or disease. ▸ stem cells, p. 206; gene therapy, p. 211

a.

b.

Figure 24.12 **Nervous System Damage.** (a) Actor Christopher Reeve, who broke his neck in a horseback riding accident in 1995, was among the most famous spinal cord injury patients. (b) Boxer Muhammad Ali (left) and actor Michael J. Fox have Parkinson disease, an illness that causes the death of certain cells in the brain.

24.6 Mastering Concepts

1. What are the functions of the spinal cord?
2. What are the major structures in the hindbrain, midbrain, and forebrain, and what are their functions?
3. What are the parts and functions of the cerebral cortex?
4. How do short- and long-term memories differ?
5. List some structures that protect the central nervous system.
6. To what extent can the nervous system heal itself?

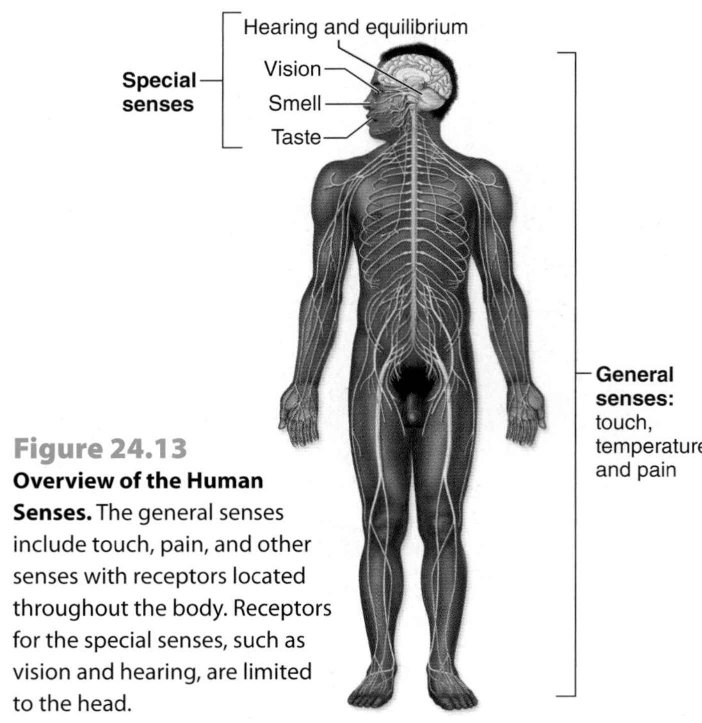

Figure 24.13 Overview of the Human Senses. The general senses include touch, pain, and other senses with receptors located throughout the body. Receptors for the special senses, such as vision and hearing, are limited to the head.

24.7 The Senses Connect the Nervous System with the Outside World

The senses are an integral part of the nervous system (figure 24.13). A **sensation** is the raw input from the peripheral nervous system that arrives at the central nervous system. For example, your eyes and hands may inform your brain that a particular object is small, round, red, and smooth. The brain integrates all of this sensory input and consults memories to form a **perception,** or interpretation of the sensations—in this case, of a tomato.

The human senses paint a complex portrait of our surroundings. Consider, for example, the woman in figure 24.14. The tips of her fingers feel the banjo strings, her eyes see the instrument, and her ears hear the music. Her skin senses the warmth of the sun. She also maintains her balance, thanks to both her ability to feel the position of her limbs and her inner ear's sense of equilibrium. Later, if she decides to have a snack, she will be able to smell and taste her food.

As rich as our own senses are, other animals can detect stimuli that are imperceptible to us. Dogs, for example, have an extremely well-developed sense of smell, which explains why these animals are so useful in sniffing out illicit drugs. Bats have an entirely different ability, called echolocation. As a bat flies, it emits high-frequency pulses of sound. The animal's large ears pick up the sound waves that bounce off of prey and other objects, and its brain analyzes these echoes to "picture" the surroundings.

Together, all of the senses help maintain homeostasis. Many of the feedback loops that maintain this state of internal constancy operate without our awareness; for example, we can't directly "feel" our blood pH or hormone concentrations. But we are aware of sights, sounds, smells, and many other stimuli. The central nervous system responds to many types of sensory input by coordinating the actions of muscles and glands, which make adjustments as necessary to maintain homeostasis.

A. Sensory Receptors Respond to Stimuli by Generating Action Potentials

All sense organs ultimately derive their information from **sensory receptor** cells that detect stimuli. The human body includes several types of sensory receptors. **Mechanoreceptors** respond to physical stimuli such as sound or touch. **Thermoreceptors** respond to temperature. **Pain receptors** detect tissue damage, extreme heat and cold, and chemicals released from damaged cells. **Photoreceptors** respond to light, and **chemoreceptors** detect chemicals.

Each of these cell types "translates" sensory information into the language of the nervous system. **Transduction** is the process by which a sensory receptor converts energy from a stimulus into action potentials. Generally, a stimulus alters the shape of a protein embedded in a sensory receptor's cell membrane, causing the membrane's permeability to ions to change. The resulting movement of ions across the membrane triggers a **receptor potential,** which is a change in the membrane potential of a sensory receptor cell (figure 24.15). The green lines in figure 24.15 depict receptor potentials that are below the cell's threshold and therefore do not trigger action potentials; the stimulus remains undetected. If the receptor potential does exceed the threshold potential, however, an action potential occurs in the sensory receptor (red line in the figure). The frequency of action potentials arriving at the brain from specific groups of receptors conveys information about the type and intensity of the stimulus.

Figure 24.14 Sensory Blend. This woman is experiencing the senses of touch, sight, and sound, among others.

B. Continuous Stimulation May Cause Sensory Adaptation

You may have noticed that your perceptions of some stimuli can change over time. Your first thought when you roll out of bed may be "I smell coffee." But by the time you stand up, pull your clothes on, and wander to the kitchen, you hardly notice the coffee odor anymore. Likewise, the steaming water in a bath tub may seem too hot at first, but it soon becomes tolerable, even pleasant.

These examples illustrate **sensory adaptation,** a phenomenon in which sensations become less noticeable with prolonged exposure to the stimulus. The explanation is that sensory receptors generate fewer action potentials under constant stimulation. Generally, the response returns only if the intensity of the stimulus changes.

Many receptors adapt quickly. Without sensory adaptation, our nervous system would constantly react to old information, and detecting new stimuli would be challenging. Pain receptors, however, are very slow to adapt. The constant awareness of pain is uncomfortable, but it also alerts us to tissue damage and prompts us to address the source of the pain.

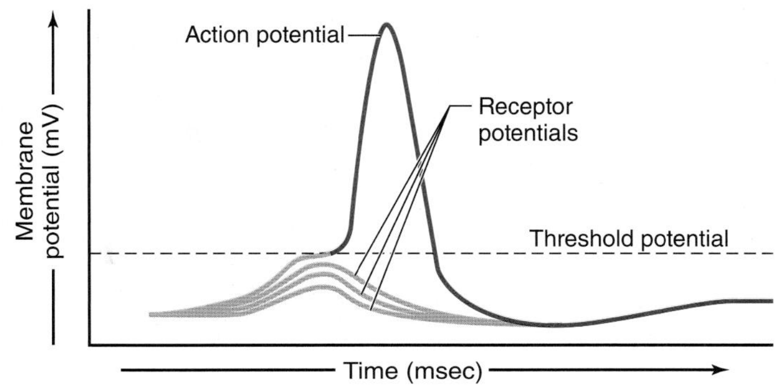

Figure 24.15 Receptor Potentials. The central nervous system detects only stimuli that provoke action potentials. Receptor potentials that do not exceed the threshold potential (green lines) do not trigger action potentials. A larger receptor potential, however, can exceed the threshold potential, stimulating an action potential (red line).

24.7 Mastering Concepts

1. Distinguish between sensation and perception.
2. What role do the senses play in maintaining homeostasis?
3. What are the major types of sensory receptors?
4. What is a receptor potential?
5. What is sensory adaptation, and how is it beneficial?

24.8 The General Senses Detect Touch, Temperature, and Pain

The general senses allow you to detect touch, temperature, or pain with any part of your skin. Each of these senses uses its own type of receptors.

The sense of touch comes from several types of mechanoreceptors (figure 24.16). The receptors all work in essentially the same way: pressure pushes the flexible sides of the receptor cell inward, generating an action potential in the nerve fiber. Most touch receptors have dendrites that are wrapped in neuroglia or connective tissue. The dendrites that snake around hair follicles, however, are "free" (unwrapped). These nerve endings sense when the hair bends.

The density of touch receptors varies across the body. As a result, the fingertips and tongue are much more sensitive to touch than, say, the skin of the lower back. This observation explains why medical professionals generally administer injections in the buttocks, shoulders, and thighs. These parts of the body have relatively few nerve endings and therefore are the least sensitive to needles and other painful stimuli.

Free nerve endings also enable the skin to sense temperature and pain. The brain integrates input from many cold and heat thermoreceptors to determine whether a stimulus is cool, hot, or somewhere in between. Pain receptors are free nerve endings that detect tissue damage. These neurons respond to the mechanical damage that follows a sharp blow, a cut, or a scrape. Pain receptors also detect extreme heat, extreme cold, and chemicals released from damaged cells.

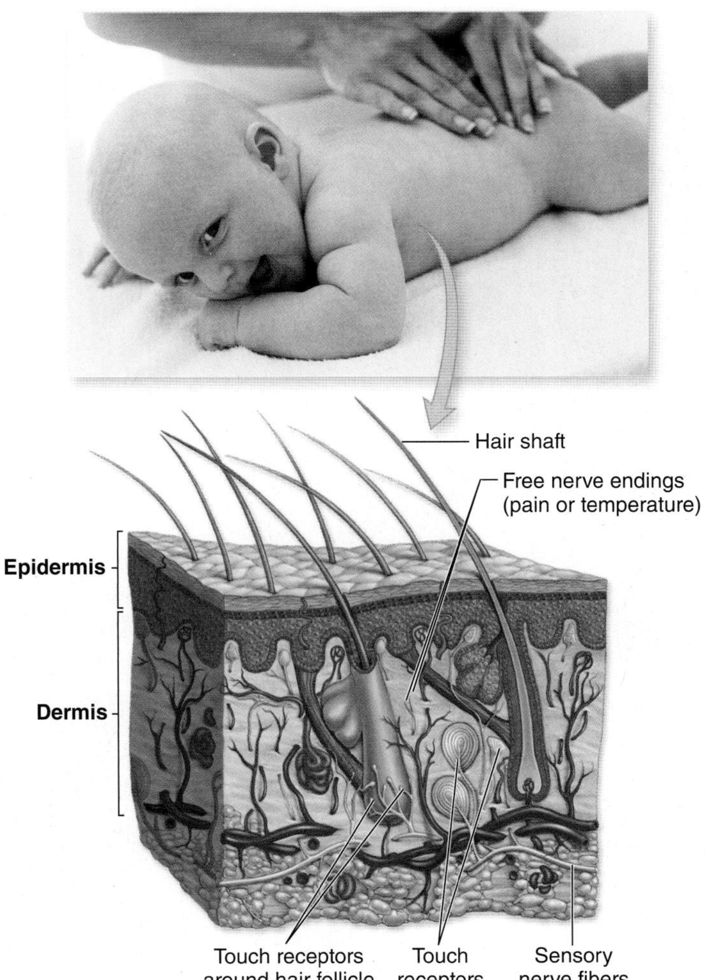

Figure 24.16 Skin Senses Many Stimuli. Sensory receptors in the skin respond to touch, temperature, and pain.

Pain is an unpleasant but important response; people who are unable to perceive pain can unknowingly injure themselves. Nevertheless, temporarily suspending the body's pain response with drugs called anesthetics can make some medical treatments tolerable. These drugs work in multiple ways. Local anesthetics such as a dentist's procaine (Novocain) stop pain-sensitive neurons from transmitting action potentials in a limited area of the body, such as one side of the mouth. General anesthetics cause a loss of consciousness that prevents the brain from perceiving pain in any part of the body.

Ultimately, a sensory receptor cell that is stimulated by touch, temperature, or pain generates action potentials. These signals travel along spinal or cranial nerves to the central nervous system, which integrates the information. We can therefore tell where on the body a sensation is originating and identify its characteristics. For example, the brain's cerebral cortex can rapidly process multiple sensory signals to perceive that the right hand is touching the hot, smooth hood of a car.

24.8 Mastering Concepts

1. Which structures provide the senses of touch, temperature, and pain?
2. How does the brain participate in the general senses?

24.9 The Senses of Smell and Taste Detect Chemicals

Chemoreception is probably the most ancient sense. Bacteria and protists use chemical cues to approach food or move away from danger, so the ability to detect external chemicals must have arisen long before animals evolved.

The senses of smell and taste both depend on the body's ability to detect chemicals. Not surprisingly, these two senses have properties in common. In each case, the stimulus molecule must dissolve in a watery solution, such as saliva or the moist lining of a nasal passage. In addition, the molecule must interact with a chemoreceptor on a sensory cell's membrane. But the two senses also differ in some ways. The nose detects odor molecules in inhaled air. We can therefore perceive scents originating from near or distant objects. Chemoreceptors in the mouth, on the other hand, can taste items only at very close range.

The sense of smell begins at the nose, which forms the entrance to the nasal cavity inside the head. Specialized olfactory receptor neurons are located high in the nasal cavity (figure 24.17). Each olfactory neuron expresses one receptor protein on its cell membrane; each receptor protein, in turn, can bind to a limited set of odorants. A molecule that enters the nose in inhaled air binds to a receptor protein, and the cell then transduces this chemical signal into receptor potentials. Each olfactory receptor cell synapses with neurons in the brain's olfactory bulb. The brain interprets the information from multiple receptors and identifies the odor.

Chemoreceptors occur not only in the nose but also in the mouth, which detects the flavors of food. The tongue's

a.

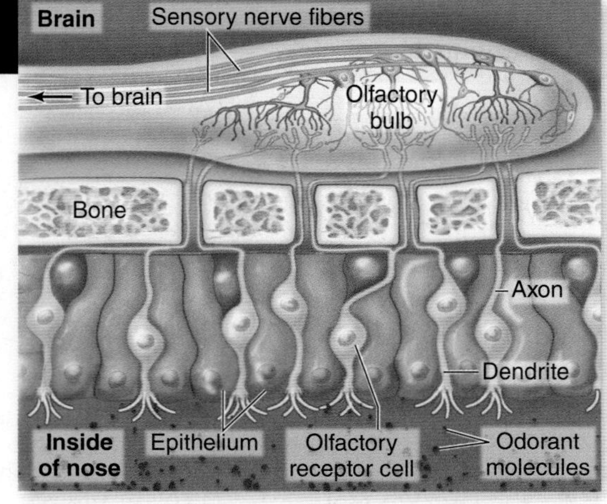

b.

Figure 24.17 The Sense of Smell. (a) Chemoreceptors in the nose detect the odor of incense. (b) An olfactory receptor cell binds an odorant molecule and transmits neural impulses to cells in the olfactory bulb. The axons of these neurons pass the information to the brain, which identifies the scent.

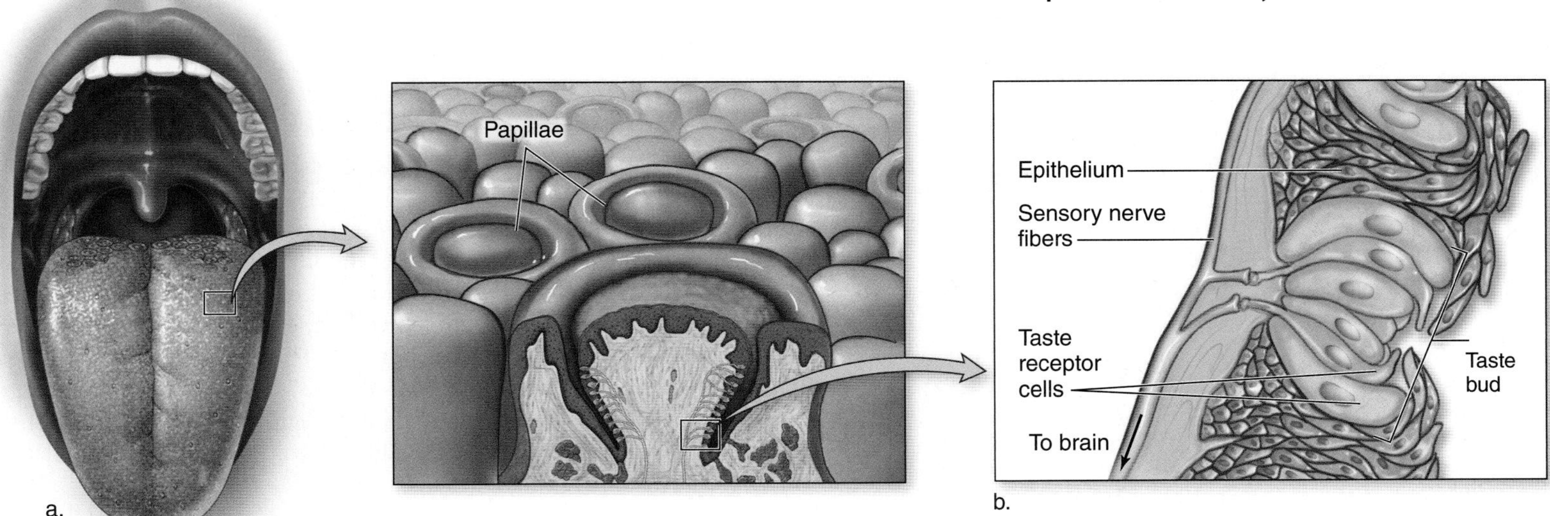

Figure 24.18
The Sense of Taste.
(a) Chemoreceptors in the mouth detect the flavor of spaghetti. (b) Taste buds on the tongue's papillae contain the taste receptor cells. These taste receptor cells synapse on sensory neurons, which convey the information to the brain.

surface is covered with papillae; these bumps house **taste buds,** the organs associated with the sense of taste (figure 24.18). Each of the mouth's 10,000 taste buds contains 50 to 150 chemoreceptor cells that generate action potentials when dissolved food molecules bind to them. At a taste bud's base, the receptor cells form synapses with sensory neurons that lead to the brain. Our sense of taste depends on the pattern and intensity of activity across all taste neurons.

Many arthropods use chemicals in communication. **Pheromones** are chemical substances that elicit specific responses in other members of the same species. For example, female silk moths release pheromones that attract males, who "smell" the chemical signal from up to several kilometers away. Female scorpions also attract mates with chemicals: males "taste" female pheromones deposited on sand. The role of chemical communication in our own species remains an open question, as described in this chapter's Burning Question.

24.9 Mastering Concepts

1. How does the brain detect and identify odors?
2. How does a taste bud function?
3. What are pheromones?

Burning Questions

Do humans have pheromones?

Advertisements for "human pheromone" colognes appeal to the desire to attract the opposite sex. Dab some on, they say, and watch your love life blossom. But are there really human pheromones?

This question is surprisingly difficult to answer, in part because human behavior is so complex; it is hard to find chemicals that elicit predictable responses. Nevertheless, at least some mammals do produce pheromones. A male hamster smeared with vaginal secretions from a female will provoke sexual advances from another male—but only if the responding male has an intact vomeronasal organ, a tiny offshoot of the olfactory system. This structure is apparently the pheromone detector.

Studies have demonstrated that pheromones from human females influence the menstrual cycles of other women. However, researchers still know little about how humans detect pheromones. We do have a vomeronasal organ, but no one has ever shown that it is functional. We therefore do not know whether the vomeronasal organ plays a role in human life or is just a vestige of our evolutionary history.

Submit your burning question to: marielle_hoefnagels @mcgraw-hill.com

24.10 Vision Depends on Light-Sensitive Cells

An **eye** is an organ that produces the sense of sight. Figure 24.19 depicts the vertebrate eye, which is composed of several layers. The **sclera** is the white, outermost layer that protects the inner structures of the eye. Toward the front of the eye, the sclera is modified into the **cornea,** a transparent curved window that bends incoming light rays. The **choroid** is the layer internal to the sclera. Behind the cornea, the choroid becomes the **iris,** which is the colored part of the eye. The iris regulates the size of the **pupil,** the hole in the middle of the iris. In bright light, the pupil is tiny, shielding the eye from excess stimulation. The pupil grows larger as light becomes dimmer.

A portion of the choroid also thickens into a structure that holds the flexible **lens,** which further bends the incoming light. Muscles regulate the curvature of the lens to focus on objects at any distance. When a person gazes at a faraway object, the lens is flattened and relaxed. To examine an article closely, however, muscles must pull the lens into a more curved shape.

Blood vessels in the choroid supply nutrients and oxygen to the **retina,** a sheet of photoreceptors that forms the innermost layer of the eye. The **optic nerve** is a cranial nerve that connects the retina to the brain. The point where the optic nerve exits the retina is called the blind spot because it lacks photoreceptors and therefore cannot sense light.

Each eyeball also contains fluid that helps bend light rays and focus them on the retina. The watery aqueous humor lies between the cornea and the lens. This fluid cleanses and nourishes the cornea and lens, and it maintains the shape of the eyeball. Behind the lens is the vitreous humor, a jellylike substance that fills most of the eyeball's volume. Light rays pass through the cornea, lens, and humors of the eye and are focused on the retina. (The Why We Care box on the facing page explains how glasses and surgery can improve poor eyesight by redirecting the light that enters the eye.)

Oddly, light has to pass through several layers of cells before reaching the photoreceptors at the back of the retina (figure 24.20). The photoreceptors are neurons called rods and cones. **Rod cells,** which are concentrated around the edges of the retina, provide black-and-white vision in dim light and enable us to see at night. **Cone cells** detect color; they are concentrated toward the center of the retina. The human eye contains about 125 million rod cells and 7 million cone cells.

Both rods and cones are studded with pigment molecules that absorb light of different wavelengths. Humans have three cone types: "blue" cones absorb shorter wavelengths of light, "green" cones absorb medium wavelengths, and "red" cones absorb long wavelengths. People who lack a cone type entirely, due to a genetic mutation, are color-blind. Because the genes encoding these pigments are on the X chromosome, red–green color blindness is more common in males than females. ▸ X-linked disorders, p. 184

When a rod or cone cell absorbs light energy, the pigment molecule changes shape and triggers receptor potentials that stimulate other neurons in the retina. Eventually, the action potentials are relayed through the optic nerve to the brain's visual cortex for processing and interpretation.

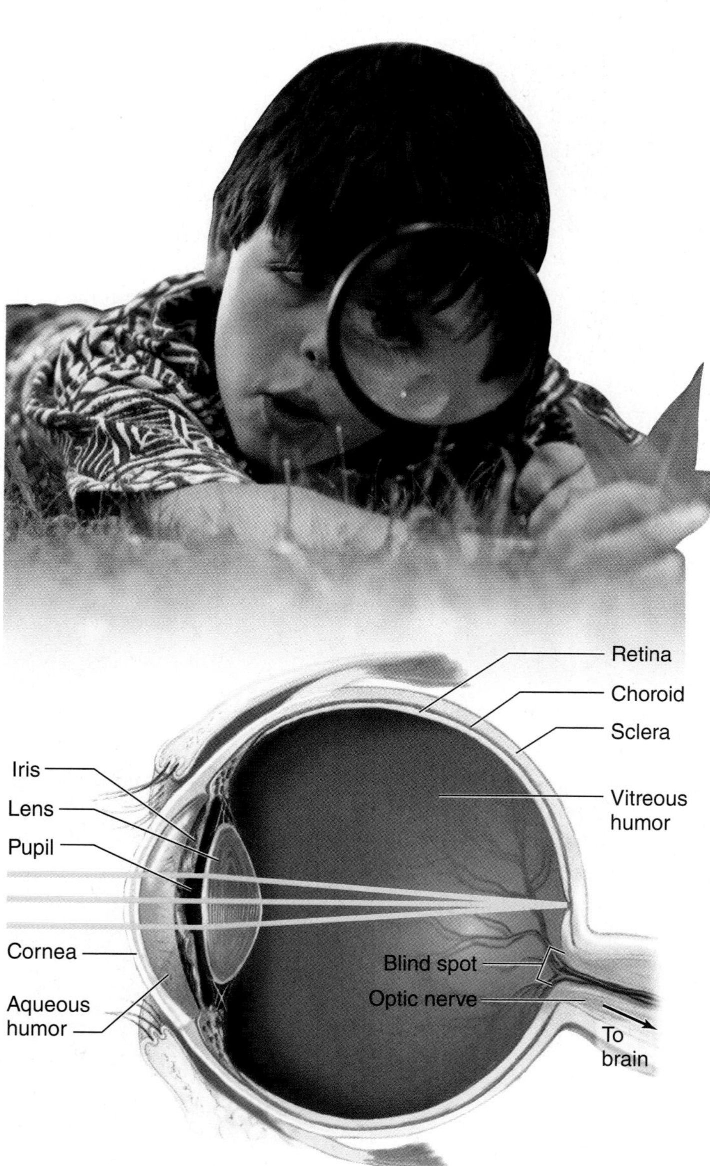

Figure 24.19 The Vertebrate Eye. Light passes through the cornea, aqueous humor, pupil, lens, and vitreous humor before striking the retina. Sensory cells in the retina transmit light information to the optic nerve.

24.10 Mastering Concepts

1. What are the parts of the vertebrate eye?
2. What are the roles of photoreceptors and pigments in vision?
3. Trace the pathway of information flow from the retina to the visual cortex of the brain.

Why We Care | Correcting Vision

The eyeball must be a certain shape for the cornea and lens to focus light rays precisely on the retina. For those of us whose eyeballs are not perfectly formed, corrective lenses (eyeglasses and contact lenses) can alter the path of light (figure 24.B).

A more recent technology for correcting vision problems is laser eye surgery, which vaporizes tiny parts of the cornea, changing the path of light to the retina.

Sometimes, the cornea becomes clouded or misshapen. Surgeons can replace the defective cornea with one taken from a cadaver. Corneal transplant surgery carries a low risk of immune system rejection because, unlike other transplantable organs, the cornea lacks blood vessels. Another common eye disorder is a cataract, in which the lens of the eye becomes opaque. Cataract surgery is a simple procedure that replaces the clouded lens with a plastic implant.

Even people with perfectly shaped eyeballs and corneas usually need reading glasses after the age of about 40. To focus on a very close object, a muscle inside the eye must curve the lens so that it can bend incoming light rays at sharper angles. As we age, the lens becomes less flexible. It therefore becomes difficult for the muscles in the eye to bend the lens enough to clearly focus on nearby objects or printed words. Laser surgery cannot correct this age-related decline in eyesight.

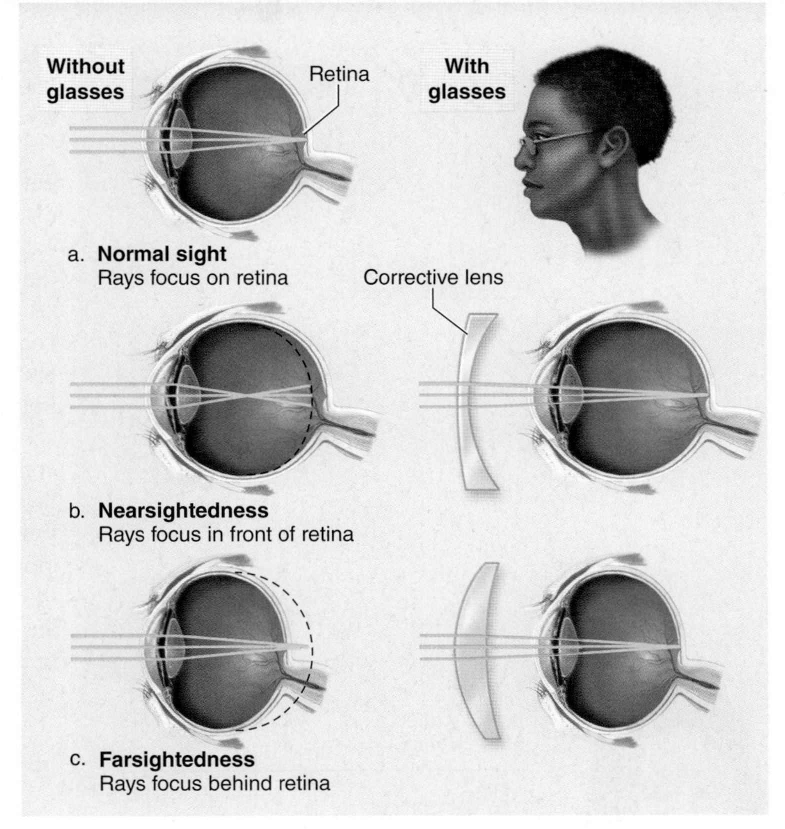

Figure 24.B Correcting Vision. Eyeglasses and contact lenses can correct many common vision problems. (a) A normally shaped eyeball focuses light rays on the retina. (b) In an elongated eyeball, light rays converge in front of the retina, impairing the ability to see distant objects (nearsightedness). (c) A short eyeball focuses light beyond the retina, and the person has difficulty seeing close objects (farsightedness).

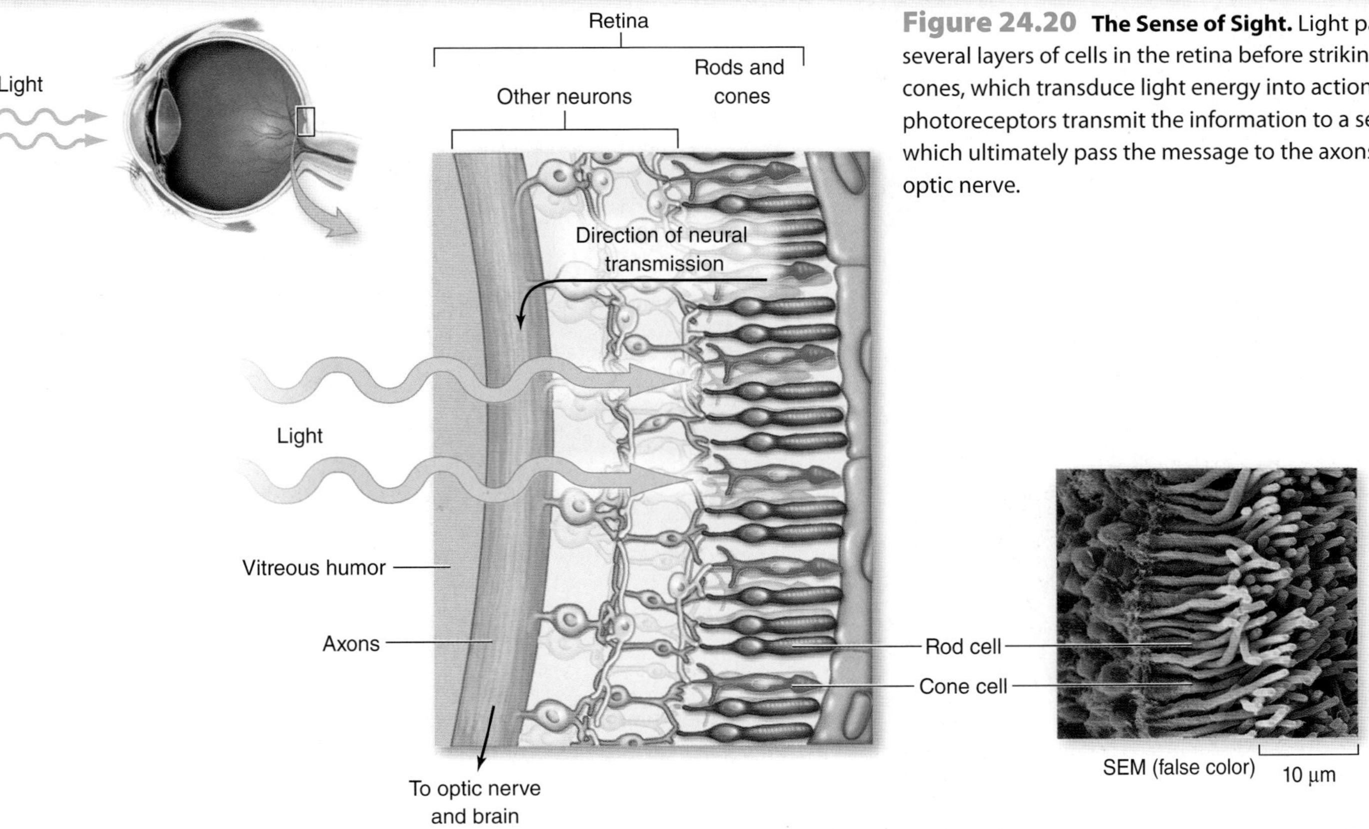

Figure 24.20 The Sense of Sight. Light passes through several layers of cells in the retina before striking the rods and cones, which transduce light energy into action potentials. These photoreceptors transmit the information to a series of neurons, which ultimately pass the message to the axons that form the optic nerve.

24.11 The Sense of Hearing Begins in the Ears

The clatter of a train, the notes of a symphony, a child's wail—what do they have in common? All are sounds that originate when something vibrates and creates repeating pressure waves in the surrounding air.

In humans, the sense of hearing begins with the fleshy outer part of the **ear,** which traps sound waves and funnels them down the **auditory canal** (ear canal) to the **eardrum** (figure 24.21). Sound pressure waves in air vibrate the eardrum, which moves three small bones in the middle ear. These bones, called the hammer, anvil, and stirrup, transmit and amplify the incoming sound.

When the stirrup moves, it pushes on the **oval window,** a membrane that connects the middle ear with the inner ear. The oval window transfers the vibration to the snail-shaped **cochlea,** where sound is transduced into neural impulses.

The spirals of the cochlea consist of three fluid-filled ducts, one of which contains the mechanoreceptors that transduce the sound to action potentials (figure 24.22). These mechanoreceptors, called **hair cells,** initiate the transduction of mechanical energy to receptor potentials. When the oval window vibrates, the fluid inside the cochlea moves, causing cilia on the hair cells to move relative to an overlying membrane. As the cilia bend, the hair cells initiate action potentials in the **auditory nerve.** The information then passes to the brain's auditory cortex for interpretation.

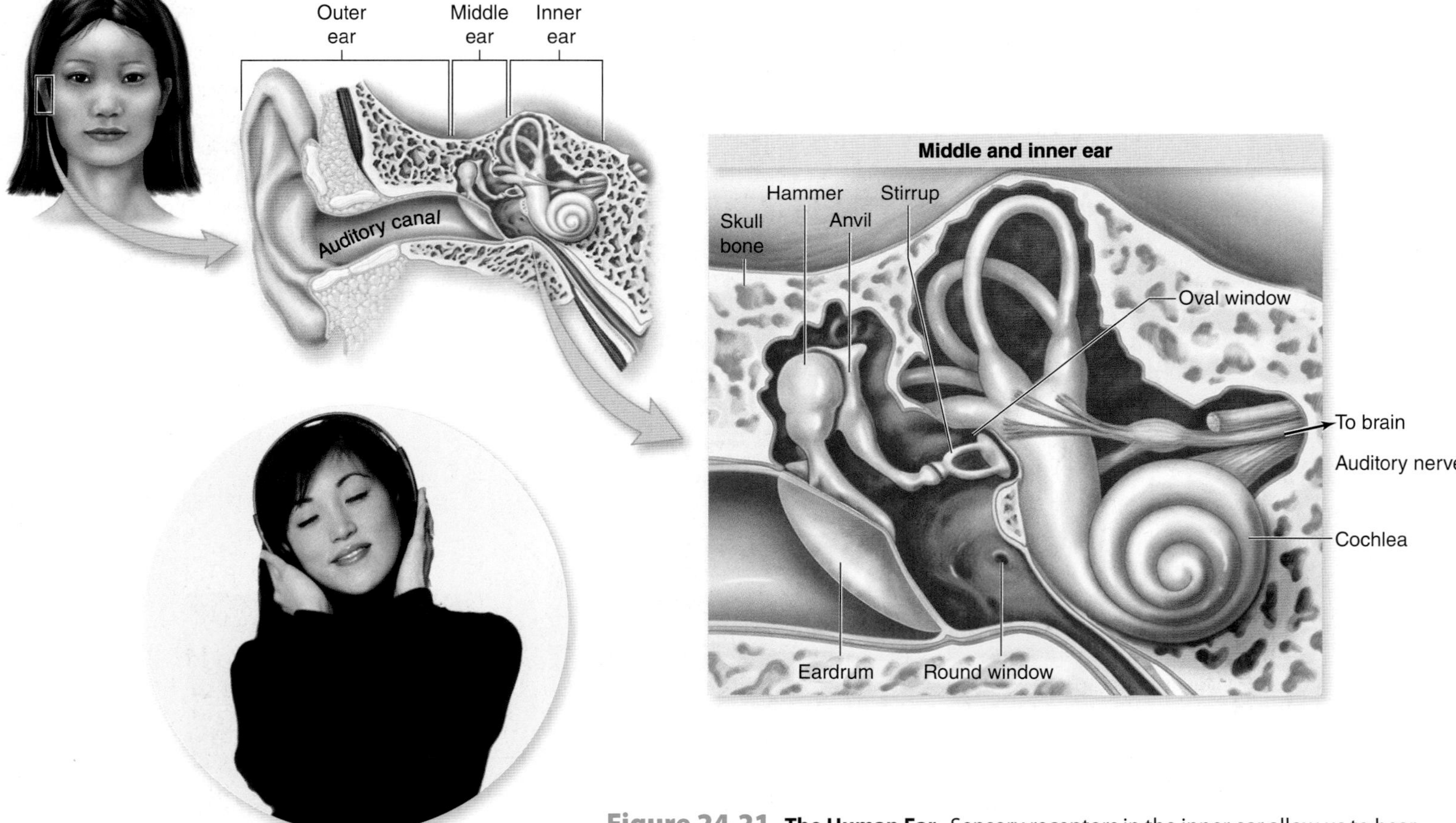

Figure 24.21 The Human Ear. Sensory receptors in the inner ear allow us to hear. Sound enters the outer ear and vibrates the three bones of the middle ear. The bones, in turn, cause vibrations in the fluid of the pea-sized cochlea in the inner ear.

Each sound generates an action potential in a different region of the cochlea. The high-pitched tinkle of a bell stimulates the base of the cochlea; the low-pitched tones of a tugboat whistle stimulate the cochlea's tip, deep inside the spiral. The brain interprets the input from different regions of the cochlea as sounds of different pitches. Sound intensity is important as well. Louder sounds stimulate more hair cells, each of which fires rapid bursts of action potentials. The brain interprets the resulting increase in the rate and number of neurons firing as an increase in loudness.

The sense of hearing requires the interaction of many parts of the ear and nervous system. Deafness can occur if any of those components fails to function correctly.

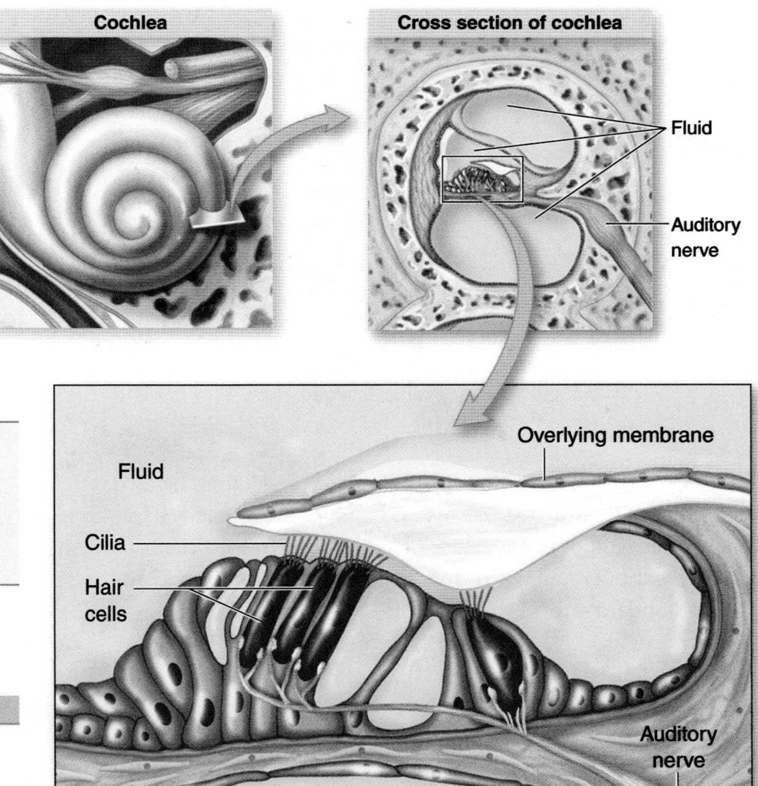

Figure 24.22 The Sense of Hearing. When the fluid inside the cochlea moves, cilia on the hair cells bend relative to the overlying membrane. These hair cells transduce sound waves into action potentials, which travel along the auditory nerve to the brain.

24.11 Mastering Concepts

1. What is the role of mechanoreceptors in the sense of hearing?
2. What are the parts of the ear, and how do they transmit sound?

Investigating Life

24.12 The Nerve of Those Clams!

No population is exempt from natural selection—not even clams. These mollusks might seem to have uneventful lives, buried in the mud along coastal waterways. But clams and humans share a common enemy: harmful algal blooms. Some of the algae living in coastal waters release potent toxins that accumulate in clams and other shellfish. When humans consume the contaminated clams, the result can be an illness called paralytic shellfish poisoning. ▸ dinoflagellates, p. 291

The same toxins can also paralyze a clam. But clams are genetically variable, and not all coastlines are equal. It therefore makes sense that natural selection should produce unique populations of clams that are adapted to their own surroundings. Theoretically, each adaptation is reflected in one or more unique DNA sequences and proteins. Linking natural selection to mutations in specific genes, however, is typically difficult. After all, each species has thousands or tens of thousands of genes, and scientists know little about how most of them function. ▸ natural selection, p. 225

The Question: One example of an exceptionally well-studied protein is the sodium channel that propagates action potentials in neurons. Can a mutation in a gene encoding a sodium channel be directly linked to an adaptation that promotes the survival of clams? A multinational research team wanted to find out. The leader of the team was Monica Bricelj, a Canadian shellfish researcher at the National Research Council Institute for Marine Biosciences in Nova Scotia. She worked with colleagues from the University of Maine, the University of Washington, and the National Oceanic and Atmospheric Administration Northwest Fisheries Science Center in Seattle, Washington.

The Approach: The researchers collected young, toxin-free softshell clams from two sites along the east coast of North America. Harmful algal blooms occur each summer at one site (Bay of Fundy), but blooms have never been known to occur at the nearby Lawrencetown Estuary site.

First, the researchers wanted to learn whether clams from the two sites are equally susceptible to algal toxins. They set up several tanks containing clams

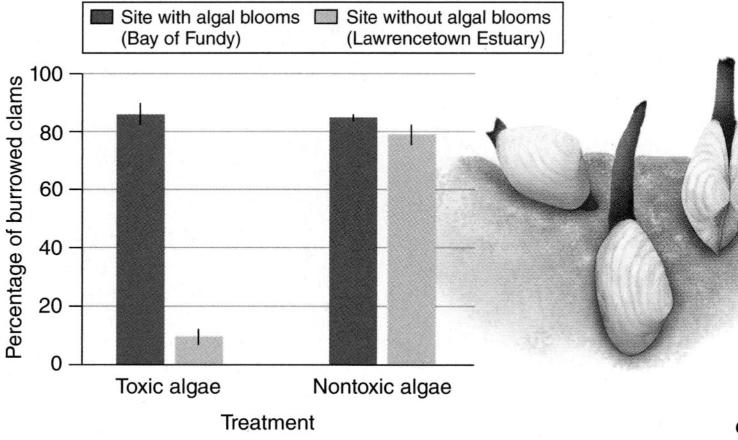

Figure 24.23 Selection for Toxin Resistance. Toxic algae did not affect clams from the Bay of Fundy, which are regularly exposed to harmful algal blooms. The toxins did, however, paralyze clams from an estuary without regular exposure to harmful algal blooms. (Error bars reflect standard errors.)

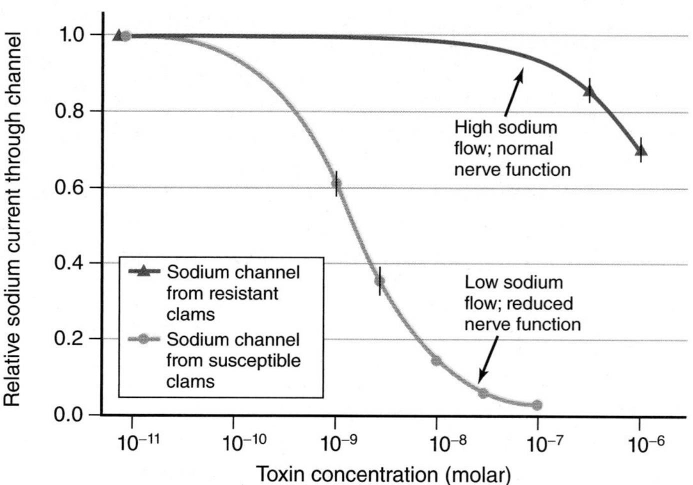

Figure 24.24 Toxin Resistance Explained. Sodium channels from toxin-resistant clams functioned at much higher toxin concentrations than did channels from susceptible clams. (Error bars reflect standard deviation; some error bars are too small to extend beyond the data point.)

and sediment. Each tank then received cells of either toxic or nontoxic algae. After 24 hours of exposure, the nontoxic algae did not affect the clams, as indicated by their ability to burrow into the sediment (figure 24.23). In contrast, the toxic algae paralyzed the muscles of most of the clams from Lawrencetown Estuary, but they did not cause paralysis in the Bay of Fundy clams. Bricelj and her colleagues therefore concluded that exposure to harmful algae has selected for toxin-resistant nervous systems in clams from the Bay of Fundy.

The team turned to molecular biology to answer the next question: how do the sodium channels in nerves from the two clam populations differ? DNA sequences revealed that the sodium channel proteins of sensitive and resistant clams differed by just one amino acid. But did that one difference explain the resistance of the Bay of Fundy clams?

To find out, the researchers grew two sets of cells in culture. One group of cells produced sodium channels identical to those of the toxin-resistant clams; the other cells produced channels like those of the susceptible mollusks. The researchers exposed both sets of cells to the toxin. If sodium continued to flow, the channel was functioning normally. But if the toxin stopped the flow of sodium, then nerve function would be impaired.

The Conclusion: The resistant channels continued to function, even at toxin concentrations that blocked sodium flow through the susceptible channels (figure 24.24). A single change in one gene therefore accounted for the difference between sensitive and resistant clams.

This study tells an unusually complete story of evolution. After all, Bricelj and her team have traced natural selection for toxin resistance all the way down to its molecular explanation: a single mutation that causes a tiny difference in the shape of sodium channels in neurons. As so often happens, a new piece of the evolutionary puzzle has emerged from an unexpected place—in this case, from the nerve of a clam.

Bricelj, V. Monica, and six coauthors. 2005. Sodium channel mutation leading to saxitoxin resistance in clams increases risk of PSP. *Nature,* vol. 434, pages 763–767.

24.12 Mastering Concepts

1. What is the evidence that the presence of algal toxins is a selective force on softshell clam populations?
2. How did Bricelj and her colleagues demonstrate that sodium channel structure explains toxin resistance in some clam populations?

Chapter Summary

24.1 The Nervous System Forms a Rapid Communication Network

- The **nervous system** and **endocrine system** work together to coordinate the feedback systems that maintain homeostasis. The nervous system's electrical signals produce much more rapid effects than the endocrine system.
- Nervous tissue consists of **neurons** and **neuroglia.**
- The vertebrate **central nervous system** consists of the **brain** and **spinal cord.** The **peripheral nervous system** conveys information between the central nervous system and the rest of the body.
- Overall, the nervous system receives sensory information, integrates it, and coordinates a response.

24.2 Neurons Are the Functional Units of a Nervous System

A. A Typical Neuron Consists of a Cell Body, Dendrites, and an Axon

- A neuron has a **cell body, dendrites** that receive impulses and transmit them toward the cell body, and an **axon** that conducts impulses away from the cell body. Fatty neuroglia wrap around portions of some axons to form the **myelin sheath.**

B. The Nervous System Includes Three Classes of Neurons

- A **sensory neuron** carries information toward the central nervous system; an **interneuron** conducts information between two neurons and coordinates responses; a **motor neuron** carries information away from the central nervous system and stimulates a muscle or gland.

24.3 Action Potentials Convey Messages

A. A Neuron at Rest Has a Negative Charge

- In a neuron at rest, the K^+ concentration is much greater inside the cell than outside, whereas the Na^+ concentration is greater outside than inside. An ion pump (the sodium–potassium pump) maintains this chemical gradient.
- The ion concentration gradient, combined with negatively charged proteins within the cell, gives the interior a negative charge, called the **resting potential.**

B. A Neuron's Membrane Potential Rises and Falls During an Action Potential

- A stimulus causes some Na^+ to enter the cell, increasing the charge inside the neuron. If enough Na^+ comes in, the membrane may reach its **threshold potential.**
- When the membrane reaches its threshold potential, an electrical change called an **action potential** begins. Na^+ and K^+ quickly redistribute across a small patch of the axon's membrane, creating a series of changes that propagate like a wave along the nerve fiber.

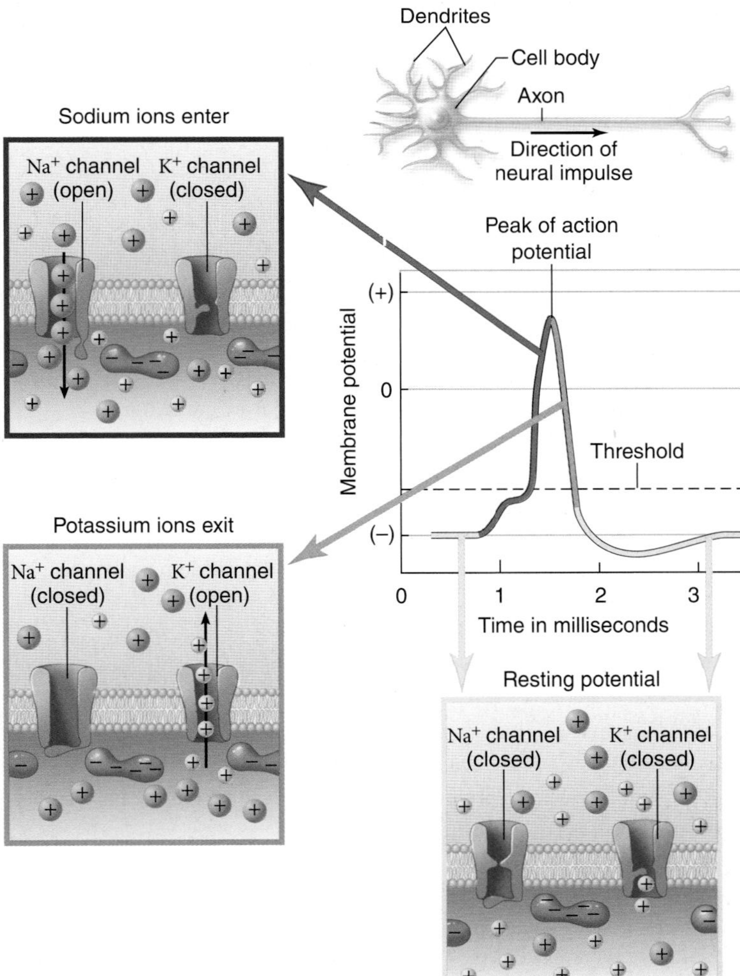

C. The Myelin Sheath Speeds Communication

- The myelin sheath increases the speed of neural impulse transmission. The neural impulse rapidly "jumps" between gaps in the myelin sheath.

24.4 Neurotransmitters Pass the Message from Cell to Cell

- A **synapse** is a junction between a neuron and another cell.
- An action potential reaching the end of an axon causes vesicles in the **synaptic terminals** of the "sending" neuron to release **neurotransmitters** into the **synaptic cleft.** These chemicals diffuse across the cleft and bind to receptors on the membrane of the cell receiving the message.
- Used neurotransmitter molecules diffuse away from the synaptic cleft, are destroyed, or are reabsorbed into the sending cell.
- An excitatory neurotransmitter makes an action potential more probable in the receiving cell; an inhibitory neurotransmitter has the opposite effect.

24.5 The Peripheral Nervous System Consists of Nerve Cells Outside the Central Nervous System

- **Nerves** are bundles of axons that convey information in the peripheral nervous system.
- The peripheral nervous system is divided into the sensory and motor pathways, and it includes all of the nerves that transmit sensations from sensory receptors and stimulate muscles and glands.
- The motor pathways of the peripheral nervous system consist of the **somatic** (voluntary) division and the **autonomic** (involuntary) division. The autonomic nervous system receives sensory information and conveys impulses to smooth muscle, cardiac muscle, and glands.
- Within the autonomic nervous system, the **sympathetic nervous system** controls physical responses to stressful events, and the **parasympathetic nervous system** restores a restful state. Both systems are always active in maintaining homeostasis.

24.6 The Central Nervous System Consists of the Spinal Cord and Brain

A. The Spinal Cord Transmits Information Between Body and Brain

- **White matter** on the periphery of the spinal cord conducts impulses to and from the brain; the central **gray matter** processes information.
- The spinal cord is a reflex center. A **reflex** is a quick, automatic, protective response.

B. The Brain Is Divided into Several Regions

- The **brainstem** consists of the midbrain and portions of the hindbrain.
- The **hindbrain** includes three main subdivisions: the **medulla oblongata,** which controls many vital functions; the **cerebellum,** which coordinates unconscious movements; and the **pons,** which bridges the medulla and higher brain regions and connects the cerebellum to the cerebrum.
- The **midbrain** conducts information between the hindbrain and the forebrain.
- The major parts of the **forebrain** are the **thalamus,** a relay station between lower and higher brain regions; the **hypothalamus,** which regulates vital physiological processes and the levels of some hormones; and the **cerebrum.** The **limbic system,** which includes the amygdala and hippocampus, also resides in the gray matter of the forebrain.
- The outer layer of the cerebrum is the **cerebral cortex,** where information is processed and integrated. The cerebrum's two **hemispheres** each receive sensory input from and direct motor responses to the opposite side of the body.

C. Many Brain Regions Participate in Memory

- Biologists have much to learn about memory, but it appears that the brain stores **short-term memories** and **long-term memories** in different ways.
- The formation of long-term memories requires an intact hippocampus, but the memories are stored in multiple lobes of the cerebral cortex.

D. Damage to the Central Nervous System Can Be Devastating

- The bones of the skull and vertebrae, **cerebrospinal fluid, blood–brain barrier,** and **meninges** protect the central nervous system.
- Trauma, infectious agents, degenerative diseases, and strokes all can damage the nervous system.

24.7 The Senses Connect the Nervous System with the Outside World

- Sense organs send information about internal and external stimuli to the central nervous system. A **sensation** is the raw input sent to the central nervous system; a **perception** is the brain's interpretation of the sensation.
- The senses help the animal body maintain homeostasis.

A. Sensory Receptors Respond to Stimuli by Generating Action Potentials

- **Sensory receptors** are sensory neurons or specialized epithelial cells that detect stimuli. Types of sensory receptors include **mechanoreceptors, thermoreceptors, pain receptors, photoreceptors,** and **chemoreceptors.**
- A sensory receptor selectively responds to a single form of energy and **transduces** it to **receptor potentials,** which change membrane potential in proportion to stimulus strength. If a receptor potential exceeds the cell's threshold, the cell generates action potentials.

B. Continuous Stimulation May Cause Sensory Adaptation

- In **sensory adaptation,** sensory receptors cease to respond to a constant stimulus.

24.8 The General Senses Detect Touch, Temperature, and Pain

- The skin's mechanoreceptors respond to touch. Free nerve endings also include thermoreceptors and pain receptors.

24.9 The Senses of Smell and Taste Detect Chemicals

- The senses of smell and taste detect chemicals dissolved in watery solutions, such as those in the nose and mouth.
- Odorant molecules bind to receptors in the olfactory epithelium of the nose.
- Humans perceive taste when chemicals stimulate receptors within **taste buds** on the tongue.
- **Pheromones** are chemicals that many animals use to communicate with others of the same species.

24.10 Vision Depends on Light-Sensitive Cells

- Photoreceptors in the **eye** contain light-sensitive pigments associated with membranes.
- The human eye's outer layer, the **sclera,** forms the transparent **cornea** in the front of the eyeball.
- The next layer, the **choroid,** supplies nutrients to the **retina.** At the front of the eye, the choroid holds the muscle that controls the shape of the **lens,** which focuses light on the photoreceptors. The **iris** adjusts the amount of light entering the eye by constricting or dilating the **pupil.**
- The innermost eye layer is the retina, and the **optic nerve** connects the retina with the brain.
- The retina's photoreceptors are **rod cells,** which provide black-and-white vision in dim light, and **cone cells,** which provide color vision in brighter light.
- Light stimulation alters the pigments embedded in membranes of rod and cone cells. The resulting change in the charge across the membrane may generate an action potential.
- Photoreceptor cells synapse with multiple layers of neurons in the retina. Eventually, axons of some of these neurons leave the retina as the optic nerve, which carries information to the visual cortex.

24.11 The Sense of Hearing Begins in the Ears

- Mechanoreceptors in the **ear** bend in response to sound waves.
- Sound enters the **auditory canal,** vibrating the **eardrum.** Three bones in the middle ear amplify these vibrations. The movements of these bones are transmitted through the **oval window,** changing the pressure in fluid within the **cochlea.** At the base of the cochlea, vibration moves cilia on **hair cells.** The **auditory nerve** transmits the impulses to the brain.
- The brain perceives the pitch of the sound through the location of the moving hair cells in the cochlea. Louder sounds generate more action potentials than softer ones.

24.12 Investigating Life: The Nerve of Those Clams!

- Exposure to harmful algal blooms has selected for clams resistant to paralytic shellfish poisoning toxins.
- Biologists have traced toxin resistance to a single difference in the amino acid sequence of a sodium channel protein in the nerves of the clams.

Multiple Choice Questions

1. Some cells of the central nervous system are located in the
   a. spinal cord.
   b. muscles.
   c. glands.
   d. Both a and c are correct.
2. What is the function of an axon?
   a. Metabolic support for the neuron
   b. Insulation that speeds impulse conduction
   c. Conduction of an impulse away from the cell body
   d. Input of signals to the nerve cell
3. Which class(es) of neuron would you expect to find in the peripheral nervous system?
   a. Interneurons
   b. Sensory neurons
   c. Motor neurons
   d. Both b and c are correct.
4. What is the likely effect of a loss of myelin along an axon?
   a. It causes the action potential to speed up because more of the membrane is exposed.
   b. It causes the action potential to slow down.
   c. It speeds up the transport of the sodium and potassium across the membrane.
   d. It increases the size of the action potential.
5. Which division of the nervous system would be responsible for a rapid heartbeat?
   a. Autonomic
   b. Sympathetic
   c. Parasympathetic
   d. Both a and b are correct.
6. The part of the human brain involved in coordinating muscle movements is the
   a. cerebrum.
   b. medulla oblongata.
   c. cerebellum.
   d. hypothalamus.
7. Which of the following is NOT among the structures that protects the central nervous system?
   a. Meninges
   b. Vertebrae
   c. Pons
   d. Cerebrospinal fluid

8. When you snuggle into bed, at first you feel the weight of the blankets on your body. Soon, however, you become unaware of the covers. What has happened?
   a. Your skin's touch receptors became unable to receive information about new stimuli.
   b. Your skin's touch receptors adapted to the feeling of the blankets.
   c. All of your body's sensory receptors became unable to receive information about new stimuli.
   d. All of your body's sensory receptors adapted to the feeling of the blankets.
9. What is the function of hair cells in the cochlea?
   a. Transduce sound waves into neural impulses
   b. Interpret and identify sounds
   c. Funnel sounds to the inner ear
   d. Prevent debris from entering the delicate inner ear

Write It Out

1. How do the nervous and endocrine systems differ in how they communicate?
2. Sketch two neurons, with one synapsing on the other. In your sketch, label the dendrites, axons, cell bodies, myelin sheath, and synapse.
3. Describe the distribution of charges in the membrane of a resting neuron.
4. What causes the switch in the distribution of charges when an axon propagates an action potential?
5. In what ways does an action potential resemble a crowd doing "the wave" in a football stadium?
6. How does the myelin sheath increase the speed at which an axon conducts a neural impulse?
7. How do neurons use neurotransmitters to communicate with other cells?
8. A scientist discovers a way to stop production of a protein required for recycling of synaptic vesicles. What will happen to the amount of neurotransmitter in the synaptic cleft?
9. List the main subdivisions of the human nervous system, along with their functions.
10. Why can the loss of reflexes be a possible indication of damage to the central nervous system?
11. How would you test the hypothesis that a nonhuman animal feels pain or thinks? Which animals would you choose to investigate this question?
12. Consider the suggestion that humans use only 10% of their brains. Given the brain's energy demands, does this claim make sense? Do studies of brain-damaged patients support or refute this statement?
13. Neuroglia outnumber neurons by about 10 to 1. In addition, neuroglia retain the ability to divide, unlike neurons. How do these two observations relate to the fact that most brain cancers begin in neuroglia?
14. How does the peripheral nervous system interact with the central nervous system to produce perceptions of stimuli?
15. What is the role of transduction in the sensory system? How does transduction occur for each of the senses described in this chapter?
16. In what ways are the senses of smell and taste similar? In what ways are they different?
17. List the structures of the human eye and their functions.
18. What are the roles of rods and cones in the sense of sight?
19. Describe one way that each sense described in this chapter can help the body maintain homeostasis.

Pull It Together

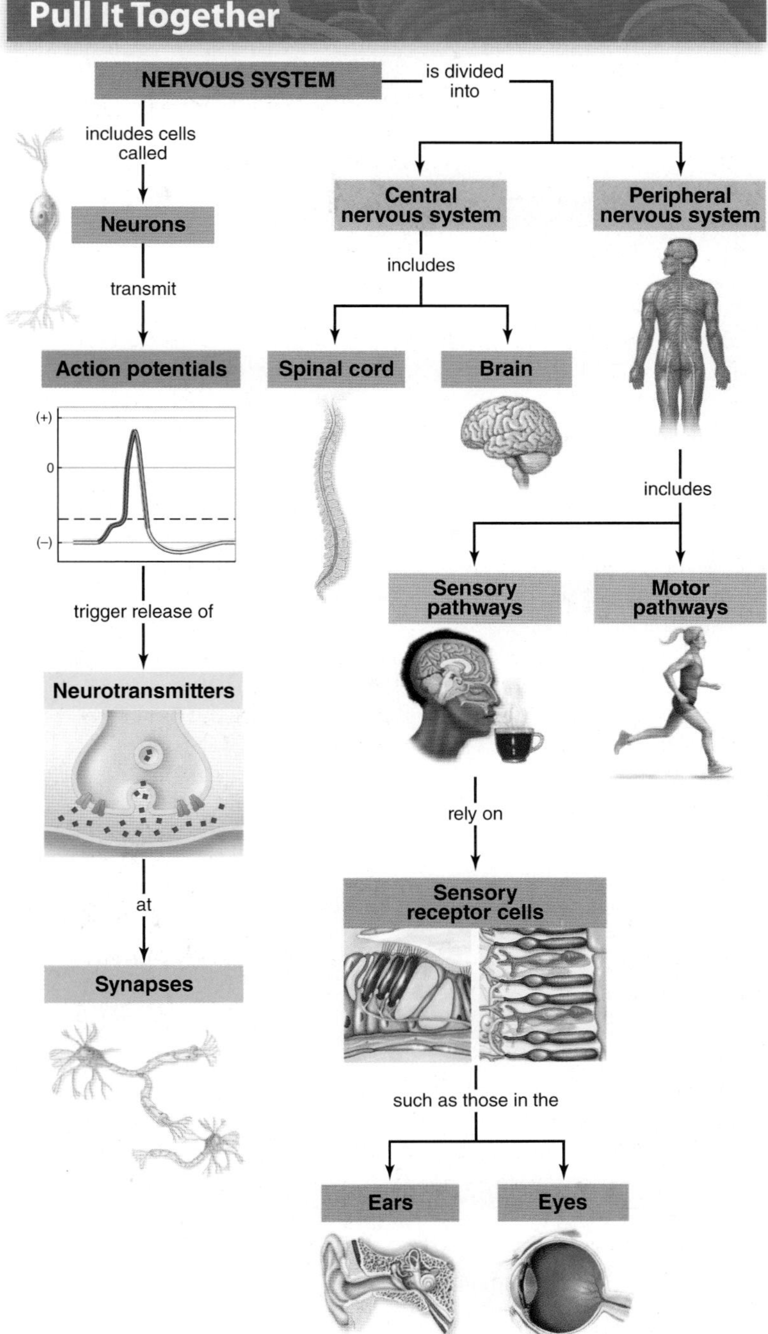

1. What are the main parts of a neuron?
2. Describe the functions of the central and peripheral nervous systems.
3. Add the somatic, autonomic, sympathetic, and parasympathetic nervous systems to this concept map.
4. Make a chart that lists the types of sensory receptors and the sense organs that use each type.

Enhance your study of this chapter with practice quizzes, animations and videos, answer keys, and downloadable study tools.
www.mhhe.com/hoefnagels

25 The Endocrine System

Hormones from the Start. Messenger molecules called hormones regulate growth and development in babies. Throughout each person's life, hormones also control metabolic rates, reproduction, and responses to stress. They help maintain homeostasis in many other ways as well.

Learning Outline

Learn How to Learn

Don't Waste Old Exams

If you are lucky, your instructor may make old exams available to your class. If so, it is usually a bad idea to simply look up and memorize the answer to each question. Instead, use the old exam as a chance to test yourself before it really counts. Put away your notes and textbook, and set up a mock exam. Answer each question without "cheating," then check how many you got right. Use the questions you got wrong—or that you guessed right—as a guide to what you should study more.

What's the Point?

The endocrine system is the body's slow communication network. Hormones, the endocrine system's communication molecules, take a leisurely route—the bloodstream—through the body. The responses may be slower than those coordinated by the nervous system, but they are just as important in maintaining homeostasis. Without the nervous and endocrine systems calling the shots, the body's other organ systems could not do their jobs.

One way to appreciate the importance of hormones is to consider what happens when they are produced in quantities that are too small or too large. A patient who fails to produce a hormone called insulin has Type 1 diabetes. If human growth hormone is lacking, the bones do not grow properly, resulting in a type of dwarfism. Too much growth hormone, on the other hand, produces a giant.

Understanding the endocrine system has led to many practical applications. Insulin injections have saved the lives of many diabetic patients, and the synthetic hormones in birth control pills have prevented countless unwanted pregnancies. This chapter introduces these hormones and many more.

25.1 The Endocrine System Uses Hormones to Communicate

Animals communicate with one another in many ways, including color displays, sounds, body language, and scents. Likewise, the cells that make up a multicellular organism's body send and receive signals; these intercellular messages coordinate the actions of the body's organ systems.

An animal's body has two main communication systems. The **nervous system,** described in chapter 24, is a network of cells that specialize in sending speedy signals that vanish as quickly as they arrive. The **endocrine system** is the other main communication system. As this chapter explains, the endocrine system does not act with the speed of neural impulses, but its chemical messages have their own advantage: staying power.

The endocrine system has two main components: glands and hormones. An **endocrine gland** consists of cells that produce and secrete hormones into the bloodstream, which carries the secretions throughout the body. A **hormone** is a biochemical that travels in the bloodstream and alters the metabolism of one or more cells.

The endocrine system would be ineffective if every hormone acted on every cell in the body. Instead, each hormone has a limited selection of **target cells** that actually respond to the hormone. Receptor proteins on or in each target cell bind to the hormone and initiate the cell's response.

Hormones are analogous to the many radio signals that stations simultaneously broadcast into the atmosphere. The receptors on the target cells, then, are like individual radios. Even when dozens of signals are present, each radio is tuned to one frequency and therefore picks up the signal of just one station. Likewise, each receptor binds to one of the many hormones that may be circulating in the bloodstream. Moreover, just as one house may contain many radios, each tuned to a different station, one cell may also have receptors for many hormones, each of which initiates a unique response.

To illustrate the power of the endocrine system, consider one stage of life that famously involves hormones: puberty. During this period, hormones transform a child's body into that of an adult. Females develop enlarged breasts and wider hips, males acquire a deeper voice and more muscular physique, and new body hair sprouts in both sexes. The same hormones also affect mood, emotions, and feelings of sexual attraction.

Hormones figure prominently into the lives of other animals, too. For example, a caterpillar undergoes a dramatic metamorphosis as it develops into a butterfly, as does a tadpole transforming into an adult frog (figure 25.1). The endocrine system's effects are not always so extreme, but they are nonetheless present throughout our lives. Some types of chemical contaminants disrupt

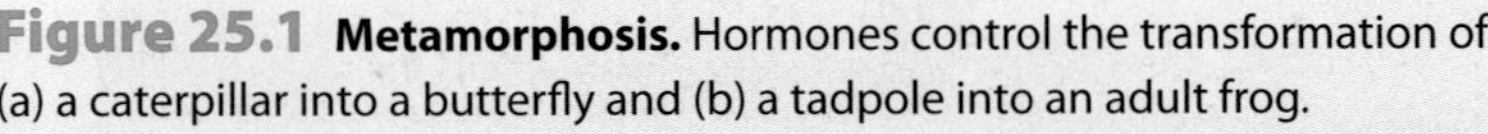

Figure 25.1 Metamorphosis. Hormones control the transformation of (a) a caterpillar into a butterfly and (b) a tadpole into an adult frog.

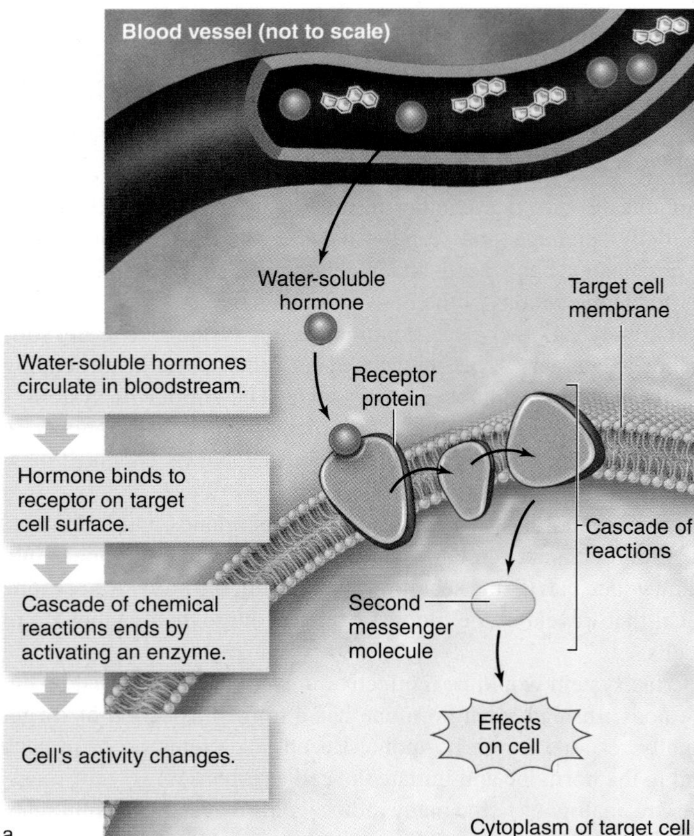

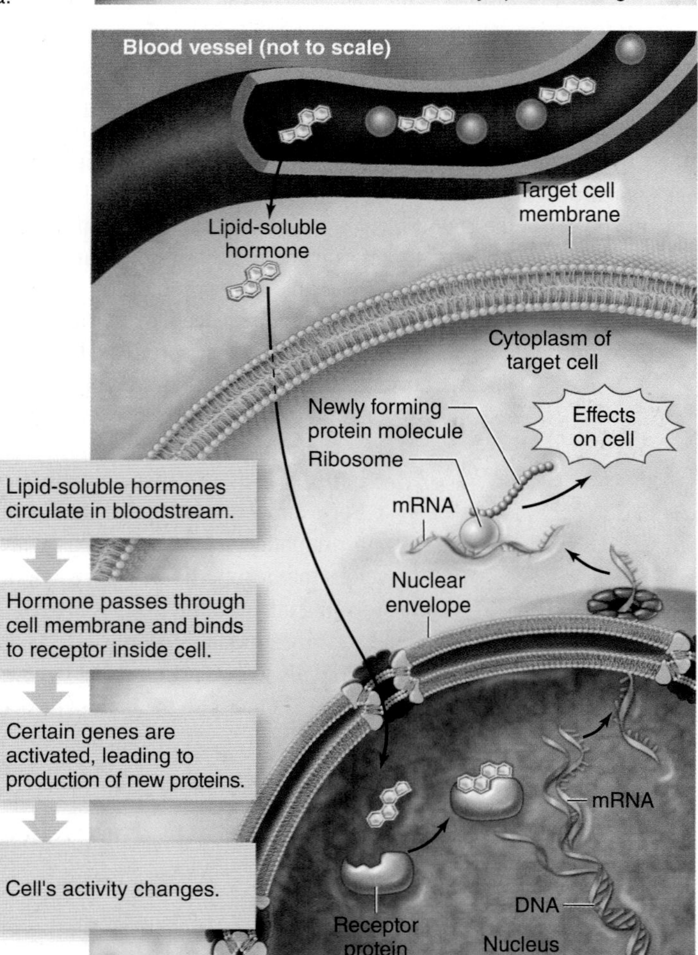

these delicate signals. The consequences can be serious and long-lasting, as described in the Burning Question box on page 519.

25.1 Mastering Concepts

1. What is the overall function of an endocrine system?
2. Describe the relationships among endocrine glands, hormones, and target cells.

25.2 Hormones Stimulate Responses in Target Cells

Just as a key fits a lock, each hormone affects only target cells bearing specific receptor molecules. The term *target cells* is a little misleading, because it implies that hormones somehow travel straight from their source to a limited set of cells. In reality, the blood circulating throughout the body contains many types of hormones at once. Each hormone's target cells are simply those with the corresponding receptors.

This section describes how the interaction between a hormone and its receptor initiates the target cell's response. The receptors may occur on the target cell's surface or inside the cytoplasm. In general, receptors for water-soluble hormones are on the cell's surface, whereas lipid-soluble hormones typically interact with internal receptors.

A. Water-Soluble Hormones Trigger Second Messenger Systems

Most water-soluble hormones are either short chains of amino acids ("peptide hormones") or proteins. These hormones, which cannot pass readily through the cell membrane's phospholipid bilayer, bind to receptors on the surface of target cells (figure 25.2a). This hormone-receptor interaction triggers a cascade of chemical reactions within the cell.

The ultimate product of the chain reaction is a **second messenger,** which is the molecule that actually provokes the cell's response. The second messenger, in turn, typically activates the enzymes that produce the hormone's effects. The entire sequence of reactions therefore has the effect of converting the external "message"—the arrival of the hormone—into an internal signal. ▸ cell membrane, p. 54

In general, water-soluble hormones act rapidly, within minutes of their release. Target cells respond quickly because all of the participating biochemicals are already in place when the hormone binds the receptor.

B. Lipid-Soluble Hormones Directly Alter Gene Expression

Some hormones are lipid-soluble. The most familiar are the **steroid hormones,** such as testosterone and estrogen. The body synthesizes these and other steroid

Figure 25.2 Target Cell Responses To Hormones. (a) Water-soluble hormones bind to receptors on the surface of target cells. A series of chemical reactions initiates the target cell's response. (b) Lipid-soluble hormones pass through cell membranes and bind to receptors in the cytoplasm or nucleus. The target cell responds by altering the expression of one or more genes.

hormones from cholesterol, which is one reason humans need at least some cholesterol in their diets. Two other lipid-soluble hormones, the thyroid hormones, are derived from a single amino acid. ▸ lipids, p. 35

Unlike peptide hormones, lipid-soluble hormones easily cross the cell membrane (figure 25.2b). Once inside the cell, the hormone may enter the nucleus and bind to a receptor associated with DNA, which triggers the production of proteins that carry out the target cell's response. Alternatively, the hormone may bind to a receptor in the cytoplasm, and the two molecules may travel together to the nucleus. Either way, response time is much slower than for peptide hormones, because the cell must produce new proteins before the hormone takes effect. ▸ DNA function, p. 114

25.2 Mastering Concepts

1. Describe the action of water- and lipid-soluble hormones.
2. Why do water-soluble hormones usually act faster than lipid-soluble hormones?

25.3 The Hypothalamus and Pituitary Gland Oversee Endocrine Control

Many organs produce hormones. The main endocrine organs in vertebrates are the hypothalamus, pituitary gland, pineal gland, thyroid gland, parathyroid glands, adrenal glands, pancreas, ovaries, and testes (figure 25.3).

Two of these structures, the hypothalamus and the pituitary gland, coordinate the rest of the endocrine system's action. The almond-sized **hypothalamus** is a part of the brain, and the **pituitary gland** is a pea-sized structure attached to a stalk extending from the hypothalamus. The hypothalamus links the nervous and endocrine systems by controlling pituitary secretions.

Endocrine System	
Main tissue types*	**Examples of locations/functions**
Epithelial	Makes up the bulk of most glands and secretes many types of hormones
Connective	Blood circulates hormones throughout the body
Nervous	Parts of the brain secrete some hormones and control release of others; some neurons secrete hormones

*See chapter 23 for descriptions.

Figure 25.3 Some Human Endocrine Glands. The endocrine system includes several glands that contain specialized hormone-secreting cells. The hormones circulate throughout the body in blood vessels, which are not shown in this figure.

Hypothalamus
(shown in green) Produces hormones that stimulate or inhibit the release of hormones from the pituitary gland

Pituitary gland
(shown in orange) Produces numerous hormones that affect target tissues directly or stimulate other endocrine glands

Pineal gland
(shown in blue) Produces melatonin

Thyroid gland
Releases thyroid hormones, which regulate metabolism

Parathyroid glands
(behind thyroid) Secrete parathyroid hormone, which helps regulate blood calcium

Adrenal glands
Produce hormones that regulate kidney function and contribute to the body's stress response

Pancreas
Releases hormones that regulate blood glucose levels

Ovaries (in female)
Produce estrogen and progesterone, which mediate monthly changes in the uterine lining and promote secondary sex characteristics

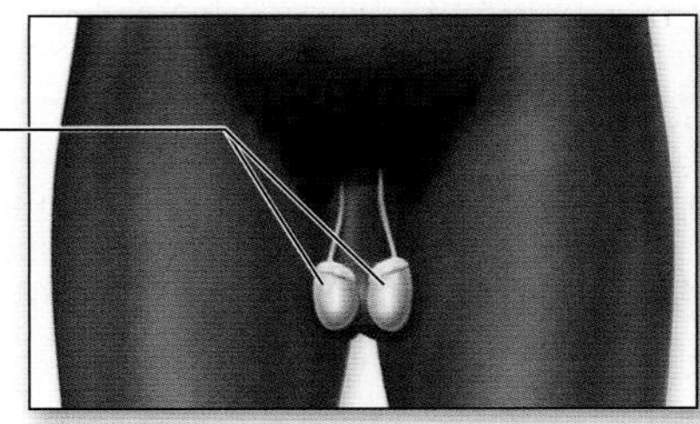

Testes (in male)
Produce testosterone, which promotes sperm maturation and secondary sex characteristics

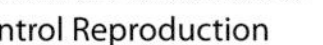

Figure 25.4 Hormones of the Hypothalamus and Pituitary: A Summary. The hypothalamus and the pituitary gland help coordinate the functioning of the other endocrine glands.

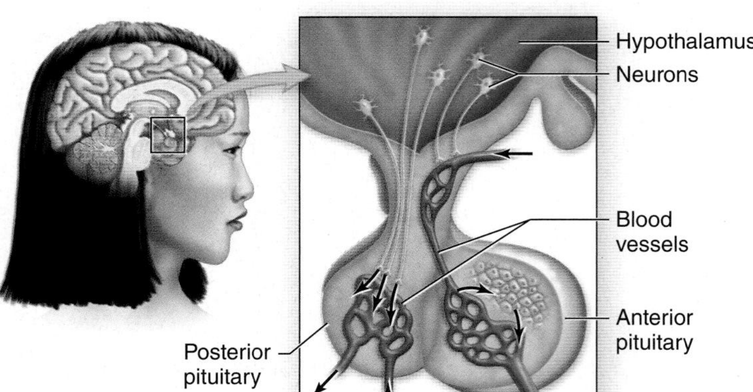

The pituitary is really two glands in one (figure 25.4): the larger **anterior pituitary** (toward the front) and the smaller **posterior pituitary** (toward the back). Anatomically, the posterior pituitary is a continuation of the hypothalamus, whereas the anterior pituitary consists of endocrine cells.

The hypothalamus controls the two parts of the pituitary in different ways. The posterior pituitary does not synthesize hormones of its own, but it does store and release two hormones that the hypothalamus produces. The hypothalamus controls the anterior pituitary in a different way—by secreting hormones that reach the anterior pituitary through a specialized system of blood vessels. These hormones either stimulate or inhibit the release of several hormones that the anterior pituitary produces. The table in figure 25.4 provides an overview of the relationships among the hypothalamus, anterior pituitary, and posterior pituitary.

Source	Hypothalamus	
Hormone	Releasing hormones	Inhibiting hormones
Type	Peptide	Peptide
Action	Stimulate release of hormones from anterior pituitary	Inhibit release of hormones from anterior pituitary

Source	Posterior pituitary		Anterior pituitary					
Hormone	Antidiuretic hormone (ADH), a.k.a. vasopressin	Oxytocin	Growth hormone (GH)	Prolactin	Thyroid stimulating hormone (TSH)	Adreno-corticotropic hormone (ACTH)	Follicle-stimulating hormone (FSH) and luteinizing hormone (LH)	Endorphins
Type	Peptide	Peptide	Protein	Protein	Protein	Peptide	Protein	Peptide
Target cells	Kidney	Mammary glands and uterus	Most cells in the body	Mammary glands	Thyroid	Adrenal cortex	Testes; Ovaries	Pain receptors in the brain
Major responses	Promotes conservation of water	Stimulates smooth muscle contraction	Stimulates tissue growth	Stimulates milk secretion	Stimulates secretion of thyroid hormones	Stimulates secretion of glucocorticoid hormones	Stimulate secretion of sex hormones; stimulate oocyte development and ovulation (in females) and sperm production (in males)	Relieve pain

A. The Posterior Pituitary Stores and Releases Two Hormones

One of the two hormones produced by the hypothalamus and released by the posterior pituitary is **antidiuretic hormone (ADH),** also called vasopressin. Among other effects, this hormone stimulates cells in the kidneys to return water to the bloodstream (rather than eliminating the water in urine). If cells in the hypothalamus detect that the body's fluids are too concentrated, the posterior pituitary releases more ADH. Additional water returns to the blood, and the body's fluids become more dilute.

Oxytocin is the other posterior pituitary hormone. When a baby suckles, sensory neurons in the mother's nipple relay the information to the brain, which stimulates the release of oxytocin. The hormone causes cells in the breast to contract, squeezing the milk through ducts leading to the nipple. Oxytocin also triggers muscle contraction in the uterus, which pushes a baby out during labor. For this reason, physicians use synthetic oxytocin to induce labor or accelerate contractions in a woman who is giving birth.

Both ADH and oxytocin also act on the vertebrate brain, playing a role in bonding, affection, and social recognition in at least some species (see section 25.6). Researchers are trying to determine whether and how these hormones participate in human social attachment and in disorders such as autism.

B. The Anterior Pituitary Produces and Secretes Six Hormones

One of the six hormones that the anterior pituitary gland produces is **growth hormone (GH).** This hormone promotes growth and development in all tissues by increasing protein synthesis and cell division rates. Levels of GH peak in the preteen years and help spark adolescent growth spurts. A severe deficiency of GH during childhood leads to pituitary dwarfism, which is associated with extremely short stature. At the other extreme, a child with too much GH becomes a pituitary giant (figure 25.5). In an adult, GH does not affect height because the long bones of the body are no longer growing. However, excess GH can cause acromegaly, a thickening of the bones in the hands and face.

Figure 25.5 Growth Hormone Abnormality. A pituitary giant, Robert Wadlow, poses with his father and young brother. At about 2.7 meters (just under 9 feet) tall, Wadlow is thought to have been the tallest person in history. He died in 1940 at age 22.

Prolactin is an anterior pituitary hormone that stimulates milk production in a woman's breasts after she gives birth. In males and in women who are not breast feeding, a hormone from the hypothalamus suppresses prolactin synthesis. In nursing mothers, however, a suckling infant triggers nerve impulses that overcome this inhibition.

The other four anterior pituitary hormones all influence hormone secretion by other endocrine glands. **Thyroid-stimulating hormone (TSH)** prompts the thyroid gland to release hormones, whereas **adrenocorticotropic hormone (ACTH)** stimulates hormone release from the adrenal glands. The remaining two anterior pituitary hormones stimulate hormone release from the ovaries and testes: **follicle-stimulating hormone (FSH)** and **luteinizing hormone (LH).** Sections 25.4 and 25.5 describe these hormones in more detail.

The anterior pituitary also produces **endorphins,** which are natural painkillers that bind to receptors on target cells in the brain. Usually, however, endorphins are not detectable in the blood, so their status as hormones is questionable.

25.3 Mastering Concepts

1. How does the hypothalamus interact with the posterior and anterior pituitary glands?
2. List the names and functions of the hormones released by the posterior and anterior pituitary glands.

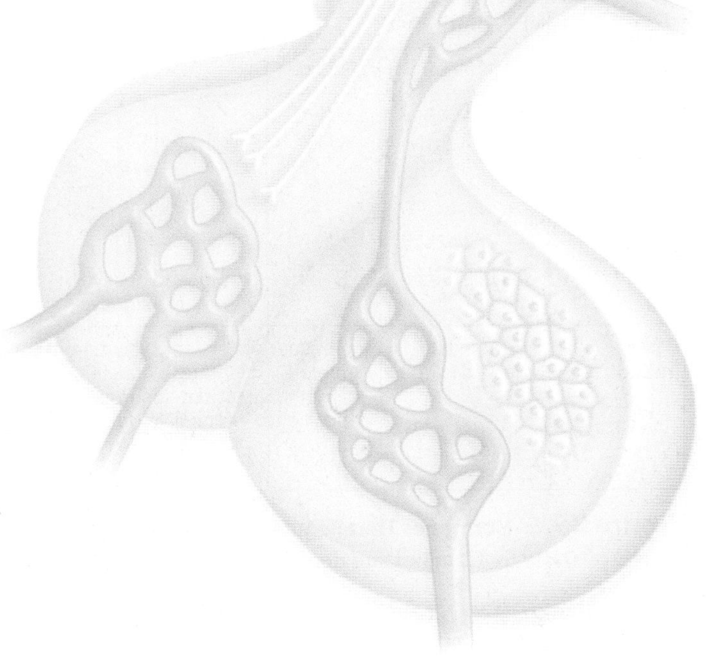

25.4 Hormones from Many Glands Regulate Metabolism

The thyroid gland, parathyroid glands, adrenal glands, and pancreas secrete hormones that influence metabolism (figure 25.6). Hormones from the anterior pituitary control many, but not all, of the activities of these glands (see figure 25.4).

A. The Thyroid Gland Sets the Metabolic Pace

The **thyroid gland** is a two-lobed structure in the neck. The lobes secrete two thyroid hormones, **thyroxine** and **triiodothyronine,** that increase the rate of metabolism in target cells. Under thyroid stimulation, the lungs exchange gases faster, the small intestine absorbs nutrients more readily, and fat levels in cells and in blood plasma decline.

The thyroid hormones illustrate how the hypothalamus and pituitary interact in negative feedback loops (figure 25.7). When blood levels of thyroid hormones are low, the hypothalamus secretes thyrotropin-releasing hormone (TRH), which stimulates the anterior pituitary to increase production of thyroid-stimulating hormone (TSH). In response, cells in the thyroid secrete thyroxine and triiodothyronine. In the opposite situation, TRH secretion slows, so the thyroid glands reduce their production of hormones.

One disorder that affects the thyroid gland is hypothyroidism, a condition in which the thyroid does not release enough hormones. The metabolic rate slows, the body burns fewer calories, and weight increases. Synthetic hormones

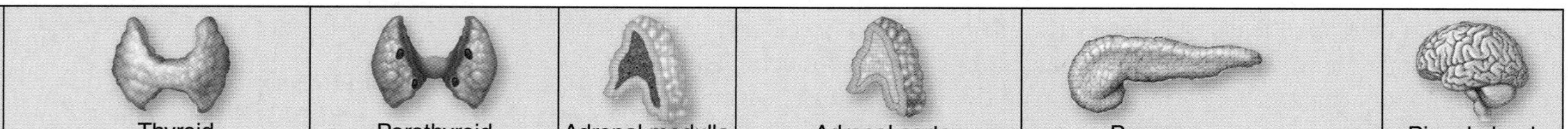

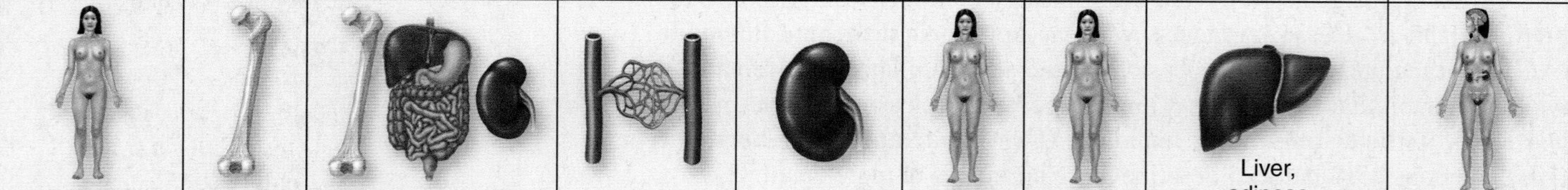

Source	Thyroid		Parathyroid	Adrenal medulla	Adrenal cortex		Pancreas		Pineal gland
Hormone	Thyroid hormones (thyroxine, triiodothyronine)	Calcitonin	Parathyroid hormone (PTH)	Epinephrine, norepinephrine	Mineralo-corticoids	Gluco-corticoids	Insulin	Glucagon	Melatonin
Type	Amine	Peptide	Peptide	Amine	Steroid	Steroid	Peptide	Peptide	Amine
Target cells	All tissues	Bone	Bone, digestive organs, kidneys	Blood vessels	Kidney	All tissues	All tissues	Liver, adipose tissue	Other endocrine glands
Major responses	Increase metabolic rate	Increases rate of calcium deposition	Releases calcium from bone, increases calcium absorption in digestive organs and kidneys	Raise blood pressure, constrict blood vessels, slow digestion	Maintain blood volume and salt balance	Increase glucose levels in blood and brain	Increases uptake of glucose	Stimulates breakdown of glycogen into glucose and of fats into fatty acids	Regulates effects of light–dark cycles

Figure 25.6 Hormones That Regulate Metabolism: A Summary. Hormones from several endocrine glands simultaneously influence many metabolic processes. (Note that "amines" are derived from amino acids. With the exception of thyroid hormones, which are lipid-soluble, amines are water-soluble.)

can treat many cases of hypothyroidism. In the past, the most common cause of hypothyroidism was iodine deficiency. Both thyroid hormones contain iodine; a deficiency of this essential element causes a goiter, or swollen thyroid gland. Today, iodine-deficient goiter is rare in nations where iodine is added to table salt.

An overactive thyroid causes hyperthyroidism. This disorder is associated with hyperactivity, an elevated heart rate, a high metabolic rate, and rapid weight loss. Graves disease is the most common type of hyperthyroidism. Both former President George H. W. Bush and his wife, Barbara, have this disorder.

Scattered cells throughout the thyroid gland produce a third hormone, **calcitonin,** which decreases blood calcium level by increasing the deposition of calcium in bone. Levels of calcitonin greatly increase during pregnancy and milk production, preventing the woman's skeleton from losing too much calcium. The overall physiological importance of calcitonin in adult humans, however, is usually minimal.

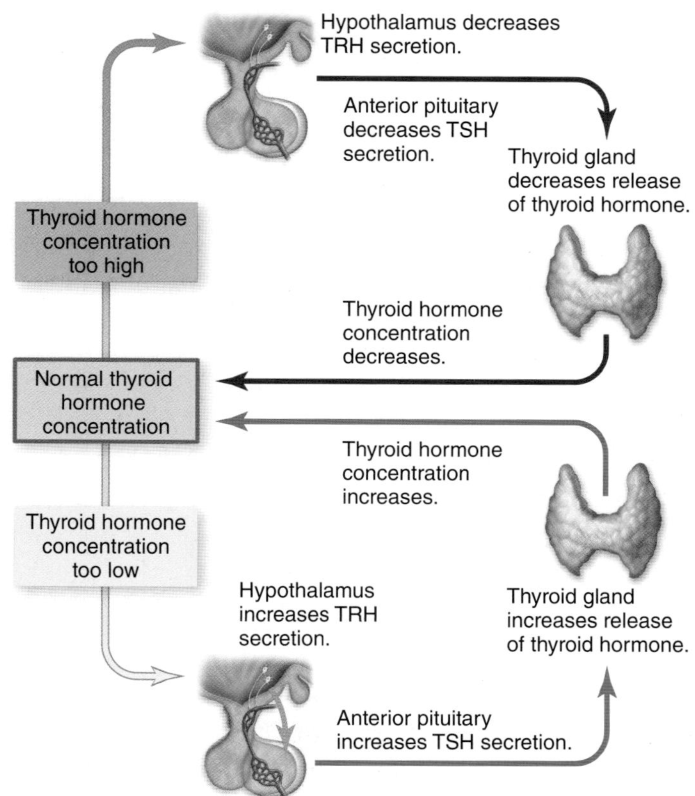

Figure 25.7 Thyroid Hormone Regulation. A negative feedback loop maintains the proper concentration of thyroid hormones in blood.

B. The Parathyroid Glands Control Calcium Level

The **parathyroid glands** are four small groups of cells embedded in the back of the thyroid gland. **Parathyroid hormone (PTH)** increases calcium levels in blood and tissue fluid by releasing calcium from bones and by enhancing calcium absorption at the digestive tract and kidneys. PTH action therefore opposes that of calcitonin.

Calcium is vital to muscle contraction, blood clotting, bone formation, and the activities of many enzymes. Underactivity of the parathyroids can therefore be fatal. Excess PTH can also be harmful if calcium leaves bones faster than it accumulates. This condition, called osteoporosis, is most common in women who have reached menopause (cessation of menstrual periods). The estrogen decrease that accompanies menopause makes bone-forming cells more sensitive to PTH, which depletes bone mass. ▸ osteoporosis, p. 530

C. The Adrenal Glands Coordinate the Body's Stress Responses

The paired, walnut-sized **adrenal glands** sit on top of the kidneys (*ad-* means near, *renal* means kidney). The **adrenal medulla** is the inner portion of each gland, and the **adrenal cortex** is the outer portion. Each region secretes different hormones, mostly in response to stress (figure 25.8).

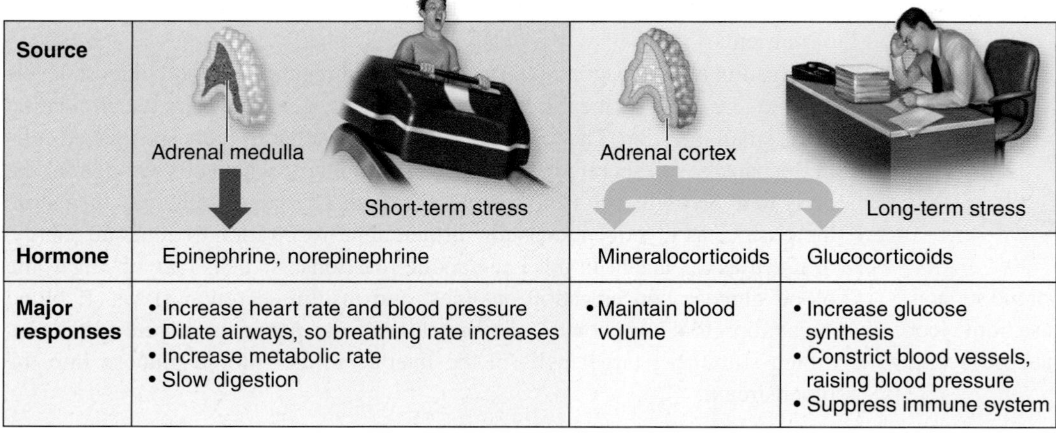

Source	Adrenal medulla — Short-term stress	Adrenal cortex — Long-term stress	
Hormone	Epinephrine, norepinephrine	Mineralocorticoids	Glucocorticoids
Major responses	• Increase heart rate and blood pressure • Dilate airways, so breathing rate increases • Increase metabolic rate • Slow digestion	• Maintain blood volume	• Increase glucose synthesis • Constrict blood vessels, raising blood pressure • Suppress immune system

Figure 25.8 Hormones of the Adrenal Glands: A Summary. The adrenal medulla secretes epinephrine and norepinephrine, which help the body respond to short-term stresses. Mineralocorticoids and glucocorticoids from the adrenal cortex enable the body to survive prolonged stress. The adrenal cortex also secretes small amounts of sex hormones (not shown).

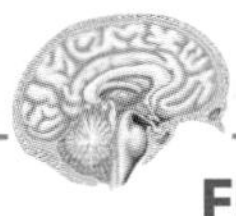

Figure It Out

Which hormone acts more slowly: cortisol or epinephrine? Why? [Hint: Consult the list of hormone types in figure 25.6.]

Answer: Cortisol; it is a steroid hormone.

The two main adrenal medulla hormones, **epinephrine** (adrenaline) and **norepinephrine** (noradrenaline), help the body respond to fear, exercise, trauma, and other short-term stresses. Signals from the sympathetic nervous system trigger release of these hormones, which cause heart rate and blood pressure to climb. In addition, the airway increases in diameter, making breathing easier. The metabolic rate increases, while digestion and other "nonessential" processes slow.

Epinephrine can save the lives of people with severe allergic reactions to bee stings or specific foods. Moments after contacting the allergen, a massive immune system reaction causes the airway to constrict. People with known allergies may therefore carry a self-injectable dose of epinephrine with them. The epinephrine temporarily reverses the effects of the allergic reaction, allowing the person to survive long enough to seek medical help. ▸ allergies, p. 602

Unlike the adrenal medulla, the adrenal cortex secretes steroid hormones, including mineralocorticoids, glucocorticoids, and even a small amount of testosterone. The **mineralocorticoids** maintain blood volume and salt balance. One example, aldosterone, stimulates the kidneys to return sodium ions and water to the blood while excreting potassium ions. This action conserves water and increases blood pressure, which is especially important in compensating for fluid loss from severe bleeding. ▸ aldosterone, p. 584

Glucocorticoids are essential in the body's response to prolonged stress. Cortisol is the most important glucocorticoid. This hormone mobilizes energy reserves by stimulating the production of glucose from amino acids. Glucocorticoids also indirectly constrict blood vessels, which slows blood loss and prevents tissue inflammation after an injury. These same effects, however, account for the unhealthy effects of chronic stress. Narrowed blood vessels can lead to heart attacks, and the suppressed immune system leaves a person vulnerable to illness.

Like other synthetic glucocorticoids, prednisone is an anti-inflammatory drug that mimics the effects of cortisol. This drug can treat arthritis, allergic reactions, and asthma, but it also suppresses the immune system. In addition, with long-term use of the drug, the adrenal cortex may stop producing its own glucocorticoid hormones. Abruptly stopping treatment may therefore cause a potentially dangerous "steroid withdrawal" condition, with symptoms including fatigue, low blood pressure, and nausea. In severe cases, the patient may go into shock, which can be fatal.

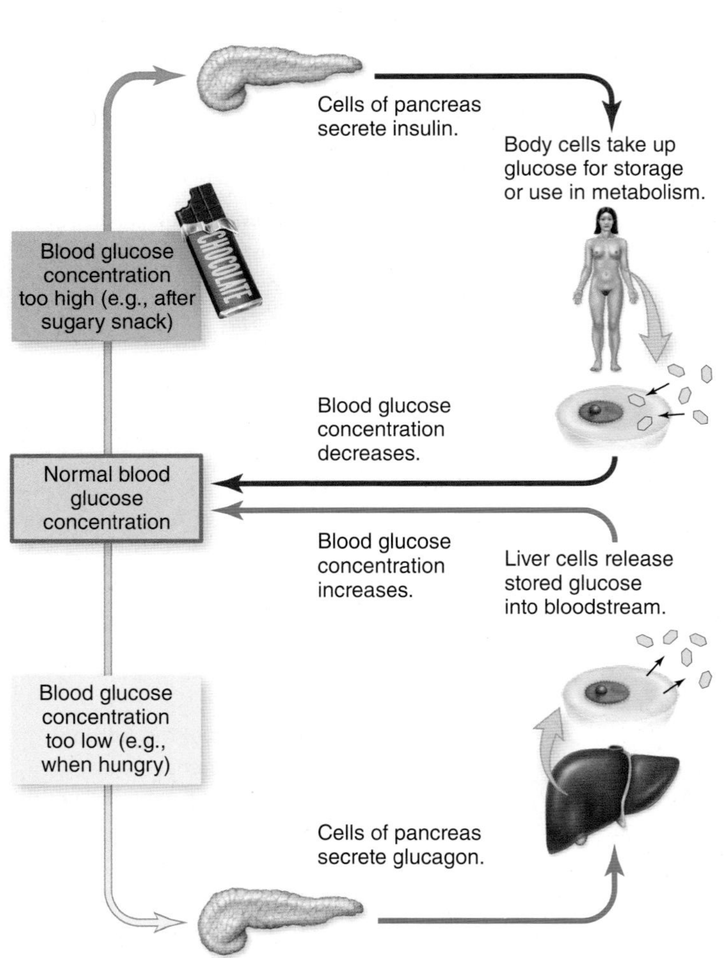

Figure 25.9 Blood Glucose Regulation. When blood sugar is high, insulin prompts the body's cells to absorb glucose from blood. Glucagon has the opposite effect, increasing blood glucose levels by stimulating the release of sugar.

D. The Pancreas Regulates Nutrient Use

The **pancreas** is an elongated gland, about the size of a hand, located beneath the stomach and attached to the small intestine. Clusters of cells in the pancreas secrete insulin and glucagon, two hormones that regulate the body's use of nutrients.

Insulin and glucagon oppose each other in regulating blood glucose levels (figure 25.9). After a meal rich in carbohydrates, glucose enters the circulation at the small intestine. The resulting rise in blood sugar triggers specialized cells in the pancreas to secrete **insulin,** which stimulates target cells throughout the body to absorb glucose from the bloodstream. The target cells may then store the glucose as glycogen, consume it in cellular respiration to generate energy, or use it as a reactant in other metabolic reactions. As cells take up sugar, the blood glucose concentration declines, and insulin secretion slows. If blood sugar dips too low, however, other cells in the pancreas secrete **glucagon,** which stimulates target cells in the liver to release stored glucose into the bloodstream.

Too Much Glucose in Blood: Diabetes Failure to regulate blood sugar can be deadly. In **diabetes,** glucose accumulates to dangerously high levels in the bloodstream. Centuries ago, before lab tests for blood sugar were available, physicians diagnosed diabetes from the sweet taste of a patient's urine.

Diabetes is a paradox: sugar pours out of the body in urine, yet the body's cells starve for lack of glucose. Symptoms include frequent urination, excessive thirst, extreme hunger, blurred vision, weakness, fatigue, irritability, nausea, and weight loss. If the diabetes remains untreated, complications may occur. For example, elevated blood glucose can eventually cause kidney failure, and damage to the peripheral nervous system may cause blindness or a loss of sensation in the hands and feet. The nerve damage, in turn, can contribute to poor healing of wounds, as undetected cuts and scrapes become infected with bacteria and fungi. Severe diabetes can eventually result in coma and death.

The accumulation of blood sugar that characterizes diabetes can occur for two reasons. In type 1 diabetes, the pancreas fails to produce insulin, so the body's cells never receive the signal to "open the door" and admit glucose. In type 2 diabetes, the body's cells fail to absorb glucose even when insulin is present; this condition is called insulin resistance. In type 2 diabetes, then, insulin "rings the doorbell," but the cell never opens the door.

Fifteen percent of affected individuals have type 1 diabetes, which usually begins in childhood or early adulthood. Typically, the underlying cause is an autoimmune disorder in which immune system cells attack the pancreas, which therefore cannot produce insulin. Type 1 diabetes is sometimes also called insulin-dependent diabetes because insulin injections can replace the missing hormone (figure 25.10). ▸ autoimmune disorders, p. 601

Type 2 diabetes is much more common, and it usually begins in adulthood. This disease is strongly associated with obesity (figure 25.11). The pie charts at the top of figure 25.11 show the rising rates of obesity in the United States over an 11-year period. The line graph at the bottom of the figure shows that over the same time span, the number of people diagnosed with type 2 diabetes nearly doubled. Moreover, nearly all type 2 diabetes patients are overweight. The exact cause–effect relationship between obesity and type 2 diabetes, however, remains unclear.

Medicines can help lower blood glucose levels, but the best way to prevent and treat type 2 diabetes is to maintain a healthy body weight by being physically active, reducing calorie intake, and choosing healthy foods (see section 28.4). Even though type 2 diabetes usually strikes in midlife, diabetes prevention should begin much earlier. After all, losing weight can be especially difficult when it requires changing dietary and exercise habits acquired over many decades.

Not Enough Glucose in Blood: Hypoglycemia The opposite of diabetes is **hypoglycemia,** in which excess insulin production or insufficient carbohydrate intake causes low blood sugar. A person with this condition feels weak, sweaty, anxious, and shaky; in severe cases, hypoglycemia can cause seizures or loss of consciousness. A healthy person might temporarily experience hypoglycemia after strenuous exercise. Frequent, small meals low in carbohydrates and high in protein can prevent insulin surges and help relieve symptoms of hypoglycemia.

E. The Pineal Gland Secretes Melatonin

The **pineal gland,** a small structure near the hypothalamus, produces the hormone **melatonin.** Darkness stimulates melatonin synthesis in the pineal gland; exposing the eye to light, on the other hand, inhibits melatonin production. The amount of melatonin in blood therefore "tells" the other cells of the body how much light the eyes are receiving. This interaction, in turn, sets the stage for the regulation of sleep–wake cycles and other circadian rhythms.

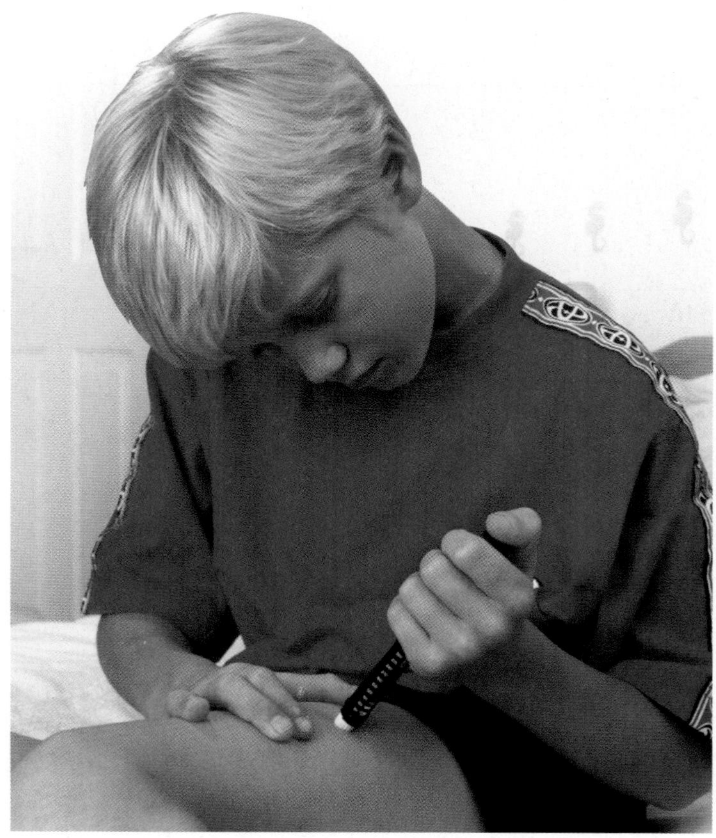

Figure 25.10 Type 1 Diabetes. This diabetic boy is injecting himself with insulin.

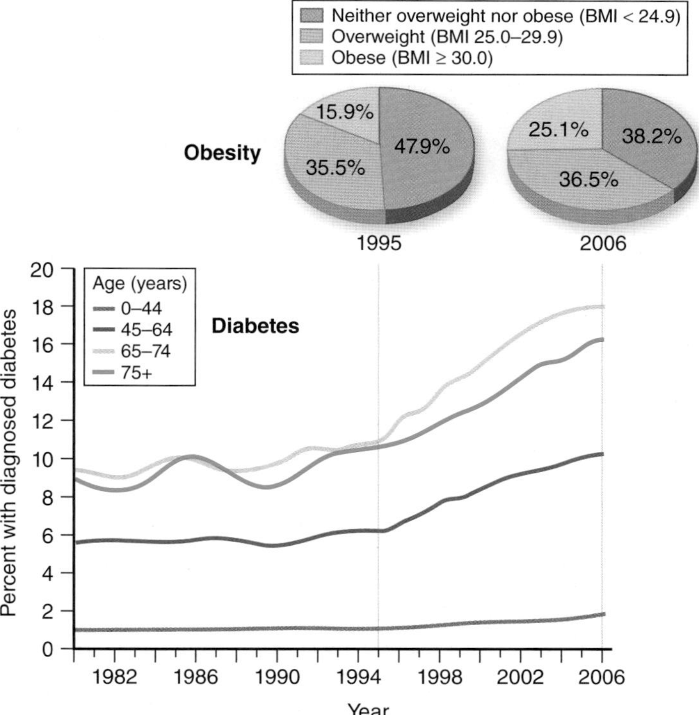

Figure 25.11 Type 2 Diabetes and Obesity. These data from the Centers for Disease Control show that the prevalence of type 2 diabetes increased along with obesity over an 11-year period.

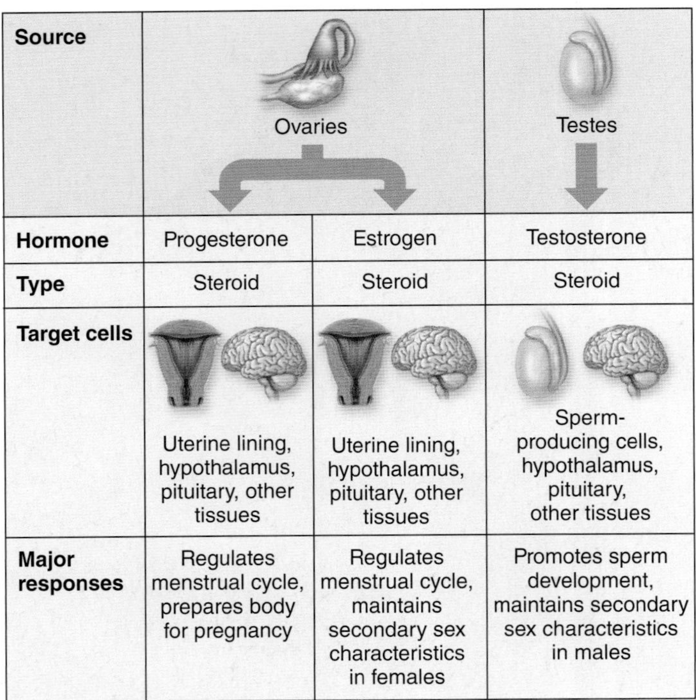

Source	Ovaries		Testes
Hormone	Progesterone	Estrogen	Testosterone
Type	Steroid	Steroid	Steroid
Target cells	Uterine lining, hypothalamus, pituitary, other tissues	Uterine lining, hypothalamus, pituitary, other tissues	Sperm-producing cells, hypothalamus, pituitary, other tissues
Major responses	Regulates menstrual cycle, prepares body for pregnancy	Regulates menstrual cycle, maintains secondary sex characteristics in females	Promotes sperm development, maintains secondary sex characteristics in males

Figure 25.12 Hormones of the Ovaries and Testes: A Summary. Hormones produced in the ovaries and testes coordinate reproduction and the development of secondary sex characteristics.

Why We Care: Anabolic Steroids in Sports

The anabolic steroids that regularly make headlines in the sporting news are synthetic forms of testosterone. Despite their notoriety, these drugs have a legitimate place in medicine. A physician might prescribe steroids for a person who produces too little testosterone, for example, or for someone with an illness that causes muscles to waste away.

Although anabolic steroids are legal only by prescription, some athletes abuse these drugs as a shortcut to greater muscle mass. Steroid users may improve strength and performance in the short term, but the drugs are harmful in the long run. In males, the body mistakes synthetic steroids for the natural hormone and lowers its own production of testosterone, causing infertility once use of the drug stops. Impotence, shrunken testicles, and the growth of breast tissue are other possible side effects. Females who abuse steroids may develop a masculine physique, a deeper voice, and facial or body hair. In adolescents, steroids hasten adulthood, stunting growth and causing early hair loss. Finally, research suggests that high doses of steroids may cause psychological side effects such as aggression, mood swings, and irritability. For all of these reasons, health professionals strongly advise against the use of illegal steroids.

A form of depression called seasonal affective disorder (SAD) may be linked to melatonin secretion that is poorly synchronized with light-dark cycles. Exposure to additional daylight (or full-spectrum light bulbs) in the morning, coupled with low doses of melatonin supplements in the afternoon, can help elevate mood by restoring the proper rhythm.

25.4 Mastering Concepts

1. What are the three hormones produced in the thyroid, and what are their functions?
2. What is the function of parathyroid hormone (PTH)?
3. How do the functions of hormones secreted by the adrenal cortex and adrenal medulla differ?
4. Describe the opposing roles of insulin and glucagon.
5. How do darkness and light affect melatonin secretion?

25.5 Hormones from the Ovaries and Testes Control Reproduction

The reproductive organs include the **ovaries** in females and the **testes** in males. These organs produce eggs and sperm, but they also secrete the steroid hormones that enable these gametes to mature (figure 25.12). In addition, hormones from the ovaries and testes promote the development of secondary sex characteristics, which are features that differentiate the sexes but do not participate directly in reproduction. This section briefly introduces the sex hormones; chapter 30 explains their role in reproduction in more detail.

In a woman of reproductive age, the levels of several sex hormones cycle approximately every 28 days. The hypothalamus produces a hormone that, in turn, stimulates the anterior pituitary to release FSH and LH into the bloodstream. At target cells in the ovary, these two hormones trigger the events that lead to ovulation. Meanwhile, the cells surrounding the egg release the sex hormones **estrogen** and **progesterone,** which exert negative feedback control on both the hypothalamus and pituitary. Estrogen also promotes development of the female secondary sex characteristics, such as breasts and wider hips, whereas progesterone helps prepare the uterus for pregnancy.

In males, FSH stimulates the early stages of sperm formation in the testes. Sperm production is completed under the influence of LH, which also prompts cells in the testes to release the sex hormone **testosterone.** This hormone stimulates the formation of male structures in the embryo and promotes later development of male secondary sex characteristics, including facial hair, deepening of the voice, and increased muscle growth (see this chapter's Why We Care box).

25.5 Mastering Concepts

1. Which organs contain target cells for FSH and LH?
2. What are the functions of estrogen, progesterone, and testosterone?

Investigating Life

25.6 Addicted to Affection

The sexual behavior of animals fascinates many people, perhaps because of what it can teach us about human relationships. In our own species, sexual attraction and feelings of love are often intertwined. Love is difficult to study in humans (and impossible to study in other animals), but scientists can examine patterns of sexual behavior in many species other than our own.

Some animals are faithful to one sexual partner for life, whereas others are much more promiscuous. One of the rarest and least understood social behaviors is monogamy. To qualify as monogamous, an animal must mate exclusively with one partner, live with its mate, help with care of the young, and defend the family against intruders. Only a tiny fraction (about 3%) of mammal species are monogamous.

Figure 25.13 **Prairie Vole.** These small rodents live in underground colonies. They are highly social and typically monogamous, so biologists study them to learn more about the genetic basis of sexual fidelity.

The Question: Two closely related species of snub-nosed rodents have given scientists the opportunity to investigate the biological basis of monogamy. Whereas prairie voles such as the one in figure 25.13 are monogamous and highly social, montane voles are promiscuous and solitary. What accounts for the difference in lifestyle? Antidiuretic hormone (ADH) apparently plays a role. In the 1990s, researchers learned that if male prairie voles were given

Burning Questions

Are plastics dangerous?

Many scientists and health professionals are concerned that some plastics—such as the baby bottle in the chapter opening photo—release harmful chemicals that may alter human development. Much of the controversy over plastics centers on a chemical called bisphenol A (BPA). Manufacturers use BPA to make shatterproof polycarbonate bottles, the linings of food cans, the sealants used in dentistry, and many other items. BPA is so common that everyone on Earth has this chemical in his or her tissues. Not only does BPA accumulate over a person's lifetime, but it can also pass from mother to fetus.

Why the concern over BPA? Research shows that at low doses, BPA acts as an endocrine-disrupting chemical. An endocrine disruptor is any substance that alters hormonal signaling, often by mimicking a natural hormone. BPA, for example, replicates the effect of the sex hormone estrogen. Other endocrine disruptors block the action of hormones, and still others stimulate or inhibit the activity of the glands that produce the hormones in the first place.

Low doses of BPA are associated with reproductive problems and developmental abnormalities in laboratory animals. But do these results apply to people? Possibly, but it's hard to say for sure. Testing for long-term effects of endocrine disruptors in humans is extremely difficult. Besides the ethical issues surrounding human experimentation, other complicating factors include the impossibility of finding BPA-free control subjects, the many stages of development at which endocrine disruptors can act, developmental differences between the sexes, and potential interactions between BPA and other endocrine disruptors.

If the problem were limited to BPA, the simple solution would be to ban this chemical and move on. But BPA is just one straw in a massive haystack. Every day, humans release thousands of pesticides, cosmetics, medications, and other products into the air, soil, and water. The environment therefore teems with chemicals that are known or potential endocrine disruptors. They are in our food and in the fatty tissues of our bodies. Determining which are harmful, in what quantities, and at which stages of life is an enormous scientific challenge. Evidence is accumulating, however, that endocrine disruptors have altered the development and reproduction of wild animals including snails, fishes, frogs, alligators, and polar bears. These widespread effects suggest that endocrine disruptors may affect humans as well.

Submit your burning question to:
marielle_hoefnagels@mcgraw-hill.com

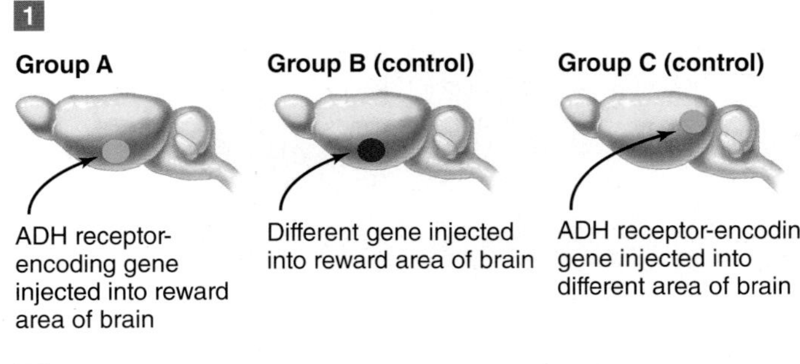

2 Each male spends 17 hours in cage with non-sexually receptive female

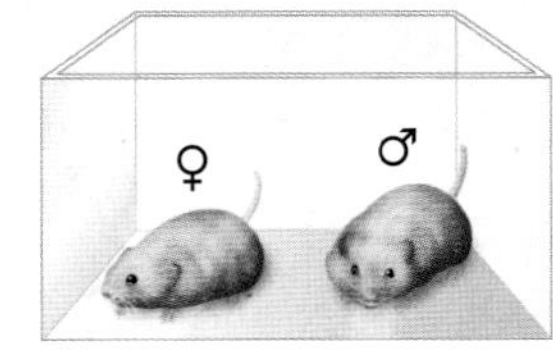

3 In a 3-hour partner-preference test, the male can choose to spend time with his "partner" or a stranger

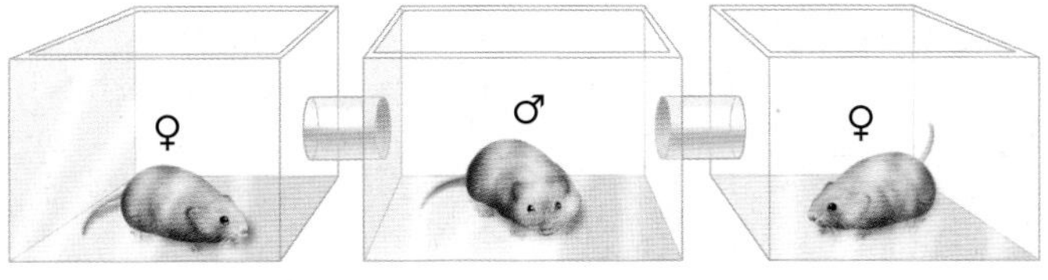

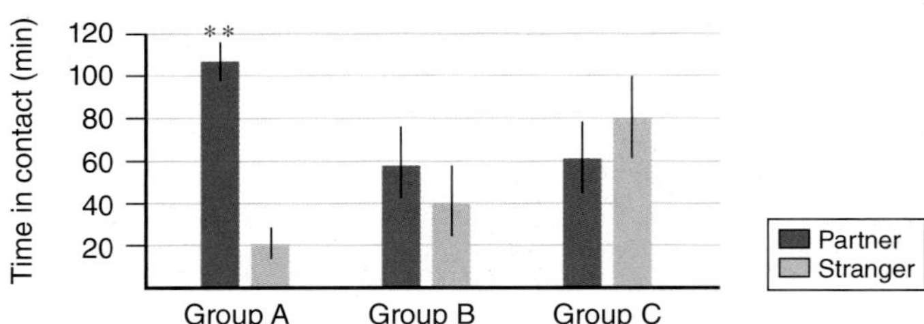

Figure 25.14 More Receptors, More Bonding. Prairie voles injected with ADH receptor genes in the reward center of the brain spent significantly more time with a female partner than with a stranger. Control voles were less likely to bond with their partners. (Asterisks indicate a statistically significant difference within a group.)

ADH, they rapidly formed social attachments, even with females they had not mated with. When ADH's effects were blocked, pair bonds did not form.

One logical explanation for the difference in sexual behavior between the two species is that the monogamous prairie voles have naturally higher levels of ADH than do the promiscuous montane voles. Yet this is not the case; both vole species have similar levels of the pair-bonding hormone. The location of receptors for ADH in the brain, however, does differ between the two species. In monogamous prairie voles, ADH receptors occur in the same brain region where addictive drugs act, and males seem to derive feelings of reward from being with their mates and young. In contrast, ADH receptors in promiscuous montane voles are located in brain regions associated with aggression.

A team of researchers, led by Lauren Pitkow and Larry Young from Emory University in Atlanta, wondered what would happen to prairie voles with extra ADH receptors in the brain areas associated with pleasure and rewards. Would the animals form social attachments even more readily?

The Approach: To find out, the researchers inserted the gene encoding the ADH receptor into a virus. They injected the modified virus into the reward areas of the brains of prairie voles, effectively increasing the number of ADH receptors (figure 25.14, step 1). Two groups of control voles also received injections. One control group received a different gene (one not related to ADH) in the reward area of the brain. Voles in the second control group received the ADH receptor gene but in a different brain area.

Afterward, each male spent 17 hours in a cage with an adult female that was not sexually receptive (figure 25.14, step 2). The voles then underwent "partner-preference" tests (figure 25.14, step 3). The researchers placed each male into a choice chamber, where he was free to spend as much time as he wanted with his female "partner" or with a different female who was a stranger to him. Male prairie voles do not ordinarily pair-bond with females after less than 24 hours together, unless they have mated. Nevertheless, the voles with the extra ADH receptors in the reward region of the brain spent much more time in contact with their partners than did either group of control voles (see the graph at the bottom of figure 25.14).

The Conclusion: The extra ADH receptors evidently made the male prairie voles especially likely to form pair bonds. Of course, it is important to remember that the evolution of complex mating behaviors required more than just one change in the brain chemistry of the vole. Nevertheless, this study is interesting because it explicitly links genes, brain chemistry, and social behavior.

This research also raises the startling possibility that a genetically modified virus can transmit genes that increase social attachment, at least in prairie voles. Could such a "love bug" infect humans, too? Researchers already know that the location of ADH receptors in the brain may play a role in human social behaviors; examples include not only sexual fidelity but also autism, a disorder in which individuals have difficulty forming social attachments. Researchers now are investigating primate ADH receptors to learn more about the biochemistry of attachment in our closest relatives.

25.6 Mastering Concepts

1. How did the researchers test the hypothesis that the number of ADH receptors in the brain's reward area influences pair-bonding?
2. Could the researchers have drawn the same conclusions if they had omitted one of the control groups? Why or why not?

Chapter Summary

25.1 The Endocrine System Uses Hormones to Communicate

- The **nervous system** and **endocrine system** specialize in the intercellular communication needed to maintain homeostasis in an animal body.
- The nervous system acts faster and more locally than the endocrine system.
- The endocrine system includes several **endocrine glands** and scattered cells, plus the **hormones** they secrete into the bloodstream. Hormones interact with **target cells** to exert their effects.

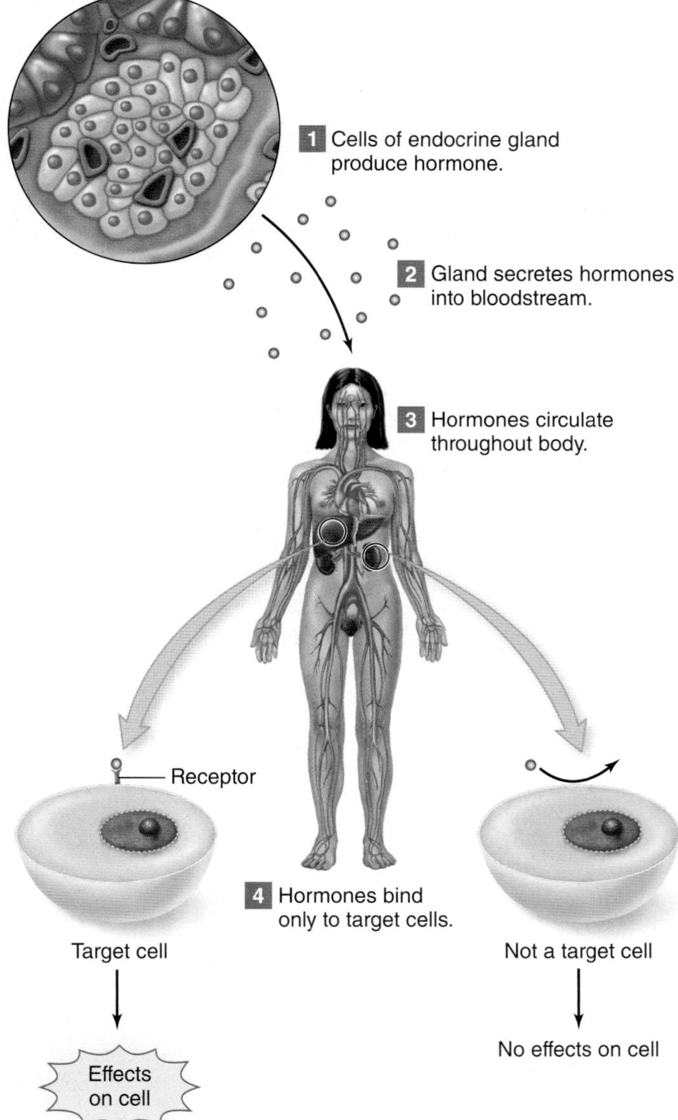
1 Cells of endocrine gland produce hormone.
2 Gland secretes hormones into bloodstream.
3 Hormones circulate throughout body.
Receptor
4 Hormones bind only to target cells.
Target cell
Not a target cell
Effects on cell
No effects on cell

25.2 Hormones Stimulate Responses in Target Cells

A. Water-Soluble Hormones Trigger Second Messenger Systems

- Water-soluble hormones such as peptides and proteins bind to the surface receptors of target cells. A **second messenger** triggers the hormone's metabolic effect.
- Water-soluble hormones act relatively rapidly.

B. Lipid-Soluble Hormones Directly Alter Gene Expression

- Most lipid-soluble **steroid hormones** cross target cell membranes and bind to receptors in the cytoplasm or nucleus. Ultimately, they activate genes that direct the synthesis of proteins, which provide the cell's response.
- Because protein production takes time, lipid-soluble hormones act relatively slowly.

25.3 The Hypothalamus and Pituitary Gland Oversee Endocrine Control

- Neurons from the **hypothalamus** influence the release of hormones from the **posterior pituitary** and **anterior pituitary** gland. These hormones influence many other processes in the body.

A. The Posterior Pituitary Stores and Releases Two Hormones

- The hypothalamus manufactures two hormones that are stored in and released from the posterior pituitary. **Antidiuretic hormone (ADH)** regulates body fluid composition, and **oxytocin** stimulates the contraction of muscles in the uterus and milk ducts.

B. The Anterior Pituitary Produces and Secretes Six Hormones

- Hormones from the hypothalamus regulate the production and release of hormones from the anterior pituitary.
- **Growth hormone (GH)** stimulates cell division, protein synthesis, and growth throughout the body.
- **Prolactin** stimulates milk production.
- **Thyroid-stimulating hormone (TSH)** prompts the thyroid gland to release hormones.
- **Adrenocorticotropic hormone (ACTH)** stimulates the adrenal cortex to release hormones.
- **Follicle-stimulating hormone (FSH)** and **luteinizing hormone (LH)** stimulate hormone release from the ovaries and testes.
- **Endorphins** are painkillers with target cells in the brain. Their status as a hormone is questionable.

25.4 Hormones from Many Glands Regulate Metabolism

A. The Thyroid Gland Sets the Metabolic Pace

- **Thyroxine** and **triiodothyronine** from the **thyroid gland** speed metabolism. The thyroid also releases **calcitonin,** which lowers the level of calcium in the blood.

B. The Parathyroid Glands Control Calcium Level

- The **parathyroid glands** secrete **parathyroid hormone (PTH),** which increases blood calcium level by releasing calcium from bone and increasing its absorption in the intestines and kidneys.

C. The Adrenal Glands Coordinate the Body's Stress Responses

- The inner portion of each **adrenal gland,** the **adrenal medulla,** secretes **epinephrine** and **norepinephrine.** These hormones ready the body to cope with a short-term emergency. The **adrenal cortex** secretes **mineralocorticoids** and **glucocorticoids,** which mobilize energy reserves during stress and maintain blood volume and blood composition.

D. The Pancreas Regulates Nutrient Use

- Cells in the **pancreas** secrete **insulin,** which stimulates cells to take up glucose. **Glucagon** increases blood glucose levels.
- In the most common types of **diabetes,** blood sugar concentrations rise to dangerous levels. Type 1 diabetes occurs when the pancreas fails to produce insulin; in type 2 diabetes, the body's cells do not respond to insulin. Type 2 diabetes is associated with obesity.
- **Hypoglycemia** is low blood sugar.

E. The Pineal Gland Secretes Melatonin

- The **pineal gland** secretes a hormone, **melatonin,** that may regulate the responses of other glands to light–dark cycles.

25.5 Hormones from the Ovaries and Testes Control Reproduction

- In females, FSH and LH stimulate the **ovaries** to secrete **estrogen** and **progesterone,** hormones that stimulate the development of female secondary sex characteristics and control the menstrual cycle.
- In males, FSH and LH stimulate the **testes** to secrete **testosterone,** which stimulates sperm cell production and the development of secondary sex characteristics.

25.6 Investigating Life: Addicted to Affection

- Monogamy is unusual among animals, but the prairie vole forms a monogamous bond with its mate. Researchers have traced pair-bonding behavior to a receptor that binds ADH in the pleasure-seeking area of the vole's brain.
- Increasing the number of ADH receptors made male voles more likely to bond with a female partner.

Multiple Choice Questions

1. Which of the following statements correctly describes a difference between the endocrine and nervous systems?
   a. The nervous system uses hormones; the endocrine system uses neurotransmitters.
   b. Only the endocrine system uses chemicals to send signals between cells.
   c. Nervous signals typically act more rapidly than endocrine signals.
   d. An endocrine signal typically affects fewer cells than a nervous signal.
2. What is a second messenger?
   a. A hormone produced only in adults
   b. A hormone that binds to the cell's exterior
   c. A molecule that initiates a hormone's effects
   d. A molecule participating in a negative feedback loop
3. The effect of a water-soluble peptide hormone such as insulin is generally quicker than that of a steroid hormone such as estrogen because
   a. peptide hormones exert changes using molecules already present in the target cell.
   b. steroid hormones trigger the synthesis of new proteins.
   c. steroid hormones cannot pass through the cell's plasma membrane.
   d. Both a and b are correct.
4. Which of the following is NOT a hormone produced in the anterior pituitary?
   a. Epinephrine
   b. Thyroid-stimulating hormone
   c. Adrenocorticotropic hormone
   d. Growth hormone
5. Treatment for high blood pressure often involves the use of medication that alters blood volume. Which of the following treatments would decrease a person's blood volume?
   a. Increase in release of thyroid-stimulating hormone
   b. Inhibition of follicle-stimulating hormone
   c. Activation of prolactin synthesis
   d. Inhibition of antidiuretic hormone
6. Besides thyroxine, the thyroid gland also produces
   a. parathyroid hormone.
   b. thyrotropin-releasing hormone.
   c. calcitonin.
   d. juvenile hormone.
7. Glucocorticoids are secreted by the
   a. thyroid. c. adrenal glands.
   b. pancreas. d. pineal gland.
8. Would an insulin injection help a person with type 2 diabetes?
   a. Yes, because the pancreas is not producing insulin.
   b. No, because the target cells do not respond to insulin.
   c. Yes, because the extra insulin will help with glucose uptake.
   d. No, because the extra insulin will trigger excess release of glucagon.
9. Secretion of melatonin is regulated by
   a. light. c. stress.
   b. temperature. d. glucose.
10. If researchers develop a new drug that blocks testosterone receptors, a likely effect is a(n)
    a. increase in body hair.
    b. reduction in testosterone production.
    c. reduction in sperm production.
    d. Both a and c are correct.

Write It Out

1. How does the endocrine system interact with the circulatory system?
2. A queen honeybee secretes a substance from a gland in her mouthparts that inhibits the development of ovaries in worker bees. Is this substance most likely a hormone, a neurotransmitter, or a pheromone (see chapter 24)? Cite a reason for your answer.
3. What prevents a hormone from affecting all body cells equally?
4. Many dairy operators inject their cows with bovine growth hormone to stimulate milk production. Cite two reasons that bovine growth hormone might not stimulate growth in people drinking the milk.
5. How do hormones regulate their own levels?
6. Compare and contrast the endocrine and nervous systems.
7. Sketch the mechanisms of water-soluble and lipid-soluble hormone function.
8. List the hormones released from the posterior pituitary and the anterior pituitary.
9. How are the pituitary and adrenal glands each really two glands in one?
10. Which hormone(s) match each of the following descriptions?
    a. Produced by a woman who is breast feeding
    b. Causes fatigue if too little is present
    c. Causes increase in blood calcium level
    d. Causes decrease in blood glucose level
    e. Synthetic steroids mimic the muscle-building effects of this hormone.
11. Describe how thyroxine, triiodothyronine, TSH, and TRH interact.
12. Ancient Egyptian doctors treated goiters with seaweed, not realizing that it was the iodine in the seaweed that was reversing the condition. Why would iodine help cure a goiter?
13. Why would a physician counsel a patient with high blood pressure to try to reduce the amount of stress in his or her life?
14. Sleep deprivation increases cortisol concentrations in the blood. Why would sleep deprivation be associated with increased risk of illness?
15. Consult chapter 24 and this chapter to create a chart comparing hormones with neurotransmitters. Include the distance over which each is active, the connection between the cell releasing signals and the receiving cell, the response speed, and the duration of the response.

16. In healthy adults, the concentration of glucose in blood is 80 to 110 milligrams per deciliter (mg/dl). After a carbohydrate-rich meal, however, the concentration may spike to 140 mg/dl.
    a. Describe the hormonal action that returns blood glucose to normal.
    b. What is the name of the condition in which the glucose concentration drops below 70 mg/dl?
    c. What is the name for the condition in which the glucose concentration before a meal is 130 mg/dl or higher?
17. Search the Internet for a diabetes risk test. What actions can you take to reduce your risk of type 2 diabetes?
18. How might insulin-producing stem cells transplanted to the pancreas help people with type 1 diabetes? Would the same treatment help people with type 2 diabetes?
19. Identify the target cells and effects of FSH, LH, estrogen, progesterone, and testosterone.
20. An endocrine disruptor is a molecule that either mimics or blocks the activity of a hormone. Propose a way to test the hypothesis that:
    a. a pesticide such as atrazine is an endocrine disruptor.
    b. endocrine disruptors have caused declines in human sperm counts.
    c. microwaving foods in plastic containers releases chemicals that act as endocrine disruptors.

Pull It Together

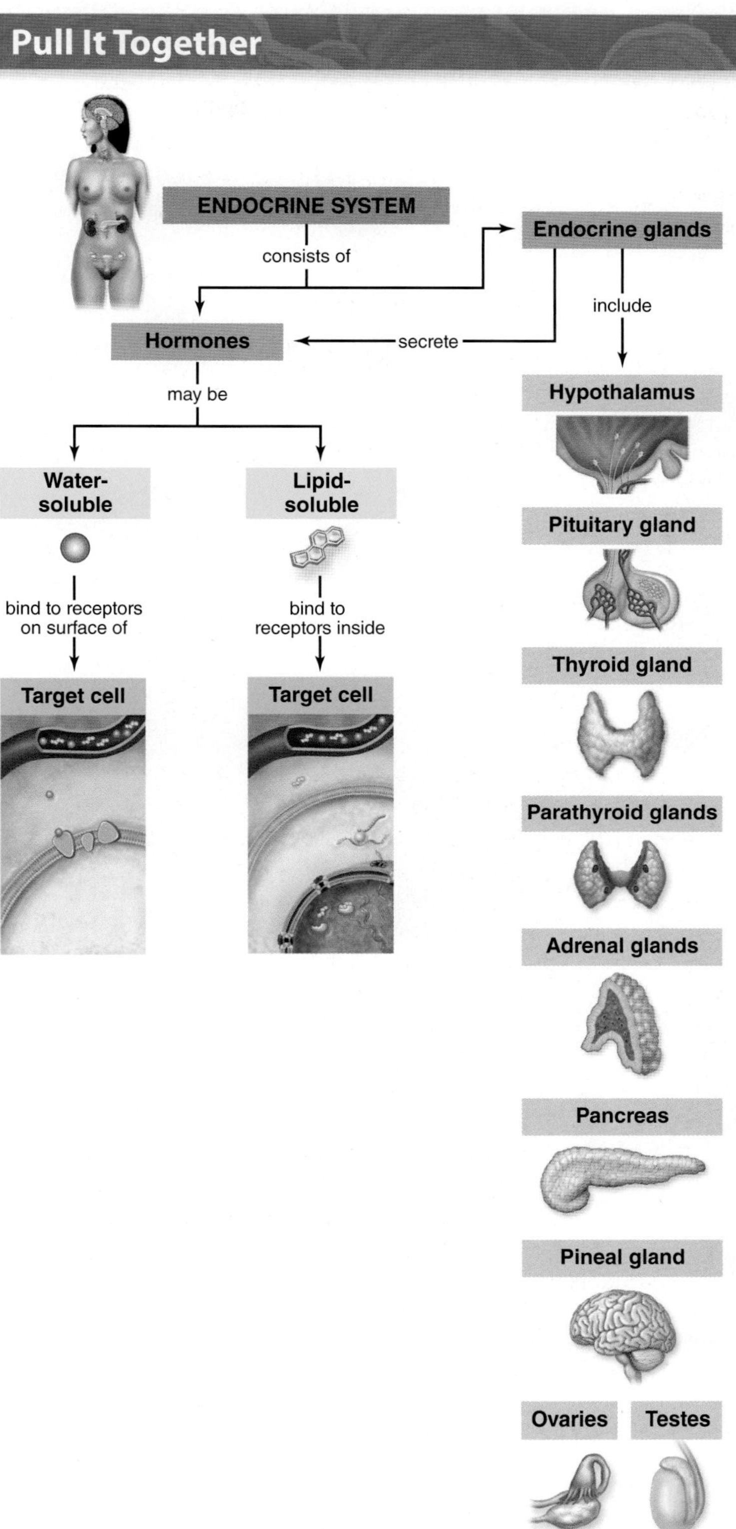

1. Describe a negative feedback loop that controls hormone secretion.
2. What brain structure connects the endocrine and nervous systems?
3. Describe the relationships among the hypothalamus, pituitary, and other endocrine glands.

26 The Skeletal and Muscular Systems

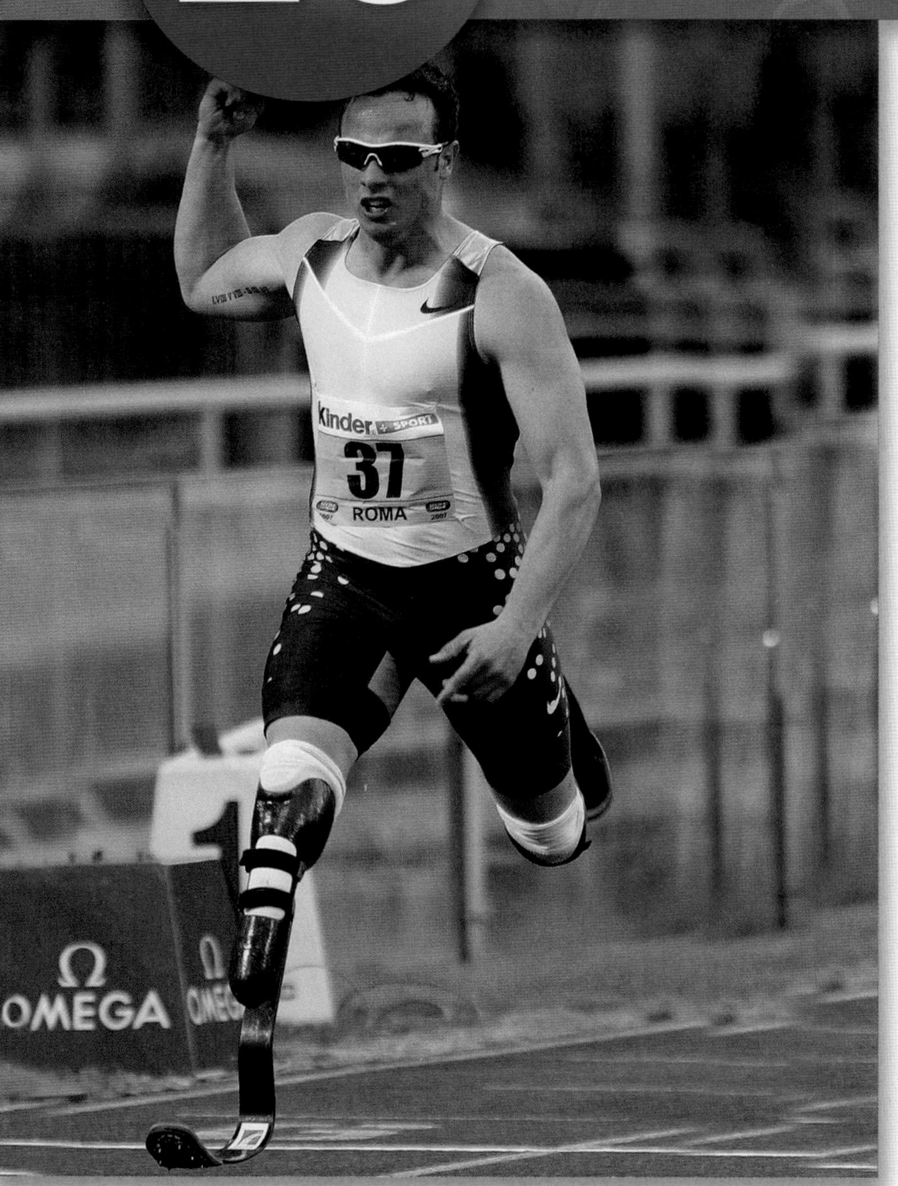

Runner. This athlete's lower legs have been replaced by prosthetics. His artificial limbs take over some of the functions of the missing bones and muscles.

Learning Outline

26.1 Skeletons Take Many Forms

26.2 The Vertebrate Skeleton Features a Central Backbone

26.3 Bones Provide Support, Protect Internal Organs, and Supply Calcium

- A. Bones Consist Mostly of Bone Tissue and Cartilage
- B. Bone Meets Bone at a Joint
- C. Bones Are Constantly Built and Degraded
- D. Bones Help Regulate Calcium Homeostasis

26.4 Muscle Movement Requires Contractile Proteins and ATP

- A. Actin and Myosin Filaments Fill Muscle Cells
- B. Sliding Filaments Are the Basis of Muscle Fiber Contraction
- C. Motor Neurons Stimulate Muscle Contraction

26.5 Muscle Fibers Generate ATP in Multiple Ways

26.6 Muscle Fiber Types Influence Athletic Performance

26.7 Investigating Life: Did a Myosin Gene Mutation Make Humans Brainier?

Learn How to Learn

Study as You Go

Last-minute cramming for exams may be a classic college ritual, but it is not usually the best strategy. If you try to memorize everything right before an exam, you may become overwhelmed and find yourself distracted by worries that you'll never learn it all. Instead, work on learning the material as the course goes along. Then, on the night before the exam, get plenty of rest, and don't forget to eat on exam day. If you are too tired or too hungry to think, you won't be able to give the exam your best shot.

What's the Point?

From Halloween skeletons to a body builder's exaggerated brawn, bones and muscles are familiar parts of an animal's body. What many people do not realize, however, is that skeletons and muscles are intimately related. As you will learn in this chapter, most muscles attach to the ends of bones. Hundreds of finely controlled muscle movements produce the range of motion possible in the human body. The nervous system coordinates the action.

The intricate relationships among nerves, bones, and muscles make it all the more amazing that surgeons can replace a missing limb or a damaged joint with a functional, if not a biological, alternative. The runner pictured on the facing page has artificial legs, and the photo above shows a replacement knee joint. These high-tech materials integrate with a patient's own flesh and bone, restoring mobility. This astonishing feat begins with a basic understanding of the skeletal and muscular systems.

26.1 Skeletons Take Many Forms

Ask a child what sets animals apart from other organisms, and he or she will likely answer "movement." This response is technically wrong—many bacteria, archaea, protists, fungi, and plants have swimming, creeping, or gliding cells. Yet the child correctly recognizes that animal movements are unmatched in their drama, versatility, and power.

The ability to hop, dig, fly, slither, scuttle, or swim comes from two closely allied, interacting organ systems: the **muscular system** and the **skeletal system,** which together function under the direction of the nervous system. In most animals, organs called **muscles** provide motion; the **skeleton** adds a firm supporting structure that muscles pull against. The skeleton also gives an animal's body shape and protects internal organs.

Figure 26.1 shows three types of skeletons. The simplest is a **hydrostatic skeleton** (*hydro-* means water), which consists of fluid constrained within a layer of flexible tissue. Many of the invertebrate animals described in chapter 17 have hydrostatic skeletons. The bell of a jellyfish, for example, consists mostly of a gelatinous substance constrained between two tissue layers. To swim, the animal rhythmically contracts the muscles acting on this hydrostatic skeleton, forcibly ejecting water from its body. Snails, squids, flatworms, earthworms, and nematodes also use hydrostatic skeletons in locomotion.

The most common type of skeleton is an **exoskeleton,** which acts as a "suit of armor" that protects the animal from the outside (*exo-* means outside). Internal muscles pull against the exoskeleton, enabling the animal to move. Animals with exoskeletons include arthropods such as crabs, lobsters, and insects. Mollusks, including clams and snails, also produce exoskeletons.

a.

b.

c.

Figure 26.1 Types of Skeletons. (a) Hydrostatic skeleton. (b) Exoskeleton. (c) Endoskeleton.

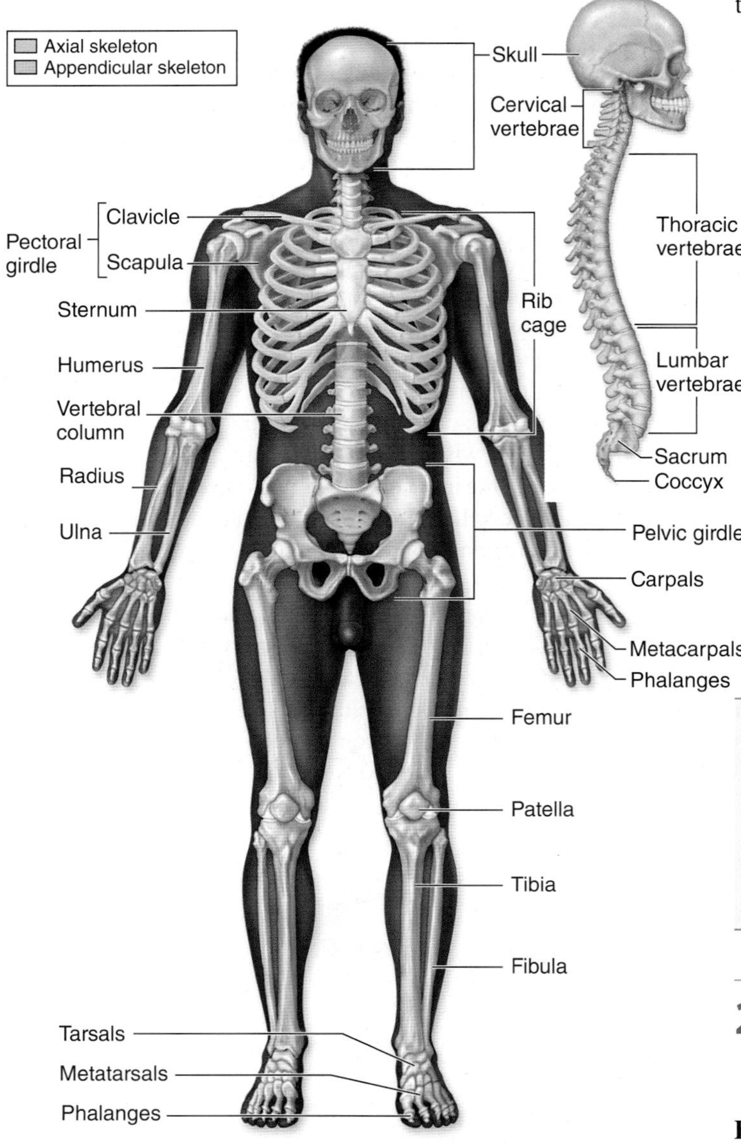

Skeletal System	
Main tissue types*	**Examples of locations/functions**
Connective	Makes up bone, cartilage, tendons, ligaments, marrow of vertebrate skeleton
Muscle	Skeletal muscle connects to movable bones, enabling voluntary movements
Nervous	Senses body position and controls muscles

*See chapter 23 for descriptions.

Figure 26.2 The Human Skeleton. The axial skeleton in humans includes bones in the head, vertebral column, and rib cage. The bones that compose and support the limbs constitute the appendicular skeleton.

Exoskeletons have advantages and disadvantages. The hard covering protects soft internal organs and provides excellent leverage for muscles. On the other hand, a growing arthropod must periodically molt; until its new skeleton has hardened, the animal's soft body is vulnerable to predators.

An **endoskeleton** is an internal support structure (*endo-* means inner). Sea stars and other echinoderms, for example, produce rigid, calcium-rich spines and internal plates. Vertebrate animals have endoskeletons made of cartilage or bone. Sharks and stingrays, for example, produce cartilage skeletons. Other fishes, and all land vertebrates, have skeletons composed primarily of bone.

Like exoskeletons, endoskeletons represent an evolutionary tradeoff. On the plus side, an internal skeleton grows with the animal, avoiding the problems associated with molting. Also, an endoskeleton makes up less of an organism's total body mass, so it can support the weight of animals as large as a whale. One disadvantage, however, is that the endoskeleton does not protect soft tissues at the body surface.

The vertebrate skeleton's capacity to change over evolutionary time is striking. Each vertebrate species has a distinctive skeleton, yet all are composed of the same types of cells and have similar arrangements. The characteristics of each species' muscles and skeleton reflect common ancestry and the selective forces in its environment. ▸▸ natural selection, p. 222; homologous structures, p. 249

26.1 Mastering Concepts

1. How do the skeletal and muscular systems interact?
2. Describe similarities and differences among the three main types of skeletons.
3. How do vertebrate skeletons reveal common ancestry?

26.2 The Vertebrate Skeleton Features a Central Backbone

Bones, the organs that compose the vertebrate skeleton, are grouped into two categories (figure 26.2). The **axial skeleton,** so named because it is located along the central axis of the body, consists of the bones in the head, vertebral column, and rib cage. The **appendicular skeleton** consists of the appendages (the limbs) and the bones that support them.

The axial skeleton shields soft body parts. The skull, which protects the brain and many of the sense organs, consists of hard, dense bones that fit together like puzzle pieces. All of the head bones are connected with immovable joints, except for the lower jaw and the middle ear. These movable jaw and ear bones enable us to chew food, speak, and hear. ▸ sense of hearing, p. 502

The **vertebral column** supports and protects the spinal cord. A human vertebral column consists of 33 vertebrae, separated by cartilage disks that cushion shocks and enhance flexibility. A "slipped," or herniated, disk occurs when these pads tear or rupture, causing a bulge that presses painfully on a nearby nerve. Scoliosis, in which the vertebral column curves to the side, is also a disorder of the axial skeleton (figure 26.3).

Attached to the human vertebral column are 12 pairs of ribs, which protect the heart and lungs. Flexible cartilage between the ribs and other bones allows muscles to elevate the ribs, a movement that is important in breathing.

In the appendicular skeleton, the **pectoral girdle** connects the forelimbs to the axial skeleton; it includes the collarbones (clavicles) and shoulder blades (scapulas). Likewise, the **pelvic girdle** attaches the hind limb bones to the axial skeleton. The hipbones join the spine in the rear and meet each other in front, creating a bowl-like pelvic cavity. (The term *pelvis* is Latin for "basin.") The bony pelvis protects the lower digestive organs, the bladder, and some reproductive structures (especially in the female).

This chapter's Why We Care box illustrates how skeletal features reveal clues that are useful to people in several professions.

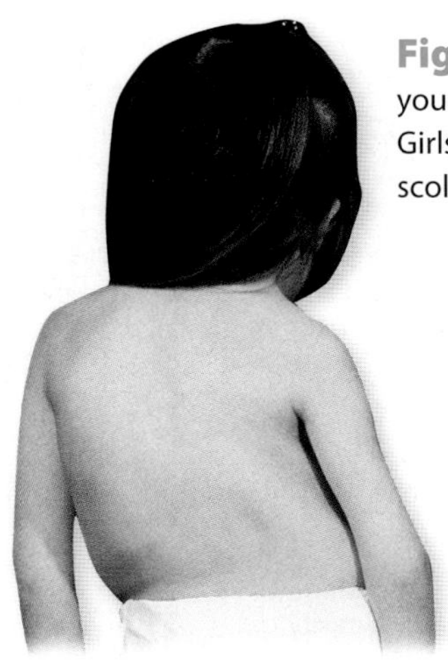

Figure 26.3 Scoliosis. This young girl's spine curves to the side. Girls are more often affected with scoliosis than boys.

26.2 Mastering Concepts

1. What are the two subdivisions of the human skeleton?
2. What are the locations of the pectoral and pelvic girdles?

26.3 Bones Provide Support, Protect Internal Organs, and Supply Calcium

The skeleton not only supports and protects the body, but it also has several other functions that may at first glance seem unrelated to one another (table 26.1). Bones connected to muscles provide movement, and bone minerals supply calcium and phosphorus to the rest of the body. Blood cells also form in the marrow inside bones.

TABLE 26.1 Functions of the Vertebrate Endoskeleton: A Summary

Function	Explanation
Support	The skeleton supports an animal's body against gravity. It largely provides the body's shape.
Movement	The vertebrate skeleton is a system of muscle-operated levers. Typically, the two ends of a skeletal (voluntary) muscle attach to different bones that connect in a structure called a joint. When the muscle contracts, one bone is pulled toward the other.
Protection of internal structures	The backbone surrounds and shields the spinal cord, the skull protects the brain, and ribs protect the heart and lungs.
Production of blood cells	Many long bones contain and protect red marrow, a tissue that produces red blood cells, white blood cells, and platelets.
Mineral storage	The skeleton stores calcium and phosphorus.

A. Bones Consist Mostly of Bone Tissue and Cartilage

A glance back at figure 26.2 reveals that bones take many shapes. Long bones make up the arms and legs, whereas the wrists and ankles consist mainly of short bones. Flat bones include the ribs and skull. Vertebrae are irregularly shaped.

Why We Care | Bony Evidence of Murder, Illness, and Evolution

Skeletons sometimes provide useful clues to past events. Hard, mineral-rich bones and teeth remain intact long after a corpse's soft body parts decay. Clues from these durable remains can help solve crimes, lend insight into human history, and shed light on evolution.

Detectives can use bones to identify the sex of a decomposed murder victim. This technique relies on the differences between male and female skeletons. Most obviously, the average male is larger than the average female. In addition, the front of the female pelvis is broader and larger than the male's, and it has a wider bottom opening that accommodates the birth of a baby. These same features allow anthropologists to determine the sex of ancient human fossils.

Bones can also reveal events and illnesses unique to each person's life. Healed breaks may indicate accidents or abuse. Egypt's King Tut, for example, suffered a severe leg break shortly before he died. Crooked joints, such as those in the hand shown in the photo, may be evidence of arthritis, and patterns of bone thickenings tell whether a person spent his or her life in hard physical labor.

The shapes and sizes of fossilized bones also reveal some of the details of human evolution. Section 17.12 explains how the skeletons and teeth of primate fossils provide clues to brain size, diet, and posture in our ancestors. Animal skeletons also tell the larger story of vertebrate evolution. For example, paleontologists can examine skeletal features to determine whether an extinct animal was terrestrial or aquatic. Air is much less supportive than water, so land-dwellers tend to have sturdier skeletons than their aquatic relatives.

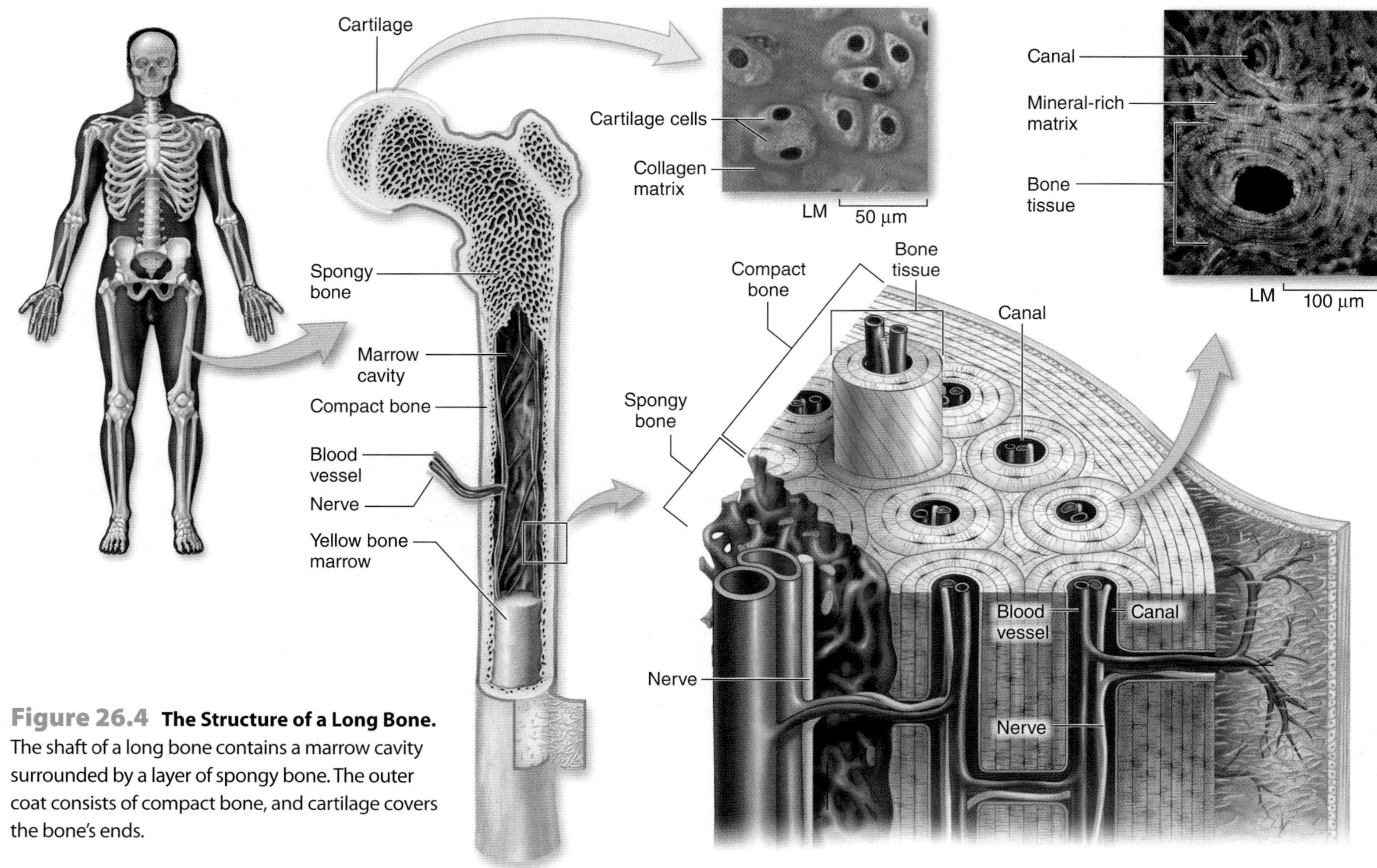

Figure 26.4 The Structure of a Long Bone. The shaft of a long bone contains a marrow cavity surrounded by a layer of spongy bone. The outer coat consists of compact bone, and cartilage covers the bone's ends.

No matter what their shape, bones are lightweight and strong because they are porous, not solid (figure 26.4). The weight of long bones is further reduced by the **marrow cavity,** a space in the shaft that contains the soft, spongy, red or yellow marrow. **Red bone marrow** is a nursery for blood cells and platelets; in adults, fatty **yellow bone marrow** replaces the red marrow in the cavities of limb bones. Yellow marrow does not produce blood, but if the body faces a severe shortage of blood cells, yellow marrow can revert to red marrow.

Besides marrow, bones also contain nerves and blood vessels. But the majority of the vertebrate skeleton consists of two types of connective tissue: bone and cartilage. Figure 26.4 offers a closer look at both of these tissues. ▸ connective tissue, p. 469

Bone tissue consists of specialized cells suspended in a hard extracellular matrix. Some bone cells secrete the matrix, which consists of collagen and minerals. Collagen is a protein that gives the bone flexibility, elasticity, and strength. The hardness and rigidity of bone comes from the minerals, primarily calcium and phosphate, that coat the collagen fibers. Other bone cells degrade the matrix at the bone surface, releasing calcium and phosphorus into the blood as needed to maintain homeostasis.

Bones include both compact and spongy bone tissue. **Compact bone** is hard and dense, with canals that house blood vessels and nervous tissue. **Spongy bone** is much lighter than compact bone, thanks to large spaces filled with red marrow. The shaft of a long bone consists mostly of compact bone overlying a layer of spongy bone. The bulbous tips also contain spongy bone.

Besides bone, cartilage is the other main connective tissue in the skeleton (see figure 26.4). This rubbery material, which covers the ends of bones, consists mostly of tough, elastic proteins. Cartilage therefore resists breakage and stretching, even when bearing great weight. Moreover, the protein network in cartilage holds a great deal of water, making it an excellent shock absorber. But cartilage lacks a blood supply. As the body moves, water within cartilage cleanses the tissue and bathes it with dissolved nutrients from nearby blood vessels. Nevertheless, the absence of a dedicated blood supply means that injured cartilage is slow to heal.

B. Bone Meets Bone at a Joint

A **joint** is an area where two bones meet. Many joints are freely movable, such as those of the knees, hips, elbows, fingers, and toes (figure 26.5). These joints consist of movable bones joined by a fluid-filled capsule of fibrous connective tissue. Together, the lubricating fluid and slippery cartilage allow bones to move against each other in a nearly friction-free environment.

Tendons and ligaments help stabilize movable joints. **Tendons** are tough bands of connective tissue that attach bone to muscle; **ligaments** are similar structures that attach bone to bone. A strain is an injury to a muscle or tendon, whereas a sprain is a stretched or torn ligament. A torn anterior cruciate ligament (ACL) is a common type of knee sprain, especially in sports such as basketball and volleyball. The ACL is one of two ligaments that criss-cross at the knee, connecting the thighbone to the shinbone. Surgical reconstruction of the ACL enables many injured athletes to return to their sports.

Arthritis is a common disorder of joints. A very severe form, rheumatoid arthritis, is an inflammation of the joint membranes, usually in the hands and feet. In the more common osteoarthritis, joint cartilage wears away. As the bone is exposed, small bumps of new bone begin to form, and the joints become stiff and painful. Osteoarthritis usually appears after age 40.

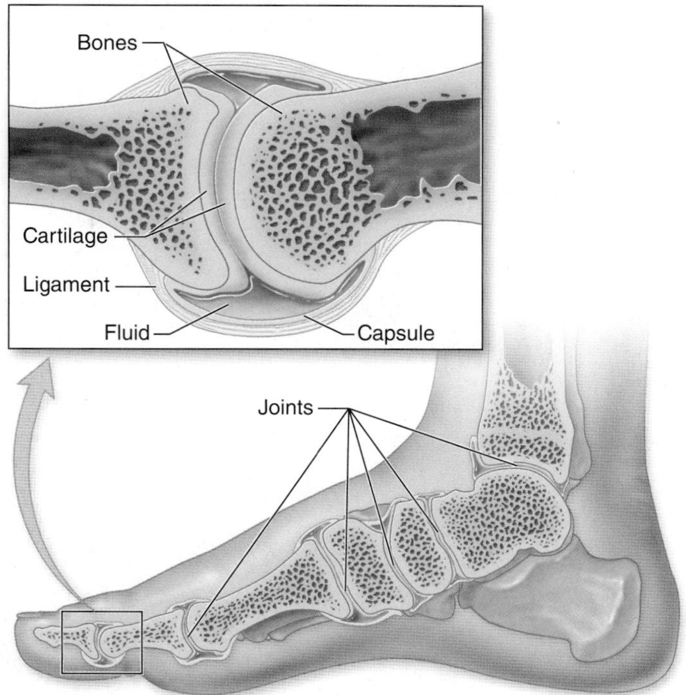

Figure 26.5 Movable Joint. A fluid-filled capsule of fibrous connective tissue surrounds a movable joint in the big toe. The lower illustration also shows other joints in the foot and ankle.

C. Bones Are Constantly Built and Degraded

The bones of a developing embryo originate as cartilage "models" (figure 26.6). As the fetus grows, each model's matrix hardens with calcium salts. After birth, bone growth becomes concentrated near the ends of the long bones in thin disks of cartilage called "growth plates." The bones continue to elongate

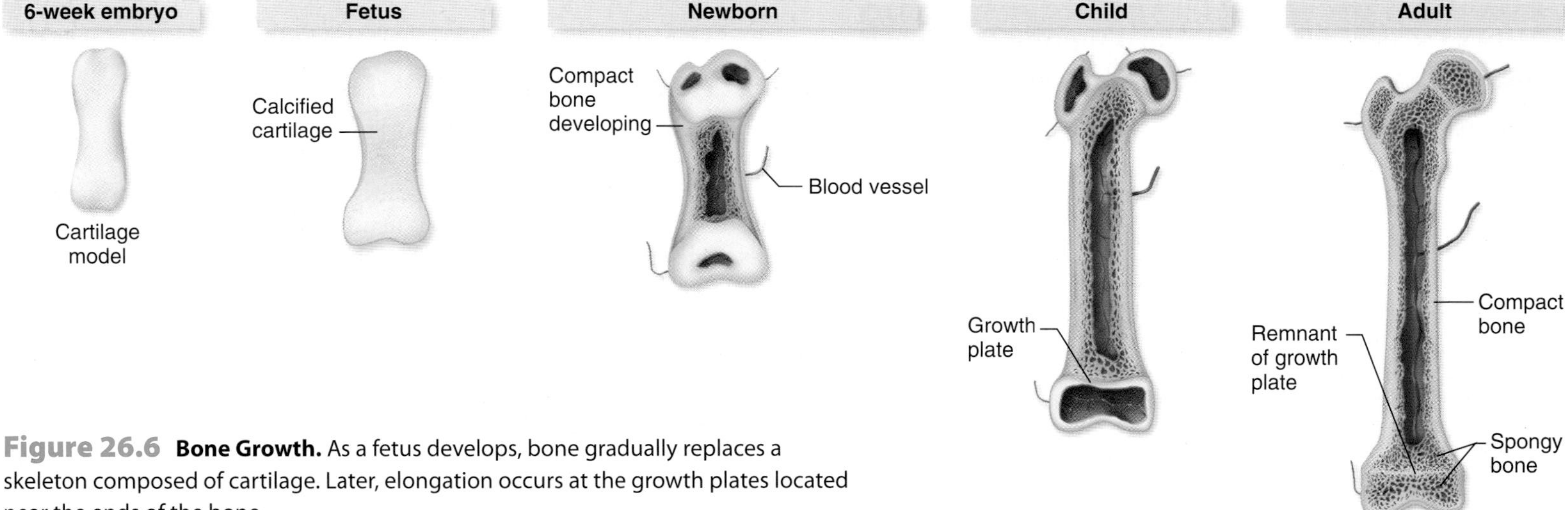

Figure 26.6 Bone Growth. As a fetus develops, bone gradually replaces a skeleton composed of cartilage. Later, elongation occurs at the growth plates located near the ends of the bone.

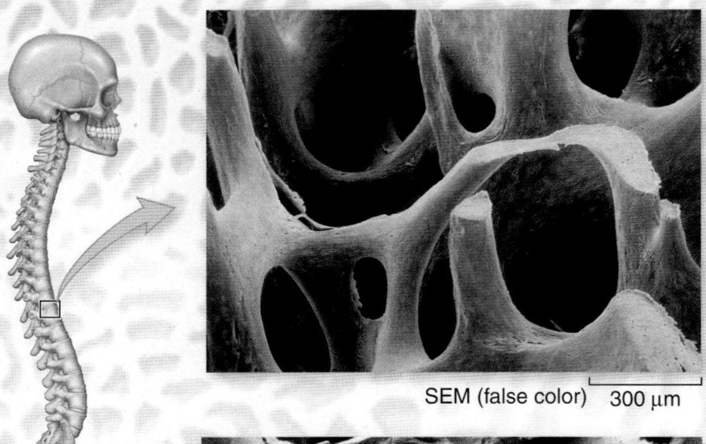

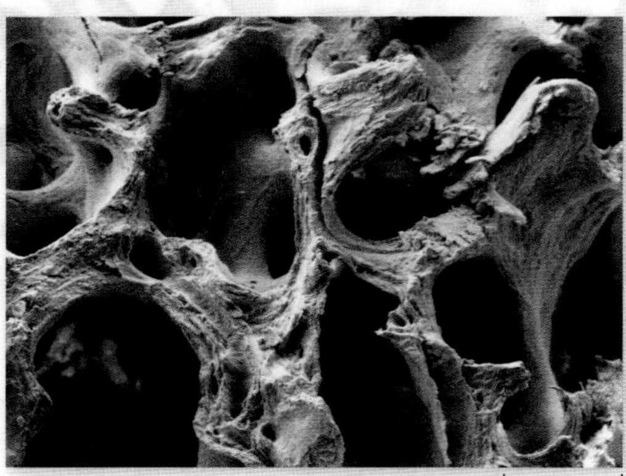

Figure 26.7 Osteoporosis. In osteoporosis, calcium loss weakens bones. The bone in the top image is normal; osteoporosis has leached away part of the bone in the bottom image.

until the late teens, when bone tissue begins to replace the cartilage growth plates. By the early twenties, bone growth is complete.

Even after a person stops growing, bone is continually being remodeled. Bones become thicker and stronger with strenuous exercise such as weight lifting. On the other hand, less-used bones lose mass. For example, astronauts lose bone density if they are in a prolonged weightless environment because their bodies don't have to work as hard as they do against Earth's gravity.

Moreover, broken bones can repair themselves. Bone cells near the site of the fracture produce new bone tissue, so that after several weeks, the injury is all but healed.

D. Bones Help Regulate Calcium Homeostasis

Throughout life, bones are a reservoir for calcium. This mineral is vital for muscle contraction, blood clotting, the activity of some enzymes, and many other essential functions. The body constantly shuttles calcium between blood and bone. Hormones from the parathyroid and thyroid glands control this exchange in a negative feedback loop. ▸▸ negative feedback loop, p. 475; parathyroid glands, p. 515

Bones sometimes lose more calcium than they add, leading to **osteoporosis,** a condition in which bones become less dense (figure 26.7). An astronaut's "disuse osteoporosis" is one example. Much more familiar, however, is the age-related osteoporosis that causes shrinking stature, back pain, and frequent fractures in the elderly.

Both men and women can suffer from osteoporosis, but the disorder is most common in females (see section 25.4B). To prevent bone loss, doctors therefore advise all women to take 1000 to 1500 milligrams of calcium daily and to exercise regularly. Several drugs can increase bone density or slow its loss.

26.3 Mastering Concepts

1. What are the main parts of a long bone?
2. Describe the structure and functions of bone tissue and cartilage.
3. What are the relationships among joints, tendons, and ligaments?
4. How are bones remodeled and repaired throughout life?
5. How do bones participate in calcium homeostasis?

26.4 Muscle Movement Requires Contractile Proteins and ATP

As we have already seen, movement relies on the interaction between bones and muscles. The human muscular system includes more than 600 **skeletal muscles,** which generate voluntary movements. (This number does not include smooth muscle and cardiac muscle, which are involuntary and are not typically considered part of the muscular system.) Table 26.2 lists some functions of skeletal muscles, and figure 26.8 identifies a few of the major skeletal muscles in a human.

Pairs of muscles often work together to generate body movements. Figure 26.9, for example, shows the biceps and triceps muscles. Tendons attach both of these muscles to the bones of the shoulder and lower arm.

TABLE 26.2 Functions of Skeletal Muscles: A Summary

Function	Explanation
Voluntary movement	Muscles attached to bones build lever systems under voluntary control.
Control of body openings	Skeletal muscles provide voluntary control of the eyelids, mouth, and anus.
Maintain posture	Muscles attached to bones keep the body upright.
Communication	Skeletal muscle movements enable facial expressions, speech, writing, and gesturing.
Maintain body temperature	Metabolic activity in skeletal muscle generates heat.

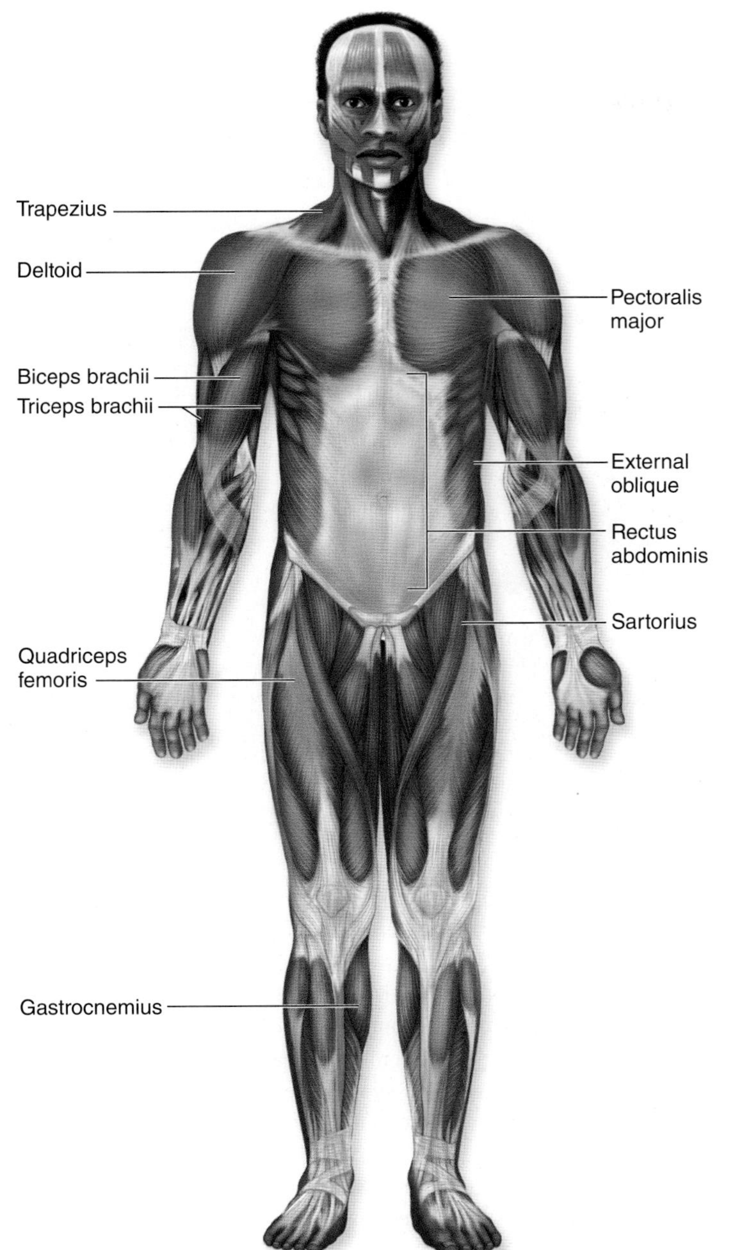

Muscular System	
Main tissue types*	**Examples of locations/functions**
Connective	Makes up tendons that attach muscles to bones; surrounds muscle cells, bundles, and whole muscles
Muscle	Connects to bones and soft tissue, enabling movement of body parts
Nervous	Senses body position and controls muscles

*See chapter 23 for descriptions.

Figure 26.8 **The Human Muscular System.** The human body has more than 600 skeletal muscles, a few of which are identified here.

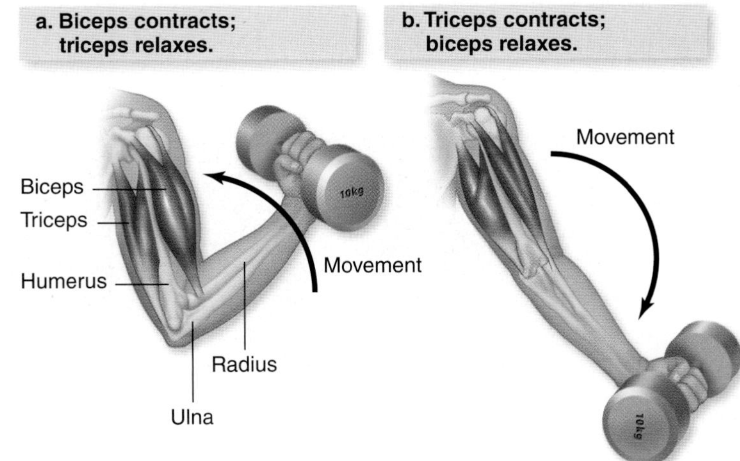

Figure 26.9 **Antagonistic Muscle Pair.** The biceps and triceps muscles work together to move the lower arm in opposite directions. (a) Contracting the biceps bends the elbow. (b) When the triceps contracts, the arm straightens.

Each contracting muscle can pull a bone in one direction but cannot push the bone the opposite way. The elbow can bend and straighten because the biceps and triceps operate in opposite directions. When you contract the biceps (the bulge that appears when you "make a muscle"), the arm bends at the elbow joint. Contraction of the triceps muscle extends the arm. Many other skeletal muscles occur in similar antagonistic pairs that permit back-and-forth movements.

A. Actin and Myosin Filaments Fill Muscle Cells

Picture a softball player swinging a bat, an action that requires the controlled contraction of many skeletal muscles in the legs, arms and torso. Each muscle moves a different body part, yet all are organized in essentially the same

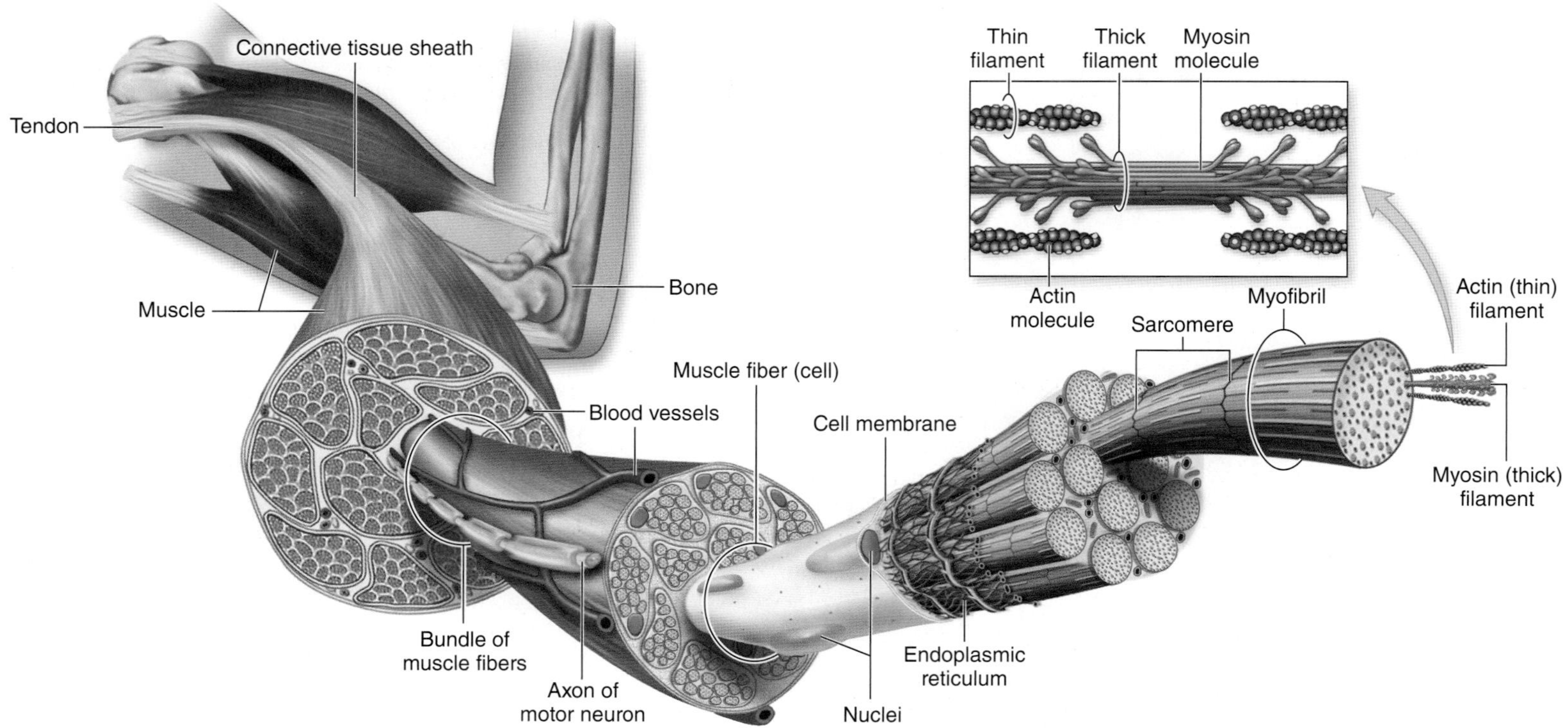

Figure 26.10 Anatomy of a Skeletal Muscle. A muscle is an organ enclosed in connective tissue, nourished by blood vessels, and controlled by nerves. Tendons attach skeletal muscles to bones. Bundles of muscle fibers make up most of the muscle's volume. Each muscle fiber is a single cell with many nuclei. Most of the cell's volume is occupied by myofibrils, which are, in turn, composed of filaments of the proteins actin and myosin.

way. Figure 26.10 illustrates several levels of muscle anatomy, zooming from the whole organ to the microscopic scale.

The left side of figure 26.10 shows a whole muscle, an organ that consists of multiple tissue types. Connective tissue, for example, makes up tendons and the sheath that wraps around each muscle. Blood vessels within the muscle deliver nutrients and oxygen while removing wastes. Nerves transmit information to and from the central nervous system (see chapter 24).

The bulk of the muscle, however, consists of skeletal muscle tissue. The cross sections in the center of figure 26.10 show that muscle tissue is composed of parallel bundles of **muscle fibers,** which are individual muscle cells. The right half of the figure focuses on one muscle cell. Each cell contains cytoplasm,

Figure 26.11 The Sliding Filament Model. (a) Myofibrils are divided into units called sarcomeres. (b–d) During muscle cell contraction, thick and thin filaments slide past one another, decreasing the length of each sarcomere.

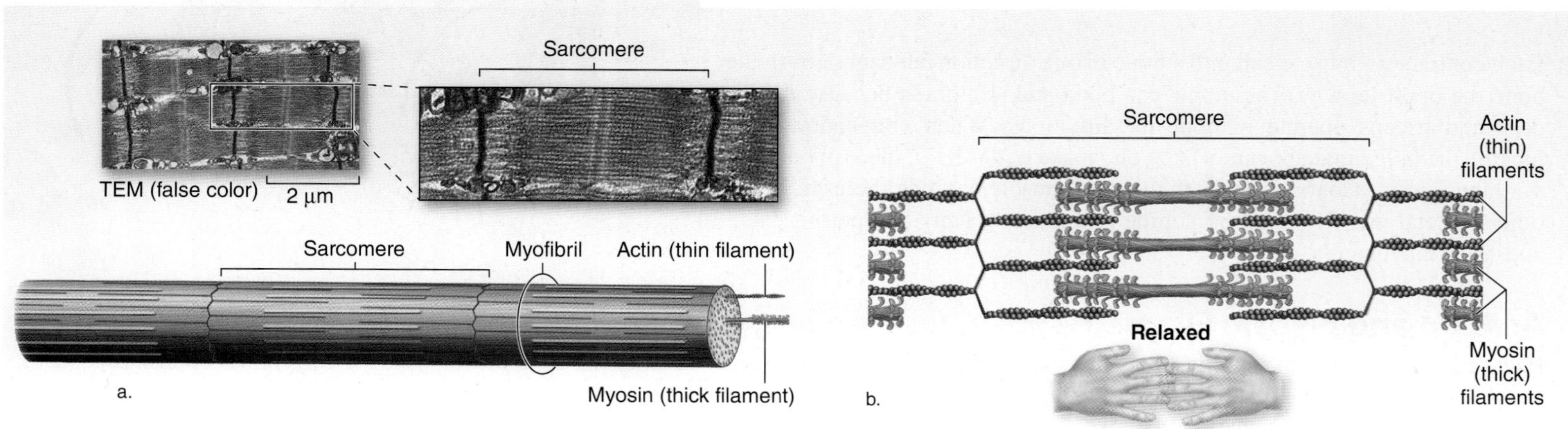

multiple nuclei, and other organelles. But most of the muscle fiber's volume is occupied by hundreds of thousands of cylindrical **myofibrils,** bundles of parallel protein filaments that run the length of the cell.

The inset at the top of figure 26.10 depicts the proteins that compose each myofibril. A **thick filament** is made of a protein called **myosin.** A **thin filament** consists primarily of two entwined strands of another protein, **actin.**

B. Sliding Filaments Are the Basis of Muscle Fiber Contraction

Skeletal muscle tissue appears striped, or striated, because of the alternating arrangement of thick and thin filaments. These striations divide each myofibril into many functional units, called **sarcomeres.** Figure 26.11 illustrates the structure and function of a sarcomere.

According to the **sliding filament model,** a muscle fiber contracts when the thin filaments slide between the thick ones. This motion shortens the sarcomere without changing the lengths of the thick or thin filaments. The overall effect is a little like fitting your fingers together to shorten the distance between your hands.

For thick and thin filaments to move past each other and contract a muscle fiber, actin and myosin must touch. The physical connection between the two types of filaments forms when the club-shaped "head" portion of each myosin molecule swings out to contact an actin molecule, forming a cross bridge (figure 26.12).

As detailed in figure 26.12, the sliding interaction between actin and myosin requires energy in the form of ATP. In step 1 of the figure, the myosin heads are not yet connected to actin. Soon, however, a myosin head forms a cross bridge by attaching to an exposed actin subunit on a thin filament (step 2). The myosin head bends, which pulls on actin and causes it to slide past myosin in the same way that an oar's motion moves a boat (step 3). The myosin head then binds a molecule of ATP and releases the actin (step 4). ATP splits into ADP and a phosphate group, prompting the myosin head to swivel back to its original position (step 5). The myosin head is now ready to contact another actin subunit farther down the thin filament. ▸ ATP, p. 72

This sliding action repeats about a hundred times per second on each of the hundreds of myosin molecules of a thick filament. Although each individual movement is minuscule, a skeletal muscle contracts quickly and forcefully due to the efforts of many thousands of "rowers."

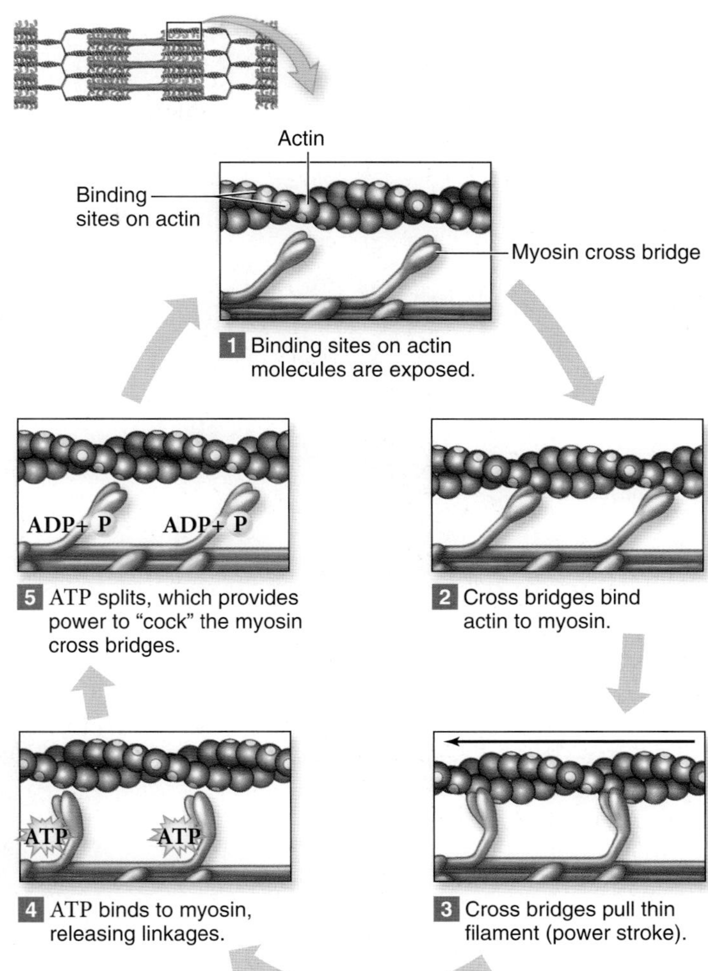

Figure 26.12 **ATP's Role in Muscle Contraction.** ATP provides the energy required for myosin filaments to "ratchet" past actin filaments as the muscle contracts.

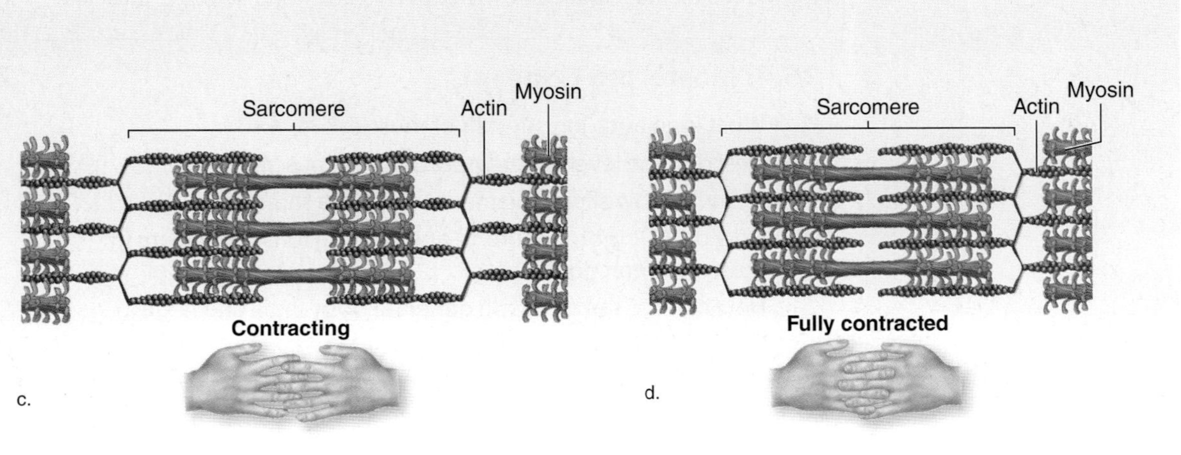

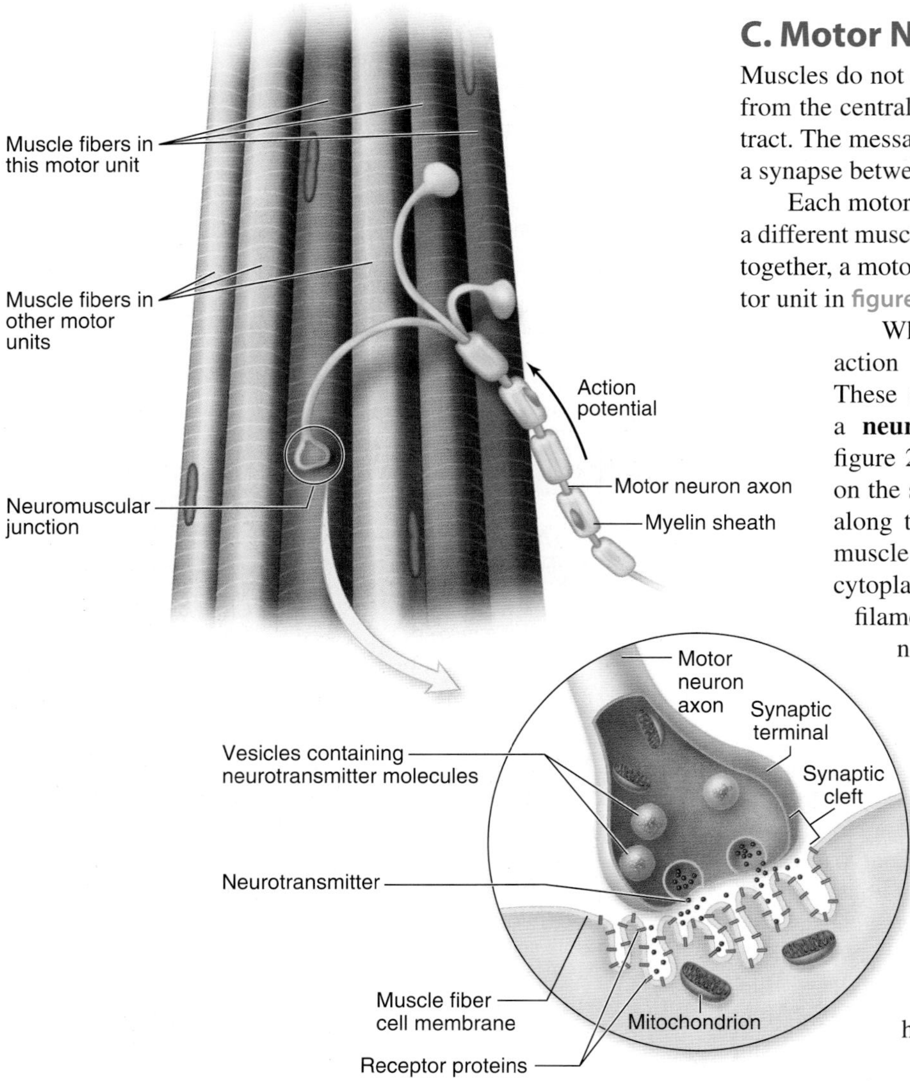

Figure 26.13 How Neurons Control Muscle Cells. One motor neuron may control multiple muscle fibers; this illustration shows a motor unit that includes three muscle cells. (The remaining muscle fibers belong to other motor units.) Each synapse between the motor neuron's axon and a muscle fiber is called a neuromuscular junction. When action potentials in the axon stimulate the release of a neurotransmitter at these synapses, the three muscle cells contract simultaneously.

C. Motor Neurons Stimulate Muscle Contraction

Muscles do not contract at random; rather, they wait for electrical stimulation from the central nervous system. A **motor neuron** delivers the signal to contract. The message is transmitted to the muscle at a **neuromuscular junction,** a synapse between a motor neuron and a muscle cell. ▸ synapse, p. 488

Each motor neuron's axon branches at its tip, with each branch leading to a different muscle fiber. One motor neuron can therefore control multiple cells; together, a motor neuron and its muscle fibers make up a **motor unit.** The motor unit in figure 26.13, for example, includes three muscle fibers.

When the central nervous system sends the signal to contract, action potentials are conveyed along the motor neuron's axon. These signals stimulate the release of a chemical message called a **neurotransmitter** at each synapse with a muscle fiber (see figure 26.13, inset). The neurotransmitters bind to receptor proteins on the surface of the muscle fiber, causing an electrical wave to race along the muscle cell membrane. This electrical signal causes the muscle fiber's endoplasmic reticulum to release calcium ions into the cytoplasm. The calcium, in turn, slightly changes the shape of the thin filament, allowing the myosin heads to bind to actin. The muscle is now free to contract. ▸ action potential, p. 486

Within one muscle, motor units vary in size from tens to hundreds of cells per motor neuron. When a neural impulse arrives, all of the fibers in a motor unit contract at the same time. A motor neuron that controls only a few muscle fibers produces fine, small-scale responses, such as the eye movements required for reading. A motor unit consisting of hundreds of muscle cells produces large, coarse movements, such as those required for throwing a ball. The more motor units activated, the stronger the force of contraction. In this way, by recruiting different combinations of motor units, the same hand can both grip a hammer and pick up a tiny nail.

Some diseases interfere with the neural signals that stimulate muscle contraction. The virus that causes polio, for example, causes paralysis by destroying motor neurons. Another disease-causing organism is the bacterium *Clostridium botulinum,* which produces botulinum toxin (commonly known as Botox). This poison blocks the release of neurotransmitters from motor neurons. Affected muscles therefore never receive the signal to contract. Ingesting botulinum in tainted foods can cause paralysis, which can be fatal. Injecting tiny amounts of Botox into the face, however, temporarily helps reduce the appearance of wrinkles by paralyzing selected muscles.

26.4 Mastering Concepts

1. What is an antagonistic pair of muscles?
2. Describe the levels of organization of a muscle.
3. Describe how sliding filaments shorten a sarcomere.
4. How do ATP, motor neurons, and calcium ions participate in muscle contraction?
5. How can the same muscle generate both small and large movements?

26.5 Muscle Fibers Generate ATP in Multiple Ways

Skeletal muscle contraction requires huge amounts of ATP to break the connection between actin and myosin. Muscle cells have several ways to produce this ATP. A resting muscle cell generates ATP in aerobic respiration, a process described in chapter 6. Muscle activity quickly depletes stored ATP, but a molecule called **creatine phosphate** replenishes it by donating a high-energy phosphate to ADP. (The Burning Question on this page discusses the value of creatine phosphate as a dietary supplement.)

After the supply of creatine phosphate is gone, aerobic respiration can continue to produce ATP for as long as the lungs and blood deliver sufficient oxygen. Otherwise, muscle cells switch to fermentation, a less efficient metabolic route that does not require O_2 but rapidly leads to lactic acid accumulation. At one time, researchers blamed lactic acid for the pain associated with muscle fatigue, but that conclusion is now being challenged.

Intense exercise may lead to a period of **oxygen debt,** during which the body requires extra O_2 to restore resting levels of ATP and to recharge the proteins that carry oxygen in blood and muscle. Heavy breathing for several minutes after intense muscle activity is a sign of oxygen debt.

Shortly after death, muscles can no longer generate any ATP at all. One consequence is rigor mortis, the stiffening of muscles that occurs within a few hours after a person dies. Without ATP, the myosin head cannot release from actin. The muscles remain in a stiff position for the next couple of days, until the protein filaments begin to decay.

26.5 Mastering Concepts

1. Describe the role of creatine phosphate in muscle metabolism.
2. What happens when a muscle cell cannot generate ATP by aerobic respiration?

Burning Questions

Is creatine a useful dietary supplement?

You may have seen jars of creatine powder on nutrition store shelves, marketed as a muscle-building aid. But does this supplement really work?

To answer this question, it helps to know that muscle cells normally contain a molecule called creatine phosphate. This compound donates its phosphate to ADP, quickly regenerating ATP soon after muscle activity starts. In theory, an increase in creatine phosphate levels should help skeletal muscle cells generate ATP, providing an energy boost during brief, intense bouts of exercise.

Although this idea seems logical, people differ in their response to creatine. For some, taking creatine powder does increase the amount of creatine phosphate inside skeletal muscle cells. But not everyone's athletic performance improves. Results vary from no effect to small gains in sprints and other short-term intense exercises.

As a note of caution, the long-term consumption of creatine powder may be harmful. Much of the extra creatine ends up in urine, indicating stress on the kidneys. The possibility of kidney toxicity requires further study.

Submit your burning question to:
marielle_hoefnagels@mcgraw-hill.com

26.6 Muscle Fiber Types Influence Athletic Performance

Most skeletal muscles contain two main types of fibers, distinguished by how quickly they contract and tire (figure 26.14). A "twitch" is a cycle of contraction and relaxation in one muscle fiber. **Slow-twitch fibers** are smaller and produce twitches of relatively long duration. Abundant capillaries bring in oxygen-rich blood, and the cells have a high content of a red pigment that stores oxygen. The O_2, in turn, supports the aerobic respiration that regenerates ATP in the fibers' plentiful mitochondria. High-endurance, slow-twitch muscles predominate in body parts that are active for extended periods, such as the flight muscles ("dark meat") of ducks and geese or the back muscles that maintain our upright posture.

Fast-twitch fibers, in contrast, are larger cells that split ATP quickly in short-duration twitches. Short bouts of rapid, powerful contraction are characteristic of fast-twitch fibers. Anaerobic pathways generate the ATP in these cells, which tire quickly. Muscles dominated by fast-twitch fibers appear white because they have few capillaries and a lower content of the red oxygen-storing pigment. The white breast muscle of a domesticated chicken, for example, can power barnyard flapping for a short time but cannot support sustained, long-distance flight.

The proportion of slow-twitch to fast-twitch fibers affects athletic performance. People with a high proportion of slow-twitch fibers excel at endurance sports, such as long-distance biking, running, and swimming. Athletes who have a higher proportion of fast-twitch fibers perform best at short, fast events, such as weight lifting, hurling the shot put, and sprinting. Genetics largely determines the balance between slow- and fast-twitch fibers in each person's muscles, although intensive training can alter this proportion in some people.

Regardless of the mix of slow- and fast-twitch fibers, regular exercise strengthens the muscular system. During the few months after a runner begins training, for example, leg muscles noticeably enlarge. This increase in muscle mass comes from the growth of individual skeletal muscle cells rather than from an increase in their number. Exercise-induced muscle growth is even more pronounced in a weight lifter, because the resistance of the weights greatly stresses the muscles. Anabolic steroids boost muscle growth by activating the genes encoding muscle proteins, but the potential side effects of illicit steroid use are serious. ▸ anabolic steroids, p. 518

A trained athlete's muscle fibers also use energy more efficiently than those of an inactive person. The athlete's cells contain more active and more numerous enzymes and more mitochondria, so his or her muscles can withstand far more exertion before oxygen debt begins. The athlete's muscles also receive more blood and store more glycogen than those of an untrained person.

Like bones, muscles can degenerate from lack of use. After just two days of inactivity, mitochondrial enzyme activity drops in skeletal muscle cells. After a week without exercise, aerobic

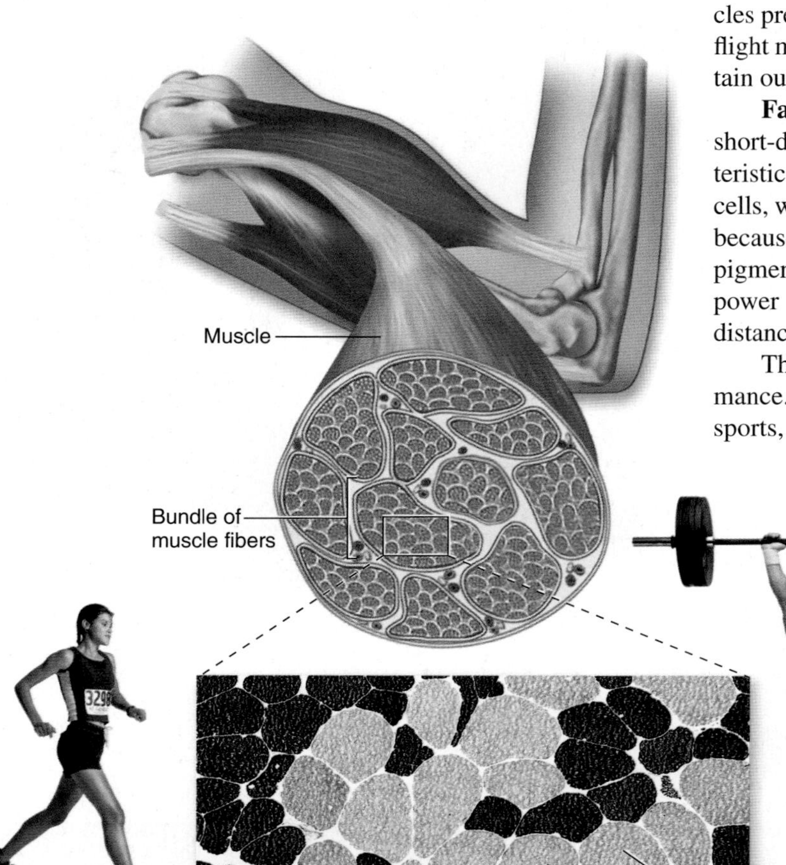

Characteristic	Slow-twitch fibers	Fast-twitch fibers
Metabolism	Aerobic	Anaerobic
Energy use	Slow, steady	Quick, explosive
Endurance	High	Low

Figure 26.14 Slow-Twitch and Fast-Twitch Fibers. This cross section shows a muscle that contains approximately equal numbers of slow-twitch (dark) and fast-twitch (light) fibers.

respiration efficiency falls by 50%. The number of small blood vessels surrounding muscle fibers declines, lowering the body's ability to deliver O_2 to the muscle. Glycogen reserves fall, and the breakdown of lactic acid occurs less efficiently. After a few months of inactivity, the benefits of regular exercise all but disappear.

Athletic ability aside, physical exertion is often followed by muscle soreness and joint pain. A soak in a hot tub can offer some relief; the Burning Question on this page explains why this technique works so well.

26.6 Mastering Concepts

1. Why do endurance sports require a high proportion of slow-twitch muscle fibers, whereas power sports require more fast-twitch muscle fibers?
2. How does exercise strengthen muscles?

Burning Questions

Why do we use heat to soothe sore muscles and joints?

Few experiences are as relaxing as slipping into a bubbling hot tub. Muscle tension subsides, and aches seem to melt away. Why does heat have this effect?

Conventional wisdom says that heat causes muscles to relax, but this answer is misleading. Technically, a muscle relaxes when actin and myosin filaments slide past one another in a way that makes the sarcomeres longer. Heat does not make muscles relax in this sense.

Instead, most of heat's soothing effects on muscles and joints are indirect. First, heat causes the proteins that make up tendons and ligaments to become more fluid and stretchier. Loosening up this connective tissue not only relieves tension on the muscles but also makes stiff joints more mobile. Second, warmth helps to relieve pain in sore, overworked muscles and joints. Heat stimulates thermoreceptors in the skin, which may override impulses from pain receptors. Third, heat may reduce the activity of motor neurons that trigger painful muscle spasms. And finally, heat increases blood flow near the body's surface. This blood speeds healing of damaged muscles in two ways: by delivering nutrients and oxygen that cells require to make repairs, and by removing the remains of damaged cells.

Submit your burning question to:
marielle_hoefnagels@mcgraw-hill.com

Investigating Life

26.7 Did a Myosin Gene Mutation Make Humans Brainier?

The old admonition not to "bite off more than you can chew" seems to apply especially well to humans. Our chewing muscles are considerably smaller than those of most primates, including chimpanzees and gorillas. We favor soft foods such as bread or cheese, and we would have a hard time chewing the bark, stems, and seeds that some of our primate relatives savor.

The Question: These differences have spurred researchers to investigate this question: How have the muscles that connect the lower jaw to the other bones of the skull evolved in humans and other primates?

The Approach: Part of the evidence that has helped scientists understand the evolution of jaw muscles came from an unexpected source. It all began with the Human Genome Project, which has allowed researchers to comb through human DNA in search of particular genes. ▸ Human Genome Project, p. 203

Hansell H. Stedman and associates from the University of Pennsylvania and the Children's Hospital of Philadelphia hoped to catalog every myosin gene in the human genome. Myosin is not just one protein; it is a family of proteins encoded by at least 40 closely related genes. Mutations in many of the myosin-encoding genes can lead to loss of muscle function and other serious disorders. Stedman's research was part of an effort to better understand diseases such as muscular dystrophy.

During a search of chromosome 7, however, the team stumbled on an inactive gene that encoded a nonfunctional myosin protein. At first, they thought the inactive gene represented a quirk in the sequences they were searching. They therefore looked at the genomes of six widely dispersed human populations originating in locations ranging from Africa to Iceland. All of the human groups had the mutated gene. The team also compared the gene to a homologous DNA sequence in seven species of nonhuman primates, including gorillas and chimpanzees. The results were clear: the researchers had discovered

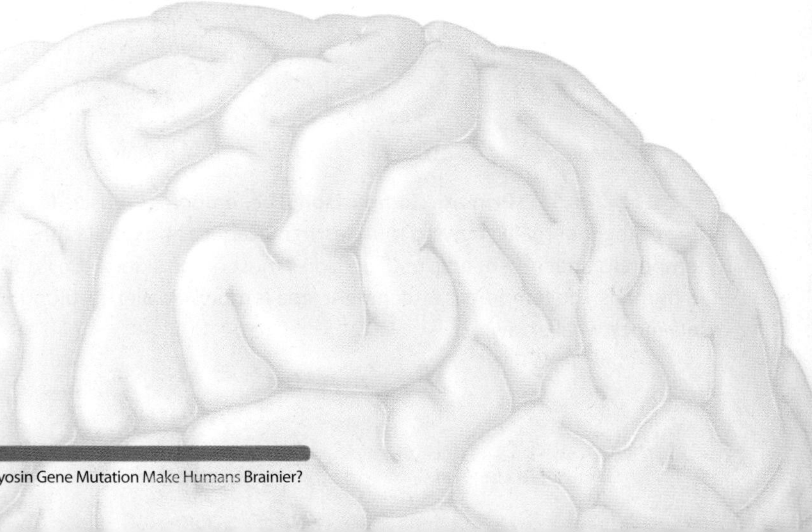

	30 40 50 60 70 80
Non-human	
Woolly monkey	CCCTCCACAGCACTGTACCCCATTTTGTCCGCTGTATTGTGCCCAATGAGTTTAAGCAGTCAG
Pigtail macaque	CCCTCCACAGCACTGTACCCCATTTTGTCCGCTGTATTGTGCCCAATGAGTTTAAGCAGTCAG
Rhesus	CCCTCCACAGCACTGTACCCCATTTTGTCCGCTGTATTGTGCCCAATGAGTTTAAGCAGTCAG
Orangutan	CCCTCCACAGCACTGTACCCCATTTTGTCCGCTGTATTGTGCCCAATGAGTTTAAGCAGTCAG
Gorilla	CCCTCCACAGCACTGTACCCCATTTTGTCCGCTGTATTGTGCCCAATGAGTTTAAGCAGTCAG
Bonobo	CCCTCCACAGCACTGTACCCCATTTTGTCCGCTGTATTGTGCCCAATGAGTTTAAGCAGTCAG
Chimpanzee	CCCTCCACAGCACTGTACCCCATTTTGTCCGCTGTATTGTGCCCAATGAGTTTAAGCAGTCAG
Human	
Africa (pygmy)	CCCTCCATAGC--CGCACCCCATTTTGTCCGCTGTATTATCCCCAATGAGTTTAAGCAATCGG
Spain (Basque)	CCCTCCATAGC--CGCACCCCATTTTGTCCGCTGTATTATCCCCAATGAGTTTAAGCAATCGG
Iceland	CCCTCCATAGC--CGCACCCCATTTTGTCCGCTGTATTATCCCCAATGAGTTTAAGCAATCGG
Japan	CCCTCCATAGC--CGCACCCCATTTTGTCCGCTGTATTATCCCCAATGAGTTTAAGCAATCGG
Russia	CCCTCCATAGC--CGCACCCCATTTTGTCCGCTGTATTATCCCCAATGAGTTTAAGCAATCGG
South America	CCCTCCATAGC--CGCACCCCATTTTGTCCGCTGTATTATCCCCAATGAGTTTAAGCAATCGG

Figure 26.15 Myosin Mutation. The DNA sequences for a small portion of the myosin gene are shown for nonhuman primates (upper seven sequences) and humans (lower six sequences). The fragments start at nucleotide #26 in the gene. Differences between the two sets of genes are highlighted with shaded boxes. The mutations in the human genes cause the encoded protein to be truncated (shortened) and nonfunctional.

a human myosin gene containing mutations that are not present in nonhuman primates (figure 26.15).

Next, the researchers discovered that in humans and macaque monkeys, only two muscles express the gene, and both participate in the up-and-down jaw movements required for chewing. Because the protein is nonfunctional in humans but functional in macaques, this finding suggested that ancient genetic mutations made our chewing muscles small and weak, at least compared with those of our closest relatives.

That result prompted Stedman's research team to learn more about the chewing apparatus in the fossilized bones of primates. Bones bear marks indicating where muscles were once attached. Until about 2 million years ago (MYA), primates had large skull bones and robust chewing muscles. These large complexes occurred in the ancestral hominines *Australopithecus* and *Paranthropus,* as well as in contemporary primates such as macaques and gorillas (figure 26.16). But more delicate chewing muscles appeared in early humans *(Homo erectus/ergaster).* ▸ human evolution, p. 347

The researchers used a "molecular clock" technique to estimate that the mutations in the myosin gene occurred approximately 2.4 MYA—before the migration of *Homo* out of Africa. The timing coincides with a significant trend in human evolution: increasing brain size. ▸ molecular clock, p. 253

The Conclusion: Stedman and his colleagues argue that the myosin mutations may have changed the chewing muscles in a way that released a constraint on the size of the brain. Enhanced brain power may have eventually led to the development of culture, profoundly changing the course of human evolution. Of course, one mutated myosin gene is, by itself, not likely to have set in motion the entire course of human history. Other changes in the skeletal and nervous systems must also have occurred to spur the evolution of the brain.

The story of this myosin gene illustrates how a seemingly routine study can have thoroughly unexpected results. After all, what began as a simple search through the human genome ended up having much wider implications for the study of human evolution. This study also points to the connections among different areas of biology. To tell their story, Stedman and his colleagues needed to understand both the muscular and the skeletal systems. In the process, they combined detailed observations of ancient fossils with modern studies of gene mutation and protein function. Their results give us something to chew on as we contemplate the evolutionary history of our own species.

Stedman, Hansell, Benjamin W. Kozyak, Anthony Nelson, et al. 2004. Myosin gene mutation correlates with anatomical changes in the human lineage. *Nature,* vol. 428, pages 415–418.

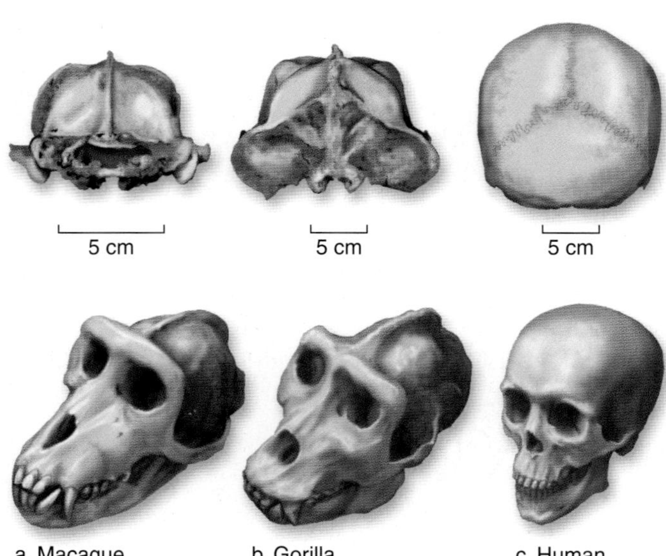

Figure 26.16 Primate Comparison. The temporalis muscle is one of the four main chewing muscles. In macaques and gorillas, the temporalis attachment area *(red)* occupies most of the side of the skull. In humans, the temporalis attachment area is much smaller, resulting in a much weaker jaw.

26.7 Mastering Concepts

1. Summarize the hypothesized relationship between the myosin gene mutation and brain size in humans and other primates.
2. Describe the lines of evidence that support this hypothesis.

Chapter Summary

26.1 Skeletons Take Many Forms

- The **muscular system** and the **skeletal system** together enable an animal to move.
- An animal's **skeleton** supports its body and protects soft tissues. **Muscles** act on the skeleton to provide motion.
- A **hydrostatic skeleton** consists of tissue containing constrained fluid. An **exoskeleton** is on the organism's exterior, and an **endoskeleton** forms inside the body.

26.2 The Vertebrate Skeleton Features a Central Backbone

- The **axial skeleton** consists of the **bones** of the head, **vertebral column,** and rib cage.
- The **appendicular skeleton** includes the limbs and the limb girdles (**pectoral** and **pelvic**) that attach them to the axial skeleton.

26.3 Bones Provide Support, Protect Internal Organs, and Supply Calcium

- Bones are strong and lightweight because they are porous. Long bones have a **marrow cavity** that contains **red bone marrow** or **yellow bone marrow.** As we age, the proportion of yellow marrow increases.

A. Bones Consist Mostly of Bone Tissue and Cartilage

- Bone tissue derives its strength from collagen and its hardness from minerals. **Compact bone** is hard and dense. **Spongy bone** has many spaces separated by a web of bony supports.
- Cartilage is a connective tissue that entraps a great deal of water, which makes it an excellent shock absorber.

B. Bone Meets Bone at a Joint

- **Joints** attach bones to each other.
- Freely moving joints consist of cartilage and a connective tissue capsule that contains lubricating fluid. **Ligaments** connect bone to bone, whereas **tendons** connect bones to muscles.

C. Bones Are Constantly Built and Degraded

- Even after growth stops, bone continually degenerates and renews itself.
- Weight-bearing exercise strengthens bones; conversely, bones weaken with disuse.

D. Bones Help Regulate Calcium Homeostasis

- Hormones control the exchange of calcium between blood and bones, maintaining homeostasis. **Osteoporosis** results when a person's bones lose more calcium than they replace.

26.4 Muscle Movement Requires Contractile Proteins and ATP

- Many **skeletal muscles** form antagonistic pairs, which enable bones to move in two directions.

A. Actin and Myosin Filaments Fill Muscle Cells

- Each skeletal **muscle fiber** is a long, cylindrical cell that contains **myofibrils** composed of two types of protein filaments. The **thick filaments** are **myosin,** and the **thin filaments** are composed primarily of **actin.**

B. Sliding Filaments Are the Basis of Muscle Fiber Contraction

- A myofibril is a chain of contractile units called **sarcomeres.** The orderly arrangement of thick and thin filaments within a sarcomere gives skeletal muscle tissue its striated (striped) appearance.

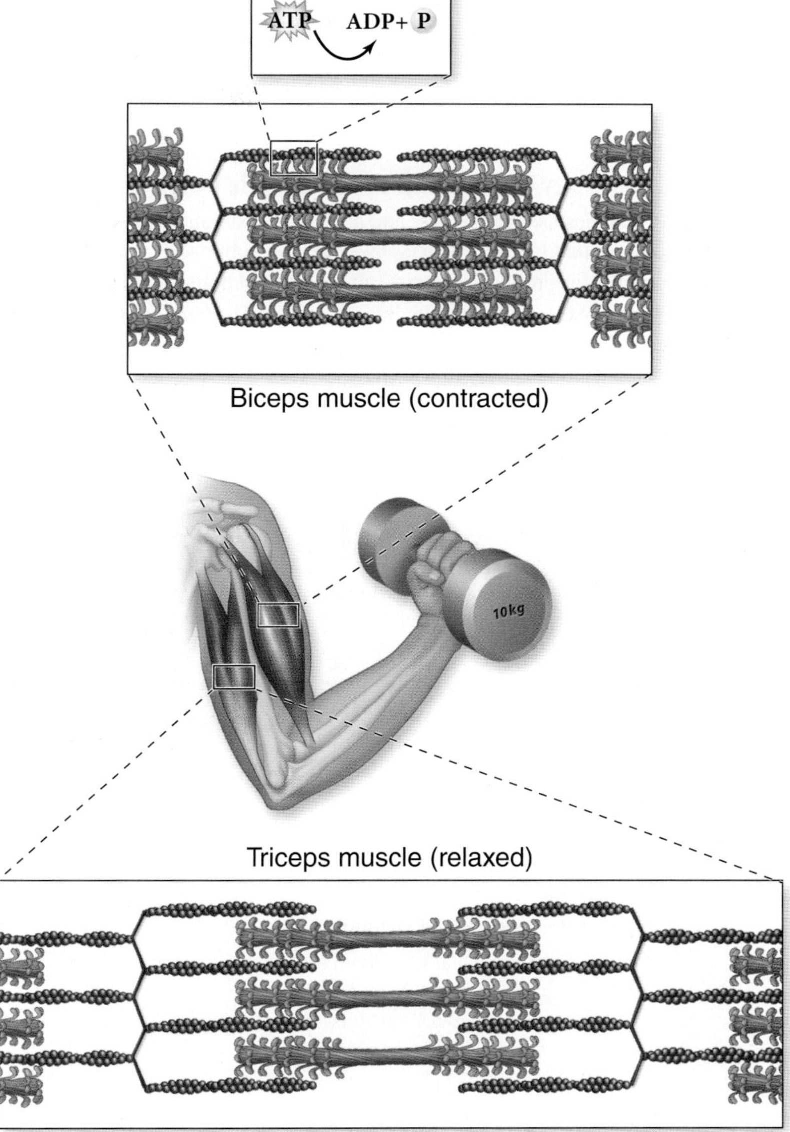

- According to the **sliding filament model,** muscle contraction occurs when thick and thin filaments move past one another. Myosin heads provide "rowing" movements as they briefly contact actin filaments.
- Muscle contraction requires ATP. When a myosin head touches actin, ATP splits. The head moves, causing the actin filament to slide past the myosin filament. A new ATP then binds to the myosin head, and the link to actin breaks. The myosin head returns to its original position, and a new connection forms farther along the filament.

C. Motor Neurons Stimulate Muscle Contraction

- A **motor neuron** and the muscle fibers it touches form a **motor unit.** When a motor neuron receives a signal from the central nervous system, it releases a **neurotransmitter** at a **neuromuscular junction.** Electrical waves then spread along the muscle cell membrane, releasing calcium ions into the cytoplasm. Calcium prompts actin filaments to change shape in a way that allows myosin to bind to it, and the muscle contracts.
- The more motor units stimulated, the greater the contraction of the muscle.

26.5 Muscle Fibers Generate ATP in Multiple Ways

- The energy that powers muscle contraction comes first from stored ATP, then from **creatine phosphate** stored in muscle cells, then from aerobic respiration, and finally from fermentation.
- **Oxygen debt** is a temporary deficiency of O_2 after intense exercise.

26.6 Muscle Fiber Types Influence Athletic Performance

- **Slow-twitch fibers** use ATP slowly and have high endurance. **Fast-twitch fibers** use ATP quickly and produce powerful contractions.
- People vary in their proportion of fast- and slow-twitch muscle fibers.
- A muscle that is exercised regularly increases in size because each muscle cell thickens. An unused muscle shrinks. Regular exercise causes changes in muscle cells that enable them to use energy more efficiently.

26.7 Investigating Life: Did a Myosin Gene Mutation Make Humans Brainier?

- Researchers examining the human genome have discovered a mutated myosin gene that is expressed only in the muscles required for chewing. Nonhuman primates lack the mutation.
- The evolution of weaker, smaller chewing muscles may have paved the way for increased brain capacity in humans.

Multiple Choice Questions

1. A hydrostatic skeleton
   a. occurs in multiple types of invertebrates.
   b. is filled with fluid.
   c. changes shape due to muscle contraction.
   d. All of the above are correct.
2. Exoskeletons differ from endoskeletons in
   a. their ability to protect an animal from the outside.
   b. their ability to grow along with an organism.
   c. their function as a framework for muscle attachment.
   d. Both a and b are correct.
3. The bones of your hand are part of the ______, whereas your backbone is part of the ______.
   a. axial skeleton; pectoral girdle
   b. appendicular skeleton; axial skeleton
   c. axial skeleton; appendicular skeleton
   d. axial skeleton; vertebral column
4. How do bones interact with blood?
   a. Bone marrow produces blood cells.
   b. Bones absorb excess calcium from blood.
   c. Bones release phosphorus to blood.
   d. All of the above are correct.
5. The function of a ligament is to connect
   a. cartilage to bone.
   b. bone to bone.
   c. bone to muscle.
   d. muscle to muscle.
6. Muscle tissue is made up of what type of cells?
   a. Sarcomeres
   b. Myofibrils
   c. Actin and myosin filaments
   d. Muscle fibers
7. Which of the following is correctly arranged in order from smallest to largest?
   a. Motor unit < sarcomere < muscle cell < actin subunit
   b. Muscle cell < actin subunit < sarcomere < motor unit
   c. Actin subunit < sarcomere < muscle cell < motor unit
   d. Sarcomere < motor unit < actin subunit < muscle cell
8. What is the primary source of energy for muscle contraction?
   a. ATP
   b. Neurotransmitters
   c. Creatine phosphate
   d. Calcium
9. Slow-twitch muscle fibers
   a. appear red, thanks to a pigment that stores oxygen.
   b. specialize in anaerobic metabolic pathways.
   c. often predominate in the muscles of endurance athletes.
   d. Both a and c are correct.
10. Which of the following is NOT a value of exercise?
    a. Increased bone density
    b. Enhanced muscle cell metabolism
    c. Increase in the number of muscle cells
    d. Increase in the size of the muscle cells

Write It Out

1. Distinguish among a hydrostatic skeleton, an exoskeleton, and an endoskeleton. What are the advantages and disadvantages of each type of skeleton? Give an example of an animal with each type.
2. Explain the observation that animals with exoskeletons and endoskeletons are better represented in the fossil record than are animals with hydrostatic skeletons. How might this difference alter scientific interpretations of the fossil record?
3. What are the components of the axial and appendicular skeletons?
4. What role does cartilage play in the vertebrate skeletal system?
5. What are the differences between spongy bone and compact bone?
6. Describe the events of bone development from embryo through adulthood.
7. How can an imbalance in calcium homeostasis lead to osteoporosis?
8. How do antagonistic muscle pairs move bones? Give an example of such a pair.
9. Describe the arrangement of actin and myosin in a muscle cell.
10. How do the effects of exercise (or lack thereof) illustrate homeostasis in bones and muscles?
11. How does the muscular system interact with the nervous system? The skeletal system? The respiratory system? The circulatory system?
12. What roles does fluid play in hydrostatic skeletons, cartilage, and movable joints?
13. Search the Internet for disorders of the skeletal or muscular system. Choose one such illness to research in more detail. Describe how the disorder interferes with bone or muscle function. What causes the disorder? Is a treatment or cure available?
14. What is the role of calcium in bones? In muscle contraction?

15. The following table shows recent men's world-record times for various running events. Graph the distance traveled against the average running speed, in meters per second. How does muscle use of ATP over time explain the graph?

Distance (m)	Time	Average m/sec
100	9.58 sec	10.44
200	19.19 sec	10.05
400	43.18 sec	9.26
800	1 min, 41.01 sec	7.91
1500	3 min, 26.00 sec	7.28
5000	12 min, 37.35 sec	6.60

Pull It Together

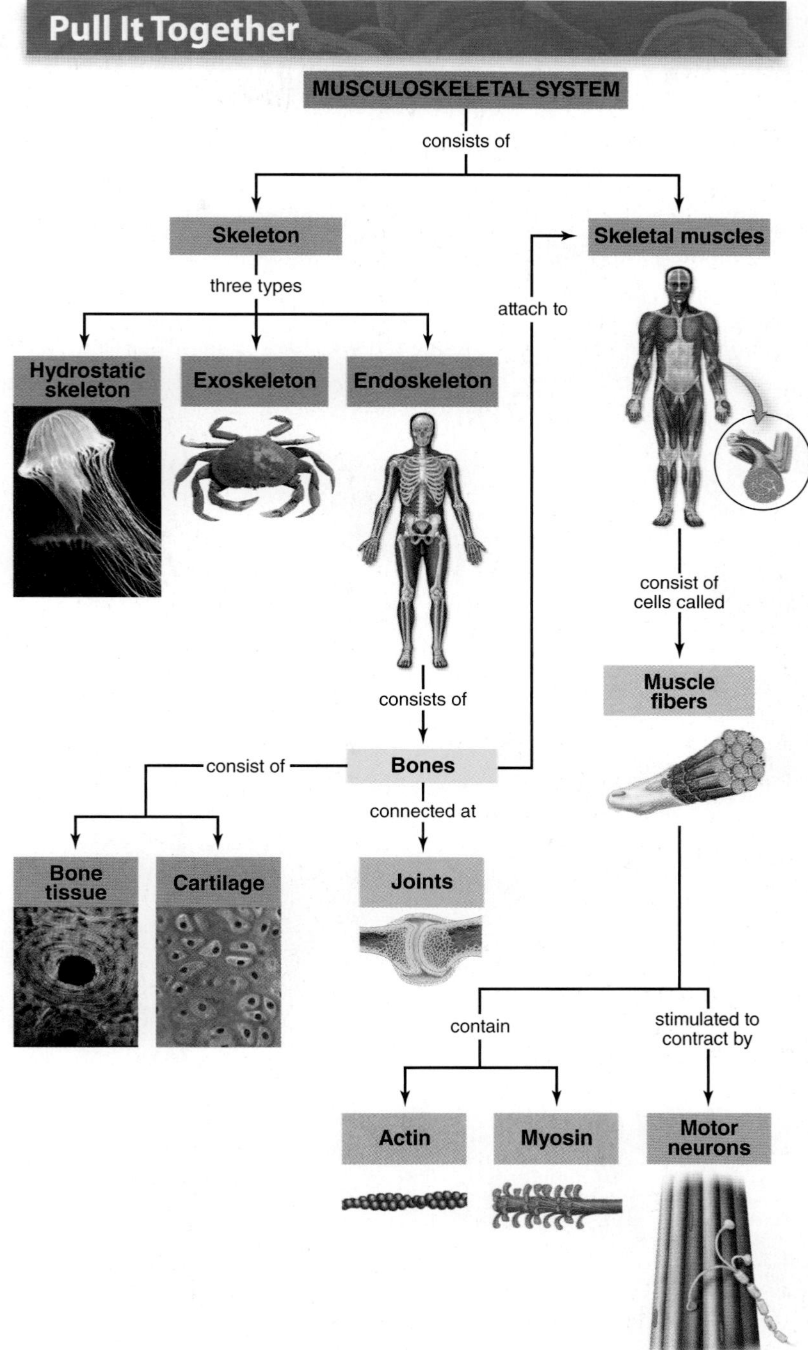

1. How do bones help maintain blood calcium concentrations?
2. How do actin and myosin interact in the sliding filament model of muscle contraction?
3. Add neurotransmitters and ATP to this concept map.
4. Add fast- and slow-twitch muscle fibers to this concept map. How do these two fiber types differ?

27 The Circulatory and Respiratory Systems

Raw Material for Artificial Blood? A technician handles a bag of hemoglobin, an oxygen-toting protein purified from human blood. The hemoglobin is being tested for use in a blood substitute.

Learning Outline

Learn How to Learn
Skipping Class?

Attending lectures is important, but you may need to skip class once in a while. How will you find out what you missed? If your instructor does not provide complete lecture notes, you may be able to copy them from a friend. Whenever you borrow someone else's notes, it's a good idea to compare them with the assigned reading to make sure they are complete and accurate. You might also want to check with the instructor if you have lingering questions about what you missed.

What's the Point?

The sight of blood is alarming to many people, and for good reason: this bright red fluid is essential to life. Powered by the heart, the bloodstream is a river that carries hormones, immune system cells, water, nutrients, and oxygen throughout the body. The same transportation network also removes waste products that cells produce. It is no wonder that a damaged heart or the loss of blood can threaten life.

Likewise, we risk death if we stop breathing for even a few minutes. Blood and breathing are closely connected. As we inhale, our lungs acquire fresh oxygen. This gas diffuses into the bloodstream at millions of tiny air sacs, each enclosed in a basket of blood vessels. At the same time, waste carbon dioxide gas diffuses out of the blood and into the lungs. Exhaled air carries this gas out of the body. This chapter describes the intimate relationship between the circulatory and respiratory systems.

27.1 Blood Has Diverse Functions

Watch a crime drama on TV, and it won't be long until a gunshot wound leaves someone lying in a pool of blood. Unless help arrives immediately, life quickly fades—a vivid reminder of blood's importance.

Blood is the fluid that the **circulatory system** transports throughout the body. This liquid carries many substances, among them the food and oxygen gas (O_2) required in aerobic cellular respiration. Without these resources, the body's cells could not generate the ATP required for life. Blood not only delivers these and other raw materials, but it also carries off wastes such as carbon dioxide (CO_2).

Besides blood, the circulatory system also includes a system of vessels that contain the blood (or a comparable fluid). The **heart** is the central pump that keeps the blood moving through these vessels.

The circulatory system has extensive connections with organ systems that exchange materials with the environment. For example, blood vessels acquire O_2 and unload CO_2 at gills, lungs, or other organs of the respiratory system. Nutrients enter the circulatory system at blood vessels near the intestines, which form part of the digestive system. Blood also circulates through the kidneys, which eliminate many water-soluble metabolic wastes (see chapter 28). Moreover, blood participates in immune reactions (see chapter 29) and helps maintain homeostasis in several ways.

Blood is a connective tissue that consists of several types of cells and cell fragments, all suspended in a liquid extracellular matrix called plasma (figure 27.1). The cell types are diverse: a cubic millimeter of blood normally contains about 5 million red blood cells, 7000 white blood cells, and 250,000 cell fragments called platelets. This section describes the functions of each component of blood; the Burning Question on page 544 explains how donating plasma and whole blood can save lives. ▸ connective tissue, p. 469

A. Plasma Carries Many Dissolved Substances

Plasma is the liquid matrix of blood. This fluid, which makes up more than half of the blood's volume, is 90% to 92% water. The function of plasma is to exchange water and dissolved substances with the fluid that surrounds the body's cells.

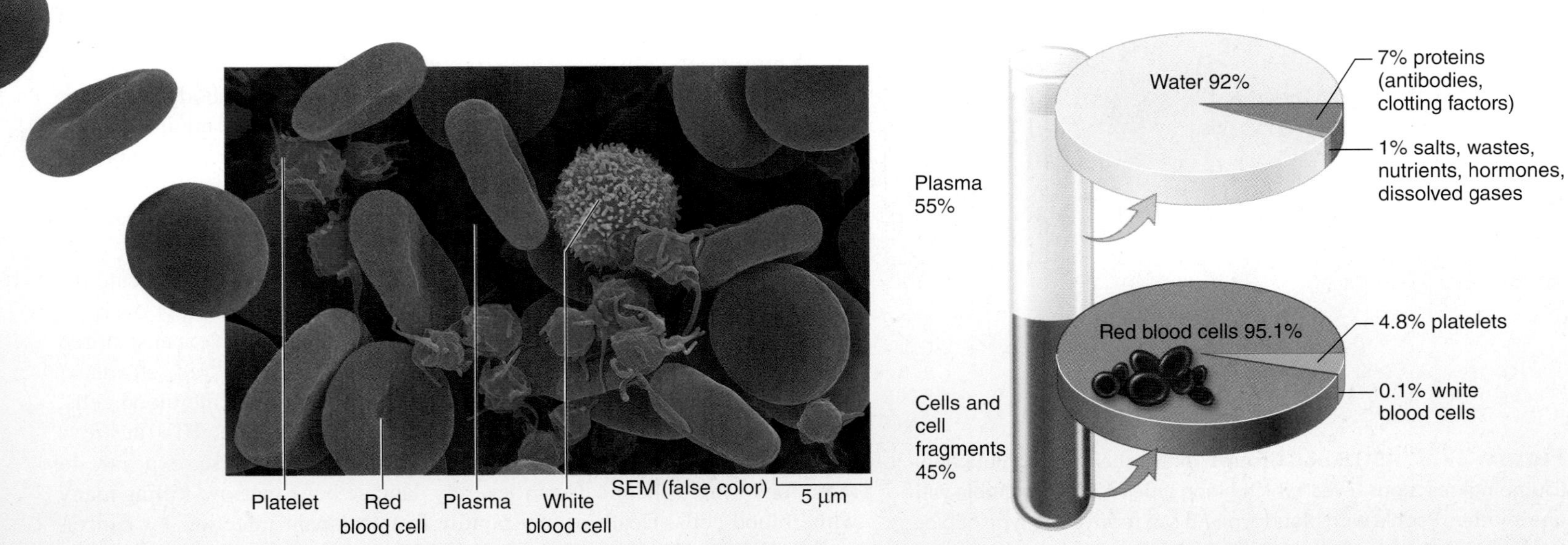

Figure 27.1 Blood Composition. Human blood is a mixture of red blood cells, white blood cells, and platelets suspended in a liquid called plasma.

Burning Questions

What is the difference between donating whole blood and donating plasma?

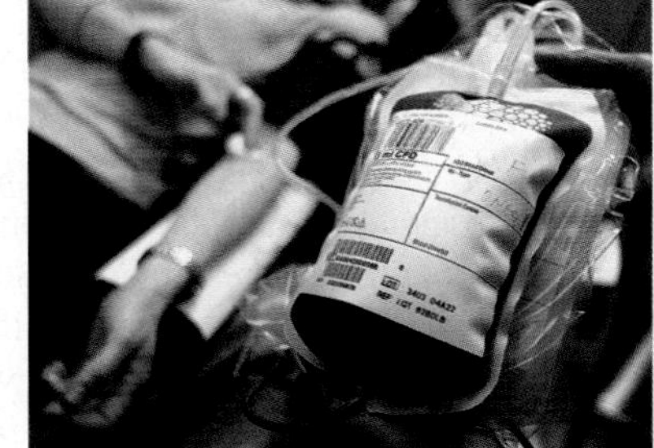

A person who "gives blood" donates 450 to 500 milliliters (about a pint) of blood to a nonprofit blood bank. After being screened for disease-causing agents, the blood may go to patients who need transfusions following trauma or surgery. More commonly, however, the blood is separated into its components, such as red blood cells, platelets, or clotting proteins. In this way, a single blood donation can help several different patients.

Plasma donation is another option. In this process, whole blood is removed from a donor's body, then a machine separates out the plasma. The red blood cells and other components are returned to the donor. The plasma center sells the plasma to pharmaceutical companies, which use it to manufacture treatments for hemophilia, hepatitis, and other diseases.

In the United States, it is illegal to pay a donor for whole blood. This law promotes a safe blood supply, because donors have no incentive to lie about illnesses that might disqualify them from donating. Plasma donors, however, can receive money. The companies that process the plasma purify each fraction separately, removing viruses and other harmful components.

Submit your burning question to:
marielle_hoefnagels@mcgraw-hill.com

Besides water, more than 70 types of dissolved proteins make up the largest component of plasma. These proteins have many functions. For example, antibodies participate in the body's immune response; high- and low-density lipoproteins transport cholesterol; and clotting factors help stop bleeding following an injury (see section 27.1D). ▸▸ antibodies, p. 595; cholesterol, p. 38

About 1% of plasma consists of dissolved salts, hormones, metabolic wastes, CO_2, nutrients, and vitamins. The concentrations of these dissolved molecules are low, but they are critical. For example, blood usually contains about 0.1% glucose; if the concentration falls to 0.06%, convulsions begin.

B. Red Blood Cells Transport Oxygen

Red blood cells are saucer-shaped disks that are packed with the pigment **hemoglobin,** a protein that carries O_2. As they fill with hemoglobin, the red blood cells of humans and some other vertebrates lose their nuclei. This adaptation maximizes the space available for hemoglobin but also means that the mature cells cannot divide.

Red blood cells originate from stem cells in red bone marrow at a rate of 2 million to 3 million per second. Mature red blood cells leave the bone marrow and enter the circulation. During its life of about 120 days, each red blood cell pounds against artery walls and squeezes through tiny capillaries. Eventually, the spleen destroys the cell and recycles most of its components. ▸ bone marrow, p. 528

Carbohydrate "markers" designated A and B may be embedded in the outer membranes of red blood cells. These markers determine each individual's blood type: A, B, AB, or O. Knowing a person's blood type is important in blood transfusions because the immune system reacts to "foreign" molecules that are not already present in the blood. Antibodies produced against incompatible blood types cause **agglutination,** a reaction in which the cells clump together (figure 27.2). Agglutination following a transfusion of incompatible blood can be fatal. ▸ ABO blood type, p. 183

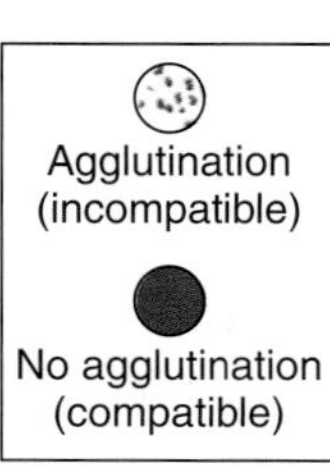

Figure 27.2 ABO Blood Groups. In this chart, the agglutination (clumping) reactions reveal which blood types are incompatible with one another. People with blood type AB can receive any type of blood; conversely, anyone can receive type O blood.

C. White Blood Cells Fight Infection

Blood also contains five types of **white blood cells,** or leukocytes. These immune system cells are larger than red blood cells, retain their nuclei, and lack hemoglobin.

White blood cells originate from stem cells in red bone marrow. Although many enter the bloodstream, most either wander in body tissues or settle in the lymphatic system. These cells participate in many immune responses. Some secrete signaling molecules that provoke inflammation, whereas others destroy microbes or produce antibodies. Chapter 29 explains the lymphatic system and the interactions of white blood cells in more detail.

White blood cell numbers that are too high or too low can indicate illness. For example, **leukemias** are cancers in which bone marrow overproduces white blood cells. The abnormal white cells form at the expense of red blood cells, so when the patient's "white cell count" rises, the "red cell count" falls. Thus, leukemia also causes anemia. Having too few white blood cells, on the other hand, leaves the body vulnerable to infection. HIV destroys T cells (a type of white blood cell), causing AIDS. Likewise, exposure to radiation or toxic chemicals can severely damage bone marrow, killing many white blood cells. Death occurs rapidly from rampant infection. ▸▸ cancer, p. 148; HIV, p. 130

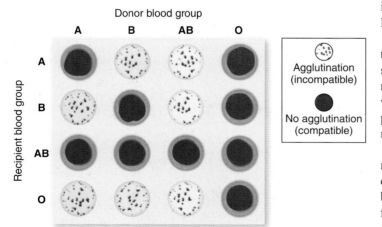

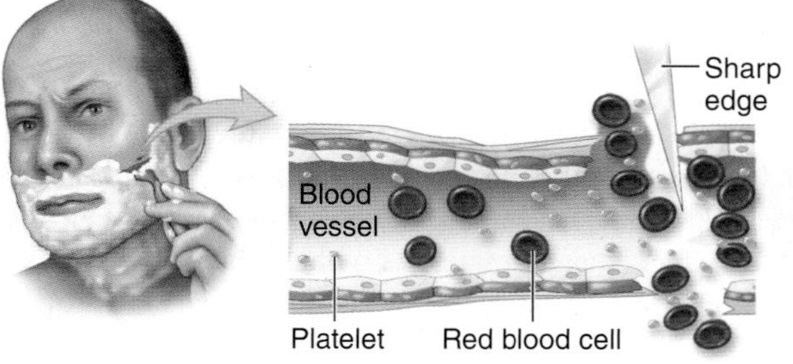

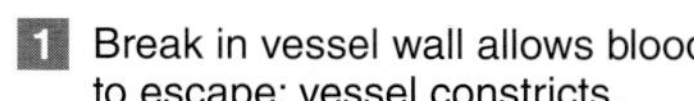

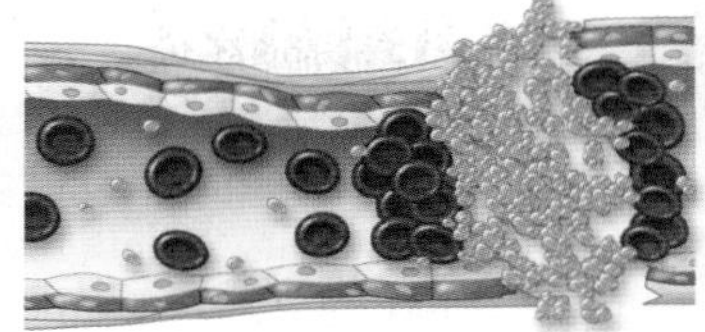

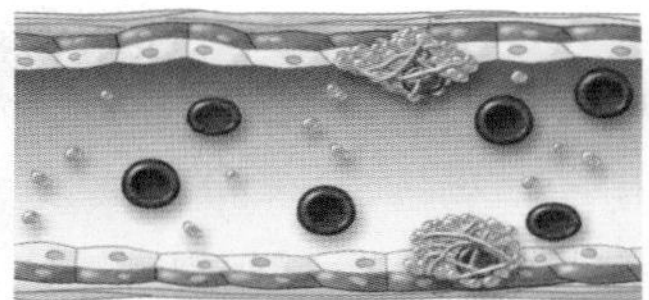

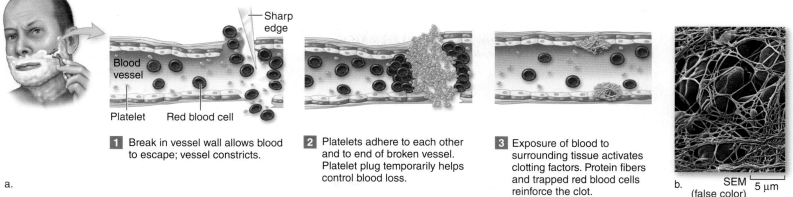

1 Break in vessel wall allows blood to escape; vessel constricts.

2 Platelets adhere to each other and to end of broken vessel. Platelet plug temporarily helps control blood loss.

3 Exposure of blood to surrounding tissue activates clotting factors. Protein fibers and trapped red blood cells reinforce the clot.

a.

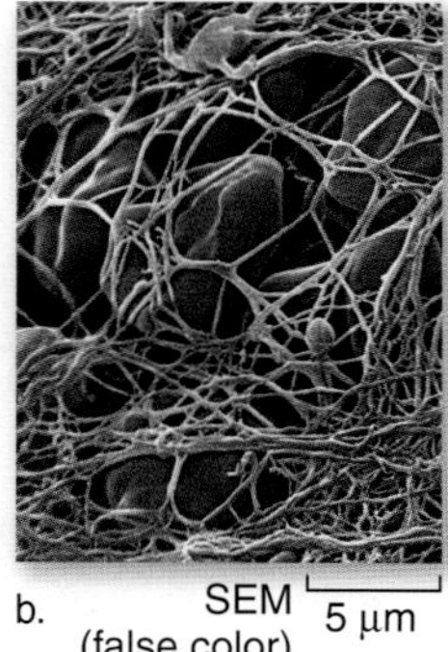

b.

Figure 27.3 Blood Clotting. (a) A cut blood vessel immediately constricts. Platelets aggregate at the injured site, forming a temporary plug. Proteins called clotting factors participate in a cascade of reactions, producing a meshwork of protein threads that strengthens the clot. (b) Red blood cells are trapped by protein threads in a clot.

D. Blood Clotting Requires Platelets and Plasma Proteins

Platelets are small, colorless cell fragments that initiate blood clotting. A platelet originates as part of a huge cell containing rows of vesicles that divide the cytoplasm into distinct regions, like a sheet of stamps. The vesicles enlarge and join together, "shedding" fragments that become platelets.

In a healthy circulatory system, platelets travel freely within the vessels. Sometimes, however, a wound nicks a blood vessel, or the blood vessel's inner lining may become obstructed. Platelets then aggregate at the site, releasing biochemicals that combine with plasma proteins called clotting factors. The resulting series of chemical reactions ends with the formation of a **blood clot**—a plug of solidified blood (figure 27.3).

Blood that clots too slowly can lead to severe blood loss. Hemophilias, for example, are inherited bleeding disorders caused by absent or abnormal clotting factors. Deficiencies of vitamins C or K can also slow clotting and wound healing. Blood that clots too readily is also extremely dangerous. In atherosclerosis, platelets may snag on rough spots in blood vessel linings. The resulting clot may stay in place or travel in the bloodstream to another location; either way, the obstruction may cut off circulation and sometimes even cause death.

Table 27.1 summarizes the functions of blood.

TABLE 27.1 Functions of Blood: A Summary

Function	Explanation
Gas exchange	Carries O_2 from lungs to tissues; carries CO_2 to the lungs to be exhaled
Nutrient transport	Carries nutrients absorbed by the digestive system throughout the body
Waste transport	Carries urea (a waste product of protein metabolism) to the kidneys for excretion in urine
Hormone transport	Carries hormones secreted by endocrine glands
Creation of interstitial fluid	Interstitial fluid that surrounds cells forms from blood plasma
Maintain homeostasis	Regulates blood pH; regulates cells' water content; generates pressure gradient that keeps plasma in capillaries; absorbs heat and dissipates it at the body's surface
Protection	Blood clots plug damaged vessels; white blood cells destroy foreign particles and participate in inflammation

27.1 Mastering Concepts

1. What are the components of blood?
2. What is the location and function of hemoglobin?
3. What are the functions of white blood cells?
4. Where do red and white blood cells originate?
5. Describe the process of blood clotting.

27.2 Animal Circulatory Systems Range from Simple to Complex

Some types of animals lack blood and a dedicated circulatory system. Flatworms, for example, use their incomplete digestive tracts not only to absorb nutrients but also in gas exchange. ▶ flatworms, p. 329

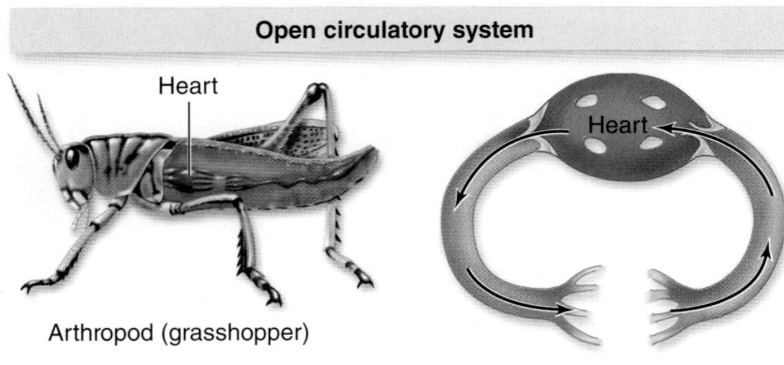

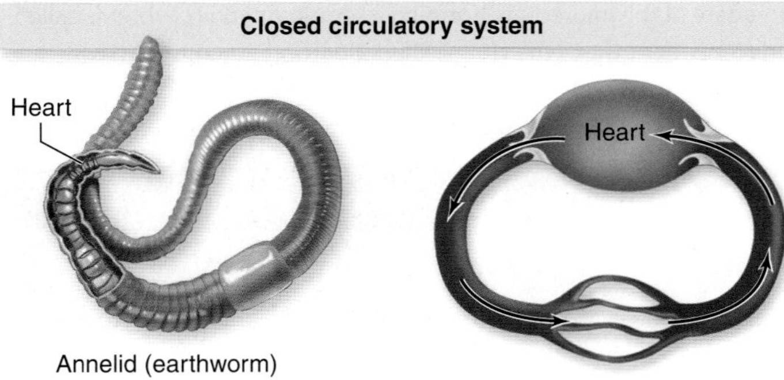

Figure 27.4 Open and Closed Circulatory Systems. In an open circulatory system, fluid leaves vessels and bathes cells directly. In a closed circulatory system, blood is confined within vessels.

Most animals, however, do have a circulatory system, which may be open or closed (figure 27.4). In an **open circulatory system,** a heart pumps fluid through short, open-ended vessels. These vessels lead to open spaces in the body cavity, where the fluid can exchange materials with the body's cells. The fluid then enters other vessels leading back to the heart. Animals with open circulatory systems include most mollusks and arthropods. In a **closed circulatory system,** blood remains within vessels that exchange materials with the fluid surrounding the body's cells. Examples of animals with closed circulatory systems include vertebrates, annelids, and some mollusks such as squids and octopuses. ▸▸▸ mollusks, p. 330; arthropods, p. 333; annelids, p. 331

Both types of circulatory systems have advantages. Open circulatory systems require fewer vessels, and the blood moves under low pressure. The energetic costs of circulation are therefore relatively low. On the other hand, blood flows at higher pressure in a closed circulatory system, so nutrient delivery and waste removal can occur more rapidly. Moreover, the vessels of a closed system can direct blood flow toward or away from specific areas of the body, depending on metabolic demands. Closed circulatory systems therefore tend to be more efficient than open systems.

All vertebrates have closed circulatory systems, but these systems do not all work the same way. Figure 27.5 shows two examples. Among the vertebrates, fishes and tadpoles have the simplest circulatory systems (see figure 27.5a). A fish's heart has just two chambers: an **atrium** where blood enters, and a **ventricle** from which blood exits. The heart pumps blood through the gills to pick up O_2 and unload CO_2. The blood then circulates to the rest of the body before returning to the heart.

Other vertebrates divide the circulatory system into two interrelated circuits united by a three- or four-chambered heart. The heart of a bird or mammal, for example, has four chambers: two atria and two ventricles (see figure 27.5b). In the **pulmonary circulation,** blood from the right side of the heart exchanges gases at the lungs and returns to the heart; in the **systemic circulation,** blood circulates from the left side of the heart to the rest of the body before returning to the right atrium.

In contrast, the heart of an adult amphibian and of most nonavian reptiles has only three chambers: two atria and one ventricle. The three-chambered heart is

Figure 27.5 Vertebrate Circulatory Systems. (a) A fish's two-chambered heart pumps blood in a single circuit around the body. (b) A bird or mammal has a four-chambered heart, maximizing the separation of the pulmonary and systemic circuits.

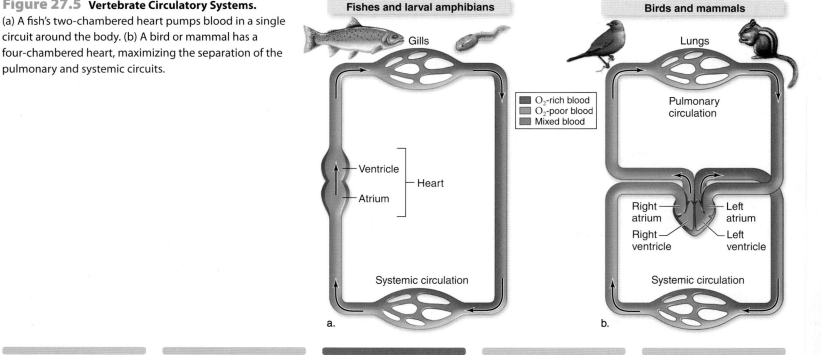

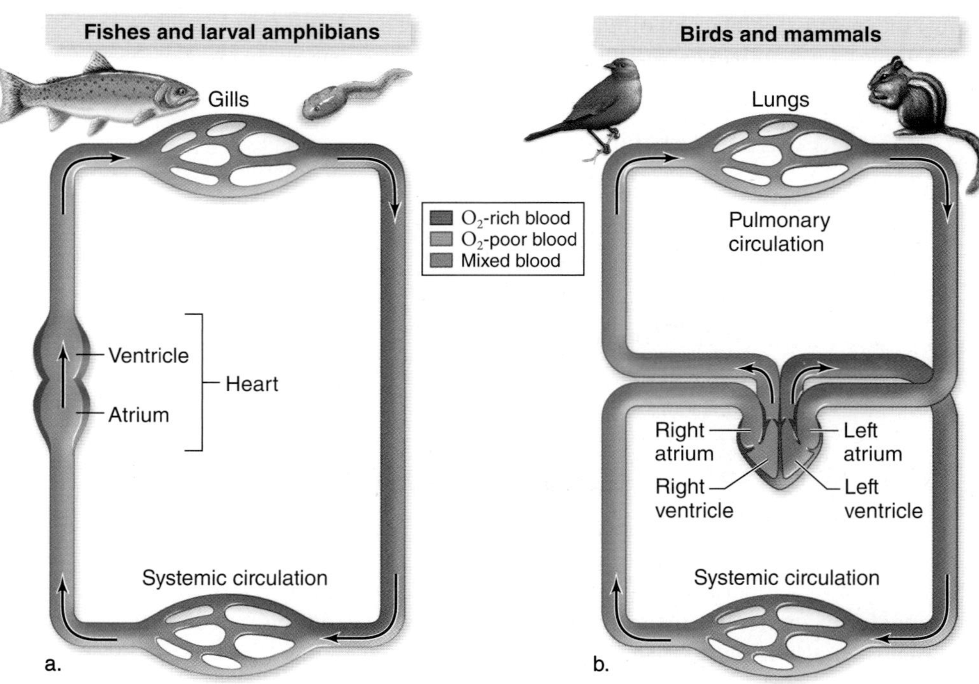

less efficient because the ventricle mixes oxygenated blood from the pulmonary circuit with oxygen-poor blood returning from the systemic circuit.

The rest of this chapter focuses on the human circulatory system and its interactions with the respiratory system.

27.2 Mastering Concepts

1. Distinguish between open and closed circulatory systems.
2. What is the difference between pulmonary and systemic circulation?

27.3 Blood Circulates Through the Heart and Blood Vessels

The plasma, cells, and platelets that make up blood circulate throughout the body in an elaborate system of blood vessels, thanks to the relentless pumping of the heart. This entire transportation network is called the **cardiovascular system** (*cardio-* refers to the heart, *vascular* to the vessels).

Figure 27.6 shows the largest of the body's blood vessels, which are classified by size and the direction of blood flow. **Arteries** are large vessels that

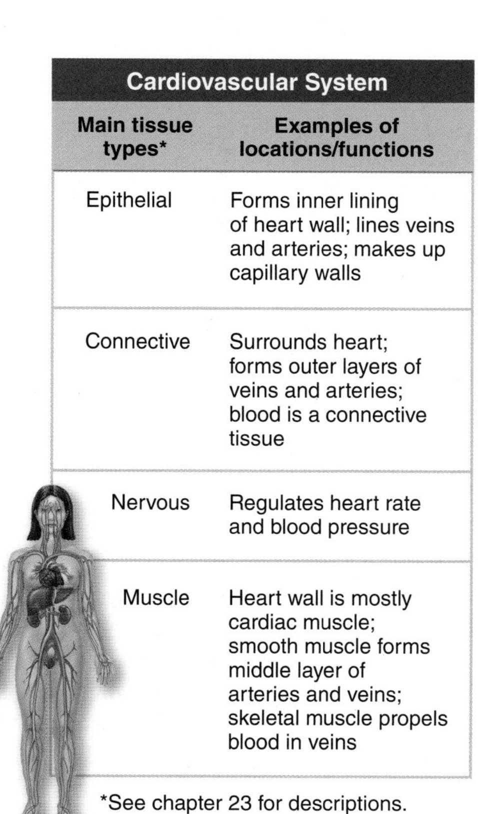

Cardiovascular System	
Main tissue types*	**Examples of locations/functions**
Epithelial	Forms inner lining of heart wall; lines veins and arteries; makes up capillary walls
Connective	Surrounds heart; forms outer layers of veins and arteries; blood is a connective tissue
Nervous	Regulates heart rate and blood pressure
Muscle	Heart wall is mostly cardiac muscle; smooth muscle forms middle layer of arteries and veins; skeletal muscle propels blood in veins

*See chapter 23 for descriptions.

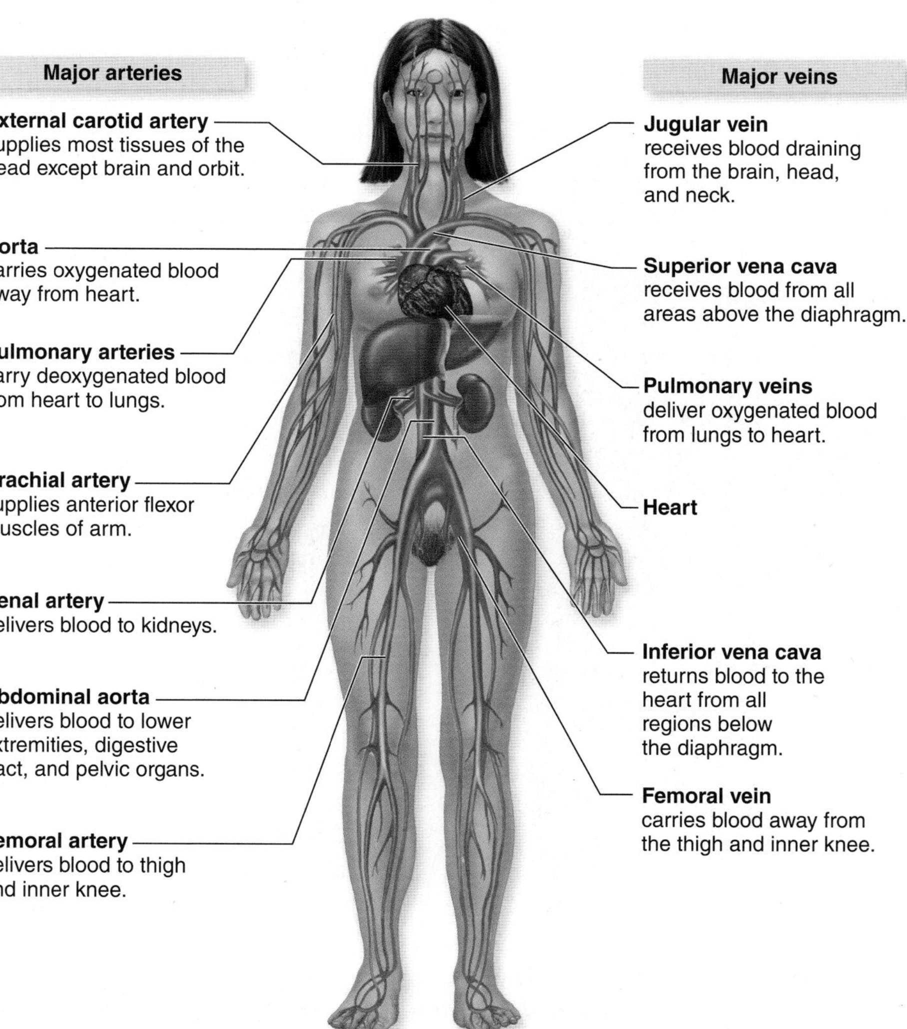
Major arteries
External carotid artery supplies most tissues of the head except brain and orbit.
Aorta carries oxygenated blood away from heart.
Pulmonary arteries carry deoxygenated blood from heart to lungs.
Brachial artery supplies anterior flexor muscles of arm.
Renal artery delivers blood to kidneys.
Abdominal aorta delivers blood to lower extremities, digestive tract, and pelvic organs.
Femoral artery delivers blood to thigh and inner knee.
Major veins
Jugular vein receives blood draining from the brain, head, and neck.
Superior vena cava receives blood from all areas above the diaphragm.
Pulmonary veins deliver oxygenated blood from lungs to heart.
Heart
Inferior vena cava returns blood to the heart from all regions below the diaphragm.
Femoral vein carries blood away from the thigh and inner knee.

Figure 27.6 Human Circulatory System.

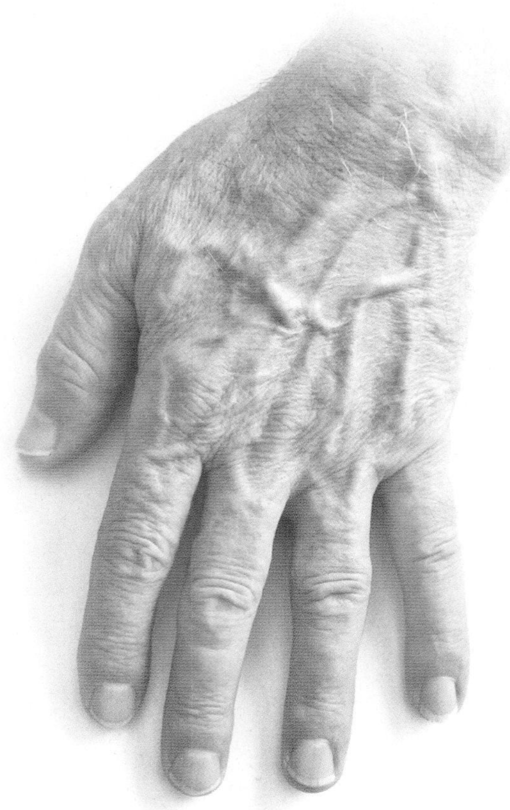

conduct blood away from the heart; the left half of the figure lists some of the body's major arteries. These branch into **arterioles,** smaller vessels that then diverge into a network of **capillaries,** the body's tiniest blood vessels.

Water and dissolved substances diffuse between each capillary and the **interstitial fluid,** the liquid that bathes the body's cells. The interstitial fluid, in turn, exchanges materials with the tissue cells.

To complete the circuit, capillaries empty into slightly larger vessels, called **venules,** which unite to form the **veins** that carry blood back to the heart. The right half of figure 27.6 lists some major veins.

Notice that in figure 27.6, arteries are red and veins are blue. This convention, coupled with the bluish appearance of blood vessels under lightly pigmented skin, has led to the misconception that the blood in veins is actually blue. In fact, blood is always red, whether it is fully oxygenated or not. Veins only appear blue because of the way that light of various wavelengths interacts with the skin. As for arteries, these blood vessels tend to be located in deeper tissues, far from the skin's surface. If arteries were visible through skin, they would appear blue, too.

27.3 Mastering Concepts

1. What is the cardiovascular system?
2. Describe the relationships among arteries, veins, arterioles, venules, and capillaries.

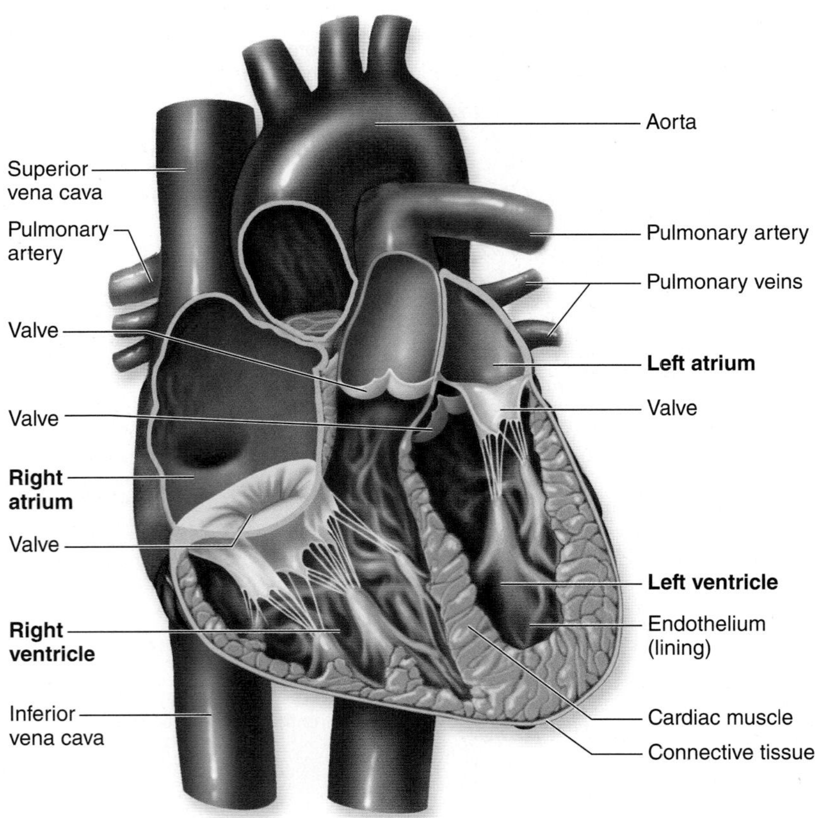

Figure 27.7 The Human Heart. This illustration depicts the four chambers, the valves, and the major blood vessels of the human heart.

27.4 The Human Heart Is a Muscular Pump

Each day, the human heart sends a volume equal to more than 7000 liters of blood through the body, and it beats more than 2.5 billion times in a lifetime. The heart of a 70-year-old person has therefore pumped enough blood to fill about 70 Olympic-sized swimming pools. This section explores the structure and function of the hard-working human heart.

A. The Heart Has Four Chambers

Figure 27.7 illustrates the fist-sized human heart. A tough connective tissue sac encloses the heart and anchors it to surrounding tissues. This protective structure consists of two tissue layers. Thanks to lubricating fluid between the two layers, the heart is free to move, even during vigorous beating.

The wall of the heart itself consists mostly of a thick layer of **cardiac muscle.** Contraction of this muscle provides the force that propels blood. The innermost lining of the heart (and of all blood vessels) consists of **endothelium,** a one-cell-thick layer of simple squamous epithelium. ▸▸ epithelial tissue, p. 469; cardiac muscle, p. 471

The human heart has four chambers: two upper atria and two lower ventricles. The atria are "primer pumps" that send blood to the ventricles, which pump the blood to the lungs or the rest of the body. Four heart valves ensure that blood moves in one direction. Two of the valves keep blood from moving back into the atrium when a ventricle contracts, and two prevent backflow into the ventricles from the arteries leaving the heart.

B. The Right and Left Halves of the Heart Deliver Blood Along Different Paths

A schematic view of the circulatory system shows the pathway of blood as it travels to and from the heart (figure 27.8). The two largest veins in the body, the superior vena cava and the inferior vena cava, deliver blood from the systemic circulation to the right atrium. From there, blood passes into the right ventricle and through the **pulmonary arteries** to the lungs, where blood picks up O_2 and unloads CO_2. The **pulmonary veins** carry oxygen-rich blood from the lungs to the left atrium of the heart, completing the pulmonary circuit.

The blood then flows from the left atrium into the left ventricle, the most powerful heart chamber. The massive force of contraction of the left ventricle sends blood into the **aorta,** the largest artery in the body. The blood then circulates throughout the body before returning to the veins that deliver blood to the right side of the heart. The systemic circuit is complete.

How does the heart muscle itself receive its blood supply? Blood does not seep from the heart's chambers directly to the cardiac muscle. Instead, two vessels that branch off of the aorta, the **coronary arteries,** supply blood to the heart muscle. A smaller vein that enters the right atrium returns blood that has been circulating within the walls of the heart. Blockage of a coronary artery can cause a heart attack.

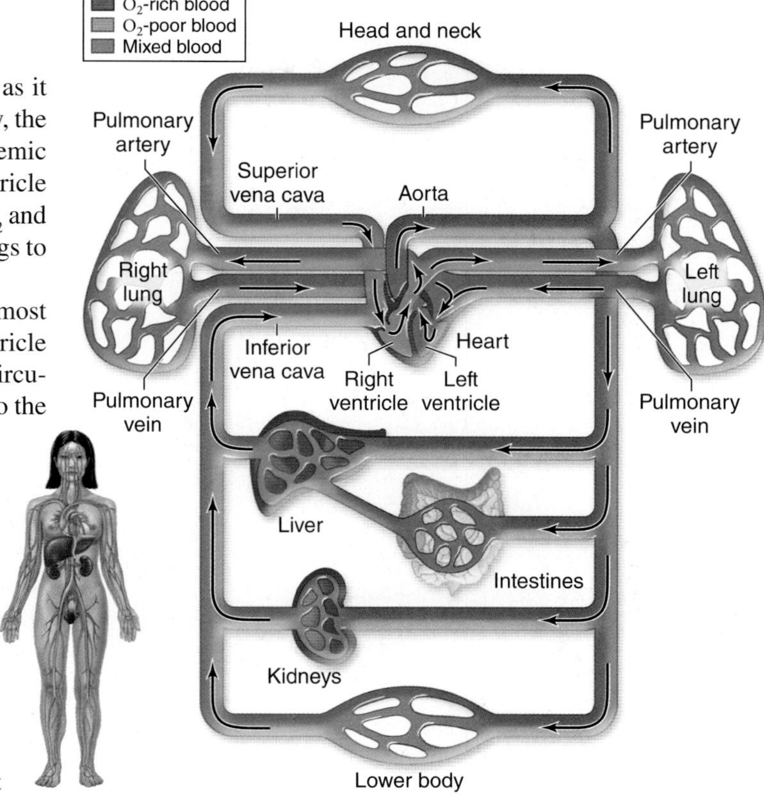

Figure 27.8 Blood's Journey in the Circulatory System. Oxygen-depleted blood leaving the right side of the heart goes to the lungs to pick up O_2. The oxygenated blood enters the left side of the heart, which pumps the blood throughout the body.

C. Cardiac Muscle Cells Produce the Heartbeat

A **cardiac cycle,** or a single beat of the heart, consists of the events that occur with each contraction and relaxation of the heart muscle.

Each heartbeat requires the forceful contraction of cardiac muscle in the wall of the heart. The sliding filament model of muscle contraction described in chapter 26 applies to cardiac muscle, just as it does to skeletal muscle. Unlike skeletal muscle, however, cardiac muscle does not require stimulation from motor neurons to contract.

Instead, cardiac muscle is "self-excitable"; many cardiac muscle cells contract in unison without input from the central nervous system. Cardiac muscle cells are interconnected, forming an almost netlike pattern (see figure 23.4). As a result, synchronized waves of action potentials can spread from cell to cell.

The signal to contract begins at the **pacemaker,** or **sinoatrial (SA) node** (figure 27.9). This region of specialized cardiac muscle cells sets the tempo of the beat (normally about 75 beats per minute). Each time the cells of the pacemaker fire, they stimulate the cardiac cells of the atria to contract. After a brief delay, which gives the ventricles time to fill, a "relay station" called the

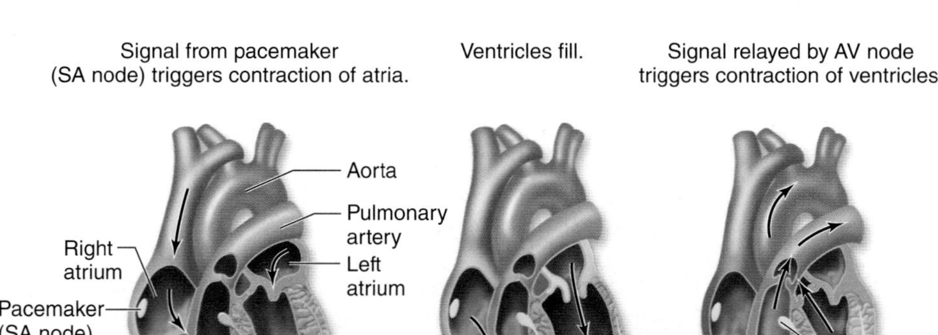

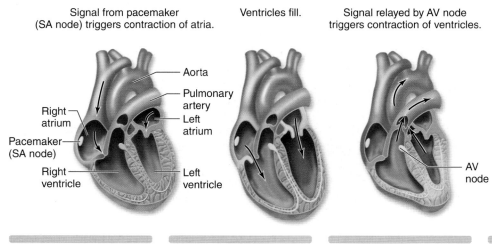

Figure 27.9 Heartbeat. Electrical signals that trigger the heartbeat start in the pacemaker (SA node), travel through the wall of the right atrium to the AV node, and pass to the ventricle walls.

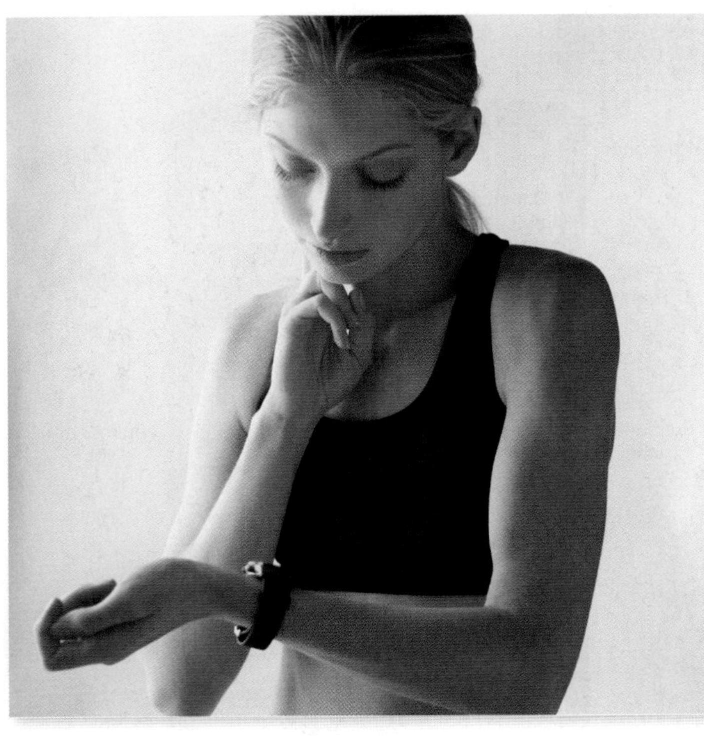

atrioventricular (AV) node sends the electrical stimulation to the ventricle walls. The cardiac cells of the ventricles then contract in unison.

The familiar "lub-dup" sound of the beating heart comes from the two sets of heart valves closing, preventing blood from flowing backward during each contraction. A heart murmur is a variation on the normal "lub-dup" sound, and it often reflects abnormally functioning valves.

D. Exercise Strengthens the Heart

After you circle the bases in a softball game, you may notice that your heart is beating faster than normal. The explanation for your elevated heart rate relates to the activity of your skeletal muscles, which require lots of ATP. Regenerating that ATP by aerobic respiration requires O_2; as we have already seen, one function of blood is to deliver this essential gas to the body's cells.

As you exercise, your heart meets the increased demand for O_2 by increasing its **cardiac output,** a measure of the volume of blood that the heart pumps each minute. Cardiac output is a function of the heart rate and the volume of blood pumped per stroke. Elevating the heart rate therefore quickly boosts cardiac output during an exercise session. With regular exercise, however, the stroke volume will also increase. An active person can therefore pump the same amount of blood at 50 beats per minute as a sedentary person's heart pumps at 75 beats per minute.

Exercise provides several other cardiovascular benefits as well. The number of red blood cells increases in response to regular exercise, and these cells are packed with more hemoglobin, delivering more O_2 to tissues. Exercise can also lower blood pressure and reduce the amount of cholesterol in blood. Moreover, regular activity spurs the development of extra blood vessels within the walls of the heart, which may help prevent a heart attack by providing alternative pathways for blood to flow to the heart muscle.

To achieve the most benefit from exercise, the heart rate must be elevated to 70% to 85% of its "theoretical maximum" for at least half an hour three times a week. One way to calculate your theoretical maximum is to subtract your age from 220 (table 27.2). If you are 18 years old, your theoretical maximum is 202 beats per minute; 70% to 85% of this value is 141 to 172 beats per minute. Tennis, skating, skiing, racquetball, vigorous dancing, hockey, basketball, biking, or brisk walking can elevate your heart rate to this level.

TABLE 27.2 Target Heart Rates by Age

Age	Theoretical Maximum Heart Rate (beats per minute)	Target Heart Rate During Exercise (beats per minute)
20	200	140–170
25	195	137–166
30	190	133–162
40	180	126–153
50	170	119–145
60	160	112–136
70	150	105–128

27.4 Mastering Concepts

1. Describe the anatomy of the heart.
2. Describe the path of blood through the heart's chambers and valves, and through the pulmonary and systemic circulations.
3. What is the function of heart valves?
4. How does the heartbeat originate and spread?
5. How does exercise affect the circulatory system?

27.5 Blood Vessels Form the Circulation Pathway

As the heart's ventricles contract, they push blood to the lungs and the rest of the body. This section describes the system of vessels through which blood travels as it delivers nutrients and removes wastes.

A. Arteries, Capillaries, and Veins Have Different Structures

As we have already seen, arteries carry blood away from the heart, whereas veins return blood to the heart. Despite these opposite functions, the walls of arteries and veins share some similarities (figure 27.10). The outermost layer is a sheath of connective tissue. The middle layer is made mostly of **smooth muscle,** and endothelium forms the innermost layer. ▸ smooth muscle, p. 471

One feature that characterizes artery walls is a thick layer of smooth muscle. The muscular walls of major arteries can withstand the high-pressure surges of blood leaving the heart. As arteries branch farther from the heart, however, their walls become thinner, and the outermost layer of connective tissue may taper away. Arterioles do retain a layer of smooth muscle that helps adjust blood pressure; section 27.5B describes how this regulation occurs.

Arterioles branch into **capillary beds,** networks of tiny blood vessels that connect an arteriole and a venule (see the lower half of figure 27.10). Capillaries are tiny but very numerous, providing extensive surface area where materials are exchanged with the interstitial fluid. Because their walls consist of a single layer of endothelial cells, nutrients and gases easily diffuse into and out of capillaries. ▸ diffusion, p. 76

From the capillary beds, blood flows into venules, which converge into veins. These vessels receive blood at low pressure. The smooth muscle layer in their walls is much reduced or even absent (see figure 27.10, upper left portion); in fact, unlike an artery, a vein collapses when empty.

If pressure in veins is so low, what propels blood back to the heart, against the force of gravity? In many veins, valves keep blood flowing in one direction (figure 27.11). As skeletal muscles contract, they squeeze veins and propel

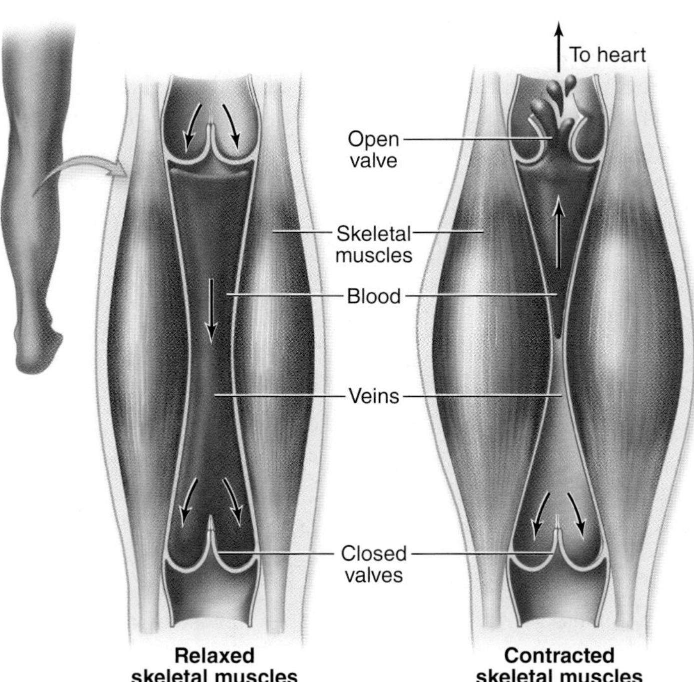

Figure 27.11 Valves in Veins. When skeletal muscles are relaxed, valves prevent blood from flowing backward in veins. Contracted skeletal muscles squeeze the veins, propelling blood through the open valves. In this illustration, the veins appear much larger than they are relative to real muscles.

Figure 27.10 Types of Blood Vessels. The walls of arteries and veins consist of connective tissue, smooth muscle, and endothelium. Arteries, which are subject to high blood pressure, are much more muscular than veins. In some veins, valves keep blood moving toward the heart. A capillary bed is a network of tiny vessels that lies between an arteriole and a venule. The capillary wall consists only of endothelium through which nutrients, wastes, and gases pass.

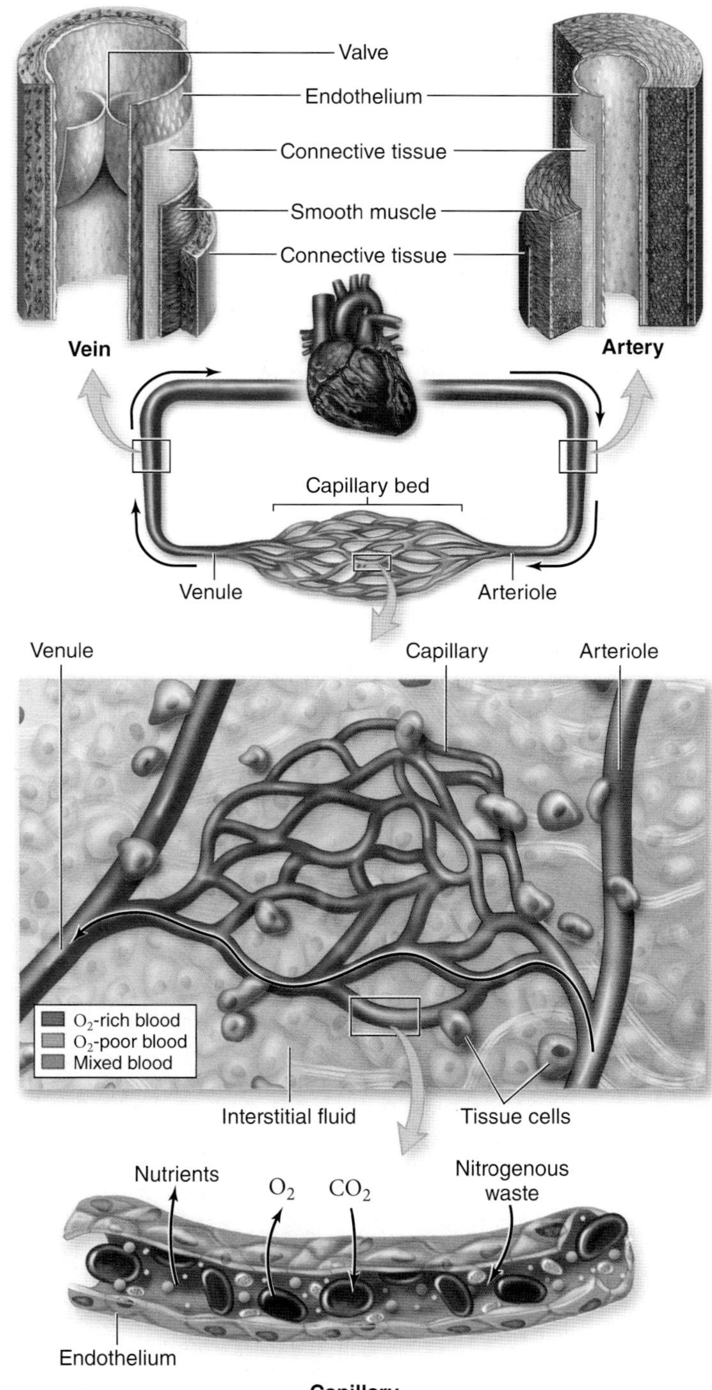

blood through the open valves in the only direction it can move: toward the heart. Varicose veins result in part from faulty valves that cause blood to pool in the veins of the lower legs. The walls of these distended blood vessels form prominent bulges under the skin.

B. Blood Pressure and Velocity Differ Among Vessel Types

A routine doctor's office visit always includes a blood pressure reading, a good indication of overall cardiovascular health. **Blood pressure** is the force that blood exerts on artery walls. As the heart drives blood through the vessels, you can feel your blood pressure as a "pulse."

A device called a sphygmomanometer measures the changes in blood pressure that occur throughout the cardiac cycle (figure 27.12). The **systolic pressure,** or upper number in a blood pressure reading, reflects the contraction of the ventricles. The **diastolic pressure,** or low point, occurs when the ventricles relax.

Blood pressure readings are in units of "millimeters of mercury," abbreviated "mm Hg"; this terminology derives from older sphygmomanometers, which measured the distance over which blood pressure could push a column of mercury. A typical blood pressure reading for a young adult is 110 mm Hg for the systolic pressure and 70 mm Hg for the diastolic pressure, expressed as "110 over 70" (written 110/70). "Normal" blood pressure, however, varies with age, sex, race, and other factors.

Blood pressure decreases with distance from the heart; that is, blood in arteries has the highest pressure, followed by capillaries and then veins. Blood velocity, however, is lowest in the capillaries. The reason is that the total cross-sectional area of capillaries is much greater than that of the arteries or veins. Just as the velocity of a river slows as the water spreads out over a delta, so does the flow of blood slow as it is divided among countless tiny capillaries. This leisurely flow of blood through the capillaries enhances nutrient and waste exchange.

Past the capillaries, venules converge into veins. The total cross-sectional area of these blood vessels is smaller than that of the capillaries. The resulting reduction in cross-sectional area helps speed blood flow back to the heart. To understand why, picture water flowing out of a hose. If you put your thumb over the nozzle, you reduce the area of the opening. What happens? The velocity of water through the nozzle increases.

Figure 27.12 Blood Pressure. (a) A sphygmomanometer measures blood pressure. The cuff is wrapped around the upper arm and inflated until no pulse is felt in the inner elbow, which signifies that circulation to the lower arm has been temporarily cut off. A stethoscope placed on the arm just below the cuff detects the sound of returning blood flow when the cuff slowly deflates. (b) The listener notes the pressure on the gauge when a thumping is first audible; this sound is the blood rushing through the arteries past the deflating cuff. The value on the gauge when the sound begins is the systolic blood pressure. The pressure reading when the sound ends is the diastolic blood pressure.

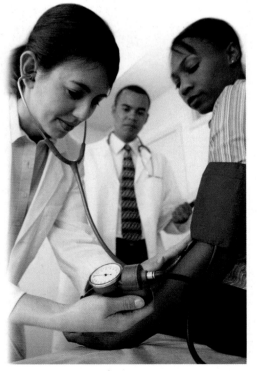

a.

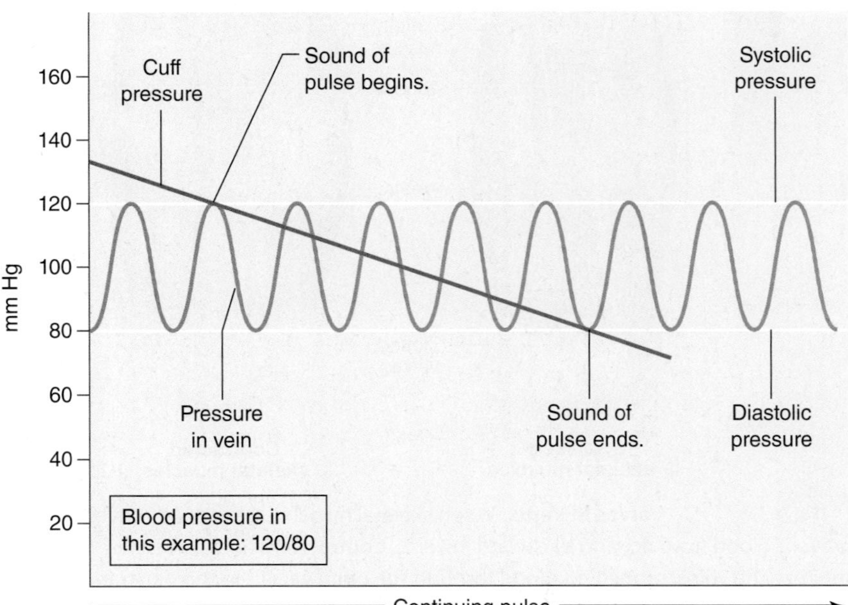

b.

Overall, a person's blood pressure reflects many factors, including blood vessel diameter, heart rate, and blood volume. The body regulates blood pressure over the long term by raising or lowering the volume of blood. Chapter 28 describes how the kidneys adjust the blood's volume by controlling the amount of fluid excreted in urine.

In the short term, blood vessel diameter and heart rate are under constant regulation by negative feedback (figure 27.13). Pressure receptors within the walls of major arteries detect blood pressure and pass that information to the medulla, in the brainstem. The medulla, via the autonomic nervous system, adjusts both heart rate and the diameter of arterioles to maintain homeostasis.
▸▸ negative feedback, p. 475; autonomic nervous system, p. 491

The role of the arterioles deserves special mention. **Vasoconstriction** is the narrowing of blood vessels that results from the contraction of smooth muscle in arteriole walls. When arteriole diameter decreases, blood pressure rises. The opposite effect, **vasodilation,** is the widening of blood vessels that occurs when the same muscles relax. Altering arteriole diameter allows the body to increase blood delivery to regions that need it most. During physical activity, for example, skeletal muscles receive additional blood at the expense of organs not in immediate use, such as those in the digestive tract.

Blood pressure that is too low or too high can cause health problems. Hypotension, which is blood pressure significantly lower than normal, may cause fainting. At the opposite end of the spectrum, consistently elevated blood pressure, or hypertension, may severely damage the circulatory system and other organs. High blood pressure affects about 31% of adults in the United States. The exact cause is usually unknown, but poor diet, smoking, and stress all increase a person's risk of developing hypertension.

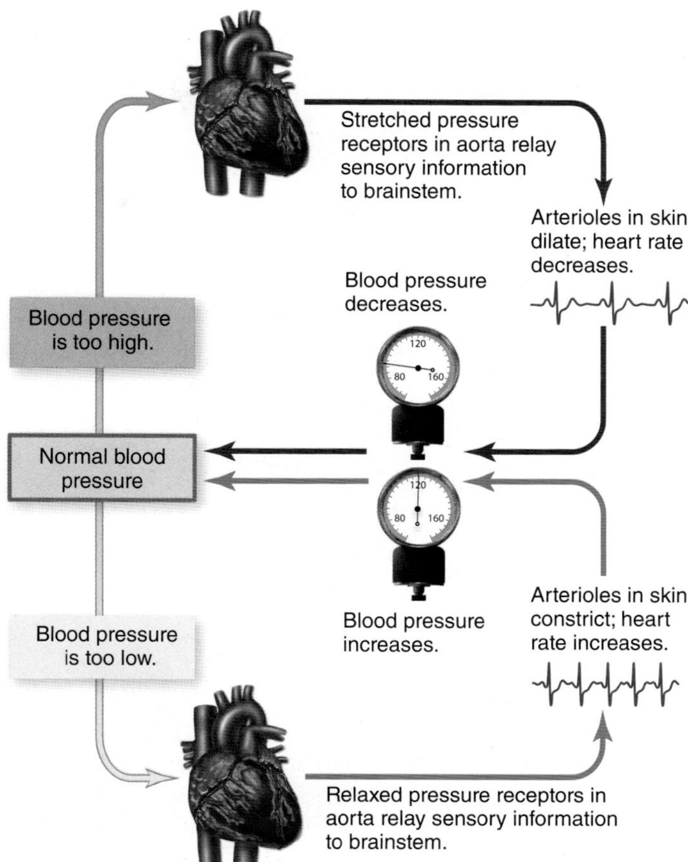

Figure 27.13 Regulation of Blood Pressure. A negative feedback loop regulates blood pressure in the short term. Stretch-sensitive neurons detect pressure in major arteries. If blood pressure climbs too high, signals from the central nervous system cause the blood vessels to dilate and the heart rate to slow. If blood pressure is too low, vessels constrict and the heart beats faster.

27.5 Mastering Concepts

1. Compare and contrast the structures of arteries, capillaries, and veins.
2. Trace the path of a red blood cell from the heart to a capillary bed in the foot and back to the heart.
3. Across the human circulatory system, how are blood pressure, blood velocity, and vessel diameter related?
4. How does the regulation of blood pressure illustrate negative feedback?

27.6 The Human Respiratory System Delivers Air to the Lungs

As we have already seen, one function of blood is to deliver O_2 to cells and to collect the CO_2 waste that cells produce. In most animals, the **respiratory system** exchanges these gases with the environment. The functions of the circulatory and respiratory systems are therefore closely connected.

Each of us breathes some 20,000 times a day. Most of the time, you inhale and exhale without thinking—unless you happen to be using your breath to fog a mirror, spin a pinwheel, or play the trumpet. Fun aside, breathing is obviously a vital function; if a person is deprived of air, death can occur within minutes.

Breathing is so automatic that it is easy to forget why we do it. Cells require ATP to power protein synthesis, movement, DNA replication, cell division, growth, reproduction, and countless other activities that require energy.

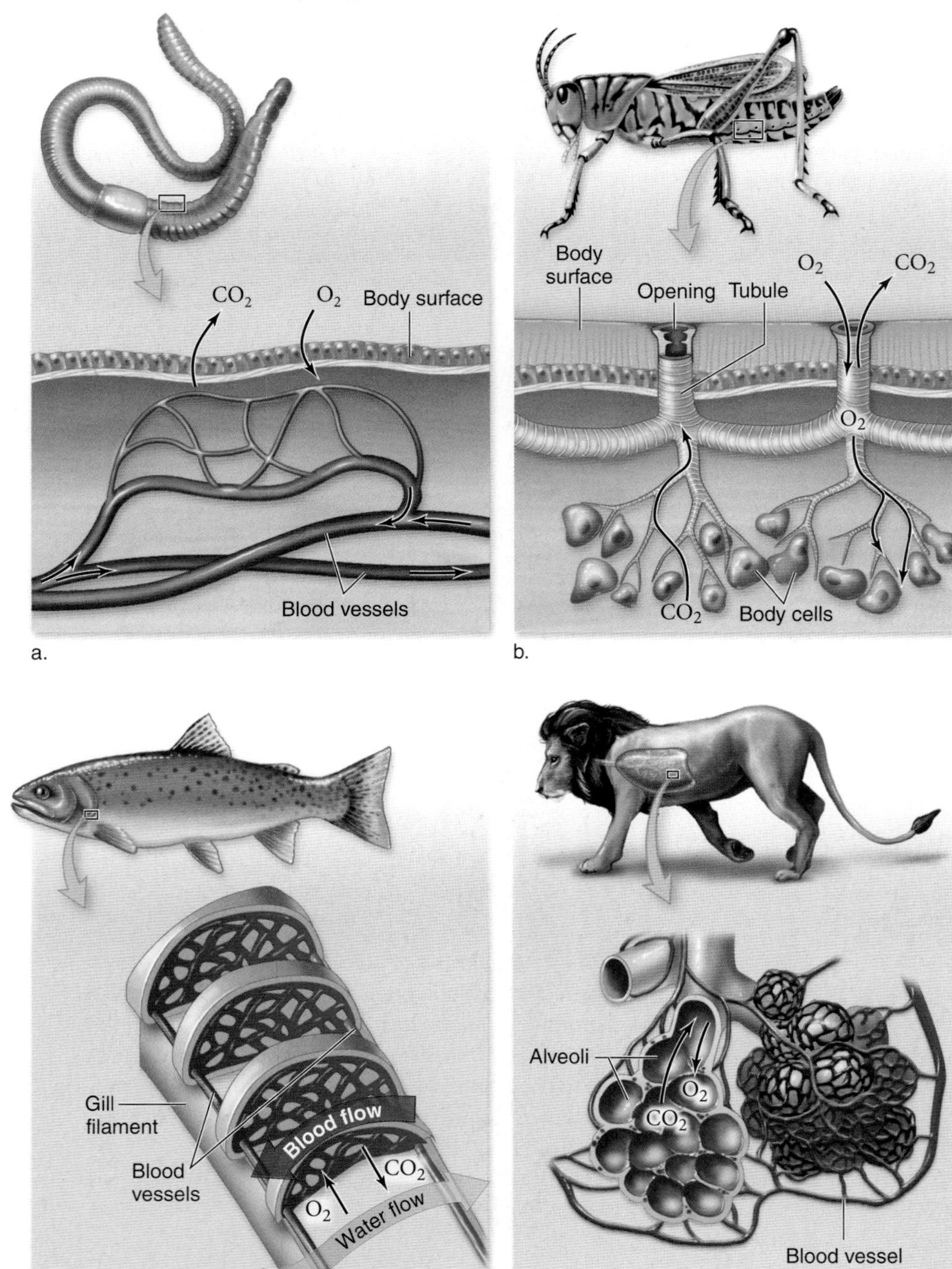

Figure 27.14 Respiratory Surfaces. Gas exchange may occur (a) across the body surface, (b) via tubules that connect the body's cells to the atmosphere, (c) at gills, or (d) in lungs.

As described in chapter 6, animal cells generate ATP in **aerobic respiration,** which consumes O_2 and generates CO_2 as a waste product. Without gas exchange, cells die. ▸ ATP, p. 72

Besides aerobic cellular respiration, the term *respiration* has two additional meanings. One is breathing (ventilation), the physical movement of air into and out of the body. Respiration can also mean the act of exchanging gases. External respiration is gas exchange between an animal's body and its environment; internal respiration is gas exchange between tissue cells and the bloodstream.

An animal's **respiratory surface** is the area of its body where external respiration occurs. In humans and other terrestrial vertebrates, the respiratory surface is inside the lungs, but other species use different surfaces (figure 27.14). Regardless of their form, however, all respiratory surfaces share three characteristics. First, their surface area must be relatively large. Not only must the respiratory surface meet the animal's demand for O_2, but it must also eliminate CO_2 fast enough to keep this waste gas from accumulating to toxic levels.

Second, an animal's respiratory surface must come into contact with either air or water; both of these substances can be a source of O_2 and a "dumping ground" for CO_2. In general, air offers two advantages over water. Air has a higher concentration of O_2 than does water; in addition, air is lighter than water. Less energy is therefore required to move air across a respiratory surface than to move an equal volume of water.

Third, respiratory surfaces consist of moist membranes across which O_2 and CO_2 diffuse. This requirement for moisture puts air-breathing organisms at a disadvantage: a respiratory surface exposed to air may dry out, rendering it useless. ▸ diffusion, p. 76

The human respiratory system is a continuous network of tubules that delivers O_2 to the circulatory system and unloads CO_2 into the lungs. Table 27.3 summarizes the functions of the respiratory system, and figure 27.15 presents an overview of its anatomy. You may find it helpful to refer to this figure as you read the rest of this section.

A. The Nose, Pharynx, and Larynx Form the Upper Respiratory Tract

The **nose,** which forms the external entrance to the nasal cavity, functions in breathing, immunity, and the sense of smell. Stiff hairs at the entrance of each nostril keep large particles out. If a particle is inhaled, a sensory cell in the nose may signal the brain to orchestrate a sneeze, which forcefully ejects the object. ▸ sense of smell, p. 498

Epithelial tissue in the nose secretes a sticky mucus that catches most airborne bacteria and dust particles that manage to bypass the hairs. Enzymes in the mucus destroy some of the would-be invaders, and immune system cells under the epithelial layer await any disease-causing organisms that penetrate the mucus.

The nasal cavity also adjusts the temperature and humidity of incoming air. Blood vessels lining the nasal cavity release heat, and mucus contributes moisture to the air. This function ensures that the respiratory surfaces deep inside the lungs remain moist.

The back of the nose and mouth leads into the **pharynx,** or throat. Both swallowed food and inhaled air pass through the pharynx. Just below and in front of the pharynx is the **larynx,** or Adam's apple, a boxlike structure that produces the voice. Stretched over the larynx are the **vocal cords,** two elastic bands of tissue that vibrate as air from the lungs passes through a slitlike opening called the **glottis.** Vibrations of the vocal cords produce the sounds of speech. A male's voice becomes deeper during puberty because the vocal cords grow longer and thicker. The cords therefore vibrate more slowly during speech, producing lower-frequency sounds that we perceive as a deeper voice.

Another function of the larynx is to direct ingested food and drink away from the respiratory system. During swallowing, a cartilage flap called the **epiglottis** covers the glottis so that food enters the digestive tract instead of the lungs.

The entire upper respiratory tract is lined with epithelium that secretes mucus. Dust and other inhaled particles trapped in the mucus are swept out by waving cilia. Coughing brings the mucus up, to be either spit out or swallowed.

TABLE 27.3 Functions of the Human Respiratory System: A Summary

Function	Explanation
Gas exchange	Lungs exchange O_2 and CO_2 with blood.
Sense of smell	Breathing moves air to the odor receptor cells in the nose.
Production of sounds, including speech	Movement of air across the vocal cords in the larynx produces sounds.
Maintaining blood pH homeostasis	Breathing volume and rate determine the concentration of CO_2 in blood, which affects blood pH.

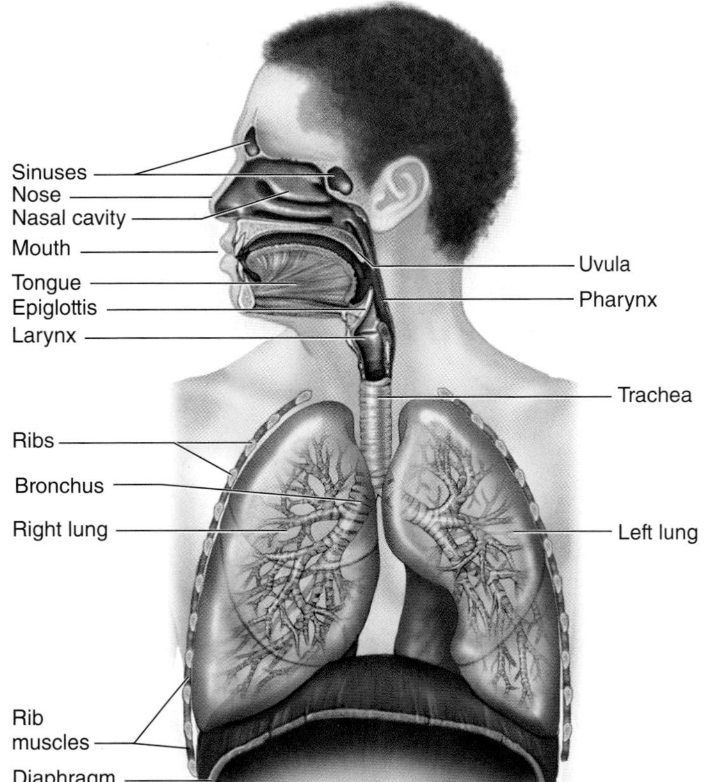

Respiratory System	
Main tissue types*	**Examples of locations/functions**
Epithelial	Enables diffusion across walls of alveoli and capillaries; secretes mucus along respiratory tract.
Connective	Blood (a connective tissue) exchanges gases with lungs; cartilage makes up part of the nose, trachea, bronchi, and larynx.
Nervous	Autonomic nervous system controls smooth muscle in bronchi.
Muscle	Smooth muscle in lungs regulates airflow to alveoli; skeletal muscle in diaphragm expands lungs.

*See chapter 23 for descriptions.

Figure 27.15 The Human Respiratory System. Inhaled air passes through the mouth and trachea and then into increasingly narrow tubes until it arrives in the alveoli, where gas exchange occurs.

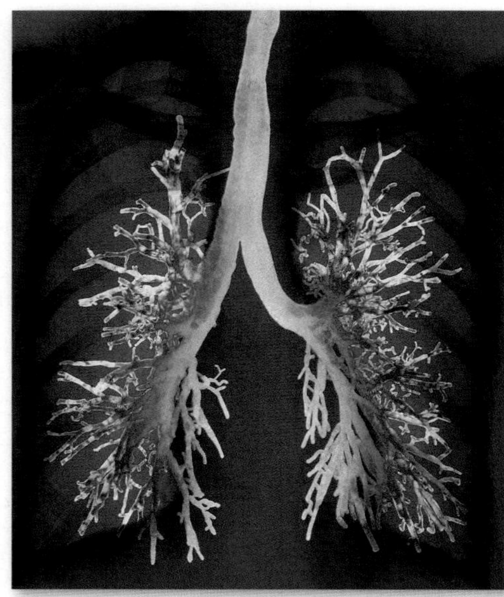

Figure 27.16 **The Bronchial Tree.** The respiratory passages of the lungs form a complex branching pattern. This is an X-ray image called a bronchogram.

B. The Lower Respiratory Tract Consists of the Trachea and Lungs

The **trachea,** or windpipe, is the tube just beneath the larynx. C-shaped rings of cartilage hold the trachea open and accommodate the expansion of the esophagus—the tube leading from the mouth to the stomach—during swallowing. You can feel these rings in the lower portion of your throat. Cilia and mucus coat the trachea's inside surface, trapping debris and moistening the incoming air.

The trachea branches into two **bronchi,** one leading to each lung. The bronchi branch repeatedly, each branch decreasing in diameter and wall thickness (figure 27.16). **Bronchioles** ("little bronchi") are the finest branches. The bronchioles have no cartilage, but their walls contain smooth muscle. The autonomic nervous system controls contraction of these muscles, adjusting airflow in response to metabolic demands.

Each bronchiole narrows into several alveolar ducts, and each duct opens into a grapelike cluster of alveoli, where gas exchange occurs (figure 27.17). Each **alveolus** is a tiny sac with a wall of epithelial tissue that is one cell layer thick. A vast network of capillaries surrounds each cluster of alveoli. Oxygen and CO_2 diffuse through the thin walls of the alveoli and the neighboring capillaries. The interface between the alveoli and the capillaries is the respiratory surface in humans, and it is enormous: the total surface area of the alveoli in one pair of lungs is about 50 times the area of the skin.

27.6 Mastering Concepts

1. What is the main function of the respiratory system?
2. What is the relationship between the circulatory and respiratory systems?
3. List the components of the upper and lower respiratory tracts.
4. Describe the relationships among the trachea, bronchi, bronchioles, and alveoli.

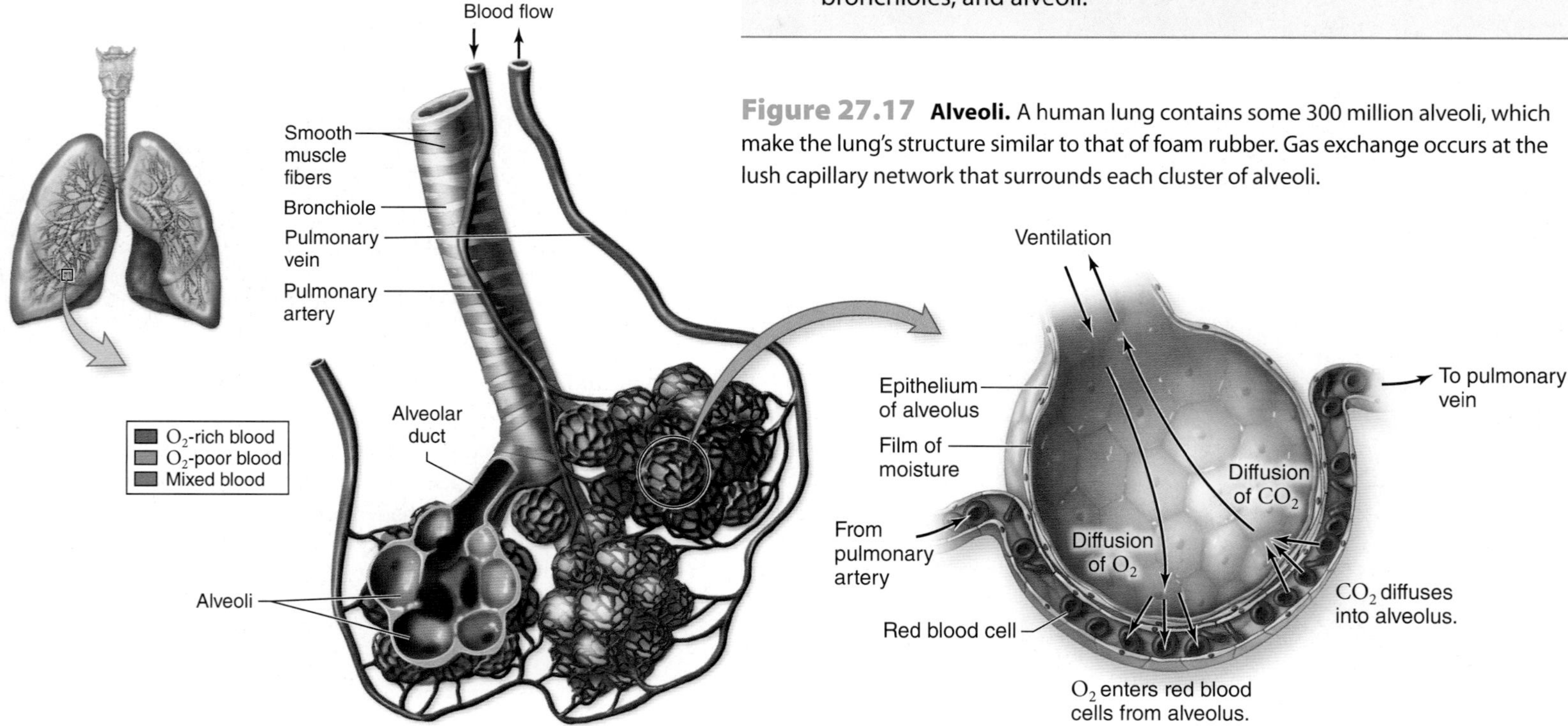

Figure 27.17 **Alveoli.** A human lung contains some 300 million alveoli, which make the lung's structure similar to that of foam rubber. Gas exchange occurs at the lush capillary network that surrounds each cluster of alveoli.

27.7 Breathing Requires Pressure Changes in the Lungs

Pay attention to your own breathing for a moment. Each **respiratory cycle** consists of one inhalation and one exhalation (figure 27.18). Each time you **inhale,** air moves into the lungs; when you **exhale,** air flows out of the lungs.

What drives this back-and-forth motion? The answer is that air flows from areas of high pressure to areas of low pressure. Therefore, air enters the body when the pressure inside the lungs is lower than the pressure outside the body. Conversely, air moves out when the pressure in the lungs is greater than the atmospheric pressure.

The body generates these pressure changes by altering the volume of the chest cavity. As a person inhales, skeletal muscles of the rib cage and diaphragm contract, expanding and elongating the chest cavity. The resulting increase in volume lowers the air pressure within the space between the lungs and the outer wall of the chest. The lungs therefore expand, lowering pressure in the alveoli. Air rushes in. Inhalation requires energy because muscle contraction uses ATP.

The muscles of the rib cage and the diaphragm then relax. The rib cage falls to its former position, the diaphragm rests up in the chest cavity again, and the elastic tissues of the lung recoil. The pressure in the lungs now exceeds atmospheric pressure, so air flows out. At rest, exhalation is passive—that is, it requires only muscle relaxation, not contraction—and therefore does not require ATP.

Hiccups briefly interrupt the respiratory cycle. In a hiccup, the diaphragm contracts unexpectedly, causing a sharp intake of air; the "hic" sound occurs as the epiglottis closes. Chapter 13's Why We Care box explores the evolutionary origin of hiccups, which have no known function.

Illness or injury may prevent contraction of the diaphragm and rib muscles, so breathing stops. Old-fashioned "iron lungs" and modern mechanical ventilators compensate for this loss of function (figure 27.19). An iron lung is an airtight chamber in which a patient lies with his or her head sticking out. Every few seconds, the air pressure inside the machine drops, drawing air into the lungs through the nose or mouth. Conversely, raising the pressure causes exhalation.

Medical professionals can test lung function by having a patient blow into a device called a spirometer. One measure of lung capacity is the **tidal volume,** or the amount of air inhaled or exhaled during a quiet breath taken at rest. In a young adult male, the tidal volume is about 500 milliliters. **Vital capacity,** on the other hand, is the total amount of air that a person can exhale after taking the deepest possible breath, some 4700 mL in a young man.

As we age, vital capacity declines. Illnesses can also interfere with a person's lung function by reducing the elasticity of the lungs, obstructing the airways, or weakening the muscles of the chest. This chapter's Why We Care box, on page 561, describes a few disorders that affect the respiratory and circulatory systems.

27.7 Mastering Concepts

1. What is the relationship between the volume of the chest cavity and the air pressure in the lungs?
2. Describe the events of one respiratory cycle.
3. Define *tidal volume* and *vital capacity*.

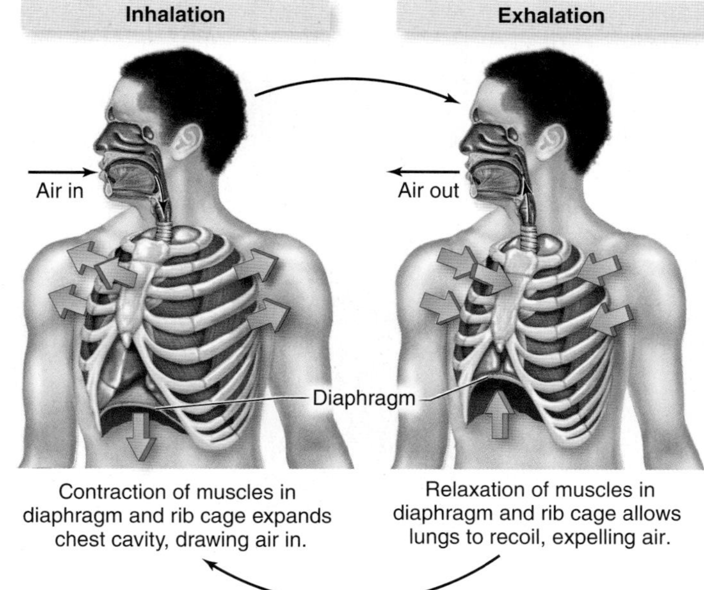

Inhalation
Exhalation
Air in
Air out
Diaphragm
Contraction of muscles in diaphragm and rib cage expands chest cavity, drawing air in.
Relaxation of muscles in diaphragm and rib cage allows lungs to recoil, expelling air.

Figure 27.18 **How We Breathe.** Inhalation requires contraction of the muscles of the diaphragm and rib cage. The expanding chest cavity has lower air pressure than the atmosphere, so air moves into the lungs. When we exhale, the diaphragm relaxes and the rib cage lowers, reversing the process and pushing air out of the lungs.

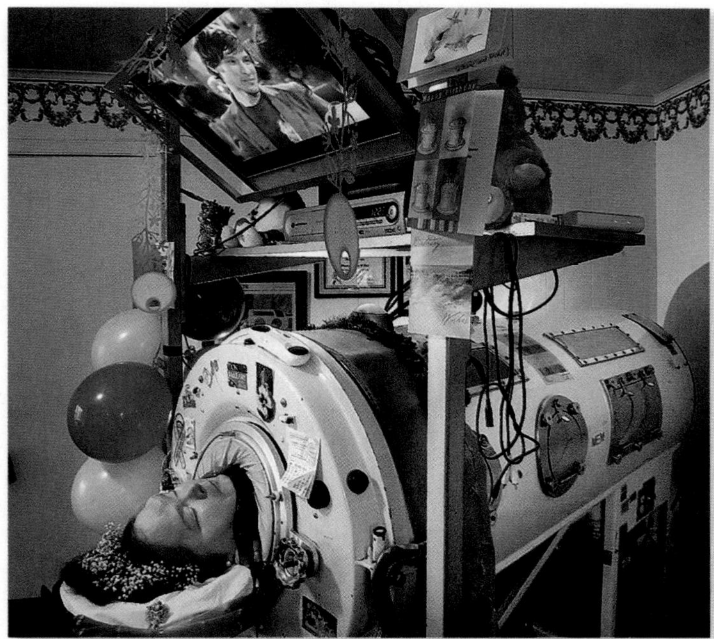

Figure 27.19 **Breathing Machine.** When this photo was taken, this 60-year-old woman had been in an iron lung for 57 years. She was a small child when she contracted polio, a viral disease that caused her muscles to deteriorate. Because her diaphragm is paralyzed, she cannot inhale on her own.

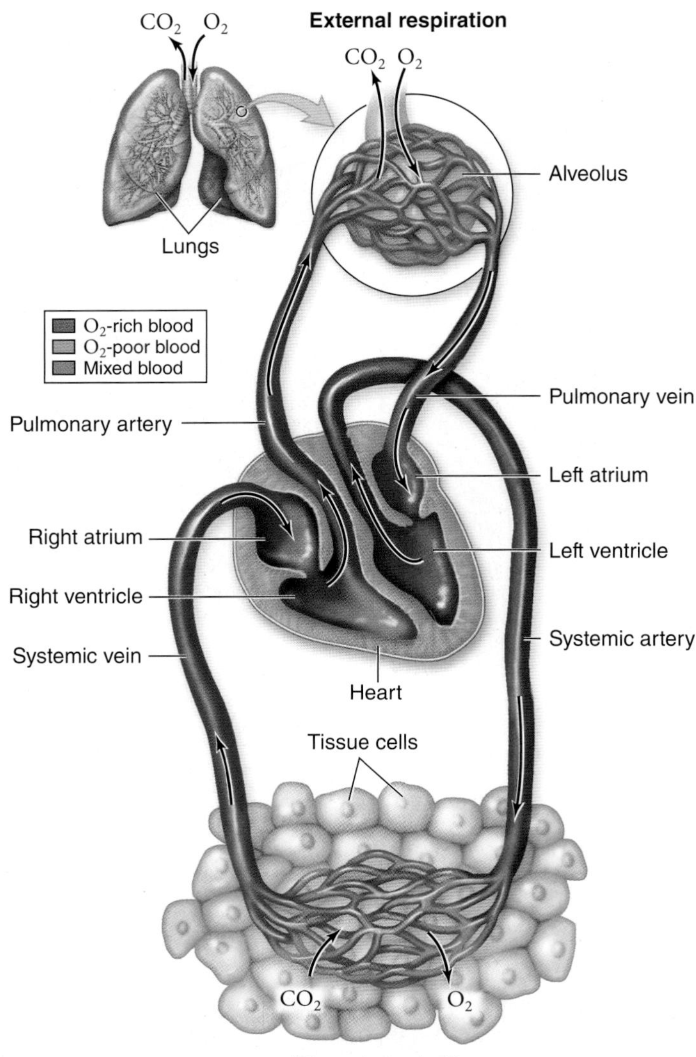

Figure 27.20 Gas Exchange at the Lungs and Tissues. CO_2 diffuses out of blood and into the alveoli of the lungs. O_2 moves in the opposite direction. In the rest of the body, O_2 diffuses out of the blood and into the tissues, while CO_2 moves into the bloodstream.

27.8 Red Blood Cells Carry Most Oxygen and Carbon Dioxide

Gas exchange in the alveoli and at the body's other tissues relies on simple diffusion (figure 27.20). In external respiration, which occurs at the lungs, O_2 diffuses down its concentration gradient from the alveoli into the blood. At the same time, CO_2 diffuses from the blood to the air in the lungs. The heart then pumps the freshly oxygenated blood to the rest of the body. In internal respiration, O_2 diffuses from blood to the tissue fluid and then into the body's respiring cells, which have the lowest O_2 level. CO_2 diffuses in the opposite direction.

Blood carries O_2 and CO_2 in different ways. Red blood cells transport at least 99% of blood O_2; the rest is dissolved in plasma. Hemoglobin attracts O_2 in red blood cells. Tucked into each hemoglobin protein are four iron atoms, each of which can combine with one O_2 molecule picked up in the lungs.

Not surprisingly, illness or death results when hemoglobin cannot bind O_2. Carbon monoxide (CO), for example, is a colorless, odorless gas in cigarette smoke and in exhaust from car engines, kerosene heaters, wood stoves, and home furnaces. CO binds to hemoglobin more readily than O_2 does. When 30% of the hemoglobin molecules carry CO instead of O_2, a person loses consciousness and may go into a coma or even die.

Red blood cells also transport about 90% to 95% of CO_2 that enters the blood. Hemoglobin carries some CO_2, but it does not bind this gas as readily as it binds O_2. Instead, an enzyme in red blood cells converts most CO_2 to bicarbonate ions (HCO_3^-). The following sequence of chemical reactions produces bicarbonate (the two double arrows indicate that the reactions are reversible):

$$CO_2 + H_2O \longleftrightarrow H_2CO_3 \text{ (carbonic acid)}$$

$$H_2CO_3 \longleftrightarrow H^+ \text{ (hydrogen ions)} + HCO_3^- \text{ (bicarbonate)}$$

Notice that the second reaction produces hydrogen ions (H^+), a byproduct that allows the brain to regulate the depth and rate of breathing (figure 27.21). During intense exercise, for example, actively respiring muscle cells release abundant CO_2 into the blood. When CO_2 levels rise, blood becomes more acidic. Receptors in the arteries and in the medulla of the brain detect this change in blood pH. In response, the brain stimulates an increase in the breathing rate. The body acquires additional O_2 and releases the excess CO_2, maintaining homeostasis in blood gas concentrations.

Perhaps surprisingly, O_2 is less important than CO_2 in regulating breathing. The level of O_2 in blood typically affects the breathing rate only if it falls dangerously low. Sometimes this O_2-regulating system fails, especially in the very young. Sudden infant death syndrome, in which a baby dies while asleep, may occur when receptors fail to detect low oxygen levels in arterial blood.

27.8 Mastering Concepts

1. Describe O_2 and CO_2 diffusion in external and internal respiration.
2. In what forms does blood transport O_2 and CO_2?
3. How does the brain regulate breathing rate?

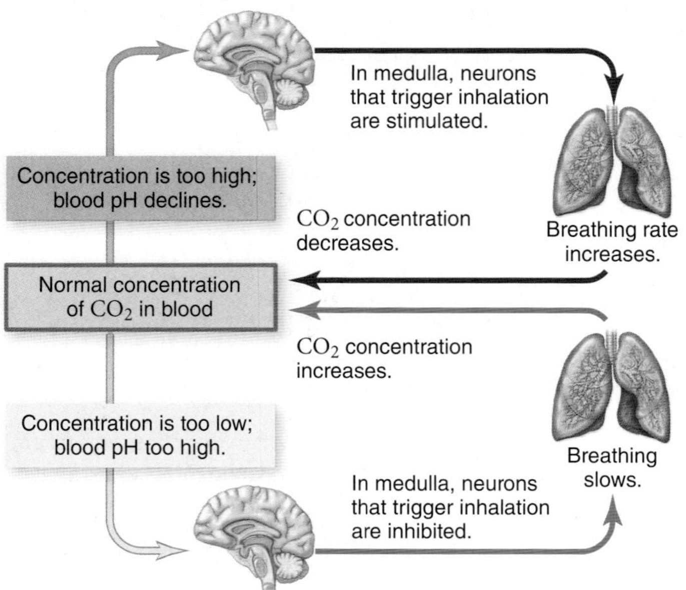

Figure 27.21 Breathing Control. Multiple receptors send information about blood pH and CO_2 concentrations to the brain. Neurons in the medulla integrate this information and regulate the contraction of rib and diaphragm muscles.

Investigating Life

27.9 In (Extremely) Cold Blood

Sometimes, an obscure discovery can turn into a big story. So it was with a report that appeared in the journal *Nature* in 1954, when a researcher named J. T. Ruud confirmed the existence of a fish with colorless blood. The animal in Ruud's report was an icefish that lives deep in the extremely cold ocean waters surrounding Antarctica (figure 27.22). The blood of the icefish is a ghostly white. Microscopic examination of the blood revealed white blood cells, but few if any red blood cells and never any hemoglobin. The story represented a biological curiosity because it contradicted the commonly held idea that all vertebrate life requires hemoglobin.

Figure 27.22 Icefish. A scuba diver approaches an icefish in the Southern Ocean near Antarctica.

The Question: Since Ruud's time, researchers have described 16 species of icefishes, none of which has hemoglobin. Interestingly, icefishes have red-blooded relatives that share their frigid habitat. The "family tree" of these fishes is well understood, based on studies of ribosomal RNA, mitochondrial DNA, and many other traits. Could these relationships help researchers answer questions about the origin of the icefishes' colorless blood?

The Approach: Biologist Thomas J. Near, of Yale University, worked with Northeastern University's Sandra K. Parker and H. William Detrich III to learn more about icefish blood. They already knew that hemoglobin consists of four polypeptides called globins; two of the chains are designated alpha, and the other two are called beta. Also, the genes encoding both alpha and beta globins had already been well-studied in many vertebrates.

Near, Parker, and Detrich collected specimens representing all 16 species of Antarctic icefishes, plus three species representing the icefishes' red-blooded relatives. The researchers extracted DNA from the fishes' cells and sequenced the regions where the globin genes are normally located. ▸ DNA sequencing, p. 203

The team discovered that the fishes fell into three categories (figure 27.23). One group consisted of the red-blooded fishes with functioning genes encoding both alpha and beta globins. The second category included 15 of the 16 icefish species. All of these fishes had just a small fragment of the alpha globin gene; the beta globin gene was missing entirely. The third category included just one icefish species, *Neopagetopsis ionah,* which had a unique gene arrangement. In this animal's DNA, both the alpha and beta genes were present but were mutated in a way that leaves the fish unable to produce hemoglobin. Surprisingly, *N. ionah* is not a "missing link" that gave rise to other icefishes, as one might expect from its globin gene configuration. Instead, *N. ionah* is right in the middle of the family tree.

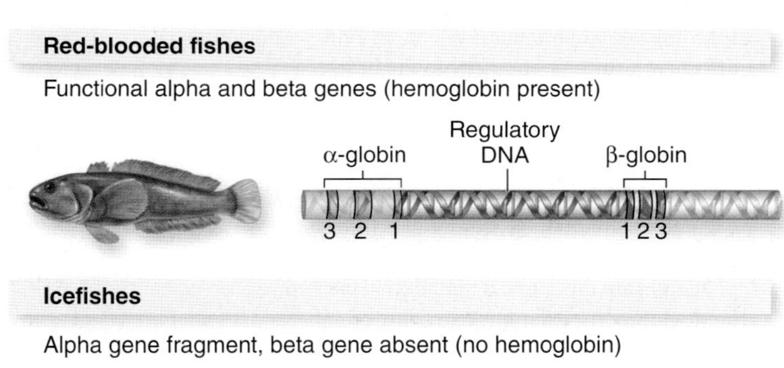

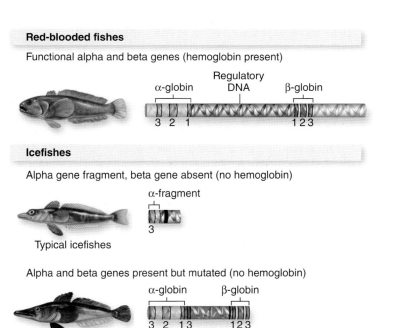

Figure 27.23 Shattered Genes. Analysis of DNA sequences revealed that red-blooded fishes have intact alpha and beta globin genes. No icefish, however, produces hemoglobin. Most icefishes have just a fragment of the alpha gene and lack the beta gene entirely. The icefish *N. ionah* has nonfunctional versions of both genes.

The Conclusion: The genetic analysis clearly explained why icefishes have colorless blood: unlike their red-blooded relatives, icefishes simply cannot produce hemoglobin. Evidently, in the very cold waters of the Antarctic, metabolic rates are so low that a lack of hemoglobin does not reduce reproductive success.

This story reminds us that scientific inquiry is a journey. What began as a report of an unusual fish in 1954 has blossomed into an in-depth study of the evolution of hemoglobin. And, although we now know exactly why icefishes have colorless blood, a new question has emerged: What accounts for *N. ionah*'s unusual globin genes? The answer may lie with future biologists—people whose desire to understand evolution is "in their blood."

Near, Thomas J., Sandra K. Parker, and H. William Detrich III. 2006. A genomic fossil reveals key steps in hemoglobin loss by the Antarctic icefishes. *Molecular Biology and Evolution,* vol. 23, no. 11, pages 2008–2016.

27.9 Mastering Concepts

1. How did researchers use DNA evidence to determine why icefishes have colorless blood?
2. Which component of blood is likely to transport most of the oxygen in an icefish?

Why We Care | The Unhealthy Circulatory and Respiratory Systems

Atherosclerosis

Fatty deposits inside the walls of coronary arteries reduce blood flow to the heart muscle. A diet high in fat and cholesterol is associated with this "hardening of the arteries," also called atherosclerosis (*athero-* is from the Greek word for "paste," and *sclerosis* means "hardness"). Atherosclerosis can cause several ailments, including chest pain, heart attack, arrhythmia, and aneurysm.

Aneurysm

Atherosclerosis can weaken the wall of an artery so much that a region of the vessel forms a pulsating, enlarging sac called an aneurysm. The artery wall may also be weakened at birth or be damaged by injury, infection, or persistently high blood pressure. The aneurysm may rupture without warning, causing massive bleeding. A burst aneurysm can be fatal, especially if it affects the aorta or an artery in the brain.

Anemias

Anemias are a collection of more than 400 disorders resulting from a decrease in the oxygen-carrying capacity of blood. A common symptom is fatigue, reflecting a shortage of O_2 at the body's cells. Some types of anemia are inherited; a mutation in the gene encoding hemoglobin, for example, can cause an inherited form of anemia called sickle cell disease. Other types of anemia are related to diet, especially an iron deficiency, which can prevent cells from producing hemoglobin. Iron-deficiency anemia is most common in women because of blood loss in menstruation. In still other forms of anemia, red blood cells may be too small, be manufactured too slowly, or die too quickly. ▸ sickle cell disease, p. 124

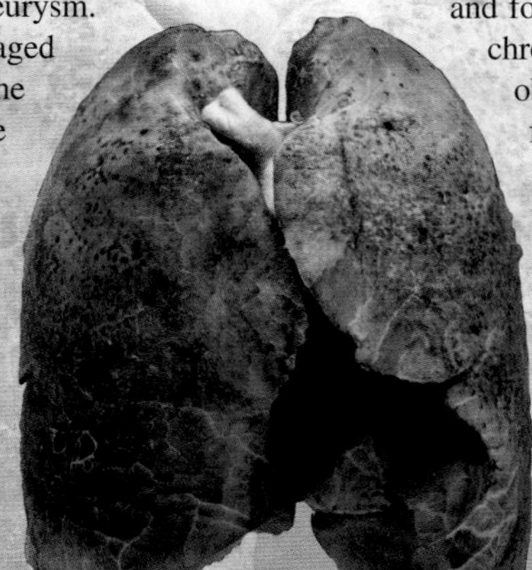

Figure 27.A Smoker's Lungs. Healthy lungs are pink, but these have turned black after years of exposure to cigarette smoke.

Asthma

During an asthma attack, spasms occur in the smooth muscle lining the lung's bronchi, slowing airflow and causing wheezing. An allergy to pollen, pet dander (skin particles from dogs or cats), or dust mites triggers most asthma attacks. Inhalant drugs that treat asthma usually relax the bronchial muscles.

The Common Cold

The viruses that cause colds infect cells in the upper respiratory tract (see chapter 7). A day or so after infection, the immune system's efforts to get rid of the invading viruses cause the typical symptoms of a cold: coughs, runny nose, and sneezes. There is no cure. Fortunately, colds are usually not a serious health problem, although clogged sinuses can invite bacterial infections.

The Effects of Smoking on Respiratory and Cardiovascular Health

Smoking is the most common preventable cause of death. Tobacco use is associated with cancers of the mouth, larynx, esophagus, jaw, and lungs; 85% of lung cancer cases occur in smokers (figure 27.A). Cigarette smoke contains chemicals that mutate DNA in lung cells; these altered cells may divide and form tumors. Patients with lung cancer experience chest pain, chronic coughing, and shortness of breath. Large tumors may obstruct the airway. Moreover, cancerous cells may break away from the tumor and spread throughout the body.

Cigarette smoke damages the lungs in other ways as well. The very first inhalation of cigarette smoke slows the beating of cilia. With time, the cilia become paralyzed, and they eventually vanish. Without cilia to remove mucus, coughing alone must clear particles from the airways. Smoking also causes excess mucus production, which favors the reproduction of disease-causing microorganisms. Smokers are therefore especially susceptible to respiratory infections.

The smoker's cough leads to emphysema and chronic bronchitis. *Emphysema,* a term derived from the Greek word for "inflate," is an abnormal accumulation of air in the lungs. Long-term exposure to cigarette smoke and other irritants causes a loss of elasticity in lung tissues. Coughing may rupture the delicate walls of the alveoli, impeding airflow and reducing the surface area for gas exchange. The patient experiences shortness of breath, an expanded chest, and hyperventilation. Emphysema is often accompanied by chronic bronchitis—that is, inflammation of the bronchi. Together, these two illnesses are called chronic obstructive pulmonary disease (COPD).

Tobacco harms the circulatory system as well. Nicotine stimulates the secretion of epinephrine and norepinephrine, increasing both heart rate and blood pressure. Nicotine also damages blood vessels and stimulates the formation of blood clots, increasing the risk of heart attack and stroke. ▸ stroke, p. 495

Cigarette smoking is clearly unhealthy, yet many people find it difficult or impossible to quit, thanks to nicotine's addictive qualities. Nevertheless, it pays to stop smoking. Cilia may reappear, and the thickening of alveolar walls can reverse, although ruptured alveoli are gone forever.

Chapter Summary

27.1 Blood Has Diverse Functions

- A **circulatory system** consists of **blood** and a **heart.** The blood delivers nutrients and oxygen gas (O_2), removes metabolic wastes such as carbon dioxide (CO_2), and transports other substances. The heart pumps the fluid throughout the body.
- Human blood is a mixture of water, proteins and other dissolved substances, cells, and cell fragments.

A. Plasma Carries Many Dissolved Substances

- **Plasma** is the fluid component of blood; it transports all other blood components.

B. Red Blood Cells Transport Oxygen

- **Red blood cells** contain abundant **hemoglobin,** a pigment that binds O_2 molecules. Red blood cells originate in red bone marrow.
- Surface markers on red blood cells react with antibodies in **agglutination** reactions that reveal a person's blood type.

C. White Blood Cells Fight Infection

- **White blood cells** provoke inflammation, destroy infectious organisms, and secrete antibodies. **Leukemia** is a type of cancer in which red bone marrow produces too many white blood cells.

D. Blood Clotting Requires Platelets and Plasma Proteins

- **Platelets** are cell fragments that collect near a wound. Damaged tissue activates plasma proteins that trigger the formation of a network of fibers, trapping additional platelets and perpetuating **blood clot** formation.

Components of Blood: A Summary

Component	Function
Plasma	Liquid component of blood; exchanges water and many dissolved substances with fluid surrounding body cells
Red blood cells	Carry O_2
White blood cells	Destroy foreign substances, initiate inflammation
Platelets	Initiate clotting

27.2 Animal Circulatory Systems Range from Simple to Complex

- In an **open circulatory system,** blood bathes tissues directly in open spaces before returning to the heart.
- In a **closed circulatory system,** such as that of vertebrates, the heart pumps blood through a continuous system of vessels.
- A fish has a two-chambered heart, with an **atrium** that receives blood and a **ventricle** that pumps blood out.
- Most land vertebrates have a three- or four-chambered heart. In these animals, the **pulmonary circulation** delivers oxygen-depleted blood to the lungs, and the **systemic circulation** brings freshly oxygenated blood to the rest of the body.

27.3 Blood Circulates Through the Heart and Blood Vessels

- The heart is the muscular pump that drives blood through the vessels of the human **cardiovascular system.**
- **Arteries** are blood vessels that carry blood away from the heart. Arteries branch into smaller **arterioles,** which lead to tiny capillaries.
- **Capillaries** exchange materials with the **interstitial fluid** surrounding the body's cells.
- Capillaries empty into **venules,** which converge into the **veins** that return blood to the heart.

27.4 The Human Heart Is a Muscular Pump

A. The Heart Contains Four Chambers

- A sac of connective tissue surrounds the heart. **Cardiac muscle** makes up most of the heart wall. **Endothelium** lines the inside of the heart and all of the body's blood vessels.
- The heart has two atria that receive blood and two ventricles that propel blood throughout the body. The heart's four valves ensure one-way blood flow.

B. The Right and Left Halves of the Heart Deliver Blood Along Different Paths

- **Pulmonary arteries** and **pulmonary veins** transport blood between the right side of the heart and the lungs.
- Blood exits the left side of the heart at the **aorta,** the artery that carries blood toward the rest of the body.
- **Coronary arteries** supply blood to the heart muscle itself.

C. Cardiac Muscle Cells Produce the Heartbeat

- A **cardiac cycle** consists of a single contraction and relaxation of the heart muscle.
- The **pacemaker,** or **sinoatrial (SA) node,** is a collection of specialized cardiac muscle cells in the wall of the right atrium. The SA node sets the heart rate. From there, the heartbeat spreads to the **atrioventricular (AV) node** and then through the ventricles.

D. Exercise Strengthens the Heart

- Exercise increases the heart's **cardiac output** and lowers blood pressure.

27.5 Blood Vessels Form the Circulation Pathway

A. Arteries, Capillaries, and Veins Have Different Structures

- The walls of arteries and veins consist of an inner layer of endothelium, a middle layer of **smooth muscle,** and an outer layer of connective tissue. Arteries have thicker, more elastic walls than veins.
- Nutrient and waste exchange occur at the **capillary beds,** where blood vessels consist of a single layer of endothelium.

B. Blood Pressure and Velocity Differ Among Vessel Types

- The pumping of the heart and the diameter of the blood vessels determine **blood pressure. Systolic pressure** reflects the force exerted on blood vessel walls when the ventricles contract. The low point of a blood pressure reading, **diastolic pressure,** occurs when the ventricles relax.
- Blood pressure is highest in the arteries and lowest in the veins. Because of their high total cross-sectional area, capillaries have the lowest blood velocity.
- The autonomic nervous system controls the heart rate. **Vasoconstriction** and **vasodilation** in the arterioles adjust the blood pressure.

27.6 The Human Respiratory System Delivers Air to the Lungs

- Cells use O_2 in **aerobic respiration** to release the energy in food and store the energy in ATP. CO_2 forms as a byproduct of respiration and must be eliminated from the body.
- **Respiratory systems** exchange O_2 and CO_2 with air or water, often in conjunction with a circulatory system that transports gases within the body.
- O_2 and CO_2 are exchanged by diffusion across a moist **respiratory surface** such as the body surface, gills, or lungs.

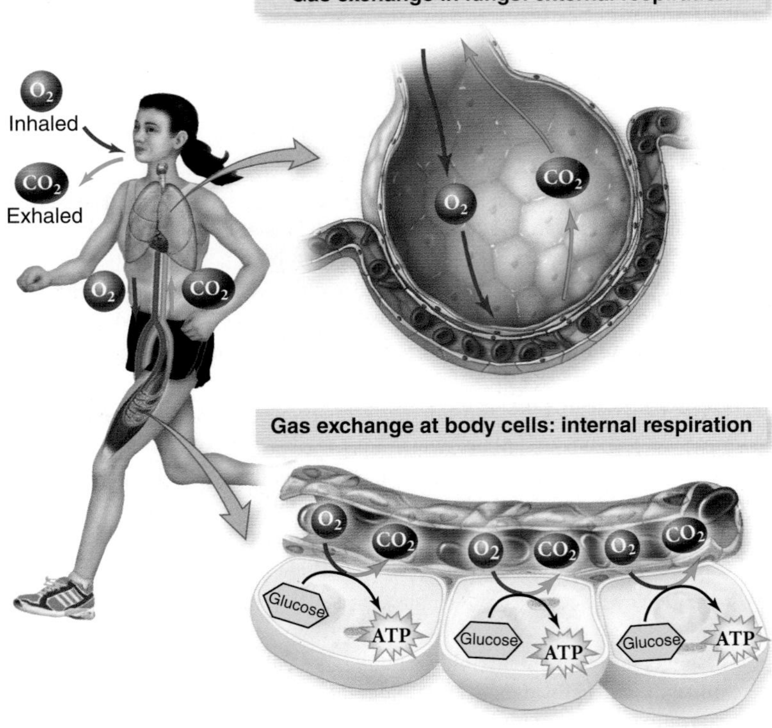

A. The Nose, Pharynx, and Larynx Form the Upper Respiratory Tract

- The **nose** purifies, warms, and moisturizes inhaled air. The air then flows through the **pharynx** and **larynx.**
- **Vocal cords** stretched over the larynx produce the voice as air passes through the **glottis.** The **epiglottis** prevents food from entering the trachea through the glottis.

B. The Lower Respiratory Tract Consists of the Trachea and Lungs

- Cartilage rings hold open the **trachea,** which branches into **bronchi** that deliver air to the lungs. The bronchi branch extensively and form smaller air tubules, **bronchioles,** which end in clusters of tiny, thin-walled, saclike **alveoli.**
- Many capillaries surround each alveolus. O_2 diffuses into the blood from the alveolar air, while CO_2 diffuses from the blood into the alveoli.

27.7 Breathing Requires Pressure Changes in the Lungs

- A **respiratory cycle** consists of one **inhalation** and one **exhalation.**
- When the diaphragm and rib cage muscles contract, the chest cavity expands. This reduces air pressure in the lungs, drawing air in. When these muscles relax and the chest cavity shrinks, the pressure in the lungs increases and pushes air out.
- Measurements of lung function include **tidal volume** and **vital capacity.**

27.8 Red Blood Cells Carry Most Oxygen and Carbon Dioxide

- Almost all oxygen transported to cells is bound to hemoglobin in red blood cells. Carbon monoxide (CO) poisoning occurs when CO prevents O_2 from binding hemoglobin.
- Some CO_2 in the blood is bound to hemoglobin or dissolved in plasma. Most CO_2, however, is transported as bicarbonate ion, generated from carbonic acid that forms when CO_2 reacts with water.
- The brain uses blood pH (an indirect measure of CO_2 concentration) to adjust the depth and rate of breathing.

27.9 Investigating Life: In (Extremely) Cold Blood

- Antarctic icefishes are unique among vertebrates in that they lack hemoglobin. Researchers have traced this unusual characteristic to major deletions in the alpha and beta hemoglobin genes.

Multiple Choice Questions

1. Which component of blood is responsible for clot formation?
   a. Red blood cells
   b. White blood cells
   c. Plasma
   d. Platelets
2. A property of an open circulatory system includes
   a. the absence of a heart.
   b. movement of fluid into spaces in the tissues of an organism.
   c. the absence of vessels.
   d. All of the above are correct.
3. Which chamber of the human heart collects the oxygenated blood from the lungs?
   a. Left atrium
   b. Left ventricle
   c. Right atrium
   d. Right ventricle
4. How would the pacemaker (SA node) of an athlete at rest differ from that of a sedentary person?
   a. It would establish a higher rate of contraction.
   b. It would not be any different.
   c. It would establish a lower rate of contraction.
   d. It would trigger a stronger contraction.
5. Which type of blood vessel uses smooth muscle contractions to help control blood flow?
   a. A capillary
   b. A venule
   c. A vein
   d. An arteriole
6. If a man suffers from high blood pressure, it is possible that his
   a. blood vessels are abnormally dilated.
   b. blood vessels are abnormally constricted.
   c. kidneys are removing too much fluid.
   d. medulla is underactive.
7. Why do humans breathe?
   a. To eliminate CO_2
   b. To support aerobic respiration in mitochondria
   c. To keep the respiratory surface dry
   d. Both a and b are correct.
8. Air flows from areas of ______ to areas of ______.
   a. high O_2 concentration; low O_2 concentration
   b. low O_2 concentration; high O_2 concentration
   c. high pressure; low pressure
   d. low pressure; high pressure
9. In humans,
   a. gas exchange occurs at the bronchi.
   b. a respiratory cycle lasts at least 1 minute.
   c. contraction of the diaphragm causes exhalation.
   d. inhaling requires more energy than exhaling.
10. What information does the brain normally use to regulate the breathing rate?
    a. Level of O_2
    b. Level of CO_2
    c. Hemoglobin content of blood
    d. Demand for ATP

Write It Out

1. Maintaining the proper proportions of cells and platelets in the blood is essential for health. What can happen when the blood contains too few or too many red blood cells? Too few or too many white blood cells? Too few or too many platelets?
2. Why can a person with type A blood not receive a transfusion of type B blood? If a person has type O blood, what blood type(s) can he or she receive in a transfusion?
3. Why is blood clotting that happens too quickly or too slowly dangerous?
4. One effect of aspirin is to prevent platelets from sticking together. Why do some people take low doses of aspirin to help prevent a heart attack?
5. How are open and closed circulatory systems similar? How are they different?
6. Describe the circulatory systems of fishes and mammals. What is the advantage of separating the pulmonary and systemic circulatory pathways?
7. Describe the events that occur during one cardiac cycle.
8. Make a chart that compares systemic arteries, capillaries, and systemic veins. Consider the following properties: structure; amount of smooth muscle; presence of valves; cross-sectional area; blood pressure; blood velocity; direction of blood flow relative to the heart; O_2 content of blood.
9. How do the body's cells receive nutrients and O_2 and dispose of wastes?
10. Why is blood pressure highest in the arteries and lowest in the veins?
11. What types of changes in blood vessels would raise blood pressure?
12. Some of the body's blood pressure receptors are located in the carotid sinus, where the carotid artery passes through the neck. If you press lightly on the carotid sinus, what do you predict should happen to your heart rate? What if you press lightly on a spot just *below* the carotid sinus? *Hint:* Figure 27.13 may help you answer this question.
13. Describe the interactions between the circulatory system and the respiratory, immune, digestive, and endocrine systems.
14. Name three ways that the circulatory system helps maintain homeostasis.
15. Section 8.7 describes the rationale behind cancer treatments that inhibit the growth of blood vessels toward a tumor. Why would tumors without a blood supply quit growing (or even shrink)?
16. What is the function of breathing?
17. What is the connection between breathing and cellular respiration?
18. An earthworm prefers moist soil. Why does this animal die if it dries out on a sidewalk?
19. How is air cleaned, warmed, and humidified before it reaches the lungs?
20. Trace the pathway of an O_2 molecule from the time it enters the nose to the time it reaches a respiring cell at the tip of your finger.
21. Describe the events that happen during inhalation and exhalation.
22. What is the difference between tidal volume and vital capacity? What does each measurement indicate about lung function?
23. Explain the diffusion gradients for O_2 and CO_2 at alveoli and at body cells.
24. How does blood transport most of the CO_2 produced by the body's cells? In what other ways is CO_2 transported?
25. One recommended treatment for anxiety-related hyperventilation (overbreathing) is to breathe into a paper bag for several minutes. After several breaths, how does the composition of air inside the bag compare with that in the atmosphere? How would breathing air from the bag help relieve hyperventilation? How might it be dangerous to breathe into a paper bag for more than a few minutes?

Pull It Together

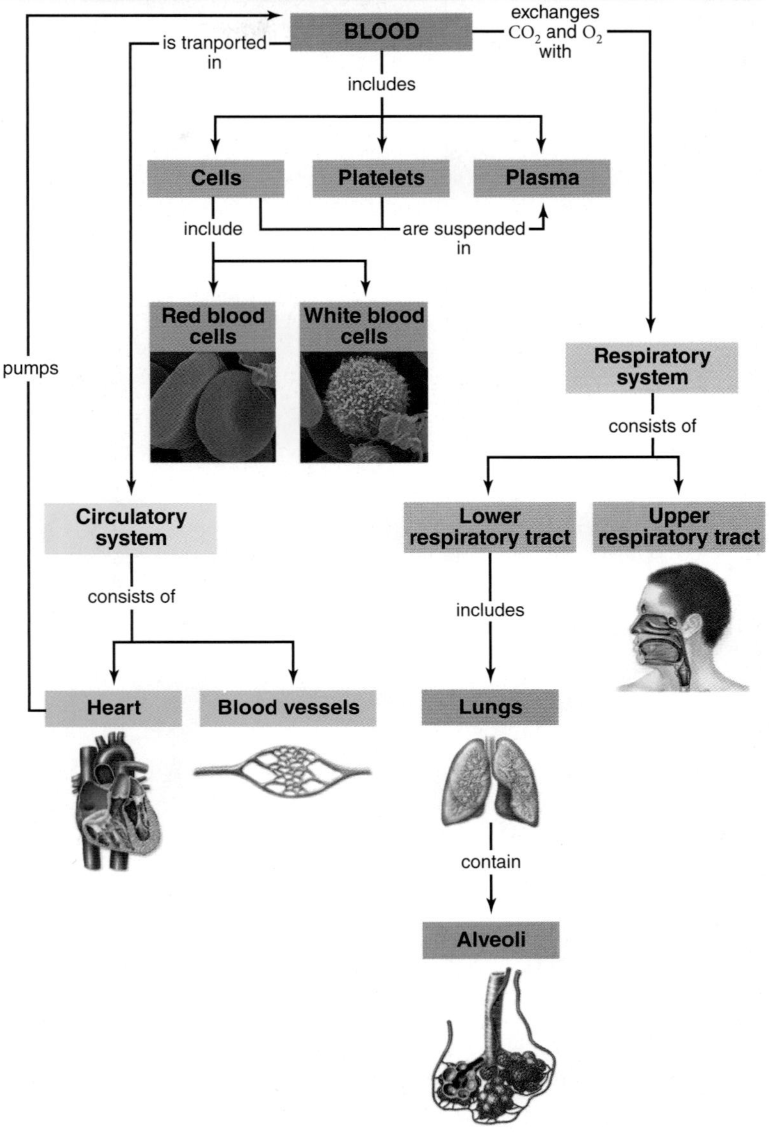

BLOOD
is tranported in
exchanges CO_2 and O_2 with
includes
Cells
Platelets
Plasma
include
are suspended in
Red blood cells
White blood cells
pumps
Respiratory system
consists of
Circulatory system
Lower respiratory tract
Upper respiratory tract
consists of
includes
Heart
Blood vessels
Lungs
contain
Alveoli

1. How do the pulmonary and systemic circulatory pathways fit into this concept map?
2. What other substances are in blood besides those listed in this concept map?
3. What are the functions of red and white blood cells?
4. Add the following terms to this concept map: *diaphragm, alveolus, interstitial fluid, brain, hemoglobin, O_2, CO_2.*
5. Describe the relationships among the parts of the upper and lower respiratory tracts.

28 Regulating Temperature, Nutrients, and Body Fluids

Food and Drink. Humans and many other types of animals need to eat and drink several times a day to maintain homeostasis.

Learning Outline

Learn How to Learn
Avoid Distractions

Despite your best intentions, constant distractions may take you away from your studies. Friends, music, TV, phone calls, text messages, video games, and the Internet all offer attractive diversions. How can you stay focused? One answer is to find your own place to study where no one can find you. Turn your phone off for a few hours; the world will get along without you while you study. And if you must use your computer, create a separate user account with settings that prevent you from visiting favorite websites during study time.

What's the Point?

The animal body's inputs and outputs are familiar: food and drink go in, and wastes come out. But what happens inside the body in the meantime?

It all begins with the digestive system, which dismantles the nutrients in food and drink. Blood vessels snaking around the intestines absorb the nutrients and distribute them throughout the body. Meanwhile, we eliminate the indigestible food as feces.

Urine has a different source: the kidneys. These organs cleanse the blood and release urine as a byproduct. This surprisingly complex fluid contains water, metabolic wastes, and many other substances. The kidneys adjust urine composition to maintain the body's delicate balance between water and salts.

Intricate networks of chemical reactions underlie all of these activities; they proceed fast enough to sustain life only within a limited temperature range. How does the body maintain its temperature? That subject is where this chapter begins.

28.1 Animal Bodies Maintain Homeostasis in Many Ways

Animals live nearly everywhere on Earth (figure 28.1). The frigid Antarctic contrasts sharply with the perpetual humidity of a tropical rain forest or with the extremely dry, scorching desert. Most animals live in more moderate environments, but each species has adaptations that enable it to regulate its internal environment—that is, to maintain homeostasis.

One example is temperature regulation. The chemical reactions that sustain life slow down at low temperatures, so an active animal must maintain a minimum body temperature. At the same time, too much heat can be fatal.

Each habitat selects for a different way of regulating body temperature. The parrots in figure 28.1, for example, live in a jungle, which is warm all year. This habitat does not strongly select for heat-saving adaptations. But nighttime temperatures can plummet in the desert. The roadrunner, a desert bird, allows its body temperature to drop during cool nights, slowing its metabolism. The next morning, the bird warms its body back up by basking in the sun. The penguin faces a much more extreme challenge. A thick layer of fat under its skin helps retain warmth, and feathers add insulation. Moreover, penguins often huddle together, conserving heat against howling Antarctic winds.

Diets vary widely as well. Parrots live on a carbohydrate-rich, low-protein diet of fruits, seeds, and other plant parts. Penguins and roadrunners, on the other hand, mostly eat other animals—fish, squid, and crustaceans for the penguins, and lizards, insects, and other small animals for the roadrunners. These diets are relatively high in protein and fat but low in carbohydrates. The digestive systems of all of these birds reflect their varied diets.

Besides regulating temperature and nutrients, an animal also maintains homeostasis in the chemical composition of its body fluids. Blood and other fluids contain water, salts, and other dissolved solutes; the balance of solutes and water is critical to life. ▸▸ ions, p. 27; water, p. 29

Many animals live in habitats that lack water or salt. In hot, dry areas, an animal must conserve enough water for cells to function. In the jungle, abundant rainfall ensures that animals have plenty of fresh water. But the same water also carries away scarce salts. Penguins have the opposite problem. They are surrounded by ocean water, and they eat a salty diet. These salts exert a powerful osmotic pressure that pulls moisture out of their cells. An animal in this habitat retains water only if it continually pumps excess salt out of its body.

Figure 28.1 Different Habitats. Penguins thrive on Antarctic ice, parrots inhabit the warm, humid tropics, and roadrunners live in the desert. The adaptations of each bird reflect its diet, the temperature of its habitat, and many other selective forces.

This chapter begins by describing how animals regulate body temperature. The next five sections turn to nutrition and the digestive system. The chapter concludes with the structure and function of the human urinary system, which helps maintain the composition of body fluids.

28.1 Mastering Concepts

1. What does it mean for an organism to maintain homeostasis?
2. How do different habitats select for unique adaptations?

28.2 Heat Gains and Losses Determine an Animal's Body Temperature

Whether an animal lives near the South Pole or the Amazonian rain forest, its body temperature must remain within certain limits. Part of the reason is that extreme temperatures alter biological molecules. Excessive heat can ruin a protein's three-dimensional shape and disrupt its function. Extreme cold solidifies lipids, inhibiting membrane function. Overall, if cells become too warm or too cool, vital biochemical reactions proceed too slowly to sustain life. ▸▸▸ protein shape, p. 40; lipids, p. 35; enzymes, p. 74

a. b.

Figure 28.2 Endotherm and Ectotherm. (a) A mouse is an endotherm; its metabolism generates most of its body heat. (b) An ectotherm such as a snake alters its behavior to manage the gain of heat from or loss of heat to the environment.

Thermoregulation is the control of body temperature, and it requires the ability to balance heat gained from and lost to the environment. In addition, an animal can maintain homeostasis by controlling how much heat its own body produces. When cells generate ATP in aerobic respiration (the topic of chapter 6), they also produce metabolic heat. The more active the animal, the higher its metabolic rate and the more heat it produces.

The main source of an animal's body heat may be internal or external (figure 28.2). An **endotherm** regulates its body temperature internally. Most endotherms maintain a relatively constant body temperature by balancing heat generated in metabolism (especially in the muscles) with heat lost to the environment. Mammals and birds are endotherms; insulation in the form of fat, feathers, or fur helps retain their body heat.

Other adaptations also help endotherms maintain a constant body temperature. The hypothalamus detects blood temperature, receives information from thermoreceptors in the skin and other organs, and controls many of the responses that maintain homeostasis (figure 28.3). In cold weather, the animal may shiver; the contraction of skeletal muscle generates heat. Blood vessels in the limbs also constrict, retaining more blood in the warmer core of the body. At the same time, muscles in the skin cause feathers or fur to stand erect, trapping an insulating air layer next to the skin. (In humans, this hair-raising response is useless because we have so little body hair. Nevertheless, goose bumps form when the hair muscles contract.) Animals may also migrate, hibernate, or huddle together to conserve heat (figure 28.4a).

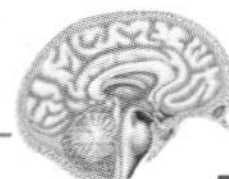

Figure It Out

As the sun sets and the external temperature gets colder, will a frog's body temperature go down, stay the same, or go up?

Answer: It will go down.

An **ectotherm** lacks an internal temperature-regulating mechanism. It thermoregulates by moving to areas where it can gain or lose heat, so its temperature varies with external conditions. The vast majority of animals are ectotherms, including all invertebrates, plus fishes, amphibians, and nonavian reptiles (see figure 28.2b). Like endotherms, ectotherms have a repertoire of heat-conserving behaviors, such as seeking sunlight, sprawling on warm rocks or roadways, building insulated burrows, and tucking wings and legs near their bodies.

So far, the focus has been on conserving heat, but animals also must maintain homeostasis when the environment is too hot (figure 28.4b). Evaporative cooling from the skin or respiratory surfaces is one way to lower body temperature. For example, humans sweat to cool off, whereas a panting coyote allows water to evaporate from the moist lining of its mouth. Likewise, an owl flutters loose skin under its throat to move air over moist surfaces in the mouth.

In addition, when the environment is warm, blood vessels in the limbs dilate and allow more blood to approach the relatively cool body surface. Tiny veins in the face and scalp also reroute blood cooled near the body's surface toward the brain. This adaptation explains why vigorous exercise causes the face of a light-skinned person to turn red.

Behavioral strategies can also help both ectotherms and endotherms to cool off. Many animals escape the sun's heat by swimming, covering themselves with cool mud, or retreating to the shade. Some burrow underground and emerge only at night; others extend their wings to promote cooling. Humans consume cold food and drinks, swim, fan ourselves, and shed extra layers of clothing.

Both ectothermy and endothermy have advantages and disadvantages. The ectotherm uses much less energy, and therefore requires less food and O_2, than an endotherm. However, an ectothermic animal must be able to obtain or escape environmental heat. An injured snake that could not squeeze into a crevice to avoid the broiling sun would cook to death. Ectotherms also become sluggish when the temperature is low, which can make it hard for them to escape from predators.

On the other hand, an endotherm maintains its body temperature even in cold weather or in the middle of the night. But this internal constancy comes at a cost. The metabolic rate of an endotherm is generally five times that of an ectotherm of similar size and body temperature. Endotherms therefore require much more food than do ectotherms. We turn next to the organ system that acquires this food: the digestive system.

28.2 Mastering Concepts

1. Describe the difference between endotherms and ectotherms.
2. What are the advantages and disadvantages of endothermy and ectothermy?

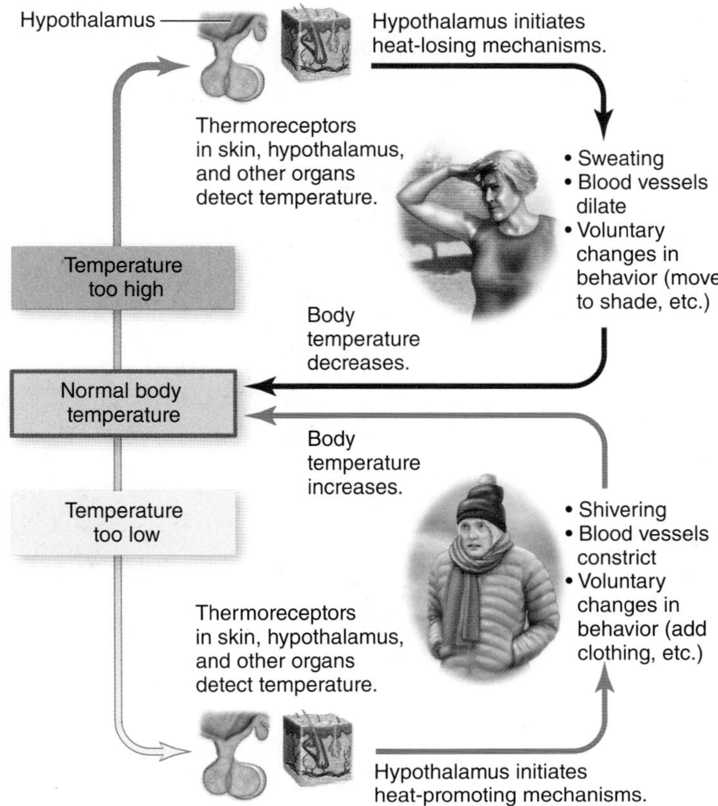

Figure 28.3 Thermoregulation in Humans. Thermoreceptors signal the hypothalamus to keep body temperature within a certain range.

a.

b.

Figure 28.4 Too Cold or Too Hot. (a) These snow monkeys are adapted to cold winters. Their thick fur retains body heat, as does their huddling behavior. (b) This panting dog loses excess heat through its mouth, while the man has employed a behavioral strategy that helps him cool off: he has shed his excess clothing.

Figure 28.5 Delicious. Eating provides the raw materials and energy required for life.

28.3 Digestive Systems Allow Animals to Maintain Nutrient and Energy Homeostasis

Is it true that "you are what you eat"? In some ways, the answer is yes. After all, the atoms and molecules that make up your body came from food that you ate (or that your mother ate before you were born). But in other ways, the answer is no. The woman in figure 28.5 may enjoy eating fruit, yet she looks and acts nothing like a mango. Clearly, food is not incorporated whole into her body, even though atoms and molecules derived from food compose her and every other animal.

The resolution of this paradox lies in the **digestive system,** the organs that ingest food, break it down, absorb the small molecules, and eliminate undigested wastes. As this section describes, some of the molecules absorbed from food do become part of the animal body, but others are used to generate the energy needed for life.

All animals, along with fungi and many other microbes, are heterotrophs. A **heterotroph** is an organism that must consume food—organic matter—to obtain carbon and energy. The opposite of a heterotroph is an **autotroph,** such as a plant or alga, which uses inorganic raw materials and an energy source such as sunlight to build its own organic molecules.

An animal's food is its source of **nutrients,** which are substances that the organism uses for metabolism, growth, maintenance, and repair of its tissues. The six main types of nutrients in food are carbohydrates, proteins, lipids, water, vitamins, and minerals (see chapter 2).

These nutrients contain two important resources. One is the potential energy stored in the chemical bonds of carbohydrates, proteins, and lipids. As described in chapter 6, cells can use each of these fuels in cellular respiration to generate ATP, the energy-rich molecule that powers most cellular activities. ▸ ATP, p. 72

The second resource that food contains is the chemical building blocks that make up the animal's body. Simple sugars, fatty acids, amino acids, nucleotides, water, vitamins, and minerals are the raw materials that build, repair, and maintain all parts of the body, from blood to bone. To the extent that your body incorporates these building blocks, you really are what you eat.

An animal's metabolic rate largely determines its need for energy and nutrients. As we have already seen, endotherms such as birds and mammals have relatively high metabolic rates because they use a lot of energy to maintain a constant body temperature.

Body size also influences the need for food. In general, the larger the animal, the more it needs to eat. When corrected for body size, however, the smallest animals typically have the highest metabolic rates. A hummingbird, for example, has a much higher surface area relative to its body mass than does an elephant. Because the tiny bird loses much more heat to the environment, it must consume much more food to maintain a constant body temperature. A hummingbird therefore eats its own weight in food every day; an elephant takes three months to do the same.

Another factor that affects metabolic rate is an animal's physiological state. Growth and reproduction require more energy and nutrients than simply maintaining the adult body. Baby animals therefore often have ravenous appetites, and a new parent may spend much of its time finding food to fuel its offsprings' rapid growth (figure 28.6).

Figure 28.6 Ravenous. These chicks are begging for the food that will fuel their rapid growth.

28.3 Mastering Concepts

1. What are two reasons that animals must eat?
2. Explain the factors that affect an animal's metabolic rate.

28.4 A Varied Diet Is Essential to Good Health

Nutrients fall into two categories. **Macronutrients** are required in large amounts. Water is a macronutrient; all living cells require water as a solvent and as a participant in many reactions. Organisms use three other macronutrients—carbohydrates, proteins, and lipids—to build cells and to generate ATP. Despite the many nonfat foods on grocery store shelves, the diet must include *all* of these nutrients, including moderate amounts of fat.

Unlike macronutrients, **micronutrients** are required in very small amounts. Two examples are vitamins and minerals, neither of which are used as fuel. Instead, these micronutrients participate in many aspects of cell metabolism. Table 28.1 provides details on the sources and functions of several vitamins and minerals. Many processed foods are fortified with vitamins and minerals, so deficiencies in developed countries are rare.

TABLE 28.1 Selected Vitamins and Minerals in the Human Diet

	Food Sources	Function(s)	Selected Deficiency Symptoms
Vitamins			
Water-Soluble Vitamins			
B complex vitamins			
Niacin	Liver, meat, peas, beans, whole grains, fish	Growth, energy use	Pellagra (diarrhea, dementia, dermatitis)
Folic acid	Liver, navy beans, dark green vegetables	Manufacture of red blood cells, metabolism	Weakness, fatigue, diarrhea, neural tube defects in fetus
Vitamin C	Citrus fruits, tomatoes, peppers, strawberries, cabbage	Antioxidant, production of connective tissue and neurotransmitters	Scurvy (weakness, gum bleeding, weight loss)
Fat-Soluble Vitamins			
Vitamin A	Liver, dairy products, egg yolk, vegetables, fruit	Night vision, new cell growth	Blindness, impaired immune function
Vitamin D	Fish liver oil, milk, egg yolk	Bone formation	Skeletal deformation (rickets)
Minerals			
Calcium	Milk products, green leafy vegetables	Electrolyte, bone and tooth structure, blood clotting, hormone release, nerve transmission, muscle contraction	Muscle cramps and twitches; weakened bones, heart malfunction
Iron	Meat, liver, fish, shellfish, egg yolk, peas, beans, dried fruit, whole grains	Part of hemoglobin and myoglobin, part of some enzymes	Anemia, learning deficits in children
Phosphorus	Meat, fish, eggs, poultry, whole grains	Bone and tooth structure; part of DNA, ATP, and cell membranes	Weakness, mineral loss from bones
Potassium	Fruits, potatoes, meat, fish, eggs, poultry, milk	Electrolyte, nerve transmission, muscle contraction, nucleic acid synthesis	Weakness, loss of appetite, muscle cramps, confusion, heart arrhythmia
Sodium	Table salt, meat, fish, eggs, poultry, milk	Electrolyte, nerve transmission, muscle contraction	Muscle cramps, nausea, weakness

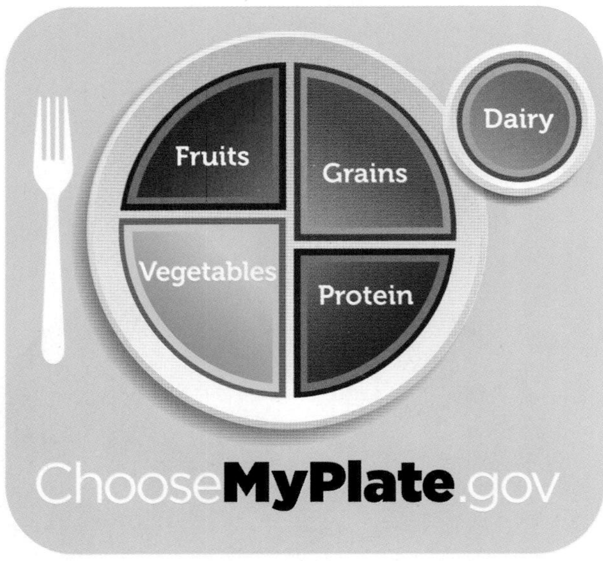

Figure 28.7 One Healthful Diet. According to the U.S. Department of Agriculture's guidelines, more than three quarters of each plate of food should consist of fruits, vegetables, and grains.

The best way to acquire the required macro- and micronutrients is to eat a varied diet. The U.S. government's dietary guidelines emphasize fruits and vegetables, grains, limited amounts of meat or other protein sources, and low-fat dairy products (figure 28.7). The Harvard School of Public Health suggests a somewhat different diet that minimizes dairy products, red meat, and starchy processed grains. Whole grains and vegetable oils, along with abundant vegetables, make up the foundation of this diet.

The food molecules that we cannot digest help maintain good health, too. Dietary fiber, for example, is composed of indigestible plant parts such as the cellulose in plant cell walls. Humans do not produce cellulose-digesting enzymes, so plant cell walls and other indigestible matter contribute only bulk—not nutrients—to food. This increased mass eases movement of the food through the digestive tract, so that harmful ingredients in food contact the walls of the intestines for a shorter period. The result is a lower incidence of colorectal cancer among people who consume abundant fiber in their food. A high-fiber diet also reduces blood cholesterol and helps regulate blood sugar. ▸ cellulose, p. 35

A balanced diet delivers many long-term health benefits, including a reduced risk of type 2 diabetes, cancer, osteoporosis, high blood pressure, and heart disease. Fortunately, packaged foods have labels that describe the nutrient content in each serving of food.

28.4 Mastering Concepts

1. Which nutrients are macronutrients and which are micronutrients?
2. How does indigestible fiber contribute to a healthy diet?

28.5 Eating Disorders Disrupt Nutrient Homeostasis

Healthy eating has two main components. First, the diet must include all of the nutrients necessary to sustain life. A second consideration is the energy content of food, which must balance a person's activity level. Overeating and undereating disrupt nutrient homeostasis.

A. Body Weight Reflects Food Intake and Activity Level

A food's energy content is measured in Calories. By definition, 1 **kilocalorie** (1 food **Calorie;** kcal) is the energy needed to raise 1 kilogram of water from 14.5°C to 15.5°C under controlled conditions.

Studies have shown that 1 gram of carbohydrate or protein yields 4 kcal, whereas 1 gram of fat yields 9 kcal. These values help explain the link between a fatty diet and weight gain; fats supply the most energy of any type of food. When we take in more Calories than we expend, weight increases; those who consume fewer Calories than they expend lose weight and may even starve. Most young adults require 2000 to 2400 Calories per day, depending on gender and level of physical activity.

What constitutes a "healthful" weight? The most common measure is the body mass index, or BMI (figure 28.8). To calculate BMI, divide a person's weight (in kilograms) by his or her squared height (in meters): BMI = weight/

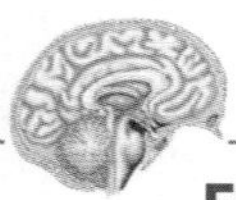

Figure It Out

Consider the following nutritional facts. Bacon cheeseburger: 23 g fat, 25 g protein, 2 g carbohydrates; large fries: 25 g fat, 6 g protein, 63 g carbohydrates; large soda: 86 g carbohydrates. How many kcal are in this meal?

Answer: 1160 kcal

(height)^2. Alternatively, multiply weight (in pounds) by 704.5, and divide by the square of the height (in inches).

Many health professionals consider a person whose BMI is less than 19 to be underweight. A BMI between 19 and 25 is healthy; an overweight person has a BMI greater than 25; and a BMI greater than 30 denotes **obesity.** Morbid obesity is defined as a BMI greater than 40. One limitation of BMI is that it cannot account for many of the details that affect health. An extremely muscular person, for example, will have a high BMI because muscle is denser than fat, yet he or she would not be considered overweight.

Another useful measure is the ratio of waist diameter to hip diameter. People whose fat accumulates at the waistline ("apples") are more susceptible to health problems such as insulin resistance than are "pears," who are bigger around the hips.

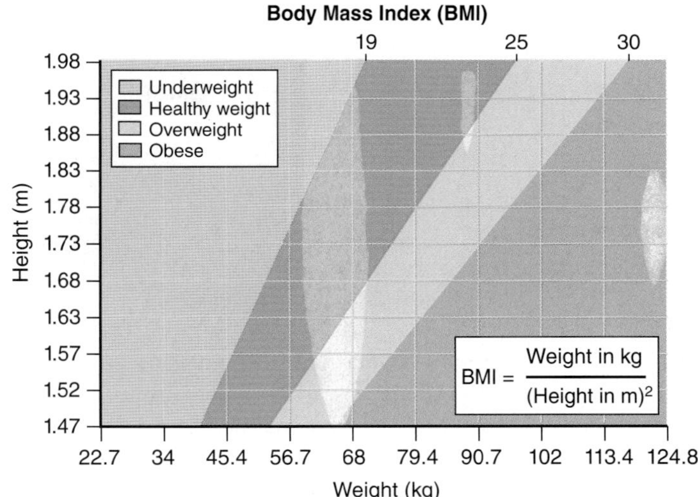

Figure 28.8 **Body Mass Index.** This chart is a quick substitute for a BMI calculation; the intersection of a person's height (in meters) and weight (in kilograms) indicates the BMI range.

B. Starvation: Too Few Calories to Meet the Body's Needs

A healthy human can survive for 50 to 70 days without food—much longer than without air or water. In some areas of the world, famine is a constant threat, and millions of people starve to death every year. Hunger strikes, inhumane treatment of prisoners, and eating disorders can also cause starvation (figure 28.9).

The starving human body essentially digests itself. After only a day without food, reserves of sugar and glycogen are gone. The body then begins extracting energy from stored fat and from muscles, the largest protein source in the body. As the muscles are depleted, the body begins to break down other proteins. Gradually, metabolism slows, blood pressure drops, the pulse weakens, and chills set in. Skin becomes dry and hair falls out as the proteins that form these structures are digested. When the body dismantles the immune system's antibody proteins, protection against infection declines. Mouth sores and anemia develop, the heart beats irregularly, and bones begin to degenerate. Near the end, the starving human is blind, deaf, and emaciated.

Anorexia nervosa, or self-imposed starvation, is refusal to maintain normal body weight. The condition affects about 1 in 250 adolescents, more than 90% of whom are female. The sufferer perceives herself as overweight and eats barely enough to survive, losing as much as 25% of her original body weight. She may further lose weight by vomiting, taking laxatives and diuretics, or exercising intensely. Intravenous feedings, psychotherapy, and nutritional counseling may help, but 15% to 21% of people with anorexia die from the disease.

Bulimia is another eating disorder that mainly affects females. Rather than avoiding food, a person with **bulimia** eats large quantities and then intentionally vomits or uses laxatives shortly afterward, a pattern called "binge and purge." A person with bulimia may or may not be underweight.

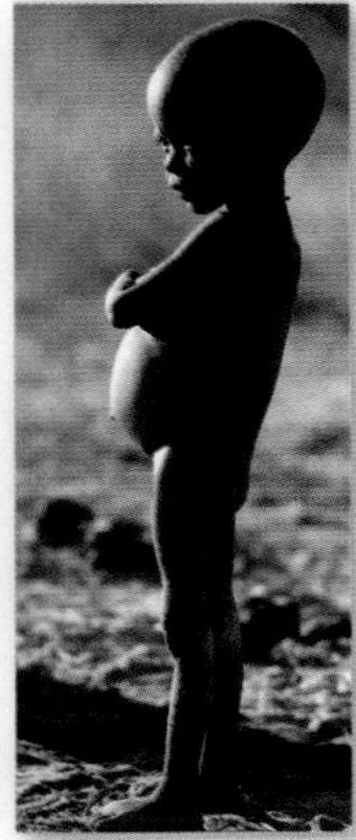

Figure 28.9 **Two Forms of Starvation.** The girl on the left suffers from anorexia nervosa, or self-imposed starvation. The malnourished girl on the right is a famine victim. Her thin legs and distended belly are signs of a severe protein deficiency.

C. Obesity: More Calories Than the Body Needs

Obesity is increasingly common in the United States, and the health consequences can be serious. People who accumulate fat around their waists are susceptible to type 2 diabetes, high blood pressure, and atherosclerosis. High body weight is also correlated with congestive heart failure, acid reflux disease, urinary incontinence, low back pain, stroke, sleep disorders, and many other health problems. In addition, obese people face a higher than average risk of cancers of the colon, breast, and uterus. ▸ diabetes, p. 517

Excess body weight accumulates when a person consumes more calories than he or she expends. For most people, the main culprits are a diet loaded

Figure 28.10 Hormone Deficiency. In a normal mouse, leptin secreted by fat cells affects target cells in the hypothalamus, helping the brain regulate appetite and metabolism. The obese mouse on the left cannot produce leptin and therefore has a ravenous appetite.

with sugar and fat, coupled with an inactive lifestyle. Nevertheless, many genes contribute to appetite, digestion, and metabolic rate, so the combination of alleles that a person inherits plays at least a small part in the risk for obesity.

Some of these genes encode hormones, which interact in complex and poorly understood ways to maintain the balance between food intake and energy expenditure. One weight-related hormone is leptin. Stored fat releases leptin into the bloodstream. At the hypothalamus, leptin interacts with receptors and triggers a signal cascade that inhibits food intake and increases metabolic activity. This action explains why leptin-deficient mice become extremely obese (figure 28.10). Leptin deficiency, however, is very rare in humans.

Scientific studies of leptin and other appetite-related hormones may someday yield new treatments for obesity. In the meantime, the concern over expanding waistlines has fueled demand for low-calorie artificial sweeteners and fats (see chapter 2). Although fad diets remain popular, the most healthful way to lose weight and reverse cardiovascular disease and diabetes is to exercise and reduce calorie intake while maintaining a balanced diet. For people who have difficulty losing weight in this way, stomach-reduction surgery and drugs that either reduce appetite or block fat absorption offer other options.

28.5 Mastering Concepts

1. Describe the relationship of body weight to calorie intake and energy expenditure.
2. What is body mass index?
3. Describe the events of starvation.
4. What are some of the causes and effects of obesity?

28.6 Most Animals Have a Specialized Digestive Tract

Biologists divide animals into categories based on what they eat and how they eat it (figure 28.11). **Herbivores,** such as cows and rabbits, eat only plants. Eagles, cats, wolves, and other **carnivores** hunt other animals for food. **Detritivores** consume decomposing organic matter; dung beetles and earthworms illustrate this diet. Finally, **omnivores** eat a broad variety of foods, including plants and animals. Humans are omnivores, as are raccoons, pigs, chickens, and many other animals.

Many animals rely on one or a few kinds of food. Some animals, such as anteaters, flycatchers, praying mantises, and most spiders, eat only insects. Other animals eat only fish or fruits. The giant panda is a leaf-eater. Because it eats only bamboo, a wild panda can survive only where that plant thrives. Animals with more flexible diets, such as raccoons, can live in a broader range of habitats.

a.

b.

c.

d.

Figure 28.11 Many Ways to Eat. (a) A giant panda munches on bamboo. (b) This leopard is eating its kill. (c) A mosquito takes a blood meal. (d) This basking shark filters food from water.

A. Acquiring Nutrients Requires Several Steps

Although diets differ, all animals have the same four-step process of obtaining and using food (figure 28.12). First, **ingestion** is the entrance of food into the digestive tract. The second stage, **digestion,** is the physical and chemical breakdown of food. In mammals, this process begins with chewing, which tears food into small pieces mixed with saliva. Chewing therefore softens food and increases the surface area exposed to digestive enzymes. In chemical digestion, enzymes split large nutrient molecules into their smaller components. In the third stage, **absorption,** the nutrients enter the cells lining the digestive tract and move into the bloodstream to be transported throughout the body (see chapter 27). Fourth, in **elimination,** the animal's body expels undigested food. **Feces** are the solid wastes that leave the digestive tract. ▸ enzymes, p. 74

One potential source of confusion is the distinction between feces and urine, both of which are animal waste products. Feces are composed partly of undigested food that never enters the body's cells. Urine, on the other hand, is a watery fluid containing dissolved nitrogen and other metabolic wastes produced by the body's cells. Section 28.10 describes how the kidneys produce urine.

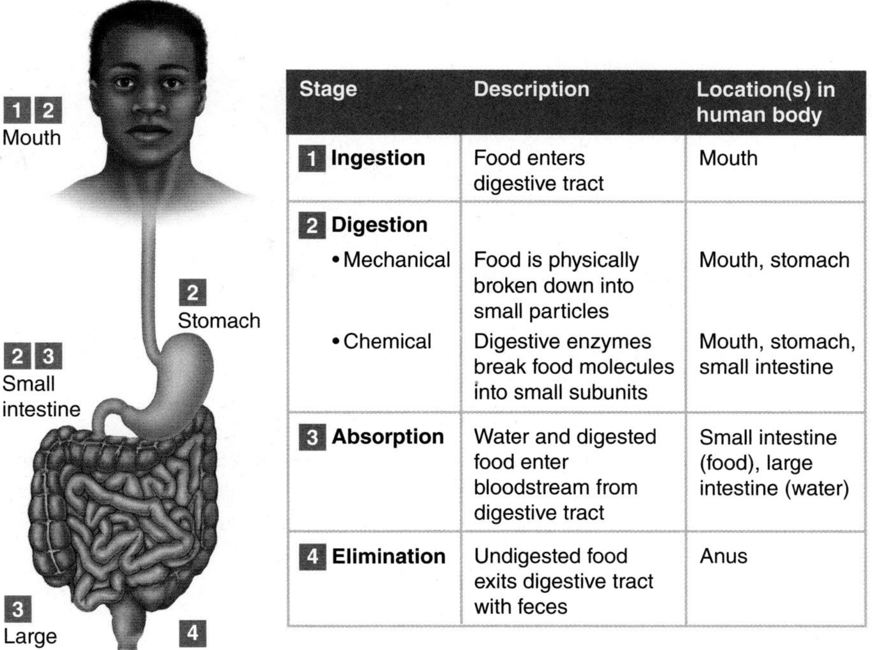

Stage	Description	Location(s) in human body
1 **Ingestion**	Food enters digestive tract	Mouth
2 **Digestion**		
• Mechanical	Food is physically broken down into small particles	Mouth, stomach
• Chemical	Digestive enzymes break food molecules into small subunits	Mouth, stomach, small intestine
3 **Absorption**	Water and digested food enter bloodstream from digestive tract	Small intestine (food), large intestine (water)
4 **Elimination**	Undigested food exits digestive tract with feces	Anus

Figure 28.12 Acquiring and Using Food. The four stages by which animals acquire and use food are ingestion, digestion, absorption, and elimination.

B. Digestive Tracts May Be Incomplete or Complete

Because heterotrophs and their food are composed of the same types of chemicals, digestive enzymes could just as easily attack an animal's body as its food. Digestion therefore occurs within specialized compartments that are protected from enzyme action.

These compartments may be inside or outside cells (figure 28.13). Sponges are the only animals that rely solely on intracellular digestion. Collar cells lining the body wall of a sponge take in nutrients and enclose the food in a food vacuole. A loaded food vacuole fuses with another sac containing digestive enzymes that break down nutrient molecules. Digestion occurs entirely inside the cell, but the process is physically separated from other functions. ▸ sponges, p. 327

Other animals use extracellular digestion, releasing enzymes into a digestive cavity connected with the outside world. The enzymes dismantle large food particles, then cells lining the cavity absorb the products of digestion.

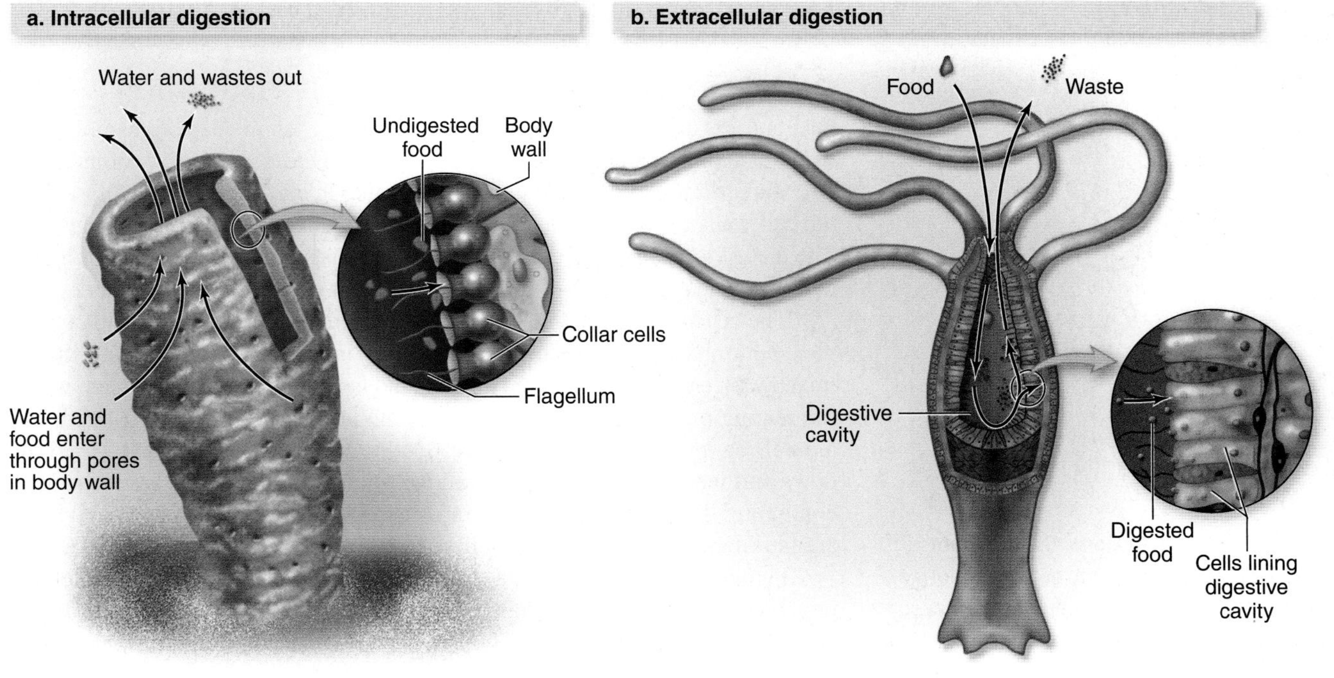

Figure 28.13 Intracellular and Extracellular Digestion. (a) A sponge uses intracellular digestion, which occurs entirely inside cells. (b) Extracellular digestion occurs in a digestive cavity containing enzymes that break down food. Cells lining the cavity absorb the digested nutrients.

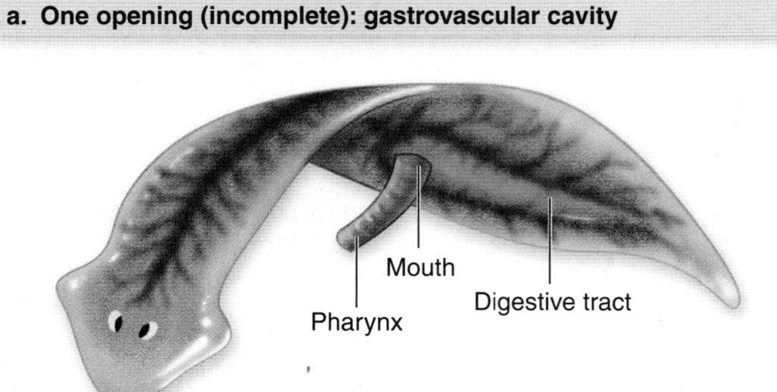

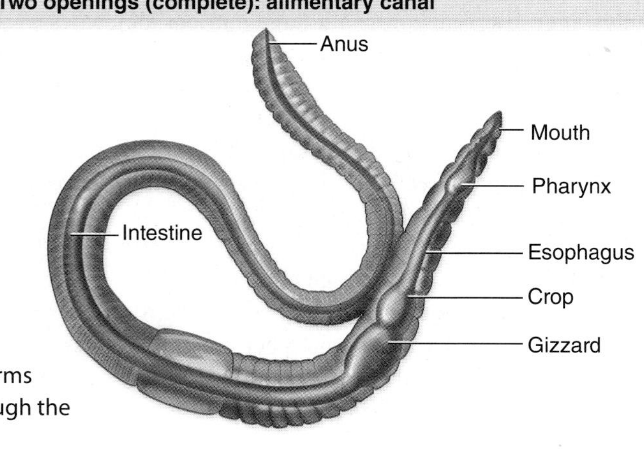

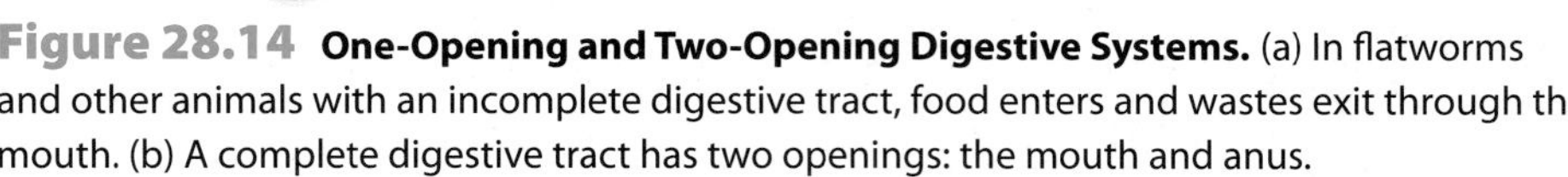
Figure 28.14 One-Opening and Two-Opening Digestive Systems. (a) In flatworms and other animals with an incomplete digestive tract, food enters and wastes exit through the mouth. (b) A complete digestive tract has two openings: the mouth and anus.

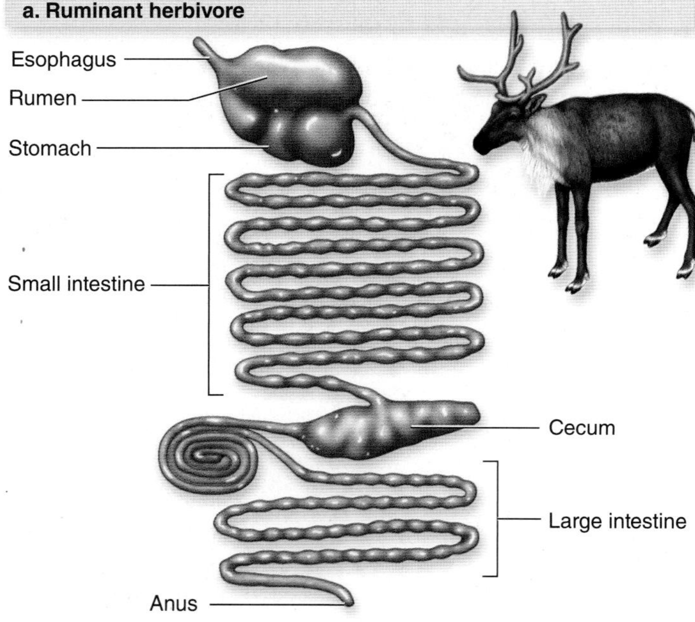

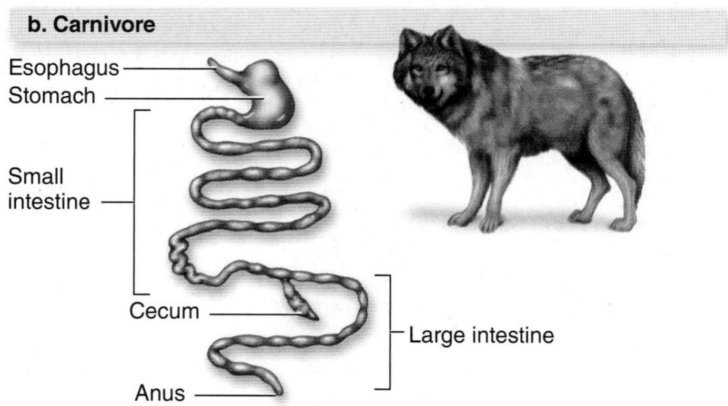

Figure 28.15 Digestive System Adaptations. (a) Ruminant herbivores have a rumen and a long digestive tract, an adaptation to a grassy diet. (b) The protein-rich diet of carnivores is easy to digest, so the digestive system is much shorter and has a reduced cecum.

Food remains outside the body's cells until it is digested and absorbed. Extracellular digestion eases waste removal because indigestible components of food never enter the cells. Instead, the digestive tract simply ejects the waste.

The cavity in which extracellular digestion occurs may have one or two openings (figure 28.14). An **incomplete digestive tract** has only one opening: a mouth that both ingests food and ejects wastes. The animal must digest food and expel the residue before the next meal can begin. This arrangement limits the potential for specialized compartments that might store, digest, or absorb nutrients. Cnidarians such as jellyfish and *Hydra* have incomplete digestive tracts, as do flatworms. In these organisms, the digestive tract is also called a **gastrovascular cavity** because it doubles as a circulatory system that distributes nutrients to the body cells. ▸▸ cnidarians, p. 328; flatworms, p. 329

Most animals have a **complete digestive tract** with two openings; the mouth is the entrance, and the **anus** is the exit. This tubelike digestive cavity is called the **alimentary canal** or **gastrointestinal (GI) tract.** Notice that food passes through in one direction. Regions of the tube can develop specialized areas that break food into smaller particles, digest it, absorb the nutrients, and eliminate wastes. A complete digestive tract therefore extracts nutrients from food more efficiently than an incomplete digestive tract.

C. Diet Influences Digestive Tract Structure

Diet and lifestyle differences select for digestive system adaptations in all animals, including mammals. Figure 28.15 shows the digestive tracts of an herbivore and a carnivore. An herbivore's diet is rich in hard-to-digest cellulose from the cell walls of plants. The long digestive tract allows extra time for digestion. The diet of a carnivore, on the other hand, consists mostly or entirely of highly digestible meat. The overall length of the digestive tract is therefore short.

The elk in figure 28.15a is a **ruminant,** which is an herbivore with a complex, four-chambered organ that specializes in the digestion of grass. Saliva mixed with chewed grass enters the first and largest chamber, the rumen, where fermenting microorganisms break the plant matter down into balls of cud. The animal regurgitates the cud into its mouth; chewing the cud breaks the food down further. When the animal swallows again, the food bypasses the rumen, continuing digestion in the remaining chambers. Cows, sheep, deer, and goats are familiar ruminants. ▸ fermentation, p. 108

Figure 28.15 also depicts another structure whose size varies with diet: the pouchlike **cecum,** which forms the entrance to the large intestine. In herbivores, the cecum is large, and it houses bacteria that break down cellulose-rich plant matter. Carnivores have a small or absent cecum. The cecum is medium-sized in omnivores, reflecting a diet based partly on plants.

28.6 Mastering Concepts

1. Define the terms *herbivore, carnivore, detritivore,* and *omnivore.*
2. What four processes does food undergo when an animal eats?
3. Distinguish between intracellular and extracellular digestion.
4. How do incomplete and complete digestive tracts differ?
5. Compare and contrast the digestive systems of an elk and a wolf.

28.7 The Human Digestive System Consists of Several Organs

The human digestive system consists of the gastrointestinal tract and accessory structures (figure 28.16). Some of the accessory structures, such as the salivary glands and pancreas, produce digestive enzymes. Two others, the liver and gallbladder, produce and store bile, which assists in fat digestion. The teeth and tongue are also accessory organs.

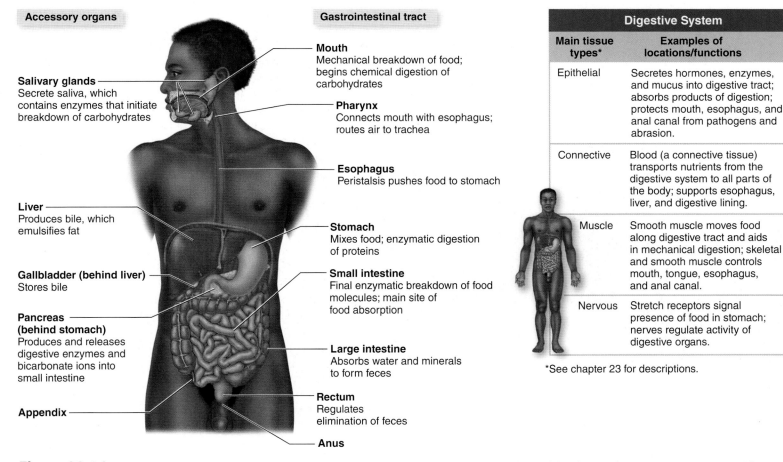

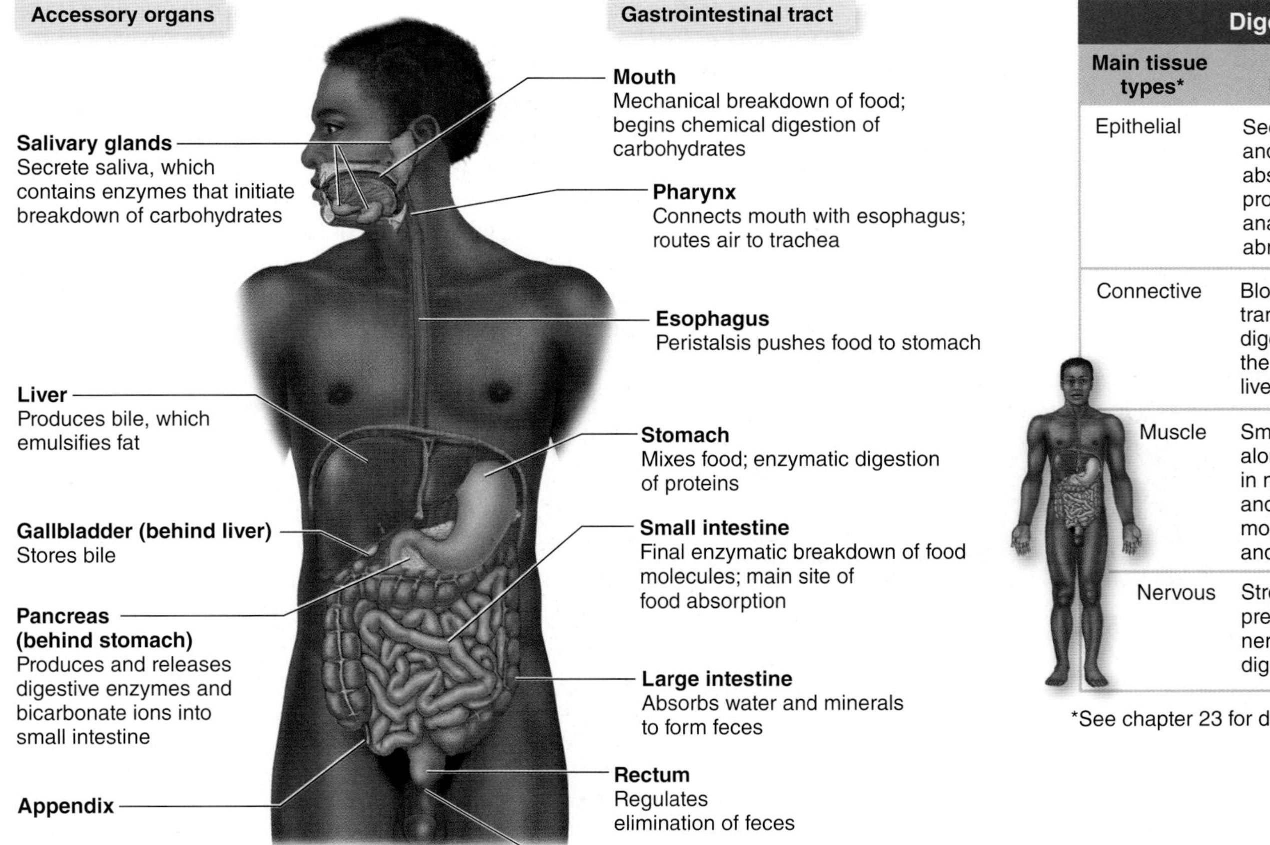
Accessory organs
Salivary glands
Secrete saliva, which contains enzymes that initiate breakdown of carbohydrates
Liver
Produces bile, which emulsifies fat
Gallbladder (behind liver)
Stores bile
Pancreas (behind stomach)
Produces and releases digestive enzymes and bicarbonate ions into small intestine
Appendix
Gastrointestinal tract
Mouth
Mechanical breakdown of food; begins chemical digestion of carbohydrates
Pharynx
Connects mouth with esophagus; routes air to trachea
Esophagus
Peristalsis pushes food to stomach
Stomach
Mixes food; enzymatic digestion of proteins
Small intestine
Final enzymatic breakdown of food molecules; main site of food absorption
Large intestine
Absorbs water and minerals to form feces
Rectum
Regulates elimination of feces
Anus

Digestive System	
Main tissue types*	**Examples of locations/functions**
Epithelial	Secretes hormones, enzymes, and mucus into digestive tract; absorbs products of digestion; protects mouth, esophagus, and anal canal from pathogens and abrasion.
Connective	Blood (a connective tissue) transports nutrients from the digestive system to all parts of the body; supports esophagus, liver, and digestive lining.
Muscle	Smooth muscle moves food along digestive tract and aids in mechanical digestion; skeletal and smooth muscle controls mouth, tongue, esophagus, and anal canal.
Nervous	Stretch receptors signal presence of food in stomach; nerves regulate activity of digestive organs.

*See chapter 23 for descriptions.

Figure 28.16 The Human Digestive System. Food breaks down as it moves through the chambers of the digestive tract. Accessory organs aid in digestion.

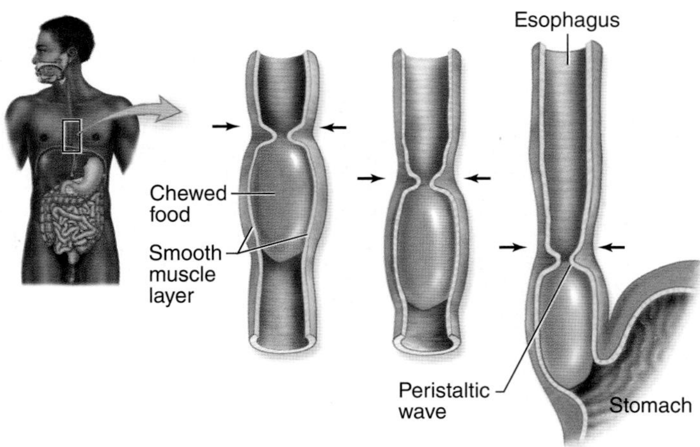

Figure 28.17 Peristalsis. Layers of smooth muscle coordinate their contractions to move food in one direction through the digestive tract.

A. Muscles Underlie the Digestive Tract

How does food make its way along an animal's digestive tract? The answer is that layers of smooth muscle underlying the entire digestive tract undergo **peristalsis,** or rhythmic waves of contraction (figure 28.17). These contractions not only propel food in one direction but also churn the food, mixing it with enzymes to form a liquid. Unlike skeletal muscle, smooth muscle contraction is involuntary: it does not require input from motor neurons. Instead, the autonomic nervous system stimulates smooth muscle to contract. ▸▸ smooth muscle tissue, p. 471; autonomic nervous system, p. 491

Muscles also control the openings between digestive organs. **Sphincters** are muscular rings that can contract to block the passage of materials. The sphincters at the mouth and anus are composed of skeletal muscle and are under voluntary control, so we can decide when to open our mouth or eliminate feces. The remaining sphincters within the digestive tract, however, are composed of involuntary smooth muscle.

B. Digestion Begins in the Mouth and Esophagus

A tour of the digestive system begins at the mouth, where the taste of food triggers salivary glands to secrete saliva. This fluid contains an enzyme that starts to break down starch into monosaccharides (sugar monomers). Meanwhile, the **teeth**—mineral-hardened structures embedded in the jaws—grasp and chew the food. Chewing is a form of mechanical digestion: water and mucus in saliva aid the teeth as they tear food into small pieces, increasing the surface area available for chemical digestion. The muscular **tongue** at the floor of the mouth mixes the food with saliva and pushes it to the back of the mouth to be swallowed.

The chewed mass of food passes first through the **pharynx,** or throat, the tube that also conducts air to the trachea. During swallowing, the **epiglottis** temporarily covers the opening to the trachea so that food enters the digestive tract instead of the lungs. From the pharynx, swallowed food and liquids pass to the **esophagus,** a muscular tube leading to the stomach. Food does not merely slide down the esophagus under the influence of gravity; instead, contracting muscles push it along in a wave of peristalsis.

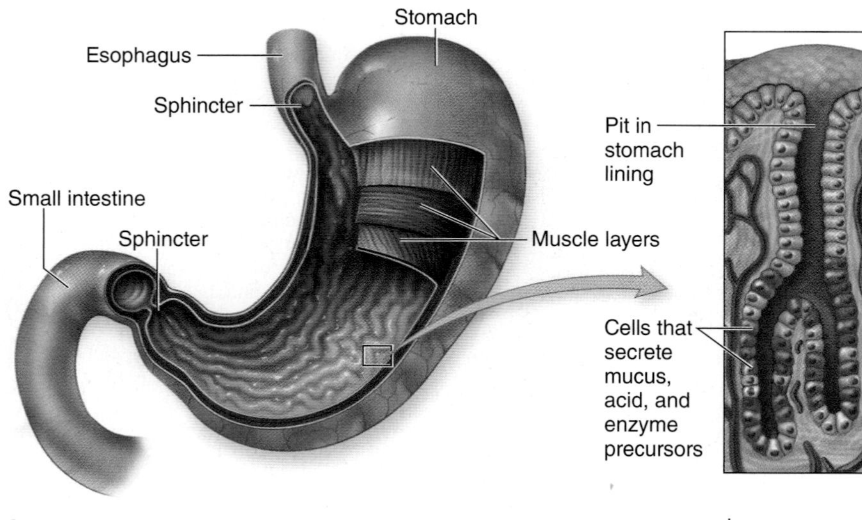

Figure 28.18 The Stomach. (a) The stomach receives food from the esophagus, mixes it with gastric juice, and passes it to the small intestine. (b) The stomach lining contains cells that secrete mucus and gastric juice.

C. The Stomach Stores, Digests, and Pushes Food

The **stomach** is a J-shaped muscular bag that receives food from the esophagus (figure 28.18). The stomach is about the size of a large sausage when empty, but when very full, it can expand to hold as much as 3 or 4 liters of food. Ridges in the stomach's lining can unfold like the pleats of an accordion to accommodate a large meal.

The stomach absorbs very few nutrients, but it can absorb some water and salts (electrolytes), a few drugs (e.g., aspirin), and, like the rest of the digestive tract, alcohol. As a result, we feel alcohol's intoxicating effects quickly.

The stomach's main function, however, is to continue the mechanical and chemical digestion of food. Swallowed chunks of food break into smaller pieces as waves of peristalsis churn the stomach's contents. At the same time, the stomach lining produces **gastric juice,** a mixture of water, mucus, salts, hydrochloric acid, and enzymes.

This gastric juice comes from specialized cells housed in pits in the lining of the stomach. Some cells produce mucus; others secrete a protein that becomes **pepsin,** an enzyme that digests proteins. Still others release hydrochloric acid. The pH of the gastric juice is therefore low, about 1.5 or 2. The acidity denatures the proteins in food, kills most disease-causing organisms, and activates pepsin so that protein digestion can begin. ▸▸ epithelial tissue, p. 469; pH, p. 32

If gastric juice breaks down protein in food, how does the stomach keep from digesting itself? First, the stomach produces little gastric juice until food is present. Second, mucus coats and protects the stomach lining. Tight junctions between cells in the stomach lining also prevent gastric juice from seeping through to the tissues below.

Chyme is the semifluid mixture of food and gastric juice in the stomach. At regular intervals, small amounts of chyme squirt through the sphincter that links the stomach and the upper part of the small intestine (the duodenum).

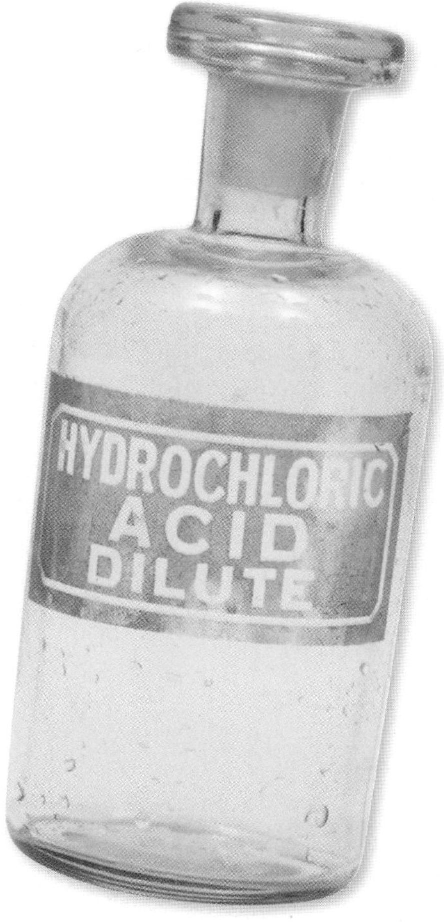

D. The Small Intestine Digests and Absorbs Nutrients

The **small intestine** is a 7-meter-long tubular organ that completes digestion and absorbs nutrients. Although narrow in comparison with the large intestine, the small intestine is the longest organ in the digestive system.

Anatomy of the Small Intestine The duodenum makes up the first 25 centimeters of the small intestine. Glands in the wall of the duodenum secrete mucus that protects and lubricates the small intestine. In addition, ducts from the pancreas and liver open into the duodenum.

The small intestine absorbs water, minerals, free amino acids, cholesterol, and vitamins without further digestion. Most molecules in food, however, require additional processing by digestive enzymes. Although most of these enzymes come from the pancreas, cells lining the small intestine produce enzymes called carbohydrases that act on short polysaccharides and disaccharides. The small intestine immediately absorbs the simple sugars that the carbohydrases release. People who lack one such enzyme, lactase, cannot digest milk sugar; this chapter's Burning Question discusses this condition.

Burning Questions

What's lactose intolerance?

Lactose, or milk sugar, is a disaccharide in milk. In an infant's small intestine, an enzyme called lactase breaks down lactose. Most people stop producing lactase after infancy; after all, milk is not typically part of an adult mammal's diet. If a person without lactase consumes milk, bacteria in the large intestine ferment the undigested sugar. Their byproducts create the symptoms of lactose intolerance: abdominal pain, gas, diarrhea, bloating, and cramps.

People with lactose intolerance can prevent these problems simply by avoiding fresh milk. Instead, they can choose fermented dairy products such as yogurt, buttermilk, and cheese; bacteria have already broken down the lactose in those foods. Taking lactase tablets can also prevent symptoms.

Interestingly, people with roots in northern Europe and a few other locations continue to produce lactase as adults, thanks to a long-ago genetic mutation that was adaptive in dairy-herding regions of the world.

Submit your burning question to:
marielle_hoefnagels@mcgraw-hill.com

The rest of the small intestine absorbs nutrients from digested food and passes them to the bloodstream. Close examination of the hills and valleys along the small intestine's lining reveals millions of **villi,** tiny fingerlike projections that absorb nutrients (figure 28.19). The epithelial cells on the surface of each villus bristle with hundreds of **microvilli,** extensions of the cell membrane. Villi and microvilli increase the surface area of the small intestine at least 600 times, allowing for the efficient extraction of nutrients from food.

The capillaries that snake throughout each villus take up the newly absorbed nutrients and water, then empty into veins that carry the nutrient-laden blood to the liver. Also inside each villus is a lymph capillary that receives digested fats. Cells throughout the body use all of these nutrients to generate energy and to build new proteins, carbohydrates, lipids, and nucleic acids.

Like the stomach, the small intestine protects itself against self-digestion by producing digestive biochemicals only when food is present. In addition, mucus protects the intestinal wall from digestive juices and neutralizes stomach acid. Nevertheless, many intestinal lining cells die in the caustic soup. Rapid division of the small intestine's epithelial cells compensates for the loss, replacing the lining every 36 hours.

The Role of the Pancreas, Liver, and Gallbladder Aside from carbohydrases, most of the digestive enzymes in the small intestine come from the **pancreas** (see figure 28.16). This accessory organ sends about a liter of pancreatic "juice" to the duodenum each day. The fluid from the pancreas contains many enzymes. Trypsin and chymotrypsin break polypeptides into amino acids; pancreatic amylase digests starch; pancreatic lipase breaks down fats; and nucleases split nucleic acids such as DNA into nucleotides. In addition to these enzymes, pancreatic juice also contains alkaline sodium bicarbonate, which neutralizes the acid from the stomach.

Fats present an interesting challenge to the digestive system. Lipase enzymes are water soluble, but fats are not. Therefore, lipase can only act at the surface of a fat droplet, where it contacts water. **Bile** is a greenish-yellow

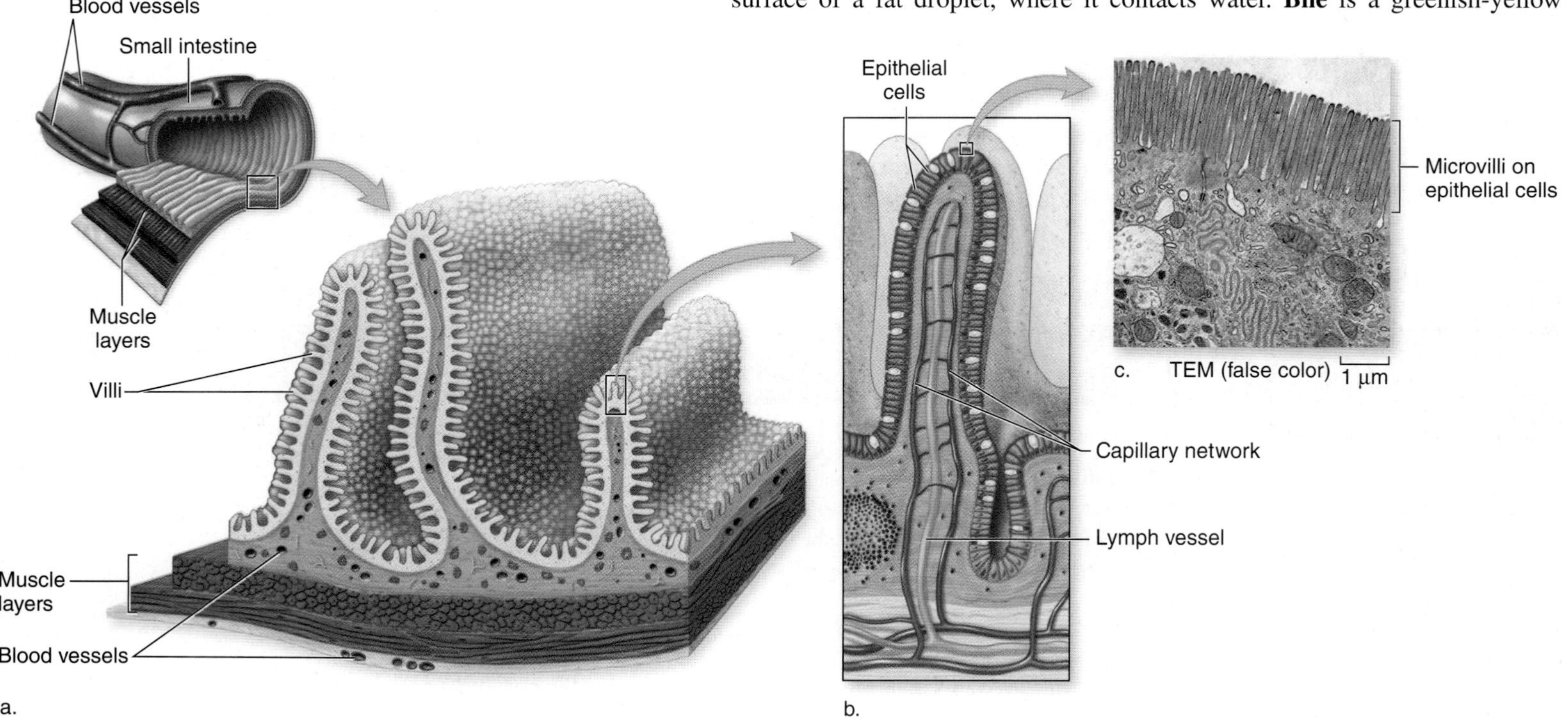

Figure 28.19 The Small Intestine. (a) Fingerlike villi project from each ridge of the small intestine's lining. (b) Within each villus, blood-filled capillaries absorb digested carbohydrates and proteins, and lymph capillaries absorb digested fats. (c) Microvilli add tremendous surface area for absorption.

biochemical that helps solve this problem by dispersing the fat into tiny globules suspended in water. The resulting mixture, called an emulsion, increases the surface area exposed to lipase.

Bile comes from the **liver,** a large accessory organ with more than 200 functions. The liver's only *direct* contribution to digestion is the production of bile. The **gallbladder** is an accessory organ that stores this bile until chyme triggers its release into the small intestine. The cholesterol in bile can crystallize, forming gallstones that partially or completely block the duct to the small intestine. Gallstones are very painful and may require removal of the gallbladder. A person can survive without this organ because surgeons simply redirect the flow of bile from the liver to the small intestine. ▸ cholesterol, p. 38

The liver's other functions include detoxifying harmful substances in the blood. Nutrient-laden blood arrives from the intestines and passes through the liver's extensive capillary beds, which remove bacteria and toxins. (In a condition called cirrhosis, scar tissue blocks this vital blood flow through the liver.) The liver gets "first dibs" on the nutrients in the blood before it is pumped to the rest of the body. This accessory organ also stores glycogen and fat-soluble vitamins and produces blood-clotting proteins.

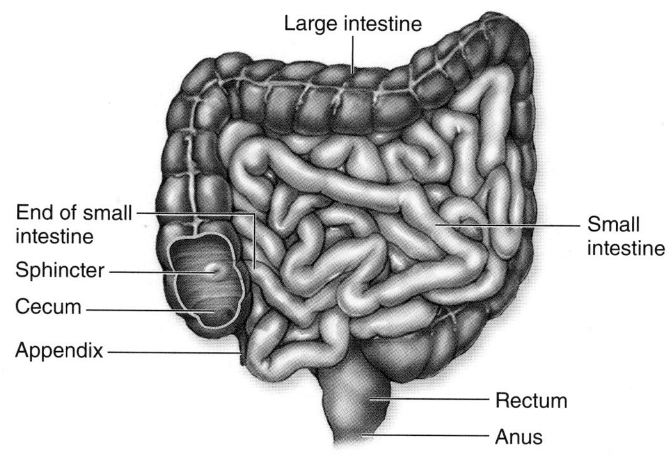

Figure 28.20 The Large Intestine. The large intestine receives chyme from the small intestine. The lining of the intestine absorbs water, salts, and minerals; whatever is left is eliminated as feces.

E. The Large Intestine Completes Nutrient and Water Absorption

The material remaining in the small intestine moves next into the **large intestine,** which extends to the anus while forming a "frame" around the small intestine (figure 28.20). At 1.5 meters long, the large intestine is much shorter than the small intestine, but its diameter is greater (about 6.5 centimeters). Its main functions are to absorb water and salts and to eliminate the remainder as feces.

The start of the large intestine is the pouchlike cecum. Dangling from the cecum is the appendix, a thin, worm-shaped tube. Trapped bacteria or undigested food can cause the appendix to become irritated, inflamed, and infected, producing severe pain. A burst appendix can spill its contents into the abdominal cavity and spread the infection. (This chapter's Why We Care box describes some other examples of illnesses affecting the gastrointestinal tract.)

The colon forms the majority of the large intestine. Here, the large intestine absorbs most of the water, electrolytes, and minerals from chyme. Veins carry blood from vessels surrounding the large intestine to the liver.

The remnants of digestion consist mostly of bacteria, undigested fiber, and intestinal cells. These materials, plus smaller amounts of other substances, collect in the rectum as solid or semisolid feces. When the rectum is full, receptor cells trigger a reflex that eliminates the feces through the anus.

Our partnership with our intestinal microbes deserves special mention. Trillions of bacteria, representing about 500 different species, are normal inhabitants of the large intestine. These microscopic residents produce the characteristic foul-smelling odors of intestinal gas and feces, but they also provide many benefits. Most notably, they help prevent infection by harmful microorganisms. They also decompose cellulose and some other nutrients, produce B vitamins and vitamin K, and break down bile and some drugs. Antibiotic drugs often kill these normal bacteria and allow other microorganisms to grow. This change in the intestinal ecosystem causes the diarrhea that sometimes accompanies treatment with antibiotics. ▸ beneficial microbes, p. 286

Interestingly, a baby is born with a microbe-free digestive tract. The infant begins acquiring its microbiota with its first meal of milk or formula. Bacteria on the mother's skin and in the environment gradually enter the baby and colonize the intestines, establishing populations that will persist throughout the person's life.

Why We Care | The Unhealthy Digestive System

The entire length of the human digestive tract is subject to numerous disorders. Some are a nuisance or easily treated, whereas others can be deadly. A few are listed here:

- **Acid reflux:** Gastric juice, normally confined to the stomach, sometimes emerges through the sphincter guarding the stomach entrance. The acid burns the esophagus, causing "heartburn."
- **Appendicitis:** The appendix can become inflamed or infected. If it ruptures, it can release bacteria into the abdominal cavity, causing serious infection and sometimes even death when left untreated.
- **Diarrhea:** If the intestines fail to absorb as much water as they should, the feces become loose and watery.
- **Constipation:** An obstructed large intestine, loss of peristalsis, dehydration, starvation, or anxiety might cause hard, dry feces that are difficult to eliminate.
- **Colon (colorectal) cancer:** Cancerous tumors may arise in the rectum, colon, or appendix. Colon cancer is a leading cause of death worldwide; a diet high in fiber aids in prevention.

28.7 Mastering Concepts

1. Explain the action and importance of peristalsis and sphincters in digestion.
2. Describe the functions of saliva, teeth, and the tongue in digestion.
3. How does food move from the mouth to the stomach?
4. Describe the mechanical and chemical digestion that occurs in the stomach.
5. What is the structure and function of the small intestine?
6. How do the pancreas, liver, and gallbladder aid digestion?
7. Describe the events that occur as food passes through the large intestine.
8. How does undigested food leave the body?

28.8 Animals Eliminate Nitrogenous Wastes and Regulate Water and Salts

As we have already seen, blood carries nutrients and water from the digestive tract to the cells that make up the rest of the body. These cells, in turn, release metabolic wastes into the bloodstream. **Excretion** is the elimination of these wastes. For example, as described in chapter 27, the respiratory system excretes CO_2, a byproduct of aerobic cellular respiration.

An animal's body also excretes nitrogen-containing (nitrogenous) wastes, which cells produce during the breakdown of proteins (figure 28.21). Proteins are composed of amino acids, which can enter the energy-generating pathways described in chapter 6. During this process, amino groups ($-NH_2$) are stripped from amino acids. In the liver, cells incorporate the nitrogen into a waste molecule called **urea.** This nitrogenous waste then moves to the bloodstream and is eliminated with water in urine.

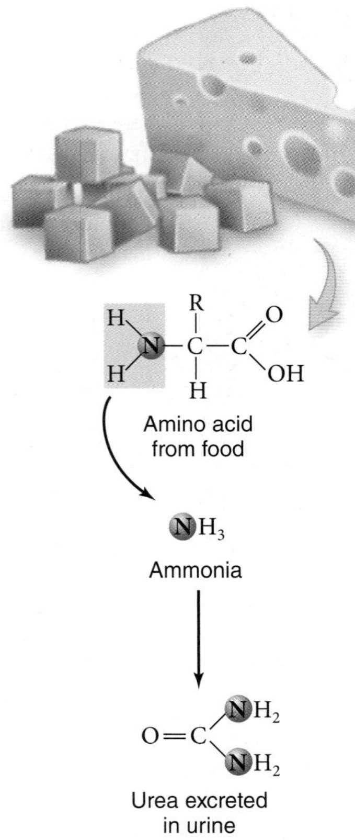

Besides eliminating urea, urine also participates in the regulation of the balance between salt and water inside the body. In most habitats, organisms must **osmoregulate;** that is, they control the concentration of ions in their body fluids as the environment changes. Osmoregulation requires managing the gain and loss of water, ions, or both.

A brief review of how water and ions move across membranes will help explain how osmoregulation works. Osmosis is the diffusion of water across a semipermeable membrane; the net direction of water movement is toward the side with the highest concentration of dissolved solutes. If a cell's external environment is saltier than the cell itself, water moves out of the cell. In the opposite situation, water moves into the cell. ▸ membrane transport, p. 75

Osmoregulation often requires cells to move ions against their concentration gradient; that is, from where they are less concentrated to where they are more concentrated. This process, called active transport, requires energy in the form of ATP. Water may follow the ions by osmosis; our kidneys exploit this mechanism to conserve water during the production of urine.

Bony fishes that live in the ocean face different challenges in osmoregulation from their counterparts in fresh water (figure 28.22). Ocean water is much saltier than a fish's cells, so the animal loses water by osmosis, mostly at the

Figure 28.21 Nitrogenous Waste. Protein breakdown yields ammonia, which the mammalian liver converts to urea for elimination in urine.

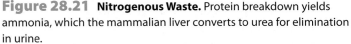

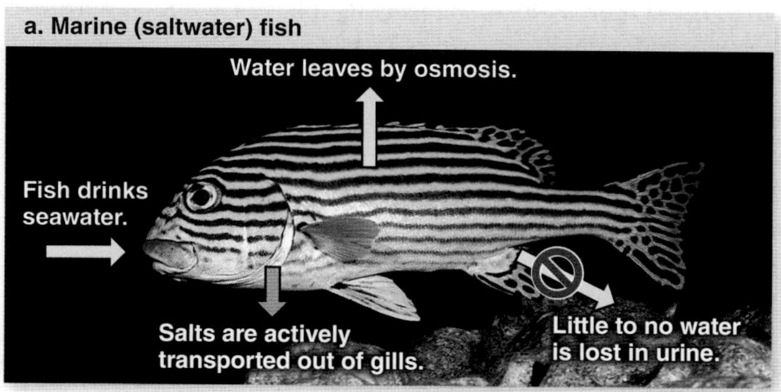

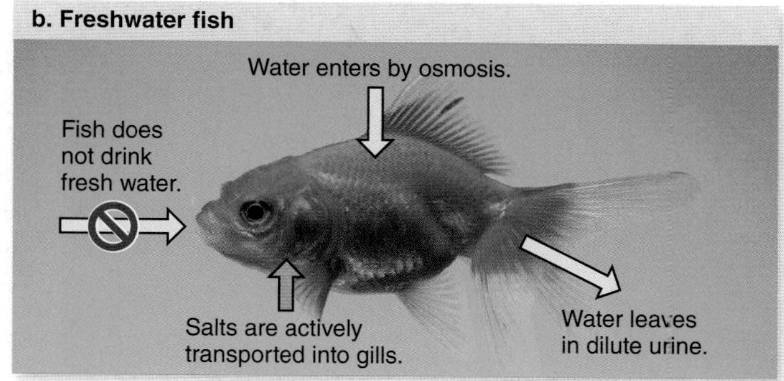

Figure 28.22 Osmoregulation in Fishes. Marine and freshwater fishes face opposite challenges in managing ions and water. (a) Seawater contains a higher solute concentration than the cells of a marine fish. The animal therefore constantly loses water by osmosis and pumps ions out by active transport. (b) Fresh water contains few dissolved solutes; a fish in that habitat therefore constantly gains water by osmosis and must use active transport to acquire essential ions.

gills. The fish therefore drinks seawater, produces little urine, and uses active transport at the gills to get rid of excess salts. In contrast, fresh water is much more dilute than the cells of a fish. A freshwater fish therefore constantly takes in water at its gills and through its skin by osmosis, while losing salts to its surroundings. Its kidneys shed excess water in dilute urine, and cells in the gills use active transport to absorb ions from water.

28.8 Mastering Concepts

1. What is the main nitrogenous waste in a mammal's urine?
2. Explain how osmoregulation occurs in marine and freshwater fish.

28.9 The Urinary System Produces, Stores, and Eliminates Urine

The human **urinary system** filters blood, eliminates nitrogenous wastes, and helps maintain the ion concentration of body fluids. The paired **kidneys** are the major excretory organs in the urinary system (figure 28.23). Located near the rear wall of the abdomen, each kidney is about the size of an adult fist and weighs about 230 grams.

As the kidneys cleanse blood, a liquid waste called **urine** forms; section 28.10 describes this process in more detail. Besides eliminating urea and other toxic substances, kidneys have other functions as well. These organs conserve water, salts, glucose, amino acids, and other valuable nutrients. They also help regulate blood pH.

One other function of the kidneys is to regulate the volume of blood. What happens if we drink too many fluids or if we lose too much moisture in sweat and breath? Rather than swelling like a balloon or drying up like a leaf, the body adjusts: the kidneys maintain the volume of blood by controlling the amount of water lost in urine. This function is important because blood volume is one factor that influences blood pressure. ▸ blood pressure, p. 552

The urine from each kidney drains into a **ureter,** a narrow muscular tube about 28 centimeters long. Waves of smooth muscle contraction squeeze the fluid along the two ureters and squirt it into the **urinary bladder,** a saclike muscular organ that collects urine.

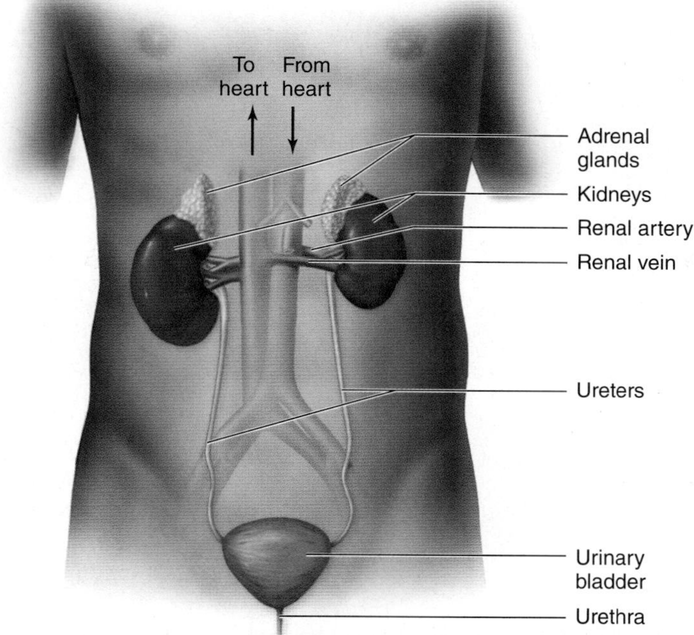

Urinary System	
Main tissue types*	**Examples of locations/functions**
Epithelial	Enables diffusion between nephron and blood; also lines ureters and bladder.
Connective	Blood (which kidneys filter) is a connective tissue.
Muscle	Smooth muscle controls flow of blood to and from nephrons; smooth and skeletal muscle sphincters control urine release.
Nervous	Sensory cells in hypothalamus coordinate negative feedback loops that maintain homeostasis.

*See chapter 23 for descriptions.

Figure 28.23 Human Urinary System. The human urinary system includes the kidneys, ureters, urinary bladder, and urethra. This generalized depiction omits the differences between male and female organs. Figures 30.4 and 30.8 show the sex differences in more detail.

The **urethra** is the tube that connects the bladder with the outside of the body. In females, the urethra opens between the clitoris and vagina. In males, the urethra extends along the length of the penis. The urethra also carries semen in males (see chapter 30). The term *urogenital tract* reflects the intimate connection between the urinary and reproductive systems.

Two sphincters must relax before urine can leave the bladder. A spinal reflex involuntarily controls the innermost sphincter, which is made of smooth muscle. The outer sphincter consists of skeletal muscle. Its relaxation is under voluntary control in most people over 2 years old.

The adult bladder can hold about 600 milliliters of urine. The accumulation of urine stimulates stretch receptors in the bladder. The receptors send impulses to the spinal cord, which stimulates sensory neurons that contract the bladder muscles, generating a strong urge to urinate. We can suppress the urge to urinate for a short time by contracting the external sphincter. Eventually, the cerebral cortex directs the sphincters to relax, and bladder muscle contractions force urine out of the body.

Weakened sphincter muscles, overactive bladder muscles, and nerve damage are among the underlying causes of urinary incontinence—the loss of bladder control. Urinary tract infections, pregnancy, prostate enlargement, spinal cord injuries, and many other conditions are associated with incontinence. Treatments include everything from behavioral changes to drugs to the surgical implantation of an artificial sphincter.

28.9 Mastering Concepts

1. List the organs that make up the human urinary system.
2. What are the functions of the kidneys?

Kidney
Renal artery
Renal vein
Ureter
a.
Nephron
Filter Tubule
Nephron
Tubule Filter
Artery
Vein
Collecting duct
b.

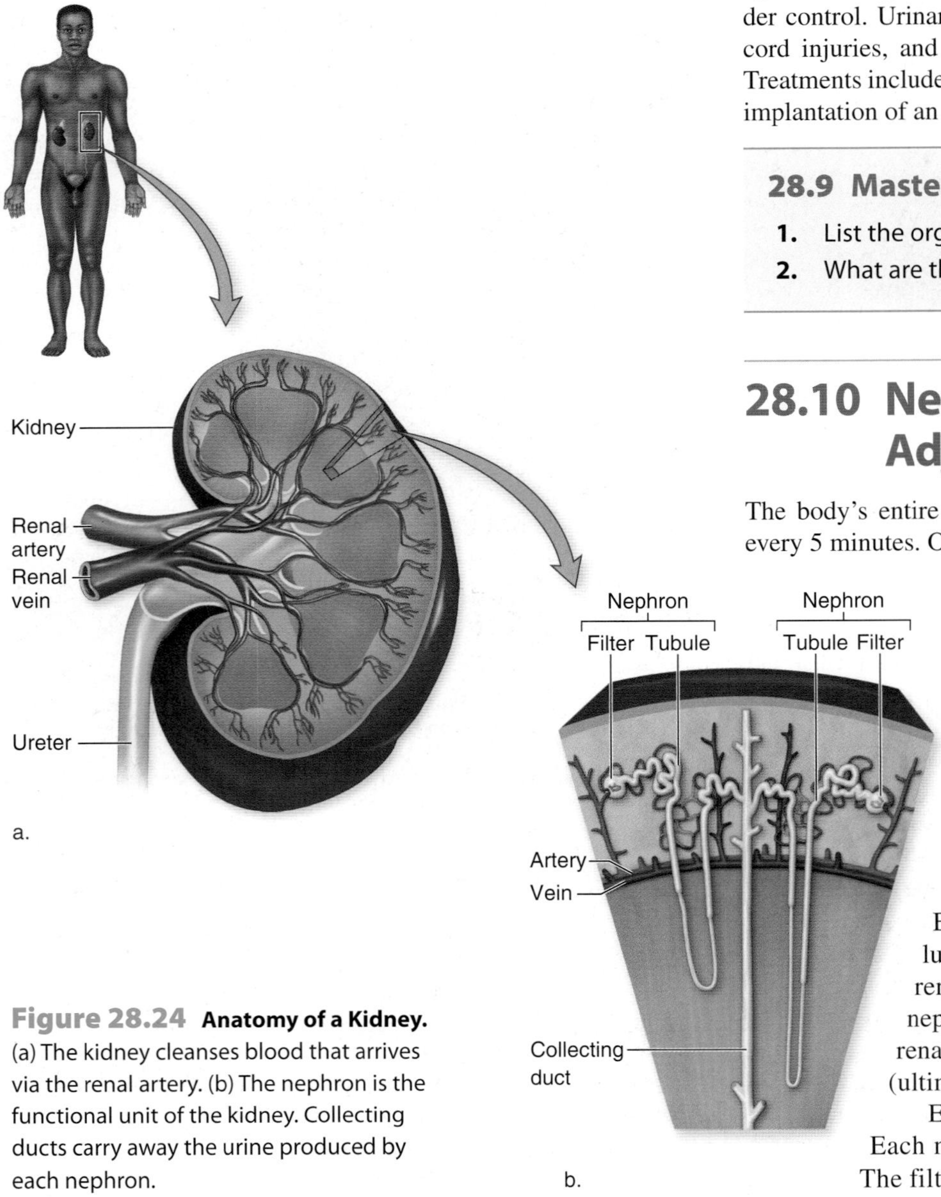

Figure 28.24 Anatomy of a Kidney. (a) The kidney cleanses blood that arrives via the renal artery. (b) The nephron is the functional unit of the kidney. Collecting ducts carry away the urine produced by each nephron.

28.10 Nephrons Remove Wastes and Adjust the Composition of Blood

The body's entire blood supply courses through the kidney's blood vessels every 5 minutes. Of the 1600 to 2000 liters of blood that pass through the kidneys each day, approximately 180 liters of fluid filter from the blood into the **nephrons**, the functional units of the kidney. Nephrons are responsible for sorting valuable body fluids from waste. Most of the fluid that the nephrons process is reabsorbed into the blood, not released in urine. As a result, a person produces only about 1.5 liters of urine daily.

A. Nephrons Interact Closely with Blood Vessels

Each kidney contains 1.3 million tubular nephrons. As illustrated in figure 28.24, each kidney receives blood via a renal artery, which branches into capillaries surrounding each nephron. The kidney's capillaries eventually converge into the renal vein, which carries cleansed blood out of the kidney and (ultimately) to the heart.

Examine the anatomy of the nephrons in figure 28.24b. Each nephron consists of two main parts: a filter and a tubule. The filter receives fluid from the blood. From there, the solution travels along the tubule, which is a winding passageway that dips toward the kidney's center before returning to the outer portion of the kidney. The entire nephron, when stretched out, is about 3 to 4 centimeters long.

A **collecting duct** receives the fluid from several nephrons. Urine from many collecting ducts empties into the funnel-like upper portion of the ureter. The fluid flows down the ureter to the urinary bladder and eventually moves out of the body through the urethra.

B. Urine Formation Includes Filtration, Reabsorption, and Secretion

The chemical composition of urine reflects three processes (figure 28.25):

1. **Filtration:** Water and dissolved substances are filtered out of the blood at the entrance to the nephron. Blood pressure drives substances across the capillary walls into the nephron. Pores in the filter allow water, urea, glucose, salts, and amino acids to pass, but large structures such as plasma proteins, blood cells, and platelets remain in the bloodstream.
2. **Reabsorption:** Useful materials such as salts, water, glucose, and amino acids return from the nephron to the blood.
3. **Secretion:** Toxins and drugs that are bound to plasma proteins are secreted into the nephron to be eliminated in urine, as are hydrogen ions (H^+) and other surplus ions.

After reabsorption and secretion, the filtrate is urine. Urine contains water, several types of ions, urea, and small amounts of other metabolic wastes. Nearly all of the glucose and amino acids present in the original filtrate, however, return to the blood. Nevertheless, the exact chemical composition of urine can vary, as described in the Burning Question on this page.

Filtration: Fluid and dissolved substances enter nephron from blood

Reabsorption: Water, glucose, ions, and other useful substances return to blood from filtrate

Secretion: Drugs, poisons, and H^+ ions are secreted from blood into filtrate

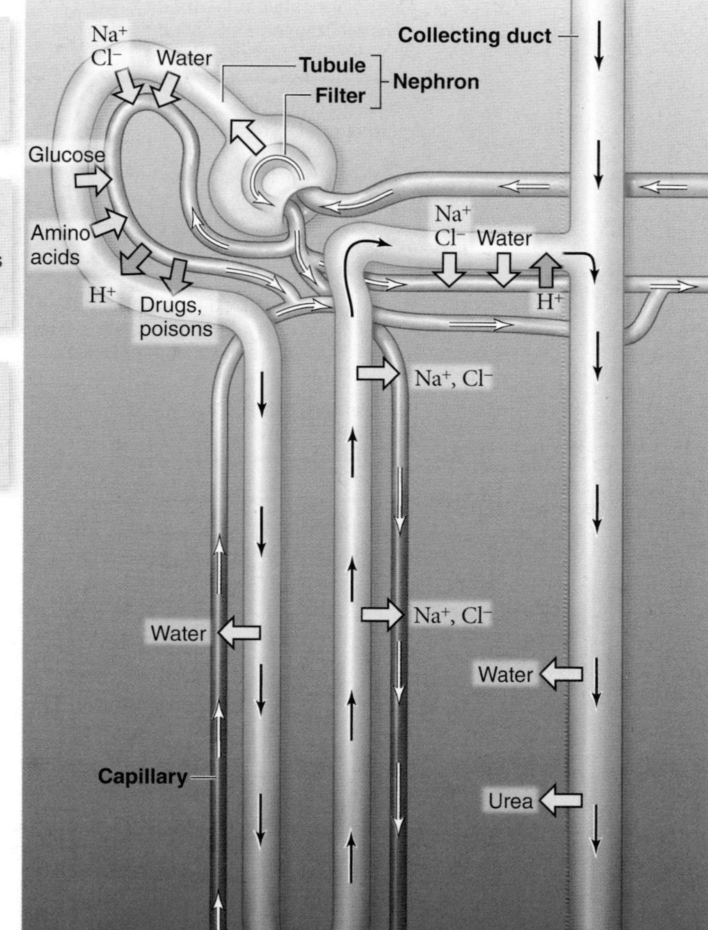

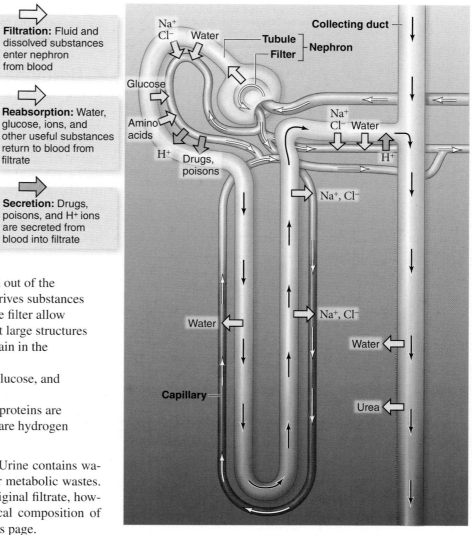

Figure 28.25 Overview of Urine Formation. Three processes contribute to urine production: filtration, reabsorption, and secretion. The nephron exchanges materials with blood along its entire length.

Burning Questions

What can urine reveal about health and diet?

Urinalysis is a routine part of many medical examinations. Laboratory tests of the chemical components of urine can reveal many health problems:

- More than a trace of glucose may be a sign of diabetes, a high-carbohydrate diet, or stress. Stress causes the adrenal glands to release excess epinephrine, which stimulates the liver to break down more glycogen into glucose. ▸ diabetes, p. 517
- Albumin may be a sign of damaged nephrons, since this plasma protein does not normally fit through the pores of the filter at the head of the nephron.
- Together, pus and an absence of glucose indicate a urinary tract infection. The pus consists of infection-fighting white blood cells along with bacteria, which consume the glucose.
- Traces of marijuana, cocaine, and other substances may appear in the urine. Athletes and employees of some organizations undergo routine drug testing.

Urine is normally pale yellow, thanks to a pigment that the liver produces as it breaks down dead blood cells. Colorless urine usually indicates excessive water intake or the ingestion of diuretics such as coffee or beer. A reddish tinge may suggest anything from bleeding in the urinary tract to beet consumption to mercury poisoning. Either vitamin C or carrot consumption can color urine orange.

Submit your burning question to:
marielle_hoefnagels@mcgraw-hill.com

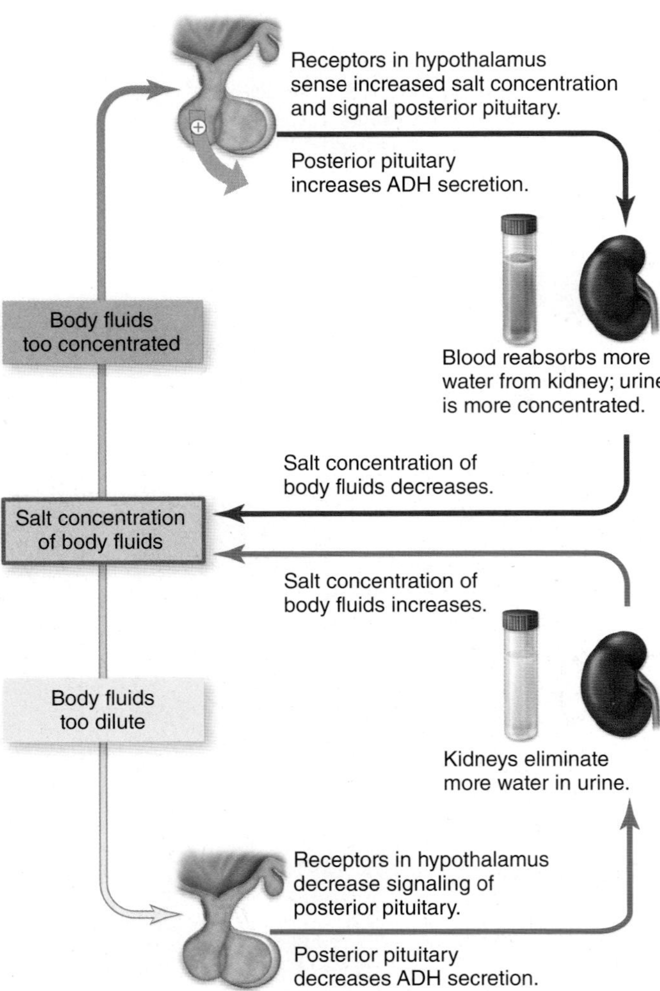
Receptors in hypothalamus sense increased salt concentration and signal posterior pituitary.
Posterior pituitary increases ADH secretion.
Body fluids too concentrated
Blood reabsorbs more water from kidney; urine is more concentrated.
Salt concentration of body fluids decreases.
Salt concentration of body fluids
Salt concentration of body fluids increases.
Body fluids too dilute
Kidneys eliminate more water in urine.
Receptors in hypothalamus decrease signaling of posterior pituitary.
Posterior pituitary decreases ADH secretion.

Figure 28.26 Osmoregulation in Humans. A feedback loop regulates the amount of water that blood reabsorbs from the kidneys.

When the nephrons fail to do their job, nitrogenous wastes and other toxins accumulate in the blood to harmful levels; in addition, a person may lose too much water and become dehydrated. Without treatment, kidney failure can be fatal.

C. Hormones Regulate Kidney Function

Kidney function adjusts continuously to maintain homeostasis. For example, we produce more concentrated urine when water is scarce. On the other hand, drinking too much water results in abundant, dilute urine.

Hormones help make these adjustments (figure 28.26). When we are dehydrated, receptor cells in the hypothalamus send impulses to the posterior pituitary gland, which secretes a peptide hormone called **antidiuretic hormone (ADH),** or vasopressin. ADH triggers the formation of additional water channels in the walls of the nephron and collecting duct. As a result, the blood reabsorbs more water, and the urine becomes very concentrated. Conversely, if blood plasma is too dilute, ADH production stops, and more water is eliminated in the urine. ▸ posterior pituitary, p. 512

A diuretic is a substance that increases the volume of urine. The ethyl alcohol in alcoholic beverages is a diuretic. Alcohol stimulates urine production partly by reducing ADH secretion, thereby decreasing reabsorption of water into the blood. By increasing water loss to urine, alcoholic beverages actually intensify thirst; dehydration also causes the discomfort of a hangover.

Hormones also act on the kidneys to regulate blood pressure. For example, when blood pressure and blood volume dip too low, the adrenal cortex releases the steroid hormone **aldosterone.** This hormone stimulates the production of sodium channels in the nephron. Na^+ ions move from the nephron into the blood, and water follows by osmosis. As a result, blood pressure rises. ▸ adrenal glands, p. 515

28.10 Mastering Concepts

1. Trace the path of blood as it moves through a kidney.
2. What is a nephron?
3. What three processes occur in urine formation?
4. What is the function of the collecting duct?
5. Describe the roles of antidiuretic hormone and aldosterone in regulating kidney function.

Figure 28.27 Pretty Bird. Feathers have many functions, including insulation, flight, and communication. Scientists are working to determine how these structures evolved.

Investigating Life

28.11 Sniffing Out the Origin of Feathers

Have you wondered about the origin of a bird's beautiful plumage (figure 28.27)? Evolutionary biologists have been working to answer this question. Existing nonavian reptiles are ectotherms, whereas birds (and mammals) are endotherms. Yet fossil and DNA evidence clearly indicate that birds arose from an ancient lineage of nonavian reptiles.

The Question: Feathers provide insulation that helps maintain a bird's body temperature. Did this adaptation evolve at the same time as the elevated metabolic rates associated with endothermy in birds?

To test this hypothesis of simultaneous evolution, scientists need to trace animal ancestry back in time. Ideally, they would examine fossils of animals from several points along the bird lineage, before and after the evolution of endothermy and feathers. But this task is easier said than done. Feathers occasionally show up in fossils, but how can we know whether an extinct animal was an endotherm or an ectotherm?

The Approach: John A. Ruben and his colleagues at Oregon State University believe they have hit on the ideal indicator of endothermy: the inside of the nose. Endothermy requires a high metabolic rate, which in turn means a huge demand for O_2 to fuel respiration. Birds therefore have elevated breathing rates relative to ectotherms. The researchers predicted that, in general, endotherms should have broader nasal cavities than ectotherms, in part to allow for this high breathing rate.

To make sure this was the case, Ruben's research team measured the cross-sectional areas of the nasal cavities of 21 living species of birds, mammals, and nonavian reptiles. In every case, the cross-sectional area of the nasal cavity was larger for an endotherm than for an ectotherm of equal size (figure 28.28). The consistent, strong relationship suggested that measuring the nasal cavity in a fossil should be a good way to learn if an extinct animal was an endotherm or an ectotherm.

The researchers therefore used modern imaging technologies to measure nasal cavities inside the fossilized skulls of three dinosaur species that lived about 70 million years ago (MYA) and are closely related to modern birds. The results indicate that the reptilian ancestors to birds probably were ectotherms. Yet fossil evidence suggests that feathers already existed by 150 MYA.

The Conclusion: Feathers are adaptations that help birds stay warm, so it is easy to assume they evolved hand-in-hand with endothermy. Ruben's team paired old-fashioned comparative anatomy with modern technology to turn this assumption on its head. Feathers apparently existed tens of millions of years before birds became endothermic; nevertheless, other studies suggest that endothermy was already present in mammalian ancestors before there was fur. Thanks to the efforts of this research team, we now have part of the answer to the puzzle—and it is right in front of our nose.

Ruben, John A., Willem J. Hillenius, Nicholas R. Geist, et al. 1996. The metabolic status of some late Cretaceous dinosaurs. *Science,* vol. 273, pages 1204–1207.

Ruben, John A., and Terry D. Jones. 2000. Selective factors associated with the origin of fur and feathers. *American Zoologist,* vol. 40, pages 585–596.

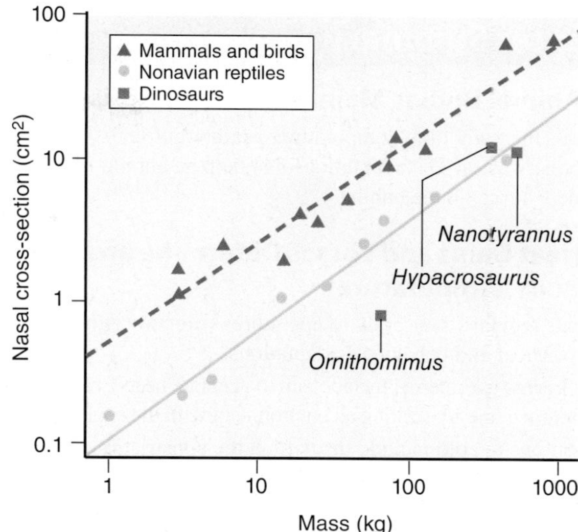

Figure 28.28 **The Nose Knows.** The nasal cavities of existing endotherms (ranging in size from herons to African cape buffaloes) have a higher cross-sectional area than those of ectotherms of equal size. Dinosaurs had nasal cavities similar in size to those of existing ectotherms.

28.11 Mastering Concepts

1. How did researchers use nasal cavities to draw their conclusions?
2. Suppose a fossil of a 100-kilogram dinosaur has a nasal cavity greater than 10 square centimeters. According to figure 28.28, would that finding affect Ruben's conclusions?

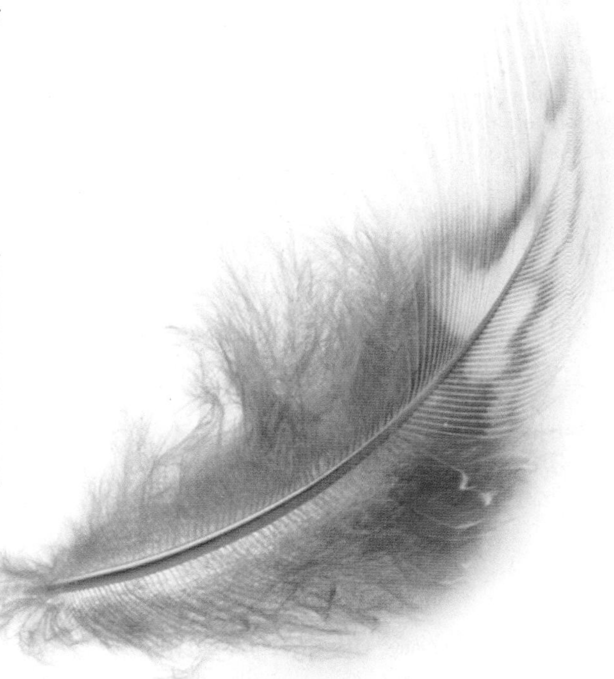

Chapter Summary

28.1 Animal Bodies Maintain Homeostasis in Many Ways

- Animals maintain body temperature, acquire nutrients, and dispose of metabolic wastes. The adaptations that help an animal maintain homeostasis vary depending on the habitat.

28.2 Heat Gains and Losses Determine an Animal's Body Temperature

- Animals regulate their body temperatures **(thermoregulate)** with physiological and behavioral adaptations.
- **Endotherms** use internal metabolism to generate heat. **Ectotherms** regulate body temperature by seeking an environment with the appropriate temperature.
- Adaptations to cold include insulation, the constriction of blood vessels near the body's surface, shivering, and hibernation.
- Evaporative cooling, routing blood toward the body surface, and behaviors that accelerate heat loss are adaptations to high temperatures.

28.3 Digestive Systems Allow Animals to Maintain Nutrient and Energy Homeostasis

- The **digestive system** acquires and dismantles food.
- Unlike plants and algae, which are **autotrophs,** animals are **heterotrophs.** The **nutrients** in food provide energy and raw materials needed for growth and maintenance.
- An animal's metabolic rate determines its need for food. Metabolic rate, in turn, reflects the animal's body temperature regulation, body size, and physiological state.

28.4 A Varied Diet Is Essential to Good Health

- Metabolism, growth, maintenance, and repair of body tissues all demand nutrients from food. **Macronutrients** include carbohydrates, proteins, fats, and water, whereas **micronutrients** include vitamins and minerals.

28.5 Eating Disorders Disrupt Nutrient Homeostasis

A. Body Weight Reflects Food Intake and Activity Level

- **Kilocalories** measure the energy food provides. Fat has more **Calories** per gram than either carbohydrate or protein.

B. Starvation: Too Few Calories to Meet the Body's Needs

- If a person does not eat enough over a long period, the body uses reserves of fat and protein to fuel essential processes. **Anorexia nervosa** and **bulimia** are eating disorders that may reduce calorie intake to dangerously low levels.

C. Obesity: More Calories Than the Body Needs

- A person who eats more calories than he or she expends will gain weight. **Obesity** is associated with many health problems.

28.6 Most Animals Have a Specialized Digestive Tract

- **Herbivores** eat plants, **carnivores** eat meat, **detritivores** consume decaying organic matter, and **omnivores** have a varied diet.

A. Acquiring Nutrients Requires Several Steps

- Food is **ingested, digested,** and **absorbed** into the bloodstream; indigestible wastes are **eliminated** as **feces.**
- In chemical digestion, enzymes dismantle large molecules into their smaller subunits.

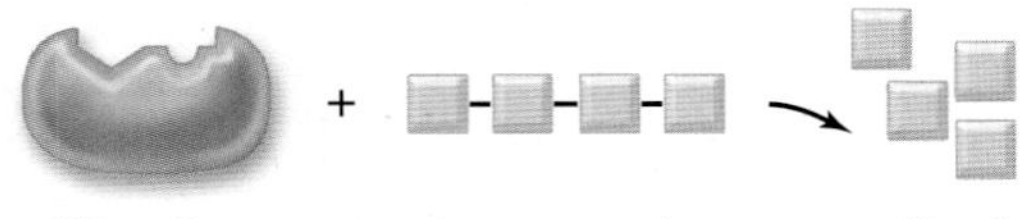

B. Digestive Tracts May Be Incomplete or Complete

- Sponges have intracellular digestion. Their cells engulf food and digest it in food vacuoles.
- Other animals use extracellular digestion, which occurs in a cavity outside cells. An **incomplete digestive tract** (also called a **gastrovascular cavity**) has one opening. A **complete digestive tract,** or **alimentary canal (gastrointestinal tract),** has two openings. Food enters through the mouth and is digested and absorbed; undigested material leaves through the **anus.**

C. Diet Influences Digestive Tract Structure

- The length of the digestive tract and size of the **cecum** are adaptations to specific diets. In **ruminants,** bacteria inhabiting the rumen help break down hard-to-digest plant matter.

28.7 The Human Digestive System Consists of Several Organs

A. Muscles Underlie the Digestive Tract

- Waves of contraction called **peristalsis** move food along the digestive tract. Muscular **sphincters** control movement from one compartment to another.

B. Digestion Begins in the Mouth and Esophagus

- In the mouth, **teeth** break food into small pieces. Salivary glands produce saliva, which moistens food and begins starch digestion.
- With the help of the **tongue,** swallowed food moves past the **pharynx** and through the **esophagus** to the stomach. The **epiglottis** prevents food from entering the trachea.

C. The Stomach Stores, Digests, and Pushes Food

- The **stomach** stores food, mixes it with **gastric juice,** and churns it into liquefied **chyme.** Hydrochloric acid in the gastric juice kills most microorganisms and denatures proteins. The protein-splitting enzyme **pepsin** begins protein digestion.

D. The Small Intestine Digests and Absorbs Nutrients

- The **small intestine** is the main site of digestion and nutrient absorption. **Villi** absorb the products of digestion; **microvilli** on each villus provide tremendous surface area.
- The **pancreas** supplies pancreatic amylase, trypsin, chymotrypsin, lipases, and nucleases to the small intestine. These enzymes break down carbohydrates, polypeptides, lipids, and nucleic acids.
- The **liver** produces **bile,** which emulsifies fat; the **gallbladder** stores the bile and releases it to the small intestine.

E. The Large Intestine Completes Nutrient and Water Absorption

- Material remaining after absorption in the small intestine passes to the **large intestine,** which absorbs water, minerals, and salts, leaving feces. Bacteria digest the remaining nutrients and produce useful vitamins that are then absorbed. Feces exit the body through the anus.

28.8 Animals Eliminate Nitrogenous Wastes and Regulate Water and Salts

- Animals **excrete** metabolic wastes. The nitrogenous waste called **urea** is a byproduct of protein breakdown.
- **Osmoregulation** is the control of ion concentrations in body fluids. Depending on its habitat, an animal may need to conserve or eliminate water and ions.

28.9 The Urinary System Produces, Stores, and Eliminates Urine

- The **urinary system** excretes nitrogenous wastes (mostly urea) and regulates water and electrolyte levels.
- The **kidneys** produce **urine.** Each kidney drains into a **ureter,** which delivers urine to the **urinary bladder** for temporary storage. Urine leaves the body through the **urethra.**

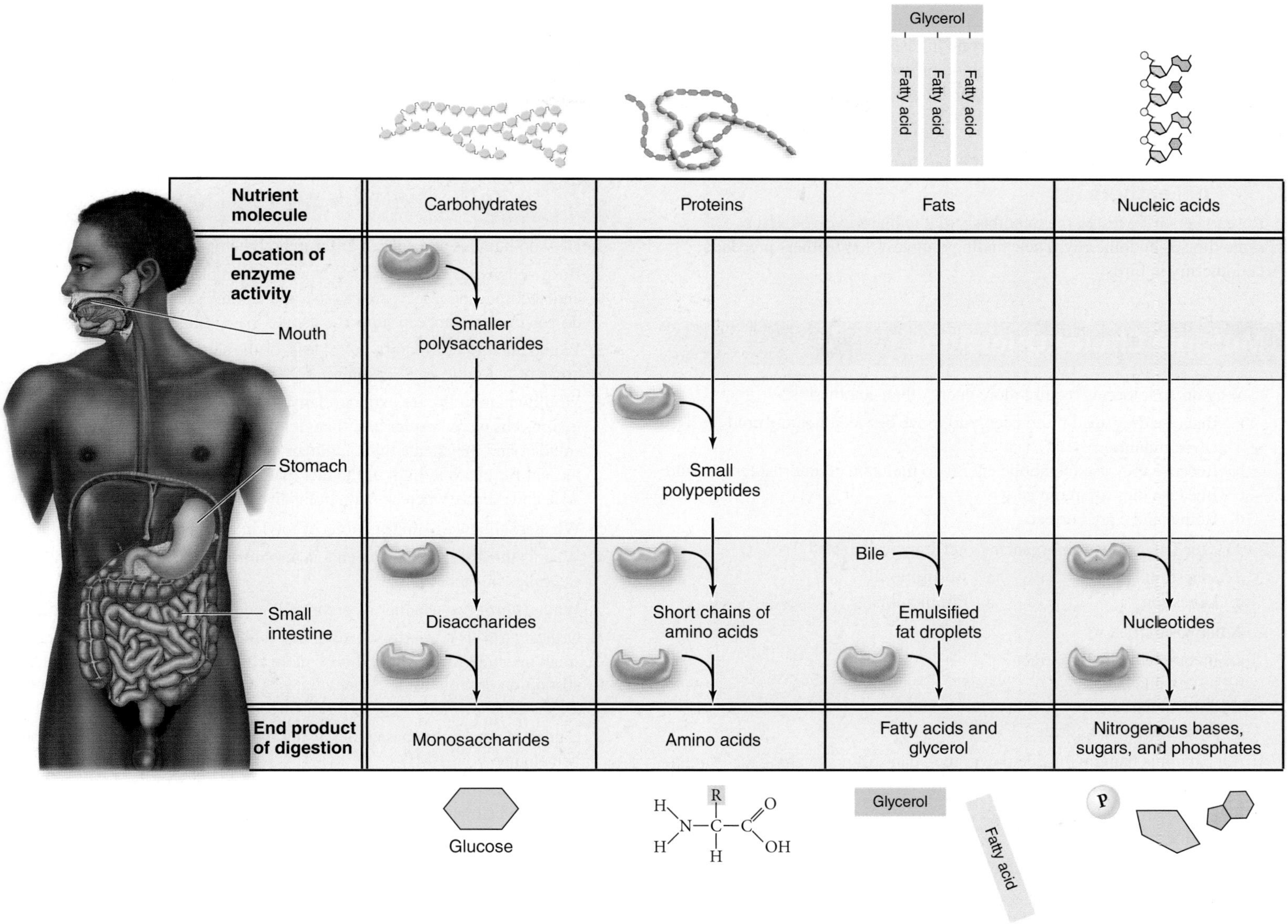

Glycerol
Fatty acid
Fatty acid
Fatty acid
Nutrient molecule
Carbohydrates
Proteins
Fats
Nucleic acids
Location of enzyme activity
Mouth
Smaller polysaccharides
Stomach
Small polypeptides
Small intestine
Disaccharides
Short chains of amino acids
Bile
Emulsified fat droplets
Nucleotides
End product of digestion
Monosaccharides
Amino acids
Fatty acids and glycerol
Nitrogenous bases, sugars, and phosphates
Glucose
Glycerol
Fatty acid
P

28.10 Nephrons Remove Wastes and Adjust the Composition of Blood

- The **nephron** sorts valuable body fluids from wastes.

A. Nephrons Interact Closely with Blood Vessels

- Each nephron receives blood from capillaries originating at the renal artery. The renal vein carries cleansed blood away from the kidney.
- The two main regions of a nephron are the filter and a winding tubule. Waste fluid moves from the nephron into a **collecting duct.**

B. Urine Formation Includes Filtration, Reabsorption, and Secretion

- Blood **filtration** occurs at the entrance to a nephron. Blood pressure forces some components of blood through the filter into the nephron.
- Along a nephron's tubule, capillaries **reabsorb** useful components such as glucose, amino acids, ions, and water. Other adjustments maintain blood pH.
- Additional wastes are **secreted** from blood into the filtrate in each nephron.
- Urine is the fluid that nephrons release into the kidney's collecting ducts.

C. Hormones Regulate Kidney Function

- **Antidiuretic hormone (ADH),** secreted by the posterior pituitary gland, regulates water reabsorption from the nephron. ADH increases the permeability of the nephron and the collecting duct, so more water is reabsorbed into the bloodstream and urine is more concentrated.

Incoming arteriole
Outgoing arteriole
Filtration
Nephron
Reabsorption
Capillary
Interstitial fluid
Secretion
Venule
Urine

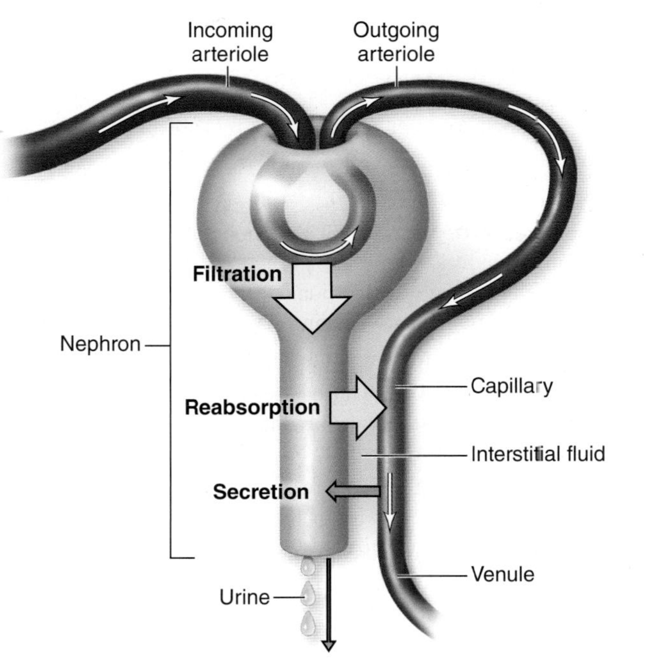

- The adrenal cortex releases **aldosterone** in response to either low Na^+ concentration in the plasma or low blood pressure. Aldosterone causes additional Na^+ to be reabsorbed into the blood; water follows by osmosis, raising blood pressure.

28.11 Investigating Life: Sniffing Out the Origin of Feathers

- Researchers have tested the hypothesis that feathers evolved at the same time as endothermy. Their findings suggest that feathers preceded endothermy in birds.

Multiple Choice Questions

1. Why do endotherms require more energy than ectotherms?
   a. Because they need more energy to move between hot and cold environments
   b. Because they use metabolic energy to maintain an internal temperature
   c. Because they are more active
   d. Both a and c are correct.
2. At which stage does an organism's cells gain nutrients?
   a. Ingestion
   b. Digestion
   c. Absorption
   d. Elimination
3. A flatworm has a(n)
   a. incomplete digestive tract.
   b. mouth and anus.
   c. alimentary canal.
   d. Both b and c are correct.
4. If a person is hanging upside down, food can still move along the esophagus to the stomach, thanks to
   a. microvilli.
   b. chyme.
   c. the epiglottis.
   d. peristalsis.
5. Making the pH of the stomach closer to neutral (pH 7) would prevent the
   a. digestion of proteins.
   b. movement of chyme to the duodenum.
   c. absorption of carbohydrates by the stomach.
   d. Both a and c are correct.
6. What is the function of bile?
   a. To break proteins into amino acids
   b. To digest fat molecules
   c. To break fat into small droplets
   d. To digest nucleic acids
7. The protein you eat is mostly
   a. incorporated into your body without modification.
   b. eliminated in feces.
   c. converted to fat before digestion.
   d. dismantled into individual amino acids.
8. What is an important function of the normal intestinal microbiota?
   a. Prevention of infection by disease-causing bacteria
   b. Production of digestive enzymes that degrade protein
   c. Decomposition of dietary fats
   d. Absorption of excess vitamins
9. What would happen to an ocean fish if it were placed in fresh water?
   a. Water would move into the organism.
   b. Ions would move into the organism.
   c. Water would move out of the organism.
   d. There would be no effect.
10. Which of the following is NOT reabsorbed into the bloodstream after filtration occurs at the head of the nephron?
    a. glucose
    b. urea
    c. water
    d. amino acids

Write It Out

1. How do humans and snakes differ in body temperature regulation?
2. Birds and insects frequently collect nectar from plants. Birds are endothermic, and insects are ectothermic. For the same investment of nectar, do you think a plant can support a greater mass of insects or of birds?
3. Would an alligator require more, less, or the same amount of food as a horse of the same size? Explain.
4. Woolly mammoths are extinct relatives of modern-day elephants. The mammoths were heavier and shaggier than elephants, their ears were smaller, and they had a thick fat layer under their skin. Explain each of these differences in light of the fact that today's elephants originate in Asia and Africa, whereas mammoths lived on the tundra.
5. What are the two main functions of food in an animal's body?
6. What is the difference between a macronutrient and a micronutrient? Give examples of each.
7. What determines whether a person will gain, lose, or maintain weight?
8. Orlistat (Alli) is a weight-loss drug that inhibits the activity of lipases in the small intestine. Why would this be more effective than a drug that blocks absorption of proteins or carbohydrates? Given that four essential vitamins are fat-soluble, what might be a side effect of blocking fat absorption?
9. Calculate your body mass index using the formula in the text. How could you change your BMI?
10. Nutritional scoring systems rate foods according to their nutritional value. The table below lists sample values from the NuVal system, which rates foods on a scale of 1 (least healthy) to 100 (healthiest). Search the Internet to learn what information researchers use in calculating the score for each food. Browse the scores for your favorite foods. Which foods that you eat have the highest scores? The lowest? How might you use these scores to adjust your shopping and eating habits?

Food	Nutritional Score
Chocolate granola bar	9
Ground beef	26
Egg	33
Canned corn	50
Whole wheat bread	81
Frozen broccoli	100

11. Fructose and glucose are both monosaccharides, but the body metabolizes these sugars differently. For example, glucose stimulates insulin release from the pancreas (see chapter 25); fructose does not. Moreover, insulin stimulates leptin release. Use this information to propose an explanation for the correlation between the skyrocketing consumption of high fructose corn syrup since 1970 and the rise in obesity during the same period.
12. What are the four stages of food use in animals, and where in the human digestive tract does each of these stages occur?
13. Compare and contrast the digestive systems of a whale and a sponge.
14. Name an organism that has each of the following: extracellular digestion; an alimentary canal; a gastrovascular cavity.
15. How is a carnivore's digestive system different from that of an herbivore?
16. How does mechanical breakdown of food speed chemical digestion?
17. Identify a part of the digestive system that includes the following: duodenum; cecum, appendix, rectum, and anus; villi and microvilli.

18. List the main parts of the human digestive system, then create a chart that compares the locations, anatomy, and functions of each part.
19. Trace the movement of food in the digestive tract from mouth to anus.
20. How does the structure of the small intestine maximize surface area?
21. What are the digestive products of carbohydrates, proteins, and fats?
22. Compare and contrast the alveoli of the lungs (see chapter 27) with the villi of the small intestine.
23. How do the circulatory and muscular systems interact with the digestive system?
24. How does it benefit an organism to have a digestive system with an extensive surface area?
25. Design an experiment to test the hypothesis that intestinal bacteria are essential to nutrient absorption in mice.
26. Many children believe that a piece of swallowed chewing gum will remain in the body for 7 years. Chewing gum is made of an indigestible polymer that does not dissolve in water. Since the gum cannot be digested, what happens to it after it is swallowed? Given your answer, does the 7-year timescale make sense? Propose an alternative prediction for how long it might take instead, and explain your reasoning.
27. Imagine you are adrift at sea. If you drink seawater, you will dehydrate much faster than if you have access to fresh water. Explain.
28. List the organs that make up the human urinary system. What is the function of each?
29. Kidney stones are calcium-rich crystals that form inside the kidney. What symptoms would you expect if the stones lodge in a ureter?
30. Shortly after you drink a large glass of water, you will feel the urge to urinate. Explain this observation. Begin by tracing the path of the water, starting at the stomach and ending with the arrival of urine in the bladder.
31. How does the kidney reduce the volume of urine to a small fraction of the volume of filtrate that enters the nephron?
32. Why is protein in the urine a sign of kidney damage? What structures in the kidney are probably affected?
33. How could very low blood pressure impair kidney function?
34. Which of the substances in the following table are excreted in urine, and which are reabsorbed into the bloodstream?

Concentrations (mg/100 mL)			
Substance	**Plasma**	**Filtrate**	**Urine**
Glucose	100	100	0
Urea	26	26	1820
Uric acid	4	4	53
Creatinine	1	1	196

35. Many pharmaceutical drugs leave the body in urine. As we age, the number of nephrons in the kidneys declines. Do you predict that an older person would need a higher or lower dose of a drug to compensate for the amount lost in urine? Explain your answer.
36. Review the action of steroid and peptide hormones in chapter 25. Which hormone should act faster, ADH or aldosterone? Why?
37. In a disease called diabetes insipidus, ADH activity is insufficient. Would a person with this disease produce more or less urine than normal? Explain.
38. Use the Internet to find a list of diseases of the kidneys or other organs of the urinary system. Select one to research further. What causes the illness you chose, and what are the symptoms? How does the disease interfere with the function of the urinary system? Is there a treatment or cure? Who is most at risk for the disease?

Pull It Together

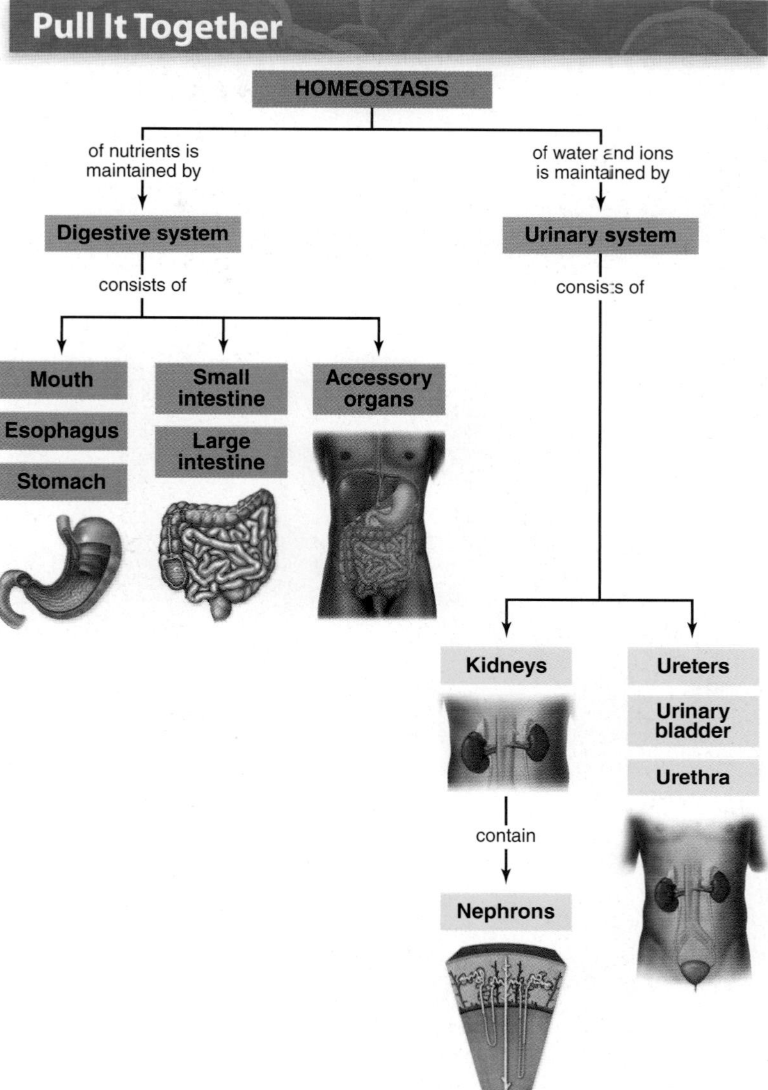

1. Add the terms *ingestion, digestion, absorption, elimination, chyme, bacteria,* and *peristalsis* to this concept map.
2. What are the accessory organs required for digestion? Add them to this concept map. What is the function of each?
3. In which organ(s) are carbohydrates, proteins, and fats digested?
4. What are the functions of filtration, secretion, and reabsorption in the nephron?
5. How do collecting ducts fit into this concept map?
6. What is the relationship among the kidneys, ureters, bladder, and urethra?
7. How do aldosterone and antidiuretic hormone influence kidney function?

Enhance your study of this chapter with practice quizzes, animations and videos, answer keys, and downloadable study tools.
www.mhhe.com/hoefnagels

29 The Immune System

Flu Outbreak. Fear of contracting influenza creates high demand for flu vaccines, which "teach" the immune system to recognize certain viruses.

Learning Outline

29.1 Many Cells, Tissues, and Organs Defend the Body
- A. White Blood Cells Play Major Roles in the Immune System
- B. The Lymphatic System Produces and Transports Many Immune System Cells
- C. The Immune System Has Two Main Subdivisions

29.2 Innate Defenses Are Nonspecific and Act Early
- A. Barriers Form the First Line of Defense
- B. Internal Innate Defenses Destroy Invaders

29.3 Adaptive Immunity Defends Against Specific Pathogens
- A. Macrophages Trigger Both Cell-Mediated and Humoral Immunity
- B. T Cells Coordinate Cell-Mediated Immunity
- C. B Cells Direct the Humoral Immune Response
- D. The Secondary Immune Response Is Stronger Than the Primary Response

29.4 Vaccines Jump-Start Immunity

29.5 Several Disorders Affect the Immune System
- A. Autoimmune Disorders Are Devastating and Mysterious
- B. People with Immunodeficiencies Are Vulnerable to Opportunistic Infections
- C. Allergies Misdirect the Immune Response

29.6 Investigating Life: The Hidden Cost of Hygiene

Learn How to Learn

Practice Your Recall

Here's an old-fashioned study tip that still works. When you finish reading a passage, close the book and write what you remember—in your own words. In this chapter, for example, you will learn about the parts of the human immune system. After you read about them, can you list and describe them without peeking at your book? Try it and find out!

What's the Point?

The immune system is unusual. Unlike most other body systems, it does not feature prominent organs like the heart, muscles, or brain. Instead, it consists of a widespread collection of cells and chemicals, and we are usually unaware of its activities.

The immune system's main job is to prevent illness. Its cells quietly patrol your body's tissues, attacking virus-infected cells, cancerous cells, and anything that does not belong to your body. What's more, the immune system "remembers" the invaders that it encountered in the past.

Most of the time, we only become aware of the immune system when something goes wrong. Its cells and chemicals may overreact and attack the body's own tissues; they may launch an allergic reaction; or they may not function at all. This chapter describes the activities and disorders of the human immune system.

29.1 Many Cells, Tissues, and Organs Defend the Body

Disease-causing agents—**pathogens**—are nearly everywhere. Viruses, bacteria, protists, fungi, and worms are in water, food, soil, and air. These pathogens can enter our bodies whenever we eat, drink, breathe, or interact with people and other animals. Yet we are not constantly sick. The explanation is that the **immune system** enables the body to recognize its own cells and to defend against infections, cancer, and foreign substances. The vertebrate immune system consists of a network of cells, defensive chemicals, and fluids that permeate the body; this section introduces them.

A. White Blood Cells Play Major Roles in the Immune System

Blood is critical to immune function. Plasma, the liquid matrix of blood, carries defensive proteins called antibodies. In addition, infection-fighting **white blood cells** (also called leukocytes) are suspended in blood plasma and occupy the interstitial fluid between cells. Stem cells in **red bone marrow,** the spongy tissue inside bones, give rise to white blood cells. ▸▸ bone marrow, p. 528; composition of blood, p. 543

White blood cells play many roles in the body's defenses (figure 29.1). About 75% of white blood cells function primarily as **phagocytes,** which are scavenger cells that engulf and destroy bacteria and debris. **Macrophages** form one important class of phagocytes. Some types of macrophages wander throughout the body; others remain in just one tissue. As described in sections 29.2 and 29.3, macrophages play multiple roles in initiating the body's defenses. ▸ phagocytosis, p. 79

The remaining white blood cells are mostly **lymphocytes,** which include several cell types. **B cells** mature in red bone marrow, then migrate to lymphoid tissues and into the blood. **T cells** originate in red bone marrow but mature in the thymus, a small immune organ in the chest ("T" is for thymus). From there, T cells migrate throughout the body. Together, B cells and T cells

Figure 29.1 White Blood Cells. (a) Human blood contains three main classes of white blood cells. (b) This phagocyte is engulfing bacteria.

White blood cell type	Example(s)	Function(s)
Phagocyte	Macrophage	Engulf bacteria and debris
Lymphocyte	B cell, T cell, natural killer cell	Coordinate immune response; attack infected or cancerous cells
Basophil	N/A	Trigger inflammation

a.

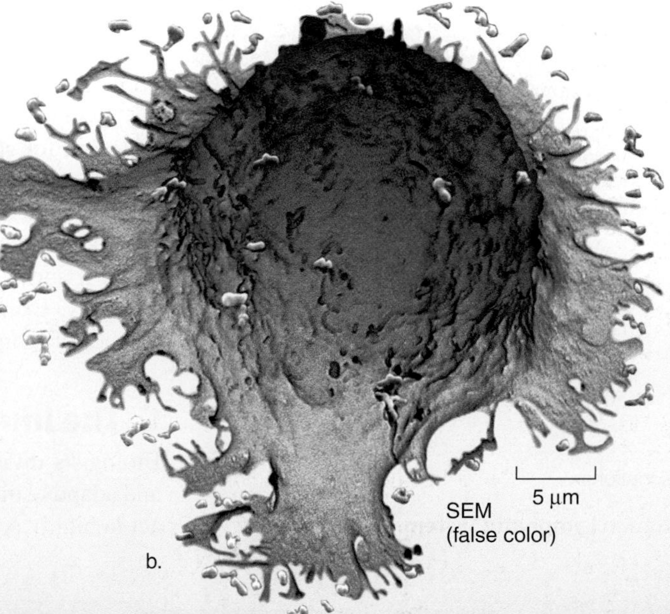

coordinate the body's responses to specific pathogens, as described in section 29.3. Another type of lymphocyte, the **natural killer cell,** attacks cancerous or virus-infected body cells.

The least common white blood cells are **basophils,** which release chemical signals that trigger inflammation and allergies. Their close relatives, **mast cells,** share similar functions. Like basophils, mast cells originate in red bone marrow. But mast cells do not circulate in blood. Rather, they settle in tissues, especially those of the skin, digestive tract, and respiratory system.

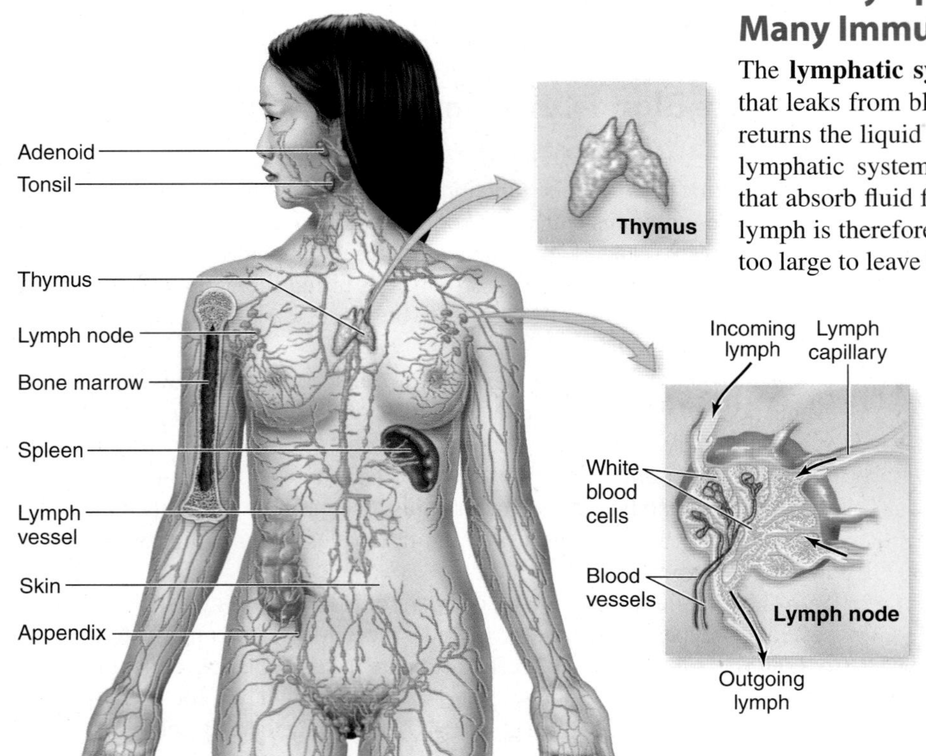

Lymphatic System	
Main tissue types*	**Examples of locations/functions**
Epithelial	Thymus, spleen, and tonsils consist partly of epithelial tissue; lines lymphatic and blood vessels; lymphoid tissue lies beneath epithelial tissues of the digestive, respiratory, and urinary tracts, guarding potential points of entry for pathogens.
Connective	Immune system cells and chemicals circulate in blood and lymph, which are connective tissues; bone marrow is connective tissue that produces lymphocytes; thymus, spleen, and lymph nodes consist partly of connective tissue.

*See chapter 23 for descriptions.

Figure 29.2 The Human Lymphatic System.

B. The Lymphatic System Produces and Transports Many Immune System Cells

The **lymphatic system** is the part of the immune system that collects fluid that leaks from blood vessels, removes bacteria, debris, and cancer cells, and returns the liquid to the blood (figure 29.2). **Lymph,** the colorless fluid of the lymphatic system, originates in **lymph capillaries**—tiny, dead-end vessels that absorb fluid from the spaces between cells. The chemical composition of lymph is therefore similar to that of blood plasma, minus the proteins that are too large to leave blood capillaries.

The cells of lymph capillaries, however, are not joined as tightly together as those of blood capillaries. Lymph capillaries therefore also admit bacteria, viruses, cancer cells, and other large particles in body tissues. These capillaries then converge into larger lymph vessels that eventually empty into veins in the chest, where the fluid returns to the blood.

Along the way, lymph passes through **lymph nodes,** kidney-shaped organs that contain millions of white blood cells. These infection-fighting cells intercept and destroy cellular debris, cancer cells, and bacteria in the lymph flow. Inside each lymph node, millions of lymphocytes engulf dead cells and pathogens circulating in lymph. Lymph nodes also release B and T cells to lymph, which carries them to the blood. When you have an infection, you can sometimes feel your enlarged lymph nodes as "swollen glands" in the neck, armpits, or groin.

The lymphatic system can also carry cancer cells that break off of tumors, seeding new tumors elsewhere in the body. A biopsy of cancerous tissue therefore often includes a sample of nearby lymph nodes. If these lymph nodes are cancer-free, abnormal cells may not have begun to invade other tissues, improving the chance of successful treatment. ▸ cancer, p. 148

Lymph nodes are the most familiar examples of lymphoid organs, a general term for structures that produce, accumulate, or aid in the circulation of lymphocytes. Red bone marrow and the thymus are lymphoid organs. Another is the **spleen,** a lymphoid organ containing masses of lymphocytes and macrophages that destroy pathogens in the blood. Scattered concentrations of lymphoid tissues also guard the mucous membranes where pathogens may enter the body. Examples include the tonsils (near the throat), the appendix, and patches of lymphoid tissue in the small intestine.

C. The Immune System Has Two Main Subdivisions

Biologists divide the human immune system into two parts: innate defenses and adaptive immunity. Together, innate defenses and adaptive immunity interact in highly coordinated ways to defend the body against pathogens.

Innate defenses provide a broad defense against any infectious agent. *Innate* refers to the fact that these defenses are always present and ready to function, as described in section 29.2. In **adaptive immunity,** the body's immune cells not only recognize specific parts of a pathogen, but they also "remember" previous encounters. Section 29.3 describes adaptive immunity in detail.

29.1 Mastering Concepts

1. List the cell types that participate in the body's defenses, along with some of their functions.
2. What is the relationship between lymph and blood?
3. What are the functions of the main lymphoid organs?
4. What are the two subdivisions of the immune system?

29.2 Innate Defenses Are Nonspecific and Act Early

The body's innate defenses include many components, as summarized in figure 29.3. These defenses are called "nonspecific" because they act against any type of invader.

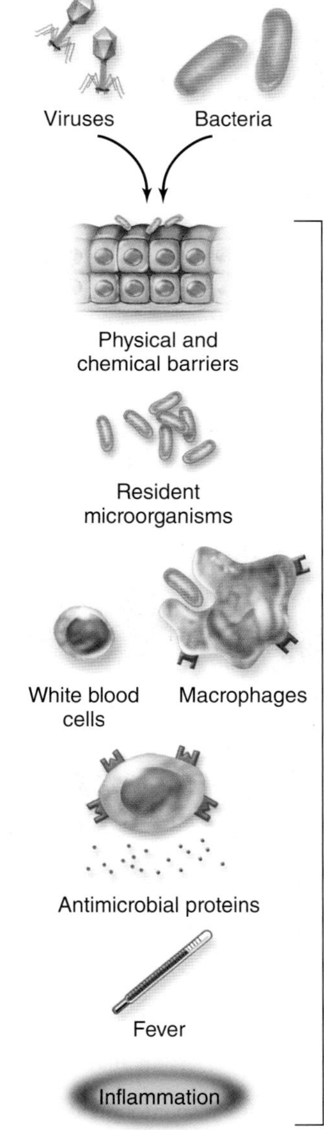

Figure 29.3 Overview of Innate Defenses. These nonspecific defenses prevent bacteria, viruses, and other pathogens from entering the body, or they attack those that do breach the physical and chemical barriers.

A. Barriers Form the First Line of Defense

Several types of physical barriers block pathogens and foreign substances from entering the body. Unpunctured skin is the most extensive and obvious wall (see the Why We Care box on page 594). Other physical barriers include mucus that traps inhaled dust particles in the nose; wax in the ears; tears that wash irritants from the eyes and contain antimicrobial substances; and cilia that sweep bacteria out of the respiratory system. In addition, strong acid destroys most of the microbes that reach the stomach. ▸▸ integumentary system, p. 476; stomach, p. 576

An often underappreciated component of this first line of defense is the body's normal microbiota. Resident microbes on the skin, in the gut, and elsewhere help prevent colonization by pathogens. ▸ beneficial microbes, p. 286

B. Internal Innate Defenses Destroy Invaders

A large collection of defensive cells and molecules awaits any microbe that manages to breach the body's external barriers.

White Blood Cells White blood cells play many roles in the body's innate defenses. Some types of phagocytes simply destroy bacteria. Macrophages are phagocytes that not only consume pathogens but also promote fever; the same cells also play a critical role in activating the body's adaptive immune response. Natural killer cells destroy cancerous or virus-infected cells. Basophils provoke inflammation, attracting additional white blood cells.

Complement Proteins and Cytokines Many antimicrobial biochemicals participate in the innate defenses. For example, white blood cells produce several types of **complement** proteins, all of which help to destroy pathogens in the body. When activated, some complement proteins trigger a chain reaction that punctures bacterial cell membranes. Others cause mast cells to release histamine, and still others attract phagocytes.

Why We Care | Severe Burns

Intact skin is the body's first line of defense against infection. Severe burns from fires, hot liquids, or corrosive chemicals, however, can damage the lower layer of the skin, giving bacteria and other pathogens direct access to the underlying tissues. As a result, burn patients face a high risk of infection. Aggressive treatment with antibiotics can help prevent this life-threatening outcome.

Burn patients also confront a second risk: dehydration. Intact skin is waterproof and therefore helps keep underlying tissues moist. If burns are extensive, body fluids evaporate rapidly through the wounds. Patients with large burns therefore receive intravenous fluids that compensate for the loss and help maintain blood volume.

Other chemical defenses include **cytokines,** messenger proteins that bind to immune cells and promote cell division, activate defenses, or otherwise alter their activity. For example, interleukins are the largest group of cytokines. Their name comes from their role in communicating (*inter-*) between leukocytes, or white blood cells (*-leukins*). In addition, cells infected by viruses release interferons, which are cytokines that alert other components of the immune system to the infection.

Fever Cytokines travel throughout the body in the bloodstream. At the hypothalamus, they can initiate a temporary increase in the set point of the body's thermostat. **Fever,** a rise in the body's temperature, is therefore a common reaction to infection. Although the shivering and chills that accompany fever feel uncomfortable, a mild fever can help fight infection. A higher body temperature kills some bacteria and viruses. Fever also counters microbial growth indirectly, because higher body temperature reduces the iron level in the blood. Bacteria and fungi require more iron as the temperature rises, so a fever stops the replication of these pathogens. Phagocytes also attack more vigorously when the temperature climbs. ▸ hypothalamus, p. 511

Inflammation **Inflammation** is an immediate, localized reaction to an injury or any pathogen that breaches the body's barriers. The area surrounding the wound or infection site becomes red, warm, swollen, and painful. Overall, inflammation recruits immune components, helps clear debris, and creates an environment hostile to microorganisms.

Figure 29.4 illustrates the events of inflammation in response to a minor injury from a splinter. Tissue damage provokes basophils and mast cells to release **histamine,** a chemical that dilates (widens) blood vessels and causes them to become more permeable to fluids and white blood cells.

As capillaries near the injury become dilated, additional blood arrives, turning the area warm and red. Plasma leaking out of the blood vessels dilutes

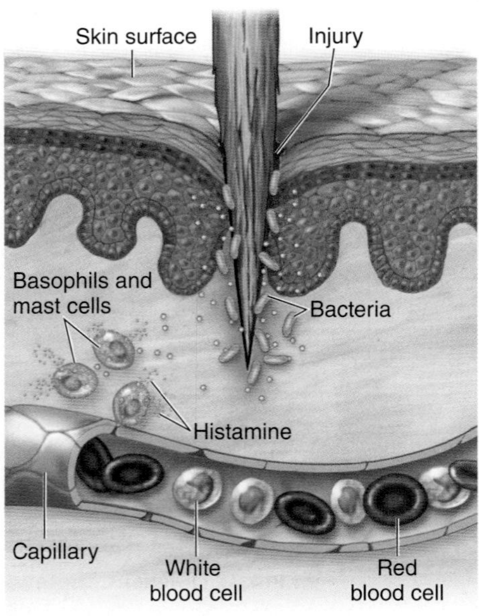

1 Damaged cells trigger mast cells and basophils to release histamine.

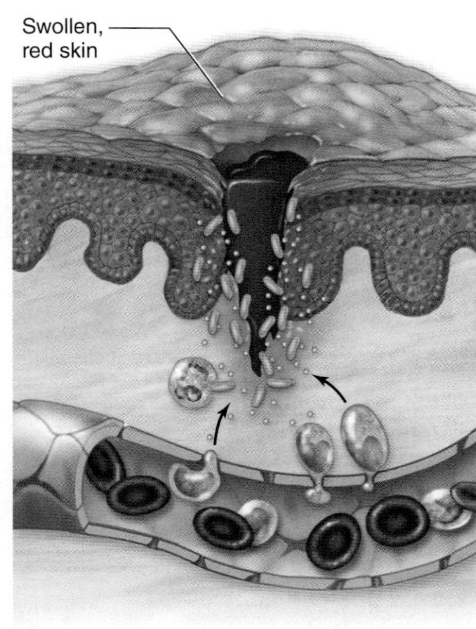

2 Histamine causes blood vessels to dilate and become more permeable. White blood cells move into the damaged area.

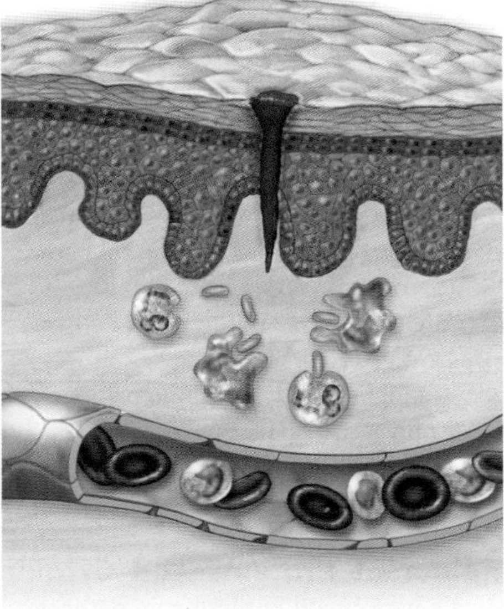

3 White blood cells engulf and destroy bacteria and damaged cells.

Figure 29.4 Inflammation. Immediately after a splinter pierces the skin, chemicals released from damaged cells initiate the inflammatory response.

the toxins secreted by bacteria and causes localized swelling. Pressure on the swollen tissues, coupled with chemical signals released from the injured cells, stimulates pain receptors in the skin. Meanwhile, macrophages and other phagocytes squeeze through the blood vessel walls and move into the area, engulfing and destroying bacteria and damaged cells. Pus may accumulate; this whitish fluid contains white blood cells, bacteria, and debris from dead cells.

In medical terminology, the suffix *-itis* indicates inflammation. For example, dermatitis (a rash) signifies inflamed skin, often resulting from contact with an irritant such as poison ivy. Appendicitis is inflammation of the appendix, usually caused by bacterial infection. Aspirin and ibuprofen reduce pain and swelling after an injury by blocking the enzymes that induce inflammation.

Inflammation may be acute or chronic. Acute inflammation is an adaptation that prevents infection after an injury. The effects usually last only a few days or less, as illustrated by the short-term discomfort of a minor burn or "paper cut." Chronic inflammation, on the other hand, may last for months or years. The persistent presence of pathogens or toxins can cause any tissue in the body to become chronically inflamed; genetic mutations may also play a role. Medical problems associated with chronic inflammation include rheumatoid arthritis, atherosclerosis, gum disease, and many other serious illnesses.

29.2 Mastering Concepts

1. What are innate defenses?
2. Describe the external barriers to infection.
3. Which white blood cells participate in innate defenses?
4. What are some examples of antimicrobial biochemicals?
5. How is fever protective?
6. Describe the events of inflammation.

29.3 Adaptive Immunity Defends Against Specific Pathogens

The innate defenses described in section 29.2 are broad-spectrum weapons. Adaptive immune responses, on the other hand, act against individual targets. Two classes of lymphocytes, B cells and T cells, provide the ammunition in these precision defenses.

The target in an adaptive immune response is an **antigen,** which is any molecule that stimulates an immune reaction by B and T cells. Most antigens are carbohydrates or proteins. Examples include parts of a bacterial cell wall or viral protein coat, proteins on the surface of a mold spore or pollen grain, and unique molecules on the surface of a cancer cell.

The word *antigen* (short for *anti*body-*gen*erating) reflects a crucial part of adaptive immunity: the production of **antibodies,** which are Y-shaped proteins that recognize specific antigens. As described later in this section, each B and T cell is genetically programmed to recognize and bind to only one target antigen. But because every foreign particle contains dozens of molecules that can act as antigens, many sets of lymphocytes respond to invasion by one pathogen.

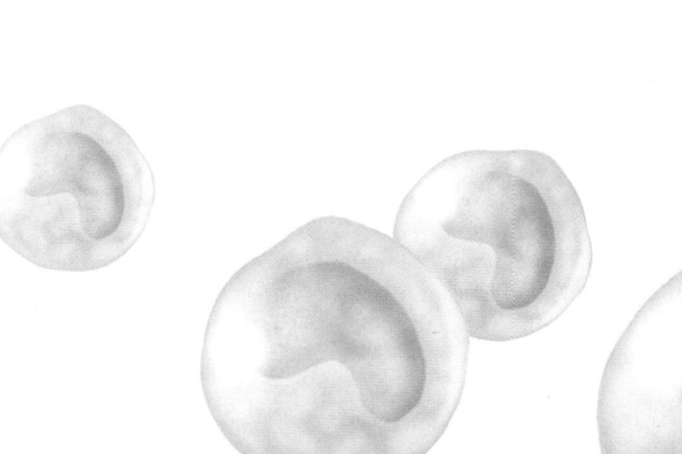

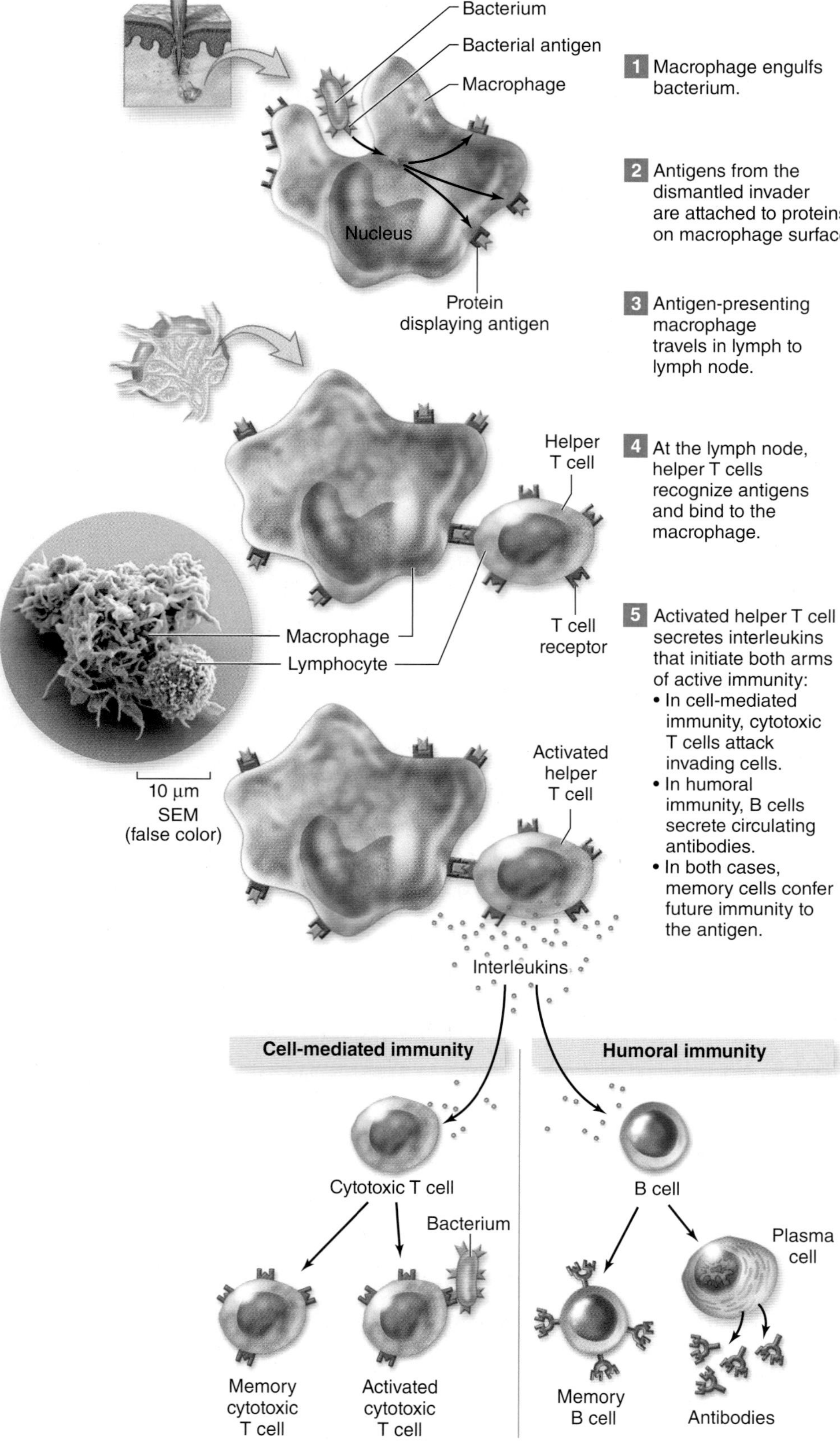
Bacterium
Bacterial antigen
Macrophage
1 Macrophage engulfs bacterium.
2 Antigens from the dismantled invader are attached to proteins on macrophage surface.
Nucleus
Protein displaying antigen
3 Antigen-presenting macrophage travels in lymph to lymph node.
Helper T cell
4 At the lymph node, helper T cells recognize antigens and bind to the macrophage.
Macrophage
Lymphocyte
T cell receptor
5 Activated helper T cell secretes interleukins that initiate both arms of active immunity:
• In cell-mediated immunity, cytotoxic T cells attack invading cells.
• In humoral immunity, B cells secrete circulating antibodies.
• In both cases, memory cells confer future immunity to the antigen.
10 μm
SEM (false color)
Activated helper T cell
Interleukins
Cell-mediated immunity
Humoral immunity
Cytotoxic T cell
B cell
Bacterium
Plasma cell
Memory cytotoxic T cell
Activated cytotoxic T cell
Memory B cell
Antibodies

Figure 29.5 Adaptive Immunity: A Summary. A macrophage engulfs a bacterium, then displays bacterial antigens on its surface. At a lymph node, a helper T cell binds to the macrophage. The activated helper T cell sets into motion the cell-mediated and humoral immune responses.

A. Macrophages Trigger Both Cell-Mediated and Humoral Immunity

One of the first cell types to respond to infection is the macrophage, which not only participates in innate defenses but also triggers adaptive immunity. The macrophage engulfs a pathogen, dismantles it, and links each antigen to a self protein on the macrophage surface (figure 29.5, steps 1 and 2).

A macrophage displaying an antigen on its surface travels in lymph to a lymph node, where the cell encounters collections of T and B cells (figure 29.5, step 3). **Helper T cells** are "master cells" of the immune system because they initiate and coordinate the adaptive immune response. When an antigen-presenting macrophage meets a helper T cell with receptors specific to the antigen it is displaying, the two cells bind (figure 29.5, step 4). This event simultaneously initiates the two arms of the adaptive immune response: cell-mediated and humoral immunity (figure 29.5, step 5).

In **cell-mediated immunity,** defensive cells attack and kill invaders by direct cell-to-cell contact. The activated helper T cell secretes cytokines that activate **cytotoxic T cells,** which destroy virus-infected, cancerous, or damaged cells. The cytokines also activate B cells specific to the same antigen and initiate **humoral immunity,** which relies primarily on secreted antibodies (the term *humoral* refers to substances that circulate in body fluids). Upon stimulation by T cells, B cells proliferate explosively and differentiate into plasma cells and memory B cells. The **plasma cells** immediately secrete huge numbers of antibodies. The **memory cells,** on the other hand, remain in the body long after the initial infection subsides, launching a quick immune response upon subsequent exposure to the antigen. In effect, memory cells "remember" antigens the immune system has already encountered.

B. T Cells Coordinate Cell-Mediated Immunity

Cytotoxic T cells provide cell-mediated immunity (figure 29.6). Receptors on the surface of a cytotoxic T cell bind to antigens on the surface of an invader or a cancer cell. The T cell then releases a protein that pokes holes in the cell's membrane and kills the invader. Cytotoxic T cells also recognize and destroy cells infected with viruses. If a T cell can kill the cell before the virus has a chance to replicate, the infection is stopped.

After the attack, memory T cells help the immune system retain a long-term "memory" of a pathogen. If the body encounters the same pathogen again, memory T cells differentiate immediately into cytotoxic T cells.

Cell-mediated immunity is one factor that complicates organ transplants. The body perceives any foreign object, including a donated kidney, heart, or skin graft,

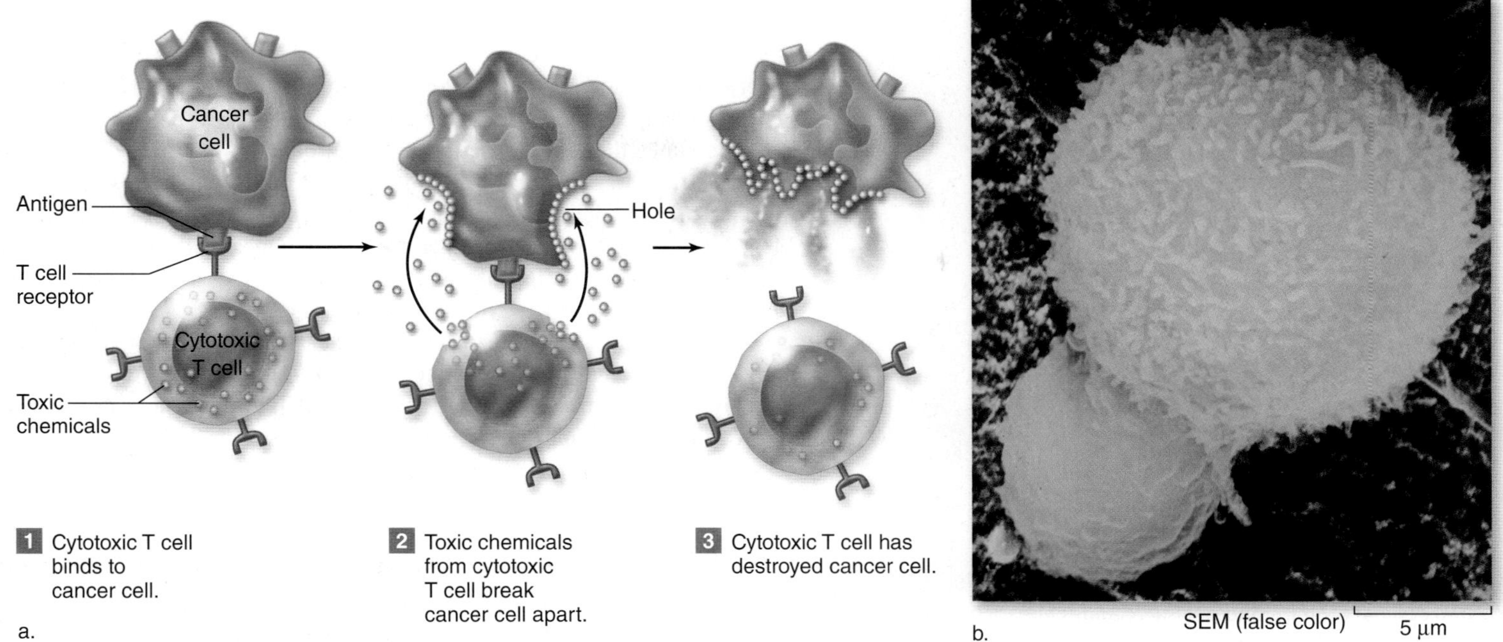

Figure 29.6 Cytotoxic T Cells. (a) An activated cytotoxic T cell binds to a cancer cell and injects a protein that pokes holes in the cancer cell's membrane. The cancer cell dies, leaving behind debris that macrophages clear away. (b) A small cytotoxic T cell (purple) attacks a large cancer cell (pink).

as something to be destroyed. Cytotoxic T cells bind to and destroy the transplanted cells, provoking tissue rejection. A regimen of drugs can suppress this immune response, but the cost is increased vulnerability to cancer and infectious disease (see section 29.5).

C. B Cells Direct the Humoral Immune Response

The humoral immune response includes millions of different B cells, each producing a unique antibody.

Antibodies Are Defensive Proteins Antibodies are the main weapons of humoral immunity (figure 29.7). These large proteins circulate freely in blood plasma, lymph, and interstitial fluid. Some antibodies also act as antigen receptors on the membranes of B cells.

The simplest antibody molecule consists of four polypeptides: two identical light (short) chains and two identical heavy (long) chains. Together, the four chains form a shape like the letter Y. Each chain has both constant and variable regions. The **constant regions** have amino acid sequences that are very similar in all antibody molecules, but the **variable regions** differ a great deal among antibodies. These variable regions determine the specific target antigen to which an antibody binds.

Antibodies are potent weapons. The binding of an antibody to an antigen can inactivate a microbe or neutralize its toxins. Antibodies can cause pathogens to clump, making them more apparent to macrophages, which then destroy the pathogens. They can coat viruses, preventing them from contacting target cells. Antibodies also activate complement proteins, which destroy microorganisms.

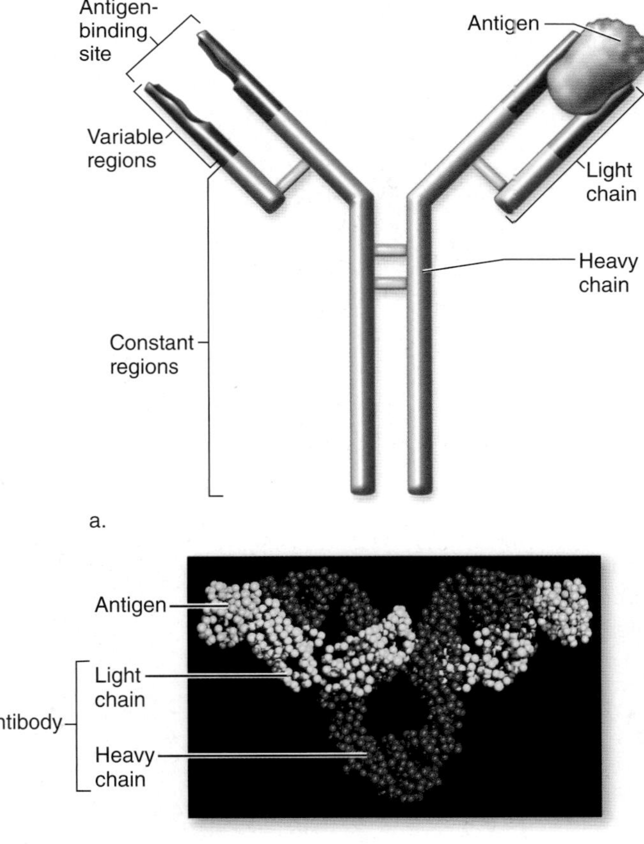

Figure 29.7 Antibody Structure. (a) The simplest antibody molecules consist of four polypeptide chains, each of which has constant (light purple) and variable (dark purple) regions. The variable portions form the antigen-binding sites. (b) A computer-generated view of an antibody molecule bound to an antigen.

Genetic Recombination Yields a Huge Variety of Antibodies and Antigen Receptors Of the human genome's 25,000 or so genes, fewer than 250 encode proteins that specifically bind to antigens. How can one person's lymphocytes produce enough unique antibody proteins and antigen

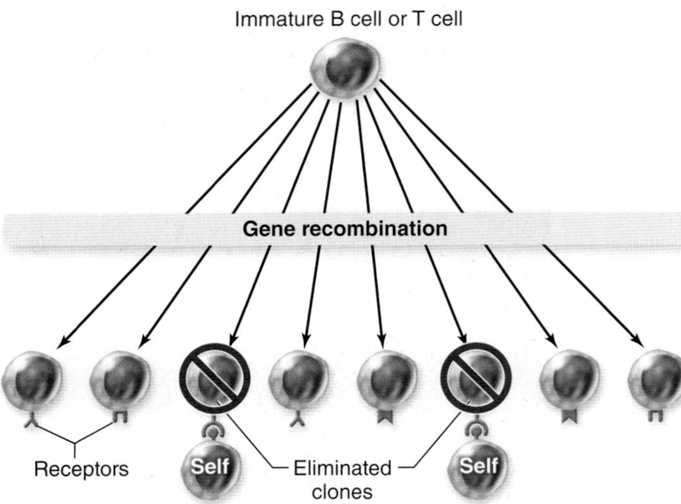

Figure 29.8 Clonal Deletion. As lymphocytes develop, they are tested against proteins and polysaccharides already present on the body's own cell surfaces. Clones that match self antigens are eliminated by programmed cell death (apoptosis).

receptor proteins to defeat millions of potential pathogens? As it turns out, generating these diverse molecules is a little like using the limited number of words in a language to compose an infinite variety of stories.

The genes that encode antibodies each contain hundreds of small DNA segments that are rearranged as lymphocytes develop. The result: countless lineages of cells that each produce a unique antigen receptor and antibody. Most lymphocytes will never encounter a pathogen with the corresponding antigen, but a few will. Thanks to genetic recombination, the immune system can respond to even newly emerging pathogens.

Some of these antigen receptors, however, will no doubt correspond to the body's own molecules ("self antigens"). In a process called **clonal deletion,** lymphocytes that recognize the body's own cell surfaces and molecules are "weeded out" by apoptosis, or programmed cell death (figure 29.8). This process begins before birth. The developing immune system somehow also learns not to attack antigens in food. ▸ apoptosis, p. 140

Clonal Selection Explains the Surge of Identical Antibodies

On the surface of each B cell is a version of the antibody that the cell will produce. Until a B cell encounters the antigen it is genetically programmed to recognize, it remains dormant. But when an antigen binds to this surface antibody, the B cell begins to activate. Cytokines from the corresponding helper T cell complete the activation.

In a process called **clonal selection,** an activated B cell divides rapidly, generating an army of memory cells and plasma cells that are clones of the original B cell (figure 29.9). The plasma

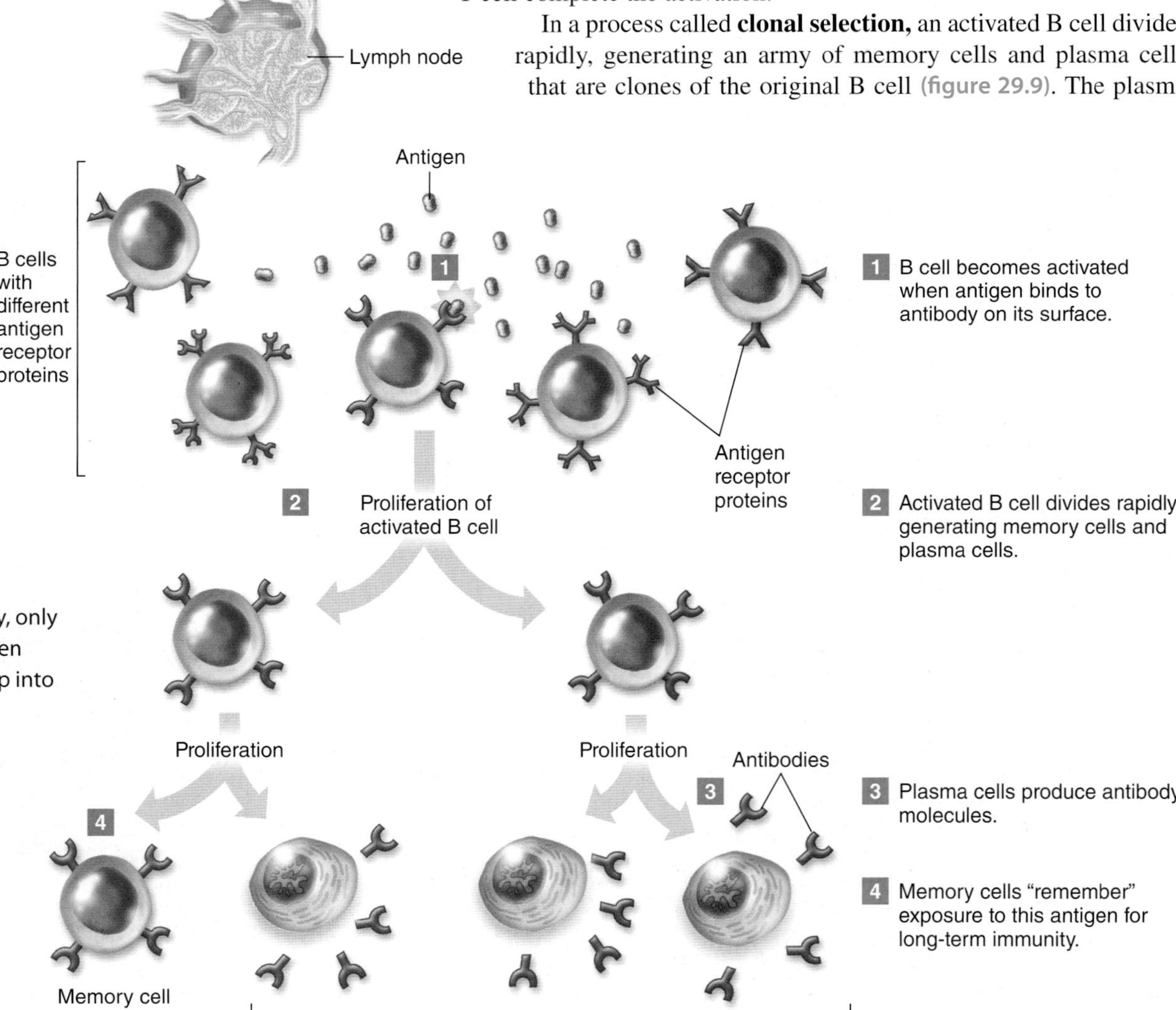

Figure 29.9 Clonal Selection. According to clonal selection theory, only the lymphocyte that binds an antigen proliferates; its descendants develop into memory cells or plasma cells.

cells are efficient protein factories, making thousands of antibody molecules each second. Although the plasma cells vanish after the infection is over, the memory cells "remember" exposure to the antigen for years or decades.

The body's immune response is complicated by the fact that each invading virus, bacterium, or other pathogen has many different antigens on its surface (figure 29.10). The immune response therefore involves multiple antibodies, each made by a specific B cell and its clones.

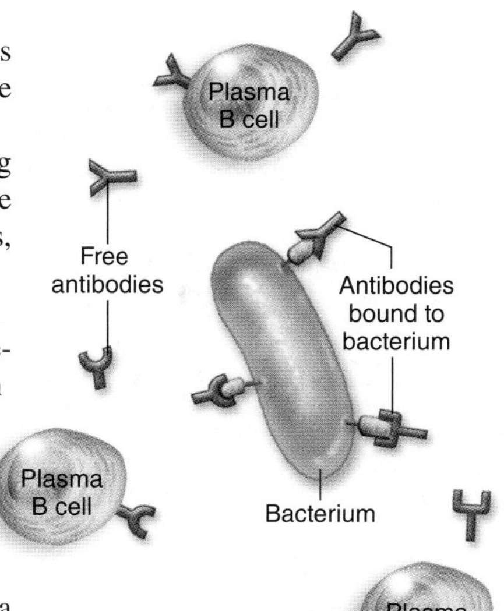

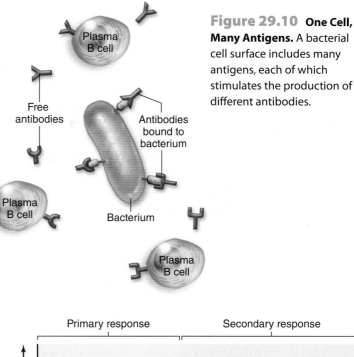

Figure 29.10 One Cell, Many Antigens. A bacterial cell surface includes many antigens, each of which stimulates the production of different antibodies.

Humoral Immunity Is Passive or Active The humoral immune response is divided into two categories: passive and active (table 29.1). In **passive immunity,** a person receives intact antibodies from another individual. For example, an infant acquires antibodies from its mother in breast milk. The administration of antivenom to a victim of a snake bite also illustrates passive immunity.

Active immunity results from the body's own production of antibodies after exposure to antigens in the environment. A person who is bitten by a tick carrying Lyme disease, for example, may begin producing antibodies against the bacteria that cause the disease.

D. The Secondary Immune Response Is Stronger Than the Primary Response

The **primary immune response** is the adaptive immune system's first reaction to a foreign antigen. Because the clonal selection process takes time, days or even weeks may elapse before antibody concentrations reach their peak. During this time, the pathogen can cause severe damage or death. If a person survives, however, the memory B cells and memory T cells leave a lasting impression—that is, immunological memory.

As a result, the **secondary immune response**—the immune system's reaction the next time it detects the same foreign antigen—is much stronger than the primary response (figure 29.11). Memory B cells transform into rapidly dividing plasma cells. Within hours, billions of antigen-specific antibodies are circulating throughout the host body, destroying the pathogen before it takes hold. Usually, there is no hint that a second infection ever occurred. As described in section 29.4, vaccines create this immunological memory without risking an initial infection.

It is important to remember that turning off an immune response once an infection has been halted is as important as turning it on. After all, powerful immune biochemicals can attack not only pathogens but also the body's healthy tissues. Immunologists continue to learn more about the precise signals that cause the immune system to "back down" after a threat is removed.

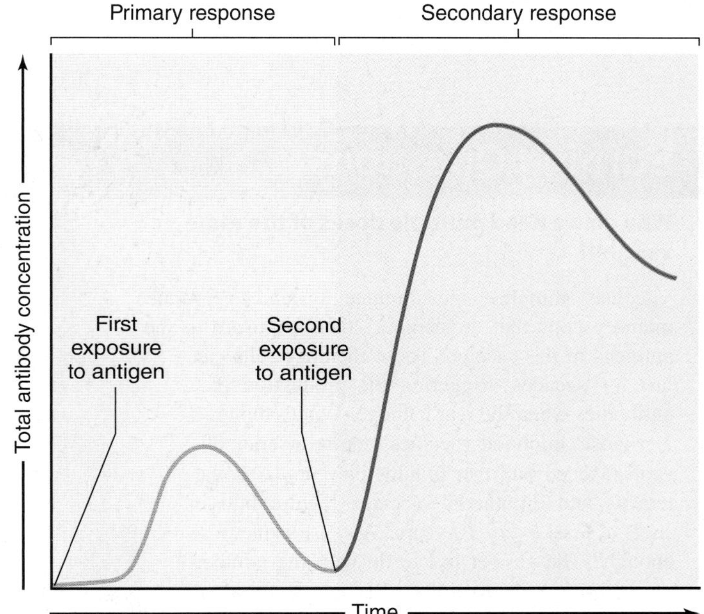

Figure 29.11 Primary and Secondary Immune Responses. The primary immune response leaves memory cells that stimulate a stronger immune response on subsequent exposure to the foreign antigen.

TABLE 29.1 Ways to Acquire Immunity: A Summary

Type	Description	Examples
Passive immunity	One individual acquires antibodies from another individual.	• Fetus acquires antibodies from mother via placenta or milk. • Dog bite victim receives injections of antibodies to rabies virus. • Snake bite victim receives intravenous antivenom (antibodies to snake venom).
Active immunity	Individual produces antibodies to an antigen.	• Having chickenpox confers future immunity to that disease ("natural" active immunity). • Influenza vaccine triggers production of memory cells specific to antigens in the vaccine ("artificial" active immunity).

29.3 Mastering Concepts

1. What is the relationship between antigens and antibodies?
2. What is the role of macrophages in adaptive immunity?
3. What are the two subdivisions of adaptive immunity, and which cell types participate in each?
4. What do cytotoxic T cells do?
5. Describe the structure and function of an antibody.
6. What happens after a B cell is stimulated?
7. Explain the difference between the primary and secondary immune responses.
8. What happens if an immune reaction persists after a pathogen is eliminated?

29.4 Vaccines Jump-Start Immunity

The immune system is remarkably effective at keeping pathogens and cancer cells from taking over our bodies. Nevertheless, humans do suffer from many incurable infectious diseases caused by viruses and other pathogens. Besides sanitation, the best way to prevent many of these illnesses is vaccination.

A **vaccine** is a substance that stimulates active immunity against a pathogen without actually causing illness. The vaccine consists partly of antigens that "teach" the recipient's immune system to recognize a pathogen. Once taken into the body, the antigens simulate a primary immune response. Memory cells linger after this initial exposure, ensuring that a subsequent encounter with the real pathogen triggers the rapid secondary immune response (see this chapter's Burning Question). Vaccination programs therefore reduce both the incidence and the spread of infectious disease.

The use of vaccines in medicine dates to the late eighteenth century, when an incurable viral disease called smallpox was ravaging the human population. The fatality rate among infected people was about 25%, and about two thirds of the survivors were left horribly scarred and sometimes blind. But in 1796, a British country physician named Edward Jenner invented a vaccine against smallpox. The preparation contained vaccinia viruses, which cause a mild infection called cowpox. The two viruses—smallpox and vaccinia—are related to each other, and they share some antigens. Exposure to the vaccinia virus therefore confers immunity to smallpox.

Over the next 150 years, vaccination greatly reduced smallpox incidence in many countries, yet the disease still raged elsewhere. In 1967, however, the vaccine became the centerpiece of a coordinated worldwide smallpox eradication campaign. By 1980, the World Health Organization declared that "smallpox is dead." The declaration heralded a milestone in medicine—the eradication of a disease. Today, all known stocks of smallpox virus reside in two labs, one in the United States and the other in Russia. Only the threat of bioterrorism maintains the demand for the smallpox vaccine among some military personnel and "first responders."

Scientists have developed vaccines against many other illnesses as well. The antigens in the vaccines take several different forms (table 29.2). Measles and mumps vaccines, for example, contain weakened viruses. Others, such as the vaccine against polio, contain inactivated viruses that cannot cause an infection. Diphtheria and tetanus vaccines incorporate a toxin that bacterial

Burning Questions

Why do we need multiple doses of the same vaccine?

Vaccines stimulate the immune system to produce memory cells that "remember" their exposure to the antigens in the vaccine. These memory cells can last for decades, triggering the production of antibodies when the real pathogen comes along. Yet most childhood vaccines require a series of shots, spaced out over months or years. And the tetanus and diphtheria vaccines require booster shots at least every 10 years. Why isn't one dose enough? The answer has to do with the number of memory cells that the body produces after exposure to the vaccine.

The vaccine's formulation helps determine the need for booster shots. A vaccine that consists of active viruses causes a mild infection that lasts for about a week. This lengthy exposure to viral antigens stimulates a robust immune response, so booster shots are not usually necessary. On the other hand, when a vaccine contains toxins or inactivated viruses, no infection occurs. The body's exposure to the antigens is therefore relatively brief, and the number of memory cells may be too small to launch an effective immune response against the pathogen. In that case, repeated shots help boost the number of memory cells over time.

Submit your burning question to:
marielle_hoefnagels@mcgraw-hill.com

pathogens produce. Still others, such as the hepatitis A and hepatitis B vaccines, incorporate only a part of the pathogen's surface. The "cervical cancer" vaccine, approved by the U.S. Food and Drug Administration in 2006, contains proteins identical to those on the human papillomavirus, a pathogen that is strongly correlated with cervical cancer.

Although vaccines have saved countless lives since Jenner's time, they cannot prevent all infectious diseases. For example, researchers have been unable to develop a vaccine against HIV, the rapidly evolving virus that causes AIDS. Influenza viruses also mutate rapidly, so each vaccine is effective for only one flu season. And it has so far proved impossible to develop one vaccine that will prevent infection by the many viruses that cause the common cold.

TABLE 29.2 Types of Vaccines

Vaccine Formulation	Examples
Live, weakened pathogen	Polio (oral vaccine), measles, mumps, rubella, chickenpox
Inactivated pathogen	Polio (injectable vaccine), influenza, hepatitis A
Inactivated toxins	Tetanus, diphtheria
Subunits of pathogens	Cholera, whooping cough (pertussis)
Recombinant vaccines; component vaccines	Lyme disease, hepatitis B, human papillomavirus

29.4 Mastering Concepts

1. What is a vaccine?
2. List the main types of vaccine formulations.
3. Why haven't scientists been able to develop vaccines against HIV and the common cold?

29.5 Several Disorders Affect the Immune System

The immune system may turn against the body's own cells, or it may fail to respond to disease-causing organisms. In addition, harmless substances sometimes trigger an immune response. (A woman's immune system can even attack her own fetus, as described in the Why We Care box on this page.)

A. Autoimmune Disorders Are Devastating and Mysterious

Ideally, the immune system does not attack the body's own cells; clonal deletion should eliminate lymphocytes corresponding to molecules already present in the body. In an **autoimmune disorder,** however, the immune system mistakenly attacks the body's molecules as if they were foreign antigens.

The resulting damage to tissues and organs may be severe. In type I diabetes, for example, antibodies attack the insulin-producing cells of the pancreas. Without insulin, the body's cells starve because they cannot absorb glucose. Another disease, rheumatoid arthritis, arises from an autoimmune attack on cells lining the skeleton's joints. Pain and joint deformity are the result.

B. People with Immunodeficiencies Are Vulnerable to Opportunistic Infections

An **immunodeficiency** is a condition in which the immune system lacks one or more essential components. A weakened immune system leaves a person vulnerable to **opportunistic pathogens** and cancers that do not normally affect

Why We Care | **Protecting a Fetus from Immune Attack**

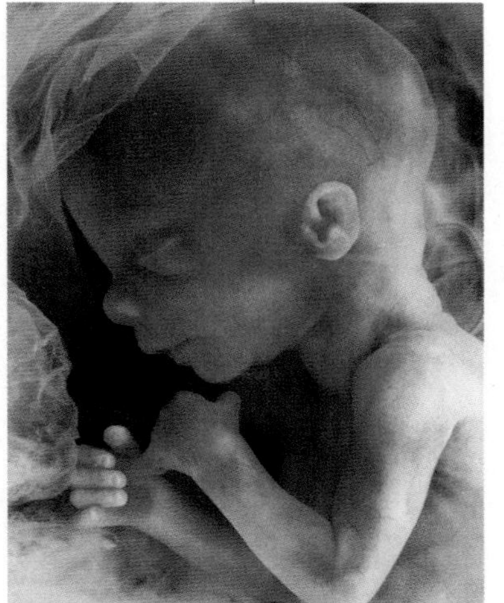

Since the immune system rejects "foreign" cells, it may seem surprising that a woman's body does not destroy her fetus. After all, the developing child is not genetically identical to its mother. In general, the female immune response dampens during pregnancy so that it doesn't reject the embryo and fetus. Full immune function returns after the woman gives birth.

One possible source of problems, however, traces to an antigen called the Rhesus (Rh) factor. Some people produce this protein on the surfaces of their red blood cells. A person can be Rh-positive (Rh^+) or Rh-negative (Rh^-). If your blood type is positive (such as "A positive"), the Rh antigen is present; if your blood is Rh-negative (such as "O negative"), your cells lack the Rh antigen. ▸ blood types, p. 183

Suppose an Rh^- woman becomes pregnant with an Rh^+ baby. Some of the fetus's cells enter the mother's bloodstream, so her immune system produces antibodies to the Rh antigen. In all subsequent Rh^+ pregnancies, these antibodies can cross the placenta and destroy the fetus's blood. A transfusion of Rh^- blood at birth can save the newborn's life, but this is rarely necessary. Instead, women receive an injection of a drug, Rho(D) immune globulin, which prevents the immune response to the Rh antigen.

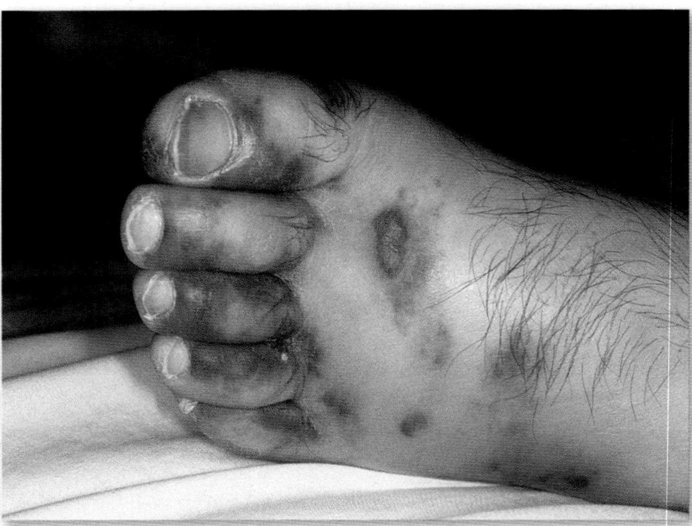

Figure 29.12 Opportunistic Illness. Kaposi sarcoma is a form of cancer that occurs mainly in people with reduced immune system function (including AIDS). The cancer is characterized by bruiselike tumors on the skin. Immunocompromised patients are susceptible to many other infectious diseases as well.

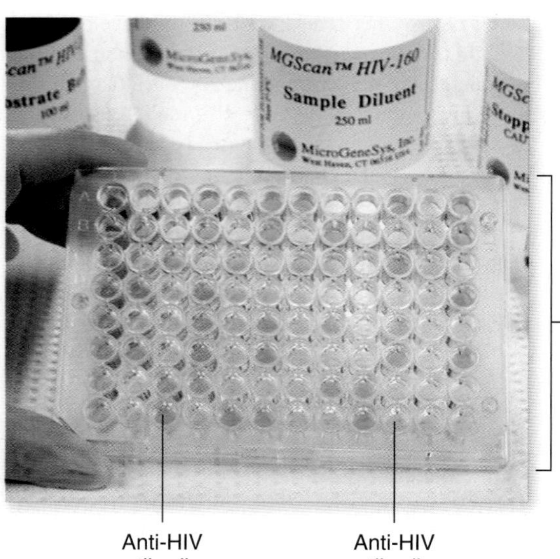

Figure 29.13 HIV Test. A person who has been exposed to HIV produces antibodies to the virus. When the person's body fluid is applied to a specially treated plate, a color change reveals the presence of these antibodies.

people with healthy immune systems (figure 29.12). Viruses such as HIV weaken the immune system, as do some inherited diseases and pharmaceutical drugs.

Human immunodeficiency virus (HIV) causes acquired immune deficiency syndrome (AIDS). Most people acquire HIV by sexual contact or by using blood-contaminated needles when injecting drugs. A mother can also transmit HIV to her baby, either during delivery or in breast milk.

When HIV enters the body, it initially targets helper T cells (see figure 7.20). HIV's genes encode the proteins and RNA needed to manufacture new viruses. Infected T cells die as they assemble and release new viral particles, which then infect additional helper T cells. As a result, the infection spreads within the body. For months to a decade or more, however, no AIDS symptoms appear, because the body can produce enough new T cells to compensate for the loss. During this latent period, B cells manufacture antibodies to the virus; rapid tests for HIV exposure detect these proteins (figure 29.13). Unfortunately, the antibodies do not halt the disease.

HIV-positive people track their disease progress with blood tests that measure the number of helper T cells. As helper T cell counts decline, the ability of cytotoxic T cells to destroy infected cells also weakens. Eventually, the immune system fails entirely, and the infections and cancers of AIDS begin.

AIDS is a consequence of a viral infection, but immune deficiency can also be inherited. Each year, a few children are born defenseless against infection due to **severe combined immunodeficiency (SCID),** a disorder in which neither T nor B cells function. David Vetter was the most famous SCID patient. Born in Texas in 1971, David had no thymus gland and spent the 12 years of his life in a vinyl bubble, awaiting a treatment that never came. Today, most children born with SCID receive bone marrow transplants before they are 3 months old. In addition, gene therapy has been used to replace faulty genes in some SCID patients. ▸ gene therapy, p. 211

Immunodeficiency is also common among organ transplant recipients. To avoid rejection of a donated organ, transplant recipients must take immune-suppressing drugs for the rest of their lives. Like other people with immunodeficiencies, these patients are vulnerable to opportunistic infections.

C. Allergies Misdirect the Immune Response

In an **allergy,** the immune system is overly sensitive, launching an exaggerated attack on a harmless substance (figure 29.14). Common **allergens,** or antigens that trigger an allergy, include foods, dust mites, pollen, pet dander, and oils in the leaves of plants such as poison ivy. The allergens activate B cells to produce antibodies. A first exposure to the allergen initiates a step called sensitization, in which antibodies bind to mast cells. On subsequent exposure, the allergens bind to the molecules attached to the mast cells, causing them to explosively release histamine and other allergy mediators.

The symptoms of an allergic response depend on where in the body the mast cells release mediators. Many mast cells are in the skin, respiratory passages, and digestive tract, so allergies often affect these organs. The result: hives, runny nose, watery eyes, asthma, nausea, vomiting, and diarrhea. Antihistamine drugs relieve these symptoms, either by preventing the release of histamine or by keeping it from binding to target cells.

Some individuals react to allergens with **anaphylactic shock,** a rapid, widespread, and potentially life-threatening reaction in which mast cells release allergy mediators throughout the body. The person may at first feel an inexplicable apprehension. Then, suddenly, the entire body itches and erupts in hives. Histamine causes blood vessels to dilate, lowering blood pressure. As blood rushes to the skin, not enough of it reaches the brain, and the person

Figure 29.14 Allergy. Pollen enters the eyes, nose, and lungs, triggering B cells to differentiate into antibody-secreting plasma cells. These antibodies attach to mast cells. When the same type of pollen is encountered again, it binds to antibodies on the mast cells. The mast cells burst, releasing histamine and other chemicals that cause the allergic reaction.

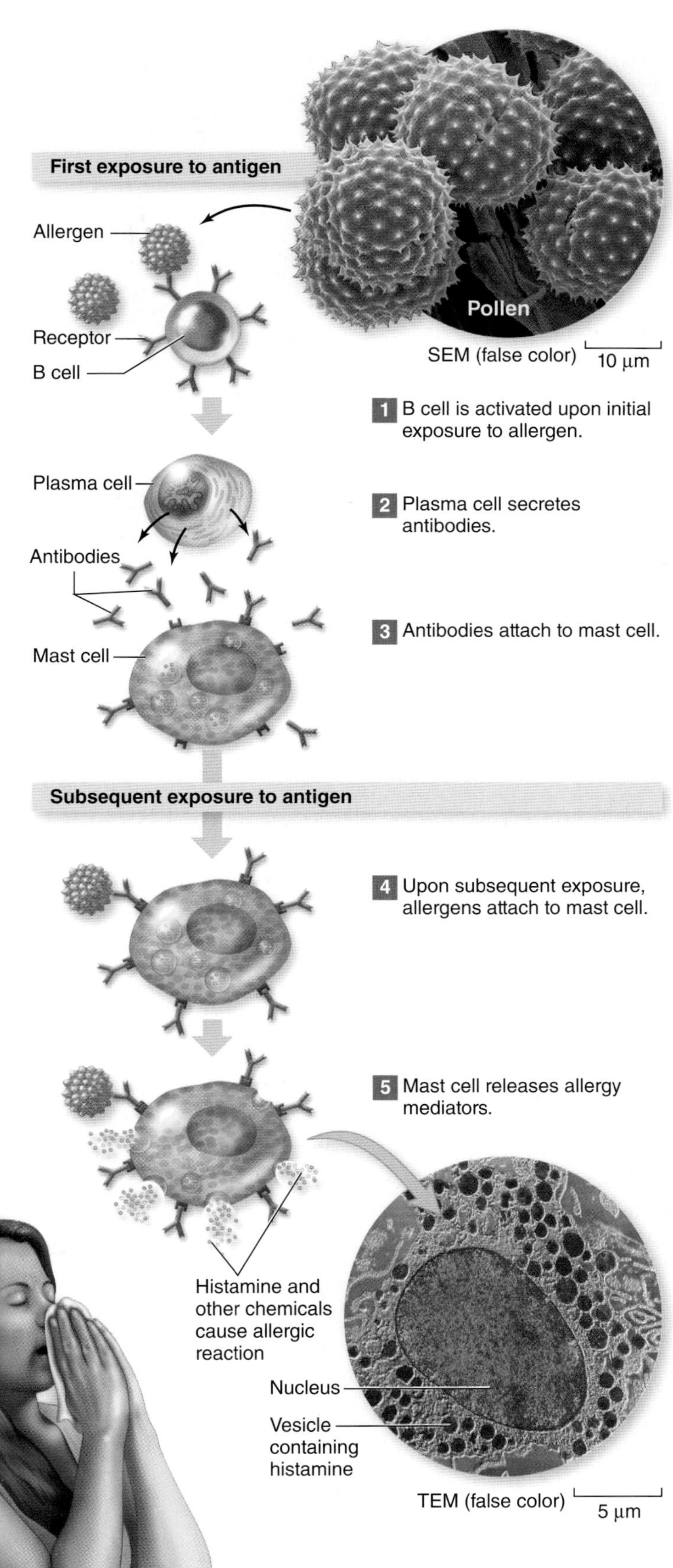
First exposure to antigen
Allergen
Receptor
B cell
Pollen
SEM (false color)
10 µm
1 B cell is activated upon initial exposure to allergen.
Plasma cell
Antibodies
2 Plasma cell secretes antibodies.
Mast cell
3 Antibodies attach to mast cell.
Subsequent exposure to antigen
4 Upon subsequent exposure, allergens attach to mast cell.
5 Mast cell releases allergy mediators.
Histamine and other chemicals cause allergic reaction
Nucleus
Vesicle containing histamine
TEM (false color)
5 µm

becomes dizzy and may lose consciousness. Breathing becomes difficult as the airways in the lungs become constricted. Meanwhile, the face, tongue, and larynx begin to swell. Unless the person receives an injection of epinephrine and sometimes an incision into the trachea to restore breathing, death can come within minutes.

Anaphylactic shock most often results from an allergy to penicillin, insect stings, or foods. Peanut allergy, for example, affects 6% of the U.S. population and is on the rise. The allergens are seed storage proteins that enter the bloodstream undigested. The fact that the initial allergic reaction to peanuts occurs at an average age of 14 months, typically after eating peanut butter, suggests that sensitization occurs even earlier, during breast feeding or before birth.

Early exposure to microorganisms and viruses may be crucial to the development of the immune system. A growing body of evidence has led to the "hygiene hypothesis," which suggests that excessive cleanliness has contributed to recent increases in the incidence of asthma and some allergies (see section 29.6). Apparently, ultraclean surroundings decrease stimulation of the immune system early in life.

29.5 Mastering Concepts

1. What events might lead to autoimmunity?
2. How do HIV and SCID lead to immunodeficiency?
3. Which cells and biochemicals participate in an allergic reaction?

Investigating Life

29.6 The Hidden Cost of Hygiene

Healthy immune function requires a delicate balance. On the one hand, the immune system must be strong enough to protect the body from dangerous pathogens. But if the immune response is too strong, we run the risk of overreacting to harmless substances—as in allergies—or launching an autoimmune attack against our own cells and tissues.

This fine balance reflects our evolutionary history. For millions of years, the human immune system has coevolved with countless bacteria, viruses, and parasitic worms. Many of these hidden residents produce substances that suppress our immune systems, an adaptation that allows them to "fly under the radar" and maintain long-term, chronic infections. Now, however, thanks to improved sanitation, vaccines, and antibiotics, people in developed nations are exposed to far less infectious

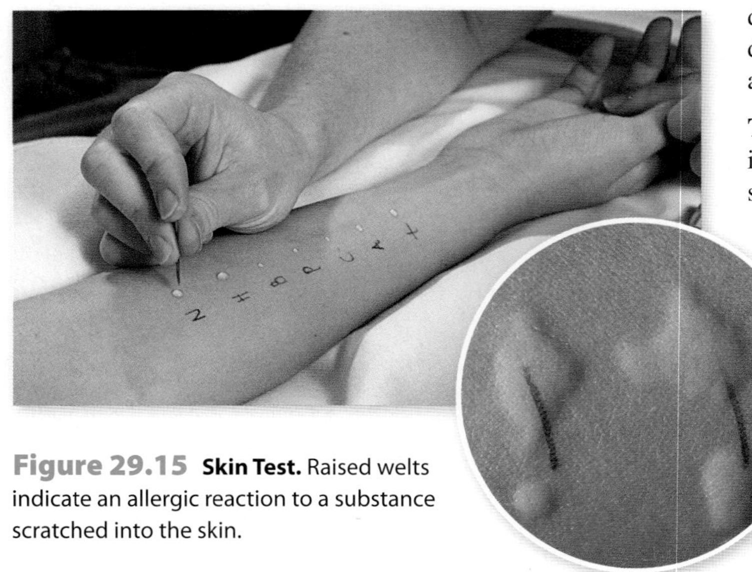

Figure 29.15 Skin Test. Raised welts indicate an allergic reaction to a substance scratched into the skin.

disease than their counterparts in developing countries. Meanwhile, people in developed countries have a relatively high incidence of allergies, asthma, and autoimmune disorders.

The Question: According to an idea called the hygiene hypothesis, eliminating pathogens from everyday life has removed a critical check on the immune system. If so, then people with chronic infections should have dampened immune systems, along with reduced incidence of allergies. Is this the case?

The Approach: A research team led by Maria Yazdanbakhsh at Leiden University in the Netherlands investigated this question. Along with colleagues from the Netherlands, the United Kingdom, Germany, and the west African nation of Gabon, Yazdanbakhsh studied the incidence of allergies and chronic worm infection among children in Gabon. The team predicted that children infected with worms would have a lower incidence of allergies than their uninfected schoolmates.

The study population consisted of 513 schoolchildren, aged 5 to 14 years. The researchers tested each child for allergies to several substances, including dust mite extract. The team scratched the potential allergen into each child's forearm. If the child was allergic to a substance, the scratched area turned red and swollen within about 10 minutes (figure 29.15). The team also checked for infection with several types of parasitic worms, including a liver fluke.

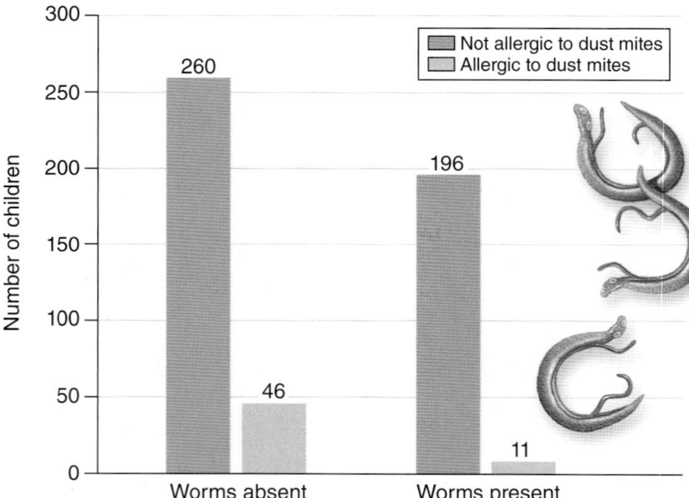

Figure 29.16 Protective Worms? Of the 306 children without parasitic worms, dust mite allergies appeared in 46 (about 15%). In contrast, of the 207 schoolchildren infected with worms, only 11 (about 5%) also had allergies.

The Conclusion: Of the 513 children, 57 tested positive for dust-mite allergies. Forty-six of these allergic children were worm-free; only 11 were infected with flukes (figure 29.16). Statistical analysis of the data indicated that harboring worms significantly lowers the risk for allergies. Worms apparently induce white blood cells to release an interleukin that dampens the overall immune response and suppresses allergies.

This study suggests the intriguing possibility that parasites might have a role to play in the fight against allergies. Biologists hope to identify which chemicals in worms stimulate immune cells to release the "braking" interleukin. The long-term outcome may be new drugs to treat immune disorders.

Anita H. J. van den Biggelaar and six coauthors, including Maria Yazdanbakhsh. 2000. Decreased atopy in children infected with *Schistosoma haematobium:* a role for parasite-induced interleukin-10. *Lancet,* vol. 356, pages 1723–1727.

29.6 Mastering Concepts

1. How did researchers investigate the worm–allergy connection?
2. How do infectious worms lower the risk for allergies?

Chapter Summary

29.1 Many Cells, Tissues, and Organs Defend the Body

- The **immune system** protects the body against **pathogens** and cancer cells.

A. White Blood Cells Play Major Roles in the Immune System

- Several types of **white blood cells** participate in immune responses.
- **Macrophages** and some other white blood cells are **phagocytes,** cells that engulf and destroy bacteria and debris.
- **B cells** and **T cells** are **lymphocytes** that mature in the **red bone marrow** and the **thymus,** respectively. **Natural killer cells** are also lymphocytes.
- **Basophils** are white blood cells that participate in inflammation; they are closely related to noncirculating **mast cells.**

B. The Lymphatic System Produces and Transports Many Immune System Cells

- The **lymphatic system** is a bridge between the circulatory and immune systems. Dead-end vessels called **lymph capillaries** collect a fluid called **lymph;** larger lymph vessels carry the fluid within the body.
- Besides the thymus, other lymph organs include the **spleen** and **lymph nodes.** Immune cells are also concentrated in the tonsils, appendix, and digestive tract.

C. The Immune System Has Two Main Subdivisions

- **Innate defenses** provide broad protection against all pathogens, whereas **adaptive immunity** is directed against specific pathogens. Only adaptive immunity produces a "memory" that protects against future exposure to a previously encountered pathogen.

29.2 Innate Defenses Are Nonspecific and Act Early

A. Barriers Form the First Line of Defense

- Intact skin, mucous membranes, tears, earwax, and cilia block pathogens.

B. Internal Innate Defenses Destroy Invaders

- White blood cells destroy bacteria and promote inflammation; natural killer cells destroy cancerous or virus-infected cells; macrophages consume pathogens, promote fever, and activate the immune response.
- **Complement** proteins interact in a cascade that ends with the destruction of bacterial cells.
- **Cytokines** are antimicrobial molecules that communicate with immune system cells and stimulate the development of a fever. Interferons and interleukins are examples of cytokines.
- The elevated body temperature of a mild **fever** helps discourage microbial replication.
- Basophils and mast cells participate in **inflammation,** which is an immediate reaction to injury. These cells release **histamine,** a biochemical that causes blood vessels to dilate.
- Redness, warmth, swelling, and pain are associated with inflammation.

29.3 Adaptive Immunity Defends Against Specific Pathogens

- Adaptive immunity is directed against specific **antigens.**

A. Macrophages Trigger Both Cell-Mediated and Humoral Immunity

- A macrophage that engulfs a pathogen links antigens from the microbe to proteins on its cell surface.
- A **helper T cell** binding to the antigen-presenting cell initiates the **cell-mediated** and **humoral** components of the adaptive immune response. Activated helper T cells activate other T cells and B cells.

B. T Cells Coordinate Cell-Mediated Immunity

- **Cytotoxic T cells** release biochemicals that kill bacteria and cells infected with viruses. Memory T cells help provide long-term immunity.

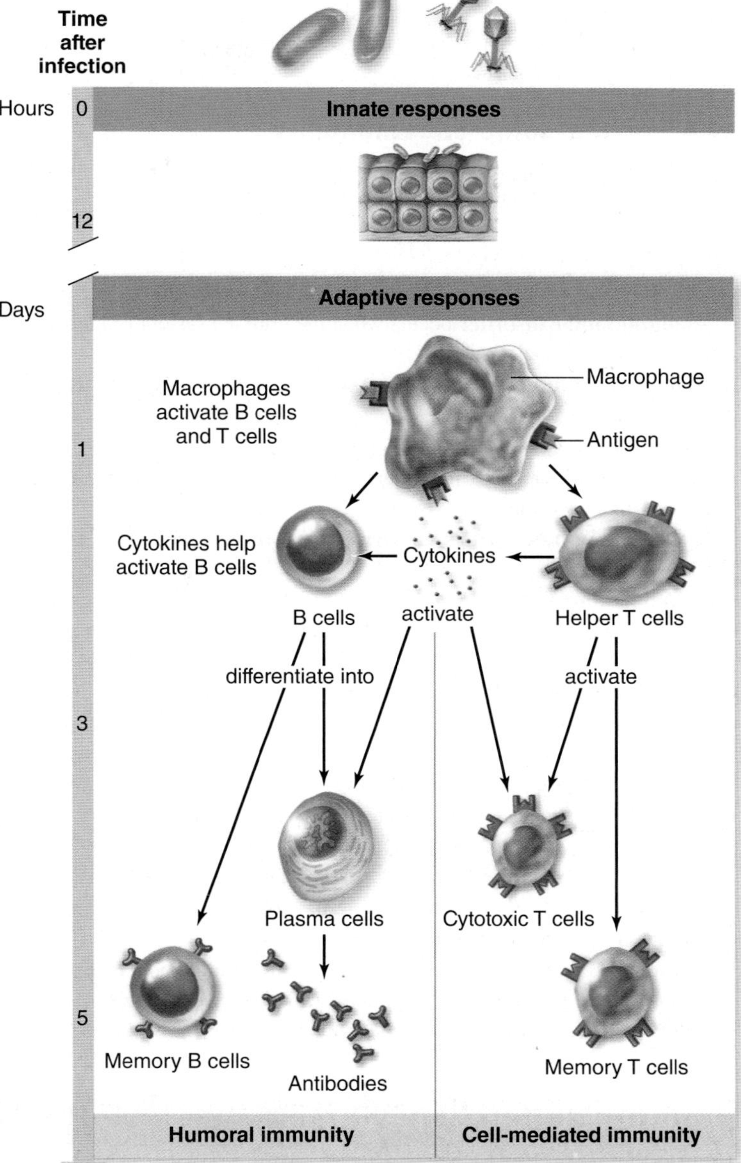

C. B Cells Direct the Humoral Immune Response

- An **antibody** is a Y-shaped protein composed of two heavy and two light polypeptide chains. Each chain has a **constant region** and a **variable region.** Antibodies bind antigens and form complexes that attract other immune system components.
- Antibodies and antigen receptors are incredibly diverse because DNA segments shuffle during early lymphocyte development. **Clonal deletion** subsequently eliminates lymphocytes corresponding to self antigens.
- In **clonal selection,** an activated B cell multiplies rapidly, generating an army of identical **plasma cells** that all churn out the same antibody. Some also differentiate into **memory cells.**
- In **passive immunity,** a person receives antibodies from someone else. In **active immunity,** a person makes his or her own antibodies.

D. The Secondary Immune Response Is Stronger Than the Primary Response

- The first encounter with an antigen provokes the **primary immune response,** which is relatively slow. Its legacy is memory cells that greatly speed the **secondary immune response** on subsequent exposure to the same antigen.

- Tissue damage can occur if the immune response does not turn off after eliminating a pathogen.

29.4 Vaccines Jump-Start Immunity

- A **vaccine** "teaches" the immune system to recognize specific components of a pathogen, bypassing the primary immune response.

29.5 Several Disorders Affect the Immune System

A. Autoimmune Disorders Are Devastating and Mysterious

- An **autoimmune disorder** occurs when the immune system produces antibodies that attack the body's own tissues.

B. People with Immunodeficiencies Are Vulnerable to Opportunistic Infections

- An **immunodeficiency** is the absence of one or more essential elements of the immune system. These disorders leave patients vulnerable to cancer and **opportunistic pathogens.**
- The **human immunodeficiency virus (HIV)** kills helper T cells, causing AIDS.
- **Severe combined immune deficiency (SCID)** is an inherited disease.
- Drugs that prevent organ transplant rejection also weaken the immune system.

C. Allergies Misdirect the Immune Response

- An **allergy** is an immune reaction to a harmless substance. An **allergen** triggers the production of antibodies, which bind mast cells. On subsequent exposure, these mast cells release allergy mediators such as histamine.
- **Anaphylactic shock** is a life-threatening allergic reaction.

29.6 Investigating Life: The Hidden Cost of Hygiene

- According to the hygiene hypothesis, reduced exposure to pathogens is associated with an increase in allergies.
- Researchers investigating the hygiene hypothesis found that Gabonese schoolchildren infected with parasitic worms had fewer allergies. The worms induce immune cells to release an allergy-suppressing interleukin.

Multiple Choice Questions

1. Which types of cells play important roles in both inflammation and allergy?
   a. Phagocytes
   b. Memory cells and plasma cells
   c. Basophils and mast cells
   d. B cells and T cells
2. Histamine acts on the ______ , causing redness and swelling.
   a. white blood cells
   b. cells lining blood vessels
   c. smooth muscle cells
   d. red blood cells
3. How do complement proteins contribute to the innate immune response?
   a. They cause bacteria to burst.
   b. They attract phagocytes to an injury.
   c. They cause mast cells to release histamine.
   d. All of the above are correct.
4. The innate immune response is characterized by its
   a. rapid response to invading pathogens.
   b. ability to "remember" pathogens it has already encountered.
   c. ability to produce antibodies.
   d. Both b and c are correct.
5. What is the function of a cytotoxic T cell?
   a. It displays antigens to a helper T cell.
   b. It secretes proteins that destroy foreign cells.
   c. It secretes cytokines that stimulate antibody production.
   d. It triggers clonal selection of B cells.
6. Antibody function requires that the shape of the ______ matches the shape of the antigen.
   a. constant region
   b. light chain
   c. variable region
   d. heavy chain
7. In what process is clonal selection important?
   a. Complement function
   b. B cell activation
   c. Inflammation
   d. Phagocytosis
8. Why is the secondary immune response so much stronger than the primary response?
   a. Because high concentrations of antibodies are already present
   b. Because the phagocytes present the antigens more rapidly
   c. Because memory cells can rapidly convert to plasma cells
   d. Because protein synthesis occurs more quickly in memory cells
9. How do vaccines prevent infectious disease?
   a. By killing bacteria and viruses
   b. By boosting overall immune function
   c. By stimulating a primary immune response
   d. By passive immunity
10. HIV causes immunodeficiency by attacking
    a. B memory cells.
    b. helper T cells.
    c. plasma cells.
    d. cytotoxic T cells.

Write It Out

1. List and describe the components of the lymphatic system.
2. Explain the observation that lymphoid tissues are scattered in the skin, lungs, stomach, and intestines.
3. How does the immune system interact with the circulatory system?
4. List the types of innate defenses.
5. Dead phagocytes are one component of pus. Why is pus a sure sign of infection?
6. How can inflammation be both helpful and harmful?
7. If you take an antiinflammatory drug after spraining your ankle, what symptoms should be reduced?
8. State the functions of antibodies, cytokines, and complement proteins.
9. What do a plasma cell and a memory cell descended from the same B cell have in common, and how do they differ?
10. In your own words, write a paragraph describing the events of adaptive immunity, beginning with a macrophage engulfing a bacterial cell and ending with the production of memory cells.
11. How do innate defenses and adaptive immunity cooperate to eradicate an infection?
12. Which do you think would be more dangerous, a deficiency of T cells or a deficiency of B cells? Explain your reasoning.
13. One benefit of sexual reproduction is a genetically variable population. This genetic variation may help a population stay "one step ahead" of pathogen populations. Describe how genetic variability can enhance immunity.
14. What is a vaccine, and how is a vaccine different from an antibiotic?

15. Explain why it might be dangerous for a person with a weakened immune system to receive a vaccine consisting of a live, weakened pathogen.
16. Influenza viruses mutate rapidly, whereas the chickenpox virus does not. Why are people encouraged to receive vaccinations against influenza every year, whereas immunity to chickenpox lasts for decades?
17. If worm infections suppress the immune system as suggested in section 29.6, do you think vaccines should be more or less effective in children infected with worms? Explain your answer.
18. What is an opportunistic infection? Explain the statement that opportunistic infections, not HIV alone, cause death in an end-stage AIDS patient.
19. How do SCID, AIDS, and allergies each relate to the function of the immune system?
20. What role do antibodies play in allergic reactions and in autoimmune disorders?
21. How might a drug advertised as a "histamine blocker" relieve allergy symptoms?
22. Explain the difference between: clonal deletion and clonal selection; a natural killer cell and a cytotoxic T cell; antibodies and antigens; cell-mediated and humoral immunity; an autoimmune disorder and an immunodeficiency.
23. Search the Internet for evidence for and against the hypothesis that autism is associated with the thimerosal preservative that was once added to childhood vaccines (keep in mind that not all websites are equally credible). Do you find the evidence for or against the hypothesis most compelling? What sort of evidence would it take to change your position to the opposite side of the issue?
24. Search the Internet for information about immune system disorders. Choose one illness to study in more detail. What are the characteristics of the disorder? Who is primarily affected? What causes the illness, and is there a treatment or cure?
25. Search the Internet for ads for commercial products that claim to "boost the immune system." Choose a product to investigate in detail. What specific claims do ads for the product make? What scientific evidence does the manufacturer offer in support of its claims? Based on what you know about the immune system, does the scientific evidence seem convincing?

Pull It Together

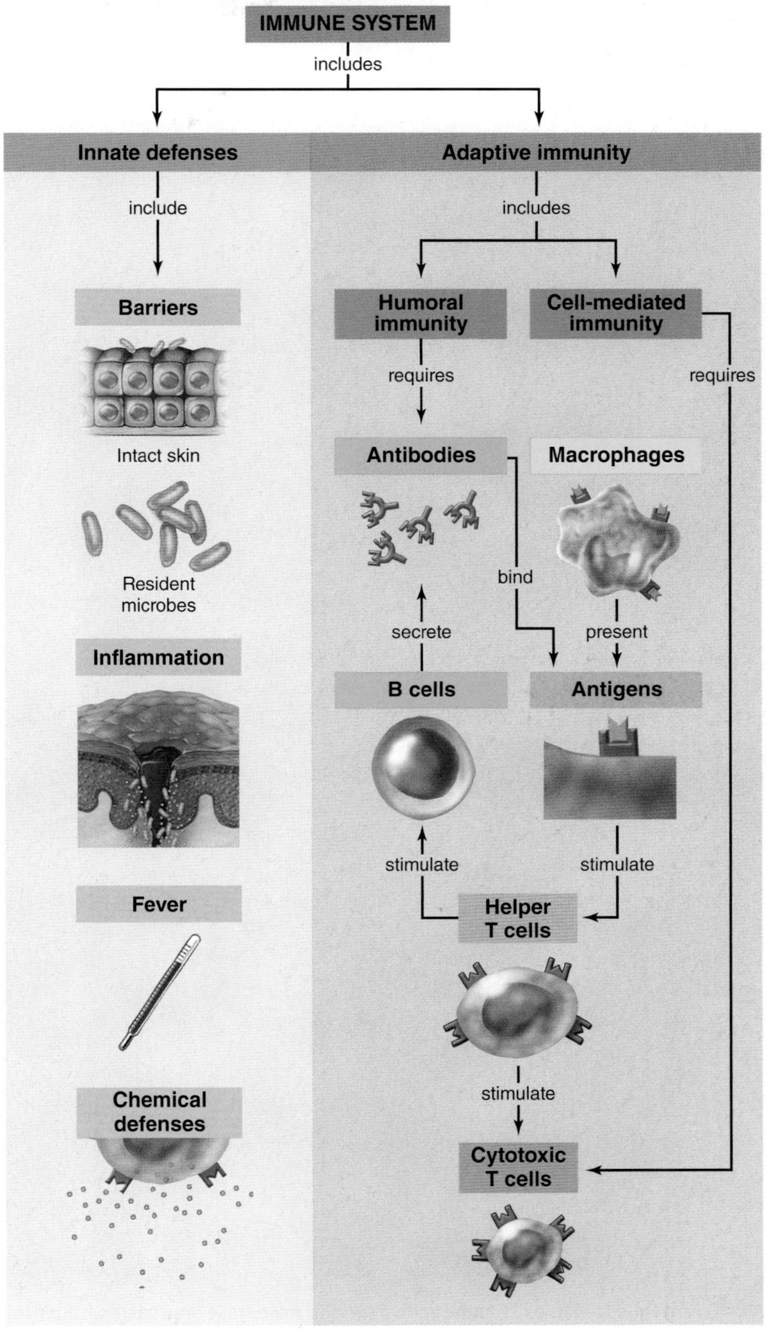

1. How do innate defenses and adaptive immunity differ?
2. What are examples of barriers that contribute to innate defenses?
3. Where do cytokines and complement proteins fit into this concept map?
4. How do cytokines interact with the adaptive immune system?
5. How do lymph and lymph nodes fit into this concept map?
6. What are the roles of memory B cells and plasma B cells?

30 Animal Reproduction and Development

A **Different Role for Males.** In some animal species, males take unusual reproductive roles. This male sea horse is giving birth.

Learning Outline

Learn How to Learn

Make Your Own Review Sheet

If you are facing a big exam, how can you make sense of everything you have learned? One way is to make your own review sheet. The best strategy will depend on what your instructor expects you to know, but here are a few ideas to try: make lists; draw concept maps that link ideas within and between chapters; draw diagrams that illustrate important processes; and write mini-essays that explain the main points in each chapter's learning outline.

What's the Point?

The animal kingdom is full of intriguing reproductive strategies. Consider, for example, the male sea horse pictured on the opposite page. These fish look unusual, with their elongated snouts and upright swimming posture. Their reproductive habits are unique as well: the males become pregnant!

As in other sexually reproducing animals, the female sea horse produces eggs. But she deposits the eggs into a brood pouch on the male's abdomen. He then fertilizes the eggs with his sperm. The young develop in the wall of his brood pouch for 2 to 4 weeks. At the end of the pregnancy, he gives birth to dozens or hundreds of miniature sea horses.

Humans are no less amazing. Sperm and egg cells come together in a woman's body. The resulting cell begins to divide, first into two cells, then four, then eight, and so on. The resulting ball of cells soon hollows out and develops an outside and an inside. Slowly, organs develop and begin to work together. After nine months, a brand new baby emerges into the world.

This chapter explores these two interrelated topics—reproduction and development—with a focus on our own species.

30.1 Animal Development Begins with Reproduction

A monarch butterfly emerges from its chrysalis; a baby bird hatches from an egg; a kitten becomes a full-grown cat. All of these familiar examples illustrate growth and development. Together, reproduction, growth, and development are shared features of all multicellular life. Chapter 22 described how flowering plants reproduce and grow; this chapter picks up the topic for animals.

A. Reproduction Is Asexual or Sexual

Like plants, animals may reproduce asexually or sexually (or both). In **asexual reproduction,** the offspring contain genetic information from only one parent. Aside from mutations that occur during replication, all offspring are identical to the parent and to one another. Animals that undergo asexual reproduction include aphids and some types of lizards. In general, asexual reproduction is advantageous in environments that do not change much over time.

Sexual reproduction requires two parents, each of which contributes half the DNA in each offspring. In many species, sexual reproduction entails high energy costs for attracting mates, copulating, and defending against rivals (see section 30.6). Nevertheless, the benefits of genetic diversity apparently outweigh these costs, especially in a changing environment. Sexual reproduction is therefore extremely common among animals. ▸ why sex? p. 155

In organisms that reproduce sexually, haploid **gametes** are the sex cells that carry the genetic information from each parent. The gametes—sperm cells from males and egg cells from females—are the products of meiosis, a specialized type of cell division. In meiosis, a diploid cell containing two sets of chromosomes divides into four haploid cells, each containing just one chromosome set. **Fertilization** is the union of two gametes; the product of fertilization is the diploid **zygote,** the first cell of the new offspring.

Sperm and egg come together in a variety of ways. In **external fertilization,** males and females release gametes into the same environment, and fertilization occurs outside the body (figure 30.1a). This strategy is especially common in aquatic animals. Salmon, for example, spawn in streams. Females lay eggs in gravelly nests, and then males shed sperm over them. Other animals with external fertilization include sponges, corals, sea urchins, and some amphibians. Unique "recognition" proteins on the surfaces of the gametes keep sperm cells from fertilizing eggs of the wrong species.

a.

b.

Figure 30.1 External and Internal Fertilization. (a) A sea urchin releases sperm cells into the water. Meanwhile, females release eggs; fertilization is external. (b) A male black-necked stilt mates with a female. Their offspring will develop inside the female's body until she lays three or four hard-shelled eggs in a nest.

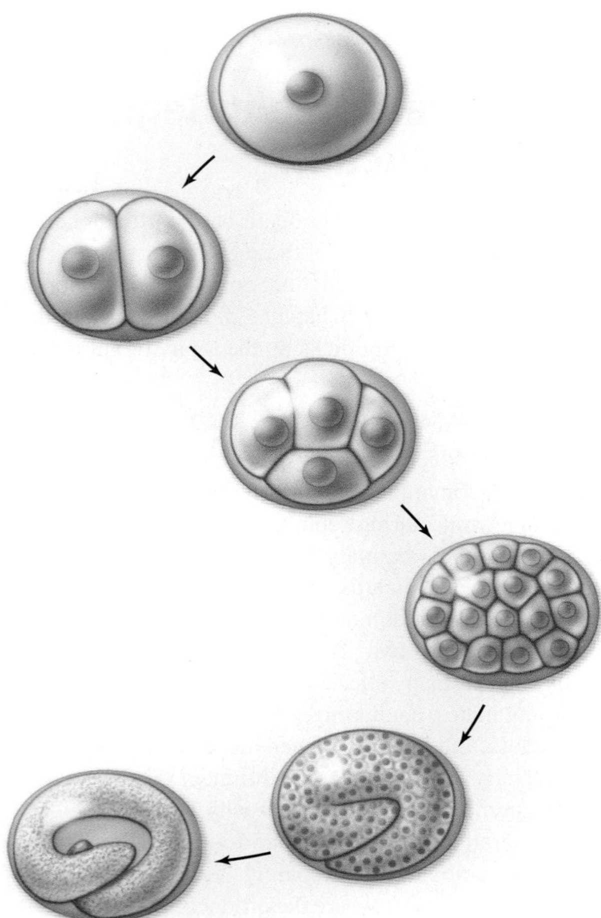

Figure 30.2 Tiny Worm. The life of the roundworm *Caenorhabditis elegans* begins as a single fertilized egg cell. Researchers understand nematode development in detail, describing and mapping the fates of all cells produced from the original zygote.

Figure 30.3 Tiny Turtle. A baby turtle emerges from its egg. Like other animals that undergo direct development, the newly hatched turtle is a miniature version of the adult.

In **internal fertilization,** a male deposits sperm inside a female's body, where fertilization occurs. Land animals, including mammals, nonavian reptiles, and birds, commonly use internal fertilization (see figure 30.1b). After copulation, the female may lay hard-shelled, fertilized eggs that provide both nutrition and a protected environment in which the young develop. A chicken egg is a familiar example. Alternatively, the female may bear live young, as humans and other mammals do.

B. Development Is Indirect or Direct

No matter what the method of fertilization, development of sexually reproducing animals begins with the zygote. That first cell begins to divide soon after fertilization is complete. As the embryonic animal grows, cells divide and die in coordinated ways to shape the body's distinctive form and function. Developmental biologists study the stages of an animal's growth as cells specialize and interact to form tissues, organs, and organ systems (figure 30.2). The similarities and differences among developing animals can yield important clues to evolution, as illustrated in figure 13.12.

One key to animal development is **differentiation,** the process by which cells in organs such as the skin, brain, eyes, and heart activate unique combinations of genes to acquire their specialized functions. Another essential process is **pattern formation,** in which genes determine the overall shape and structure of the animal's body, such as the number of segments or the placement of limbs. ▸ control of gene expression, p. 121

Differentiation and pattern formation involve complex interactions between the DNA inside cells and external signals such as hormones. These interactions ultimately regulate the formation of each structure. Section 7.6 described the importance of homeotic genes in establishing the correct placement of a developing animal's parts. Scientists first discovered homeotic genes by studying mutant flies with legs growing out of their heads. Since that time, additional studies have verified that homeotic genes orchestrate development in humans and all other animal species.

Although many details of animal development remain undiscovered, clear patterns do emerge on a broader scale. For example, biologists distinguish between indirect and direct development. An animal that undergoes **indirect development** spends the early part of its life as a **larva,** an immature stage that looks different from the adult. A caterpillar, for example, is a larva that looks nothing like its butterfly parents; likewise, a tadpole resembles a fish, not the adult frog or salamander that it will grow up to become. Caterpillars, tadpoles, and other larvae often spend most of their time eating and growing. Then, during a process called **metamorphosis,** the larva matures into an adult.

Humans, horses, and many other animals undergo **direct development:** at birth, an infant resembles a smaller version of its parents. The hatching turtle in figure 30.3, for example, looks like an adult, except for its small size.

This chapter combines reproduction and development, starting with the reproductive anatomy of human males and females. Before you begin, you may find it helpful to review mitosis (chapter 8), meiosis (chapter 9), and the basics of hormone function (chapter 25). The second half of the chapter describes human prenatal development; that is, how a fertilized egg grows into a fully formed infant.

30.1 Mastering Concepts

1. What is the difference between asexual and sexual reproduction?
2. How is internal fertilization different from external fertilization?
3. How do genes participate in differentiation and pattern formation?
4. Differentiate between indirect and direct development.

30.2 Males Produce Sperm Cells

Both the male and female **reproductive systems** consist of the organs that produce and transport gametes. Each system includes primary sex organs: the paired **gonads** (testes or ovaries), which contain the **germ cells** that give rise to gametes. Secondary sex organs include the network of tubes that transport the gametes.

In both sexes, hormones control reproduction and promote the development of **secondary sex characteristics,** features that distinguish the sexes but do not participate directly in reproduction. Examples include wider hips and enlarged breasts in adult females and facial hair and deep voices in adult males.

Although the male and female reproductive systems share some similarities, there are also obvious differences. This section details the features and processes that are unique to males.

A. Male Reproductive Organs Are Inside and Outside the Body

Figure 30.4 illustrates the human male reproductive system. The paired **testes** (singular: testis) are the male gonads. The testes lie in a sac called the **scrotum.** Their location outside of the abdominal cavity allows the testes to maintain a temperature about 3°C cooler than the rest of the body, which is necessary for sperm to develop properly. Muscles surrounding each testis can bring the scrotum closer to the body, conserving warmth when the temperature is too cold. Conversely, if conditions are too warm, the scrotum descends away from the body.

A maze of small ducts carries developing sperm to the left or right **epididymis,** a tightly coiled tube that receives and stores sperm from one testis. From each epididymis, sperm cells move into a **vas deferens,** a duct that travels upward out of the scrotum, bends behind the bladder, and connects with the

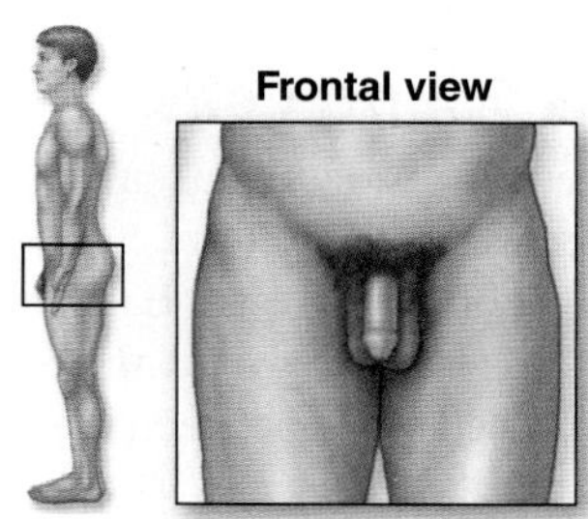

Reproductive System (Male)	
Main tissue types*	**Examples of locations/functions**
Epithelial	Lines ducts of reproductive tract; produces sperm cells in seminiferous tubules; produces secretions in accessory glands.
Connective	Makes up walls of testes; makes up erectile tissue in penis.
Nervous	Penis contains sensory nerve fibers and nerve endings; hypothalamus secretes hormones that affect the anterior pituitary.
Muscle	Smooth muscle surrounds ducts of reproductive tract, propelling sperm out of the body.

*See chapter 23 for descriptions.

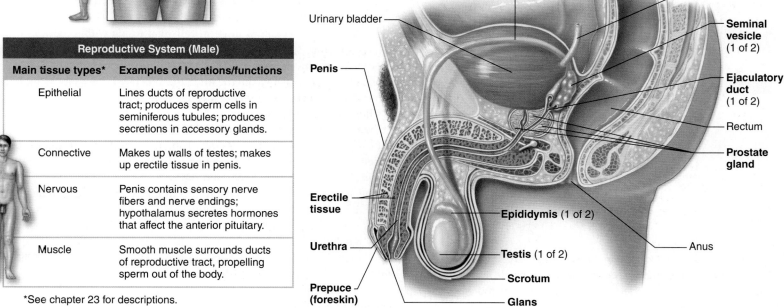

Figure 30.4 The Human Male Reproductive System. The paired testes manufacture sperm cells, which travel through a series of ducts before exiting the body via the urethra in the penis.

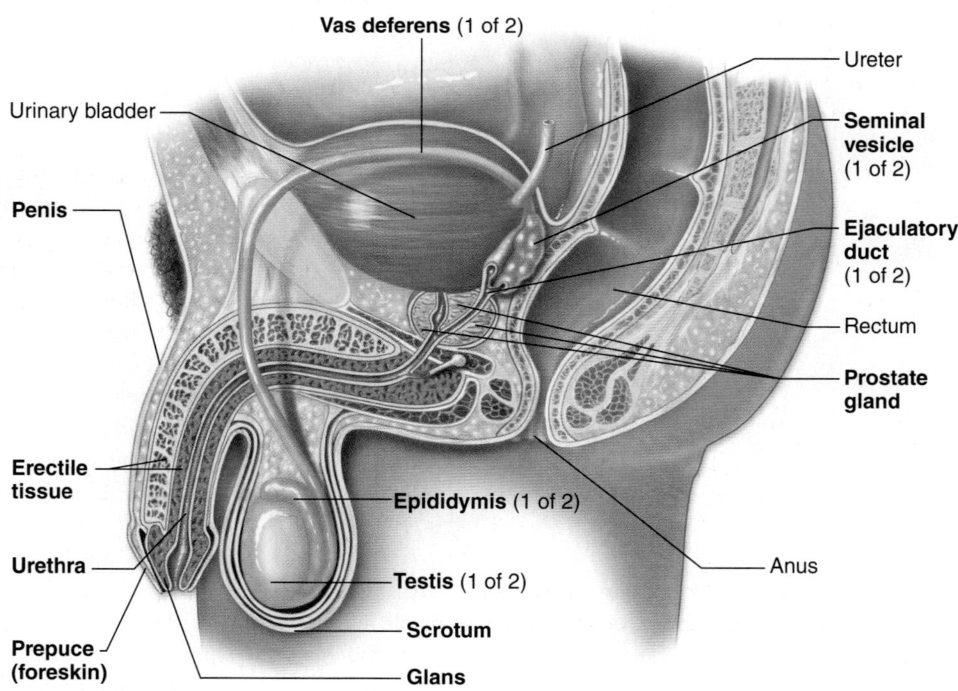

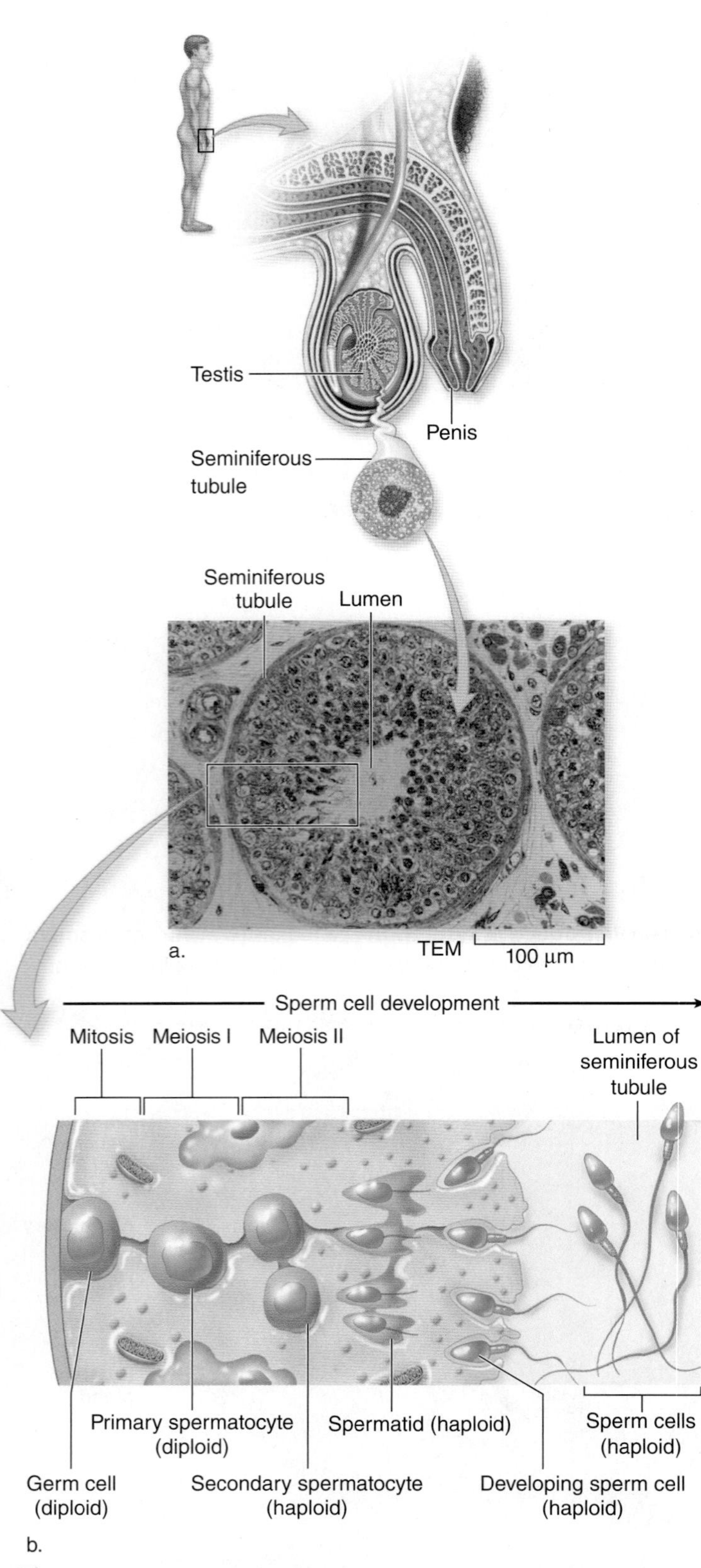

Figure 30.5 Sperm Production. (a) Anatomy of a testis. (b) In the walls of the seminiferous tubules, diploid germ cells divide mitotically. Some of the daughter cells undergo meiosis, giving rise to four haploid cells that mature into sperm cells.

left or right **ejaculatory duct.** The two ejaculatory ducts empty into the **urethra,** the tube that extends the length of the cylindrical **penis** and carries both urine and semen out of the body. Although the two fluids share the urethra, a healthy male cannot urinate when sexually aroused because a ring of smooth muscle temporarily seals the exit from the urinary bladder.

Semen, the fluid that carries sperm cells, includes secretions from several accessory glands. The two **seminal vesicles,** one of which opens into each vas deferens, secrete most of the fluid in semen. The secretions include fructose (a sugar that supplies energy) and prostaglandins. Prostaglandins are hormone-like lipids that may stimulate contractions in the female reproductive tract, helping to propel sperm. In addition, the single, walnut-sized **prostate gland** wraps around part of the urethra and contributes a thin, milky, alkaline fluid that activates the sperm to swim.

During sexual arousal, the penis becomes erect, enabling it to penetrate the vagina and deposit semen in the female reproductive tract. At the peak of sexual stimulation, a pleasurable sensation called **orgasm** occurs, accompanied by rhythmic muscular contractions along the reproductive tract. These contractions eject the semen through the urethra and out the penis. **Ejaculation** is the discharge of semen from the penis. One human ejaculation typically delivers more than 100 million sperm cells.

Two cancers of the male reproductive system originate in the prostate gland and testes. Prostate cancer is the second most common type of cancer in men (behind lung cancer). The resulting prostate enlargement constricts the urethra and may interfere with urination and ejaculation. Prostate cancer usually strikes men older than 50; noncancerous (benign) prostate enlargement affects many older men as well. ▸ cancer, p. 148

In testicular cancer, which usually occurs in men younger than 40, mutated germ cells in the testes divide out of control, forming lumps that may be detected in a self-examination. Testicular cancer has a very high cure rate, if detected before it spreads to other parts of the body.

B. Spermatogenesis Yields Sperm Cells

Spermatogenesis, the production of sperm, is a continuous process that begins when a male reaches puberty and continues throughout life.

Figure 30.5 illustrates the internal anatomy of a testis. Each testis contains about 200 tightly coiled, 50-centimeter-long **seminiferous tubules,** which produce the sperm cells. Endocrine cells fill the spaces between the seminiferous tubules and secrete male sex hormones.

Sperm production begins with germ cells that reside within the wall of a seminiferous tubule (see figure 30.5b). The germ cells are diploid, so their nuclei contain 46 chromosomes. When a germ cell divides mitotically, one daughter cell remains in the tubule wall; the other cell becomes a diploid **primary spermatocyte** that accumulates cytoplasm and moves closer to the tubule's lumen (central cavity).

In the wall of the seminiferous tubule, the primary spermatocyte undergoes the first division of meiosis, yielding two haploid **secondary spermatocytes.** These cells undergo meiosis II, forming four round, haploid cells called **spermatids** that each contain 23 chromosomes.

As the spermatids move into the lumen of the seminiferous tubule, they complete their differentiation into mature sperm cells. They separate into individual cells and develop flagella, although they will not be able to swim until they reach the epididymis. They also lose much of their cytoplasm, acquire a streamlined shape, and package their DNA into a distinct head (figure 30.6). Mitochondria just below the head region generate the ATP the sperm needs to move toward an egg cell. The caplike **acrosome** covers the head and releases enzymes that will help the sperm penetrate the egg cell.

The entire process, from germ cell to mature sperm cell, takes 74 days in humans. ▸ ATP, p. 72

C. Hormones Influence Male Reproductive Function

Hormones play a critical role in male reproduction (figure 30.7). In the brain, the hypothalamus secretes **gonadotropin-releasing hormone (GnRH).** This water-soluble hormone travels in the bloodstream to the anterior pituitary, where it stimulates the release of two other water-soluble hormones: **follicle-stimulating hormone (FSH)** and **luteinizing hormone (LH).** Blood carries FSH and LH throughout the body. ▸ water-soluble hormones, p. 510

LH induces endocrine cells in the testes to release the steroid hormone **testosterone** and other male sex hormones (androgens). In the presence of FSH, testosterone affects the body in multiple ways. In adolescents, the hormone stimulates the development of secondary sex characteristics. The testes and penis begin to enlarge at puberty, and hair grows on the face, in the armpits, and at the groin. Testosterone also stimulates the secretion of growth hormone, causing a growth spurt that increases height, boosts muscle mass, and deepens the voice. In adults, testosterone stimulates sperm production, sustains the libido, and controls the activity of the prostate gland. ▸ steroid hormones, p. 510

Negative feedback loops maintain homeostasis in the concentrations of these hormones. A negative feedback loop also helps explain one well-known consequence of abusing anabolic steroids: infertility or low sperm counts (see chapter 25's Why We Care box). The body mistakes the synthetic steroids for testosterone, causing the testes to produce less of the real sex hormone. Without testosterone, sperm do not form. ▸ negative feedback, p. 475

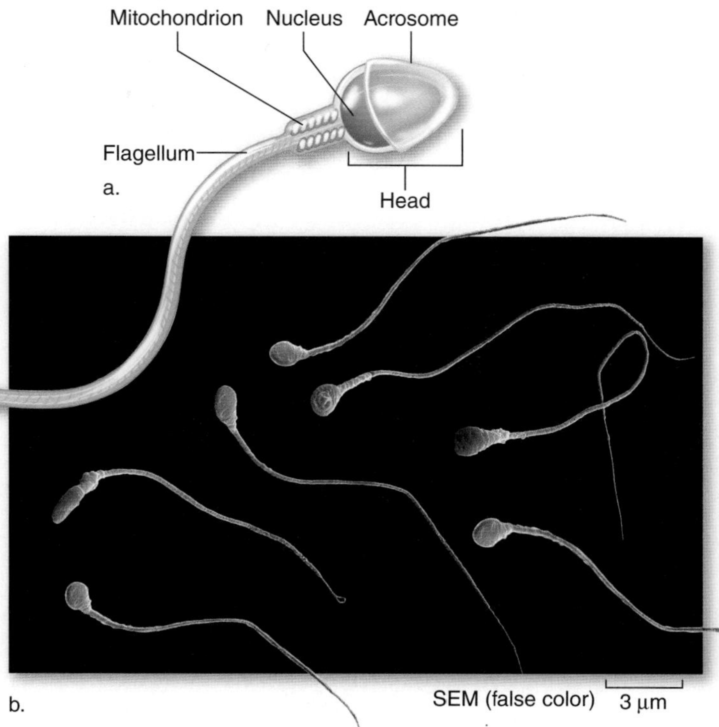

Figure 30.6 Human Sperm. (a) The DNA in a sperm cell is in the nucleus, which enters the egg cell. The long flagellum propels the sperm. (b) Scanning electron micrograph of human sperm cells.

30.2 Mastering Concepts

1. What are the relationships among gonads, germ cells, gametes, and the zygote?
2. Describe the role of each part of the male reproductive system.
3. Where in the testes do sperm develop?
4. What are the stages of spermatogenesis?
5. What are the parts of a mature sperm cell?
6. How do hormones regulate sperm production?

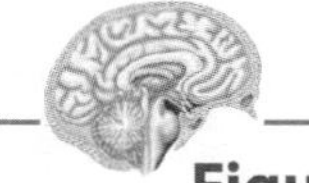

Figure It Out

Suppose that a single ejaculate contains 240 million sperm cells. How many primary spermatocytes must enter meiosis to produce this many sperm cells, and how many secondary spermatocytes are produced along the way?

Answer: 60 million primary spermatocytes; 120 million secondary spermatocytes.

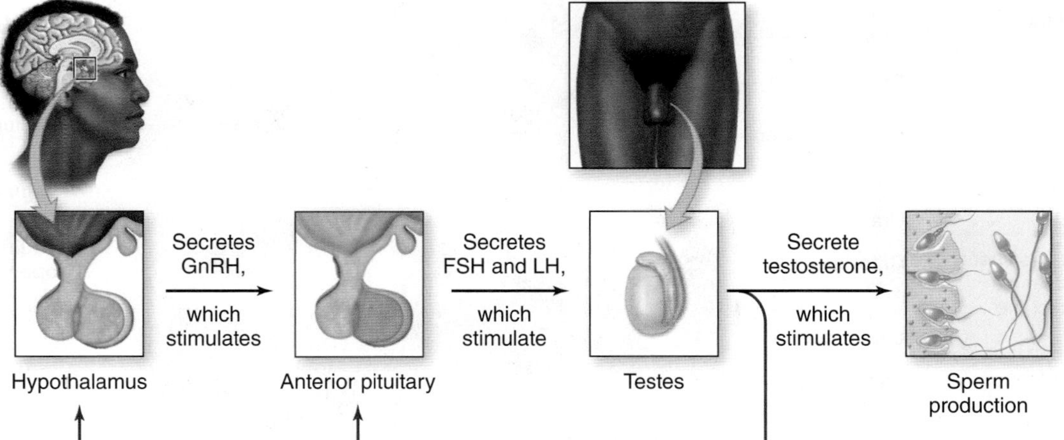

Figure 30.7 Male Reproductive Hormones. Hormones from the hypothalamus initiate a cascade that leads to sperm production in the testes. In a negative feedback loop, testosterone production regulates hormone release from the hypothalamus and anterior pituitary.

30.3 Females Produce Egg Cells

Egg cell production in females is somewhat more complicated than is sperm formation in males for at least two reasons. First, in females, meiosis begins before birth, pauses, and resumes at sexual maturity. Meiosis does not complete until after a sperm cell fertilizes the egg cell. Second, egg cell production is cyclical, under the control of several interacting hormones whose levels fluctuate monthly during a woman's reproductive years. Keep these differences in mind while reading this section.

A. Female Reproductive Organs Are Inside the Body

Female sex cells develop within the **ovaries,** paired gonads in the abdomen (figure 30.8). Ovaries produce both egg cells and sex hormones. They do not contain ducts comparable to the seminiferous tubules of the male's testes. Instead, within each ovary of a newborn female are about a million oocytes, the cells that give rise to mature egg cells. Each oocyte is nestled in a fluid-filled **follicle.**

Approximately once a month, beginning at puberty, one ovary releases the single most mature oocyte. Beating cilia sweep the mature oocyte into the fingerlike projections of one of the two **uterine tubes** (also called fallopian tubes or oviducts). If sperm are present, fertilization occurs in a uterine tube. The tube carries the oocyte or zygote into a muscular saclike organ, the **uterus.** During pregnancy, the fetus develops inside the uterus, also called the womb. The **endometrium,** or inner lining of the uterus, has a rich blood supply that is important in both menstruation and pregnancy.

The **cervix** is the necklike narrowing at the lower end of the uterus. The cervix opens into the **vagina,** the tube that leads outside the body. The vagina receives the

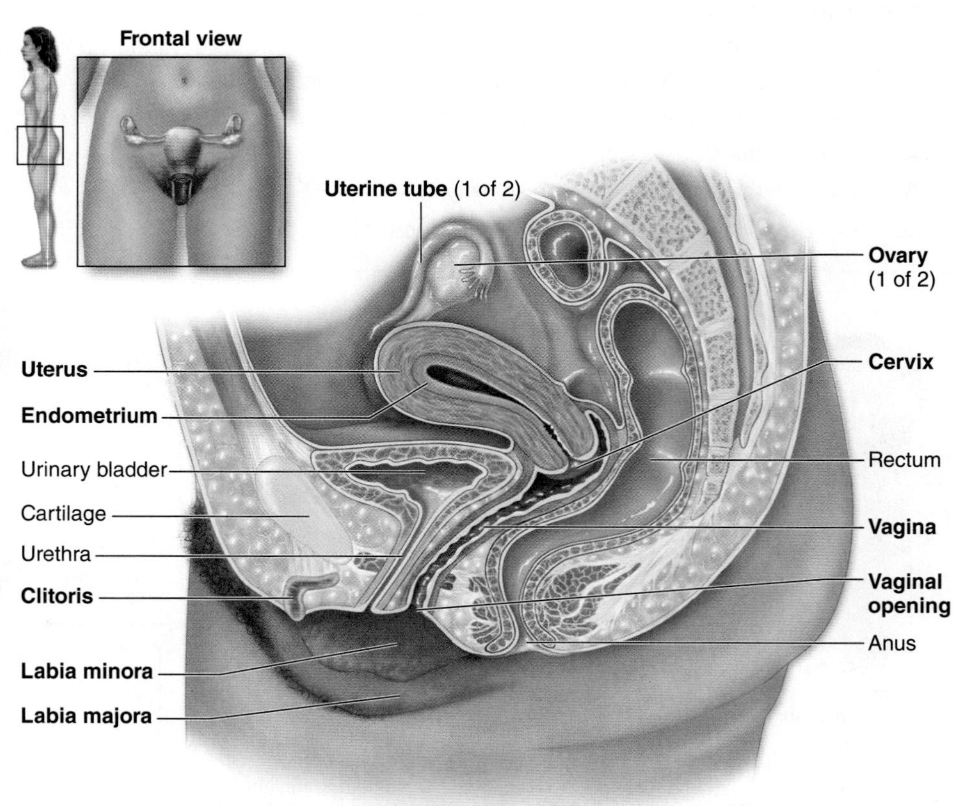

Figure 30.8 The Human Female Reproductive System. One of the two ovaries releases an oocyte each month. This egg cell is drawn into a nearby uterine tube. If a sperm cell fertilizes the oocyte, the offspring develops in the uterus and is delivered through the vagina.

Reproductive System (Female)	
Main tissue types*	**Examples of locations/functions**
Epithelial	Lines uterus, uterine tubes, and vagina; produces oocytes in ovaries; forms external surface of umbilical cord.
Connective	Makes up walls of ovaries, uterus, and vagina.
Nervous	Clitoris contains sensory nerve fibers and nerve endings; hypothalamus secretes hormones that affect the anterior pituitary.
Muscle	Smooth muscle surrounds uterine tubes, uterus, and vagina.

*See chapter 23 for descriptions.

penis during intercourse, and it is also the birth canal. Like many other areas of the body, the vagina harbors a community of resident microorganisms. These bacteria lower the pH of the vagina, which helps keep other microbes—including harmful bacteria and the yeast *Candida albicans*—from taking over. Taking antibiotics can disrupt this microbial community and create an opportunity for *Candida* to overgrow, causing a vaginal yeast infection. ▶ beneficial microbes, p. 286

Two pairs of fleshy folds protect the vaginal opening on the outside: the labia majora (major lips) and the thinner, underlying flaps of tissue they protect, called the labia minora (minor lips). The **clitoris** is a 2-centimeter-long structure at the upper junction of both pairs of labia. Rubbing the clitoris stimulates females to experience orgasm. Together, the labia, clitoris, and vaginal opening constitute the **vulva,** or external female genitalia.

The female secondary sex characteristics include the wider and shallower shape of the pelvis, the accumulation of fat around the hips, a higher pitched voice than that of the male, and the breasts. Each **breast** contains fatty tissue, collagen, and milk ducts. The nipple delivers milk to the nursing infant.

Cancers of the female reproductive system often develop in the breasts, cervix, or ovaries. Breast cancer is the most common cancer type in women. The abnormally dividing cells may originate in the milk-forming tissues or in the milk ducts of the breast. Some, but not all, forms of breast cancer have a strong genetic component. A family history is also the leading risk factor for ovarian cancer, which usually originates in the outer lining of the ovary. In contrast, nearly all cases of cervical cancer are associated with the human papillomavirus (see section 30.4). Pap tests detect the abnormal cells of cervical cancer. In 2006, the U.S. Food and Drug Administration approved for girls and young women a "cervical cancer vaccine" that contains proteins of the human papillomavirus. ▶ vaccines, p. 600

B. Oogenesis Yields Egg Cells

The making of an egg cell—**oogenesis**—begins with a diploid germ cell containing 46 chromosomes (figure 30.9). Each germ cell grows, accumulates cytoplasm, replicates its DNA, and divides mitotically, becoming two **primary oocytes.** The

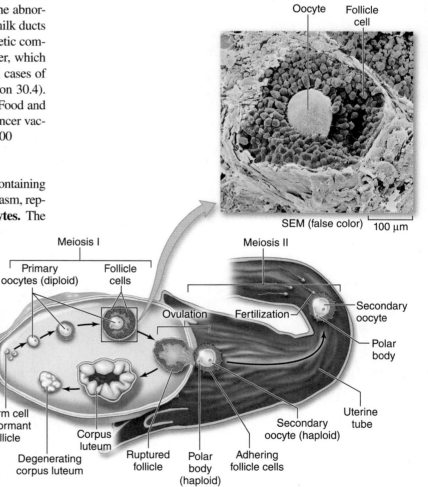

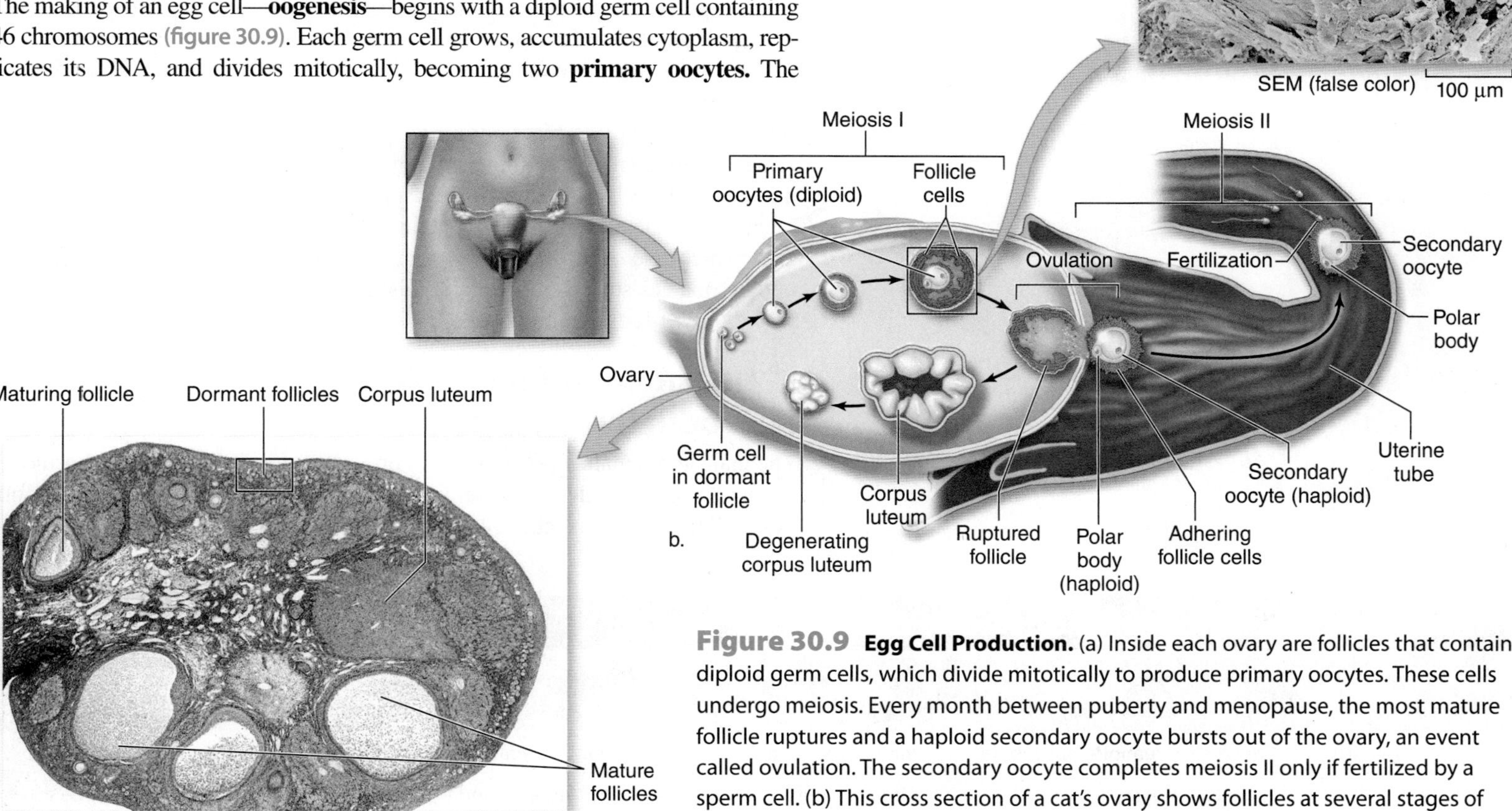

Figure 30.9 Egg Cell Production. (a) Inside each ovary are follicles that contain diploid germ cells, which divide mitotically to produce primary oocytes. These cells undergo meiosis. Every month between puberty and menopause, the most mature follicle ruptures and a haploid secondary oocyte bursts out of the ovary, an event called ovulation. The secondary oocyte completes meiosis II only if fertilized by a sperm cell. (b) This cross section of a cat's ovary shows follicles at several stages of development. The uterine tube is not shown in this photo.

subsequent divisions of meiosis partition the cytoplasm unequally, so that oogenesis (unlike spermatogenesis) produces cells of different sizes. By the end of meiosis I, the primary oocyte has divided into a small haploid **polar body** and a larger haploid **secondary oocyte,** each containing 23 chromosomes.

Ovulation is the release of a secondary oocyte from its follicle. As the follicle ruptures, the egg cell emerges from the ovary's surface and enters the nearby uterine tube. Following ovulation, the now-ruptured follicle transforms into a gland called a **corpus luteum.** Meanwhile, meiosis halts at metaphase II and does not resume unless fertilization occurs. In that case, the secondary oocyte again divides unequally to produce a small additional polar body and the mature haploid egg cell (or ovum), which contains 23 chromosomes and a large amount of cytoplasm. The polar body produced in meiosis I may divide into two additional polar bodies, or it may decompose.

The egg cell, in receiving most of the cytoplasm, contains all of the biochemicals and organelles that the zygote will use until its own DNA begins to function. The polar bodies normally play no further role in development. Rarely, however, sperm can fertilize polar bodies, and a mass of tissue that does not resemble an embryo grows until the woman's body rejects it. A fertilized polar body accounts for about 1 in 100 miscarriages.

From puberty to menopause (the cessation of menstrual periods), monthly hormonal cues prompt an ovary to release one secondary oocyte into a uterine tube. If a sperm penetrates the oocyte membrane, meiosis in the oocyte completes, and the two nuclei combine to form the diploid zygote. If the secondary oocyte is not fertilized, it leaves the body with the endometrium in the menstrual flow.

In some ways, oogenesis is similar to spermatogenesis (table 30.1). Each process starts with a diploid germ cell that eventually gives rise to the haploid gametes. Also, both testes and ovaries contain gametes in various stages of development. Of course, the two processes also differ. For example, spermatogenesis gives rise to four equal-sized sperm cells, whereas in females, one germ cell yields one functional egg cell and three smaller polar bodies.

Also, the timetable for oogenesis differs greatly from that of spermatogenesis. A male takes about 74 days to produce a sperm cell. In contrast, oogenesis stretches from before birth until after puberty. The ovaries of a 3-month-old female fetus contain 2 million or more primary oocytes. From then on, the number declines. At birth, a million primary oocytes are present, their development arrested in prophase I. Only about 400,000 remain by the time of puberty, after which one or a few oocytes complete meiosis I each month. These secondary oocytes stop meiosis again, this time at metaphase II. Meiosis is completed only if fertilization occurs.

C. Hormones Influence Female Reproductive Function

The male and female reproductive systems rely on many of the same hormones (figure 30.10). Females, however, produce these hormones in different quantities and on a different schedule.

TABLE 30.1 Spermatogenesis and Oogenesis Compared

Process	Diploid Starting Cell	Product of Mitosis (Diploid)	Products of Meiosis I (Haploid)	Products of Meiosis II (Haploid)
Spermatogenesis	Germ cell in seminiferous tubule	Primary spermatocyte	Two secondary spermatocytes	Four equal-sized spermatids
Oogenesis	Germ cell in ovary	Primary oocyte	One large secondary oocyte + one small polar body	One large egg cell + three small polar bodies

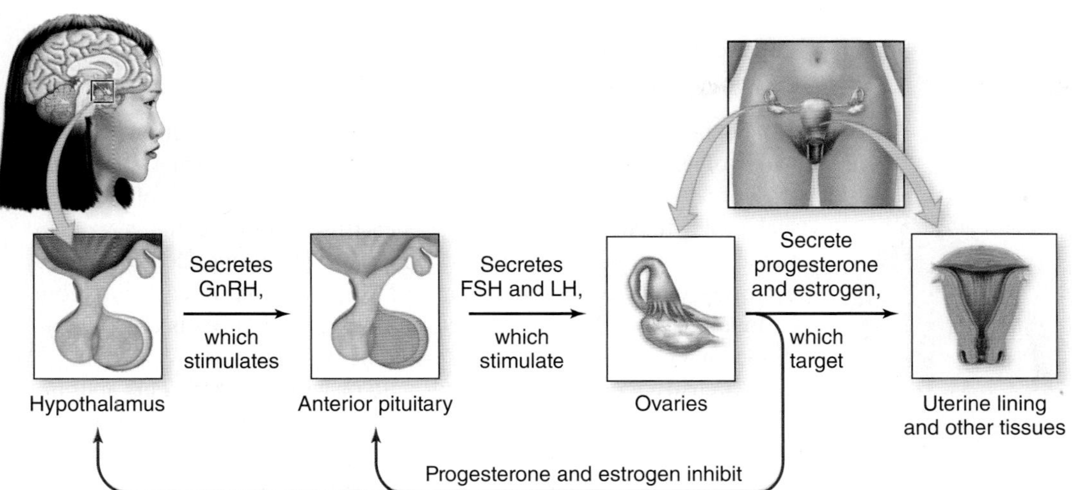

Figure 30.10 Female Reproductive Hormones. Hormones from the hypothalamus initiate a cascade that regulates the activities of the ovaries and the uterine lining. Progesterone and estrogen, in turn, regulate hormone release from the hypothalamus and anterior pituitary in a negative feedback loop.

In females, hormonal fluctuations produce two interrelated cycles. The **ovarian cycle** controls the timing of oocyte maturation in the ovaries, and the **menstrual cycle** prepares the uterus for pregnancy. Figure 30.11 tracks changes in the follicle, the uterine lining, and the levels of four hormones during the ovarian and menstrual cycles.

Menstruation begins on the first day of the menstrual cycle. Low blood levels of two sex hormones, **estrogen** and **progesterone,** signal the hypothalamus to secrete GnRH. This hormone prompts the anterior pituitary to release FSH and LH into the bloodstream. In the ovaries, receptors on the surfaces of follicle cells bind to FSH, stimulating follicles to mature and to release estrogen.

Estrogen has two seemingly contradictory roles in the ovarian cycle. At low concentrations, estrogen inhibits the release of both LH and FSH. But at around day 14 of the cycle, a spike in estrogen accumulation triggers the release of additional LH and FSH from the anterior pituitary. This LH surge in the bloodstream triggers ovulation and transforms the ruptured follicle into a corpus luteum.

The corpus luteum, in turn, secretes progesterone and estrogen, which have multiple effects. These two hormones act together to promote the thickening of the endometrium, preparing the uterus for possible pregnancy. Progesterone and estrogen also feed back to the hypothalamus, inhibiting the production of GnRH, LH, and FSH. Over the next several days, the corpus luteum degenerates into an inactive scar made of collagen.

If pregnancy does not occur, levels of progesterone and estrogen gradually decline (section 30.5 describes what happens if pregnancy does occur). The reduced levels of these hormones no longer maintain the endometrium, which then exits the body through the cervix and vagina as menstrual flow. Lowered progesterone and estrogen levels also release their inhibition of GnRH, LH, and FSH in the brain, and the cycle begins anew.

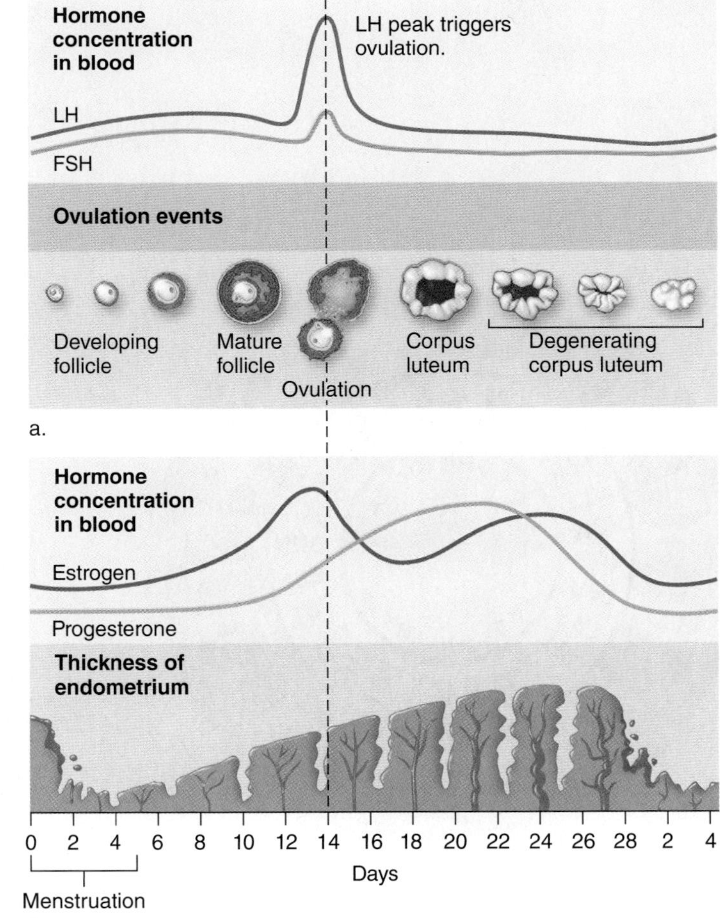

Figure 30.11 The Ovarian and Menstrual Cycles. (a) In the ovarian cycle, elevated concentrations of FSH stimulate follicle maturation. A burst of LH triggers ovulation and converts the follicle into a corpus luteum, which releases estrogen and progesterone. These hormones inhibit LH and FSH production. (b) The menstrual cycle begins with release of the uterine lining. As estrogen rises and ovulation occurs, the endometrium thickens; meanwhile, progesterone prepares the lining for pregnancy. If fertilization does not occur, estrogen and progesterone secretion from the corpus luteum ceases, and the cycle begins anew.

D. Hormonal Fluctuations Can Cause Discomfort

Fluctuating concentrations of hormones trigger a variety of conditions that are unique to women (figure 30.12). One example is premenstrual syndrome (PMS), a collection of symptoms that appears in the second half of the menstrual cycle. In the days before her menstrual period begins, a woman may experience headache, breast tenderness, cramping, depression, irritability, or dozens of other signs of PMS. The cause of each symptom is unknown, but the correlation with hormonal changes is clear. Over-the-counter drugs provide relief from many symptoms.

Menstrual cramps may occur with or without PMS. This abdominal pain arises from smooth muscle contractions in the uterus. The function of these contractions is to help the menstrual fluid exit the uterus; heavy bleeding is correlated with severe cramps.

As a woman nears the end of her reproductive years, her hormonal fluctuations cease. Ironically, the estrogen withdrawal that accompanies menopause can cause symptoms as well. For example, hot flashes affect most women going through menopause. A hot flash, which typically lasts a few minutes, is a temporary sensation of heat in the face and upper body, coupled with flushed skin and sweating. The cause is unknown, but researchers speculate that the withdrawal of estrogen somehow affects the temperature set point of the hypothalamus.

Figure 30.12 Shifting Hormones. Hormonal fluctuations cause premenstrual syndrome, cramps, and hot flashes.

E. Contraceptives Prevent Pregnancy

Pregnancy requires the union of sperm and egg; **contraception** is the use of devices or practices that work "against conception"; that is, they prevent pregnancy. Table 30.2 summarizes some of the most common methods, each of which has advantages and disadvantages.

Besides abstinence, the most effective contraceptives are surgical; next are those that adjust hormone concentrations in the woman's body. Birth control pills, patches, vaginal rings, injections, and implants all contain a synthetic form of progesterone, which mimics the hormonal effects of pregnancy. If used correctly, each of these methods prevents ovulation and therefore precludes fertilization.

Other birth control methods kill sperm, block the meeting of sperm and oocyte, or prevent a developing embryo from implanting in the lining of the uterus. Only latex condoms, however, simultaneously prevent pregnancy and protect against sexually transmitted diseases—the subject of section 30.4.

30.3 Mastering Concepts

1. What is the role of each part of the female reproductive system?
2. Where do egg cells develop?
3. What are the stages of oogenesis?
4. What is the role of polar bodies in oogenesis?
5. How do hormones regulate the ovarian and menstrual cycles?
6. List examples of hormone-induced female problems.
7. Describe some of the most common contraceptives.

TABLE 30.2 Birth Control Methods

Method	Mechanism	Likelihood of Success (%)
Barriers and Spermicides		
Condom and spermicide	Condom keeps sperm out of vagina; spermicide kills sperm that escape	95–98
Diaphragm and spermicide	Blocks cervix and kills sperm	83–97
Hormonal		
Combination birth control pill or patch (estrogen and progesterone)	Prevents ovulation and implantation, thickens cervical mucus	90–100
Minipill (progesterone only)	Blocks implantation, deactivates sperm, thickens cervical mucus	87–100
Subdermal implant (progesterone only)	Prevents ovulation, thickens cervical mucus	99.8
Behavioral		
Rhythm method	No intercourse during fertile times, as inferred from body temperature and other clues	79–87
Withdrawal	Removal of penis from vagina before ejaculation	75–91
Surgical		
Vasectomy	Cuts vas deferentia, so sperm cells never reach urethra	99.85
Tubal ligation	Cuts uterine tubes, so oocytes never reach uterus	99.6
Other		
Intrauterine device, with or without progesterone	Prevents implantation of preembryo	95–99

30.4 Sexual Activity May Transmit Disease

Disease-causing viruses, bacteria, protists, and fungi lurk everywhere: in food, air, water, and, of course, in and on the human body. Some of these microbes cause **sexually transmitted diseases (STDs),** which spread to new hosts during sexual contact. Interestingly, humans are not the only ones to suffer from STDs. Other animal species have STDs of their own; so do plants, which can pass viroids in pollen. ▸ viroids, p. 132

Vaginal intercourse, oral sex, and anal sex all can provide direct, person-to-person transmission for a wide variety of disease-causing agents. Table 30.3 lists a sampling of some of the most common STDs.

In the United States, the most common STD is genital warts, which can be caused by more than 40 strains of the human papillomavirus (HPV). These viruses infect millions of new hosts every year. Many infections remain symptomless, but others trigger the growth of visible bumps on the genitals. Some of these viruses also cause cervical cancer; in fact, nearly all cervical cancer tumors test positive for DNA from HPV.

Another STD that infects millions of people each year is trichomoniasis, caused by a protist called *Trichomonas vaginalis* (see figure 15.26b). Males can transmit this organism, usually without visible symptoms. Infected women may notice unusual vaginal discharge along with pain, irritation, and itching.

Chlamydia, a third common STD, is caused by the bacterium *Chlamydia trachomatis*. Symptoms might include discharge from the penis or vagina and pain or a burning sensation when urinating. Chlamydia, however, is sometimes

TABLE 30.3 Examples of Sexually Transmitted Diseases

Disease	Agent	Treatment
Viruses		
HIV/AIDS	Human immunodeficiency virus (HIV)	Combination of drugs that reduce viral replication
Genital warts	Human papillomavirus (HPV)	Removal of warts
Genital herpes	Herpes simplex virus	Medications that reduce outbreak frequency and duration
Hepatitis B	Hepatitis B virus	None
Bacteria		
Chlamydia	*Chlamydia trachomatis*	Antibiotics
Gonorrhea	*Neisseria gonorrhoeae*	Antibiotics
Syphilis	*Treponema pallidum*	Antibiotics
Protists		
Trichomoniasis	*Trichomonas vaginalis*	Antiprotozoan drugs
Fungi		
Candidiasis	*Candida albicans*	Antifungal drugs

called a "silent disease" because some 75% of infected women and 50% of infected men are symptomless.

Infections with HPV, trichomoniasis, chlamydia, and other agents listed in table 30.3 often remain invisible, but that does not mean they are harmless. For example, in addition to the risk of cervical cancer associated with HPV, untreated chlamydia infections in women can spread to the uterine tubes. Pelvic inflammatory disease, one possible complication, can cause pain and infertility. Moreover, syphilis, gonorrhea, and chlamydia can pass to infants during childbirth.

Most STDs are also associated with an elevated risk for acquiring and transmitting HIV. One explanation is that many STDs cause sores through which viral particles can enter or leave the body. A second reason is that any infection can cause inflammation and other defensive reactions. As described in chapter 29, these responses attract the types of white blood cells that HIV infects. Efforts to prevent STDs in general can therefore also help reduce infections by HIV in particular.

The best way to prevent sexually transmitted diseases is to abstain from any type of sexual activity. The second best way is to develop a long-term, monogamous relationship with a partner who has recently been tested for STDs and is therefore known to be disease-free. The third best way is to properly use a latex condom throughout a sexual encounter. In addition, vaccines can protect against some sexually transmitted viruses, including HPV and hepatitis B.

30.4 Mastering Concepts

1. List and describe three common STDs.
2. Describe two reasons that a symptomless infection with an STD can be harmful.

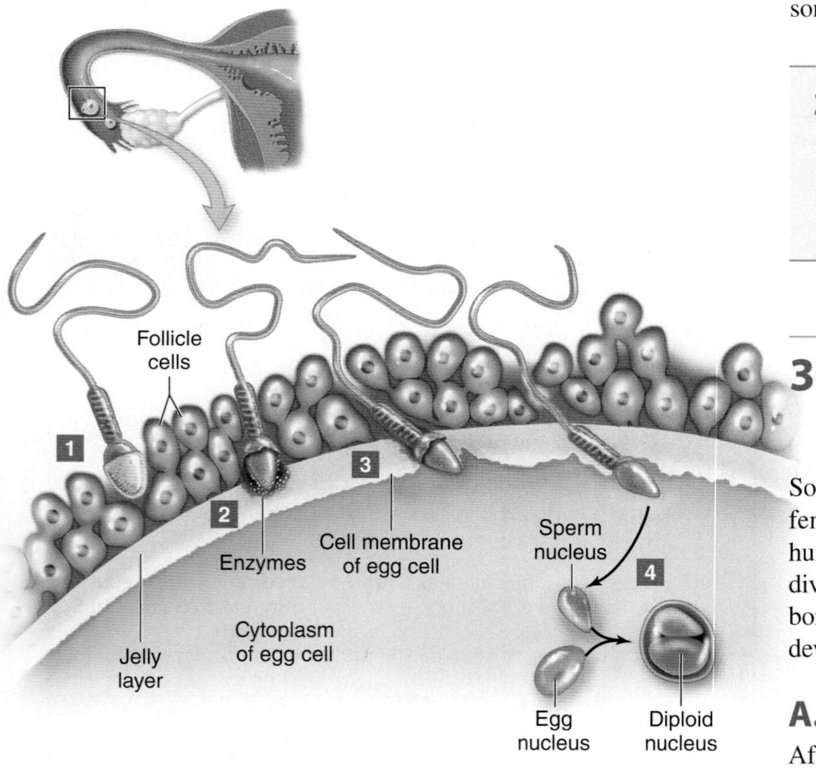

30.5 The Human Infant Begins Life as a Zygote

So far, this chapter has described gamete production in the human male and female reproductive systems. This section now turns to the development of a human baby. As you shall see, fertilization produces the zygote; this single cell divides many times as it develops into a preembryo, embryo, fetus, and newborn baby. The Why We Care box on page 623 explains how problems during development can cause birth defects.

A. Fertilization Initiates Pregnancy

After intercourse, sperm cells swim toward the oocyte. Of the 100 million sperm that begin the journey, only about 200 arrive at the egg cell's location in the uterine tube.

Those that make it must penetrate two layers to contact the ovum. An outer layer of follicle cells surrounds a thin, clear "jelly layer" of proteins and carbohydrates that encases the oocyte (figure 30.13). On contact with the cells surrounding the oocyte, each sperm's acrosome bursts, spilling enzymes that digest the jelly layer.

Fertilization begins when the outer membrane of one sperm cell touches that of the secondary oocyte. At that time, changes across the oocyte surface prevent other sperm from fertilizing the same egg cell. As the sperm's head

Follicle cells
Jelly layer
Enzymes
Cell membrane of egg cell
Cytoplasm of egg cell
Sperm nucleus
Egg nucleus
Diploid nucleus

1 Sperm squeezes between follicle cells adhering to egg cell.

2 Sperm's acrosome bursts, releasing enzymes that digest jelly layer surrounding egg cell.

3 Sperm cell membrane fuses with egg cell membrane.

4 Sperm cell nucleus enters egg cell and fuses with its nucleus.

Figure 30.13 Fertilization. A sperm cell contacts an egg cell, releasing enzymes that help its nucleus enter the oocyte.

TABLE 30.4 Assisted Reproductive Technologies

Technology	Description
Artificial insemination	Donated sperm is placed in a woman's reproductive tract.
Oocyte donation	A donor's oocyte is placed in a woman's reproductive tract with the prospective father's sperm.
In vitro fertilization (IVF)	Sperm fertilizes an oocyte in a laboratory dish; the preembryo is placed in a woman's uterus.
Intracytoplasmic sperm injection (ICSI)	Variant of *in vitro* fertilization in which a sperm cell is injected directly into an egg.
Gamete intrafallopian transfer (GIFT)	Oocytes are collected and placed with sperm into a woman's uterine tube; fertilization occurs in the woman's body.
Zygote intrafallopian transfer (ZIFT)	Sperm fertilizes an oocyte in a laboratory dish; the preembryo is placed in a woman's uterine tube.

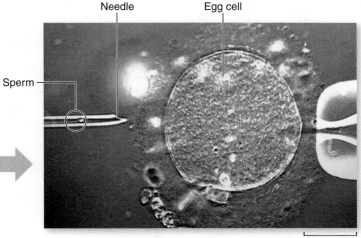

Needle
Egg cell
Sperm
LM 12 μm

enters the secondary oocyte, the sperm's DNA is released. Meanwhile, the female cell completes meiosis. The sperm and egg DNA combine, completing zygote formation. This diploid cell has 23 pairs of chromosomes; one chromosome of each pair comes from each parent. ▸ homologous chromosomes, p. 156

Occasionally a woman ovulates two or more egg cells at once, and a different sperm fertilizes each one. If all the zygotes complete development, the result is twins, triplets, quadruplets, or even higher-order multiple births. Because each zygote results from a separate sperm and egg cell, the siblings will not be genetically identical, and they may be of different sexes. At the opposite end of the spectrum are couples that have trouble conceiving any child at all; table 30.4 lists a few examples of how technology can help. ▸ multiple births, p. 162

B. The Preembryonic Stage Ends with Implantation

The first 2 weeks of prenatal development have a variety of names, but we will call this period the **preembryonic stage.**

About 36 hours after fertilization, the zygote divides for the first time, beginning a period of mitotic cell division called **cleavage** (figure 30.14). The result is a solid ball of 16 or more cells. The mass of cells reaches the uterus 3 to 6 days after fertilization. The ball of cells then hollows out, its center filling with fluid that seeps in from the uterus. This fluid-filled ball of cells is called a **blastocyst.** The few cells inside the blastocyst form the **inner cell mass,** the cells that will develop into the embryo itself. (The inner cell mass is also the source of embryonic stem cells.)

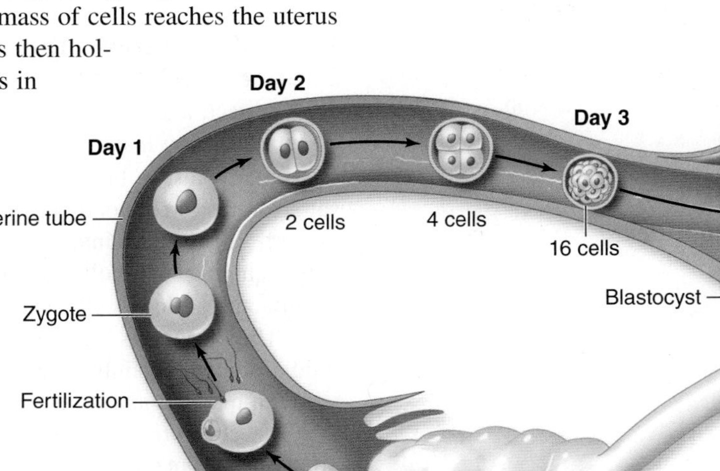

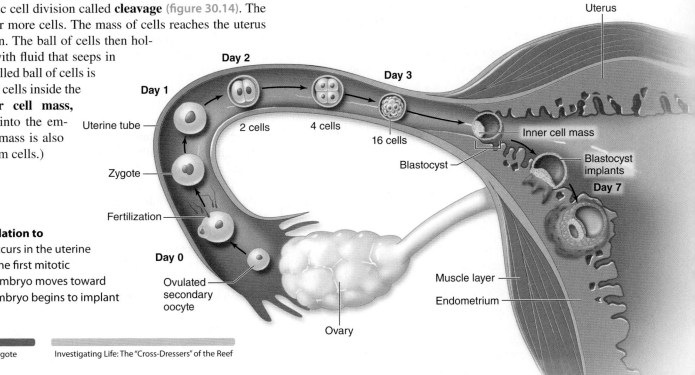

Figure 30.14 From Ovulation to Implantation. Fertilization occurs in the uterine tube, producing the zygote. The first mitotic divisions occur while the preembryo moves toward the uterus. By day 7, the preembryo begins to implant in the uterine lining.

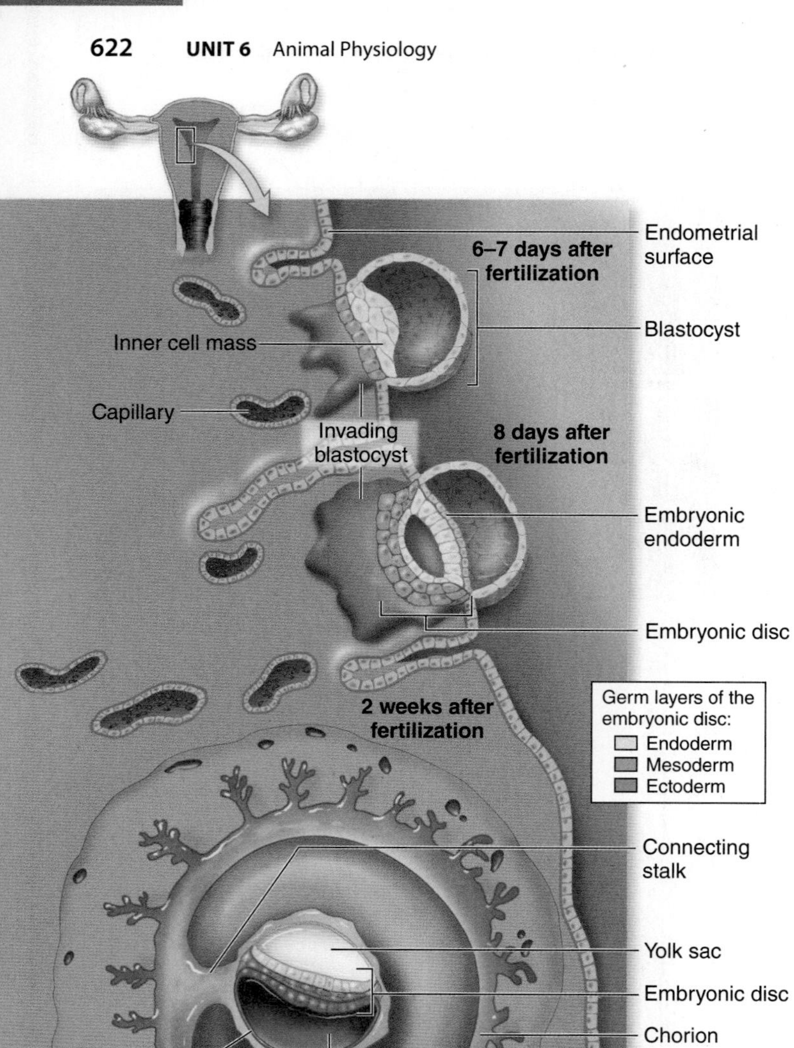

Figure 30.15 Implantation and Gastrulation. About a week after fertilization, the inner cell mass settles against the uterine lining. The blastocyst sends extensions into the endometrium. Meanwhile, the enlarging preembryo begins to fold into the three primary germ layers. Implantation is complete 2 weeks after fertilization.

In a process called **implantation,** the blastocyst becomes embedded in the lining of the uterus (figure 30.15). Implantation occurs within a week of fertilization. The outer layer of the blastocyst not only secretes digestive enzymes that eat through the outer layer of the uterine lining, but it also sends projections into the uterine lining. Until the placenta forms, the preembryo obtains nutrients from these digested endometrial cells. ▸ stem cells, p. 206

The blastocyst now secretes **human chorionic gonadotropin (hCG),** the hormone that is the basis of pregnancy tests. For a while, hCG keeps the cells of the corpus luteum producing progesterone, which prevents menstruation and further ovulation. In this way, the blastocyst helps to ensure its own survival; if the uterine lining were shed, the blastocyst would leave the woman's body, too. The blastocyst produces hCG for about 10 weeks.

During the second week of development, the blastocyst completes implantation. A space called the amniotic cavity forms within a sac called the amnion (see figure 30.15). The inner cell mass flattens and forms the **embryonic disc,** which will develop into the embryo.

As the preembryo continues to develop, one layer of the embryonic disc becomes **ectoderm,** and an inner layer becomes **endoderm.** Soon, a middle **mesoderm** layer forms from the ectoderm. (As you will see, each of these layers develops into different organs during the embryonic stage.) The **gastrula** is the resulting three-layered structure. The formation of the gastrula is called gastrulation, and its start marks the end of the preembryonic stage at about 2 weeks postfertilization (see figure 30.15). Although the woman has not yet missed her menstrual period, she might notice effects of her shifting hormones, such as swollen, tender breasts and fatigue. By now, her urine contains enough hCG for an at-home pregnancy test to detect. ▸ germ layers, p. 325

The preembryo may split during the first 2 weeks of development, forming identical twins. Depending on when the split occurs, the twins may or may not share the same amnion and placenta; the later the split, the more structures the twins will share. If a preembryo splits after day 12 of pregnancy, the twins are unlikely to separate completely, and they may be conjoined.

C. Organs Take Shape During the Embryonic Stage

The **embryonic stage** lasts from the end of the second week until the end of the eighth week. During this stage of development, cells in all three layers continue to divide and differentiate, forming the body's organs.

Four Membranes, the Placenta, and the Umbilical Cord Support the Embryo Four thin layers of tissue, called membranes, support, protect, and nourish the embryo. Their presence is an important clue to our evolutionary history because each occurs not only in humans but also in other mammals, in birds, and in nonavian reptiles. One membrane, the **yolk sac,** manufactures blood cells until about the sixth week; in addition, parts of the yolk sac develop into the intestines and germ cells. By the third week, an outpouching of the yolk sac forms the **allantois,** another membrane. It, too, manufactures blood cells, and it gives rise to blood vessels in the umbilical cord. The **amnion** is the transparent sac that contains the amniotic fluid. This fluid cushions the embryo, allows it to shift its position, and maintains a constant temperature and pressure. ▸ amnion, p. 340

The **chorion** is the outermost membrane. **Chorionic villi** are fingerlike projections from the chorion that extend into the uterine lining. These structures establish the beginning of the **placenta,** a structure that will connect the developing embryo with its mother's uterus (figure 30.16). One side of the placenta comes from the embryo; the other side consists of endometrial tissue and blood from the pregnant woman's circulation. Cells collected from amniotic fluid, or sampled chorionic villi cells, are used in many prenatal medical tests.

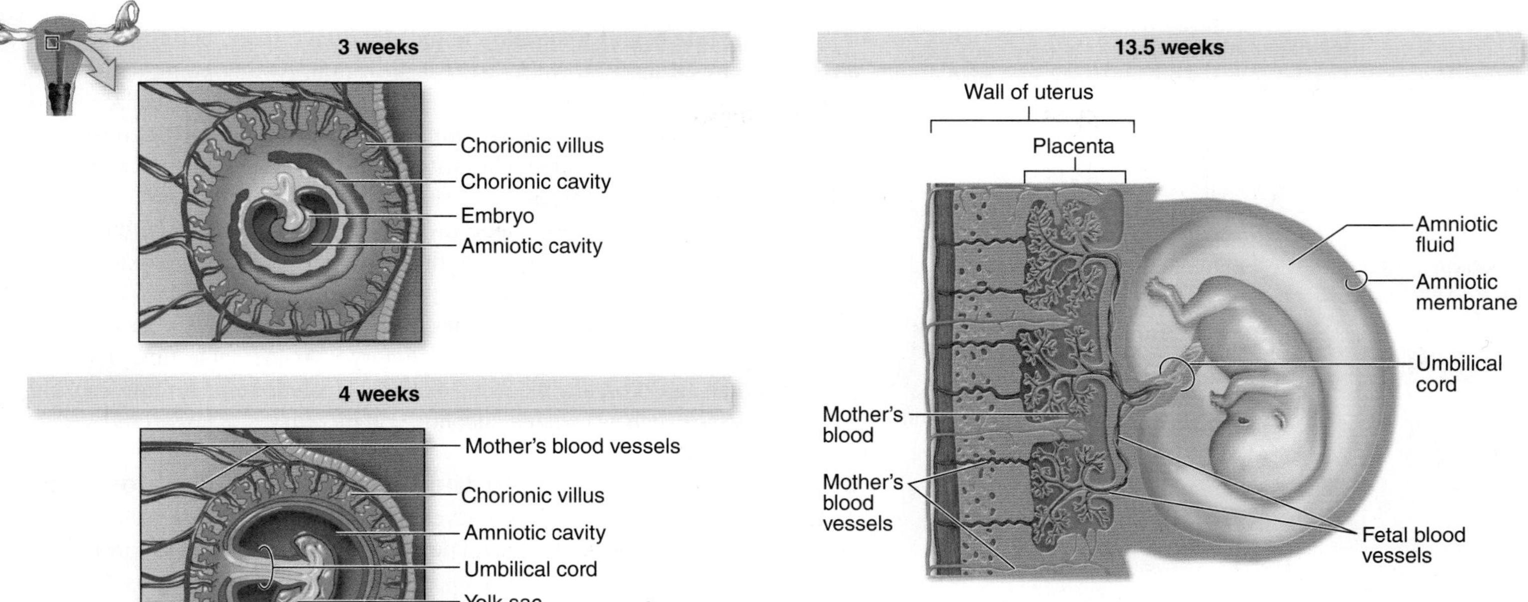

Figure 30.16 Development of the Placenta. As an embryo develops, it produces chorionic villi that extend into the uterine lining. Eventually, blood vessels from the embryo grow into the chorionic villi and exchange materials with pools of maternal blood across a thin membrane.

Why We Care | Birth Defects

About 97% of newborns are apparently normal, but birth defects occasionally occur. A birth defect is any abnormality that causes death or disability in a child. About two thirds of birth defects stem from a disruption during the embryonic period, because developing organs are especially sensitive to damage. The brain is vulnerable throughout prenatal development; this sensitivity explains why many birth defect syndromes include mental retardation.

Listed below are a few examples of conditions that can cause birth defects.

- **Alcohol:** A child with fetal alcohol syndrome has impaired intellect, ranging from minor learning disabilities to mental retardation. Physicians therefore advise all pregnant women to avoid alcohol.
- **Caffeine:** The caffeine in coffee, tea, soft drinks, and chocolate constricts blood vessels in the placenta, reducing blood flow to the fetus. Caffeine also crosses the placenta and accumulates in the fetal brain. Heavy caffeine consumption during pregnancy is associated with low birth weight and a small head size in the newborn.
- **Cigarettes:** Smoking during pregnancy increases the risk of miscarriage, stillbirth, and prematurity. Carbon monoxide from cigarette smoke crosses the placenta and robs the fetus of oxygen.
- **Illicit drugs:** A pregnant woman's use of cocaine, heroin, methamphetamine, and other illicit drugs is associated with poor fetal growth and low birth weight.
- **Prescription drugs:** Some prescription drugs cause birth defects. During the late 1950s, for example, physicians prescribed thalidomide as a treatment for morning sickness in pregnant women. The drug caused severe limb shortening in the children of these women (figure 30.A).
- **Excess or insufficient vitamins:** Too much vitamin A can cause miscarriages and defects of the heart, nervous system, and face. Vitamin deficiencies can also cause birth defects. Spina bifida, for example, is associated with insufficient folic acid in the mother's diet. ▸ vitamins, p. 569
- **Starvation:** Inadequate nutrition during pregnancy increases the incidence of miscarriage and damages the placenta, causing low birth weight, short stature, tooth decay, delayed sexual development, learning disabilities, and possibly mental retardation. Starvation while in the uterus greatly raises the risk of developing obesity, type 2 diabetes, and other conditions later in life. ▸ starvation, p. 571
- **Viral infection:** HIV infects 15% to 30% of infants born to HIV-positive women. Fetuses infected with HIV are at risk for low birth weight, prematurity, and stillbirth. In addition, the virus that causes rubella (German measles) causes deafness, cataracts, and heart disease; herpes simplex viruses can infect the fetal nervous system and cause neurological disabilities such as mental retardation or cerebral palsy.

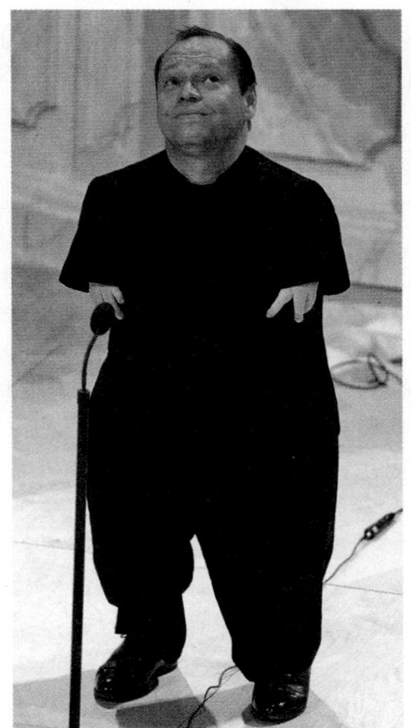

Figure 30.A The Effects of Thalidomide. The limb bones in Grammy award-winning baritone Thomas Quasthoff's arms and legs are unusually short, and his hands resemble flippers. His mother took thalidomide to combat morning sickness early in pregnancy.

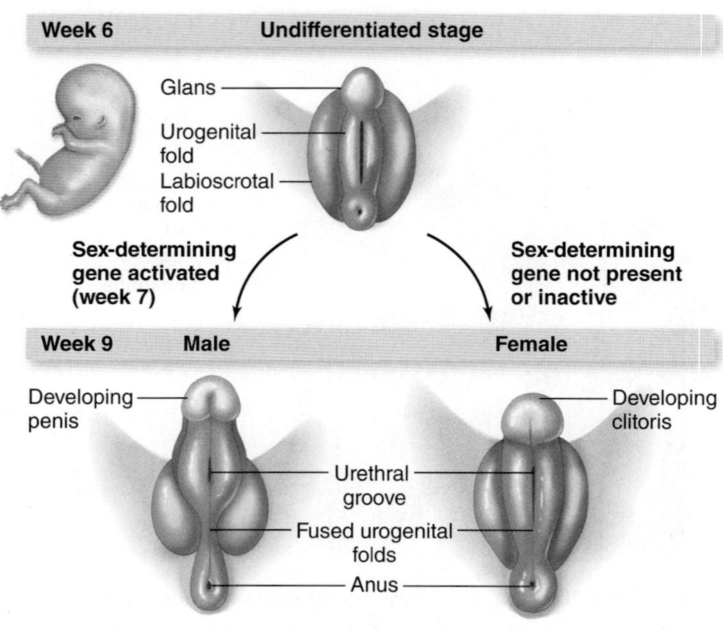

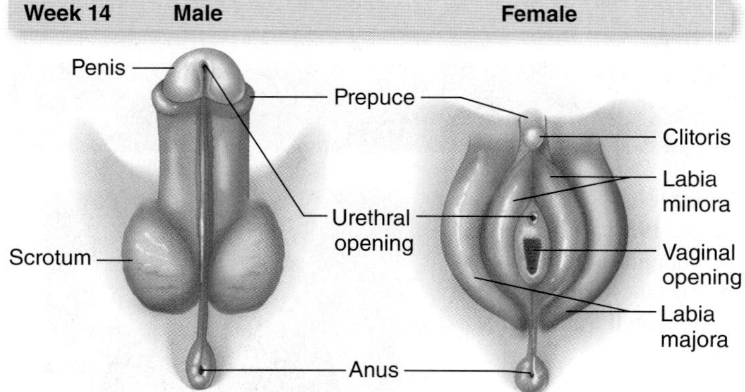

Figure 30.17 Development of Male and Female Genitalia. Until about week 7 of development, embryos have undifferentiated sex organs. If the sex-determining gene on the Y chromosome is activated, development continues as a male. Otherwise, female genitals develop.

The placenta begins to develop in the embryonic stage, but it is not completely developed until 10 weeks after fertilization. At that point, substances can diffuse across the chorionic villi cells between the woman's circulatory system and the fetus. Arteries and veins in the **umbilical cord** connect the embryo or fetus to the placenta. Umbilical cord blood is a rich source of stem cells used to treat an ever-expanding list of disorders.

The placenta blocks most large proteins and red blood cells, but many other substances can cross between mother and embryo. Carbon dioxide, urea, and other wastes from the embryo pass to the mother's blood. Glucose, amino acids, oxygen, ions, and some antibodies from the mother travel in the opposite direction, nourishing and protecting the embryo. At the same time, harmful substances can also cross the placenta; examples include some disease-causing agents and drugs such as cocaine, alcohol, and nicotine.

Organ Formation Begins in the Third Week of Development

As the placenta and umbilical cord develop, so does the embryo itself. Beginning during the third week of prenatal development, distinct organs form. Over several months, ectoderm cells develop into the nervous system, sense organs, outer skin layers, hair, nails, and skin glands. Splits in the mesoderm form the coelom, which becomes the chest and abdominal cavities. Mesoderm cells develop into bone, muscle, blood, the inner skin layer, and the reproductive organs. Endoderm cells form the organs of the digestive and respiratory systems. ▸ coelom, p. 326

Between the third and the fifth week after fertilization, many changes shape the organ systems of the developing embryo. The ectoderm differentiates into the central nervous system. At about the same time, a reddish bulge containing the heart appears; it begins to beat around day 22. Blood cells begin to form and to fill developing blood vessels. Immature lungs and kidneys appear. Small buds appear that will develop into arms and legs. The embryo also develops a distinct head and jaw and early evidence of eyes, ears, and nose. A woman carrying this embryo, which is now only about 6 millimeters long, may suspect that she is pregnant because her menstrual period is about 2 weeks late.

All early embryos have unspecialized reproductive structures. At week 7, however, a sex-determining gene on the Y chromosome is activated in male embryos. Hormones then begin to stimulate development of male reproductive organs and glands. If there is no Y chromosome (or if the sex-determining gene never switches on), female reproductive structures develop (figure 30.17). Overall, many enzymes and membrane proteins participate in sex determination. This chapter's Burning Question describes how abnormalities in these molecules cause a condition called intersex.

During the seventh and eighth weeks, a cartilage skeleton appears. The placenta is now almost fully formed and functional, secreting estrogen and progesterone that maintain the blood-rich uterine lining. The embryo is about the size and weight of a paper clip. By the end of the eighth week, all organ systems are in place, and the embryonic stage of prenatal development is complete. The offspring is now a fetus.

D. Organ Systems Become Functional in the Fetal Stage

The third stage of prenatal development is the **fetal stage,** lasting from the beginning of the ninth week through the full 38 weeks of development. The fetal stage therefore begins near the end of the first trimester (3-month period) of pregnancy and ends 9 months after fertilization. During this time, the fetus grows considerably (figure 30.18). Organs begin to function and coordinate, forming organ systems.

As the first trimester progresses, the body proportions of the fetus begin to appear more like those of a newborn. Bone begins to form and will eventually replace most of the cartilage, which is softer. Soon, as nerves and muscles begin to coordinate their actions, the fetus will move its arms and legs. Physical differences between the sexes are usually detectable by ultrasound after the twelfth week. From this time, the fetus sucks its thumb, kicks, and makes fists and faces, and baby teeth begin to form in the gums. More than half of all pregnant women experience the nausea and vomiting of morning sickness in their first trimester.

During the second trimester, body proportions become even more like those of a newborn. By the fourth month, the fetus has hair, eyebrows, lashes, nipples, and nails. Bone continues to replace the cartilage skeleton. The fetus's muscle movements become stronger, and the woman may begin to feel a slight fluttering in her abdomen. By the end of the fifth month, the fetus curls into the classic head-to-knees position. As the second trimester ends, the woman feels distinct kicks and jabs and may even detect a fetal hiccup. The fetus is now about 30 centimeters long.

In the final trimester, fetal brain cells rapidly connect into networks, and organs differentiate further and grow. A layer of fat develops beneath the skin. The digestive and respiratory systems mature last, which is why infants born prematurely often have difficulty digesting milk and breathing. The fetus may move vigorously, causing back pain and frequent urination in the woman as it presses against her bladder. About 266 days (38 weeks) after a single sperm burrowed into an oocyte, a baby is ready to be born.

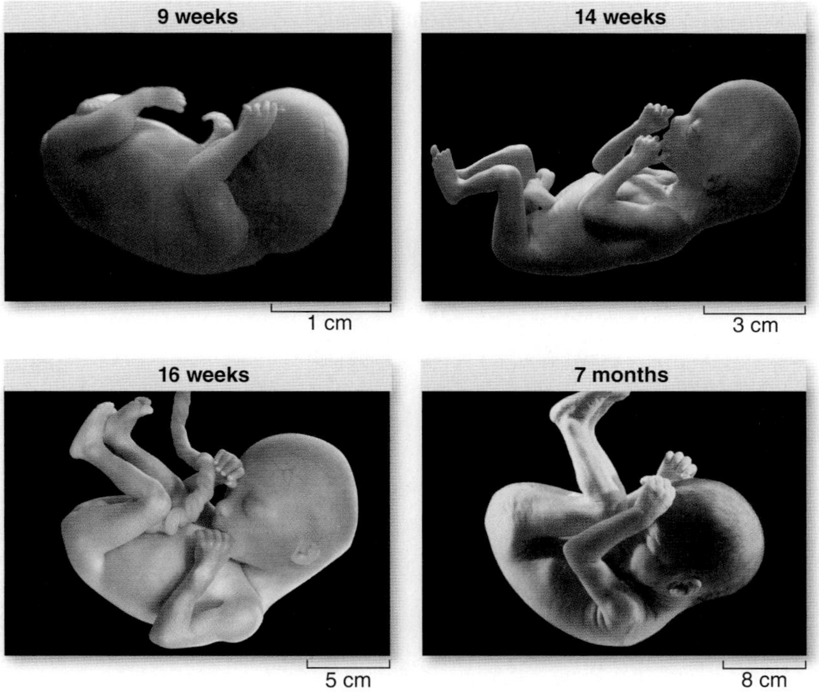

9 weeks

1 cm

14 weeks

3 cm

16 weeks

5 cm

7 months

8 cm

Figure 30.18 **The Fetal Stage.** These photographs show the development of a fetus from 9 weeks to 7 months after fertilization.

E. Muscle Contractions in the Uterus Drive Childbirth

A pregnant woman performs strenuous work in the hours before a child is born, which explains why the process of giving birth is called **labor.** The first sign of labor may be an abrupt leaking of amniotic fluid as the fetus presses down and ruptures the amniotic sac ("water breaking"). Labor may also begin with a discharge of blood and mucus from the vagina, or a woman may feel mild contractions in her lower abdomen about every 20 minutes.

Burning Questions

Do human hermaphrodites exist?

Many people believe that there are just two kinds of people: males and females. But the truth is considerably more interesting. After all, the development of the genitals depends on interactions among multiple genes, hormones, and embryonic tissues. Any error in this complex sequence of events can lead to unexpected results.

In a child conceived as a boy, genes on the Y chromosome signal the embryonic gonads to produce testosterone and other masculinizing hormones (androgens). If cells in the early embryo have a membrane receptor that binds to the androgens, the fetus develops normal male genitals. Sometimes, however, a child inherits a mutated version of the gene encoding the receptor. The gonads produce androgens, but the target tissues cannot bind to the hormones because the receptor is misshapen or absent. This condition, called androgen insensitivity syndrome, has varying degrees of severity. The child (conceived as a male) may develop genitals that are ambiguous or appear female.

Androgen insensitivity syndrome is just one of many so-called *intersex* conditions, in which a person's anatomy does not match the "standard" male or female. Others include 5-alpha reductase deficiency, Klinefelter syndrome, and Turner syndrome. Intersex conditions affect people who are genetically male (XY) or female (XX) or who have sex chromosome abnormalities (such as XO or XXY). ▸ sex chromosome abnormalities, p. 166

Although it is tempting to confuse the terms *intersex* and *hermaphrodite,* they are not the same. A true hermaphrodite, such as an earthworm, has both male and female reproductive organs. In humans, such a condition is exceedingly uncommon; when it does occur, the gonads rarely if ever function.

Submit your burning question to:
marielle_hoefnagels@mcgraw-hill.com

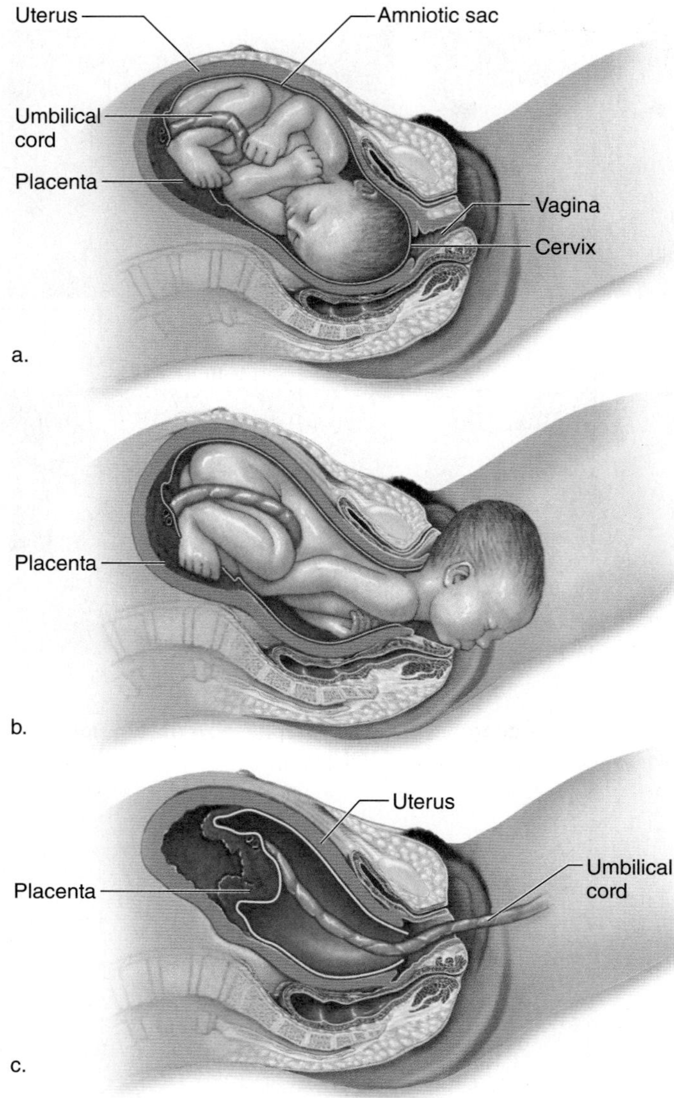

Figure 30.19 Childbirth. (a) About 2 weeks before birth, the fetus "drops" in the woman's pelvis, and the cervix may begin to dilate. (b) At the onset of labor, the amniotic sac may break as the baby begins to emerge. (c) The baby is pushed out of the birth canal, followed by the placenta.

As labor proceeds, hormones prompt the smooth muscle that makes up the wall of the uterus to contract with increasing frequency and intensity. During the first stage of labor, the cervix dilates (opens) a little more each time the baby's head presses against it. By the end of the first stage of labor, the cervix stretches open to about 10 centimeters. The second stage of labor is delivery (figure 30.19), during which the baby typically descends head-first through the cervix and vagina. In the third and last stage of labor, the uterus expels the placenta.

The events of childbirth illustrate **positive feedback,** in which a process reinforces itself (as opposed to negative feedback, in which a process counteracts an existing condition). At the onset of labor, the cervix begins to stretch. Sensory receptors at the cervix relay the message to the hypothalamus, which triggers release of the hormone oxytocin from the posterior pituitary. Oxytocin travels in the bloodstream and stimulates muscles in the uterus to contract, pushing the baby out (for this reason, physicians sometimes use synthetic oxytocin to induce labor). As the baby emerges, the cervix stretches farther and stimulates more oxytocin production, which intensifies the uterine contractions, and so on. When the baby is born, other hormonal changes stop the cycle.

Not all births go according to plan. For example, about 3% of babies have a "breech presentation," in which the baby's feet, knees, or buttocks appear first instead of the head. Breech deliveries are more difficult than head-first deliveries and account for some cesarean sections ("C-sections"). In this procedure, a surgeon removes the child from the uterus through an incision in the abdomen. About one fourth of all babies in the United States are delivered by cesarean section, either by choice or because the life of the mother or baby is at risk.

Sometimes, a pregnancy ends with a premature birth. An infant is premature if it is born before completing 35 weeks (about 8 months) of gestation. A fetus born before 22 weeks of gestation is not viable, but babies born after that time may survive. Premature infants are at risk for many health problems, so they typically spend their first weeks or months in incubators at a neonatal intensive care unit. The incubators control the temperature and protect the infants from infection.

30.5 Mastering Concepts

1. What are the events of fertilization?
2. What are the relationships among the zygote, blastocyst, inner cell mass, and gastrula?
3. What is implantation, and when does it occur?
4. Which supportive structures develop during the embryonic period? What are their functions?
5. When do sex differences appear, and what triggers them?
6. What are the events of the second and third trimesters?
7. Which events make up the three stages of labor?

Investigating Life

30.6 The "Cross-Dressers" of the Reef

Across the animal kingdom, many paths lead to reproductive success. For example, bighorn sheep battle head-to-head to determine which will win the exclusive "right" to mate with a female. But fighting ability is not the only way to measure fitness. If a female mates with many males in a short period, the competition shifts to a much smaller field: her reproductive tract. Only one sperm will fertilize each egg cell. Which will it be?

Sometimes, numbers decide the winner. Males that produce the most sperm are most likely to fertilize an egg cell, just as the owner of several raffle tickets has a better chance of winning a prize than someone who buys only one. But behavior also often plays a role. In some species, for example, a male may try to block other males from approaching a female he has already mated with; in effect, the male prevents his rivals from buying raffle tickets. Males also do the equivalent of destroying raffle tickets that others have purchased. That is, they remove other males' sperm before depositing their own.

Sperm competition has selected for unusual behavioral adaptations in a squidlike mollusk called the Australian giant cuttlefish *(Sepia apama)*. These animals, which grow to nearly a meter long, usually live alone. During the winter mating season, however, they congregate by the hundreds of thousands on the reefs of southern Australia. ▸ mollusks, p. 330

The two cuttlefish sexes look different from each other (figure 30.20). A female has shorter arms than a male, and her skin has dark patches on a white background. The male's arms are longer and whiter, and he displays moving patterns of zebralike stripes on his skin during courtship rituals.

When a female accepts a male's mating attempt, the two animals align head-to-head, and he inserts a sperm packet into a pouch near her mouth. He also tries to flush out the sperm packets that other males have deposited. After mating, she retreats to her den. She removes eggs, one by one, from her mantle cavity and passes each through her sperm pouch to be fertilized.

The Question: With a sex ratio of at least four males to every female, the competition for mates is fierce. What reproductive strategies has natural selection favored in male cuttlefish?

The Approach: A study led by Marié-Jose Naud of Australia's Flinders University and Roger Hanlon of the Marine Biological Laboratory at Woods Hole, Massachusetts, showed that mate-guarding is one successful strategy. That is, the largest males mate with females and guard them afterward, fighting off rivals to prevent subsequent insemination of their mates. Direct observation, followed by DNA analysis, revealed that males who guarded a female for up to 40 minutes after mating fertilized significantly more eggs than those who guarded for less than 20 minutes (figure 30.21).

Nevertheless, smaller males do get to mate. How do they gain access to females? A team of Australian biologists, led by Mark Norman, noticed that some males are female impersonators. A small male can disguise himself as a female by hiding the arms that reveal his sex and changing his skin color. (The ploy is so realistic that other males, including other female impersonators, often try to mate with the mimic.) Norman's team observed more than 20 examples of sexual mimicry, but they were unable to tell how often mimics slipped past a guard, approached a female, mated, and successfully fertilized eggs.

Hanlon, Naud, and their colleagues began to answer these questions. They videotaped cuttlefish sexual encounters on the reef, but they also used DNA analysis to determine which male fathered each female's first laid egg (figure 30.22). They found that impersonators deceived a guarding male and approached a female about 30 times out of 62 attempts. Five of the 30 mimics tried to mate with the female. The guard male interrupted one attempt, and the female rejected another, but three were successful. DNA analysis showed that two of these three female impersonators fertilized the first egg laid after mating. The third did not. Because females store sperm, however, the team could not rule out the possibility that sperm from the third mimic fertilized a subsequent egg.

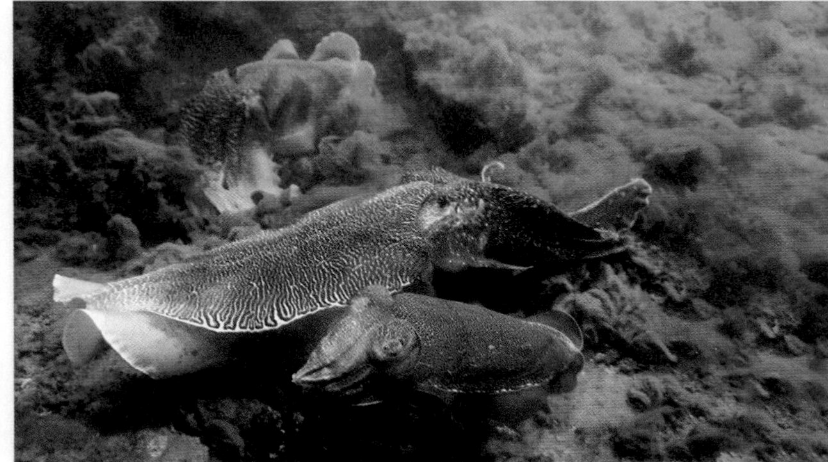

Figure 30.20 The Australian Giant Cuttlefish. In this species, males are substantially larger than females.

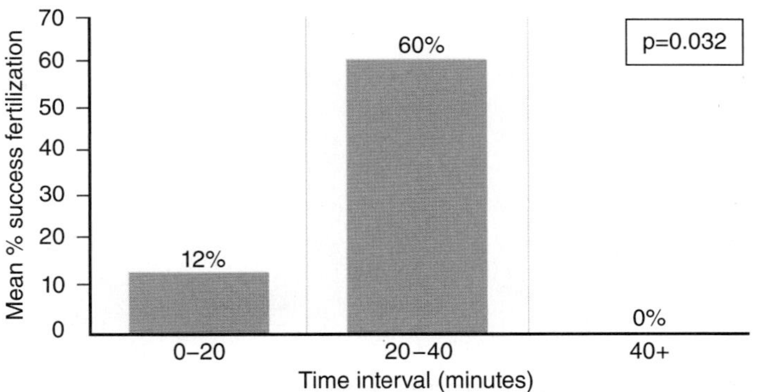

Figure 30.21 Mate Guarding Works. Researchers timed the mate-guarding activities of 22 male cuttlefish and used DNA to determine the paternity of the resulting fertilized eggs. On average, males who guarded their mates from 20 to 40 minutes (n=10) had greater reproductive success than those who guarded for less than 20 minutes (n=8) or more than 40 minutes (n=4). The P-value indicates that these values are significantly different from one another.

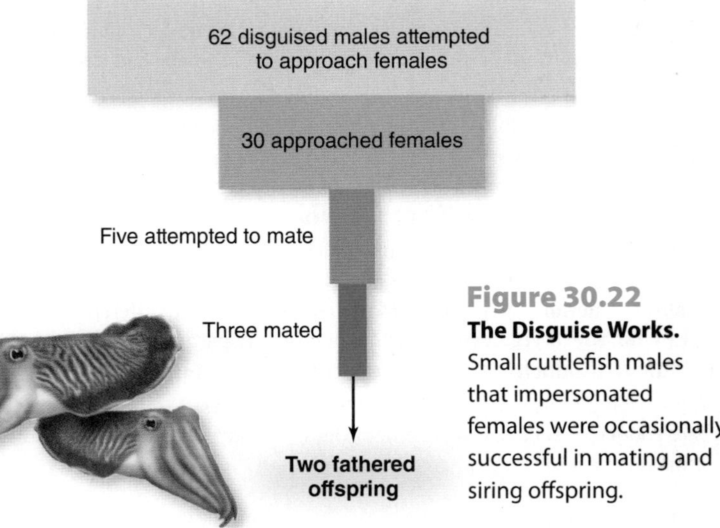

Figure 30.22 The Disguise Works. Small cuttlefish males that impersonated females were occasionally successful in mating and siring offspring.

The Conclusion: Even within the same species, there may be more than one path to reproductive success. In polygamous animals such as the cuttlefish, natural selection favors the male with the most successful sperm—and he may not be the largest or the strongest individual. True, the browniest males can fight off rivals and preserve their own access to a female, but the fierce competition and constant distractions often leave females with additional mating opportunities. A small male has little chance of winning a head-to-head competition with a larger rival, but he does have another tool—deception. Thanks to his changeable skin, even a small cuttlefish has a shot at winning in the great raffle of life.

Hanlon, Roger T., Marié-Jose Naud, Paul W. Shaw, and Jonathan N. Havenhand. 2005. Transient sexual mimicry leads to fertilization. *Nature,* vol. 433, page 212.

Naud, Marié-Jose, Roger T. Hanlon, Karina C. Hall, et al. 2004. Behavioural and genetic assessment of reproductive success in a spawning aggregation of the Australian giant cuttlefish, *Sepia apama. Animal Behaviour,* vol. 67, pages 1043–1050.

Norman, Mark D., Julian Finn, and Tom Tregenza. 1999. Female impersonation as an alternative reproductive strategy in giant cuttlefish. *Proceedings of the Royal Society of London B.,* vol. 266, pages 1347–1349.

30.6 Mastering Concepts

1. List two questions that Hanlon and Naud investigated.
2. How would you test the hypothesis that the offspring of a mate-guarding male is more likely to guard his mate than the offspring of a "sneaker" male? What does this hypothesis assume about the inheritance of mate guarding?

Chapter Summary

30.1 Animal Development Begins with Reproduction

A. Reproduction Is Asexual or Sexual

- **Asexual reproduction** does not require a partner and yields identical offspring.
- In **sexual reproduction,** two haploid **gametes** unite and form a **zygote,** the first cell of a new offspring. **Fertilization** may occur in the environment **(external fertilization)** or inside an animal's body **(internal fertilization).**

B. Development Is Indirect or Direct

- Development requires **differentiation,** the formation of specialized cells. In **pattern formation,** the animal takes on its overall shape and structure.
- Animals that undergo **indirect development** have a **larva** stage that does not resemble the adult. **Metamorphosis** transforms the larva into an adult.
- In **direct development,** young animals resemble miniature adults.

30.2 Males Produce Sperm Cells

- The **reproductive systems** of both males and females include **gonads,** which house the **germ cells** that give rise to gametes. Other sex organs deliver or nurture the gametes. Males and females have different **secondary sex characteristics,** features that do not directly participate in reproduction.

A. Male Reproductive Organs Are Inside and Outside the Body

- Developing sperm originate within the paired **testes.** Also inside the testes are endocrine cells that secrete hormones. A pouch called the **scrotum** contains the testes.
- Sperm travel through the **epididymis, vas deferens,** and **ejaculatory duct,** then they exit the body with **semen** through the **urethra** (within the **penis**) during **orgasm** and **ejaculation.**
- The **prostate gland** and **seminal vesicles** add secretions to semen.

B. Spermatogenesis Yields Sperm Cells

- **Spermatogenesis** occurs in the **seminiferous tubules** of the testes. The process begins with a diploid germ cell, which divides mitotically to yield a stem cell and a **primary spermatocyte.** The first meiotic division produces two haploid **secondary spermatocytes.** In meiosis II, the secondary spermatocytes divide, yielding four **spermatids.** The spermatids develop into mature sperm cells.
- A mature sperm cell has a flagellum and a head that contains the chromosomes. A caplike **acrosome** covers the head.

C. Hormones Influence Male Reproductive Function

- **Gonadotropin-releasing hormone (GnRH)** from the hypothalamus stimulates the anterior pituitary gland to release **follicle-stimulating hormone (FSH)** and **luteinizing hormone (LH).** In males, these hormones affect the testes, triggering the release of **testosterone** necessary for sperm formation and the development of secondary sex characteristics.

30.3 Females Produce Egg Cells

A. Female Reproductive Organs Are Inside the Body

- Egg cells (and their nourishing **follicle cells**) originate in the **ovaries.** Each month after puberty, an egg cell emerges from an ovary. The **uterine tube** collects the egg cell and delivers it to the **uterus.** A blood-rich

endometrium lines the inside of the uterus. The **cervix** leads to the **vagina,** which connects the uterus with the outside of the body.

- The **vulva,** or external genitalia, consists of the labia, **clitoris,** and vaginal opening. **Breasts** deliver milk to infants.

B. Oogenesis Yields Egg Cells

- In **oogenesis,** germ cells divide mitotically to form two **primary oocytes.** In meiosis I, the cytoplasm of the primary oocyte divides unevenly as it splits into one large, haploid **secondary oocyte** and a much smaller **polar body.** In meiosis II, the secondary oocyte again divides unequally, yielding the large ovum and another small polar body.
- After **ovulation,** the ruptured follicle develops into the **corpus luteum.**
- Meiosis in the female begins before birth and completes at fertilization.

C. Hormones Influence Female Reproductive Function

- The ovaries secrete **estrogen** and **progesterone,** hormones that stimulate development of female sexual characteristics. GnRH, FSH, LH, estrogen, and progesterone control the **ovarian cycle** and the **menstrual cycle.**
- Following ovulation, the corpus luteum secretes hormones that prepare the body for pregnancy. If pregnancy does not occur, the endometrium is shed in menstrual flow.

D. Hormonal Fluctuations Can Cause Discomfort

- Premenstrual syndrome, menstrual cramps, and hot flashes are associated with changing hormone concentrations.

E. Contraceptives Prevent Pregnancy

- **Contraception** is the use of behaviors, barriers, hormones, spermicidal chemicals, or other devices that prevent pregnancy.

30.4 Sexual Activity May Transmit Disease

- A **sexually transmitted disease (STD)** spreads via sexual contact. Viruses and bacteria cause most STDs, which may cause infertility.

30.5 The Human Infant Begins Life as a Zygote

A. Fertilization Initiates Pregnancy

- In fertilization, a sperm cell burrows through the two layers surrounding a secondary oocyte. The two united cells constitute the diploid zygote.

B. The Preembryonic Stage Ends with Implantation

- The **preembryonic stage** lasts from fertilization until the end of the second week of development.
- After fertilization, **cleavage** divides the zygote into a ball of cells. Between days 3 and 6, the ball arrives at the uterus and hollows to form a **blastocyst.** An outer layer of cells and an **inner cell mass** form. The blastocyst secretes **human chorionic gonadotropin (hCG),** which prevents menstruation. **Implantation** occurs between days 6 and 14.
- During the second week, the amniotic cavity forms as the inner cell mass flattens, forming the **embryonic disc. Ectoderm** and **endoderm** form, and then **mesoderm** appears, establishing the three primary germ layers of the **gastrula.**

C. Organs Take Shape During the Embryonic Stage

- The **embryonic stage** lasts from the second week through the eighth week of development.
- During this period, **chorionic villi** extending from the **chorion** start to develop into the **placenta.** The **yolk sac, allantois,** and **umbilical cord** form as the **amnion** swells with fluid.

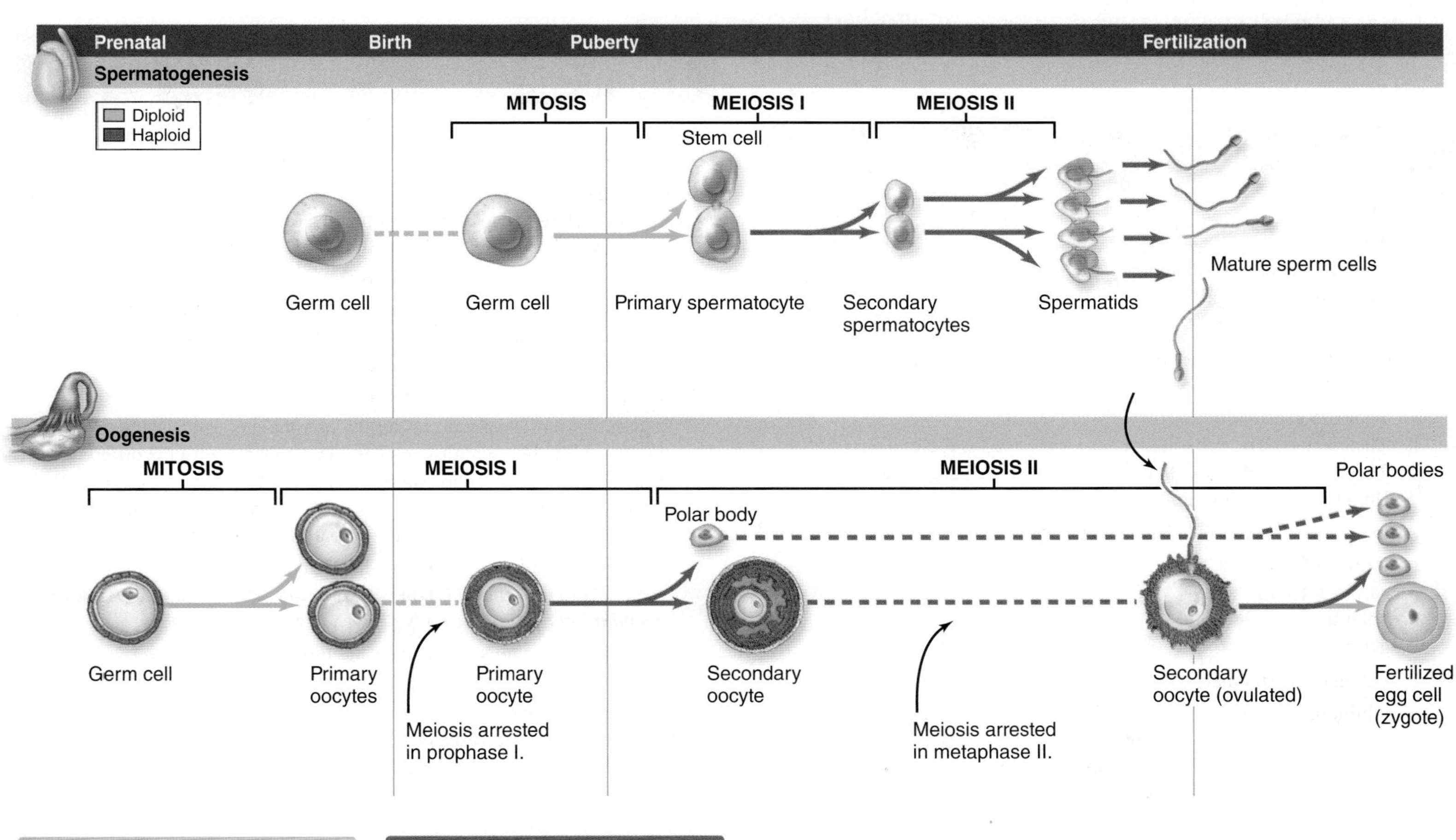

- Organs form throughout the embryonic stage, including arm and leg buds, the heart, facial structures, skin, sex organs, and the skeleton.

D. Organ Systems Become Functional in the Fetal Stage

- Structures continue to elaborate during the **fetal stage,** which lasts from the ninth week of development until birth.

E. Muscle Contractions in the Uterus Drive Childbirth

- **Labor,** or childbirth, begins as the fetus presses against the cervix. In a **positive feedback** loop, cervical stretching triggers the release of oxytocin, which stimulates uterine contractions that push the baby farther out, causing even more stretching. Eventually, the mother expels the baby and the placenta.

Name	Duration	Description
Zygote	About 24 hours after ovulation	Fertilized egg cell
Preembryonic stage	From first cell division until implantation (about 2 weeks)	Solid ball of cells differentiates into blastocyst and then gastrula
Embryonic stage	From implantation until about 8 weeks after fertilization	Germ layers differentiate into organ systems
Fetal stage	From end of eighth week until birth (end of first trimester, plus second and third trimesters)	Organ systems become functional

30.6 Investigating Life: The "Cross-Dressers" of the Reef

- In Australian giant cuttlefish, females store sperm from multiple males. Natural selection favors males that prevent rivals from fertilizing the female's eggs. In addition, some males disguise themselves as females, increasing their opportunities to mate.

Multiple Choice Questions

1. What is a zygote?
   a. The male gamete
   b. The product of fertilization
   c. The female germ cell
   d. The female gamete
2. What is the relationship between a primary spermatocyte and a germ cell?
   a. They are genetically identical.
   b. The spermatocyte is haploid and the germ cell is diploid.
   c. The spermatocyte has a flagellum; the germ cell does not.
   d. Both b and c are correct.
3. After ovulation, the follicle becomes a
   a. dormant follicle.
   b. corpus luteum.
   c. polar body.
   d. germ cell.
4. In both males and females, the main function of GnRH is to
   a. inhibit the production of sex hormones.
   b. stimulate the release of LH and FSH.
   c. inhibit the development of the corpus luteum.
   d. stimulate the development of the embryo.
5. Why can't a fertilized polar body develop into a fetus?
   a. Because it has too few chromosomes
   b. Because it has too many chromosomes
   c. Because it lacks cytoplasm and organelles
   d. Because it carries excess flagella
6. Which of the following STDs can be treated with an antiviral drug?
   a. Genital herpes
   b. Trichomoniasis
   c. Chlamydia
   d. All of the above are correct.
7. The acrosome reaction allows a sperm cell to penetrate the
   a. jelly layer encasing the oocyte.
   b. cervix, which blocks access to the uterus.
   c. plasma membrane of the secondary oocyte.
   d. Both a and b are correct.
8. How does the size of the blastocyst compare to that of the gastrula and zygote?
   a. Larger than the gastrula but smaller than the zygote
   b. Larger than both the gastrula and the zygote
   c. Smaller than the gastrula but larger than the zygote
   d. Smaller than both the gastrula and the zygote
9. The umbilical cord's function is to
   a. transport nutrients to the fetal digestive system.
   b. connect each ovary to the other reproductive organs.
   c. connect the developing fetus to the placenta.
   d. transfer nutrients from uterine tube to the uterus.
10. The hormones that determine the development of male or female reproductive structures first become active during
   a. fertilization.
   b. the preembryonic stage.
   c. the embryonic stage.
   d. the fetal stage.

Write It Out

1. What are the advantages and disadvantages of asexual and sexual reproduction? Of internal and external fertilization?
2. How are the human male and female reproductive tracts similar, and how are they different? How are the structures of the testis and ovary similar and different?
3. Make a chart that lists the major hormones involved in human reproduction. Complete the chart by listing the organ that releases each hormone; the location of target cells; and whether each hormone acts in males, females, or both.
4. How are the timetables different for oogenesis and spermatogenesis?
5. Point mutations usually occur during interphase of mitosis, but most chromosomal abnormalities arise during meiosis. Given the differences between gamete production in males and females, why is it reasonable to predict that more point mutations occur during sperm production and more chromosomal abnormalities appear in egg cells?
6. Is each of the following cell types haploid or diploid? How does each cell type relate to the others? *Germ cell; primary spermatocyte; spermatid; secondary oocyte; polar body derived from a primary oocyte*
7. How do the structures of the male and female human gametes aid them in performing their functions?
8. A vasectomy is a surgical procedure in which a physician cuts the vas deferens. Does a vasectomy stop sperm production entirely, block testosterone production, block sperm delivery to the urethra, or prevent ejaculation? Explain your answer.

9. Use the Internet to learn more about sexually transmitted diseases. Choose one to study in detail. What type of infectious agent causes the disease? What are the symptoms and long-term consequences of infection? Is a treatment available? Who is most affected?
10. How does menstruation stop when a woman becomes pregnant?
11. This chapter used the term *villus* in describing part of the chorion; the same term appeared in chapter 28's description of the small intestine. How are the chorionic and intestinal villi similar and different in structure and function?
12. Arrange these structures in order from youngest to oldest: gastrula, zygote, fetus, blastocyst.
13. Fetal red blood cells contain a version of hemoglobin (an oxygen-binding protein) that is slightly different from that in adult red blood cells. Given the relationship between fetus and mother, which hemoglobin do you predict should have a higher affinity for oxygen? Explain your answer.
14. Consult a website that describes and illustrates fetal development. What technology do you think would be necessary to enable a fetus born in the fourth month to survive in a laboratory setting?
15. What are the events of childbirth?
16. What kinds of studies and information would be necessary to determine whether exposure to a particular chemical can cause birth defects a year later? How would such an analysis differ if it were a man or a woman who was exposed?
17. One risk factor for developing breast cancer or ovarian cancer is a family history of either disease. Researchers have identified some alleles associated with inherited breast and ovarian cancers, making genetic tests possible. If a female close to you had a family history of either cancer, what considerations would help her decide whether to have her DNA tested for these alleles?
18. Use this textbook or the Internet to learn more about human cloning and stem cell therapies. How does each topic relate to human reproduction and development? Why are these techniques controversial?

Pull It Together

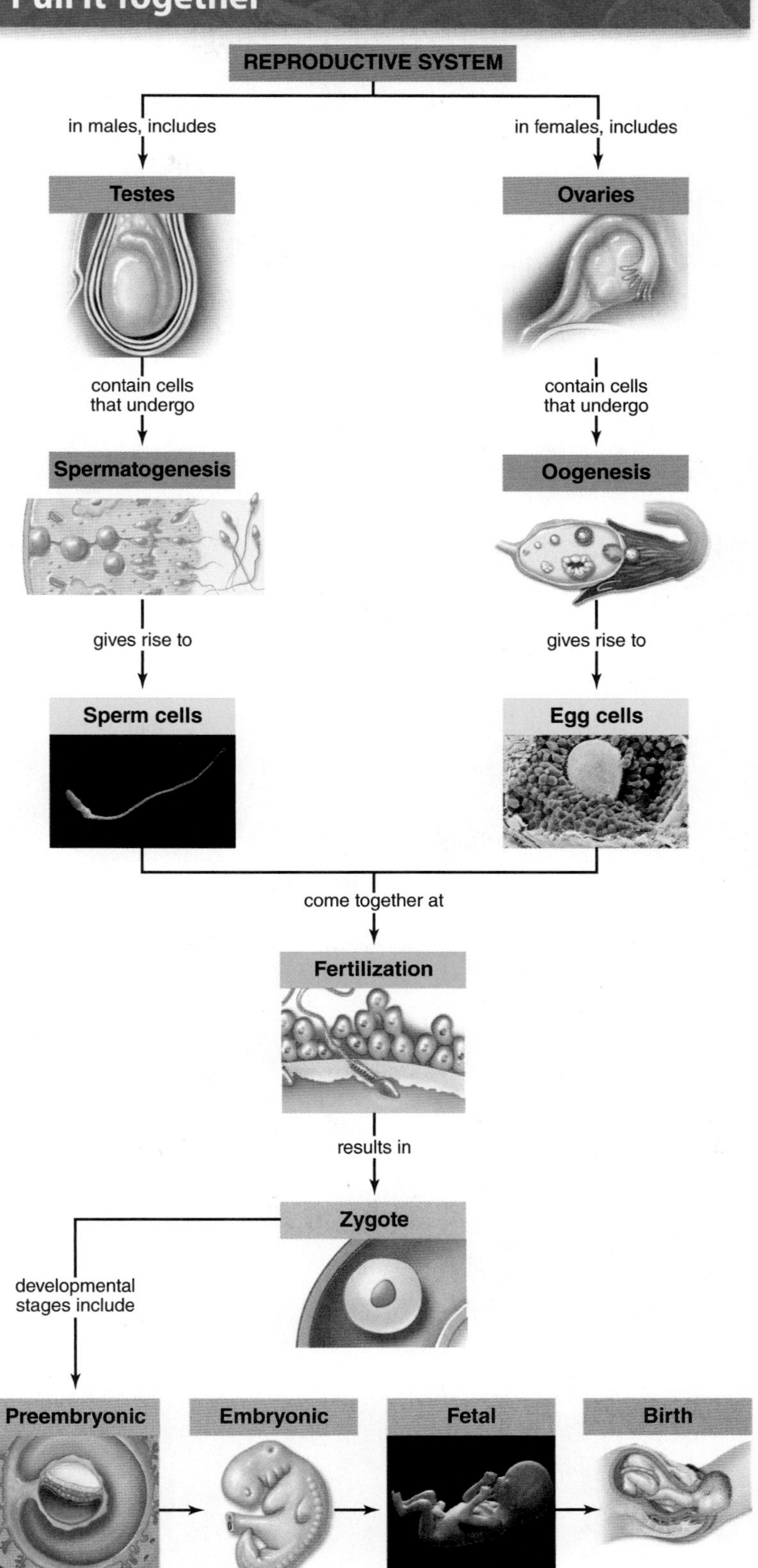

1. How are spermatogenesis and oogenesis similar, and how are they different?
2. What are the events of fertilization?
3. What are the events of the main developmental stages?
4. Add the terms *placenta, follicle, polar body, gonad, gamete, meiosis,* and *mitosis* to this concept map.

Appendix A *Answers to Multiple Choice Questions*

Chapter 1
1. d 2. b 3. c 4. a 5. d 6. c 7. b 8. d 9. c 10. a

Chapter 2
1. d 2. b 3. c 4. c 5. a 6. b 7. d 8. a 9. d 10. d

Chapter 3
1. b 2. c 3. b 4. d 5. a 6. c 7. b 8. c 9. a 10. b

Chapter 4
1. b 2. d 3. a 4. c 5. a 6. c 7. a 8. d 9. b 10. b

Chapter 5
1. c 2. c 3. d 4. b 5. c 6. d 7. b 8. c 9. b 10. d

Chapter 6
1. a 2. c 3. b 4. d 5. c 6. c 7. b 8. d 9. d 10. a

Chapter 7
1. d 2. d 3. a 4. c 5. d 6. a 7. d 8. a 9. c 10. c

Chapter 8
1. a 2. d 3. b 4. c 5. b 6. b 7. a 8. a 9. c 10. c

Chapter 9
1. c 2. b 3. a 4. d 5. d 6. a 7. c 8. a 9. c 10. a

Chapter 10
1. d 2. b 3. d 4. a 5. b 6. b 7. c 8. a 9. c 10. c 11. d

Chapter 11
1. c 2. a 3. c 4. b 5. c or d 6. c 7. c 8. a 9. d 10. b

Chapter 12
1. c 2. c 3. d 4. d 5. c 6. b 7. c 8. c 9. a 10. b

Chapter 13
1. d 2. d 3. c 4. c 5. c 6. b 7. a 8. c 9. a

Chapter 14
1. a 2. c 3. a 4. c 5. b 6. d 7. b 8. c 9. b 10. b

Chapter 15
1. d 2. c 3. a 4. c 5. b

Chapter 16
1. d 2. a 3. b 4. d 5. b 6. d 7. c 8. b

Chapter 17
1. b 2. b 3. d 4. a 5. b 6. c 7. c 8. d 9. d 10. b 11. b 12. a 13. d 14. c 15. b 16. c 17. a

Chapter 18
1. d 2. a 3. b 4. d 5. d 6. c 7. b 8. c

Chapter 19
1. b 2. c 3. c 4. d 5. c 6. d

Chapter 20
1. a 2. b 3. b 4. c 5. b 6. d

Chapter 21
1. c 2. b 3. b 4. c 5. a 6. a 7. a 8. d 9. b 10. c

Chapter 22
1. b 2. c 3. a 4. b 5. c 6. b 7. d 8. a 9. b 10. d

Chapter 23
1. d 2. b 3. d 4. c 5. d 6. c 7. b 8. a 9. b 10. d

Chapter 24
1. a 2. c 3. d 4. b 5. d 6. c 7. c 8. b 9. a

Chapter 25
1. c 2. c 3. d 4. a 5. d 6. c 7. c 8. b 9. a 10. c

Chapter 26
1. d 2. d 3. b 4. d 5. b 6. d 7. c 8. a 9. d 10. c

Chapter 27
1. d 2. b 3. a 4. c 5. d 6. b 7. d 8. c 9. d 10. b

Chapter 28
1. b 2. c 3. a 4. d 5. a 6. c 7. d 8. a 9. a 10. b

Chapter 29
1. c 2. b 3. d 4. a 5. b 6. c 7. b 8. c 9. c 10. b

Chapter 30
1. b 2. a 3. b 4. b 5. c 6. a 7. a 8. c 9. c 10. c

Appendix B *A Brief Guide to Statistical Significance*

Experiments often yield numerical data, such as the height of a plant or the incidence of illness in vaccinated children (see, for example, figure 1.9). But how are we to know whether an observed difference between two samples is "real"? For example, if we do find that 100 vaccinated children become sick slightly less often than 100 unvaccinated ones, how can we make sure that this outcome does not simply reflect random variation between samples of 100 children?

A statistical analysis can help. The dictionary definition of *statistics* is "the science that deals with the collection, analysis, and interpretation of numerical data, often using probability theory." Note that the analysis is grounded in probability theory, a branch of mathematics that deals with random events. A statistical test is therefore a mathematical tool that assesses variation, with the goal of determining whether any observed differences between treatments could be explained by the variation that random events would produce.

Researchers use many types of statistical tests, depending on the type of data collected and the design of the experiment. A description of these tests is beyond the scope of this appendix. For now, it is enough to understand that in each statistical test, the researcher computes a value (the "test statistic") that takes into account the sample size and the variability in the data. The researcher then determines the likelihood that the observed test statistic could be explained by chance alone.

An imaginary experiment will help you understand the role of variability in accepting or rejecting a hypothesis. Suppose that you have two friends, Pat and Kris, both of whom play softball. Pat claims to be able to hit a ball farther than Kris, but Kris disagrees. You therefore set up a test of the null hypothesis, which is that Pat and Kris can hit the ball equally far. You ask both of your friends to hit the ball one time, and Pat's ball does go farther. But Kris wants to re-do the test. This time, Kris's ball goes farther. Evidently, two hits apiece is not sufficient for you to settle the matter.

You therefore decide to improve the experiment (figure B.1). This time, each player gets to hit 10 balls, and you use a tape measure to determine how far each ball traveled from home plate. Figure B.2 shows two possible outcomes of the contest. In each scenario, Pat's average distance is 63 meters, compared with 49 meters for Kris. Pat therefore appears to be the better hitter.

But look more closely at the data. In Outcome 1, the hitting distances are much less variable than they are in Outcome 2. How does this variability influence our conclusions about Pat and Kris?

The answer lies in statistical tests. The goal of each statistical test is to calculate the probability that an observed outcome would arise *if the null hypothesis were true*. This probability is called the P value. The lower the P value, the greater the chance that the difference between two treatments is "real."

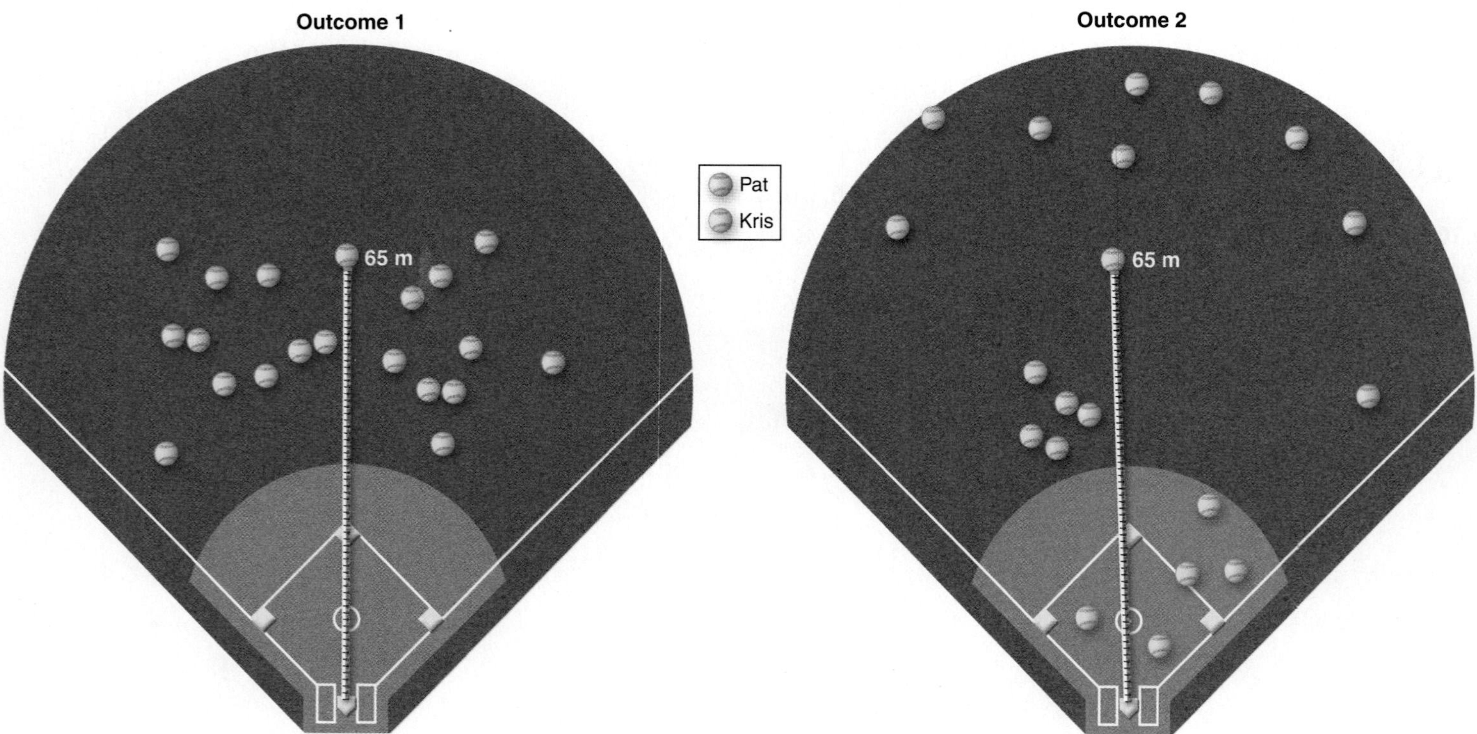

Figure B.1 Hitting Competition. These illustrations show two possible outcomes in a hitting contest between Pat and Kris. Note that the batting distances in Outcome 1 were much less variable than they were in Outcome 2.

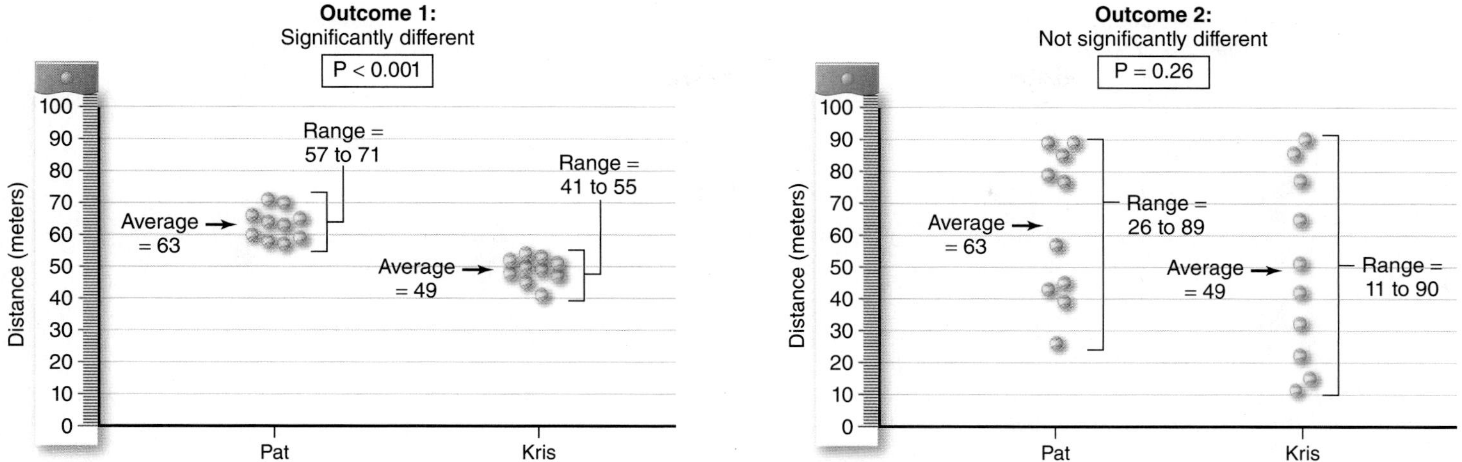

Figure B.2 Statistical Significance. In Outcome 1, the difference between Pat and Kris is considered highly significant at P<0.001; in Outcome 2, however, the variability in hitting distances means that the difference between the two batters is not statistically significant.

Generally, biologists accept a P value of 0.05 or smaller as being statistically significant. In other words, a difference between two treatments is statistically significant when the probability that we would observe that result by chance alone is 5% or less. Moreover, a P value of 0.01 or smaller is considered highly significant. Note that the meaning of the word *significant* is different from its use in everyday language. Ordinarily, "significant" means "important." Not so in statistics, where "significant" simply means "likely to be true," and "highly significant" means "very likely to be true."

Returning to our experiment, the null hypothesis is that Pat and Kris are equally good hitters. The amount of variability in Outcome 1 was small, and the calculated value of our test statistic suggests that we can reject this null hypothesis with a P value of <0.001. In other words, there is a 99.999% chance that Pat really is a better hitter than Kris and that our results are not simply due to chance (see figure B.2). In Outcome 2, however, the hitting distances were much more variable, and the calculated P value is 0.26. We therefore cannot reject the null hypothesis with confidence. After all, given these data, the chance that Pat really is the better batter is only 74%. In science, a 26% chance of incorrectly rejecting the null hypothesis is unacceptably high.

Scientists often include information about statistical analyses along with their data (figure B.3). The most common technique is to graph the average for each treatment and then add error bars that reflect the amount of variability in the data. The longer the error bar, the greater the amount of variability and the less confident we are in the accuracy of our result.

An error bar usually indicates either the standard error or the 95% confidence interval; you may wish to consult a statistics reference to learn more about each. Because these two measures have slightly different meanings, researchers should always note the type of error bar depicted on a graph.

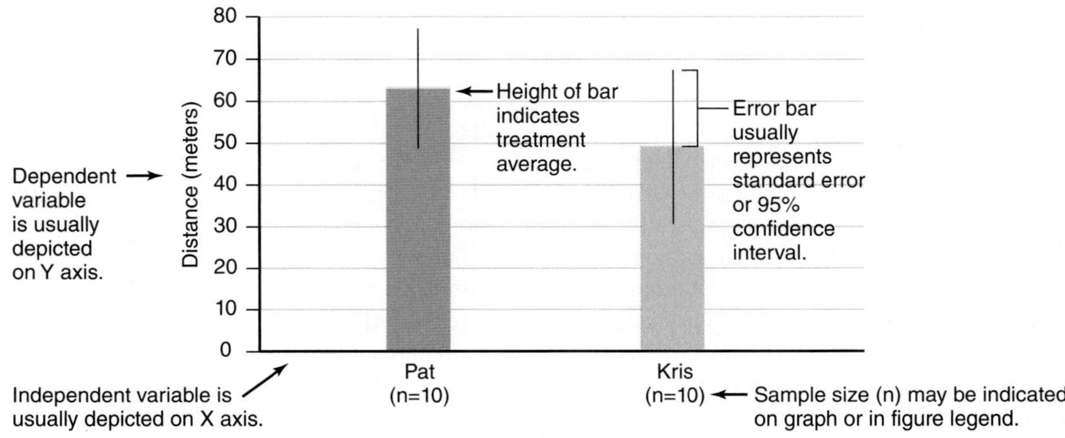

Figure B.3 Representing Statistics on a Graph. The basic parts of a bar graph include the axes, treatment averages, and error bars.

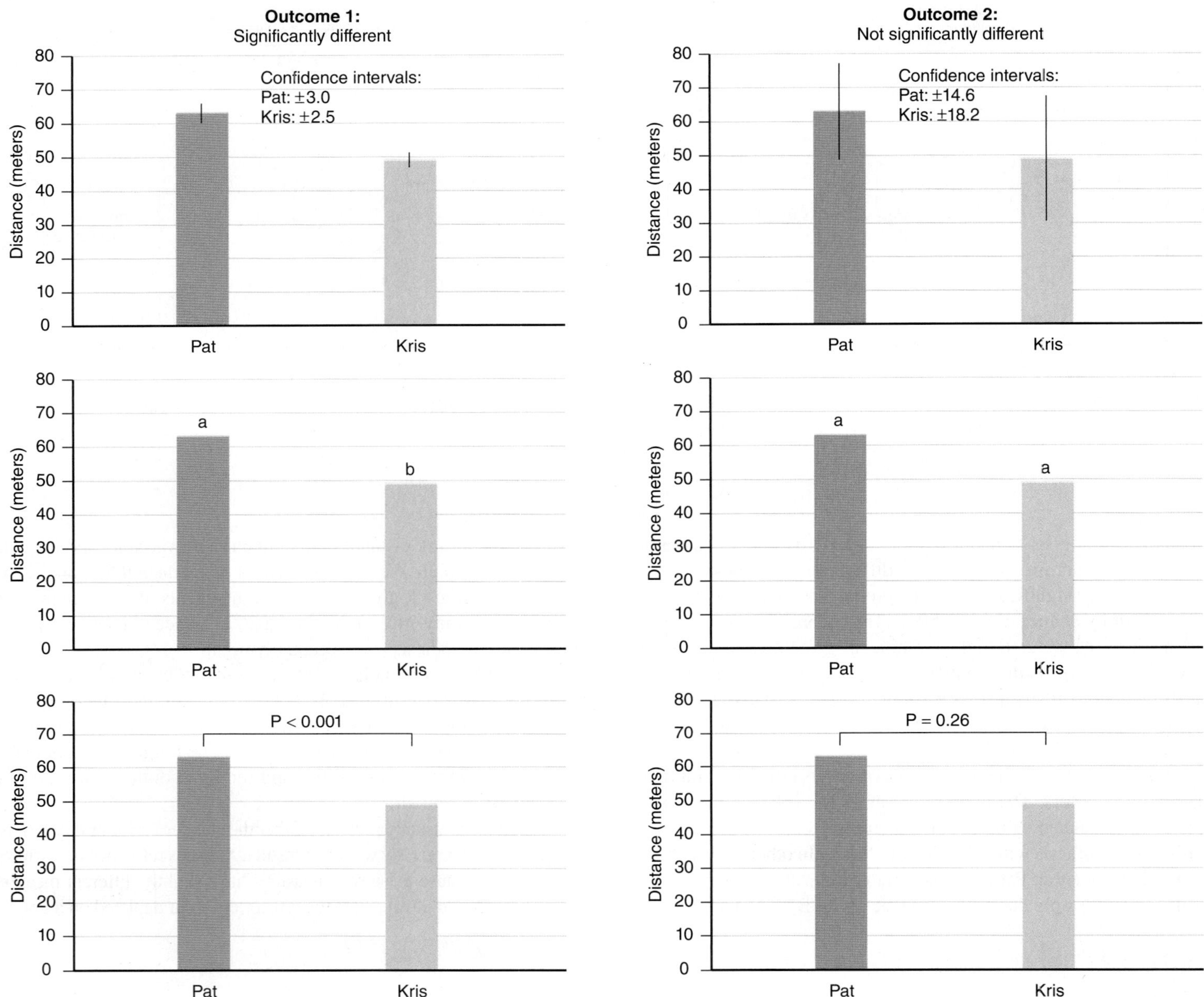

Figure B.4 Three Ways to Represent Statistics. Error bars, letters, and P values are all ways to indicate whether the difference between two treatments is statistically significant.

Figure B.4 shows three common ways to indicate whether an observed difference is statistically significant. Examine the error bars on the top pair of graphs in figure B.4. These bars indicate the 95% confidence intervals that were calculated for the two possible outcomes in our hitting competition. Because the data in Outcome 1 are much less variable than for Outcome 2, the error bars for Outcome 1 are smaller than for Outcome 2. The overlapping error bars for Outcome 2 indicate that the difference between Pat and Kris is not statistically significant.

Figure B.4 also shows that researchers sometimes use other methods to illustrate which data points are significantly different from one another. The middle pair of graphs in figure B.4 shows one approach. In Outcome 1 of our batting experiment, Pat was a significantly better hitter than Kris, so the bars depicting their averages are topped with different letters (*a* and *b*). In Outcome 2, however, Pat and Kris were not significantly different, so their bars have the same letter, *a*. A third possibility is to simply report the P values between pairs of treatments; the last pair of graphs in figure B.4 illustrates this strategy.

Appendix C *Metric Units and Conversions*

Metric Prefixes

Symbol	Prefix	Increase or Decrease	
G	giga	One billion	1,000,000,000
M	mega	One million	1,000,000
k	kilo	One thousand	1,000
h	hecto	One hundred	100
da	deka (or deca)	Ten	10
d	deci	One-tenth	0.1
c	centi	One-hundredth	0.01
m	milli	One-thousandth	0.001
μ	micro	One-millionth	0.000001
n	nano	One-billionth	0.000000001

Metric Units and Conversions

	Metric Unit	Metric to English Conversion	English to Metric Conversion
Length	1 meter (m)	1 km = 0.62 mile 1 m = 1.09 yards = 39.37 inches 1 cm = 0.394 inch 1 mm = 0.039 inch	1 mile = 1.609 km 1 yard = 0.914 m 1 foot = 0.305 m = 30.5 cm 1 inch = 2.54 cm
Mass	1 gram (g) 1 metric ton (t) = 1,000,000 g = 1,000 kg	1 t = 1.102 tons (U.S.) 1 kg = 2.205 pounds 1 g = 0.0353 ounce	1 ton (U.S.) = 0.907 t 1 pound = 0.4536 kg 1 ounce = 28.35 g
Volume (liquids)	1 liter (l)	1 l = 1.06 quarts 1 ml = 0.034 fluid ounce	1 gallon = 3.79 l 1 quart = 0.95 l 1 pint = 0.47 l 1 fluid ounce = 29.57 ml
Temperature	Degrees Celsius (°C)	°C = (°F − 32)/1.8	°F = (°C × 1.8) + 32
Energy and Power	1 joule (J)	1 J = 0.239 calorie 1 kJ = 0.239 kilocalorie ("food calorie")	1 calorie = 4.186 J 1 kilocalorie ("food calorie") = 4186 J
Time	1 second (sec)		

Appendix D *Periodic Table of the Elements*

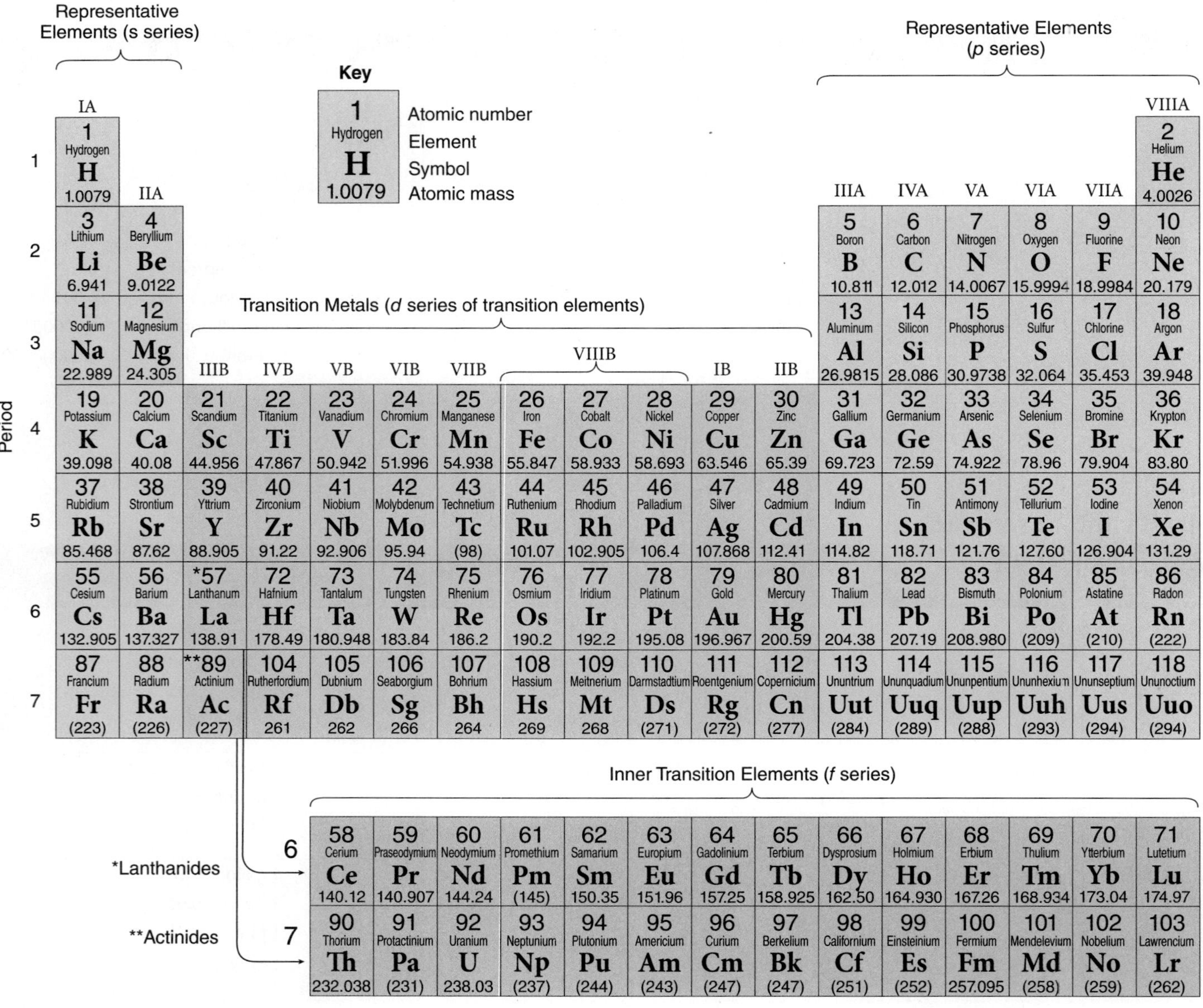

Period	IA	IIA	IIIB	IVB	VB	VIB	VIIB	VIIIB	VIIIB	VIIIB	IB	IIB	IIIA	IVA	VA	VIA	VIIA	VIIIA
1	1 Hydrogen H 1.0079																	2 Helium He 4.0026
2	3 Lithium Li 6.941	4 Beryllium Be 9.0122											5 Boron B 10.811	6 Carbon C 12.012	7 Nitrogen N 14.0067	8 Oxygen O 15.9994	9 Fluorine F 18.9984	10 Neon Ne 20.179
3	11 Sodium Na 22.989	12 Magnesium Mg 24.305											13 Aluminum Al 26.9815	14 Silicon Si 28.086	15 Phosphorus P 30.9738	16 Sulfur S 32.064	17 Chlorine Cl 35.453	18 Argon Ar 39.948
4	19 Potassium K 39.098	20 Calcium Ca 40.08	21 Scandium Sc 44.956	22 Titanium Ti 47.867	23 Vanadium V 50.942	24 Chromium Cr 51.996	25 Manganese Mn 54.938	26 Iron Fe 55.847	27 Cobalt Co 58.933	28 Nickel Ni 58.693	29 Copper Cu 63.546	30 Zinc Zn 65.39	31 Gallium Ga 69.723	32 Germanium Ge 72.59	33 Arsenic As 74.922	34 Selenium Se 78.96	35 Bromine Br 79.904	36 Krypton Kr 83.80
5	37 Rubidium Rb 85.468	38 Strontium Sr 87.62	39 Yttrium Y 88.905	40 Zirconium Zr 91.22	41 Niobium Nb 92.906	42 Molybdenum Mo 95.94	43 Technetium Tc (98)	44 Ruthenium Ru 101.07	45 Rhodium Rh 102.905	46 Palladium Pd 106.4	47 Silver Ag 107.868	48 Cadmium Cd 112.41	49 Indium In 114.82	50 Tin Sn 118.71	51 Antimony Sb 121.76	52 Tellurium Te 127.60	53 Iodine I 126.904	54 Xenon Xe 131.29
6	55 Cesium Cs 132.905	56 Barium Ba 137.327	*57 Lanthanum La 138.91	72 Hafnium Hf 178.49	73 Tantalum Ta 180.948	74 Tungsten W 183.84	75 Rhenium Re 186.2	76 Osmium Os 190.2	77 Iridium Ir 192.2	78 Platinum Pt 195.08	79 Gold Au 196.967	80 Mercury Hg 200.59	81 Thalium Tl 204.38	82 Lead Pb 207.19	83 Bismuth Bi 208.980	84 Polonium Po (209)	85 Astatine At (210)	86 Radon Rn (222)
7	87 Francium Fr (223)	88 Radium Ra (226)	**89 Actinium Ac (227)	104 Rutherfordium Rf 261	105 Dubnium Db 262	106 Seaborgium Sg 266	107 Bohrium Bh 264	108 Hassium Hs 269	109 Meitnerium Mt 268	110 Darmstadtium Ds (271)	111 Roentgenium Rg (272)	112 Copernicium Cn (277)	113 Ununtrium Uut (284)	114 Ununquadium Uuq (289)	115 Ununpentium Uup (288)	116 Ununhexium Uuh (293)	117 Ununseptium Uus (294)	118 Ununoctium Uuo (294)

Inner Transition Elements (*f* series)

	Period														
*Lanthanides	6	58 Cerium Ce 140.12	59 Praseodymium Pr 140.907	60 Neodymium Nd 144.24	61 Promethium Pm (145)	62 Samarium Sm 150.35	63 Europium Eu 151.96	64 Gadolinium Gd 157.25	65 Terbium Tb 158.925	66 Dysprosium Dy 162.50	67 Holmium Ho 164.930	68 Erbium Er 167.26	69 Thulium Tm 168.934	70 Ytterbium Yb 173.04	71 Lutetium Lu 174.97
**Actinides	7	90 Thorium Th 232.038	91 Protactinium Pa (231)	92 Uranium U 238.03	93 Neptunium Np (237)	94 Plutonium Pu (244)	95 Americium Am (243)	96 Curium Cm (247)	97 Berkelium Bk (247)	98 Californium Cf (251)	99 Einsteinium Es (252)	100 Fermium Fm 257.095	101 Mendelevium Md (258)	102 Nobelium No (259)	103 Lawrencium Lr (262)

Appendix E *Amino Acid Structures*

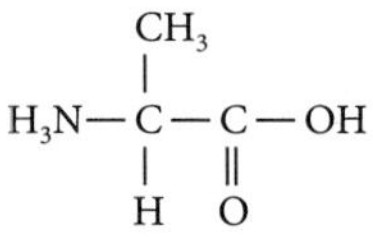

Alanine
(Ala; A)

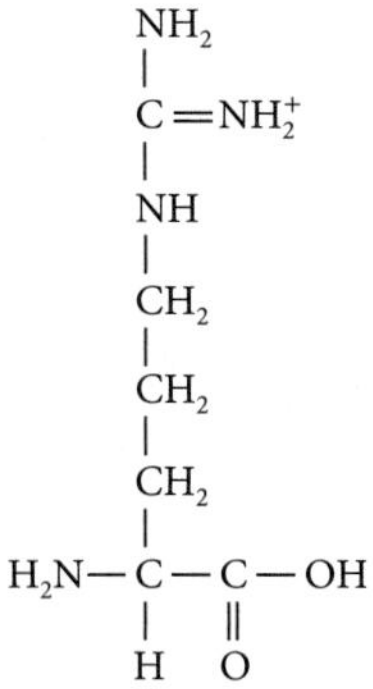

Arginine
(Arg; R)

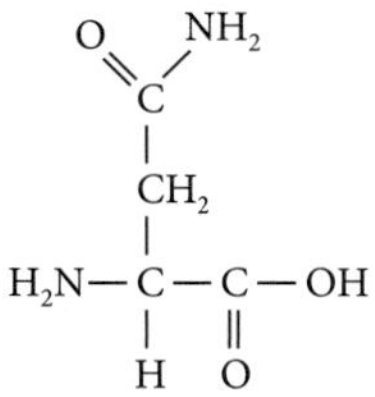

Asparagine
(Asn; N)

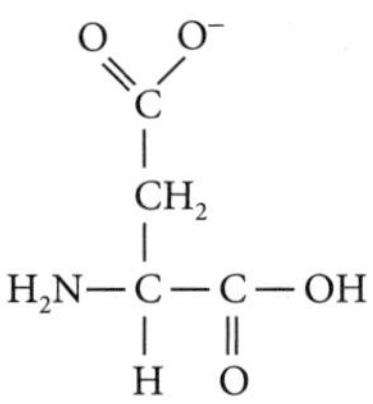

Aspartic
acid (Asp; D)

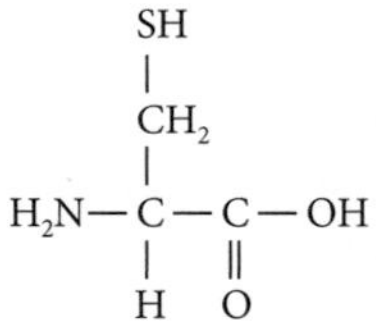

Cysteine
(Cys; C)

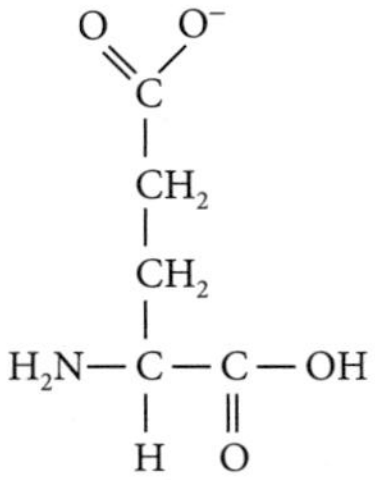

Glutamic
acid (Glu; E)

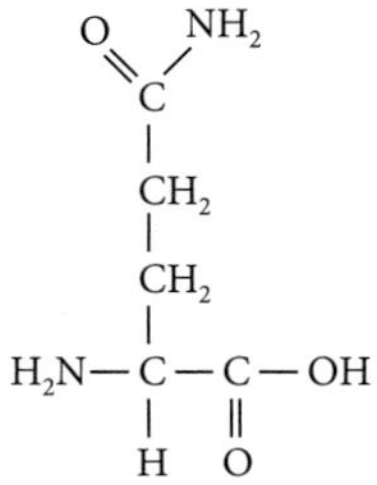

Glutamine
(Gln; Q)

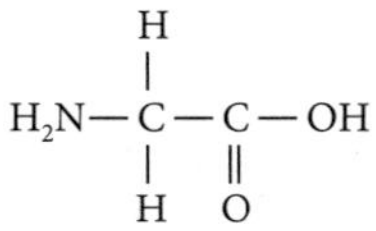

Glycine
(Gly; G)

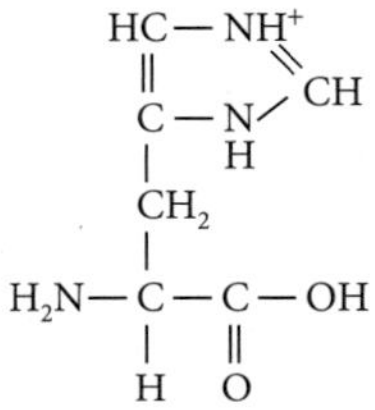

Histidine
(His; H)

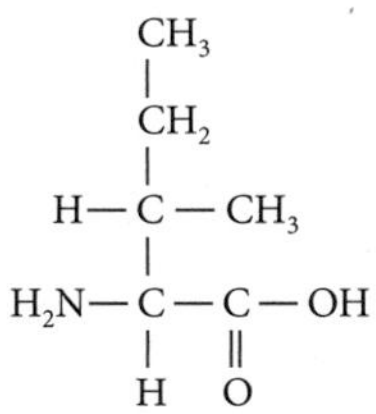

Isoleucine
(Ile; I)

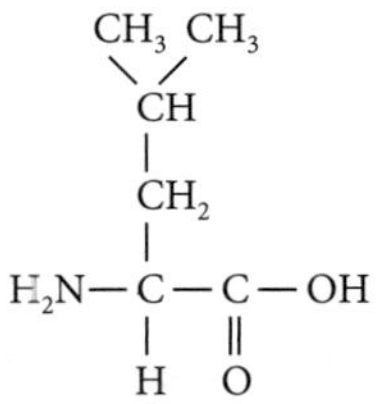

Leucine
(Leu; L)

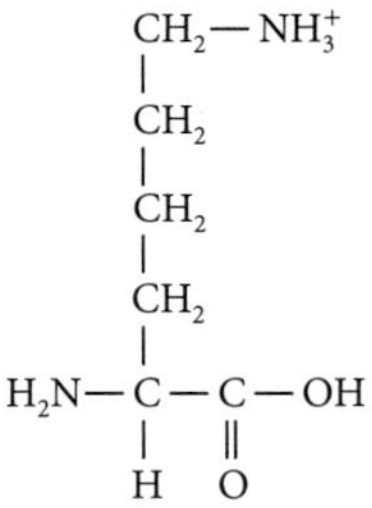

Lysine
(Lys; K)

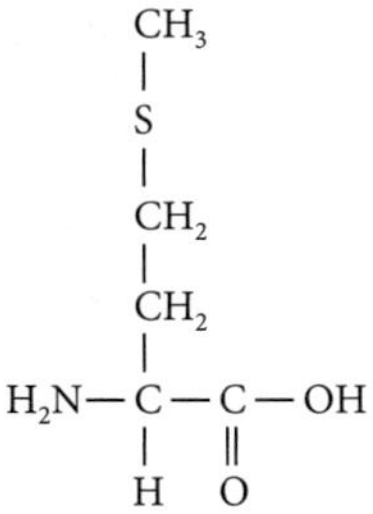

Methionine
(Met; M)

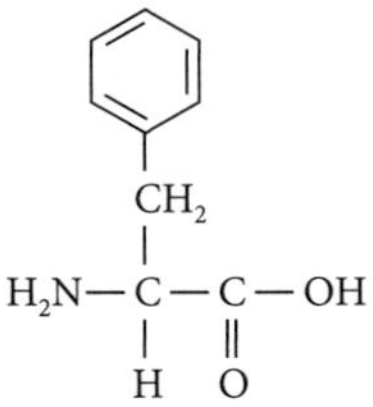

Phenylalanine
(Phe; F)

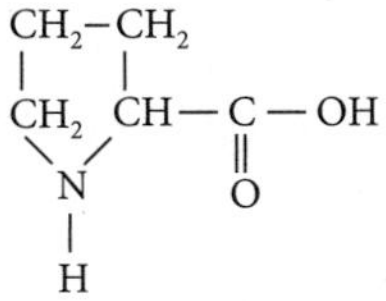

Proline
(Pro; P)

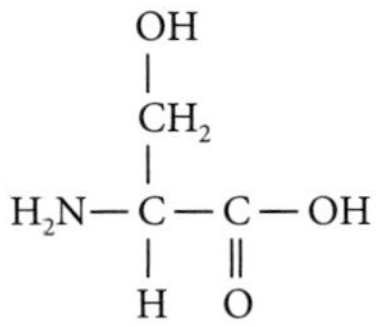

Serine
(Ser; S)

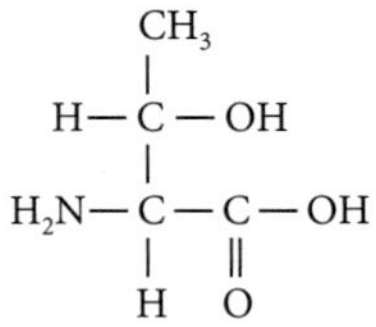

Threonine
(Thr; T)

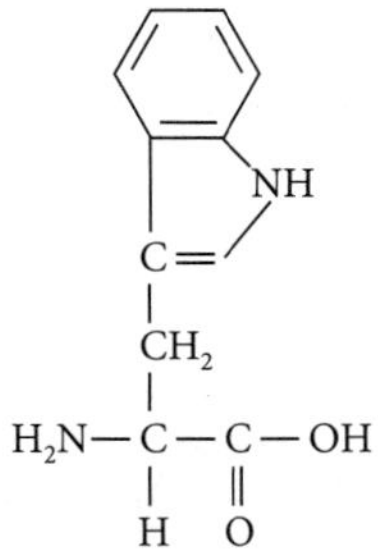

Tryptophan
(Trp; W)

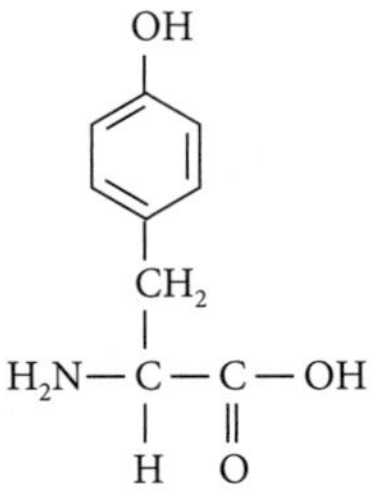

Tyrosine
(Tyr; Y)

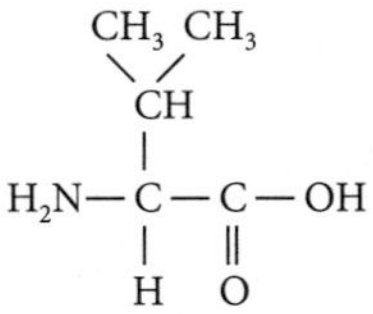

Valine
(Val; V)

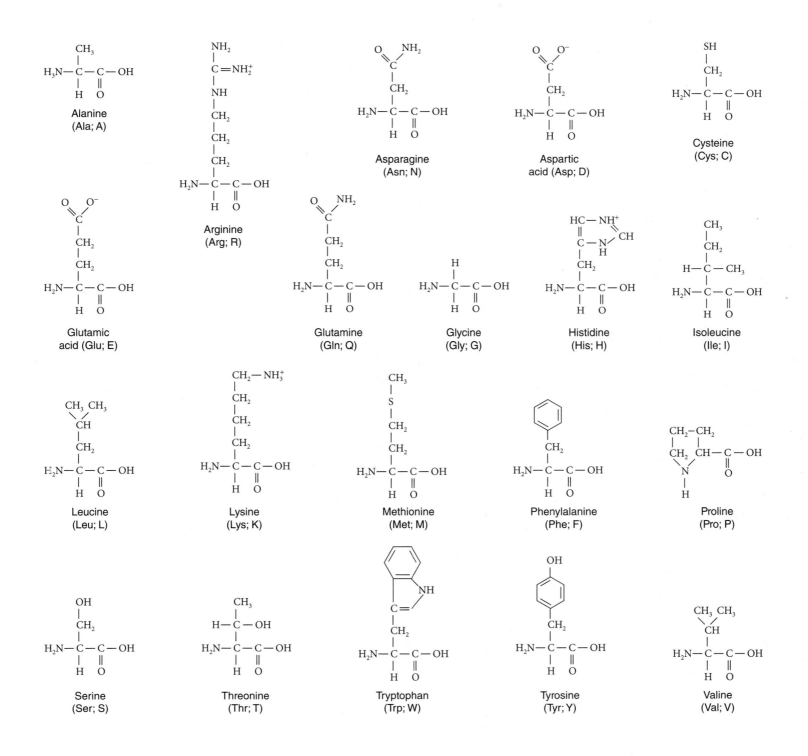

Glossary

A

abiotic: nonliving

abscisic acid: plant hormone that inhibits seed germination and plant growth

absolute dating: determining the age of a fossil in years

absorption: the process of taking in and incorporating nutrients or energy

accessory pigment: photosynthetic pigment other than chlorophyll *a* that extends the range of light wavelengths useful in photosynthesis

acetyl CoA: molecule that enters the Krebs cycle in cellular respiration; product of partial oxidation of pyruvate

acid: a molecule that releases hydrogen ions into a solution

acid deposition: low pH precipitation or particles that form when air pollutants react with water in the upper atmosphere

acrosome: structure covering the head of a sperm cell; contains enzymes that enable the sperm to penetrate the layers surrounding an oocyte

actin: protein that forms thin filaments in muscle cells; also forms part of the cytoskeleton

action potential: all-or-none electrochemical change across the cell membrane of a neuron; the basis of a nerve impulse

activation energy: energy required for a chemical reaction to begin

active immunity: immunity generated by an organism's production of antibodies

active site: the part of an enzyme to which substrates bind

active transport: movement of a substance across a membrane against its concentration gradient, using a carrier protein and energy from ATP

adaptation: inherited trait that permits an organism to survive and reproduce

adaptive immunity: defense system in vertebrates that recognizes and remembers specific antigens

adenosine triphosphate (ATP): a molecule whose high-energy phosphate bonds power many biological processes

adrenal cortex: outer portion of an adrenal gland; secretes mineralocorticoids, glucocorticoids, and small amounts of sex hormones

adrenal gland: one of two endocrine glands atop the kidneys

adrenal medulla: inner portion of an adrenal gland; secretes epinephrine and norepinephrine

adrenocorticotropic hormone (ACTH): hormone produced in the anterior pituitary

adult stem cell: cell that can give rise to a limited subset of cells in the body

aerobic respiration: complete oxidation of glucose to CO_2 in the presence of O_2, producing ATP

age structure: distribution of age classes in a population

agglutination: clumping together of cells

alcoholic fermentation: metabolic pathway in which NADH reduces the pyruvate from glycolysis, producing ethanol and CO_2

aldosterone: mineralocorticoid hormone produced in the adrenal cortex

alga: aquatic, photosynthetic protist

alimentary canal: two-opening digestive tract; also called gastrointestinal (GI) tract

alkaline: having a pH greater than 7

allantois: extraembryonic membrane that forms as an outpouching of the yolk sac

allele: one of two or more alternative forms of a gene

allele frequency: number of copies of one allele, divided by the number of alleles in a population

allergen: antigen that triggers an allergic reaction

allergy: exaggerated immune response to a harmless substance

allopatric speciation: formation of new species after a physical barrier separates a population into groups that cannot interbreed

alternation of generations: the sexual life cycle of plants and many green algae, which alternates between a diploid sporophyte stage and a haploid gametophyte stage

alveolus (pl. alveoli): microscopic air sac in the mammalian lungs, where gas exchange occurs

amino acid: an organic molecule consisting of a central carbon atom bonded to a hydrogen atom, an amino group, a carboxyl group, and an R group

amino group: a nitrogen atom single-bonded to two hydrogen atoms

amnion: extraembryonic membrane that contains amniotic fluid

amniote: a vertebrate in which protective membranes surround the embryo (amnion, chorion, and allantois); reptiles and mammals

amniotic egg: reptile or monotreme egg containing fluid and nutrients within membranes that protect the embryo

amoeboid protozoan: unicellular protist that produces pseudopodia

amphibian: tetrapod vertebrate that can live on land but requires water to reproduce

analogous: similar in function but not in structure because of convergent evolution, not common ancestry

anaphase: stage of mitosis in which the spindle pulls sister chromatids toward opposite poles of the cell

anaphase I: anaphase of meiosis I, when spindle fibers pull homologous chromosomes toward opposite poles of the cell

anaphase II: anaphase of meiosis II, when centromeres split and spindle fibers pull sister chromatids toward opposite poles of the cell

anaphylactic shock: rapid, widespread, severe allergic reaction

anatomy: the study of an organism's structure

ancestral character: characteristic already present in the ancestor of a group being studied

anchoring (or adhering) junction: connection between two adjacent animal cells; anchors intermediate filaments in a single spot on the cell membrane

angiosperm: a seed plant that produces flowers and fruits; includes monocots and eudicots

annelid: segmented worm; phylum Annelida

anorexia nervosa: eating disorder characterized by refusal to maintain normal body weight

antenna pigment: photosynthetic pigment that passes photon energy to the reaction center of a photosystem

anterior pituitary: the front part of the pituitary gland

anther: pollen-producing structure at tip of stamen

antibody: protein that binds to an antigen

anticodon: a three-base portion of a tRNA molecule; the anticodon is complementary to one codon

antidiuretic hormone (ADH): hormone released from the posterior pituitary; also called vasopressin

antigen: molecule that elicits an immune reaction by B and T cells

anus: exit from a complete digestive tract

aorta: the largest artery leaving the heart

apical dominance: the suppression of the growth of lateral buds by the intact terminal bud of a plant

apical meristem: meristem at the tip of a root or shoot

apicomplexan: non-motile protist with cell containing an apical complex; obligate animal parasite

apoptosis: programmed cell death that is a normal part of development

appendicular skeleton: the limb bones and the bones that support them in the vertebrate skeleton

arachnid: type of chelicerate arthropod; spiders, ticks, mites, and scorpions

Archaea: one of two domains of prokaryotes

arteriole: small artery

artery: vessel that carries blood away from the heart

arthropod: segmented animal with an exoskeleton and jointed appendages; phylum Arthropoda

artificial selection: selective breeding strategy in which a human allows only organisms with desired traits to reproduce

asexual reproduction: form of reproduction in which offspring arise from only one parent

atom: a particle of matter; composed of protons, neutrons, and electrons

atomic mass: the average mass of all isotopes of an element

atomic number: the number of protons in an atom's nucleus

ATP: adenosine triphosphate; a molecule whose high-energy phosphate bonds power many biological processes

ATP synthase: enzyme complex that admits protons through a membrane, where they trigger phosphorylation of ADP to ATP

atrioventricular (AV) node: specialized cardiac muscle cells that delay the heartbeat, giving the ventricles time to fill

atrium: heart chamber that receives blood

auditory canal: ear canal; funnels sounds from the outer ear to the eardrum

auditory nerve: nerve fibers that connect the cochlea and vestibular apparatus to the brain

autoimmune disorder: immune reaction to the body's own cells

autonomic nervous system: in the peripheral nervous system, motor pathways that lead to smooth muscle, cardiac muscle, and glands

autosomal dominant: inheritance pattern of a dominant allele on an autosome

autosomal recessive: inheritance pattern of a recessive allele on an autosome

autosome: a nonsex chromosome

autotroph: organism that produces organic molecules by acquiring carbon from inorganic sources; primary producer

auxin: plant hormone that promotes cell elongation in stems and fruits

axial skeleton: the central axis of a vertebrate skeleton; consists of the bones of the head, vertebral column, and rib cage

axillary bud: undeveloped shoot in the angle between stem and petiole

axon (nerve fiber): a neuron extension that transmits messages away from the cell body and toward another cell

B

B cell: type of lymphocyte that produces antibodies

bacillus (pl. bacilli): rod-shaped prokaryote

background extinction rate: steady, gradual loss of species through natural competition or loss of genetic diversity

Bacteria: one of two domains of prokaryotes

bacteriophage (phage): a virus that infects bacteria

bark: tissues outside the vascular cambium

base: a molecule that either releases hydroxide ions into a solution or removes hydrogen ions from it

basidiomycete: fungus that produces sexual spores on a basidium

basophil: type of white blood cell that triggers inflammation and allergy

benign tumor: mass of abnormal cells that does not have the potential to spread

bilateral symmetry: body form in which only one plane divides the animal into mirror image halves

bile: digestive biochemical that emulsifies fats

binary fission: type of asexual reproduction in which a prokaryotic cell divides into two identical cells

biodiversity: the variety of life on Earth

biogeochemical cycle: geological and biological processes that recycle elements vital to life

biogeography: the study of the distribution patterns of species across the planet

biological species: a population, or group of populations, whose members can interbreed and produce fertile offspring

biomagnification: increasing concentrations of a chemical in higher trophic levels

biome: one of several major types of ecosystems

biosphere: part of Earth where life can exist

biotic: living

bird: tetrapod vertebrate with feathers, wings, and an amniotic egg

birth rate: the number of new individuals produced per 1000 individuals per unit time

bivalve: type of mollusk

blade: flattened part of a leaf

blastocyst: preembryonic stage consisting of a fluid-filled ball of cells

blastula: stage of early animal embryonic development; a sphere of cells surrounding a fluid-filled cavity

blood: type of connective tissue consisting of cells and platelets suspended in a liquid matrix

blood clot: plug of solidified blood

blood-brain barrier: close-knit cells that form capillaries in the brain, limiting the substances that can enter

blood pressure: force that blood exerts against artery walls

bone: type of connective tissue consisting of cells embedded in a mineralized matrix; also, in the vertebrate skeleton, an organ consisting of bone tissue, cartilage, and other tissues

bony fish: jawed fish with a skeleton made of bone; ray-finned fishes and lobe-finned fishes

bottleneck: sudden reduction in the size of a population

brain: a distinct concentration of nervous tissue, often encased within a skull, at the anterior end of an animal

brainstem: continuation of the spinal cord into the vertebrate hindbrain

breast: milk-producing organ in female mammals

bronchiole: small branched airway that connects bronchi to alveoli

bronchus (pl. bronchi): one of two large tubes that branch from the trachea

brown alga: multicellular photosynthetic aquatic protist with swimming spores and brownish accessory pigments

bryophyte: plant that lacks vascular tissue; includes liverworts, hornworts, and mosses

buffer system: weak acid/base pair that resists changes in pH

bulimia: eating disorder in which a person eats large quantities and then intentionally vomits or uses laxatives shortly afterward

bulk element: an element that an organism requires in large amounts

bundle-sheath cell: thick-walled plant cell surrounding veins; site of Calvin cycle in C_4 plants

C

C_3 pathway: the Calvin cycle

C_4 pathway: a carbon fixation pathway in which CO_2 combines with a three-carbon molecule to form a four-carbon compound

caecilian: type of amphibian

calcitonin: thyroid hormone that decreases blood calcium levels

Calorie: one kilocalorie

calorie: the energy required to raise the temperature of 1 gram of water by 1°C under standard conditions

Calvin cycle: in photosynthesis, a metabolic pathway in which CO_2 is fixed and incorporated into a three-carbon carbohydrate

calyx: collective term for the sepals of a flower

CAM pathway: carbon fixation that occurs at night; CO_2 is later released for use in the Calvin cycle during the day

cancer: class of diseases characterized by uncontrolled division of cells that invade or spread to other tissues

capillary: tiny blood vessel that connects an arteriole with a venule

capillary bed: network of capillaries

carbohydrate: compound containing carbon, hydrogen, and oxygen in a ratio 1:2:1

carbon fixation: the initial incorporation of carbon from CO_2 into an organic compound

carbon reactions: the reactions of photosynthesis that use ATP and NADPH to synthesize carbohydrates from carbon dioxide

carboxyl group: a carbon atom double-bonded to an oxygen and single-bonded to a hydroxyl group

cardiac cycle: sequence of contraction and relaxation that makes up the heartbeat

cardiac muscle: involuntary muscle tissue composed of branched, striated, single-nucleated contractile cells

cardiac output: the volume of blood that the heart pumps each minute

cardiovascular system: circulatory system

carnivore: animal that eats animals

carpel: leaflike structure enclosing an angiosperm's ovule(s)

carrying capacity: maximum number of individuals that a habitat can support indefinitely

cartilage: type of connective tissue consisting of cells surrounded by a rubbery collagen matrix

cartilaginous fish: jawed fish with a skeleton made of cartilage; sharks, skates, and rays

cecum: the entrance to the large intestine

cell: smallest unit of life that can function independently

cell body: enlarged portion of a neuron that contains most of the organelles

cell cycle: sequence of events that occur in an actively dividing cell

cell membrane: the boundary of a cell, consisting of proteins embedded in a phospholipid bilayer

cell plate: in plants, the materials that begin to form the wall that divides two cells

cell theory: the ideas that all living matter consists of cells, cells are the structural and functional units of life, and all cells come from preexisting cells

cell wall: a rigid boundary surrounding cells of many prokaryotes, protists, plants, and fungi

cell-mediated immunity: branch of adaptive immune system in which defensive cells kill invaders by direct cell-cell contact

cellular slime mold: protist in which feeding stage consists of individual cells that come together as a multicellular "slug" when food runs out

centipede: type of mandibulate arthropod

central nervous system (CNS): the brain and spinal cord

centromere: small section of a chromosome where sister chromatids attach to each other

centrosome: part of the cell that organizes microtubules

cephalization: development of sensory structures and a brain at the head end of an animal

cephalopod: type of mollusk

cerebellum: area of the hindbrain that coordinates subconscious muscular responses

cerebral cortex: outer layer of the cerebrum

cerebrospinal fluid: fluid that bathes and cushions the central nervous system

cerebrum: region of the forebrain that controls intelligence, learning, perception, and emotion

cervix: lower, narrow part of the uterus

chaparral: Mediterranean shrubland

charophyte: type of green alga thought to be most closely related to terrestrial plants

chelicerate: arthropod with clawlike mouthparts (chelicerae); horseshoe crabs and arachnids

chemical bond: attractive force that holds atoms together

chemical reaction: interaction in which some bonds break and new bonds form, rearranging atoms and causing one substance to change into another

chemoreceptor: sensory receptor that responds to chemicals

chemotroph: organism that derives energy by oxidizing inorganic or organic chemicals

chiton: type of mollusk

chlorophyll *a*: green pigment that plants, algae, and cyanobacteria use to harness the energy in sunlight

chloroplast: organelle housing the reactions of photosynthesis in eukaryotes

chordate: animal that at some time during its development has a notochord, hollow nerve cord, pharyngeal pouches or slits, and a postanal tail; phylum Chordata

chorion: outermost extraembryonic membrane

chorionic villus: fingerlike projection extending from the chorion to the uterine lining

choroid: middle layer of the eyeball, between the sclera and the retina

chromatid: one of two identical DNA molecules that make up a replicated chromosome

chromatin: collective term for all of the DNA and its associated proteins in the nucleus of a eukaryotic cell

chromosome: a continuous molecule of DNA wrapped around protein in the nucleus of a eukaryotic cell; also, the genetic material of a prokaryotic cell

chyme: semifluid mass of food and gastric juice that moves from the stomach to the small intestine

chytridiomycete (chytrid): microscopic fungus that produces motile zoospores

ciliate: protist with cilia-covered cell surface

cilium (pl. cilia): one of many short, movable protein projections extending from a cell

circulatory system: organ system that distributes blood (or a comparable fluid) throughout the body

clade: monophyletic group of organisms consisting of a common ancestor and all of its descendants

cladistics: phylogenetic system that defines groups by distinguishing between ancestral and derived characters

cladogram: treelike diagram built using shared derived characteristics

cleavage: period of rapid cell division following fertilization

cleavage furrow: in animals, the initial indentation between two daughter cells in mitosis

climax community: community that persists indefinitely if left undisturbed

clitoris: small, highly sensitive female sexual organ

clonal deletion: elimination of lymphocytes with receptors for self antigens

clonal selection: rapid division of a stimulated B cell, generating memory B cells and plasma cells that are clones of the original B cell

closed circulatory system: circulatory system in which blood remains confined to vessels

club moss: type of seedless vascular plant

cnidarian: animal with radial symmetry, two germ layers, a jellylike interior, and cnidocytes; phylum Cnidaria

cnidocyte: cell in cnidarians that can fire a toxic barb in predation or defense

coccus (pl. cocci): spherical prokaryote

cochlea: spiral-shaped part of the inner ear, where vibrations are translated into nerve impulses

codominance: mode of inheritance in which two alleles are fully expressed in a heterozygote

codon: a triplet of mRNA bases that specifies a particular amino acid

coelacanth: type of lobe-finned fish

coelom: fluid-filled animal body cavity that forms completely within mesoderm

coevolution: genetic change in one species selects for subsequent change in another species

cohesion: the attraction of water molecules to one another

cohesion-tension theory: theory that explains how water moves under tension in xylem

collecting duct: tubule in the kidney into which nephrons drain urine

collenchyma: elongated living plant cells with thick, elastic cell walls

commensalism: type of symbiosis in which one member benefits without affecting the other member

community: group of interacting populations that inhabit the same region

compact bone: solid, hard bone tissue consisting of tightly packed cylindrical units

companion cell: in phloem, a parenchyma cell adjacent to a sieve tube element

competition: struggle between organisms for the same limited resource

competitive exclusion principle: the idea that two or more species cannot indefinitely occupy the same niche

competitive inhibition: change in an enzyme's activity occurring when an inhibitor binds to the active site, competing with the enzyme's normal substrate

complement: group of proteins that help destroy pathogens

complementary: in DNA and RNA, the precise pairing of purines (A and G) to pyrimidines (C, T, and U)

complete digestive tract: digestive tract through which food passes in one direction from mouth to anus

compound: a molecule including different elements

compound leaf: leaf that is divided into leaflets

concentration gradient: difference in solute concentrations between two adjacent regions

cone: a pollen- or ovule-bearing structure in many gymnosperms

cone cell: photoreceptor cell in the retina that detects colors

conifer: type of gymnosperm

connective tissue: animal tissue consisting of widely spaced cells in a distinctive extracellular matrix

conservation biology: study of the preservation of biodiversity

constant region: amino acid sequence that is the same for all antibodies

consumer (heterotroph): organism that uses organic sources of energy and carbon

contraception: use of devices or practices that prevent pregnancy

control: untreated group used as a basis for comparison with a treated group in an experiment

convergent evolution: the evolution of similar adaptations in organisms that do not share the same evolutionary lineage

coral reef: underwater deposit of calcium carbonate formed by colonies of coral animals

cork cambium: lateral meristem that produces cork cells and parenchyma in woody plant

cornea: in the eye, a modified portion of the sclera that forms a transparent curved window that admits light

corolla: collective term for the petals of a flower

coronary artery: artery that provides blood to the heart muscle

corpus luteum: gland formed from a ruptured ovarian follicle that has recently released an oocyte

cortex: ground tissue between epidermis and vascular tissue in roots and stems

cotyledon: seed leaf in angiosperms

covalent bond: type of chemical bond in which two atoms share electrons

cranium: part of the skull that encloses the brain

creatine phosphate: molecule stored in muscle fibers; donates its high-energy phosphate to ADP, regenerating ATP

crista (pl. cristae): fold of the inner mitochondrial membrane along which many of the reactions of cellular respiration occur

crocodilian: type of reptile

crossing over: exchange of genetic material between homologous chromosomes during prophase I of meiosis

crustacean: type of mandibulate arthropod

culture: the knowledge, beliefs, and behaviors that humans transmit from generation to generation

cuticle: waterproof layer covering the aerial epidermis of a plant

cycad: type of gymnosperm

cytokine: messenger protein synthesized in immune cells that influences the activity of other immune cells

cytokinesis: distribution of cytoplasm into daughter cells in cell division

cytokinin: plant hormone that stimulates cell division

cytoplasm: the watery mixture that occupies much of a cell's volume. In eukaryotic cells, it consists of all materials, including organelles, between the nuclear envelope and the cell membrane

cytoskeleton: framework of protein rods and tubules in eukaryotic cells

cytotoxic T cell: lymphocyte that kills invading cells by binding them and releasing chemicals

D

death rate: the number of deaths per 1000 individuals per unit time

decomposer: organism that consumes wastes and dead organic matter, returning inorganic nutrients to the ecosystem

deforestation: removal of tree cover from a previously forested area

dehydration synthesis: formation of a covalent bond between two molecules by the loss of water

denaturation: modification of a protein's shape so that its function is destroyed

dendrite: thin neuron branch that receives neural messages and transmits information to the cell body

denitrification: conversion of nitrites and nitrates to N_2

density-dependent factor: population-limiting condition whose effects increase when populations are large

density-independent factor: population-limiting condition that acts irrespective of population size

dependent variable: response that may be under the influence of an independent variable

derived character: characteristic not found in the ancestor of a group being studied

dermal tissue: tissue covering a plant's surface

dermis: layer of connective tissue that lies beneath the epidermis in vertebrate skin

desert: type of terrestrial biome; very low precipitation

determinate growth: growth that halts at maturity

detritivore: animal that eats decomposing organic matter

detritus: feces and dead organic matter

deuterostome: clade of bilaterally symmetrical animals in which the first opening in the gastrula develops into the anus

diabetes: disease resulting from an inability to produce or use insulin

diastolic pressure: lower number in a blood pressure reading; reflects relaxation of the ventricles

diatom: photosynthetic aquatic protist with a two-part silica wall

differentiation: process by which cells acquire specialized functions

diffusion: movement of a substance from a region where it is highly concentrated to an area where it is less concentrated

digestion: the physical and chemical breakdown of food

digestive system: organ system that dismantles food, absorbs nutrient molecules, and eliminates indigestible wastes

dihybrid cross: mating between two individuals that are heterozygous for two genes

dinoflagellate: unicellular aquatic protist with two flagella of unequal length; many have cellulose plates

diploid cell: cell containing two full sets of chromosomes, one from each parent; also called $2n$

direct development: gradual development of a juvenile animal into an adult, without an intervening larval stage

directional selection: form of natural selection in which one extreme phenotype is fittest, and the environment selects against the others

disaccharide: a simple sugar that consists of two bonded monosaccharides

disruptive selection: form of natural selection in which the two extreme phenotypes are fittest

DNA (deoxyribonucleic acid): genetic material consisting of a double helix of nucleotides

DNA polymerase: enzyme that adds new DNA nucleotides and corrects mismatched base pairs in DNA replication

DNA probe: a single-stranded sequence of nucleotides that is complementary to a known region of DNA

DNA profiling: biotechnology tool that uses DNA to detect genetic differences between individuals

DNA technology: the manipulation of genes for a practical purpose

domain: broadest (most inclusive) taxonomic category

dominant allele: allele that is expressed whenever it is present

dorsal, hollow nerve cord: tubular nerve cord that forms dorsal to the notochord; one of the four characteristics of chordates

double fertilization: in angiosperms, one sperm nucleus fertilizes the egg and another fertilizes the polar nuclei

E

ear: sense organ of hearing and equilibrium

eardrum: structure that transmits sound from air to the middle ear

echinoderm: unsegmented deuterostome with a five-part body plan, radial symmetry in adults, and a spiny outer covering; phylum Echinodermata

ecological footprint: measure of the land area needed to support one or more humans

ecology: study of relationships among organisms and the environment

ecosystem: a community and its nonliving environment

ectoderm: outermost germ layer in an animal embryo

ectotherm: animal that lacks an internal mechanism that keeps its temperature within a narrow range; invertebrates, fishes, amphibians, and nonavian reptiles

ejaculation: discharge of semen through the penis

ejaculatory duct: tube that deposits sperm into the urethra

electromagnetic spectrum: range of naturally occurring radiation

electron: a negatively charged particle that orbits the atom's nucleus

electron transport chain: membrane-bound molecular complex that shuttles electrons to slowly extract their energy

electronegativity: an atom's tendency to attract electrons

electrophoresis: technique that uses an electric field to sort DNA fragments by size

element: a pure substance consisting of atoms containing a characteristic number of protons

elimination: the expulsion of waste from the body

embryo sac: mature female gametophyte in angiosperms

embryonic disc: in the preembryo, a flattened, two-layered mass of cells that develops into the embryo

embryonic stage: stage of human development lasting from the end of the second week until the end of the eighth week of gestation

embryonic stem cell: stem cell that can give rise to all types of cells in the body

emergent property: quality that results from interactions of a system's components

endangered species: a species facing a high risk of extinction in the near future

endocrine gland: concentration of hormone-producing cells in an animal

endocrine system: organ system consisting of glands and cells that secrete hormones

endocytosis: form of transport in which the cell membrane engulfs extracellular material

endoderm: innermost germ layer in an animal embryo

endodermis: the innermost cell layer of root cortex

endomembrane system: eukaryotic organelles that exchange materials in transport vesicles

endometrium: inner uterine lining

endophyte: fungus that colonizes a plant without triggering disease symptoms

endoplasmic reticulum: interconnected membranous tubules and sacs in a eukaryotic cell

endorphin: pain-killing protein produced in the anterior pituitary

endoskeleton: skeleton on the inside of an animal

endosperm: triploid tissue that stores food for the embryo in an angiosperm seed

endospore: dormant, thick-walled structure that enables some bacteria to survive harsh conditions

endosymbiont theory: the idea that mitochondria and chloroplasts originated as free-living bacteria engulfed by other prokaryotic cells

endothelium: layer of epithelial tissue that lines blood vessels and the heart

endotherm: animal that maintains its body temperature by using heat generated from its own metabolism; birds and mammals

energy: the ability to do work

energy shell: group of electron orbitals that share the same energy level

entropy: randomness or disorder

envelope: the membrane layer surrounding the protein coat of some viruses

enzyme: an organic molecule that catalyzes a chemical reaction without being consumed

epidermis: in animals, the outermost layer of skin; in plants, cells covering the leaves, stems, and roots

epididymis: tube that receives and stores sperm from one testis

epiglottis: cartilage that covers the glottis, routing food to the digestive tract during swallowing

epinephrine (adrenaline): hormone secreted by the adrenal medulla; also can act as a neurotransmitter

epithelial tissue (epithelium): animal tissue consisting of tightly packed cells that form linings, coverings, and glands

equilibrium species: species consisting of long-lived, late-maturing individuals that have few offspring, with each receiving heavy parental investment

esophagus: muscular tube that leads from the pharynx to the stomach

essential nutrient: substance vital for an organism's metabolism, growth, and reproduction

estrogen: steroid hormone produced in ovaries of female vertebrates

estuary: area where fresh water in a river meets the salty water of an ocean

ethylene: volatile plant hormone that ripens fruit

eudicot: one of the two main clades of angiosperms

euglenoid: unicellular flagellated protist with an elongated cell

eukaryote: organism composed of one or more cells containing a nucleus and other membrane-bounded organelles

eutrophication: addition of nutrients to a body of water

evaporation: the conversion of a liquid to a vapor (gas)

evolution: descent with modification; change in allele frequencies in a population over time

excretion: elimination of metabolic wastes

exhalation: movement of air out of the lungs

exocytosis: form of transport in which vesicles containing cell secretions fuse with the cell membrane

exon: portion of an mRNA that is translated after introns are removed

exoskeleton: skeleton on the outside of an animal

experiment: a test of a hypothesis under controlled conditions

exponential growth: population growth pattern in which the number of new individuals is proportional to the size of the population

external fertilization: release of gametes by males and females into the same environment

extinction: disappearance of a species

extracellular matrix: nonliving substances that surround animal cells; includes ground substance and fibers

eye: organ that detects light and produces the sense of sight

F

F_1 (first filial) generation: the offspring of the P generation in a genetic cross

F_2 (second filial) generation: the offspring of the F_1 generation in a genetic cross

facilitated diffusion: form of passive transport in which a substance moves down its concentration gradient with the aid of a transport protein

facultative anaerobe: organism that can live with or without O_2

$FADH_2$: electron carrier molecule used in respiration

fast-twitch fiber: large muscle cell that produces twitches of short duration

fatty acid: long-chain hydrocarbon terminating with a carboxyl group

feather: in birds, an epidermal outgrowth composed of keratin

feces: solid waste that leaves the digestive tract

fermentation: metabolic pathway in the cytoplasm in which NADH from glycolysis reduces pyruvate

fertilization: the union of two gametes

fetal stage: stage of human development lasting from the beginning of the ninth week of gestation through birth

fever: rise in the body's temperature

fibrous root system: branching root system arising from a plant's stem

filtration: removal of water and solutes from the blood, as occurs at the glomerulus

fish: vertebrate animal with fins and external gills

fitness: an organism's contribution to the next generation's gene pool

flagellated protozoan: unicellular heterotrophic protist with one or more flagella

flagellum (pl. flagella): a long whiplike appendage that a cell uses for motility

flatworm: unsegmented worm lacking a coelom; phylum Platyhelminthes

flower: reproductive structure in angiosperms; produces pollen and eggs

fluid mosaic: two-dimensional structure of movable phospholipids and proteins that form biological membranes

fluke: type of parasitic flatworm

follicle cell: nourishing cell surrounding an oocyte

follicle-stimulating hormone (FSH): reproductive hormone produced in the anterior pituitary

food chain: series of organisms that successively eat each other

food web: network of interconnecting food chains

foot: ventral muscular structure that provides movement in mollusks

foraminiferan: amoeboid protozoan with a calcium carbonate shell

forebrain: front part of the vertebrate brain

fossil: any evidence of an organism from more than 10,000 years ago

founder effect: genetic drift that occurs when a small, nonrepresentative group of individuals leaves their ancestral population and begins a new settlement

frameshift mutation: type of mutation in which nucleotides are added or deleted by any number other than a multiple of three, altering the reading frame

free-living flatworm: planarian or marine flatworm

frog: type of amphibian

fruit: seed-containing structure in angiosperms

Fungi: kingdom containing mostly multicellular eukaryotes that are heterotrophs by external digestion

G

G_1 phase: gap stage of interphase in which the cell grows and carries out its basic functions

G_2 phase: gap stage of interphase in which the cell synthesizes and stores membrane components and spindle proteins

gallbladder: organ that stores bile from the liver and releases it into the small intestine

gamete: a sex cell; sperm or egg cell

gametophyte: haploid, gamete-producing stage of the plant life cycle

gap junction: connection between two adjacent animal cells that allows cytoplasm to flow between them

gastric juice: mixture of water, mucus, salts, hydrochloric acid, and enzymes produced at the stomach lining

gastrointestinal (GI) tract: two-opening digestive tract; also called alimentary canal

gastropod: type of mollusk

gastrovascular cavity: digestive chamber with a single opening

gastrula: stage of early animal embryonic development during which three tissue layers form

gene: sequence of DNA that encodes a specific protein or RNA molecule

gene pool: all of the genes and their alleles in a population

gene therapy: treatment that replaces a faulty gene in a cell with a functioning version of the gene

genetic code: correspondence between specific nucleotide sequences and amino acids

genetic drift: change in allele frequencies that occurs purely by chance

genome: all the genetic material in an organism

genotype: an individual's combination of alleles for a particular gene

genotype frequency: number of individuals of one genotype, divided by the number of individuals in the population

genus: taxonomic category that groups closely related species

geologic timescale: a division of Earth's history into eons, eras, periods, and epochs defined by major geological or biological events

germ cell: cell that gives rise to gametes in an animal

germination: resumption of growth after seed dormancy is broken

gibberellin: plant hormone that promotes shoot elongation

ginkgo: type of gymnosperm

gland: organ that secretes substances into the bloodstream or into a duct

global climate change: long-term changes in Earth's weather patterns

glomeromycete: fungus lacking sexual spores; forms mycorrhizae

glottis: slitlike opening between the vocal cords

glucagon: pancreatic hormone that raises blood sugar level by stimulating liver cells to break down glycogen into glucose

glucocorticoid: hormone secreted by the adrenal cortex

glycerol: a three-carbon molecule that forms the backbone of triglycerides and phospholipids

glycolysis: a metabolic pathway occurring in the cytoplasm of all cells; one molecule of glucose splits into two molecules of pyruvate

gnetophyte: type of gymnosperm

Golgi apparatus: a system of flat, stacked, membrane-bounded sacs that packages cell products for export

gonad: gland that manufactures hormones and gametes in animals; ovary or testis

gonadotropin-releasing hormone (GnRH): reproductive hormone produced in the hypothalamus

gradualism: theory that proposes that evolutionary change occurs gradually, in a series of small steps

granum (pl. grana): a stack of flattened thylakoid discs in a chloroplast

gravitropism: directional growth response to gravity

gray matter: nervous tissue in the central nervous system; consists mostly of neuron cell bodies, dendrites, and synapses

green alga: photosynthetic protist that has pigments, starch, and cell walls similar to those of land plants

greenhouse effect: increase in surface temperature caused by carbon dioxide and other atmospheric gases

ground tissue: plant tissue that makes up most of the primary plant body; composed mostly of parenchyma cells

growth hormone (GH): hormone produced in the anterior pituitary

guard cells: pair of cells flanking a stoma

gymnosperm: a plant with seeds that are not enclosed in a fruit; includes conifers, *Ginkgo*, gnetophytes, and cycads

H

habitat: physical place where an organism normally lives

hagfish: jawless animal with a cranium but not vertebrae

hair cell: mechanoreceptor that initiates sound transduction in the cochlea

half-life: the time it takes for half the atoms in a sample of a radioactive substance to decay

haploid cell: cell containing one set of chromosomes; also called *n*

Hardy–Weinberg equilibrium: situation in which allele frequencies do not change from one generation to the next

heart: muscular organ that pumps blood (or a comparable fluid) throughout the body

heartwood: dark-colored, nonfunctioning secondary xylem in woody plant

helper T cell: lymphocyte that coordinates activities of other immune system cells

hemisphere: one of two halves of the cerebrum

hemoglobin: pigment that carries oxygen in red blood cells

herbaceous plant: plant with a green, nonwoody stem at maturity

herbivore: animal that eats plants

heterotroph: organism that obtains carbon and energy by eating another organism; consumer

heterozygous: possessing two different alleles for a particular gene

hindbrain: lower, posterior portion of the vertebrate brain

histamine: biochemical that dilates blood vessels and increases their permeability; involved in inflammation and allergies

homeostasis: the ability of an organism to maintain a stable internal environment despite changes in the external environment

homeotic: describes any gene that, when mutated, leads to organisms with structures in the wrong places

hominid: any of the "great apes" (orangutans, gorillas, chimpanzees, and humans)

hominine: extinct or modern human

hominoid: any ape, including humans

homologous: similar in structure or position because of common ancestry

homologous pair: two chromosomes that look alike and have the same sequence of genes

homozygous: possessing two identical alleles for a particular gene

hormone: biochemical synthesized in small quantities in one place and transported to another

hornwort: type of bryophyte

horseshoe crab: type of chelicerate arthropod

horsetail: type of seedless vascular plant

human chorionic gonadotropin (hCG): hormone secreted by an embryo; prevents menstruation

human immunodeficiency virus (HIV): virus that causes acquired immune deficiency syndrome (AIDS)

humoral immunity: branch of adaptive immune system in which B cells secrete antibodies in response to a foreign antigen

hydrogen bond: weak chemical bond between opposite partial charges on two molecules or within one large molecule

hydrolysis: splitting a molecule by adding water

hydrophilic: attracted to water

hydrophobic: repelled by water

hydrostatic skeleton: skeleton consisting of constrained fluid in a closed body compartment

hypertonic: describes a solution in which the solute concentration is greater than on the other side of a semipermeable membrane

hypha (pl. hyphae): a fungal filament; the basic structural unit of a multicellular fungus

hypoglycemia: low blood sugar caused by excess insulin or insufficient carbohydrate intake

hypothalamus: small forebrain structure beneath the thalamus that controls homeostasis and links the nervous and endocrine systems

hypothesis: a testable, tentative explanation based on prior knowledge

hypotonic: describes a solution in which the solute concentration is less than on the other side of a semipermeable membrane

I

immune system: organ system consisting of cells that defends the body against infections, cancer, and foreign substances

immunodeficiency: condition in which the immune system lacks one or more components

impact theory: idea that mass extinctions were caused by impacts of extraterrestrial origin

implantation: embedding of the blastocyst into the uterine lining

incomplete digestive tract: digestive tract with one opening that takes in food and ejects wastes

incomplete dominance: mode of inheritance in which a heterozygote's phenotype is intermediate between the phenotypes of the two homozygotes

independent variable: a factor that is hypothesized to influence a dependent variable

indeterminate growth: growth that persists indefinitely

indirect development: development of a juvenile animal into an adult while passing through intervening larval stages

inflammation: immediate, localized reaction to an injury or any pathogen that breaches the body's barriers

ingestion: the act of taking food into the digestive tract

inhalation: movement of air into the lungs

innate defense: cell or substance that provides generalized protection against all infectious agents

inner cell mass: cells in the blastocyst that develop into the embryo

insect: type of mandibulate arthropod

insulin: pancreatic hormone that lowers blood sugar level by stimulating body cells to take up glucose from the blood

integumentary system: organ system consisting of skin and its outgrowths

intermediate filament: component of the cytoskeleton; intermediate in size between a microtubule and a microfilament

intermembrane compartment: the space between a mitochondrion's two membranes

internal fertilization: use of a copulatory organ to deposit sperm inside a female's body

interneuron: neuron that connects one neuron to another in the central nervous system

internode: stem area between two points of leaf attachment

interphase: stage preceding mitosis or meiosis, when the cell carries out its functions, replicates its DNA, and grows

interstitial fluid: liquid that bathes cells in a vertebrate's body

intertidal zone: region along a coastline between the high and low tide marks

intron: portion of an mRNA molecule that is removed before translation

invasive species: introduced species that establishes a breeding population in a new location and spreads widely from the original point of introduction

invertebrate: animal without a backbone

ion: an atom or group of atoms that has lost or gained electrons, giving it an electrical charge

ionic bond: attraction between oppositely charged ions

iris: colored part of the eye; regulates the size of the pupil

isotonic: condition in which a solute concentration is the same on both sides of a semipermeable membrane

isotope: any of the forms of an element, each having a different number of neutrons in the nucleus

J

jaws: bones that frame the entrance to the mouth

joint: area where two bones meet

J-shaped curve: plot of exponential growth over time

K

karyotype: a size-ordered chart of the chromosomes in a cell

keystone species: a species whose effect on community structure is disproportionate to its biomass

kidney: excretory organ in the vertebrate urinary system

kilocalorie (kcal): one thousand calories; one food Calorie.

kinetic energy: energy being used to do work; energy of motion

kingdom: taxonomic category below domain

Krebs cycle: stage in cellular respiration that completely oxidizes the products of glycolysis

L

labor: the process of childbirth

***lac* operon:** in *E. coli*, three lactose-degrading genes plus the promoter and operator that control their transcription

lactic acid fermentation: metabolic pathway in which NADH from glycolysis reduces pyruvate, producing lactic acid

lamprey: type of jawless fish

lancelet: type of invertebrate chordate

large intestine: part of the digestive tract that connects the small intestine to the anus

larva: in animal development, an immature stage that does not resemble the adult of the species

larynx: boxlike structure in front of the pharynx

latent: describes an infection in which viral genetic material in a host cell does not cause symptoms

lateral line: network of canals that extends along the sides of fishes and houses receptor organs that detect vibrations

lateral meristem: meristem whose daughter cells thicken a root or stem

law of independent assortment: Mendel's law stating that during gamete formation, the segregation of the alleles for one gene does not influence the segregation of the alleles for another gene

law of segregation: Mendel's law stating that the two alleles of each gene are packaged into separate gametes

leaf: flattened organ that carries out photosynthesis

leech: type of annelid

lens: structure in the eye that bends incoming light

leukemia: cancer in which bone marrow overproduces white blood cells

lichen: association of a fungus and a green alga or cyanobacterium

life history: the events of an organism's life, especially those that are related to reproduction

life table: chart that shows the probability of surviving to any given age

ligament: band of fibrous connective tissue that connects bone to bone across a joint

ligase: enzyme that catalyzes formation of covalent bonds in the DNA sugar-phosphate backbone

light reactions: photosynthetic reactions that harvest light energy and store it in molecules of ATP or NADPH

lignin: tough, complex molecule that strengthens the walls of some plant cells

limbic system: collection of forebrain structures involved in emotion and memory

linkage group: group of genes that tend to be inherited together because they are on the same chromosome

linkage map: diagram of gene order and spacing on a chromosome, based on crossover frequencies

linked genes: genes on the same chromosome

lipid: hydrophobic organic molecule consisting mostly of carbon and hydrogen

liver: organ that produces bile, detoxifies blood, stores glycogen and fat-soluble vitamins, synthesizes blood proteins, and monitors blood glucose level

liverwort: type of bryophyte

lizard: type of reptile

lobe-finned fish: type of bony fish; coelacanths and lungfishes

logistic growth: the leveling-off of a population in response to environmental resistance

long-term memory: memory that can last from hours to a lifetime

lung: sac-like structure where gas exchange occurs in air-breathing vertebrates

lungfish: type of lobe-finned fish

luteinizing hormone (LH): reproductive hormone produced in the anterior pituitary

lymph: fluid in lymph vessels

lymph capillary: dead-end vessel that collects lymph

lymph node: lymphatic structure located along lymph capillary; contains white blood cells that help fight infection

lymphatic system: organ system consisting of lymphoid organs and lymph vessels that recover excess tissue fluid and aid in immunity

lymphocyte: type of white blood cell; T cell, B cell, or natural killer cell

lysogenic infection: type of viral infection in which the genetic material of a virus is replicated along with the host cell's chromosome

lysosome: organelle in a eukaryotic cell that buds from the Golgi apparatus and enzymatically dismantles molecules, bacteria, and worn-out cell parts

lytic infection: type of viral infection in which a virus enters a cell, replicates, and causes the host cell to burst (lyse) as it releases the new viruses

M

macroevolution: large-scale evolutionary change

macronutrient: nutrient required in large amounts

macrophage: type of phagocyte

malignant tumor: mass of abnormal cells that has the potential to invade adjacent tissues and spread throughout the body

mammal: amniote with hair and mammary glands

mammary gland: milk-producing gland in mammals

mandibulate: arthropod with jawlike mouthparts (mandibles); crustaceans, insects, centipedes, and millipedes

mantle: dorsal fold of tissue that secretes a shell in most mollusks

marrow cavity: space in a bone shaft that contains marrow

marsupial: mammal that bears live young after a short gestation

mass extinction: the disappearance of many species over relatively short expanses of time

mass number: the total number of protons and neutrons in an atom's nucleus

mast cell: immune system cell that triggers inflammation and allergy

matrix: the inner compartment of a mitochondrion

matter: substance that takes up space and is made of atoms

mechanoreceptor: sensory receptor sensitive to physical deflection

Mediterranean shrubland: type of terrestrial biome; rainy winters and dry summers (also called chaparral)

medulla oblongata: part of the brainstem nearest the spinal cord

medusa: free-swimming form of a cnidarian

megaspore: in seed plants, spore that gives rise to female gametophyte

meiosis: division of genetic material that halves the chromosome number and yields genetically variable gametes

melatonin: hormone produced in the pineal gland

memory cell: lymphocyte produced in an initial infection; launches a rapid immune response upon subsequent exposure to an antigen

meninges: membranes that cover and protect the central nervous system

menstrual cycle: hormonal cycle that prepares the uterus for pregnancy

meristem: localized region of active cell division in a plant

mesoderm: embryonic germ layer between ectoderm and endoderm in an animal embryo

mesophyll: photosynthetic ground tissue in leaves

messenger RNA (mRNA): a molecule of RNA that encodes a protein

metabolism: the biochemical reactions of a cell

metamorphosis: developmental process in which an animal changes drastically in body form during the transition between juvenile and adult

metaphase: stage of mitosis in which chromosomes are aligned down the center of a cell

metastasis: spreading of cancer

metaphase I: metaphase of meiosis I, when homologous chromosome pairs align down the center of a cell

metaphase II: metaphase of meiosis II, when replicated chromosomes align down the center of a cell

microevolution: relatively short-term changes in allele frequencies within a population or species

microfilament: component of the cytoskeleton; made of the protein actin

micronutrient: nutrient required in small amounts

microspore: in seed plants, a spore that gives rise to a male gametophyte

microtubule: component of the cytoskeleton; made of subunits of the protein tubulin

microvillus (pl. microvilli): extension of the plasma membrane of an epithelial cell of a villus

midbrain: part of the brain between the forebrain and hindbrain

millipede: type of mandibulate arthropod

mineral: essential element other than C, H, O, or N

mineralocorticoid: hormone secreted by the adrenal cortex

mitochondrion: organelle that houses the reactions of cellular respiration in eukaryotes

mitosis: division of genetic material that yields two genetically identical cells

mitotic spindle: a structure of microtubules that aligns and separates chromosomes in mitosis

modern evolutionary synthesis: the idea that genetic mutations create the variation upon which natural selection acts

molecular clock: application of the rate at which DNA mutates to estimate when two types of organisms diverged from a shared ancestor

molecule: two or more atoms joined by chemical bonds

mollusk: unsegmented animal with a soft body, mantle, muscular foot, and visceral mass; phylum Mollusca

monocot: one of the two main clades of angiosperms

monohybrid cross: mating between two individuals that are heterozygous for the same gene

monomer: a single unit of a polymer

monosaccharide: a sugar molecule that contains five or six carbon atoms

monotreme: egg-laying mammal

moss: type of bryophyte

motor neuron: neuron that transmits a message from the central nervous system toward a muscle or gland

motor unit: a motor neuron and all of the muscle fibers it contacts

muscle: organ that powers movements in animals by contracting; consists of muscle tissue and other tissue types

muscle fiber: muscle cell

muscle tissue: animal tissue consisting of contractile cells that provide motion

muscular system: organ system consisting of skeletal muscles whose contractions form the basis of movement and posture

mutagen: any external agent that causes a mutation

mutant: a genotype, phenotype, or allele that is not the most common in a population or that has been altered from the "typical" (wild type) condition

mutation: a change in a DNA sequence

mutualism: type of symbiosis that improves the fitness of both partners

mycelium: assemblage of hyphae that forms an individual fungus

mycorrhiza: mutually beneficial association of a fungus and the roots of a plant

myelin sheath: fatty material that insulates some nerve fibers in vertebrates, speeding nerve impulse transmission

myofibril: cylindrical subunit of a muscle fiber, consisting of parallel protein filaments

myosin: protein that forms thick filaments in muscle cells

N

NADH: molecule that carries electrons in glycolysis and respiration

NADPH: molecule that carries electrons in photosynthesis

natural killer cell: type of lymphocyte that participates in innate defenses

natural selection: differential reproduction of organisms based on inherited traits

negative feedback: pathway in which the product of a reaction inhibits the enzyme that controls its formation; also, an action that maintains homeostasis by countering an existing condition

nephron: functional unit of the kidney

nerve: bundle of nerve fibers (axons) bound together in a sheath of connective tissue

nervous system: organ system that specializes in rapid communication

nervous tissue: tissue type whose cells (neurons and neuroglia) form a communication network

net primary production: energy available to consumers in a food chain, after cellular respiration and heat loss by producers

neuroglia: one of two cell types in nervous tissue

neuromuscular junction: synapse of a neuron onto a muscle cell

neuron: one of two cell types in nervous tissue

neurotransmitter: chemical passed from a neuron to receptors on another neuron or on a muscle or gland cell

neutral: neither acidic nor basic; not electrically charged

neutron: a particle in an atom's nucleus that is electrically neutral

niche: all resources a species uses for survival, growth, and reproduction

nitrification: conversion of ammonia to nitrites and nitrates

nitrogen fixation: conversion of N_2 to NH_4^+, a form of nitrogen that plants can use

nitrogenous base: a nitrogen-containing compound that forms part of a nucleotide

node: point at which leaves attach to a stem

nodule: root growth housing nitrogen-fixing bacteria

noncompetitive inhibition: change in an enzyme's shape occurring when an inhibitor binds to a site other than the active site

nondisjunction: failure of chromosomes to separate at anaphase I or anaphase II of meiosis

nonpolar covalent bond: a covalent bond in which atoms share electrons equally

norepinephrine (noradrenaline): hormone secreted by the adrenal medulla; also can act as a neurotransmitter

nose: organ that forms the entrance to the nasal cavity inside the head; functions in breathing and olfaction

notochord: flexible rod that forms the framework of the vertebral column and induces formation of the neural tube; one of the four characteristics of chordates

nuclear envelope: the two membranes bounding a cell's nucleus

nuclear pore: a hole in the nuclear envelope

nucleic acid: a long polymer of nucleotides; DNA or RNA

nucleoid: the part of a prokaryotic cell where the DNA is located

nucleolus: a structure within the nucleus where components of ribosomes are assembled

nucleosome: the basic unit of chromatin; consists of DNA wrapped around eight histone proteins

nucleotide: building block of a nucleic acid; consists of a phosphate group, a nitrogenous base, and a five-carbon sugar

nucleus: central part of an atom; also, the membrane-bounded sac that contains DNA in a eukaryotic cell

nutrient: any substance that an organism uses for metabolism, growth, maintenance, and repair of its tissues

O

obesity: unhealthy amount of body fat; body mass index greater than 30

obligate aerobe: organism that requires O_2 for generating ATP

obligate anaerobe: organism that must live in the absence of O_2

oligochaete: type of annelid

omnivore: animal that eats many types of food, including plants and animals

oogenesis: the production of egg cells

open circulatory system: circulatory system in which blood circulates freely through the body cavity

operator: in an operon, the DNA sequence between the promoter and the protein-encoding regions

operon: group of related bacterial genes plus a promoter and operator that control the transcription of the entire group at once.

opportunistic pathogen: infectious agent that cannot cause disease in a healthy individual

opportunistic species: species consisting of short-lived, early-maturing individuals that have many offspring, with each receiving little parental investment

optic nerve: nerve fibers that connect the retina to the brain

orbital: volume of space where a particular electron is likely to be

organ: two or more tissues that interact and function as an integrated unit

organ system: two or more physically or functionally linked organs

organelle: compartment of a eukaryotic cell that performs a specialized function

organic molecule: compound containing both carbon and hydrogen

organism: a single living individual

orgasm: pleasurable sensation, accompanied by involuntary muscle contractions, associated with sexual activity

osmoregulation: control of an animal's ion concentration

osmosis: simple diffusion of water through a semipermeable membrane

osteoporosis: condition in which bones become less dense

outgroup: basis for comparison in a cladistics analysis

oval window: membrane between the middle ear and the inner ear

ovarian cycle: hormonal cycle that controls the timing of oocyte maturation in the ovaries

ovary: the base of a flower's carpel, which encloses one or more ovules; in animals, the female gonad

overexploitation: harvesting a species faster than it can reproduce

ovulation: release of an oocyte from an ovarian follicle

ovule: egg-bearing structure that develops into a seed in gymnosperms and angiosperms

oxidation: the loss of one or more electrons by a participant in a chemical reaction

oxidation-reduction (redox) reaction: chemical reaction in which one reactant is oxidized and another is reduced

oxygen debt: after vigorous exercise, a period in which the body requires extra oxygen to restore ATP and creatine phosphate to muscle and to recharge oxygen-carrying proteins

oxytocin: hormone released from the posterior pituitary

ozone layer: atmospheric zone rich in ozone gas (O_3), which absorbs the sun's ultraviolet radiation

P

P (parental) generation: the first generation (true-breeding) in a genetic cross

pacemaker: specialized cardiac cells that set the tempo of the heartbeat

pain receptor: sensory receptor that detects mechanical damage, temperature extremes, or chemicals released from damaged cells

paleontology: the study of fossil remains or other clues to past life

pancreas: gland between the spleen and the small intestine; produces hormones, digestive enzymes, and bicarbonate

parasitism: type of symbiosis in which one member increases its fitness at the expense of the other

parasympathetic nervous system: part of the autonomic nervous system that opposes the sympathetic nervous system; dominates during relaxed times

parathyroid gland: one of four small groups of cells behind the thyroid gland

parathyroid hormone (PTH): hormone produced in the parathyroid gland

parenchyma: unspecialized plant cells that make up majority of ground tissue

parental chromosome: chromosome containing genetic information from only one parent

passive immunity: immunity generated when an organism receives antibodies from another organism

passive transport: movement of a solute across a membrane without the direct expenditure of energy

pathogen: disease-causing agent

pattern formation: developmental process that establishes the body's overall shape and structure

pectoral girdle: bones that connect the forelimbs to the axial skeleton

pedigree: chart showing family relationships and phenotypes

peer review: evaluation of scientific results by experts before publication in a journal

pelvic girdle: bones that connect the hind limbs to the axial skeleton

penis: male organ of copulation and urination

pepsin: enzyme that begins the digestion of proteins in the stomach

peptide bond: a covalent bond between adjacent amino acids; results from dehydration synthesis

peptidoglycan: material in bacterial cell wall

perception: the brain's interpretation of a sensation

periodic table: chart that lists elements according to their properties

peripheral nervous system: neurons that transmit information to and from the central nervous system

peristalsis: waves of muscle contraction that propel food along the digestive tract

peroxisome: membrane-bounded sac that houses enzymes that break down fatty acids and dispose of toxic chemicals

persistent organic pollutant: carbon-based chemical pollutants that remain in ecosystems for long periods

petal: flower part interior to sepals

petiole: stalk that supports a leaf blade

pH scale: a measurement of how acidic or basic a solution is

phagocyte: cell that engulfs and digests foreign material and cell debris

phagocytosis: form of endocytosis in which the cell engulfs a large particle

pharyngeal pouch (or slit): opening in the pharynx of a chordate embryo; one of the four characteristics of chordates

pharynx: tube just behind the oral and nasal cavities; the throat

phenotype: observable characteristic of an organism

pheromone: volatile chemical an organism releases that elicits a response in another member of the species

phloem: vascular tissue that transports sugars and other dissolved organic substances in plants

phloem sap: solution of water, minerals, sucrose, and other biochemicals in phloem

phospholipid: molecule consisting of glycerol attached to two hydrophobic fatty acids and a hydrophilic phosphate group

phospholipid bilayer: double layer of phospholipids that forms in water; forms the majority of a biological membrane

photic zone: region in a water body where light is sufficient for photosynthesis

photon: a packet of light or other electromagnetic radiation

photoperiod: day length

photoreceptor: molecule or cell that detects quality and quantity of light

photorespiration: a metabolic pathway in which rubisco reacts with O_2 instead of CO_2, counteracting photosynthesis

photosynthesis: biochemical reactions that enable organisms to harness sunlight energy to manufacture organic molecules

photosystem: cluster of pigment molecules and proteins in a chloroplast's thylakoid membrane

phototroph: organism that derives energy from sunlight

phototropism: directional growth response to unidirectional light

phylogenetics: field of study that attempts to explain the evolutionary relationships among species

physiology: the study of the functions of organisms and their parts

phytoplankton: microscopic photosynthetic organisms that drift in water

pilus (pl. pili): short projection made of protein on a prokaryotic cell

pineal gland: small gland in the brain that secretes melatonin

pioneer species: the first species to colonize an area devoid of life

pith: ground tissue inside a ring of vascular bundles in roots and stems

pituitary gland: pea-sized endocrine gland attached to the hypothalamus

placebo: inert substance used as an experimental control

placenta: structure that connects the developing fetus to the maternal circulation in placental mammals

placental mammal: mammal in which the developing fetus is nourished by a placenta

Plantae: kingdom consisting of multicellular, eukaryotic autotrophs

plasma: watery, protein-rich fluid that forms the matrix of blood

plasma cell: B cell that secretes large quantities of one antibody

plasmid: small circle of double-stranded DNA separate from a cell's chromosome

plasmodesma (pl. plasmodesmata): connection between plant cells that allows cytoplasm to flow between them

plasmodial slime mold: protist in which feeding stage consists of a plasmodium containing many nuclei

plate tectonics: theory that Earth's surface consists of several plates that move in response to forces acting deep within the planet

platelet: cell fragment that orchestrates clotting in blood

pleiotropy: multiple phenotypic effects of one genotype

point mutation: type of mutation in which one DNA base substitutes for another

polar body: small cell produced in female meiosis

polar covalent bond: a covalent bond in which electrons are attracted more to one atom's nucleus than to the other

polar nucleus: one of two nuclei fertilized to yield endosperm in angiosperms

pollen: immature male gametophyte in seed plants (gymnosperms and angiosperms)

pollen sac: pollen-producing cavity in anther

pollination: transfer of pollen to female reproductive part

pollution: physical, chemical or biological change in the environment that harms organisms

polychaete: type of annelid

polygenic: caused by more than one gene

polymer: a long molecule composed of similar subunits (monomers)

polymerase chain reaction (PCR): biotechnology tool that rapidly produces millions of copies of a DNA sequence of interest

polyp: sessile form of a cnidarian

polypeptide: a long polymer of amino acids

polyploid cell: cell with extra chromosome sets

polysaccharide: carbohydrate consisting of hundreds of monosaccharides

pons: oval mass in the brainstem where white matter connects the forebrain to the medulla and cerebellum

population: interbreeding members of the same species occupying the same region

population density: number of individuals of a species per unit area or volume of habitat

positive feedback: a process that reinforces an existing condition

postanal tail: muscular tail that extends past the anus; one of the four characteristics of chordates

posterior pituitary: the back part of the pituitary gland

postzygotic reproductive barrier: separation of species due to selection against hybrid offspring

potential energy: stored energy available to do work

predator: animal that eats other animals

prediction: anticipated outcome of the test of a hypothesis

preembryonic stage: first two weeks of human development

preimplantation genetic diagnosis (PGD): technique in which DNA from one cell is used to determine whether an embryo carries a genetic disease

pressure flow theory: theory that explains how phloem sap moves from source to sink

prey: animal that a predator eats

prezygotic reproductive barrier: separation of species due to factors that prevent the formation of a zygote

primary growth: growth from apical meristems

primary immune response: immune system's response to its first encounter with a foreign antigen

primary oocyte: in oogenesis, a diploid cell that undergoes the first meiotic division and yields a haploid polar body and a haploid secondary oocyte

primary producer: species forming the base of a food web; autotroph

primary spermatocyte: a diploid cell that undergoes the first meiotic division and yields two haploid secondary spermatocytes

primary structure: the amino acid sequence of a protein

primary succession: appearance of organisms in an area previously devoid of life

primate: mammal with opposable thumbs, eyes in front of the skull, a relatively large brain, and flat nails instead of claws; includes prosimians, simians, and hominoids

prion: infectious protein particle

producer (autotroph): organism that uses inorganic sources of energy and carbon

product: the result of a chemical reaction

product rule: the chance of two independent events occurring equals the product of the individual chances of each event

progesterone: steroid hormone produced in ovaries of female vertebrates

prokaryote: a cell that lacks a nucleus and other membrane-bounded organelles; bacteria and archaea

prolactin: hormone produced in the anterior pituitary

promoter: a control sequence at the start of a gene; attracts RNA polymerase and (in eukaryotes) transcription factors

prophage: DNA of a lysogenic bacteriophage that is inserted into a host cell's chromosome

prophase: stage of mitosis when chromosomes condense and the mitotic spindle begins to form

prophase I: prophase of meiosis I, when chromosomes condense and become visible, and crossing over occurs

prophase II: prophase of meiosis II, when chromosomes condense and become visible

prosimian: type of primate; a lemur, aye-aye, loris, tarsier, or bush baby

prostate gland: male structure that produces a milky, alkaline fluid that activates sperm

protein: a polymer consisting of amino acids and folded into its functional three-dimensional shape

protein coat: structural component that surrounds the genetic material of a virus

protist: eukaryotic organism that is not a plant, fungus, or animal

proton: a particle in an atom's nucleus carrying a positive charge

protostome: clade of bilaterally symmetrical animals in which the first opening in the gastrula develops into the mouth

protozoan: unicellular protist that is heterotrophic and (usually) motile

pseudocoelom: fluid-filled animal body cavity lined by endoderm and mesoderm

pulmonary artery: artery that leads from the right ventricle to the lungs

pulmonary circulation: blood circulation between the heart and lungs

pulmonary vein: vein that leads from the lungs to the left atrium

punctuated equilibrium: theory that life's history has been characterized by bursts of rapid evolution interrupting long periods of little change

Punnett square: diagram that uses the genotypes of the parents to reveal the possible results of a genetic cross

pupil: opening in the iris that admits light into the eye

pyramid of energy: diagram depicting energy stored at each trophic level at a given time

pyruvate: the three-carbon product of glycolysis

Q

quaternary structure: the shape arising from interactions between multiple polypeptide subunits of the same protein

R

R group: an amino acid side chain

radial symmetry: body form in which any plane passing through the body from the mouth to the opposite end divides the body into mirror images

radioactive isotope: atom that emits particles or rays as its nucleus disintegrates

radiometric dating: type of absolute dating that uses known rates of radioactive decay to date fossils

radula: a chitin-rich, tonguelike strap in many mollusks

rain shadow: downwind side of a mountain, with a drier climate than the upwind side

ray-finned fish: type of bony fish

reabsorption: renal tubule's return of useful substances to the blood

reactant: a starting material in a chemical reaction

reaction center: a molecule of chlorophyll *a* (and associated proteins) that participates in the light reactions of photosynthesis

receptacle: attachment point for flower parts

receptor potential: localized change in membrane potential (a graded potential) in a sensory receptor

recessive allele: allele whose expression is masked if a dominant allele is present

recombinant chromosome: chromosome containing genetic information from both parents as a result of crossing over

recombinant DNA: genetic material spliced together from multiple sources

red alga: multicellular, photosynthetic, marine protist with red or blue accessory pigments

red bone marrow: marrow that gives rise to blood cells and platelets

red blood cell: disc-shaped blood cell that contains hemoglobin

reduction: the gain of one or more electrons by a participant in a chemical reaction

reflex: type of innate behavior; an instantaneous, automatic response to a stimulus

relative dating: placing a fossil into a sequence of events without assigning it a specific age

repressor: in an operon, a protein that binds to the operator and prevents transcription

reproductive system: organ system that produces and transports gametes and may nurture developing offspring

reptile: tetrapod vertebrate with an amniote egg and a dry scaly body covering

resource partitioning: use of the same resource in different ways or at different times by multiple species

respiratory cycle: one inhalation followed by one exhalation

respiratory surface: part of an animal's body that exchanges gases with the environment

respiratory system: organ system that acquires oxygen gas and releases carbon dioxide

resting potential: electrical potential inside a neuron not conducting a nerve impulse

restriction enzyme: enzyme that cuts double-stranded DNA at a specific base sequence

retina: sheet of photoreceptors that forms the innermost layer of the eye

ribosomal RNA (rRNA): a molecule of RNA that, along with proteins, forms a ribosome

ribosome: a structure built of RNA and protein where mRNA anchors during protein synthesis

ribulose bisphosphate (RuBP): the five-carbon molecule that reacts with CO_2 in the Calvin cycle

RNA (ribonucleic acid): nucleic acid typically consisting of a single strand of nucleotides

RNA polymerase: enzyme that uses a DNA template to produce a molecule of RNA

RNA world: the idea that the first independently replicating life form was RNA

rod cell: photoreceptor in the retina that provides black-and-white vision

root: belowground part of most plants

root cap: cells that protect the root apical meristem from abrasion

rough endoplasmic reticulum: ribosome-studded portion of the ER where secreted proteins are synthesized

roundworm: unsegmented worm with a pseudocoelom; phylum Nematoda

rubisco: enzyme that adds CO_2 to ribulose bisphosphate in the carbon reactions of photosynthesis

ruminant: herbivore with a four-chambered organ specialized for grass digestion

S

S phase: the synthesis phase of interphase, when DNA replicates

S-shaped curve: plot of logistic growth over time

salamander: type of amphibian

sample size: number of subjects in each experimental group

sapwood: light-colored, functioning secondary xylem in woody plant

sarcomere: one of many repeated units in a myofibril of a muscle cell

saturated fatty acid: a fatty acid with single bonds between all carbon atoms

savanna: type of terrestrial biome; grassland with scattered trees

scientific method: a systematic approach to understanding the natural world based on evidence and testable hypotheses

sclera: the outermost layer of the eye; the white of the eye

sclerenchyma: rigid plant cells that support mature plant parts

scrotum: the sac containing the testes

second messenger: molecule that translates information from a cell's exterior into an effect inside the cell

secondary growth: increase in girth from cell division in lateral meristem

secondary immune response: immune system's response to subsequent encounters with a foreign antigen

secondary oocyte: haploid cell that undergoes the second meiotic division and yields a haploid polar body and a haploid egg cell

secondary sex characteristic: trait that distinguishes the sexes but does not participate directly in reproduction

secondary spermatocyte: haploid cell that undergoes the second meiotic division and yields two haploid spermatids

secondary structure: a "substructure" within a protein, resulting from hydrogen bonds between parts of the peptide backbone

secondary succession: change in a community's species composition following a disturbance

secretion: addition of substances to the fluid in a renal tubule

seed: in gymnosperms and angiosperms, a plant embryo packaged with a food supply inside a tough outer coat

seed coat: protective outer layer of seed

seedless vascular plant: plant with vascular tissue but not seeds; includes true ferns, club mosses, whisk ferns, and horsetails

segmentation: division of an animal body into repeated subunits

selective permeability: the property that enables a membrane to admit some substances and exclude others

semen: fluid that carries sperm cells out of the body

seminal vesicle: structure that contributes fluid, fructose, and prostaglandins to semen

seminiferous tubule: tubule within a testis where sperm form and mature

sensation: information that reaches the central nervous system about a stimulus

sensory adaptation: lessening of sensation with prolonged exposure to a stimulus

sensory neuron: neuron that transmits information from a stimulated body part to the central nervous system

sensory receptor: cell that detects stimulus information

sepal: part of the outermost whorl of a flower

severe combined immunodeficiency (SCID): inherited immune system disorder in which neither T cells nor B cells function

sex chromosome: a chromosome that carries genes that determine sex

sex-linked: describes genes or traits on the X or Y chromosome

sexual dimorphism: difference in appearance between males and females

sexual reproduction: the combination of genetic material from two individuals to create a third individual

sexual selection: type of natural selection resulting from variation in the ability to obtain mates

sexually transmitted disease (STD): illness that spreads during sexual contact

shoot: aboveground part of a plant

short tandem repeat (STR): short repeated DNA sequence that varies in length among individuals in a population

short-term memory: memory only available for a few moments

sieve tube element: conducting cell that makes up sieve tube in phloem

simian: type of primate; a monkey

simple diffusion: form of passive transport in which a substance moves down its concentration gradient without the use of a transport protein

simple leaf: leaf with an undivided blade

sink: plant part that does not photosynthesize

sinoatrial (SA) node: specialized cardiac muscle cells that set the pace of the heartbeat; the pacemaker

skeletal muscle: voluntary muscle tissue consisting of long, unbranched, striated cells containing multiple nuclei; also, an organ composed of bundles of skeletal muscle cells and other tissue types that generates voluntary movements between pairs of bones

skeletal system: organ system consisting of bones and ligaments that support body structures and that attach to muscles

skeleton: structure that supports an animal's body

skin: the outer surface of the body

sliding filament model: sliding of actin and myosin past each other to shorten a muscle cell

slow-twitch fiber: small muscle fiber that produces twitches of long duration

small intestine: the part of the digestive tract that connects the stomach with the large intestine; site of most chemical digestion and absorption

smog: type of air pollution that forms a visible haze in the lower atmosphere

smooth endoplasmic reticulum: portion of the ER that produces lipids and detoxifies poisons

smooth muscle: involuntary muscle tissue consisting of nonstriated, spindle-shaped cells

snake: type of reptile

sodium-potassium pump: protein that uses energy from ATP to transport Na^+ out of cells and K^+ into cells

solute: a chemical that dissolves in a solvent, forming a solution

solution: a mixture of a solute dissolved in a solvent

solvent: a chemical in which other substances dissolve, forming a solution

somatic cell: body cell that does not give rise to gametes

somatic cell nuclear transfer: technique used to clone a mammal from an adult cell

somatic nervous system: in the peripheral nervous system, motor pathways carrying signals to skeletal (voluntary) muscles

source: plant part that produces or releases sugar

speciation: formation of one or more new species

species: a distinct type of organism

species evenness: measure of biodiversity; the proportion of the community that each species occupies

species richness: measure of biodiversity; the number of species in a community

spermatid: haploid cell produced after meiosis II in spermatogenesis

spermatogenesis: the production of sperm

sphincter: muscular ring that contracts to close an opening

spinal cord: tube of nervous tissue that extends through the vertebral column

spirillum (pl. spirilla): spiral-shaped prokaryote

spleen: abdominal organ that produces and stores lymphocytes and destroys worn-out red blood cells

sponge: simple animal lacking true tissues and gastrulation; phylum Porifera

spongy bone: bone tissue with large spaces between a web of bony struts

spore: reproductive cell of a plant or fungus

sporophyte: diploid, spore-producing stage of the plant life cycle

stabilizing selection: form of natural selection in which extreme phenotypes are less fit than the optimal intermediate phenotype

stamen: male flower part interior to petals

standardized variable: any factor held constant for all subjects in an experiment

statistically significant: unlikely to be attributed to chance

statolith: starch-containing plastid in root cap cell that functions as a gravity detector

stem: part of a plant that supports leaves

steroid hormone: a lipid-soluble hormone that can freely diffuse through a cell membrane and bind to a receptor inside the cell

sterol: lipid consisting of four interconnected carbon rings

stigma: in angiosperms, pollen-receiving tip of style

stoma (pl. stomata): pore in a plant's epidermis through which gases are exchanged with the atmosphere

stomach: J-shaped compartment in the digestive tract; receives food from the esophagus

stroma: the fluid inner region of the chloroplast

style: in angiosperms, the stalklike upper part of a carpel

substitution mutation: replacement of one nucleotide in a gene with another

succession: change in the species composition of a community over time

survivorship curve: graph of the proportion of individuals that survive to a particular age

symbiosis: one species living in or on another

sympathetic nervous system: part of the autonomic nervous system that opposes the parasympathetic nervous system; mobilizes the body to respond quickly to environmental stimuli

sympatric speciation: formation of a new species within the habitat boundaries of a parent species

synapse: junction at which a neuron communicates with another cell

synaptic cleft: space into which neurotransmitters are released between two cells at a synapse

synaptic terminal: enlarged tip of an axon; contains synaptic vesicles

systematics: field of study that includes taxonomy and phylogenetics

systemic circulation: blood circulation between the heart and the rest of the body, except the lungs

systolic pressure: upper number in a blood pressure reading; reflects contraction of the ventricles

T

T cell: type of lymphocyte that coordinates adaptive immune response and destroys infected cells

taiga: type of terrestrial biome; the northern coniferous forest (also called boreal forest)

tapeworm: type of parasitic flatworm

taproot: large central root that persists throughout the life of a plant

target cell: cell that expresses receptors for a particular hormone

taste bud: cluster of cells that detect chemicals in food

taxon: a group of organisms at any rank in the taxonomic hierarchy

taxonomy: the science of describing, naming, and classifying organisms

telophase: stage of mitosis in which chromosomes arrive at opposite poles and nuclear envelopes form

telophase I: telophase of meiosis I, when homologs arrive at opposite poles

telophase II: telophase of meiosis II, when chromosomes arrive at opposite poles and nuclear envelopes form

temperate coniferous forest: type of terrestrial biome; coniferous trees dominate

temperate deciduous forest: type of terrestrial biome; deciduous trees dominate

temperate grassland: type of terrestrial biome; grazing, fire, and drought restrict tree growth

template strand: the strand that is transcribed in a DNA double helix

tendon: band of fibrous connective tissue that attaches a muscle to a bone

terminator: sequence in DNA that signals where the gene's coding region ends

tertiary structure: the overall shape of a polypeptide, resulting mostly from interactions between amino acid R groups and water

test cross: a mating of an individual of unknown genotype to a homozygous recessive individual; offspring phenotypes reveal the unknown genotype

testis (pl. testes): male gonad

testosterone: steroid hormone produced in the testes of male vertebrates

tetrapod: vertebrate with four limbs

thalamus: forebrain structure that relays sensory input to the cerebrum

theory: well-supported scientific explanation

thermoreceptor: sensory receptor that responds to temperature

thermoregulation: control of an animal's body temperature

thick filament: in muscle cells, a filament composed of myosin

thigmotropism: directional growth response to touch

thin filament: in muscle cells, a filament composed of actin

threshold potential: potential to which a neuron's membrane must be depolarized to trigger an action potential

thylakoid: disclike structure that makes up the inner membrane of a chloroplast

thylakoid space: the inner compartment of the thylakoid

thymus: lymphoid organ in the upper chest where T cells learn to distinguish foreign antigens from self antigens

thyroid gland: gland in the neck that secretes thyroid hormones and calcitonin

thyroid-stimulating hormone: hormone produced in the anterior pituitary

thyroxine: one of two thyroid hormones; increases the rate of cellular metabolism

tidal volume: volume of air inhaled or exhaled during a normal breath

tight junction: connection between two adjacent animal cells that prevents fluid from flowing past the cells

tissue: group of cells that interact and provide a specific function

tongue: muscular structure on the floor of the mouth

tooth: mineral-hardened structure embedded in the jaw

trace element: an element that an organism requires in small amounts

trachea (pl. tracheae): in vertebrates, the respiratory tube just beneath the larynx; the "windpipe." In invertebrates, a branched tubule that brings air in close contact with cells, facilitating gas exchange

tracheid: long, narrow conducting cell in xylem

transcription: production of RNA using DNA as a template

transcription factor: in a eukaryotic cell, a protein that binds a gene's promoter and regulates transcription

transduction: transfer of DNA from one cell to another via a virus; also, conversion of energy from one form to another

transfer RNA (tRNA): a molecule of RNA that binds an amino acid at one site and an mRNA codon at its anticodon site

trans fat: unsaturated fat with straight fatty acid tails

transgenic: containing DNA from multiple species

translation: assembly of an amino acid chain according to the sequence of nucleotides in mRNA

transpiration: evaporation of water from a leaf

triglyceride: lipid consisting of one glycerol bonded to three fatty acids

triiodothyronine: one of two thyroid hormones; increases the rate of cellular metabolism

trilobite: extinct type of arthropod

trophic level: an organism's position along a food chain

tropical rain forest: type of terrestrial biome; year-round high temperatures and precipitation

tropism: orientation toward or away from a stimulus

true-breeding: always producing offspring identical to the parent for one or more traits; homozygous

true fern: type of seedless vascular plant

tumor: abnormal mass of tissue resulting from cells dividing out of control

tundra: type of terrestrial biome; low temperature and short growing season

tunicate: type of invertebrate chordate

turgor pressure: the force of water pressing against the cell wall

turtle: type of reptile

U

umbilical cord: ropelike structure that connects an embryo or fetus with the placenta

unsaturated fatty acid: a fatty acid with at least one double bond between carbon atoms

urea: nitrogenous waste derived from ammonia

ureter: muscular tube that transports urine from the kidney to the bladder

urethra: tube that transports urine (and semen in males) out of the body

urinary bladder: muscular sac where urine collects

urinary system: organ system that filters blood and helps maintain concentrations of body fluids

urine: liquid waste produced by kidneys

uterine tube: tube that conducts an oocyte from an ovary to the uterus

uterus: muscular, saclike organ where embryo and fetus develop

V

vaccine: substance that initiates a primary immune response so that when an infectious agent is encountered, the secondary immune response can rapidly deactivate it

vacuole: membrane-bounded storage sac in a cell, especially the large central vacuole in a plant cell

vagina: conduit from the uterus to the outside of the body

valence shell: outermost occupied energy shell of an atom

variable: any changeable element in an experiment

variable region: amino acid sequence that is different for every antibody

vas deferens: tube that transports sperm from an epididymis to an ejaculatory duct

vascular bundle: collection of xylem, phloem, parenchyma, and sclerenchyma in plants

vascular cambium: lateral meristem that produces secondary xylem and phloem

vascular tissue: conducting tissue for water, minerals, and organic substances in plants

vasoconstriction: decrease in the diameter of a blood vessel

vasodilation: increase in the diameter of a blood vessel

vegetative plant parts: nonreproductive parts (roots, stems, and leaves)

vein: vascular bundle inside leaf; also, a vessel that returns blood to the heart

ventricle: heart chamber that pumps blood out of the heart

venule: small vein

vertebra: one unit of the vertebral column; composed of bone or cartilage that supports and protects the spinal cord

vertebral column: bone or cartilage that supports and protects the spinal cord

vertebrate: animal with a backbone

vesicle: a membrane-bounded sac that transports materials within a cell

vessel element: short, wide conducting cell in xylem

vestigial: having no apparent function in one organism, but homologous to a functional structure in another species

villus (pl. villi): tiny projection on the inner lining of the small intestine

viroid: infectious RNA molecule

virus: infectious agent that consists of genetic information enclosed in a protein coat

visceral mass: part of a mollusk that contains the digestive and reproductive systems

vital capacity: maximum volume of air that can be forced out of the lungs during one breath

vocal cord: elastic tissue band that covers the larynx and vibrates as air passes, producing sound

vulnerable species: species facing a high risk of extinction in the distant future

vulva: external female genitalia

W

water mold: filamentous, heterotrophic protist; also called an oomycete

water vascular system: system of canals in echinoderms; provides locomotion and osmotic balance

wavelength: the distance a photon moves during a complete vibration

whisk fern: type of seedless vascular plant

white blood cell: one of five types of blood cells that help fight infection

white matter: nervous tissue in the central nervous system; consists of myelinated axons

wild-type: the most common phenotype, genotype, or allele

wood: secondary xylem

woody plant: plant with stems and roots made of wood and bark

X

X inactivation: turning off all but one X chromosome in each cell of a mammal (usually female) early in development

X-linked: describes traits controlled by genes on the X chromosome

xylem: vascular tissue that transports water and dissolved minerals in plants

xylem sap: solution of water and dissolved minerals in xylem

Y

yellow bone marrow: fatty marrow that replaces red bone marrow as bones age

yolk sac: extraembryonic membrane that forms beneath the embryonic disc and manufactures blood cells

Z

zygomycete: fungus that produces zygospores

zygote: the fused egg and sperm that develops into a diploid individual

Credits

Photographs

Chapter 1

Opener: © t14/ZUMA Press/Newscom; p. 3 (corn): © Corbis (RF); 1.1: © SMC Images/The Image Bank/Getty Images; 1.2 (population): © Gregory G. Dimijian, M.D./Photo Researchers; 1.2 (community): © Todd Gustafson/Danita Delimont; 1.2 (ecosystem): © Manoj Shah/The Image Bank/Getty Images; 1.2 (biosphere): © Corbis (RF); p. 6 (nest): © Siede Preis/ Getty Images (RF); 1.5a: © Dennis Kunkel/Phototake; 1.5b: © Brand X Pictures/Getty Images (RF); 1.5c: © Corbis Animals in Action CD; 1.6a-b: © Michael and Patricia Fogden/Animals Animals - Earth Scenes; 1.7a (inset): © Ron Occalea/The Medical File/Peter Arnold/ Photolibrary; 1.7a: © Dennis Kunkel Microscopy, Inc.; 1.8 (bacteria): © Kwangshin Kim/Photo Researchers; 1.8 (archaea): © Ralph Robinson/Visuals Unlimited; 1.8 (protista): © Melba Photo Agency/PunchStock (RF); 1.8 (animalia): Courtesy of The National Human Genome Research Institute; 1.8 (fungi): © Corbis (RF); 1.8 (plantae): © Photo by Keith Weller/USDA; p. 10 (snake): © Ann Manner/Photodisc/Getty Images (RF); p. 11 (journals): © McGraw-Hill Companies, Inc./ Jill Braaten, photographer; 1.10a: U.S. fish & Wildlife Service/J&K Hollingsworth; 1.10b: © Corbis (RF); 1.12: © Geoff McIlleron: Firefly Images/Photographersdirect. com; p. 14 (pills): © Stockbyte/Getty Images (RF); p. 15 (rat): © Photodisc Collection/Getty Images (RF); p. 15 (sweetener): © Martin Bond/Photo Researchers; p. 16 (woman): © Getty Images/Photodisc (RF); 1.13 (moth): © Mitsuhiko Imamori/Minden Pictures; 1.13 (Darwin): © Richard Milner; 1.13 (Wallace): © Hulton Archive/ Getty Images; p. 17 (Origin of Species): © Bettmann/ Corbis; p. 19 (earth): © Corbis (RF); p. 19 (leaves): © Photo by Keith Weller/USDA; p. 19 (bacteria): © Kwangshin Kim/Photo Researchers; p. 19 (archaea): © Ralph Robinson/Visuals Unlimited; p. 19 (bee): Courtesy of The National Human Genome Research Institute; p. 19 (coffe tasters): © Corbis (RF)

Chapter 2

Opener: © Zero Creatives/Getty Images (RF); p. 21 (dog): © Photodisc/Getty Images (RF); p. 23: © Steve Cole/ Getty Images (RF); 2.5a: © Pixtal/SuperStock (RF); 2.5b: © F. Schussler/PhotoLink (RF)/Getty Images; 2.5c: © Getty Images (RF); 2.5d: © Jonelle Weaver/ Getty Images (RF); p. 26: © Pier/Getty Images (RF); 2.7: © Corbis (RF); 2.8: © The McGraw-Hill Companies, Inc./Jacques Cornell photographer; 2.9: © Steve Allen/Brand X Pictures/Alamy (RF); 2.10: © Herman Eisenbeiss/Photo Researchers; 2.11: © Getty Images/ flickr (RF); p. 31: © Ingram Publishing/SuperStock (RF); p. 33: © Stockdisc/PunchStock (RF); p. 34 (grocer): © Masterfile (RF); p. 34 (plate): © Ingram Publishing/Alamy (RF); 2.16c (top): © Dennis Kunkel Microscopy, Inc.; 2.16c (middle): © Gary Gaugler/Visuals Unlimited; 2.16c (bottom): © Marshall Sklar/SPL/Photo Researchers; p. 37: © Burke/Triolo/Brand X Pictures (RF); 2.17 (butter): © D. Hurst/Alamy (RF); 2.17 (oil): © The McGraw-Hill Companies, Inc./Jacques Cornell photographer; 2.18: © BananaStock/PunchStock (RF); p. 39: © Comstock/Jupiter Images (RF); 2.25: © Scott Camazine/Alamy

Chapter 3

Opener: © Thomas Deerinck/Visuals Unlimited, Inc.; p. 49: © AP Photo/The Columbian, Janet L. Mathews; 3.2a: © Comstock (RF)/Alamy; 3.2a (inset): © Michael Abbey/Visuals Unlimited; 3.2b: © Inga Spence/Visuals Unlimited; 3.2b (inset): © Dr. Dennis Kunkel/Visuals Unlimited; 3.2c: © Inga Spence/Visuals Unlimited; 3.2c (inset): © Microworks Color/Phototake; 3.2d: © Inga Spence/Visuals Unlimited; 3.2d (inset): © Steve Gschmeissner/SPL/Photo Researchers; 3.3b: © Wim van Egmond/Visuals Unlimited; 3.5b: © Dr. Martin Oeggerli/ Visuals Unlimited; p. 55: © GlowImages/Alamy (RF); p. 56 (candy): © Getty Images/Digital Vision (RF); p. 56 (piglet): © Tim Flach/Getty Images; 3.12b: © David M. Phillips/The Population council/Science Source/Photo Researchers; 3.13: © Prof. J. L. Kemeny/ISM/Phototake; 3.14, 3.16: © Biophoto Associates/Photo Researchers; 3.17: © Dr. Donald Fawcett/Visuals Unlimited; 3.18: © Biophoto Associates/Photo Researchers; 3.19: © Bill Longcore/Photo Researchers; 3.20a: © Innerspace Imaging/Photo Researchers; 3.20b: © Francois Paquet-Durand/Photo Researchers; 3.20c: © Edwin A. Reschke/ Peter Arnold/Photolibrary; 3.20d: © Kevin & Betty Collins/Visuals Unlimited; 3.22a: © D.W. Fawcett/Photo Researchers; 3.22b: © Dr. Tony Brain/Photo Researchers; 3.23a: © BioPhoto Associates/Photo Researchers; 3.25a-b: Courtesy Prof. Jeffery Errington; p. 65 (ameoba): © Wim van Egmond/Visuals Unlimited; p. 65 (e-coli): © Dr. Martin Oeggerli/Visuals Unlimited; p. 65 (bee): Courtesy of The National Human Genome Research Institute; p. 65 (leaf): © Photo by Keith Weller/USDA; p. 65 (bacteria): © Kwangshin Kim/Photo Researchers; p. 65 (archaea): © Ralph Robinson/Visuals Unlimited; p. 65 (paramecium): © Michael Abbey/Visuals Unlimited; p. 65 (streptococcus): © David McCarthy/Photo Researchers; p. 67 (bacteria): © Kwangshin Kim/Photo Researchers; p. 67 (archaea): © Ralph Robinson/Visuals Unlimited

Chapter 4

Opener: © Scott Markewitz/Getty Images; p. 69: © Comstock Images (RF); 4.3 (both): © Ryan McVay/ Getty Images; 4.4 (top): © Blair Seitz/Photo Researchers; 4.4 (bottom): © ImageSource/Corbis (RF); p. 74: © Stockdisc/PunchStock (RF); 4.15a-c: © Dr. David M. Phillips/Visuals Unlimited; 4.16a-b: © Nigel Cattlin/ Photo Researchers; 4.18: © Biology Media/Photo Researchers; p. 80: © Richard Hutchings/The McGraw-Hill Companies; p. 81: CDC/ Janice Haney Carr

Chapter 5

Opener: © Christian Kober/Getty Images; p. 85 (sprout): © Corbis (RF); 5.1: Electron micrograph by Wm. P. Wergin, courtesy of Eldon H. Newcomb, University of Wisconsin-Madison; 5.4 (leaves): © Steve Raymer/NGS Image Collection; 5.4 (mesophyll): Electron micrograph by Wm. P. Wergin, courtesy of Eldon H. Newcomb, University of Wisconsin-Madison; 5.5: KN Ferreira, TM Iverson, K Maghlaoui, J Barber, S Iwata, "Architecture of the photosynthetic oxygen-evolving center." SCIENCE, 19 March 2004: Vol. 303 no. 5665 pp. 1831-1838. © 2004 Reprinted with permission.; p. 90 (leaves): © Corbis (RF); p. 92 (dandelion): © image100/Corbis (RF); p. 93 (leaf): © Brand X Pictures/PunchStock (RF); 5.10 (left): © Tony Sweet/Digital Vision (RF)/Getty Images; 5.10 (middle): © Joeseph Sohm-Visions of America/Getty Images (RF); 5.10 (right): © Digital Vision (RF)/Getty Images; 5.11: Mary E. Rumpho, Elizabeth J. Summer, and James R. Manhart, "Solar-Powered Sea Slugs. Mollusc/Algal Chloroplast Symbiosis." Plant Physiology, May 2000, Vol. 123, pp. 29-38; 5.12: Rumpho, Mary E. et al. "Horizontal gene transfer of the algal nuclear gene psbO to the photosynthetic sea slug Elysia chlorotica." PNAS November 18, 2008; vol. 105, no. 46: 17867-17871. Used by permission © 2011 National Academy of Sciences, U.S.A.

Chapter 6

Opener: © Three Images/Lifesize/Getty Images; p. 98 (bird): © Getty Images/Purestock (RF); 6.1: © Thomas Deerinck, NCMIR/SPL/Photo Researchers; 6.3 (leaves): © Steve Raymer/NGS Image Collection; 6.3 (mesophyll): Electron micrograph by Wm. P. Wergin, courtesy of Eldon H. Newcomb, University of Wisconsin-Madison; p. 103 (poison): © Corbis (RF); p. 105: © Photodisc/ Getty Images (RF); 6.9: © Digital Vision (RF)/Getty Images; 6.10 (champagne): © Brand X Pictures (RF)/ PunchStock; 6.10 (lifting weights): © Corbis (RF); 6.11 (both): © Marc Gibernau, CNRS

Chapter 7

Opener: © Dr. Gopal Murti/Visuals Unlimited; p. 113 (poster): © Universal Pictures/Photofest; 7.1a-b: © Science Source/Photo Researchers; 7.1c: © Bettmann/ Corbis; 7.1d: © Photodisc/Photolibrary (RF); 7.8: © Tom Pantages/Phototake; 7.10: © Kiseleva and Donald Fawcett/Visuals Unlimited; p. 120 (mushroom): © Jean-Louis Le Moigne/Peter Arnold/Photolibrary; 7.14a: © Andrew Syred/SPL/Photo Researchers; 7.14b: © Science VU/Dr. F. R. Turner/Visuals Unlimited; 7.15a: © Micro Discovery/Corbis; 7.15b: © Dr. Gopal Murti/SPL/Photo Researchers; 7.16a: © Erich Schlegel/ Dallas Morning News/Corbis; 7.16b: © Pallava Bagla/ Corbis; 7.16c: © Scott Olson/Getty Images; 7.17a: © Dr. O. Bradfute/Peter Arnold/Photolibrary; 7.17b: © Eye of Science/Photo Researchers; 7.17c: © E.O.S./ Gelderblom/Photo Researchers; 7.17d: © NIAID/Peter Arnold/Photolibrary; 7.17e: © George Musil/Visuals Unlimited; p. 128: © Photodisc/Photolibrary (RF); 7.21 (left): © Nigel Cattlin/Photo Researchers; 7.21 (right): © Science VU/Visuals Unlimited; 7.22: © Getty Images/ Science Photo Library (RF); 7.23: Theodore Diener/

USDA Plant Virology Laboratory; 7.24 (cow): © Pixtal/age fotostock (RF); 7.24 (tissue): © Ralph Eagle Jr./Photo Researchers; p. 133: © Dave and Les Jacobs/Blend Images LLC; 7.25 (mouse): © Naturfoto Honal/Corbis; 7.25 (monkey): © A & M Shah/Animals Animals - Earth Scenes; 7.25 (gorilla): © Paul Souders/Corbis; 7.25 (chimp): © Creatas (RF)/PunchStock; 7.25 (human): © Creatas (RF)/PictureQuest

Chapter 8

Opener: © PhotoAlto/Getty Images (RF); p. 139: © Steve Gschmeissner/SPL/Getty Images (RF); 8.2a: © Brad Smith, University of Michigan NICHD: NO1-HD-6-3257; 8.2b: © Image Source (RF)/Getty Images; 8.2c: © Hans Pfletschinger/Photolibrary; 8.2d: Centers for Disease Control and Prevention (CDC); p. 143: © TLF Design/Alamy (RF); 8.6: © Clouds Hill Imaging Ltd./Corbis; p. 145: © Steven P. Lynch/The Mcgraw-Hill Companies (RF); 8.9 (animal all): © Ed Reschke/Peter Arnold/Photolibrary; 8.9 (plant all): © Ed Reschke; 8.10a: © Dr. David Phillips/Visuals Unlimited; 8.10b: © R. Calentine/Visuals Unlimited; p. 150 (sunscreen): © Stockbyte/Getty Images (RF); p 150 (cell division): © Steve Gschmeissner/SPL/Getty Images (RF); p. 153: © Clouds Hill Imaging Ltd./Corbis

Chapter 9

Opener: © IT Stock/age fotostockk (RF); p. 155: © Corbis (RF); 9.1a (all): © Carolina Biological Supply Company/Phototake; 9.1b: © Jane Burton/Getty Images; 9.2 (all): © CNRI/Photo Researchers; 9.4: © Francis Leroy, Biocosmos/Photo Researchers; 9.6 (all): © Ed Reschke/Peter Arnold/Photolibrary; p. 160: © D. Normark/PhotoLink/Getty Images (RF); p. 162: © Nancy R. Cohen/Getty Images (RF); 9.9 (identical): © Barbara Penoyar/Getty Images (RF); 9.9 (fraternal): © Image Source Black (RF)/Getty Images; 9.12a (both): © CNRI/Photo Researchers; 9.12b: © George Doyle/Stockbyte (RF)/Getty Images; 9.14: Courtesy of Dr. Pamela S. Soltis

Chapter 10

Opener: © Punchstock/Sockbyte (RF); p. 171 (puppies): © Punchstock/BananaStock (RF); 10.1a: © CNRI/Photo Researchers; 10.2: © James King-Holmes/Photo Researchers; p. 174 (cola): © Pixtal/SuperStock (RF); p. 174 (ingredients label): © David Tietz/Editorial Image, LLC; 10.10: © Pat Pendarvis; 10.18 (both): © Andrew Syred/Photo Researchers; 10.20a: © William E. Ferguson; 10.20b: © Horst Schaefer/Peter Arnold/Photolibrary; p. 187: © Image Source Pink (RF)/Getty Images; 10.21a: © Rick Wilking/Reuters/Corbis; 10.21b: © Stringer Brazil/Reuters; 10.21c: © BSIP/Photo Researchers; 10.22: © Carolyn A. McKeone/Photo Researchers; 10.23: © Sarah Leen/National Geographic Image Collection; 10.24: © Nigel Cattlin/Visuals Unlimited; p. 192 & p. 195: © CNRI/Photo Researchers

Chapter 11

Opener: © AP Photo/Ben Margot; p. 199: © Edward Kinsman/Photo Researchers; p. 200: Stephen Ausmus/USDA; 11.5: © Josh Westrich/zefa/Corbis; 11.6: © David Tietz/Editorial Image, LLC; 11.8a: © Congressional Quarterly/Getty Images; 11.8b: © Getty Images; 11.10: © Inga Spence/Visuals Unlimited; 11.11: © AP Photo/Paul Clements; 11.13a: © RAJAU/PHANIE/Photo Researchers; 11.13b: © Andreu Dalmau/epa/Corbis; p. 212: © Corbis (RF); 11.15: © Creatas (RF)/PunchStock; p. 214: © Creatas/PunchStock; p. 217 (fish): © Edward Kinsman/Photo Researchers; p. 217 (cells): © Rajau/Phanie/Photo Researchers

Chapter 12

Opener: © rubberball/Getty Images (RF); p. 219: © C Squared Studios/Getty Images (RF); 12.1 (left): © Stockdisc/PunchStock (RF); 12.1 (right): © Red Chopsticks/Getty Images (RF); 12.2 (Aristotle): © Science Source/Photo Researchers; 12.2 (Buffon): © The Print Collector/Imagestate; 12.2 (Lamarck): © Bettmann/Corbis; 12.2 (Lyell): © Corbis; 12.2 (Darwin): © Richard Milner; 12.2 (Wallace): © Hulton Archive/Getty Images; p. 222: © Sergey Galushko/Alamy (RF); 12.3: © Jeff Greenberg/Peter Arnold/Photolibrary; 12.4: © David Zurick (RF); 12.6 (Darwin): © Richard Milner; 12.6 (sequencing): © Josh Westrich/zefa/Corbis; p. 225 (bug): © IT Stock/PunchStock (RF); 12.7a: © Garrett W. Ellwood/NBAE via Getty Images; 12.7b: © Perennou Nuridsany/Photo Researchers; 12.8a: © Dennis Kunkel Microscopy, Inc.; 12.8a (inset): © Ron Occalea/The Medical File/Peter Arnold/Photolibrary; 12.9: © Image Source (RF)/PunchStock; 12.10: © Dr. John Alcock/Visuals Unlimited; 12.11a: © John Cancalosi/Peter Arnold/Photolibrary; 12.11b: © B.A.E. Inc./Alamy (RF); p. 228: © Creatas/PunchStock (RF); 12.15a: © James Warwick/Getty Images; 12.15b: © Michael S. Yamashita/Corbis; 12.15c: © Sumio Harada/Minden Pictures; p. 233 (prison): © Philip Gordon/Photolibrary; p. 233 (bird): © Jeremy Woodhouse/Photodisc/Getty Images (RF); 12.17b: Courtesy of Dr. Victor A. McKusick/Johns Hopkins Hospital; p. 241 (beetles): Dennis Sheridan © David Liebman PinkGuppy; p. 241 (rams): © Sumio Harada/Minden Pictures

Chapter 13

Openers: © O. Louis Mazzatenta/NGS Image Collection; p. 243: © McGraw-Hill Higher Education/Carlyn Iverson, photographer; 13.1 (archaefructus): Ge Sun, David L. Dilcher, Shaoling Zheng and Zhekun Zhou. "In Search of the First Flower: A Jurassic Angiosperm, Archaefructus, from Northeast China." SCIENCE, 27 November 1998; Vol. 282, No. 5394, pages 1601-1772. © 1998 Reprinted with permission.; 13.1 (pet. wood): © PhotoLink/Getty Images (RF); 13.1 (embryo): © University of the Witwatersrand/epa/Corbis; 13.3: © Jean-Claude Carton/Bruce Coleman/Photoshot; 13.1 (coprolite): © Sinclair Stammers/Photo Researchers; 13.4: © Staffan Widstrand/Nature Picture Library; 13.1 (trilobite): © Siede Preis/Getty Images (RF); 13.9a: © E.R. Degginger/Animals Animals - Earth Scenes; 13.1 (fish): © Phil Degginger/Carnegie Museum/Alamy (RF); 13.9b: © Science Vu/Visuals Unlimited; 13.1 (leaf): © Biophoto Associates/Photo Researchers; 13.10a: © Francesco Tomasinelli/The Lighthouse/Visuals Unlimited; 13.1 (triceratops): © Francois Gohier/Photo Researchers; 13.10b: © Francesco Tomasinelli/The Lighthouse/Visuals Unlimited; 13.10c: © Dante Fenolio/Photo Researchers; 13.12 (fish): © Dr. Richard Kessel/Visuals Unlimited; 13.12 (mouse): © Steve Gschmeissner/Photo Researchers; 13.12 (alligator): USGS/Southeast Ecological Science Center; p. 252: © Ingram Publishing/Alamy (RF); p. 254: © Comstock/PunchStock (RF); 13.16a: © Dr. Hussam Zaher; p. 257 (trilobite): © Siede Preis/Getty Images (RF); p. 257 (embryo): © Steve Gschmeissner/Photo Researchers; p. 257 (canyon): © Jeff Greenberg/Peter Arnold/Photolibrary

Chapter 14

Opener: © Klaus Nigge/National Geographic/Getty Images; p. 259: © Getty Images (RF); 14.1 (bacteria): © S. Lowry/University Ulster/Getty Images; 14.1 (tree): © Corbis (RF); 14.1 (bird): © Erich Kuchling/Westend61/Getty Images (RF); 14.2: © IT Stock Free/Alamy (RF); p. 262 (mosquito): USDA; p. 262 (mule): © D. Normark/PhotoLink/Getty Images (RF); 14.5 (Galápagos tortoise): © Tui De Roy/Minden Pictures; 14.5 (Chatham Island tortoise): © Ardea/Watson, M./Animals Animals - Earth Scenes; 14.5 (giant tortoise): © Gibson, Mickey/Animals Animals - Earth Scenes; 14.6: © Robyn Beck/AFP/Getty Images; 14.6 (fish): © Stone Nature Photography/Alamy; 14.12 (inset): © Francois Gohier/Photo Researchers; p. 268: © U.S. Fish & Wildlife Service/Luther C. Goldman; 14.15 (all): Courtesy of Toby Bradshaw and Doug Schemske; p. 273 (sperm): © Francis Leroy, Biocosmos/Photo Researchers; p. 273 (bird): Photo courtesy of USDA Natural Resources Conservation Service; p. 275 (fossil): © Francois Gohier/Photo Researchers

Chapter 15

Opener: © NPS photo by William S. Keller (RF); p. 277: © The mcGraw-Hill companies, Inc./John Thoeming, photographer; 15.5: © Hiroya Minakuchi/Minden Pictures; 15.6 (bacteria): © Kwangshin Kim/Photo Researchers; 15.6 (archaea): © Ralph Robinson/Visuals Unlimited; 15.7 (volvox): © Wim van Egmond/Visuals Unlimited; 15.8a: © David M. Phillips/Visuals Unlimited; 15.8b: © SciMAT/Photo Researchers; 15.8c: © Ed Reschke/Peter Arnold/Photolibrary; 15.9: © Michael Abbey/Photo Researchers; 15.10a: © John Walsh/Photo Researchers; 15.10b: © Dr Gopal Murti/Photo Researchers; 15.11 (mud pool): © Ralph C. Eagle, Jr./Photo Researchers; 15.11 (archaea): © Eye of Science/Photo Researchers; 15.12: © Dr. John D. Cunningham/Visuals Unlimited; 15.12 (inset): © Science VU/Visuals Unlimited; p. 286 (taking pill): © Keith Brofsky/Getty Images (RF); 15.13: © Ingram Publishing/SuperStock (RF); 15.13 (inset): Centers for Disease Control and Prevention (CDC); 15.14a: © Joe Munroe/Photo Researchers; 15.14b: © David Wrobel/Visuals Unlimited; 15.14c: © Jonathan A. Meyers/Photo Researchers; p. 287: © Photodisc/Alamy (RF); 15.17b: © M. Abbey/Visuals Unlimited; 15.18: © Melba Photo Agency/PunchStock (RF); p. 291 (algae): © Michael Marten/Photo Researchers; 15.19: © Dr. David M. Phillips/Visuals Unlimited; 15.20 (diatoms): © Carolina Biological Supply Company/Phototake; 15.20 (single diatom): © Steve Gschmeissner/Photo Researchers; 15.21: © Ralph A. Clevenger/Corbis; 15.22: © Daniel W. Gatshall/Visuals Unlimited; 15.23 (spirogyra): © Tom Stack/Tom Stack & Associates; 15.23 (micrasterias): © Wim van Egmond/Visuals Unlimited; 15.23 (desmid): © M. I. Walker/Photo Researchers; 15.24: © W.E. Fry, Plant Pathology, Cornell University; 15.25 (both): © Carolina Biological Supply Company/Phototake; 15.26a: © Eric V. Grave/Photo Researchers; 15.26b: © Dr. Dennis Kunkel/Visuals Unlimited; 15.26c: © Eye of Science/Photo Researchers; 15.27a: © Manfred Kage/Peter Arnold/Photolibrary; 15.27b: © Wim van Egmond/Visuals Unlimited/Corbis;

15.28: © Michael Abbey/Visuals Unlimited; 15.29: © Corbis (RF); p. 297: © Photodisce/Getty Images (RF); 15.33: © Ed Young/Corbis; 15.34a: © Nigel Cattlin/ Visuals Unlimited; 15.34a (inset): © Biodisc/Visuals Unlimited; 15.34b: © Emanuele Biggi/Getty Images; 15.34c: © Lee Berger, James Cook University; 15.34c (frog): © Dr. Janalee Caldwell; 15.35a: © Joseph B. Morton; 15.35b (left): © Dr. John D. Cunningham/ Visuals Unlimited; 15.35b (right): © R.L. Peterson/ Biological Photo Service; 15.36: © William H. Mullins/ Photo Researchers; 15.36 (inset): © V. Ahmadijian/ Visuals Unlimited; 15.37: © Robert van der Hilst/Corbis; p. 303 (proteus): © Dr. Fred Hossler/Visuals Unlimited; p. 303 (archaea): © Ralph Robinson/Visuals Unlimited; p. 303 (volvox): © Wim van Egmond/Visuals Unlimited; p. 303 (cacao): © Robert van der Hilst/Corbis; p. 303 (mushroom): © Corbis (RF); p. 303 (bee): Courtesy of The National Human Genome Research Institute

Chapter 16

Opener: © G. R. "Dick" Roberts/Natural Sciences Image Library; p. 305: © S. Solum/PhotoLink/Getty Images (RF); 16.1: © Dr. John D. Cunningham/Visuals Unlimited; 16.3: © Photo by Keith Weller/USDA; 16.4 (peas): © Corbis (RF); 16.4 (vascular tissue): © Dr. John D. Cunningham/Visuals Unlimited; 16.4 (cuticle): © M. I. Walker/Photo Researchers; p. 308 & p. 309: © Creatas/ PunchsStock (RF); 16.7a: © Edward S. Ross; 16.7b: © William E. Ferguson; 16.7c: © Steven P. Lynch/The Mcgraw-Hill Companies (RF); 16.8: © Ed Reschke; 16.9a: © John Gates/Visuals Unlimited; 16.9b: © Michel Viard/Peter Arnold/Photolibrary; 16.9c: © W. Ormerod/ Visuals Unlimited; 16.9d: © Ed Reschke; 16.9e: © Rod Planck/Photo Researchers; 16.10 (spores): © David M. Dennis/Animals Animals - Earth Scenes; 16.10 (gametophyte): © Stan Elems/Visuals Unlimited; 16.11a (top): © Walter H. Hodge/Peter Arnold/Photolibrary; 16.11a (bottom): © Pat Pendarvis; 16.11b (top): © Richard Shiell/Animals Animals - Earth Scenes; 16.11b (bottom): © G. R. "Dick" Roberts/Natural Sciences Image Library; 16.11c (top): © Jack Dykinga/Nature Picture Library; 16.11c (bottom): © Ed Reschke/Peter Arnold/Photolibrary; 16.11d (top): © Gerald & Buff Corsi/Visuals Unlimited; 16.11d (bottom): © Edward S. Ross; p. 315: © Westend61/Alamy (RF); 16.13a: © Hans Reinhard/OKAPIA/Photo Researchers; 16.13b: © Richard Weiss/Peter Arnold/Photolibrary; 16.13c: © Dwight Kuhn; 16.13d: © Pat Pendarvis; p. 317: © Burke/Triolo Productions/Getty Images (RF); p. 318 (corn): © C Squared Studios/Getty Images (RF); 16.15: Courtesy of K. Schaefer; p. 321 (vascular tissue): © Dr. John D. Cunningham/Visuals Unlimited; p. 321 (pine cone): © Ed Reschke/Peter Arnold/Photolibrary; p. 321 (peas): © Corbis (RF); p. 321 (bryopyite): © Edward S. Ross; p. 321 (fern): © Rod Planck/Photo Researchers; p. 321 (tree): © Jack Dykinga/Nature Picture Library; p. 321 (flower cluster): © Dwight Kuhn

Chapter 17

Opener: © Alex Wild/Visuals Unlimited; p. 323: © Digital Vision/PunchStock; 17.2: © A.J. Copley/ Visuals Unlimited; 17.3: Courtesy of The National Human Genome Research Institute; 17.5 (all): © Herve Conge/ Phototake; p. 336: © Purestock/Getty Images (RF); 17.8 (sponge): © Getty Images (RF); 17.8 (fire sponge): © Diane R. Nelson (RF); 17.9 (jellyfish): © Kevin Schafer/Alamy (RF); 17.9 (hydra): © T. E. Adams/ Visuals Unlimited; 17.9 (multiple coral): © Comstock Images/PictureQuest (RF); 17.9 (individual coral): © Leslie Newman & Andrew Flowers/Photo Researchers; 17.9 (anemone): © Russell Illig/Getty Images (RF); 17.10 (marine flatworm): © Leslie Newman & Andrew Flowers/Photo Researchers; 17.10 (flatworm): © Carolina Biological Supply Company/Phototake; 17.10 (liver fluke): © Volker Steger/Photo Researchers; 17.10 (tapeworm): © Andrew Syred/Photo Researchers; 17.11 (chiton): © Kjell B. Sandved/Photo Researchers; 17.11 (bivalve): © Andrew J. Martinez/Photo Researchers; 17.11 (snail): © Digital Vision Ltd. (RF); 17.11 (slug): © Steven P. Lynch/The Mcgraw-Hill Companies (RF); 17.11 (octopus): © Fred Bavendam/Minden Pictures; 17.11 (squid): © Comstock Images/PictureQuest (RF); 17.12 (earthworm): © E.R. Degginger/Bruce Coleman/ Photoshot; 17.12 (leech): © Edward Kinsman/Photo Researchers; 17.12 (polychaete): © Marty Snyderman/ Visuals Unlimited; 17.13 (C. elegans): © Sinclair Stammers/Photo Researchers; 17.13 (elephantiasis): © R. Umesh Chandran, TDR, WHO/Photo Researchers; 17.13 (inset): © David Spears/Phototake; p. 334: © Creatas/PunchStock; 17.15: © Francois Gohier/ Photo Researchers; 17.16a: © Nature's Images/Photo Researchers; 17.16b: Centers for Disease Control and Prevention (CDC); 17.16c: © Corbis (RF); 17.16d: © Digital Vision/Punchstock (RF); 17.17a: © De Agostini Picture Library/Getty Images; 17.17b: © G/C Merker/ Visuals Unlimited; 17.18a: © (Zigmond) Carmella Leszczynski/Animals Animals - Earth Scenes; 17.18b: © Pete Atkinson/Photographer's Choice (RF)/Getty Images; 17.19a: © Design Pics Inc./Alamy (RF); 17.19b: © Thomas Shahan/Getty Images; p. 337 (follicle Mites): © Andrew Syred/Photo Researchers; 17.20 (juvenile seastar): © Wim van Egmond/Visuals Unlimited; 17.20 (starfish): © E.R. Degginger/Animals Animals - Earth Scenes; 17.20 (sand dollar): © Marty Snyderman/Visuals Unlimited; 17.20 (sea cucumber): © Nancy Sefton/ Photo Researchers; 17.20 (starfish): © E.R. Degginger/ Animals Animals - Earth Scenes; 17.20 (sea urchin): © Andrew J. Martinez/Photo Researchers; 17.23: © Creatas (RF)/PunchStock; 17.24 (tunicate - blue): © Nancy Sefton/Photo Researchers; 17.24 (tunicates - orange): © Janna Nichols; 17.24 (lancelet): © Oxford Scientific/Photolibrary; 17.25 (hagfish): © Tom McHugh/ Photo Researchers; 17.25 (slime): © James McCullagh/ Visuals Unlimited, Inc.; p. 342 (school of fish): © Jeff Hunter/Photographer's Choice RF/Getty Images; 17.26 (lamprey): © Russ Kinne/Photo Researchers; 17.26 (sting ray): © Hal Beral/Visuals Unlimited; 17.26 (shark): © W. Gregory Brown/Animals Animals - Earth Scenes; 17.26 (snappers): © Corbis (RF); 17.26 (lungfish): © Peter E. Smith/Natural Sciences Images Library; 17.26 (coelacanth): © Peter Scoones/Planet Earth Pictures/Getty Images; 17.27 (frog): © Creatas (RF)/PunchStock; 17.27 (caecilian): © E.D. Brodie Jr.; 17.27 (salamander): © Suzanne L. Collins & Joseph T. Collins/Photo Researchers; 17.28 (turtle): © Ed Reschke/ Peter Arnold/Photolibrary; 17.28 (lizard): © Creatas (RF)/PunchStock; 17.28 (snake): © Joe McDonald/ Animals Animals - Earth Scenes; 17.28 (alligator): © Joe McDonald/Animals Animals - Earth Scenes; 17.28 (ostrich): © Panoramic Images/Getty Images; 17.29 (platypus): © Fritz Prenzel/Animals Animals - Earth Scenes; 17.29 (echidna): © Phil Savoie/Nature Picture Library; 17.29 (kangaroo): © Martin Harvey/Gallo Images/Corbis; 17.29 (opossum): © Frank Lukasseck/ Getty Images; 17.29 (human): © Blend Images/Getty Images (RF); 17.29 (dolphin): © Creatas/PunchStock (RF); 17.29 (bat): © S. Dalton/Animals Animals - Earth Scenes; 17.30 (baboon): © Puresotck/PunchStock (RF); 17.30 (human): © Martial Colomb/Getty Images (RF); 17.32 (left): Skulls Unlimited International, Inc © David Liebman Pink Guppy; 17.32 (right): © Manfred Kage/ Peter Arnold/Photolibrary; p. 348: © Andersen Ross/ Getty Images (RF); 17.33 (chimp skull & teeth): Skulls Unlimited International, Inc © David Liebman Pink Guppy; 17.33 (Homo sapiens skull): © Ralph Hutchings/ Visuals Unlimited; 17.33 (Homo sapiens teeth): © The McGraw-Hill Companies, Inc./Photo by Christine Eckel; 17.35: © John Reader/Photo Researchers; 17.37: © Tetra Images/Getty Images (RF); 17.38 (Ichthyostega): © DEA Picture Library/Photolibrary; 17.39: © Ted Daeschler/ VIREO/Academy of Natural Sciences; p. 359 (sponge): © Getty Images (RF); p. 359 (hydra): © T. E. Adams/ Visuals Unlimited; p. 359 (liver fluke): © Volker Steger/ Photo Researchers; p. 359 (snail): © Digital Vision Ltd. (RF); p. 359 (earthworm): © E.R. Degginger/Bruce Coleman/Photoshot; p. 359 (roundworm): © Sinclair Stammers/Photo Researchers; p. 359 (centipede): © G/C Merker/Visuals Unlimited; p. 359 (starfish): © E.R. Degginger/Animals Animals - Earth Scenes; p. 359 (salamander): © Suzanne L. Collins & Joseph T. Collins/ Photo Researchers

Chapter 18

Opener: © Getty Images; p. 361: CDC/Janice Haney Carr; 18.1 (biosphere): © Corbis (RF); 18.1 (ecosystem): © Manoj Shah/The Image Bank/Getty Images; 18.1 (community): © Todd Gustafson/Danita Delimont; 18.1 (population): © Gregory G. Dimijian, M.D./Photo Researchers; 18.2a: © John A. Novak/Animals Animals - Earth Scenes; 18.2b: © PhotoAlto/PunchStock (RF); p. 363: © Ingram Publishing (RF); p. 364: © Corbis (RF); 18.4: © Kevin Schafer/Corbis; 18.7: © Ronald Wittek/ Getty Images; 18.10a: © Digital Vision/PunchStock (RF); 18.10b: Courtesy of John McColgan, Alaska Fire Service/ Bureau of Land Management; p. 369 (bird feeder): © Duncan Usher/Foto Natura/Minden Pictures; 18.11a: © Inga Spence/Visuals Unlimited; 18.11b: © Fabio Colombini Medeiros/Animals Animals - Earth Scenes; 18.12a: © Flat Earth Images (RF); 18.12b: © DLILLC/ Corbis (RF); 18.13: © Reinhard/ARCO/Nature Picture Library; p. 371: © Phil Degginger/Alamy (RF); p. 374 (water): © Imagemore Co., Ltd./Corbis (RF); 18.18: © James Jordan Photography/Getty Images (RF); p. 374 (firefly): © Phil Degginger/Alamy; p. 377 (penquins): © John A. Novak/Animals Animals - Earth Scenes; p. 378 (palm): © Flat Earth Images (RF); p. 378 (rice): © Inga Spence/Visuals Unlimited/Getty Images; p. 378 (deer): © Corbis Animals in Action CD; p. 378 (lions): © Beverly Joubert/National Geographic/Getty Images

Chapter 19

Opener: © Norm Thomas/Photo Researchers; p. 379: © Ingram Publishing/SuperStock (RF); 19.1a: © David Hall/Photo Researchers; 19.1b: © IT Stock Free/Alamy (RF); 19.1c: © Kristy-Anne Glubish/Design Pics (RF)/ Corbis; 19.3: NASA; p. 382: © Corbis (RF); 19.8 (taiga): © Thomas Kitchin/Photo Researchers; 19.8 (coniferous forest): © Comstock/PunchStock (RF); 19.8 (deciduous forest): © Digital Archive Japan/Alamy (RF); 19.8

(grassland): © PhotoDisc/Getty Images (RF); 19.8 (rain forest): © Frans Lanting/Corbis; 19.8 (tundra): © Michael DeYoung/Corbis; 19.8 (chaparral): © Andrew Brown; Ecoscene/Corbis; 19.8 (desert): © Ed Reschke; 19.8 (savanna): © Arthur Morris/Corbis; 19.8 (arctic): © Corbis (RF); 19.9 (oligotrophic lake): © ML Sinibaldi/Corbis; 19.9 (eutrophic lake): © The McGraw-Hill Companies, Inc./Pat Watson, photographer; 19.9 (stream): © Creatas/PunchStock (RF); 19.9 (river): © Corbis (RF); 19.9 (ocean): © Bryan Mullenix/Getty Images (RF); 19.9 (estuarie): © Joe/Arrington/Visuals Unlimited; 19.9 (intertidal): © D. Brown/Animals Animals - Earth Scenes; 19.9 (reef): © Digital Vision/Getty Images (RF); 19.10: © Mark Hamblin/Photolibrary; 19.13: © Dr. Parvinder Sethi (RF); 19.14: © Steven P. Lynch/The Mcgraw-Hill Companies (RF); 19.15a: © Kevin Schafer/The Image Bank/Getty Images; 19.15b: © Thomas Marent/Visuals Unlimted; 19.15c: © Simon D. Pollard/Photo Researchers; 19.16: © Beverly Joubert/National Geographic/Getty Images; 19.17: © Mark Moffett/Minden Pictures; 19.18: © Johnny Johnson/Photographer's Choice/Getty Images; p. 392: © Peter Arnold, Inc./Alamy; 19.21: © Jerry Dodrill/Aurora/Getty Images; p. 394: © C Squared Studios/Getty Images (RF); 19.26: © Corbis (RF); p. 397 (birds): © Stockbyte (RF); 19.27: © Corbis (RF); P. 398: © Brand X Pictures/PunchStock (RF); p. 399: © Michael T. Sedam/Corbis (RF); p. 402: © Photo24/Getty Images (RF); 19.32: © Digital Vision/Getty Images (RF); p. 403: © Ingram Publishing/SuperStock (RF); 19.34: Courtesy Marilyn J. Roossinck. Luis M. Márquez, Regina S. Redman, Russell J. Rodriguez, and Marilyn J. Roossinck. "A virus in a fungus in a plant: three-way symbiosis required for thermal tolerance." SCIENCE, 26 January 2007: Vol. 315. no. 5811, pp. 513 - 515. © 2007 Reprinted with permission.; p. 407 (ecosystem): © Manoj Shah/The Image Bank/Getty Images; p. 407 (mountains): © Corbis (RF); p. 407 (community): © Todd Gustafson/Danita Delimont; p. 407 (bison): © PhotoDisc/Getty Images (RF); p. 407 (scavengers): © Mark Hamblin/Photolibrary; p. 407 (ants): © Mark Moffett/Minden Pictures; p. 407 (bear): © Digital Vision/Getty Images (RF); p. 407 (caribou): © Thomas Kitchin/Photo Researchers; p. 407 (lake): © ML Sinibaldi/Corbis; p. 407 (reef): © Digital Vision/Getty Images (RF)

Chapter 20

Openers: Claire Fackler, NOAA National Marine Sanctuaries; p. 409: © Keren Su/Stone/Getty Images; 20.2a: Photo by Lynn Betts, courtesy of USDA Natural Resources Conservation Service; 20.2b: © Wayne Lawler; Ecoscene/Corbis; 20.2c: © Corbis (RF); 20.3: © David Falk/Getty Images (RF); 20.4: © Ed Kashi/Corbis; 20.6: © Digital Vision/PunchStock (RF); 20.7: © Reuters/Corbis; 20.8: © Oliver Strewe/Stone/Getty Images; 20.10b: © Corbis (RF); p. 416 (both): NASA; 20.11: © USGS/Canadian Coast Guard, photo by Patrick Kelley; 20.12a: © George Grall/National Geographic/Getty Images; 20.12b: © Steve St. John/Getty Images (RF); 20.13: © China Photos/Getty Images News; 20.14: © CC Lockwood/Animals Animals - Earth Scenes; p. 419 (capitol): © Brand X Pictures/PunchStock (RF); 20.16: © Dr. John D. Cunningham/Visuals Unlimited; 20.17: © Comstock/PunchStock (RF); 20.18: © Patrick Landmann/Photo Researchers; p. 422 (girl): © PhotoDisc/Getty Images (RF); p. 422 (forest): © Pepiera Tom/Iconotec.com (RF); 20.19: © Thomas Marent,/Visuals Unlimited/Corbis; p. 425 (loss): © Wayne Lawler; Ecoscene/Corbis; p. 425 (smog): © Reuters/Corbis; p. 425 (by-catch): © CC Lockwood/Animals Animals - Earth Scenes; p. 425 (bear): © USGS/Canadian Coast Guard, photo by Patrick Kelley; p. 425 (rhino): © Comstock/PunchStock (RF); p. 425 (invasive): © George Grall/National Geographic/Getty Images; p. 425 (DNA): © Photodisc/Photolibrary (RF); p. 425 (pelt): © China Photos/Getty Images News

Chapter 21

Opener: © David Sieren/Visuals Unlimited; p. 427: © G.C. Kelly/Photo Researchers; p. 428 (label): © David Tietz/Editorial Image, LLC; 21.3a: © Nigel Cattlin/Photo Researchers; 21.3b: © Nigel Cattlin/Visuals Unlimited; 21.4: © Wally Eberhart/Visuals Unlimited; p. 430 (cactus): © Robert Glusic/Corbis (RF); 21.5 (parenchyma): © Dr. Ken Wagner/Visuals Unlimited; 21.5 (collenchyma): © Biophoto Associates/Photo Researchers; 21.5 (sclerenchyma): © Carolina Biological Supply Company/Phototake; 21.5 (xylem): © Dr. Richard Kessel & Dr. Gene Shih/Visuals Unlimited; 21.5 (phloem): © George Wilder/Visuals Unlimited; 21.6: © Dr. Gerald Van Dyke/Visuals Unlimited; 21.8a: © Steven P. Lynch/The Mcgraw-Hill Companies (RF); 21.8b: © Dr. Jack Bostrack/Visuals Unlimited; 21.10a-b: © Dwight Kuhn; p. 435: © Richard Carlton/Visuals Unlimited; 21.12a: © The McGraw-Hill Companies, Inc./Al Telser, photographer; 21.12b: © Dr. Brad Mogen/Visuals Unlimited; 21.13: © Dr. Jeremy Burgess/Photo Researchers; 21.14: © Jack M. Bostrack/Visuals Unlimited; 21.15: © Dr. John D. Cunningham/Visuals Unlimited; 21.17b: © Siede Preis/Getty Images (RF); 21.17c: © Herve Conge/Phototake; 21.B: © Frederick Mckinney/Photographer's Choice RR/Getty Images; p. 442: © Burke Triolo Productions/Getty Images (RF); 21.20: © Ingram Publishing (RF); 21.21: © Mark Boulton/Alamy; 21.22: © David Sieren/Visuals Unlimited; p. 447 (ground tissue): © Steven P. Lynch/The Mcgraw-Hill Companies (RF); p. 447 (dermal): © Dr. Gerald Van Dyke/Visuals Unlimited; p. 447 (parenchyma): © Dr. Ken Wagner/Visuals Unlimited

Chapter 22

Opener: © Konrad Wothe/Minden Pictures; p. 449: © Stephen Dalton/Photo Researchers; 22.1a-b: © Steven P. Lynch/The Mcgraw-Hill Companies (RF); p. 451: © Burke/Triolo Productions/Getty Images (RF); 22.4a: © Corbis (RF); 22.4b: © MedioImages/Getty Images (RF); 22.4c: © Merlin D. Tuttle/Bat Conservation International/Photo Researchers; 22.4d-e: © Leonard Lessin/Photo Researchers; 22.4f: © Dr. Jeremy Burgess/Photo Researchers; 22.7a: © John D. Cunningham/Visuals Unlimited; 22.7b: © Steven P. Lynch/The Mcgraw-Hill Companies (RF); 22.8 (all): © Brent Seabrook; TA22.1 (cherry & pineapple): © Ingram Publishing (RF)/Alamy; TA22.1 (strawberry): © Corbis (RF); 22.9a: © Rod Planck/Photo Researchers; 22.9b: © Scott Camazine/Photo Researchers; 22.9c: © Adam Hart-Davis/SPL/Photo Researchers; p. 456 (boy): © Deborah Jaffe/Getty Images (RF); p. 456 (sprout): © Corbis (RF); 22.10a: © Dwight Kuhn; 22.10b: © Ed Reschke; 22.11: © Nigel Cattlin/Visuals Unlimited; p. 459 (flowers): © David G. Clark; 22.12: © Sylvan Wittwer/Visuals Unlimited; 22.13: © Kent Knudson/PhotoLink/Getty Images (RF); 22.14: © Martin Shields/Photo Researchers; 22.17a: © C. Calentine/Visuals Unlimited; 22.17b: © BioPhot; 22.18: © William E. Ferguson; 22.19: © Jupiterimages/ImageSource (RF); p. 465 (flower): © Leonard Lessin/Photo Researchers; p. 465 (pollen): © Dr. Jeremy Burgess/Photo Researchers

Chapter 23

Opener: © James King-Holmes/Photo Researchers; p. 467 (penguin): © DLILLC (RF)/Corbis; p. 468 (liposuction): © image100/Corbis (RF); 23.2 (simple squamous & cuboidal): © Ed Reschke/Peter Arnold/Photolibrary; 23.2 (simple columnar): © Eckel DAI (RF); 23.2 (stratified squamous): © Dr. Fred Hossler/Visuals Unlimited; 23.3 (loose & blood): © The McGraw-Hill Companies, Inc./Al Telser, photographer; 23.3 (dense, adipose, & bone): © The McGraw-Hill Companies, Inc./Dennis Strete, photographer; 23.3 (cartilage): © Chuck Brown/Photo Researchers; 23.4 (skeletal & smooth): © Ed Reschke; 23.4 (cardiac): © Manfred Kage/Peter Arnold/Photolibrary; 23.5: © Stan Elems/Visuals Unlimited; 23.6: © Digital Vision/Getty Images; p. 475: © Bettmann/Corbis; 23.10: © Lee Davenport/McGraw-Hill; 23.11: © Corbis (RF); p. 481 (epithelial): © Dr. Fred Hossler/Visuals Unlimited; p. 481 (connective): © The McGraw-Hill Companies, Inc./Al Telser, photographer; p. 481 (muscle): © Manfred Kage/Peter Arnold/Photolibrary; p. 481 (nervous): © Stan Elems/Visuals Unlimited

Chapter 24

Opener: © Cary Wolinsky/Getty Images; p. 483: © Digital Vision (RF); 24.2: © Dr. John D. Cunningham/Visuals Unlimited; 24.6: ER Lewis, YY Zeevi and TE Everhart; p. 490: © Comstock Images/Alamy (RF); 24.8: © Manfred Kage/Peter Arnold/Photolibrary; 24.10: © AFP/Getty Images; 24.11: © McGraw-Hill Companies, Inc./Gary He, phototgrapher; 24.12a: © Pool/Getty Images; 24.12b: © AP Photo/Kenneth Lambert; 24.14: © RubberBall Productions/Getty Images (RF); 24.16: © Bananastock/PictureQuest (RF); 24.17: © Corbis (RF); 24.18: © White Rock/Getty Images (RF); p. 499 (ad): © David Tietz/Editorial Image, LLC; 24.19: © Comstock/Getty Images (RF); 24.20: © Photo Quest Ltd/Science Photo Library/Corbis (RF); 24.21: © Rubberball Productions (RF); p. 503: © Isabelle Rozenbaum & Frederic Cirou/PhotoAlto/PunchStock (RF)

Chapter 25

Opener: © Bananastock/PunchStock (RF); p. 509: © Getty Images (RF); 25.1a (both): © The McGraw-Hill Companies/Ken Cavanagh, photographer; 25.1b: © Robert Clay/Alamy (RF); 25.5: © AP Photo; 25.10: © Saturn Stills/Photo Researchers; 25.13: © Gary Meszaros/Visuals Unlimited; p. 519: © Corbis (RF)

Chapter 26

Opener: © Claudio Peri/epa/Corbis; p. 525: © MedicalRF.com/Corbis; 26.1a (jellyfish): © Gabriel Bouys/AFP/Getty Images; 26.1b (crab): © Photodisc/Getty Images (RF); 26.1c (fish): © Jim Wehtje/Getty Images (RF); 26.3: © Southern Illinois University/Photo Researchers; p. 527 (x-ray): © Image Source/Getty Images (RF); 26.4 (cartilage): © Chuck Brown/Photo Researchers; 26.4 (bone): © Ed Reschke; 26.7 (healthy): © Prof. P.M.

Motta/Univ. "La Sapienza", Rome/Photo Researchers; 26.7 (diseased): © Dee Breger/Photo Researchers; 26.11: © Biology Pics/Photo Researchers; p. 535: © Photodisc Inc./ Getty Images (RF); p. 535 (creatine): © Alan Mather/ Alamy; 26.14 (runner): © RubberBall/Getty Images (RF); 26.14 (fiber): © G.W. Willis/Visuals Unlimited; 26.14 (weight lifter): © Jack Mann/Photodisc/Getty Images (RF); p. 537 (man): © liquidlibrary/PictureQuest (RF); p. 541 (jellyfish): © Gabriel Bouys/AFP/Getty Images; p. 541 (crab): © Photodisc/Getty Images (RF); p. 541 (bone): © Ed Reschke; p. 541 (cartilage): © Chuck Brown/Photo Researchers

Chapter 27

Opener: © Paul Kitagaki Jr/ZUMA Press/Corbis; p. 543 (top): © Photodisc/Getty Images (RF); 27.1: © Dr. Dennis Kunkel/Visuals Unlimited; p. 544 (blood): © Toby Melville/Reuters/Corbis; 27.3b: © Dr. David Phillips/Visuals Unlimited; p. 548: © Ingram Publishing/ SuperStock (RF); p. 550: © Duncan Smith/Getty Images (RF); 27.12: © Blend Images (RF); 27.16: © Innerspace Imaging/Photo Researchers; 27.19: © AP Photo/The Tennessean, John Partipilo; 27.22: © Rick Price/Corbis; p. 560: © Ralph Hutchings/Visuals Unlimited; p. 563 (blood cells): © Dr. Dennis Kunkel/Visuals Unlimited

Chapter 28

Opener: © Ingram Publishing (RF); p. 565 (top): © C Squared Studios/Getty Images (RF); 28.1 (penguins): © Johnny Johnson/The Image Bank/Getty Images; 28.1 (parrots): © IT Stock (RF)/PunchStock; 28.1 (roadrunner): © U.S. Fish & Wildlife Service/Gary Karamer, photographer; 28.2 (mouse): © John A.L. Cooke/Animals Animals - Earth Scenes; 28.2 (snake): © IT Stock (RF)/ PunchStock; 28.4a: © Akira Kaede/Digital Vision (RF)/ Getty Images; 28.4b: © Dynamic Graphics/PictureQuest (RF); 28.5: © Stockbyte/PunchStock (RF); 28.6: © Digital Vision/PunchStock (RF); p. 569: © Ken Karp/McGraw-Hill Companies; 28.9 (anorexia): © AP Photo/The Grand Island Independent, Barrett Stinson; 28.9 (starvation): © AP Photo/Brennan Linsley; 28.10: © Science VU/ Jackson/Visuals Unlimited; 28.11a: © Digital Vision/ PunchStock (RF); 28.11b: © PhotoAlto/PunchStock (RF); 28.11c: Centers for Disease Control and Prevention (CDC); 28.11d: © image100/PunchStock (RF); p. 577 (HCl): © Ingram Publishing/SuperStock (RF); p. 577 (milk): © Burke/Triolo Productions (RF)/Getty Images; 28.19c: Courtesy of David H. Alpers, M.D.; p. 579 (medicine): © Michael Matisse/Getty Images (RF); 28.22a-b: © Brand X Pictures/PunchStock (RF); p. 583 (samples): © Corbis (RF); 28.27: © Pat Pendarvis; p. 585: © Patrick Blake/Alamy (RF)

Chapter 29

Opener: © Getty Images; p. 591 (girl): © Jose Luis Pelaez Inc/Getty Images (RF); 29.1: © Dr. David M. Phillips/Visuals Unlimited; p. 594: © Corbis (RF); p. 595: © Getty Images (RF); 29.5: © Dr. Olivier Schwartz, Institute Pasteur/SPL/Photo Researchers; 29.6b: © Dr. Andrejs Liepins/Photo Researchers; 29.7b: © Len Lessin/ Peter Arnold/Photolibrary; p. 600: © TRBfoto/Getty Images (RF); p. 601: © Brand X Pictures/PunchStock (RF); 29.12: © Dr. Ken Greer/Visuals Unlimited; 29.13: © Hank Morgan/Photo Researchers; 29.14 (top): © David Scharf/Peter Arnold/Photolibrary; 29.14 (bottom): © Institut Pasteur/Phototake; 29.15: © Paul Rapson/Photo Researchers; 29.15 (inset): © SIU/Visuals Unlimited

Chapter 30

Opener: © Dr. Paul Zahl/Photo Researchers; p. 609 (mother): © Nancy Ney/Digital Vision/Getty Images (RF); 30.1a: © Andrew J. Martinez/Photo Researchers; 30.1b: © Tim Fitzharris/Minden Pictures; 30.3: © Daniel Heuclin/Photo Researchers; 30.5a: Larry Johnson, Dept. of Veterinary Anatomy and Public Health; 30.6b: © Eye of Science/Photo Researchers; 30.9a: © Victor P. Eroschenko (RF); 30.9b: © Prof. P.M. Motta, G. Macchiarelli, S.A. Nottola/Photo Researchers; 30.12: © Image Source/ PunchStock (RF); p. 618 (birth control): © Getty Images (RF); p. 621: © Science Photo Library (RF)/Getty Images; p. 623: © AP Photo/Peer Grimm, Pool; 30.18 (all): © Ralph Hutchings/Visuals Unlimited; 30.20: © Georgette Douwma/Photo Researchers; p. 631 (sperm): © Eye of Science/Photo Researchers; p. 631 (egg): © Prof. P.M. Motta, G. Macchiarelli, S.A. Nottola/Photo Researchers; p. 631 (fetus): © Ralph Hutchings/Visuals Unlimited

Index

Note: Page numbers followed by an f indicate figures; numbers followed by a t indicate tables.

A

B

C

D

E

F

N

Q

R

S

T

U

V

W

X

Y

Z